College Accounting

Chapters 1–29

Other McGraw-Hill textbooks available by these authors include:

John J. Wild, Ken W. Shaw, and Barbara Chiappetta
Fundamental Accounting Principles, 19th Edition
ISBN: 0077303202
MHID: 9780077303204

John J. Wild, Ken W. Shaw, and Barbara Chiappetta
Principles of Financial Accounting, 19th Edition
ISBN: 0077303210
MHID: 9780077303211

John J. Wild, Ken W. Shaw, and Barbara Chiappetta
Financial and Managerial Accounting: Information for Decisions, 3rd Edition
ISBN: 0077303504
MHID: 9780077303501

John J. Wild
Financial Accounting Fundamentals, 2009 Edition
ISBN: 0073379573
MHID: 9780073379579

John J. Wild and Ken W. Shaw
Managerial Accounting, 2010 Edition
ISBN: 0073379581
MHID: 9780073379586

John J. Wild
Financial Accounting: Information for Decisions, 5th Edition
ISBN: 0073527017
MHID: 9780073527017

2

edition

College Accounting

Chapters 1–29

John J. Wild
University of Wisconsin at Madison

Vernon J. Richardson
University of Arkansas

Ken W. Shaw
University of Missouri at Columbia

McGraw-Hill
Irwin

McGraw-Hill Irwin

COLLEGE ACCOUNTING
Published by McGraw-Hill/Irwin, a business unit of The McGraw-Hill Companies, Inc., 1221
Avenue of the Americas, New York, NY, 10020. Copyright © 2011, 2008 by The McGraw-Hill
Companies, Inc. All rights reserved. No part of this publication may be reproduced or distributed
in any form or by any means, or stored in a database or retrieval system, without the prior written
consent of The McGraw-Hill Companies, Inc., including, but not limited to, in any network or other
electronic storage or transmission, or broadcast for distance learning.

Some ancillaries, including electronic and print components, may not be available to customers
outside the United States.

This book is printed on acid-free paper.

1 2 3 4 5 6 7 8 9 0 DOW/DOW 1 0 9 8 7 6 5 4 3 2 1 0

ISBN   978-0-07-813667-2 (chapters 1–29)
MHID   0-07-813667-9 (chapters 1–29)
ISBN   978-0-07-726873-2 (chapters 1–14)
MHID   0-07-726873-3 (chapters 1–14)

Vice president and editor-in-chief: *Brent Gordon*
Editorial director: *Stewart Mattson*
Publisher: *Tim Vertovec*
Executive editor: *Steve Schuetz*
Director of development: *Ann Torbert*
Senior development editor: *Christina A. Sanders*
Vice president and director of marketing: *Robin J. Zwettler*
Marketing manager: *Michelle Heaster*
Vice president of editing, design and production: *Sesha Bolisetty*
Managing editor: *Lori Koetters*
Lead production supervisor: *Carol A. Bielski*
Lead designer: *Matthew Baldwin*
Senior photo research coordinator: *Lori Kramer*
Photo researcher: *Sarah Evertson*
Lead media project manager: *Brian Nacik*
Cover design: *Matthew Baldwin*
Interior design: *Matthew Baldwin*
Cover image: *© Getty Images*
Typeface: *10.5/12 Times Roman*
Compositor: *Aptara®, Inc.*
Printer: *R. R. Donnelley*

Library of Congress Cataloging-in-Publication Data
Wild, John J.
    College accounting : chapters 1–29 / John J. Wild, Vernon J. Richardson,
Ken W. Shaw.—2nd ed.
        p. cm.
    Includes index.
    ISBN-13: 978-0-07-813667-2 (chapters 1–29 : alk. paper)
    ISBN-10: 0-07-813667-9 (chapters 1–29 : alk. paper)
    ISBN-13: 978-0-07-726873-2 (chapters 1–14 : alk. paper)
    ISBN-10: 0-07-726873-3 (chapters 1–14 : alk. paper)
    1. Accounting. I. Richardson, Vernon J. II. Shaw, Ken W. III. Title.
HF5635.W693 2011
657—dc22

                                            2009041924

www.mhhe.com

To my wife **Gail** and children, **Kimberly, Jonathan, Stephanie**, and **Trevor**.

To my parents, **Jay** and **Lavona Richardson**.

To my wife **Linda** and children, **Erin**, **Emily**, and **Jacob**.

College Accounting

Dear Friends and Colleagues,

We all struggle with many of the same teaching challenges: motivating students to learn, making accounting relevant to them, integrating technology, and covering crucial material. We wrote this book intending to give our students and us the means to confront each of those challenges.

One problem with many college accounting books is that their dated examples and boring companies fail to engage students. As instructors, we are responsible for bringing accounting to life through interesting and contemporary examples of exciting companies and industries. This book's chapter-opening vignettes and its many examples showcase successful, dynamic entrepreneurs that excite and engage students. Discussions of ethics, fraud, and the Sarbanes-Oxley Act further engage students. We also illustrate many key accounting concepts using the financial statements of Best Buy, RadioShack, and other well-recognized companies.

We all believe that our students must be able to prepare and interpret accounting information to successfully enter the business world. We use short learning sessions, with clear examples and objectives, to ensure student success. To help students transition, we show students where and how business decisions draw on accounting knowledge.

Students today learn in ways beyond reading chapters and attending classes. Important developments in technology are creating new avenues for learning accounting. Working together, this book's publisher and we developed new tools to reach and sustain students throughout the course. An exciting example of those tools is Connect Accounting™ or Connect Accounting Plus™ (which includes an interactive eBook). Connect Accounting is our application of the accounting adage that "perfect practice makes perfect." Other highly successful tools include the book's Online Learning Center and Carol Yacht's Quickbooks Guide.

This is an exciting time to be an accounting instructor. We welcome your thoughts on how we can continue to engage today's accounting students and prepare them for tomorrow's business world.

John   Vern   Ken

John J. Wild is a professor of accounting and the Robert and Monica Beyer Distinguished Professor at the University of Wisconsin at Madison. He previously held appointments at Michigan State University and the University of Manchester in England. He received his BBA, MS, and PhD from the University of Wisconsin.

Professor Wild teaches accounting courses at both the undergraduate and graduate levels. He has received the Mabel W. Chipman Excellence-in-Teaching Award, the departmental Excellence-in-Teaching Award, and the Teaching Excellence Award from the 2003 and 2005 business graduates at the University of Wisconsin. He also received the Beta Alpha Psi and Roland F. Salmonson Excellence-in-Teaching Award from Michigan State University. Professor Wild is a past KPMG Peat Marwick National Fellow and is a recipient of fellowships from the American Accounting Association and the Ernst and Young Foundation.

Professor Wild is an active member of the American Accounting Association and its sections. He has served on several committees of these organizations, including the Outstanding Accounting Educator Award, Wildman Award, National Program Advisory, Publications, and Research Committees. Professor Wild is author of *Fundamental Accounting Principles, Financial Accounting,* and *Financial Statement Analysis*, published by McGraw-Hill/Irwin. His research appears in The Accounting Review, Journal of Accounting Research, Journal of Accounting and Economics, Contemporary Accounting Research, Journal of Accounting, Auditing and Finance, Journal of Accounting and Public Policy, and other journals. He is past associate editor of Contemporary Accounting Research and has served on several editorial boards including The Accounting Review.

Professor Wild, his wife, and four children enjoy travel, music, sports, and community activities.

Vernon J. Richardson is Professor of Accounting and the S. Robson Walton Distinguished Chair in the Sam M. Walton College of Business at the University of Arkansas. He currently serves as Accounting department chair. He received his B.S., Masters of Accountancy, and MBA from Brigham Young University and a Ph.D. in accounting from the University of Illinois at Urbana-Champaign. He has taught students at the University of Arkansas, University of Illinois, Brigham Young University, University of Kansas, and the China Europe International Business School (Shanghai).

Professor Richardson is a member of the American Accounting Association. He currently serves as the president of the American Accounting Association Information Systems section. Professor Richardson has published articles in the Accounting Review, the Journal of Accounting and Economics, Journal of Accounting and Public Policy, Journal of Business, Finance, and Accounting, Financial Analysts Journal, MIS Quarterly, Journal of Operations Management, Journal of Marketing, and the American Business Law Journal.

Professor Richardson, his wife, and their twelve children all enjoy music, traveling, sports, and watching movies.

Ken W. Shaw is an associate professor of accounting and the Deloitte Professor at the University of Missouri at Columbia. He previously was on the faculty at the University of Maryland at College Park. He received an accounting degree from Bradley University and an MBA and PhD from the University of Wisconsin. He is a Certified Public Accountant with work experience in public accounting.

Professor Shaw teaches financial accounting at the undergraduate and graduate levels. He was voted the "Most Influential Professor" by the 2005 and 2006 School of Accountancy graduating classes, won the Williams-Keepers Teaching Excellence Award in 2007, and won O'Brien Excellence in Teaching Awards in 2003 and 2008. He is also the advisor to his school's chapter of the Association of Certified Fraud Examiners.

Professor Shaw is an active member of the American Accounting Association and its sections. He has served on committees of these organizations and presented his research papers at national and regional meetings. Professor Shaw is co-author of *Fundamental Accounting Principles*, *Financial and Managerial Accounting*, and *Managerial Accounting* published by McGraw-Hill/Irwin. Professor Shaw's research appears in the Accounting Review; the Journal of Accounting Research; Contemporary Accounting Research; Journal of Financial and Quantitative Analysis; Strategic Management Journal; Journal of the American Taxation Association; Journal of Accounting, Auditing, and Finance; Journal of Business, Finance, and Accounting; Journal of Financial Research; Research in Accounting Regulation; and other journals. He currently serves on the editorial boards of Issues in Accounting Education and the Journal of Business Research.

In his leisure time, Professor Shaw enjoys tennis, cycling, music, and coaching his children's sports teams.

College Accounting

Help get your students on the path to success. *College Accounting (CA)* will help your students succeed by leading them through engaging accounting content and providing state-of-the-art technology.

One of the greatest challenges students confront in a college accounting course is seeing the relevance of materials. *CA* tackles this issue head-on with **engaging content** and a **motivating style**. Students are motivated when reading materials that are **clear and relevant**. *CA* chapter-opening vignettes showcase dynamic, successful, entrepreneurial individuals and companies guaranteed to **interest and excite readers**. This text's featured companies—Best Buy and RadioShack—engage students with their annual reports, which are great vehicles for **learning** financial statements. Further, this book's coverage of the accounting cycle fundamentals is widely praised for its **clarity and effectiveness**.

CA also delivers **state-of-the-art technology** to help students succeed. **Connect Accounting** provides students with instant grading and feedback for assignments that are completed online. **Connect Accounting Plus** integrates an online version of the textbook with our popular Connect Accounting system. *CA* also offers accounting students portable **iPod-ready content**.

We're confident you'll agree that *CA* **will lead your students on the path to succeed**.

Engaging Content

College Accounting 2e by Wild, Richardson, and Shaw brings excitement to your College Accounting course in its extensive use of small business examples, integration of computerized learning tools, superior end-of-chapter material, and a highly engaging pedagogical design. *College Accounting* motivates students with real-world applications and examples including motivating chapter openers featuring real entrepreneurs. The text also includes the financial statements of Best Buy and RadioShack to further engage students by applying knowledge learned in the course directly to a familiar company.

Cutting-Edge Technology

College Accounting offers the most advanced and comprehensive technology on the market in a seamless, easy-to-use platform. As students learn in different ways, *CA* provides a technology smorgasbord that helps students learn more effectively and efficiently. Connect Accounting, eBook options, and iPod content are some of the options available. Connect Accounting Plus takes learning to another level by integrating an online version of the textbook with all the power of Connect Accounting. Technology offerings include the following:

- Connect Accounting
- Connect Accounting Plus
- iPod content
- Quickbooks Templates
- Online Learning Center
- ALEKS for the Accounting Cycle
- ALEKS for Financial Accounting

McGraw-Hill Connect Accounting

Less Managing. More Teaching. Greater Learning.

McGraw-Hill Connect Accounting is an online assignment and assessment solution that connects students with the tools and resources they'll need to achieve success. McGraw-Hill Connect Accounting helps prepare students for their future by enabling faster learning, more efficient studying, and higher retention of knowledge.

McGraw-Hill Connect Accounting features

Connect Accounting offers a number of powerful tools and features to make managing assignments easier, so faculty can spend more time teaching. With Connect Accounting, students can engage with their coursework anytime and anywhere, making the learning process more accessible and efficient. Connect Accounting offers you the features described below.

Simple assignment management

With Connect Accounting, creating assignments is easier than ever, so you can spend more time teaching and less time managing. The assignment management function enables you to:

- Create and deliver assignments easily with selectable end-of-chapter questions and test bank items.
- Streamline lesson planning, student progress reporting, and assignment grading to make classroom management more efficient than ever.
- Go paperless with the eBook and online submission and grading of student assignments.

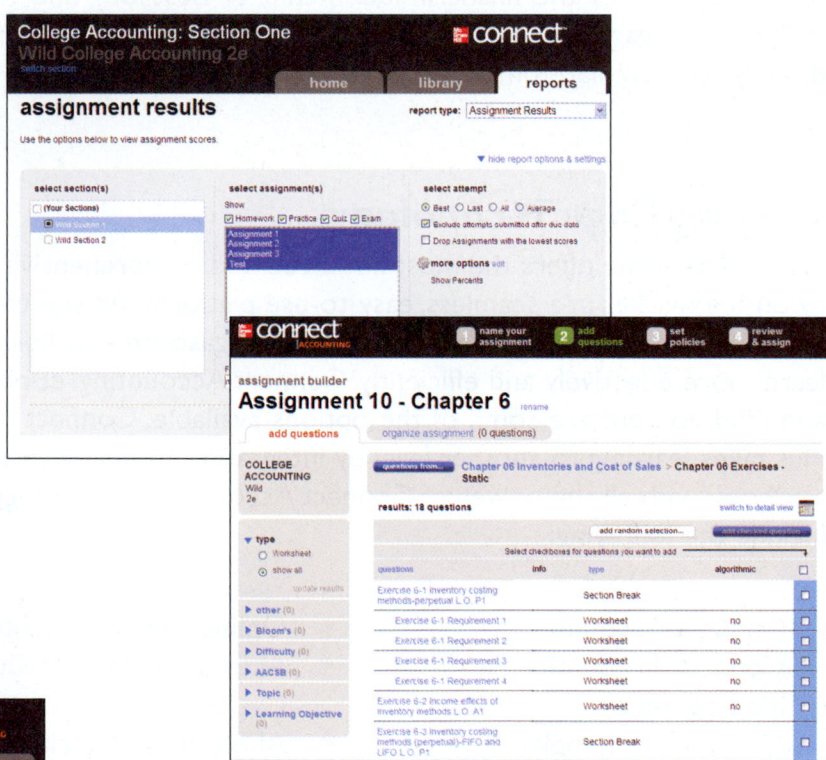

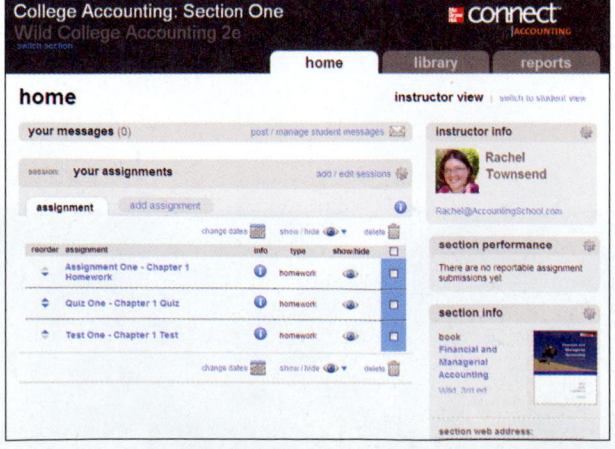

Smart grading

When it comes to studying, time is precious. Connect Accounting helps students learn more efficiently by providing feedback and practice material when they need it, where they need it. When it comes to teaching, your time also is precious. The grading function enables you to:

- Have assignments scored automatically, giving students immediate feedback on their work and side-by-side comparisons with correct answers.
- Access and review each response; manually change grades or leave comments for students to review.
- Reinforce classroom concepts with practice tests and instant quizzes.

Student study center

The Connect Accounting Student Study Center is the place for students to access additional resources. The Student Study Center:

- Offers students quick access to lectures, practice materials, eBooks, and more.
- Provides instant practice material and study questions, easily accessible on the go.

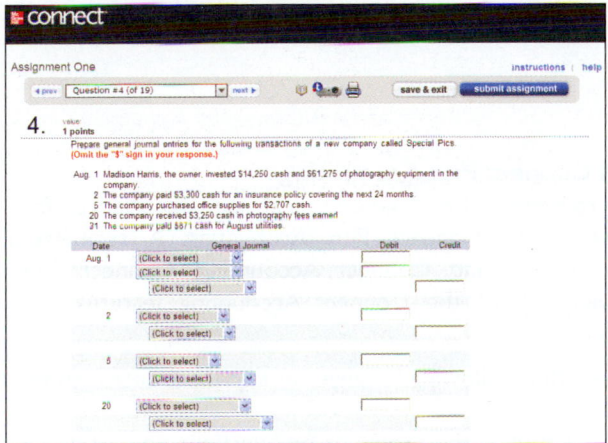

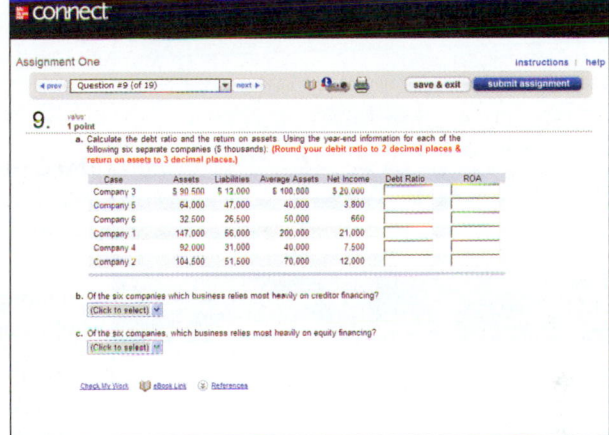

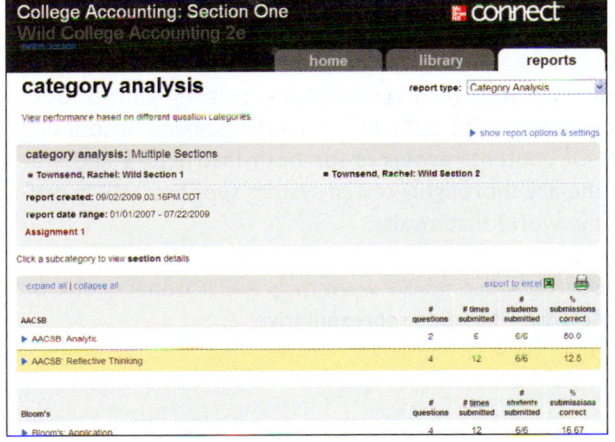

Student progress tracking

Connect Accounting keeps instructors informed about how each student, section, and class is performing, allowing for more productive use of lecture and office hours. The progress-tracking function enables you to:

- View scored work immediately and track individual or group performance with assignment and grade reports.
- Access an instant view of student or class performance relative to learning objectives.
- Collect data and generate reports required by many accreditation organizations, such as AACSB and AICPA.

Lecture capture

Increase the attention paid to lecture discussion by decreasing the attention paid to note taking. For an additional charge Lecture Capture offers new ways for students to focus on the in-class discussion, knowing they can revisit important topics later. Lecture Capture enables you to:

- Record and distribute your lecture with a click of the button.
- Record and index PowerPoint presentations and anything shown on your computer so it is easily searchable, frame by frame.
- Offer access to lectures anytime and anywhere by computer, iPod, or mobile device.
- Increase intent listening and class participation by easing students' concerns about note-taking. Lecture Capture will make it more likely you will see students' faces, not the tops of their heads.

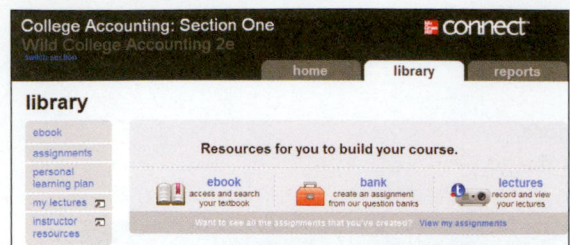

Instructor library

The Connect Accounting Instructor Library is your repository for additional resources to improve student engagement in and out of class. You can select and use any asset that enhances your lecture. The Connect Accounting Instructor Library includes the Solutions Manual, Instructor's Resource Manual, Test Bank, and PowerPoint lecture slides.

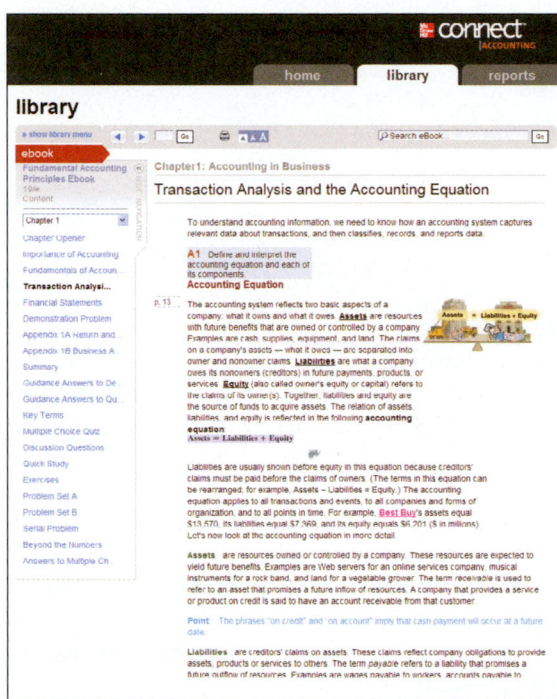

McGraw-Hill Connect Plus Accounting

McGraw-Hill reinvents the textbook learning experience for the modern student with Connect Plus Accounting. A seamless integration of an eBook and Connect Accounting, Connect Plus Accounting provides all of the Connect Accounting features plus the following:

- An integrated eBook, allowing for anytime, anywhere access to the textbook.
- Dynamic links between the problems or questions you assign to your students and the location in the eBook where that problem or question is covered.
- A powerful search function to pinpoint and connect key concepts in a snap.

In short, Connect Accounting offers you and your students powerful tools and features that optimize your time and energies, enabling you to focus on course content, teaching, and student learning. Connect Accounting also offers a wealth of content resources for both instructors and students. This state-of-the-art, thoroughly tested system supports you in preparing students for the world that awaits.

For information about Connect, go to www.mcgrawhillconnect.com, or contact your local McGraw-Hill sales representative.

Tegrity Campus: Lectures 24/7

Tegrity Campus is a service that makes class time available 24/7 by automatically capturing every lecture. With a simple one-click start-and-stop process, you capture all computer screens and corresponding audio in a format that is easily searchable, frame by frame. Students can replay any part of any class with easy-to-use browser-based viewing on a PC or Mac, an iPod, or other mobile device. Educators know that the more students can see, hear, and experience class resources, the better they learn. In fact, studies prove it. Tegrity Campus's unique search feature helps students efficiently find what they need, when they need it, across an entire semester of class recordings. Help turn your students' study time into learning moments immediately supported by your lecture. With Tegrity Campus, you also increase intent listening and class participation by easing students' concerns about note-taking. Lecture Capture will make it more likely you will see students' faces, not the tops of their heads.

To learn more about Tegrity, watch a 2-minute Flash demo at http://tegritycampus.mhhe.com.

Assurance of Learning Ready

Many educational institutions today are focused on the notion of assurance of learning, an important element of some accreditation standards. College Accounting is designed specifically to support your assurance of learning initiatives with a simple, yet powerful solution. Each test bank question for College Accounting maps to a specific chapter learning outcome/objective listed in the text. You can use our test bank software, EZ Test and EZ Test Online, or in Connect Accounting to easily query for learning outcomes/objectives that directly relate to the learning objectives for your course. You can then use the reporting features of EZ Test to aggregate student results in similar fashion, making the collection and presentation of assurance of learning data simple and easy.

AACSB Statement

The McGraw-Hill Companies is a proud corporate member of AACSB International. Understanding the importance and value of AACSB accreditation, *College Accounting*, 2nd edition recognizes the curricula guidelines detailed in the AACSB standards for business accreditation by connecting selected questions in the test bank to the six general knowledge and skill guidelines in the AACSB standards. The statements contained in *College Accounting*, 2nd edition are provided only as a guide for the users of this textbook. The AACSB leaves content coverage and assessment within the purview of individual schools, the mission of the school, and the faculty. While *College Accounting*, 2nd edition and the teaching package make no claim of any specific AACSB qualification or evaluation, we have within *College Accounting*, 2nd edition labeled selected questions according to the six general knowledge and skills areas.

McGraw-Hill Customer Care Contact Information

At McGraw-Hill, we understand that getting the most from new technology can be challenging. That's why our services don't stop after you purchase our products. You can e-mail our Product Specialists 24 hours a day to get product training online. Or you can search our knowledge bank of Frequently Asked Questions on our support Website. For Customer Support, call 800-331-5094 or visit www.mhhe.com/support. One of our Technical Support Analysts will be able to assist you in a timely fashion.

ALEKS®

ALEKS® for the Accounting Cycle and ALEKS® for Financial Accounting

Available from McGraw-Hill over the World Wide Web, ALEKS (Assessment and LEarning in Knowledge Spaces) provides precise assessment and individualized instruction in the fundamental skills your students need to succeed in accounting.

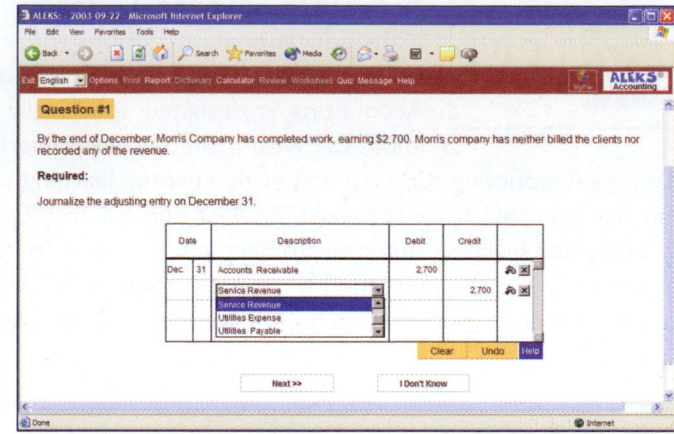

ALEKS motivates your students because ALEKS can tell what a student knows, doesn't know, and is most ready to learn next. ALEKS does this using the ALEKS Assessment and Knowledge Space Theory as an artificial intelligence engine to exactly identify a student's knowledge of accounting. When students focus on precisely what they are ready to learn, they build the confidence and learning momentum that fuel success.

To learn more about adding ALEKS to your principles course, visit www.business.aleks.com.

How Can Students Study on the Go Using Their iPod?

iPod Content

Harness the power of one of the most popular technology tools students use today—the Apple iPod. Our innovative approach allows students to download audio and video presentations right into their iPod and take learning materials with them wherever they go. Students just need to visit the Online Learning Center at **www.mhhe.com/wildCA2e** to download our iPod content. For each chapter of the book they will be able to download audio-narrated lecture presentations designed for use on various versions of iPods.

It makes review and study time as easy as putting in headphones.

How Can Text-Related Web Resources Enhance My Course?

Online Learning Center (OLC)

We offer an Online Learning Center (OLC) that follows *College Accounting* chapter by chapter. It doesn't require any building or maintenance on your part. It's ready to go the moment you and your students type in the URL: www.mhhe.com/wildCA2e. As students study and learn from *College Accounting*, they can visit the Student Edition of the OLC Website to work with a multitude of helpful tools:

- Generic Template Working Papers
- Chapter Learning Objectives
- Interactive Chapter Quizzes
- PowerPoint® Presentations
- Narrated PowerPoint® Presentations
- iPod Content
- Excel Template Assignments

A secured Instructor Edition stores essential course materials to save you prep time before class. Everything you need to run a lively classroom and an efficient course is included. All resources available to students, plus . . .

- Sample Syllabi
- Test Bank
- Instructor's Manual
- Solutions Manual
- Solutions to Excel Template Assignments

The OLC Website also serves as a doorway to other technology solutions, like course management systems.

Learning Objectives

Each chapter opens with Learning Objectives that are highlighted throughout the chapter body and end-of-chapter materials. These Learning Objectives give students direction on the concepts that they are building on and focus their learning. The chapter opener also provides "A Look Back," "A Look at This Chapter," and "A Look Ahead" to inform students where they are, where they were, and where they will be going to help better direct them on their journey through *College Accounting*.

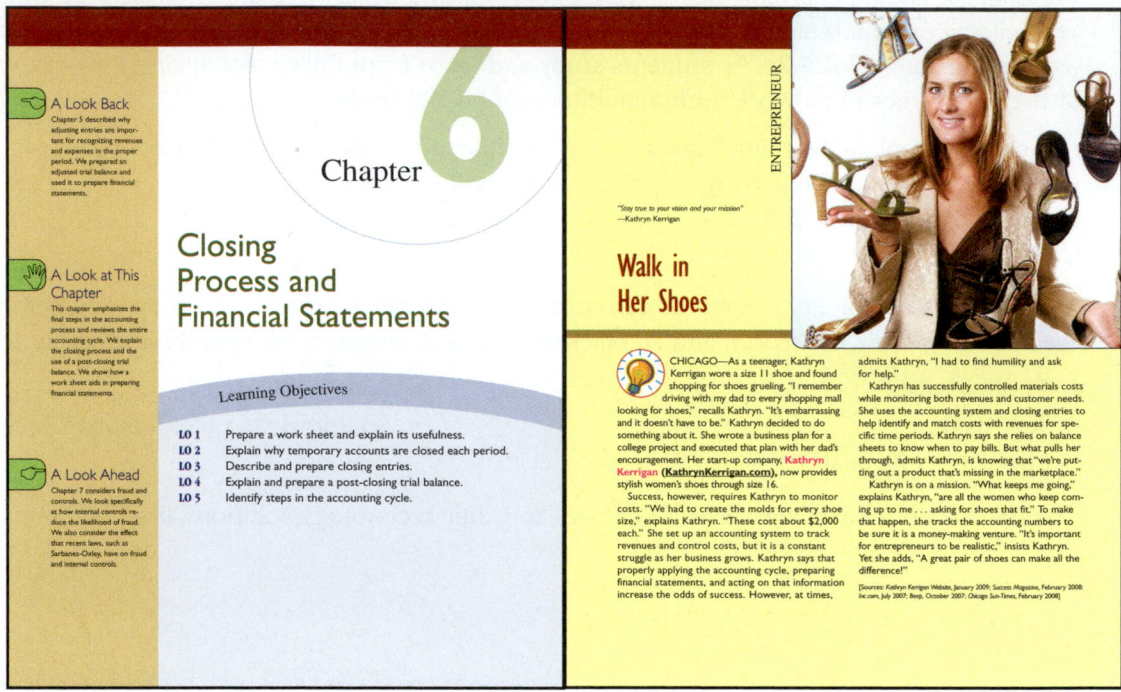

Whether we prepare, analyze, or apply accounting information, one skill remains essential: decision making. To help develop good decision-making habits and to illustrate the relevance of accounting, *College Accounting* uses a unique pedagogical framework comprised of a variety of approaches, giving students insight into every aspect of business decision making. Many later chapters also include a tool, such as ratio analysis, that uses accounting data to better understand company operations. An "In the News" feature offers information relevant to students entering the business world.

IN THE NEWS

Perpetual Accounting   **Wal-Mart** uses a network of information links with its point-of-sale cash registers to coordinate sales, purchases, and distribution. Its supercenters, for instance, ring up to 15,000 separate sales on heavy days. By using cash register information, the company can fix pricing mistakes quickly and capitalize on sales trends.

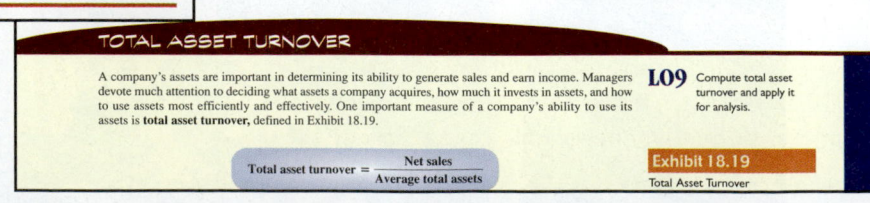

TOTAL ASSET TURNOVER

A company's assets are important in determining its ability to generate sales and earn income. Managers devote much attention to deciding what assets a company acquires, how much it invests in assets, and how to use assets most efficiently and effectively. One important measure of a company's ability to use its assets is **total asset turnover**, defined in Exhibit 18.19.

LO9   Compute total asset turnover and apply it for analysis.

$$\text{Total asset turnover} = \frac{\text{Net sales}}{\text{Average total assets}}$$

Exhibit 18.19
Total Asset Turnover

Chapter Preview with Flow Chart

This feature provides a handy textual/visual guide at the start of each chapter. Students can begin their reading with a clear understanding of what they will learn and when, which allows them to stay more focused and organized along the way.

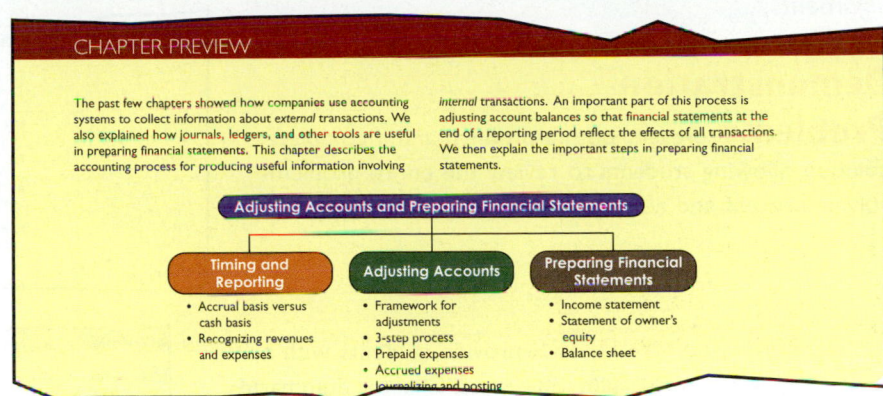

How You Doin'?

These short question/answer features reinforce the material immediately preceding them. They allow the reader to pause and reflect on the topics described, then receive immediate feedback before going on to new topics. Answers are provided at the end of each chapter.

Marginal Student Annotations

These annotations provide students with additional hints, tips, and examples to help them more fully understand the concepts and retain what they have learned. The annotations also include notes on global implications of accounting and further examples.

FastForward

FastForward is a case that takes students through the Accounting Cycle, Chapters 2–6. The FastForward icon is placed in the margin whenever this case is discussed.

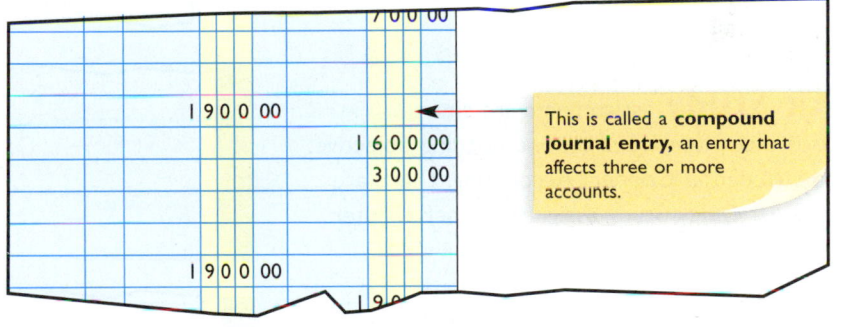

How are chapter concepts

Once a student has finished reading the chapter, how well he or she retains the material can depend greatly on the questions, exercises, and problems that reinforce it. This book leads the way in comprehensive, accurate end-of-chapter assignments.

Demonstration Problems present both a problem and a complete solution, allowing students to review the entire problem-solving process and achieve success.

Chapter Summaries provide students with a review organized by learning objectives. Chapter Summaries recap each learning objective.

Key Terms are bolded in the text and repeated at the end of the chapter with definitions and page numbers indicating their location. The book also includes a complete Glossary of Key Terms.

Multiple Choice Quizzes

In response to review and focus group feedback, the authors have created Multiple Choice Quizzes that quickly test chapter knowledge before a student moves on to complete Quick Studies, Exercises, and Problems.

Quick Study assignments are short exercises that often focus on one learning objective. All are included in Connect Accounting. There are usually 8–10 Quick Study assignments per chapter.

Exercises are one of this book's many strengths and a competitive advantage. There are about 10–15 per chapter and all are included in Connect Accounting.

Problem Sets A & B

are proven problems that can be assigned as homework or for in-class projects. All problems are coded according to one or more learning objectives, and items from Problem Set A are included in Connect Accounting.

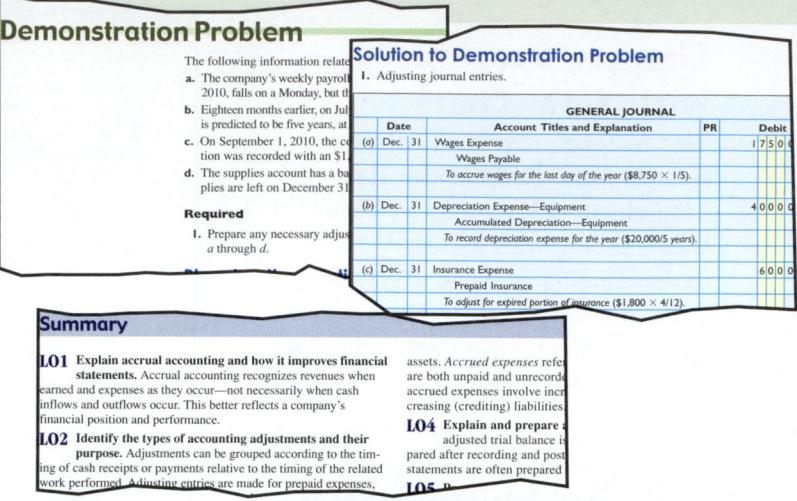

Demonstration Problem

The following information relate
a. The company's weekly payroll
2010, falls on a Monday, but th
b. Eighteen months earlier, on Jul
is predicted to be five years, at
c. On September 1, 2010, the co
tion was recorded with an $1.
d. The supplies account has a ba
plies are left on December 31

Required
1. Prepare any necessary adjus
a through *d*.

Solution to Demonstration Problem
1. Adjusting journal entries.

GENERAL JOURNAL

	Date		Account Titles and Explanation	PR	Debit	
(a)	Dec.	31	Wages Expense		1 7 5 0 0	
			Wages Payable			
			To accrue wages for the last day of the year ($8,750 × 1/5).			
(b)	Dec.	31	Depreciation Expense—Equipment		4 0 0 0 0	
			Accumulated Depreciation—Equipment			
			To record depreciation expense for the year ($20,000/5 years).			
(c)	Dec.	31	Insurance Expense		6 0 0 0	
			Prepaid Insurance			
			To adjust for expired portion of insurance ($1,800 × 4/12).			

Summary

LO1 Explain accrual accounting and how it improves financial statements. Accrual accounting recognizes revenues when earned and expenses as they occur—not necessarily when cash inflows and outflows occur. This better reflects a company's financial position and performance.

LO2 Identify the types of accounting adjustments and their purpose. Adjustments can be grouped according to the timing of cash receipts or payments relative to the timing of the related work performed. Adjusting entries are made for prepaid expenses,

assets. *Accrued expenses* refer
are both unpaid and unrecorde
accrued expenses involve incr
creasing (crediting) liabilities

LO4 Explain and prepare a
adjusted trial balance is
pared after recording and post
statements are often prepared

LO5 P

Key Terms

Accrual basis accounting (p. 104) Accounting system that recognizes revenues when earned and expenses as they occur; the basis for GAAP.
Accrued expenses (p. 109) Costs incurred in a period that are both unpaid and unrecorded; adjusting entries for recording accrued expenses involve increasing expenses and increasing liabilities.
Adjusted trial balance (p. 110) List of accounts and balances prepared after period-end adjustments are recorded and posted.
Adjusting entry (p. 106) Journal entry at the end of an accounting period to bring an asset or liability account to its proper amount and

Contra account (p. 108
having an opposite norm
other account's balance.
Depreciation (p. 108) E
and equipment to period
expense of using the asse
Fiscal year (p. 105) Co
chosen as the organizatio
Interim financial state

Multiple Choice Quiz   Answers on p. 125

Additional Multiple Choice Quizzes are available at the book's Website.

1. A company forgot to record accrued and unpaid employee wages of $350,000 at period-end. This oversight would
   a. Understate net income by $350,000.
   b. Overstate net income by $350,000.
   c. Have no effect on net income.
   d. Overstate assets by $350,000.
   e. Understate assets by $350,000.

     a. $4,000
     b. $8,000
     c. $12,000
     d. $20,000
     e. $24,000

2. Prior to recording adjusting entries, the Office Supplies account has a $450 debit balance. A physical count of supplies shows $125 of unused supplies still available. The required adjusting entry is:

4. A company purchases a deli
   2010. The truck is estimated
   zero salvage value. The com
   of depreciation. How much
   on the

connect

QUICK STUDY

QS 5–1
Computing accrual income and cash income **LO1**

In its first year of operations, Case Co. earned $60,000 in revenues and received $52,000 cash from these customers. The company recorded expenses of $37,500 but had not paid $6,000 of them by the end of the year. The company also prepaid $3,250 cash for next year's insurance premium. Calculate Case Co.'s first year net income under (a) the cash basis and (b) the accrual basis of accounting.

connect

EXERCISES

Exercise 5–1
Determining assets and expenses for accrual and cash accounting **LO1**

On November 1, 2009, a company paid a $15,300 premium on a 36-month insurance policy for coverage beginning on that date. Refer to that policy and fill in the blanks in the following table.

Balance Sheet Prepaid Insurance Asset Using			Insurance Expense Using		
	Accrual Basis	Cash Basis		Accrual Basis	Cash Basis
Dec. 31, 2009	$_____	$_____	2009	$_____	$_____
Dec. 31, 2010	_____	_____	2010	_____	_____
Dec. 31, 2011	_____	_____	2011	_____	_____
Dec. 31, 2012	_____	_____	2012	_____	_____
			Total	$_____	$_____

Check 2011 insurance expense:
Accrual, $5,100; Cash, $0. Dec. 31,
2011, asset: Accrual, $4,250; Cash, $0.

PROBLEM SET A

Problem 5–1A
Preparing adjusting entries, adjusted trial balance, and financial statements
LO3 LO4 LO5

eXcel
mhhe.com/wildCA2e

Wells Technical Institute (WTI), a sc
pay tuition directly to the school. WT
trial balance as of December 31, 2010
tries on December 31, 2010, follow.

Additional Information
a. An analysis of the school's insura
b. A count shows that teaching supp
c. Annual depreciation on the equip
d. Annual depreciation on the profes
e. The school's two employees are p
   at the rate of $100 per day for eac
f. The balance in the Prepaid Rent a

as of December 31, 2010. The Institute
rectly to the business and offers exten-
al balance are items *a* through *f* that re-

PROBLEM SET B

Problem 5–1B
Preparing adjusting entries, adjusted trial balance, and financial statements **LO3 LO4 LO5**

Beyond the Numbers exercises ask students to use accounting figures and understand their meaning. Students also learn how accounting applies to a variety of business situations. These creative and fun exercises are divided into sections:

- Reporting in Action
- Comparative Analysis
- Ethics Challenge
- Workplace Communication
- Taking It To The Net
- Teamwork in Action
- Entrepreneurs in Business
- Your Ethics Call
- You Call It

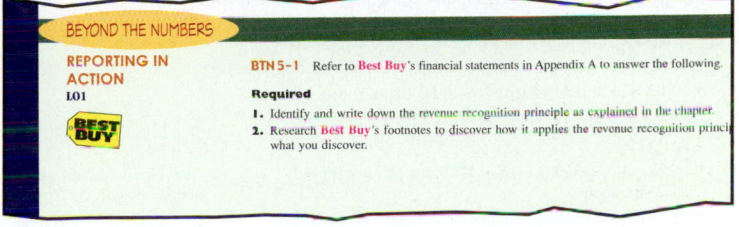

Serial Problems use a continuous running case study to illustrate chapter concepts in a familiar context. Serial Problems can be followed continuously from the first chapter or picked up at any later point in the book; enough information is provided to ensure students can get right to work.

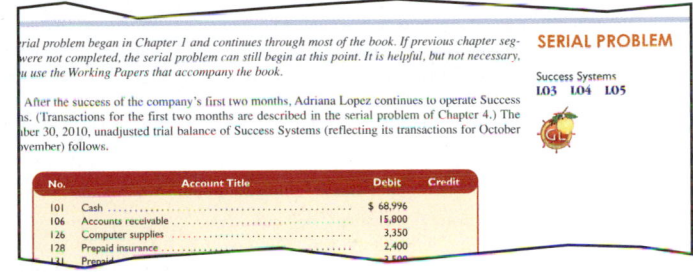

Appendix on Accounting Principles discusses a rules-based versus a principles-based accounting system. It also describes the objectives, characteristics, and assumptions of accounting principles.

The End of the Chapter Is Only the Beginning

Our valuable and proven assignments aren't just confined to the book. From problems that require technological solutions to materials found exclusively online, this book's end-of-chapter material is fully integrated with its technology package.

- Quick Studies, Exercises, and Problems available on Connect Accounting (see page ix) are marked with an icon.

- Problems supported by the Quickbooks Software are marked with an icon.

- The Online Learning Center (OLC) includes Personal Interactive Quizzes and Excel template assignments.

- Problems supported with Microsoft Excel template assignments are marked with an icon.

mhhe.com/wildCA2e

Put Away Your Red Pen

We pride ourselves on the accuracy of this book's assignment materials. Independent research reports that instructors and reviewers point to the accuracy of this book's assignment materials as one of its key competitive advantages.

The authors extend a special thanks to accuracy checker Anna Boulware, St. Charles Community College.

Enhancements for College Accounting 2e

This edition's revisions are driven by feedback from instructors and students. Many of the revisions are summarized here. Feedback suggests that this is the book instructors want to teach from and students want to learn from. General revisions include:

- Updated design-visual graphics and text layout
- New and revised entrepreneurial elements throughout text
- Revised end of chapter material throughout text
- New feature company, Best Buy, with Annual Report, and comparison to RadioShack

Chapter 1

- Updated Opener, **LoveSac,** with revised entrepreneurial assignment
- Improved discussion and graphic on users of accounting information
- Updated graphic on accounting salaries
- New discussion on experience and education requirements for entry-level accounting jobs
- Expanded discussion on sources of ethical guidance
- New discussion of organization structures
- New discussion of types of businesses
- New graphic on recent publicized accounting scandals
- New reference to the Public Company Accounting Oversight Board
- New information on real-world companies' use of accounting principles
- Revised end-of-chapter material, including 7 new questions

Chapter 2

- New Opener, **SPANX,** with new entrepreneurial assignment
- Simplified discussion of 3-step process for analyzing transactions
- New exhibit on links between financial statements
- New discussion of financial statement headings and alternative names
- Clarified discussion of items that impact owner's equity
- Revised end-of-chapter material, including 15 new questions

Chapter 3

- Updated Opener, **Cake Love,** with revised entrepreneurial assignment
- Clarified discussion of T-accounts
- New simplified 3-step process for determining postings to T-accounts
- Enhanced discussion of normal balances
- Enhanced discussion on prepayments
- Increased clarity of exhibit illustrating expanded accounting equation
- Increased clarity of exhibit illustrating the rules of debit and credit
- Revised end-of-chapter material, including 10 new questions

Chapter 4

- Updated Opener, **Vosges Haut Chocolate,** with revised entrepreneurial assignment
- Enhanced exhibit on the recording process
- Clarified discussion and added exhibit comparing the T-account with the general ledger account
- Simplified discussion of the journalizing and posting process
- New exhibits on the journalizing and posting process
- Enhanced discussion of correcting errors
- Revised end-of-chapter material, including 14 new questions

Chapter 5

- New Opener, **PopCap Games**, with revised entrepreneurial assignment
- New discussion of accrual basis versus cash basis accounting
- New exhibit comparing effects of accrual basis versus cash basis accounting
- New discussion of why certain accounts are adjusted
- New exhibit on framework for adjustments
- Simplified 3-step adjusting process and examples
- New exhibits on journalizing and posting adjusting entries
- Revised end-of-chapter material, including 11 new questions

Chapter 6

- New Opener, **Kathryn Kerrigan**, with revised entrepreneurial assignment
- New discussion on the benefits and uses of a work sheet
- New discussion of preparing pro-forma financial statements
- Simplified discussion on preparing the work sheet
- New graphic on sorting accounts to financial statement columns on the work sheet
- New graphic on how to determine income or loss from work sheet totals
- Clarified discussion on how to balance the work sheet for either income or loss
- New discussion and exhibit on treatment of additional owner investment
- New discussion of handling errors on the work sheet
- Simplified discussion of the closing process
- Enhanced graphic on closing process
- Enhanced exhibit showing the use of the work sheet in the closing process
- Revised end-of-chapter material, including 6 new questions
- Two new practice sets covering the full accounting cycle

Chapter 7

- New Opener, **Dylan's Candy Bar**, with revised entrepreneurial assignment
- New graphic, ways to detect fraud
- New discussion on fraud detection
- New exhibit, fraud red flags
- Added examples of real fraud cases

Chapter 8

- Updated Opener, **Wildflower Linen**, with revised entrepreneurial assignment
- New exhibit illustrating signature card document
- New section and exhibit on blank and restrictive endorsements
- New graphic and explanation of non-sufficient funds and overdraft fees
- Revised end-of-chapter material, including 8 new questions

Chapter 9

- New Opener, **Feed Granola Company**, with revised entrepreneurial assignment
- New discussion of independent contractors
- Enhanced discussion of self-employment taxes
- New illustration of Social Security taxes that exceed the maximum earnings limit
- New illustration of the Medicare tax
- Updated with new minimum wage (as of July 24, 2009)
- Updated with 2009 tax withholding tables

Chapter 10

- Updated Opener, **1-800-GOT-JUNK**, with revised entrepreneurial assignment
- Added new How You Doin'? questions
- Simplified discussion of federal unemployment taxes and credit for state unemployment taxes
- Simplified journal entries for federal and state unemployment taxes

Chapter 11

- Updated Opener, **Life is Good**, with revised entrepreneurial assignment
- Enhanced examples of wholesalers and retailers
- Enhanced discussion of cash receipts journal with associated end of chapter assignments

Chapter 12

- Updated Opener, **CoCaLo**, with revised entrepreneurial assignment
- Chapter now begins with section on Accounting for Merchandise Purchases
- Enhanced discussion of cash disbursements journal with associated end of chapter assignments
- Revised end-of-chapter material, including 10 new questions
- Two new practice sets covering special journals and subsidiary ledgers

Chapter 13

- **New Opener**, **BigBadToyStore**, with new entrepreneurial assignment
- Continues Z-Mart example from previous merchandising chapters for continuity and clarity
- New discussion and computation examples of net sales, net purchases, cost of goods sold, and gross profit
- Simplified presentation of the work sheet for merchandisers
- New discussion of adjustment for merchandise inventory
- New exhibits on journalizing and posting adjustments for merchandise inventory
- Simplified chart and discussion of framework for adjustments
- Simplified discussion of adjusting journal entries for a merchandiser
- Simplified discussion of unearned revenues and their adjustment
- New second Demonstration Problem added
- Revised end-of-chapter material, including 15 new questions

Chapter 14

- **New Opener**, **RockBottomGolf,** with revised entrepreneurial assignment
- Continued Z-Mart example from previous merchandising chapters for continuity and clarity
- Simplified work sheet presentation and exhibit
- New section on statement of owner's equity
- New table showing items that impact owner's equity and their information sources
- Simplified closing entries section
- New section on post-closing trial balance
- New exhibit, postings to Income Summary account
- New exhibit on use of work sheet in preparing closing entries
- Revised end-of-chapter material, including 14 new questions

Chapter 15

- **New Opener**, **Under Armor,** with revised entrepreneurial assignment
- Updated exhibit on accounts receivable for selected companies
- New exhibit on differences in methods to account for uncollectible accounts
- New exhibit on days in receivables across different industries

Chapter 16

- **Updated Opener**, **TOKYOPOP**, with revised entrepreneurial assignment
- Added interest computation formula throughout chapter for easy reference and clarity
- Enhanced section on times interest earned ratio

Chapter 17

- **New Opener**, **Beauty Encounter**, with new entrepreneurial assignment
- Updated section on analysis of inventory management
- Revised end-of-chapter materials, including an assignment that evaluates if Wal-Mart lives up to its reputation of quick inventory turnover

Chapter 18

- **New Opener**, **Sambazon**, with revised entrepreneurial assignment
- Updated exhibit on plant assets of selected companies, as a percent of assets.
- Section now focuses on depletion of natural resources

Chapter 19

- **New Opener**, **Samanta Shoes**, with new entrepreneurial assignment
- Updated real-world examples including those for Macadamia Orchards and Big River
- New example of partnership accounting using Trump Entertainment Resorts

Chapter 20

- **New Opener**, **Inogen**, with revised entrepreneurial assignment
- Revised end-of-chapter material, including new capital structure comparisons between Best Buy and RadioShack

Chapter 21

- **Updated Opener**, **Crocs**, with revised entrepreneurial assignment
- Simplified discussion of taxable income
- Updated Tax Tables with 2009 Tax Rates
- Updated example of Statement of Stockholder's Equity from Apple Computer
- Added news of recent stock split at feature company, Crocs
- Simplified discussion of dividend yield

Chapter 22

- **New Opener**, **Rap Snacks**, with new entrepreneurial assignment
- Enhanced discussion on the basics of bonds
- Streamlined discussion of bond retirement before maturity
- Added new example of bond retirement by conversion
- Streamlined discussion of other types of long-term financing
- Debt-to-equity Ratio discussion, features new Six Flags example

Chapter 23

- **Updated Opener**, **Ashtae Products**, with revised entrepreneurial assignment
- Added list of the required financial statements for statement of cash flows preparation
- Added discussion to the indirect vs. direct method of preparing statement of cash flows

Chapter 24

- **Updated Opener**, **Motley Fool**, with revised entrepreneurial assignment
- Chapter completely revised, combining Chapters 24 and 25 of the prior edition into one all-new chapter
- Revised discussion of horizontal and vertical analysis
- New ratio analysis compares Best Buy to RadioShack and industry averages for comparative benchmark analysis
- Revised end-of-chapter material

Chapter 25

- **New Opener**, **Kernel Seasons**, with revised entrepreneurial assignment
- New discussion on the IMA's road-map for resolving ethical dilemmas
- Updated real-world examples including that for Apple's iPhone and Briggs Stratton
- Reformatted several exhibits for improved clarity
- Added balance sheet to exhibit that shows cost flows across accounting reports
- New exercise on how inventory fraud impacts Best Buy

Chapter 26

- **New Opener**, **Sprinturf**, with new entrepreneurial assignment
- Brought chapter forward, so Job Order Cost Accounting is now covered prior to Departmental Accounting
- Streamlined explanation of closing over- and underapplied overhead
- New discussion of employee fraud schemes involving disbursements
- New discussion of employee fraud schemes involving payroll and clock cards

Chapter 27

- **Updated Opener**, **Jungle Jim's International Market**
- Revised end-of-chapter material, including a new Internet exercise involving Best Buy's Corporate Responsibility reporting

Chapter 28

- **New Opener**, **Martin Guitar Company**, with new entrepreneurial assignment
- Revised exhibits showing variance calculations for increased simplicity
- Expanded discussion of analyzing variances for added insight
- New assignment on benchmarking

Chapter 29

- **New Opener**, **Prairie Sticks Bat Company**, with revised entrepreneurial assignment

Supplements

Instructor

Instructor's Resource CD-ROM

ISBN: 9780077268817
MHID: 0077268814

This is your all-in-one resource. It allows you to create custom presentations from your own materials or from the following text-specific materials provided in the CD's asset library:

- Instructor's Resource Manual
- Solutions Manual. *Prepared by John J. Wild, Vernon J. Richardson, and Ken W. Shaw.*
- Test Bank, Computerized Test Bank. *Prepared by Linda Muren and Veronica Czekaj, Cuyahoga Community College.*
- PowerPoint® Presentations allow for revision of lecture slides, and include a viewer, allowing screens to be shown with or without the software. *Prepared by Jason Bess, Stautzenberger College.*
- Excel Template Assignments
- Link to PageOut

Student

Study Guide and Working Papers

Vol. 1, Chapters 1–14
ISBN: 9780077268855
MHID: 0077268857

Written by John J. Wild, Vernon J. Richardson and Ken W. Shaw.

Electronic Study Guide and Excel Working Papers CD

Chapters 1–29
ISBN: 9780077268787
MHID: 0077268784

Written by John J. Wild, Vernon J. Richardson, and Ken W. Shaw.

Study Guide and Working Papers delivered in Excel spreadsheets. Excel Working Papers are available on CD-ROM and can be bundled with the printed Working Papers; see your representative for information. The Study Guide covers each chapter and appendix with reviews of the learning objectives, outlines of the chapters, summaries of chapter materials, and additional problems with solutions.

QuickBooks Pro2010 Student Guide and Templates

ISBN: 9780077399443
MHID: 0077399447

Prepared by Carol Yacht.

To better prepare students for accounting in the real world, select end-of-chapter material in the text is tied to Quickbooks software. The accompanying student guide provides a step-by-step walkthrough for students on how to complete the problem in the software.

The authors extend special thanks to the supplement authors and accuracy checkers:

Test Bank: Linda Muren and Veronica Czekaj, Cuyahoga Community College

PowerPoint Presentations: Jason Bess, Stautzenberger College

Online Quizzes: Anna Boulware, St. Charles Community College

Supplement accuracy and quality assurance: Helen Roybark, Radford University; Beth Woods, Accuracy Counts; Lorie Darche, Southwest Florida College

The authors and McGraw-Hill/Irwin would like to recognize the following instructors for their valuable feedback and involvement in the development of *College Accounting 2e*. We are thankful for their suggestions, counsel, and encouragement.

Cornelia Alsheimer-Barthel, Santa Barbara City College

Jack Aschkenazi, American Intercontinental University Online

Marjorie Ashton, Truckee Meadows Community College

Jeanne Bedell, Keiser University

Sean Bell, Advanced Career Training

Jason Bess, Stautzenberger College

Juanita Garza Blankenship, Del Mar College

Sara Bottomley, Indiana Business College

Anna Boulware, St. Charles Community College

Judith Brierley, Seminole Community College

Peggy Brock, Central New Mexico Community College

Rebecca F. Brown, Des Moines Area Community College

Joan Cook, Milwaukee Area Technical College

Dean Danielson, San Joaquin Delta College

Lorie Darche, Southwest Florida College

Susan Snow Davis, Green River Community College

Vincent DeBiase II, San Joaquin Valley College

Carol Easley, National College

Steven Ernest, Baton Rouge Community College

Vanessa Escalante, LA College International

Richard Firth, Colorado Technical University

Mark Fronke, Cerritos College

Marina Grau, Houston Community College

Betty Habershon, Prince George's Community College

Toni Hartley, Laurel Business Institute

Christina Hata, MiraCosta College

Keith Hendrick, DeKalb Technical College

YuanRong Jia-Reid, Huntington Junior College

Dennis Jirkovsky, Indiana Business College and Longview Community College

Vern Jorgensen, Southwestern College

Dmitriy Kalyagin, Chabot College

Rosemary Keasey, Butler County Community College

Donna Kimmerling, Indiana Business College

Barbara Krause, South Hills School of Business

Kimberly Lamb, Stautzenberger College

Greg Lauer, North Iowa Area Community College-Mason

David Laurel, South Texas College

Harold Lea, Fashion Institute of Design

Mary E. Leslie, Grossmont College

Lolita Lockett, Jones College

Delores Loedel, MiraCosta College

Thomas Lynch, Hocking College

James B. Meir, Cleveland State Community College

Julie Miller-Millmann, Chippewa Valley Tech College

Anita Morgan, Colorado Technical University Online

Cathy Nash, Dekalb Technical College

Joe Nicassio, Westmoreland County Community College

Sharon Owens, Westwood College

Gary Reynolds, Ozarks Technical Community College

Brenda Richter, Santa Barbara City College

Alberta E. Robinson, Indiana Business College

Amanda J. Salinas, Palo Alto College

Jan Sedely, Ohio Business College

Elizabeth Serapin, Columbia Southern University

Gabrielle Serrano, Elgin Community College

Daniel P. Small, J. Sargeant Reynolds Community College

Lauren Smith, Front Range Community College

Joan Thomas, National College

Bill Thompson, Full Sail Real World Education

Patricia Walczk, Lansing Community College

Roger Waller, San Joaquin Delta Community College

Elry Wallman, Institute of Business and Medical Careers

We would like to thank the entire McGraw-Hill/Irwin *College Accounting* team, including Stewart Mattson, Tim Vertovec, Steve Schuetz, Christina Sanders, Lori Koetters, Matthew Baldwin, Carol Bielski, Lori Kramer, and Brian Nacik as well as Aaron Downey from Matrix Productions. We also thank the great marketing and sales support staff, including Kathleen Klehr, Michelle Heaster, Sankha Basu, and Abbey Woodward. Many talented educators and professionals worked hard to create the supplements for this book, and for their efforts we're grateful. Finally, many more people we either did not meet or whose efforts we did not personally witness nevertheless helped to make this book everything that it is, and we thank them all.

John Wild   Vernon Richardson   Ken Shaw

Brief Contents

*Appendixes C and D are not printed in the text; they are available on the book's Website, mhhe.com/wildCA2e.

Contents

26 Job Order Cost Accounting 712

27 Departmental and Responsibility Accounting 748

28 Budgets and Standard Costing 776

29 Relevant Costing for Managerial Decisions 804

College Accounting

A Look at This Chapter

Accounting plays a crucial role in the information age. In this chapter, we discuss the importance of accounting to different types of organizations and describe its many users and uses. We explain that ethics are crucial to accounting. We also describe the meaning and source of generally accepted accounting principles.

A Look Ahead

Chapter 2 introduces the accounting equation and how it helps to describe business transactions. Chapters 2 through 6 show (via the accounting cycle) how financial statements reflect business activities.

Chapter

Introduction to Accounting

Learning Objectives

LO 1   Explain the purpose and importance of accounting in the information age.

LO 2   Identify users and uses of accounting.

LO 3   Identify career opportunities in accounting and related fields.

LO 4   Explain why ethics are crucial to accounting.

LO 5   Explain the meaning of generally accepted accounting principles.

LO 6   Identify the groups that establish generally accepted accounting principles.

LO 7   Identify the three types of ownership structures.

A **short article** launches each chapter showing the relevance of accounting for a real entrepreneur. An **Entrepreneurs In Business** problem at the end of the assignments returns to this article with a mini-case.

"Ask everyone to give you money... remember, you hold the opportunity for them"
—Shawn Nelson

Love, Peace, and Profits

SALT LAKE CITY—Trying to get comfortable while watching TV, Shawn Nelson thought "a huge beanbag thing" would be far more relaxing than his old couch. So he made one—a big one! Seven feet across and shaped like a baseball, Shawn's creation was the talk of friends and neighbors. Shortly after making and selling a few "huge beanbag things," Shawn knew it needed a better name. Drawing on the 1960s retro spirit of "love and peace," Shawn named his invention the **LoveSac** and his company (**LoveSac.com**) was born.

Yet LoveSac's launch was anything but smooth. Shawn began by working out of his mother's basement. He then set up shop at trade shows and even the local drive-in cinema. He got his first big break when **Limited Too** called after seeing his display at a trade show. "I answered the phone," says Shawn, "Twelve thousand Sacs? Sure, no problem." Who was he kidding?

Shawn's debt swelled to over $50,000 as he worked 19-hour days and slept in the aged building in which he manufactured the Sacs. "It nearly broke me emotionally, physically, mentally," Shawn recalls.

"We finished the order but ate up all our profits." Without profits his business, too, would soon be retro. So Shawn approached furniture retailers to ask if they would carry Sacs. "Shawn can still hear the laughter," states LoveSac's Website.

Just when things seemed bleakest, Shawn's cousin suggested he open a retail location. Desperate, Shawn took a three-month lease in a shopping mall. His goal: sell one SuperSac per day. This would cover rent and pay him and his cousin a $5 hourly wage. Shawn then developed a transaction-based accounting system to get a handle on orders and sales.

Incredibly, customers crowded into his store within days of opening. Four weeks later and just before Christmas, customers were lined up outside the door waiting for Sacs to arrive from the factory. By Christmas Eve, Shawn's store was nearly sold out. Today, Shawn has more than 20 stores projected to generate over $30 million in sales. With results like that we'd all love Sacs!

[Sources: *LoveSac Website,* January 2009; *CNBC Business Nation interview,* February 2008; *Entrepreneur,* November 2004; *LA Confidential,* Fall 2004; *Life & Style Weekly,* June 2005.]

*A **Preview** opens each chapter with a summary of topics covered.*

Today's world is one of information—its preparation, communication, analysis, and use. Accounting is at the heart of this information age. Knowledge of accounting provides career opportunities and the insight to take advantage of them. This book introduces concepts, procedures, and analyses that help us make better decisions. In this chapter we describe accounting, the users and uses of accounting information, and career opportunities in accounting. We also emphasize the importance of ethics for accounting.

Introduction to Accounting

Importance of Accounting	**Opportunities in Accounting**	**Fundamentals of Accounting**
• Accounting information uses • Accounting information users	• Entry-level jobs • Careers in accounting • Accounting certifications	• Ethics is key • Generally accepted accounting principles • Ownership structures

Importance of Accounting

LO1 Explain the purpose and importance of accounting in the information age.

We live in an information age—a time of communication and immediate access to data, news, facts, and commentary. Information affects how we live, whom we associate with, and our opportunities. To fully benefit from the available information, we need knowledge of how the information system collects, processes, and reports information to decision makers.

Accounting Information Uses

Providing information about what businesses own, what they owe, and how they perform is an important aim of accounting. **Accounting** is an information and measurement system that identifies, records, and communicates information about an organization's business activities. *Identifying* business activities requires selecting transactions relevant to an organization. Examples are the sale of iPods by **Apple** and the receipt of ticket fees by **TicketMaster**. *Recording* business activities requires keeping a chronological log of transactions measured in dollars and classified and summarized in a useful format. *Communicating* business activities requires preparing accounting reports such as financial statements. It also requires analyzing and interpreting such reports. (The financial statements and notes of **Best Buy** and **RadioShack** are shown in Appendix A of this book.) Exhibit 1.1 summarizes accounting activities.

Real company names are printed in bold magenta.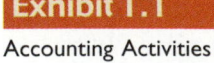

All aspects of business involve accounting. The most common contact with accounting is through credit approvals, checking accounts, tax forms, and payroll. These experiences tend to focus on the recordkeeping role of accounting. **Recordkeeping,** or **bookkeeping,** is the recording of transactions and events, either manually or electronically. This is just one part of accounting.

Exhibit 1.1

Accounting Activities

Identifying	Recording	Communicating
Select transactions and events	Input, measure, and classify	Prepare, analyze, and interpret

Accounting also identifies and communicates information on transactions and events, and it includes the crucial processes of analysis and interpretation.

Technology is a key part of modern business and plays a major role in accounting. Accounting software packages like *QuickBooks* and *Simply Accounting* reduce the time, effort, and cost of recordkeeping while improving clerical accuracy.

Accounting Information Users

Accounting is often called the *language of business* because all organizations set up an accounting information system to communicate information to help people make better decisions. Exhibit 1.2 shows that accounting users can be divided into two groups: internal users and external users.

Internal users

- Owners
- Managers
- Internal auditors
- Sales staff
- Budget officers
- Controllers

External users

- Lenders
- Shareholders
- Governments
- Consumer groups
- External auditors
- Customers

Exhibit 1.2

Users of Accounting Information

Infographics reinforce key concepts through visual learning.

Internal Information Users   **Internal users** of accounting information are those directly involved in managing and operating an organization. They use the information to help improve the efficiency and effectiveness of an organization. **Managerial accounting** is the area of accounting that serves the decision-making needs of internal users. Internal reports are not subject to the same rules as external reports and instead are designed with the special needs of internal users in mind.

Several types of internal users rely on accounting reports, including:

Owners   As the owner of **LoveSac**, Shawn Nelson needs accounting data to answer questions like:

- Are we keeping our production costs low enough?
- Should we expand into clothing and other accessories?
- Should we open more retail outlets?
- Do we need to borrow money?

Managers   As a business grows, its owner often must assign managers to certain duties.

- *Purchasing managers* need to know what, when, and how much to purchase.
- *Marketing managers* use reports about sales and costs to target customers; set prices; and monitor customer needs, tastes, and price concerns.
- *Human resource managers* need information about employees' payroll, benefits, performance, and compensation.
- *Production managers* depend on information to monitor costs and ensure quality.
- *Distribution managers* need reports for timely, accurate, and efficient delivery of products.
- *Service managers* need to know the costs and benefits of looking after products and services.
- *Research and development managers* need information about projected costs and revenues of any proposed changes in products and services.

Internal auditors   Internal auditors design and test their employer's internal controls. *Internal controls* are procedures designed to protect company property, ensure reliable reports, promote efficiency, and ensure employees follow company policies. Examples are good records, physical controls (locks, passwords, guards), and independent reviews.

LO2 Identify users and uses of accounting.

External Information Users   **External users** of accounting information are *not* directly involved in running the organization. They include shareholders (investors), lenders, directors, customers, suppliers, regulators, lawyers, brokers, and the press. External users have limited access to an organization's information. Yet their business decisions depend on information that is reliable, relevant, and comparable.

Financial accounting is the area of accounting aimed at serving external users by providing them with financial statements. These statements are known as *general-purpose financial statements*. The term *general-purpose* refers to the broad range of purposes for which external users rely on these statements.

Each external user has special information needs depending on the types of decisions to be made, including the following:

Capital providers

- *Lenders* (creditors) loan money or other resources to a business. Banks often are lenders. Lenders look for information to help them assess whether a business is likely to repay its loans with interest.
- *Shareholders* (investors) are the owners of a corporation. They use accounting reports in deciding whether to buy, hold, or sell stock. Shareholders typically elect a *board of directors* to oversee their interests in an organization. Since directors are responsible to shareholders, their information needs are similar.

External auditors

- *External* (independent) *auditors* examine financial statements to verify that they are prepared according to generally accepted accounting principles. Their work is overseen by the Public Company Accounting Oversight Board (PCAOB).

Labor unions

- *Labor unions* use financial statements to judge the fairness of wages, assess job prospects, and bargain for better wages.

Regulators

- The Internal Revenue Service (IRS) requires organizations to file accounting reports in computing taxes.
- Utility boards use accounting information to set utility rates.
- The Securities and Exchange Commission (SEC) requires reports for companies that sell their stock to the public.

Business associates

- *Suppliers* use accounting information to judge the soundness of a customer before making sales on credit.
- *Customers* use financial reports to assess the staying power of potential suppliers.

IN THE NEWS

In The News highlight relevant items from practice.

They Fought the Law   Our economic and social welfare depends on reliable accounting information. A few managers in recent years forgot that and are now paying their dues. They include L. Dennis Kozlowski of **Tyco**, convicted of falsifying accounting records; Bernard Ebbers of **WorldCom**, convicted of an $11 billion accounting scandal, and Andrew Fastow of **Enron**, guilty of hiding debt and inflating income.

Entrepreneurs, particularly in small companies, perform many of the tasks demanded of both external and internal users, and thus rely heavily on accounting information.

HOW YOU DOIN'?   Answers—p. 13

1. What is the purpose of accounting?
2. What is the relation between accounting and recordkeeping?
3. Who are the internal and external users of accounting information?
4. Identify at least five types of managers who are internal users of accounting information.
5. What are internal controls and why are they important?

How You Doin'? is a chance to stop and reflect on key points.

Opportunities in Accounting

Entry-Level Jobs

Accounting offers many types of jobs. Typical education and experience requirements for common entry-level jobs are described in Exhibit 1.3 below.

L03 Identify career opportunities in accounting and related fields.

Job Title	Education	Experience
Accounting clerk	1–2 accounting courses	Little or none
Bookkeeper	1–2 years of accounting courses	Some as an accounting clerk
Accountant	Two-year or four-year college degree	Little or none

Exhibit 1.3

Common Entry-Level Jobs

Career Paths

Accounting has four broad areas of opportunities: financial, managerial, taxation, and accounting-related. Exhibit 1.4 lists selected opportunities in each area.

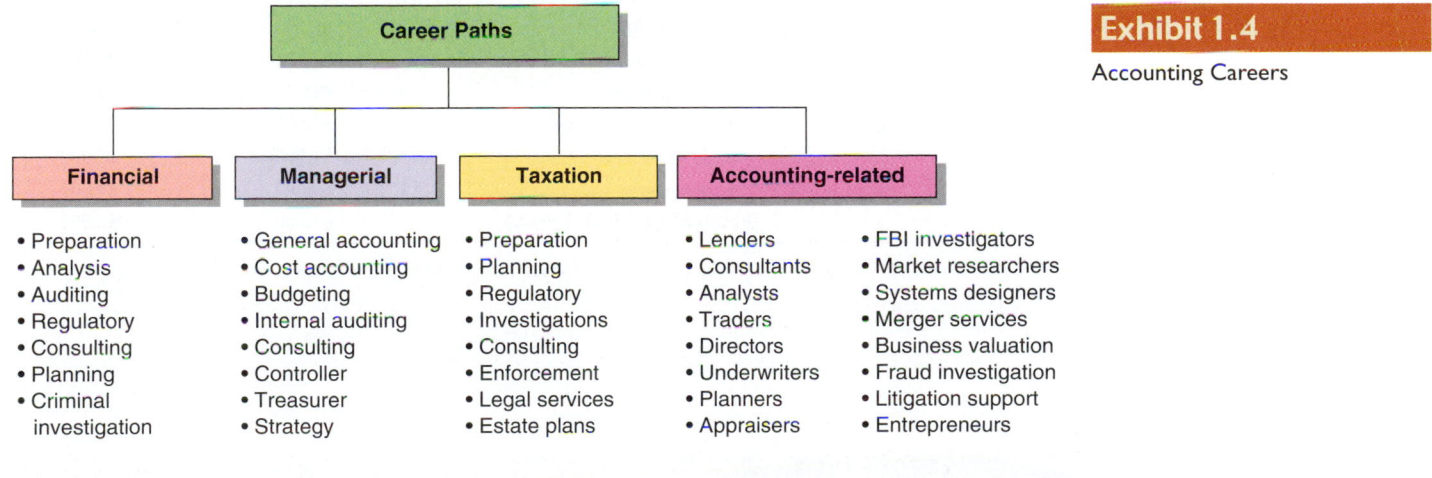

Exhibit 1.4

Accounting Careers

The majority of accounting opportunities are in *private accounting,* as shown in Exhibit 1.5. *Public accounting* offers the next largest number of opportunities. Private accountants are employed by a single company. Public accountants provide auditing, tax, and consulting work for

Exhibit 1.5

Accounting Jobs by Area

Graphical displays are often used to illustrate key points.

Private accounting 60%

Public accounting 25%

Government, not-for-profit and education 15%

other companies for service fees. Still other opportunities exist in government (and not-for-profit) agencies, including business regulation and investigation of law violations.

Certifications

Accounting specialists are highly regarded. Their professional standing often is denoted by a certificate. Employers look for specialists with designations such as certified book-keeper (CB), certified payroll professional (CPP), personal financial specialist (PFS), certified fraud examiner (CFE), and certified forensic accountant (CrFA). Certified public accountants (CPAs) must meet education and experience requirements, pass an examination, and exhibit ethical character. Many accounting specialists hold certificates in addition to or instead of the CPA. Two of the most common are the certificate in management accounting (CMA) and the certified internal auditor (CIA).

Individuals with accounting knowledge are always in demand. Benefit packages can include flexible work schedules, telecommuting options, career path alternatives, casual work environments, extended vacation time, and child and elder care.

Demand for accounting specialists is booming. Exhibit 1.6 reports average annual salaries for several accounting positions. Salary variation depends on location, company size, professional designation, experience, and other factors. For example, salaries for full-charge bookkeepers average $57,500 per year. Likewise, annual salaries for accounting clerks averages $37,500.

Exhibit 1.6

Accounting Salaries for Selected Fields

Field	Title (experience)	2007 Salary	2012 Estimate*
Public Accounting	Partner	$190,000	$242,500
	Manager (6–8 years)	94,500	120,500
	Senior (3–5 years)	72,000	92,000
	Junior (0–2 years)	51,500	65,500
Private Accounting	CFO	232,000	296,000
	Controller/Treasurer	147,500	188,000
	Manager (6–8 years)	87,500	111,500
	Senior (3–5 years)	72,500	92,500
	Junior (0–2 years)	49,000	62,500
Recordkeeping	Full-charge bookkeeper	57,500	73,500
	Accounts manager	51,000	65,000
	Payroll manager	54,500	69,500
	Accounting clerk (0–2 years)	37,500	48,000

*Estimates assume a 5% compounded annual increase over 2007 levels. For updated salary data go to www.aicpa.org, Abbott-Langer.com, or Kforce.com.

HOW YOU DOIN'?

Answers—p. 13

6. What career opportunities exist in the taxation area?

7. What types of certificates are available in accounting?

Fundamentals of Accounting

Accounting is guided by concepts and principles. This section describes two key fundamentals of accounting.

LO4 Explain why ethics are crucial to accounting.

Ethics—A Key Concept

The goal of accounting is to provide useful information for decisions. For information to be useful, it must be trusted. This demands ethics in accounting. **Ethics** are beliefs that distinguish right from wrong. They are accepted standards of good and bad behavior.

Identifying the ethical path is sometimes difficult. The preferred path is a course of action that avoids casting doubt on one's decisions. For example, accounting users are less likely to trust an auditor's report if the auditor's pay depends on the success of the client being audited. To avoid such concerns, ethical rules are often set. For example, external auditors are banned from direct investment in their client and cannot accept pay that depends on figures in the client's reports. Exhibit 1.7 gives guidelines for making ethical decisions.

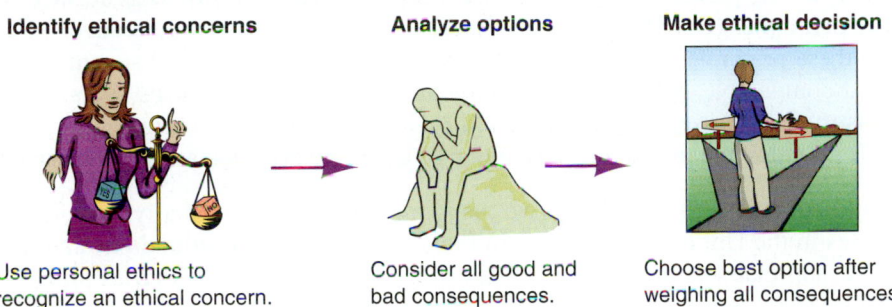

Identify ethical concerns	Analyze options	Make ethical decision
Use personal ethics to recognize an ethical concern.	Consider all good and bad consequences.	Choose best option after weighing all consequences.

Exhibit 1.7

Guidelines for Ethical Decision Making

Providers of accounting information often face ethical choices as they prepare financial reports. These choices can affect the price a buyer pays and the wages paid to workers. They can even affect the success of products and services. Misleading information can lead to a wrongful closing of a division that harms workers, customers, and suppliers. There is an old saying worth remembering: *Good ethics are good business.*

Accountants have many sources of ethical guidance. For example, the American Institute of Certified Public Accountants' *Code of Professional Ethics* is available at **www.aicpa.org**. The Institute of Management Accountants' *Statement of Ethical Professional Practice* (at **www.imanet.org**) provides guidance on ethical principles and how to resolve ethical conflicts. The **Sarbanes-Oxley Act** requires each issuer of securities to disclose whether it has adopted a code of ethics for its senior officers and the contents of that code. This act also requires that financial statements filed with the SEC be certified by the CEO and CFO as fairly representing the company's financial performance and position. Violators can receive a $5 million fine and/or up to 20 years in prison. Nevertheless, accounting abuses occur, as the listing below of some recent accounting scandals shows.

Company	Alleged Accounting Abuses
Enron	Inflated income, hid debt, and bribed officials
WorldCom	Understated expenses to inflate income and hid debt
Fannie Mae	Inflated income
Adelphia Communications	Understated expenses to inflate income and hid debt
AOL Time Warner	Inflated revenues and income
Xerox	Inflated income
Bristol-Myers Squibb	Inflated revenues and income
Nortel Networks	Understated expenses to inflate income
Global Crossing	Inflated revenues and income
Tyco	Hid debt, and CEO evaded taxes
Halliburton	Inflated revenues and income
Qwest Communications	Inflated revenues and income

IN THE NEWS

Virtuous Returns Virtue is not always its own reward. Compare the S&P 500 with the Domini Social Index (DSI), which covers 400 companies that have especially good records of social responsibility. We see that returns for companies with socially responsible behavior are at least as high as those of the S&P 500.

Copyright © 2007 by KLD Research & Analytics, Inc. The "Domini 400 Social Index" is a service mark of KLD Research & Analytics.

Graphical displays are often used to illustrate key points.

Generally Accepted Accounting Principles

LO5 Explain the meaning of generally accepted accounting principles.

Financial accounting practice is governed by concepts and rules known as **generally accepted accounting principles (GAAP).** To use and interpret financial statements effectively, we need to understand these principles. GAAP aims to make information in financial statements relevant, reliable, and comparable. *Relevant information* affects the decisions of its users. *Reliable information* is trusted by users. *Comparable information* is helpful in contrasting organizations. Appendix B provides a more detailed discussion of generally accepted accounting principles.

LO6 Identify the groups that establish generally accepted accounting principles.

Setting Accounting Principles Two main groups establish generally accepted accounting principles in the United States. The **Financial Accounting Standards Board (FASB)** is the private group that sets both broad and specific principles. The **Securities and Exchange Commission (SEC)** is the government group that establishes reporting requirements for companies that issue stock to the public.

In today's global economy, there is increased demand by external users for comparability in accounting reports. This often arises when companies wish to raise money from lenders and investors in different countries. To that end, the **International Accounting Standards Board (IASB)** issues *International Financial Reporting Standards (IFRS)* that identify preferred accounting practices. The IASB hopes to create more harmony among accounting practices of different countries. If standards are harmonized, one company can potentially use a single set of financial statements in all financial markets. Many countries' standard setters support the IASB, and differences between U.S. GAAP and IASB's practices are fading. Yet, the IASB does not have authority to impose its standards on companies.

Rules–Based versus Principles–Based U.S. accounting practices are often viewed as *rules-based*. This means that companies apply technical, specific, and detailed rules in preparing financial statements. A *principles-based* approach is sometimes argued as preferable. A principles-based system would develop and apply broad, fundamental concepts for reporting. Companies would have more flexibility in preparing principles-based reports. For example, a broad principle might be that a company must report all debt it might have to repay. Certain executives of **Enron** were able to mislead investors by not reporting some of its debt. While many of Enron's reports technically followed rules-based standards, the reports failed to adequately disclose its debts.

IN THE NEWS

Principles and Scruples Auditors, directors, and lawyers are using principles to improve accounting reports. Examples include accounting restatements at **Navistar**, financial restatements at **Nortel**, accounting reviews at **Echostar**, and expense adjustments at **Electronic Data Systems**. Principles-based accounting has led accounting firms to drop clients deemed too risky. Examples include **Grant Thornton**'s resignation as auditor of **Fremont General** due to alleged failures in providing information when promised, and **Ernst and Young**'s resignation as auditor of **Catalina Marketing** due to alleged accounting errors.

8. What three-step guidelines can help people make ethical decisions?

9. Why are ethics and social responsibility valuable to organizations?

10. Why are ethics crucial in accounting?

11. Who sets U.S. accounting rules?

12. How are U.S. companies affected by international accounting standards?

Ownership Structures

The **business entity assumption** means that a business is accounted for separately from other business and from its owners. This is necessary for making good business decisions. Businesses generally are of one of three major legal forms: *proprietorships, partnerships,* and *corporations.* In this book you will learn the accounting for each of these different business types.

LO7 Identify the three types of ownership structures.

1. A **sole proprietorship,** or simply **proprietorship,** is a business owned by one person. No special legal requirements must be met to start a proprietorship. It is a separate entity for accounting purposes, but it is *not* a separate legal entity from its owner. This means, for example, that a court can order an owner to sell personal belongings to pay a proprietorship's debt. This *unlimited liability* of a proprietorship is a disadvantage. However, an advantage is that a proprietorship's income is not subject to a business income tax but is instead reported and taxed on the owner's personal income tax return. Business characteristics are summarized in Exhibit 1.8.

Characteristic	Proprietorship	Partnership	Corporation
Business entity	yes	yes	yes
Legal entity	no	no	yes
Limited liability	no*	no*	yes
Unlimited life	no	no	yes
Business taxed	no	no	yes
One owner allowed	yes	no	yes

Exhibit 1.8

Characteristics of Businesses

* Proprietorships and partnerships that are set up as LLCs provide limited liability.

2. A **partnership** is a business owned by two or more people called *partners.* Like a proprietorship, no special legal requirements must be met in starting a partnership. The only requirement is an agreement between partners to run a business together. The agreement can be either oral or written and usually indicates how income and losses are to be shared. A partnership, like a proprietorship, is *not* legally separate from its owners. This means that each partner's share of profits is reported and taxed on that partner's tax return. It also means *unlimited liability* for its partners. However, several types of partnerships limit liability. The most common of these, a *limited liability company (LLC),* offers the limited liability of a corporation and the tax treatment of a partnership (and proprietorship).

3. A **corporation** is a business legally separate from its owners, meaning it is responsible for its own acts and its own debts. Separate legal status means that a corporation can conduct business with the rights, duties, and responsibilities of a person. A corporation acts through its managers, who are its legal agents. Separate legal status also means that its owners, who are called **shareholders** (or **stockholders**), are not personally liable for corporate acts and debts. This limited liability is its main advantage. A main disadvantage is what's called *double taxation*—meaning that (1) the corporation's income is taxed and (2) any distribution of income to the corporation's owners through dividends is taxed as part of the owners' personal income.

Types of Businesses Businesses can also be classified by the type of product or service they provide. A **service business** provides services to customers. These could include computer repair, catering, tax preparation, and many others. A **merchandising business** buys products from other companies and then resells them to consumers. **Best Buy**, **RadioShack**, and **Target** are well-known merchandisers. **Manufacturing businesses,** like **LoveSac**, make products to sell to either merchandisers and/or consumers. We will study the accounting for each of these business types in this book.

HOW YOU DOIN'?
Answers—p. 13

13. Why is the business entity assumption important?

14. What are the three basic forms of business organization?

15. What is the name given the owners of a corporation? What is the name given to the ownership units of a corporation?

---

*The **Demonstration Problem** is a review of key chapter content. Planning the Solution offers strategies in solving the problem.*

Demonstration Problem

After months of planning, Polly Guthrie opens SuperSub, a sandwich shop. Because this is her first time running a business, Polly is wondering who will use her financial statements.

Required

List four potential external or internal users of SuperSub's financial statements. Explain how they might use these statements.

Planning the Solution

- Look back at the list of possible external and internal users on pages 5 and 6 and think about how each might use SuperSub's financial statements.
- Consider any user that might use and need SuperSub's financial statements.

Solution to Demonstration Problem

Interested users would include:

1. Polly Guthrie, owner and internal user. Polly will use the financial statements to see where she is earning and spending her money. She can also use her financial statements to predict and budget for future sales and costs.
2. Internal Revenue Service, external user. This regulator will need to see SuperSub's accounting reports to compute and monitor the accurate payment of income tax.
3. Lenders (or a bank), external user. Owners periodically need loans to operate or expand their businesses. The bank often requests financial statements, which it can use to assess whether SuperSub will be able to repay its loans.
4. Suppliers (creditors), external user. Suppliers of the foodstuffs like assurance that they will get paid promptly. They will often ask for financial statements or additional financial information to get the information they need.

*A **Summary** organized by learning objectives concludes each chapter.*

Summary

LO1 **Explain the purpose and importance of accounting in the information age.** Accounting is an information and measurement system that aims to identify, record, and communicate relevant, reliable, and comparable information about business activities. It helps assess opportunities, products, investments, and social and community responsibilities.

LO2 **Identify users and uses of accounting.** Users of accounting are both internal and external. Some users and uses of accounting include (a) managers in controlling, monitoring, and planning; (b) lenders for measuring the risk and repayment of loans; (c) shareholders for assessing the return and risk of stock; (d) directors for overseeing management; and (e) employees for judging employment opportunities.

LO3 **Identify career opportunities in accounting and related fields.** Opportunities in accounting include financial, managerial, and tax accounting. They also include accounting-related fields such as lending, consulting, managing, and planning.

LO4 **Explain why ethics are crucial to accounting.** The goal of accounting is to provide useful information for decision making. For information to be useful, it must be trusted. This demands ethical behavior in accounting.

LO5 **Explain the meaning of generally accepted accounting principles.** Generally accepted accounting principles are a common set of standards applied by accountants. Accounting principles aid in producing relevant, reliable, and comparable information.

LO6 **Identify the groups that establish generally accepted accounting principles.** Generally accepted accounting principles (GAAP) are established by two main groups in the United States: the Financial Accounting Standards Board (FASB) and the Securities and Exchange Commission (SEC). The FASB is a private entity that sets financial accounting principles. The SEC is the governmental entity that establishes financial reporting requirements for companies that issue stock to the public.

LO7 **Identify the three types of ownership structures.** Proprietorships, partnerships, and corporations are the three main types of ownership structures. A proprietorship is a business owned by one person, while a partnership is owned by two or more partners. Proprietorships and partnerships are not separate legal entities from their owners. Corporations are separate legal entities from their owners, who are called shareholders.

Guidance Answers to   HOW YOU DOIN'?

1. Accounting is an information and measurement system that identifies, records, and communicates relevant information to help people make better decisions.

2. Recordkeeping, also called *bookkeeping,* is the recording of financial transactions and events, either manually or electronically. Recordkeeping is essential to data reliability; but accounting is this and much more. Accounting includes identifying, measuring, recording, reporting, and analyzing business events and transactions.

3. External users of accounting include lenders, shareholders, directors, customers, suppliers, regulators, lawyers, brokers, and the press. Internal users of accounting include managers, officers, and other internal decision makers involved with strategic and operating decisions.

4. Internal users (managers) include those from research and development, purchasing, human resources, production, distribution, marketing, and servicing.

5. Internal controls are procedures designed to protect assets, ensure reliable accounting reports, promote efficiency, and encourage adherence to company policies. Internal controls are crucial for relevant and reliable information.

6. Tax preparation, tax planning, and tax enforcement are among the various career opportunities in the taxation area.

7. Some of the certificates that exist in accounting include: certified public accountant (CPA), certified management accountant (CMA), certified internal auditor (CIA), certified fraud examiner (CFE), certified bookkeeper (CB), certified payroll professional (CPP), and personal financial specialist (PFS).

8. Ethical guidelines are threefold: (1) identify ethical concerns using personal ethics, (2) analyze options considering all good and bad consequences, and (3) make ethical decisions after weighing all consequences.

9. Ethics and social responsibility yield good behavior, and they often result in higher income and a better working environment.

10. For accounting to provide useful information for decisions, it must be trusted. Trust requires ethics in accounting.

11. Two major participants in setting rules include the SEC and the FASB.

12. Most U.S. companies are not directly affected by international accounting standards. International standards are put forth as preferred accounting practices. However, stock exchanges and other parties are increasing the pressure to narrow differences in worldwide accounting practices. International accounting standards are playing an important role in that process.

13. Users desire information about the performance of a specific entity. If information is mixed between two or more entities, its usefulness decreases.

14. The three basic forms of business organization are sole proprietorships, partnerships, and corporations.

15. Owners of corporations are called *shareholders* (or *stockholders*). Corporate ownership is divided into units called *shares* (or *stock*). The most basic of corporate shares is common stock (or capital stock).

A list of key terms with page references concludes each chapter (a complete glossary is at the end of the book).

Key Terms

Accounting (p. 4) Information and measurement system that identifies, records, and communicates relevant information about a company's business activities.

Business entity assumption (p. 11) Concept that assumes a business will be accounted for separately from its owner(s) and any other entity.

Corporation (p. 11) Business that is a separate legal entity under state or federal laws with owners called *shareholder* or *stockholders.*

Ethics (p. 9) Codes of conduct by which actions are judged as right or wrong, fair or unfair, honest or dishonest.

External users (p. 6) Persons using accounting information who are not directly involved in running the organization.

Financial accounting (p. 6) Area of accounting mainly aimed at serving external users.

Financial Accounting Standards Board (FASB) (p. 10) Independent group of full-time members responsible for setting accounting rules.

Generally accepted accounting principles (GAAP) (p. 10) Rules that specify acceptable accounting principles.

Internal users (p. 5) Persons using accounting information who are directly involved in managing the organization.

International Accounting Standards Board (IASB) (p. 10) Group that identifies preferred accounting practices and encourages global acceptance; issues International Financial Reporting Standards (IFRS).

Managerial accounting (p. 5) Area of accounting mainly aimed at serving the decision-making needs of internal users; also called *management accounting.*

Manufacturing business (p. 12) A business that makes products for sale.

Merchandising business (p. 12) A business that buys goods from manufacturers and then sells them to consumers.

Partnership (p. 11) Unincorporated association of two or more persons to pursue a business for profit as co-owners.

Proprietorship (p. 10) Business owned by one person that is not organized as a corporation.

Recordkeeping (p. 4) Part of accounting that involves recording transactions and events, either manually or electronically; also called *bookkeeping.*

Sarbanes-Oxley Act (p. 9) Created the *Public Company Accounting Oversight Board,* regulates analyst conflicts, imposes corporate governance requirements, enhances accounting and control disclosures, impacts insider transactions and executive loans, establishes new types of criminal conduct, and expands penalties for violations of federal securities laws.

Securities and Exchange Commission (SEC) (p. 10) Federal agency Congress has charged to set reporting rules for organizations that sell ownership shares to the public.

Service business (p. 11) A business that provides services to customers.

Shareholders (p. 11) Owners of a corporation; also called *stockholders.*

Multiple Choice Quiz   Answers on p. 19   mhhe.com/wildCA2e

Additional Multiple Choice Quizzes are available at the book's Website.

1. Accounting is an information and measurement system that _____ information about an organization's business activities.
   a. Translates
   b. Records
   c. Chooses
   d. Prints out
2. External users of financial information include:
   a. Purchasing managers
   b. Service managers
   c. The chief executive officer
   d. Lenders
3. Typical accounting specialists with designations include all of the following except:
   a. Certified Financial Analyst (CFA)
   b. Certified Public Accountant (CPA)
   c. Certified Bookkeeper (CB)
   d. Certified Payroll Professional (CPP)
4. Generally accepted accounting principles do not aim to make information in financial statements:
   a. Reasonable
   b. Relevant
   c. Reliable
   d. Comparable
5. The Financial Accounting Standards Board is the:
   a. Governmental group that sets financial accounting principles.
   b. International group that identifies preferred international accounting principles.
   c. Private group that sets both broad and specific accounting principles.
   d. Governmental group that sets standards for state and local governmental financial statements.

Discussion Questions

1. What is the purpose of accounting in society?
2. Technology is increasingly used to process accounting data. Why then must we study and understand accounting?
3. Identify at least four kinds of external users and describe how they use accounting information.
4. What are at least three questions business owners and managers might be able to answer by looking at accounting information?
5. Identify three actual businesses that offer services and three actual businesses that offer products.
6. Describe the internal role of accounting for organizations.

7. Identify three types of services typically offered by accounting professionals.

8. What type of accounting information might be useful to the marketing managers of a business?

9. Why is accounting described as a service activity?

10. What are some accounting-related professions?

11. How do ethics rules affect auditors' choice of clients?

12. What work do tax accounting professionals perform in addition to preparing tax returns?

13. Refer to the financial statements of **Best Buy** in Appendix A near the end of the book. Look at the consolidated statements of earnings (income statement). How many years are included and what are their dates?

Connect Accounting repeats assignments via the Web, which allows instructors to monitor, promote, and assess student learning. It can be used in practice, homework, or exam mode.

Quick Study exercises give readers a brief test of key elements.

(*a*) Define these accounting-related acronyms: GAAP, SEC, FASB and IASB. (*b*) Briefly explain the importance of the knowledge base or organization that is referred to for each of the accounting-related acronyms.

QUICK STUDY

QS 1–1
Identifying accounting terms
LO5   LO6

Identify the following users as either external users (E) or internal users (I).

a. Customers E   **d.** Business press E   **g.** Shareholders E   **j.** FBI and IRS E

b. Suppliers E   **e.** Managers I   **h.** Lenders E   **k.** Consumer group E

c. Brokers E   **f.** District attorney E   **i.** Controllers I   **l.** Sales staff I

QS 1–2
Identifying accounting users   **LO2**

An important responsibility of many accounting professionals is to design and implement internal control procedures for organizations. Explain the purpose of internal control procedures. Provide two examples of internal controls applied by companies.

QS 1–3
Explaining internal control   **LO2**

Identify at least three main areas of opportunities for accounting professionals. For each area, identify at least three job possibilities linked to accounting.

QS 1–4
Accounting opportunities   **LO3**

Accounting professionals must sometimes choose between two or more acceptable methods of accounting for business transactions and events. Explain why these situations can involve difficult matters of ethical concern.

QS 1–5
Identifying ethical concerns   **LO4**

Using the information provided in the chapter, determine what the 2012 estimate of salaries is for the following selected accounting fields:

QS 1–6
Identifying career opportunities
LO3

Accounting Position	Expected 2012 Salary
Controller/treasurer	$?
Private accounting (senior)	$?
Payroll manager	$?
Public accounting (manager)	$?

QS 1–7
Generally accepted accounting
principles   **L05**

Generally accepted accounting principles aim to make information relevant, reliable, and comparable. Choose the correct definition on the right for each of these terms:

1. Relevant
2. Reliable
3. Comparable

a. Information is both broad and specific
b. Information is helpful in contrasting organizations
c. The information affects the decisions of its users.
d. Information is trusted by users

QS 1–8
Ownership structures   **L07**

Businesses generally are of three major legal forms. List and briefly describe these three alternative legal forms of business ownership structure.

EXERCISES

connect

Exercise 1–1
Describing accounting
responsibilities   **L02   L03**

Many accounting professionals work in one of the following three areas.

A. Financial accounting   **B.** Managerial accounting   **C.** Tax accounting

Identify the area of accounting that is most involved in each of the following responsibilities.

___B___ 1. Internal auditing.
___A___ 2. External auditing.
___B___ 3. Cost accounting.
___B___ 4. Budgeting.

___C___ 5. Investigating violations of tax laws.
___C___ 6. Planning transactions to minimize taxes.
___A___ 7. Preparing external financial statements.
___A___ 8. Reviewing reports for SEC compliance.

Exercise 1–2
Identifying accounting
users and uses   **L02**

Much of accounting is directed at serving the information needs of those users that are external to an organization. Identify at least three external users of accounting information and indicate two questions they might seek to answer through their use of accounting information.

Exercise 1–3
Identifying ethical concerns   **L04**

Assume the following roles and describe a situation in which ethical considerations play an important part in guiding your decisions and actions.

a. You are a student in an introductory accounting course.
b. You are a manager with responsibility for several employees.
c. You are an accounting professional preparing tax returns for clients.
d. You are an accounting professional with audit clients that are competitors in business.

Exercise 1–4
Learning the language of business
L03   L04   L05   L06

Match each of the numbered descriptions 1 through 7 with the term or phrase it best reflects. Indicate your answer by writing the letter for the term or phrase in the blank provided.

A. Audit   **C.** Ethics   **E.** SEC   **G.** IASB
B. GAAP   **D.** Tax accounting   **F.** Public accountants

___C___ 1. Principles that determine whether an action is right or wrong.
___F___ 2. Accounting professionals who provide services to many clients.
___D___ 3. An accounting area that includes planning future transactions to minimize taxes paid.
___A___ 4. An examination of an organization's accounting system and records that adds credibility to financial statements.
___E___ 5. Government group that establishes reporting requirements for companies that issue stock to the public.
___B___ 6. Concepts and rules that govern financial accounting practice.
___G___ 7. Group that issues preferred international accounting practices.

Exercise 1–5
Ownership structures   **L07**

Following are descriptions of several different business organizations. Determine whether the description refers to a sole proprietorship, partnership, or corporation.

a. Ownership of Zander Company is divided into 1,000 shares of stock. C
b. Wallingford is owned by Trent Malone, who is personally liable for the company's debts. SP

c. Elijah Fong and Ava Logan own Financial Services, a financial services provider. Neither Fong nor Logan has personal responsibility for the debts of Financial Services.   C

d. Dylan Bailey and Emma Kayley own Speedy Packages, a courier service. Both are personally liable for the debts of the business.   P

e. IBC Services does not have separate legal existence apart from the one person who owns it.   SP

f. Physio Products does not pay income taxes and has one owner.   SP

g. Aaliyah Services pays its own income taxes and has two owners.   C

Accounting specialists are often denoted by certifications. Several of these are mentioned in the chapter. Write the full name of each of the certifications below:

a. CMA   **d.** CB   **g.** CPP

b. CPA   **e.** PFS

c. CFE   **f.** CIA

Exercise 1–6
Professional certifications   **LO3**

---

connect™

The following is a list of selected users of accounting information. Match the appropriate user A through E to the following information needs 1 through 5.

A. Suppliers   **C.** Shareholders   **E.** Employees

B. Lenders   **D.** Production managers

___D___ **1.** Monitor costs and ensure quality.

___A___ **2.** Judge the soundness of a customer before making sales on credit.

___E___ **3.** Assessing employment opportunities.

___B___ **4.** Assessing whether a loan is likely to be repaid.

___C___ **5.** Deciding whether to buy, hold, or sell stock.

PROBLEM SET A

Problem 1–1A
Identifying accounting users   **LO2**

The following is a list of broad opportunities in accounting. Match the appropriate broad opportunity A through D to the specific accounting opportunity 1 through 8.

A. Financial   **C.** Taxation

B. Managerial   **D.** Accounting-related

___D___ **1.** Appraiser   ___D___ **5.** Litigation support

___C___ **2.** Estate planning   ___B___ **6.** Internal audit

___A___ **3.** External audit   ___A___ **7.** Financial statement preparation

___B___ **4.** Budgeting   ___C___ **8.** Tax planning

Problem 1–2A
Identify opportunities in accounting   **LO3**

The following is a list of selected internal users of accounting information. Match the appropriate user A through E to the following information needs 1 through 5.

A. Research and development managers   **C.** Distribution managers   **E.** Service managers

B. Human resource managers   **D.** Purchasing managers

___D___ **1.** Assessing when and how much to purchase.

___E___ **2.** Judge the costs and benefits of looking after products and services.

___C___ **3.** Monitor timely, accurate, and efficient delivery of products and services.

___B___ **4.** Assessing employees' payroll, benefits, performance, and compensation.

___A___ **5.** Measuring projected costs and revenues of any proposed changes in products and services.

PROBLEM SET B

Problem 1–1 B
Identifying accounting users   **LO2**

The following is a list of accounting terms. Match the appropriate accounting term A through D to its definition 1 through 4.

A. Accounting   **C.** Managerial accounting

B. Bookkeeping   **D.** Financial accounting

Problem 1–2B
Definition of accounting terms
LO1   LO2

_____ D ____ **1.** Area of accounting aimed at serving external users by providing them with financial statements.

_____ A ____ **2.** Information and measurement system that identifies, records, and communicates information about an organization's business activities.

_____ B ____ **3.** The recording of transactions and events, either manually or electronically.

_____ C ____ **4.** Area of accounting that serves the decision-making needs of internal users.

The serial problem starts in this chapter and continues throughout most chapters of the book. It is most readily solved if you use the Working Papers that accompany this book.

SERIAL PROBLEM

Success Systems

SP 1   On October 1, 2010, Adriana Lopez launched a computer services company, **Success Systems,** that is organized as a proprietorship and provides consulting services, computer system installations, and custom program development. Lopez will prepare the company's first set of financial statements on December 31, 2010.

Required

List at least five potential internal and external users of Success Systems' financial statements. Explain why each user would be interested in the financial statements.

Beyond the Numbers (BTN) is a special problem section aimed to refine communication, conceptual, analysis, and research skills. It includes many activities helpful in developing an active learning environment.

BEYOND THE NUMBERS

REPORTING IN ACTION
LO1

BTN 1–1   Find **Best Buy**'s annual report included in Appendix A near the end of the book.

Required

List at least three likely users of Best Buy's financial statements and how they would use financial statements.

ETHICS CHALLENGE
LO4

BTN 1–2   Managerial accounting professionals follow a code of ethics. As a member of the Institute of Management Accountants, the managerial accountant must comply with Standards of Ethical Conduct.

Required

1. Identify, print, and read the *Statement of Ethical Professional Practice* posted at **www.IMAnet.org**. (Search using "ethical professional practice.")

2. What four overarching ethical principles underlie the IMA's statement?

3. Describe the courses of action the IMA recommends in resolving ethical conflicts.

WORKPLACE COMMUNICATION
LO6

BTN 1–3   The Financial Accounting Standards Board (FASB) sets accounting standards. The FASB's mission is described at its Website (**FASB.org**) under the tab "About FASB."

Required

Prepare a half-page report outlining the mission of the FASB. Identify the ways it has set out to accomplish that mission.

TAKING IT TO THE NET
LO2

BTN 1–4   Find **Best Buy**'s most current financial statements by going to their Website (**BestBuy.com**) and click on the link "For Our Investors" at the bottom of the page. Click on "Annual Reports" in the right column. Click on the most recent "Form 10-K" tab.

Required

1. What is the date of this annual report?
2. What are the titles of the financial statements included in this report?

BTN 1-5   Teamwork is important in today's business world. Successful teams schedule convenient meetings, maintain regular communications, and cooperate with and support their members. This assignment aims to establish support/learning teams, initiate discussions, and set meeting times.

Required

1. Form teams and open a team discussion to determine a regular time and place for your team to meet between each scheduled class meeting. Notify your instructor via a memorandum or e-mail message as to when and where your team will hold regularly scheduled meetings.
2. Develop a list of telephone numbers and/or e-mail addresses of your teammates.

TEAMWORK IN ACTION
L01

BTN 1-6   Refer to this chapter's opening feature about **LoveSac**. Assume that Shawn Nelson decides to open a new manufacturing facility to meet customer demand. To open the new facility, Shawn would have to get a loan from a bank.

Required

1. Which external users would be interested in reviewing LoveSac's financial statements? Why?
2. What specific information would a loan officer want to review before extending a loan to LoveSac?

ENTREPRENEURS IN BUSINESS
L02

BTN 1-7   You and a friend develop a new design for in-line skates that improves speed and performance by 25 to 40 percent. You plan to form a business to manufacture and market these skates. You and your friend want to minimize taxes, but your prime concern is potential lawsuits from individuals who might be injured on these skates. What form of organization do you set up?

YOU CALL IT — ENTREPRENEUR

1. b
2. d
3. a

4. a
5. c

ANSWERS TO MULTIPLE CHOICE QUIZ

A Look Back

Chapter 1 explained the importance of accounting to different types of organizations. We also described the use and users of accounting information.

A Look at This Chapter

This chapter explains the accounting equation and how it helps to describe business transactions. We also show how accounting information is reflected in financial statements.

A Look Ahead

Chapter 3 further describes the analysis of business transactions. We also introduce and explore the basics of double-entry accounting.

Chapter 2

Accounting for Business Transactions

Learning Objectives

LO 1 Define the accounting equation and each of its components.

LO 2 Analyze business transactions using the accounting equation.

LO 3 Identify and prepare basic financial statements and explain how they interrelate.

"It has been a dream come true"
—Sara Blakely

The Bottom Line

ATLANTA—"Working as a sales trainer by day and performing stand-up comedy at night, I didn't know the first thing about the pantyhose industry," admits Sara Blakely. "Except, I dreaded wearing most pantyhose." One night Sara cut the feet out of her pantyhose to wear with white pants and open-toed shoes, and at that moment, Sara knew she had a unique idea. Sara took $5,000 in savings and launched **SPANX (Spanx.com)**, a manufacturer of footless pantyhose, slimming intimates, hosiery, and other women's apparel.

To pursue her business ambitions, Sara studied business activities and learned the value of accounting information. She established recordkeeping processes, transaction analysis, inventory accounting, and financial statement reporting. I had to get a handle on my financial situation, says Sara, as I wanted to remain self-funded. To this day, Sara remains self-funded and has a reliable accounting system to help her make good business decisions.

I had to account for product costs, office expenses, supplier payments, patent fees, and other expenses, says Sara. At the same time, Sara expanded sales and struggled to stay profitable. "I had no money to advertise, so I hit the road," laughs Sara. "For the entire first year, I did in-store rallies . . . staying all day introducing customers to Spanx."

In her first three months, Sara sold over 50,000 pairs of footless pantyhose. Today, just seven short years from her launch, Sara reports over $150 million in retail sales. "We are still a small company of women," claims Sara, "obsessed with inventing and improving comfortable undergarments." Sara continues to track and account for all revenues and expenses. She maintains that success requires proper accounting for and analysis of the financial side.

The bigger message of SPANX, says Sara, is promoting comfort and confidence for women. Insists Sara, "We believe all women deserve the opportunity to make the most of their assets!"

[Sources: *SPANX Website*, January 2009; *Entrepreneur*, May 2007; *Smart Money*, September 2002; *TV Guide*, July 2007; *Financial Times*, 2006; *ABC Television*, 2007]

Accounting identifies, records, and communicates information about an organization's business activities. In this chapter, we introduce the accounting equation as a means of identifying and recording business transactions. We also introduce basic financial statements that communicate accounting information about the company's performance and financial position.

Accounting for Business Transactions

Transaction Analysis
- Accounting equation
- Transactions and the accounting equation

Financial Statements
- Income statement
- Statement of owner's equity
- Balance sheet

Transaction Analysis and the Accounting Equation

LO1 Define the accounting equation and each of its components.

To understand accounting information, we need to know how an accounting system captures relevant data about transactions, and then classifies, records, and reports data. In this section, we introduce the accounting equation and then show how the accounting equation represents each business transaction.

Accounting Equation

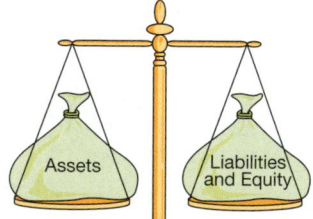

The accounting system reflects two basic aspects of a company: what it owns and what it owes. **Assets** are resources with future benefits that are owned or controlled by a company. The claims on a company's assets—what it owes—are separated into owner and nonowner claims. **Liabilities** are what a company owes its nonowners (creditors) in future payments, products, or services. **Equity** (also called owner's equity or capital) refers to the claims of its owner(s). Together, liabilities and equity are the source of funds to acquire assets. The relation of assets, liabilities, and equity is reflected in the following **accounting equation:**

$$\text{Assets} = \text{Liabilities} + \text{Equity}$$

Liabilities are usually shown before equity in this equation because creditors' claims must be paid before the claims of owners. (The terms in this equation can be rearranged; for example, Assets − Liabilities = Equity.) The accounting equation applies to all transactions and events, to all companies and forms of organization, and to all points in time. Let's now look at the accounting equation in more detail.

Assets   **Assets** are resources owned or controlled by a company that are expected to yield future benefits. Examples of assets include Web servers for an online services company, musical instruments for a rock band, land for a vegetable grower, and cash in the company's bank account. The term *receivable* refers to an asset that promises a future inflow of resources. A company that provides a service or product on credit is said to have an account receivable from that customer. The phrases *on credit* and *on account* imply that cash payment will occur at a future date. Other typical assets include supplies, equipment, land, and buildings.

Liabilities   **Liabilities** are creditors' claims on assets. **Creditors** are individuals and organizations that own the right to receive payment from a company. These claims reflect obligations

IN THE NEWS

Web Info   Most organizations maintain Websites that include accounting data—see **Best Buy (BestBuy.com)** as an example. The SEC keeps an online database called **EDGAR (www.sec.gov/edgar.shtml)**, which has accounting information for thousands of companies that issue stock to the public. Information services such as **Finance.Google.com** and **Finance.Yahoo.com** offer additional online data and analysis.

to provide assets, products, or services to others. The term *payable* refers to a liability that promises a future outflow of resources. Examples are wages payable to workers, accounts payable to suppliers, loans (or notes) payable to banks, and taxes payable to the government.

Equity   **Equity** is the owner's claim on assets. Equity is equal to assets minus liabilities. This is the reason equity is also called *net assets* or *residual equity*.

Equity for a proprietorship (or partnership)—commonly called owner's equity—increases and decreases as follows: owner investments and revenues *increase* equity, whereas owner withdrawals and expenses *decrease* equity. **Owner investments** are assets an owner puts into the company and are included under the generic account **Owner, Capital. Owner withdrawals** are assets an owner takes from the company for personal use.

Revenues increase equity and are the assets earned from a company's earnings activities. Examples are consulting services provided, sales of products, facilities rented to others, and commissions from services. **Expenses** decrease equity and are the cost of assets or services used to earn revenues. Examples are costs of employee time, use of supplies, and advertising, utilities, and insurance services from others. At any point in time, equity is the accumulated revenues and owner investments minus the accumulated expenses and owner withdrawals since the company began. This breakdown of equity yields the following **expanded accounting equation.**

$$\text{Assets} = \text{Liabilities} + \underbrace{\text{Owner, Capital} - \text{Owner, Withdrawals} + \text{Revenues} - \text{Expenses}}_{\text{Equity}}$$

Net income occurs when revenues exceed expenses. Net income increases equity. A **net loss** occurs when expenses exceed revenues, which decreases equity. Owner investments and withdrawals are not included in net income.

Transactions and the Accounting Equation

A transaction is defined as a business activity that affects the accounting equation. **External transactions** are exchanges of value between two entities, which yield changes in the accounting equation. An example is a company's payment of its electric bill. **Internal transactions** are exchanges within an entity; they can also affect the accounting equation. An example is a company's use of its supplies, which are reported as expenses when used. **Events** refer to those happenings that affect an entity's accounting equation *and* can be reliably measured. They include natural events such as floods and fires that destroy assets and create losses. They do not include, for example, the signing of service or product contracts, which by themselves do not impact the accounting equation.

An **account** is a record within an accounting system in which increases and decreases are entered and stored. Specific asset, liability, equity, revenue, and expense items are recorded in separate accounts. This section uses the accounting equation and accounts to analyze 11 selected transactions and events of FastForward, a start-up consulting (service) business, in its first month

LO2   Analyze business transactions using the accounting equation.

of operations. We focus on two questions when analyzing the effects of a transaction on the accounting equation.

1. Which accounts are affected by the transaction?
2. How is the accounting equation affected?

Remember that each transaction and event leaves the accounting equation in balance and that assets *always* equal the sum of liabilities and equity.

Starting the Business   On December 1, Chuck Taylor forms a consulting business, focused on assessing the performance of athletic footwear and accessories, which he names FastForward. He sets it up as a proprietorship; he owns and manages the business. The marketing plan for the business is to focus primarily on consulting with sports clubs, amateur athletes, and others who place orders for athletic footwear and accessories with manufacturers.

Transaction 1: Investment by Owner
Chuck Taylor invests $30,000 cash in FastForward.
Taylor personally invests $30,000 cash in the new company and deposits the cash in a bank account opened under the name of FastForward. The accounts in this transaction are Cash (an asset) and C. Taylor, Capital (owner's equity). (Owner investments are always included under the title "Owner name," Capital). Both accounts increase by $30,000 as a result of this transaction. After this transaction, Fastforward's assets equal its equity, and the accounting equation is in balance.The effect of this transaction on FastForward is reflected in the accounting equation as follows.

	Assets	=	Liabilities	+	Equity
	Cash	=			C. Taylor, Capital
(1)	+$30,000	=			+$30,000

Transaction 2: Purchase Supplies for Cash
FastForward pays $2,500 cash for supplies.
FastForward uses $2,500 of its cash to buy supplies of brand name athletic footwear for performance testing over the next few months. This transaction is an exchange of cash, an asset, for another kind of asset, supplies. It merely changes the form of assets from cash to supplies. The decrease in cash exactly equals the increase in supplies. Fastforward's total assets and owner's equity each remain at $30,000 after this transaction. The supplies of athletic footwear are assets because of the expected future benefits from the test results of their performance. This transaction is reflected in the accounting equation as follows:

	Assets			=	Liabilities	+	Equity
	Cash	+	Supplies	=			C. Taylor, Capital
Old Bal.	$30,000			=			$30,000
(2)	−2,500	+	$2,500				
New Bal.	$27,500	+	$ 2,500	=			$30,000
		$30,000				$30,000	

Transaction 3: Purchase Equipment for Cash
FastForward pays $26,000 cash for equipment.
FastForward spends $26,000 to acquire equipment for testing athletic footwear. Like transaction 2, transaction 3 is an exchange of one asset, cash, for another asset, equipment. The equipment

is an asset because of its expected future benefits from testing athletic footwear. This purchase changes the makeup of assets but does not change the asset total. The accounting equation remains in balance. Transactions 2 and 3 illustrate a fundamental idea in accounting: *Payments of cash are not always expenses.*

		Assets				=	Liabilities	+	Equity
	Cash	+	Supplies	+	Equipment	=			C. Taylor, Capital
Old Bal.	$27,500	+	$2,500			=			$30,000
(3)	−26,000			+	$26,000				
New Bal.	$ 1,500	+	$2,500	+	$ 26,000	=			$30,000
			$30,000						$30,000

Transaction 4: Purchase Supplies on Credit

FastForward purchases $7,100 of supplies on credit.
Taylor decides he needs more supplies of athletic footwear and accessories. These additional supplies total $7,100, but as we see from the accounting equation in transaction 3, FastForward has only $1,500 in cash. Taylor arranges to purchase the supplies on credit from CalTech Supply Company. Thus, FastForward acquires supplies in exchange for a promise to pay for them later. This purchase increases assets by $7,100 in supplies, and liabilities (called *accounts payable*) increase by the same amount. The effects of this purchase follow:

		Assets				=	Liabilities	+	Equity
	Cash	+	Supplies	+	Equipment	=	Accounts Payable	+	C. Taylor, Capital
Old Bal.	$1,500	+	$2,500	+	$26,000	=			$30,000
(4)		+	7,100				+$7,100		
New Bal.	$1,500	+	$9,600	+	$26,000	=	$ 7,100	+	$30,000
			$37,100					$37,100	

Transaction 5: Provide Services for Cash

FastForward provides consulting services and immediately collects $4,200 cash.
FastForward earns revenues by consulting with clients about test results on athletic footwear and accessories. In one of its first jobs, FastForward provides consulting services to an athletic club and immediately collects $4,200 cash. The accounting equation reflects this increase in cash of $4,200 and in equity of $4,200. This increase in equity is shown in the far right column under Revenues because the cash received is earned by providing consulting services. Using separate accounts to record revenues and owner investments (transaction 1) helps in preparing accurate financial statements.

		Assets				=	Liabilities	+		Equity		
	Cash	+	Supplies	+	Equipment	=	Accounts Payable	+	C. Taylor, Capital	+		Revenues
Old Bal.	$1,500	+	$9,600	+	$26,000	=	$7,100	+	$30,000			
(5)	+4,200									+		$4,200
New Bal.	$5,700	+	$9,600	+	$26,000	=	$7,100	+	$30,000	+		$ 4,200
			$41,300						$41,300			

Transactions 6 and 7: Payment of Expenses in Cash

FastForward pays $1,000 in cash for December rent.
FastForward pays $700 cash for employee salaries.

In transaction 6, FastForward pays $1,000 rent to the landlord of the building where its facilities are located. Paying this amount allows FastForward to occupy the space for the month of December. In transaction 7, FastForward pays the biweekly $700 salary of the company's only employee. Both transactions 6 and 7 are December expenses for FastForward. The costs of both rent and salary are expenses, as opposed to assets, because their benefits are used in December (they have no future benefits after December). The accounting equation shows that both transactions reduce cash and equity. The far right column identifies these decreases as Expenses.

By definition, increases in expenses yield decreases in equity.

	Assets					=	Liabilities	+				Equity		
	Cash	+	Supplies	+	Equipment	=	Accounts Payable	+	C. Taylor, Capital	+	Revenues	−	Expenses
Old Bal.	$5,700	+	$9,600	+	$26,000	=	$7,100	+	$30,000	+	$4,200		
(6)	−1,000											−	$1,000
Bal.	4,700	+	9,600	+	26,000	=	7,100	+	30,000	+	4,200	−	1,000
(7)	− 700											−	700
New Bal.	$4,000	+	$9,600	+	$26,000	=	$7,100	+	$30,000	+	$4,200	−	$ 1,700

$39,600 $39,600

Transaction 8: Provide Services and Facilities for Credit

FastForward provides consulting services of $1,600 and rents its test facilities for $300. The customer is billed $1,900 for these services.

FastForward provides consulting services of $1,600 and rents its test facilities for $300 to an amateur sports club. The rental involves allowing club members to try recommended footwear and accessories at FastForward's testing grounds. The sports club is billed for the $1,900 total. This transaction results in a new asset, called *accounts receivable,* which means the client has not yet paid the $1,900 bill. Since FastForward has already provided the consulting services and the rental, FastForward considers the full $1,900 as Revenues. These two revenue items increase equity as shown in the Revenues column of the accounting equation below. Transaction 8 reveals another important concept: *Revenues do not require immediate receipt of cash.*

	Assets								=	Liabilities	+			Equity		
	Cash	+	Accounts Receivable	+	Supplies	+	Equipment	=	Accounts Payable	+	C. Taylor, Capital	+	Revenues	−	Expenses
Old Bal.	$4,000	+		+	$9,600	+	$26,000	=	$7,100	+	$30,000	+	$4,200	−	$1,700
(8)		+	$1,900									+	1,600		
												+	300		
New Bal.	$4,000	+	$ 1,900	+	$9,600	+	$26,000	=	$7,100	+	$30,000	+	$6,100	−	$1,700

$41,500 $41,500

Transaction 9: Receipt of Cash from Accounts Receivable

FastForward receives $1,900 cash from the customer billed in transaction 8.
The client in transaction 8 (the amateur sports club) pays $1,900 to FastForward 10 days after it is billed for consulting services. This transaction 9 does not change the total amount of assets and does not affect liabilities or equity. It converts the receivable (an asset) to cash (another asset). It does not create new revenue. Revenue was recognized when FastForward rendered the services in transaction 8, not when the cash is now collected. Transaction 9 shows that *receipt of cash is not always a revenue.* The new balances follow:

	Assets									=	Liabilities	+		Equity			
	Cash	+	Accounts Receivable	+	Supplies	+	Equipment	=		Accounts Payable	+	C. Taylor, Capital	+	Revenues	−	Expenses
Old Bal.	$4,000	+	$1,900	+	$9,600	+	$26,000	=		$7,100	+	$30,000	+	$6,100	−	$1,700
(9)	+1,900	−	1,900													
New Bal.	$5,900	+	$ 0	+	$9,600	+	$26,000	=		$7,100	+	$30,000	+	$6,100	−	$1,700
			$41,500										$41,500			

Transaction 10: Payment of Accounts Payable

FastForward pays its supplier $900 cash toward the account payable from transaction 4.
FastForward pays CalTech Supply $900 cash as partial payment for its earlier $7,100 purchase of supplies (transaction 4), leaving $6,200 unpaid. The accounting equation shows that this transaction decreases FastForward's cash by $900 and decreases its liability to CalTech Supply by $900. Equity does not change. This event does not create an expense even though cash flows out of FastForward. Instead, the expense is recorded when FastForward uses the supplies. (We show this and other adjustments in later chapters).

	Assets								=	Liabilities	+		Equity			
	Cash	+	Accounts Receivable	+	Supplies	+	Equipment	=	Accounts Payable	+	C. Taylor, Capital	+	Revenues	−	Expenses
Old Bal.	$5,900	+	$ 0	+	$9,600	+	$26,000	=	$7,100	+	$30,000	+	$6,100	−	$1,700
(10)	− 900								− 900						
New Bal.	$5,000	+	$ 0	+	$9,600	+	$26,000	=	$6,200	+	$30,000	+	$6,100	−	$1,700
			$40,600									$40,600			

Transaction 11: Withdrawal of Cash by Owner

Chuck Taylor withdraws $200 cash from FastForward for personal use.
The owner of FastForward withdraws $200 cash for personal use. Withdrawals are accounted for as a decrease in equity. Withdrawals are not expenses because they are not part of the company's earning process. Since withdrawals are not company expenses, they are not used in computing net income.

By definition, increases in withdrawals yield decreases in equity.

	Assets								=	Liabilities	+		Equity					
	Cash	+	Accounts Receivable	+	Supplies	+	Equipment	=	Accounts Payable	+	C. Taylor, Capital	−	C. Taylor, Withdrawals	+	Revenues	−	Expenses
Old Bal.	$5,000	+	$ 0	+	$9,600	+	$26,000	=	$6,200	+	$30,000			+	$6,100	−	$1,700
(11)	− 200											− $200				
New Bal.	$4,800	+	$ 0	+	$9,600	+	$26,000	=	$6,200	+	$30,000	−	$200	+	$6,100	−	$1,700
			$40,400										$40,400				

Summary of Transactions

We summarize in Exhibit 2.1 the effects of these 11 transactions of FastForward using the accounting equation. Two points should be noted. First, the accounting equation remains in balance after each transaction. Second, transactions can be analyzed by their effects on components of the accounting equation. For example, in transactions 2, 3, and 9, one asset increased while another asset decreased by equal amounts.

Exhibit 2.1

Summary of Transactions Using the Accounting Equation

	Cash	+	Accounts Receivable	+	Supplies	+	Equipment	=	Accounts Payable	+	C. Taylor, Capital	−	C. Taylor, Withdrawals	+	Revenues	−	Expenses
(1)	$30,000							=			$30,000						
(2)	− 2,500			+	$2,500												
Bal.	27,500			+	2,500			=			30,000						
(3)	−26,000					+	$26,000										
Bal.	1,500			+	2,500	+	26,000	=			30,000						
(4)				+	7,100				+$7,100								
Bal.	1,500			+	9,600	+	26,000	=	7,100	+	30,000						
(5)	+ 4,200													+	$4,200		
Bal.	5,700			+	9,600	+	26,000	=	7,100	+	30,000			+	4,200		
(6)	− 1,000															−	$1,000
Bal.	4,700			+	9,600	+	26,000	=	7,100	+	30,000			+	4,200	−	1,000
(7)	− 700															−	700
Bal.	4,000			+	9,600	+	26,000	=	7,100	+	30,000			+	4,200	−	1,700
(8)		+	$1,900											+	1,600		
														+	300		
Bal.	4,000	+	1,900	+	9,600	+	26,000	=	7,100	+	30,000			+	6,100	−	1,700
(9)	+ 1,900	−	1,900														
Bal.	5,900	+	0	+	9,600	+	26,000	=	7,100	+	30,000			+	6,100	−	1,700
(10)	− 900								− 900								
Bal.	5,000	+	0	+	9,600	+	26,000	=	6,200	+	30,000			+	6,100	−	1,700
(11)	− 200											−	$200				
Bal.	$ 4,800	+	$ 0	+	$ 9,600	+	$ 26,000	=	$ 6,200	+	$ 30,000	−	$ 200	+	$6,100	−	$1,700

HOW YOU DOIN'?   Answers—p. 33

1. When is the accounting equation in balance, and what does that mean?
2. How can a transaction not affect any liability and equity accounts?
3. Describe a transaction that increases equity and another transaction that decreases equity.
4. Identify a transaction that decreases both assets and liabilities.

IN THE NEWS

Women Entrepreneurs   The Center for Women's Business Research reports that women-owned businesses, such as **SPANX**, are growing and that they

- Total approximately 11 million and employ nearly 20 million workers.
- Generate $2.5 trillion in annual sales and tend to embrace technology.
- Are philanthropic—70% of owners volunteer at least once per month.
- Are more likely funded by individual investors (73%) than venture firms (15%).

Financial Statements

This section shows how three basic financial statements are prepared from the analysis of business transactions. The financial statements and their purposes are:

LO3 Identify and prepare basic financial statements and explain how they interrelate.

1. **Income statement**—describes a company's revenues and expenses along with the resulting net income or loss over a period of time due to earnings activities. This statement is sometimes called a *profit and loss statement,* or *P&L.*

2. **Statement of owner's equity**—explains changes in owner's equity from net income (or loss) and from any owner investments and withdrawals over a period of time. This statement is also called the *statement of changes in owner's equity.*

3. **Balance sheet**—describes a company's financial position (types and amounts of assets, liabilities, and equity) at a point in time.

Exhibit 2.2 shows the links between financial statements across time. A balance sheet reflects financial position at a *point in time.* The income statement and the statement of owner's equity reflect activity over a *period of time.* Information from these two financial statements updates the balance sheet at the next *point in time.*

Exhibit 2.2

Links between Financial Statements across Time

```
              ┌──────────────┐
              │   Income     │
              │  statement   │
              └──────────────┘
┌──────────────┐  ┌──────────────┐  ┌──────────────┐
│  Beginning   │  │  Statement   │  │   Ending     │
│   balance    │  │     of       │  │   balance    │
│    sheet     │  │   owner's    │  │    sheet      │
│              │  │   equity     │  │              │
└──────────────┘  └──────────────┘  └──────────────┘
Point in time     Period of time     Point in time
```

We prepare these financial statements using the 11 selected transactions of FastForward from Exhibit 2.1. Note, a financial statement's heading lists the 3 W's: **Who**—name of organization; **What**—name of statement; and **When**—statement's point in time or period of time.

Income Statement

The income statement shows the profitability of business operations over a period of time. FastForward's income statement for December is shown at the top of Exhibit 2.3. Information about revenues and expenses is from the Equity columns of Exhibit 2.1. Revenues are reported first on the income statement. They include consulting revenues of $5,800 from transactions 5 and 8 and rental revenue of $300 from transaction 8. Expenses are reported after revenues. (Here we list larger amounts first, but we can sort expenses in different ways.) Rent and salary expenses are from transactions 6 and 7. Expenses reflect the costs to generate the revenues reported. Net income (or loss) is reported at the bottom of the income statement. During the month of December, FastForward had net income, or profit, of $4,400. Notice that owner's investments and withdrawals are *not* part of income.

Exhibit 2.3

Financial Statements and Their Links

> A single ruled line denotes an addition or subtraction. Final totals are double underlined.

> Arrow lines show how the statements interrelate. ① Net income is used to update equity (capital) ② Ending capital is used to prepare the balance sheet.

FASTFORWARD
Income Statement
For Month Ended December 31, 2010

Revenues		
Consulting revenue	$ 5,800	
Rental revenue	300	
Total revenues		$ 6,100
Expenses		
Rent expense	1,000	
Salaries expense	700	
Total expenses		1,700
Net income		**$ 4,400**

FASTFORWARD
Statement of Owner's Equity
For Month Ended December 31, 2010

C. Taylor, Capital, December 1, 2010		$ 0
Plus: Investments by owner	$30,000	
Net income	4,400	34,400
		34,400
Less: Withdrawals by owner		200
C. Taylor, Capital, December 31, 2010		**$34,200**

FASTFORWARD
Balance Sheet
December 31, 2010

Assets		Liabilities	
Cash	$ 4,800	Accounts payable	$ 6,200
Supplies	9,600		
Equipment	26,000	**Equity**	
		C. Taylor, Capital	34,200
Total assets	$ 40,400	Total liabilities and equity	$ 40,400

Statement of Owner's Equity

The statement of owner's equity reports information about how equity changes over the reporting period. This statement shows beginning capital, events that increase it (owner investments and net income), and events that decrease it (owner withdrawals and net loss). FastForward's statement of owner's equity is the second report in Exhibit 2.3. The beginning capital balance is measured as of the start of business on December 1. It is zero because FastForward did not exist before then. An existing business reports the beginning balance as of the end of the prior reporting period (such as from November 30). FastForward's statement shows that Taylor's initial investment created $30,000 of equity. It also shows the $4,400 of net income earned during the period. This links the income statement to the statement of owner's equity (see line ①). The statement also reports Taylor's $200 cash withdrawal and FastForward's end-of-period capital balance of $34,200. This ending capital is carried over and reported on the balance sheet. This links the statement of owner's equity to the balance sheet (see line ②).

Balance Sheet

The balance sheet reports the type and amounts of assets, liabilities, and owner's equity at a point in time. FastForward's balance sheet is the third report in Exhibit 2.3. This statement refers to FastForward's financial condition at the close of business on December 31. The left side of the balance sheet lists FastForward's assets: cash, supplies, and equipment. The upper right side of the balance sheet shows that FastForward owes $6,200 to creditors. Any other liabilities (such as a bank loan) would be listed here. The equity (capital) balance is $34,200. Note again the link between the ending balance of the statement of owner's equity and the equity balance here—see line ②.

HOW YOU DOIN'?   Answers—p. 33

5. Explain the link between the income statement and the statement of owner's equity.

6. Describe the link between the balance sheet and the statement of owner's equity.

Demonstration Problem

After several months of planning, Jasmine Worthy started a haircutting business called Expressions. The following events occurred during its first month of business.

a. On August 1, Worthy invested $3,000 cash and $15,000 of equipment in Expressions.

b. On August 2, Expressions paid $600 cash for furniture for the shop.

c. On August 3, Expressions paid $500 cash to rent space in a strip mall for August.

d. On August 4, it purchased $1,200 of equipment on credit for the shop (using an account payable).

e. On August 5, Expressions opened for business. Cash received from services provided in the first week and a half of business (ended August 15) is $825.

f. On August 15, it provided $100 of haircutting services on account.

g. On August 17, it received a $100 check for services previously rendered on account on August 15.

h. On August 17, it paid $125 cash to an assistant for working during the grand opening.

i. Cash received from services provided during the second half of August is $930.

j. On August 31, it paid $400 toward the account payable entered into on August 4.

k. On August 31, Worthy made a $900 cash withdrawal for personal use.

Required

1. Arrange the following asset, liability, and equity titles in a table similar to the one in Exhibit 2.1: Cash; Accounts Receivable; Furniture; Store Equipment; Accounts Payable; J. Worthy, Capital; J. Worthy, Withdrawals; Revenues; and Expenses. Show the effects of each transaction using the accounting equation.

2. Prepare an income statement for August.

3. Prepare a statement of owner's equity for August.

4. Prepare a balance sheet as of August 31.

Planning the Solution

- Set up a table like Exhibit 2.1 with the appropriate columns for accounts.
- Analyze each transaction and show its effects as increases or decreases in the appropriate columns. Be sure the accounting equation remains in balance after each transaction.
- Prepare the income statement, and identify revenues and expenses. List those items on the statement, compute the difference, and label the result as *net income* or *net loss*.
- Use information in the Equity columns to prepare the statement of owner's equity.
- Use information in the last row of the transactions table to prepare the balance sheet.

Solution to Demonstration Problem

1.

	Assets									=	Liabilities	+					Equity			
	Cash	+	Accounts Receiv- able	+	Furni- ture	+	Store Equip- ment		=	Accounts Payable	+	J. Worthy, Capital	−	J. Worthy, Withdrawals	+	Revenues	−	Expenses
a.	$3,000						$15,000					$18,000						
b.	− 600			+	$600													
Bal.	2,400	+		+	600	+	15,000	=				18,000						
c.	− 500																−	$500
Bal.	1,900	+		+	600	+	15,000	=				18,000					−	500
d.						+	1,200			+$1,200								
Bal.	1,900	+		+	600	+	16,200	=	1,200	+		18,000					−	500
e.	+ 825														+	$ 825		
Bal.	2,725	+		+	600	+	16,200	=	1,200	+		18,000			+	825	−	500
f.		+	$100												+	100		
Bal.	2,725	+	100	+	600	+	16,200	=	1,200	+		18,000			+	925	−	500
g.	+ 100	−	100															
Bal.	2,825	+	0	+	600	+	16,200	=	1,200	+		18,000			+	925	−	500
h.	− 125																−	125
Bal.	2,700	+	0	+	600	+	16,200	=	1,200	+		18,000			+	925	−	625
i.	+ 930														+	930		
Bal.	3,630	+	0	+	600	+	16,200	=	1,200	+		18,000			+	1,855	−	625
j.	− 400									− 400								
Bal.	3,230	+	0	+	600	+	16,200	=	800	+		18,000			+	1,855	−	625
k.	− 900												−	$900				
Bal.	$ 2,330	+	$ 0	+	$600	+	$ 16,200	=	$ 800	+		$ 18,000	−	$900	+	$1,855	−	$625

2.

EXPRESSIONS Income Statement For Month Ended August 31		
Revenues		
Haircutting services revenue		$1,855
Expenses		
Rent expense	$500	
Wages expense	125	
Total expenses		625
Net income		$1,230

3.

EXPRESSIONS Statement of Owner's Equity For Month Ended August 31		
J. Worthy, Capital, August 1*		$ 0
Plus: Investments by owner	$18,000	
Net income	1,230	19,230
		19,230
Less: Withdrawals by owner		900
J. Worthy, Capital, August 31		$18,330

* If Expressions had been an existing business from a prior period, the beginning capital balance would equal the Capital account balance from the end of the prior period.

4.

EXPRESSIONS Balance Sheet August 31			
Assets		**Liabilities**	
Cash	$ 2,330	Accounts payable	$ 800
Furniture	600	**Equity**	
Store equipment	16,200	J. Worthy, Capital	18,330
Total assets	$19,130	Total liabilities and equity	$19,130

Summary

LO1 **Define the accounting equation and each of its components.** The accounting equation is: Assets = Liabilities + Equity. Assets are resources owned by a company. Liabilities are creditors' claims on assets. Equity is the owner's claim on assets (*the residual*). The expanded accounting equation is: Assets = Liabilities + [Owner Capital − Owner Withdrawals + Revenues − Expenses].

LO2 **Analyze business transactions using the accounting equation.** A *transaction* is an exchange of value between two parties. Examples include exchanges of products, services, money, and

rights to collect money. Transactions always have at least two effects on one or more components of the accounting equation. This equation is always in balance.

LO3 **Identify and prepare basic financial statements and explain how they interrelate.** Three basic financial statements report on an organization's activities: balance sheet, income statement, and statement of owner's equity. Net income from the income statement updates equity on the statement of owner's equity. Ending owner's equity is reported on the ending balance sheet.

Guidance Answers to HOW YOU DOIN'?

1. The accounting equation is: Assets = Liabilities + Equity. This equation is always in balance, both before and after each transaction. This means that a company's assets are equal to the claims on those assets.

2. A transaction that changes the makeup of assets would not affect liability and equity accounts. FastForward's transactions 2, 3, and 9 are examples. Each exchanges one asset for another.

3. Earning revenue by performing services, as in FastForward's transaction 5, increases equity (and assets). Incurring expenses while servicing clients, such as in transactions 6 and 7, decreases equity (and assets). Other examples include owner investments that increase equity and owner withdrawals that decrease equity.

4. Paying a liability with an asset reduces both asset and liability totals. One example is FastForward's transaction 10 that reduces a payable by paying cash.

5. An income statement reports a company's revenues and expenses along with the resulting net income or loss. A statement of owner's equity shows changes in equity, including that from net income or loss. Both statements report transactions occurring over a period of time.

6. The balance sheet describes a company's financial position (assets, liabilities, and equity) at a point in time. The equity amount in the balance sheet is obtained from the statement of owner's equity.

Key Terms

Account (p. 23) Record within an accounting system in which increases and decreases are entered and stored in a specific asset, liability, equity, revenue, or expense.

Accounting equation (p. 22) Equality involving a company's assets, liabilities, and equity; Assets = Liabilities + Equity; also called *balance sheet equation*.

Assets (p. 22) Resources a business owns or controls that are expected to provide current and future benefits to the business.

Balance sheet (p. 29) Financial statement that lists types and dollar amounts of assets, liabilities, and equity at a specific date.

Creditors (p. 22) Individuals and organizations that are entitled to receive payment from a company.

Equity (p. 23) Owner's claim on the assets of a business; equals the residual interest in an entity's assets after deducting liabilities; also called *net assets*.

Events (p. 23) Those happenings that affect an entity's accounting equation *and* can be reliably measured.

Expanded accounting equation (p. 23) Assets = Liabilities + Equity; Equity equals [Owner capital − Owner withdrawals + Revenues − Expenses].

Expenses (p. 23) Outflows or using up of assets as part of operations of a business to generate sales.

External transactions (p. 23) Exchanges of value between one entity and another entity.

Income statement (p. 29) Financial statement that subtracts expenses from revenues to yield a net income or loss over a specified period of time; also includes any gains or losses.

Internal transactions (p. 23) Activities within an organization that can affect the accounting equation.

Liabilities (p. 22) Creditors' claims on an organization's assets; involves a probable future payment of assets, products, or services that a company is obliged to make due to past transactions or events.

Net income (p. 23) Amount earned after subtracting all expenses necessary for and matched with sales for a period; also called *income*, *profit*, or *earnings*.

Net loss (p. 23) Excess of expenses over revenues for a period.

Owner, Capital (p. 23) Account showing the owner's claim on company assets; equals owner investments plus net income (or less net losses) minus owner withdrawals since the company's inception; also referred to as *equity*.

Owner investment (p. 23) Assets put into the business by the owner.

Owner withdrawals (p. 23) Payment of cash or other assets from a proprietorship or partnership to its owner or owners.

Revenues (p. 23) Gross increase in equity from a company's business activities that earn income; also called *sales*.

Statement of owner's equity (p. 29) Report of changes in equity over a period; adjusted for increases (owner investment and net income) and for decreases (withdrawals and net losses).

Multiple Choice Quiz   Answers on p. 43   mhhe.com/wildCA2e

Additional Multiple Choice Quizzes are available at the book's Website.

1. When supplies are paid for with cash, which accounts increase or decrease?
 a. Supplies increase; cash increases.
 b. Supplies increase; accounts payable increases.
 c. Supplies increase; cash neither increases nor decreases.
 d. Supplies increase; cash decreases.

2. When supplies are purchased on account, which accounts increase or decrease?
 a. Supplies increase; accounts payable increases.
 b. Supplies increase; accounts receivable increases.
 c. Supplies increase; accounts payable decreases.
 d. Supplies increase; equity decreases.

3. If the assets of a company increase by $100,000 during the year and its liabilities increase by $35,000 during the same year, then the change in equity of the company during the year must have been:
 a. An increase of $135,000.
 b. A decrease of $135,000.
 c. A decrease of $65,000.
 d. An increase of $65,000.
 e. An increase of $100,000.

4. A company borrows $50,000 cash from Third National Bank. How does this transaction affect the accounting equation for this company?

 a. Assets increase by $50,000; liabilities increase by $50,000; no effect on equity.
 b. Assets increase by $50,000; no effect on liabilities; equity increases by $50,000.
 c. Assets increase by $50,000; liabilities decrease by $50,000; no effect on equity.
 d. No effect on assets; liabilities increase by $50,000; equity increases by $50,000.
 e. No effect on assets; liabilities increase by $50,000; equity decreases by $50,000.

5. Geek Squad performs services for a customer and bills the customer for $500. How would Geek Squad record this transaction?
 a. Accounts receivable increase by $500; revenues increase by $500.
 b. Cash increases by $500; revenues increase by $500.
 c. Accounts receivable increase by $500; revenues decrease by $500.
 d. Accounts receivable increase by $500; accounts payable increase by $500.
 e. Accounts payable increase by $500; revenues increase by $500.

Discussion Questions

1. Define (*a*) *assets*, (*b*) *liabilities*, (*c*) *equity*, and (*d*) *net assets*.
2. What events or transactions change equity?
3. What do accountants mean by the term *revenue*?
4. Define *net income* and explain its computation.
5. Identify the three basic financial statements of a business.
6. What information is reported in an income statement?
7. Give two examples of expenses a business might incur.
8. What is the purpose of the statement of owner's equity?

9. What information is reported in a balance sheet?
10. Refer to the financial statements of **Best Buy** in Appendix A near the end of the book. To what level are dollar amounts rounded? What time period does its income statement cover?
11. Refer to the financial statements for **RadioShack** in Appendix A near the end of the book. What time period does its balance sheet cover? To what level are dollar amounts rounded?

connect

a. Total assets of Charter Company equal $700,000 and its equity is $420,000. What is the amount of its liabilities? $280,000

b. Total assets of Martin Marine equal $500,000 and its liabilities and equity amounts are equal to each other. What is the amount of its liabilities? What is the amount of its equity? $250,000 each

QUICK STUDY

QS 2–1
Applying the accounting equation
LO1

Use the accounting equation to compute the missing financial statement amounts (a), (b), and (c).

Company	Assets	=	Liabilities	+	Equity
1	$75,000		$ (a)35,000		$40,000
2	$ (b)50,000		$25,000		$70,000
3	$85,000		$20,000		$ (c) 65,000

QS 2–2
Applying the accounting equation
LO1

Indicate in which financial statement each item would most likely appear: income statement (I), balance sheet (B), or statement of owner's equity (E).

a. Assets B   c. Equipment B   e. Liabilities B   g. Total liabilities and equity B

b. Withdrawals E   d. Expenses I   f. Revenues I

QS 2–3
Identifying items with financial statements LO3

Use RadioShack's December 31, 2007, financial statements, in Appendix A near the end of the book, to answer the following:

a. Identify the dollar amounts of RadioShack's 2007 (1) total assets, (2) total liabilities, and (3) total equity.

b. Using RadioShack's amounts from part a, verify that Assets = Liabilities + Equity.

QS 2–4
Identifying and computing assets, liabilities, and equity LO1

Explain how the transactions below impact the accounting equation.

a. Collect $4,000 cash from a customer for consulting services provided. A↑, E↑

b. Bill a customer $2,800 for consulting services provided.
A↑, E↑

QS 2–5
Using the accounting equation
LO2

Explain how the transactions below impact the accounting equation.

a. Pay $1,800 cash for employee wages. cash (A) ↓, E (expenses) ↓

b. Pay $10,000 cash for office equipment.
cash ↓ (A), office equipment (A) ↑

QS 2–6
Using the accounting equation
LO2

Explain how the transactions below impact the accounting equation.

a. Owner invests $50,000 cash in her new business. cash (A) ↑, owner's investment (E) ↑

b. Owner withdraws $4,000 cash from the business for personal use.
cash (A) ↓, owner's withdrawal (E) ↓

QS 2–7
Using the accounting equation
LO2

Explain how the transactions below impact the accounting equation.

a. Pay $1,200 in cash for supplies. cash (A) ↓, supplies (A) ↑

b. Purchase $2,000 of office supplies on credit. office supplies (A) ↑, AP (L) ↑

QS 2–8
Using the accounting equation
LO2

EXERCISES

Exercise 2-1
Using the accounting equation
LO1

Determine the missing amount from each of the separate situations a, b, and c below.

	Assets	=	Liabilities	+	Equity
a.	? 65,000	=	$20,000	+	$45,000
b.	$100,000	=	$34,000	+	? 66,000
c.	$154,000	=	? 114,000	+	$40,000

Exercise 2-2
Classifying accounts
LO1   LO2

Classify each of the following accounts as an asset (A), liability (L), or equity (E) account.

_____ L_ **1.** Accounts Payable   _____ A_ **5.** Supplies

_____ L_ **2.** Loan (or Notes) Payable   _____ A_ **6.** Equipment

_____ A_ **3.** Accounts Receivable   _____ E_ **7.** Rod Smith, Capital

_____ A_ **4.** Cash

Exercise 2-3
Identifying effects of transactions
on the accounting equation
LO1   LO2

Provide an example of a transaction that creates the described effects for the separate cases *a* through *g*.

a. Decreases an asset and decreases equity.

b. Increases an asset and increases a liability.

c. Decreases a liability and increases a liability.

d. Decreases an asset and decreases a liability.

e. Increases an asset and decreases an asset.

f. Increases a liability and decreases equity.

g. Increases an asset and increases equity.

Exercise 2-4
Using the accounting equation
LO1   LO2

Answer the following questions. (*Hint:* Use the accounting equation.)

a. Cadence Office Supplies has assets equal to $123,000 and liabilities equal to $47,000 at year-end. What is the total equity for Cadence at year-end? $76,000

b. At the beginning of the year, Addison Company's assets are $300,000 and its equity is $100,000. During the year, assets increase $80,000 and liabilities increase $50,000. What is the equity at the end of the year? $130,000

Check (c) Beg. equity, $60,000

c. At the beginning of the year, Quasar Company's liabilities equal $70,000. During the year, assets increase by $60,000, and at year-end assets equal $190,000. Liabilities decrease $5,000 during the year. What are the beginning and ending amounts of equity? $60,000 $125,000

Exercise 2-5
Identifying effects of transactions
using the accounting equation
LO1   LO2

Leora Holden began a professional practice on June 1 and plans to prepare financial statements at the end of each month. During June, Holden (the owner) completed these transactions.

a. Owner invested $60,000 cash along with equipment that had a $15,000 market value.

b. Paid $1,500 cash for rent of office space for the month.

c. Purchased $10,000 of additional equipment on credit (payment due within 30 days).

d. Completed work for a client and immediately collected the $2,500 cash earned.

e. Completed work for a client and sent a bill for $8,000 to be received within 30 days.

f. Purchased additional equipment for $6,000 cash.

g. Paid an assistant $3,000 cash as wages for the month.

h. Collected $5,000 cash on the amount owed by the client described in transaction *e*.

i. Paid $10,000 cash to settle the liability created in transaction *c*.

j. Owner withdrew $1,000 cash for personal use.

Required

Check Net income, $6,000

Create a table like the one in Exhibit 2.1, using the following headings for columns: Cash; Accounts Receivable; Equipment; Accounts Payable; Holden, Capital; Holden, Withdrawals; Revenues; and Expenses. Then use additions and subtractions to show the effects of the transactions on individual items of the accounting equation. Show new balances after each transaction.

The following table shows the effects of five transactions (*a* through *e*) on the assets, liabilities, and equity of Trista's Boutique. Write short descriptions of what likely happened in each transaction.

Exercise 2-6
Identifying effects of transactions on accounting equation
LO1   LO2

	Assets				=	Liabilities	+	Equity	
	Cash	+ Accounts Receivable	+ Office Supplies	+ Land	=	Accounts Payable	+ Trista, Capital	+ Revenues	
	$ 21,000	+ $ 0	+ $3,000	+ $ 19,000	=	$ 0	+ $43,000	+ $ 0	
a.	− 4,000			+ 4,000					
b.			+ 1,000			+1,000			
c.		+ 1,900						+ 1,900	
d.	− 1,000					−1,000			
e.	+ 1,900	− 1,900							
	$ 17,900	+ $ 0	+ $4,000	+ $ 23,000	=	$ 0	+ $43,000	+ $1,900	

On October 1, Keisha King organized Real Answers, a new consulting firm. On October 31, the company's records show the following items and amounts. Use this information to prepare an October income statement for the business.

Exercise 2-7
Preparing an income statement   LO3

Cash	$11,500	Cash withdrawals by owner	$ 2,000
Accounts receivable	12,000	Consulting fees earned	14,000
Office supplies	24,437	Rent expense	2,520
Land	46,000	Salaries expense	5,600
Office equipment	18,000	Telephone expense	760
Accounts payable	25,037	Miscellaneous expenses	580
Owner investments	84,360		

Check   Net income, $4,540

Use the information in Exercise 2-7 to prepare an October statement of owner's equity for Real Answers.

Exercise 2-8
Preparing a statement of owner's equity   LO3

Use the information in Exercise 2-7 (if completed, you can also use your solution to Exercise 2-8) to prepare an October 31 balance sheet for Real Answers.

Exercise 2-9
Preparing a balance sheet   LO3
Check   Total assets, $111,937

The following is selected financial information for Elko Energy Company for the year ended December 31, 2010: revenues, $55,000; expenses, $40,000; net income, $15,000.

Exercise 2-10
Preparing an income statement
LO3

Required

Prepare the 2010 income statement for Elko Energy Company.

The following is selected financial information for Amity Company as of December 31, 2010: liabilities, $44,000; equity, $46,000; assets, $90,000.

Exercise 2-11
Preparing a balance sheet   LO3

Required

Prepare the balance sheet for Amity Company as of December 31, 2010.

Following is selected financial information for Kasio Co. for the year ended December 31, 2010.

Exercise 2-12
Preparing a statement of owner's equity   LO3

K. Kasio, Capital, Dec. 31, 2010	$14,000	K. Kasio, Withdrawals	$1,000
Net income	8,000	K. Kasio, Capital, Dec. 31, 2009	7,000

Required

Prepare the 2010 statement of owner's equity for Kasio.

Exercise 2-13
Preparing a statement of
owner's equity   **LO3**

Following is selected financial information of First Act for the year ended December 31, 2010.

I. Firstact, Capital, Dec. 31, 2010	$47,000	I. Firstact, Withdrawals	$ 7,000
Net income	5,000	I. Firstact, Capital, Dec. 31, 2009	49,000

Required

Prepare the 2010 calendar-year statement of owner's equity for First Act.

Exercise 2-14
Analyzing effects of transactions
LO1   LO2

Isabel Lopez started Biz Consulting, a new business, and completed the following transactions during its
first year of operations.

a. I. Lopez invests $70,000 cash and office equipment valued at $10,000 in the business.

b. Purchased a $20,000 building to use as an office. Biz paid $20,000 in cash.

c. Purchased office equipment for $15,000 cash.

d. Purchased $1,200 of office supplies credit.

Required

1. Create a table like the one in Exhibit 2.1, using the following headings for the columns: Cash; Office
   Supplies; Office Equipment; Building; Accounts Payable; I. Lopez, Capital.

2. Use additions and subtractions to show the effects of these transactions on individual items of the
   accounting equation. Show new balances after each transaction.

Exercise 2-15
Preparing financial statements **LO3**

Isabel Lopez's consulting business, Biz Consulting, reports the following accounting equation balances on
December 31, 2010, the end of its first year of operations.

Assets					=	Liabilities	+	Equity			
Cash	**+ Accounts Receivable**	**+ Office Supplies**	**+ Office Equipment**	**+ Building**	**= Accounts Payable**	**+**		**+ I. Lopez, Capital**	**− I. Lopez, Withdrawals**	**+ Revenues**	**− Expenses**
Bal. $34,525	+ $1,000	+ $1,200	+ $26,700	+ $150,000	= $132,200			+ $80,000	− $3,275	+ $6,800	− $2,300

Required

Check   (2) I. Lopez Capital,
          December 31, $81,225

1. Compute net income for 2010.

2. Prepare a statement of owner's equity for 2010 and a balance sheet as of December 31, 2010.

Problem Set B located at the end of Problem Set A is provided for each problem to reinforce the learning process.

connect™

PROBLEM SET A

Problem 2-1A
Computing missing information
using accounting knowledge and
the accounting equation
LO1   LO2

The following financial statement information is from five separate companies.

	Company A	Company B	Company C	Company D	Company E
December 31, 2009					
Assets	$55,000	$34,000	$24,000	$60,000	$119,000
Liabilities	24,500	21,500	9,000	40,000	?
December 31, 2010					
Assets	58,000	40,000	?	85,000	113,000
Liabilities	?	26,500	29,000	24,000	70,000
During year 2010					
Owner investments	6,000	1,400	9,750	?	6,500
Net income	8,500	?	8,000	14,000	20,000
Owner cash withdrawals	3,500	2,000	5,875	0	11,000

Required

1. Answer the following questions about Company A.

   a. What is the amount of equity on December 31, 2009? $30,500

   b. What is the amount of equity on December 31, 2010? $41,500

Check   (1b) $41,500

   c. What is the amount of liabilities on December 31, 2010? $16,500

2. Answer the following questions about Company B.
   a. What is the amount of equity on December 31, 2009? $12,500
   b. What is the amount of equity on December 31, 2010? $13,500
   c. What is net income for year 2010? $14,100
3. Calculate the amount of assets for Company C on December 31, 2010. $91,500
4. Calculate the amount of owner investments for Company D during year 2010. $47,000
5. Calculate the amount of liabilities for Company E on December 31, 2009. $91,500

Check (2c) $1,600
(3) $55,875

Identify how each of the following separate transactions affects financial statements. For the balance sheet, identify how each transaction affects total assets, total liabilities, and total equity. For the income statement, identify how each transaction affects net income. For increases, place a "+" in the column or columns. For decreases, place a "−" in the column or columns. If both an increase and a decrease occur, place a "+/−" in the column or columns. The first transaction is completed as an example.

Problem 2–2A
Identifying effects of transactions on financial statements
LO1 LO2

		Balance Sheet			Income Statement
	Transaction	Total Assets	Total Liab.	Total Equity	Net Income
1	Owner invests cash in business	+		+	
2	Receives cash for services provided	+		+	+
3	Pays cash for employee wages	−		−	−
4	Owner withdraws cash	−		−	
5	Provides services on credit	+		+	+
6	Buys office equipment for cash	+/−			
7	Collects cash on receivable from (6)	+/−			

Holden Graham started The Graham Co., a new business that began operations on May 1. Graham Co. completed the following transactions during that first month.

Problem 2–3A
Analyzing transactions and preparing financial statements
LO2 LO3

mhhe.com/wildCA2e

May	1	H. Graham invested $40,000 cash in the business.
	1	Rented a furnished office and paid $2,200 cash for May's rent.
	3	Purchased $1,890 of office equipment on credit.
	5	Paid $750 cash for this month's cleaning services.
	8	Provided consulting services for a client and immediately collected $5,400 cash.
	12	Provided $2,500 of consulting services for a client on credit.
	15	Paid $750 cash for an assistant's salary for the first half of this month.
	20	Received $2,500 cash payment for the services provided on May 12.
	22	Provided $3,200 of consulting services on credit.
	25	Received $3,200 cash payment for the services provided on May 22.
	26	Paid $1,890 cash for the office equipment purchased on May 3.
	27	Purchased $80 of advertising in this month's (May) local paper on credit.
	28	Paid $750 cash for an assistant's salary for the second half of this month.
	30	Paid $300 cash for this month's telephone bill.
	30	Paid $280 cash for this month's utilities.
	31	Graham withdrew $1,400 cash for personal use.

Required

1. Arrange the following asset, liability, and equity titles in a table like Exhibit 2.1: Cash; Accounts Receivable; Office Equipment; Accounts Payable; H. Graham, Capital; H. Graham, Withdrawals; Revenues; and Expenses.

2. Show effects of the transactions on the accounts of the accounting equation by recording increases and decreases in the appropriate columns. Do not determine new account balances after each transaction. Determine the final total for each account and verify that the equation is in balance.

3. Prepare an income statement for May, a statement of owner's equity for May, and a May 31 balance sheet.

Check (2) Ending balances: Cash, $42,780; Expenses, $5,110

(3) Net income, $5,990; Total assets, $44,670

Problem 2-4A

Analyzing transactions and
preparing financial statements
LO2   LO3

mhhe.com/wildCA2e

Helga Ander started a new business and completed these transactions during December.

Dec. 1   Helga Ander transferred $65,000 cash from a personal savings account to a checking account
           in the name of Ander Electric.
       2   Rented office space and paid $1,000 cash for the December rent.
       3   Purchased $13,000 of electrical equipment by paying $4,800 cash and agreeing to pay the
           $8,200 balance in 30 days.
       5   Purchased office supplies by paying $800 cash.
       6   Completed electrical work and immediately collected $1,200 cash for the work.
       8   Purchased $2,530 of office equipment on credit.
      15   Completed electrical work on credit in the amount of $5,000.
      18   Purchased $350 of office supplies on credit.
      20   Paid $2,530 cash for the office equipment purchased on December 8.
      24   Billed a client $900 for electrical work completed.
      28   Received $5,000 cash for the work completed on December 15.
      29   Paid the assistant's salary of $1,400 cash for this month.
      30   Paid $540 cash for this month's utility bill.
      31   Ander withdrew $950 cash for personal use.

Required

1. Arrange the following asset, liability, and equity titles in a table like Exhibit 2.1: Cash; Accounts
   Receivable; Office Supplies; Office Equipment; Electrical Equipment; Accounts Payable; H. Ander,
   Capital; H. Ander, Withdrawals; Revenues; and Expenses.

Check   (2) Ending balances: Cash,
$59,180, Accounts Payable, $8,550

2. Use additions and subtractions to show the effects of each transaction on the accounts in the accounting equation. Show new balances after each transaction.

        (3) Net income, $4,160;
Total assets, $76,760

3. Use the increases and decreases in the columns of the table from part 2 to prepare an income statement
   and a statement of owner's equity for the month. Also prepare a balance sheet as of the end of the month.

PROBLEM SET B

Problem 2-1B

Computing missing information
using accounting knowledge
LO1   LO2

The following financial statement information is from five separate companies.

	Company V	Company W	Company X	Company Y	Company Z
December 31, 2009					
Assets	$54,000	$ 80,000	$141,500	$92,500	$144,000
Liabilities	25,000	60,000	68,500	51,500	?
December 31, 2010					
Assets	59,000	100,000	186,500	?	170,000
Liabilities	36,000	?	65,800	42,000	42,000
During year 2010					
Owner investments	5,000	20,000	?	48,100	60,000
Net income	?	40,000	18,500	24,000	32,000
Owner cash withdrawals	5,500	2,000	0	20,000	8,000

Required

1. Answer the following questions about Company V.
   a. What is the amount of equity on December 31, 2009? $29,000
   b. What is the amount of equity on December 31, 2010? $23,000
   c. What is the net income or loss for the year 2010? $22,500

Check   (1b) $23,000

2. Answer the following questions about Company W.
   a. What is the amount of equity on December 31, 2009? $ 20,000
   b. What is the amount of equity on December 31, 2010? $ 78,000

(2c) $22,000

   c. What is the amount of liabilities on December 31, 2010? $22,000

3. Calculate the amount of owner investments for Company X during 2010. $102,200

(4) $135,100

4. Calculate the amount of assets for Company Y on December 31, 2010. $135,100

5. Calculate the amount of liabilities for Company Z on December 31, 2009. $100,000

Identify how each of the following separate transactions affects financial statements. For the balance sheet, identify how each transaction affects total assets, total liabilities, and total equity. For the income statement, identify how each transaction affects net income. For increases, place a "+" in the column or columns. For decreases, place a "−" in the column or columns. If both an increase and a decrease occur, place "+/−" in the column or columns. The first transaction is completed as an example.

Problem 2–2B

Identifying effects of transactions on financial statements

LO1   LO2

		Balance Sheet			Income Statement
	Transaction	Total Assets	Total Liab.	Total Equity	Net Income
1	Owner invests cash in business	+		+	
2	Pays cash for salaries	−		−	−
3	Provides services for cash	+		+	+
4	Pays cash for rent	−		−	−
5	Buys store equipment for cash	+/−			
6	Owner withdraws cash	−		−	
7	Provides services on credit	+		+	+
8	Collects cash on receivable from (7)	+/−			

Holly Nikolas launched a new business, Holly's Maintenance Co., that began operations on June 1. The following transactions were completed by the company during that first month.

Problem 2–3B

Analyzing transactions and preparing financial statements

LO2   LO3

June 1   H. Nikolas invested $130,000 cash in the business.
     2   Rented a furnished office and paid $6,000 cash for June's rent.
     4   Purchased $2,400 of equipment on credit.
     6   Paid $1,150 cash for the next week's advertising of the opening of the business.
     8   Completed maintenance services for a customer and immediately collected $850 cash.
    14   Completed $7,500 of maintenance services for City Center on credit.
    16   Paid $800 cash for an assistant's salary for the first half of the month.
    20   Received $7,500 cash payment for services completed for City Center on June 14.
    21   Completed $7,900 of maintenance services for Paula's Beauty Shop on credit.
    24   Completed $675 of maintenance services for Build-It Coop on credit.
    25   Received $7,900 cash payment from Paula's Beauty Shop for the work completed on June 21.
    26   Made payment of $2,400 cash for the equipment purchased on June 4.
    28   Paid $800 cash for an assistant's salary for the second half of this month.
    29   Nikolas withdrew $4,000 cash for personal use.
    30   Paid $150 cash for this month's telephone bill.
    30   Paid $890 cash for this month's utilities.

Required

1. Arrange the following asset, liability, and equity titles in a table like Exhibit 2.1: Cash; Accounts Receivable; Equipment; Accounts Payable; H. Nikolas, Capital; H. Nikolas, Withdrawals; Revenues; and Expenses.

2. Show the effects of the transactions on the accounts of the accounting equation by recording increases and decreases in the appropriate columns. Do not determine new account balances after each transaction. Determine the final total for each account and verify that the equation is in balance.

Check   (2) Ending balances: Cash, $130,060; Expenses, $9,790

(3) Net income, $7,135; Total assets, $133,135

3. Prepare a June income statement, a June statement of owner's equity, and a June 30 balance sheet.

Truro Excavating Co., owned by Raul Truro, began operations in July and completed the following transactions during that first month.

Problem 2–4B

Analyzing transactions and preparing financial statements

LO2   LO3

July 1   R. Truro invested $80,000 cash in the business.
     2   Rented office space and paid $700 cash for the July rent.
     3   Purchased excavating equipment for $5,000 by paying $1,000 cash and agreeing to pay the $4,000 balance in 30 days.
     6   Purchased office supplies for $600 cash.
     8   Completed work for a customer and immediately collected $7,600 cash for the work.

10   Purchased $2,300 of office equipment on credit.
15   Completed work for a customer on credit in the amount of $8,200.
17   Purchased $3,100 of office supplies on credit.
23   Paid $2,300 cash for the office equipment purchased on July 10.
25   Billed a customer $5,000 for work completed.
28   Received $8,200 cash for the work completed on July 15.
30   Paid an assistant's salary of $1,560 cash for this month.
31   Paid $295 cash for this month's utility bill.
31   Truro withdrew $1,800 cash for personal use.

Required

1. Arrange the following asset, liability, and equity titles in a table like Exhibit 2.1: Cash; Accounts Receivable; Office Supplies; Office Equipment; Excavating Equipment; Accounts Payable; R. Truro, Capital; R. Truro, Withdrawals; Revenues; and Expenses.

Check   (2) Ending balances: Cash, $87,545; Accounts Payable, $7,100

2. Use additions and subtractions to show the effects of each transaction on the accounts in the accounting equation. Show new balances after each transaction.

(3) Net income, $18,245; Total assets, $103,545

3. Use the increases and decreases in the columns of the table from part 2 to prepare an income statement, and a statement of owner's equity. Also prepare a balance sheet as of the end of the month.

SERIAL PROBLEM

Success Systems

(This serial problem started in Chapter 1 and continues through most of the chapters. If the Chapter 1 segment was not completed, the problem can begin at this point. It is helpful, but not necessary, to use the Working Papers that accompany this book.)

SP 2   On October 1, 2010, Adriana Lopez started a computer services company, **Success Systems,** that provides consulting services, computer system installations, and custom program development. Lopez expects to prepare the company's first set of financial statements on December 31, 2010.

Required

Create a table like the one in Exhibit 2.1 using the following headings for columns: Cash; Accounts Receivable; Computer Supplies; Computer System; Office Equipment; Accounts Payable; A. Lopez, Capital; A. Lopez, Withdrawals; Revenues; and Expenses. Then use additions and subtractions to show the effects of the October transactions for Success Systems on the individual items of the accounting equation. Show new balances after each transaction.

Oct. 1   Adriana Lopez invested $75,000 cash, a $25,000 computer system, and $10,000 of office equipment in the business.
      3   Purchased $1,600 of computer supplies on credit from Corvina Office Products.
      6   Billed Easy Leasing $6,200 for services performed in installing a new Web server.
      8   Paid $1,600 cash for the computer supplies purchased from Corvina Office Products on October 3.
     12   Billed Easy Leasing another $1,950 for services performed.
     15   Received $6,200 cash from Easy Leasing toward its account.
     17   Paid $900 cash to repair computer equipment damaged when moving it.
     20   Paid $1,790 cash for an advertisement in the local newspaper.
     22   Received $1,950 cash from Easy Leasing toward its account.
     28   Billed Clark Company $7,300 for services performed.
     31   Paid $1,050 cash for Michelle Jones's wages for seven days of work this month.
     31   Lopez withdrew $4,000 cash for personal use.

Check   Ending balances: Cash, $73,810; Revenues, $15,450; Expenses, $3,740

BEYOND THE NUMBERS

REPORTING IN ACTION

L01

BTN 2-1   Key financial figures for **Best Buy**'s fiscal year ended March 1, 2008, follow.

Key Figure	In Millions
Liabilities + Equity	$12,758
Net income	1,407
Revenues	40,023

Required

1. What is the total amount of assets invested in **Best Buy**?

2. How much are total expenses for Best Buy for the year ended March 1, 2008?

BTN 2-2   WorldCom committed fraud by accounting for some expenses as if they were assets.

ETHICS CHALLENGE
LO1   LO2

Required

1. Using the accounting equation, show the accounting for an expense and the accounting for an asset (assume $1,000 cash is paid in each instance). Does the accounting equation balance in both instances?

2. What ethical concerns would you have if your business accounted for an expense as if it were an asset?

BTN 2-3   Refer to this chapter's opening feature about **SPANX**. Assume that the founder, Sara Blakely, is having difficulty assessing how well her business has performed over the past year. Write Sara Blakely a half-page memo to explain which financial statement will provide her the best information on her company's performance and which particular number she should focus on.

WORKPLACE COMMUNICATION
LO3

BTN 2-4   Visit the EDGAR database at (www.SEC.gov). Under "Filings and Forms" click on "Search for Company Filings." Access the Form 10-K report of **Rocky Mountain Chocolate Factory** (ticker RMCF) filed on May 14, 2007, covering its 2007 fiscal year.

TAKING IT TO THE NET
LO3

Required

1. Item 6 of its 10-K report provides comparative financial highlights of RMCF for the years 2004–2007. How would you describe the revenue trend for RMCF over this five-year period?

2. Has RMCF been profitable (see net income) over this four-year period? Support your answer.

BTN 2-5   Divide the class into teams and play **Monopoly**™. Each team takes 10 turns. Each team starts with $1,500 of owners' capital, in cash.

TEAMWORK IN ACTION
LO1   LO2

Required

1. Each team accounts for its first 10 transactions using the accounting equation. Use a table like Exhibit 2.1.

2. Each team presents its accounting equation entries to one other team.

BTN 2-6   Assume that Sara Blakely of SPANX wants to expand her business. She is considering financing her expansion in one of two ways: (1) contributing more of her own cash to the business or (2) borrowing cash from a bank.

ENTREPRENEURS IN BUSINESS
LO2   LO3

Required

Identify the issues that Blakely should consider when trying to decide on the method for financing the expansion.

BTN 2-7   You open a wholesale business selling entertainment equipment to retail outlets. You find that most of your customers demand to buy on credit. How can you use the balance sheets of these customers to help you decide which ones to extend credit to?

YOU CALL IT— ENTREPRENEUR

---

1. d

2. a

3. d;

4. a

5. a

ANSWERS TO MULTIPLE CHOICE QUIZ

Assets	=	Liabilities	+	Equity
+$100,000	=	+35,000	+	?

Change in equity = $100,000 − $35,000 = $65,000

A Look Back

Chapter 2 introduced the accounting equation and accounts for various transactions. We also introduced the basic financial statements.

A Look at This Chapter

This chapter introduces double-entry accounting. We explain the analysis and recording of transactions using debits and credits and T-accounts. We show how a trial balance is used to check the accuracy of debits and credits.

A Look Ahead

Chapter 4 introduces the general journal and general ledger. We show how transactions are journalized (recorded) in a general journal and then posted in a general ledger.

Chapter

Applying Double-Entry Accounting

Learning Objectives

LO 1 Describe a T-account and its use in recording transactions.

LO 2 Define debits and credits and explain their role in double-entry accounting.

LO 3 Post transactions in T-accounts.

LO 4 Prepare and explain the use of a trial balance.

LO 5 Prepare financial statements from a trial balance.

"Each individual problem you face is totally surmountable"—Warren Brown

Making Dough

WASHINGTON, DC—Warren Brown started baking cakes to reduce stress, but his friends' appetites demanded more. "Friends were jumping on the bed" saying how much they loved the cakes and insisting that I set up shop, says Warren.

Starting small, Warren baked cakes from scratch using all-natural ingredients in his apartment for hours after work each evening. He sold his sweet concoctions mostly to co-workers and friends, and even held a cake open house at the local art gallery. But Warren was determined to grow his business. He took a course in entrepreneurship at his local community college, and there he discovered the importance of accounting.

Launching his fledgling cake business presented Warren with many challenges. He borrowed $125,000 from the Small Business Administration to buy the equipment to get his business started. He established inventory accounting, transaction analysis, and accounting entries. Rapidly changing prices for his cake ingredients require Warren to closely monitor his selling prices and costs to enable a profit. "Everything feels like a disaster when it's right in your face," says Warren. "You just have to be calm, look at what you're doing, and fix the problem." Warren fixed the problems and unveiled his shop called **Cake Love** (**CakeLove.com**). "I opened up this tiny retail, walk-up bakery . . . [to sell] goodies that are baked from scratch," Warren recalls.

Today, Cake Love entices customers with the scents of fresh bakery at each of its six locations. Warren's Love Café offers customers an inviting place to lounge for hours with free wireless Internet and comfy chairs. "I want it to be relaxed and comfortable," says Warren. "People can bring their work, their kids, their friends, and just relax."

Warren continues to experiment with new treats. "I'm always getting better, improving my skills," he said. Warren also shows a keen appetite for using accounting information to make good business decisions. "But," says Warren, "I love eating what I make more."

"The bigger message of Cake Love is finding your passion and working to reach your goals," says Warren. That's a slice of advice worth more than any amount of dough.

[Sources: *Cake Love Website,* January 2009; *Black Enterprise,* September 2004; *Georgetown Voice,* March 2005; *National Public Radio (NPR) Website,* May 2005; *Inc.com,* April 2005; *Modern Baking,* November 1, 2004; Diamondback online, February 21, 2007.]

Financial statements report on the financial performance and condition of an organization. A main goal of this chapter is to illustrate how transactions are recorded and how they are reflected in financial statements. Debits and credits are introduced and identified as a tool in helping analyze and process transactions.

Applying Double-Entry Accounting

Analyzing and Recording Transactions
- The T-account
- Double-entry
- An illustration

Preparing and Using a Trial Balance
- Trial balance preparation
- Trial balance use

Analyzing and Recording Transactions

In Chapter 2, we introduced the accounting equation, Assets = Liabilities + Equity, as a way to understand what resources the organization owns and who has rights to those resources. However, organizations do not record their transactions in accounting equation form. Instead, they record increases and decreases in individual accounts.

The T-Account

LO1 Describe a T-account and its use in recording transactions.

An account is a record of increases and decreases in a specific asset, liability, equity, revenue, or expense item due to an organization's transactions. A **T-account** is a tool used to understand the effects of these transactions. Its name comes from its shape like the letter T. The layout of a T-account (shown in Exhibit 3.1) is (1) the account title on top, (2) a left, or **debit,** side, and (3) a right, or **credit,** side. We can think of the terms *debit* and *credit* as accounting terms for left and right. In addition, to debit an account means to post a dollar amount on the left side of the T-account. To credit an account means to post a dollar amount on the right side of the T-account. This is true for all types of accounts.

Exhibit 3.1

The T-Account

Account Title	
(Left side)	(Right side)
Debit	**Credit**

In Chapter 2, we accounted for the December transactions of FastForward using the accounting equation. As an illustration of the use of the T-account, we show how increases and decreases in cash are accounted for. The T-account for FastForward's Cash account, reflecting its first 11 transactions (from Exhibit 2.1), is shown in Exhibit 3.2. (Only nine of FastForward's first 11 transactions impact its Cash account). We include descriptions of each transaction for illustration purposes. T-accounts usually include only numbers.

LO2 Define debits and credits and explain their role in double-entry accounting.

Exhibit 3.2

Computing the Balance for a T-Account

Cash			
Investment by owner	30,000	Purchase of supplies	2,500
Consulting services revenue earned	4,200	Purchase of equipment	26,000
Collection of account receivable	1,900	Payment of rent	1,000
Footing	**36,100**	Payment of salary	700
		Payment of account payable	900
		Withdrawal by owner	200
		Footing	**31,300**
Balance	**4,800**		

Note that the numbers in a T-account are not identified with either plus or minus signs. In the next section we explain how the accountant knows how debits and credits impact individual accounts. At this point, simply understand that increases in cash are shown on the left (or debit) side and decreases in cash are shown on the right (or credit) side. The increases in FastForward's Cash account total $36,100, and the decreases total $31,300. These totals are called **footings.** To foot a column of numbers means to compute the total of that column. The difference between total debits and total credits for an account, including any beginning balance, is the **account balance.** When the sum of debits exceeds the sum of credits, the account has a *debit balance*. It has a *credit balance* when the sum of the credits exceeds the sum of debits. When the sum of debits equals the sum of credits, the account has a zero balance. Since the total increases (debits) exceed the total decreases (credits) for FastForward's Cash account, its ending balance in cash is a debit balance of $4,800, (computed as $36,100 minus $31,300).

Double-Entry Accounting

Double-entry accounting requires that each transaction be recorded in at least two accounts. It also means the *total amount debited must equal the total amount credited* for each transaction. Thus, the sum of the debits for all entries must equal the sum of the credits for all entries, and the sum of debit account balances must equal the sum of credit account balances. This means the accounting equation is in balance.

The system for recording debits and credits follows from the usual accounting equation—see Exhibit 3.3. Two points are important here. First, accounts on the left side of the accounting equation (assets) increase with entries in the left side of the T-account (debits). Accounts on the

"Total debits equal total credits for each entry."

Assets		=	Liabilities		+	Equity	
Debit for increases	Credit for decreases		Debit for decreases	Credit for increases		Debit for decreases	Credit for increases
+	−		−	+		−	+

Exhibit 3.3

Debits and Credits in the Accounting Equation

right side of the accounting equation (liabilities and equity) increase with entries on the right side of the T-account (credits). Second, an account's **normal balance** is the side of the account on which increases are recorded. Thus, the left side is the *normal balance* side for assets, and the right side of the T-account is the *normal balance* side for liabilities and equity. This matches their layout in the accounting equation where assets are on the left side of this equation, and liabilities and equity are on the right.

Recall that equity increases from revenues and owner investments and it decreases from expenses and owner withdrawals. These important equity relations are conveyed by expanding the accounting equation to include debits and credits in double-entry form as shown in Exhibit 3.4. The abbreviation "Dr." is for debit, and the abbreviation "Cr." is for credit.

Exhibit 3.4

Debit and Credit Effects for Expanded Accounting Equation

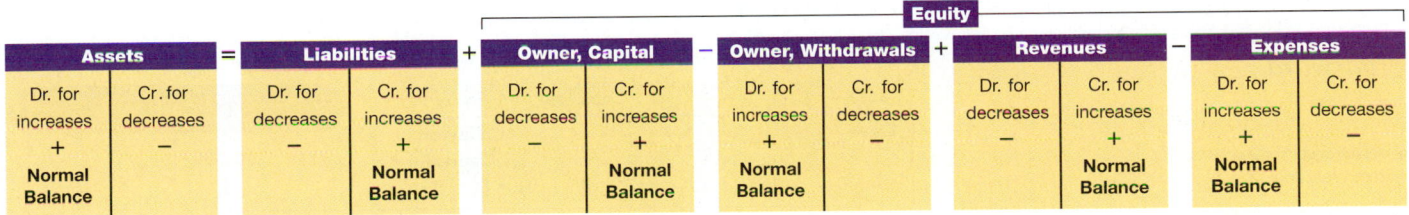

						Equity							
Assets		=	Liabilities		+	Owner, Capital		−	Owner, Withdrawals		+	Revenues		−	Expenses	
Dr. for increases	Cr. for decreases		Dr. for decreases	Cr. for increases		Dr. for decreases	Cr. for increases		Dr. for increases	Cr. for decreases		Dr. for decreases	Cr. for increases		Dr. for increases	Cr. for decreases
+	−		−	+		−	+		+	−		−	+		+	−
Normal Balance				Normal Balance			Normal Balance		Normal Balance				Normal Balance		Normal Balance	

Increases (credits) to capital and revenues *increase* equity; increases (debits) to withdrawals and expenses *decrease* equity. The normal balance of each account (asset, liability, capital, withdrawals, revenue, or expense) refers to the left or right (debit or credit) side where *increases* are recorded.

Recording Transactions—An Illustration

LO3 Post transactions in T-accounts.

We return to the activities of FastForward to show how to record transactions in T-account form. Study each transaction thoroughly before proceeding to the next. The first 11 transactions are from Chapter 2, and we analyze five additional December transactions of FastForward (numbered 12 through 16) that were omitted earlier.

Here is a simple three-step process to follow to record a transaction in T-account form. We use the letters *TAP* to stand for the steps: Transaction, Analysis, and Post.

1. *Transaction:* Determine which accounts are affected by the transaction.
2. *Analysis:* Analyze the transaction using the accounting equation.
   a. Label the affected accounts as either assets, liabilities, or equity (including revenues and expenses).
   b. Determine whether the transaction increases or decreases the affected accounts.
   c. Verify the accounting equation remains in balance.
3. *Post:* Using the rules of debit and credit, post the transactions to T-accounts. To **post** means to make an entry in an account. We summarize the rules of debit and credit in Exhibit 3.5.

Exhibit 3.5

Debit and Credit Rules

Accounts	Debit and Credit Rules	
	Increase (normal bal.)	Decrease
Asset	Debit	Credit
Liability	Credit	Debit
Capital	Credit	Debit
Withdrawals	Debit	Credit
Revenue	Credit	Debit
Expense	Debit	Credit

1. Investment by Owner

FASTForward

Total debits equal total credits for each transaction.

Transaction: Chuck Taylor invests $30,000 cash in FastForward.

Analysis:

Assets	=	Liabilities	+	Equity
Cash				**C. Taylor, Capital**
+30,000	=	0	+	30,000

Cash and C. Taylor, Capital increase by $30,000. Cash is debited and C. Taylor, Capital is credited.

Post in T-accounts:

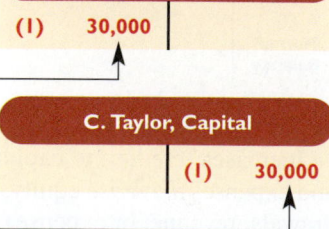

Cash	
(1) 30,000	

C. Taylor, Capital	
	(1) 30,000

2. Purchase Supplies for Cash

Transaction: FastForward pays $2,500 cash for supplies.

Analysis:

Post in T-accounts:

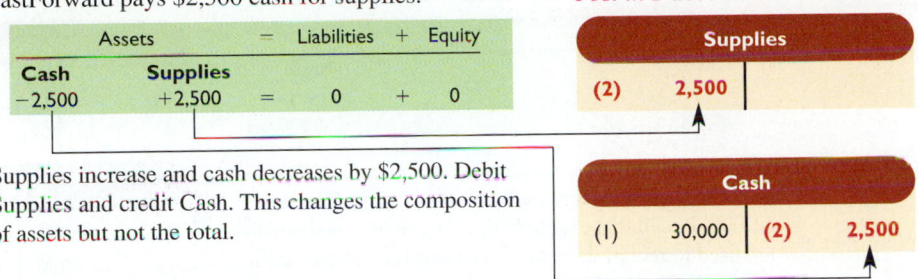

Supplies increase and cash decreases by $2,500. Debit Supplies and credit Cash. This changes the composition of assets but not the total.

3. Purchase Equipment for Cash

Transaction: FastForward pays $26,000 cash for equipment.

Analysis:

Post in T-accounts:

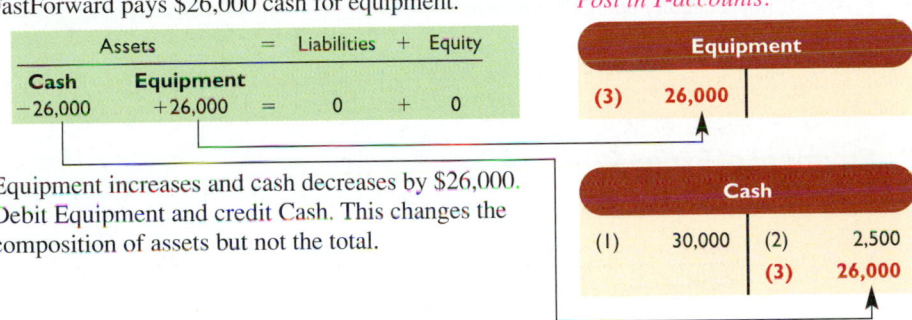

Equipment increases and cash decreases by $26,000. Debit Equipment and credit Cash. This changes the composition of assets but not the total.

4. Purchase Supplies on Credit

Transaction: FastForward purchases $7,100 of supplies on credit from a supplier.

Analysis:

Post in T-accounts:

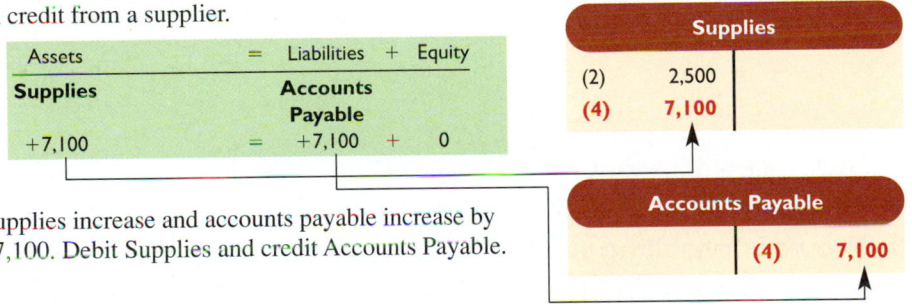

Supplies increase and accounts payable increase by $7,100. Debit Supplies and credit Accounts Payable.

5. Provide Services for Cash

Transaction: FastForward provides consulting services and immediately collects $4,200 cash.

Analysis:

Post in T-accounts:

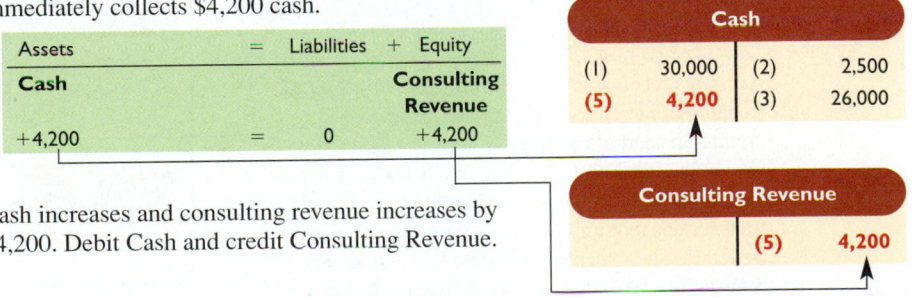

Cash increases and consulting revenue increases by $4,200. Debit Cash and credit Consulting Revenue.

6. Payment of Expense in Cash

Transaction: FastForward pays $1,000 cash for December rent.

Analysis:

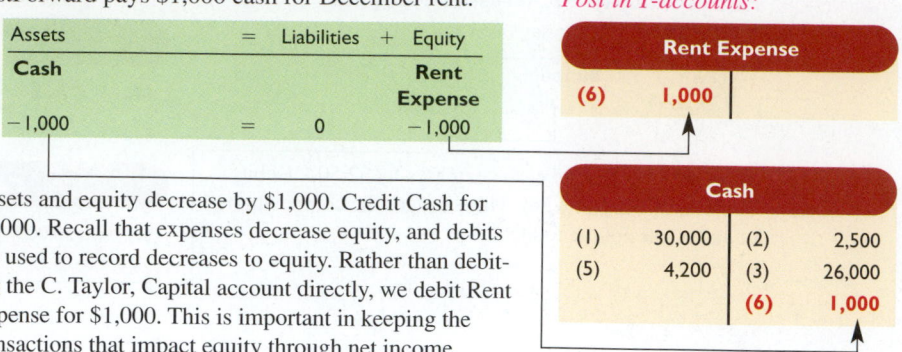

Post in T-accounts:

Assets and equity decrease by $1,000. Credit Cash for $1,000. Recall that expenses decrease equity, and debits are used to record decreases to equity. Rather than debiting the C. Taylor, Capital account directly, we debit Rent Expense for $1,000. This is important in keeping the transactions that impact equity through net income (revenues and expenses) separate from the owner transactions (withdrawals and contributions) that impact equity but not net income.

7. Payment of Expense in Cash

Transaction: FastForward pays $700 cash for employee salaries.

Analysis:

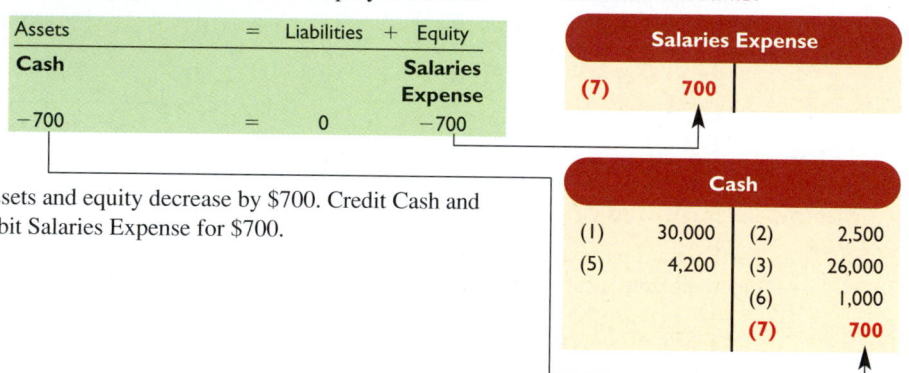

Post in T-accounts:

Assets and equity decrease by $700. Credit Cash and debit Salaries Expense for $700.

8. Provide Consulting and Rental Services on Credit

Transaction: FastForward provides consulting services of $1,600 and rents its test facilities for $300. The customer is billed $1,900 for these services.

Analysis:

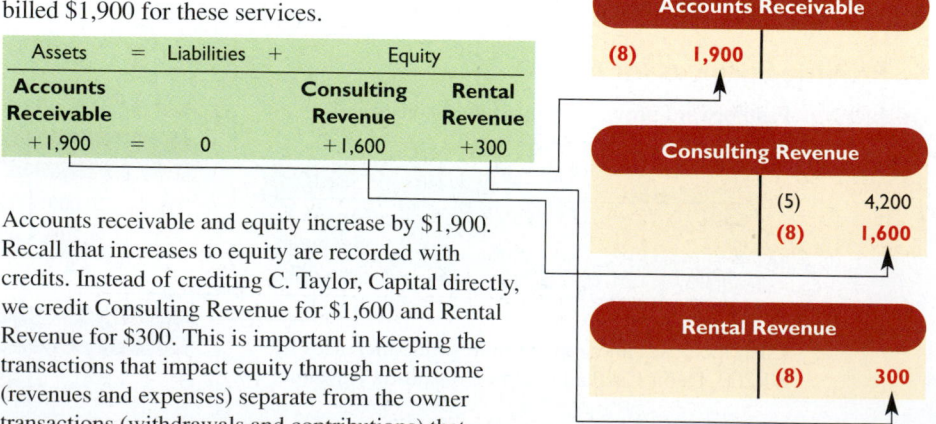

Post in T-accounts:

Accounts receivable and equity increase by $1,900. Recall that increases to equity are recorded with credits. Instead of crediting C. Taylor, Capital directly, we credit Consulting Revenue for $1,600 and Rental Revenue for $300. This is important in keeping the transactions that impact equity through net income (revenues and expenses) separate from the owner transactions (withdrawals and contributions) that impact equity but not net income.

9. Receipt of Cash on Account

Transaction: FastForward receives $1,900 cash from the client billed in transaction 8.

Analysis:

Post in T-accounts:

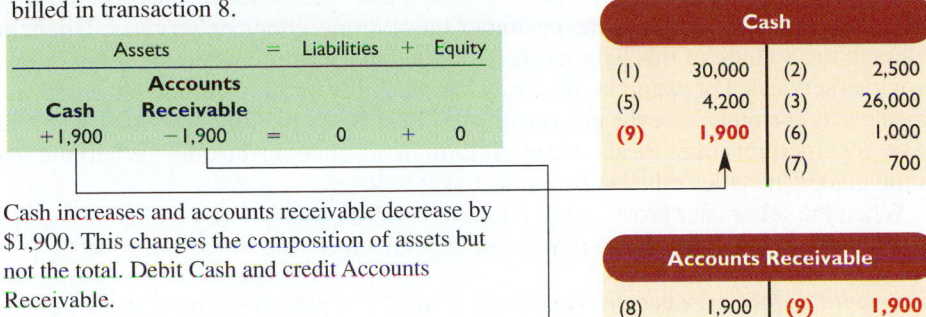

Cash increases and accounts receivable decrease by $1,900. This changes the composition of assets but not the total. Debit Cash and credit Accounts Receivable.

10. Partial Payment of Accounts Payable

Transaction: FastForward pays the supplier $900 cash toward the account payable from transaction 4.

Analysis:

Post in T-accounts:

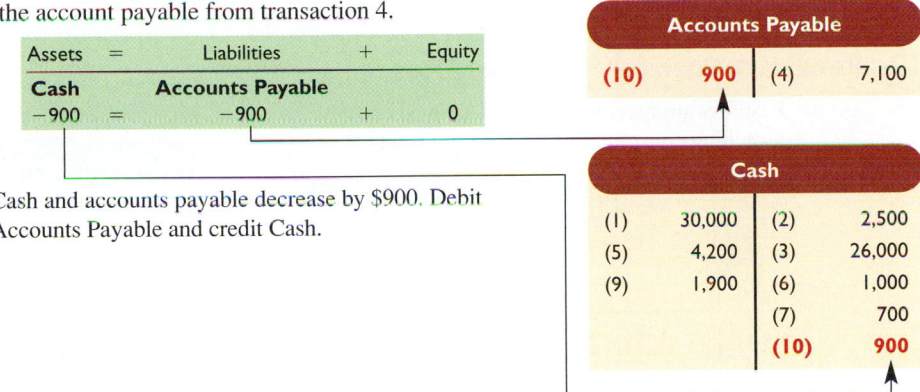

Cash and accounts payable decrease by $900. Debit Accounts Payable and credit Cash.

11. Withdrawal of Cash by Owner

Transaction: Chuck Taylor withdraws $200 cash from FastForward for personal use.

Analysis:

Post in T-accounts:

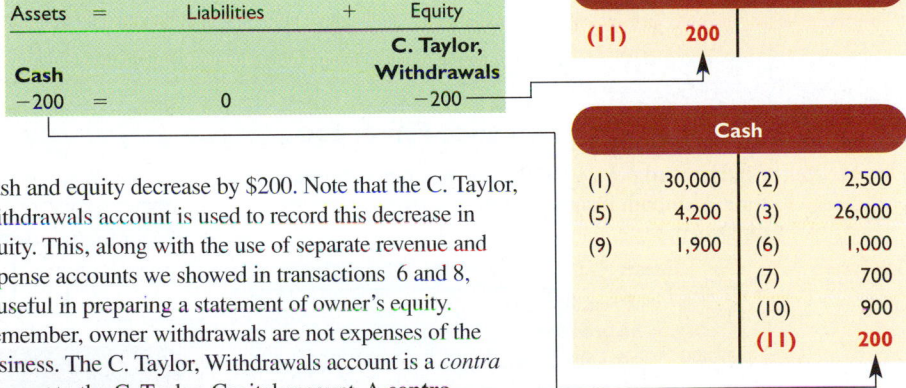

Cash and equity decrease by $200. Note that the C. Taylor, Withdrawals account is used to record this decrease in equity. This, along with the use of separate revenue and expense accounts we showed in transactions 6 and 8, is useful in preparing a statement of owner's equity. Remember, owner withdrawals are not expenses of the business. The C. Taylor, Withdrawals account is a *contra account* to the C. Taylor, Capital account. A **contra account** is an account linked with another account. Its normal balance is opposite that of the linked account's balance.

Prepayments   So far we have used the transactions from Chapter 2 to show how to post transactions to T-accounts. We now introduce five additional transactions of FastForward for December. The first two of these transactions illustrate how to account for *prepayments* of cash.

Cash collected before services are provided Sometimes customers pay in advance for products or services to be provided later. Examples include magazine subscriptions collected in advance by a publisher, gift certificates by stores, and season ticket sales by sports teams. When this happens, the seller owes the customer those future goods or services. **Unearned revenue** refers to the amount of this liability that is settled in the future when the seller delivers goods or provides services. For example, Best Buy has a liability of $332 million for unredeemed gift certificates; as customers use the gift certificates, Best Buy's liability decreases. The Chicago Bears have unearned revenues of about $60 million in advance ticket sales. When the team plays its home games, it settles this liability to its ticket holders.

When the seller later provides the goods or services, this liability will be reduced and revenue will be recorded. We show this process in later chapters.

Cash paid before services are received Sometimes a business pays in advance for goods or services to be provided later. Common examples of these prepaid amounts include prepaid rent and prepaid insurance. **Prepaid assets** (also called *prepaid expenses*) refers to amounts a business has paid in advance for future goods or services. These prepayments are assets, since the business expects future benefits from the prepayments. These prepaid assets become expenses as the goods or services are provided, a process we show in later chapters.

12. Receipt of Cash for Future Services

Transaction: FastForward receives $3,000 cash in advance of providing consulting services to a customer.

Analysis:

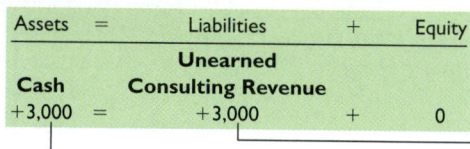

Assets	=	Liabilities	+	Equity
		Unearned		
Cash		**Consulting Revenue**		
+3,000	=	+3,000	+	0

Accepting $3,000 cash obligates FastForward to perform future services. Unearned revenue is a liability created when customers pay in advance for services (or products). Cash increases and liabilities increase by $3,000. Debit Cash and credit Unearned Consulting Revenue.

Post in T-accounts:

Cash			
(1)	30,000	(2)	2,500
(5)	4,200	(3)	26,000
(9)	1,900	(6)	1,000
(12)	**3,000**	(7)	700
		(10)	900
		(11)	200

Unearned Consulting Revenue			
		(12)	**3,000**

13. Pay Cash for Future Insurance Coverage

Transaction: FastForward pays $2,400 cash (insurance premium) for a 24-month insurance policy. Coverage begins on December 1.

Analysis:

Assets		=	Liabilities	+	Equity
	Prepaid				
Cash	**Insurance**				
−2,400	+2,400	=	0	+	0

This prepayment provides FastForward with insurance coverage over the next 24 months. This insurance coverage is an asset. The asset prepaid insurance increases by $2,400, and cash decreases by $2,400. This changes the composition of assets but not the total. Debit Prepaid Insurance and credit Cash.

Post in T-accounts:

Prepaid Insurance			
(13)	**2,400**		

Cash			
(1)	30,000	(2)	2,500
(5)	4,200	(3)	26,000
(9)	1,900	(6)	1,000
(12)	3,000	(7)	700
		(10)	900
		(11)	200
		(13)	**2,400**

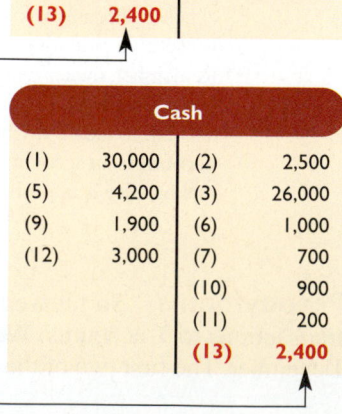

14. Purchase Supplies for Cash

Transaction: FastForward pays $120 cash for supplies.

Analysis:

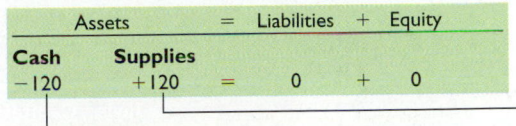

Assets		=	Liabilities	+	Equity
Cash	**Supplies**				
−120	+120	=	0	+	0

Supplies increase and cash decreases by $120. This changes the composition of assets but not the total. Debit Supplies and credit Cash.

Post in T-accounts:

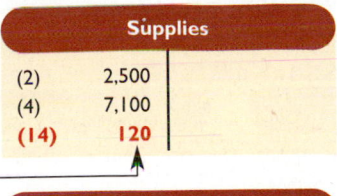

Supplies

(2)	2,500
(4)	7,100
(14)	**120**

Cash

(1)	30,000	(2)	2,500
(5)	4,200	(3)	26,000
(9)	1,900	(6)	1,000
(12)	3,000	(7)	700
		(10)	900
		(11)	200
		(13)	2,400
		(14)	**120**

15. Payment of Expense in Cash

Transaction: FastForward pays $230 cash for December utilities expense.

Analysis:

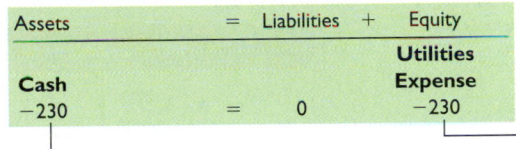

Assets	=	Liabilities	+	Equity
				Utilities Expense
Cash				
−230	=	0		−230

Cash decreases and equity decreases by $230. Remember that we use expense accounts to record transactions that decrease equity through net income. As debits reduce equity, debit Utilities Expense and credit Cash.

Post in T-accounts:

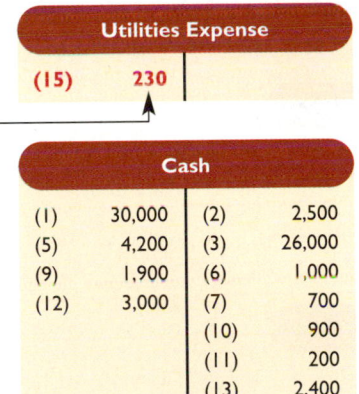

Utilities Expense

(15)	**230**

Cash

(1)	30,000	(2)	2,500
(5)	4,200	(3)	26,000
(9)	1,900	(6)	1,000
(12)	3,000	(7)	700
		(10)	900
		(11)	200
		(13)	2,400
		(14)	120
		(15)	**230**

16. Payment of Expense in Cash

Transaction: FastForward pays $700 cash in employee salaries for work performed in the latter part of December.

Analysis:

Assets	=	Liabilities	+	Equity
Cash				**Salaries Expense**
−700	=	0		−700

Cash decreases and equity decreases (through expenses) by $700. Debit Salaries Expense and credit Cash.

Post in T-accounts:

Salaries Expense

(7)	700
(16)	**700**

Cash

(1)	30,000	(2)	2,500
(5)	4,200	(3)	26,000
(9)	1,900	(6)	1,000
(12)	3,000	(7)	700
		(10)	900
		(11)	200
		(13)	2,400
		(14)	120
		(15)	230
		(16)	**700**

Exhibit 3.6

T-Accounts for FastForward

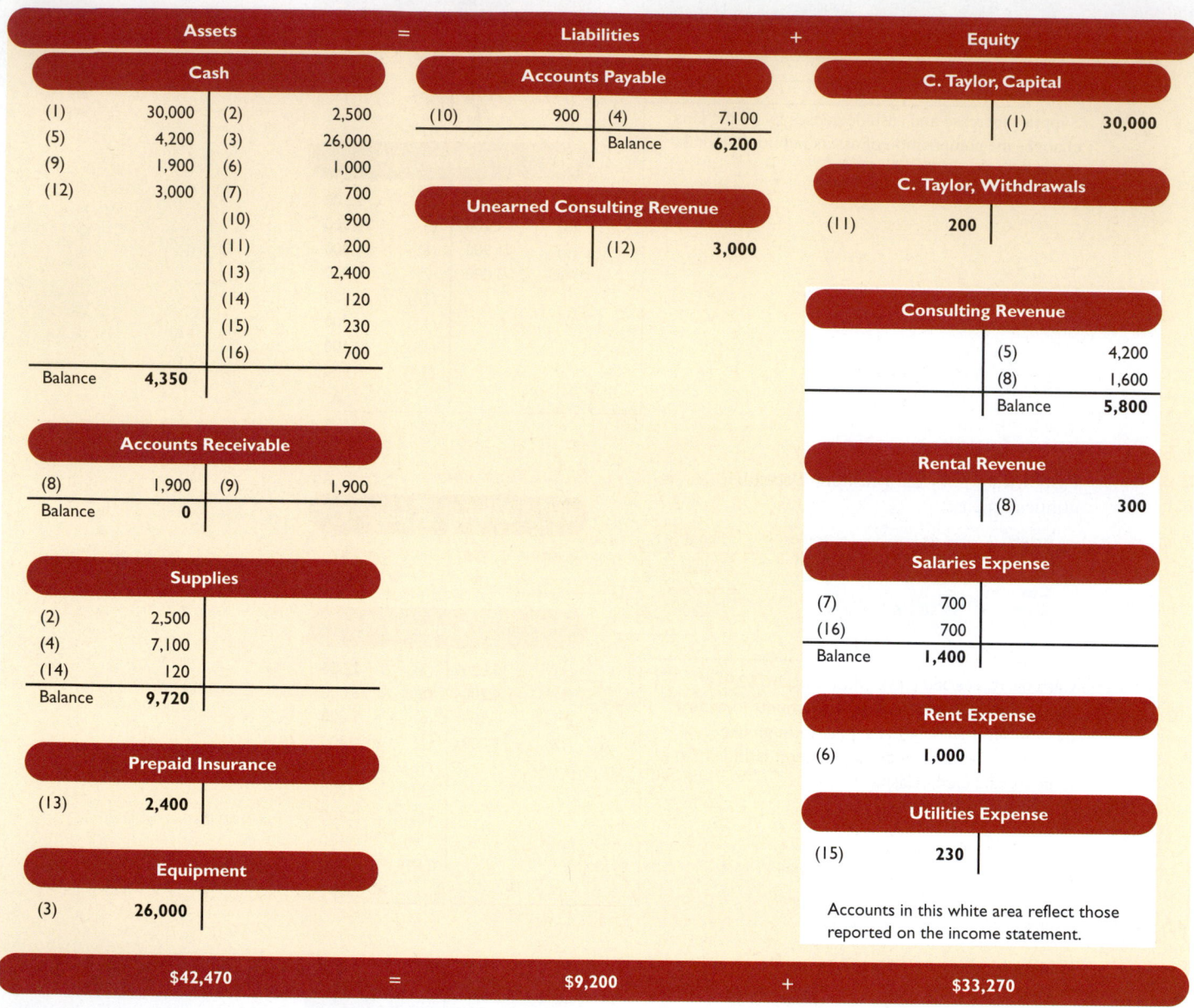

Assets		=	Liabilities		+	Equity	

Cash

(1)	30,000	(2)	2,500
(5)	4,200	(3)	26,000
(9)	1,900	(6)	1,000
(12)	3,000	(7)	700
		(10)	900
		(11)	200
		(13)	2,400
		(14)	120
		(15)	230
		(16)	700
Balance	4,350		

Accounts Receivable

(8)	1,900	(9)	1,900
Balance	0		

Supplies

(2)	2,500		
(4)	7,100		
(14)	120		
Balance	9,720		

Prepaid Insurance

(13)	2,400

Equipment

(3)	26,000

Accounts Payable

(10)	900	(4)	7,100
		Balance	6,200

Unearned Consulting Revenue

		(12)	3,000

C. Taylor, Capital

		(1)	30,000

C. Taylor, Withdrawals

(11)	200	

Consulting Revenue

		(5)	4,200
		(8)	1,600
		Balance	5,800

Rental Revenue

		(8)	300

Salaries Expense

(7)	700	
(16)	700	
Balance	1,400	

Rent Expense

(6)	1,000	

Utilities Expense

(15)	230	

Accounts in this white area reflect those reported on the income statement.

$42,470	=	$9,200	+	$33,270

Summary of T-Account Illustration

Exhibit 3.6 shows the T-accounts of FastForward after all 16 transactions are posted to T-accounts and ending balances are computed. The numbers in brackets in each of the T-accounts refer to the transaction number from our illustration. The accounts are grouped according to the accounting equation: assets, liabilities, and equity. Note several important points. First, as with each transaction, the ending account balances must obey the accounting equation. Specifically, total assets equal $42,470 ($4,350 + $0 + $9,720 + $2,400 + $26,000); total liabilities equal $9,200 ($6,200 + $3,000); and total equity equals $33,270 ($30,000 − $200 + $5,800 + $300 − $1,400 − $1,000 − $230). These numbers prove the accounting equation: Assets of $42,470 = Liabilities of $9,200 + Equity of $33,270. Second, the capital, withdrawals, revenue, and expense accounts reflect the transactions that change equity. Third, the revenue and expense account balances will be summarized and reported in the income statement.

HOW YOU DOIN'?   Answers—p. 61

4. What types of transactions increase equity? What types decrease equity?

5. Why are accounting systems called *double entry*?

6. For each transaction, double-entry accounting requires which of the following: (*a*) Debits to asset accounts must create credits to liability or equity accounts, (*b*) a debit to a liability account must create a credit to an asset account, or (*c*) total debits must equal total credits.

7. An owner invests $15,000 cash along with equipment having a market value of $23,000 in a company. Describe how T-accounts will be used to record this transaction.

8. Matt Waller receives $3,000 cash for his consulting services provided. Describe how T-accounts will be used to record this transaction.

Trial Balance

Double-entry accounting requires the sum of debit account balances to equal the sum of credit account balances. A trial balance is used to verify this. A **trial balance** is a list of accounts and their balances at a point in time. The accounts are usually ordered according to the accounting equation in Exhibit 3.4. Account balances are reported in the appropriate debit or credit column of a trial balance. Exhibit 3.7 shows the trial balance for FastForward after its 16 transactions have been recorded in T-accounts. (This is an *unadjusted* trial balance—Chapter 5 explains the necessary adjustments.) A trial balance is *not* a financial statement but a mechanism for checking the equality of debits and credits. Financial statements do not have debit and credit columns.

Preparing a Trial Balance

Preparing a trial balance involves three steps:

LO4 Prepare and explain the use of a trial balance.

1. List each account title and its amount (from the T-accounts) in the trial balance. If an account has a zero balance, list it with a zero in its normal balance column (or omit it entirely). Investigate any accounts that do not have normal balances, as this could indicate errors.

2. Compute the total of debit balances and the total of credit balances.

3. Verify (*prove*) total debit balances equal total credit balances.

The total of debit balances equals the total of credit balances for the trial balance in Exhibit 3.7. Equality of these two totals does not guarantee that no recording errors were made. For example, the column totals will still be equal when a debit or credit of a correct amount is made to a wrong account. Another error that does not cause unequal column totals is when equal debits and credits of an incorrect amount are recorded.

Searching for and Correcting Errors   If the trial balance does not balance (its column totals are not equal), the error (or errors) must be found. Follow these steps to search for an error:

1. Verify that the trial balance columns are correctly added.

2. Verify that account balances are accurately entered from the T-account to the trial balance.

3. Check to see whether a debit (or credit) balance is mistakenly listed in the trial balance as a credit (or debit).

4. Recompute each account balance in the T-accounts.

5. Verify that the debits equal the credits for each transaction.

At this point the error should be uncovered.[1]

---

[1] *Transposition* occurs when two digits are switched, or transposed, within a number. If transposition is the only error, it yields a difference between the two trial balance totals that is evenly divisible by 9. For example, assume that a $691 debit in an entry is incorrectly posted to the ledger as $619. Total credits are then larger than total debits by $72 ($691 − $619). The $72 error is evenly divisible by 9 (72/9 = 8). The first digit of the quotient (in our example it is 8) equals the difference between the digits of the two transposed numbers (the 9 and the 1).

Exhibit 3.7

Trial Balance (unadjusted)

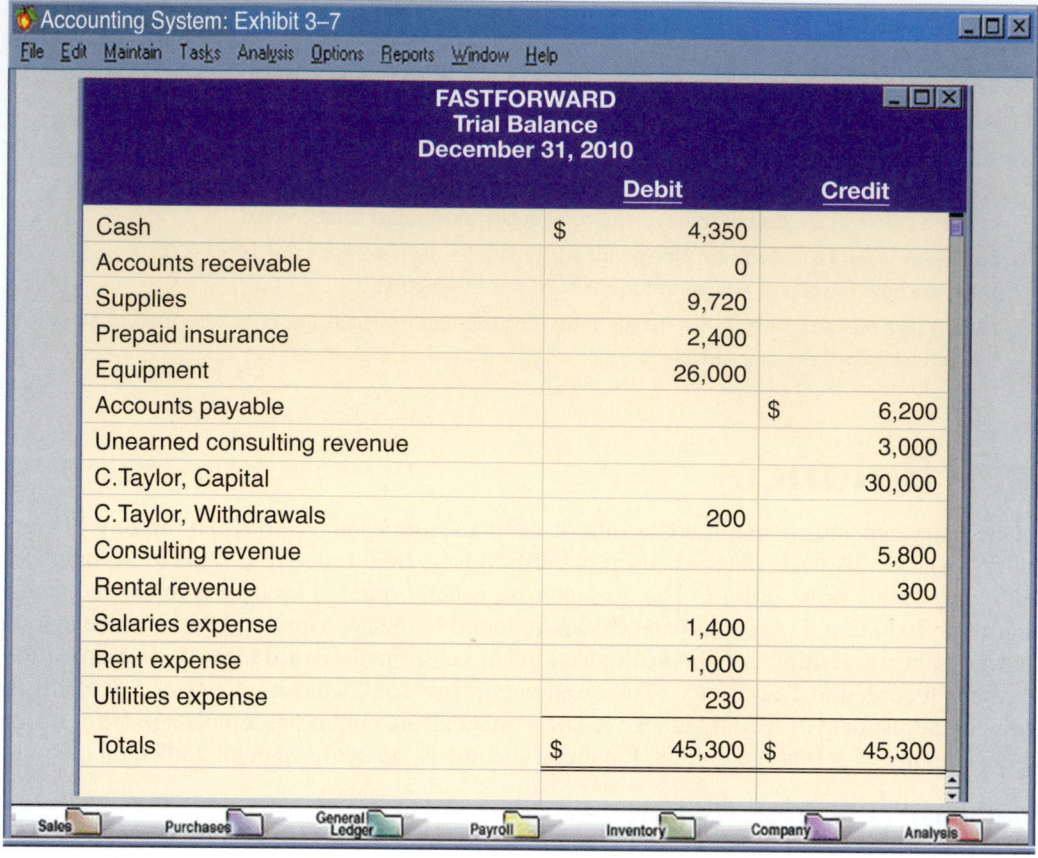

Accounting System: Exhibit 3–7		
File Edit Maintain Tasks Analysis Options Reports Window Help		

FASTFORWARD
Trial Balance
December 31, 2010

	Debit	Credit
Cash	$ 4,350	
Accounts receivable	0	
Supplies	9,720	
Prepaid insurance	2,400	
Equipment	26,000	
Accounts payable		$ 6,200
Unearned consulting revenue		3,000
C.Taylor, Capital		30,000
C.Taylor, Withdrawals	200	
Consulting revenue		5,800
Rental revenue		300
Salaries expense	1,400	
Rent expense	1,000	
Utilities expense	230	
Totals	$ 45,300	$ 45,300

Sales   Purchases   General Ledger   Payroll   Inventory   Company   Analysis

Using a Trial Balance to Prepare Financial Statements

LO5 Prepare financial statements from a trial balance.

This section shows how to prepare *financial statements* from the trial balance in Exhibit 3.7 and information on the December transactions of FastForward. The statements differ from those in Chapter 2 because of several additional transactions. These statements are also more precisely called *unadjusted statements* because we need to make some further accounting adjustments (described in Chapter 5).

Income Statement   An income statement reports a company's revenues earned minus its expenses over a period of time. FastForward's income statement for December is shown at the top of Exhibit 3.8. Information about revenues and expenses is taken from the trial balance in Exhibit 3.7. The income statement reports total revenues ($6,100) and total expenses ($2,630). Net income (revenues minus expenses) of $3,470 is reported at the bottom of the statement. Owner investments and withdrawals are *not* part of income.

Statement of Owner's Equity   The statement of owner's equity reports information about how equity changes over the reporting period. FastForward's statement of owner's equity is the second report in Exhibit 3.8. It shows the $30,000 owner investment, the $3,470 of net income, the $200 withdrawal, and the $33,270 end-of-period (capital) balance. (The beginning balance in the statement of owner's equity is rarely zero; an exception is for the first period of operations. The beginning capital balance in January 2011 is $33,270, which is December 2010's ending balance.)

Balance Sheet   The balance sheet reports the financial position of a company at a point in time, usually at the end of a month, quarter, or year. FastForward's balance sheet is the third

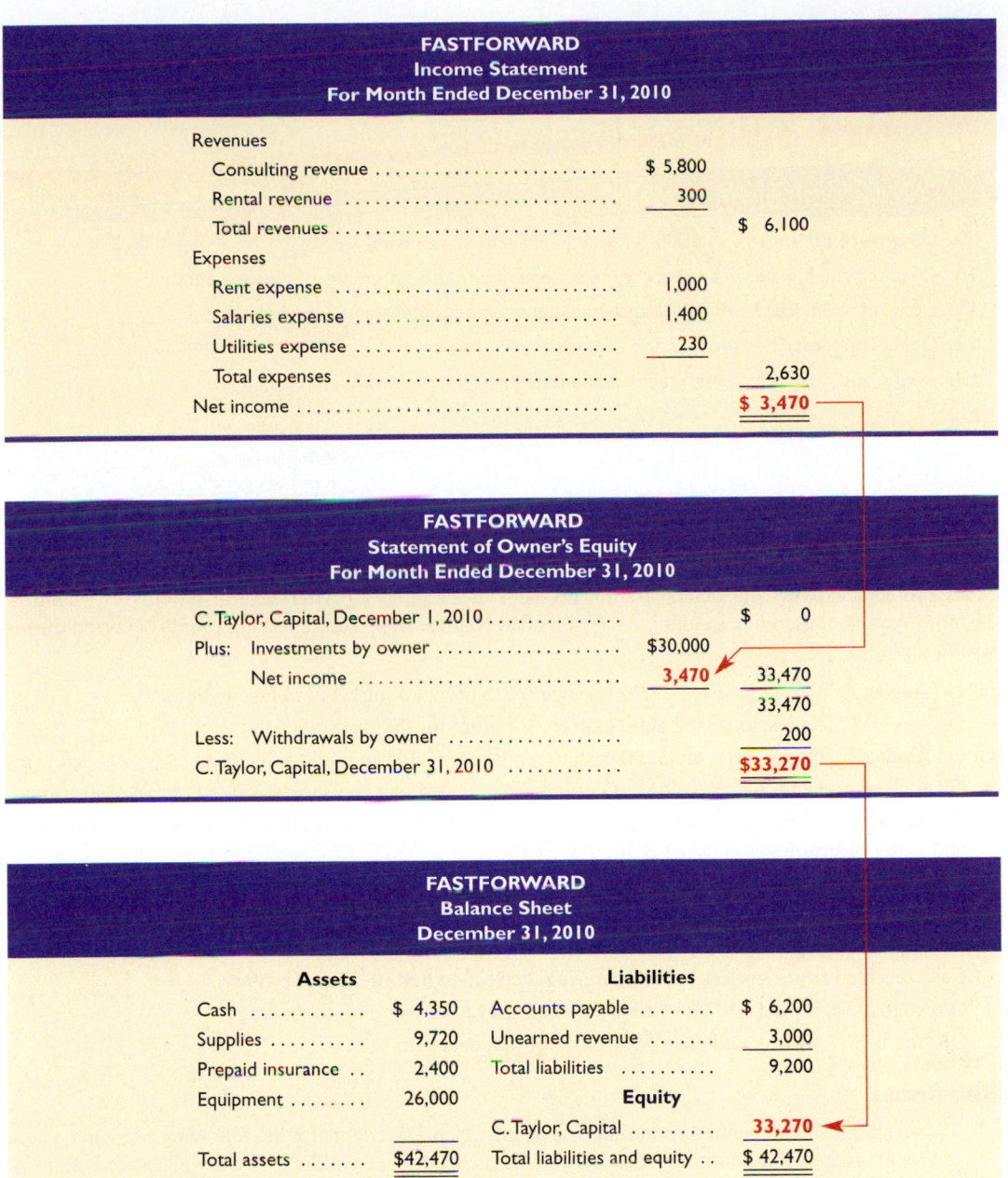

Exhibit 3.8

Financial Statements and Their Links

FASTFORWARD
Income Statement
For Month Ended December 31, 2010

Revenues		
Consulting revenue	$ 5,800	
Rental revenue	300	
Total revenues		$ 6,100
Expenses		
Rent expense	1,000	
Salaries expense	1,400	
Utilities expense	230	
Total expenses		2,630
Net income		$ 3,470

FASTFORWARD
Statement of Owner's Equity
For Month Ended December 31, 2010

C. Taylor, Capital, December 1, 2010		$ 0
Plus: Investments by owner	$30,000	
Net income	3,470	33,470
		33,470
Less: Withdrawals by owner		200
C. Taylor, Capital, December 31, 2010		$33,270

FASTFORWARD
Balance Sheet
December 31, 2010

Assets		Liabilities	
Cash	$ 4,350	Accounts payable	$ 6,200
Supplies	9,720	Unearned revenue	3,000
Prepaid insurance	2,400	Total liabilities	9,200
Equipment	26,000	**Equity**	
		C. Taylor, Capital	33,270
Total assets	$42,470	Total liabilities and equity	$ 42,470

Arrow lines show how the statements are linked. Net income for the period updates the owner's equity at the end of the period. The ending owner's equity appears on the balance sheet at the end of the period.

report in Exhibit 3.8. This statement refers to financial condition at the close of business on December 31, 2010. The left side of the balance sheet lists FastForward's assets: cash, supplies, prepaid insurance, and equipment. The upper right side of the balance sheet shows that it owes $6,200 to creditors and $3,000 in services to customers who paid in advance. The equity section shows an ending capital balance of $33,270. Note the link between the ending balance of C. Taylor, on the statement of owner's equity and its disclosure on the balance sheet. This means that FastForward's financial performance for December updates its financial position at the end of December. This updating is a key feature of accounting.

Presentation Issues Dollar signs are not used in T-accounts, but they do appear in financial statements. The usual practice is to put dollar signs beside only the first and last numbers in a column. **Best Buy**'s financial statements in Appendix A show this. Companies also commonly round amounts in reports to the nearest dollar, or even to a higher level. Best Buy is typical of many large companies in that it rounds dollar amounts in its financial statements to the nearest million. This decision is based on the perceived impact of rounding for users' business decisions.

HOW YOU DOIN'?   Answers—p. 61

9. Where are dollar signs typically entered in financial statements?

10. Describe the link between the income statement and the statement of owner's equity.

11. Explain the link between the balance sheet and the statement of owner's equity.

12. Define and describe revenues and expenses.

13. Define and describe assets, liabilities, and equity.

Demonstration Problem

(This problem extends the demonstration problem of Chapter 2.) After several months of planning, Jasmine Worthy started a haircutting business called Expressions. The following events occurred during its first month.

a. On August 1, Worthy invested $3,000 cash and $15,000 of equipment in Expressions.

b. On August 2, Expressions paid $600 cash for furniture for the shop.

c. On August 3, Expressions paid $500 cash to rent space in a strip mall for August.

d. On August 4, it purchased $1,200 of equipment on credit for the shop (using an account payable).

e. On August 5, Expressions opened for business. Cash received from services provided in the first week and a half of business (ended August 15) is $825.

f. On August 15, it provided $100 of haircutting services on account.

g. On August 17, it received a $100 check for services previously rendered on account.

h. On August 17, it paid $125 to an assistant for working during the grand opening.

i. Cash received from services provided during the second half of August is $930.

j. On August 31, it paid $400 toward the account payable entered into on August 4.

k. On August 31, Worthy withdrew $900 cash for personal use.

Required

1. Post each transaction in the appropriate T-account. Open T-accounts for the following accounts: Cash; Accounts Receivable; Furniture; Store Equipment; Accounts Payable; J. Worthy, Capital; J. Worthy, Withdrawals; Haircutting Services Revenue; Wages Expense; Rent Expense.

2. Prepare a trial balance from the T-accounts as of August 31.

3. Prepare an income statement for August.

4. Prepare a statement of owner's equity for August.

5. Prepare a balance sheet as of August 31.

Planning the Solution

- Analyze each transaction.
- Post each transaction in the appropriate T-accounts.
- Calculate each ending account balance and list the accounts with their balances on a trial balance.
- Verify that the total debits in the trial balance equal the total credits.
- To prepare the income statement, identify revenues and expenses. List those items on the statement, compute the difference between total revenues and total expenses, and label the result as net income or net loss.
- Use information in the trial balance to prepare the statement of stockholder's equity.
- Use information in the trial balance to prepare the balance sheet.

Solution to Demonstration Problem

1. Post each transaction to the appropriate T-account.

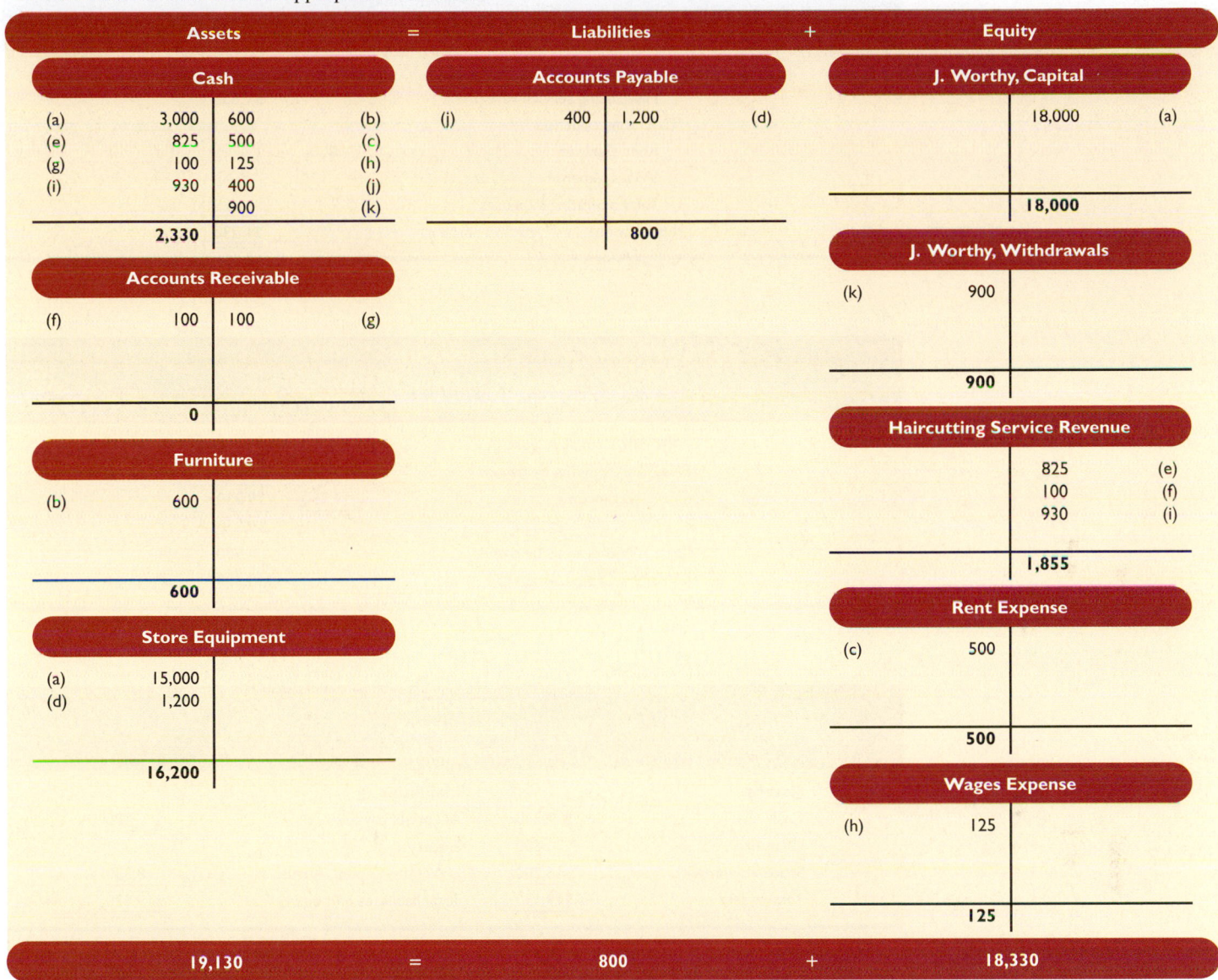

2. Prepare a trial balance from the T-accounts.

EXPRESSIONS Trial Balance August 31, 2010		
	Debit	**Credit**
Cash	$ 2,330	
Accounts receivable	0	
Furniture	600	
Store equipment	16,200	
Accounts payable		$ 800
J. Worthy, Capital, August 1		18,000
J. Worthy, Withdrawals	900	
Haircutting service revenue		1,855
Wages expense	125	
Rent expense	500	
Totals	$20,655	$20,655

3.

EXPRESSIONS Income Statement For Month Ended August 31, 2010		
Revenues		
Haircutting service revenue		$1,855
Operating expenses		
Rent expense	$500	
Wages expense	125	
Total operating expenses		625
Net income		$1,230

4.

EXPRESSIONS Statement of Owner's Equity For Month Ended August 31, 2010			
J. Worthy, Capital, August 1		$ 0	
Plus: Investments by owner	$18,000		
Net income	1,230	19,230	
		19,230	
Less: Withdrawals by owner		900	
J. Worthy, Capital, August 31		$18,330	

5.

EXPRESSIONS Balance Sheet August 31, 2010			
Assets		**Liabilities**	
Cash	$ 2,330	Accounts payable	$ 800
Furniture	600	**Equity**	
Store equipment	16,200	J. Worthy, Capital, August 31	18,330
Total assets	$19,130	Total liabilities and equity	$19,130

Summary

LO1 **Describe a T-account and its use in recording transactions.** A T-account is a tool to show the effects of transactions and events on accounts. A T-account has both a left (debit) and right (credit) side.

LO2 **Define debits and credits and explain their role in double-entry accounting.** *Debit* refers to left, and *credit* refers to right. Debits increase assets, expenses, and withdrawals while credits decrease them. Credits increase liabilities, owner capital, and revenues; debits decrease them. Double-entry accounting means each transaction affects at least two accounts and has at least one debit and one credit. The system for recording debits and credits follows from the accounting equation. The left side of an account is the normal balance for assets, withdrawals, and expenses, and the right side is the normal balance for liabilities, capital, and revenues.

LO3 **Post transactions in T-accounts.** We analyze transactions using concepts of double-entry accounting. This analysis is performed by determining a transaction's effects on accounts. Posting is the process of entering dollar amounts for transactions in the appropriate debit or credit side of the affected T-accounts.

LO4 **Prepare and explain the use of a trial balance.** A trial balance is a list of accounts, showing their debit or credit balances in separate columns. The trial balance is useful in preparing financial statements and in revealing recordkeeping errors.

LO5 **Prepare financial statements from a trial balance.** The balance sheet, the statement of owner's equity and the income statement use the trial balance for their preparation.

1.

Assets	Liabilities	Equity
a,c,e	b,d	—

2. A T-account is a tool to record increases and decreases in a specific asset, liability, equity, revenue, or expense.

3. No. Debit and credit both can mean increase or decrease. The particular meaning in a circumstance depends on the *type of account*. For example, a debit increases the balance of asset, withdrawals, and expense accounts, but it decreases the balance of liability, capital, and revenue accounts.

4. Equity is increased by revenues and by owner investments. Equity is decreased by expenses and owner withdrawals.

5. The name *double entry* is used because all transactions affect at least two accounts. There must be at least one debit in one account and at least one credit in another account.

6. Answer is (*c*).

7. Debit Cash for $15,000, debit Store Equipment for $23,000, and credit Owner, Capital for $38,000.

8. Debit Cash for $3,000 and credit Consulting Services Revenue for $3,000.

9. At a minimum, dollar signs are placed beside the first and last numbers in a column. It is also common to place dollar signs beside any amount that appears after a ruled line to indicate that an addition or subtraction has occurred.

10. An income statement reports a company's revenues and expenses along with the resulting net income or loss. A statement of owner's equity reports changes in equity, including that from net income or loss. Both statements report transactions occurring over a period of time.

11. The balance sheet describes a company's financial position (assets, liabilities, and equity) at a point in time. The capital amount in the balance sheet is obtained from the statement of owner's equity.

12. Revenues are inflows of assets in exchange for products or services provided to customers as part of the main operations of a business. Expenses are outflows or the using up of assets that result from providing products or services to customers.

13. Assets are the resources a business owns or controls that carry expected future benefits. Liabilities are the obligations of a business, representing the claims of others against the assets of a business. Equity reflects the owner's claims on the assets of the business after deducting liabilities.

Key Terms

Account balance (p. 47) Difference between total debits and total credits (including the beginning balance for an account.

Contra account (p. 51) An account linked with another account. Its normal balance is opposite that of the other account's balance.

Credit (p. 46) Recorded on the right side; an entry that decreases asset and expense accounts, and increases liability, revenue and most equity accounts; abbreviated Cr.

Debit (p. 46) Recorded on the left side; an entry that increases asset and expense accounts, and decreases liability, revenue, and most equity accounts; abbreviated Dr.

Double-entry accounting (p. 47) Accounting system in which each transaction affects at least two accounts and has at least one debit and one credit.

Footing (p. 47) The total of a column of numbers.

Normal balance (p. 47) The side of a T-account on which increases are recorded. Asset accounts have normal debit balances. Liability and equity accounts have normal credit balances.

Post (p. 47) Make an entry in an account.

Prepaid assets (p. 52) Asset created when a company pays in advance for products or services to be received later. Also called prepaid expenses.

T-account (p. 46) Tool used to show the effects of transactions and events on individual accounts.

Trial balance (p. 55) List of accounts and their balances at a point in time; total debit balances equal total credit balances.

Unearned revenue (p. 52) Liability created when customers pay in advance of products or services to be provided later; earned when the products or services are later delivered.

Multiple Choice Quiz   Answers on p. 71   mhhe.com/wildCA2e

Additional Multiple Choice Quizzes are available at the book's Website.

1. Asset and expense accounts normally have
  a. Zero balances
  b. Credit balances
   c. Debit balances
  d. Negative balances

2. The accounting equation requires that if assets have a balance of $1 million and equity has a balance of $600,000, then liabilities must equal
  a. $600,000
  b. $1,600,000
  c. $0
  d. $400,000

3. Kirk Hinrich starts a new business by making an investment of $600,000 cash. Using the double-entry method, this increase in cash should be accounted for by
  a. Debiting Cash
  b. Crediting Cash
  c. Debiting Accounts Receivable
  d. Crediting Inventory

4. To record the payment of wages to its employees, Roy Beach Co. would
  a. Debit Wage Expense, debit Cash
  b. Debit Wage Expense, credit Cash
  c. Debit Cash, credit Wage Expense
  d. Credit Cash, credit Wage Expense

5. On May 1, Mattingly Lawn Service collected $2,500 cash from a customer in advance of five months of lawn service. Mattingly records this increase in liability as a
  a. Credit to Unearned Lawn Service Fees for $2,500.
  b. Debit to Lawn Service Fees Earned for $2,500.
  c. Credit to Cash for $2,500.
  d. Debit to Unearned Lawn Service Fees for $2,500.
  e. Credit to Capital for $2,500.

Discussion Questions

1. Provide the names of two (a) asset accounts, (b) liability accounts, and (c) equity accounts.

2. What is the normal balance for an asset account? What is the normal balance for a liability account?

3. What is an unearned revenue account? Why would customers pay in advance for services (or products) not yet received?

4. If assets are valuable resources and asset accounts have debit balances, why do expense accounts also have debit balances?

5. Why does the recordkeeper prepare a trial balance?

6. Identify the three basic financial statements of a business.

7. What information is reported in an income statement?

8. Why does the user of an income statement need to know the time period that it covers?

9. What information is reported in a balance sheet?

10. Define (a) assets, (b) liabilities, (c) equity, and (d) net assets.

11. Which financial statement is sometimes called the statement of financial position?

12. Review the **Best Buy** balance sheet in Appendix A. Identify three accounts on its balance sheet that carry debit balances and three accounts on its balance sheet that carry credit balances.

QUICK STUDY

QS 3–1
Identifying financial statement items
LO5

Identify the financial statement(s) where each of the following items appears. Use I for income statement, E for statement of owner's equity, and B for balance sheet.
  a. Cash withdrawal by owner
  b. Office equipment
  c. Accounts payable
  d. Cash
  e. Utilities expenses
  f. Office supplies
  g. Prepaid rent
  h. Unearned fees
  i. Service fees earned

QS 3–2
Linking debit or credit with
normal balance   **LO2**

Using Exhibit 3.4 as a guide, indicate whether a debit or credit *decreases* the normal balance of each of the following accounts.
  a. Repair Services Revenue
  b. Interest Payable
  c. Accounts Receivable
  d. Salaries Expense
  e. Owner Capital
  f. Prepaid Insurance
  g. Buildings
  h. Interest Revenue
  i. Owner Withdrawals
  j. Unearned Revenue
  k. Accounts Payable
  l. Office Supplies

QS 3–3
Analyzing debit or credit
by account   **LO2**

Using Exhibit 3.4 as a guide, identify whether a debit or credit yields the indicated change for each of the following accounts.
  a. To increase Land
  b. To decrease Cash
  c. To increase Utilities Expense
  d. To increase Fees Earned
  e. To decrease Unearned Revenue
  f. To decrease Prepaid Insurance
  g. To increase Accounts Payable
  h. To decrease Accounts Receivable
  i. To increase Owner Capital
  j. To increase Store Equipment

Identify the normal balance (debit or credit) for each of the following accounts.

a. Office Supplies   **d.** Wages Expense   **g.** Wages Payable

b. Owner Withdrawals   **e.** Cash   **h.** Building

c. Fees Earned   **f.** Prepaid Insurance   **i.** Owner Capital

QS 3–4
Identifying normal balance   **LO2**

Post the following transactions to the appropriate T-accounts and compute the ending balance in each account.

a. On January 13, DeShawn Tyler opens a landscaping business called Elegant Lawns by investing $70,000 cash along with equipment having a $30,000 value.

b. On January 21, Elegant Lawns purchases office supplies on credit for $280.

c. On January 29, Elegant Lawns receives $7,800 cash for performing landscaping services.

d. On January 30, Elegant Lawns receives $1,000 cash in advance of providing landscaping services to a customer.

QS 3–5
Posting to T-accounts   **LO3**

Indicate the financial statement on which each of the following items appears. Use I for income statement, E for statement of owner's equity, and B for balance sheet.

a. Services Revenue   **e.** Equipment   **h.** Depreciation Expense

b. Wages Payable   **f.** Prepaid Insurance   **i.** Owner Withdrawals

c. Accounts Receivable   **g.** Buildings   **j.** Office Supplies

d. Salaries Expense

QS 3–6
Classifying accounts in financial statements   **LO1 LO5**

Post the following transactions to the appropriate T-accounts.

a. Owner invests $10,000 cash to start an auto repair shop.

b. Received $3,500 cash for providing repair services.

c. Paid $1,700 cash for this month's rent.

d. Owner withdraws $500 cash for personal use.

QS 3–7
Posting to T-accounts   **LO3**

Foot the cash T-account below and compute its ending balance.

QS 3–8
Footing T-accounts   **LO3**

Cash	
40,000	15,000
7,800	6,200
1,000	

---

connect

For each of the following (1) identify the type of account as an asset, liability, equity, revenue, or expense, (2) enter *debit* (*Dr.*) or *credit* (*Cr.*) to identify the kind of entry that would increase the account balance, and (3) identify the normal balance of the account.

a. Accounts Payable   **e.** Owner Capital   **i.** Equipment

b. Postage Expense   **f.** Accounts Receivable   **j.** Fees Earned

c. Prepaid Insurance   **g.** Owner Withdrawals   **k.** Wages Expense

d. Land   **h.** Cash   **l.** Unearned Revenue

EXERCISES

Exercise 3–1
Identifying type and normal balances of accounts   **LO1 LO2**

Record the transactions below for Amena Company by recording debit and credit amounts directly in the following T-accounts: Cash; Accounts Receivable; Office Supplies; Office Equipment; Accounts Payable; A. Amena, Capital; A. Amena, Withdrawals; Fees Earned; and Rent Expense. Use the letters *a* through *i* to identify transactions in the T-accounts. Determine the ending balance of each T-account.

a. Ahmad Amena, owner, invested $13,325 cash in the business.

b. Purchased office supplies for $475 cash.

Exercise 3–2
Recording effects of transactions in T-accounts   **LO1 LO2 LO3**

c. Purchased $6,235 of office equipment on credit.

d. Received $2,000 cash as fees for services provided to a customer.

e. Paid $6,235 cash to settle the payable for the office equipment purchased in transaction *c*.

f. Billed a customer $3,300 as fees for services provided.

g. Paid $775 cash for the monthly rent.

h. Collected $2,300 cash toward the account receivable created in transaction *f*.

Check   Cash ending balance, $9,340

i. Ahmad Amena withdrew $800 cash for personal use.

Exercise 3–3
Preparing a trial balance
LO3   LO4

After recording the transactions of Exercise 3-2 in T-accounts and calculating the ending balance of each account, prepare a trial balance. Use May 31, 2010, as its report date.

Exercise 3–4
Analyzing revenue transactions
LO1   LO2   LO3

Examine the following transactions and identify those that create revenues for Valdez Services, a company owned by Brina Valdez. Use T-accounts to record the transactions that create revenues. Explain why the other transactions did not create revenues.

a. Brina Valdez invests $39,350 cash in the business.

b. Provided $2,300 of services on credit.

c. Provided services to a client and immediately received $875 cash.

d. Received $10,200 cash from a client in payment for services to be provided next year.

e. Received $3,500 cash from a client in partial payment of an account receivable.

f. Borrowed $120,000 cash from the bank by signing a promissory note.

Exercise 3–5
Analyzing expense transactions
LO1   LO2   LO3

Examine the following transactions and identify those that create expenses for Valdez Services. Use T-accounts to record the transactions that create expenses. Explain why the other transactions did not create expenses.

a. Paid $12,200 cash for office supplies that were purchased on account more than 1 year ago.

b. Paid $1,233 cash for the receptionist's salary for the two weeks just completed.

c. Paid $39,200 cash for equipment.

d. Paid $870 cash for this month's utilities.

e. Owner (B. Valdez) withdrew $4,500 cash for personal use.

Exercise 3–6
Analyzing changes in equity   **LO3**

Compute the missing amount in each of the following separate companies *a* through *d*.

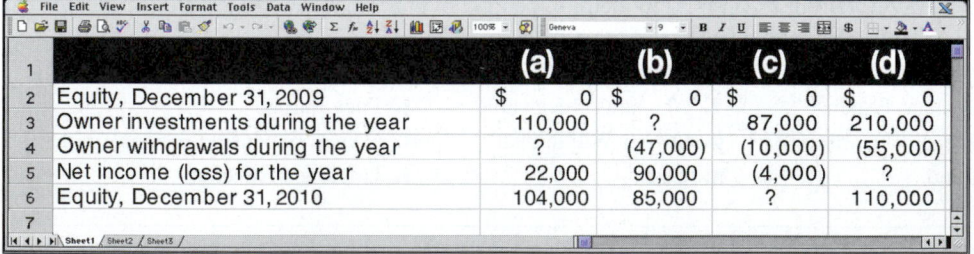

	(a)	(b)	(c)	(d)
Equity, December 31, 2009	$ 0	$ 0	$ 0	$ 0
Owner investments during the year	110,000	?	87,000	210,000
Owner withdrawals during the year	?	(47,000)	(10,000)	(55,000)
Net income (loss) for the year	22,000	90,000	(4,000)	?
Equity, December 31, 2010	104,000	85,000	?	110,000

Exercise 3–7
Interpreting and describing transactions from T-accounts   **LO3**

Assume the following T-accounts reflect Belle Co.'s accounts and that seven transactions are posted to them. Provide a short description of each of the seven transactions *a* through *g* of Belle Co. Include dollar amounts in your descriptions.

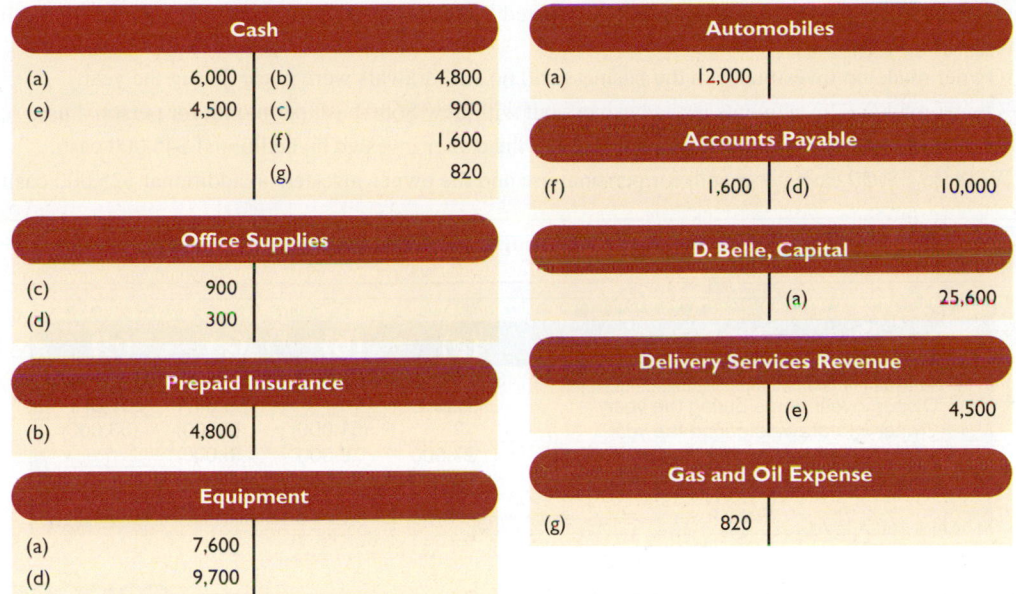

Refer to the T-accounts in Exercise 3-7. Compute ending balances and prepare Belle Company's income statement and statement of owner's equity for the month ended December 31, 2010.

Exercise 3–8
Preparing an income statement and statement of owner's equity
LO5

Refer to the T-accounts in Exercise 3-7. Compute ending balances and prepare Belle Company's balance sheet. Assume the balance sheet is dated December 31, 2010. (*Hint:* The December 31, 2010, D. Belle, Capital account balance is $29,280.)

Exercise 3–9
Preparing a balance sheet   **LO5**

On October 1, Diondre Shabazz organized a new consulting firm called Tech Talk. On October 31, the company's records show the following accounts and amounts. Use this information to prepare an October income statement for the business.

Exercise 3–10
Preparing an income statement   **LO5**

Cash	$ 12,614	D. Shabazz, Withdrawals	$ 2,000
Accounts receivable	25,648	Consulting fees earned	25,620
Office supplies	4,903	Rent expense	6,859
Land	69,388	Salaries expense	12,405
Office equipment	27,147	Telephone expense	560
Accounts payable	12,070	Miscellaneous expenses	280
D. Shabazz, Capital	124,114		

Check   Net income, $5,516

Use the information in Exercise 3-10 to prepare an October statement of owner's equity for Tech Talk. (The owner invested $124,114 to launch the company.)

Exercise 3–11
Preparing a statement of owner's equity   **LO5**

Use the information in Exercise 3-10 (if completed, you can also use your solution to Exercise 3-11) to prepare an October 31 balance sheet for Tech Talk.

Exercise 3–12
Preparing a balance sheet   **LO5**

A company had the following assets and liabilities at the beginning and end of a recent year.

Exercise 3–13
Computing net income   **LO5**

	Assets	Liabilities
Beginning of the year	$131,000	$56,159
End of the year	180,000	72,900

Determine the net income earned or net loss incurred by the business during the year for each of the following *separate* cases:

a. Owner made no investments in the business and no withdrawals were made during the year.

b. Owner made no investments in the business but withdrew $650 cash per month for personal use.

c. No withdrawals were made during the year but the owner invested an additional $45,000 cash.

d. Withdrew $650 cash per month for personal use and the owner invested an additional $25,000 cash.

Exercise 3-14

Analyzing changes in a company's equity   **LO3**

Compute the missing amount in each of the following separate companies *a* through *d*.

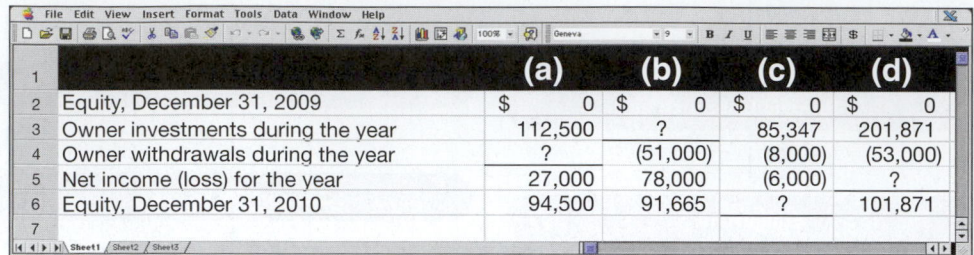

	(a)	(b)	(c)	(d)
Equity, December 31, 2009	$ 0	$ 0	$ 0	$ 0
Owner investments during the year	112,500	?	85,347	201,871
Owner withdrawals during the year	?	(51,000)	(8,000)	(53,000)
Net income (loss) for the year	27,000	78,000	(6,000)	?
Equity, December 31, 2010	94,500	91,665	?	101,871

connect™

PROBLEM SET A

Problem 3-1A

Posting transactions to T-accounts; preparing a trial balance

LO2   LO3   LO4

mhhe.com/wildCA2e

Denzel Brooks opens a Web consulting business called Venture Consultants and completes the following transactions in March.

March 1   Brooks invested $150,000 cash along with $22,000 of office equipment in the business.
2   Prepaid $6,000 cash for six months' rent for an office. (*Hint:* Debit Prepaid Rent (an asset) for $6,000.)
3   Made credit purchases of office equipment for $3,000 and office supplies for $1,200.
6   Completed services for a client and immediately received $4,000 cash.
9   Completed a $7,500 project for a client, who must pay within 30 days.
12   Paid $4,200 cash to settle the account payable created on March 3.
19   Paid $5,000 cash for the premium on a 12-month insurance policy.
22   Received $3,500 cash as partial payment for the work completed on March 9.
25   Completed work for another client for $3,820 on credit.
29   Brooks withdrew $5,100 cash for personal use.
30   Purchased $600 of additional office supplies on credit.
31   Paid $500 cash for this month's utility bill.

Required

1. Open the following T-accounts—Cash; Accounts Receivable; Office Supplies; Prepaid Insurance; Prepaid Rent; Office Equipment; Accounts Payable; D. Brooks, Capital; D. Brooks, Withdrawals; Services Revenue; and Utilities Expense. Post the transactions in the T-accounts.

2. Prepare a trial balance as of the end of March.

Problem 3-2A

Posting transactions to T-accounts; preparing a trial balance; preparing financial statements

LO1   LO2   LO3   LO4   LO5

Kendis Lanelle opened a computer consulting business called Viva Consultants and completed the following transactions in the first month of operations.

April 1   Lanelle invested $80,000 cash along with office equipment valued at $26,000 in the business.
2   Prepaid $9,000 cash for 12 months' rent for office space. (*Hint:* Debit Prepaid Rent (an asset) for $9,000.)
3   Made credit purchases for $8,000 in office equipment and $3,600 in office supplies.
6   Completed services for a client and immediately received $4,000 cash.
9   Completed a $6,000 project for a client, who must pay within 30 days.
13   Paid $11,600 cash to settle the account payable created on April 3.
19   Paid $2,400 cash for the premium on a 12-month insurance policy. (*Hint:* Debit Prepaid Insurance (an asset) for $2,400.)
22   Received $4,400 cash as partial payment for the work completed on April 9.
25   Completed work for another client for $2,890 on credit.
28   Lanelle withdrew $5,500 cash for personal use.
29   Purchased $600 of additional office supplies on credit.
30   Paid $435 cash for this month's utility bill.

Required

1. Open the following T-accounts—Cash; Accounts Receivable; Office Supplies; Prepaid Insurance; Prepaid Rent; Office Equipment; Accounts Payable; K. Lanelle, Capital; K. Lanelle, Withdrawals; Services Revenue; and Utilities Expense. Post the transactions in the T-accounts.

2. Prepare a trial balance as of April 30.

3. Prepare an income statement for the month of April.

4. Prepare a statement of owner's equity for the month of April.

5. Prepare a balance sheet as of April 30.

Check   (1) Ending balances: Cash, $59,465; Accounts Receivable, $4,490; Accounts Payable, $600

(2) Total debits, $119,490

AE Consulting reports the following trial balance as of December 31, 2010, the end of its first month of operations.

Problem 3–3A
Preparing financial statements
LO4   LO5

AE CONSULTING Trial Balance December 31		
	Debit	**Credit**
Cash	$ 39,670	
Accounts receivable	2,750	
Office supplies	1,700	
Office equipment	48,100	
Building	165,000	
Land	40,000	
Accounts payable		$169,100
A. Emitt, Capital		120,800
A. Emitt, Withdrawals	2,900	
Fees earned		14,350
Salaries expense	3,500	
Utilities expense	630	
Total	$304,250	$304,250

Required

1. Prepare an income statement for the month.

2. Prepare a statement of owner's equity for the month.

3. Prepare a balance sheet as of the end of the month.

Diella Management Services opens for business and completes these transactions in November.

PROBLEM SET B

Nov. 1   Cicely Diella, the owner, invested $30,000 cash along with $15,000 of office equipment in the business.

Problem 3–1B
Posting transactions to T-accounts, preparing a trial balance
LO2   LO3   LO4

2   Prepaid $4,500 cash for six months' rent for an office. (*Hint:* Debit Prepaid Rent (an asset) for $4,500.)

4   Made credit purchases of office equipment for $2,500 and of office supplies for $600.

8   Completed work for a client and immediately received $3,400 cash.

12   Completed a $10,200 project for a client, who must pay within 30 days.

13   Paid $3,100 cash to settle the payable created on November 4.

19   Paid $1,800 cash for the premium on a 24-month insurance policy.

22   Received $5,200 cash as partial payment for the work completed on November 12.

24   Completed work for another client for $1,750 on credit.

28   Cicely Diella withdrew $5,300 cash for personal use.

29   Purchased $249 of additional office supplies on credit.

30   Paid $831 cash for this month's utility bill.

Required

1. Open the following T-accounts—Cash; Accounts Receivable; Office Supplies; Prepaid Insurance; Prepaid Rent; Office Equipment; Accounts Payable; C. Diella, Capital; C. Diella, Withdrawals; Services Revenue; and Utilities Expense. Post the transactions in the T-accounts.
2. Prepare a trial balance as of the end of November.

Problem 3-2B

Posting transactions to T-accounts
preparing a trial balance; preparing
financial statements

LO1   LO2   LO3   LO4   LO5

Johnson Management Services opens for business and completes these transactions in September.

Sept. 1   John Johnson, the owner, invests $38,000 cash along with office equipment valued at $15,000 in the business.
2   Prepaid $9,000 cash for 12 months' rent for office space. (*Hint:* Debit Prepaid Rent (an asset) for $9,000.)
4   Made credit purchases for $8,000 in office equipment and $2,400 in office supplies.
8   Completed work for a client and immediately received $3,280 cash.
12   Completed a $15,400 project for a client, who must pay within 30 days.
13   Paid $10,400 cash to settle the payable created on September 4.
19   Paid $1,900 cash for the premium on an 18-month insurance policy. (*Hint:* Debit Prepaid Insurance (an asset) for $1,900.)
22   Received $7,700 cash as partial payment for the work completed on September 12.
24   Completed work for another client for $2,100 on credit.
28   John Johnson withdrew $5,300 cash for personal use.
29   Purchased $550 of additional office supplies on credit.
30   Paid $860 cash for this month's utility bill.

Required

1. Open the following T-accounts—Cash; Accounts Receivable; Office Supplies; Prepaid Insurance; Prepaid Rent; Office Equipment; Accounts Payable; J. Johnson, Capital; J. Johnson, Withdrawals; Service Fees Earned; and Utilities Expense. Post the transactions in the T-accounts.
2. Prepare a trial balance as of the end of September.
3. Prepare an income statement for the month of September.
4. Prepare a statement of owner's equity for the month of September.
5. Prepare a balance sheet as of September 30.

Problem 3-3B

Preparing financial statements

LO5

Witter Consulting provides the following trial balance as of June 30, 2010, the end of its first month of operations.

WITTER CONSULTING Trial Balance June 30	Debit	Credit
Cash	$ 34,570	
Accounts receivable	2,500	
Office supplies	2,200	
Office equipment	48,500	
Building	165,000	
Land	50,000	
Accounts payable		$173,300
D. Witter, Capital		121,800
D. Witter, Withdrawals	2,700	
Fees earned		14,500
Salaries expense	3,500	
Utilities expense	630	
Total	$309,600	$309,600

Required

1. Prepare an income statement for the month.

2. Prepare a statement of owner's equity for the month.

3. Prepare a balance sheet as of the end of the month.

(This serial problem started in Chapter 1 and continues through most of the chapters. If the Chapter 1 segment was not completed, the problem can begin at this point. It is helpful, but not necessary, to use the Working Papers that accompany this book.)

SERIAL PROBLEM

Success Systems
LO2   LO3

SP 3   On October 1, 2010, Adriana Lopez launched a computer services company called **Success Systems,** which provides consulting services, computer system installations, and custom program development. Lopez adopts the calendar year for reporting purposes and expects to prepare the company's first set of financial statements on December 31, 2010. The company uses the following accounts:

Account	Account
Cash	A. Lopez, Capital
Accounts Receivable	A. Lopez, Withdrawals
Computer Supplies	Computer Services Revenue
Prepaid Insurance	Wages Expense
Prepaid Rent	Advertising Expense
Office Equipment	Mileage Expense
Computer Equipment	Miscellaneous Expenses
Accounts Payable	Repairs Expense—Computer

Required

1. Post each of the following transactions to the appropriate T-accounts.

Oct. 1   Lopez invested $75,000 cash, a $25,000 computer system, and $10,000 of office equipment in the business.
2   Paid $3,500 cash for four months' rent. (*Hint:* Debit Prepaid Rent for $3,500.)
3   Purchased $1,600 of computer supplies on credit from Corvina Office Products.
5   Paid $2,400 cash for one year's premium on a property and liability insurance policy. (*Hint:* Debit Prepaid Insurance for $2,400.)
6   Billed Easy Leasing $6,200 for services performed in installing a new Web server.
8   Paid $1,600 cash for the computer supplies purchased from Corvina Office Products on October 3.
12   Billed Easy Leasing another $1,950 for services performed.
15   Received $6,200 cash from Easy Leasing on its account.
17   Paid $900 cash to repair computer equipment that was damaged when moving it.
20   Paid $1,790 cash for an advertisement in the local newspaper.
22   Received $1,950 cash from Easy Leasing on its account.
28   Billed Clark Company $7,300 for services performed.
31   Paid $1,050 cash for Michelle Jones's wages for seven days' work.
31   Lopez withdrew $4,000 cash for personal use.
Nov. 1   Reimbursed Lopez in cash for business automobile mileage allowance (Lopez logged 1,200 miles at $0.32 per mile).
2   Received $3,600 cash from Edge Corporation for computer services performed.
5   Purchased computer supplies for $1,750 cash from Corvina Office Products.
8   Billed Gomez Co. $6,500 for services performed.
18   Received $5,000 cash from Clark Company as partial payment of the October 28 bill.
22   Donated $300 cash to the United Way in the company's name.
24   Completed work for Alex's Engineering Co. and sent it a bill for $7,000.
28   Reimbursed Lopez in cash for business automobile mileage (1,500 miles at $0.32 per mile).
30   Paid $2,100 cash for Michelle Jones's wages for 14 days' work.
30   Lopez withdrew $2,500 cash for personal use.

2. Prepare a trial balance (dated November 30, 2010) from the ending balances of the T-accounts from part 1.

BEYOND THE NUMBERS

<table>
<tr>
<td>

REPORTING IN ACTION

LO5

</td>
<td>

BTN 3–1   Refer to **Best Buy**'s financial statements in Appendix A for the following questions.

Required

1. What amount of cash does Best Buy report for each of the years ended March 1, 2008, and March 3, 2007?
2. Did Best Buy's cash balance increase or decrease during the year ended March 1, 2008?

</td>
</tr>
<tr>
<td>

ETHICS CHALLENGE

LO5

</td>
<td>

BTN 3–2   Craig Thorne works in a public accounting firm and hopes to eventually be a partner. The management of Allnet Company invites Thorne to prepare a bid to audit Allnet's financial statements. In discussing the audit fee, Allnet's management suggests a fee range in which the amount depends on the reported profit of Allnet. The higher its profit, the higher will be the audit fee paid to Thorne's firm.

Required

1. Identify the parties potentially affected by this audit and the fee plan proposed.
2. What are the ethical factors in this situation? Explain.
3. Would you recommend that Thorne accept this audit fee arrangement? Why or why not?
4. Describe some ethical considerations guiding your recommendation.

</td>
</tr>
<tr>
<td>

WORKPLACE COMMUNICATION

LO5

</td>
<td>

BTN 3–3   Lila Corentine is an aspiring entrepreneur and your friend. She is having difficulty understanding the purposes of financial statements and how they fit together across time.

Required

Write a one-page memorandum to Corentine explaining the purposes of the three basic financial statements and how they are linked across time.

</td>
</tr>
<tr>
<td>

TAKING IT TO THE NET

</td>
<td>

BTN 3–4   Search the Web for answers to the following questions on accounting careers. One suitable Website is CareerOneStop (**www.CareerOneStop.org**). For documentation print copies of the Website information accessed.

1. Identify the number of listings for accounting positions and the various accounting job titles.
2. Identify the number of listings for other job titles, with examples, that require or prefer accounting knowledge/experience but are not specifically accounting positions.
3. Specify the salary range for the accounting and accounting-related positions if provided.
4. Identify a job that appeals to you, the reason for its appeal, and its requirements.

</td>
</tr>
<tr>
<td>

TEAMWORK IN ACTION

LO2   LO3

</td>
<td>

BTN 3–5   The expanded accounting equation consists of assets, liabilities, capital, withdrawals, revenues, and expenses. It can be used to reveal insights into changes in a company's financial position.

Required

1. Form *learning teams* of six (or more) members. Each team member must select one of the six components and each team must have at least one expert on each component: (*a*) assets, (*b*) liabilities, (*c*) capital, (*d*) withdrawals, (*e*) revenues, and (*f*) expenses.
2. Form *expert teams* of individuals who selected the same component in part 1. Expert teams are to draft a report that each expert will present to his or her learning team addressing the following:
   a. Identify for its component the (i) increase and decrease side of the account and (ii) normal balance side of the account.
   b. Describe a transaction, with amounts, that increases its component.

</td>
</tr>
</table>

c. Using the transaction and amounts in (*b*), verify the equality of the accounting equation.

d. Describe a transaction, with amounts, that decreases its component.

e. Using the transaction and amounts in (*d*), verify the equality of the accounting equation.

3. Each expert should return to his/her learning team. In rotation, each member presents his/her expert team's report to the learning team. Team discussion is encouraged.

BTN 3-6   Assume Warren Brown of Cake Love wishes to expand but needs a $30,000 loan. The bank requests Warren to prepare a balance sheet. Warren has not kept formal records but is able to provide the following accounts and their amounts as of December 31, 2010:

ENTREPRENEURS IN BUSINESS

LO5

Cash	$ 3,600	Accounts Receivable	$9,600	Prepaid Insurance	$ 1,500
Prepaid Rent	9,400	Store Supplies	6,600	Equipment	50,000
Accounts Payable	17,800			Total Equity*	62,900
Annual net income	40,000				

* The total equity amount reflects all owner investments, withdrawals, revenues, and expenses as of December 31, 2010.

Required

1. Prepare a balance sheet as of December 31, 2010, for Cake Love.

2. Do you think the prospects of Cake Love repaying a $30,000 bank loan are good? Why or why not?

---

1. c; Assets and expenses normally have debit balances.

2. d; Assets = Liabilities + Equity.

3. a; The cash investment should be accounted for as a debit to cash (and a credit to K. Hinrich, Capital).

4. b; The accountant would debit Wage Expense and credit Cash.

5. a; Debit Cash for $2,500 and credit Unearned Lawn Service Fees for $2,500.

ANSWERS TO MULTIPLE CHOICE QUIZ

A Look Back

Chapter 3 explained the analysis and recording of transactions. We showed how to apply and interpret T-accounts, double-entry accounting, and trial balances.

A Look at This Chapter

This chapter continues our focus on the accounting process. We introduce source documents as inputs for analysis and describe a company's chart of accounts. We also explain how transactions are journalized and posted to the general ledger.

A Look Ahead

Chapter 5 explains the need to adjust accounts. We describe the various types of adjustments and the adjusted trial balance. We show how the adjusted trial balance is used to prepare financial statements.

Chapter 4

Preparing the General Journal and General Ledger

Learning Objectives

LO 1	Explain the steps in processing transactions.
LO 2	Describe source documents and their purpose.
LO 3	Describe a chart of accounts.
LO 4	Record transactions in a general journal.
LO 5	Post entries to a general ledger.
LO 6	Prepare financial statements from a trial balance.
LO 7	Explain how to correct errors in the general journal and general ledger.

"You just have to do it. There are no limitations."
—Katrina Markoff

Culinary Adventures

CHICAGO—"My heritage is Macedonian," says Katrina Markoff, "and my love of cooking has been with me from childhood. I began to think, why not combine international spices and chocolate?" Markoff ultimately created a chocolate confectionary company, **Vosges Haut Chocolat [VosgesChocolate.com],** with an "East-meets-West" feel. "I noticed a lack of creativity in chocolate," says Markoff. "They were all gold boxes with chocolate that tasted lousy and had raspberry and strawberry filling."

With ingredients such as wasabi, balsamic vinegar, jasmine flower, curry, and anise, you won't confuse her chocolate with any others. "When I tell people stories about the ingredients," says Markoff, "they tend to slow down and pay attention to what they're putting in their mouths."

Markoff is also a businessperson. "I couldn't help it," says Markoff, "my mother is an entrepreneur." That business sense mixed with her culinary skills gives her unique insights. Last year's sales were almost $12 million. The company's current best seller is "Mo's Bacon Bar," which contains pieces of apple-wood smoked bacon, she explains. Such results foretell further growth. "I'd like to just keep expanding," Markoff says.

Markoff insists that a timely and reliable accounting system is crucial for Vosges Haut Chocolat's success. This system gives Markoff the financial statement information that has enabled her company to obtain the necessary financing to feed its growth. This chapter focuses on the accounting system underlying financial statements.

The accounting system also gives her information on key expenses. She personally inspects and purchases each spice, flower, and chocolate used. "Right now, I'm trying out a Jamaican-style truffle, flavored with rum and allspice." Once new products meet her culinary standards, they are appropriately priced.

"We want people to experience chocolate through the use of their senses—all six!" exclaims Markoff. One of her newer products is the Aztec collection that combines chocolate with spices of the vanilla bean, ancho chili pepper, Ceylon cinnamon, and cashews. Adds Markoff, both chocolate and spices have a long history as aphrodisiacs. Now we're cooking!

[Sources: *Vosges Haut Chocolat Website,* January 2009; *Inc.* magazine, April 2005; *Entrepreneur,* 2002; Chocomap, January 2007; *Entrepreneur,* May 2008; *The Wall Street Journal,* D1, February 14, 2008.

Knowledge of how the accounting system processes transactions into financial statements is important. The goal of this chapter is to illustrate how transactions are recorded in a general journal and then posted to a general ledger. The chapter also shows how general ledger account balances are used to prepare financial statements.

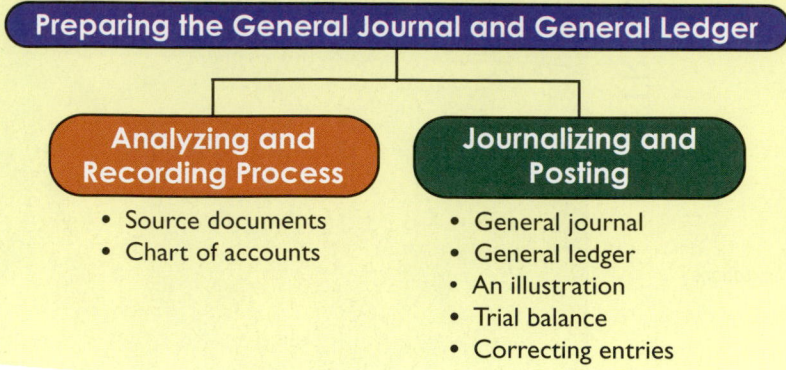

Preparing the General Journal and General Ledger

Analyzing and Recording Process
- Source documents
- Chart of accounts

Journalizing and Posting
- General journal
- General ledger
- An illustration
- Trial balance
- Correcting entries

Analyzing and Recording Process

LO1 Explain the steps in processing transactions.

In Chapter 3 we used T-accounts and the accounting equation as tools to understand transactions. Businesses don't use T-accounts to maintain their books; instead, the accounting process for analyzing and recording transactions and events follows the steps shown in Exhibit 4.1.

Exhibit 4.1

Steps in Processing Transactions

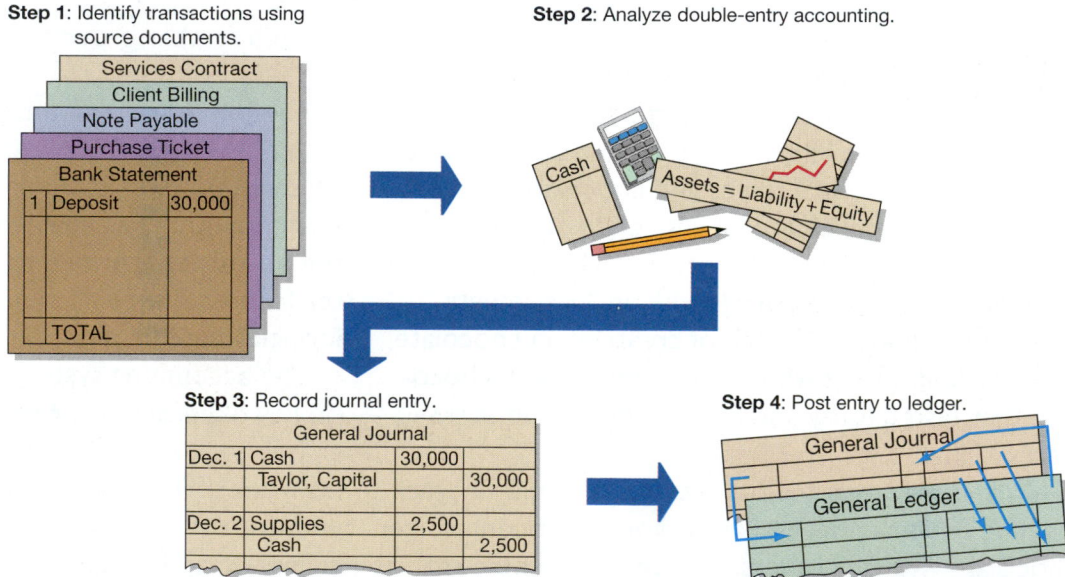

Steps 1 and 2—involving transaction analysis and double-entry accounting—were introduced in Chapters 2 and 3. This chapter extends that discussion and focuses on steps 3 and 4 of the accounting process. Step 3 is to record each transaction in a journal. A **journal** gives a complete record of each transaction in one place. It also shows debits and credits for each transaction. The process of recording transactions in a journal is called **journalizing.** Step 4 is to transfer (or *post*) entries from the journal to the ledger. The process of transferring journal entry information to the ledger is called **posting.** We can summarize this process with the letters *TARP,* which stand for: Transaction, Analysis, Record, and Post. The complete collection of all accounts in an accounting information system is called a **ledger** (or **general ledger**).

A journal is often referred to as the *book of original entry.* The ledger is referred to as the *book of final entry* because financial statements are prepared from it.

Business transactions and events are the starting points. Relying on source documents, transactions and events are analyzed using the accounting equation to understand how they affect accounts. These effects are recorded in accounting records, informally referred to as the *accounting books,* or simply the *books.* Additional steps such as posting and then preparing a trial balance help summarize and classify the effects of transactions and events. Ultimately, the accounting process provides information in useful reports or financial statements to decision makers.

Source Documents

Source documents identify and describe transactions entering the accounting process. They are the sources of accounting information and can be in either hard copy or electronic form. Examples are sales invoices, checks, purchase orders, bills from suppliers, employee earnings records, and bank statements (as shown in Exhibit 4.2). To illustrate, when an item is purchased on credit, the seller usually prepares at least two copies of a sales invoice. One copy is given to the buyer. Another copy, often sent electronically, is used by the seller to record the sale. Sellers use invoices for recording sales and for control; buyers use them for recording purchases and for monitoring purchasing activity. Many cash registers record information for each sale on a tape or electronic file locked inside the register. This record can be used as a source document for recording sales in the accounting records. Source documents, especially if obtained from outside the organization, provide objective and reliable evidence about transactions and their amounts.

LO2 Describe source documents and their purpose.

Exhibit 4.2

Sampling of Source Documents

A. Sales invoice (for goods or services provided)

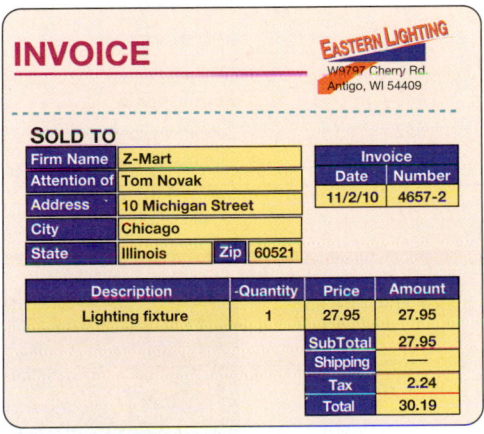

B. Cash register summary (detail of cash receipts)

C. Processed check images (detail of cash payments)

E. Deposit ticket (record of bank deposits)

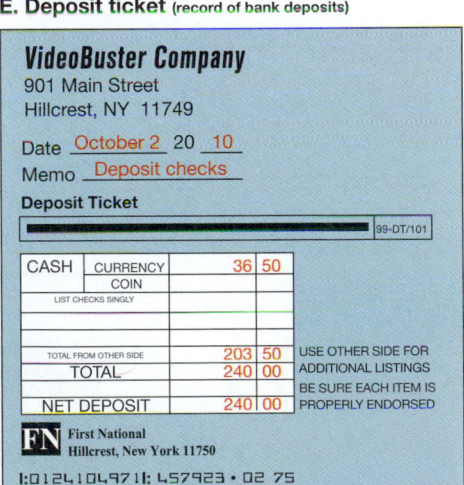

D. Bill from supplier (for goods or services received)

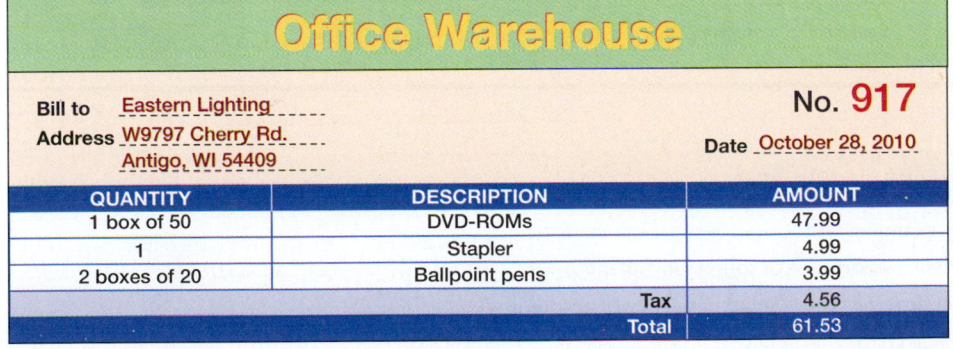

LO3 Describe a chart of accounts.

Chart of Accounts

To know which account is affected in a transaction, we must know which accounts a particular company uses. A company's size and diversity of operations affect the number of accounts needed. A small company can get by with as few as 20 or 30 accounts; a large company can require several thousand. The **chart of accounts** is a list of all accounts a company uses and includes an identification number assigned to each account. A small business might use the following numbering system for its accounts:

101–199	Asset accounts
201–299	Liability accounts
301–399	Equity accounts
401–499	Revenue accounts
501–699	Expense accounts

These numbers provide a three-digit code that is useful in recordkeeping. In this case, the first digit assigned to asset accounts is a 1, the first digit assigned to liability accounts is a 2, and so on. The second and third digits relate to the accounts' subcategories. Exhibit 4.3 shows a *partial* chart of accounts for FastForward, the focus company of Chapters 2 and 3. Different companies use different account titles. An example of the variety of accounts and their titles can be seen by looking at the chart of accounts located before the index at the back of the book.

Exhibit 4.3

Partial Chart of Accounts for FastForward

Account Number	Account Name
101	Cash
106	Accounts receivable
126	Supplies
128	Prepaid insurance
167	Equipment
201	Accounts payable
236	Unearned consulting revenue

Account Number	Account Name
301	C. Taylor, Capital
302	C. Taylor, Withdrawals
403	Consulting revenue
406	Rental revenue
622	Salaries expense
637	Insurance expense
640	Rent expense
652	Supplies expense
690	Utilities expense

IN THE NEWS

Sporting Accounts   The **Miami Heat** have the following major revenue and expense accounts:

Revenues	Expenses
Basketball ticket sales	Team salaries
TV & radio broadcast fees	Game costs
Advertising revenues	NBA franchise costs
Basketball playoff receipts	Promotional costs

HOW YOU DOIN'?   Answers—p. 89

1. Identify examples of accounting source documents.
2. Explain the importance of source documents.
3. What determines the number and types of accounts a company uses?
4. Describe a chart of accounts.

Journalizing and Posting

The General Journal

The process of journalizing transactions requires an understanding of a journal. While companies can use various journals, every company uses a **general journal.** It can be used to record any transaction. Exhibit 4.4 provides an example. The general journal contains columns to record:

1. Date of transaction.
2. Titles of affected accounts.
3. Dollar amount of each debit.
4. Dollar amount of each credit.
5. Posting reference.

Computerized journals are often designed to look like a manual journal page and also include error-checking routines that ensure debits equal credits for each entry. Shortcuts allow record-keepers to select account names and numbers from pull-down menus.

LO4 Record transactions in a general journal.

GENERAL JOURNAL				Page 1
Date	**Account Titles and Explanation**	**PR**	**Debit**	**Credit**

Exhibit 4.4

Sample General Journal

Journalizing Transactions   To record entries in a general journal, use this four-step process.

1. Date the transaction: Enter the year at the top of the first column and the month and day on the first line of each journal entry.
2. Enter titles of accounts **debited** and then enter amounts in the Debit column on the same line. Account titles are taken from the chart of accounts and are aligned with the left margin of the Account Titles and Explanation column.
3. Enter titles of accounts **credited** and then enter amounts in the Credit column on the same line. Account titles are from the chart of accounts and are indented from the left margin of the Account Titles and Explanation column to distinguish them from debited accounts.
4. Enter a brief explanation of the transaction on the line below the entry (it often references a source document). This explanation is indented about half as far as the credited account titles to avoid confusing it with accounts.

There are no exact rules for writing journal entry explanations. An explanation should be short yet describe why an entry is made.

We use the 16 transactions of FastForward from Chapter 3 to show how to journalize transactions. These transactions are summarized in Exhibit 4.5. A detailed journalizing example using FastForward's first transaction in December follows:

Transaction 1

Chuck Taylor invests $30,000 cash in FastForward on December 1.

Step 1: Enter the date in the date column. Enter the year at the top of the first column and then enter the month and the day.

Date	Account Titles and Explanation	PR	Debit	Credit
2010 Dec. 1				

Step 2: Enter the titles of the accounts debited and enter the debit amount in the Debit column on the same line. Note that dollar signs are not used in journals.

Date		Account Titles and Explanation	PR	Debit	Credit
2010 Dec.	1	Cash		30 0 0 0 00	

Step 3: Enter the titles of the accounts credited and enter the credit amount in the credit column on the same line. Indent the credit account title from the left margin of the Account Titles and Explanation column.

Date		Account Titles and Explanation	PR	Debit	Credit
2010 Dec.	1	Cash		30 0 0 0 00	
		C. Taylor, Capital			30 0 0 0 00

Step 4: Enter an explanation, indented about half as far the credited account title.

Date		Account Titles and Explanation	PR	Debit	Credit
2010 Dec.	1	Cash		30 0 0 0 00	
		C. Taylor, Capital			30 0 0 0 00
		Investment by owner.			

Exhibit 4.5

FastForward's December Transactions

Date		Transaction
(1) Dec. 1		Chuck Taylor invests $30,000 cash in FastForward.
(2) Dec. 2		FastForward pays $2,500 cash for supplies.
(3) Dec. 3		FastForward pays $26,000 cash for equipment.
(4) Dec. 4		FastForward purchases $7,100 of supplies on credit.
(5) Dec. 5		FastForward provides consulting services and immediately collects $4,200 in cash.
(6) Dec. 6		FastForward pays $1,000 cash for December rent.
(7) Dec. 12		FastForward pays $700 cash for employee salaries.
(8) Dec. 13		FastForward provides consulting services of $1,600 and rents its test facilities for $300. The customer is billed $1,900 for these services.
(9) Dec. 19		FastForward receives $1,900 cash from the client billed in transaction 8.
(10) Dec. 20		FastForward pays the supplier $900 cash toward the account payable from transaction 4.
(11) Dec. 21		Chuck Taylor withdraws $200 cash from FastForward for personal use.
(12) Dec. 22		FastForward receives $3,000 cash in advance of providing consulting services to a customer.
(13) Dec. 23		FastForward pays $2,400 cash (insurance premium) for a 24-month insurance policy. Coverage begins on December 1.
(14) Dec. 23		FastForward pays $120 cash for supplies.
(15) Dec. 23		FastForward pays $230 cash for December utilities expense.
(16) Dec. 26		FastForward pays $700 cash in employee salaries for work performed in the latter part of December.

FastForward's transactions are journalized in Exhibit 4.6. Review this carefully. We identify each transaction with its number (1–16) in our example; this information is not usually seen in journals.

A blank line is left between each journal entry for clarity. When a transaction is first recorded, the **posting reference (PR) column** is left blank (in a manual system). Later, when posting entries to the general ledger, the identification numbers of the individual ledger accounts are entered in the PR column. We show how to post journal entries to the general ledger next.

GENERAL JOURNAL Page 1

	Date		Account Titles and Explanation	PR	Debit	Credit
(1)	2010 Dec.	1	Cash		30 000 00	
			C. Taylor, Capital			30 000 00
			Investment by owner.			
(2)	Dec.	2	Supplies		2 500 00	
			Cash			2 500 00
			Purchased supplies for cash.			
(3)	Dec.	3	Equipment		26 000 00	
			Cash			26 000 00
			Purchased equipment for cash.			
(4)	Dec.	4	Supplies		7 100 00	
			Accounts Payable			7 100 00
			Purchased supplies on credit.			
(5)	Dec.	5	Cash		4 200 00	
			Consulting Revenue			4 200 00
			Provide services for cash.			
(6)	Dec.	6	Rent Expense		1 000 00	
			Cash			1 000 00
			Payment of rent expense in cash.			
(7)	Dec.	12	Salaries Expense		700 00	
			Cash			700 00
			Payment of salaries expense in cash.			
(8)	Dec.	13	Accounts Receivable		1 900 00	
			Consulting Revenue			1 600 00
			Rental Revenue			300 00
			Provide rental and consulting services on credit.			
(9)	Dec.	19	Cash		1 900 00	
			Accounts Receivable			1 900 00
			Receipt of cash on account.			
(10)	Dec.	20	Accounts Payable		900 00	
			Cash			900 00
			Payment of accounts payable (partial).			
(11)	Dec.	21	C. Taylor, Withdrawals		200 00	
			Cash			200 00
			Withdrawal of cash by owner.			
(12)	Dec.	22	Cash		3 000 00	
			Unearned Consulting Revenue			3 000 00
			Receipt of cash for future services.			
(13)	Dec.	23	Prepaid Insurance		2 400 00	
			Cash			2 400 00
			Cash payment for insurance coverage.			

This is called a **compound journal entry,** an entry that affects three or more accounts.

Exhibit 4.6

Journal Entries for FastForward Transactions

[continued on next page]

[continued from previous page]

(14)	Dec.	23	Supplies			1 2 0 00	
			Cash				1 2 0 00
			Purchased supplies for cash.				
(15)	Dec.	23	Utilities Expense			2 3 0 00	
			Cash				2 3 0 00
			Payment of utilities expense in cash.				
(16)	Dec.	26	Salaries Expense			7 0 0 00	
			Cash				7 0 0 00
			Payment of salaries expense in cash.				

The General Ledger

The general journal gives a complete record of each transaction in one place. To determine the current balance of each specific account, however, information in the journal must be transferred (or posted) to each account.

Balance Column Account   The T-accounts that were introduced in Chapter 3 are a simple way to show how the accounting process works. However, actual accounting systems need more structure, and therefore use **balance column accounts** in ledgers. We compare T-accounts to the balance column accounts found in ledgers in Exhibit 4.7, using the first few transactions for FastForward. The T-account is a useful classroom tool which represents the more formal balance column account.

Exhibit 4.7

Comparing T-account with Balance Column account

Cash		
30,000		2,500
4,200		26,000
Balance	**5,700**	

	Cash				Account No. 101	
Date	**Explanation**	**PR**	**Debit**	**Credit**	**Balance**	
2010						
Dec. 1		G1	30,000		30,000	
Dec. 2		G1		2,500	27,500	
Dec. 3		G1		26,000	1,500	
Dec. 10		G1	4,200		**5,700**	

The balance column account format is similar to a T-account in having columns for debits and credits. It differs from a T-account by including the account number (101) from FastForward's chart of accounts, transaction date, posting reference (PR), and explanation columns. It also has a column with the running balance of the account after each entry is recorded. To illustrate, FastForward's Cash account in Exhibit 4.7 is debited on December 1 for the $30,000 owner investment, yielding a $30,000 debit balance. The account is credited on December 2 for $2,500, yielding a $27,500 debit balance. On December 3, it is credited again, this time for $26,000, and its debit balance is reduced to $1,500. The Cash account is debited for $4,200 on December 10, and its debit balance increases to $5,700.

The heading of the Balance column does not show whether it is a debit or credit balance. Instead, an account is assumed to have a *normal balance*. Unusual events can sometimes temporarily give an account an abnormal balance. An *abnormal balance* refers to a balance on the side where decreases are recorded. For example, a customer might mistakenly overpay a bill. This gives that customer's account receivable an abnormal (credit) balance. An abnormal balance is often identified by circling it or by entering it in red or some other unusual color in manual systems. An abnormal balance might be shown in brackets in a computerized system. A zero balance for an account is usually shown by writing zeros or a dash in the Balance column to avoid confusion between a zero balance and one omitted in error. Explanations are typically included in ledger accounts only for unusual transactions or events.

Posting Journal Entries   Step 4 of processing transactions is to post journal entries to ledger accounts (see Exhibit 4.1). To ensure that the ledger is up-to-date, entries are posted as soon as possible. This might be daily, weekly, or when time permits. All entries must be posted to the ledger before financial statements are prepared to ensure that account balances are up-to-date. When entries are posted to the ledger, the debits in journal entries are transferred into ledger accounts as debits, and credits are transferred into ledger accounts as credits. The steps to post a journal entry to a general ledger account are:

LO5   Post entries to a general ledger.

1. Identify the ledger account that is debited in the journal entry and enter the date of the transaction in the date column.
2. Enter the debit amount in the debit column.
3. Update the balance of the ledger account.
4. Enter the journal and page in the PR column of the ledger. For example, the letter G shows the journal entry came for the General Journal; the number 1 indicates the journal entry came from page 1 of that journal.

In the ledger

5. Enter the general ledger account number in the PR column of the journal. This creates a link between the general ledger and the journal entry in the general journal. This link is a useful cross-reference for tracing an amount from one record to another. Also, if an accountant is interrupted during the posting process, PR numbers enable the accountant or others to determine where to resume.

In the journal

Next, to complete the posting of that entry, repeat the above process for the credit part of the journal entry.

In Exhibit 4.8 we provide a detailed example of the posting process using FastForward's first journal entry from December 1.

Posting a Debit

1. Enter the year, 2010, and the date (December 1) of FastForward's first transaction in the Cash account in the ledger.
2. Enter the $30,000 debit to cash in the debit column of the Cash account.

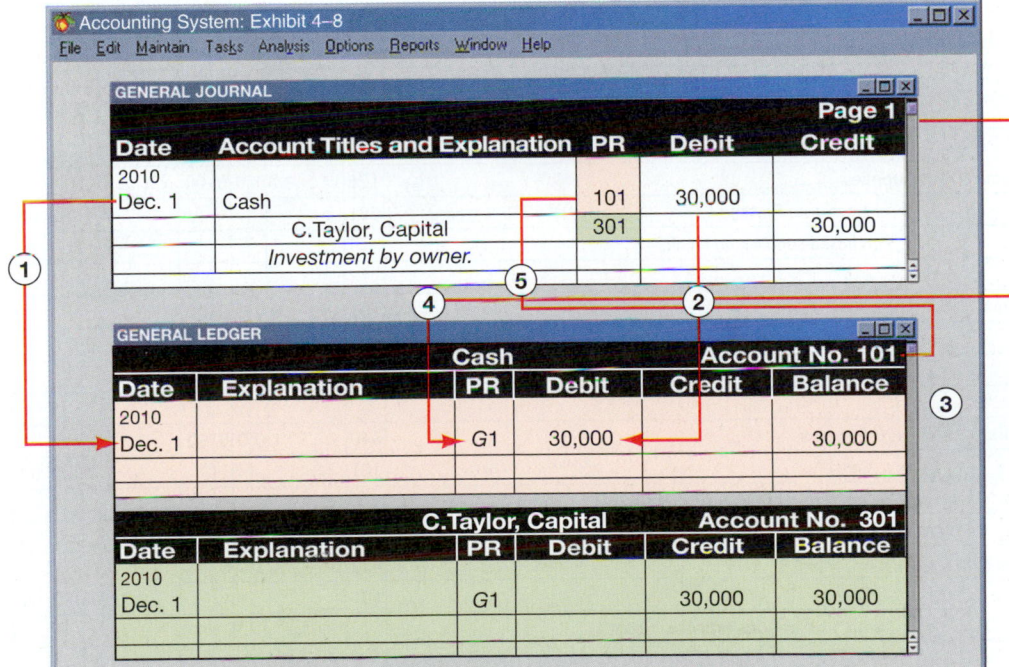

Exhibit 4.8

Posting an Entry to the Ledger

Arrow lines show the posting steps for the *debit* of this journal entry. The steps are similar for the *credit* of this journal entry. Step ③ occurs only in the ledger.

3. Update the balance of the Cash account to $30,000.

In the ledger
4. Enter *G*1 in the PR column, indicating the journal entry is from page 1 of the general journal.

In the journal
5. Put 101, the account number for the Cash general ledger account, in the PR column of the journal.

Posting a Credit

1. Enter the year, 2010, and the date (December 1) of FastForward's first transaction in the C. Taylor, Capital, account in the ledger.
2. Enter the $30,000 credit in the credit column of the C. Taylor, Capital, account.
3. Update the balance of the C. Taylor, Capital, account to $30,000.

In the ledger
4. Enter *G*1 in the PR column, indicating the journal entry is from page 1 of the general journal.

In the journal
5. Put 301, the account number for the C. Taylor, Capital, general ledger account, in the PR column of the journal.

Journalizing and Posting—An Illustration

We return to the activities of FastForward to show how to journalize and post their first 16 transactions. We first show the 16 transactions as journal entries in the general journal (Exhibit 4.9). Note that account numbers are included in the "PR" column, indicating the entries have been

Exhibit 4.9

Journal Entries for FastForward Transactions, after Posting to General Ledger

	Date		Account Titles and Explanation	PR	Debit	Credit
			GENERAL JOURNAL			Page 1
(1)	2010 Dec.	1	Cash	101	30 000 00	
			C. Taylor, Capital	301		30 000 00
			Investment by owner.			
(2)	Dec.	2	Supplies	126	2 500 00	
			Cash	101		2 500 00
			Purchased supplies for cash.			
(3)	Dec.	3	Equipment	167	26 000 00	
			Cash	101		26 000 00
			Purchased equipment for cash.			
(4)	Dec.	4	Supplies	126	7 100 00	
			Accounts Payable	201		7 100 00
			Purchased supplies on credit.			
(5)	Dec.	5	Cash	101	4 200 00	
			Consulting Revenue	403		4 200 00
			Provide services for cash.			
(6)	Dec.	6	Rent Expense	640	1 000 00	
			Cash	101		1 000 00
			Payment of rent expense in cash.			
(7)	Dec.	12	Salaries Expense	622	700 00	
			Cash	101		700 00
			Payment of salaries expense in cash.			

[continued on next page]

[continued from previous page]

					Debit		Credit	
(8)	Dec.	13	Accounts Receivable	106	1 9 0 0 00			
			Consulting Revenue	403			1 6 0 0 00	
			Rental Revenue	406			3 0 0 00	
			Provide rental and consulting services on credit.					
(9)	Dec.	19	Cash	101	1 9 0 0 00			
			Accounts Receivable	106			1 9 0 0 00	
			Receipt of cash on account.					
(10)	Dec.	20	Accounts Payable	201	9 0 0 00			
			Cash	101			9 0 0 00	
			Payment of accounts payable (partial).					
(11)	Dec.	21	C. Taylor, Withdrawals	302	2 0 0 00			
			Cash	101			2 0 0 00	
			Withdrawal of cash by owner.					
(12)	Dec.	22	Cash	101	3 0 0 0 00			
			Unearned Consulting Revenue	236			3 0 0 0 00	
			Receipt of cash for future services.					
(13)	Dec.	23	Prepaid Insurance	128	2 4 0 0 00			
			Cash	101			2 4 0 0 00	
			Cash payment for insurance coverage.					
(14)	Dec.	23	Supplies	126	1 2 0 00			
			Cash	101			1 2 0 00	
			Purchased supplies for cash.					
(15)	Dec.	23	Utilities Expense	690	2 3 0 00			
			Cash	101			2 3 0 00	
			Payment of utilities expense in cash.					
(16)	Dec.	26	Salaries Expense	622	7 0 0 00			
			Cash	101			7 0 0 00	
			Payment of salaries expense in cash.					

posted to the general ledger. We then show the results of posting these transactions to ledger accounts (Exhibit 4.10).

The general ledger accounts in Exhibit 4.10 do not include a column for explanations. Explanations are typically included in ledger accounts only for unusual transactions or events. If an explanation is needed, it can be added in the date column, directly below the date of the unusual transaction or event.

The fundamental concepts of the manual (pencil-and-paper) system we illustrate are identical to those of a computerized accounting system. However, posting is automatic and immediate in a computerized system. Accounting software also typically includes features that reduce the chance for errors, for example computing updated account balances and ensuring all journal entries have equal debits and credits.

Trial Balance

After all entries have been posted, a trial balance is prepared to ensure the equality of debits and credits in the general ledger. All of the accounts in the ledger are entered into the trial balance, typically in account number order. The balance for each account is obtained from the last row of

Exhibit 4.10

General Ledger for FastForward

Cash   Account No. 101

Date	PR	Debit	Credit	Balance
Dec. 1	G1	30,000		30,000
2	G1		2,500	27,500
3	G1		26,000	1,500
5	G1	4,200		5,700
6	G1		1,000	4,700
12	G1		700	4,000
19	G1	1,900		5,900
20	G1		900	5,000
21	G1		200	4,800
22	G1	3,000		7,800
23	G1		2,400	5,400
23	G1		120	5,280
23	G1		230	5,050
26	G1		700	4,350

Accounts Receivable   Account No. 106

Date	PR	Debit	Credit	Balance
Dec. 13	G1	1,900		1,900
19	G1		1,900	0

Supplies   Account No. 126

Date	PR	Debit	Credit	Balance
Dec. 2	G1	2,500		2,500
4	G1	7,100		9,600
23	G1	120		9,720

Prepaid Insurance   Account No. 128

Date	PR	Debit	Credit	Balance
Dec. 23	G1	2,400		2,400

Equipment   Account No. 167

Date	PR	Debit	Credit	Balance
Dec. 3	G1	26,000		26,000

Accounts Payable   Account No. 201

Date	PR	Debit	Credit	Balance
Dec. 4	G1		7,100	7,100
20	G1	900		6,200

Unearned Consulting Revenue   Account No. 236

Date	PR	Debit	Credit	Balance
Dec. 22	G1		3,000	3,000

C. Taylor, Capital   Account No. 301

Date	PR	Debit	Credit	Balance
Dec. 1	G1		30,000	30,000

C. Taylor, Withdrawals   Account No. 302

Date	PR	Debit	Credit	Balance
Dec. 21	G1	200		200

Consulting Revenue   Account No. 403

Date	PR	Debit	Credit	Balance
Dec. 5	G1		4,200	4,200
13	G1		1,600	5,800

Rental Revenue   Account No. 406

Date	PR	Debit	Credit	Balance
Dec. 13	G1		300	300

Salaries Expense   Account No. 622

Date	PR	Debit	Credit	Balance
Dec. 12	G1	700		700
26	G1	700		1,400

Rent Expense   Account No. 640

Date	PR	Debit	Credit	Balance
Dec. 6	G1	1,000		1,000

Utilities Expense   Account No. 690

Date	PR	Debit	Credit	Balance
Dec. 23	G1	230		230

LO6 Prepare financial statements from a trial balance.

information for that account in the ledger and entered in the trial balance. As in Chapter 3, if the total debits do not equal the total credits in the trial balance, the accountant must determine why. In Exhibit 4.11 we provide FastForward's trial balance, prepared from the general ledger accounts in Exhibit 4.10 as of the end of December. You will notice it is the same as the trial balance we prepared from T-accounts in Chapter 3. The income statement, statement of owner's equity, and balance sheet shown in Exhibit 4.11 can then be prepared from this trial balance. We showed in detail how to prepare these three financial statements in Chapter 3.

Exhibit 4.11

Preparing Financial Statements from Trial Balance

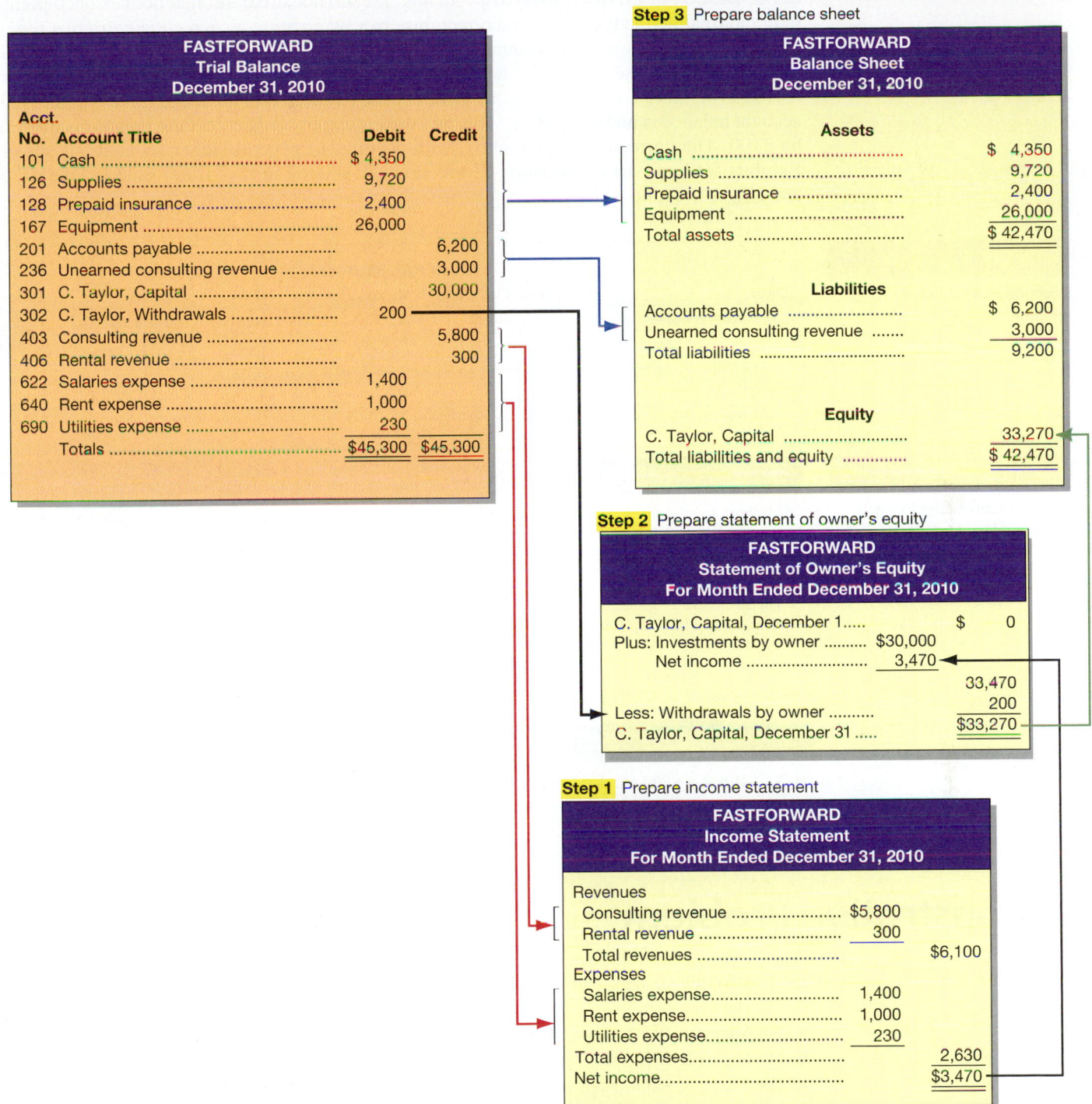

Step 3 Prepare balance sheet

FASTFORWARD
Trial Balance
December 31, 2010

Acct. No.	Account Title	Debit	Credit
101	Cash	$ 4,350	
126	Supplies	9,720	
128	Prepaid insurance	2,400	
167	Equipment	26,000	
201	Accounts payable		6,200
236	Unearned consulting revenue		3,000
301	C. Taylor, Capital		30,000
302	C. Taylor, Withdrawals	200	
403	Consulting revenue		5,800
406	Rental revenue		300
622	Salaries expense	1,400	
640	Rent expense	1,000	
690	Utilities expense	230	
	Totals	$45,300	$45,300

FASTFORWARD
Balance Sheet
December 31, 2010

Assets

Cash	$ 4,350
Supplies	9,720
Prepaid insurance	2,400
Equipment	26,000
Total assets	$ 42,470

Liabilities

Accounts payable	$ 6,200
Unearned consulting revenue	3,000
Total liabilities	9,200

Equity

C. Taylor, Capital	33,270
Total liabilities and equity	$ 42,470

Step 2 Prepare statement of owner's equity

FASTFORWARD
Statement of Owner's Equity
For Month Ended December 31, 2010

C. Taylor, Capital, December 1		$ 0
Plus: Investments by owner	$30,000	
Net income	3,470	
		33,470
Less: Withdrawals by owner		200
C. Taylor, Capital, December 31		$33,270

Step 1 Prepare income statement

FASTFORWARD
Income Statement
For Month Ended December 31, 2010

Revenues		
Consulting revenue	$5,800	
Rental revenue	300	
Total revenues		$6,100
Expenses		
Salaries expense	1,400	
Rent expense	1,000	
Utilities expense	230	
Total expenses		2,630
Net income		$3,470

Correcting Errors in the Journal and the Ledger

Errors sometimes occur in journal entries. When they occur, we must correct them. How we correct the error depends on whether it is discovered before or after the journal entry is posted.

LO7 Explain how to correct errors in the general journal and general ledger.

Error Discovered before Posting   In this case, the error can be corrected in a manual system by drawing a line through the incorrect information. The correct information is written above it to create a record of change for the auditor. Many computerized systems allow the operator to replace the incorrect information directly.

Error Discovered after Posting   In this case, do not strike through both erroneous entries in the journal and ledger. Instead, correct this error by creating a *correcting entry* that removes the amount from the wrong account and records it in the correct account. As an example, suppose a $100 purchase of supplies is journalized with an incorrect debit to Equipment and a correct $100 credit to Cash, and then this incorrect entry is posted to the ledger. The Supplies ledger account balance is understated by $100, and the Equipment ledger account balance is overstated by $100. The correcting journal entry, with postings to general ledger accounts, is shown in Exhibits 4.12 and 4.13. The word "Correcting" is entered in the "Date" column in each general ledger account.

Exhibit 4.12

Correcting Journal Entry

GENERAL JOURNAL					
Date	**Account Titles and Explanation**	**PR**	**Debit**		**Credit**
2010 July 28	Supplies	126	1 0 0 00		
	Equipment	167			1 0 0 00
	To correct error where equipment was incorrectly debited.				

Exhibit 4.13

Effects of a Correcting Journal Entry on Ledger Accounts

General Ledger											
Supplies			**Account No. 126**			**Equipment**			**Account No. 167**		
Date	**PR**	**Debit**	**Credit**	**Balance**		**Date**	**PR**	**Debit**	**Credit**	**Balance**	
2010 July 28						2010 July 15	G1	800		800	
Correcting	G1	100		100		22	G1	100		900	
						28					
						Correcting	G1		100	800	

HOW YOU DOIN'?

Answer—p. 89

5. Assume a $500 purchase of prepaid insurance is journalized with an incorrect debit to Supplies, and this incorrect entry is posted to the ledger. Prepare the correcting journal entry.

Demonstration Problem

(This problem extends the demonstration problem of Chapters 2 and 3.) After several months of planning, Jasmine Worthy started a haircutting business called Expressions. The following events occurred during its first month.

a. On August 1, Worthy invested $3,000 cash and $15,000 of equipment in Expressions.

b. On August 2, Expressions paid $600 cash for furniture for the shop.

c. On August 3, Expressions paid $500 cash to rent space in a strip mall for August.

d. On August 4, it purchased $1,200 of equipment on credit for the shop (using an account payable).

e. On August 5, Expressions opened for business. Cash received from services provided in the first week and a half of business (ended August 15) is $825.

f. On August 15, it provided $100 of haircutting services on account.

g. On August 17, it received a $100 check for services previously rendered on account.

h. On August 17, it paid $125 to an assistant for working during the grand opening.

i. Cash received from services provided during the second half of August is $930.

j. On August 31, it paid $400 on the account payable entered into on August 4.

k. On August 31, Worthy withdrew $900 cash for personal use.

Required

1. Open the following ledger accounts in balance column format (account numbers are in parentheses): Cash (101); Accounts Receivable (102); Furniture (161); Store Equipment (165); Accounts Payable (201); J. Worthy, Capital (301); J. Worthy, Withdrawals (302); Haircutting Services Revenue (403); Wages Expense (623); and Rent Expense (640). Prepare general journal entries for the transactions.

2. Post the journal entries from (1) to the ledger accounts.

3. Prepare a trial balance as of August 31.

Extended Analysis

4. In the coming months, Expressions will experience a greater variety of business transactions. Identify which accounts are debited and which are credited for the following transactions. (*Hint:* We must use some accounts not opened in part 1.)

   a. Purchase supplies with cash.

   b. Pay cash for future insurance coverage.

   c. Receive cash for services to be provided in the future.

   d. Purchase supplies on account.

Planning the Solution

- Analyze each transaction and use the debit and credit rules to prepare a journal entry for each.
- Post each debit and each credit from journal entries to their ledger accounts and cross-reference each amount in the PR columns of the journal and ledger.
- Calculate each account balance and list the accounts with their balances on a trial balance.
- Verify that total debits in the trial balance equal total credits.
- Analyze the future transactions to identify the accounts affected and apply debit and credit rules.

Solution to Demonstration Problem

1. General journal entries:

		GENERAL JOURNAL			
Date		Account Titles and Explanation	PR	Debit	Credit
2010 Aug.	1	Cash	101	3 0 0 0 00	
		Store Equipment	165	15 0 0 0 00	
		J. Worthy, Capital	301		18 0 0 0 00
		Owner's investment.			
	2	Furniture	161	6 0 0 00	
		Cash	101		6 0 0 00
		Purchased furniture for cash.			
	3	Rent Expense	640	5 0 0 00	
		Cash	101		5 0 0 00
		Paid rent for August.			
	4	Store Equipment	165	1 2 0 0 00	
		Accounts Payable	201		1 2 0 0 00
		Purchased additional equipment on credit.			
	15	Cash	101	8 2 5 00	
		Haircutting Services Revenue	403		8 2 5 00
		Cash receipts from first half of August.			
	15	Accounts Receivable	102	1 0 0 00	
		Haircutting Services Revenue	403		1 0 0 00
		To record revenue for services provided on account.			

[continued on next page]

[continued from previous page]

					Debit		Credit	
17	Cash	101		1 0 0 00		
	Accounts Receivable	102				1 0 0 00
	To record cash received as payment on account.					
17	Wages Expense	623		1 2 5 00		
	Cash	101				1 2 5 00
	Paid wages to assistant.					
31	Cash	101		9 3 0 00		
	Haircutting Services Revenue	403				9 3 0 00
	Cash receipts from second half of August.					
31	Accounts Payable	201		4 0 0 00		
	Cash	101				4 0 0 00
	Paid an installment on the account payable.					
31	J. Worthy, Withdrawals	302		9 0 0 00		
	Cash	101				9 0 0 00
	Cash withdrawal by owner.					

2. Post journal entries from part 1 to the ledger accounts:

General Ledger

Cash   Account No. 101

Date	PR	Debit	Credit	Balance
Aug. 1	G1	3,000		3,000
2	G1		600	2,400
3	G1		500	1,900
15	G1	825		2,725
17	G1	100		2,825
17	G1		125	2,700
31	G1	930		3,630
31	G1		400	3,230
31	G1		900	2,330

Accounts Receivable   Account No. 102

Date	PR	Debit	Credit	Balance
Aug. 15	G1	100		100
17	G1		100	0

Furniture   Account No. 161

Date	PR	Debit	Credit	Balance
Aug. 2	G1	600		600

Store Equipment   Account No. 165

Date	PR	Debit	Credit	Balance
Aug. 1	G1	15,000		15,000
4	G1	1,200		16,200

Accounts Payable   Account No. 201

Date	PR	Debit	Credit	Balance
Aug. 4	G1		1,200	1,200
31	G1	400		800

J. Worthy, Capital   Account No. 301

Date	PR	Debit	Credit	Balance
Aug. 1	G1		18,000	18,000

J. Worthy, Withdrawals   Account No. 302

Date	PR	Debit	Credit	Balance
Aug. 31	G1	900		900

Haircutting Services Revenue Account No. 403

Date	PR	Debit	Credit	Balance
Aug. 15	G1		825	825
15	G1		100	925
31	G1		930	1,855

Wages Expense   Account No. 623

Date	PR	Debit	Credit	Balance
Aug. 17	G1	125		125

Rent Expense   Account No. 640

Date	PR	Debit	Credit	Balance
Aug. 3	G1	500		500

3. Prepare a trial balance from the ledger:

EXPRESSIONS Trial Balance August 31		
	Debit	**Credit**
Cash	$ 2,330	
Accounts receivable	0	
Furniture	600	
Store equipment	16,200	
Accounts payable		$ 800
J. Worthy, Capital		18,000
J. Worthy, Withdrawals	900	
Haircutting services revenue		1,855
Wages expense	125	
Rent expense	500	
Totals	$20,655	$20,655

4a. Supplies *debited*
      Cash *credited*

4b. Prepaid Insurance *debited*
      Cash *credited*

4c. Cash *debited*
      Unearned Services Revenue *credited*

4d. Supplies *debited*
      Accounts Payable *credited*

Summary

LO1 **Explain the steps in processing transactions.** The accounting process identifies business transactions and events, analyzes and records their effects, and summarizes and prepares information useful in making decisions. Transactions and events are the starting points in the accounting process. Source documents help in their analysis. The effects of transactions and events are recorded in journals. Posting along with a trial balance helps summarize and classify these effects.

LO2 **Describe source documents and their purpose.** Source documents identify and describe transactions and events. Examples are sales tickets, checks, purchase orders, bills, and bank statements. Source documents provide objective and reliable evidence, making information more useful.

LO3 **Describe a chart of accounts.** The chart of accounts is a list of all accounts and usually includes an identification number assigned to each account.

LO4 **Record transactions in a general journal.** Transactions are recorded in a journal. The journal includes columns for dates, account titles and explanations, debit amounts, credit amounts, and a posting reference column.

LO5 **Post entries to a general ledger.** Each entry in a journal is posted to a ledger. The ledger provides information that is used to produce financial statements. Balance column accounts are widely used and include columns for debits, credits, and the account balance. A posting reference column provides a link between the ledger and the entry in the journal.

LO6 **Prepare financial statements from a trial balance.** A trial balance is prepared from the general ledger, and then used to prepare the income statement, statement of owner's equity, and the balance sheet.

LO7 **Explain how to correct errors in the general journal and general ledger.** If an error in a journal entry is discovered before the error is posted, it can be corrected by drawing a line through the incorrect information. If an error in a journal entry is not discovered until after it is posted, correct this error with a *correcting entry* that removes the amount from the erroneous accounts and records it to the correct accounts.

Guidance Answers to HOW YOU DOIN'?

1. Examples of source documents are sales tickets, checks, purchase orders, charges to customers, bills from suppliers, employee earnings records, and bank statements.

2. Source documents serve many purposes, including recordkeeping and internal control. Source documents, especially if obtained from outside the organization, provide objective and reliable evidence about transactions and their amounts.

3. A company's size and diversity affect the number of accounts in its accounting system. The types of accounts depend on

information the company needs to both effectively operate and report its activities in financial statements.

4. A chart of accounts is a list of all of a company's accounts and their identification numbers.

5. The Supplies ledger account balance is overstated by $500 and the Prepaid Insurance ledger account balance is understated by $500. The correcting journal entry is: debit Prepaid Insurance and credit Supplies (both for $500).

Key Terms

Balance column account (p. 80) Account with debit and credit columns for recording entries and another column for showing the balance of the account after each entry.

Chart of accounts (p. 76) List of accounts used by a company; includes an identification number for each account.

Compound journal entry (p. 79) An entry that affects three or more accounts.

General journal (p. 77) All-purpose journal for recording the debits and credits of transactions and events.

Journal (p. 74) Record in which transactions are entered before they are posted to ledger accounts; also *book of original entry.*

Journalizing (p. 74) Process of recording transactions in a journal.

Ledger (p. 74) Record containing all accounts (with amounts) for a business; also called *general ledger.*

Posting (p. 74) Process of transferring journal entry information to a ledger; computerized systems automate this process.

Posting reference (PR) column (p. 78) A column in journals and ledgers in which individual ledger account numbers are entered when entries are posted to those ledger accounts.

Source documents (p. 75) Source of information for accounting entries that can be in either paper or electronic form; also called *business papers.*

Multiple Choice Quiz

Answers on p. 101　　　mhhe.com/wildCA2e

Additional Multiple Choice Quizzes A and B are available at the book's Website.

1. The process of transferring debits and credits from the journal to the ledger is called
   a. Transferring
   b. Posting
   c. Journalizing
   d. Referencing

2. Unearned revenue exists when customers pay in advance for products or services and is accounted for as a(n)
   a. Asset
   b. Revenue
   c. Expense
   d. Liability

3. Amalia Company received its utility bill for the current period of $700 and immediately paid it. Its journal entry to record this transaction includes a
   a. Credit to Utility Expense for $700.
   b. Debit to Utility Expense for $700.
   c. Debit to Accounts Payable for $700.
   d. Debit to Cash for $700.
   e. Credit to Capital for $700.

4. Liang Shue contributed $250,000 cash and land worth $500,000 to open his new business, Shue Consulting. Which of the following journal entries does Shue Consulting make to record this transaction?

	Debit	Credit
a. Cash Assets	750,000	
L. Shue, Capital		750,000
b. L. Shue, Capital	750,000	
Assets		750,000
c. Cash	250,000	
Land	500,000	
L. Shue, Capital		750,000
d. L. Shue, Capital	750,000	
Cash		250,000
Land		500,000

5. A trial balance prepared at year-end shows total credits exceed total debits by $765. This discrepancy could have been caused by
   a. An error in the general journal where a $765 increase in Accounts Payable was recorded as a $765 decrease in Accounts Payable.
   b. The ledger balance for Accounts Payable of $7,650 being entered in the trial balance as $765.
   c. A general journal error where a $765 increase in Accounts Receivable was recorded as a $765 increase in Cash.
   d. The ledger balance of $850 in Accounts Receivable was entered in the trial balance as $85.
   e. An error in recording a $765 increase in Cash as a credit.

Discussion Questions

1. Discuss the steps in processing business transactions.
2. What kinds of transactions can be recorded in a general journal?
3. Are debits or credits typically listed first in general journal entries? Are the debits or the credits indented?
4. Should a transaction be recorded first in a journal or the ledger? Why?
5. If an incorrect amount is journalized and posted to the accounts, how should the error be corrected?
6. If assets are valuable resources and asset accounts have debit balances, why do expense accounts also have debit balances?
7. What is the difference between a T-account and a general ledger account?

connect™

Identify the items from the following list that are likely to serve as source documents.

a. Sales ticket

b. Income statement

c. Trial balance

d. Telephone bill

e. Invoice from supplier

f. Company revenue account

g. Balance sheet

h. Prepaid insurance

i. Bank statement

QUICK STUDY

QS 4–1

Identifying source documents

LO2

Prepare journal entries for each of the following selected transactions.

a. On January 13, DeShawn Tyler opens a landscaping business called Elegant Lawns by investing $70,000 cash along with equipment having a $30,000 value.

b. On January 21, Elegant Lawns purchases office supplies on credit for $280.

c. On January 29, Elegant Lawns receives $7,800 cash for performing landscaping services.

d. On January 30, Elegant Lawns receives $1,000 cash in advance of providing landscaping services to a customer.

QS 4–2

Preparing journal entries   LO4

Refer to QS 4-2. Post each of the journal entries to the correct T-accounts.

QS 4–3

Posting to T-accounts   LO5

Goro Co. bills a client $62,000 for services provided and agrees to accept the following two items in full payment: (1) $10,000 cash, and (2) computer equipment worth $52,000. What journal entry should Goro make to record this transaction?

QS 4–4

Compound journal entry   LO4

A trial balance has total debits of $20,000 and total credits of $24,500. Which one of the following errors would create this imbalance? Explain.

a. A $2,250 debit to Rent Expense in a journal entry is incorrectly posted to the ledger as a $2,250 credit.

b. A $4,500 debit to Salaries Expense in a journal entry is incorrectly posted to the ledger as a $4,500 credit.

c. A $2,250 credit to Consulting Fees Earned in a journal entry is incorrectly posted to the ledger as a $2,250 debit.

QS 4–5

Identifying a posting error   LO7

On August 4, 2010, a company incorrectly debits Rent Expense instead of Salaries Expense when recording payroll for the month. On August 30, the error is discovered while preparing the trial balance. Propose a correcting journal entry to correct the books. If the error had not been discovered, how would the company's income statement have been affected?

QS 4–6

Preparing a correcting journal entry   LO7

Prepare journal entries for the following selected transactions and post them to the appropriate general ledger accounts. In posting the entries, use account numbers from the chart of accounts at the back of the book, and assume the journal entries are made on page 4 of the general journal.

a. Harley Vance invests $60,000 of cash along with fitness equipment valued at $25,000 in her startup business named HV Fitness.

b. Vance withdraws $2,800 cash for personal use.

QS 4–7

Journalizing and posting owner transactions   LO4   LO5

QS 4-8
Journalizing and posting
transactions   **LO4   LO5**

Prepare journal entries for the following selected transactions of JK Design and post them to the appropriate general ledger accounts. In posting the entries, use account numbers from the chart of accounts at the back of the book, and assume the journal entries are made on page 4 of the general journal.

a. Completed $6,250 of design work for a client, who agrees to pay within 30 days.

b. Received $4,000 cash as partial payment from the customer in transaction *a*.

c. Paid $1,800 cash salary to an assistant.

QS 4-9
Journalizing transactions   **LO4**

Prepare journal entries for the following selected transactions of Custom Cabinets.

a. Purchased $2,000 of office supplies on credit.

b. Provided services to a client and collected $8,000 cash.

c. Paid $635 in cash for this month's utilities.

d. Paid $2,000 in cash to settle the payable created in transaction *a*.

connect

EXERCISES

Exercise 4-1
Preparing general journal entries
LO4

Prepare general journal entries for the following transactions of a new business called Pose-for-Pics.

Aug. 1 Madison Harris, the owner, invested $6,500 cash and $33,500 of photography equipment in the business.
   2 Paid $2,100 cash for an insurance policy covering the next 24 months.
   5 Purchased office supplies for $880 cash.
   20 Received $3,000 cash in photography fees earned.
   29 Paid $675 cash for August utilities.

Exercise 4-2
Preparing T-accounts (ledger)
and a trial balance   **LO5**

Use the information in Exercise 4-1 to prepare an August 31 trial balance for Pose-for-Pics. Open these T-accounts: Cash; Office Supplies; Prepaid Insurance; Photography Equipment; M. Harris, Capital; Photography Fees Earned; and Utilities Expense. Post the general journal entries to these T-accounts (which will serve as the ledger), and prepare a trial balance.

Exercise 4-3
Preparing an income statement
LO6

On October 1, Diondre Shabazz organized a new consulting firm called OnTech. On October 31, the company's general ledger shows the following items and amounts. Use this information to prepare an October income statement for the business.

Cash	$11,360	D. Shabazz, Withdrawals	$ 2,000
Accounts receivable	14,000	Consulting fees earned	14,000
Office supplies	3,250	Rent expense	3,550
Patents	46,000	Salaries expense	7,000
Office equipment	18,000	Telephone expense	760
Accounts payable	8,500	Miscellaneous expenses	580
D. Shabazz, Capital	84,000		

Check   Net income, $2,110

Exercise 4-4
Preparing a statement of
owner's equity   **LO6**

Use the information in Exercise 4-3 to prepare an October statement of owner's equity for OnTech.

Use the information in Exercise 4-3 (if completed, you can also use your solution to Exercise 4-4) to prepare an October 31 balance sheet for OnTech.

Exercise 4-5
Preparing a balance sheet   **LO6**

Assume the following T-accounts reflect Belle Co.'s general ledger and that seven transactions *a* through *g* are posted to them. Use information from the T-accounts to prepare general journal entries for each of the seven transactions (a) through (g). Provide a short description of each transaction.

Exercise 4-6
Preparing general journal entries
LO4

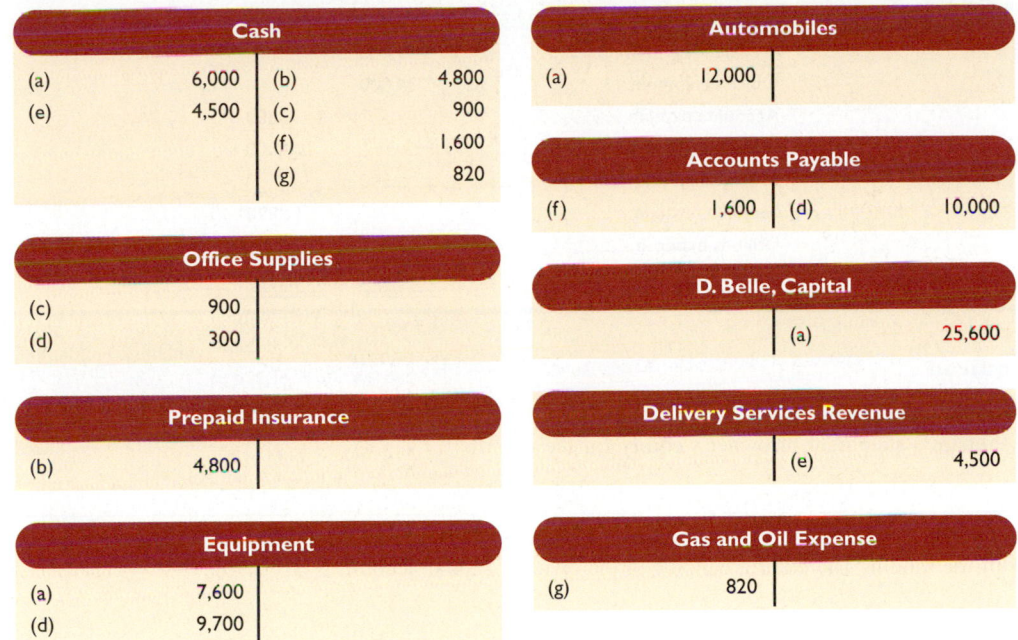

Bonnie Stradling opened a computer consulting business called Stradling Consultants and completed the following transactions in the first month of operations.

Exercise 4-7
Preparing journal entries   **LO4**

April 1   Bonnie invested $80,000 cash along with office equipment valued at $26,000 in the business.
2   Prepaid $9,000 cash for 12 months' rent for office space. (*Hint:* Debit Prepaid Rent for $9,000.)
3   Made credit purchases for $8,000 in office equipment and $3,600 in office supplies. Payment is due within 10 days.
6   Completed services for a client and immediately received $4,000 cash.
9   Completed a $6,000 project for a client, who must pay within 30 days.
13   Paid $11,600 cash to settle the account payable created on April 3.
19   Paid $2,400 cash for the premium on a 12-month insurance policy. (*Hint:* Debit Prepaid Insurance for $2,400.)
22   Received $4,400 cash as partial payment for the work completed on April 9.
25   Completed work for another client for $2,890 on credit.
28   Bonnie withdrew $5,500 cash for personal use.
29   Purchased $600 of additional office supplies on credit.
30   Paid $435 cash for this month's utility bill.

Required

Prepare general journal entries to record these transactions (use the account titles listed below). Cash (101); Accounts Receivable (106); Office Supplies (124); Prepaid Insurance (128); Prepaid Rent (131); Office Equipment (163); Accounts Payable (201); B. Stradling, Capital (301); B. Stradling, Withdrawals (302); Services Revenue (403); and Utilities Expense (690).

Exercise 4-8
Preparing financial statements from the trial balance   **LO6**

After posting the journal entries from Exercise 4-7 to general ledger accounts, Stradling Consultants reports the following trial balance.

STRADLING CONSULTANTS Trial Balance April 30		
	Debit	**Credit**
Cash	$ 59,465	
Accounts receivable	4,490	
Office supplies	4,200	
Prepaid insurance	2,400	
Prepaid rent	9,000	
Office equipment	34,000	
Accounts payable		$ 600
B. Stradling, Capital		106,000
B. Stradling, Withdrawals	5,500	
Services revenue		12,890
Utilities expense	435	
Total	$119,490	$119,490

Required

1. Prepare an income statement for the month.

2. Prepare a statement of owner's equity for the month.

Check   Ending owner's equity, $112,955

Exercise 4-9
Preparing a balance sheet from the trial balance   **LO6**

Refer to the trial balance in Exercise 4-8 and prepare a balance sheet for Stradling Consultants as of the end of the month. The ending balance in the owner's capital account is $112,955.

Exercise 4-10
Chart of accounts   **LO3**

Using the chart of accounts provided at the back of this book, determine the account names and their account numbers that would be used to record the following transactions.

a. Owner invests cash and office equipment in a new business.

b. Purchase office supplies on credit.

c. Provide services to a client and collect cash.

d. Pay cash for utilities expenses.

e. Provide services to a client, who agrees to pay within 30 days.

f. Owner withdraws cash for personal use.

Exercise 4-11
Preparing journal entries   **LO4**

Kamilos Management Services opens for business and completes these transactions in September.

Sept.   1   Tom Kamilos, the owner, invests $38,000 cash along with office equipment valued at $15,000 in the business.

2   Prepaid $9,000 cash for 12 months' rent for office space. (*Hint:* Debit Prepaid Rent for $9,000.)

4   Made credit purchases for $8,000 in office equipment and $2,400 in office supplies. Payment is due within 10 days.

8   Completed work for a client and immediately received $3,280 cash.

12   Completed a $15,400 project for a client, who must pay within 30 days.

13   Paid $10,400 cash to settle the payable created on September 4.

19   Paid $1,900 cash for the premium on an 18-month insurance policy. (*Hint:* Debit Prepaid Insurance for $1,900.)

22   Received $7,700 cash as partial payment for the work completed on September 12.

24   Completed work for another client for $2,100 on credit.

28   Tom Kamilos withdrew $5,300 cash for personal use.

29   Purchased $550 of additional office supplies on credit.

30   Paid $860 cash for this month's utility bill.

Required

Prepare general journal entries to record these transactions (use account titles listed below). Cash (101); Accounts Receivable (106); Office Supplies (124); Prepaid Insurance (128); Prepaid Rent (131); Office Equipment (163); Accounts Payable (201); T. Kamilos, Capital (301); T. Kamilos, Withdrawals (302); Service Fees Earned (401); and Utilities Expense (690).

After posting the journal entries from Exercise 4-11, Kamilos Management Services reports the following trial balance.

Exercise 4–12
Preparing financial statements from the trial balance   **LO6**

KAMILOS MANAGEMENT SERVICES
Trial Balance
September 30

	Debit	Credit
Cash	$21,520	
Accounts receivable	9,800	
Office supplies	2,950	
Prepaid insurance	1,900	
Prepaid rent	9,000	
Office equipment	23,000	
Accounts payable		$ 550
T. Kamilos, Capital		53,000
T. Kamilos, Withdrawals	5,300	
Service fees earned		20,780
Utilities expense	860	
Totals	$74,330	$74,330

Required

1. Prepare an income statement for the month.

2. Prepare a statement of owner's equity for the month.

Check   Ending T. Kamilos, Capital $67,620

Refer to the trial balance provided in Exercise 4-12 and prepare a balance sheet as of the end of the month. The ending balance in the owner's capital account is $67,620.

Exercise 4–13
Preparing a balance sheet from the trial balance   **LO6**

---

connect

Aracel Engineering completed the following transactions in the month of June.

PROBLEM SET A

Problem 4–1A
Preparing and posting journal entries; preparing a trial balance
LO3   LO4   LO5

a. Jenna Aracel, the owner, invested $100,000 cash, office equipment with a value of $5,000, and $60,000 of drafting equipment to launch the business.

b. Purchased land worth $6,300 for an office by paying $6,300 cash.

c. Purchased a portable building with $55,000 cash and moved it onto the land acquired in b.

d. Paid $3,000 cash for the premium on a 12-month insurance policy.

e. Completed and delivered a set of plans for a client and collected $6,200 cash.

f. Purchased $9,500 of additional drafting equipment by paying $9,500 cash.

g. Completed $14,000 of engineering services for a client. This amount is to be received in 30 days.

h. Purchased $1,150 of additional office equipment on credit.

i. Completed engineering services for $22,000 on credit.

j. Received a bill for rent of equipment that was used on a recently completed job. The $1,000 rent cost must be paid within 30 days.

k. Collected $7,000 cash in partial payment from the client described in transaction g.

l. Paid $1,200 cash for wages to a drafting assistant.

m. Paid $1,150 cash to settle the account payable created in transaction h.

n. Paid $925 cash for minor repairs to its drafting equipment.

o. Jenna Aracel withdrew $9,480 cash for personal use.

p. Paid $1,200 cash for wages to a drafting assistant.

q. Paid $2,500 cash for advertisements in the local newspaper during June.

Required

1. Prepare general journal entries to record these transactions (use the account titles listed in part 2).

2. Open the following ledger accounts—their account numbers are in parentheses (use the balance column format): Cash (101); Accounts Receivable (106); Prepaid Insurance (108); Office Equipment (163); Drafting Equipment (164); Building (170); Land (172); Accounts Payable (201); J. Aracel, Capital (301); J. Aracel, Withdrawals (302); Engineering Fees Earned (402); Wages Expense (601); Equipment Rental Expense (602); Advertising Expense (603); and Repairs Expense (604). Post the journal entries from part 1 to the accounts and enter the balance after each posting.

3. Prepare a trial balance as of the end of June.

Problem 4-2A
Preparing and posting journal entries; preparing a trial balance

LO3   LO4   LO5

mhhe.com/wildCA2e

Kasey Reese opens a consulting business called Cougar Consulting and completes the following transactions in March.

March	1	Reese invested $150,000 cash along with $22,000 of office equipment in the business.
	2	Prepaid $6,000 cash for six months' rent for an office. (*Hint:* Debit Prepaid Rent for $6,000.)
	3	Made credit purchases of office equipment for $3,000 and office supplies for $1,200. Payment is due within 10 days.
	6	Completed services for a client and immediately received $4,000 cash.
	9	Completed a $7,500 project for a client, who must pay within 30 days.
	12	Paid $4,200 cash to settle the account payable created on March 3.
	19	Paid $5,000 cash for the premium on a 12-month insurance policy.
	22	Received $3,500 cash as partial payment for the work completed on March 9.
	25	Completed work for another client for $3,820 on credit.
	29	Reese withdrew $5,100 cash for personal use.
	30	Purchased $600 of additional office supplies on credit.
	31	Paid $500 cash for this month's utility bill.

Required

1. Prepare general journal entries to record these transactions (use the account titles listed in part 2).

2. Open the following ledger accounts—their account numbers are in parentheses (use the balance column format): Cash (101); Accounts Receivable (106); Office Supplies (124); Prepaid Insurance (128); Prepaid Rent (131); Office Equipment (163); Accounts Payable (201); K. Reese, Capital (301); K. Reese, Withdrawals (302); Services Revenue (403); and Utilities Expense (690). Post the journal entries from part 1 to the ledger accounts and enter the balance after each posting.

3. Prepare a trial balance as of the end of March.

Problem 4-3A
Preparing financial statements from the trial balance   **LO6**

Below is the trial balance for HV Consulting for the month ended September 30.

HV CONSULTING Trial Balance September 30		
	Debit	**Credit**
Cash	$ 12,665	
Accounts receivable	2,250	
Office supplies	2,000	
Office equipment	50,900	
Automobiles	16,500	
Building	160,000	
Land	40,000	
Accounts payable		$ 5,600
H. Venedict, Capital		271,500
H. Venedict, Withdrawals	2,800	
Fees earned		14,250
Salaries expense	3,600	
Utilities expense	635	
Total	$291,350	$291,350

Required

1. Prepare an income statement for the month.

2. Prepare a statement of owner's equity for the month.

3. Prepare a balance sheet as of the end of the month.

After all journal entries have been posted, Levi Hancock finds that errors have been made in recording some company transactions. Help Levi prepare correcting journal entries for each of the following errors.

Problem 4-4A

Correcting errors with journal entries   **LO7**

1. The following journal entry was made to record the purchase of supplies for $700 cash.

| Equipment | 700 | |
| Cash | | 700 |

2. The following journal entry was made to record the cash payment of $1,850 for prepaid rent.

| Prepaid Insurance | 1,850 | |
| Cash | | 1,850 |

3. The following journal entry was made to record the cash receipt of $2,000 for consulting services.

| Accounts Receivable | 2,000 | |
| Consulting Services Revenue | | 2,000 |

4. The following journal entry was made to record the cash payment of $1,375 for utilities expense.

| Utilities Expense | 1,375 | |
| Accounts Payable | | 1,375 |

At the beginning of April, Bernadette Grechus launched a custom computer solutions company called Softworks. The company had the following transactions during April.

PROBLEM SET B

a. Bernadette Grechus invested $75,000 cash, office equipment with a value of $5,750, and $30,000 of computer equipment in the company.

Problem 4-1B

Preparing and posting journal entries; preparing a trial balance   **LO3   LO4   LO5**

b. Purchased land worth $22,000 for an office by paying $22,000 cash.

c. Purchased a portable building with $34,500 cash and moved it onto the land acquired in *b*.

d. Paid $5,000 cash for the premium on a two-year insurance policy.

e. Provided services to a client and immediately collected $4,600 cash.

f. Purchased $4,500 of additional computer equipment by paying $4,500 cash.

g. Completed $4,250 of services for a client. This amount is to be received within 30 days.

h. Purchased $950 of additional office equipment on credit.

i. Completed client services for $10,200 on credit.

j. Received a bill for rent of a computer testing device that was used on a recently completed job. The $580 rent cost must be paid within 30 days.

k. Collected $8,800 cash from the client described in transaction *i*.

l. Paid $1,800 cash for wages to an assistant.

m. Paid $950 cash to settle the payable created in transaction *h*.

n. Paid $608 cash for minor repairs to the company's computer equipment.

o. Grechus withdrew $6,230 cash for personal use.

p. Paid $1,800 cash for wages to an assistant.

q. Paid $750 cash for advertisements in the local newspaper during April.

Required

1. Prepare general journal entries to record these transactions (use account titles listed in part 2).

2. Open the following ledger accounts—their account numbers are in parentheses (use the balance column format): Cash (101); Accounts Receivable (106); Prepaid Insurance (108); Office Equipment

Check   (2) Ending balances: Cash, $10,262; Accounts Receivable, $5,650; Accounts Payable, $580

(163); Computer Equipment (164); Building (170); Land (172); Accounts Payable (201); B. Grechus, Capital (301); B. Grechus, Withdrawals (302); Fees Earned (402); Wages Expense (601); Computer Rental Expense (602); Advertising Expense (603); and Repairs Expense (604). Post the journal entries from part 1 to the accounts and enter the balance after each posting.

3. Prepare a trial balance as of the end of April.

(3) Trial balance totals, $130,380

Problem 4–2B
Preparing and posting journal entries; preparing a trial balance
LO3   LO4   LO5

Barry Wells Management Group opens for business and completes these transactions in November.

Nov.	1	Barry Wells, the owner, invested $30,000 cash along with $15,000 of office equipment in the business.
	2	Prepaid $4,500 cash for six months' rent for an office. (*Hint:* Debit Prepaid Rent for $4,500.)
	4	Made credit purchases of office equipment for $2,500 and of office supplies for $600. Payment is due within 10 days.
	8	Completed work for a client and immediately received $3,400 cash.
	12	Completed a $10,200 project for a client, who must pay within 30 days.
	13	Paid $3,100 cash to settle the payable created on November 4.
	19	Paid $1,800 cash for the premium on a 24-month insurance policy.
	22	Received $5,200 cash as partial payment for the work completed on November 12.
	24	Completed work for another client for $1,750 on credit.
	28	Barry Wells withdrew $5,300 cash for personal use.
	29	Purchased $249 of additional office supplies on credit.
	30	Paid $831 cash for this month's utility bill.

Required

1. Prepare general journal entries to record these transactions (use account titles listed in part 2).

Check *(2) Ending balances: Cash, $23,069; Accounts Receivable, $6,750; Accounts Payable, $249*

2. Open the following ledger accounts—their account numbers are in parentheses (use the balance column format): Cash (101); Accounts Receivable (106); Office Supplies (124); Prepaid Insurance (128); Prepaid Rent (131); Office Equipment (163); Accounts Payable (201); B. Wells, Capital (301); B. Wells, Withdrawals (302); Services Revenue (403); and Utilities Expense (690). Post the journal entries from part 1 to the ledger accounts and enter the balance after each posting.

(3) Total debits, $60,599

3. Prepare a trial balance as of the end of November.

Problem 4–3B
Preparing financial statements from the trial balance   **LO6**

Below is the trial balance for Nuncio Consulting for the month ended June 30.

NUNCIO CONSULTING Trial Balance June 30		
	Debit	**Credit**
Cash	$17,860	
Accounts receivable	2,000	
Office supplies	500	
Office equipment	15,600	
Automobiles	8,000	
Building	40,000	
Land	7,500	
Accounts payable		$ 1,200
A. Nuncio, Capital		86,500
A. Nuncio, Withdrawals	1,100	
Fees earned		7,400
Salaries expense	2,000	
Utilities expense	540	
Total	$95,100	$95,100

Required

1. Prepare an income statement for the month.

2. Prepare a statement of owner's equity for the month.

3. Prepare a balance sheet as of the end of the month.

After all journal entries have been posted, Kasey Beck finds that errors have been made in recording some company transactions. Help Kasey prepare correcting journal entries for each of the following errors.

Problem 4–4B
Correcting errors with
journal entries   LO7

1. The following journal entry was made to record the purchase of equipment for $1,450 cash.

Supplies	1,450	
Cash		1,450

2. The following journal entry was made to record the cash purchase of $870 for prepaid rent.

Rent Expense	870	
Cash		870

3. The following journal entry was made to record the cash payment of $1,780 for utilities expense.

Salaries Expense	1,780	
Cash		1,780

4. The following journal entry was made to record $2,000 for consulting services on account.

Cash	2,000	
Consulting Services Revenue		2,000

(This serial problem started in Chapter 1 and continues through most of the chapters. If previous chapter segments were not completed, the problem can begin at this point. It is helpful, but not necessary, to use the Working Papers that accompany this book.)

SERIAL PROBLEM

Success Systems
LO3   LO4   LO5

SP 4   On October 1, 2010, Adriana Lopez launched a computer services company called Success Systems, which provides consulting services, computer system installations, and custom program development. Lopez adopts the calendar year for reporting purposes and expects to prepare the company's first set of financial statements on December 31, 2010. The company's initial chart of accounts follows.

Account	No.	Account	No.
Cash	101	A. Lopez, Capital	301
Accounts Receivable	106	A. Lopez, Withdrawals	302
Computer Supplies	126	Computer Services Revenue	403
Prepaid Insurance	128	Wages Expense	623
Prepaid Rent	131	Advertising Expense	655
Office Equipment	163	Mileage Expense	676
Computer Equipment	167	Miscellaneous Expenses	677
Accounts Payable	201	Repairs Expense—Computer	684

Required

1. Prepare journal entries to record each of the following transactions for Success Systems.

Oct. 1   Lopez invested $75,000 cash, a $25,000 computer system, and $10,000 of office equipment in the business.

      2   Paid $3,500 cash for four months' rent. (*Hint:* Debit Prepaid Rent for $3,500.)

      3   Purchased $1,600 of computer supplies on credit from Corvina Office Products.

      5   Paid $2,400 cash for one year's premium on a property and liability insurance policy. (*Hint:* Debit Prepaid Insurance for $2,400.)

      6   Billed Easy Leasing $6,200 for services performed in installing a new Web server.

8	Paid $1,600 cash for the computer supplies purchased from Corvina Office Products on October 3.
12	Billed Easy Leasing another $1,950 for services performed.
15	Received $6,200 cash from Easy Leasing on its account.
17	Paid $900 cash to repair computer equipment that was damaged when moving it.
20	Paid $1,790 cash for an advertisement in the local newspaper.
22	Received $1,950 cash from Easy Leasing on its account.
28	Billed Clark Company $7,300 for services performed.
31	Paid $1,050 cash for Michelle Jones's wages for seven days' work.
31	Lopez withdrew $4,000 cash for personal use.

Nov.	1	Reimbursed Lopez in cash for business automobile mileage allowance (Lopez logged 1,200 miles at $0.32 per mile).
	2	Received $3,600 cash from Edge Corporation for computer services performed.
	5	Purchased computer supplies for $1,750 cash from Corvina Office Products.
	8	Billed Gomez Co. $6,500 for services performed.
	18	Received $5,000 cash from Clark Company as partial payment of the October 28 bill.
	22	Donated $300 cash to the United Way in the company's name.
	24	Completed work for Alex's Engineering Co. and sent it a bill for $7,000.
	28	Reimbursed Lopez in cash for business automobile mileage (1,500 miles at $0.32 per mile).
	30	Paid $2,100 cash for Michelle Jones's wages for 14 days' work.
	30	Lopez withdrew $2,500 cash for personal use.

Check   (2) Cash, Nov. 30 bal., $68,996

        (3) Trial bal. totals, $142,550

2. Open ledger accounts (in balance column format) and post the journal entries from part 1 to them.

3. Prepare a trial balance (dated November 30, 2010) from the ending balances in the ledger accounts from part 1.

BEYOND THE NUMBERS

REPORTING IN ACTION
LO2

BTN 4-1   **Best Buy** sells consumer electronics in its retail outlets and from its online stores.

Required

Based on your understanding of Best Buy, identify at least four types of source documents that Best Buy would likely use in its operations.

ETHICS CHALLENGE
LO2

BTN 4-2   Your manager requires that you, as cashier, immediately enter each sale. Recently, lunch hour traffic has increased and the assistant manager asks you to avoid delays by taking customers' cash and making change without entering sales. The assistant manager says she will add up cash and enter sales after lunch. She says that, in this way, the register will always match the cash amount when the manager arrives at three o'clock. What do you do?

Required

Discuss the advantages to the process proposed by the assistant manager and the concerns you have with the proposal. Decide what you would do.

WORKPLACE COMMUNICATION
LO4   LO5

BTN 4-3   Mark Ellingson is an aspiring entrepreneur and your friend. He is having difficulty understanding the link between the general journal and the general ledger.

Required

Write a half-page memorandum to Ellingson explaining how the general journal and the general ledger are linked to each other.

TAKING IT TO THE NET
LO4   LO5   LO7

BTN 4-4   **Quickbooks** is an accounting software program with both a general journal and general ledger. Access Quickbooks' Website (**QuickBooks.com**) and review the various Quickbooks' software programs to answer the following requirements.

Required

1. Which Quickbooks' program would be most appropriate for a small business? Which would be most appropriate for a large business?
2. Many of the examples given in this chapter assumed manual journal entries, where journal entries are recorded and then later posted. How would a computerized program be different? How would the correction of errors differ?

BTN 4–5   Refer to the chapter's opening feature about Katrina Markoff and her **Vosges Haut Chocolat** company.

ENTREPRENEURS IN BUSINESS

L03

Required

What are some examples of accounts you would expect to see in the Vosges Haut Chocolat company chart of accounts?

---

1. b
2. d
3. b; debit Utility Expense for $700, and credit Cash for $700.
4. c; debit Cash for $250,000, debit Land for $500,000, and credit L. Shue, Capital for $750,000.
5. d

ANSWERS TO MULTIPLE CHOICE QUIZ

A Look Back

Chapters 3 and 4 explained the analysis and recording of transactions. We showed how to apply and interpret T-accounts, double-entry accounting, ledgers, postings, and trial balances.

A Look at This Chapter

This chapter introduces the need to adjust accounts. Adjusting accounts is important for recognizing revenues and expenses in the proper period. We describe the adjusted trial balance and how it is used to prepare financial statements.

A Look Ahead

Chapter 6 highlights the completion of the accounting cycle. We explain the important final steps in the accounting process. These include closing procedures and the post-closing trial balance. We show how a work sheet can aid in this process.

Chapter 5

Adjusting Accounts and Preparing Financial Statements

Learning Objectives

LO 1 Explain accrual accounting and how it improves financial statements.

LO 2 Identify the types of accounting adjustments and their purpose.

LO 3 Prepare and explain adjusting entries.

LO 4 Explain and prepare an adjusted trial balance.

LO 5 Prepare financial statements from an adjusted trial balance.

"Get a good accountant"
—Jason Kapalka (from left: John Vechey, Brian Feite, Jason Kapalka)

High Score

SEATTLE—Jason Kapalka met John Vechey and Brian Feite, both 19 at the time, after the two had created an online game. "We hit it off really well," explains Jason. "We were all a little unhappy with our jobs. We thought, 'Hey, we could start our own company.'" Their startup company, **PopCap Games (PopCap.com),** is a creator and provider of downloadable games. Jason recalls that their friends considered them crazy.

Undaunted, the three scraped together the little cash they had. Jason explains that each worked out of their respective apartments to save money. "We survived," admits Jason, "because we didn't have many expenses." The young trio quickly developed a system to account for everything, including cash, revenues, receivables, and payables. They also adjusted to the deferral and accrual of revenues and expenses. Setting up a good accounting system is an important part of success, explains Jason. "Don't wait until . . . everything is a big mess."

Most of PopCap's sales are paid for in advance of game delivery. This means few uncollectible accounts.

The team also defers payment of their expenses to the time permitted—which is good management. "We're trying to keep a very simple business model," insists Jason. The team continues to fine-tune their accounting system as they remain focused on revenues, income, assets, and liabilities. "No matter what you do," argues Jason, "there's always something that you haven't done."

Financial statements preparation and analysis are a process that the three continue to work on. Although they insist on timely and accurate accounting reports, Jason says "it really helped us to keep things simple." To help make it simple, they took time to understand accounting adjustments and their effects. It is part of the larger picture. "You're not going to get breaks unless you're working hard."

Today, PopCap is a success story. "Now we can afford Mac and Cheese, and the occasional bottle of water," laughs Jason. "Life is good!"

[Sources: *PopCap Website,* January 2009; *Entrepreneur,* February 2008; *Wired,* March 2008; *2o2p Magazine,* September 2006; *Washington Post,* March 2008]

The past few chapters showed how companies use accounting systems to collect information about *external* transactions. We also explained how journals, ledgers, and other tools are useful in preparing financial statements. This chapter describes the accounting process for producing useful information involving *internal* transactions. An important part of this process is adjusting account balances so that financial statements at the end of a reporting period reflect the effects of all transactions. We then explain the important steps in preparing financial statements.

Adjusting Accounts and Preparing Financial Statements

Timing and Reporting
- Accrual basis versus cash basis
- Recognizing revenues and expenses

Adjusting Accounts
- Framework for adjustments
- 3-step process
- Prepaid expenses
- Accrued expenses
- Journalizing and posting adjusting entries
- Adjusted trial balance

Preparing Financial Statements
- Income statement
- Statement of owner's equity
- Balance sheet

Timing and Reporting

This section describes how the use of accrual basis accounting impacts the recording of revenues and expenses.

Accrual Basis versus Cash Basis

LO1 Explain accrual accounting and how it improves financial statements.

After external transactions and events are recorded, several accounts still need adjustment before their balances appear in financial statements. This need arises because internal transactions and events remain unrecorded. **Accrual basis accounting** uses the adjusting process to recognize revenues when earned and expenses when incurred (matched with revenues). Sometimes cash is received before (or after) the revenue is earned. Likewise, sometimes cash is paid before an expense is incurred. **Cash basis accounting** recognizes revenue when cash is received and records expenses when cash is paid. This means that cash basis net income is the difference between cash receipts and cash payments. It is commonly held that accrual accounting better reflects business performance than does cash basis accounting.

As an example, FastForward's insurance costs $100 per month, but FastForward paid $2,400 in advance for 24 months of insurance coverage beginning on December 1, 2010. Accrual accounting requires FastForward to record $100 of insurance expense per month. Exhibit 5.1 illustrates this allocation of insurance cost across these three years. The accrual basis balance sheet reports any unexpired insurance as a Prepaid Insurance asset. For example, FastForward would report an asset of $2,300 at the end of 2010.

Exhibit 5.1

Accrual Basis Accounting for Allocating Prepaid Insurance to Expense

Transaction: Purchase 24 months' insurance beginning December 2010

Insurance Expense 2010			
Jan $0	Feb $0	Mar $0	Apr $0
May $0	June $0	July $0	Aug $0
Sept $0	Oct $0	Nov $0	Dec $100

Insurance Expense 2011			
Jan $100	Feb $100	Mar $100	Apr $100
May $100	June $100	July $100	Aug $100
Sept $100	Oct $100	Nov $100	Dec $100

Insurance Expense 2012			
Jan $100	Feb $100	Mar $100	Apr $100
May $100	June $100	July $100	Aug $100
Sept $100	Oct $100	Nov $100	Dec $0

Alternatively, a cash basis income statement for December 2010 reports insurance expense of $2,400, as shown in Exhibit 5.2. The cash basis income statements for years 2011 and 2012 show no insurance expense. Also, the cash basis balance sheet never reports an insurance asset.

Exhibit 5.2

Cash Accounting for Allocating Prepaid Insurance to Expense

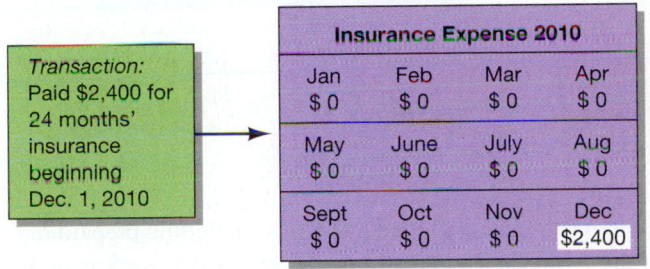

Transaction:
Paid $2,400 for 24 months' insurance beginning Dec. 1, 2010

Insurance Expense 2010			
Jan $ 0	Feb $ 0	Mar $ 0	Apr $ 0
May $ 0	June $ 0	July $ 0	Aug $ 0
Sept $ 0	Oct $ 0	Nov $ 0	Dec $2,400

Insurance Expense 2011			
Jan $ 0	Feb $ 0	Mar $ 0	Apr $ 0
May $ 0	June $ 0	July $ 0	Aug $ 0
Sept $ 0	Oct $ 0	Nov $ 0	Dec $0

Insurance Expense 2012			
Jan $ 0	Feb $ 0	Mar $ 0	Apr $ 0
May $ 0	June $ 0	July $ 0	Aug $ 0
Sept $ 0	Oct $ 0	Nov $ 0	Dec $0

Recognizing Revenues and Expenses

To provide timely information, accountants prepare reports at regular intervals. The **time period assumption** assumes a business's activities can be divided into specific periods, such as a month or year. Reports covering a one-year period are called **annual financial statements.** Annual financial statements can be for a **fiscal year** made up of any 12 consecutive months, and are not always for a calendar year ending on December 31. **Interim financial statements** cover one, three, or six months of activity.

We use the time period assumption to divide a company's activities into specific time periods, but not all activities are complete when financial statements are prepared. Thus, adjustments often are required to get correct account balances.

We rely on two principles in the adjusting process: revenue recognition and matching. The **revenue recognition principle** requires that revenue be recorded when earned. Most companies earn revenue when they provide services and products to customers. A major goal of the adjusting process is to have revenue recognized (reported) in the time period when it is earned.

The **matching principle** aims to record expenses in the same accounting period as the revenues that are earned as a result of these expenses. This matching of expenses with the revenue benefits is a major part of the adjusting process.

Matching expenses with revenues often requires us to predict certain events. When we use financial statements, we must understand that they require estimates and therefore include measures that are not always precise. **Walt Disney**'s annual report explains that its production costs from movies, such as *Pirates of the Caribbean,* are matched to revenues based on a ratio of current revenues from the movie divided by its predicted total revenues.

HOW YOU DOIN'?   Answers—p. 115

1. What two accounting principles most directly drive the adjusting process?

2. If your company pays a $4,800 premium on April 1, 2010, for two years' insurance coverage, how much insurance expense is reported in 2011 using cash basis accounting? Using accrual basis accounting?

Adjusting Accounts

In this section we suggest a framework for considering the types of adjustments that must be made at the end of the reporting period.

LO2 Identify the types of accounting adjustments and their purpose.

Framework for Adjustments

Adjustments are necessary for transactions that extend over more than one accounting period. It is helpful to group adjustments by the timing of cash receipt or cash payment in relation to when the work is performed. Exhibit 5.3 identifies types of adjustments.

Exhibit 5.3

Types of Adjustments

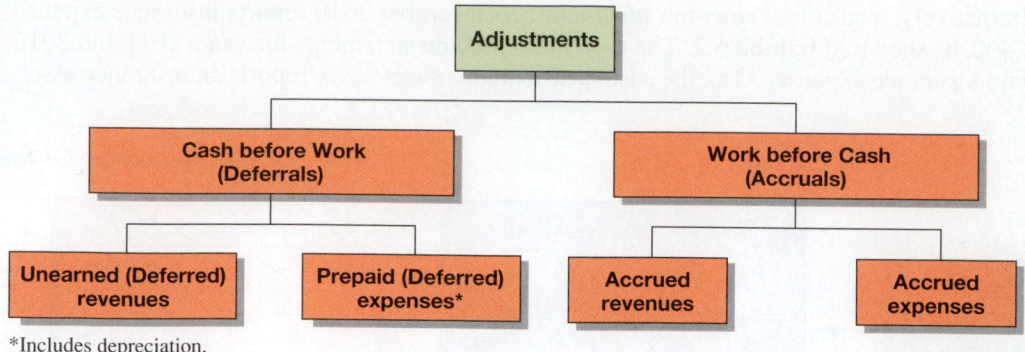

*Includes depreciation.

The left side of this exhibit shows unearned revenues and prepaid expenses (including prepaid rent and depreciation), which reflect transactions when cash is paid or received *before* work is done. They are also called *deferrals* because the recognition of an expense (or revenue) is *deferred* until after the related work is done. The right side of this exhibit shows accrued revenues and accrued expenses, which reflect transactions when work is done before cash is paid or received.

Adjusting entries are necessary for each of these so that revenues, expenses, assets, and liabilities are correctly reported. It is helpful to remember that each adjusting entry affects one or more income statement accounts *and* one or more balance sheet accounts (but never the Cash account). Adjusting entries are posted to general ledger accounts just like other general journal entries. In this chapter we show the adjustments for prepaid expenses and accrued expenses. In Chapter 13 we show the adjustments for unearned revenues and accrued revenues.

LO3 Prepare and explain adjusting entries.

FASTForward

3-Step Adjusting Process

Adjusting accounts is a three-step process:

Step 1: **Determine the current account balance.**

Step 2: **Determine what the current account balance should be.**

Step 3: **Record the adjusting journal entry to get from step 1 to step 2.**

Prepaid (Deferred) Expenses

Prepaid expenses refer to items *paid for* before receiving their benefits. Prepaid expenses are assets. When these assets are used, their costs become expenses. Adjusting entries for prepaid assets increase expenses and decrease assets as shown in the T-accounts of Exhibit 5.4. Such adjustments reflect transactions and events that use up prepaid expenses (including passage of time). To illustrate the accounting for prepaid expenses, this section focuses on prepaid insurance, supplies, and depreciation.

Exhibit 5.4

Adjusting for Prepaid Expenses

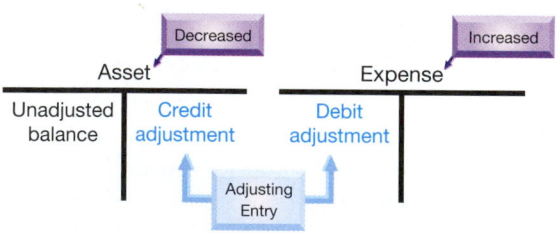

Prepaid Insurance   We use our three-step process for this and all accounting adjustments.

Step 1:   We determine the current balance of FastForward's prepaid insurance to be its payment of $2,400 for 24 months of insurance benefits beginning on December 1, 2010. The balance in insurance expense is $0.

Step 2:   As time passes, the benefits of the insurance gradually expire and some of the Prepaid Insurance asset becomes expense. For instance, one month's insurance coverage expires by December 31, 2010. This expense is $100, or $2,400/24.

Step 3:   The adjusting entry to record this expense and reduce the asset, along with postings to T-accounts, follows:

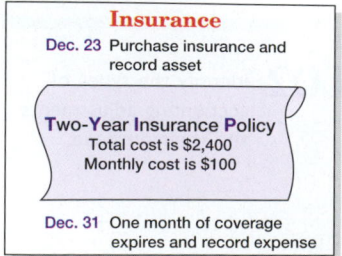

Insurance

Dec. 23 Purchase insurance and record asset

Two-Year Insurance Policy
Total cost is $2,400
Monthly cost is $100

Dec. 31 One month of coverage expires and record expense

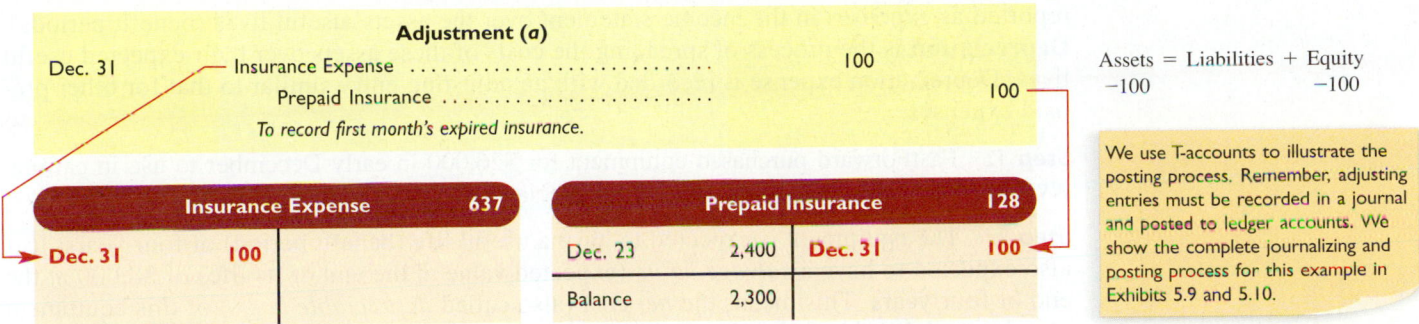

Adjustment (a)

Dec. 31	Insurance Expense	100	
	Prepaid Insurance		100
	To record first month's expired insurance.		

Assets = Liabilities + Equity
−100   −100

Insurance Expense		637
Dec. 31	**100**	

Prepaid Insurance			128
Dec. 23	2,400	**Dec. 31**	**100**
Balance	2,300		

We use T-accounts to illustrate the posting process. Remember, adjusting entries must be recorded in a journal and posted to ledger accounts. We show the complete journalizing and posting process for this example in Exhibits 5.9 and 5.10.

After adjusting and posting, the $100 balance in Insurance Expense and the $2,300 balance in Prepaid Insurance are ready for reporting in financial statements.

Supplies   Supplies are a prepaid expense requiring adjustment.

Step 1:   Recall that FastForward purchased $9,720 of supplies in December and used some of them during the month. When financial statements are prepared at December 31, the cost of supplies used during December must be included in computing net income.

Step 2:   On December 31 FastForward counts its *unused* supplies and finds $8,670 remaining of the $9,720 supplies. The $1,050 difference between these two amounts ($9,720 − $8,670) is December's supplies expense.

Step 3:   The adjusting entry to record this expense and reduce the Supplies asset account, along with T-account postings, follows:

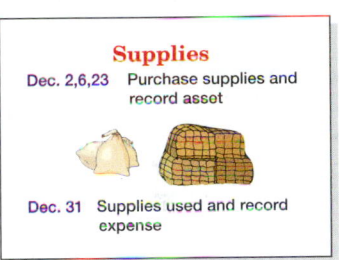

Supplies

Dec. 2,6,23   Purchase supplies and record asset

Dec. 31   Supplies used and record expense

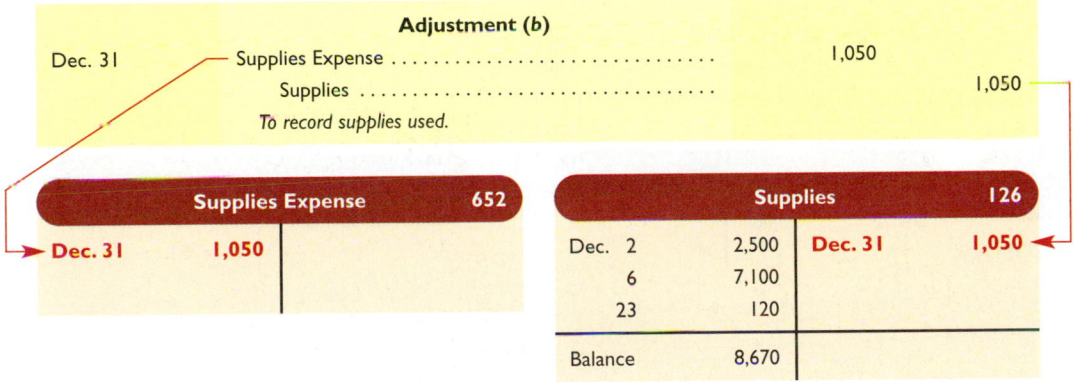

Adjustment (b)

Dec. 31	Supplies Expense	1,050	
	Supplies		1,050
	To record supplies used.		

Assets = Liabilities + Equity
−1,050   −1,050

Supplies Expense		652
Dec. 31	**1,050**	

Supplies			126
Dec. 2	2,500	**Dec. 31**	**1,050**
6	7,100		
23	120		
Balance	8,670		

The balance of the Supplies account is $8,670 after posting—equaling the cost of the remaining supplies.

Other Prepaid Expenses   Other prepaid expenses, like Prepaid Rent, are accounted for exactly like Insurance and Supplies. Also, note that some prepaid expenses are both paid for and fully used up within a single accounting period. One example is when a company pays monthly rent on one of the first few days each month. This payment creates a prepaid asset early in each month that fully expires by the end of that month. In these special cases we can record the cash paid with a debit to an expense account instead of an asset account.

Depreciation   A special category of prepaid expenses is **plant assets,** which refers to long-term tangible assets used to produce and sell products and services. Plant assets are expected to provide benefits for more than one period. Examples of plant assets are buildings, machines, vehicles, and fixtures. All plant assets, with the exception of land, eventually wear out or decline in usefulness. The costs of using these assets are deferred and are gradually reported as expenses in the income statement over the assets' useful lives (benefit periods). **Depreciation** is the process of spreading the costs of these assets over their expected useful lives. Depreciation expense is recorded with an adjusting entry similar to that for other prepaid expenses.

Step 1: FastForward purchased equipment for $26,000 in early December to use in earning revenue. This equipment's cost must be depreciated.

Step 2: The equipment is expected to have a useful life (benefit period) of four years. It is also expected to have a *salvage value* (expected value at the end of its life) of $8,000 at the end of four years. This means the *net* cost (also called *depreciable basis*) of this equipment over its useful life is $18,000 (equal to $26,000 − $8,000). There are many methods to allocate this $18,000 net cost to expense over the equipment's four-year useful life. FastForward uses a method called **straight-line depreciation,** which allocates equal amounts of the asset's net cost to depreciation during its useful life. The monthly depreciation expense is computed as:

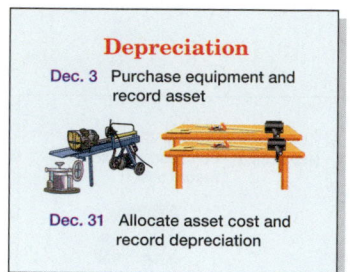

Depreciation

Dec. 3   Purchase equipment and record asset

Dec. 31   Allocate asset cost and record depreciation

$$\text{Monthly depreciation expense} = \frac{\text{Cost} - \text{Salvage value}}{\text{Useful life}}$$

$$= \frac{(\$26,000 - 8,000)}{48 \text{ months}} = \$375 \text{ per month}$$

Step 3: The adjusting entry to record monthly depreciation expense, along with T-account postings follows:

Assets = Liabilities + Equity
−375   −375

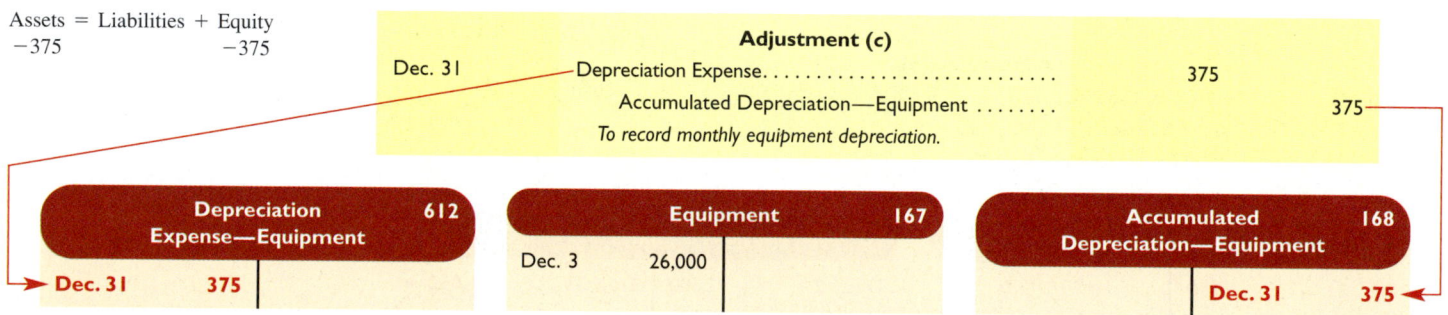

Adjustment (c)

Dec. 31	Depreciation Expense...........................	375	
	Accumulated Depreciation—Equipment		375
	To record monthly equipment depreciation.		

Depreciation Expense—Equipment	612	Equipment	167	Accumulated Depreciation—Equipment	168
Dec. 31 375		Dec. 3 26,000			Dec. 31 375

After posting the adjustment, the Equipment account ($26,000) less its Accumulated Depreciation ($375) account equals $25,625. The $375 balance in the Depreciation Expense account is reported in the December income statement.

Accumulated depreciation is kept in a separate contra account, not in the Equipment account. A **contra account** is an account linked with another account. Its normal balance is opposite of, and is reported as a subtraction from, that other account's balance.

A contra account allows balance sheet readers to know both the full costs of assets and the total amount of accumulated depreciation. By knowing both these amounts, decision makers can better assess a company's capacity and its need to replace assets. For example, FastForward's December 31 balance sheet shows both the $26,000 original cost of equipment and the $375 balance in the accumulated depreciation contra account. This information reveals that the equipment is close to new. If FastForward reports equipment only at its net amount of $25,625, users cannot assess the equipment's age or its need for replacement. The title of the contra account, *Accumulated Depreciation,* indicates that this account includes total depreciation expense for all prior periods for which the asset was used. To illustrate how Accumulated Depreciation increases as the asset's useful life expires, the Equipment and the Accumulated Depreciation accounts appear as in Exhibit 5.5 on February 29, 2011, after three months of adjusting entries.

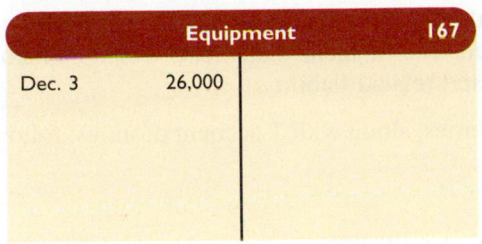

The $1,125 balance in the accumulated depreciation account is subtracted from its related $26,000 asset cost. The difference ($24,875) between these two balances is the cost of the asset that has not yet been depreciated. This difference is called the **book value,** or *net amount,* which equals the asset's cost less its accumulated depreciation. These account balances are reported in the assets section of FastForward's February 29, 2011, balance sheet in Exhibit 5.6.

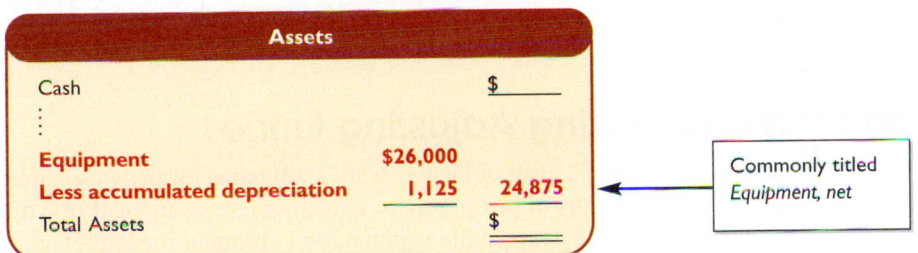

Accrued Expenses

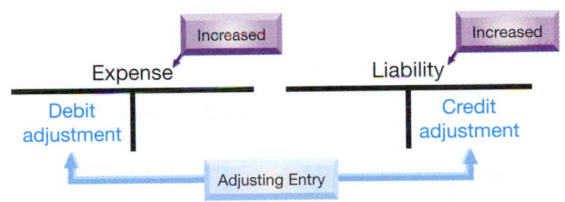

Accrued expenses refer to costs that occur in a period but are both unpaid and unrecorded at the end of the period. Accrued expenses must be reported on the income statement in the period they occur. Adjusting entries for recording accrued expenses involves increasing expenses and increasing liabilities as shown in Exhibit 5.7. Common examples of accrued expenses are salaries, interest, rent, and taxes. We use salaries to show how to adjust accounts for accrued expenses.

Accrued Salaries Expense   FastForward's employee earns $70 per day, or $350 for a five-day workweek beginning on Monday and ending on Friday.

Step 1:   Its employee is paid every two weeks on Friday. On December 12 and 26, the salary is paid, recorded in the journal, and posted to the ledger. The balance in Salaries Payable is $0.

Step 2:   The calendar in Exhibit 5.8 shows three working days after the December 26 payday (29, 30, and 31). This means the employee has earned three days' salary by the close of

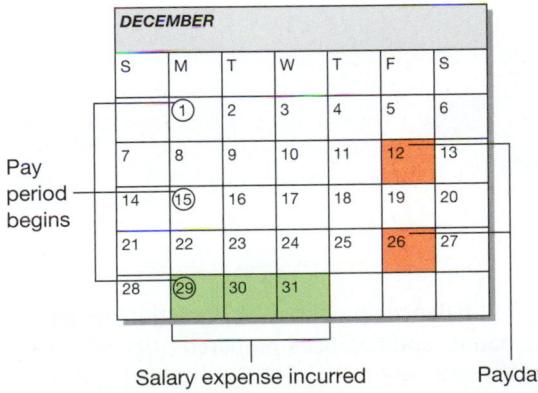

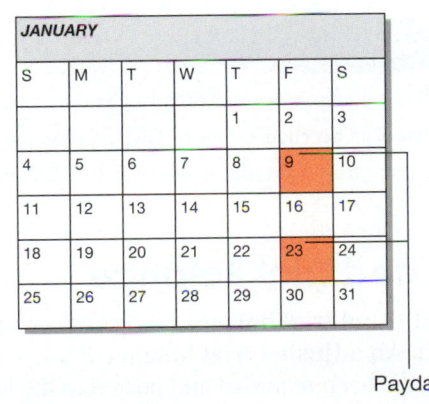

business on Wednesday, December 31. This equals \$210, computed as 3 days × \$70 per day. Yet, this salary cost has not been paid nor recorded. The financial statements would be incomplete if FastForward fails to record this expense and related liability.

Step 3:   The adjusting entry to record accrued salaries, along with T-account postings, follows:

Assets = Liabilities + Equity
+210   −210

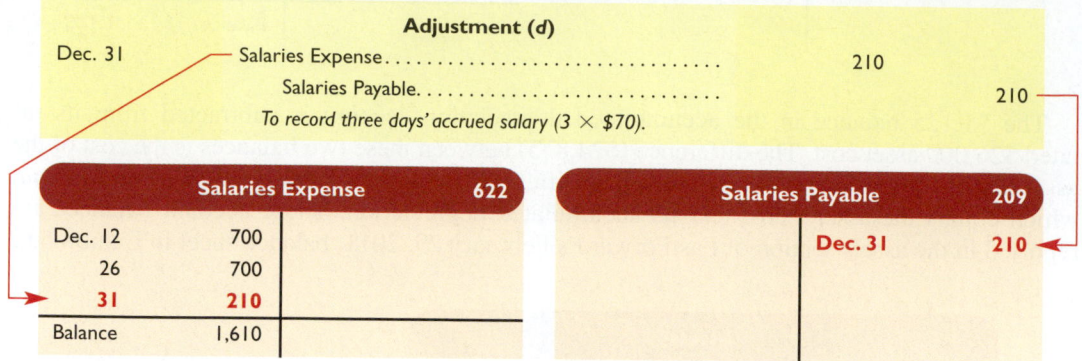

Journalizing and Posting Adjusting Entries

In Exhibit 5.9 we show how to journalize all of FastForward's adjusting entries in a general journal. Exhibit 5.10 then shows the results of posting these adjusting entries in FastForward's general ledger. The abbreviation "Adj." appears in the explanation column of the ledger accounts to note the amount is from an adjusting journal entry.

Exhibit 5.9

Recording Adjusting Entries in the General Journal

The title "Adjusting Entries" can be written at the beginning of a series of adjusting entries, rather than writing detailed explanations below each journal entry.

	Date		Account Titles and Explanation	PR	Debit	Credit
			GENERAL JOURNAL			Page 1
			Adjusting Entries			
(a)	Dec. 2010	31	Insurance Expense	637	1 0 0 00	
			Prepaid Insurance	128		1 0 0 00
(b)	Dec.	31	Supplies Expense	652	1 0 5 0 00	
			Supplies	126		1 0 5 0 00
(c)	Dec.	31	Depreciation Expense	612	3 7 5 00	
			Accumulated Depreciation-Equipment	168		3 7 5 00
(d)	Dec.	31	Salaries Expense	622	2 1 0 00	
			Salaries Payable	209		2 1 0 00

HOW YOU DOIN'?   Answers—p. 115

3. What is a contra account? Explain its purpose.

4. What is an accrued expense? Give an example.

5. Describe how a prepaid expense arises. Give an example.

Adjusted Trial Balance

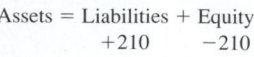 Explain and prepare an adjusted trial balance.

An **unadjusted trial balance** is a list of accounts and balances prepared *before* adjustments are recorded. An **adjusted trial balance** is a list of accounts and balances prepared *after* adjusting entries have been recorded and posted to the ledger.

Exhibit 5.10
General Ledger after Posting Adjusting Entries

Asset Accounts

Cash   Acct. No. 101

Date	Explan.	PR	Debit	Credit	Balance
2010					
Dec. 1		G1	30,000		30,000
2		G1		2,500	27,500
3		G1		26,000	1,500
5		G1	4,200		5,700
6		G1		1,000	4,700
12		G1		700	4,000
19		G1	1,900		5,900
20		G1		900	5,000
21		G1		200	4,800
22		G1	3,000		7,800
23		G1		2,400	5,400
23		G1		120	5,280
23		G1		230	5,050
26		G1		700	**4,350**

Accounts Receivable   Acct. No. 106

Date	Explan.	PR	Debit	Credit	Balance
2010					
Dec. 13		G1	1,900		1,900
19		G1		1,900	**0**

Supplies   Acct. No. 126

Date	Explan.	PR	Debit	Credit	Balance
2010					
Dec. 2		G1	2,500		2,500
4		G1	7,100		9,600
23		G1	120		9,720
31	Adj.	G1		1,050	**8,670**

Prepaid Insurance   Acct. No. 128

Date	Explan.	PR	Debit	Credit	Balance
2010					
Dec. 23		G1	2,400		2,400
31	Adj.	G1		100	**2,300**

Equipment   Acct. No. 167

Date	Explan.	PR	Debit	Credit	Balance
2010					
Dec. 3		G1	26,000		**26,000**

Accumulated Depreciation— Equipment   Acct. No. 168

Date	Explan.	PR	Debit	Credit	Balance
2010					
Dec. 31	Adj.	G1		375	**375**

Liability and Equity Accounts

Accounts Payable   Acct. No. 201

Date	Explan.	PR	Debit	Credit	Balance
2010					
Dec. 4		G1		7,100	7,100
20		G1	900		**6,200**

Salaries Payable   Acct. No. 209

Date	Explan.	PR	Debit	Credit	Balance
2010					
Dec. 31	Adj	G1		210	**210**

Unearned Consulting Revenue   Acct. No. 236

Date	Explan.	PR	Debit	Credit	Balance
2010					
Dec. 22		G1		3,000	**3,000**

C. Taylor, Capital   Acct. No. 301

Date	Explan.	PR	Debit	Credit	Balance
2010					
Dec. 1		G1		30,000	**30,000**

C. Taylor, Withdrawals   Acct. No. 302

Date	Explan.	PR	Debit	Credit	Balance
2010					
Dec. 21		G1	200		**200**

Revenue and Expense Accounts

Consulting Revenue   Acct. No. 403

Date	Explan.	PR	Debit	Credit	Balance
2010					
Dec. 5		G1		4,200	4,200
13		G1		1,600	**5,800**

Rental Revenue   Acct. No. 406

Date	Explan.	PR	Debit	Credit	Balance
2010					
Dec. 13		G1		300	**300**

Depreciation Expense— Equipment   Acct. No. 612

Date	Explan.	PR	Debit	Credit	Balance
2010					
Dec. 31	Adj.	G1	375		**375**

Salaries Expense   Acct. No. 622

Date	Explan.	PR	Debit	Credit	Balance
2010					
Dec. 12		G1	700		700
26		G1	700		1,400
31	Adj.	G1	210		**1,610**

Insurance Expense   Acct. No. 637

Date	Explan.	PR	Debit	Credit	Balance
2010					
Dec. 31	Adj.	G1	100		**100**

Rent Expense   Acct. No. 640

Date	Explan.	PR	Debit	Credit	Balance
2010					
Dec. 6		G1	1,000		**1,000**

Supplies Expense   Acct. No. 652

Date	Explan.	PR	Debit	Credit	Balance
2010					
Dec. 31	Adj.	G1	1,050		**1,050**

Utilities Expense   Acct. No. 690

Date	Explan.	PR	Debit	Credit	Balance
2010					
Dec. 23		G1	230		**230**

Exhibit 5.11

Unadjusted and Adjusted
Trial Balances

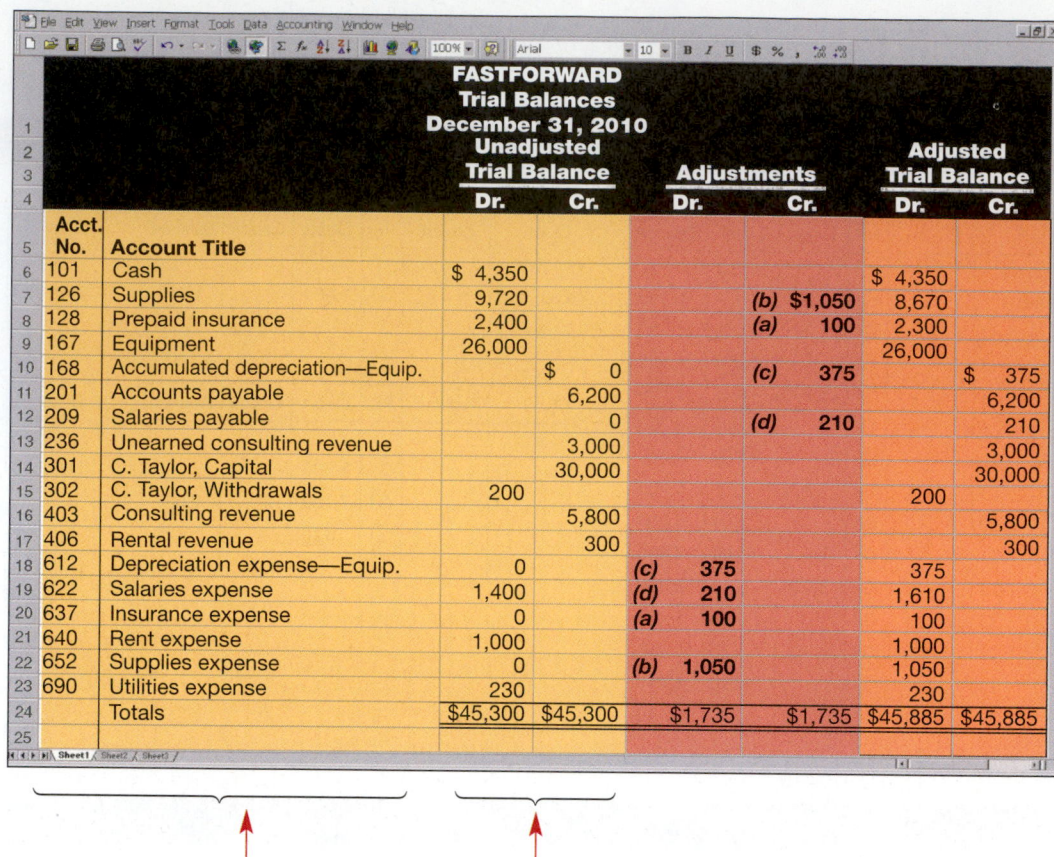

C. Taylor, Capital balance is not updated in the adjusted trial balance.

List all accounts from the ledger and those expected to arise from adjusting entries.

Enter all amounts available from ledger accounts. Column totals must be equal.

Exhibit 5.11 shows both the unadjusted and the adjusted trial balances for FastForward at December 31, 2010. The order of accounts in the trial balance usually matches the order in the chart of accounts. Several new accounts arise from the adjusting entries. Each adjustment (see middle columns) is identified by a letter in parentheses that links it to an adjusting entry explained earlier. Each amount in the Adjusted Trial Balance columns is computed by taking that account's amount from the Unadjusted Trial Balance columns and adding or subtracting any adjustment(s). To illustrate, Supplies has a $9,720 Dr. balance in the unadjusted columns. Subtracting the $1,050 Cr. amount shown in the adjustments columns yields an adjusted $8,670 Dr. balance for Supplies. Notice that the amounts in the Adjusted Trial Balance column agree with their ending balances in the general ledger, shown in Exhibit 5.10. Not all accounts require adjustment each period, so some accounts have blanks in the adjustments columns.

Preparing Financial Statements

L05 Prepare financial statements from an adjusted trial balance.

We can prepare financial statements directly from information in the *adjusted* trial balance. Exhibit 5.12 shows how revenue and expense balances are transferred from the adjusted trial balance to the income statement (red lines). The net income and the withdrawals amount are then used to prepare the statement of owner's equity (black lines). Asset and liability balances on the adjusted trial balance are then transferred to the balance sheet (blue lines). The ending capital is determined on the statement of owner's equity and transferred to the balance sheet (green line). The ending capital balance is computed; it *does not* come from the adjusted trial balance.

Even though balance sheet accounts are listed first in a trial balance, we usually prepare financial statements in the following order: income statement, statement of owner's equity, and balance sheet. This order makes sense since the balance sheet uses information from the statement of owner's equity, which in turn uses information from the income statement.

Exhibit 5.12

Preparing Financial Statements (Adjusted Trial Balance from Exhibit 5.11)

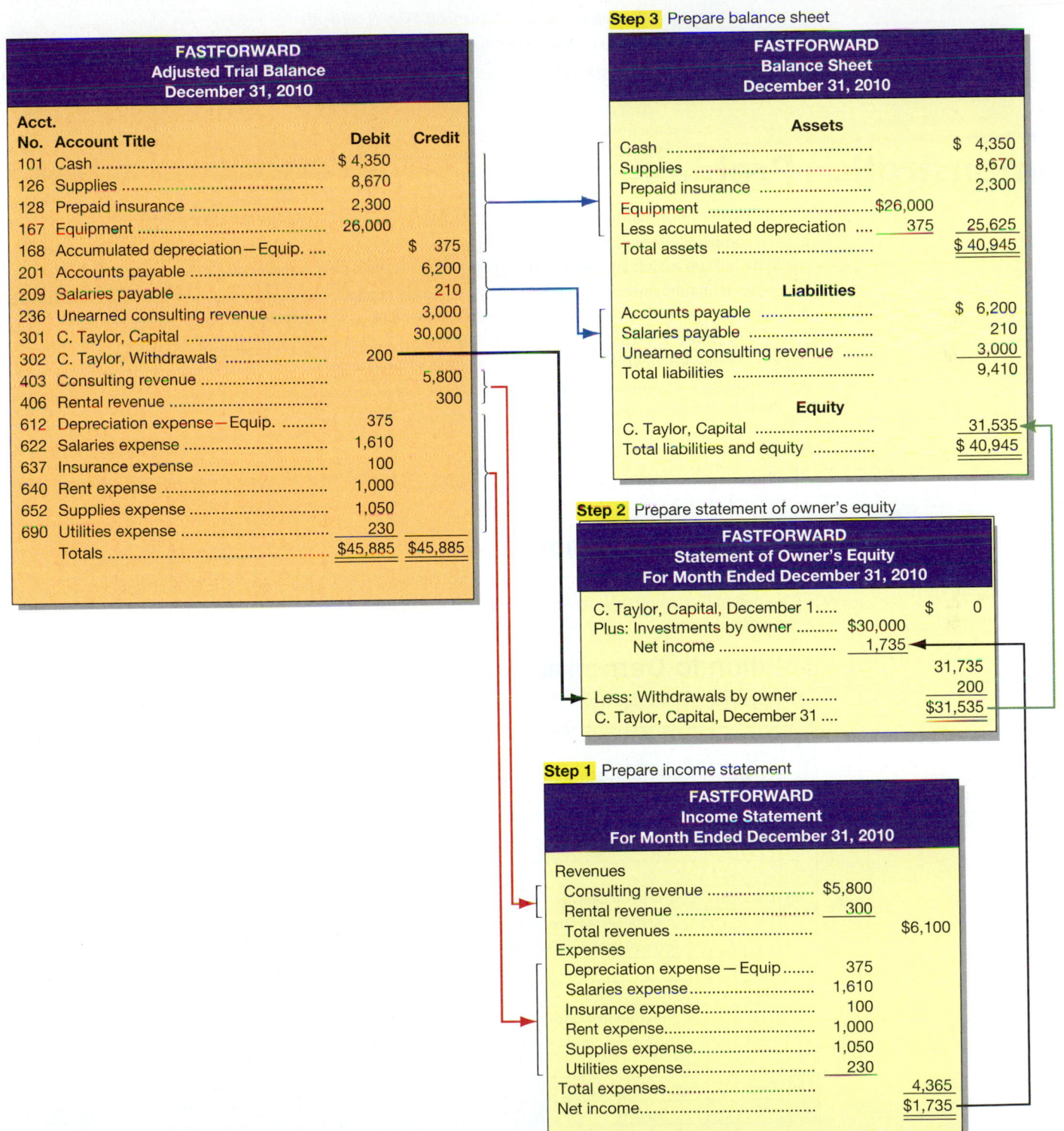

Step 3 Prepare balance sheet

FASTFORWARD
Adjusted Trial Balance
December 31, 2010

Acct. No.	Account Title	Debit	Credit
101	Cash	$ 4,350	
126	Supplies	8,670	
128	Prepaid insurance	2,300	
167	Equipment	26,000	
168	Accumulated depreciation—Equip.		$ 375
201	Accounts payable		6,200
209	Salaries payable		210
236	Unearned consulting revenue		3,000
301	C. Taylor, Capital		30,000
302	C. Taylor, Withdrawals	200	
403	Consulting revenue		5,800
406	Rental revenue		300
612	Depreciation expense—Equip.	375	
622	Salaries expense	1,610	
637	Insurance expense	100	
640	Rent expense	1,000	
652	Supplies expense	1,050	
690	Utilities expense	230	
	Totals	$45,885	$45,885

FASTFORWARD
Balance Sheet
December 31, 2010

Assets

Cash		$ 4,350
Supplies		8,670
Prepaid insurance		2,300
Equipment	$26,000	
Less accumulated depreciation	375	25,625
Total assets		$ 40,945

Liabilities

Accounts payable	$ 6,200
Salaries payable	210
Unearned consulting revenue	3,000
Total liabilities	9,410

Equity

C. Taylor, Capital	31,535
Total liabilities and equity	$ 40,945

Step 2 Prepare statement of owner's equity

FASTFORWARD
Statement of Owner's Equity
For Month Ended December 31, 2010

C. Taylor, Capital, December 1		$ 0
Plus: Investments by owner	$30,000	
Net income	1,735	
		31,735
Less: Withdrawals by owner		200
C. Taylor, Capital, December 31		$31,535

Step 1 Prepare income statement

FASTFORWARD
Income Statement
For Month Ended December 31, 2010

Revenues		
Consulting revenue	$5,800	
Rental revenue	300	
Total revenues		$6,100
Expenses		
Depreciation expense — Equip.	375	
Salaries expense	1,610	
Insurance expense	100	
Rent expense	1,000	
Supplies expense	1,050	
Utilities expense	230	
Total expenses		4,365
Net income		$1,735

6. Jordan Air has the following information in its unadjusted and adjusted trial balances.

	Unadjusted		Adjusted	
	Debit	Credit	Debit	Credit
Prepaid insurance	$6,200		$5,900	
Salaries payable		$ 0		$1,400

What are the adjusting entries that Jordan Air likely recorded?

7. What accounts are taken from the adjusted trial balance to prepare an income statement?

8. In preparing financial statements from an adjusted trial balance, what statement is usually prepared second?

Demonstration Problem

The following information relates to Fanning's Electronics on December 31, 2010.

a. The company's weekly payroll is $8,750, paid each Friday for a five-day workweek. Assume December 31, 2010, falls on a Monday, but the employees will not be paid their wages until Friday, January 4, 2011.

b. Eighteen months earlier, on July 1, 2009, the company purchased equipment that cost $20,000. Its useful life is predicted to be five years, at which time the equipment is expected to be worthless (zero salvage value).

c. On September 1, 2010, the company purchased a 12-month insurance policy for $1,800. The transaction was recorded with an $1,800 debit to Prepaid Insurance.

d. The supplies account has a balance of $2,500 before adjustment. A count reveals that only $675 of supplies are left on December 31.

Required

1. Prepare any necessary adjusting entries on December 31, 2010, in relation to transactions and events *a* through *d*.

Planning the Solution

- Analyze each situation to determine which accounts need to be updated with an adjustment.
- Use the three-step process to compute the amount of each adjustment and prepare the necessary adjusting journal entries.

Solution to Demonstration Problem

1. Adjusting journal entries.

This solution provides explanations for each adjusting entry. The accountant can instead write "Adjusting Entries" at the beginning of a series of adjusting entries.

		GENERAL JOURNAL			Page 9	
	Date	**Account Titles and Explanation**	**PR**	**Debit**		**Credit**
(a)	Dec. 31	Wages Expense		1 7 5 0 00		
		Wages Payable				1 7 5 0 00
		To accrue wages for the last day of the year ($8,750 × 1/5).				
(b)	Dec. 31	Depreciation Expense—Equipment		4 0 0 0 00		
		Accumulated Depreciation—Equipment				4 0 0 0 00
		To record depreciation expense for the year ($20,000/5 years).				
(c)	Dec. 31	Insurance Expense		6 0 0 00		
		Prepaid Insurance				6 0 0 00
		To adjust for expired portion of insurance ($1,800 × 4/12).				
(d)	Dec. 31	Supplies Expense		1 8 2 5 00		
		Supplies				1 8 2 5 00
		To record supplies used ($2,500 − $675).				

Summary

LO1 **Explain accrual accounting and how it improves financial statements.** Accrual accounting recognizes revenues when earned and expenses as they occur—not necessarily when cash inflows and outflows occur. This better reflects a company's financial position and performance.

LO2 **Identify the types of accounting adjustments and their purpose.** Adjustments can be grouped according to the timing of cash receipts or payments relative to the timing of the related work performed. Adjusting entries are made for prepaid expenses, unearned revenues, accrued expenses, and accrued revenues.

LO3 **Prepare and explain adjusting entries.** *Prepaid expenses* refer to items paid for in advance of receiving their benefits. Prepaid expenses are assets. Adjusting entries for prepaids involve increasing (debiting) expenses and decreasing (crediting)

assets. *Accrued expenses* refer to costs incurred in a period that are both unpaid and unrecorded. Adjusting entries for recording accrued expenses involve increasing (debiting) expenses and increasing (crediting) liabilities.

LO4 **Explain and prepare an adjusted trial balance.** An adjusted trial balance is a list of accounts and balances prepared after recording and posting adjusting entries. Financial statements are often prepared from the adjusted trial balance.

LO5 **Prepare financial statements from an adjusted trial balance.** Revenue and expense balances are reported on the income statement. Asset, liability, and equity balances are reported on the balance sheet. We usually prepare statements in the following order: income statement, statement of owner's equity, and balance sheet.

Guidance Answers to HOW YOU DOIN'?

1. The revenue recognition and the matching principle lead most directly to the adjusting process.

2. No expense is reported in 2011 under cash basis accounting. Under cash basis accounting, all $4,800 is reported as expense in April 2010 when paid. Under accrual basis accounting $2,400 (computed as $4,800/24 × 12) is reported as expense in 2011.

3. A contra account is an account that is subtracted from the balance of a related account. Use of a contra account provides more information than simply reporting a net amount.

4. An accrued expense is a cost incurred in a period that is both unpaid and unrecorded prior to adjusting entries. One example is salaries earned but not yet paid at period-end.

5. A prepaid expense arises when items have been paid for in advance of receiving their benefits. Examples are prepaid insurance, prepaid rent, and supplies.

6. The probable adjusting entries of Jordan Air are:

Insurance Expense	300	
Prepaid Insurance		300
To record insurance expired.		
Salaries Expense	1,400	
Salaries Payable		1,400
To record accrued salaries.		

7. Revenue accounts and expense accounts.

8. Statement of owner's equity.

Key Terms

Accrual basis accounting (p. 104) Accounting system that recognizes revenues when earned and expenses as they occur; the basis for GAAP.

Accrued expenses (p. 109) Costs incurred in a period that are both unpaid and unrecorded; adjusting entries for recording accrued expenses involve increasing expenses and increasing liabilities.

Adjusted trial balance (p. 110) List of accounts and balances prepared after period-end adjustments are recorded and posted.

Adjusting entry (p. 106) Journal entry at the end of an accounting period to bring an asset or liability account to its proper amount and update the related expense or revenue account.

Annual financial statements (p. 105) Financial statements covering a one-year period; often based on a calendar year, but any consecutive 12-month (or 52-week) period is acceptable.

Book value (p. 109) Asset's acquisition cost less its accumulated depreciation; also sometimes used synonymously as the *carrying value* of an account.

Cash basis accounting (p. 104) Accounting system that recognizes revenues when cash is received and recognizes expenses as cash is paid; not consistent with GAAP.

Contra account (p. 108) Account linked with another account and having an opposite normal balance; reported as a subtraction from the other account's balance.

Depreciation (p. 108) Expense created by allocating the cost of plant and equipment to periods in which the asset is used; represents the expense of using the asset.

Fiscal year (p. 105) Consecutive 12-month (or 52-week) period chosen as the organization's annual accounting period.

Interim financial statements (p. 105) Financial statements covering periods of less than one year; usually based on one-, three-, or six-month periods.

Matching principle (p. 105) Prescribes expenses to be reported in the same period as the revenues earned as a result of those expenses.

Plant assets (p. 107) Tangible long-lived assets used to produce or sell products and services; also called *property, plant and equipment (PP&E)* or *fixed assets*.

Prepaid expenses (p. 106) Items paid for in advance of receiving their benefits; classified as assets.

Revenue recognition principle (p. 105) Prescribes that revenue is recognized on the income statement in the period it is earned.

Straight-line depreciation method (p. 108) Method that allocates an equal portion of the depreciable cost of plant asset (cost minus salvage value) to each accounting period in its useful life.

Time period assumption (p. 105) Assumption that an organization's activities can be divided into specific time periods such as months or years.

Unadjusted trial balance (p. 110) List of accounts and balances prepared before accounting adjustments are recorded and posted.

Multiple Choice Quiz
Answers on p. 125   **mhhe.com/wildCA2e**

Additional Multiple Choice Quizzes are available at the book's Website.

1. A company forgot to record accrued and unpaid employee wages of $350,000 at period-end. This oversight would
   a. Understate net income by $350,000.
   b. Overstate net income by $350,000.
   c. Have no effect on net income.
   d. Overstate assets by $350,000.
   e. Understate assets by $350,000.

2. Prior to recording adjusting entries, the Office Supplies account has a $450 debit balance. A physical count of supplies shows $125 of unused supplies still available. The required adjusting entry is:
   a. Debit Office Supplies $125; Credit Office Supplies Expense $125.
   b. Debit Office Supplies $325; Credit Office Supplies Expense $325.
   c. Debit Office Supplies Expense $325; Credit Office Supplies $325.
   d. Debit Office Supplies Expense $325; Credit Office Supplies $125.
   e. Debit Office Supplies Expense $125; Credit Office Supplies $125.

3. On May 1, 2010, a two-year insurance policy was purchased for $24,000 with coverage to begin immediately. What is the amount of insurance expense that appears on the company's income statement for the year ended December 31, 2010?

   a. $4,000
   b. $8,000
   c. $12,000
   d. $20,000
   e. $24,000

4. A company purchases a delivery truck for $39,000 on July 1, 2010. The truck is estimated to have a useful life of 6 years and zero salvage value. The company uses the straight-line method of depreciation. How much depreciation expense is recorded on the truck for the year ended December 31, 2010?
   a. $3,500
   b. $3,250
   c. $4,000
   d. $6,500
   e. $7,000

5. A company purchased a machine for $80,000 on January 1, 2008. Straight-line depreciation expense on the machine is $8,000 per year. The machine's book value on December 31, 2010, is
   a. $0.
   b. $24,000.
   c. $56,000.
   d. $72,000.
   e. $80,000.

Discussion Questions

1. What is the difference between the cash basis and the accrual basis of accounting?

2. Why is the accrual basis of accounting generally preferred over the cash basis?

3. What is a prepaid expense and where is it reported in the financial statements?

4. What type of assets require adjusting entries to record depreciation?

5. What contra account is used when recording and reporting the effects of depreciation? Why is it used?

6. Review the balance sheet of **Best Buy** in Appendix A. Identify the asset accounts that require adjustment before annual financial statements can be prepared. What would be the effect on the income statement if these asset accounts were not adjusted?

QUICK STUDY

QS 5-1
Computing accrual income and cash income   **LO1**

In its first year of operations, Case Co. earned $60,000 in revenues and received $52,000 cash from these customers. The company recorded expenses of $37,500 but had not paid $6,000 of them by the end of the year. The company also prepaid $3,250 cash for next year's insurance premium. Calculate Case Co.'s first year net income under (a) the cash basis and (b) the accrual basis of accounting.

Classify the following adjusting entries as involving prepaid expenses (PE) or accrued expenses (AE).

a. _____ To record employee wages earned but not yet paid (nor recorded).

b. _____ To record annual depreciation expense.

c. _____ To record the cost of supplies used.

QS 5-2
Types of adjusting entries **LO2**

Adjusting entries affect at least one balance sheet account and at least one income statement account. For the following entries, identify the account to be debited and the account to be credited. Indicate which of the accounts is the income statement account and which is the balance sheet account.

a. Entry to record wage expenses incurred but not yet paid (nor recorded).

b. Entry to record expiration of prepaid insurance.

c. Entry to record annual depreciation expense.

QS 5-3
Recording and analyzing adjusting entries **LO3**

---

a. On July 1, 2010, Lamis Company paid $1,200 for six months of insurance coverage. No adjustments have been made to the Prepaid Insurance account, and it is now December 31, 2010. Prepare the journal entry to reflect expiration of the insurance as of December 31, 2010.

b. Shandi Company has a Supplies account balance of $500 on January 1, 2010. During 2010, it purchased $2,000 of supplies. As of December 31, 2010, $800 of supplies are available. Prepare the adjusting journal entry to correctly report the balance of the Supplies account and the Supplies Expense account as of December 31, 2010.

QS 5-4
Adjusting prepaid expenses **LO3**

---

a. Chika Company purchases $20,000 of equipment on January 1, 2010. The equipment is expected to last five years and be worth $2,000 at the end of that time. Prepare the journal entry to record one year's depreciation expense for the equipment as of December 31, 2010. Use the straight-line method.

b. What is the book value of the equipment on December 31, 2010?

QS 5-5
Adjusting for depreciation **LO3**

An employee gets paid $500 for a five-day workweek. At the end of July, she has worked one day for which she has not been paid. What adjusting journal entry must her employer make to correctly record salaries expense for July?

QS 5-6
Accruing salaries **LO3**

The following information is taken from Brooke Company's unadjusted and adjusted trial balances.

	Unadjusted		Adjusted	
	Debit	Credit	Debit	Credit
Prepaid insurance	$4,100		$3,700	
Salaries payable		$ 0		$800

Given this information, what were the adjusting journal entries?

QS 5-7
Interpreting adjusting entries **LO3**

In the blank space beside each adjusting entry, enter the letter of the explanation A through C that most closely describes the entry.

A. To record this period's depreciation expense.

B. To record amounts earned but not yet paid.

C. To record this period's use of a prepaid expense.

QS 5-8
Classifying adjusting entries **LO3**

			Debit	Credit
_____	1.	Insurance Expense	3,180	
		Prepaid Insurance		3,180
_____	2.	Depreciation Expense	38,217	
		Accumulated Depreciation		38,217
_____	3.	Salaries Expense	13,280	
		Salaries Payable		13,280

connect™

EXERCISES

Exercise 5-1
Determining assets and expenses for accrual and cash accounting
LO1

Check 2011 insurance expense: Accrual, $5,100; Cash, $0. Dec. 31, 2011, asset: Accrual, $4,250; Cash, $0.

On November 1, 2009, a company paid a $15,300 premium on a 36-month insurance policy for coverage beginning on that date. Refer to that policy and fill in the blanks in the following table.

	Balance Sheet Prepaid Insurance Asset Using			Insurance Expense Using	
	Accrual Basis	Cash Basis		Accrual Basis	Cash Basis
Dec. 31, 2009	$_____	$_____	2009	$_____	$_____
Dec. 31, 2010	_____	_____	2010	_____	_____
Dec. 31, 2011	_____	_____	2011	_____	_____
Dec. 31, 2012	_____	_____	2012	_____	_____
			Total	$_____	$_____

Exercise 5-2
Preparing adjusting entries **LO3**

Check (c) Dr. Office Supplies Expense, $3,882;

(d) Dr. Insurance Expense, $5,800

Prepare adjusting journal entries for the year ended (date of) December 31, 2010, for each of these separate situations.

a. Depreciation on the company's equipment for 2010 is computed to be $18,000.

b. The Prepaid Insurance account had a $6,000 debit balance at December 31, 2010, before adjusting for the costs of any expired coverage. An analysis of the company's insurance policies showed that $1,100 of unexpired insurance coverage remains.

c. The Office Supplies account had a $700 debit balance on December 31, 2009, and $3,480 of office supplies was purchased during the year. The December 31, 2010, count showed $298 of supplies available.

d. The Prepaid Insurance account had a $6,800 debit balance at December 31, 2010, before adjusting for the costs of any expired coverage. An analysis of insurance policies showed that $5,800 of coverage had expired.

e. Wage expenses of $3,200 have been incurred but are not paid as of December 31, 2010.

Exercise 5-3
Preparing adjusting entries **LO3**

Check (d) Dr. Insurance Expense, $2,800

For each of the following separate cases, prepare adjusting entries required of financial statements for the year ended (date of) December 31, 2010.

a. Wages of $8,000 are earned by workers but not paid as of December 31, 2010.

b. Depreciation on the company's equipment for 2010 is $18,531.

c. The Office Supplies account had a $240 debit balance on December 31, 2009. During 2010, $5,239 of office supplies is purchased. A count of supplies at December 31, 2010, shows $487 of supplies available.

d. The Prepaid Insurance account had a $4,000 balance on December 31, 2009. An analysis of insurance policies shows that $1,200 of unexpired insurance benefits remain at December 31, 2010.

Exercise 5-4
Adjusting and paying accrued wages **LO3**

Lopez Management has five part-time employees, each of whom earns $250 per day. They are normally paid on Fridays for work completed Monday through Friday of the same week. They were paid in full on Friday, December 28, 2010. The next week, the five employees worked only four days because New Year's Day was an unpaid holiday. Show (a) the adjusting entry that would be recorded on Monday, December 31, 2010, and (b) the journal entry that would be made to record payment of the employees' wages on Friday, January 4, 2011.

Exercise 5-5
Determining cost flows through accounts **LO3**

Determine the missing amounts in each of these four separate situations a through d.

	a	b	c	d
Supplies available—prior year-end	$ 400	$1,200	$1,260	?
Supplies purchased during the current year	2,800	6,500	?	$3,000
Supplies available—current year-end	650	?	1,350	700
Supplies expense for the current year	?	1,200	8,400	4,588

Total weekly salaries expense for all employees is $10,000. This amount is paid at the end of the day on Friday of each five-day workweek. April 30 falls on Tuesday of this year, which means that the employees had worked two days since the last payday. The next payday is May 3.

What is the required adjusting journal entry as of April 30? What is the journal entry needed to record payment of the salaries on May 3?

Exercise 5-6

Adjusting and paying accrued expenses **LO3**

Arnez Co.'s annual accounting period ends on December 31, 2010. The following information concerns the adjusting entries to be recorded as of that date.

a. The Office Supplies account started the year with a $4,000 balance. During 2010, the company purchased supplies for $13,400, which was added to the Office Supplies account. The amount of supplies available at December 31, 2010, totaled $2,554.

b. An analysis of the company's insurance policies provided the following facts.

Exercise 5-7

Preparing adjusting journal entries **LO3**

Policy	Date of Purchase	Months of Coverage	Total Cost
A	April 1, 2009	24	$14,400
B	April 1, 2010	36	12,960
C	August 1, 2010	12	2,400

The total cost for each policy was paid in full (for all months) at the purchase date, and the Prepaid Insurance account was debited for the full cost. (Year-end adjusting entries for Prepaid Insurance were properly recorded in all prior years.)

c. The company has 15 employees, who earn a total of $1,960 in salaries each working day. They are paid each Monday for their work in the five-day workweek ending on the previous Friday. Assume that December 31, 2010, is a Tuesday, and all 15 employees worked the first two days of that week. Because New Year's Day is a paid holiday, they will be paid salaries for five full days on Monday, January 6, 2011.

d. The company purchased a building on January 1, 2010. It cost $960,000 and is expected to have a $45,000 salvage value at the end of its predicted 30-year life. Annual depreciation is $30,500.

Required

Use the information to prepare adjusting entries as of December 31, 2010.

Check (b) Dr. Insurance Expense, $11,440 (d) Dr. Depreciation Expense, $30,500

Natsu Co.'s annual accounting period ends on October 31, 2010. The following information concerns the adjusting entries that need to be recorded as of that date.

a. The Office Supplies account started the fiscal year with a $600 balance. During the fiscal year, the company purchased supplies for $4,570, which was added to the Office Supplies account. The supplies available at October 31, 2010, totaled $800.

b. An analysis of the company's insurance policies provided the following facts.

Exercise 5-8

Recording adjusting journal entries **LO3**

Policy	Date of Purchase	Months of Coverage	Total Cost
A	April 1, 2009	24	$6,000
B	April 1, 2010	36	7,200
C	August 1, 2010	12	1,320

The total cost for each policy was paid in full (for all months) at the purchase date, and the Prepaid Insurance account was debited for the full cost. (Year-end adjusting entries for Prepaid Insurance were properly recorded in all prior fiscal years.)

c. The company has four employees, who earn a total of $1,000 for each workday. They are paid each Monday for their work in the five-day workweek ending on the previous Friday. Assume that

October 31, 2010, is a Monday, and all five employees worked the first day of that week. They will be paid salaries for five full days on Monday, November 7, 2010.

d. The company purchased a building on November 1, 2009, that cost $175,000 and is expected to have a $40,000 salvage value at the end of its predicted 25-year life. Annual depreciation is $5,400.

Check *(b)* Dr. Insurance Expense, $5,350; *(d)* Dr. Depreciation Expense, $5,400.

Required

Use the information to prepare adjusting entries as of October 31, 2010.

PROBLEM SET A

Problem 5-1A
Preparing adjusting entries, adjusted trial balance, and financial statements

LO3   LO4   LO5

mhhe.com/wildCA2e

Wells Technical Institute (WTI), a school owned by Tristana Wells, provides training to individuals who pay tuition directly to the school. WTI also offers training to groups in off-site locations. Its unadjusted trial balance as of December 31, 2010, follows. Descriptions of items *a* through *f* that require adjusting entries on December 31, 2010, follow.

Additional Information

a. An analysis of the school's insurance policies shows that $2,400 of coverage has expired.

b. A count shows that teaching supplies costing $2,800 are available at year-end 2010.

c. Annual depreciation on the equipment is $13,200.

d. Annual depreciation on the professional library is $7,200.

e. The school's two employees are paid weekly. As of the end of the year, two days' salaries have accrued at the rate of $100 per day for each employee.

f. The balance in the Prepaid Rent account represents rent for December.

WELLS TECHNICAL INSTITUTE Unadjusted Trial Balance December 31, 2010	Debit	Credit
Cash	$ 34,000	
Accounts receivable	0	
Teaching supplies	8,000	
Prepaid insurance	12,000	
Prepaid rent	3,000	
Professional library	35,000	
Accumulated depreciation—Professional library		$ 10,000
Equipment	80,000	
Accumulated depreciation—Equipment		15,000
Accounts payable		38,500
Salaries payable		0
T. Wells, Capital		90,000
T. Wells, Withdrawals	50,000	
Tuition fees earned		123,900
Training fees earned		40,000
Depreciation expense—Professional library	0	
Depreciation expense—Equipment	0	
Salaries expense	50,000	
Insurance expense	0	
Rent expense	33,000	
Teaching supplies expense	0	
Advertising expense	6,000	
Utilities expense	6,400	
Totals	$ 317,400	$ 317,400

Required

1. Using Exhibit 5.11 as a guide, create a seven-column sheet with the following headings:

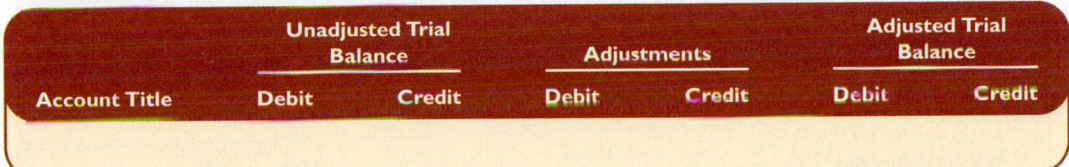

Account Title	Unadjusted Trial Balance		Adjustments		Adjusted Trial Balance	
	Debit	Credit	Debit	Credit	Debit	Credit

2. Enter the account titles and balances in the unadjusted trial balance columns onto your sheet.

3. Prepare the necessary adjusting journal entries for items *a* through *f* and record them in the adjustments column. Assume that adjusting entries are made only at year end.

4. Compute adjusted account balances and enter the balances in the adjusted trial balance columns.

5. Prepare Wells Technical Institute's income statement and statement of owner's equity for the year 2010 and prepare its balance sheet as of December 31, 2010. The owner made no additional investments during the year.

Check   (4) Adj. Trial balance totals $338,200; (5) Net income, $37,100; Ending T. Wells, Capital $77,100

The adjusted trial balance for Chiara Company as of December 31, 2010, follows.

Problem 5-2A
Preparing financial statements from the adjusted trial balance
LO5

	Debit	Credit
Cash	$ 30,000	
Accounts receivable	52,000	
Office supplies	16,000	
Automobiles	168,000	
Accumulated depreciation—Automobiles		$ 50,000
Equipment	138,000	
Accumulated depreciation—Equipment		18,000
Land	78,000	
Accounts payable		90,000
Salaries payable		19,000
R. Chiara, Capital		255,800
R. Chiara, Withdrawals	46,000	
Fees earned		484,000
Depreciation expense—Automobiles	26,000	
Depreciation expense—Equipment	18,000	
Salaries expense	188,000	
Wages expense	40,000	
Office supplies expense	34,000	
Advertising expense	58,000	
Repairs expense—Automobiles	24,800	
Totals	$916,800	$916,800

Required

Use the information in the adjusted trial balance to prepare (*a*) the income statement for the year ended December 31, 2010; (*b*) the statement of owner's equity for the year ended December 31, 2010; and (*c*) the balance sheet as of December 31, 2010. The owner made no additional investments during the year.

Check   (c) Total assets, $414,000

Following is the unadjusted trial balance for Augustus Institute as of December 31, 2010. The Institute provides one-on-one training to individuals who pay tuition directly to the business and offers extension training to groups in off-site locations. Shown after the trial balance are items *a* through *f* that require adjusting entries as of December 31, 2010.

PROBLEM SET B

Problem 5-1B
Preparing adjusting entries, adjusted trial balance, and financial statements   **LO3   LO4   LO5**

```
Microsoft Excel - Book1                                                          _ 8 X
File Edit View Insert Format Tools Data Accounting Window Help                    _ 8 X
```

AUGUSTUS INSTITUTE
Unadjusted Trial Balance
December 31, 2010

Account	Debit	Credit
Cash	$ 60,000	
Accounts receivable	0	
Teaching supplies	70,000	
Prepaid insurance	19,000	
Prepaid rent	3,800	
Professional library	12,000	
Accumulated depreciation—Professional library		$ 2,500
Equipment	40,000	
Accumulated depreciation—Equipment		20,000
Accounts payable		39,800
Salaries payable		0
C. Augustus, Capital		71,500
C. Augustus, Withdrawals	20,000	
Tuition fees earned		129,200
Training fees earned		68,000
Depreciation expense—Professional library	0	
Depreciation expense—Equipment	0	
Salaries expense	44,200	
Insurance expense	0	
Rent expense	29,600	
Teaching supplies expense	0	
Advertising expense	19,000	
Utilities expense	13,400	
Totals	$ 331,000	$ 331,000

`Sheet1  Sheet2  Sheet3`

Additional Information

a. An analysis of the Institute's insurance policies shows that $9,500 of coverage has expired.

b. An inventory count shows that teaching supplies costing $20,000 are available at year-end 2010.

c. Annual depreciation on the equipment is $5,000.

d. Annual depreciation on the professional library is $2,400.

e. The Institute's only employee is paid weekly. As of the end of the year, three days' salaries have accrued at the rate of $150 per day.

f. The balance in the Prepaid Rent account represents rent for December.

Required

1. Using Exhibit 5.11 as a guide, create a seven-column sheet with the following headings:

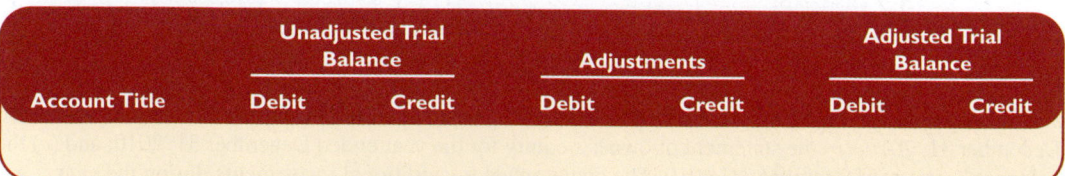

	Unadjusted Trial Balance		Adjustments		Adjusted Trial Balance	
Account Title	Debit	Credit	Debit	Credit	Debit	Credit

2. Enter the account titles and balances in the unadjusted trial balance columns onto your sheet.

3. Prepare the necessary adjusting journal entries for items *a* through *f* and record them in the adjustments column. Assume that adjusting entries are made only at year end.

4. Compute adjusted account balances and enter the balances in the adjusted trial balance columns.

5. Prepare Augustus Institute's income statement and statement of owner's equity for the year 2010, and prepare its balance sheet as of December 31, 2010. The owner made no additional investments during the year.

Check   (4) Adj. trial balance totals, $338,850; (5) Net income, $19,850; Ending C. Augustus, Capital, $71,350

The adjusted trial balance for Speedy Courier as of December 31, 2010, follows.

Problem 5-2B
Preparing financial statements
from the adjusted trial balance
LO5

	Debit	Credit
Cash	$ 58,000	
Accounts receivable	120,000	
Office supplies	22,000	
Trucks	134,000	
Accumulated depreciation—Trucks		$ 58,000
Equipment	270,000	
Accumulated depreciation—Equipment		200,000
Land	100,000	
Accounts payable		276,000
Salaries payable		28,000
L. Horace, Capital		125,000
L. Horace, Withdrawals	50,000	
Delivery fees earned		611,800
Depreciation expense—Trucks	29,000	
Depreciation expense—Equipment	48,000	
Salaries expense	74,000	
Wages expense	300,000	
Office supplies expense	31,000	
Advertising expense	27,200	
Repairs expense—Trucks	35,600	
Totals	$1,298,800	$1,298,800

Required

Use the information in the adjusted trial balance to prepare (*a*) the income statement for the year ended December 31, 2010, (*b*) the statement of owner's equity for the year ended December 31, 2010, and (*c*) the balance sheet as of December 31, 2010. The owner made no additional investments during the year.

Check   (c) Total assets $446,000

This serial problem began in Chapter 1 and continues through most of the book. If previous chapter segments were not completed, the serial problem can still begin at this point. It is helpful, but not necessary, that you use the Working Papers that accompany the book.

SERIAL PROBLEM

Success Systems
LO3   LO4   LO5

SP 5   After the success of the company's first two months, Adriana Lopez continues to operate Success Systems. (Transactions for the first two months are described in the serial problem of Chapter 4.) The November 30, 2010, unadjusted trial balance of Success Systems (reflecting its transactions for October and November) follows.

No.	Account Title	Debit	Credit
101	Cash	$ 68,996	
106	Accounts receivable	15,800	
126	Computer supplies	3,350	
128	Prepaid insurance	2,400	
131	Prepaid rent	3,500	
163	Office equipment	10,000	
164	Accumulated depreciation—Office equipment		$ 0
167	Computer equipment	25,000	
168	Accumulated depreciation—Computer equipment		0
201	Accounts payable		0
210	Wages payable		0
236	Unearned computer services revenue		0
301	A. Lopez, Capital		110,000
302	A. Lopez, Withdrawals	6,500	
403	Computer services revenue		32,550

[continued on next page]

[continued from previous page]

612	Depreciation expense—Office equipment	0	
613	Depreciation expense—Computer equipment	0	
623	Wages expense	3,150	
637	Insurance expense	0	
640	Rent expense	0	
652	Computer supplies expense	0	
655	Advertising expense	1,790	
676	Mileage expense	864	
677	Miscellaneous expenses	300	
684	Repairs expense—Computer	900	
	Totals	$142,550	$142,550

Success Systems had the following transactions and events in December 2010.

Dec. 2   Paid $1,200 cash to Hilldale Mall for Success Systems' share of mall advertising costs.
     3   Paid $500 cash for minor repairs to the company's computer.
     4   Received $7,000 cash from Alex's Engineering Co. for the receivable from November.
   10   Paid cash to Michelle Jones for six days of work at the rate of $150 per day.
   14   Notified by Alex's Engineering Co. that Success's bid of $9,000 on a proposed project has been accepted. Alex's paid a $2,500 cash advance to Success Systems.
   15   Purchased $2,100 of computer supplies on credit from Cain Office Products.
   16   Sent a reminder to Gomez Co. to pay the fee for services recorded on November 8.
   20   Completed a project for Chang Corporation and received $3,620 cash.
22–26   Took the week off for the holidays.
   26   Received $3,000 cash from Gomez Co. on its receivable.
   26   Reimbursed Lopez's business automobile mileage (800 miles at $0.32 per mile).
   27   Lopez withdrew $2,000 cash for personal use.

The following additional facts are collected for use in making adjusting entries prior to preparing financial statements for the company's first three months:

a. The December 31 count of computer supplies shows $775 still available.

b. Three months have expired since the 12-month insurance premium was paid in advance.

c. As of December 31, Michelle Jones has not been paid for four days of work at $150 per day.

d. The company's computer is expected to have a five-year life with no salvage value.

e. The office equipment is expected to have a four-year life with no salvage value.

f. Three of the four months' prepaid rent has expired.

Required

1. Prepare journal entries to record each of the December transactions and events for Success Systems. Post those entries to the accounts in the ledger.

2. Prepare adjusting entries to reflect *a* through *f*. Post those entries to the accounts in the ledger.

3. Prepare an adjusted trial balance as of December 31, 2010.

4. Prepare an income statement for the three months ended December 31, 2010.

5. Prepare a statement of owner's equity for the three months ended December 31, 2010.

6. Prepare a balance sheet as of December 31, 2010.

Check   (3) Adjusted trial balance totals, $153,245

(6) Total assets, $122,635

BEYOND THE NUMBERS

REPORTING IN ACTION

LO1

BTN 5–1   Refer to **Best Buy**'s financial statements in Appendix A to answer the following.

Required

1. Identify and write down the revenue recognition principle as explained in the chapter.

2. Research **Best Buy**'s footnotes to discover how it applies the revenue recognition principle. Report what you discover.

BTN 5-2   At year-end the president of your company asks you, the accountant, not to record accrued expenses until next year because they will not be paid until then. The president also directs you to record in current year revenue a prepayment from a customer for services that won't be provided until next year. Your company would report a net income instead of a net loss if you carry out the president's instructions. What do you do?

ETHICS CHALLENGE
LO3

BTN 5-3   Access the **Gap**'s Website (**gap.com**) to answer the following requirements.

Required

1. What are Gap's main brands?

2. Access Gap's 2008 annual report either at the company's Website (or at **www.SEC.gov**). What is Gap's fiscal year-end?

3. What is Gap's net sales for the period ended February 2, 2008?

4. What is Gap's net income for the period ended February 2, 2008?

**TAKING IT TO
THE NET**
LO5

BTN 5-4   Two types of adjustments are described in the chapter: (1) prepaid expenses and (2) accrued expenses.

Required

1. Form *learning teams* of two (or more) members. Each team member must select one of the two adjustments as an area of expertise (each team must have at least one expert in each area).

2. Form *expert teams* from the individuals who have selected the same area of expertise. Expert teams are to discuss and write a report that each expert will present to his or her learning team addressing the following:

  a. Description of the adjustment and why it's necessary.

  b. Example of a transaction or event, with dates and amounts, that requires adjustment.

  c. Adjusting entry(ies) for the example in requirement *b*.

  d. Status of the affected account(s) before and after the adjustment in requirement *c*.

  e. Effects on financial statements of not making the adjustment.

3. Each expert should return to his or her learning team. In rotation, each member should present his or her expert team's report to the learning team. Team discussion is encouraged.

**TEAMWORK
IN ACTION**
LO2   LO3

BTN 5-5   Review the opening feature of this chapter dealing with **PopCap Games**.

Required

1. Assume that PopCap sells a $300 gift certificate to a customer, collecting the $300 cash in advance. Prepare the journal entry for the collection of $300 cash under (*a*) cash basis accounting and (*b*) accrual basis accounting.

2. PopCap understands that many companies carry inventories, and the owners are thinking of carrying an inventory of games on CDs. The owners desire your advice on the pros and cons of carrying such inventory. Provide at least one reason for and one reason against carrying inventories.

**ENTREPRENEURS
IN BUSINESS**
LO1

BTN 5-6   A small publishing company signs a well-known athlete to write a book. The company pays the athlete $500,000 to sign plus future book royalties. A note to the company's financial statements says that "prepaid expenses include $500,000 in author signing fees to be matched against future expected sales." Is this accounting for the signing bonus acceptable? How does it affect your analysis?

YOU CALL IT
LO2

---

1. b; the forgotten adjusting entry is: *dr.* Wages Expense, *cr.* Wages Payable.

2. c; Supplies used = $450 − $125 = $325

3. b; Insurance expense = $24,000 × (8/24) = $8,000; adjusting entry is: *dr.* Insurance Expense for $8,000, *cr.* Prepaid Insurance for $8,000.

4. b; $3,250 = [($39,000 − $0)/6 years] × ½ year

5. c; Book value = $80,000 − (3 × $8,000) = $56,000

**ANSWERS TO
MULTIPLE CHOICE
QUIZ**

Chapter

A Look Back

Chapter 5 described why adjusting entries are important for recognizing revenues and expenses in the proper period. We prepared an adjusted trial balance and used it to prepare financial statements.

A Look at This Chapter

This chapter emphasizes the final steps in the accounting process and reviews the entire accounting cycle. We explain the closing process and the use of a post-closing trial balance. We show how a work sheet aids in preparing financial statements.

A Look Ahead

Chapter 7 considers fraud and controls. We look specifically at how internal controls reduce the likelihood of fraud. We also consider the effect that recent laws, such as Sarbanes-Oxley, have on fraud and internal controls.

Closing Process and Financial Statements

Learning Objectives

LO 1 Prepare a work sheet and explain its usefulness.

LO 2 Explain why temporary accounts are closed each period.

LO 3 Describe and prepare closing entries.

LO 4 Explain and prepare a post-closing trial balance.

LO 5 Identify steps in the accounting cycle.

"Stay true to your vision and your mission"
—Kathryn Kerrigan

Walk in Her Shoes

CHICAGO—As a teenager, Kathryn Kerrigan wore a size 11 shoe and found shopping for shoes grueling. "I remember driving with my dad to every shopping mall looking for shoes," recalls Kathryn. "It's embarrassing and it doesn't have to be." Kathryn decided to do something about it. She wrote a business plan for a college project and executed that plan with her dad's encouragement. Her start-up company, **Kathryn Kerrigan (KathrynKerrigan.com)**, now provides stylish women's shoes through size 16.

Success, however, requires Kathryn to monitor costs. "We had to create the molds for every shoe size," explains Kathryn. "These cost about $2,000 each." She set up an accounting system to track revenues and control costs, but it is a constant struggle as her business grows. Kathryn says that properly applying the accounting cycle, preparing financial statements, and acting on that information increase the odds of success. However, at times, admits Kathryn, "I had to find humility and ask for help."

Kathryn has successfully controlled materials costs while monitoring both revenues and customer needs. She uses the accounting system and closing entries to help identify and match costs with revenues for specific time periods. Kathryn says she relies on balance sheets to know when to pay bills. But what pulls her through, admits Kathryn, is knowing that "we're putting out a product that's missing in the marketplace."

Kathryn is on a mission. "What keeps me going," explains Kathryn, "are all the women who keep coming up to me . . . asking for shoes that fit." To make that happen, she tracks the accounting numbers to be sure it is a money-making venture. "It's important for entrepreneurs to be realistic," insists Kathryn. Yet she adds, "A great pair of shoes can make all the difference!"

[Sources: *Kathryn Kerrigan Website*, January 2009; *Success Magazine*, February 2008; *Inc.com*, July 2007; *Beep*, October 2007; *Chicago Sun-Times*, February 2008]

Earlier chapters described how transactions and events are analyzed, journalized, and posted. We also described important adjustments that are necessary in preparing financial statements. This chapter explains the closing process that readies revenue, expense, and withdrawal accounts for the next reporting period and updates the capital account. A work sheet is shown to be a useful tool for that process and in preparing financial statements.

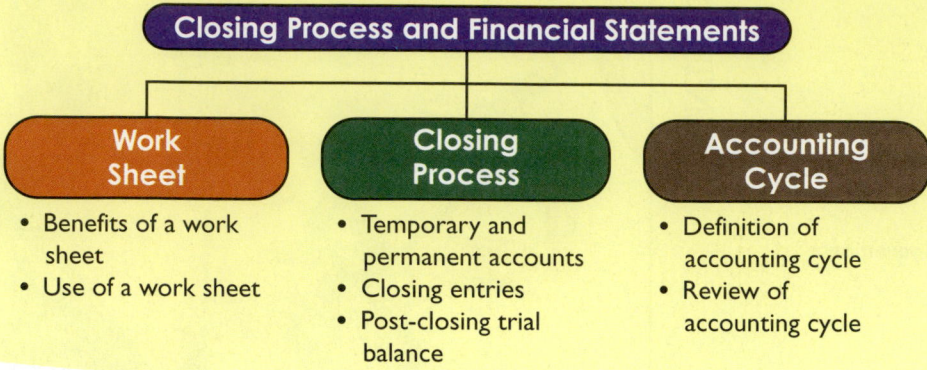

Closing Process and Financial Statements

Work Sheet
- Benefits of a work sheet
- Use of a work sheet

Closing Process
- Temporary and permanent accounts
- Closing entries
- Post-closing trial balance

Accounting Cycle
- Definition of accounting cycle
- Review of accounting cycle

Work Sheet as a Tool

In Chapter 5 we showed how to prepare financial statements from an adjusted trial balance. This approach is good when the number of accounts and/or adjustments is low. Accountants often use various analyses and internal documents when preparing formal reports and financial statements. Internal documents are often called **working papers.** One widely used working paper is the **work sheet,** which helps accountants prepare financial statements and aids in the closing process.

Benefits of a Work Sheet

LO1 Prepare a work sheet and explain its usefulness.

A work sheet is *not* a required report, yet using a manual or electronic work sheet has several potential benefits. Specifically, a work sheet

- Aids the preparation of financial statements.
- Reduces the possibility of errors when working with many accounts and adjustments.
- Links accounts and adjustments to their impacts in financial statements.
- Assists in planning and organizing an audit of financial statements—as it can be used to reflect any adjustments necessary.
- Helps in preparing interim (monthly and quarterly) financial statements when the journalizing and posting of adjusting entries are postponed until year-end.
- Shows the effects of proposed or "what-if" transactions.
- Aids in closing temporary accounts.

Since a work sheet is *not* a required report or an accounting record, its format is flexible and can be modified by its user to fit his/her preferences. In this chapter we show a common format for the work sheet.

Use of a Work Sheet

When a work sheet is used to prepare financial statements, it is constructed at the end of a period before the adjusting process. The complete work sheet includes a list of the accounts, their balances and adjustments, and their sorting into financial statement columns. It provides two columns each for the unadjusted trial balance, the adjustments, the adjusted trial balance, the income statement, and the balance sheet (including the statement of owner's equity).

To describe and interpret the work sheet, we use the information from FastForward. Preparing the work sheet has five important steps. Each step, 1 through 5, is color-coded and explained with reference to Exhibit 6.1.

① Step 1. Enter Unadjusted Trial Balance

Refer to Exhibit 6.1. The first step in preparing a work sheet is to list the title of every account and its account number that is expected to appear on its financial statements. This includes all accounts in the ledger plus any new ones expected from adjusting entries. Most adjusting entries—including expenses from salaries, supplies, depreciation, and insurance—are predictable and recurring. The unadjusted balance for each account is then entered in the appropriate Debit or Credit column of the unadjusted trial balance columns. The totals of these two columns must be equal. Exhibit 6.1 shows FastForward's work sheet after completing this first step.

② Step 2. Enter Adjustments

Refer to Exhibit 6.1a (turn over first transparency). The second step in preparing a work sheet is to enter adjustments in the Adjustments columns. The adjustments shown are the same ones shown in Chapter 5. An identifying letter links the debit and credit of each adjusting entry. This is called *keying* the adjustments. **After preparing a work sheet, adjusting entries must still be entered in the journal and posted to the ledger.** The Adjustments columns provide the information for those entries.

③ Step 3. Prepare Adjusted Trial Balance

Refer to Exhibit 6.1b (turn over second transparency). The adjusted trial balance is prepared by combining the adjustments with the unadjusted balances for each account. To avoid omitting the transfer of an account balance, start with the first line (cash) and continue in account order. As an example, the Prepaid Insurance account has a $2,400 debit balance in the Unadjusted Trial Balance columns. This $2,400 debit is combined with the $100 credit in the Adjustments columns to give Prepaid Insurance a $2,300 debit in the Adjusted Trial Balance columns. The totals of the Adjusted Trial Balance columns confirm the equality of debits and credits.

④ Step 4. Sort Adjusted Trial Balance Amounts to Financial Statements

Refer to Exhibit 6.1c (turn over third transparency). This step involves sorting account balances from the adjusted trial balance to their proper financial statement columns as follows:

Accounts	Sorted to Column
Expenses	Income Statement Debit
Revenues	Income Statement Credit
Assets	Balance Sheet and Statement of Owner's Equity Debit
Withdrawals	Balance Sheet and Statement of Owner's Equity Debit
Liabilities	Balance Sheet and Statement of Owner's Equity Credit

⑤ Step 5. Total Statement Columns, Compute Income or Loss, and Balance Columns

Refer to Exhibit 6.1d (turn over fourth transparency). Compute totals for each financial statement column. At this point, debit and credit totals will probably not equal. Use the difference in the totals of the Income Statement columns to determine whether the business has a net income or a net loss:

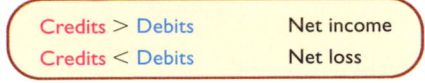

Credits > Debits	Net income
Credits < Debits	Net loss

For example, for Fastforward the Income Statement Credit column total of $6,100 is greater than the Income Statement Debit column total of $4,365. The difference of $1,735 is

[text continued on p. 131]

Exhibit 6.1

Work Sheet with Unadjusted Trial Balance

File Edit View Insert Format Tools Data Window Help

FastForward
Work Sheet
For Month Ended December 31, 2010

No.	Account	Unadjusted Trial Balance Dr.	Cr.	Adjustments Dr.	Cr.	Adjusted Trial Balance Dr.	Cr.	Income Statement Dr.	Cr.	Balance Sheet & Statement of Owner's Equity Dr.	Cr.
101	Cash	4,350									
126	Supplies	9,720									
128	Prepaid insurance	2,400									
167	Equipment	26,000									
168	Accumulated depreciation—Equip.		0								
201	Accounts payable		6,200								
209	Salaries payable		0								
236	Unearned consulting revenue		3,000								
301	C. Taylor, Capital		30,000								
302	C. Taylor, Withdrawals	200									
403	Consulting revenue		5,800								
406	Rental revenue		300								
612	Depreciation expense—Equip.	0									
622	Salaries expense	1,400									
637	Insurance expense	0									
640	Rent expense	1,000									
652	Supplies expense	0									
690	Utilities expense	230									
	Totals	45,300	45,300								

Sheet1 / Sheet2 / Sheet3

List all accounts from the ledger and those expected to arise from adjusting entries.

Enter all amounts available from ledger accounts. Column totals must be equal.

A work sheet collects and summarizes information used to prepare adjusting entries, financial statements, and closing entries.

FastForward's net income for the month. In the case of *net income* do the following on the work sheet:

- Enter the net income in the Income Statement Debit column, in the Net income row.
- Enter the net income in the Net income row in the Balance Sheet and Statement of Owner's Equity Credit column. Adding net income to the Credit column implies this amount will increase owner's equity.
- Compute new column totals for the Income Statement Debit and Balance Sheet and Statement of Owner's Equity Credit columns. Total debits should now equal total credits.

For example, after entering net income of $1,735 in the work sheet, FastForward's Income Statement columns each total $6,100, and its Balance Sheet and Statement of Owner's Equity columns each total $41,520.

In the case of *net loss* do the following on the work sheet:

- Enter the net loss in the Income Statement Credit column, in the Net income row.
- Enter the net loss in the Net income row in the Balance Sheet and Statement of Owner's Equity Debit column. Carrying the net loss to the Debit column implies this amount will reduce owner's equity.
- Compute new column totals for the Income Statement Credit and Balance Sheet and Statement of Owner's Equity Debit columns. Total debits should now equal total credits.

Updating owner's equity   Note that owner's equity is not updated on the work sheet. Instead, ending owner's capital is computed using amounts from the work sheet—beginning owner's capital plus net income minus withdrawals. This is done in the Statement of Owner's Equity (see Exhibit 6.3).

Additional owner investments   Care must be taken in reporting owner's equity when the owner makes additional investments during the year. In this case, the ending balance of owner's equity in the ledger would equal last year's ending owner's equity *plus* the additional owner investments during the year. The accountant reviews the activity in the owner's equity general ledger account to find these separate amounts. Exhibit 6.2 provides an example.

Owner, Capital					Acct. No. 301
Date	Explanation	PR	Debit	Credit	Balance
2010					
Nov. 30	Balance				40,000
Dec. 28	Additional owner investment	GI		5,000	45,000

Exhibit 6.2

Owner's Equity Ledger Account with Additional Owner Investment

In this case, the Statement of Owner's Equity for December would begin with the $40,000 beginning balance, and the next row of the statement would show the $5,000 additional investment.

If the Balance Sheet columns don't balance   The totals of the last two work sheet columns *must* balance after adding the net income or loss. If they do not, errors have been made. Perform the following steps to find the errors:

1. Add the column totals again.
2. Make sure the net income or loss has been sorted to the correct column.
3. Add the Income Statement columns again and make sure they equal and you have computed the correct net income.

IN THE NEWS

Accoun-tech   An electronic work sheet using spreadsheet software such as Excel allows us to easily change numbers, assess the impact of alternative strategies, and quickly prepare financial statements at less cost. It can also increase the available time for analysis and interpretation.

Work Sheet Applications and Analysis

A work sheet does not replace financial statements. It is a tool we can use at the end of an accounting period to help organize data and prepare financial statements. FastForward's financial statements are shown in Exhibit 6.3. Its income statement amounts are taken from the Income

Exhibit 6.3

Financial Statements Prepared from the Work Sheet

FASTFORWARD
Income Statement
For Month Ended December 31, 2010

Revenues		
Consulting revenue	$ 5,800	
Rental revenue	300	
Total revenues		$ 6,100
Expenses		
Depreciation expense—Equipment	375	
Salaries expense	1,610	
Insurance expense	100	
Rent expense	1,000	
Supplies expense	1,050	
Utilities expense	230	
Total expenses		4,365
Net income		$ 1,735

FASTFORWARD
Statement of Owner's Equity
For Month Ended December 31, 2010

Net income increases ending owner's capital.

C. Taylor, Capital, December 1		$ 0
Add: Investment by owner	$30,000	
Net income	1,735	31,735
		31,735
Less: Withdrawals by owner		200
C. Taylor, Capital, December 31		$31,535

FASTFORWARD
Balance Sheet
December 31, 2010

Assets

Cash		$ 4,350
Supplies		8,670
Prepaid insurance		2,300
Equipment	$26,000	
Less: Accumulated depreciation—Equipment	375	25,625
Total assets		$40,945

Liabilities

Accounts payable		$ 6,200
Salaries payable		210
Unearned consulting revenue		3,000
Total liabilities		9,410

Equity

Ending owner's capital appears on the balance sheet.

C. Taylor, Capital		31,535
Total liabilities and equity		$40,945

Statement columns of the work sheet. Similarly, amounts for its balance sheet and its statement of owner's equity are taken from the Balance Sheet & Statement of Owner's Equity columns of the work sheet.

A work sheet is also useful to journalize adjusting entries as the information is in the Adjustments columns. It is important to remember that a work sheet is not a journal. This means that even when a work sheet is prepared, it is necessary to both journalize adjustments and post them to the ledger.

Work sheets can also help in analyzing proposed, or what-if, transactions. This is done by entering financial statement amounts in the Unadjusted columns. Proposed transactions are then entered into the Adjustments columns. We then compute adjusted amounts from the proposed transactions. The extended amounts in the last four columns of the work sheet then show the financial statement effects of these proposed transactions. These financial statement columns yield **pro forma financial statements** because they show the statements *as if* the proposed transactions happened.

HOW YOU DOIN'?   Answers—p. 141

1. Where do we get the amounts to enter in the Unadjusted Trial Balance columns of a work sheet?

2. What are the advantages of using a work sheet to help prepare adjusting entries?

Closing Process

The **closing process** is an important step at the end of an accounting period *after* financial statements are completed. The purpose of the closing process is to:

LO2 Explain why temporary accounts are closed each period.

- Set revenue, expense, and owner withdrawal accounts to zero. This is done so these accounts can properly measure income and withdrawals in the *next* period.
- Update the owner capital account balance to its proper ending balance.

The closing process involves three tasks:

Task 1:   Identify accounts used in the closing process.

Task 2:   Journalize and post closing entries.

Task 3:   Prepare a post-closing trial balance.

We discuss these tasks next.

Temporary and Permanent Accounts

Temporary (or *nominal*) **accounts** accumulate data for one accounting period. They include all revenue and expense accounts, the owner withdrawal account, and the Income Summary account (discussed below). They are temporary because they start with balances of zero at the beginning of a period, they record transactions and events for that period, and then are closed to have zero balances at the end of the period. For example, FastForward's net income of $1,735 for this period cannot also be included in its net income for the next period; starting each period with zero balances in revenue and expense accounts ensures proper income measurement. **Permanent** (or *real*) **accounts** carry their balances into the next period and generally consist of all balance sheet accounts. For example, FastForward's ending cash balance of $4,350 on December 31 will be its beginning cash balance on January 1 of the next year. A simple rule applies to the closing process: *Only temporary accounts are closed.*

Income Summary   **Income Summary** is a temporary account used only in the closing process. Note, Income Summary does not appear in our work sheet in Exhibit 6.1, and it is

Temporary Accounts

| Revenues |
| Expenses |
| Owner Withdrawals |
| Income Summary |

Permanent Accounts

| Assets |
| Liabilities |
| Owner Capital |

not used for recording transactions during the year. The Income Summary account has these features:

■ It starts the closing process with a zero balance.
■ It is credited for the sum of all the revenue accounts for the period.
■ It is debited for the sum of all the expense accounts for the period.
■ It is closed to the owner capital account.
■ It ends the closing process with a zero balance. Just before it is closed, its balance is equal to the net income or loss for that period.

Owner, Capital   The Owner, Capital account is the only permanent account that appears in the closing process. This is so this account can be updated to reflect that period's performance. Recall that the balance for Owner, Capital on the work sheet *is not* its ending balance; closing journal entries are necessary to obtain the correct ending balance of Owner, Capital in the ledger.

Recording Closing Entries

To record and post **closing entries** is to transfer the ending balances in the temporary accounts to the Owner, Capital account. To close a temporary account means to make an entry to reduce its account balance to zero. If all accounts have normal balances, revenue accounts are closed with debit entries and expense and withdrawal accounts are closed with credit entries. The four-step closing process is shown in Exhibit 6.4.

Exhibit 6.4

The Four-Step Closing Process

Accounts Being Closed	Closing Entry Made to
1. Revenue accounts	Cr. Income Summary
2. Expense accounts	Dr. Income Summary
3. Income Summary account	To Owner, Capital*
4. Withdrawals account	Dr. Owner, Capital

* Cr. for net income. Dr. for net loss.

After completing steps 1 and 2, the income statement accounts are now ready for the next period. After completing steps 3 and 4, the balance in the Owner, Capital account in the general ledger equals the ending amount shown on the Statement of Owner's Equity. Exhibits 6.5 and 6.6 illustrate the four-step closing process for FastForward, using ending balances in the Income Statement and Balance Sheet and Statement of Owner's Equity columns from the work sheet in Exhibit 6.1d. We next use this work sheet information to explain the four-step closing process.

LO3 Describe and prepare closing entries.

Step 1: Close Credit Balances in Revenue Accounts to Income Summary   The first closing entry transfers credit balances in revenue accounts to the Income Summary account. We bring accounts with credit balances to zero by debiting them. For FastForward, this journal entry is step 1 in Exhibit 6.6. This entry closes revenue accounts and leaves them with zero balances. The accounts are now ready to record revenues when they occur in the next period. The $6,100 credit entry to Income Summary equals total revenues for the period.

Step 2: Close Debit Balances in Expense Accounts to Income Summary   The second closing entry transfers debit balances in expense accounts to the Income Summary account. We bring expense accounts' debit balances to zero by crediting them. With a balance of zero, these accounts are ready to record expenses for the next period. This second closing entry for FastForward is step 2 in Exhibit 6.6. Exhibit 6.5 shows that posting this entry gives each expense account a zero balance. The sum of these expense account debit balances before closing is $4,365 ($375 + 1,610 + 100 + 1,000 + 1,050 + 230). This amount is debited to Income Summary and represents total expenses for the period.

It is possible to close revenue and expense accounts directly to owner's capital. Computerized accounting systems do this.

Step 3: Close Income Summary to Owner's Capital   After steps 1 and 2, the balance (credit) of Income Summary is equal to December's net income of $1,735. The third closing entry transfers the balance of the Income Summary account to the capital account. This entry closes the Income Summary account and is step 3 in Exhibit 6.6. The Income Summary account has a zero balance after posting this entry. It continues to have a zero

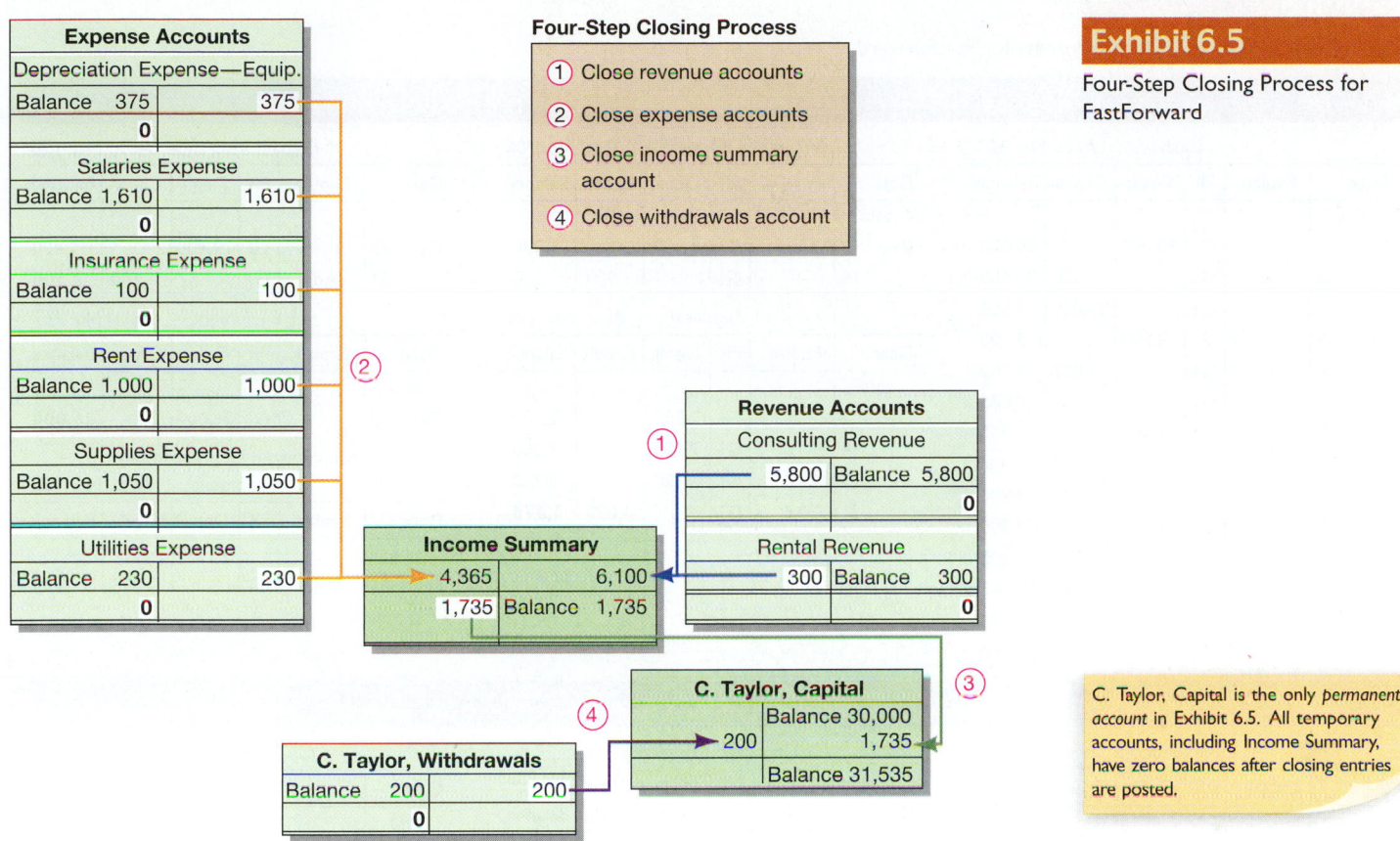

Exhibit 6.5

Four-Step Closing Process for FastForward

C. Taylor, Capital is the only *permanent* account in Exhibit 6.5. All temporary accounts, including Income Summary, have zero balances after closing entries are posted.

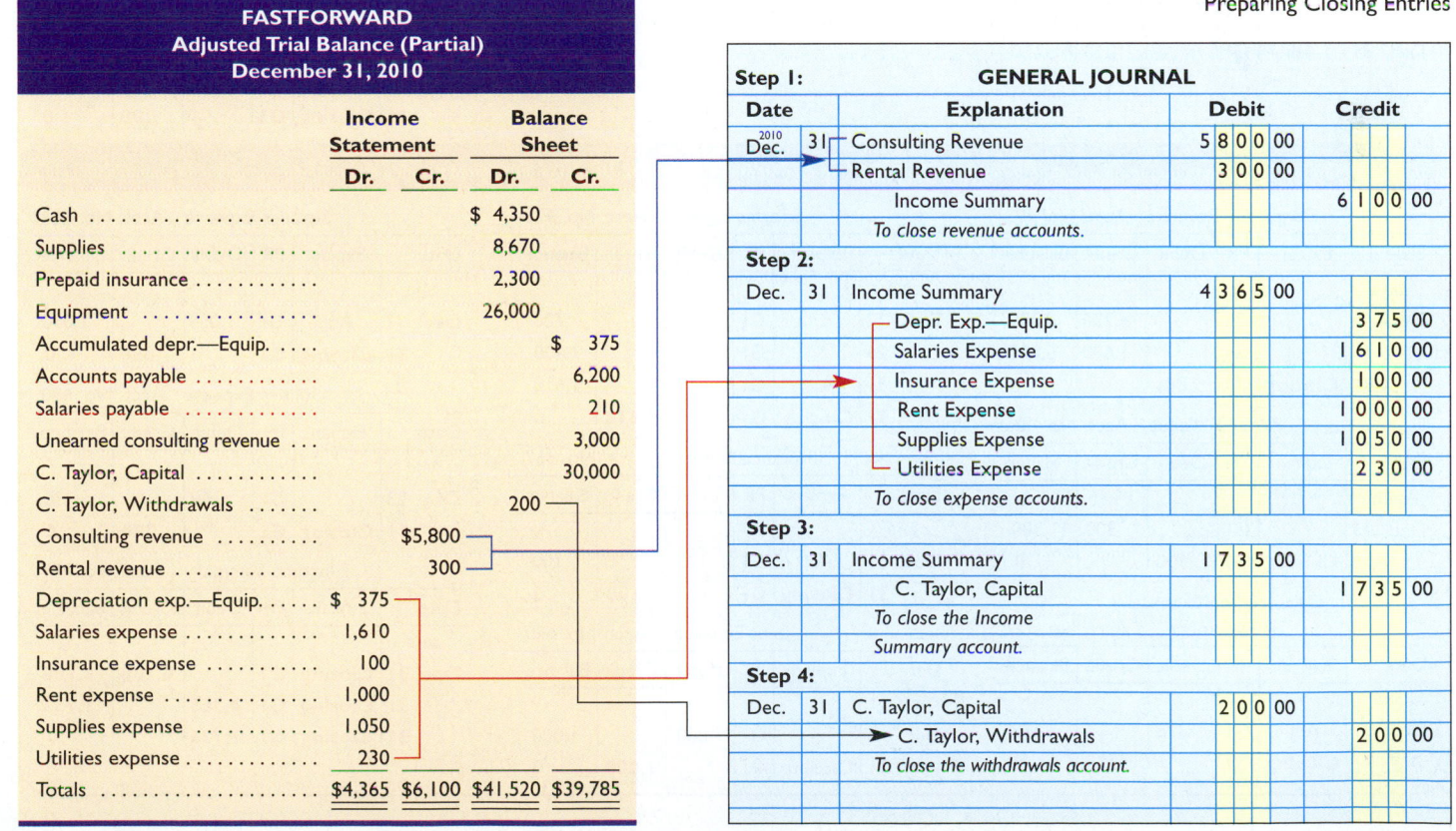

Exhibit 6.6

Preparing Closing Entries

Exhibit 6.7

General Ledger after the Closing Process for FastForward

Asset Accounts

Cash Acct. No. 101

Date	Explan.	PR	Debit	Credit	Balance
2010					
Dec. 1		G1	30,000		30,000
2		G1		2,500	27,500
3		G1		26,000	1,500
5		G1	4,200		5,700
6		G1		1,000	4,700
12		G1		700	4,000
19		G1	1,900		5,900
20		G1		900	5,000
21		G1		200	4,800
22		G1	3,000		7,800
23		G1		2,400	5,400
23		G1		120	5,280
23		G1		230	5,050
26		G1		700	**4,350**

Accounts Receivable Acct. No. 106

Date	Explan.	PR	Debit	Credit	Balance
2010					
Dec. 13		G1	1,900		1,900
19		G1		1,900	**0**

Supplies Acct. No. 126

Date	Explan.	PR	Debit	Credit	Balance
2010					
Dec. 2		G1	2,500		2,500
4		G1	7,100		9,600
23		G1	120		9,720
31	Adj.	G1		1,050	**8,670**

Prepaid Insurance Acct. No. 128

Date	Explan.	PR	Debit	Credit	Balance
2010					
Dec. 23		G1	2,400		2,400
31	Adj.	G1		100	**2,300**

Equipment Acct. No. 167

Date	Explan.	PR	Debit	Credit	Balance
2010					
Dec. 3		G1	26,000		**26,000**

Accumulated Depreciation—Equipment Acct. No. 168

Date	Explan.	PR	Debit	Credit	Balance
2010					
Dec. 31	Adj.	G1		375	**375**

Liability and Equity Accounts

Accounts Payable Acct. No. 201

Date	Explan.	PR	Debit	Credit	Balance
2010					
Dec. 4		G1		7,100	7,100
20		G1	900		**6,200**

Salaries Payable Acct. No. 209

Date	Explan.	PR	Debit	Credit	Balance
2010					
Dec. 31	Adj	G1		210	**210**

Unearned Consulting Revenue Acct. No. 236

Date	Explan.	PR	Debit	Credit	Balance
2010					
Dec. 22		G1		3,000	**3,000**

C. Taylor, Capital Acct. No. 301

Date	Explan.	PR	Debit	Credit	Balance
2010					
Dec. 1		G1		30,000	30,000
31	Closing	G1		1,735	31,735
31	Closing	G1	200		31,735

C. Taylor, Withdrawals Acct. No. 302

Date	Explan.	PR	Debit	Credit	Balance
2010					
Dec. 21		G1	200		200
31	Closing	G1		200	0

Revenue and Expense Accounts (including Income Summary)

Consulting Revenue Acct. No. 403

Date	Explan.	PR	Debit	Credit	Balance
2010					
Dec. 5		G1		4,200	4,200
13		G1		1,600	5,800
31	Closing	G1	5,800		0

Rental Revenue Acct. No. 406

Date	Explan.	PR	Debit	Credit	Balance
2010					
Dec. 13		G1		300	300
31	Closing	G1	300		0

Depreciation Expense—Equipment Acct. No. 612

Date	Explan.	PR	Debit	Credit	Balance
2010					
Dec. 31	Adj.	G1	375		375
31	Closing	G1		375	0

Salaries Expense Acct. No. 622

Date	Explan.	PR	Debit	Credit	Balance
2010					
Dec. 12		G1	700		700
26		G1	700		1,400
31	Adj.	G1	210		1,610
31	Closing	G1		1,610	0

Insurance Expense Acct. No. 637

Date	Explan.	PR	Debit	Credit	Balance
2010					
Dec. 31	Adj.	G1	100		100
31	Closing	G1		100	0

Rent Expense Acct. No. 640

Date	Explan.	PR	Debit	Credit	Balance
2010					
Dec. 6		G1	1,000		1,000
31	Closing	G1		1,000	0

Supplies Expense Acct. No. 652

Date	Explan.	PR	Debit	Credit	Balance
2010					
Dec. 31	Adj.	G1	1,050		1,050
31	Closing	G1		1,050	0

Utilities Expense Acct. No. 690

Date	Explan.	PR	Debit	Credit	Balance
2010					
Dec. 23		G1	230		230
31	Closing	G1		230	0

Income Summary Acct. No. 901

Date	Explan.	PR	Debit	Credit	Balance
2010					
Dec. 31	Closing	G1		6,100	6,100
31	Closing	G1	4,365		1,735
31	Closing	G1	1,735		0

balance until the closing process again occurs at the end of the next period. (If a net loss occurred because expenses exceeded revenues, the third entry is reversed: debit Owner, Capital and credit Income Summary.)

Step 4: Close Withdrawals Account to Owner's Capital   The fourth closing entry transfers any debit balance in the withdrawals account to the owner's capital account—see step 4 in Exhibit 6.6. This entry gives the withdrawals account a zero balance, and the account is now ready to accumulate next period's withdrawals. This entry also reduces the capital account balance to the $31,535 amount reported on the balance sheet.

Post-Closing Trial Balance

Exhibit 6.7 shows the entire ledger of FastForward as of December 31 after adjusting and closing entries are posted. (The transaction and adjusting entries are in Chapters 3, 4, and 5.) The temporary accounts (revenues, expenses, and withdrawals) have ending balances equal to zero. The final task in the closing process is to ensure that debit and credit balances equal for the *permanent* accounts in the general ledger.

A **post-closing trial balance** is a list of permanent accounts and their balances from the ledger after all closing entries have been journalized and posted. It lists the balances for all accounts not closed. These accounts comprise a company's assets, liabilities, and equity, which are those in the balance sheet. The aim of a post-closing trial balance is to verify that (1) total debits equal total credits for permanent accounts and (2) all temporary accounts have zero balances. FastForward's post-closing trial balance is shown in Exhibit 6.8. The post-closing trial balance usually is the last step in the accounting process.

LO4   Explain and prepare a post-closing trial balance.

FASTFORWARD Post-Closing Trial Balance December 31, 2010	Debit	Credit
Cash	$ 4,350	
Supplies	8,670	
Prepaid insurance	2,300	
Equipment	26,000	
Accumulated depreciation—Equipment		$ 375
Accounts payable		6,200
Salaries payable		210
Unearned consulting revenue		3,000
C. Taylor, Capital		31,535
Totals	$41,320	$41,320

Exhibit 6.8

Post-Closing Trial Balance

The post-closing trial balance does not include revenues, expenses, or owner withdrawals. All of those accounts have zero balances after closing.

Accounting Cycle

Chapters 2 through 6 can be usefully summarized by examining the accounting cycle. The term **accounting cycle** refers to the steps from processing transactions through preparing financial statements. It is called a *cycle* because the steps are repeated each reporting period. Exhibit 6.9 shows the nine steps in the cycle, beginning with analyzing transactions and ending with a post-closing trial balance. Steps 1 through 3 usually occur regularly as a company enters into transactions. Steps 4 through 9 are done at the end of a period.

LO5   Identify steps in the accounting cycle.

HOW YOU DOIN'?   Answers—p. 141

3. What are the major steps in preparing closing entries?

4. Why are revenue and expense accounts called *temporary*? Can you identify and list any other temporary accounts?

5. What accounts are listed on the post-closing trial balance?

Exhibit 6.9

Steps in the Accounting Cycle*

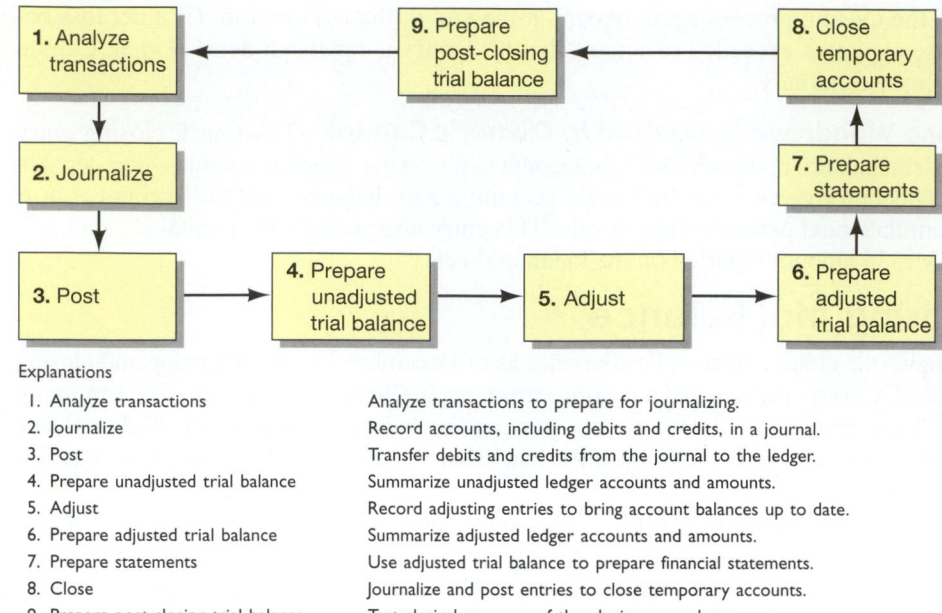

Explanations

1. Analyze transactions	Analyze transactions to prepare for journalizing.
2. Journalize	Record accounts, including debits and credits, in a journal.
3. Post	Transfer debits and credits from the journal to the ledger.
4. Prepare unadjusted trial balance	Summarize unadjusted ledger accounts and amounts.
5. Adjust	Record adjusting entries to bring account balances up to date.
6. Prepare adjusted trial balance	Summarize adjusted ledger accounts and amounts.
7. Prepare statements	Use adjusted trial balance to prepare financial statements.
8. Close	Journalize and post entries to close temporary accounts.
9. Prepare post-closing trial balance	Test clerical accuracy of the closing procedures.

*Steps 4, 6, and 9 can be done on a work sheet. A work sheet is useful in *planning* adjustments, but adjustments (step 5) must always be journalized and posted. Steps 3, 4, 6, and 9 are automatic with a computerized system.

Demonstration Problem

The partial work sheet of Midtown Repair Company at December 31, 2010, follows.

	Adjusted Trial Balance		Income Statement		Balance Sheet and Statement of Owner's Equity	
	Debit	**Credit**	**Debit**	**Credit**	**Debit**	**Credit**
Cash	95,600					
Prepaid insurance	16,000					
Prepaid rent	4,000					
Equipment	170,000					
Accumulated depreciation—Equipment		57,000				
Accounts payable		52,000				
C. Trout, Capital		178,500				
C. Trout, Withdrawals	30,000					
Repair services revenue		180,800				
Consulting revenue		14,800				
Depreciation expense—Equipment	28,500					
Wages expense	85,000					
Rent expense	48,000					
Insurance expense	6,000					
Totals	483,100	483,100				

Required

1. Complete the work sheet by extending the adjusted trial balance totals to the appropriate financial statement columns.
2. Prepare closing entries for Midtown Repair Company. Assume you are using page 7 of the General Journal.
3. Set up the Income Summary and the C. Trout, Capital account in the general ledger (in balance column format) and post the closing entries to these accounts.
4. Determine the balance of the C. Trout, Capital account to be reported on the December 31, 2010, balance sheet.
5. Prepare an income statement, statement of owner's equity, and balance sheet as of December 31, 2010.

Planning the Solution

- Extend the adjusted trial balance account balances to the appropriate financial statement columns.
- Prepare entries to close the revenue accounts to Income Summary, to close the expense accounts to Income Summary, to close Income Summary to the capital account, and to close the withdrawals account to the capital account.
- Post the first and second closing entries to the Income Summary account. Examine the balance of income summary and verify that it agrees with the net income shown on the work sheet.
- Post the third and fourth closing entries to the capital account.
- Use the work sheet's two right-most columns and your answer in part 4 to prepare the balance sheet.

Solution to Demonstration Problem

1. Completing the work sheet.

	Adjusted Trial Balance		Income Statement		Balance Sheet and Statement of Owner's Equity	
	Debit	**Credit**	**Debit**	**Credit**	**Debit**	**Credit**
Cash	95,600				95,600	
Prepaid insurance	16,000				16,000	
Prepaid rent	4,000				4,000	
Equipment	170,000				170,000	
Accumulated depreciation—Equipment		57,000				57,000
Accounts payable		52,000				52,000
C. Trout, Capital		178,500				178,500
C. Trout, Withdrawals	30,000				30,000	
Repair services revenue		180,800		180,800		
Consulting revenue		14,800		14,800		
Depreciation expense—Equipment	28,500		28,500			
Wages expense	85,000		85,000			
Rent expense	48,000		48,000			
Insurance expense	6,000		6,000			
Totals	483,100	483,100	167,500	195,600	315,600	287,500
Net income			28,100			28,100
Totals			195,600	195,600	315,600	315,600

2. Closing entries.

		GENERAL JOURNAL			Page 7	
Date		**Explanation**	**Debit**		**Credit**	
2010 Dec.	31	Repair Services Revenue	180 800 00			
		Consulting Revenue	14 800 00			
		Income Summary			195 600 00	
		To close revenue accounts.				
Dec.	31	Income Summary	167 500 00			
		Depreciation Expense—Equipment			28 500 00	
		Wages Expense			85 000 00	
		Rent Expense			48 000 00	
		Insurance Expense			6 000 00	
		To close expense accounts.				
Dec.	31	Income Summary	28 100 00			
		C. Trout, Capital			28 100 00	
		To close the Income Summary account.				
Dec.	31	C. Trout, Capital	30 000 00			
		C. Trout, Withdrawals			30 000 00	
		To close the withdrawals account.				

* We exclude posting reference details in the general journal above.

3. Set up the Income Summary and the capital ledger accounts and post the closing entries.

INCOME SUMMARY						Account No. 901
Date		**Explanation**	**PR**	**Debit**	**Credit**	**Balance**
2010 Jan.	1	Beginning balance				0 00
Dec.	31	Close revenue accounts	G7		195 600 00	195 600 00
	31	Close expense accounts	G7	167 500 00		28 100 00
	31	Close income summary	G7	28 100 00		0 00

C. TROUT, CAPITAL						Account No. 301
Date		**Explanation**	**PR**	**Debit**	**Credit**	**Balance**
2010 Jan.	1	Beginning balance				178 500 00
Dec.	31	Close Income Summary	G7		28 100 00	206 600 00
	31	Close C. Trout, Withdrawals	G7	30 000 00		176 600 00

4. The final capital balance of $176,600 (from part 3) will be reported on the December 31, 2010, balance sheet. The final capital balance reflects the increase due to the net income earned during the year and the decrease for the owner's withdrawals during the year.

5. Prepare financial statements.

MIDTOWN REPAIR COMPANY Income Statement For Year Ended December 31, 2010		
Revenues		
Repair services revenue	$180,800	
Consulting revenue	14,800	
Total revenues		$195,600
Expenses		
Depreciation expense—Equipment	28,500	
Wages expense	85,000	
Rent expense	48,000	
Insurance expense	6,000	
Total expenses		167,500
Net income		$ 28,100

MIDTOWN REPAIR COMPANY Statement of Owner's Equity For Year Ended December 31, 2010		
C. Trout, Capital, December 31, 2009		$178,500
Add: Investment by owner	$ 0	
Net income	28,100	28,100
		206,600
Less: Withdrawals by owner		30,000
C. Trout, Capital, December 31, 2010		$176,600

MIDTOWN REPAIR COMPANY
Balance Sheet
December 31, 2010

Assets

Cash		$ 95,600
Prepaid insurance		16,000
Prepaid rent		4,000
Equipment	$170,000	
Less: Accumulated depreciation—Equipment	57,000	113,000
Total assets		$228,600

Liabilities

Accounts payable	$ 52,000

Equity

C. Trout, Capital	176,600
Total liabilities and equity	$228,600

Summary

LO1 **Prepare a worksheet and explain its usefulness.** A work sheet can be a useful tool in preparing and analyzing financial statements. It is helpful at the end of a period in preparing adjusting entries, an adjusted trial balance, and financial statements. A work sheet usually contains five pairs of columns: Unadjusted Trial Balance, Adjustments, Adjusted Trial Balance, Income Statement, and Balance Sheet & Statement of Owner's Equity.

LO2 **Explain why temporary accounts are closed each period.** Temporary accounts are closed at the end of each accounting period for two main reasons. First, the closing process updates the capital account to include the effects of all transactions and events recorded for the period. Second, it prepares revenue, expense, and withdrawals accounts for the next reporting period by giving them zero balances.

LO3 **Describe and prepare closing entries.** Closing entries involve four steps: (1) close credit balances in revenue accounts to Income Summary, (2) close debit balances in expense accounts to Income Summary, (3) close Income Summary to the capital account, and (4) close the withdrawals account to owner's capital.

LO4 **Explain and prepare a post-closing trial balance.** A post-closing trial balance is a list of permanent accounts and their balances after all closing entries have been journalized and posted. Its purpose is to verify that (1) total debits equal total credits for permanent accounts and (2) all temporary accounts have zero balances.

LO5 **Identify steps in the accounting cycle.** The accounting cycle consists of 9 steps: (1) analyze transactions, (2) journalize, (3) post, (4) prepare an unadjusted trial balance, (5) adjust accounts, (6) prepare an adjusted trial balance, (7) prepare statements, (8) close temporary accounts, and (9) prepare a post-closing trial balance.

1. Amounts in the Unadjusted Trial Balance columns are taken from current account balances in the ledger. The balances for new accounts expected to arise from adjusting entries can be left blank or set at zero.

2. A work sheet offers the advantage of listing on one page all necessary information to make adjusting entries.

3. The major steps in preparing closing entries are to close (1) credit balances in revenue accounts to Income Summary, (2) debit balances in expense accounts to Income Summary, (3) Income Summary to owner's capital, and (4) any withdrawals account to owner's capital.

4. Revenue and expense accounts are called *temporary* because they are opened and closed each period. The Income Summary and owner's withdrawals accounts are also temporary.

5. Permanent accounts make up the post-closing trial balance, which consist of asset, liability, and equity accounts.

Key Terms

Accounting cycle (p. 137) Recurring steps performed each accounting period, starting with analyzing transactions and continuing through the post-closing trial balance.

Closing entries (p. 134) Entries recorded at the end of each accounting period to transfer end-of-period balances in revenue, expense, and withdrawal accounts to the capital account.

Closing process (p. 133) Necessary end-of-period steps to prepare the accounts for recording the transactions of the next period.

Income Summary (p. 133) Temporary account used only in the closing process to which the balances of revenue and expense accounts are transferred; its balance is transferred to the capital account.

Permanent accounts (p. 133) Accounts that reflect activities related to one or more future periods; balance sheet accounts whose balances are not closed; also called *real accounts*.

Post-closing trial balance (p. 137) List of permanent accounts and their balances from the ledger after all closing entries are journalized and posted.

Pro forma financial statements (p. 133) Statements that show the effects of proposed transactions and events as if they had occurred.

Temporary accounts (p. 133) Accounts used to record revenues, expenses, and withdrawals; they are closed at the end of each period; also called *nominal accounts*.

Work sheet (p. 128) Spreadsheet used to draft an unadjusted trial balance, adjusting entries, adjusted trial balance, and financial statements.

Working papers (p. 128) Analyses and other internal documents prepared by accountants when organizing information for formal reports and financial statements.

Multiple Choice Quiz   Answers on p. 155   mhhe.com/wildCA2e

Additional Multiple Choice Quizzes are available at the book's Website.

1. G. Venda, owner of Venda Services, withdrew $25,000 from the business during the current year. The entry to close the withdrawals account at the end of the year is:

a.	G. Venda, Withdrawals	25,000	
	G. Venda, Capital		25,000
b.	Income Summary	25,000	
	G. Venda, Capital		25,000
c.	G. Venda, Withdrawals	25,000	
	Cash		25,000
d.	G. Venda, Capital	25,000	
	Salary Expense		25,000
e.	G. Venda, Capital	25,000	
	G. Venda, Withdrawals		25,000

2. The following information is available for the R. Kandamil Company before closing the accounts. After all of the closing entries are made, what will be the balance in the R. Kandamil, Capital account?

Total revenues	$300,000
Total expenses	195,000
R. Kandamil, Capital	100,000
R. Kandamil, Withdrawals	45,000

   a. $360,000
   b. $250,000

   c. $160,000
   d. $150,000
   e. $60,000

3. Which of the following is a permanent account?
   a. Income Summary
   b. Sales Revenue
   c. Utilities Expense
   d. Rent Expense
   e. Cash

4. A work sheet's Income Statement debit column totals $92,000 and its Income Statement credit column totals $86,700 at the end of the year. Based on this, the company made
   a. Net loss of $5,300 for the year
   b. Net income of $5,300 for the year
   c. Total revenues of $92,000 for the year
   d. Total expenses of $86,700 for the year

5. The temporary account used only in the closing process to hold the amounts of revenues and expenses before the net difference is added or subtracted from the owner's capital account is called the
   a. Closing account.
   b. Nominal account.
   c. Income Summary account.
   d. Balance Column account.
   e. Contra account.

Discussion Questions

1. What accounts are affected by closing entries? What accounts are not affected?

2. What two purposes are accomplished by recording closing entries?

3. What are the steps in recording closing entries?

4. What is the purpose of the Income Summary account?

5. Explain whether an error has occurred if a post-closing trial balance includes a Depreciation Expense account.

6. What tasks are aided by a work sheet?

7. Why are the debit and credit entries in the Adjustments columns of the work sheet identified with letters?

8. What are the overall benefits of a work sheet?

connect

Gloriosa Company began the current period with a $28,000 credit balance in the M. Gloriosa, Capital account. At the end of the period, the company's adjusted account balances include the following temporary accounts with normal balances.

Service fees earned	$45,000	Interest revenue	$6,000
Salaries expense	29,000	M. Gloriosa, Withdrawals	7,200
Depreciation expense	9,000	Utilities expense	3,000

After closing the revenue and expense accounts, what will be the balance of the Income Summary account? After all closing entries are journalized and posted, what will be the balance of the M. Gloriosa, Capital account?

QUICK STUDY

QS 6-1
Determining effects of closing entries **LO2 LO3**

List the following steps of the accounting cycle in their proper order.

a. Posting the journal entries.
b. Journalizing and posting adjusting entries.
c. Preparing the adjusted trial balance.
d. Journalizing and posting closing entries.
e. Analyzing transactions and events.
f. Preparing the financial statements.
g. Preparing the unadjusted trial balance.
h. Journalizing transactions and events.
i. Preparing the post-closing trial balance.

QS 6-2
Identifying the accounting cycle
LO5

The following information is taken from the work sheet for Warton Company as of December 31, 2010. Using this information, determine the amount for B. Warton, Capital that should be reported on its December 31, 2010, balance sheet.

	Income Statement		Balance Sheet and Statement of Owner's Equity	
	Dr.	Cr.	Dr.	Cr.
B. Warton, Capital				72,000
B. Warton, Withdrawals			39,000	
Totals	122,000	181,000		

QS 6-3
Interpreting a work sheet **LO1**

In preparing a work sheet, indicate the financial statement Debit column to which a normal balance in the following accounts should be extended. Use I for the Income Statement Debit column and B for the Balance Sheet and Statement of Owner's Equity Debit column.

_____ **a.** Equipment
_____ **b.** Owner, Withdrawals
_____ **c.** Prepaid rent
_____ **d.** Depreciation expense—Equipment
_____ **e.** Accounts receivable
_____ **f.** Insurance expense

QS 6-4
Applying a work sheet **LO1**

List the following steps in preparing a work sheet in their proper order by writing numbers 1–5 in the blank spaces provided.

a. _____ Total the statement columns, compute net income (loss), and complete work sheet.
b. _____ Extend adjusted balances to appropriate financial statement columns.
c. _____ Prepare an unadjusted trial balance on the work sheet.
d. _____ Prepare an adjusted trial balance on the work sheet.
e. _____ Enter adjustments data on the work sheet.

QS 6-5
Ordering work sheet steps **LO1**

The ledger of Claudell Company includes the following unadjusted normal balances: Prepaid Rent $1,000 and Wages Expense $25,000. Adjusting entries are required for (a) rent expense of $200 and (b) accrued wages expense of $700. Enter the unadjusted balances of Prepaid Rent and Wages Expense and the necessary adjustments on a partial work sheet and complete the work sheet for these accounts. Use Exhibit 6.1 as a guide.

QS 6-6
Preparing a partial work sheet
LO1

The ledger of Mai Company includes the following accounts with normal balances: D. Mai, Capital $9,000; D. Mai, Withdrawals $800; Services Revenue $13,000; Wages Expense $8,400; and Rent Expense $1,600. Prepare the necessary closing entries from the available information at December 31.

QS 6-7
Prepare closing entries from the ledger **LO3**

QS 6-8
Identify post-closing accounts
LO4

Identify the accounts listed in QS 6-7 that would be included in a post-closing trial balance.

EXERCISES

Exercise 6-1
Preparing and posting
closing entries   **LO3**

Use the year-end information from the following ledger accounts (assume that all accounts have normal balances) to prepare closing journal entries and then post those entries to the appropriate ledger accounts. Assume the closing entries are made on page 2 of a general journal.

General Ledger

M. Muncel, Capital — Acct. No. 301

Date	PR	Debit	Credit	Balance
Dec. 31				40,000

M. Muncel, Withdrawals — Acct. No. 302

Date	PR	Debit	Credit	Balance
Dec. 31				22,000

Services Revenue — Acct. No. 401

Date	PR	Debit	Credit	Balance
Dec. 31				76,000

Depreciation Expense — Acct. No. 603

Date	PR	Debit	Credit	Balance
Dec. 31				15,000

Salaries Expense — Acct. No. 622

Date	PR	Debit	Credit	Balance
Dec. 31				20,000

Insurance Expense — Acct. No. 637

Date	PR	Debit	Credit	Balance
Dec. 31				4,400

Rent Expense — Acct. No. 640

Date	PR	Debit	Credit	Balance
Dec. 31				8,400

Income Summary — Acct. No. 901

Date	PR	Debit	Credit	Balance

Check M. Muncel, Capital (ending balance), $46,200

Exercise 6-2
Preparing closing entries and a
post-closing trial balance
LO3   LO4

The adjusted trial balance for Salonika Marketing Co. follows. Complete the four right-most columns of the table by first entering information for the four closing entries (keyed *1* through *4*) and second by completing the post-closing trial balance.

No.	Account Title	Adjusted Trial Balance Dr.	Cr.	Closing Entry Information Dr.	Cr.	Post-Closing Trial Balance Dr.	Cr.
101	Cash	$ 9,200					
106	Accounts receivable	25,000					
153	Equipment	42,000					
154	Accumulated depreciation—Equipment		$ 17,500				
193	Franchise	31,000					
201	Accounts payable		15,000				
209	Salaries payable		4,200				
233	Unearned fees		3,600				
301	E. Salonika, Capital		68,500				
302	E. Salonika, Withdrawals	15,400					
401	Marketing fees earned		80,000				
611	Depreciation expense—Equipment	12,000					
622	Salaries expense	32,500					
640	Rent expense	13,000					
677	Miscellaneous expenses	8,700					
901	Income summary						
	Totals	$188,800	$188,800				

The following adjusted trial balance contains the accounts and balances of Cruz Company as of December 31, 2010, the end of its fiscal year. (1) Prepare the December 31, 2010, closing entries for Cruz Company. (2) Prepare the December 31, 2010, post-closing trial balance for Cruz Company.

Exercise 6–3

Preparing closing entries and a post-closing trial balance

LO2   LO3   LO4

No.	Account Title	Debit	Credit
101	Cash	$19,000	
126	Supplies	13,000	
128	Prepaid insurance	3,000	
167	Equipment	24,000	
168	Accumulated depreciation—Equipment		$ 7,500
301	T. Cruz, Capital		47,600
302	T. Cruz, Withdrawals	7,000	
404	Services revenue		44,000
612	Depreciation expense—Equipment	3,000	
622	Salaries expense	22,000	
637	Insurance expense	2,500	
640	Rent expense	3,400	
652	Supplies expense	2,200	
	Totals	$99,100	$99,100

Check   (2) T. Cruz, Capital (ending), $51,500; Total debits, $59,000

Use the following December 31, 2010, adjusted trial balance of Wilson Trucking Company to prepare the (1) income statement, (2) statement of owner's equity, and (3) balance sheet for the year ended December 31, 2010. The K. Wilson, Capital account balance is $175,000 at December 31, 2009.

Exercise 6–4

Preparing financial statements

LO1

Account Title	Debit	Credit
Cash	$ 8,000	
Accounts receivable	17,500	
Office supplies	3,000	
Trucks	172,000	
Accumulated depreciation—Trucks		$ 36,000
Land	85,000	
Accounts payable		65,000
Wages payable		4,000
K. Wilson, Capital		175,000
K. Wilson, Withdrawals	20,000	
Trucking fees earned		130,000
Depreciation expense—Trucks	23,500	
Salaries expense	61,000	
Office supplies expense	8,000	
Repairs expense—Trucks	12,000	
Totals	$410,000	$410,000

These 14 accounts are from the Adjusted Trial Balance columns of a company's 10-column work sheet. In the blank space beside each account, write the letter of the appropriate financial statement column (A, B, C, or D) to which a normal account balance is extended on the work sheet.

A. Debit column for the Income Statement columns.

B. Credit column for the Income Statement columns.

C. Debit column for the Balance Sheet and Statement of Owner's Equity columns.

D. Credit column for the Balance Sheet and Statement of Owner's Equity columns.

Exercise 6–5

Extending adjusted account balances on a work sheet

LO1

_____	**1.** Unearned Revenue		_____	**8.** Accounts Receivable	
_____	**2.** Machinery		_____	**9.** Accumulated Depreciation	
_____	**3.** Owner, Withdrawals		_____	**10.** Office Supplies	
_____	**4.** Depreciation Expense		_____	**11.** Insurance Expense	
_____	**5.** Accounts Payable		_____	**12.** Cash	
_____	**6.** Service Fees Revenue		_____	**13.** Rent Expense	
_____	**7.** Owner, Capital		_____	**14.** Wages Payable	

Exercise 6-6

Extending accounts in a work sheet   **LO1**

The Adjusted Trial Balance columns of a 10-column work sheet for Planta Company follow. Complete the work sheet by extending the account balances into the appropriate financial statement columns and by entering the amount of net income for the reporting period.

No.	Account Title	Debit	Credit
101	Cash	$ 7,000	
106	Accounts receivable	27,200	
153	Trucks	42,000	
154	Accumulated depreciation—Trucks		$ 17,500
183	Land	32,000	
201	Accounts payable		15,000
209	Salaries payable		4,200
233	Unearned fees		3,600
301	F. Planta, Capital		65,500
302	F. Planta, Withdrawals	15,400	
401	Plumbing fees earned		84,000
611	Depreciation expense—Trucks	6,500	
622	Salaries expense	38,000	
640	Rent expense	13,000	
677	Miscellaneous expenses	8,700	
	Totals	$189,800	$189,800

Check   Net income, $17,800

Exercise 6-7

Completing the income statement columns and preparing closing entries   **LO1**   **LO3**

These partially completed Income Statement columns from a 10-column work sheet are for Brown's Bike Rental Company. (1) Use the information to determine the amount that should be entered on the net income line of the work sheet. (2) Prepare the company's closing entries. The owner, H. Brown, did not make any withdrawals this period.

Account Title	Debit	Credit
Rent earned		120,000
Salaries expense	46,300	
Insurance expense	7,400	
Office supplies expense	16,000	
Bike repair expense	4,200	
Depreciation expense—Bikes	20,500	
Totals		
Net income		
Totals		

Check   Net income, $25,600

Exercise 6-8

Preparing a work sheet and recording closing entries

LO1   **LO3**

The following unadjusted trial balance contains the accounts and balances of Dylan Delivery Company as of December 31, 2010, its first year of operations.

(1) Use the following information about the company's adjustments to complete a 10-column work sheet for Dylan Delivery Company.

a. Unrecorded depreciation on the trucks at the end of the year is $40,000.

b. An additional $1,000 of salaries must be accrued at year-end.

c. The cost of unused office supplies still available at year-end is $2,000.

(2) Prepare the year-end closing entries for Dylan Delivery Company, and determine the capital amount to be reported on its year-end balance sheet.

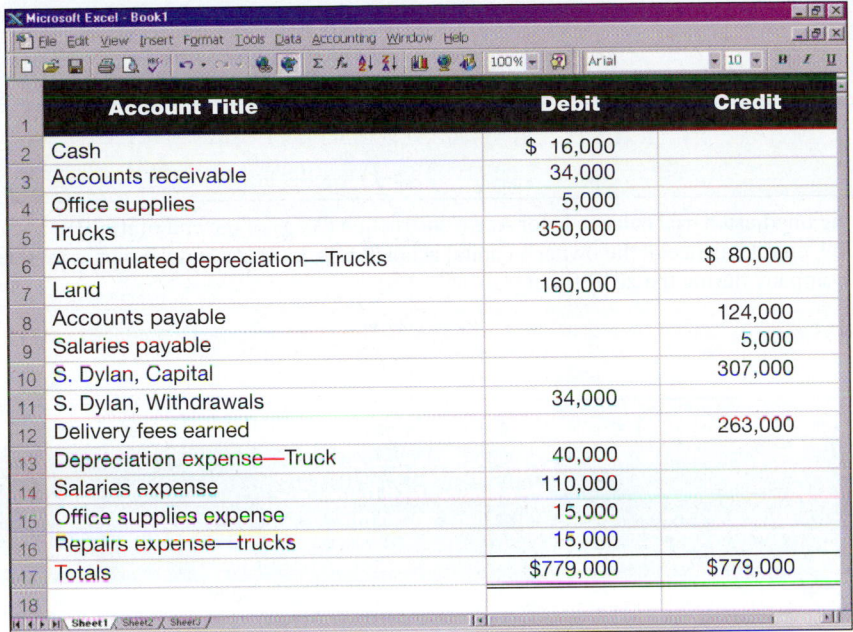

Account Title	Debit	Credit
Cash	$ 16,000	
Accounts receivable	34,000	
Office supplies	5,000	
Trucks	350,000	
Accumulated depreciation—Trucks		$ 80,000
Land	160,000	
Accounts payable		124,000
Salaries payable		5,000
S. Dylan, Capital		307,000
S. Dylan, Withdrawals	34,000	
Delivery fees earned		263,000
Depreciation expense—Truck	40,000	
Salaries expense	110,000	
Office supplies expense	15,000	
Repairs expense—trucks	15,000	
Totals	$779,000	$779,000

Check Adj. trial balance totals, $820,000; Net income, $39,000

connect

The adjusted trial balance of Karise Repairs on December 31, 2010, follows.

	KARISE REPAIRS		
	Adjusted Trial Balance		
	December 31, 2010		
No.	**Account Title**	**Debit**	**Credit**
101	Cash	$ 14,000	
124	Office supplies	1,300	
128	Prepaid insurance	2,050	
167	Equipment	50,000	
168	Accumulated depreciation—Equipment		$ 5,000
201	Accounts payable		14,000
210	Wages payable		600
301	C. Karise, Capital		33,000
302	C. Karise, Withdrawal	16,000	
401	Repair fees earned		90,950
612	Depreciation expense—Equipment	5,000	
623	Wages expense	37,500	
637	Insurance expense	800	
640	Rent expense	10,600	
650	Office supplies expense	3,600	
690	Utilities expense	2,700	
	Totals	$143,550	$143,550

PROBLEM SET A

Problem 6-1A
Preparing trial balances, closing entries, and financial statements
LO1   LO3   LO4   LO5

mhhe.com/wildCA2e

Required

1. Prepare an income statement and a statement of owner's equity for the year 2010, and a balance sheet at December 31, 2010. There are no owner investments in 2010.

2. Prepare closing journal entries.

3. Prepare a post-closing trial balance.

Problem 6-2A

Preparing a work sheet, adjusting and closing entries, and financial statements   **L01   L03**

The following unadjusted trial balance is for Ace Construction Co. as of the end of its 2010 fiscal year. The June 30, 2009, credit balance of the owner's capital account was $53,660, and the owner invested $35,000 cash in the company during the 2010 fiscal year.

File Edit View Insert Format Tools Data Window Help			
ACE CONSTRUCTION CO. **Unadjusted Trial Balance** **June 30, 2010**			
No.	**Account Title**	**Debit**	**Credit**
101	Cash	$ 18,500	
126	Supplies	9,900	
128	Prepaid insurance	7,200	
167	Equipment	132,000	
168	Accumulated depreciation—Equipment		$ 26,250
201	Accounts payable		31,800
208	Rent payable		0
210	Wages payable		0
301	V. Ace, Capital		88,660
302	V. Ace, Withdrawals	33,000	
401	Construction fees earned		132,100
612	Depreciation expense—Equipment	0	
623	Wages expense	49,610	
637	Insurance expense	0	
640	Rent expense	12,000	
652	Supplies expense	0	
684	Repairs expense	10,710	
690	Utilities expense	5,890	
	Totals	$ 278,810	$ 278,810

Required

1. Using Exhibit 6.1 as a guide, prepare a 10-column work sheet for fiscal year 2010, starting with the unadjusted trial balance and including adjustments based on these additional facts.

   a. The supplies available at the end of fiscal year 2010 had a cost of $3,300.

   b. The cost of expired insurance for the fiscal year is $3,800.

   c. Annual depreciation on equipment is $8,400.

   d. The June utilities expense of $650 is not included in the unadjusted trial balance because the bill arrived after the trial balance was prepared. The $650 amount owed needs to be recorded.

   e. The company's employees have earned $1,800 of accrued wages at fiscal year-end.

   f. The rent expense incurred and not yet paid or recorded at fiscal year-end is $500.

2. Use the work sheet to enter the adjusting entries, then journalize the adjusting entries.

3. Prepare an adjusted trial balance.

4. Extend the adjusted trial balance amounts to the proper financial statement column of the work sheet.

5. Prepare closing entries.

6. Prepare the income statement and the statement of owner's equity for the year ended June 30 and the balance sheet at June 30, 2010.

Check   (3) Total assets, $122,550; Total liabilities, $34,750; Net income, $32,140

Holt Company's adjusted trial balance on December 31, 2010, follows.

HOLT COMPANY
Adjusted Trial Balance
December 31, 2010

No.	Account Title	Debit	Credit
101	Cash	$ 14,450	
125	Store supplies	5,140	
128	Prepaid insurance	1,200	
167	Equipment	31,000	
168	Accumulated depreciation—Equipment		$8,000
201	Accounts payable		1,500
210	Wages payable		2,700
301	P. Holt, Capital		35,650
302	P. Holt, Withdrawals	15,000	
401	Repair fees earned		54,700
612	Depreciation expense—Equipment	2,000	
623	Wages expense	26,400	
637	Insurance expense	600	
640	Rent expense	3,600	
651	Store supplies expense	1,200	
690	Utilities expense	1,960	
	Totals	$102,550	$102,550

PROBLEM SET B

Problem 6-1B
Preparing trial balances, closing entries, and financial statements
L01   L03   L04   L05

Required

1. Prepare an income statement and a statement of owner's equity for the year 2010, and a balance sheet at December 31, 2010. There are no owner investments in 2010.

2. Prepare closing journal entries.

3. Prepare a post-closing trial balance.

Check   (1) Ending capital balance, $39,590

(3) P-C trial balance totals, $51,790

The following unadjusted trial balance is for Power Demolition Company as of the end of its April 30, 2010, fiscal year. The April 30, 2009, credit balance of the owner's capital account was $46,900, and the owner invested $40,000 cash in the company during the 2010 fiscal year.

Problem 6-2B
Preparing a work sheet, adjusting and closing entries, and financial statements   **L01   L03**

	No.	Account Title	Debit	Credit
3	101	Cash	$ 7,000	
4	126	Supplies	16,000	
5	128	Prepaid insurance	12,600	
6	167	Equipment	200,000	
7	168	Accumulated depreciation—Equipment		$ 14,000
8	201	Accounts payable		36,800
9	208	Rent payable		0
10	210	Wages payable		0
11	301	J. Bonair, Capital		86,900
12	302	J. Bonair, Withdrawals	12,000	
13	401	Demolition fees earned		187,000
14	612	Depreciation expense—Equipment	0	
15	623	Wages expense	44,700	
16	637	Insurance expense	0	
17	640	Rent expense	13,200	
18	652	Supplies expense	0	
19	684	Repairs expense	14,400	
20	690	Utilities expense	4,800	
21		Totals	$ 324,700	$ 324,700

POWER DEMOLITION COMPANY
Unadjusted Trial Balance
April 30, 2010

Required

1. Using Exhibit 6.1 as a guide, prepare a 10-column work sheet for fiscal year 2010, starting with the unadjusted trial balance and including adjustments based on these additional facts.

  a. The supplies available at the end of fiscal year 2010 had a cost of $7,900.

  b. The cost of expired insurance for the fiscal year is $10,600.

  c. Annual depreciation on equipment is $7,000.

  d. The April utilities expense of $800 is not included in the unadjusted trial balance because the bill arrived after the trial balance was prepared. The $800 amount owed needs to be recorded.

  e. The company's employees have earned $2,000 of accrued wages at fiscal year-end.

  f. The rent expense incurred and not yet paid or recorded at fiscal year-end is $3,000.

2. Enter the adjusting entry information in the work sheet; then journalize adjusting entries.

3. Prepare an adjusted trial balance.

4. Extend the adjusted trial balance amounts to the proper financial statement column of the work sheet.

5. Prepare closing entries.

6. Prepare the income statement and the statement of owner's equity for the year ended April 30, and the balance sheet at April 30, 2010.

Check (3) Total assets, $195,900; Total liabilities, $42,600; Net income, $78,400

PRACTICE SET 1

Adventure Travel
Applying the accounting cycle
LO3   LO4   LO5

mhhe.com/wildCA2e

On April 1, 2010, Jiro Nozomi created a new travel agency, Adventure Travel. The following transactions occurred during the company's first month.

April	1	Nozomi invested $30,000 cash and computer equipment worth $20,000 in the business.
	2	Rented furnished office space by paying $1,800 cash for the first month's (April) rent. (Hint: Adventure Travel debited Rent Expense for this payment.)
	3	Purchased $1,000 of office supplies for cash.
	10	Paid $2,400 cash for the premium on a 12-month insurance policy. Coverage begins on April 11.
	14	Paid $1,600 cash for two weeks' salaries earned by employees.
	24	Collected $8,000 cash on commissions from airlines on tickets obtained for customers.
	26	Paid another $1,600 cash for two weeks' salaries earned by employees.

27   Paid $350 cash for minor repairs to the company's computer.
27   Paid $750 cash for this month's telephone bill.
28   Nozomi withdrew $1,500 cash for personal use.

The company's chart of accounts follows:

101	Cash	405	Commissions Earned
106	Accounts Receivable	612	Depreciation Expense—Computer Equip.
124	Office Supplies	622	Salaries Expense
128	Prepaid Insurance	637	Insurance Expense
167	Computer Equipment	640	Rent Expense
168	Accumulated Depreciation—Computer Equip.	650	Office Supplies Expense
209	Salaries Payable	684	Repairs Expense
301	J. Nozomi, Capital	688	Telephone Expense
302	J. Nozomi, Withdrawals	901	Income Summary

Required

1. Use the balance column format to set up each ledger account listed in the chart of accounts.

2. Prepare journal entries to record the transactions for April and post them to the ledger accounts.

3. Prepare an unadjusted trial balance as of April 30.

4. Use the following information to journalize and post adjusting entries for the month:

   a. Two-thirds of one month's insurance coverage has expired. (Round your answer to the nearest dollar).

   b. At the end of the month, $600 of office supplies are still available.

   c. This month's depreciation on the computer equipment is $500.

   d. Employees earned $420 of unpaid and unrecorded salaries as of month-end.

5. Prepare the income statement and the statement of owner's equity for the month of April and the balance sheet at April 30, 2010.

6. Prepare journal entries to close the temporary accounts and post these entries to the ledger.

7. Prepare a post-closing trial balance.

Check (3) Unadj. trial balance totals, $58,000

(4a) Dr. Insurance Expense, $133

(5) Net income, $447; J. Nozomi, Capital (4/30/2010), $48,947, Total assets, $49,367

(7) P-C trial balance totals, $49,867

On July 1, 2010, Lula Plume created a new self-storage business, Safe Storage Co. The following transactions occurred during the company's first month.

July 1   Plume invested $30,000 cash and buildings worth $150,000 in the business.
      2   Rented equipment by paying $2,000 cash for the first month's (July) rent. (Hint: Safe Storage debited Rent Expense for this payment.)
      5   Purchased $2,400 of office supplies for cash.
     10   Paid $7,200 cash for the premium on a 12-month insurance policy. Coverage begins on July 11.
     14   Paid an employee $1,000 cash for two weeks' salary earned.
     24   Collected $9,800 cash for storage fees from customers.
     26   Paid another $1,000 cash for two weeks' salary earned by an employee.
     27   Paid $950 cash for minor repairs to a leaking roof.
     27   Paid $400 cash for this month's telephone bill.
     28   Plume withdrew $2,000 cash for personal use.

The company's chart of accounts follows:

101	Cash	401	Storage Fees Earned
106	Accounts Receivable	606	Depreciation Expense—Buildings
124	Office Supplies	622	Salaries Expense
128	Prepaid Insurance	637	Insurance Expense
173	Buildings	640	Rent Expense
174	Accumulated Depreciation—Buildings	650	Office Supplies Expense
209	Salaries Payable	684	Repairs Expense
301	L. Plume, Capital	688	Telephone Expense
302	L. Plume, Withdrawals	901	Income Summary

PRACTICE SET 2

Safe Storage Co.

Applying the accounting cycle

LO3   LO4   LO5

Required

1. Use the balance column format to set up each ledger account listed in the chart of accounts.
2. Prepare journal entries to record the transactions for July and post them to the ledger accounts.
3. Prepare an unadjusted trial balance as of July 31.
4. Use the following information to journalize and post adjusting entries for the month:
    a. Two-thirds of one month's insurance coverage has expired. (Round your answer to the nearest dollar).
    b. At the end of the month, $1,525 of office supplies are still available.
    c. This month's depreciation on the buildings is $1,500.
    d. An employee earned $100 of unpaid and unrecorded salary as of month-end.
5. Prepare the income statement and the statement of owner's equity for the month of July and the balance sheet at July 31, 2010.
6. Prepare journal entries to close the temporary accounts and post these entries to the ledger.
7. Prepare a post-closing trial balance.

Check (3) Unadj. trial balance totals, $189,800

(4a) Dr. Insurance Expense, $400

(5) Net income, $1,575; L. Plume, Capital (7/31/2010), $179,575; Total assets, $179,675

(7) P-C trial balance totals, $181,175

SERIAL PROBLEM

Success Systems

LO3 LO4

(This serial problem began in Chapter 1 and continues through most of the book. If previous chapter segments were not completed, the serial problem can begin at this point. It is helpful, but not necessary, that you use the Working Papers that accompany the book.)

SP 6 The December 31, 2010, adjusted trial balance of Success Systems (reflecting its transactions from October through December of 2010) follows.

No.	Account Title	Debit	Credit
101	Cash	$ 80,260	
106	Accounts receivable	5,800	
126	Computer supplies	775	
128	Prepaid insurance	1,800	
131	Prepaid rent	875	
163	Office equipment	10,000	
164	Accumulated depreciation—Office equipment		$ 625
167	Computer equipment	25,000	
168	Accumulated depreciation—Computer equipment		1,250
201	Accounts payable		2,100
210	Wages payable		600
236	Unearned computer services revenue		2,500
301	A. Lopez, Capital		110,000
302	A. Lopez, Withdrawals	8,500	
403	Computer services revenue		36,170
612	Depreciation expense—Office equipment	625	
613	Depreciation expense—Computer equipment	1,250	
623	Wages expense	4,650	
637	Insurance expense	600	
640	Rent expense	2,625	
652	Computer supplies expense	4,675	
655	Advertising expense	2,990	
676	Mileage expense	1,120	
677	Miscellaneous expenses	300	
684	Repairs expense—Computer	1,400	
901	Income summary		0
	Totals	$153,245	$153,245

Required

1. Record and post the necessary closing entries for Success Systems.

2. Prepare a post-closing trial balance as of December 31, 2010.

Check   Post-closing trial balance totals, $124,510

BTN 6–1   Refer to **Best Buy**'s financial statements in Appendix A to answer the following.

REPORTING IN ACTION

LO2   LO3

Required

1. For the fiscal year ended March 1, 2008, what amount is credited to Income Summary to summarize its revenues earned?

2. For the fiscal year ended March 1, 2008, what is the balance of its Income Summary account before it is closed?

BTN 6–2   On January 20, 2011, Tamira Nelson, the accountant for Picton Enterprises, is feeling pressure to complete the annual financial statements. The company president has said he needs up-to-date financial statements to share with the bank on January 21 at a dinner meeting that has been called to discuss Picton's obtaining loan financing for a special building project. Tamira knows that she will not be able to gather all the needed information in the next 24 hours to prepare the entire set of adjusting entries that must be posted before the financial statements accurately portray the company's performance and financial position for the fiscal period ended December 31, 2010. Tamira ultimately decides to estimate several expense accruals at the last minute. When deciding on estimates for the expenses, she uses low estimates because she does not want to make the financial statements look worse than they are. Tamira finishes the financial statements before the deadline and gives them to the president without mentioning that several account balances are estimates that she provided.

ETHICS CHALLENGE

LO5

Required

1. Identify several courses of action that Tamira could have taken instead of the one she took.

2. If you were in Tamira's situation, what would you have done? Briefly justify your response.

BTN 6–3   Assume that one of your classmates states that a company's books should be ongoing and therefore not closed until that business is terminated. Write a one-half-page memo to this classmate explaining the concept of the closing process by drawing analogies between (1) a scoreboard for an athletic event and the revenue and expense accounts of a business or (2) a sports team's record book and the capital account. (*Hint:* Think about what would happen if the scoreboard is not cleared before the start of a new game.)

WORKPLACE COMMUNICATION

LO2   LO3

BTN 6–4   Go to the American institute of Professional Bookkeepers Website, located at <u>www.aipb.org</u>. Click on "certification" and then on "Certified Bookkeeper Survey." Using information from this survey, answer the following questions:

TAKING IT TO THE NET

1. What are the requirements for a bookkeeper to become a Certified Bookkeeper?

2. What are the six primary topics covered on the Certified Bookkeeper examination?

3. What percentage of Certified Bookkeepers recommend certification to other bookkeepers?

BTN 6-5   The unadjusted trial balance and information for the accounting adjustments of Noseworthy Investigators follow. Form teams of four members each. Then, within each four-person team, form two-person groups. Each group involved in this project is to assume two of the four responsibilities listed. After completing each of these responsibilities, the team should work together to prove the accounting equation.

Unadjusted Trial Balance		
Account Title	**Debit**	**Credit**
Cash	$16,000	
Supplies	12,000	
Prepaid insurance	3,000	
Equipment	25,000	
Accumulated depreciation—Equipment		$ 7,000
Accounts payable		3,000
D. Noseworthy, Capital		34,000
D. Noseworthy, Withdrawals	6,000	
Investigation fees earned		33,000
Rent expense	15,000	
Totals	$77,000	$77,000

Additional Year-End Information

a. Insurance that expired in the current period amounts to $2,200.

b. Equipment depreciation for the period is $4,000.

c. Unused supplies total $5,000 at period-end.

Responsibilities

Two team members work together to complete the following tasks:

1. Determine the necessary adjusting journal entries.

2. Use this adjusting information to determine the adjusted balances to extend to the balance sheet columns of a work sheet for Noseworthy. Also determine total assets and total liabilities.

Two other team members work together to complete the following tasks:

3. Using the adjusting information obtained from the other two team members, determine the adjusted balances of Noseworthy's revenue and expense accounts.

4. Prepare closing journal entries. Provide the other team members with the ending capital account balance.

The entire team should then prove the accounting equation using post-closing balances. If the equation does not balance, work as a team to resolve the error. The team's goal is to complete the task as quickly and accurately as possible.

BTN 6-6   Review the chapter's opening feature on Kathryn Kerrigan and her shoe business.

1. Why is it important for Kathryn Kerrigan to match costs and revenues in a specific time period? How do closing entries help in this regard?

2. What objectives are met when Kathryn Kerrigan applies closing procedures at the end of each accounting period?

BTN 6-7   You make a printout of the electronic work sheet used to prepare financial statements. There is no depreciation adjustment, yet you own a large amount of equipment. Does the absence of depreciation adjustment concern you?

YOU CALL IT

1. e

4. a

2. c

5. c

3. e

ANSWERS TO MULTIPLE CHOICE QUIZ

A Look Back

Chapter 6 explained the final steps in the accounting cycle. We described the closing process and showed how a work sheet aids in preparing financial statements.

A Look at This Chapter

This chapter extends our study of accounting to fraud and internal control. We explain workplace fraud and describe internal control procedures that can help prevent it.

A Look Ahead

Chapter 8 focuses on cash and control of cash. We discuss control features of banking activities and petty cash systems.

Chapter 7

Fraud, Ethics, and Controls

Learning Objectives

LO 1 Define workplace fraud and explain the four elements common to all fraud schemes.

LO 2 Describe the three major types of workplace fraud.

LO 3 Define internal control and identify its purpose and principles.

LO 4 Explain how technology impacts an internal control system.

LO 5 Describe the limitations of internal control.

LO 6 Explain provisions of the Sarbanes-Oxley Act that are designed to detect and curtail fraud.

LO 7 *Appendix 7A*—Describe the use of documentation and verification to control cash disbursements.

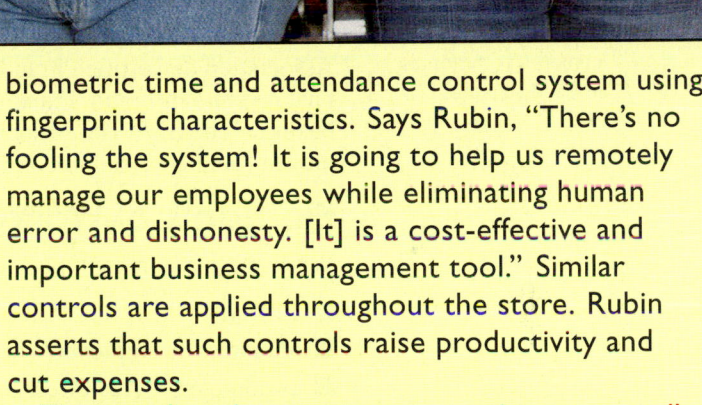

"It's a creative outlet for me . . . it doesn't feel like work"—Dylan Lauren (Jeff Rubin on left)

Sweet Success

NEW YORK—A 10-foot chocolate bunny named Jeffrey greets you as you enter the store—that should be warning enough! This elite designer candy store, christened **Dylan's Candy Bar (DylansCandyBar.com),** is the brainchild of co-founders Dylan Lauren and Jeff Rubin (the bunny is named for him). This sweet-lovers heaven offers more than 5,000 different choices of sweets from all over the world. It has become a hip hang-out for locals and tourists—and it has made candy cool. Says Lauren, "Park Avenue women come in, and the first thing they ask for is Gummi bears. They love that it's very childhood, nostalgic."

Although marketing is an important part of its success, Lauren and Rubin's management of internal controls and cash is equally impressive. Several control procedures monitor its business activities and safeguard its assets. An example is the biometric time and attendance control system using fingerprint characteristics. Says Rubin, "There's no fooling the system! It is going to help us remotely manage our employees while eliminating human error and dishonesty. [It] is a cost-effective and important business management tool." Similar controls are applied throughout the store. Rubin asserts that such controls raise productivity and cut expenses.

The store's cash management practices are equally impressive, including controls over cash receipts and payments. Internal controls are crucial when on a busy day its store brings in more than a thousand customers, and their cash. Moreover, expansion is already underway in Orlando and Houston. Through it all, Lauren says it is "totally fun."

[Sources: *Dylan's Candy Bar Website,* January 2009; *Entrepreneur,* June 2005; *USA Today,* October 26, 2001; *Duke Magazine,* January–February 2004; *CNN.com,* November 2005; *CandyAddict.com,* June 2007]

We all are aware of reports and experiences of theft and fraud. These affect us in several ways: We lock doors, chain bikes, review sales receipts, and buy alarm systems. A company also takes actions to safeguard, control, and manage what it owns. Experience tells us that small companies are most vulnerable, usually due to weak internal controls. This chapter discusses workplace fraud. Management must set up policies and procedures to safeguard a company's assets. To do so, management *and* employees must understand and apply principles of internal control. This chapter describes these principles and how to apply them.

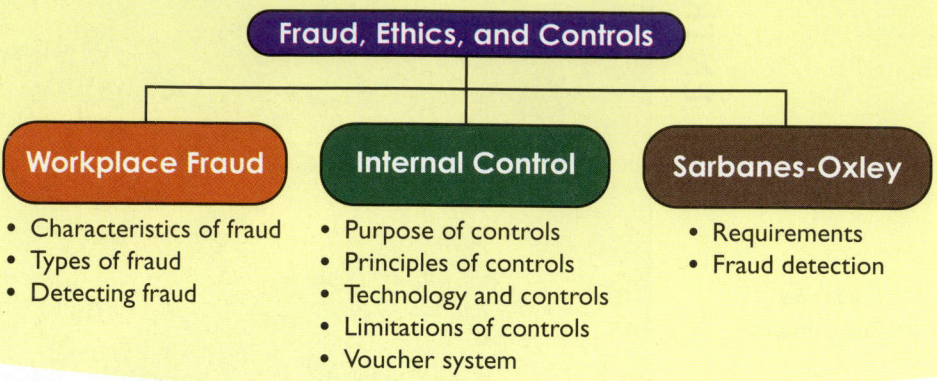

Workplace Fraud

Workplace fraud involves the use of one's job for personal gain, through the deliberate misuse of the employer's assets. Such fraud includes, for example, theft of the employer's cash or other assets, overstating reimbursable expenses, payroll schemes, and financial statement frauds. Workplace fraud affects all business and it is costly: A 2008 *Report to the Nation* from the Association of Certified Fraud Examiners estimates the average U.S. business loses 7% of its annual revenues to fraud. Fraud is particularly costly for small businesses because it can lead to the business's demise. The Association of Certified Fraud Examiners (**acfe.com**) estimates that employee fraud costs small companies more than $100,000 per incident.

LO1 Define workplace fraud and explain the four elements common to all fraud schemes.

Elements of Workplace Fraud Schemes

While there are many types of fraud schemes, all workplace fraud

- ◼ Is secret.
- ◼ Violates the employee's duties to his employer.
- ◼ Is done to provide direct or indirect benefit to the employee.
- ◼ Costs the employer money.

For example, in a billing fraud, an employee sets up a bogus supplier. The employee then secretly prepares bills from the supplier and pays these bills from the employer's checking account. The employee cashes the checks sent to the bogus supplier and uses them for his or her own personal benefit. Later in this chapter we discuss how a system of internal control can help the employer prevent this and other types of fraud schemes.

Major Types of Workplace Fraud

LO2 Describe the three major types of workplace fraud.

According to the Association of Certified Fraud Examiners' *2008 Report to the Nation*, most workplace frauds fall into three broad types:

1. **Asset misappropriation.** This type involves the theft or misuse of the employer's resources. For example, the employee might steal cash or inventory, disburse payroll checks to bogus employees, or pay invoices to phony suppliers. Other common schemes include accepting cash payments from customers but not recording sales, filing false expense reports, and claiming overtime for hours not worked.

2. **Corruption.** These schemes involve an employee's wrongful use of influence in a business transaction with the result that the employee receives financial gain at the expense of

the employer. Bribery is often part of corruption schemes; for example, an employee might bribe another party to take part in a fraudulent invoice scheme.

3. **Fraudulent financial statements.** Falsification of the employer's financial statements commonly includes recording fictitious revenues, overstating certain asset values, and hiding certain liabilities or expenses.

Exhibit 7.1 shows the percentage of reported frauds by type and their related losses. The percentages sum to more than 100 percent as a fraud occurrence might involve more than one type. Asset misappropriation is the most commonly reported fraud, but fraudulent financial statements cause the greatest losses in dollars.

Reported Frauds	Percentage of Reported Frauds	Loss per Occurrence
Asset misappropriation	88.7%	$ 150,000
Corruption	27.4%	$ 375,000
Fraudulent financial statements	10.3%	$2,000,000

Percentages in this chart sum to more than 100% as several cases involve more than one type of fraud.

Detecting Fraud   Exhibit 7.2 provides information on the percentage of fraud cases detected by various methods. Tips, often received through anonymous hotlines, are the most common way frauds are detected. Most of these tips come from employees of the defrauded business, suggesting employee education might be useful in fighting fraud. Customers and suppliers are also good sources of tips. Many frauds are detected by internal controls and internal audits, which we discuss in detail in this chapter. About 9 percent of frauds are detected by external auditors, typically in the course of their testing the firm's internal controls and other processes. Still, many frauds are detected simply by accident.

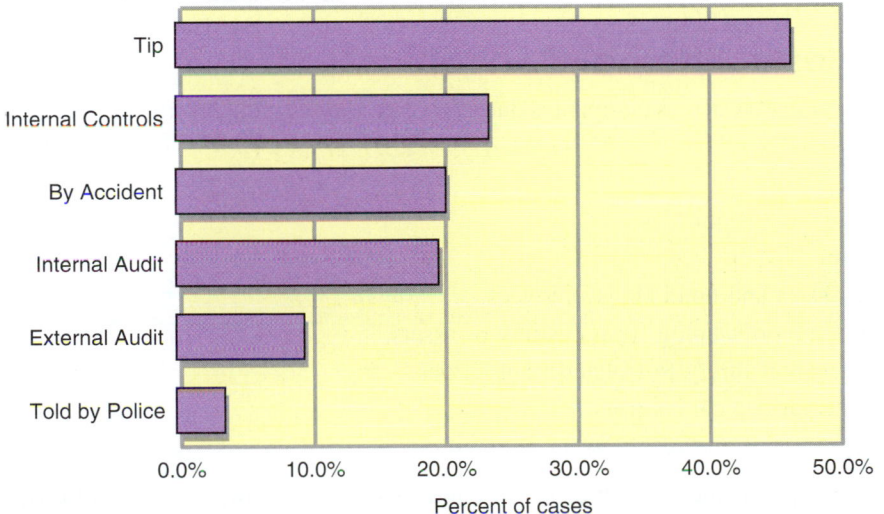

People committing fraud ("fraudsters") often leave behavioral clues. Knowledge of these clues can help employees identify suspicious behaviors that could indicate fraud. Common examples of red flags exhibited by fraudsters include:

■ Employee paid an average salary buys fancy cars, clothes, boats, or homes.

■ Employee is facing serious financial hardships, such as medical bills, loan or credit card payments.

■ Employee won't share duties or take vacations—might indicate fear of fraud being uncovered.

■ Employee is unusually irritable or defensive.

■ Employee is too close with suppliers—might indicate they are a fraud "team."

Internal Control

This section describes internal control. We also discuss how technology impacts internal control and the limitations of control procedures.

Purpose of Internal Control

LO3 Define internal control and identify its purpose and principles.

Managers (or owners) of small businesses often control the entire operation. These managers usually purchase all assets, hire and manage employees, negotiate all contracts, and sign all checks. They know from personal contact and observation whether the business is actually receiving the assets and services paid for. Most companies, however, cannot maintain this close personal supervision. They must use formal procedures to control business activities.

Managers use an internal control system to monitor and control business activities. An **internal control system** is the policies and procedures managers use to:

- Protect assets.
- Ensure reliable accounting.
- Promote efficient operations.
- Urge adherence to company policies.

Managers like internal control systems because they can prevent avoidable losses, help managers plan operations, and monitor company and employee performance. Internal controls do not provide guarantees against loss, but they lower the company's risk of loss.

IN THE NEWS

What's the Password?   Good internal control prevents unauthorized access to assets and accounting records by requiring passwords. It takes a password, for instance, to boot up most office PCs, log onto a network, and access voice mail, e-mail, and most online services.

Principles of Internal Control

Internal controls vary across companies due to factors like the nature of the business and its size. Certain fundamental internal control principles apply to all companies. The **principles of internal control** are to

1. Establish responsibilities.
2. Maintain adequate records.
3. Insure assets and bond key employees.
4. Separate recordkeeping from custody of assets.
5. Divide responsibility for related transactions.
6. Apply technological controls.
7. Perform regular and independent reviews.

This section explains these seven principles and describes how internal control procedures reduce the risk of workplace fraud and theft. These procedures also increase the reliability and accuracy of accounting records.

Establish Responsibilities   Responsibility for a task should be clearly established and assigned to one person. When a problem occurs in a company where responsibility is not identified, determining who is at fault is difficult. For instance, if two salesclerks share the same cash register and there is a cash shortage, neither clerk can be held accountable. To prevent this problem, one clerk might be given responsibility for handling all cash sales. Alternately, a company can use a register with separate cash drawers for each clerk. Most of us have waited at a retail counter during a shift change while employees swap cash drawers. Many companies have a mandatory vacation policy for employees who handle cash. When another employee must cover for the one on vacation, it is more difficult to hide cash frauds.

Maintain Adequate Records Good recordkeeping helps protect assets and ensures that employees use prescribed procedures. Reliable records provide information that managers use to monitor company activities. When detailed records are kept, for instance, equipment is unlikely to be lost or stolen without detection. Similarly, transactions are less likely to be entered in wrong accounts if a chart of accounts is set up and carefully used. Preprinted forms and internal documents are also useful. When sales slips are properly designed, for instance, sales personnel can record needed information efficiently with less chance of errors or delays to customers. When sales slips are prenumbered and controlled, each one issued is the responsibility of one salesperson. This prevents the salesperson from pocketing cash by making a sale and destroying the sales slip. Computerized point-of-sale systems achieve the same control results.

Insure Assets and Bond Key Employees Assets should be adequately insured against loss. Employees handling large amounts of cash and easily transferable assets should be bonded. An employee is *bonded* when a company purchases an insurance policy, or a bond, against losses from theft by that employee. Bonding reduces the risk of loss and discourages theft. Bonded employees know an independent bonding company is unlikely to be sympathetic with an employee involved in theft.

Separate Recordkeeping from Custody of Assets A person who controls or has access to an asset must not keep that asset's accounting records. This reduces the risk of theft or waste of an asset because the person with control over it knows that another person keeps its records. Also, a recordkeeper who does not have access to the asset has no reason to falsify records. To steal an asset and hide the theft from the records, two or more people must *collude* (agree in secret to commit the fraud).

IN THE NEWS

Tag Control A novel technique exists for marking physical assets. It involves embedding a less than one-inch-square tag of fibers that creates a unique optical signature recordable by scanners. Manufacturers hope to embed tags in everything from compact discs and credit cards to designer clothes.

Divide Responsibility for Related Transactions Good internal control divides responsibility for a transaction or a series of related transactions between two or more individuals or departments. This ensures that the work of one individual acts as a check on the other. This *separation of duties* is not a call for duplication of work. Each employee or department should perform unduplicated work. Examples of transactions with divided responsibility are placing purchase orders, receiving merchandise, and paying **vendors** (sellers or suppliers). These tasks should not be given to one individual or department. Assigning responsibility for two or more of these tasks to one party increases mistakes and perhaps fraud. Having an independent person, for example, check incoming goods for quality and quantity encourages more care and attention to detail than having the person who placed the order do the checking. Added protection can result from having a third person approve payment of the invoice. A company can even designate a fourth person with authority to write checks as another protective measure.

Apply Technological Controls Cash registers, check protectors, time clocks, and personal identification scanners are examples of devices that can improve internal control. Technology often improves the effectiveness of controls. A cash register with a locked-in tape or electronic file makes a record of each cash sale. A check protector perforates the amount of a check into its face and makes it difficult to alter the amount. A time clock registers the exact time an employee both arrives at and leaves from the job. Personal scanners limit access to only authorized individuals. These and other technological controls are an effective part of many internal control systems.

IN THE NEWS

About Face Face-recognition software snaps a digital picture of a person's face and converts key facial features—say, the distance between the eyes—into a series of numerical values. These can be stored on an ID or ATM card as a simple bar code to prohibit unauthorized access.

Perform Regular and Independent Reviews Personnel changes, time pressures, and technological advances present risks of errors or fraud. To counter these factors, regular reviews of internal control systems are needed to ensure that procedures are followed. These reviews are preferably done by internal auditors not directly involved in the activities. Many companies also pay for audits by independent, external auditors. Losses from fraud are lower in businesses with an internal audit department.

Technology and Internal Control

LO4 Explain how technology impacts an internal control system.

Technology impacts internal control systems in several important ways. Technology allows us quicker access to databases and information. Used effectively, this greatly improves managers' abilities to monitor and control business activities. This section also describes other technological impacts.

Information on Internet fraud can be found at these Websites:
- fraud.org
- sec.gov/investor/pubs/cyberfraud.htm
- ftc.gov/bcp/consumer/shtm

Reduced Processing Errors Technology reduces errors in processing information. If the software and data entry are correct, the risk of mechanical and mathematical errors is nearly eliminated. However, less human involvement in data processing can cause data entry errors to go undiscovered. Also, errors in software can produce consistent but erroneous processing of transactions. Continually checking and monitoring all types of systems are important.

More Extensive Testing of Records A company's review and audit of electronic records can include more extensive testing when information is easily and rapidly accessed. When accounting records are kept manually, auditors and others likely select only small samples of data to test. When data are accessible with computer technology, however, auditors can quickly analyze large samples or even the entire database.

IN THE NEWS

Identity Check There's a new security device—a person's ECG (electrocardiogram) reading—that is as unique as a fingerprint and a lot harder to lose or steal than a PIN. ECGs can be read through fingertip touches. An ECG also shows that a living person is actually there, whereas fingerprint and facial recognition software can be fooled.

Limited Evidence of Processing With computers, fewer hard-copy items of documentary evidence are available for review. Yet technologically advanced systems can provide new evidence. They can, for instance, record who made the entries, the date and time, the source of the entry, and so on. Technology can also be designed to require the use of passwords or other identification before access to the system is granted. This means that internal control depends more on the design and operation of the information system and less on the analysis of its resulting documents.

Crucial Separation of Duties Technology often eliminates or consolidates some jobs. A company with a reduced workforce risks losing its crucial separation of duties. To minimize risk of error and fraud, the person who designs and programs the information system must not be the one who operates it. The company must also separate control over computer programs and files from the activities related to cash receipts and disbursements. For instance, a computer operator should not control check-writing activities. Separation of duties can be especially difficult and costly in small companies with few employees.

IN THE NEWS

Mystery Movie The Association of Certified Fraud Examiners' Website reports: A movie theater manager stole $30,000. During slow times, when he thought he was not being observed, the manager would print a customer's ticket but keep it for himself and allow the customer to enter the movie without a ticket. During busy times, the manager would then resell the tickets he had withheld and pocket the cash. The manager was caught by an alert employee who happened to see what he was doing.

Increased E-Commerce Technology has encouraged the growth of e-commerce. **Amazon.com** and **eBay** are examples of companies that successfully use e-commerce. Most companies have some e-commerce transactions. All such transactions involve at least three risks. (1) *Credit card number theft* is a risk of using, transmitting, and storing such data online. This increases the cost of e-commerce. (2) *Computer viruses* are harmful programs that attach themselves to innocent files for purposes of infecting other files and programs. (3) *Impersonation* online can result in charges of sales to bogus accounts, purchases of inappropriate materials, and the unknowing release of confidential information to hackers. Companies use both *firewalls* and *encryption* to combat some of these risks—firewalls are points of entry to a system that require passwords to continue, and encryption is a mathematical process to rearrange contents that cannot be read without the process code. Each year millions of Americans have their privacy compromised.

"Worst case of identity theft I've ever seen!"

Copyright 2004 by Randy Glasbergen. www.glasbergen.com

Limitations of Internal Control

All internal control policies and procedures have limitations which usually arise from either (1) the human element or (2) the cost-benefit principle.

L05 Describe the limitations of internal control.

Internal controls are applied by people. This human element creates several potential limitations that we can categorize as either (1) human error or (2) human fraud. *Human error* can occur from negligence, fatigue, misjudgment, or confusion. *Human fraud* involves intent by people to defeat internal controls, such as *management override,* for personal gain. Fraud also includes collusion to thwart the separation of duties. Dollar losses from fraud more than triple when two or more people collude. The human element highlights the importance of establishing an *internal control environment* to convey management's commitment to internal control policies and procedures.

The second major internal control is the *cost-benefit principle.* The costs of internal controls must not exceed their benefits. Analysis of costs and benefits must consider the impact on morale. Most companies, for instance, can legally read employees' e-mails, yet few do unless they have evidence of potential harm to the company. The same holds for drug testing, phone tapping, and hidden cameras. The bottom line is that managers must establish internal control policies and procedures with a net benefit to the company.

A Hacker's Guide to Cyberspace

Pharming Viruses attached to e-mails and Websites load software onto your PC that monitors key strokes; when you sign on to financial Websites, it steals your passwords.

Phishing Hackers send e-mails to you posing as banks; you are asked for information using fake Websites where they reel in your passwords and personal data.

WI-Phishing Cybercrooks set up wireless networks hoping you use them to connect to the Web; your passwords and data are stolen as you use their network.

Bot-Networking Hackers send remote-control programs ("bots") to your PC that take control to send out spam and viruses; they then even rent your bot to other cybercrooks.

Typo-Squatting Hackers set up Websites with addresses similar to legit outfits; when you make a typo and hit their sites, they infect your PC with viruses or take them over as bots.

HOW YOU DOIN'?

Answers—p. 170

1. Principles of internal control suggest that (choose one): (*a*) Responsibility for a series of related transactions (such as placing orders, receiving and paying for merchandise) should be assigned to one employee; (*b*) Responsibility for individual tasks should be shared by more than one employee so that one serves as a check on the other; or (*c*) Employees who handle considerable cash and easily transferable assets should be bonded.

2. What are some impacts of computing technology on internal control?

Voucher System of Control

Most large thefts occur from payment of phony invoices. A **voucher system** is a set of procedures and approvals designed to control payments and the acceptance of obligations. A **voucher** is an internal document (or file). The voucher system of control establishes procedures for

■ Verifying, approving, and recording obligations for eventual cash payment.

■ Issuing checks for payment of verified, approved, and recorded obligations.

A reliable voucher system follows standard procedures for every transaction. This applies even when multiple purchases are made from the same supplier.

IN THE NEWS

Cyber Setup   The FTC is on the cutting edge of cybersleuthing. Opportunists in search of easy money are lured to **WeMarket4U.net/netops**. Take the bait and you get warned—and possibly targeted. The top 4 fraud complaints as compiled by the Internet Crime Complaint Center are shown to the right.

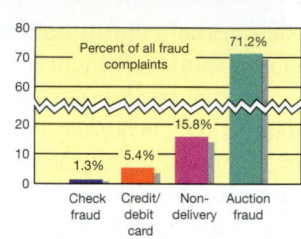

> Establish responsibilties

> Divide responsibility; separate recordkeeping from asset custody; bond key employees

> Maintain adequate records.

Voucher systems illustrate internal control principles. A voucher system often limits the type of obligations that a department or individual can incur. In a large retail store, for instance, only a purchasing department should be authorized to incur obligations for merchandise inventory. Another key factor is that procedures for purchasing, receiving, and paying for merchandise are divided among several departments (or individuals). These employees are often bonded to insure against loss from theft. These departments include the one requesting the purchase, the purchasing department, the receiving department, and the accounting department. To coordinate and control responsibilities of these departments, a company uses several different business documents. Exhibit 7.3 shows how documents are accumulated in a voucher. This specific example begins with a *purchase requisition* and concludes with a *check* drawn against cash. Appendix 7A describes each document entering and leaving a voucher system. It also describes the internal control objective served by each document.

A voucher system should be applied to all expenditures. To illustrate, when a company receives a monthly telephone bill, it should review and verify the charges, prepare a voucher (file), and insert the bill. This transaction is then recorded with a journal entry. If the amount is currently

Exhibit 7.3

Document Flow in a Voucher System

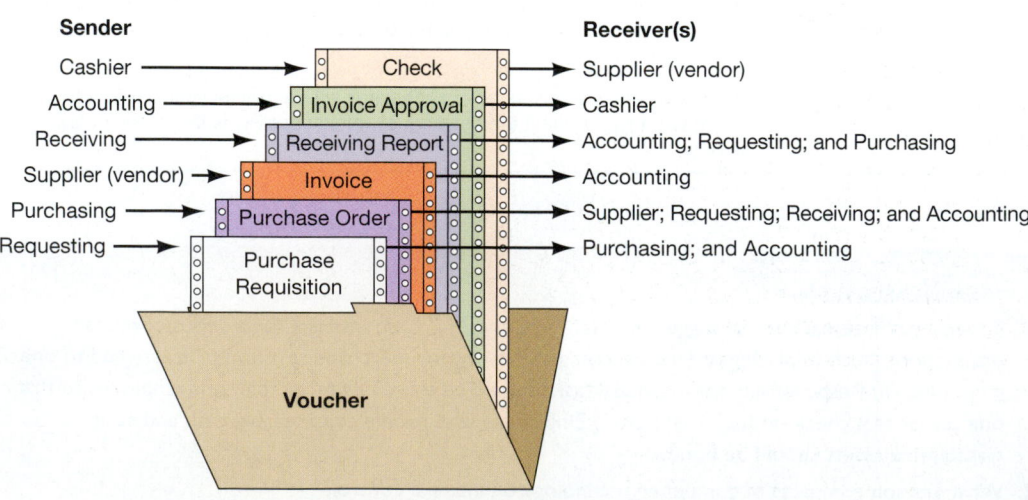

due, a check is issued. If not, the voucher is filed for payment on its due date. If no voucher is prepared, verifying the invoice and its amount after several days or weeks can be difficult. Also, without records, a dishonest employee could collude with a dishonest supplier to get more than one payment for an obligation, payment for excessive amounts, or payment for goods and services not received. An effective voucher system helps prevent such frauds.

IN THE NEWS

Phony Consulting   From the Association of Certified Fraud Examiners' Website: A purchasing agent for a large company set up a vendor file in his wife's maiden name, then approved more than $1 million in company payments to her. The supporting documentation consisted of the wife's invoices for "consulting services," but those services were never performed. A fellow employee, suspicious of the agent's recent purchase of a new boat and car, caught on to the scheme and turned him in.

The Sarbanes–Oxley Act

Congress passed the Sarbanes-Oxley Act in 2002. This act has several provisions designed to reduce financial fraud. Adherence to the act's provisions is required for U.S. public companies. However, privately held and small businesses can also benefit from many of the control features in the act. Next we discuss some of the act's provisions that might be useful as part of a system of internal control to reduce fraud.

L06 Explain provisions of the Sarbanes-Oxley Act that are designed to detect and curtail fraud.

Requirements of the Sarbanes-Oxley Act

The act requires each annual report to include an *internal control* report, which must:

- State managers' responsibility for establishing and maintaining adequate internal controls for financial reporting.
- Assess the effectiveness of those controls.

In addition, the company's external auditor must test the company's internal control system with respect to financial reporting. This independent review provides an important external check on the company's financial statements.

Each company's chief executive officer (CEO) and chief financial officer (CFO) must certify that the financial statements fairly present the operations and financial condition of the company. This fixes responsibility for the company's financial reports with high-level executives who should have knowledge of the company's accounting.

The act also requires publicly traded companies to establish procedures for "the confidential, anonymous submission by employees of complaints regarding the company's accounting or internal controls."

Fraud Detection   Evidence in the Association of Certified Fraud Examiners 2008 *Report to the Nation* suggests anonymous tips are a company's best way to detect fraud. About 46% of all detected frauds were detected by tips, leading frauds detected by internal audit (about 19%), and frauds detected by accident (about 20%).

Evidence suggests that several of the Sarbanes-Oxley related controls are helpful in reducing fraud. Exhibit 7.4 compares average loss per fraud occurrence for public companies, based on whether they have anonymous fraud hotlines and whether management certifies the financial statements. Though not required, controls like these are also helpful in reducing fraud losses of private companies.

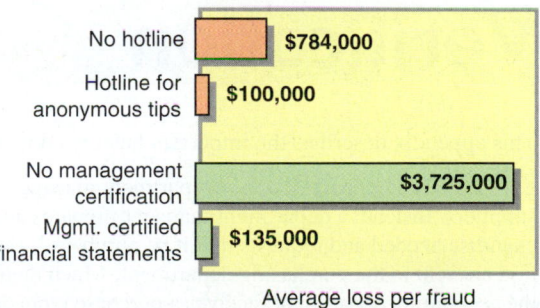

	Average loss per fraud
No hotline	$784,000
Hotline for anonymous tips	$100,000
No management certification	$3,725,000
Mgmt. certified financial statements	$135,000

Exhibit 7.4

Sarbanes-Oxley Controls and Average Loss per Fraud

Answers—p. 170

HOW YOU DOIN'?

3. Should all companies require a voucher system? At what point in a company's growth would you recommend a voucher system?

4. What type of company must follow the provisions of the Sarbanes-Oxley Act?

5. What is a company's best way to detect fraud?

Demonstration Problem

Shaw Company applies the following practices for internal control purposes.

1. Each sales clerk uses his or her own cash drawer. The cash drawer can be opened only by swiping an employee identification card.

2. The company's cash registers keep a record of each transaction in an electronic file. The company's manager reviews these files daily.

3. The company's manager issues prenumbered sales slips to salespersons. Salespersons must submit their sales slips to the manager after making a sale. The manager verifies that all sales slips are accounted for each month.

4. The company buys goods for resale from a manufacturer. Each purchase must be approved by a manager. The company's receiving department employees check incoming goods for quantity and quality. The company purchases a bond on each of its receiving department employees. The manager cannot receive goods, and the receiving department employees cannot make purchase orders. Neither the manager nor any of the receiving department employees are allowed to make accounting journal entries.

Required

Identify which of the seven principles of internal control is being applied in each of the above scenarios. More than one principle of internal control might apply to a scenario.

Solution to Demonstration Problem

	Scenario Number			
	1	2	3	4
■ Establish responsibilities	x			
■ Maintain adequate records			x	
■ Insure assets and bond key employees				x
■ Separate recordkeeping from custody of assets				x
■ Divide responsibility for related transactions				x
■ Apply technological controls	x	x		
■ Perform regular and independent reviews			x	x

APPENDIX

7A Documentation and Verification

LO7

Describe the use of documentation and verification to control cash disbursements.

This appendix describes the important business documents of a voucher system of control.

Purchase Requisition   Department managers are usually not allowed to place orders directly with suppliers. Instead, a department manager prepares and signs a **purchase requisition,** which lists the merchandise needed and requests that it be purchased—see Exhibit 7A.1. Two copies of the purchase requisition are sent to the purchasing department, which then sends one copy to the accounting department. When the accounting department receives a purchase requisition, it creates and maintains a voucher for this transaction. The requesting department keeps a third copy.

```
                    Purchase Requisition          No. 917
                          Z-Mart

  From ___ Sporting Goods Department ___   Date _____ October 28, 2010 ___
  To ____ Purchasing Department _____    Preferred Vendor ___ Trex _____

  Request purchase of the following item(s):

    Model No.   Description                        Quantity
    CH 015      Challenger X7                      1
    SD 099      SpeedDemon                         1

  Reason for Request _____ Replenish inventory _____
  Approval for Request _____ J.Z. _____

  For Purchasing Department use only: Order Date _10/30/10_  P.O. No. ___P98___
```

Purchase Order

A **purchase order** is a document the purchasing department uses to place an order with a vendor. A purchase order authorizes a vendor to ship ordered merchandise at the stated price and terms—see Exhibit 7A.2. When the purchasing department receives a purchase requisition, it prepares at least five copies of a purchase order. The copies are distributed as follows: *copy 1* to the vendor as a purchase request and as authority to ship merchandise; *copy 2,* along with a copy of the purchase requisition, to the accounting department, where it is entered in the voucher and used in approving payment of the invoice; *copy 3* to the requesting department to inform its manager that action is being taken; *copy 4* to the receiving department without order quantity so it can compare with goods received and provide independent count of goods received; and *copy 5* retained on file by the purchasing department.

It is important to note that a voucher system is designed to uniquely meet the needs of a specific business. Thus, you should read this appendix as one example of a common voucher system design, but *not* the only design.

```
                       Purchase Order            No. P98
                          Z-Mart
                     10 Michigan Street
                  Chicago, Illinois 60521

  To:  Trex                       Date _____ 10/30/10 _____
       W9797 Cherry Road          FOB _____ Destination _____
       Antigo, Wisconsin 54409    Ship by  As soon as possible
                                  Terms _____ 2/15, n/30 _____

  Request shipment of the following item(s):

    Model No.   Description      Quantity   Price    Amount
    CH 015      Challenger X7    1          490      490
    SD 099      SpeedDemon       1          710      710

  All shipments and invoices must    Ordered by
  include purchase order number
                                     _____ J.W. _____
```

Invoice

An **invoice** is an itemized statement of goods prepared by the vendor listing the customer's name, items sold, sales prices, and terms of sale. An invoice is also a bill sent to the buyer from the supplier. From the vendor's point of view, it is a *sales invoice*. The buyer, or **vendee**, treats it as a *purchase invoice*. When receiving a purchase order, the vendor ships the ordered merchandise to the buyer and includes or mails a copy of the invoice covering the shipment to the buyer. The invoice is sent to the buyer's accounting department where it is placed in the voucher.

Receiving Report

Many companies have a separate department to receive all merchandise and purchased assets. When each shipment arrives, this receiving department counts the goods and checks them for damage and agreement with the purchase order. It then prepares four or more copies of a **receiving report,** which is used within the company to notify the appropriate persons that ordered goods have been received and to describe the quantities and condition of the goods. One copy is sent to accounting and placed in the voucher. Copies are also sent to the requesting department and the purchasing department to notify them that the goods have arrived. The receiving department retains a copy in its files.

Invoice Approval   When a receiving report arrives, the accounting department should have copies of the following documents in the voucher: purchase requisition, purchase order, and invoice. With the information in these documents, the accounting department can record the purchase and approve its payment. In approving an invoice for payment, it checks and compares information across all documents. To facilitate this checking and to ensure that no step is omitted, it often uses an **invoice approval,** also called *check authorization*—see Exhibit 7A.3. An invoice approval is a checklist of steps necessary for approving an invoice for recording and payment. It is a separate document either filed in the voucher or preprinted (or stamped) on the voucher.

Exhibit 7A.3

Invoice Approval

Invoice Approval			
Document		By	Date
Purchase requisition	917	72	10/28/10
Purchase order	P98	9W	10/30/10
Receiving report	R85	SK	11/3/10
Invoice:	4657		11/12/10
Price		9k	11/12/10
Calculations		9k	11/12/10
Terms		9k	11/12/10
Approved for payment		BC	

As each step in the checklist is approved, the person initials the invoice approval and records the current date. Final approval implies the following steps have occurred:

1. **Requisition check:** Items on invoice are requested per purchase requisition.
2. **Purchase order check:** Items on invoice are ordered per purchase order.
3. **Receiving report check:** Items on invoice are received, per receiving report.
4. **Invoice check: Price:** Invoice prices are as agreed with the vendor.
   Calculations: Invoice has no mathematical errors.
   Terms: Terms are as agreed with the vendor.

Voucher   Once an invoice has been checked and approved, the voucher is complete. A complete voucher is a record summarizing a transaction. Once the voucher certifies a transaction, it authorizes recording an obligation. A voucher also contains approval for paying the obligation on an appropriate date. The physical form of a voucher varies across companies. Many are designed so that the invoice and other related source documents are placed inside the voucher, which can be a folder.

Completion of a voucher usually requires a person to enter certain information on both the inside and outside of the voucher. Typical information required on the inside of a voucher is shown in Exhibit 7A.4,

Exhibit 7A.4

Inside of a Voucher

Z-Mart
Chicago, Illinois   Voucher No. 5268

Date   Oct. 28, 2010
Pay to   Trex
City   Antigo   State   Wisconsin

For the following: (attach all invoices and supporting documents)

Date of Invoice	Terms	Invoice Number and Other Details	Terms
Nov. 2, 2010	2/15, n/30	Invoice No. 4657	1,200
		Less discount	24
		Net amount payable	1,176

Payment approved

N. O. Neal

Auditor

and that for the outside is shown in Exhibit 7A.5. This information is taken from the invoice and the supporting documents filed in the voucher. A complete voucher is sent to an authorized individual (often called an *auditor*). This person performs a final review, approves the accounts and amounts for debiting (called the *accounting distribution*), and authorizes recording of the voucher.

Exhibit 7A.5

Outside of a Voucher

		Voucher No. 5268	
Accounting Distribution			
Account Debited	Amount	Due Date	November 12, 2010
Purchases	1,200	Pay to	Trex
Store Supplies		City	Antigo
Office Supplies		State	Wisconsin
Sales Salaries			
Other		Summary of charges:	
		Total charges	1,200
		Discount	24
		Net payment	1,176
		Record of payment:	
Total Vouch. Pay. Cr.	1,200	Paid	
		Check No.	

After a voucher is approved and recorded (in a journal called a **voucher register**), it is filed by its due date. A check is then sent on the payment date from the cashier, the voucher is marked "paid," and the voucher is sent to the accounting department and recorded (in a journal called the **check register**). The person issuing checks relies on the approved voucher and its signed supporting documents as proof that an obligation has been incurred and must be paid. The purchase requisition and purchase order confirm the purchase was authorized. The receiving report shows that items have been received, and the invoice approval form verifies that the invoice has been checked for errors. There is little chance for error and even less chance for fraud without collusion unless all the documents and signatures are forged.

Summary

LO1 Define workplace fraud and explain the four elements common to all fraud schemes. Workplace fraud involves the use of one's job for personal gain, through deliberate misuse of the employer's assets. All workplace fraud is secret, violates the employee's job duties, provides financial benefit to the employee, and costs the employer money.

LO2 Describe the three major types of workplace fraud. Asset misappropriation, corruption, and fraudulent financial statements are the three major types of workplace fraud.

LO3 Define internal control and identify its purpose and principles. An internal control system consists of the policies and procedures managers use to protect assets, ensure reliable accounting, promote efficient operations, and urge adherence to company policies. It can prevent avoidable losses and help managers both plan operations and monitor company and human performance. Principles of good internal control include establishing responsibilities, maintaining adequate records, insuring assets and bonding employees, separating recordkeeping from custody of assets, dividing responsibilities for related transactions, applying technological controls, and performing regular independent reviews.

LO4 Explain how technology impacts an internal control system. Technology improves managers' abilities to monitor and control business activities. It also allows for more extensive testing of records. However, technological systems often produce less hard-copy evidence to review. Technology often eliminates jobs, making separation of duties more difficult, particularly in small companies.

LO5 Describe the limitations of internal control. Internal control systems are limited by the human element and the cost-benefit principle. Human error and/or human fraud, particularly collusion, limit the effectiveness of internal control systems. The cost-benefit principle states that the costs of internal controls must not exceed their benefits. In considering costs the employer must consider the effects of certain controls on employee morale.

LO6 Explain provisions of the Sarbanes-Oxley Act that are designed to detect and curtail fraud. The Sarbanes-Oxley Act requires each annual report to include an internal control report that states managers' responsibility for maintaining adequate internal controls for financial reporting. The company must also assess the effectiveness of its internal controls.

LO7^A **Describe the use of documentation and verification to control cash disbursements.** A voucher system is a set of procedures and approvals designed to control cash disbursements and acceptance of obligations. The voucher system of control relies on several important documents, including the voucher and its supporting files. A key factor in this system is that only approved departments and individuals are authorized to incur certain obligations.

Guidance Answers to HOW YOU DOIN'?

1. (*c*)
2. Technology reduces processing errors. It also allows more extensive testing of records, limits the amount of hard evidence, and highlights the importance of separation of duties.

3. Not all companies need a voucher system. A voucher system is used when an owner/manager can no longer control purchasing procedures through personal supervision and direct participation.
4. U.S. public companies.
5. Anonymous tips.

Key Terms

Check register (p. 169) Another name for a cash disbursements journal when the journal has a column for check numbers.

Internal control system (p. 160) All policies and procedures used to protect assets, ensure reliable accounting, promote efficient operations, and urge adherence to company policies.

Invoice (p. 167) Itemized record of goods, prepared by the vendor that lists the customer's name, items sold, sales prices, and terms of sale.

Invoice approval (p. 168) Document containing a checklist of steps necessary for approving the recording and payment of an invoice; also called *check authorization.*

Principles of internal control (p. 160) Principles prescribing management to establish responsibility, maintain records, insure assets, separate recordkeeping from custody of assets, divide responsibility for related transactions, apply technological controls, and perform reviews.

Purchase order (p. 168) Document used by the purchasing department to place an order with a seller (vendor).

Purchase requisition (p. 166) Document listing merchandise needed by a department and requesting it be purchased.

Receiving report (p. 167) Form used to report that ordered goods are received and to describe the quantity and condition.

Vendee (p. 167) Buyer of goods or services.

Vendor (p. 161) Seller of goods or services.

Voucher (p. 164) Internal file used to store documents and information to control cash disbursements and to ensure that a transaction is properly authorized and recorded.

Voucher register (p. 169) Journal (referred to as *book of original entry*) in which all vouchers are recorded after they have been approved.

Voucher system (p. 164) Procedures and approvals designed to control cash disbursements and acceptance of obligations.

Workplace fraud (p. 158) The deliberate misuse of an employer's assets for an employee's personal gain.

Multiple Choice Quiz   Answers on p. 175   mhhe.com/wildCA2e

Additional Multiple Choice Quizzes are available at the book's Website.

1. When two clerks share the same cash register, it is a violation of which internal control principle?
   a. Establish responsibilities.
   b. Maintain adequate records.
   c. Insure assets.
   d. Bond key employees.
   e. Apply technological controls.

2. The impact of technology on internal controls includes
   a. Reduced processing errors.
   b. Elimination of the need for regular audits.
   c. Elimination of the need to bond employees.
   d. More efficient separation of duties.
   e. Elimination of fraud.

3. The most serious limitation of internal control is
   a. Computer error.
   b. Human fraud or human error.
   c. Cost-benefit principle.

   d. Cybercrime.
   e. Management fraud.

4. A set of procedures and approvals that is designed to control cash disbursements and the acceptance of obligations is referred to as a(n):
   a. Internal cash system.
   b. Petty cash system.
   c. Cash disbursement system.
   d. Voucher system.
   e. Cash control system.

5. The source by which the greatest percentage of workplace fraud schemes is detected is
   a. Tips from customers and vendors.
   b. Internal auditors.
   c. Accident.
   d. Tips from employees.
   e. Independent auditors.

Discussion Questions

1. List the four common elements of all workplace frauds.
2. List the three major types of workplace frauds.
3. List the seven broad principles of internal control.
4. Internal control procedures are important in every business, but at what stage in the development of a business do they become especially critical?
5. Why should responsibility for related transactions be divided among different departments or individuals?
6. Why should the person who keeps the records of an asset not be the person responsible for its custody?
7. When a store purchases merchandise, why are individual departments not allowed to directly deal with suppliers?
8. What are the limitations of internal controls?
9. What are the three main methods of detecting workplace fraud?

connect

An internal control system consists of all policies and procedures used to protect assets, ensure reliable accounting, promote efficient operations, and urge adherence to company policies.

1. What is the main objective of internal control procedures? How is that objective achieved?
2. Why should recordkeeping for assets be separated from custody over those assets?
3. Why should the responsibility for a transaction be divided between two or more individuals or departments?

QUICK STUDY

QS 7–1
Internal control objectives LO3

A good system of internal control separates the recordkeeping from the control of assets.

1. Explain why this separation of duties can be effective.
2. Which limitation of internal control might limit 'separation of duties' from preventing fraud?
3. How can technology impact a company's ability to separate duties?

QS 7–2
Internal control
LO3 LO4 LO5

For each of the independent cases below, identify the principle of internal control that is violated, and recommend what should be done to remedy the violation.

1. In order to save money, Regal Company has decided to drop its property insurance on assets and to stop bonding the cashiers who handle less than $10,000 in cash each day.
2. Wang Company records each sale on prenumbered invoices. These invoices are left in an open drawer for any employee to access. No employee at Wang Company examines whether all the invoices are accounted for after employees take them from the open drawer.
3. Gerald McNichols, the owner of McNichols Company, prides himself on hiring only the most competent employees. McNichols believes that since these employees are highly competent and that he trusts them completely and wants to keep employee morale high, there is no need for anyone to review the employees' performance.

QS 7–3
Internal control procedures LO3

Management uses a voucher system to help control and monitor cash disbursements. Identify at least four key documents that are part of a voucher system of control.

QS 7–4^A
Documents in a voucher system
LO7

Identify and explain provisions of the Sarbanes-Oxley Act that are designed to prevent fraud.

QS 7–5
Sarbanes-Oxley LO6

EXERCISES

Exercise 7-1
Analyzing internal control
LO2 LO3

Franco Company is a rapidly growing start-up business. Its recordkeeper, who was hired one year ago, left town after the company's manager discovered that a large sum of money had disappeared over the past six months. An audit disclosed that the recordkeeper had written and signed several checks made payable to her fiancé and then recorded the checks as salaries expense. The fiancé, who cashed the checks but never worked for the company, left town with the recordkeeper. As a result, the company incurred an uninsured loss of $184,000. Evaluate Franco's internal control system and indicate which principles of internal control appear to have been ignored. Which type of workplace fraud has been committed?

Exercise 7-2
Principles of internal control
LO3

Match each of the following transactions 1 through 10 with the applicable internal control principle A through G (some answers refer to more than one principle).

A. Establish responsibility.

B. Maintain adequate records.

C. Insure assets and bond employees.

D. Separate recordkeeping from custody of assets.

E. Divide responsibility for related transactions.

F. Apply technological controls.

G. Perform regular and independent reviews.

_____ **1.** Cashier does not have access to the cash register recorded tape or file.

_____ **2.** A company uses a voucher system.

_____ **3.** No two clerks share the same cash drawer.

_____ **4.** The bookkeeper prepares and signs checks.

_____ **5.** A company uses a computerized point of sale system.

_____ **6.** A company hires CPAs to perform an audit.

_____ **7.** A company buys an insurance policy to protect against employee theft.

_____ **8.** A company has separate departments for purchasing, receiving, and accounts payable.

_____ **9.** A company has an internal auditor on staff.

_____ **10.** A company uses a check protector.

Exercise 7-3ᴬ
Voucher system   **LO7**

The voucher system of control is designed to control cash disbursements and the acceptance of obligations.

1. The voucher system of control establishes procedures for what two processes?

2. What types of expenditures should be overseen by a voucher system of control?

3. When is the voucher initially prepared? Explain.

Exercise 7-4ᴬ
Documents in a voucher system
LO7

Match each document in a voucher system in column one with its description in column two.

Document

1. Purchase requisition

2. Purchase order

3. Invoice

4. Receiving report

5. Invoice approval

6. Voucher

Description

A. An itemized statement of goods prepared by the vendor listing the customer's name, items sold, sales prices, and terms of sale.

B. An internal file used to store documents and information to control cash disbursements and to ensure that a transaction is properly authorized and recorded.

C. A document used to place an order with a vendor that authorizes the vendor to ship ordered merchandise at the stated price and terms.

D. A checklist of steps necessary for the approval of an invoice for recording and payment; also known as a check authorization.

E. A document used by department managers to inform the purchasing department to place an order with a vendor.

F. A document used to notify the appropriate persons that ordered goods have arrived, including a description of the quantities and condition of goods.

connect™

For each of these five separate cases, identify the principle(s) of internal control that is violated. Recommend what the business should do to ensure adherence to principles of internal control.

1. Halton Company records each sale on a preprinted invoice. Since sometimes invoices are spoiled when they are prepared, the invoices are not prenumbered, but the sales clerk writes the next number onto each invoice.

2. Julia and Justine are cashiers at Tico Company. Justine often processes transactions from Julia's cash drawer when Julia is at lunch.

3. Nori Nozumi posts all patient charges and payments at the Hopeville Medical Clinic. Each night Nori backs up the computerized accounting system to a tape and stores the tape in a locked file at her desk.

4. Benedict Shales prides himself on hiring quality workers who require little supervision. As office manager, Benedict gives his employees full discretion over their tasks and for years has seen no reason to perform independent reviews of their work.

5. Cala Farah's manager has told her to reduce costs. Cala decides to raise the deductible on the plant's property insurance from $5,000 to $10,000. This cuts the property insurance premium in half. In a related move, she decides that bonding the plant's employees is a waste of money since the company has not experienced any losses due to employee theft. Cala saves the entire amount of the bonding insurance premium by dropping the bonding insurance.

PROBLEM SET A

Problem 7-1A
Analyzing internal control **LO3**

It is important that companies assess their risks of workplace fraud. Managers must also possess the skills to identify workplace fraud and the skills to establish internal controls to effectively reduce the risks of such fraud.

Required

For each of the following five separate cases, identify which of the three major types of workplace fraud is likely to occur. Recommend internal controls that are effective in reducing the likelihood of such fraud.

1. As part of his computer programming duties, Martin Gomez adds new employees to his company's payroll system. Martin also manages the payroll and signs payroll checks. Martin recently added several fictitious employees to the payroll.

2. Green Oaks Racquet Club uses a manual system to record which member uses its tennis courts. Members often pay for their court times with cash, which is deposited nightly. The manager of Green Oaks notices that several nightly deposits are at unexpectedly low amounts.

3. Haynes Company pays its accountant a bonus based on its financial performance. The accountant overstated the company's revenues in its most recent income statement.

4. An accounts payable clerk has been processing invoices with inflated prices from a certain supplier. In return, the clerk receives 20% of the invoice price as a kickback.

5. Custom Electronics is a major wholesaler of computers, stereos, and other expensive electronic equipment. The inventory is stored in a warehouse that is often left unlocked. Its inventory manager notices that a large number of iPods are missing.

Problem 7-2A
Workplace fraud and internal controls
LO2 LO3 LO6

For each of these five separate cases, identify the principle(s) of internal control that is violated. Recommend what the business should do to ensure adherence to principles of internal control.

1. Latisha Tally is the company's computer specialist and oversees its computerized payroll system. Her boss recently asked her to put password protection on all office computers. Latisha has put a password in place that allows only the boss access to the file where pay rates are changed and personnel are added or deleted from the payroll.

2. Marker Theater has a computerized order-taking system for its tickets. The system is active all week and backed up every Friday night.

3. Sutton Company has two employees handling acquisitions of inventory. One employee places purchase orders and pays vendors. The second employee receives the merchandise.

4. The owner of Super Pharmacy uses a check protector to perforate checks, making it difficult for anyone to alter the amount of the check. The check protector is on the owner's desk in an office that contains company checks and is normally unlocked.

PROBLEM SET B

Problem 7-1B
Analyzing internal control **LO3**

5. Lavina Company is a small business that has separated the duties of cash receipts and cash disbursements. The employee responsible for data base programming and data entry also writes checks to pay for purchases.

Problem 7–2B
Workplace fraud and internal controls

LO2 LO3 LO6

It is important that companies assess their risks of workplace fraud. Managers must also possess the skills to identify workplace fraud and the skills to establish internal controls to effectively reduce the risks of such fraud.

Required

For each of the following five separate cases, identify which of the three major types of workplace fraud is likely to occur. Recommend internal controls that are effective in reducing the likelihood that such fraud occurs.

1. As part of her computer programming duties, Brandi Marks adds new suppliers to her company's accounts payable system. Brandi also manages accounts payable and signs checks payable to suppliers. Brandi recently added several new suppliers to the accounts payable system.

2. Peña Company has its employees write down their hours worked in a manual ledger. One employee consistently claims more unscheduled overtime hours than any other employee.

3. Gibson Company pays its accountant a bonus based on its financial performance. The accountant understated the company's expenses in its most recent income statement.

4. An employee refuses to buy goods from a potential supplier unless that supplier hires the employee's wife.

5. Ace Electronics is a major wholesaler of electronic equipment. The company's inventory manager is responsible for ordering inventory and paying suppliers. Recently, warehouse employees reported several large shipments of cell phones missing.

BEYOND THE NUMBERS

REPORTING IN ACTION
LO2   LO5

BTN 7–1   Workplace fraud affects **Best Buy**. Refer to Best Buy's financial statements in Appendix A to answer the following:

1. Explain how inventory losses (such as theft) impact how Best Buy reports merchandise inventory on its balance sheet.

2. In which income statement account does Best Buy report inventory losses?

ETHICS CHALLENGE
LO2   LO3

BTN 7–2   The owner of a start-up information services company requires all employees to take at least one week of vacation per year. Why does the employer require this "forced vacation" policy?

WORKPLACE COMMUNICATION
LO6

BTN 7–3   Assume you are the owner of a small business. You are planning on borrowing money from a local bank. What are some features of the Sarbanes-Oxley Act that you could adopt to help persuade the banker that your financial statements are not fraudulent?

TAKING IT TO THE NET
LO1   LO2   LO3

BTN 7–4   Visit the Association of Certified Fraud Examiners Website at **acfe.com**. Research the fraud facts (refer to the 2008 *Report to the Nation,* see fraud resource center—under publications—*Report to the Nation*) presented at this site and fill in the blanks in the following statements.

1. It is estimated that ____% of U.S. organizations' revenues are lost as a result of occupational fraud and abuse. Applied to the U.S. gross domestic product, this translates to losses of approximately $____ billion.

2. Small businesses are the most vulnerable to occupational fraud and abuse. The average scheme in a small business causes $_____ in losses. The average scheme in the largest companies costs $_____.

3. The most common method for detecting occupational fraud is through tips from _____, customers, vendors, and anonymous sources. The second most common method of discovery is _____.

4. The typical occupational fraud perpetrator is a first-time offender. Only _____% of occupational fraudsters in this study were known to have prior convictions for fraud-related offenses.

5. All occupational frauds fall into one of three categories: _____, corruption, or _____ statements.

6. Over _____% of occupational frauds involve asset misappropriations. Cash is the targeted asset _____% of the time.

7. Corruption schemes account for _____% of all occupational frauds, and they cause over $_____ in losses, on average.

8. Fraudulent statements are the most costly form of occupational fraud with median losses of $_____ million per scheme.

9. Frauds committed by employees cause median losses of $_____, while frauds committed by owners cause median losses of $_____.

10. Losses caused by perpetrators older than 60 are _____ times higher than losses caused by employees 25 and younger.

BTN 7-5 Organize the class into teams. Each team must prepare a list of 10 internal controls a consumer could observe in a typical retail department store. When called upon, the team's spokesperson must be prepared to share controls identified by the team that have not been shared by another team's spokesperson.

TEAMWORK IN ACTION
LO3   LO4

BTN 7-6 Review the opening feature of this chapter that highlights Dylan Lauren and Jeff Rubin and their company **Dylan's Candy Bar**.

ENTREPRENEURS IN BUSINESS
LO3   LO5

Required

1. List the seven principles of internal control and explain how Dylan and Jeff could implement each of them in their candy store.

2. Do you believe that they will need to add additional controls as their business expands? Explain.

---

1. a	**4.** d
2. a	**5.** d
3. b	

ANSWERS TO MULTIPLE CHOICE QUIZ

A Look Back

Chapter 7 focused on fraud, ethics, and controls. We described control procedures that can reduce fraud.

A Look at This Chapter

This chapter focuses on cash and its control. We explain the control of and accounting for cash receipts and payments. These controls include banking activities, petty cash funds, and bank reconciliations.

A Look Ahead

Chapter 9 focuses on employee payroll. We show how the employer records employee payroll and deductions.

Chapter 8

Cash and Cash Controls

Learning Objectives

LO 1   Define cash and describe three guidelines for control of cash.

LO 2   Describe controls for cash receipts.

LO 3   Describe controls for cash disbursements.

LO 4   Explain and record petty cash fund transactions.

LO 5   Identify banking activities as controls of cash.

LO 6   Describe a bank statement.

LO 7   Prepare and explain a bank reconciliation.

"You must follow through on your promises and do the best work you can"
—Youngsong Martin

Dressing Up for Business

BUENA PARK, CA—Youngsong Martin found the plain, dreary look of most social and business events extremely disappointing. She recalls, "I was too familiar with the institutional look of those metal-rimmed chairs in banquet halls and ballrooms, drab folding chairs at many outdoor events, and the rather ordinary tablecloths and napkins." Martin reacted by launching **Wildflower Linen** (**WildflowerLinens.com**) to provide custom table linens, chair covers, and sashes to dress up banquets, meetings, weddings, and special events of all sorts.

"I derive more pleasure than I had imagined," explains Martin. "It has been a dream come true to 'dress' entire events." Martin also enjoys the service side and getting "to know customers on a more personal level."

But the business side is where Martin needed the most help. "You don't really realize what's involved with running a business until you actually do it," says Martin. "I definitely needed help with the management and financial aspects." In particular, Martin needed help with internal controls, including controls over cash receipts, disbursements, petty cash, and bank reconciliations. The online order system is linked with cash and the banking system that requires careful management.

"It's one thing to think you know where your money's going," stresses Martin. "But it's quite another to actually write expenses down and see how they affect your operations." Martin says she must "analyze expenses and determine if they are necessary to help keep my business growing. It's almost like I'm getting an MBA." With nearly 40 employees and growing revenue, Martin has dressed up her business with more than just linens.

[Sources: *Wildflower Linen Website,* May 2009; *SCORE.org Website,* June 2009]

Cash is a necessary asset of every business. Cash is the most liquid of all assets and can be easily hidden or moved. Experience tells us that small businesses are most vulnerable, usually due to weak controls over cash. It is important that the business owner have a system of control over cash. This chapter describes controls to safeguard cash.

Cash and Cash Controls

Control of Cash
- Cash and liquidity
- Control of receipts
- Control of disbursements

Banking Activities as Controls
- Basic bank services
- Bank statement
- Bank reconciliation

Control of Cash

Cash and Liquidity

LO1 Define cash and describe three guidelines for control of cash.

Good accounting systems help manage cash and control access to it. **Liquidity** refers to a company's ability to pay its near-term obligations. Cash and similar assets are called **liquid assets** because they can be readily used to settle such obligations. A company needs liquid assets to effectively operate.

Cash includes currency and coins along with the amounts on deposit in bank accounts. Cash also includes items that are acceptable for deposit in bank accounts, such as checks and money orders. Cash is a business's most liquid asset. A system of cash control should meet three basic guidelines:

1. Handling cash is separate from recordkeeping of cash.
2. Cash receipts are promptly deposited in a bank.
3. Cash payments are made by check.

The first guideline separates duties to reduce errors and the potential for fraud. With duties separated, two or more people must work together to steal cash and hide this action in the accounting records. The second and third guidelines produce a timely, independent bank record of cash receipts and payments and reduce the chance of cash theft or loss. Independent bank records of cash receipts and cash payments are useful in controlling cash, as we discuss in the next two sections.

Control of Cash Receipts

LO2 Describe controls for cash receipts.

Control of cash receipts ensures that cash received is properly recorded and deposited. Cash receipts arise from cash sales, collections of customer accounts, receipts of interest earned, bank loans, sales of assets, and owner investments. This section explains control over two important types of cash receipts: over-the-counter and by mail.

Over-the-Counter Cash Receipts   Over-the-counter cash sales should be recorded on a cash register at the time of each sale. To help ensure that correct amounts are entered, each register should be located so customers can read the amounts entered. Clerks also should enter each sale before wrapping merchandise and give the customer a receipt for each sale. Each cash register should provide a permanent, locked-in record of each sale (sometimes referred to as a *cash register tape*).

Access to cash should be separate from its recordkeeping. For over-the-counter cash receipts, this separation begins with the cash sale. The clerk who has access to cash in the register should not have access to its locked-in record in the register. At the end of the clerk's work period, the

IN THE NEWS

Perpetual Accounting   **Wal-Mart** uses a network of information links with its point-of-sale cash registers to coordinate sales, purchases, and distribution. Its supercenters, for instance, ring up to 15,000 separate sales on heavy days. By using cash register information, the company can fix pricing mistakes quickly and capitalize on sales trends.

clerk should count the cash in the register, record the amount, and turn over the cash and a record of its amount to the company cashier. The cashier, like the clerk, has access to the cash but should not have access to accounting records (or the cash register tape). A third employee, often a supervisor, compares the record of total register transactions (or the cash register tape) with the cash receipts reported by the cashier. This record is the basis for a journal entry recording over-the-counter cash receipts. The third employee has access to the records for cash but not to the actual cash. The clerk and the cashier have access to cash but not to the accounting records. None of them can make a mistake or divert cash without the difference being revealed—see the following diagram.

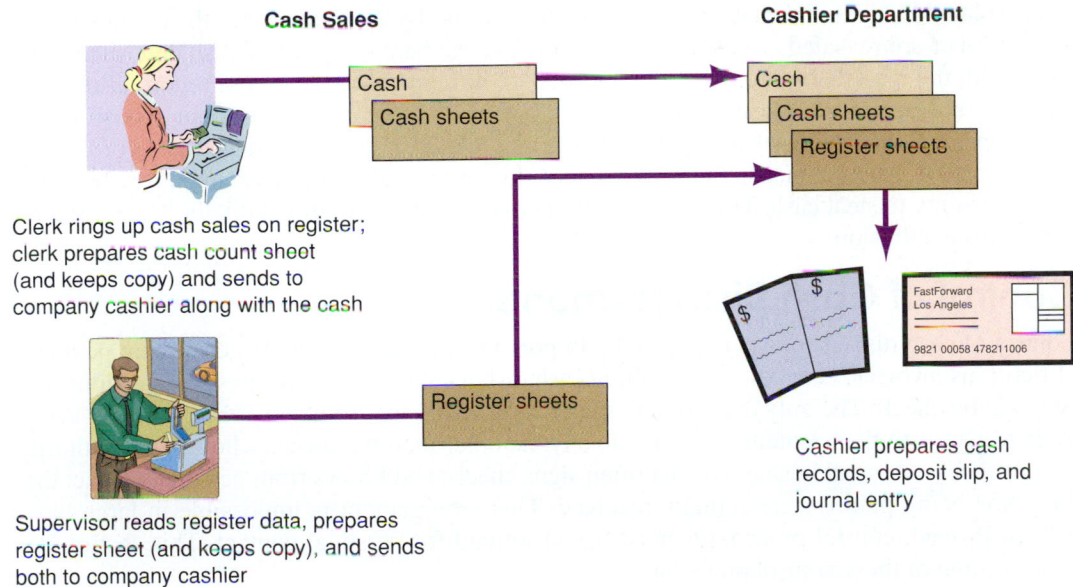

Cash over and short.   Although a clerk is careful, customers can be given the wrong change. This means that at the end of a work period, the cash in a cash register might not equal the record of cash receipts. This difference is reported in the **Cash Over and Short** account, which records the income statement effects of cash overages and cash shortages. A credit entry to Cash Over and Short increases income, while a debit to Cash Over and Short decreases income. To illustrate, if a cash register's record shows $550 but the count of cash in the register is $555, the entry to record cash sales and its overage is

Cash	555	
Cash Over and Short		5
Sales		550
To record cash sales and a cash overage.		

Assets = Liabilities + Equity
+555   + 5
                        +550

Instead, if a cash register's record shows $625 but the count of cash in the register is $621, the entry to record cash sales and its shortage is:

Assets = Liabilities + Equity
+621   −   4
                      +625

Cash	621	
Cash Over and Short	**4**	
Sales		625
To record cash sales and a cash shortage.		

Since customers more often dispute being shortchanged than being given too much change, the Cash Over and Short account usually has a debit balance at the end of an accounting period. A debit balance reflects an expense.

Cash Receipts by Mail

Control of cash receipts that arrive by mail starts with opening the mail. Two people should be present for opening the mail. If so, theft of cash receipts by mail requires collusion between these two employees. The person(s) opening the mail enters a list (in triplicate) of money received. This list includes a record of each sender's name, the amount, and an explanation of why the money is sent. The first copy is sent with the money to the cashier. A second copy is sent to the recordkeeper. A third copy is kept by the clerks who opened the mail. The cashier deposits the money in a bank, and the recordkeeper records the amounts received in the accounting records.

This process reflects good cash control. When the bank balance is reconciled by another person (explained later in the chapter), errors or acts of fraud by the mail clerks, the cashier, or the recordkeeper are revealed. They are revealed because the bank's record of cash deposited must agree with the records from each of the three. Also, if the mail clerks do not report all receipts correctly, customers will question their account balances. If the cashier does not deposit all receipts, the bank balance does not agree with the recordkeeper's cash balance. The recordkeeper and the person who reconciles the bank balance do not have access to cash and therefore have no opportunity to steal cash. This system makes errors and fraud highly unlikely. The exception is employee collusion.

> Collusion implies that two or more individuals know of or are involved with the activities of the other(s).

Control of Cash Disbursements

LO3 Describe controls for cash disbursements.

Control of cash disbursements is especially important as most large thefts occur from payment of fictitious invoices. One key to controlling cash disbursements is to require all expenditures to be made by check. The only exception is small payments made from petty cash. Another key is to deny access to the accounting records to anyone other than the owner who has the authority to sign checks. A small business owner often signs checks and knows from personal contact that the items being paid for are actually received. This arrangement is impossible in large businesses. Instead, control procedures must be substituted for personal contact. This section describes some of these control procedures.

Petty Cash System of Control

A basic principle for controlling cash disbursements is that all payments must be made by check. An exception is made for **petty cash** disbursements, which are the small payments required for items such as postage, courier fees, minor repairs, and low-cost supplies. To avoid the time and cost of writing checks for small amounts, a company sets up a petty cash fund to make small payments. A petty cash fund is used only for business expenses.

Operating a petty cash fund.   Establishing a petty cash fund requires estimating the total amount of small payments likely to be made during a short period such as a week or month. A check is then drawn by the company cashier for an amount slightly in excess of this estimate. This check is recorded with a debit to the Petty Cash account (an asset) and a credit to Cash. The check is cashed, and the cash is given to an employee designated as the *petty cashier*. The petty cashier keeps this cash safe, makes payments from the fund, and keeps records of it in a secure place called the *petty cashbox*.

LO4 Explain and record petty cash fund transactions.

When each cash disbursement is made, the person receiving payment should sign a prenumbered *petty cash receipt*—see Exhibit 8.1. The petty cash receipt is then put in the petty cashbox with the remaining money. The sum of all receipts plus the remaining cash should always equal the total fund amount. A $100 petty cash fund, for instance, contains any combination of cash and petty cash receipts that totals $100 (examples are $80 cash plus $20 in receipts, or $10 cash plus $90 in receipts). Each disbursement reduces cash and increases the amount of receipts in the petty cashbox.

Petty Cash Receipt		No. 9
Z-Mart		
For ___ Freight charges ___	Date ___ 11/5/10 ___	
Charge to ___ Transportation-In ___	Amount ___ $6.75 ___	
Approved by ___ *Jim Gillo* ___	Received by ___ *Dick Fitch* ___	

Exhibit 8.1

Petty Cash Receipt

Cash should be added to the petty cash fund when the fund nears zero and at the end of an accounting period when financial statements are prepared. The petty cashier sorts the paid receipts by the type of expense and then totals the receipts. The petty cashier gives all paid receipts to the company cashier, who stamps all receipts *paid* so they cannot be reused, files them for record-keeping, and gives the petty cashier a check for their total. When this check is cashed and the money placed in the petty cashbox, the total money in the petty cashbox equals its original amount. The fund is now ready for a new cycle of petty cash payments.

Illustrating a petty cash fund.   To illustrate, assume Z-Mart establishes a petty cash fund on November 1 and designates one of its office employees as the petty cashier. A $75 check is drawn, cashed, and the cash given to the petty cashier. The entry to record the setup of this petty cash fund is

Nov. 1	Petty Cash	75	
	Cash		75
	To establish a petty cash fund.		

Assets = Liabilities + Equity
+75
−75

After the petty cash fund is established, the *Petty Cash account is not debited or credited again unless the amount of the fund is changed. (Reducing the balance or eliminating a petty cash fund would require a credit to Petty Cash).*

Next, assume that Z-Mart's petty cashier makes several November payments from petty cash. Each person who received payment signs a receipt. On November 27, after making a $26.50 cash payment for tile cleaning, only $3.70 cash remains in the fund. The petty cashier summarizes and totals the petty cash receipts as shown in Exhibit 8.2. (This report can also include receipt number and names of those who approved and received cash payments.)

Z-MART			
Petty Cash Payments Report			
Miscellaneous Expenses			
Nov. 2	Washing windows	$20.00	
Nov. 27	Tile cleaning	26.50	$46.50
Transportation-In			
Nov. 5	Transport of merchandise purchased	6.75	
Nov. 20	Transport of merchandise purchased	8.30	15.05
Delivery Expense			
Nov. 18	Customer's package delivered		5.00
Office Supplies Expense			
Nov. 15	Purchase of office supplies immediately used		4.75
Total	....		**$71.30**

Exhibit 8.2

Petty Cash Payments Report

Transportation costs for inventory purchases are added to the Transportation-In account that becomes part of the merchandise inventory cost. The petty cash payments report and all receipts are given to the company cashier in exchange for a $71.30 check to reimburse the fund. The petty cashier cashes the check and puts the $71.30 cash in the petty cashbox. The recordkeeper makes this entry:

Assets = Liabilities + Equity
−71.30   −46.50
                          −15.05
                          − 5.00
                          − 4.75

Nov. 27	Miscellaneous Expenses................................	46.50	
	Transportation-In.....................................	15.05	
	Delivery Expense......................................	5.00	
	Office Supplies Expense..............................	4.75	
	Cash..		71.30
	To reimburse petty cash.		

Increasing or decreasing a petty cash fund. To illustrate, assume Z-Mart *increases* its petty cash fund from $75 to $100, after making the November 27 entry above. The entry to increase the fund is

Assets = Liabilities + Equity
+25.00
−25.00

Nov. 27	Petty Cash	25	
	Cash...		25
	To increase the petty cash fund amount.		

Cash over and short. Sometimes a petty cashier fails to get a receipt for payment or over-pays for the amount due. When this occurs and the fund is later reimbursed, the petty cash payments report plus the cash remaining will not equal the fund balance. This mistake causes the fund to be *short*. This shortage is recorded as an expense in the reimbursing entry with a debit to the Cash Over and Short account. (An overage in the petty cash fund is recorded with a credit to Cash Over and Short in the reimbursing entry.) To illustrate, the entry to reimburse a $200 petty cash fund when its payments report shows $178 in miscellaneous expenses and $15 cash remains is:

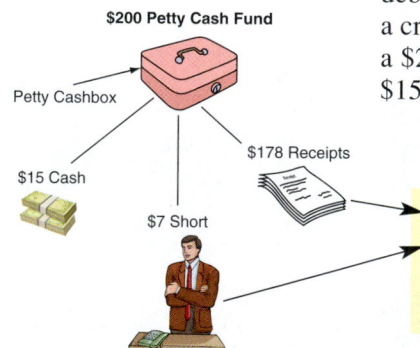

$200 Petty Cash Fund

Petty Cashbox

$15 Cash

$178 Receipts

$7 Short

	Miscellaneous Expenses..	178	
	Cash Over and Short...	**7**	
	Cash..		185
	To reimburse petty cash.		

Alternatively, if Z-Mart *decreases* the petty cash fund from $75 to $55 on November 27, the entry is to (1) credit Petty Cash for $20 (decreasing the fund from $75 to $55) and (2) debit Cash for $20 (reflecting the $20 transfer from Petty Cash to Cash).

In summary, to avoid errors in recording petty cash reimbursement, follow these steps:

Event	Petty Cash	Cash	Expenses
Set up fund	Dr.	Cr.	—
Reimburse fund ..	—	Cr.	Dr.
Increase fund	Dr.	Cr.	—
Decrease fund ...	Cr.	Dr.	—

1. Prepare petty cash payments report.
2. Compute cash needed by subtracting cash remaining from total fund amount.
3. Record journal entry.
4. Check to make sure "Dr. = Cr." in entry. Any difference is recorded in Cash Over and Short.

HOW YOU DOIN'? Answers—p. 192

1. Why are some cash payments made from a petty cash fund, and not by check?
2. Why should a petty cash fund be reimbursed at the end of an accounting period?
3. Identify at least two results of reimbursing a petty cash fund.

Banking Activities as Controls

Banks provide many services, including helping companies control cash. Banks safeguard cash and provide detailed and independent records of cash transactions. This section describes these services and the banking documents that help control cash.

Basic Bank Services

LO5 Identify banking activities as controls of cash.

This section explains basic bank services—such as the bank account, the bank deposit, and checking—that help control cash.

Bank Account, Deposit, and Check A *bank account* is a record set up by a bank for a customer. It permits a customer to deposit money for safekeeping and helps control withdrawals. To limit access to a bank account, all persons authorized to write checks on the account must sign a **signature card** (Exhibit 8.3), which bank employees use to verify signatures on checks. Many companies have more than one bank account to serve different needs and to handle special transactions such as payroll.

Exhibit 8.3

Signature Card

Standard Bankers System, Inc.
Branch
Account Number
☐ Savings ☐ Current ☐ STD ☐ FDR ☐ FCY ☐ Others ....
For Individual Accounts
Name
Signature
Name
Signature
Name
Signature
Name
Signature
Mode of Operation: ☐ Singly ☐ Either or Survivor ☐ Jointly ☐ Any Two
Others: Pls. specify

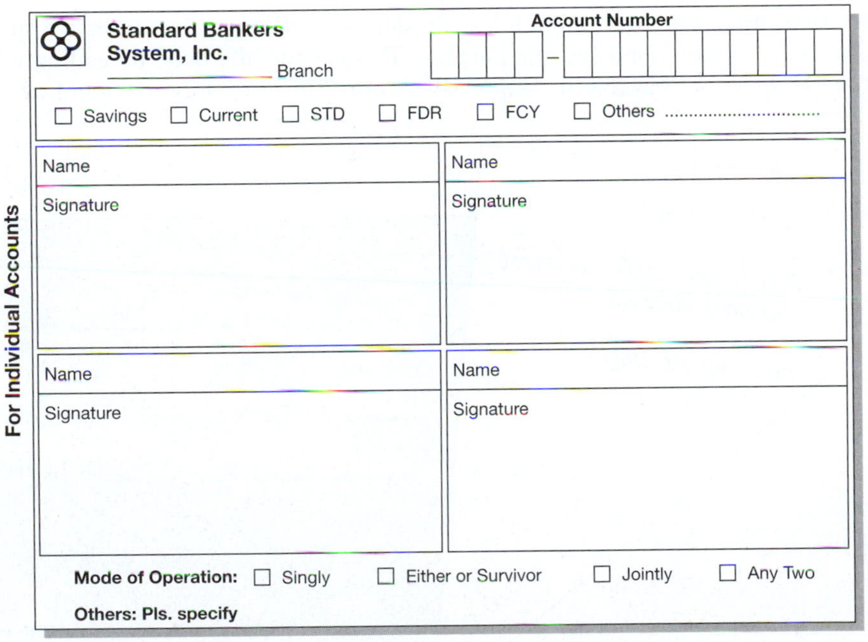

Each bank deposit is supported by a **deposit ticket,** which lists items such as currency, coins, and checks deposited along with their dollar amounts. The bank gives the customer a copy of the deposit ticket or a deposit receipt as proof of the deposit. Exhibit 8.4 shows one type of deposit ticket.

Exhibit 8.4

Deposit Ticket

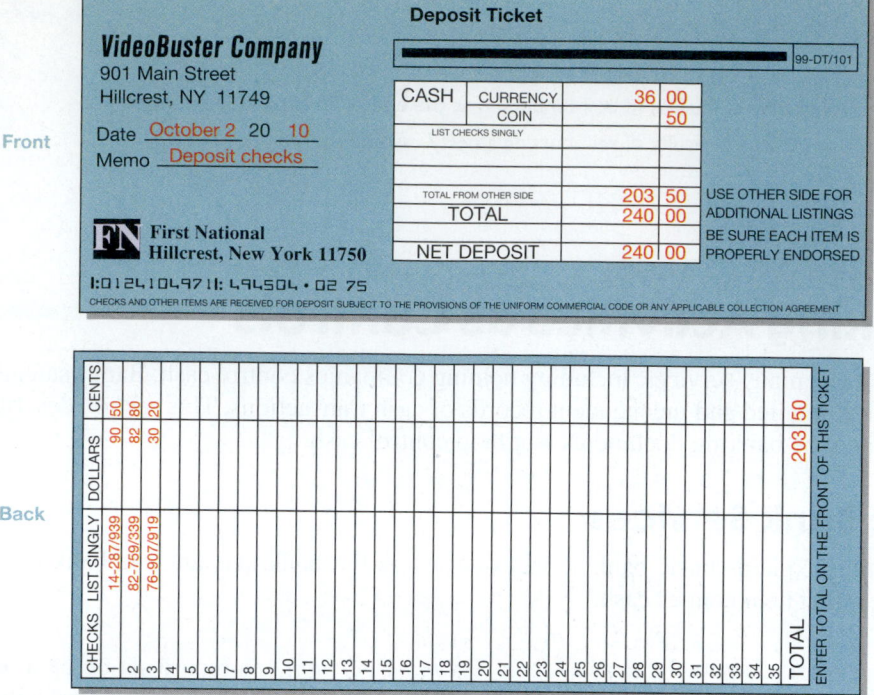

A check being deposited must be endorsed by the depositor. The **endorsement** is a written authorization transferring ownership of the check, generally to a bank. There are two basic types of endorsements:

1. **Blank endorsement**—the depositor signs the back of the check and the check is payable to the bearer of the check.
2. **Restrictive endorsement** (Exhibit 8.5)—the depositor transfers the check to a specific person, business, or bank for a specific purpose. This is generally done by adding words such as "For Deposit" or "Payable to James Myers only" to restrict the payment of the check.

Exhibit 8.5

Restrictive Endorsement

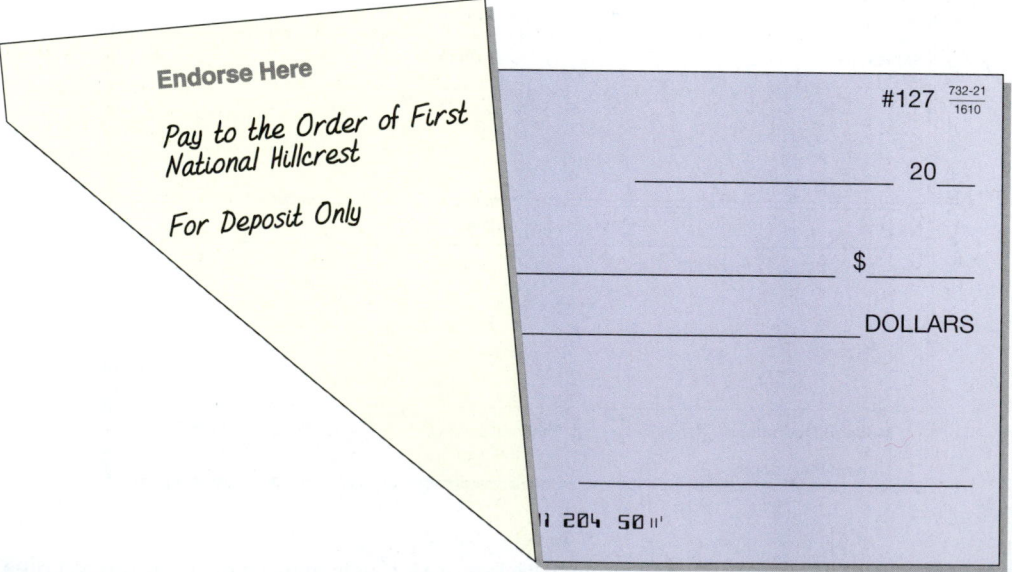

A **check** is used to withdraw money from a bank account. A check involves three parties: a *maker* who signs the check, a *payee* who receives the check, and a *bank* (or *payer*) on which the check is drawn. The bank provides a customer with checks that are numbered and imprinted

IN THE NEWS

Web-bank   Many companies balance checkbooks and pay bills online. Customers value the convenience of banking services anytime, anywhere. Services include the ability to stop payment on a check, move money between accounts, get up-to-date balances, and identify cleared checks and deposits.

with the name and address of both the customer and bank. Exhibit 8.6 shows one type of check, accompanied by an optional *remittance advice* explaining the payment. When a remittance advice is unavailable, the *memo* line is often used for a brief explanation.

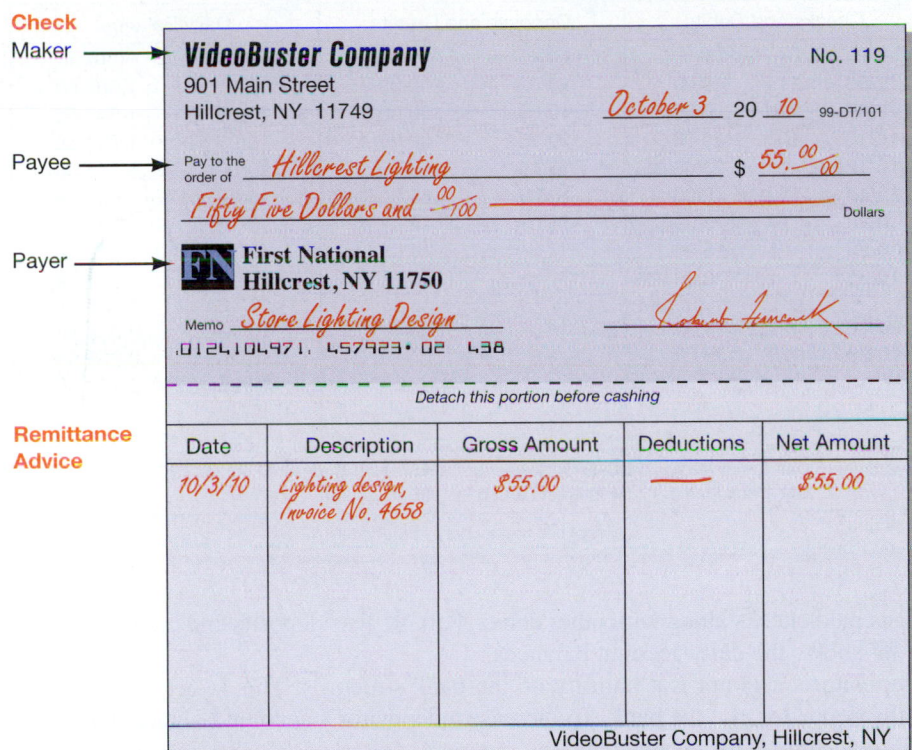

Exhibit 8.6

Check with Remittance Advice

Electronic Funds Transfer   **Electronic funds transfer (EFT)** is the electronic transfer of cash from one party to another. No paper documents are used. Banks simply transfer cash from one account to another with a journal entry. Companies are increasingly using EFT because it is easy and low cost. For instance, it can cost up to 50 cents to process a check through the banking system, whereas EFT cost is near zero. Items such as payroll, rent, utilities, insurance, and interest payments are commonly handled by EFT. The bank statement lists cash withdrawals by EFT with the checks and other deductions. Cash receipts by EFT are listed with deposits and other additions. A bank statement is sometimes a depositor's only notice of an EFT.

Bank Statement

Usually once a month, the bank sends each depositor a **bank statement** showing the activity in the account. Different banks use different formats for their bank statements, but all include the following information:

LO6   Describe a bank statement.

1. Beginning-of-period balance of the depositor's account.
2. Checks and other debits decreasing the account during the period.
3. Deposits and other credits increasing the account during the period.
4. End-of-period balance of the depositor's account.

This information reflects the bank's records. Exhibit 8.7 shows a bank statement. Identify each of these four items in that statement. Part ❶ of Exhibit 8.7 summarizes changes in the account.

Exhibit 8.7

Bank Statement

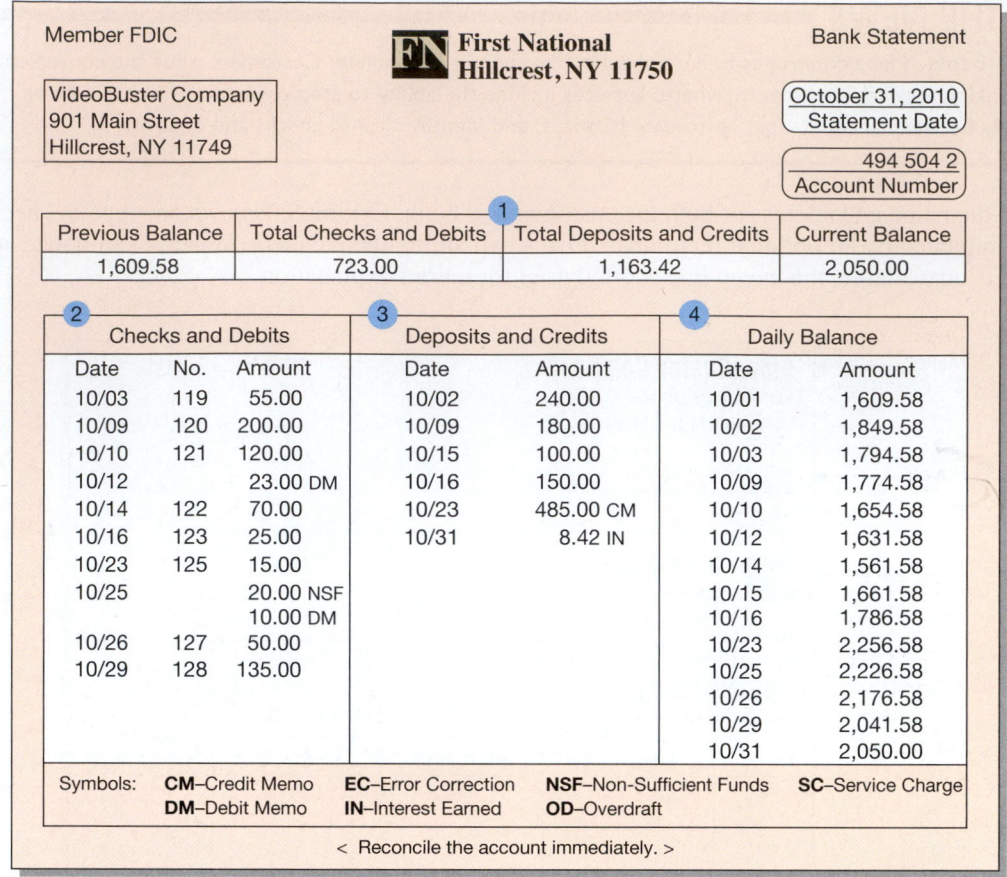

| Member FDIC | | **FN First National** | | Bank Statement |
| | | **Hillcrest, NY 11750** | | |

VideoBuster Company
901 Main Street
Hillcrest, NY 11749

October 31, 2010
Statement Date

494 504 2
Account Number

Previous Balance	Total Checks and Debits	Total Deposits and Credits	Current Balance
1,609.58	723.00	1,163.42	2,050.00

Checks and Debits			Deposits and Credits		Daily Balance	
Date	No.	Amount	Date	Amount	Date	Amount
10/03	119	55.00	10/02	240.00	10/01	1,609.58
10/09	120	200.00	10/09	180.00	10/02	1,849.58
10/10	121	120.00	10/15	100.00	10/03	1,794.58
10/12		23.00 DM	10/16	150.00	10/09	1,774.58
10/14	122	70.00	10/23	485.00 CM	10/10	1,654.58
10/16	123	25.00	10/31	8.42 IN	10/12	1,631.58
10/23	125	15.00			10/14	1,561.58
10/25		20.00 NSF			10/15	1,661.58
		10.00 DM			10/16	1,786.58
10/26	127	50.00			10/23	2,256.58
10/29	128	135.00			10/25	2,226.58
					10/26	2,176.58
					10/29	2,041.58
					10/31	2,050.00

| Symbols: | **CM**–Credit Memo | **EC**–Error Correction | **NSF**–Non-Sufficient Funds | **SC**–Service Charge |
| | **DM**–Debit Memo | **IN**–Interest Earned | **OD**–Overdraft | |

< Reconcile the account immediately. >

Part ② lists paid checks along with other debits. Part ③ lists deposits and credits to the account, and part ④ shows the daily account balances.

The depositor's account is a liability on the bank's records. This is because the money belongs to the depositor, not the bank. To increase a depositor's account balance, the bank *credits* that liability account. This means that debit memos from the bank produce *credits* on the depositor's books, and credit memos from the bank produce *debits* on the depositor's books.

The bank statement includes a list of the depositor's canceled checks (or the actual canceled checks) along with any debit or credit memoranda affecting the account. **Canceled checks** are checks the bank has paid and deducted from the customer's account during the period. Other deductions that can appear on a bank statement include (1) bank service charges and fees, (2) checks deposited that are uncollectible, (3) corrections of previous errors, (4) withdrawals through automated teller machines (ATMs), and (5) periodic payments set up in advance by a depositor. (Most company checking accounts do not allow ATM withdrawals because the company wants to make all disbursements by check.) Except for service charges, the bank notifies the depositor of each deduction with a debit memorandum when the bank reduces the balance. A copy of each debit memorandum is usually sent with the statement.

Transactions that increase the depositor's account include amounts the bank collects on behalf of the depositor and the corrections of previous errors. Credit memoranda notify the depositor of all increases when they are recorded. A copy of each credit memorandum is often sent with the bank statement. Banks that pay interest on checking accounts credit it to the depositor's account each period. In Exhibit 8.7, the bank credits $8.42 of interest to the account as shown at the bottom of the "Deposits and Credits" column.

Bank Reconciliation

LO7 Prepare and explain a bank reconciliation.

When a company deposits all cash receipts and makes all cash payments (except petty cash) by check, the bank statement helps prove the accuracy of its cash records. This is done using a **bank reconciliation,** which is a report explaining any differences between the checking account balance according to the depositor's records and the balance reported on the bank statement.

Purpose of Bank Reconciliation   The balance of a checking account reported on the bank statement rarely equals the balance in the depositor's accounting records. This is usually due to information that one party has that the other does not. We must therefore prove the accuracy of both the depositor's records and those of the bank. This means we must *reconcile* the two balances and explain or account for any differences in them. Among the reasons the bank statement balance might differ from the depositor's book balance are these:

■ **Outstanding checks. Outstanding checks** are checks written (or drawn) by the depositor, deducted on the depositor's records, and sent to payees, but not yet received by the bank for payment at the bank statement date.

■ **Deposits in transit** (also called **outstanding deposits**). **Deposits in transit** are deposits made and recorded by the depositor but not yet recorded on the bank statement. For example, companies can make deposits (in the night depository) at the end of a business day after the bank is closed. If such a deposit occurred on a bank statement date, it would not appear on this period's statement. The bank would record such a deposit on the next business day, and it would appear on the next period's bank statement.

■ **Deductions for uncollectible items and for services.** A company sometimes deposits another party's check that is uncollectible (usually meaning the balance in the other party's account is not large enough to cover the check). This is called a *non-sufficient funds (NSF)* check. The bank would have initially credited (increased) the depositor's account for the amount of the check. When the bank learns the check is uncollectible, it debits (reduces) the depositor's account for the amount of that check. Other possible bank charges to a depositor's account that are first reported on a bank statement include printing new checks and service fees.

■ **Additions for collections and for interest.** Banks sometimes act as collection agents for their depositors by collecting notes and other items. Banks can also receive electronic funds transfers to the depositor's account. When a bank collects an item, it is added to the depositor's account, less any service fee. The bank also sends a credit memorandum to notify the depositor of the transaction. When the memorandum is received, the depositor should record it; yet it sometimes remains unrecorded until the bank reconciliation is prepared. The bank statement also includes a credit for any interest earned.

■ **Errors.** Both banks and depositors can make errors. Bank errors might not be discovered until the depositor prepares the bank reconciliation. Also, depositor errors can be discovered when the bank balance is reconciled. Error testing includes: (a) comparing deposits on the bank statement with deposits in the accounting records and (b) comparing canceled checks on the bank statement with checks recorded in the accounting records.

Illustration of a Bank Reconciliation   We follow nine steps in preparing the bank reconciliation. It is helpful to refer to the bank reconciliation in Exhibit 8.8 when studying steps ① through ⑨.

Forms of Check Fraud (CkFraud.org)

- Forged signatures—legitimate blank checks with fake payer signature
- Forged endorsements—stolen check that is endorsed and cashed by someone other than the payee
- Counterfeit checks—fraudulent checks with fake payer signature
- Altered checks—legitimate check altered (such as changed payee or amount) to benefit perpetrator
- Check kiting—deposit check from one bank account (without sufficient funds) into a second bank account

---

Exhibit 8.8

Bank Reconciliation

VIDEOBUSTER
Bank Reconciliation
October 31, 2010

①	Bank statement balance		$ 2,050.00	⑤	Book balance	$ 1,404.58
②	Add			⑥	Add	
	Deposit of Oct. 31 in transit		145.00		Collect $500 note less $15 fee $485.00	
			2,195.00		Interest earned 8.42	493.42
						1,898.00
③	Deduct			⑦	Deduct	
	Outstanding checks				Check printing charge 23.00	
	No. 124 .... $150.00				NSF check plus service fee ... 30.00	53.00
	No. 126 .... 200.00	350.00				
④	**Adjusted bank balance**		**$1,845.00**	⑧	**Adjusted book balance**	**$1,845.00**

⑨ Balances are equal (reconciled)

(1) Identify the bank statement balance of the cash account (*balance per bank*). VideoBuster's bank balance is $2,050.

(2) Identify and list any unrecorded deposits and any bank errors understating the bank balance. Add them to the bank balance. VideoBuster's $145 deposit placed in the bank's night depository on October 31 is not recorded on its bank statement.

(3) Identify and list any outstanding checks and any bank errors overstating the bank balance. Outstanding checks are identified by comparing canceled checks on the bank statement with checks recorded. Deduct them from the bank balance. VideoBuster's comparison of canceled checks with its books shows two checks outstanding: No. 124 for $150 and No. 126 for $200.

(4) Compute the *adjusted bank balance,* also called the *corrected* or *reconciled balance.*

(5) Identify the company's book balance of the cash account (*balance per book*). VideoBuster's book balance is $1,404.58.

(6) Identify and list any unrecorded credit memoranda from the bank, any interest earned, and errors understating the book balance. Add them to the book balance. Enclosed with VideoBuster's bank statement is a credit memorandum showing the bank collected a note receivable for the company on October 23. The note's proceeds of $500 (minus a $15 collection fee) are credited to the company's account. VideoBuster's bank statement also shows a credit of $8.42, not yet recorded, for interest earned on the average cash balance.

(7) Identify and list any unrecorded debit memoranda from the bank, any service charges, and errors overstating the book balance. Deduct them from the book balance. Debits on VideoBuster's bank statement that are not yet recorded include (a) a $23 charge for check printing and (b) an NSF check for $20 plus a related $10 processing fee. (The NSF check is dated October 16 and was included in the book balance.)

(8) Compute the *adjusted book balance,* also called *corrected* or *reconciled balance.*

(9) Verify that the two adjusted balances from steps 4 and 8 are equal. If so, they are reconciled. If not, check for accuracy and missing data until the balances are equal.

IN THE NEWS

Not-So-Free Banking   **Bankrate.com** surveys indicate non-sufficient funds and overdraft program fees have risen significantly from 2005 to 2008, with the average fee now at $28.95 per transaction, an increase of more than 7% in the past three years. Bank and credit union income from non-sufficient funds and overdraft program fees exceed $34.7 billion in the United States. (**Bretton-woods.com**, 2009)

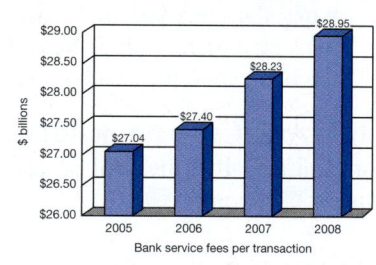

Bank service fees per transaction

Adjusting Entries from a Bank Reconciliation

A bank reconciliation often identifies unrecorded items that need recording by the company. In VideoBuster's reconciliation, the adjusted balance of $1,845 is the correct balance as of October 31. But the company's accounting records show a $1,404.58 balance. We must prepare journal entries to adjust the book balance to the correct balance. *It is important to remember that only the items reconciling the book balance require adjustment.* A review of Exhibit 8.8 indicates that four entries are required for VideoBuster. Adjusting entries could also be combined into one compound entry.

Collection of note.   The first entry records the proceeds of its note receivable collected by the bank and the expense of having the bank perform that service. A note receivable is a written promise to pay from a customer.

Oct. 31	Cash	485	
	Collection Expense	15	
	Notes Receivable		500
	To record the collection fee and proceeds		
	for a note collected by the bank.		

Assets = Liabilities + Equity
+485   −15
−500

Interest earned. The second entry records interest credited to its account by the bank.

Oct. 31	Cash	8.42	
	Interest Revenue		8.42
	To record interest earned on the cash		
	balance in the checking account.		

Assets = Liabilities + Equity
+8.42   +8.42

Check printing. The third entry records expenses for the check printing charge.

Oct. 31	Miscellaneous Expenses	23	
	Cash		23
	Check printing charge.		

Assets = Liabilities + Equity
−23   −23

NSF check. The fourth entry records the NSF check that is returned as uncollectible. The $20 check was originally received from T. Woods in payment of his account and then deposited. (The company debited Cash and credited Accounts Receivable.) The bank charged $10 for handling the NSF check and deducted $30 total from VideoBuster's account. The entry must reverse the effects of the original entry made when the check was received and must record (add) the $10 bank fee to the amount owed by T. Woods.

Oct. 31	Accounts Receivable—T. Woods	30	
	Cash		30
	To charge Woods' account for $20 NSF check		
	and $10 bank fee.		

Assets = Liabilities + Equity
+30
−30

After these four entries are recorded, the book balance of cash is adjusted to the correct amount of $1,845 (computed as $1,404.58 + $485 + $8.42 − $23 − $30). The Cash T-account to the side shows the same computation.

Cash			
Beg. bal.	1,404.58		
6	485.00	7	23.00
6	8.42	7	30.00
Adj. bal.	1,845.00		

HOW YOU DOIN'?   Answers—p. 192

4. What is a bank statement?

5. What is the meaning of the phrase *to reconcile a bank balance*?

6. Why do we reconcile the bank statement balance of cash and the depositor's book balance of cash?

7. List at least two items affecting the bank balance side of a bank reconciliation and indicate whether the items are added or subtracted.

8. List at least three items affecting the book balance side of a bank reconciliation and indicate whether the items are added or subtracted.

Demonstration Problem 1

Prepare a bank reconciliation for Jamboree Enterprises for the month ended November 30, 2010. The following information is available to reconcile Jamboree Enterprises' book balance of cash with its bank statement balance as of November 30, 2010:

a. After all posting is complete on November 30, the company's book balance of Cash has a $16,380 debit balance, but its bank statement shows a $38,520 balance.

b. Checks No. 2024 for $4,810 and No. 2026 for $5,000 are outstanding.

c. In comparing the canceled checks on the bank statement with the entries in the accounting records, it is found that Check No. 2025 in payment of rent is correctly drawn for $1,000 but is erroneously entered in the accounting records as $880.

d. The November 30 deposit of $17,150 was placed in the night depository after banking hours on that date, and this amount does not appear on the bank statement.

e. In reviewing the bank statement, a check written by Jumbo Enterprises in the amount of $160 was erroneously drawn against Jamboree's account.

f. A credit memorandum enclosed with the bank statement indicates that the bank collected a $30,000 note and $900 of related interest on Jamboree's behalf. This transaction was not recorded by Jamboree prior to receiving the statement.

g. A debit memorandum for $1,100 lists a $1,100 NSF check received from a customer, Marilyn Welch. Jamboree had not recorded the return of this check before receiving the statement.

h. Bank service charges for November total $40. These charges were not recorded by Jamboree before receiving the statement.

Planning the Solution

- Set up a bank reconciliation with a bank side and a book side (as in Exhibit 8.8). Leave room to both add and deduct items. Each column will result in a reconciled, equal balance.

- Examine each item *a* through *h* to determine whether it affects the book or the bank balance and whether it should be added or deducted from the bank or book balance.

- After all items are analyzed, complete the reconciliation and arrive at a reconciled balance between the bank side and the book side.

- For each reconciling item on the book side, prepare an adjusting entry. Additions to the book side require an adjusting entry that debits Cash. Deductions on the book side require an adjusting entry that credits Cash.

Solution to Demonstration Problem 1

JAMBOREE ENTERPRISES
Bank Reconciliation
November 30, 2010

Bank statement balance		$38,520	Book balance		$16,380
Add			Add		
Deposit of Nov. 30	$17,150		Collection of note	$30,000	
Bank error (Jumbo)	160	17,310	Interest earned	900	30,900
		55,830			47,280
Deduct			Deduct		
Outstanding checks			NSF check (M. Welch)	1,100	
No. 2024	4,810		Recording error (# 2025)	120	
No. 2026	5,000	9,810	Service charge	40	1,260
Adjusted bank balance		**$46,020**	**Adjusted book balance**		**$46,020**

REQUIRED ADJUSTING ENTRIES FOR JAMBOREE				
Nov.	30	Cash	30 9 0 0 00	
		Notes Receivable		30 0 0 0 00
		Interest Revenue		9 0 0 00
		To record collection of note with interest.		
Nov.	30	Accounts Receivable—M. Welch	1 1 0 0 00	
		Cash		1 1 0 0 00
		To reinstate account due from an NSF check.		
Nov.	30	Rent Expense	1 2 0 00	
		Cash		1 2 0 00
		To correct recording error on check no. 2025.		
Nov.	30	Bank Service Charges	4 0 00	
		Cash		4 0 00
		To record bank service charges.		

Demonstration Problem 2

Bacardi Company established a $150 petty cash fund with Dean Martin as the petty cashier. When the fund balance reached $19 cash, Martin prepared a petty cash payments report, which follows.

Petty Cash Payments Report				
Receipt No.	**Account Charged**		**Approved by**	**Received by**
12	Delivery Expense	$ 29	Martin	A. Smirnoff
13	Transportation-In	18	Martin	J. Daniels
15	(Omitted)	32	Martin	C. Carlsberg
16	Miscellaneous Expense	41	(Omitted)	J. Walker
	Total	$120		

Required

1. Identify four internal control weaknesses from the payments report.
2. Prepare general journal entries to record:
   a. Establishment of the petty cash fund.
   b. Reimbursement of the fund. (Assume for this part only that petty cash receipt no. 15 was issued for miscellaneous expenses.)
3. What is the Petty Cash account balance immediately before reimbursement? Immediately after reimbursement?

Solution to Demonstration Problem 2

1. Four internal control weaknesses are
   a. Petty cash ticket no. 14 is missing. Its omission raises questions about the petty cashier's management of the fund.
   b. The $19 cash balance means that $131 has been withdrawn ($150 − $19 = $131). However, the total amount of the petty cash receipts is only $120 ($29 + $18 + $32 + $41). The fund is $11 short of cash ($131 − $120 = $11). Was petty cash receipt no. 14 issued for $11? Management should investigate.
   c. The petty cashier (Martin) did not sign petty cash receipt no. 16. This omission could have been an oversight on his part or he might not have authorized the payment. Management should investigate.

> **d.** Petty cash receipt no. 15 does not indicate which account to charge. This omission could have been an oversight on the petty cashier's part. Management could check with C. Carlsberg and the petty cashier (Martin) about the transaction. Without further information, debit Miscellaneous Expense.

2. Petty cash general journal entries.

    a. Entry to establish the petty cash fund.   **b.** Entry to reimburse the fund.

Petty Cash	150	
Cash		150

Delivery Expense	29	
Transportation-In	18	
Miscellaneous Expense ($41 + $32)	73	
Cash Over and Short	11	
Cash		131

3. The Petty Cash account balance *always* equals its fund balance, in this case $150. This account balance does not change unless the fund is increased or decreased.

Summary

LO1 **Define cash and describe three guidelines for control of cash.** Cash includes currency, coins, amounts on deposit in bank accounts, and checks acceptable for deposit in bank accounts. Guidelines for control of cash include (1) separation of the handling of cash from its recordkeeping, (2) cash receipts should be promptly deposited in a bank, and (3) cash payments should be made by check.

LO2 **Describe controls for cash receipts.** Control of over-the-counter cash receipts includes use of a cash register, customer review, use of receipts, a permanent transaction record locked-in the cash register, and separation of access to cash from its recordkeeping. Control of cash receipts by mail includes at least two people assigned to open mail and a listing of each sender's name, amount paid, and an explanation.

LO3 **Describe controls for cash disbursements.** Except for very small dollar transactions, all expenditures should be made by check. A petty cash system is used to account for small dollar transactions. Employees who sign checks should not have access to accounting records.

LO4 **Explain and record petty cash fund transactions.** Petty cash payments are for amounts for items such as postage, delivery fees, minor repairs, and supplies. A petty cashier safeguards the petty cash, makes payments from the petty cash fund, and keeps petty cash receipts and records. A Petty Cash account is debited only when the fund is established or increased in amount. When the fund is replenished, petty cash disbursements are recorded with debits to expense (or asset) accounts and a credit to cash.

LO5 **Identify banking activities as controls of cash.** A bank account is a record set up by a bank, allowing a customer to endorse checks and to deposit money for safekeeping and to draw checks on it. A bank deposit ticket proves money was deposited into a bank account. A check tells the bank to pay money from a customer's (*maker*) account to a recipient (*payee*).

LO6 **Describe a bank statement.** A bank statement shows activity in a bank account. Each bank statements lists the beginning-of-period account balance, checks and other debits decreasing the account during the period, deposits and other credits increasing the account during the period, and the end-of-period account balance.

LO7 **Prepare and explain a bank reconciliation.** A bank reconciliation proves the accuracy of the customer's and the bank's records. The bank statement balance is adjusted for items such as outstanding checks and unrecorded deposits made on or before the bank statement date but not reflected on the bank statement. The book balance is adjusted for items like service charges, bank collections for the customer, and interest earned on the account.

1. If all cash payments are made by check, numerous checks for small amounts must be written. Since this practice is expensive and time-consuming, a petty cash fund is often established for making small (immaterial) cash payments.

2. If the petty cash fund is not reimbursed at the end of an accounting period, the transactions involving petty cash are not yet recorded and the petty cash asset is overstated.

3. First, petty cash transactions are recorded when the petty cash fund is reimbursed. Second, reimbursement provides cash to allow the fund to continue being used. Third, reimbursement identifies any cash shortage or overage in the fund.

4. A bank statement is a report prepared by the bank describing the activities in a depositor's account.

5. To reconcile a bank balance means to explain the difference between the cash balance in the depositor's accounting records and the cash balance on the bank statement.

6. The purpose of the bank reconciliation is to determine whether the bank or the depositor has made any errors and whether the bank has entered any transactions affecting the account that the depositor has not recorded.

7. Unrecorded deposits—added
Outstanding checks—subtracted

8. Interest earned—added   Debit memos—subtracted
Credit memos—added   NSF checks—subtracted
                         Bank service charges—subtracted

Key Terms

Bank reconciliation (p. 186) Report that explains the difference between the book (company) balance of cash and the cash balance reported on the bank statement.

Bank statement (p. 185) Bank report on the depositor's beginning and ending cash balances, and a listing of its changes, for a period.

Blank endorsement (p. 184) Depositor signs the back of the check and the check is payable to the bearer of the check.

Canceled checks (p. 186) Checks that the bank has paid and deducted from the depositor's account.

Cash (p. 178) Includes currency, coins, and amounts on deposit in bank checking or savings accounts.

Cash Over and Short (p. 179) Income statement account used to record cash overages and cash shortages arising from errors in cash receipts or payments.

Check (p. 184) Document signed by a depositor instructing the bank to pay a specific amount to a designated recipient.

Deposits in transit (p. 187) Deposits recorded by the company but not yet recorded by its bank.

Deposit ticket (p. 183) Lists items such as currency, coins, and checks deposited and their corresponding dollar amounts.

Electronic funds transfer (EFT) (p. 185) Use of electronic communication to transfer cash from one party to another.

Endorsement (p. 184) A written authorization transferring ownership of a check.

Liquid assets (p. 178) Resources such as cash that are easily converted into other assets or used to pay for goods, services, or liabilities.

Liquidity (p. 178) Availability of resources to meet short-term cash requirements.

Outstanding checks (p. 187) Checks written and recorded by the depositor but not yet paid by the bank at the bank statement date.

Petty cash (p. 180) Small amount of cash in a fund to pay minor expenses.

Restrictive endorsement (p. 184) The depositor transfers the check to a specific person, business, or bank for a specific purpose.

Signature card (p. 183) Includes the signatures of each person authorized to sign checks on the bank account.

Multiple Choice Quiz   Answers on p. 203   mhhe.com/wildCA2e

Additional Multiple Choice Quizzes are available at the book's Website.

1. A company needs to replenish its $500 petty cash fund. Its petty cash box has $75 cash and petty cash receipts of $420. The journal entry to replenish the fund includes
   a. A debit to Cash for $75.
   b. A credit to Cash for $75.
   c. A credit to Petty Cash for $420.
   d. A credit to Cash Over and Short for $5.
   e. A debit to Cash Over and Short for $5.

2. The following information is available for Hapley Company:
   - The November 30 bank statement shows a $1,895 balance.
   - The general ledger shows a $1,742 balance at November 30.
   - A $795 deposit placed in the bank's night depository on November 30 does not appear on the November 30 bank statement.
   - Outstanding checks amount to $638 at November 30.
   - A customer's $335 note was collected by the bank in November. A collection fee of $15 was deducted by the bank and the difference deposited in Hapley's account.
   - A bank service charge of $10 is deducted by the bank and appears on the November 30 bank statement.

   How will the customer's note appear on Hapley's November 30 bank reconciliation?
   a. $320 appears as an addition to the book balance of cash.
   b. $320 appears as a deduction from the book balance of cash.
   c. $320 appears as an addition to the bank balance of cash.
   d. $320 appears as a deduction from the bank balance of cash.
   e. $335 appears as an addition to the bank balance of cash.

3. Using the information from question 2, what is the reconciled balance on Hapley's November 30 bank reconciliation?
   a. $2,052
   b. $1,895
   c. $1,742
   d. $2,201
   e. $1,184

4. Using the information from question 2, how will the $10 bank service charge appear on Hapley's November 30 bank reconciliation?
   a. $10 appears as an addition to the book balance of cash.
   b. $10 appears as an addition to the bank balance of cash.
   c. $10 appears as a deduction from the book balance of cash.
   d. $10 appears as a deduction from the bank balance of cash.
   e. The service charge will not appear on the November 30 bank reconciliation.

5. Using the information from question 2, the journal entries to adjust Hapley's book balance of cash to the bank's balance of cash on November 30 will include a
   a. Debit to Cash for the $10 bank service charge.
   b. Credit to Cash for $638 of outstanding checks.
   c. Debit to Cash for $795 of deposits in transit.
   d. Debit to Cash for $320 for collection of note, net of bank collection fees.
   e. Debit to Cash for the $153 difference between the bank's balance of Cash and the book balance of Cash.

Discussion Questions

1. Why should responsibility for related transactions be divided among different individuals?

2. Why should the person who keeps the cash records not have access to cash?

3. Which of the following assets is most liquid? Which is least liquid? Inventory, building, accounts receivable, or cash.

4. What is a petty cash receipt? Who should sign it?

5. Which type of endorsement should be used to entitle the check to be payable to the bearer of the check?

6. Why should cash receipts be deposited on the day of receipt?

7. **Best Buy**'s statement of cash flows in Appendix A describes changes in cash and cash equivalents for the year ended March 1, 2008. What amount is provided (used) by investing activities? What amount is provided (used) by financing activities?

8. Refer to **RadioShack**'s balance sheet in Appendix A. How does its cash compare with its other current assets (both in amount and percent) as of December 31, 2007. Compare and assess the cash amount at December 31, 2007, with its amount at December 31, 2006.

connect™

QUICK STUDY

QS 8-1
Cash and liquidity   **L01**

Good accounting systems help to manage cash and control access to it.

1. What items are included in the category of cash?

2. What does the term *liquidity* refer to?

QS 8-2
Control of cash
L01   L02   L03

A good system of cash control helps protect both cash receipts and cash disbursements.

1. What are three basic guidelines that help achieve this protection?

2. Identify a control system for cash disbursements.

QS 8-3
Petty cash accounting   **L04**

1. The petty cash fund of the Brooks Agency is established at $85. At the end of the current period, the fund contained $14.80 and had the following receipts: film rentals, $21.30, refreshments for meetings, $30.85 (both expenditures to be classified as Entertainment Expense); postage, $8.95; and printing, $9.10. Prepare journal entries to record (*a*) establishment of the fund and (*b*) reimbursement of the fund at the end of the current period.

2. Identify the two events that cause a Petty Cash account to be credited in a journal entry.

QS 8-4
Bank reconciliation   **L07**

1. For each of the following items, indicate whether its amount (i) affects the bank or book side of a bank reconciliation and (ii) represents an addition or a subtraction in a bank reconciliation.

   a. Interest on cash balance   **d.** Outstanding checks   **g.** Unrecorded deposits

   b. Bank service charges   **e.** Credit memos

   c. Debit memos   **f.** NSF checks

2. Which of the items in part 1 require an adjusting journal entry in the depositor's books?

QS 8-5
Petty cash accounting   **L04**

What are the four steps to avoid errors in recording petty cash reimbursement?

QS 8-6
Deposit ticket preparation   **L05**

Given the following facts, prepare a deposit ticket. Use Exhibit 8.4 as a guide.

Company Name:	Ned's Necklaces	
Date:	July 28, 2010	
Currency:	$35.00	
Coin:	$1.53	
Checks:	Account	Amount
	14-267	$13.50
	15-2263	$37.50
	4-98	$10.00

Given the following facts, prepare a check and check stub. Use Exhibit 8.6 as a guide.

QS 8–7
Check and check stub preparation
LO5

Date:	August 25, 2010
Payee:	Tony's Pizza
Amount:	$53.33
Description:	Company Party
Signature:	Mark Ellingson, Ellingson Electronics

connect ━━━━━━━━━━━━━━━━━━━━━━━━━━━━━━━━

Franco Company is a rapidly growing start-up business. Its recordkeeper, who was hired one year ago, left town after the company's manager discovered that a large sum of money had disappeared over the past six months. An audit disclosed that the recordkeeper had written and signed several checks made payable to her fiancé and then recorded the checks as salaries expense. The fiancé, who cashed the checks but never worked for the company, left town with the recordkeeper. As a result, the company incurred an uninsured loss of $184,000. Evaluate Franco's cash control system and indicate which guidelines of cash control appear to have been ignored.

EXERCISES

Exercise 8–1
Analyzing cash control   **LO3**

Some of Crown Company's cash receipts from customers are received by the company with the regular mail. Crown's recordkeeper opens these letters and deposits the cash received each day. (a) Identify any internal control problem(s) in this arrangement. (b) What changes do you recommend?

Exercise 8–2
Control of cash receipts by mail
LO2

What control procedures would you recommend in each of the following situations?

1. A concession company has one employee who sells sunscreen, T-shirts, and sunglasses at the beach. Each day, the employee is given enough sunscreen, shirts, and sunglasses to last through the day and enough cash to make change. The money is kept in a box at the stand.

2. An antique store has one employee who is given cash and sent to garage sales each weekend. The employee pays cash for this merchandise that the antique store resells.

Exercise 8–3
Control recommendations   **LO1**

Palmona Co. establishes a $200 petty cash fund on January 1. On January 8, the fund shows $38 in cash along with receipts for the following expenditures: postage, $74; photocopy expenses, $29; delivery expenses, $16; and miscellaneous expenses, $43. Prepare journal entries to (1) establish the fund on January 1, (2) reimburse it on January 8, and (3) both reimburse the fund and increase it to $450 on January 8, assuming no entry in part 2. (*Hint:* Make two separate entries for part 3.)

Exercise 8–4
Petty cash fund accounting
LO4

Check   (2) Cr. Cash $162

Waupaca Company establishes a $350 petty cash fund on September 9. On September 30, the fund shows $104 in cash along with receipts for the following expenditures: printing expenses, $40; postage expenses, $123; and miscellaneous expenses, $80. The petty cashier could not account for a $3 shortage in the fund. Prepare (1) the September 9 entry to establish the fund, (2) the September 30 entry to reimburse the fund, and (3) an October 1 entry to increase the fund to $400.

Exercise 8–5
Petty cash fund with a shortage
LO4
Check   (2) Cr. Cash $246 and (3) Cr. Cash $50

Prepare a table with the following headings for a monthly bank reconciliation dated September 30.

Exercise 8–6
Bank reconciliation   **LO6   LO7**

Bank Balance		Book Balance		Not Shown on the Reconciliation
Add	Deduct	Add	Deduct	

For each item 1 through 10, place an x in the appropriate column to indicate whether the item should be added to or deducted from the book or bank balance, or whether it should not appear on the reconciliation. At the left side of your table, number the items to correspond to the following list.

1. NSF check from customer returned on September 25 but not yet recorded by this company.

2. Interest earned on the September cash balance in the bank.

3. Deposit made on September 5 and processed by the bank on September 6.

4. Checks written by another depositor but charged against this company's account.

5. Bank service charge for September.

6. Checks outstanding on August 31 that cleared the bank in September.

7. Check written against the company's account and cleared by the bank; erroneously not recorded on the company books.

8. Checks written and mailed to payees on October 2.

9. Checks written by the company and mailed to payees on September 30.

10. Night deposit made on September 30 after the bank closed.

Exercise 8-7
Adjusting entries for bank reconciliation   **LO7**

List the items in Exercise 8-6 that require adjusting journal entries and indicate whether the Cash balance should be debited or credited.

Exercise 8-8
Bank reconciliation   **LO7**

Del Gato Clinic deposits all cash receipts on the day they are received and it makes all cash payments by check. At the close of business on June 30, 2010, its Cash account shows an $11,589 debit balance. Del Gato Clinic's June 30 bank statement shows $10,555 on deposit in the bank. Prepare a bank reconciliation for Del Gato Clinic using the following information:

a. Outstanding checks as of June 30 total $1,829.

b. The June 30 bank statement included a $16 debit memorandum for bank services.

c. Check No. 919, listed with the canceled checks, was correctly drawn for $467 in payment of a utility bill on June 15. Del Gato Clinic mistakenly recorded it with a debit to Utilities Expense and a credit to Cash in the amount of $476.

Check   Reconciled bal., $11,582

d. The June 30 cash receipts of $2,856 were placed in the bank's night depository after banking hours and were not recorded on the June 30 bank statement.

Exercise 8-9
Adjusting entries from bank reconciliation   **LO7**

Prepare the adjusting journal entries that Del Gato Clinic must record as a result of preparing the bank reconciliation in Exercise 8-8.

---

connect

PROBLEM SET A

Problem 8-1A
Analyzing cash control

LO1   **LO2**   **LO3**

For each of these five separate cases, identify the basic control guidelines(s) that is violated. Recommend what the business should do for better control.

1. Chi Han records all incoming customer cash receipts for his employer and posts the customer payments to their respective accounts.

2. At Tico Company, Julia and Justine alternate lunch hours. Julia is the petty cash cashier, but if someone needs petty cash when she is at lunch, Justine fills in as cashier.

3. Nori Nozumi personally opens all the mail for Hopeville Medical Clinic and performs monthly bank reconciliations.

4. Benedict Shales prides himself on hiring quality workers who require little supervision. As office manager, Benedict allows his bookkeeper to sign checks for the business.

5. Cala Farah deposits cash receipts for Green Meadows Video once each week.

Problem 8-2A
Establish, reimburse, and increase petty cash   **LO4**

Nakashima Gallery had the following petty cash transactions in February of the current year.

Feb. 2   Wrote a $400 check, cashed it, and gave the proceeds and the petty cashbox to Chloe Addison, the petty cashier.

5   Purchased bond paper for the copier for $14.15 that is immediately used.

12   Paid $7.95 postage to express mail a contract to a client.

14   Reimbursed Adina Sharon, the manager, $68 for business mileage on her car.

20   Purchased stationery for $67.77 that is immediately used.

23   Paid a courier $20 to deliver merchandise sold to a customer, terms FOB destination.

27   Paid $54 for postage expenses.

28   The fund had $166.02 remaining in the petty cash box. Sorted the petty cash receipts by accounts affected and exchanged them for a check to reimburse the fund for expenditures.

28   The petty cash fund amount is increased by $100 to a total of $500.

Required

1. Prepare the journal entry to establish the petty cash fund.
2. Prepare a petty cash payments report for February with these categories: delivery expense, mileage expense, postage expense, and office supplies expense. Sort the payments into the appropriate categories and total the expenditures in each category.
3. Prepare the journal entries for part 2 to both (*a*) reimburse and (*b*) increase the fund amount.

Check   (3a) Cr. Cash $233.98

Kiona Co. set up a petty cash fund for payments of small amounts. The following transactions involving the petty cash fund occurred in May (the last month of the company's fiscal year).

Problem 8-3A
Establish, reimburse, and adjust petty cash   **LO4**

QB

May 1   Prepared a company check for $300 to establish the petty cash fund.
     15   Prepared a company check to replenish the fund for the following expenditures made since May 1.
           a.   Paid $88 for janitorial services.
           b.   Paid $53.68 for miscellaneous expenses.
           c.   Paid postage expenses of $53.50.
           d.   Paid $47.15 to *The County Gazette* (the local newspaper) for an advertisement.
           e.   Counted $62.15 remaining in the petty cash box.
     16   Prepared a company check for $200 to increase the fund to $500.
     31   The petty cashier reports that $288.20 cash remains in the fund. A company check is drawn to replenish the fund for the following expenditures made since May 15.
           f.   Paid postage expenses of $147.36.
           g.   Reimbursed the office manager for business mileage, $23.50.
           h.   Paid $34.75 to deliver merchandise to a customer.
     31   The company decides that the May 16 increase in the fund was too large. It reduces the fund by $100, leaving a total of $400.

Required

1. Prepare journal entries to establish the fund on May 1, to replenish it on May 15 and on May 31, and to reflect any increase or decrease in the fund balance on May 16 and May 31.

Check   (1) Cr. to Cash: May 15, $237.85; May 16, $200

Analysis Component

2. Explain how the company's financial statements are affected if the petty cash fund is not replenished and no entry is made on May 31.

The following information is available to reconcile Branch Company's book balance of cash with its bank statement cash balance as of July 31, 2010.

Problem 8-4A
Prepare a bank reconciliation and record adjustments   **LO7**

a. After all posting is complete on July 31, the company's Cash account has a $27,497 debit balance, but its July bank statement shows a $27,233 cash balance.

b. Check No. 3031 for $1,482 and Check No. 3040 for $558 were outstanding on the June 30 bank reconciliation. Check No. 3040 is listed with the July canceled checks, but Check No. 3031 is not. Also, Check No. 3065 for $382 and Check No. 3069 for $2,281, both written in July, are not among the canceled checks on the July 31 statement.

c. In comparing the canceled checks on the bank statement with the entries in the accounting records, it is found that Check No. 3056 for July rent was correctly written and drawn for $1,270 but was erroneously entered in the accounting records as $1,250.

d. A credit memorandum enclosed with the July bank statement indicates the bank collected $8,000 cash on a noninterest-bearing note for Branch, deducted a $45 collection fee, and credited the remainder to its account. Branch had not recorded this event before receiving the statement.

e. A debit memorandum for $805 lists a $795 NSF check plus a $10 NSF charge. The check had been received from a customer, Evan Shaw. Branch has not yet recorded this check as NSF.

f. Enclosed with the July statement is a $25 debit memorandum for bank services. It has not yet been recorded because no previous notification had been received.

g. Branch's July 31 daily cash receipts of $11,514 were placed in the bank's night depository on that date, but do not appear on the July 31 bank statement.

Required

1. Prepare the bank reconciliation for this company as of July 31, 2010.
2. Prepare the journal entries necessary to bring the company's book balance of cash into conformity with the reconciled cash balance as of July 31, 2010.

Check   (1) Reconciled balance, $34,602; (2) Cr. Note Receivable $8,000

Analysis Component

3. Assume that the July 31, 2010, bank reconciliation for this company is prepared and some items are treated incorrectly. For each of the following errors, explain the effect of the error on (i) the adjusted bank statement cash balance and (ii) the adjusted cash account book balance.

a. The company's unadjusted cash account balance of $27,497 is listed on the reconciliation as $27,947.

b. The bank's collection of the $8,000 note less the $45 collection fee is added to the bank statement cash balance on the reconciliation.

Problem 8–5A

Prepare a bank reconciliation and record adjustments   **LO6   LO7**

mhhe.com/wildCA2e

Chavez Company most recently reconciled its bank statement and book balances of cash on August 31 and it reported two checks outstanding, No. 5888 for $1,028.05 and No. 5893 for $494.25. The following information is available for its September 30, 2010, reconciliation.

From the September 30 Bank Statement

Previous Balance	Total Checks and Debits	Total Deposits and Credits	Current Balance
16,800.45	9,620.05	11,272.85	18,453.25

Checks and Debits			Deposits and Credits		Daily Balance	
Date	No.	Amount	Date	Amount	Date	Amount
09/03	5888	1,028.05	09/05	1,103.75	08/31	16,800.45
09/04	5902	719.90	09/12	2,226.90	09/03	15,772.40
09/07	5901	1,824.25	09/21	4,093.00	09/04	15,052.50
09/17		600.25 NSF	09/25	2,351.70	09/05	16,156.25
09/20	5905	937.00	09/30	12.50 IN	09/07	14,332.00
09/22	5903	399.10	09/30	1,485.00 CM	09/12	16,558.90
09/22	5904	2,090.00			09/17	15,958.65
09/28	5907	213.85			09/20	15,021.65
09/29	5909	1,807.65			09/21	19,114.65
					09/22	16,625.55
					09/25	18,977.25
					09/28	18,763.40
					09/29	16,955.75
					09/30	18,453.25

From Chavez Company's Accounting Records

Cash Receipts Deposited				Cash Disbursements		
Date			Cash Debit	Check No.		Cash Credit
Sept.	5		1,103.75	5901		1,824.25
	12		2,226.90	5902		719.90
	21		4,093.00	5903		399.10
	25		2,351.70	5904		2,060.00
	30		1,682.75	5905		937.00
			11,458.10	5906		982.30
				5907		213.85
				5908		388.00
				5909		1,807.65
						9,332.05

Cash						Acct. No. 101
Date		Explanation	PR	Debit	Credit	Balance
Aug.	31	Balance				15,278.15
Sept.	30	Total receipts	R12	11,458.10		26,736.25
	30	Total disbursements	D23		9,332.05	17,404.20

Additional Information

Check No. 5904 is correctly drawn for $2,090 to pay for computer equipment; however, the recordkeeper misread the amount and entered it in the accounting records with a debit to Computer Equipment and a credit to Cash of $2,060. The NSF check shown in the statement was originally received from a customer, S. Nilson, in payment of her account. Its return has not yet been recorded by the company. The credit memorandum is from the collection of a $1,500 note for Chavez Company by the bank. The bank deducted a $15 collection fee. The collection and fee are not yet recorded.

Required

1. Prepare the September 30, 2010, bank reconciliation for this company.

2. Prepare the journal entries to adjust the book balance of cash to the reconciled balance.

Check (1) Reconciled balance, $18,271.45 (2) Cr. Note Receivable $1,500

Analysis Component

3. The bank statement reveals that some of the prenumbered checks in the sequence are missing. Describe three situations that could explain this.

For each of these five separate cases, identify the basic control guideline(s) that is violated. Recommend what the business should do for better control.

1. Lavina Company is a small business that has separated the duties of cash receipts and cash disbursements. The employee responsible for cash disbursements reconciles the bank account monthly.

2. Latisha Tally personally opens all the mail for Professional Systems and performs monthly bank reconciliations.

3. Jim Sutton prides himself on hiring quality workers who require little supervision. As office manager, Jim allows his bookkeeper to sign checks for the business.

4. Victor Vu deposits cash receipts for Quality Lawncare once each week.

5. Gates' Dog Salon uses a petty cash system. Jill is the petty cash cashier, but she allows other employees to access the petty cash drawer if she is away from her desk.

PROBLEM SET B

Problem 8–1B
Analyzing internal control **LO1**

Blues Music Center had the following petty cash transactions in March of the current year.

March   5 Wrote a $250 check, cashed it, and gave the proceeds and the petty cashbox to Jen Rouse, the petty cashier.
    11 Paid $10.75 delivery charges on merchandise sold to a customer.
    12 Purchased file folders for $14.13 that are immediately used.
    14 Reimbursed Bob Geldof, the manager, $11.65 for office supplies purchased and used.
    18 Purchased printer paper for $20.54 that is immediately used.
    28 Paid postage expenses of $18.
    30 Reimbursed Geldof $56.80 for business car mileage.
    31 Cash of $119.13 remained in the fund. Sorted the petty cash receipts by accounts affected and exchanged them for a check to reimburse the fund for expenditures.
    31 The petty cash fund amount is increased by $50 to a total of $300.

Problem 8–2B
Establish, reimburse, and increase petty cash **LO4**

Required

1. Prepare the journal entry to establish the petty cash fund.

2. Prepare a petty cash payments report for March with these categories: delivery expense, mileage expense, postage expense, and office supplies expense. Sort the payments into the appropriate categories and total the expenses in each category.

3. Prepare the journal entries for part 2 to both (*a*) reimburse and (*b*) increase the fund amount.

Check (2) Total expenses $131.87

(3a) Cr. Cash $130.87

Moya Co. establishes a petty cash fund for payments of small amounts. The following transactions involving the petty cash fund occurred in January (the last month of the company's fiscal year).

Jan.   3 A company check for $150 is written and made payable to the petty cashier to establish the petty cash fund.
    14 A company check is written to replenish the fund for the following expenditures made since January 3.

Problem 8–3B
Establishing, reimbursing, and adjusting petty cash **LO4**

      a. Purchased office supplies for $14.29 that are immediately used up.

      b. Paid $19.60 COD shipping charges on merchandise purchased for resale. Hint: Debit "Transportation-In."

      c. Paid $38.57 to All-Tech for minor repairs to a computer.

      d. Paid $12.82 for items classified as miscellaneous expenses.

      e. Counted $62.28 remaining in the petty cash box.

15   Prepared a company check for $50 to increase the fund to $200.

31   The petty cashier reports that $17.35 remains in the fund. A company check is written to replenish the fund for the following expenditures made since January 14.

      f. Paid $50 to *The Smart Shopper* for an advertisement in January's newsletter.

      g. Paid $48.19 for postage expenses.

      h. Paid $78 to Smooth Delivery for delivery of merchandise.

31   The company decides that the January 15 increase in the fund was too little. It increases the fund by another $50, leaving a total of $250.

Required

Check (1) Cr. to Cash: Jan. 14,
$87.72; Jan. 15, $50

1. Prepare journal entries to establish the fund on January 3, to replenish it on January 14 and January 31, and to reflect any increase or decrease in the fund balance on January 15 and 31.

Analysis Component

2. Explain how the company's financial statements are affected if the petty cash fund is not replenished and no entry is made on January 31.

Problem 8-4B

Prepare a bank reconciliation and record adjustments **LO7**

The following information is available to reconcile Severino Co.'s book balance of cash with its bank statement cash balance as of December 31, 2010.

a. After posting is complete, the December 31 cash balance according to the accounting records is $32,878.30, and the bank statement cash balance for that date is $46,822.40.

b. Check No. 1273 for $4,589.30 and Check No. 1282 for $400.00, both written and entered in the accounting records in December, are not among the canceled checks. Two checks, No. 1231 for $2,289.00 and No. 1242 for $410.40, were outstanding on the most recent November 30 reconciliation. Check No. 1231 is listed with the December canceled checks, but Check No. 1242 is not.

c. When the December checks are compared with entries in the accounting records, it is found that Check No. 1267 had been correctly drawn for $3,456 to pay for office supplies but was erroneously entered in the accounting records as $3,465.

d. Two debit memoranda are enclosed with the statement and are unrecorded at the time of the reconciliation. One debit memorandum is for $762.50 and dealt with an NSF check for $745 received from a customer, Titus Industries, in payment of its account. The bank assessed a $17.50 fee for processing it. The second debit memorandum is a $99.00 charge for check printing. Severino did not record these transactions before receiving the statement.

e. A credit memorandum indicates that the bank collected $19,000 cash on a note receivable for the company, deducted a $20 collection fee, and credited the balance to the company's Cash account. Severino did not record this transaction before receiving the statement.

f. Severino's December 31 daily cash receipts of $9,583.10 were placed in the bank's night depository on that date, but do not appear on the December 31 bank statement.

Required

Check (1) Reconciled balance,
$51,005.80; (2) Cr. Note Receivable
$19,000

1. Prepare the bank reconciliation for this company as of December 31, 2010.

2. Prepare the journal entries necessary to bring the company's book balance of cash into conformity with the reconciled cash balance as of December 31, 2010.

Analysis Component

3. Explain the nature of the communications conveyed by a bank when the bank sends the depositor (*a*) a debit memorandum and (*b*) a credit memorandum.

Problem 8-5B

Prepare a bank reconciliation and record adjustments **LO6 LO7**

Shamara Systems Co. most recently reconciled its bank balance on April 30 and reported two checks outstanding at that time, No. 1771 for $781.00 and No. 1780 for $1,425.90. The following information is available for its May 31, 2010, reconciliation.

From the May 31 Bank Statement

Previous Balance	Total Checks and Debits	Total Deposits and Credits	Current Balance
18,290.70	13,094.80	16,566.80	21,762.70

Checks and Debits			Deposits and Credits		Daily Balance	
Date	No.	Amount	Date	Amount	Date	Amount
05/01	1771	781.00	05/04	2,438.00	04/30	18,290.70
05/02	1783	382.50	05/14	2,898.00	05/01	17,509.70
05/04	1782	1,285.50	05/22	1,801.80	05/02	17,127.20
05/11	1784	1,449.60	05/25	7,350.00 CM	05/04	18,279.70
05/18		431.80 NSF	05/26	2,079.00	05/11	16,830.10
05/25	1787	8,032.50			05/14	19,728.10
05/26	1785	63.90			05/18	19,296.30
05/29	1788	654.00			05/22	21,098.10
05/31		14.00 SC			05/25	20,415.60
					05/26	22,430.70
					05/29	21,776.70
					05/31	21,762.70

From Shamara Systems' Accounting Records

Cash Receipts Deposited

Date		Cash Debit
May	4	2,438.00
	14	2,898.00
	22	1,801.80
	26	2,079.00
	31	2,727.30
		11,944.10

Cash Disbursements

Check No.		Cash Credit
1782		1,285.50
1783		382.50
1784		1,449.60
1785		63.90
1786		353.10
1787		8,032.50
1788		644.00
1789		639.50
		12,850.60

Cash   **Acct. No. 101**

Date		Explanation	PR	Debit	Credit	Balance
Apr.	30	Balance				16,083.80
May	31	Total receipts	R7	11,944.10		28,027.90
	31	Total disbursements	D8		12,850.60	15,177.30

Additional Information

Check No. 1788 is correctly drawn for $654 to pay for May utilities; however, the recordkeeper misread the amount and entered it in the accounting records with a debit to Utilities Expense and a credit to Cash for $644. The bank paid and deducted the correct amount. The NSF check shown in the statement was originally received from a customer, W. Sox, in payment of her account. The company has not yet recorded its return. The credit memorandum is from a $7,400 note that the bank collected for the company. The bank deducted a $50 collection fee and deposited the remainder in the company's account. The collection and fee have not yet been recorded.

Required

1. Prepare the May 31, 2010, bank reconciliation for Shamara Systems.
2. Prepare the journal entries to adjust the book balance of cash to the reconciled balance.

Analysis Component

3. The bank statement reveals that some of the prenumbered checks in the sequence are missing. Describe three possible situations to explain this.

Check (1) Reconciled balance, $22,071.50; (2) Cr. Note Receivable $7,400

SERIAL PROBLEM

Success Systems

LO7

(This serial problem began in Chapter 1 and continues through most of the book. If previous chapter segments were not completed, the serial problem can begin at this point. It is helpful, but not necessary, that you use the Working Papers that accompany the book.)

SP 8   Adriana Lopez receives the March bank statement for Success Systems on April 11, 2011. The March 31 bank statement shows an ending cash balance of $86,896. A comparison of the bank statement with the general ledger Cash account, No. 101, reveals the following.

a. Lopez notices that the bank erroneously cleared a $470 check against her account that she did not issue. The check documentation included with the bank statement shows that this check was actually issued by a company named Sierra Systems.

b. On March 25, the bank issued a $50 debit memorandum for the safety deposit box that Success Systems agreed to rent from the bank beginning March 25.

c. On March 26, the bank issued a $75 debit memorandum for printed checks that Success Systems ordered from the bank.

d. On March 31, the bank issued a credit memorandum for $33 interest earned on Success Systems's checking account for the month of March.

e. Lopez notices that the check she issued for $192 on March 31, 2011, has not yet cleared the bank.

f. Lopez verifies that all deposits made in March do appear on the March bank statement.

g. The general ledger Cash account, No. 101, shows an ending cash balance per books as $87,266 (prior to any reconciliation).

Required

1. Prepare a bank reconciliation for Success Systems for the month ended March 31, 2011.

2. Prepare any necessary adjusting entries. Use Miscellaneous Expenses, No. 677, for any bank charges. Use Interest Revenue, No. 404, for any interest earned on the checking account for the month of March.

BEYOND THE NUMBERS

REPORTING IN ACTION

LO1

BTN 8-1   Refer to **Best Buy**'s financial statements in Appendix A to answer the following.

1. For both fiscal year-ends March 1, 2008, and March 3, 2007, identify the total amount of cash and cash equivalents. Determine the percent this amount represents of total current assets, total current liabilities, total shareholders' equity, and total assets for both years. Comment on any trends.

2. For fiscal years ended March 1, 2008, and March 3, 2007, use the information in the statement of cash flows to determine the percent change between the beginning and ending year amounts of cash and cash equivalents.

ETHICS CHALLENGE

LO1   LO2   LO3

BTN 8-2   Harriet Knox, Ralph Patton, and Marcia Diamond work for a family physician, Dr. Gwen Conrad, who is in private practice. Dr. Conrad is knowledgeable about office management practices and has segregated the cash receipt duties as follows. Knox opens the mail and prepares a triplicate list of money received. She sends one copy of the list to Patton, the cashier, who deposits the receipts daily in the bank. Diamond, the recordkeeper, receives a copy of the list and posts payments to patients' accounts. About once a month the office clerks have an expensive lunch they pay for as follows. First, Patton endorses a patient's check in Dr. Conrad's name and cashes it at the bank. Knox then destroys the remittance advice accompanying the check. Finally, Diamond posts payment to the customer's account as a miscellaneous credit. The three justify their actions by their relatively low pay and knowledge that Dr. Conrad will likely never miss the money.

Required

1. Who is the best person in Dr. Conrad's office to reconcile the bank statement?

2. Would a bank reconciliation uncover this office fraud?

3. What are some procedures to detect this type of fraud?

4. Suggest additional controls that Dr. Conrad could implement.

BTN 8-3   You make a surprise count of a $300 petty cash fund. You arrive at the petty cashier when she is on the telephone. She politely asks that you return after lunch so that she can finish her business on the telephone. You agree and return after lunch. In the petty cashbox, you find 14 new $20 bills with consecutive serial numbers plus receipts totaling $20. What is your evaluation?

Required

Explain your evaluation. Provide a response in memorandum format.

WORKPLACE COMMUNICATION
LO4

BTN 8-4   Visit the Association of Certified Fraud Examiners Website at <u>acfe.com</u>. Review the cash frauds (refer to the 2008 *Report to the Nation;* see Fraud resource center—under publications—and answer the following questions.

Required

1. What percentage of asset misappropriation schemes involve cash?
2. Fraudsters who steal cash generally must access the money at one of three points within the victim's organization. What are the three points?
3. What are the five types of fraudulent disbursement schemes? What is the most common form of cash scheme? Which type of fraudulent disbursements has the high median dollar loss per occurrence?

TAKING IT TO THE NET
LO1   LO2   LO3

BTN 8-5   Refer to the chapter opener on **Wildflower Linens**. Identify and describe several cash controls that Wildflower Linens likely uses.

ENTREPRENEURS IN BUSINESS
LO2   LO3

1. e; The entry follows.

Debits to expenses (or assets)	420
Cash Over and Short	5
Cash	425

4. c
5. d

ANSWERS TO MULTIPLE CHOICE QUIZ

2. a; recognizes cash collection of note by bank.
3. a; the bank reconciliation follows.

Bank Reconciliation November 30			
Balance per bank statement	$1,895	Balance per books	$1,742
Add: Deposit in transit	795	Add: Note collected (net fee)	320
Deduct: Outstanding checks	(638)	Deduct: Service charge	(10)
Reconciled balance	$2,052	Reconciled balance	$2,052

A Look Back

Chapter 8 focused on cash. We showed how petty cash systems, bank reconciliations, and banking activities can help the business owner control cash.

A Look at This Chapter

This chapter emphasizes employee payroll. We show how to compute payroll deductions to comply with laws. We also show how the employer uses a payroll register and employee earnings records to record and control its payroll.

A Look Ahead

Chapter 10 explains how the employer pays taxes. It also shows the tax documents the employer must file to comply with laws.

Chapter 9

Employee Earnings, Deductions, and Payroll

Learning Objectives

LO 1	Describe the laws that affect employee payroll.
LO 2	Compute employee gross pay.
LO 3	Compute employee deductions for taxes and net pay.
LO 4	Record employee payroll information in a payroll register.
LO 5	Journalize payroll transactions in a general journal.
LO 6	Prepare an earnings record for each employee.
LO 7	Explain how an employer can control payroll.

"Get a clear vision and stick to it"
—Jason Osborn

Granola Gurus

NEW YORK—Jason Osborn never planned to be an entrepreneur. "It was sort of an accident," explains Osborn. "I was looking for a healthy snack food as an alternative to cookies and brownies." Osborn started cooking with granola and his concoctions caught on. After sharing it with his buddy, Jason Wright, the two decided to launch **Feed Granola Company (FeedGranola.com),** a provider of granola snacks made with organic multi-grains.

"We started peddling it . . . to a few different coffee shops and one natural health food store," recalls Osborn. "That created a small demand and we realized we had a viable product." Adds Wright, "I had no idea that I would have a granola company one day!" Their commitment to healthy food carries over to the financial side. The two especially focus on the important task of managing liabilities for payroll, supplies, employee benefits, vacations, training, and taxes. Both insist that effective management of liabilities, especially payroll and employee benefits, is crucial to success. They stress that monitoring and controlling payroll costs are a must.

To help control costs, Osborn describes how they began by trading their granola products for kitchen space. "We partnered with a meal delivery service and bartered to use their kitchen space," explains Osborn. "We'd bake our granola during the night when they weren't using it and we paid for the usage in granola. That's how we paid rent."

The two continue to monitor liabilities and their payment patterns. "Trying to balance receivables versus payables is always a big challenge," explains Wright. "When you are a small, growing company, cash flow is always a problem." The two insist that accounting for and monitoring payroll costs, the labor laws, and payroll taxes are key to a successful startup. Their company now generates sufficient income to pay for liabilities and produces revenue growth for expansion. "We want to expand our product line," says Osborn. "[Soon] we'll be available in almost every region of the country."

[Sources: *Feed Granola Website,* January 2009; *BusinessWeek,* September 2007; *Inc.com,* July and October 2007; *The Wall Street Journal,* May 2008]

In this chapter we discuss the laws that require the employer to withhold amounts from employee pay for taxes. These amounts are additional liabilities in the journal entry to record wages. We also show how the employer can use payroll registers and employee earnings records to comply with laws and control payroll expenses.

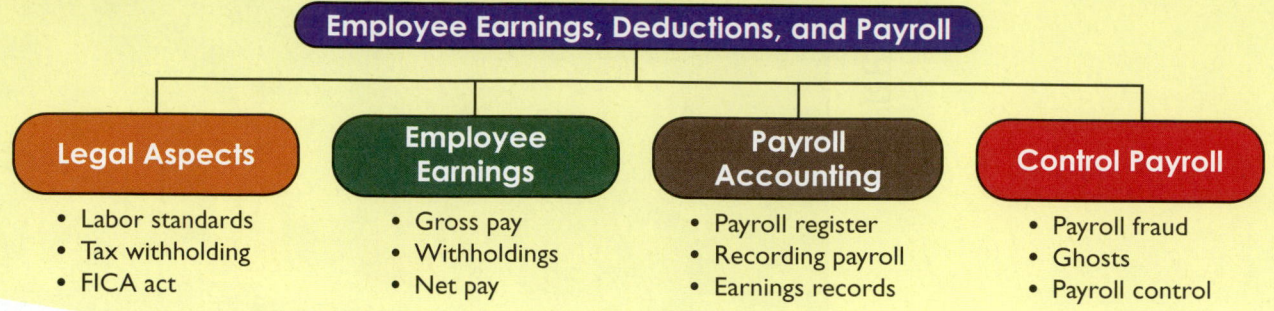

Employee Earnings, Deductions, and Payroll			
Legal Aspects	**Employee Earnings**	**Payroll Accounting**	**Control Payroll**
• Labor standards • Tax withholding • FICA act	• Gross pay • Withholdings • Net pay	• Payroll register • Recording payroll • Earnings records	• Payroll fraud • Ghosts • Payroll control

Legal Aspects of Employee Payroll

Most employees and employers pay federal and state payroll taxes. Laws require employers to also prepare and submit reports that explain how they computed tax payments. Governments can impose penalties if the employer does not follow payroll tax laws. Law requires employers to withhold amounts from employees' pay for taxes. An **employee** is someone whose work is under the direction of the employer, such as a bookkeeper or secretary. The employer controls what work the employee is to do and how it should be done. For example, employees are typically trained to perform tasks a certain way. An **independent contractor** performs a job for the employer, but decides how to do the work. Independent contractors typically do not receive training from the employer. The employer does not withhold any money for taxes for independent contractors. Using independent contractors can help businesses lower their payroll costs. However, the employer must be careful in classifying employees as independent contractors to withstand potential audit by the Internal Revenue Service.

Fair Labor Standards Act

LO1 Describe the laws that affect employee payroll.

This law applies to firms engaged in business across states. It sets a minimum wage, currently $7.25 per hour (as of July 24, 2009), and sets 40 hours as the most an employee can be required to work in a week at the normal pay rate. Employees that work more than 40 hours in a week receive overtime pay. This pay is at least one and one-half times their normal pay rate for those overtime hours.

Federal and State Income Tax Withholding

Each employee fills out an **Employee's Withholding Allowance Certificate (Form W-4)** as shown in Exhibit 9.1. The employer withholds a different amount of federal taxes for each employee. These amounts depend on the employee's marital status, his or her **gross pay,** and the number of withholding allowances the employee claims. Gross pay is the total amount an employee earns before deductions such as taxes. A **withholding allowance** lowers the amount of an employee's gross pay that is taxed. Each employee gets one personal allowance, one for a spouse if they are married, and one for each child or dependent. The more allowances an employee claims, the less tax the employer withholds.

For example, Robert Austin is an employee of Phoenix Sales and Service, a landscape design company. He is single (box 3) and has no dependents. He chooses one withholding allowance (box 5) and elects to have no additional amounts withheld from his paycheck (box 6). Employees who did not pay any taxes in the previous year and do not expect to pay taxes in the current year do not have taxes withheld from their paychecks. They write "Exempt" in box 7 on their W-4.

Exhibit 9.1

Employee's Withholding
Allowance Certificate (W-4)

Cut here and give Form W-4 to your employer. Keep the top part for your records.

Form **W-4**	**Employee's Withholding Allowance Certificate**	OMB No. 1545-0010

Department of the Treasury
Internal Revenue Service   ▶ Whether you are entitled to claim a certain number of allowances or exemption from withholding is subject to review by the IRS. Your employer may be required to send a copy of this form to the IRS.

1 Type or print your first name and middle initial	Last name	2 Your social security number
Robert J.	Austin	333 : 22 : 9999

Home address (number and street or rural route)
18 Roosevelt Blvd., Apt. C

3   ☑ Single   ☐ Married   ☐ Married, but withhold at higher Single rate.
Note. If married, but legally separated, or spouse is a nonresident alien, check the "Single" box.

City or town, state, and ZIP code
Tempe, AZ 86322

4   If your last name differs from that shown on your social security card, check here. You must call 1-800-772-1213 for a new card.   ▶ ☐

5   Total number of allowances you are claiming (from line H above or from the applicable worksheet on page 2) . . . . | 5 | 1 |
6   Additional amount, if any, you want withheld from each paycheck . . . . | 6 | $0 |

7   I claim exemption from withholding for 2009, and I certify that I meet both of the following conditions for exemption.
• Last year I had a right to a refund of all federal income tax withheld because I had no tax liability and
• This year I expect a refund of all federal income tax withheld because I expect to have no tax liability.
If you meet both conditions, write "Exempt" here . . . . ▶ | 7 |

Under penalties of perjury, I declare that I have examined this certificate and to the best of my knowledge and belief, it is true, correct, and complete.

Employee's signature
(Form is not valid
unless you sign it.) ▶ *Robert J. Austin*   Date ▶ 01/01/09

8 Employer's name and address [Employer, Complete lines 8 and 10 only if sending to the IRS.]	9 Office code (optional)	10 Employer identification number (EIN)
Phoenix Sales & Service, 1214 Mill Road, Phoenix, AZ 85621		86 : 3214587

For Privacy Act and Paperwork Reduction Act Notice, see page 2.   Cat. No. 102200   Form **W-4** (2009)

Federal Insurance Contributions Act (FICA)

The federal Social Security system pays benefits to qualified workers. Employers usually separate **FICA** taxes into two groups: (1) retirement, disability, and survivors, and (2) medical. The first group is called *Social Security benefits* and it is paid for with *Social Security taxes*. The second group is called *Medicare benefits* and it is paid for with *Medicare taxes*.

Law requires employers to withhold FICA taxes from employees to pay for this system. For the year 2009, the amount withheld from each employee's pay for Social Security taxes is 6.2% of the first $106,800 the employee earns during the calendar year. The most an individual employee could pay for Social Security tax in 2009 is $6,621.60 (0.062 × $106,800). The Medicare tax for 2009 is 1.45% of *all* amounts the employee earns. There is no upper limit on the amount of Medicare tax an employee could pay. For any changes in tax rates or maximum earnings levels, check the IRS Website at **www.IRS.gov** or the Social Security Administration Website at **www.SSA.gov**.

To illustrate the calculation of the Social Security and Medicare (FICA) taxes, assume the following income for Kelly Wheeler:

	Gross Earnings	
Pay Period	**Current**	**Year-to-Date**
December 5–11, 2009	$2,100	$105,850
December 12–18, 2009	2,150	108,000

During the pay period December 12–18, 2009, Wheeler's earnings for the calendar year went over the $106,800 Social Security maximum earnings limit by $1,200:

Year-to-date earnings	$108,000
Social Security earnings maximum for 2009	106,800
Portion of Kelly's December 12–18, 2009, earnings not subject to Social Security tax.	$ 1,200

Therefore, $1,200 of his earnings would not be subject to the Social Security tax. The Social Security tax on Wheeler's December 12–18, 2009, earnings would be:

Gross earnings.	$2,150.00
Portion of Kelly's earnings not subject to Social Security tax	1,200.00
Portion of Kelly's earnings subject to Social Security tax.	$ 950.00
Social Security tax rate	6.2%
Social Security tax	$ 58.90

All earnings are subject to the Medicare tax. Therefore, the Social Security tax on Wheeler's December 12–18, 2009, earnings would be:

Gross earnings	$2,150.00
Medicare tax rate	1.45%
Medicare tax	$ 31.18

Kelly Wheeler's total Social Security and Medicare (FICA) taxes for the December 12–18, 2009, pay period would be:

Social Security tax.	$58.90
Medicare tax	31.18
Total Social Security and Medicare taxes	$90.08

Self–Employment Tax   Persons who operate their own businesses as sole proprietors or independent contractors pay **self-employment tax.** A self-employed person must pay both the employee and employer FICA taxes. The self-employment tax rates are 12.4% (6.2% $\times$ 2) for Social Security and 2.9% (1.45% $\times$ 2) for Medicare. So, the most a self-employed person could pay for Social Security taxes in 2009 is $13,243.20 (2 $\times$ 0.062 $\times$ $106,800). There is no upper limit on the amount of Medicare tax a self-employed person could pay. Currently, people who earn $400 or more from self-employment must pay self-employment tax. This also applies to individuals who operate a part-time business in addition to a regular job.

Employee Earnings and Withholdings

Three steps are needed to determine how much to pay an employee each pay period:

1. Compute employee gross pay.
2. Determine the total amount of withholdings to deduct from gross pay.
3. Compute net pay by subtracting total withholdings from gross pay.

This section explains how we compute employee gross pay and net pay, and how withholdings impact employee pay.

Compute Employee Gross Pay

LO2 Compute employee gross pay.

Generally, management and administrative workers receive a salary. A **salary** is a fixed amount of compensation paid or received on a regular basis—every two weeks, monthly, or annually. Skilled or unskilled labor generally receive wages. **Wages** are money paid or received for work or services by the hour, day, or week or by the number of units produced.

Many employers pay wages for each hour worked. The employer must keep records of the number of hours each employee works on each day during a pay period. This can be done with a time sheet or a time clock. For example, see Exhibit 9.2 for Robert Austin's time sheet for the week ending January 7, 2009.

Time Sheet

EMPLOYEE ID No.	EMPLOYEE NAME	WEEK ENDING
AR101	Robert Austin	January 7, 2009

DAY	TIME IN	TIME OUT	TIME IN	TIME OUT	REGULAR	OVERTIME
Mon	7:30	11:30	12:30	4:30	8	
Tues	8:05	12:00	1:00	5:05	8	
Wed	8:00	12:00	12:30	4:30	8	
Thurs	7:45	11:45	12:45	4:45	8	
Fri	7:15	12:15	12:45	3:45	8	
				Total Hours	40	

Enter your time in HH:MM format

Exhibit 9.2

Employee Time Sheet

If Robert Austin earns a wage of $10 per hour worked, his gross pay for the week of January 7, 2009, is $400 (40 × $10). John Diaz, another employee of Phoenix Sales and Service, turns in a time card for the week of January 7, 2009, that shows he worked 40 regular hours and 2 overtime hours. If John Diaz's normal pay rate is $14 per hour, and he is paid one and one-half times his normal pay rate for overtime, his gross pay for the week ending January 7, 2009, is computed as:

Regular pay	40 hours × $14 per hour =	$560
Overtime premium	2 hours × $21 per hour =	42
Total gross pay		$602

Compute Withholdings from Employee Gross Pay

Payroll deductions, commonly called *withholdings,* are amounts withheld from an employee's gross pay. Required deductions result from law and include income taxes and Social Security taxes. Voluntary deductions, at an employee's option, include pension and health contributions, union dues, and charitable giving. Exhibit 9.3 summarizes the typical employee payroll deductions.

L03 Compute employee deductions for taxes and net pay.

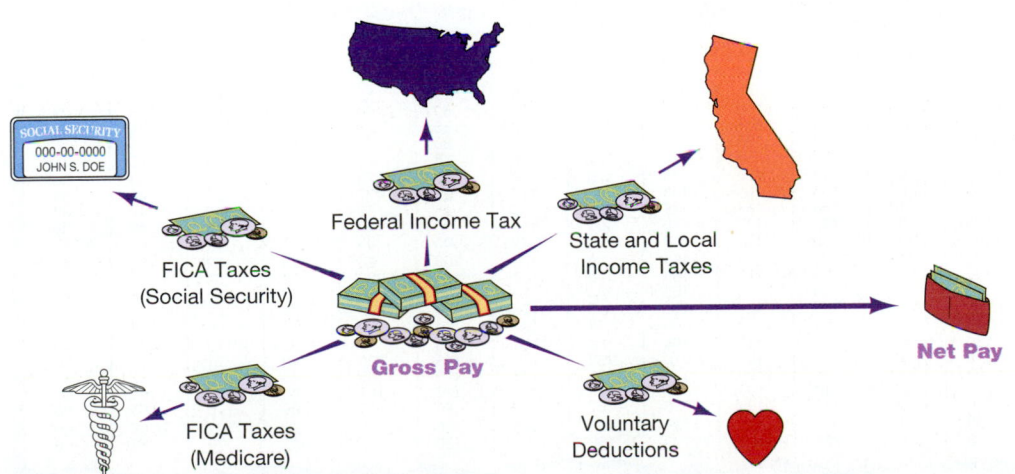

Exhibit 9.3

Payroll Deductions

Federal Income Tax Withholding   The employer uses a withholding table (called **Circular E**) from the IRS to compute the amount of federal taxes to withhold. Circular E is available for free from **www.IRS.gov**. Separate withholding tables are provided for single or married persons, and for different pay periods (for example, weekly or monthly). Exhibit 9.4 provides a part of a

Exhibit 9.4

Withholding Table Example—
Single Persons Paid Weekly

SINGLE Persons—WEEKLY Payroll Period
(For Wages Paid Through December 2009)

If the wages are—		And the number of withholding allowances claimed is—										
At least	But less than	0	1	2	3	4	5	6	7	8	9	10
		The amount of income tax to be withheld is—										
$400	$410	$37	$26	$16	$6	$0	$0	$0	$0	$0	$0	$0
410	420	38	28	17	7	0	0	0	0	0	0	0
420	430	40	29	19	8	1	0	0	0	0	0	0
430	440	41	31	20	10	2	0	0	0	0	0	0
440	450	43	32	22	11	3	0	0	0	0	0	0
450	460	44	34	23	13	4	0	0	0	0	0	0
460	470	46	35	25	14	5	0	0	0	0	0	0
470	480	47	37	26	16	6	0	0	0	0	0	0
480	490	49	38	28	17	7	0	0	0	0	0	0
490	500	50	40	29	19	8	1	0	0	0	0	0
500	510	52	41	31	20	10	2	0	0	0	0	0
510	520	53	43	32	22	11	3	0	0	0	0	0
520	530	55	44	34	23	13	4	0	0	0	0	0
530	540	56	46	35	25	14	5	0	0	0	0	0
540	550	58	47	37	26	16	6	0	0	0	0	0
550	560	59	49	38	28	17	7	0	0	0	0	0
560	570	61	50	40	29	19	8	1	0	0	0	0
570	580	62	52	41	31	20	10	2	0	0	0	0
580	590	64	53	43	32	22	11	3	0	0	0	0
590	600	65	55	44	34	23	13	4	0	0	0	0
600	610	67	56	46	35	25	14	5	0	0	0	0
610	620	68	58	47	37	26	16	6	0	0	0	0
620	630	70	59	49	38	28	17	7	0	0	0	0
630	640	71	61	50	40	29	19	8	1	0	0	0
640	650	73	62	52	41	31	20	10	2	0	0	0
650	660	74	64	53	43	32	22	11	3	0	0	0
660	670	76	65	55	44	34	23	13	4	0	0	0
670	680	77	67	56	46	35	25	14	5	0	0	0
680	690	79	68	58	47	37	26	16	6	0	0	0
690	700	80	70	59	49	38	28	17	7	0	0	0
700	710	83	71	61	50	40	29	19	8	1	0	0
710	720	85	73	62	52	41	31	20	10	2	0	0
720	730	88	74	64	53	43	32	22	11	3	0	0
730	740	90	76	65	55	44	34	23	13	4	0	0
740	750	93	77	67	56	46	35	25	14	5	0	0
800	810	108	90	76	65	55	44	34	23	13	4	0
810	820	110	93	77	67	56	46	35	25	14	5	0
820	830	113	95	79	68	58	47	37	26	16	6	0
830	840	115	98	80	70	59	49	38	28	17	7	0
840	850	118	100	83	71	61	50	40	29	19	8	1
900	910	133	115	98	80	70	59	49	38	28	17	7
910	920	135	118	100	83	71	61	50	40	29	19	8
920	930	138	120	103	85	73	62	52	41	31	20	10
930	940	140	123	105	88	74	64	53	43	32	22	11
940	950	143	125	108	90	76	65	55	44	34	23	13
950	960	145	128	110	93	77	67	56	46	35	25	14
960	970	148	130	113	95	79	68	58	47	37	26	16
970	980	150	133	115	98	80	70	59	49	38	28	17
980	990	153	135	118	100	83	71	61	50	40	29	19
990	1,000	155	138	120	103	85	73	62	52	41	31	20
1,010	1,020	160	143	125	108	90	76	65	55	44	34	23
1,020	1,030	163	145	128	110	93	77	67	56	46	35	25
1,030	1,040	165	148	130	113	95	79	68	58	47	37	26
1,040	1,050	168	150	133	115	98	80	70	59	49	38	28
1,050	1,060	170	153	135	118	100	83	71	61	50	40	29
1,060	1,070	173	155	138	120	103	85	73	62	52	41	31
1,070	1,080	175	158	140	123	105	88	74	64	53	43	32
1,080	1,090	178	160	143	125	108	90	76	65	55	44	34
1,090	1,100	180	163	145	128	110	93	77	67	56	46	35
1,100	1,110	183	165	148	130	113	95	79	68	58	47	37
1,110	1,120	185	168	150	133	115	98	80	70	59	49	38
1,120	1,130	188	170	153	135	118	100	83	71	61	50	40
1,130	1,140	190	173	155	138	120	103	85	73	62	52	41
1,140	1,150	193	175	158	140	123	105	88	74	64	53	43
1,150	1,160	195	178	160	143	125	108	90	76	65	55	44
1,160	1,170	198	180	163	145	128	110	93	77	67	56	46
1,170	1,180	200	183	165	148	130	113	95	79	68	58	47
1,180	1,190	203	185	168	150	133	115	98	80	70	59	49
1,190	1,200	205	188	170	153	135	118	100	82	71	61	50
1,200	1,210	208	190	173	155	138	120	103	85	73	62	52
1,210	1,220	210	193	175	158	140	123	105	87	74	64	53
1,220	1,230	213	195	178	160	143	125	108	90	76	65	55
1,230	1,240	215	198	180	163	145	128	110	92	77	67	56
1,240	1,250	218	200	183	165	148	130	113	95	79	68	58

Exhibit 9.5

Withholding Table Example—
Married Persons Paid Weekly

MARRIED Persons—WEEKLY Payroll Period
(For Wages Paid Through December 2009)

If the wages are— At least	But less than	0	1	2	3	4	5	6	7	8	9	10
		The amount of income tax to be withheld is—										
$400	$410	$10	$3	$0	$0	$0	$0	$0	$0	$0	$0	$0
410	420	11	4	0	0	0	0	0	0	0	0	0
420	430	12	5	0	0	0	0	0	0	0	0	0
430	440	13	6	0	0	0	0	0	0	0	0	0
440	450	14	7	0	0	0	0	0	0	0	0	0
450	460	15	8	1	0	0	0	0	0	0	0	0
460	470	16	9	2	0	0	0	0	0	0	0	0
470	480	17	10	3	0	0	0	0	0	0	0	0
480	490	19	11	4	0	0	0	0	0	0	0	0
490	500	20	12	5	0	0	0	0	0	0	0	0
500	510	22	13	6	0	0	0	0	0	0	0	0
510	520	23	14	7	0	0	0	0	0	0	0	0
520	530	25	15	8	1	0	0	0	0	0	0	0
530	540	26	16	9	2	0	0	0	0	0	0	0
540	550	28	17	10	3	0	0	0	0	0	0	0
550	560	29	19	11	4	0	0	0	0	0	0	0
560	570	31	20	12	5	0	0	0	0	0	0	0
570	580	32	22	13	6	0	0	0	0	0	0	0
580	590	34	23	14	7	0	0	0	0	0	0	0
590	600	35	25	15	8	1	0	0	0	0	0	0
600	610	37	26	16	9	2	0	0	0	0	0	0
610	620	38	28	17	10	3	0	0	0	0	0	0
620	630	40	29	19	11	4	0	0	0	0	0	0
630	640	41	31	20	12	5	0	0	0	0	0	0
740	750	58	47	37	26	16	9	2	0	0	0	0
750	760	59	49	38	28	17	10	3	0	0	0	0
760	770	61	50	40	29	19	11	4	0	0	0	0
770	780	62	52	41	31	20	12	5	0	0	0	0
780	790	64	53	43	32	22	13	6	0	0	0	0
790	800	65	55	44	34	23	14	7	0	0	0	0
800	810	67	56	46	35	25	15	8	1	0	0	0
810	820	68	58	47	37	26	16	9	2	0	0	0
820	830	70	59	49	38	28	17	10	3	0	0	0
830	840	71	61	50	40	29	19	11	4	0	0	0
840	850	73	62	52	41	31	20	12	5	0	0	0
850	860	74	64	53	43	32	22	13	6	0	0	0
860	870	76	65	55	44	34	23	14	7	0	0	0
870	880	77	67	56	46	35	25	15	8	1	0	0
880	890	79	68	58	47	37	26	16	9	2	0	0
890	900	80	70	59	49	38	28	17	10	3	0	0
900	910	82	71	61	50	40	29	19	11	4	0	0
910	920	83	73	62	52	41	31	20	12	5	0	0
920	930	85	74	64	53	43	32	22	13	6	0	0
930	940	86	76	65	55	44	34	23	14	7	0	0
940	950	88	77	67	56	46	35	25	15	8	1	0
950	960	89	79	68	58	47	37	26	16	9	2	0
960	970	91	80	70	59	49	38	28	17	10	3	0
970	980	92	82	71	61	50	40	29	19	11	4	0
980	990	94	83	73	62	52	41	31	20	12	5	0
990	1,000	95	85	74	64	53	43	32	22	13	6	0
1,000	1,010	97	86	76	65	55	44	34	23	14	7	0
1,010	1,020	98	88	77	67	56	46	35	25	15	8	1
1,020	1,030	100	89	79	68	58	47	37	26	16	9	2
1,030	1,040	101	91	80	70	59	49	38	28	17	10	3
1,090	1,100	110	100	89	79	68	58	47	37	26	16	9
1,100	1,110	112	101	91	80	70	59	49	38	28	17	10
1,110	1,120	113	103	92	82	71	61	50	40	29	19	11
1,120	1,130	115	104	94	83	73	62	52	41	31	20	12
1,130	1,140	116	106	95	85	74	64	53	43	32	22	13
1,140	1,150	118	107	97	86	76	65	55	44	34	23	14
1,150	1,160	119	109	98	88	77	67	56	46	35	25	15
1,160	1,170	121	110	100	89	79	68	58	47	37	26	16
1,170	1,180	122	112	101	91	80	70	59	49	38	28	17
1,180	1,190	124	113	103	92	82	71	61	50	40	29	19
1,190	1,200	125	115	104	94	83	73	62	52	41	31	20
1,200	1,210	127	116	106	95	85	74	64	53	43	32	22
1,210	1,220	128	118	107	97	86	76	65	55	44	34	23
1,220	1,230	130	119	109	98	88	77	67	56	46	35	25
1,230	1,240	131	121	110	100	89	79	68	58	47	37	26

Circular E withholding table for single persons paid weekly. Exhibits 9.5, 9.6, and 9.7 show additional excerpts from the withholding table. IRS withholding tables are based on projecting weekly (or other period) pay into an annual amount.

From his W-4 form, Robert Austin is a single employee who claims one withholding allowance. He is paid each week. Robert's gross pay was $400 for the week ending January 7, 2009. To determine Robert's federal tax withholding, use the withholding table in Exhibit 9.4. Scan the "If wages are" columns until "at least $400 but less than $410" is found. This range includes the $400 of income Robert earned this week. Then find the column for 1 withholding allowance and scan down the table to the row found earlier. Based on Robert's gross pay of $400 and his one withholding

Exhibit 9.6

Withholding Table Example—
Single Persons Paid Monthly

SINGLE Persons—MONTHLY Payroll Period
(For Wages Paid Through December 2009)

If the wages are—		And the number of withholding allowances claimed is—										
At least	But less than	0	1	2	3	4	5	6	7	8	9	10
		The amount of income tax to be withheld is—										
1,840	1,880	176	130	85	39	5	0	0	0	0	0	0
1,880	1,920	182	136	91	45	9	0	0	0	0	0	0
1,920	1,960	188	142	97	51	13	0	0	0	0	0	0
1,960	2,000	194	148	103	57	17	0	0	0	0	0	0
2,000	2,040	200	154	109	63	21	0	0	0	0	0	0
2,040	2,080	206	160	115	69	25	0	0	0	0	0	0
2,080	2,120	212	166	121	75	29	0	0	0	0	0	0
2,120	2,160	218	172	127	81	35	2	0	0	0	0	0
2,160	2,200	224	178	133	87	41	6	0	0	0	0	0
2,200	2,240	230	184	139	93	47	10	0	0	0	0	0
2,240	2,280	236	190	145	99	53	14	0	0	0	0	0
2,280	2,320	242	196	151	105	59	18	0	0	0	0	0
2,320	2,360	248	202	157	111	65	22	0	0	0	0	0
2,360	2,400	254	208	163	117	71	26	0	0	0	0	0
2,400	2,440	260	214	169	123	77	32	0	0	0	0	0

Exhibit 9.7

Withholding Table Example—
Married Persons Paid Monthly

MARRIED Persons—MONTHLY Payroll Period
(For Wages Paid Through December 2009)

If the wages are—		And the number of withholding allowances claimed is—										
At least	But less than	0	1	2	3	4	5	6	7	8	9	10
		The amount of income tax to be withheld is—										
$0	$1,320	$0	$0	$0	$0	$0	$0	$0	$0	$0	$0	$0
1,320	1,360	3	0	0	0	0	0	0	0	0	0	0
1,360	1,400	7	0	0	0	0	0	0	0	0	0	0
1,400	1,440	11	0	0	0	0	0	0	0	0	0	0
1,440	1,480	15	0	0	0	0	0	0	0	0	0	0
1,480	1,520	19	0	0	0	0	0	0	0	0	0	0
1,520	1,560	23	0	0	0	0	0	0	0	0	0	0
1,560	1,600	27	0	0	0	0	0	0	0	0	0	0
1,600	1,640	31	0	0	0	0	0	0	0	0	0	0
1,640	1,680	35	4	0	0	0	0	0	0	0	0	0
1,680	1,720	39	8	0	0	0	0	0	0	0	0	0
4,800	4,840	490	444	399	353	307	262	216	171	125	79	47
4,840	4,880	496	450	405	359	313	268	222	177	131	85	51
4,880	4,920	502	456	411	365	319	274	228	183	137	91	55
4,920	4,960	508	462	417	371	325	280	234	189	143	97	59
4,960	5,000	514	468	423	377	331	286	240	195	149	103	63
5,000	5,040	520	474	429	383	337	292	246	201	155	109	67
5,040	5,080	526	480	435	389	343	298	252	207	161	115	71
5,080	5,120	532	486	441	395	349	304	258	213	167	121	76
5,120	5,160	538	492	447	401	355	310	264	219	173	127	82
5,160	5,200	544	498	453	407	361	316	270	225	179	133	88
5,200	5,240	550	504	459	413	367	322	276	231	185	139	94

allowance, Phoenix Sales and Service will withhold $26 for federal taxes from Robert's gross pay for the week of January 7, 2009.

State Income Tax Withholding   States withhold income taxes based on either withholding tables or a percentage of the amount withheld for federal taxes. In our examples we assume the state income tax withholding is 8 percent of the dollar amount withheld for federal income tax. Phoenix Sales and Service will withhold $2.08 (0.08 × $26) from Robert's pay for Arizona state income tax.

FICA Withholding   As of January 7, 2009, Robert Austin has earned less than the $106,800 annual maximum for Social Security taxes. Phoenix Sales and Service will withhold $24.80 (0.062 × $400) from his gross pay for FICA Social Security taxes. Phoenix Sales and Service will also withhold $5.80 (0.0145 × $400) from his gross pay for Medicare taxes.

Voluntary Deductions   The required deductions above result from laws. Employees can choose to have other amounts withheld from their pay. These voluntary deductions can include contributions for retirement and health plans, union dues, and gifts to charity. In this example Robert Austin has not chosen any voluntary deductions.

Compute Net Pay

An employee's **net pay,** also called *take-home pay,* is gross pay minus all withholdings. For the week of January 7, 2009, Robert Austin's net pay is computed as

Gross pay	$400.00
Minus deductions for:	
Federal income tax withholding	(26.00)
State income tax withholding	(2.08)
FICA—Social Security	(24.80)
FICA—Medicare	(5.80)
Net pay	$341.32

IN THE NEWS

A growing number of companies let employees collect their pay in "payroll cards." These cards are like debit cards and allow the employee to withdraw cash from ATMs or make purchases. They are particularly useful for employees who do not have bank accounts or whose small bank account balances would generate high fees. The use of "paperless" payroll can lower payroll processing costs by up to 75%.

HOW YOU DOIN'?

Answers—p. 219

1. A company pays its one employee $3,000 per month. This company's Social Security tax rate is 6.2% of the first $106,800; and its Medicare tax rate is 1.45% of all amounts earned. The company's March payroll will include what amount for employee Social Security and Medicare taxes?

2. Identify whether the employer or employee or both incur each of the following: (a) FICA taxes, and (b) withheld income taxes.

3. An employee worked 45 hours in a pay period. She earns $16 per hour and one and one-half her normal hourly wage for all overtime hours. What is her gross pay?

Payroll Accounting

This section describes payroll accounting, including the purpose and importance of a payroll register, the recording of payroll, and the use of banking services in dispensing payroll.

Payroll Register

LO4 Record employee payroll information in a payroll register.

A **payroll register** is often used to keep a record of pay period dates, hours worked, gross pay, deductions, and net pay of each employee for each pay period. Exhibit 9.8 shows the payroll register for Phoenix Sales and Service as of January 7, 2009. For each employee, the register includes whether they are single (S) or married (M) and the number of withholding allowances they chose on their Form W-4. This information is used with each employee's gross pay, and the withholding tables from Circular E, to determine the correct amount of tax to withhold for federal income taxes. This amount is reported in the "Federal Income Tax" column. In our example, withholdings for state purposes are 8% of the amount withheld for federal income tax; the amount is shown in the "State Income Tax" column in the payroll register.

Phoenix Sales and Service collects time sheets from each of its employees, verifies their accuracy, and records the number of hours worked in the "Hours Worked This Pay Period" column. Each employee's hourly wage is entered into the "Hourly Wage" column, and employee gross earnings (regular and overtime) are computed as we showed earlier for Robert Austin and John Diaz.

The payroll register also reports the gross pay used to compute Social Security, Medicare, and the employer's unemployment taxes (in the "Taxable Earnings For" columns). These amounts can be different. For example, once an employee has earned at least $7,000 during a year, the employer stops paying unemployment tax for that employee. (We discuss employer payroll taxes, including

Only employers pay unemployment taxes.

Exhibit 9.8

Phoenix Sales and Service Payroll Register for Week Ended January 7, 2009

Payroll Register

Employee Name	Marital Status and Allowances	Beginning Cumulative Gross Earnings	Hours Worked This Pay Period	Hourly Wage	EARNINGS THIS PERIOD			Ending Cumulative Gross Earnings
					Regular	Overtime	Gross	
Austin, Robert	S-1	0.00	40	10.00	400.00	00.00	400.00	400.00
Cross, Judy	S-2	0.00	41	14.00	560.00	21.00	581.00	581.00
Diaz, John	M-0	0.00	42	14.00	560.00	42.00	602.00	602.00
Kiefe, Kay	M-2	0.00	40	14.00	560.00	00.00	560.00	560.00
Miller, Lee	M-0	0.00	40	14.00	560.00	00.00	560.00	560.00
Sears, Dale	S-0	0.00	40	14.00	560.00	00.00	560.00	560.00
Total					3,200.00	63.00	3,263.00	3,263.00

TAXABLE EARNINGS FOR			EMPLOYEE DEDUCTIONS FOR				PAYMENT INFORMATION	
Social Security	Medicare	Unemployment	Social Security	Medicare	Federal Income Tax	State Income Tax	Net Pay	Check Number
400.00	400.00	400.00	24.80	5.80	26.00	2.08	341.32	9001
581.00	581.00	581.00	36.02	8.42	43.00	3.44	490.12	9002
602.00	602.00	602.00	37.32	8.73	37.00	2.96	515.99	9003
560.00	560.00	560.00	34.72	8.12	12.00	0.96	504.20	9004
560.00	560.00	560.00	34.72	8.12	31.00	2.48	483.68	9005
560.00	560.00	560.00	34.72	8.12	61.00	4.88	451.28	9006
3,263.00	3,263.00	3,263.00	202.30	47.31	210.00	16.80	2,786.59	

unemployment, in the next chapter.) The employer also stops withholding Social Security tax for any employee who has earned at least $106,800 during the year.

Since this is the first pay period of the year for Phoenix Sales and Service, none of its employees has reached these income maximums. Social Security taxes are entered for each employee in the "Social Security" column. Medicare taxes are entered for each employee in the "Medicare" column. Finally, each employee's net pay (gross pay minus all deductions) is computed and reported in the "Net Pay" column.

Recording and Settling Payroll

LO5 Journalize payroll transactions in a general journal.

The payroll register provides the data to prepare the journal entry to record the payroll in the general ledger accounts. For the pay period ending January 7, 2009, Phoenix Sales and Service records the following journal entry in the general journal.

Assets = Liabilities + Equity
+202.30   −3,263.00
+47.31
+210.00
+16.80
+2,786.59

Jan.	7	Wage Expense	3 2 6 3 00	
		FICA—Social Security Taxes Payable (6.2%)		2 0 2 30
		FICA—Medicare Taxes Payable (1.45%)		4 7 31
		Employee Federal Income Taxes Payable		2 1 0 00
		Employee State Income Taxes Payable		1 6 80
		Accrued Wages Payable		2 7 8 6 59
		To record payroll for week ending January 7.		

Paying Employees To safeguard its cash, Phoenix Sales and Service should pay its employees by check or electronic funds transfer. Exhibit 9.9 shows the *payroll check* for Robert Austin. Included with the check is a detachable *statement of earnings* that shows Robert's gross pay, deductions, and net pay. Robert Austin should keep this statement of earnings for his records and deposit his paycheck in a bank. The payroll clerk enters the check number (9001) in the payroll register.

Companies with few employees often pay them with checks drawn on the company's regular bank account. Companies with many employees often use a special **payroll bank account** to pay employees. The payroll bank account is only used to pay employee payroll. If a payroll bank account is used, the company either (1) draws one check for the total payroll on the regular bank account and deposits it in the payroll bank account or (2) electronically transfers funds to the payroll bank account. Individual employee payroll checks are then drawn on the payroll bank account. This helps control the company's cash and helps in reconciling the regular bank account.

EMPLOYEE NO.	EMPLOYEE NAME		SOCIAL SECURITY NO.	PAY PERIOD END	CHECK DATE
AR101	Robert Austin		333-22-9999	1/7/09	1/7/09

ITEM	RATE	HOURS	TOTAL	ITEM	THIS CHECK	YEAR TO DATE
Regular	10.00	40.00	400.00	Gross	400.00	400.00
				Fed. Income tax	-26.00	-26.00
				FICA-Soc. Sec.	-24.80	-24.80
				FICA-Medicare	-5.80	-5.80
				State Income tax	-2.08	-2.08

HOURS WORKED	GROSS THIS PERIOD	GROSS YEAR TO DATE	NET CHECK	CHECK No.
40.00	400.00	400.00	$329.44	9001

(Detach and retain for your records)

PHOENIX SALES & SERVICE   Phoenix Bank and Trust   **9001**
1214 Mill Road   Phoenix, AZ 85621
Phoenix, AZ 85621   3312-87044
602-555-8900

CHECK NO.	DATE	AMOUNT
9001	Jan 7, 2009	***************$341.32*

Three Hundred Forty–One and 32/100 Dollars

PAY TO THE ORDER OF   Robert Austin
18 Roosevelt Blvd., Apt C
Tempe, AZ 86322

Mary Wills
AUTHORIZED SIGNATURE

Exhibit 9.9

Payroll Check and Statement of Earnings

Paying Employees from the Regular Bank Account   Each Phoenix Sales and Service employee will receive a check for net pay. If the employees are paid from the company's regular checking account, the company makes the following entry in the general journal.

Jan.	7	Accrued Wages Payable		2 7 8 6 59	
		Cash—R. Austin			3 4 1 32
		Cash—J. Cross			4 9 0 12
		Cash—J. Diaz			5 1 5 99
		Cash—K. Kiefe			5 0 4 20
		Cash—L. Miller			4 8 3 68
		Cash—D. Sears			4 5 1 28
		To pay payroll for pay period ending January 7, 2009.			

Assets = Liabilities + Equity
−341.32   −2,786.59
−490.12
−515.99
−504.20
−483.68
−451.28

Paying Employees from a Special Payroll Bank Account   If instead Phoenix Sales and Service uses a special payroll bank account, the following journal entries will be made in the general journal.

Jan.	7	Cash—Payroll Bank Account		2 7 8 6 59	
		Cash			2 7 8 6 59
		To transfer cash to the payroll bank account.			
Jan.	7	Accrued Wages Payable		2 7 8 6 59	
		Cash—Payroll Bank Account			2 7 8 6 59
		To pay payroll for pay period ending January 7, 2009.			

Assets = Liabilities + Equity
+2,786.59
−2,786.59

Assets = Liabilities + Equity
−2,786.59   −2,786.59

HOW YOU DOIN'?   Answers—p. 219

4. What two items determine the amount deducted from an employee's wages for federal income taxes?

5. What amount of income tax is withheld from the salary of an employee who is single with three withholding allowances and earnings of $645 in a week? (*Hint:* Use the wage bracket withholding table from Exhibit 9.4.)

6. Which of the following steps are executed when a company draws one check for total payroll and deposits it in a special payroll bank account? (*a*) Write a check to the payroll bank account for the total payroll and record it with a debit to Accrued Wages Payable and a credit to Cash. (*b*) Deposit a check (or transfer funds) for the total payroll in the payroll bank account. (*c*) Issue individual payroll checks drawn on the payroll bank account. (*d*) All of the above.

Employee Earnings Records

LO6 Prepare an earnings record for each employee.

Law requires employers to maintain **employee earnings records.** These records summarize each employee's earnings, deductions, net pay, and total earnings during each calendar year. Information in these records is used to prepare quarterly and annual tax reports (discussed in the next chapter). Exhibit 9.10 provides an employee earnings record for Robert Austin for the month ended March 31, 2009. For this exhibit we assume Robert Austin works 40 hours in each of the 8 weeks from January 1, 2009, through February 24, 2009, and then works 40 hours in each of the four weeks in March. This means his gross pay is $400 each week. The next pay period ends on Sunday, April 1, 2009.

Exhibit 9.10

Employee Earnings Report

PHOENIX SALES AND SERVICE
Employee Earnings Report
For Month Ended March 31, 2009

EMPLOYEE ID No.	EMPLOYEE NAME	EMPLOYEE SS No.
AR101	Austin, Robert	333-22-9999

		EMPLOYEE DEDUCTIONS				
Date	Gross Pay	Federal Income Tax	State Income Tax	FICA-Social Security	FICA-Medicare	Net Pay
Beg. balance	3,200.00	208.00	16.64	198.40	46.40	2,730.56
3/4/2009	400.00	26.00	2.08	24.80	5.80	341.32
3/11/2009	400.00	26.00	2.08	24.80	5.80	341.32
3/18/2009	400.00	26.00	2.08	24.80	5.80	341.32
3/25/2009	400.00	26.00	2.08	24.80	5.80	341.32
Total: 3/4/09 through 3/25/09	1,600.00	104.00	8.32	99.20	23.20	1,365.28
Year-to-date total for Robert Austin	4,800.00	312.00	24.96	297.60	69.60	4,095.84

The amount in the year-to-date gross pay column in each individual employee earnings report is entered into the "Beginning Cumulative Gross Earnings" column of the payroll register in Exhibit 9.8 at the beginning of each pay period. This alerts the accountant of those employees with year-to-date income higher than the maximum amounts for Social Security or unemployment taxes. For example, $4,800 would be entered into the payroll register for the week ending April 1, 2009, for Robert Austin.

Control over Payroll

LO7 Explain how an employer can control payroll.

Payroll activities present important risks for the business owner. First, there are often fines and penalties for not following the many laws impacting payroll. For example, a 100% penalty can be levied, with interest, on any unpaid employee withholding taxes. The government can even close a company, take its assets, and pursue legal actions against those involved. Second, the employer must maintain confidential and sensitive data on employees; for example, their Social Security numbers. Employees can become victims of identity theft if this information falls into the wrong hands. Third, the employer must be careful not to pay employees for hours not worked or to pay fictitious employees. For example, poor controls led the United States Army to pay nearly $10 million to deserters, fictitious soldiers, and other unauthorized entities.

Payroll Fraud

Employee fraud is costly. The Association of Certified Fraud Examiners (www.acfe.com) estimates that employee fraud costs small companies more than $190,000 per incident. Many employee frauds involve payroll schemes. Joseph Wells discusses three common types of payroll fraud (*Occupational Fraud and Abuse,* Austin, TX (Obsidian Publishing Co., Inc., 1997) and "Keep Ghosts Off the Payroll," 2002 article at www.acfe.com.):

Ghost Employees   A ghost employee is a reference to a name of an individual included on the payroll register who is not an employee of the company. The ghost might be a former employee or a fictitious employee created by a payroll clerk. Wells estimates that the average loss to an employer victimized by a ghost employee payroll fraud is $275,000.

Overstated Hours Worked and Salary Rates   Employees might overstate the number of hours they worked on their time cards. Dishonest payroll clerks might inflate their own or other employees' pay rates. Wells estimates that the average loss to an employer victimized by a false hours or pay rate fraud is $30,000.

Overstated Salespersons' Commissions   Salespeople might overstate the amount of sales they made. Wells estimates that the average loss to an employer victimized by a commission payroll fraud is $200,000.

Payroll Control

Several procedures can help the employer reduce payroll risks. First, the employer must be careful in employee hiring and assign only the most-trusted employees to payroll activities. Second, the employer should review and verify all time sheets. Third, all employee payroll data should be kept in locked files. Only the payroll clerk and the employer should have access to these files. Fourth, any changes to employees' withholdings or voluntary deductions must be supported by authorization forms signed by the employee. The employer must keep these forms in locked files.

   The employer also must separate certain payroll duties. The signer of the payroll checks should verify the data for each employee in the payroll register. Payroll checks should not be distributed by the payroll clerk who prepared them. The payroll clerk should not reconcile the bank account.

HOW YOU DOIN'?   Answer—p. 219

7. What type of payroll fraud has the highest average dollar loss?

Demonstration Problem

A1 Lawns reports the information below related to its employees for the week ending June 7, 2009. A1 pays its employees one and one-half times their normal hourly wage for all hours worked beyond 40 hours per week. Each of A1 Lawns' employees is single.

Employee	Hours Worked	Hourly Wage	Withholding Allowances
S. House	40	$14.25	2
E. James	46	$15.00	2
R. Johnson	44	$12.13	1

Required

1. Compute each employee's gross pay for the week.
2. Compute the amounts A1 Lawns must withhold from its employees' pay for the week ending June 7, 2009, for
   a. Federal income taxes (use wage bracket withholding tables in Exhibit 9.4).
   b. State income taxes (assume A1 Lawns withholds 8% of the amount of federal income taxes withheld).

   c. Social Security taxes. Assume no employee's year-to-date earnings exceed the Social Security maximum.

   d. Medicare taxes.

3. Compute net pay for the week for each employee.

4. Prepare the journal entry to record the payroll for the week.

5. Prepare the journal entry to pay the payroll assuming two separate scenarios:

   a. A1 Lawns does not use a special payroll bank account, and

   b. A1 Lawns uses a special payroll bank account.

Planning the Solution

- For 1, multiply hours worked (up to 40) by the employee's hourly wage, and add to that the product of any hours worked over 40 multiplied by one and one-half times the employee's hourly wage.
- For 2, use wage bracket withholding tables and tax rules to compute each employee's deductions.
- For part 3, for each employee, subtract your answer in part 2 from your answer in part 1.
- For 4 and 5 determine the accounts affected and then record the entries.

Solution to Demonstration Problem

1. Gross pay for each employee is computed as:

S. House	40 × $14.25	= $570.00
E. James	(40 × $15.00) + (6 × $22.50)	= $735.00
R. Johnson	(40 × $12.13) + (4 × $18.20)	= $558.00

2. Employee deductions:

   a. Withholdings

	Federal Income Tax[a]	State Income Tax[b]	Social Security[c]	Medicare[d]	Total
S. House	$41.00	$3.28	$35.34	$ 8.27	$ 87.89
E. James	65.00	5.20	45.57	10.66	126.43
R. Johnson	49.00	3.92	34.60	8.09	95.61

   [a] From federal wage bracket withholding tables in Exhibit 9.4.

   [b] Dollar amount withheld for federal income tax × 8%.

   [c] Gross pay × 6.2%.

   [d] Gross pay × 1.45%.

3. Net pay = Gross pay minus total deductions; computations follow:

S. House	$570.00 − $ 87.89	= $482.11
E. James	$735.00 − $126.43	= $608.57
R. Johnson	$558.00 − $ 95.61	= $462.39

4.

June	7	Wage Expense	1 8 6 3 00	
		FICA—Social Security Taxes Payable (6.2%)		1 1 5 51
		FICA—Medicare Taxes Payable (1.45%)		2 7 02
		Employee Federal Income Taxes Payable		1 5 5 00
		Employee State Income Taxes Payable		1 2 40
		Accrued Wages Payable		1 5 5 3 07
		To record payroll for week ending June 7, 2009.		

5. a. Payroll paid from general bank account.

June	7	Accrued Wages Payable	1 5 5 3 07	
		Cash—S. House		4 8 2 11
		Cash—E. James		6 0 8 57
		Cash—R. Johnson		4 6 2 39
		To pay payroll for pay period ending June 7, 2009.		

b. Payroll paid from special payroll bank account.

June	7	Cash—Payroll Bank Account	1 5 5 3 07	
		Cash		1 5 5 3 07
		To transfer cash to the payroll bank account.		
June	7	Accrued Wages Payable	1 5 5 3 07	
		Cash—Payroll Bank Account.		1 5 5 3 07
		To pay payroll for pay period ending June 7, 2009.		

Summary

LO1 Describe the laws that affect employee payroll. Law requires employers to withhold amounts from employee pay for Social Security taxes, Medicare taxes, and for federal and state income taxes.

LO2 Compute employee gross pay. Gross pay is the amount of compensation the employee earned during the period before deductions for items like taxes. It is commonly computed as the employee's hourly wage rate multiplied by the number of hours the employee worked during the pay period.

LO3 Compute employee deductions for taxes and net pay. Employees pay 6.2% of their gross pay (up to $106,800) for Social Security taxes and 1.45% of their income for Medicare taxes. Based on the number of withholding allowances the employee chooses, the employee's marital status, and gross pay, the employer computes federal and state income tax withholdings from tax tables.

LO4 Record employee payroll information in a payroll register. A payroll register is often used to keep a record of pay period dates, hours worked, gross pay, deductions, and net pay of each

employee for each pay period. The payroll register provides information the accountant can use to make journal entries and prepare tax documents.

LO5 Journalize payroll transactions in a general journal. The accountant debits Wage Expense for the total gross pay and credits tax liability accounts for amounts owed, and Accrued Wages Payable for employees' net pay. Paying the payroll results in a debit to Accrued Wages Payable and a credit to Cash.

LO6 Prepare an earnings record for each employee. Employee earnings records summarize each employee's earnings, deductions, net pay, and total earnings during each calendar year. This information is used in computing taxes and in preparing tax documents required by law.

LO7 Explain how an employer can control payroll. The employer can control payroll by hiring trustworthy employees, maintaining confidential records in locked files, and by separating important payroll duties.

Guidance Answers to HOW YOU DOIN'?

1. $(0.062 \times \$3,000) + (0.0145 \times \$3,000) = \underline{\$229.50}$

2. (a) FICA taxes are incurred by both employee and employer.
(b) Withheld income taxes are incurred by the employee.

3. $(40 \times \$16) + (5 \times \$24) = \$760.$

4. An employee's gross earnings, number of withholding allowances, and marital status determine the deduction for federal income taxes.

5. $41

6. (d)

7. The ghost employee scheme, with an average loss of $275,000.

Key Terms

Circular E (p. 210) IRS federal income tax withholding tables.

Employee (p. 206) Someone whose work is under the direction of an employer.

Employee earnings records (p. 216) Record of an employee's net pay, gross pay, deductions, and year-to-date payroll information.

Employee's Withholding Allowance Certificate (Form W-4) (p. 206) A form which shows an employee's withholding allowances.

Federal Insurance Contributions Act (FICA) Taxes (p. 207) Taxes assessed on both employers and employees; for Social Security and Medicare programs.

Gross pay (p. 206) Total compensation earned by an employee.

Independent contractor (p. 206) Someone who does a job for an employer, but decides how to do the work.

Net pay (p. 213) Gross pay less all deductions; also called *take-home pay*.

Payroll bank account (p. 214) Bank account used solely for paying employees; each pay period an amount equal to the total

employees' net pay is deposited in it and the payroll checks are drawn on it.

Payroll deductions (p. 209) Amounts withheld from an employee's gross pay; also called *withholdings*.

Payroll register (p. 213) Record for a pay period that shows the pay period dates, regular and overtime hours worked, gross pay, net pay, and deductions.

Salary (p. 208) A fixed amount of compensation paid or received on a regular basis, such as every two weeks, monthly, or annually.

Self-employment tax (p. 208) Social Security and Medicare taxes for persons who operate their own businesses. Currently, the self-employment tax rates are 12.4% on the first $106,800 of income for Social Security and 2.9% on all income for Medicare.

Wages (p. 208) Money paid or received for work or services by the hour, day, or week or by the number of units produced.

Withholding allowance (p. 206) This determines the amount of federal income taxes to withhold from an employee's pay.

Multiple Choice Quiz   Answers on p. 229   mhhe.com/wildCA2e

Additional Multiple Choice Quizzes are available at the book's Website.

1. An employee earned $50,000 during the year. FICA tax for social security is 6.2% and FICA tax for Medicare is 1.45%. The employee's share of FICA taxes is
   a. Zero, since the employee's pay exceeds the FICA limit.
   b. Zero, since FICA is not an employee tax.
   c. $3,100
   d. $725
   e. $3,825

2. Which of the following taxes is not withheld from employee's pay?
   a. Social security taxes.
   b. Unemployment taxes.
   c. Federal income taxes.
   d. State income taxes.
   e. Medicare taxes.

3. An employee worked 48 hours in the last weekly pay period. She is paid a normal wage of $12 per hour and is paid one and one-half times her normal hourly wage for all hours worked beyond 40 hours. For this pay period her *gross pay* is
   a. $480
   b. $576
   c. $624
   d. $720
   e. $864

4. A single employee claiming 4 withholding allowances earns $710 per week. If she is paid weekly, what amount will be withheld from her pay for federal income tax withholdings? (Use the withholding table in Exhibit 9.4).
   a. $64
   b. $102
   c. $50
   d. $40
   e. $56

5. A company uses a special bank account to pay its payroll. If total gross pay for a pay period was $3,500 and total net pay for the same period was $2,750, the journal entry to pay the payroll will include a
   a. credit to Cash for $3,500.
   b. credit to Cash—Payroll Bank Account for $3,500.
   c. debit to Cash—Payroll Bank Account for $2,750 and a credit to Cash for $2,750.
   d. credit to Cash—Payroll Bank Account for $2,750.
   e. debit to Wage Expense for $2,750 and a credit to Cash for $2,750.

Discussion Questions

1. What is the combined amount (in percent) of the employee and employer Social Security tax rate?

2. What is the current maximum annual level of salary used to compute an employee's Social Security taxes?

3. What is the current Medicare tax rate? This rate is applied to what maximum level of salary and wages?

4. What determines the amount deducted from an employee's wages for federal income taxes?

5. Which payroll taxes are the employee's responsibility and which are the employer's responsibility?

6. What are examples of items employees might voluntarily choose to have deducted from their pay?

7. What is a tax withholding table?

8. What amount of income tax is withheld from the salary of an employee who is single with two withholding allowances and earns $725 per week? What if the employee earned $625 and has no withholding allowances? (Use Exhibit 9.4.)

9. What are employee earnings records? Why do employers maintain employee earnings records?

10. What risks do payroll activities pose for employers?

11. Give three examples of common payroll fraud schemes that are costly to employers.

12. What procedures can an employer use to control payroll fraud?

connect™

Compute *gross pay* for each of the following employees. An overtime rate of one and one-half times the normal hourly wage is paid for each hour worked beyond 40 hours.

	Hourly Rate	No. of Hours Worked
Mike Mura	$11	42
Pedro Chavez	$14	50

QUICK STUDY

QS 9–1
Computing gross pay   LO2

Nouri Hitzu's year-to-date earnings before this pay period were $45,000. Nouri's gross pay for this weekly pay period was $845. What amounts will be withheld from Nouri's pay for this period for federal income taxes? Nouri is married and claims a total of two withholding allowances. Nouri is paid weekly. (Use the tax withholding table in Exhibit 9.5).

QS 9–2
Computing tax withholdings
LO3

Refer to QS 9-2. What amount must Nouri's employer withhold from Nouri's pay for Social Security (6.2%) taxes and Medicare (1.45%) taxes?

QS 9–3
Computing FICA taxes   LO3

An employee earned $3,450 for the current period. Calculate the total and individual amounts to be withheld for Social Security (6.2%), Medicare (1.45%), and federal income tax (15%) assuming the entire employee's pay is subject to FICA taxes.

QS 9–4
Computing FICA taxes   LO3

Dextra Computing's payroll register reports that Ramesh Jain's year-to-date earnings before this weekly pay period were $115,000. Ramesh earned $1,240 this weekly pay period. Ramesh is single and claims one withholding allowance. How much should be withheld from Ramesh's pay for federal income tax withholdings, Social Security taxes, and Medicare taxes? (Use the tax withholding table in Exhibit 9.4.)

QS 9–5
Computing withholdings   LO3

Major Co. has five employees, each of whom earns $2,500 per month and have been employed since January 1. FICA Social Security taxes are 6.2% of the first $106,800 paid to each employee, and FICA Medicare taxes are 1.45% of gross pay. Federal income tax withholding is 15% of gross pay. State income tax withholding is 8% of the dollar amount withheld for federal income tax purposes. Prepare the March 31 journal entry to record the March wage expense and related liabilities.

QS 9–6
Record employer payroll taxes
LO2   LO3   LO5

Refer to QS 9-6. Prepare the journal entries to pay the March 31 payroll, assuming Major Co. uses a special payroll bank account.

QS 9–7
Journalize payroll transactions
LO5

A self-employed worker earned $47,000 during the year. The FICA tax for Social Security is 6.2% and the FICA tax for Medicare is 1.45%. How much should this worker pay for FICA taxes?

QS 9–8
Computing FICA taxes   LO3

EXERCISES

Exercise 9–1
Computing payroll taxes and income tax withholdings   **LO3**

BMX Co. has one employee, Keesha Parks, and the company is subject to the following taxes:

Tax	Rate	Applied To
FICA—Social Security	6.20%	First $106,800
FICA—Medicare	1.45	All gross pay

Compute BMX's amounts for FICA taxes and federal income tax withholdings as applied to Keesha's gross earnings for September under each of three separate situations (*a*), (*b*), and (*c*). (Use the withholding tables in Exhibit 9.6 and Exhibit 9.7.).

	Gross Pay through August	Gross Pay for September	Marital Status	Withholding Allowances
a.	$ 6,800	$ 900	M	2
b.	19,200	2,200	S	1
c.	104,800	5,000	M	4

Exercise 9–2
Payroll-related journal entries

LO5

Using the data in situation *b* of Exercise 9-1, prepare the employer's September 30 journal entries to record (1) salary expense and its related payroll liabilities for this employee and (2) payment of the payroll. BMX does not use a special payroll bank account.

Exercise 9–3
Computing federal tax withholdings   **LO3**

Use withholding tables from Exhibits 9.4 and 9.5 to compute the amount of federal tax withheld from the weekly pay of the following employees:

Name	Gross Pay	Withholding Allowances	Marital Status
Keisha	$520	1	Single
James	600	3	Single
Tyrell	476	4	Married
Emily	817	2	Married

Exercise 9–4
Net pay and tax computations

LO3

The payroll records of One Click Software show the following information about Keisha LeShon, an employee, for the weekly pay period ending September 30, 2009. LeShon is single and claims one allowance. Compute her Social Security tax (6.2%), Medicare tax (1.45%), federal income tax withholding, state income tax (0.5%), and net pay for the current pay period. The state income tax is 0.5 percent on the first $9,000 earned. (Use the wage bracket withholding table in Exhibit 9.4 for the amount of federal income tax to withhold.)

Total (gross) earnings for current pay period	$ 725
Cumulative earnings of previous pay periods	9,600

Check   Net pay, $595.54

Exercise 9–5
Gross and net pay computation
LO2   **LO3**

Lucinda Florita, an unmarried employee, works 48 hours in the week ended January 12. Her pay rate is $14 per hour, and her wages are subject to no deductions other than FICA—Social Security, FICA—Medicare, and federal income taxes. She claims two withholding allowances. Compute her regular pay, overtime pay (overtime premium is 50% of the regular rate for hours in excess of 40 per week), and gross pay. Then compute her FICA tax deduction (use 6.2% for the Social Security portion and 1.45% for the Medicare portion), income tax deduction (use the wage bracket withholding table in Exhibit 9.4), total deductions, and net pay.

Check   Net Pay, $608.30

Exercise 9–6
Computing net pay   **LO3**

Phildell Phoenix is paid monthly. For the month of January of the current year, he earned gross pay of $8,288. FICA tax for Social Security is 6.2% and the FICA tax for Medicare is 1.45%. The amount of federal income tax withheld from his earnings was $1,375.17. Phildell contributes $125 of his monthly pay to a retirement plan and has $25 of union dues deducted from his monthly pay. Compute Phildell's net pay for the month.

Match each of the following terms A through G with the appropriate definitions 1 through 7.

Exercise 9–7
Payroll terms   **LO3   LO4**

A. FICA taxes

B. Payroll register

C. Withholding allowance

D. Gross pay

E. Wage bracket withholding table

F. Net pay

G. Payroll bank account

_____ **1.** A record for a pay period that shows the pay period dates, regular and overtime hours worked, gross pay, net pay, and deductions.

_____ **2.** A special bank account used solely for paying employees; each pay period an amount equal to the total employees' net pay is deposited and the employees' payroll checks are drawn on that account.

_____ **3.** Total compensation earned by an employee.

_____ **4.** Gross pay less all deductions.

_____ **5.** A number that is used to reduce the amount of federal income tax withheld from an employee's pay.

_____ **6.** A table of amounts of income tax to be withheld from employees' wages.

_____ **7.** Taxes assessed on both employer and employees under the Federal Insurance Contributions Act. These taxes fund Social Security and Medicare.

connect

Paloma Co. pays its employees each week. Its employees' gross pay is subject to these taxes:

PROBLEM SET A

Problem 9–1A
Payroll expenses, withholdings, and taxes   **LO2   LO3**

Tax	Rate	Applied To
FICA—Social Security	6.20%	First $106,800
FICA—Medicare	1.45	All gross pay

The company is preparing its payroll calculations for the week ended August 25. Payroll records show the following information for the company's four employees.

		Gross Pay	Current Week	
	Name	**through 8/18**	**Gross Pay**	**Income Tax Withholding**
3	Dahlia	$106,000	$2,800	$284
4	Trey	31,700	1,000	145
5	Kiesha	6,850	550	39
6	Chee	1,250	500	30

In addition to gross pay, each employee must pay one-half of the $34 per employee weekly health insurance premium. Dahlia contributes 5% of her weekly gross pay to a retirement plan. Trey and Chee each contribute $25 per week to the local United Way.

Required

Compute the following for the week ended August 25 (round amounts to the nearest cent):

1. Each employee's FICA withholdings for Social Security.

2. Each employee's FICA withholdings for Medicare.

3. Each employee's health insurance premium deduction.

4. Each employee's other voluntary deductions.

5. Each employee's net (take-home) pay.

Check   (5) Total net pay, $3,846.97

Problem 9-2A
Entries for payroll transactions
LO3   LO4

On January 8, the end of the first weekly pay period of the year, Regis Company's payroll register showed that its employees earned $22,760 of office salaries and $65,840 of sales salaries. Withholdings from the employees' salaries include FICA Social Security taxes at the rate of 6.2%, FICA Medicare taxes at the rate of 1.45%, $12,860 of federal income taxes, $1,340 of medical insurance deductions, and $840 of union dues.

Required

1. Calculate FICA Social Security taxes payable and FICA Medicare taxes payable. Prepare the journal entry to record Regis Company's January 8 employee payroll expenses and liabilities.
2. Prepare the journal entry to pay the January 8 payroll. Regis uses a special payroll bank account.

Problem 9-3A
Payroll entries, deductions, and net pay
LO1   LO2   LO3   LO5

The payroll records of Swift Company provided the following data for the weekly pay period ended December 7:

Employee	Earnings to End of Previous Week	Gross Pay	Marital Status	No. of Allowances	Medical Insurance Deduction	Union Dues	United Way
Ronald Arthur . . .	$54,000	$1,200	Married	3	$125	$15	$15
John Baines	40,500	900	Single	2	135	15	30
Ted Carter	45,000	1,000	Married	2	150	–0–	20

The FICA Social Security tax rate is 6.2% and the FICA Medicare tax rate is 1.45% on all of this week's wages paid to each employee. The state income tax equals 8 percent of the amount withheld for federal income tax purposes. (Use the withholding tables in Exhibits 9.4 and 9.5.)

Required

1. Prepare a payroll register similar to that in Exhibit 9.8 for Swift Company for the pay period ending December 7. Your payroll register should have columns for employee name, gross pay, federal income tax withheld, state income tax withheld, Social Security tax, Medicare tax, and deductions for medical insurance, union dues, and United Way contributions, and net pay.
2. Prepare the journal entry to record the December 7 payroll.
3. Prepare the journal entry to pay the December 7 payroll. Swift Company does not use a special payroll bank account.

Problem 9-4A
Payroll deductions, net pay, payroll register
LO2   LO3   LO4

Mackenzie Price operates Downtown Salon and Spa. Information on her three employees for the payroll period (week) ending June 1, 2009, is provided below. Each employee receives one and one-half times the normal hourly pay rate for any hour worked beyond 40 in a week. The FICA Social Security tax rate is 6.2% on the first $106,800 of each employee's gross pay and the FICA Medicare tax rate is 1.45% on all of this week's wages paid to each employee. Federal income tax withholdings are computed from withholding tables and state income tax withholdings are assumed to be 8% of the amount withheld for federal income tax. (Use the withholding tables in Exhibits 9.4 and 9.5.)

Employee	Earnings to End of Previous Week	Hours Worked	Regular Hourly Rate	Marital Status	No. of Allowances
Emily Jacobs	$20,800	46	$20.00	S	1
Shu Ming	14,560	40	14.00	M	5
Carter Johns	16,120	48	15.50	M	2

Required

1. Enter each employee's name, year-to-date earnings before this pay period, marital status, regular hourly rate, hours worked, and number of withholding allowances in a payroll register. Hours worked beyond 40 are considered overtime hours.
2. Compute the regular, overtime, and total gross pay for each employee for this pay period. Enter these amounts in the payroll register.
3. Compute the amounts of FICA taxes to be withheld from each employee's pay and enter these amounts in the payroll register.

4. Determine the amount of federal income tax to withhold from each employee's gross pay. Use the withholding tables in Exhibits 9.4 and 9.5. Enter these amounts in the payroll register.

5. Determine the amount of state income tax to withhold from each employee's gross pay. Enter these amounts in the payroll register.

6. Compute each employee's net pay and enter it into the payroll register.

7. Total the payroll register.

Refer to Problem 9-4A. Before the pay period ending June 1, 2009, the individual employee earnings record for Emily Jacobs reports the following:

Problem 9–5A
Payroll deductions, employee earnings records
L02 L03 L06

			DOWNTOWN SALON AND SPA				
			Employee Earnings Report				
			For Month Ended May 25, 2009				

Employee
Name   Jacobs, Emily
SS No.   344-88-9999

			Employee Deductions				
			Federal Income Tax	State Income Tax	FICA— Social Security	FICA— Medicare	
Reference	Date	Gross Pay	Federal Income Tax	State Income Tax	FICA— Social Security	FICA— Medicare	Net Pay
Beg. Balance		20,800	2,834	226.72	1,289.60	301.60	16,148.08
	6/01/2009						
	6/08/2009						
	6/15/2009						
	6/22/2009						
	6/29/2009						
Total of 6/01/2009 through 6/29/2009							
Year-to-date total for Emily Jacobs							

Social Security taxes of 6.2% and Medicare taxes of 1.45% are deducted from each employee's gross pay. Tax withholding tables are used to compute amounts to withhold for federal income taxes. State income tax withheld equals 8% of the dollar amount of federal income taxes withheld.

Required

1. Refer to Problem 9-4A and enter the payroll information for the pay period ending June 1, 2009, in an individual employee earnings record for Emily Jacobs.

2. Assume that Emily Jacobs works exactly 40 hours in each of the payroll periods ending June 8, June 15, June 22, and June 29 of 2009. Compute the amounts to withhold from Emily's weekly net pay for Social Security taxes, Medicare taxes, federal income tax withholdings, and state income tax withholdings.

3. Enter the amounts computed in requirement 2 in Emily Jacobs's individual employee earnings record.

4. Compute the total amounts of gross pay, federal income tax withholdings, state income tax withholdings, Social Security taxes, Medicare taxes, and net pay for Emily Jacobs for the month of June 1 through June 29, 2009. Enter these amounts in Emily Jacobs's individual employee earnings record.

5. Update the year-to-date totals of gross pay, federal income tax withholdings, state income tax withholdings, Social Security taxes, Medicare taxes, and net pay on Emily Jacobs's individual employee earnings record through June 29, 2009.

Fishing Guides Co. pays its employees each week. Employees' gross pay is subject to these taxes.

PROBLEM SET B

Problem 9–1B
Payroll expenses, withholdings, and taxes **L02 L03**

Tax	Rate	Applied To
FICA—Social Security	6.20%	First $106,800
FICA—Medicare	1.45%	All gross pay

The company is preparing its payroll calculations for the week ended September 30. Payroll records show the following information for the company's four employees.

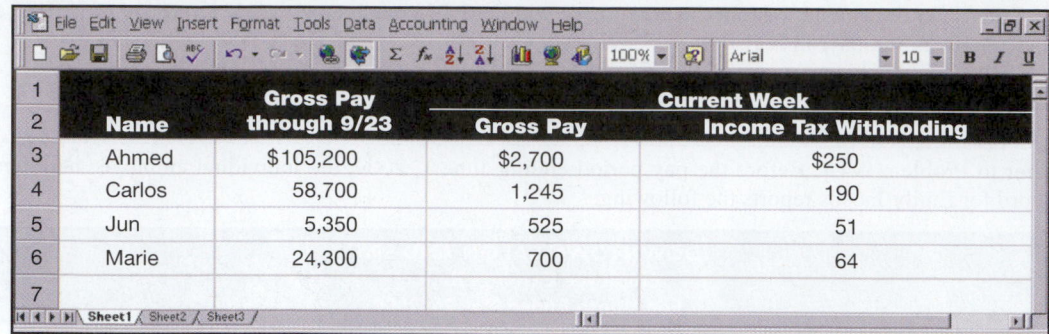

	Name	Gross Pay through 9/23	Current Week	
			Gross Pay	Income Tax Withholding
3	Ahmed	$105,200	$2,700	$250
4	Carlos	58,700	1,245	190
5	Jun	5,350	525	51
6	Marie	24,300	700	64

In addition to gross pay, each employee must pay one-half of the $40 per employee weekly health insurance premium. Ahmed contributes 5% of his weekly gross pay to a retirement plan. Carlos contributes $15 per week to charity. Jun pays $5 per week in union dues.

Required

Compute the following for the week ended September 30 (round amounts to the nearest cent):

1. Each employee's FICA withholdings for Social Security.

2. Each employee's FICA withholdings for Medicare.

3. Each employee's health insurance premium deduction.

4. Each employee's other voluntary deductions.

Check   (5) Total net pay $4,052.70   **5.** Each employee's net (take-home) pay.

Problem 9-2B

Entries for payroll transactions
LO3   **LO5**

Tavella Company's first weekly pay period of the year ends on January 8. On that date, the column totals in Tavella's payroll register indicate its sales employees earned $34,745, its office employees earned $21,225, and its delivery employees earned $1,030. The employees are to have withheld from their wages FICA Social Security taxes at the rate of 6.2%, FICA Medicare taxes at the rate of 1.45%, $8,625 of federal income taxes, $1,160 of medical insurance deductions, and $138 of union dues.

Required

Check   (1) Cr. Accrued Wages Payable, $42,716.50

1. Calculate FICA Social Security taxes payable and FICA Medicare taxes payable. Prepare the journal entry to record Tavella Company's January 8 employee payroll expenses and liabilities.

2. Prepare the journal entry to pay the January 8 payroll. Tavella uses a special payroll bank account.

Problem 9-3B

Payroll entries, deductions, net pay **LO3**   **LO4**   **LO5**

The payroll records of JK Landscape Design provided the following data for the weekly pay period ended October 7:

Employee	Earnings to End of Previous Week	Gross Pay	Marital Status	No. of Allowances	Medical Insurance Deduction	Union Dues	United Way
Roland Ames ...	$44,000	$1,100	Single	3	$ 85	$10	$25
Jan Barnes	30,500	780	Married	1	150	–0–	20
Todd Crane	35,000	985	Married	5	150	–0–	30

The FICA Social Security tax rate is 6.2% and the FICA Medicare tax rate is 1.45% on all of this week's wages paid to each employee. Use withholding tables in Exhibits 9.4 and 9.5 to find the amount of federal income tax to withhold and assume state income tax is 8% of the dollar amount of federal income tax withheld.

Required

1. Prepare a payroll register similar to that in Exhibit 9.8 for JK Landscape Design for the pay period ending October 7. Your payroll register should have columns for employee name, gross pay, federal income tax withheld, state income tax withheld, Social Security tax, Medicare tax, and deductions for medical insurance, union dues, and United Way contributions, and net pay.

2. Prepare the journal entry to record the October 7 payroll.

3. Prepare the journal entry to pay the October 7 payroll. JK Landscape Design does not use a special payroll bank account.

Merle Perkins operates A1 Auto Repair. Information on his three employees for the payroll period (week) ending June 1, 2009, is provided below. Each employee receives one and one-half times the normal hourly pay rate for any hour worked beyond 40 in a week. The FICA Social Security tax rate is 6.2% on the first $106,800 of each employee's gross pay and the FICA Medicare tax rate is 1.45% on all of this week's wages paid to each employee. Federal income tax withholdings are computed from withholding tables and state income tax withholdings are assumed to be 8% of the amount withheld for federal income tax. (Use the withholding tables in Exhibits 9.4 and 9.5.)

Problem 9-4B
Payroll deductions, net pay, payroll register LO2 LO3 LO4

Employee	Earnings to End of Previous Week	Hours Worked	Regular Hourly Rate	Marital Status	No. of Allowances
Andre Jones	$21,600	42	$21.00	S	2
Xiu Yi	12,480	35	15.00	M	3
Duane Wells	19,320	46	17.50	M	4

Required

1. Enter each employee's name, year-to-date earnings before this pay period, marital status, regular hourly rate, hours worked, and number of withholding allowances in a payroll register. Hours worked beyond 40 are considered overtime hours.

2. Compute the regular, overtime, and total gross pay for each employee for this pay period. Enter these amounts in the payroll register.

3. Compute the amounts of FICA taxes to be withheld from each employee's pay and enter these amounts in the payroll register.

4. Determine the amount of federal income tax to withhold from each employee's gross pay. Use the withholding tables in Exhibits 9.4 and 9.5. Enter these amounts in the payroll register.

5. Determine the amount of state income tax to withhold from each employee's gross pay. Enter these amounts in the payroll register.

6. Compute each employee's net pay and enter it into the payroll register.

7. Total the payroll register.

Refer to Problem 9-4B. Before the pay period ending June 1, 2009, the individual employee earnings record for Andre Jones reports the following:

Problem 9-5B
Payroll deductions, employee earnings records
LO2 LO3 LO6

		A1 AUTO REPAIR Employee Earnings Report For Month Ended May 25, 2009					

Employee
Name   Jones, Andre
SS No.   333-55-9999

				Employee Deductions			
Reference	Date	Gross Pay	Federal Income Tax	State Income Tax	FICA— Social Security	FICA— Medicare	Net Pay
Beg. Balance		21,600	2,943	235.44	1,339.20	313.20	16,769.16
	6/01/2009						
	6/08/2009						
	6/15/2009						
	6/22/2009						
	6/29/2009						
Total of 6/01/2009 through 6/29/2009							
Year-to-date total for Andre Jones							

Social Security taxes of 6.2% and Medicare taxes of 1.45% are deducted from each employee's gross pay. Tax withholding tables are used to compute amounts to withhold for federal income taxes. State income tax withheld equals 8% of the dollar amount of federal income taxes withheld.

Required

1. Refer to Problem 9-4B and enter the payroll information for the pay period ending June 1, 2009, in an individual employee earnings record for Andre Jones.

2. Assume that Andre Jones works exactly 40 hours in each of the payroll periods ending June 8, June 15, June 22, and June 29 of 2009. Compute the amounts to withhold from Andre's weekly net pay for Social Security taxes, Medicare taxes, federal income tax withholdings, and state income tax withholdings.

3. Enter the amounts computed in requirement 2 in Andre Jones's individual employee earnings record.

4. Compute the total amounts of gross pay, federal income tax withholdings, state income tax withholdings, Social Security taxes, Medicare taxes, and net pay for Andre Jones for the month of June 1 through June 29, 2009. Enter these amounts in Andre Jones's individual employee earnings record.

5. Update the year-to-date totals of gross pay, federal income tax withholdings, state income tax withholdings, Social Security taxes, Medicare taxes, and net pay on Andre Jones's individual employee earnings record through June 29, 2009.

SERIAL PROBLEM

Success Systems

(This serial problem began in Chapter 1 and continues through most of the book. If previous chapter segments were not completed, the serial problem can begin at this point. It is helpful, but not necessary, for you to use the Working Papers that accompany the book.)

SP 9   Michelle Jones earned $150 per day for the 8 days in the most recent pay period ending on February 26.

Required

1. Assume that Michelle Jones is an unmarried employee. Her wages are subject to no deductions other than FICA Social Security taxes, FICA Medicare taxes, and federal income taxes. Her federal income taxes for this pay period total $189. Compute her gross pay and net pay for the eight days' work paid on February 26.

2. Record the journal entry to reflect the payroll payment to Michelle Jones as computed in part 1. Success Systems does not use a payroll bank account.

BEYOND THE NUMBERS

REPORTING IN ACTION
L05

BTN 9-1   Refer to the financial statements of **Best Buy** in Appendix A to answer the following:

Required

1. What payroll-related liability does Best Buy report at March 1, 2008?
2. In what income statement accounts does Best Buy report its payroll and benefit costs?

Fast Forward

3. Access Best Buy's financial statements for fiscal years ending after March 1, 2008, at its Website (**www.BestBuy.com**) or the SEC's EDGAR database (**www.SEC.gov**). What payroll-related liability does Best Buy report for years ending after March 1, 2008?

ETHICS CHALLENGE
L01

BTN 9-2   You take a summer job working for a family friend as a Web page designer for a small information technology service. On your first payday, the owner slaps you on the back, gives you full payment in cash, winks, and adds: "No need to pay those high taxes, eh."

Required

What action, if any, do you take? Explain.

BTN 9-3   An owner of a growing business hires you as a consultant. He is concerned about rising pay-roll costs, and also concerned about payroll fraud. Currently, his payroll clerk collects time sheets and computes gross pay and deductions. The payroll clerk also adds new employees to the payroll system and makes all changes to employees' withholdings and voluntary deductions. Once the payroll is processed, the payroll clerk signs and distributes the payroll checks.

WORKPLACE COMMUNICATION
LO7

Required

Prepare a set of written recommendations to the business owner to strengthen the owner's control over payroll procedures. Your answer should be in a memorandum format.

BTN 9-4   Access the February 25, 2008, filing of the December 31, 2007, annual 10-K report of McDonald's Corporation (Ticker: MCD), which is available from **www.SEC.gov**.

TAKING IT TO THE NET
LO1

Required

1. Identify the amount of accrued payroll and other liabilities on McDonald's balance sheet as of December 31, 2007.
2. What amount does McDonald's report for payroll and other benefits costs for its company-operated restaurants on its 2007 income statement? Expressed as a percentage of sales, discuss how payroll and benefit costs for company-operated restaurants changed from the year ending 2006 to the year ending 2007.

BTN 9-5   Divide your team into four groups. Each group will select one employee for whom to calcu-late the Social Security Tax for the Zmud Company 11/30 weekly payroll. Recall that in 2009 there is a maximum earnings base of $106,800 per year for which the social security tax is assessed. Adi's gross weekly earnings are $2,700 with $104,200 earned through 11/23. Bob's gross weekly earnings are $1,445 with $59,700 earned through 11/23. Marcia's gross weekly earnings are $825 with $5,350 earned through 11/23. Gary's gross weekly earnings are $1,700 with $24,300 earned through 11/23.

TEAMWORK IN ACTION
LO2   LO3

Combine the social security tax from each group to arrive at a total social security tax for the Zmud company's 11/30 payroll.

BTN 9-6   Review the chapter's opening feature about Jason Osborn and Jason Wright and their start-up company, **Feed Granola Company**.

Both owners stress that controlling payroll liabilities is a must for success in business. What are some procedures both Jasons can use to reduce the chance that Feed Granola Company is hurt by a payroll fraud scheme?

ENTREPRENEURS IN BUSINESS
LO7

1. e; $50,000 × (.062 + .0145) = $3,825
2. b
3. c; (40 × $12) + (8 × $18) = $624
4. c
5. d

ANSWERS TO MULTIPLE CHOICE QUIZ

Chapter 10

Employer Payroll Tax Reporting

A Look Back

Chapter 9 focused on employee payroll and deductions. We showed how to compute employee tax deductions to comply with laws. We also showed how the employer records and controls its payroll.

A Look at This Chapter

This chapter emphasizes the employer's payroll reporting. We show how the employer computes and pays its payroll taxes and prepares tax documents to comply with laws.

A Look Ahead

Chapter 11 explains the accounting for merchandise sales and accounts receivable. We analyze and record merchandise sales transactions and explain the use of a sales and cash receipts journal.

Learning Objectives

LO 1 Describe laws that impact an employer's payroll obligations.

LO 2 Compute employer FICA taxes and record them in a general journal.

LO 3 Journalize an employer's deposit of federal income taxes and FICA taxes withheld, and prepare a deposit coupon.

LO 4 Prepare Form 941, Employer's Quarterly Federal Tax Return.

LO 5 Prepare Form W-2, Employee's Wage and Tax Statement, and Form W-3, Transmittal of Wage and Tax Statements.

LO 6 Compute an employer's state and federal unemployment taxes and record them in a general journal.

LO 7 Prepare unemployment tax returns.

LO 8 Compute and record workers' compensation insurance premiums for an employer.

"1-800-GOT-JUNK brings together great people to build a business that we can all be proud of"
—CEO, Brian Scudamore

One Man's Junk

Brian Scudamore was waiting in a McDonald's drive-thru when he realized his future was junk. With his last $700, Brian bought a used pickup truck and began hauling junk—old couches, appliances, household clutter—any nonhazardous material that two people can lift. "With a vision of creating the 'FedEx' of junk removal, I became a fulltime JUNKMAN," explains Brian. "My father was not impressed in the least."

He is now. Brian's vision resulted in him starting **1-800-GOT-JUNK** (**1800gotjunk.com**), the world's largest junk removal service. The company's approach is simple: Use clean, shiny trucks that serve as mobile billboards and employ professional, courteous drivers who are always on time. Develop a culture that is young, fun, and focused on employee growth, and "build a business that we can be proud of." With revenues of over $100 million in 2007, multiple "Best Company to Work For" awards, and a presence in 47 of North America's 50 top cities, the company has much to be proud of.

Unlike many entrepreneurs who attempt to minimize risk by outsourcing to independent contractors, Scudamore took a different approach. "I hired my first employee, a good friend of mine, a week after I started. I always believed in hiring people versus contract or consultants. I felt that if I wasn't willing to make the investment then I was questioning my own faith in the business."

Brian's investments in his 2,600 employees include five weeks of vacation per year, full health benefits, flex time, and a generous profit-sharing program that pays out 25% of company profits. While these employer-provided benefits are costly, Brian believes they help drive his company's success. "I've always said a great company is all about people."

Brian's goal is $1 billion in revenues by the end of 2012. Not bad for his initial investment of $700.

[Sources: *1-800-GOT-JUNK Website*, February 2009; *Wikipedia*, February 2009]

Keeping accurate payroll records and reports is essential to a company's success. Many laws impact the employer's payroll obligations. The employer can be assessed large penalties for not complying with these laws. This chapter shows how the employer computes its tax liabilities and prepares necessary tax documents to comply with laws.

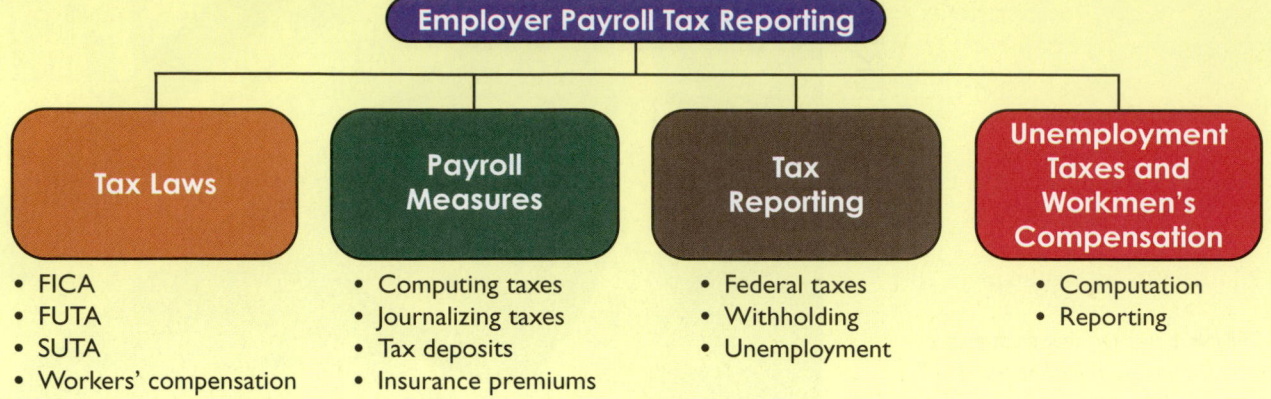

Laws Impacting Employer's Payroll Tax

Employer Identification Number

Each employee of a business has a unique Social Security number. Likewise, each business has its own **employer identification number (EIN).** The business uses its EIN for reporting its income and taxes. The business obtains its EIN by completing **Form SS-4,** available from **www.IRS.gov**. Form SS-4 is an Internal Revenue Service form that asks for general information about the business, including its name, location, main activity, and estimated number of employees.

Employer FICA Tax

LO1 Describe laws that impact an employer's payroll obligations.

Under the **Federal Insurance Contributions Act (FICA),** the employer must pay the same amounts as its employees do for Social Security and Medicare taxes. For 2009 the employer pays 6.2% of each employee's annual gross pay, up to a maximum annual gross pay of $106,800, for Social Security taxes. The employer also pays 1.45% of each employee's annual gross pay for Medicare taxes. There is no limit on Medicare taxes. Remember that self-employed persons pay both the employee and employer FICA taxes. This means the total FICA tax rate for self-employed individuals is 15.3%.

Federal and State Unemployment Tax Acts

The federal government works with states to provide a joint federal and state unemployment insurance program. These programs pay unemployment benefits to qualified workers. Each state runs its own program. The employer pays for the cost of this program. No amounts are withheld from employees.

Federal Unemployment Taxes (FUTA)   For 2009, employers pay FUTA taxes of as much as 6.2% of the first $7,000 earned by each employee in that year. This amount can be reduced by a credit of up to 5.4% of unemployment taxes paid to a state program. So, the net federal unemployment tax is often only 0.8% (gross FUTA rate of 6.2% less credit for state unemployment tax of 5.4%) of the first $7,000 of each employee's annual gross pay.

State Unemployment Taxes (SUTA)   In most states, the base rate for SUTA taxes is 5.4% of the first $7,000 paid to each employee during the year. For example, an employer with 50 employees who each earns more than $7,000 per year will pay $18,900 (0.054 × 50 × $7,000) of SUTA taxes. This base rate is adjusted for the employer's **merit rating.** The state assigns a merit rating that reflects the company's stability in employing workers. A company with low employee turnover receives a high merit rating and pays less than 5.4%. For example, the company with the same 50 employees from above might get a high merit rating and pay SUTA taxes of only 1%. This company would pay a total of only $3,500 (0.01 × 50 × $7,000) for SUTA taxes. This unemployment tax savings of $15,400 ($18,900 − $3,500) results from having a stable workforce with low employee turnover.

Workers' Compensation Insurance

Most states require employers to provide **workers' compensation insurance** for their employees. Workers' compensation provides benefits for employees who are injured on the job. The employer pays a premium, either to the state or to private insurance companies. The premium depends on the type of work the employees perform. Since construction work is considered more risky than secretarial work, an employer would pay a higher premium on its construction workers than on its secretaries. For example, the employer might pay a premium of $0.15 per each $100 of wages for a secretary, but pay $4 per each $100 of wages for a construction worker.

Employers with a small number of employees pay an estimated premium at the beginning of the year. This estimated premium is based on the company's estimated total wages for the upcoming year. At the end of the year, the actual premium is computed based on that year's total wages. The employer then either receives a refund or pays an additional premium.

HOW YOU DOIN'?   Answers—p. 247

1. What are the limits on an employee's annual pay for computing the employer's (a) Social Security tax; (b) Medicare tax; (c) federal unemployment tax; and (d) state unemployment tax?

2. Indicate whether the employer or employee or both incur each of the following: (a) FICA taxes; (b) FUTA taxes; (c) SUTA taxes; and (d) withheld income taxes.

3. A company pays its one employee $3,000 per month. The company's FUTA rate is 0.8% on the first $7,000 earned; its SUTA rate is 4.0% on the first $7,000; its Social Security tax rate is 6.2% of the first $106,800; and its Medicare tax rate is 1.45% of all amounts earned. What is the employer's total payroll tax expense for March?

Employer's Payroll Taxes

Computing Employer's FICA Tax

We return to our example of Phoenix Sales and Service, begun in Chapter 9. Phoenix Sales and Service must pay the same FICA tax amount it withholds from its employees' pay. For Robert Austin, and the week ending January 7, 2009, Phoenix Sales and Service must pay $24.80 for Social Security taxes and $5.80 for Medicare taxes. A partial payroll register for Phoenix Sales and Service is shown in Exhibit 10.1. From its payroll register, the total amounts Phoenix Sales and Service owes for FICA taxes for all of its employees for the period ending January 7, 2009, are $202.30 (Social Security) and $47.31 (Medicare).

LO2 Compute employer FICA taxes and record them in a general journal.

General Journal Entry to Record Employer FICA Tax

The general journal entry to record Phoenix Sales and Service Social Security and Medicare payroll taxes for the week ending January 7, 2009, is:

Jan.	09	Payroll Tax Expense	2 4 9 61		
		Employer FICA—Social Security Taxes Payable		2 0 2 30	
		Employer FICA—Medicare Taxes Payable		4 7 31	
		To record employer Social Security and Medicare payroll taxes.			

Assets = Liabilities +   Equity
          +202.30   −249.61
          +47.31

Exhibit 10.1

Phoenix Sales and Service Partial Payroll Register

(continued across top of next page)

Partial Payroll Register

Employee Name	Marital Status and Allowances	Beginning Cumulative Gross Earnings	Hours Worked This Pay Period	Hourly Wage	EARNINGS			Ending Cumulative Gross Earnings
					Regular	Overtime	Gross	
Austin, Robert	S-1	0.00	40	10.00	400.00	00.00	400.00	400.00
Cross, Judy	S-2	0.00	41	14.00	560.00	21.00	581.00	581.00
Diaz, John	M-0	0.00	42	14.00	560.00	42.00	602.00	602.00
Keife, Kay	M-2	0.00	40	14.00	560.00	00.00	560.00	560.00
Miller, Lee	M-0	0.00	40	14.00	560.00	00.00	560.00	560.00
Sears, Dale	S-0	0.00	40	14.00	560.00	00.00	560.00	560.00
Total	Week of January 7, 2009				3,200.00	63.00	3,263.00	3,263.00
Total	Month of January 2009				12,800.00	252.00	13,052.00	13,052.00
Total	First Quarter of 2009				41,600.00	819.00	42,419.00	42,419.00
Total	Year Ending December 31, 2009				166,400.00	3,276.00	169,676.00	169,676.00

Payroll Tax Deposits

Timing of Payroll Tax Deposits   The Internal Revenue Service (IRS) requires employers to deposit payroll taxes either monthly or semiweekly (once or twice each week). New companies deposit monthly. For other companies, the IRS has a **look-back rule** to classify depositors. The IRS looks back to a one-year period that begins on July 1 and ends on June 30. To determine an employer's status for 2009, the IRS looks back to find the total amount of Social Security, Medicare, and federal income taxes the business paid from July 1, 2007, through June 30, 2008. If this amount is less than $50,000, the IRS classifies the business as a monthly depositor. If this amount is more than $50,000, the IRS classifies the business as a semiweekly depositor. A company's depositor status is reevaluated every year. In our example, Phoenix Sales and Service is classified as a monthly depositor. A monthly depositor must deposit its employee and employer FICA taxes and employees' federal income tax withholdings by the 15th of the next month.

If the employers' total tax liability is less than $2,500 in a quarter, no deposit is required for that quarter. In this case the employer includes a check for its tax liabilities with its tax returns.

IN THE NEWS

A company's delay or failure to pay withholding taxes to the government has severe consequences. For example, a 100% penalty can be levied, with interest, on the unpaid balance. The government can even close a company, take its assets, and pursue legal action against those involved.

Computing and Recording Payroll Tax Deposits

Federal tax withholdings.   By law, the employer must deposit federal tax withholdings on a timely basis in a **federal depository bank.** A federal depository bank is authorized to accept deposits of amounts payable to the federal government. These banks can either be **Federal Reserve Banks** or **authorized depositories.** A Federal Reserve Bank can accept payroll deposits from any business. An authorized depository can accept payroll deposits from its own checking account customers.

The company uses information from its payroll register to make tax deposits. Assume that Phoenix Sales and Service employee wages and deductions for the remaining three weekly

TAXABLE EARNINGS FOR			EMPLOYEE DEDUCTIONS FOR				PAYMENT INFORMATION	
Social Security	Medicare	Unemployment	Social Security	Medicare	Federal Income Tax	State Income Tax	Net Pay	Check Number
400.00	400.00	400.00	24.80	5.80	26.00	2.08	341.32	9001
581.00	581.00	581.00	36.02	8.42	43.00	3.44	490.12	9002
602.00	602.00	602.00	37.32	8.73	37.00	2.96	515.99	9003
560.00	560.00	560.00	34.72	8.12	12.00	0.96	504.20	9004
560.00	560.00	560.00	34.72	8.12	31.00	2.48	483.68	9005
560.00	560.00	560.00	34.72	8.12	61.00	4.88	451.28	9006
3,263.00	3,263.00	3,263.00	202.30	47.31	210.00	16.80	2,786.59	
13,052.00	13,052.00	13,052.00	809.20	189.24	840.00	67.20	11,146.36	
42,419.00	42,419.00	40,200.00	2,629.90	615.03	2,730.00	218.40	36,225.67	
169,676.00	169,676.00	42,000.00	10,519.60	2,460.12	10,920.00	873.60	144,902.68	

payroll periods in January are exactly the same as those for the week of January 7, 2009. The "Total Month of January 2009" row in Exhibit 10.1 reports the following withholdings:

Employees' federal income taxes	$ 840.00
Employee FICA—Social Security taxes	809.20
Employee FICA—Medicare taxes	189.24
Employer FICA—Social Security taxes (match employee amount)	809.20
Employer FICA—Medicare taxes (match employee amount)	189.24
Total	$2,836.88

Form 8109.   The total of $2,836.88 must be deposited in a federal depository bank. The company can make the tax payment either by electronic funds transfer or by check. Companies with annual federal tax deposits above $200,000 must use electronic funds transfers. If the tax payment is made by check, the accountant prepares a **Form 8109,** Federal Tax Deposit Coupon. These preprinted deposit coupons are obtained from the Internal Revenue Service.

If the company does not have a current supply of Forms 8109 or is a new entity, it completes **Form 8109-B.** Exhibit 10.2 presents Form 8109-B for Phoenix Sales and Service for the month

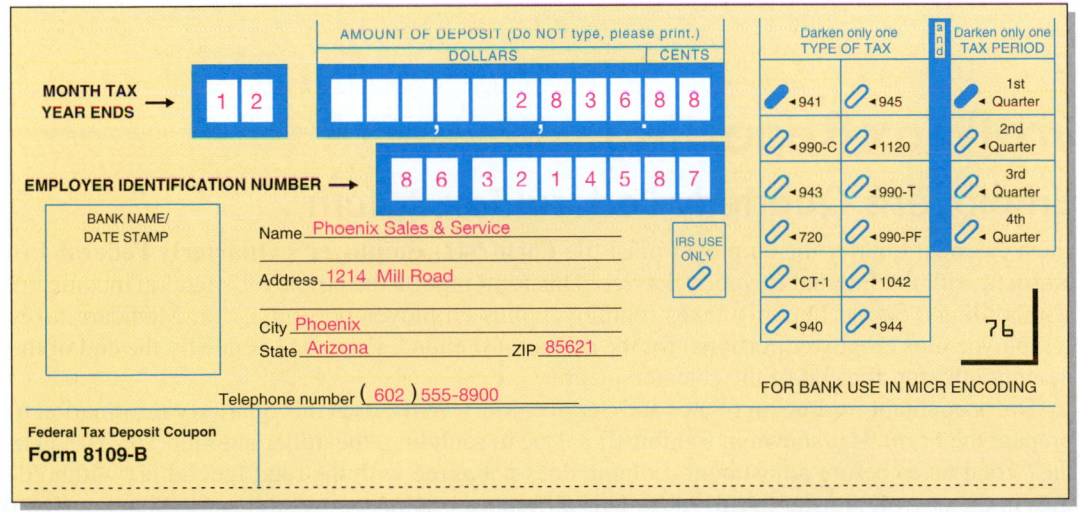

Exhibit 10.2

Form 8109-B, Federal Tax Deposit Coupon

LO3 Journalize an employer's deposit of federal income taxes and FICA taxes withheld, and prepare a deposit coupon.

of January. The company has a calendar year-end, so the accountant writes "12" in the "Month Tax Year Ends" box. The accountant also enters the company's EIN and the dollar amount ($2,836.88) of the tax deposit. Finally, the accountant darkens the "941" and "1st quarter" ovals, since the company is depositing federal taxes it will report on Form 941 (see below) and the deposit is for a month in the first quarter of the year.

General Journal Entry to Record Payroll Tax Deposit　Phoenix Sales and Service's accountant then makes the following entry in its general journal.

Assets = Liabilities + Equity
−2,836.88　　−840.00
　　　　　　−809.20
　　　　　　−189.24
　　　　　　−809.20
　　　　　　−189.24

Jan.	31	Employee Federal Income Taxes Payable	8 4 0 00	
		Employee FICA—Social Security Taxes Payable	8 0 9 20	
		Employee FICA—Medicare Taxes Payable	1 8 9 24	
		Employer FICA—Social Security Taxes Payable	8 0 9 20	
		Employer FICA—Medicare Taxes Payable	1 8 9 24	
		Cash		2 8 3 6 88
		Deposit January payroll tax withholdings.		

February and March Payroll Records　Assume that February has four weekly payroll periods and March has five weekly payroll periods. Also assume that employee wages and deductions for each weekly payroll period in February and March are exactly the same as those reported in the payroll register for the week ending January 7, 2009. The accountant for Phoenix Sales and Service has updated the company's payroll register and individual employee earnings records and made all the necessary journal entries for payroll. Then, the "Total First Quarter of 2009" row in Exhibit 10.1 reports the following withholdings:

Employees' federal income taxes	$2,730.00
Employee FICA—Social Security taxes	2,629.90
Employee FICA—Medicare taxes	615.03
Employer FICA—Social Security taxes (match employee amount)	2,629.90
Employer FICA—Medicare taxes (match employee amount)	615.03
Total	$9,219.86

Employer's Payroll Tax Reporting

Employer's Quarterly Federal Tax Return

LO4 Prepare Form 941, Employer's Quarterly Federal Tax Return.

Each calendar quarter the employer must file **Form 941, Employer's Quarterly Federal Tax Return,** with the Internal Revenue Service. This form reports the employer's federal income tax withholdings, Social Security taxes (employee plus employer portions), and Medicare taxes (employee plus employer portions) for the quarter just ended. Form 941 is due by the end of the next month after the end of the calendar quarter.

The accountant for Phoenix Sales and Service, Mary Wills, uses this quarterly information to prepare the Form 941, shown in Exhibit 10.3. Due to rounding, the dollar amount ($9,220.11) in the "Total taxes before adjustment" column does not agree with the total federal tax withholdings in the payroll register ($9,219.86). This difference is adjusted by adding $0.25 in box 7a of Form 941.

Exhibit 10.3

Form 941, Employer's Quarterly
Federal Tax Return

Form **941**   **Employer's Quarterly Federal Tax Return**   9901
Department of the Treasury — Internal Revenue Service

OMB No. 1545-0029

Employer identification number   8 6 – 3 2 1 4 5 8 7

Name (not your trade name)   Mary Wills

Trade name (if any)   Phoenix Sales & Service

Address   1214   Mill Road
Number   Street   Suite or room number

Phoenix   AZ   85821
City   State   ZIP code

Read the seperate instructions before you fill out this form. Please type or print within the boxes.

Report for this Quarter ...
(Check one.)

☑ 1: January, February, March

☐ 2: April, May, June

☐ 3: July, August, September

☐ 4: October, November, December

Part 1: Answer these questions for this quarter.

1 Number of employees who received wages, tips, or other compensation for the pay period including: *Mar. 12* (Quarter 1), *June 12* (Quarter 2), *Sept. 12* (Quarter 3), *Dec. 12* (Quarter 4)   1   6

2 Wages, tips, and other compensation   2   42,419.00

3 Total income tax withheld from wages, tips, and other compensation   3   2,730.00

4 If no wages, tips, and other compensation are subject to social security or Medicare tax .   ☐ Check and go to line 6.

5 Taxable social security and Medicare wages and tips:

	Column 1		Column 2
5a Taxable social security wages	42,419.00	× .124 =	5,259.96
5b Taxable social security tips	0.00	× .124 =	0.00
5c Taxable Medicare wages & tips	42,419.00	× .029 =	1,230.15

5d Total social security and Medicare taxes (*Column 2,* lines 5a + 5b + 5c = line 5d) .   5d   6,490.11

6 Total taxes before adjustments (lines 3 + 5d = line 6)   6   9,220.11

7 Tax adjustments (If your answer is a negative number, write it in brackets.):

7a Current quarter's fractions of cents . . . .   (.25)

7b Current quarter's sick pay . . . .

7c Current quarter's adjustments for tips and group-term life insurance   .

7d Current year's income tax withholding (Attach Form 941c) . .   .

7e Prior quarters' social security and Medicare taxes (Attach Form 941c)   .

7f Special additions to federal income tax (reserved use) . . .   .

7g Special additions to social security and Medicare (reserved use)   .

7h Total adjustments (Combine all amounts: lines 7a through 7g.) . . . . . .   7h   (.25)

8 Total taxes after adjustments (Combine lines 6 and 7h.)   8   9,219.86

9 Advance earned income credit (EIC) payments made to employees   9   0.00

10 Total taxes after adjustment for advance **EIC** (lines 8 – 9 = line 10)   10   9,219.86

11 Total deposits for this quarter, including overpayment applied from a prior quarter . .   11   9,219.86

12 Balance due (lines 10 – 11 = line 12) Make checks payable to the *United States Treasury* .   12   0.00

13 Overpayment (If line 11 is more than line 10, write the difference here.)   0.00   Check one ☐ Apply to next return.
☐ Send a refund.

Next ⟶

Refer to www.IRS.gov for revised
versions of this form.

(continued)

Exhibit 10.3

(concluded)

9902

Name (not your trade name)	Employer identification number
Mary Wills	86-3214587

Part 2: Tell us about your deposit schedule for this quarter.

If you are unsure about whether you are a monthly schedule depositor or a semiweekly schedule depositor, see *Pub. 15 (Circular E)*, section 11.

14　[A] [Z]　Write the state abbreviation for the state where you made your deposits OR write "MU" if you made your deposits in *multiple* states.

15　Check one: ☐　Line 10 is less than $2,500. Go to Part 3.

☑　You were a monthly schedule depositor for the entire quarter. Fill out your tax liability for each month. Then go to Part 3.

Tax liability:	Month 1	2,836.88
	Month 2	2,836.88
	Month 3	3,546.10
	Total	9,219.86	Total must equal line 10.

☐　You were a semiweekly schedule depositor for any part of this quarter. Fill out *Schedule B (Form 941): Report of Tax Liability for Semiweekly Schedule Depositors*, and attach it to this form.

Part 3: Tell us about your business. If a question does NOT apply to your business, leave it blank.

16　If your business has closed and you do not have to file returns in the future　.　.　.　.　.　.　.　☐ Check here, and

enter the final date you paid wages　[　/　/　].

17　If you are a seasonal employer and you do not have to file a return for every quarter of the year　.　.　☐ Check here.

Part 4: May we contact your third-party designee?

Do you want to allow an employee, a paid tax preparer, or another person to discuss this return with the IRS? See the instructions for details.

☐ Yes.　Designee's name

Phone　(　　　)　　–　　　　Personal Identification Number (PIN) [ ][ ][ ][ ][ ]

☑ No.

Part 5: Sign here

Under penalties of perjury, I declare that I have examined this return, including accompanying schedules and statements, and to the best of my knowledge and belief, it is true, correct, and complete.

✗ Sign your name here　*Mary Wills*

Print name and title　Mary Wills, Accountant

Date　04 / 30 /2009　Phone (602) 555 – 8900

Part 6: For paid preparers only (optional)

Preparer's signature	
Firm's name	
Address	EIN
	ZIP Code
Date　/　/　Phone (　)　–	SSN/PTIN

☐ Check if you are self-employed.

Employer's Annual Withholding Reporting

LO5 Prepare Form W-2, Employee's Wage and Tax Statement, and Form W-3, Transmittal of Wage and Tax Statements.

Form W-2　The employer must provide a **Form W-2, Wage and Tax Statement,** to each employee by January 31 after the calendar year ends. Form W-2 reports each employee's total earnings and deductions for the year just ended. This information comes from each employee's individual earnings record, shown in Chapter 9.

Exhibit 10.4 shows a Form W-2 for 2009 for Robert Austin. The amounts in Exhibit 10.4 assume Robert Austin's payroll information is exactly the same for each of the 52 weeks in 2009. For example, his total "wages, tips, and other compensation" of $20,800 (box 1) equals $400 (his weekly wage from Exhibit 10.1) times 52 weeks. The employer prepares several copies of Form W-2 for each employee. The employer sends one copy of Form W-2 for each employee to the Social Security Administration, one copy to the state tax department, and several copies to the employee for his or her federal and state tax returns. The employer also keeps a copy of Form W-2 for each employee.

Exhibit 10.4

Form W-2, Wage and Tax Statement

a Control number AR101	22222	OMB No. 1545-0008	
b Employer identification number (EIN) 86-3214587		1 Wages, tips, other compensation 20,800.00	2 Federal income tax withheld 1,352.00
c Employer's name, address, and ZIP code Phoenix Sales & Service 1214 Mill Road Phoenix, AZ 85621		3 Social security wages 20,800.00	4 Social security tax withheld 1,289.60
		5 Medicare wages and tips 20,800.00	6 Medicare tax withheld 301.60
		7 Social security tips	8 Allocated tips
d Employee's social security number 333-22-9999		9 Advance EIC payment	10 Dependent care benefits
e Employee's first name and initial Robert J.	Last name Austin	11 Nonqualified plans	12a
18 Roosevelt Blvd., Apt. C Tempe, AZ 86322		13 Statutory employee / Retirement plan / Third-party sick pay	12b
		14 Other	12c
f Employee's address and ZIP code			12d

15 State	Employer's state ID number	16 State wages, tips, etc.	17 State income tax	18 Local wages, tips, etc.	19 Local income tax	20 Locality name
AZ	12-345678	20,800.00	108.16			

Form **W-2** Wage and Tax Statement

Department of the Treasury—Internal Revenue Service

Copy 1—For State, City, or Local Tax Department

Form W-3 The employer also submits **Form W-3, Transmittal of Wage and Tax Statements,** with the W-2 Forms it sends to the Social Security Administration. Form W-3 reports the total wage and withholding information for all of the company's employees. Form W-3 is due by the last day of February after each calendar year-end. Exhibit 10.5 presents the Form W-3 for Phoenix Sales and Service for 2009.

Exhibit 10.5

Form W-3, Transmittal of Wage and Tax Statements

DO NOT STAPLE OR FOLD

a Control number	33333	For Official Use Only ▶ OMB No. 1545-0008	
b Kind of Payer: 941 [✓], Military [ ], 943 [ ], CT-1 [ ], Hshld. emp. [ ], Medicare govt. emp. [ ], Third-party sick pay [ ]		1 Wages, tips, other compensation 169,676.00	2 Federal income tax withheld 10,920.00
		3 Social security wages 169,676.00	4 Social security tax withheld 10,519.60
c Total number of Forms W-2 6	d Establishment number	5 Medicare wages and tips 169,676.00	6 Medicare tax withheld 2,460.12
e Employer identification number (EIN) 86-3214587		7 Social security tips	8 Allocated tips
f Employer's name Phoenix Sales & Service		9 Advance EIC payments	10 Dependent care benefits
		11 Nonqualified plans	12 Deferred compensation
		13 For third-party sick pay use only	
1214 Mill Road, Phoenix, AZ 85621 g Employer's address and ZIP code		14 Income tax withheld by payer of third-party sick pay	
h Other EIN used this year			
15 State AZ	Employer's state ID number 12-345678	16 State wages, tips, etc. 169,676.00	17 State income tax 873.60
		18 Local wages, tips, etc.	19 Local income tax
Contact person Mary Wills		Telephone number (602) 555-8900	For Official Use Only
Email address MWills@pss.com		Fax number (602) 555-8901	

Under penalties of perjury, I declare that I have examined this return and accompanying documents, and, to the best of my knowledge and belief, they are true, correct, and complete.

HOW YOU DOIN'? Answers—p. 247

4. For each of the following separate cases, determine how frequently (monthly or semiweekly) the employer must deposit payroll taxes for 2010: (a) a new business expects to pay $55,000 in payroll taxes during 2010; (b) a business had payroll taxes of $42,000 during the period July 1, 2008, through June 30, 2009; (c) a business had payroll taxes of $91,500 during the period July 1, 2008, through June 30, 2009

5. How frequently does the employer report federal payroll taxes? What tax form is used?

6. What is a Form W-2? A Form W-3?

Federal (FUTA) and State (SUTA) Unemployment Taxes

Federal and state unemployment taxes are computed at the end of each quarter. Deposits for FUTA taxes are due on the last day of the next month after the end of a quarter. The company uses either electronic funds transfer or prepares a Form 8109, Federal Tax Deposit coupon.

It is important to remember three points regarding unemployment taxes. First, unemployment taxes usually apply to only the first $7,000 of each employee's earnings during a year. The payroll clerk must keep individual employee earnings records up-to-date and be alert to employees' earnings passing this limit. Second, companies with a relatively stable employment history can pay a lower SUTA tax rate. Third, the employer receives a credit for SUTA taxes paid, and this lowers the employer's FUTA tax rate.

Computing Employer's Unemployment Taxes

LO6 Compute an employer's state and federal unemployment taxes and record them in a general journal.

Phoenix Sales and Service has a good merit rating, so it pays 2.7% of the first $7,000 earned by each employee for SUTA taxes. It receives a credit for these payments and so pays only 0.8% of the first $7,000 earned by each employee for FUTA taxes. Note that the company's FUTA tax rate is reduced by the full credit of 5.4%, even though its actual SUTA rate was only 2.7%.

For the first quarter of 2009, Phoenix Sales and Service payroll register in Exhibit 10.1 reports total earnings subject to unemployment taxes of $40,200. Each employee's total pay for FUTA and SUTA taxes is the lesser of their gross pay or $7,000. Assuming each employee earns the same gross pay in the remaining 12 weekly pay periods as he or she did for the week of January 7, 2009, this amount is computed as follows:

Employee	Weekly Gross Pay	× 13 =	Total Quarterly Gross Pay	Total Pay for FUTA and SUTA
Austin, Robert	$400.00		$5,200.00	$ 5,200.00
Cross, Judy	581.00		7,553.00	7,000.00
Diaz, John	602.00		7,826.00	7,000.00
Keife, Kay	560.00		7,280.00	7,000.00
Miller, Lee	560.00		7,280.00	7,000.00
Sears, Dale	560.00		7,280.00	7,000.00
				$40,200.00

Phoenix Sales and Service computes the total amounts it owes for FUTA and SUTA taxes for the first quarter of 2009 as:

> Federal Unemployment Taxes: $0.008 \times \$40,200.00 = \$ \ 321.60$
> State Unemployment Taxes: $\ \ 0.027 \times \$40,200.00 = \ \underline{1,085.40}$
> Total Unemployment Tax Expense $\ \ \underline{\underline{\$1,407.00}}$

General Journal Entry to Record Unemployment Taxes

The accountant then makes the following two general entries in the general journal.

Apr.	10	Payroll Tax Expense	3 2 1 60	
		Federal Unemployment Taxes Payable		3 2 1 60
		Employer's federal unemployment taxes for first quarter.		
Apr.	10	Payroll Tax Expense	1 0 8 5 40	
		State Unemployment Taxes Payable		1 0 8 5 40
		Employer's state unemployment taxes for the first quarter.		

Assets = Liabilities + Equity
+321.60 −321.60

Assets = Liabilities + Equity
+1,085.40 −1,085.40

Reporting Employer's Unemployment Taxes

FUTA and SUTA taxes are typically due by the end of the next month following the end of the quarter.

LO7 Prepare unemployment tax returns.

Reporting State Unemployment Taxes

Phoenix Sales and Service must now do two things to meet the SUTA deadline. First, it files an **Employer's Quarterly Unemployment Tax Report** for unemployment taxes owed the state of Arizona and includes a check for $1,085.40. This report is shown in Exhibit 10.6. The dollar amounts in boxes 1, 3, and 4 all agree with amounts in the company's payroll register and individual employee earnings records. Phoenix Sales and Service did not owe any additional amounts for interest, penalties, or job training taxes. Second, it deposits $321.60 in a federal depository bank, as we showed earlier.

Reporting Federal Unemployment Taxes

The employer files **Form 940, or Form 940-EZ, Employer's Annual Federal Unemployment Tax Return** by January 31 after the year ends. This deadline is extended to February 10 if the employer has made all tax deposits during the year on time. The employer uses Form 940-EZ if it pays unemployment taxes to only one state.

Assume that Phoenix Sales and Service hires no new workers during 2009. As we illustrated earlier, five of the company's six employees' gross pay exceeds the $7,000 annual limit by the end of the first quarter of 2009. Robert Austin's gross pay also passes this limit during 2009. So, for 2009 Phoenix Sales and Service has total wages subject to FUTA tax of $42,000 (6 × $7,000). The company pays a total of $336 in FUTA taxes for the year

Exhibit 10.6

Employer's Quarterly
Unemployment Tax Report

These forms vary by state, and
are available through state
governments.

ARIZONA DEPARTMENT OF ECONOMIC SECURITY
PO BOX 52027
PHOENIX, AZ 85072-2027
Telephone (602) 248-9354

ARIZONA ACCOUNT NUMBER
CALENDAR QUARTER ENDING
TO AVOID PENALTY MAIL BY
FEDERAL ID NO.

For Online Filling: **www.azui.com**

USE BLACK INK ONLY

PLEASE RETURN ORIGINAL

UNEMPLOYMENT TAX AND WAGE REPORT

A. NUMBER OF EMPLOYEES -
Report for each month, the number of full and part-time covered workers who worked during or received pay subject to UI Taxes for the payroll period which includes the 12th of the month.

6

6

6

B. WAGES - List all employees in Social Security Number order, or alphabetically by last name. Please use white paper in the same format for additional employees. If you have six or more employees, consider reporting via magnetic media. Ask for "Arizona Magnetic Media Reporting" (PAU-430). We support diskette and cartridge media. Or consider online reporting at **www.azui.com.**

C. WAGE SUMMARY - See Reverse For Instructions

1.	**TOTAL WAGES PAID IN QUARTER** From Section B. Wage Listing	42,419 00
2.	**SUBTRACT EXCESS WAGES** Cannot exceed Line 1 - see instructions	2,219 00
3.	**TAXABLE WAGES PAID** Up to $7000 per Employee - Line 1 minus line 2	40,200 00
4.	**TAX DUE** Line 3 × Tax Rate of The decimal equivalant = .027	1,085 40
5.	**ADD INTEREST DUE** 1% of Tax Due for each month payment is late	0 00
6.	**ADD PENALTY FOR LATE REPORT** 0.10% of Line 1 ($35 min / $200 max)	0 00
7.	**ADD JOB TRAINING TAX DUE** 0.10% of Line 3	0 00
8.	**TOTAL PAYMENT DUE** If the sum of lines 4 & 7 is equal to or less than $9.99, payment of the taxes due is not required.	1,085 40
9.	**SUBTRACT ANY CREDIT BALANCE** If a balance is listed, subtract from Line 8.	
10.	**AMOUNT PAID** Make check Payable to DES-Unemployment Tax	1,085 40

LIEN MAY BE FILED WITHOUT FURTHER NOTICE ON DELINQUENT TAXES.

1. Employee Social Security Number	2. Employee Name (*Last, First*)	3. Total Wages Paid in Quarter
333 - 22 - 9999	Austin, Robert	5,200.00
299 - 11 - 9201	Cross, Judy	7,553.00
444 - 11 - 9090	Diaz, John	7,826.00
909 - 11 - 3344	Keife, Kay	7,280.00
444 - 56 - 3211	Miller, Lee	7,280.00

	TOTAL WAGES THIS PAGE	35,139.00
Signature *Mary Wills*	TOTAL WAGES ALL PAGES	42,419.00*

Title: Accountant   Prepared by: Mary Wills

Date: 04/10/2009   Telephone: (602) 555-8900

PHOTO COPY FOR YOUR RECORDS

*Dale Sears' wages of $7,280.00 would be reported on a separate page.

($42,000 × 0.008). The company pays a total of $1,134 in SUTA taxes for the year ($42,000 × 0.027). By no later than January 31, 2010, the accountant files the Form 940-EZ shown in Exhibit 10.7.

General Journal Entry to Record Employer's Payment of Unemployment Taxes   After these tasks are done, the following entry is made in Phoenix Sales and Service's general journal. The employer does not file quarterly tax reports for FUTA taxes. These taxes are reported only annually. We show an example for Phoenix Sales and Service for 2009 next.

Apr.	10	Federal Unemployment Taxes Payable	321 60	
		Cash		321 60
		Remit employer's federal unemployment taxes for the first quarter.		
Apr.	10	State Unemployment Taxes Payable	1085 40	
		Cash		1085 40
		Remit employer's state unemployment taxes for the first quarter.		

Assets	=	Liabilities	+	Equity
−321.60		−321.60		

Assets	=	Liabilities	+	Equity
−1,085.40		−1,085.40		

HOW YOU DOIN'?

Answers—p. 247

7. A company has 10 employees. This company's FUTA rate is 0.8% on the first $7,000 earned; its SUTA rate is 2.5% on the first $7,000. Each employee earns over $7,000 in 2009, and the employer's total gross pay is $200,000. What amount of (*a*) FUTA taxes and (*b*) SUTA taxes will the employer pay in 2010?

8. How frequently does an employer report state and federal unemployment taxes?

Exhibit 10.7

Form 940-EZ, Employer's Annual Federal Unemployment (FUTA) Tax Return

Form **940-EZ** Department of the Treasury Internal Revenue Service

Employer's Annual Federal Unemployment (FUTA) Tax Return

▶ **See the separate Instructions for Form 940-EZ for information on completing this form.**

OMB No. 1545-1110

T / FF / FD / FP / I / T

You must complete this section.

Name (as distinguished from trade name): Mary Wills
Calendar year: 2009
Trade name, if any: Phoenix Sales & Service
Employer identification number (EIN): 86-3214587
Address (number and street): 1214 Mill Road
City, state, and ZIP code: Phoenix, AZ 85621

*Answer the questions under **Who May Use Form 940-EZ** on page 2. If you cannot use Form 940-EZ, you must use Form 940.*

A Enter the amount of contributions paid to your state unemployment fund (see the separate instructions) ▶ $ 1,134 | 00
B (1) Enter the name of the state where you have to pay contributions ▶ Arizona
(2) Enter your state reporting number as shown on your state unemployment tax return. ▶ 12-345678

If you will not have to file returns in the future, check here (see **Who Must File** in separate instructions) **and complete and sign the return.** ▶ ☐
If this is an Amended Return, check here (see **Amended Returns** in the separate instructions) ▶ ☐

Part I Taxable Wages and FUTA Tax

		Line	Amount	
1	Total payments (including payments shown on lines 2 and 3) during the calendar year for services of employees	1	169,676	00
2	Exempt payments. (Explain all exempt payments, attaching additional sheets if necessary.) ▶	2		
3	Payments of more than $7,000 for services. Enter only amounts over the first $7,000 paid to each employee **(see the separate instructions)**	3	127,676	00
4	Add lines 2 and 3	4	127,676	00
5	**Total taxable wages** (subtract line 4 from line 1) ▶	5	42,000	00
6	**FUTA tax.** Multiply the wages on line 5 by .008 and enter here. **(If the result is over $500, also complete Part II.)**	6	336	00
7	Total FUTA tax deposited for the year, including any overpayment applied from a prior year	7	336	00
8	**Balance due** (subtract line 7 from line 6). Pay to the "United States Treasury." ▶ If you owe more than $500, see **Depositing FUTA tax** in the separate instructions.	8	0	00
9	**Overpayment** (subtract line 6 from line 7). Check if it is to be: ☐ **Applied to next return** or ☐ **Refunded** ▶	9		

Part II Record of Quarterly Federal Unemployment Tax Liability (Do not include state liability.) **Complete only if line 6 is over $500.**

Quarter	First (Jan. 1 – Mar. 31)	Second (Apr. 1 – June 30)	Third (July 1 – Sept. 30)	Fourth (Oct. 1 – Dec. 31)	Total for year
Liability for quarter	321.60	14.40			336.00

Third–Party Designee Do you want to allow another person to discuss this return with the IRS (see the separate instructions)? ☐ **Yes.** Complete the following. ☑ **No**
Designee's name ▶ Phone no. ▶ ( ) Personal identification number (PIN) ▶

Under penalties of perjury, I declare that I have examined this return, including accompanying schedules and statements, and, to the best of my knowledge and belief, it is true, correct, and complete, and that no part of any payment made to a state unemployment fund claimed as a credit was, or is to be, deducted from the payments to employees.

Signature ▶ *Mary Wills* Title (Owner, etc.) ▶ Accountant Date ▶ 01/14/2010

For Privacy Act and Paperwork Reduction Act Notice, see the separate instructions. ▼ **DETACH HERE** ▼ Cat. No. 10983G Form **940-EZ**

Refer to www.IRS.gov for revised versions of this form.

Workers' Compensation Insurance

Computing Estimated Workers' Compensation Insurance Premium

LO8 Compute and record workers' compensation insurance premiums for an employer.

Phoenix Sales and Service has two types of workers: office workers and landscapers. The company pays a workers' compensation premium of $0.30 per $100 of office worker wages and $2.50 per $100 of landscapers' wages. Based on previous experience at the beginning of 2009, Phoenix Sales and Service estimates its total wages in 2009 will be $160,000. The company also estimates $53,000 of its total wages will be paid to office workers, and $107,000 will be paid to landscapers. It computes estimated workers' compensation insurance premiums for 2009 as follows:

> Office workers ($53,000/100) × $0.30 = $ 159.00
> Landscapers   ($107,000/100) × $2.50 =   2,675.00
> Total $2,834.00

General Journal Entry to Record Estimated Workers' Compensation Insurance Premium

Phoenix Sales and Service pays this premium in January 2009. The company makes the following entry in the general journal.

Assets = Liabilities + Equity
-2,834.00   -2,834.00

Jan.	14	Workers' Compensation Insurance Expense	2834 00	
		Cash		2834 00
		Estimated workers' compensation insurance premium for 2009.		

Computing Actual Workers' Compensation Insurance Premium

After the end of 2009, the payroll clerk updates the individual employee earnings records, as we showed in Chapter 9. Assume that these records show the following actual total wages for Phoenix Sales and Service employees for the year ending December 31, 2009.

> Office workers . . . . $ 49,920
> Landscapers   119,756

The actual workers' compensation insurance premium for Phoenix Sales and Service for 2009 is

> Office workers ($49,920/100) × $0.30 = $ 149.76
> Landscapers   ($119,756/100) × $2.50 =   2,993.90
> Total $3,143.66

General Journal Entry to Adjust Workers' Compensation Insurance Premium for Actual Wages

The company's estimated workers' compensation insurance premium for 2009 ($2,834.00) was too low. It pays the difference of $309.66 ($3,143.66 − $2,834.00) and makes the following journal entry.

Assets   = Liabilities +   Equity
-309.66   -309.66

Dec.	31	Workers' Compensation Insurance Expense	309 66	
		Cash		309 66
		Pay additional workers' compensation insurance premium		
		based on actual wages paid in 2009.		

Answers—p. 247

HOW YOU DOIN'?

9. A company has office staff and construction workers. The company pays workers' compensation insurance premiums of $0.20 per $100 of office staff wages and $3.00 per $100 of construction worker wages. The company estimates it will pay $65,000 in total pay to office workers and $218,000 in total pay to construction workers in 2009. What amount of estimated workers' compensation insurance premium will the company pay at the beginning of 2009?

10. What journal entry will the company in question 9 make to record the payment of its estimated workers' compensation insurance premium at the beginning of 2009?

11. Assume the company in question 9 actually pays $66,000 in total pay to office staff and $209,400 in total pay to construction workers during 2009. What journal entry will the company make to adjust its 2009 workers' compensation expense for actual 2009 wages?

Demonstration Problem

The Cutting Edge hair salon pays its employees monthly. Employees' gross pay is subject to the following taxes.

Tax	Rate	Applied to
FICA—Social Security	6.20%	First $106,800
FICA—Medicare	1.45	All gross pay
FUTA	0.80	First $7,000
SUTA	2.00	First $7,000

The company reports the following in its payroll register for its three employees for the month ending September 30, 2009.

	Gross Pay through 8/31	Current Month Gross Pay	Federal Income Tax Withholding
Brianna	$17,940	$1,840	$298
Juan	4,625	1,500	243
Shi	5,600	1,680	272
Total	$28,165	$5,020	$813

Required

1. Compute the following employer payroll taxes for the month ending September 30, 2009: (a) FICA—Social Security, (b) FICA—Medicare, (c) FUTA, and (d) SUTA.

2. Prepare the journal entries to record The Cutting Edge's payroll taxes for the month ending September 30, 2009. Assume $813 of federal income tax withheld has already been recorded with a debit to Payroll Taxes Expense and a credit to Employee Federal Income Taxes Payable.

3. The Cutting Edge deposits its payroll taxes monthly. Prepare the journal entry to record the company's payroll tax deposit for September.

4. Assume The Cutting Edge pays its FUTA and SUTA taxes monthly. Prepare the journal entry to record the payment of the company's FUTA and SUTA taxes for September.

Planning the Solution

- For 1, determine if any employee's gross pay through 8/31 is above the annual limits for any of the payroll taxes. Determine the amount of total income for the month subject to each tax. Multiply this income amount by the appropriate tax rate.
- For parts 2, 3, and 4, determine the accounts affected and then record the entries.

Solution to Demonstration Problem

1. No employee's gross pay through 8/31 exceeds the limit ($106,800) for FICA—Social Security tax. Brianna's gross pay through 8/31 does exceed the limit for FUTA and SUTA taxes, so The Cutting Edge does not owe FUTA or SUTA taxes on her pay for September. Shi's gross pay for September, when added to her gross pay through 8/31, causes her to exceed the FUTA and SUTA limit. The Cutting Edge pays FUTA and SUTA taxes on only $1,400 of Shi's September gross pay. The September payroll taxes are:

   a. FICA—Social Security $5,020 × 6.2% = $311.24

   b. FICA—Medicare $5,020 × 1.45% = $72.79

   c. FUTA $2,900* × 0.8% = $23.20

   d. SUTA $2,900 × 2.0% = $58.00

   *Juan's gross pay of $1,500 + $1,400 of Shi's gross pay.

2.

Payroll Tax Expense	465.23	
Employer FICA—Social Security Taxes Payable ...		311.24
Employer FICA—Medicare Taxes Payable........		72.79
Federal Unemployment Taxes Payable...........		23.20
State Unemployment Taxes Payable		58.00

3.

Employee Federal Income Taxes Payable.............	813.00	
Employer FICA—Social Security Taxes Payable	311.24	
Employer FICA—Medicare Taxes Payable............	72.79	
Cash		1,197.03

4.

Federal Unemployment Taxes Payable................	23.20	
State Unemployment Taxes Payable	58.00	
Cash		81.20

Summary

LO1 Describe laws that impact employer's payroll obligations.
Law requires employers to match their employees' Social Security and Medicare taxes. Employers must also pay federal and state unemployment taxes and workers' compensation insurance premiums.

LO2 Compute employer FICA taxes and record them in a general journal. The employer pays 6.2% of each employee's annual gross pay (up to $106,800) for Social Security taxes and 1.45% of their annual gross pay for Medicare taxes. The accountant debits Payroll Tax Expense and credits Employer FICA—Social Security Tax Payable and Employer—FICA Medicare Tax Payable.

LO3 Journalize an employer's deposit of federal income taxes and FICA taxes withheld and prepare a deposit coupon.
The employer must periodically deposit amounts withheld from employee pay in a federal depository. This is done by either electronic funds transfer or by completing a Form 8109. The accountant debits Employer FICA—Social Security Tax Payable and Employer FICA—Medicare Tax Payable and credits Cash.

LO4 Prepare Form 941, Employer's Quarterly Federal Tax Return. The accountant files this federal tax form within one month after each quarter ends. It reports on the employer's Federal Unemployment Taxes for the quarter.

LO5 Prepare Form W-2, Employee's Wage and Tax Statement, and Form W-3, Transmittal of Wage and Tax Statements.

After each calendar year-end the employer sends each employee a Form W-2, which summarizes the employee's wages and deductions for the year just ended. The employer transmits copies of these W-2's to the Social Security Administration and includes a Form W-3 that summarizes all the individual W-2's.

LO6 Compute an employer's state and federal unemployment taxes and record them in a general journal. The employer pays unemployment taxes of up to 6.2% of employee gross pay. Employers with stable employment histories and low turnover typically pay lower SUTA rates. Employers also receive credits for SUTA taxes and often pay FUTA taxes of only 0.8% of their employee's annual gross pay. The accountant debits Payroll Tax Expense and credits Federal Unemployment Taxes Payable and State Unemployment Taxes Payable.

LO7 Prepare unemployment tax returns. The employer files a quarterly state unemployment tax return. Federal unemployment taxes are reported annually on Form 940, the Employer's Federal Unemployment Tax Return.

LO8 Compute and record workers' compensation insurance premiums for an employer. Most states require the employer to provide benefits or pay insurance premiums for employees injured while on the job. Premium amounts are based on total estimated salary amounts and how hazardous the job is.

Guidance Answers to HOW YOU DOIN'?

1. The annual limits are: (a) $106,800, (b) none, (c) $7,000, and (d) $7,000.

2. (a) FICA taxes are incurred by both employee and employer. (b) FUTA taxes are incurred by the employer. (c) SUTA taxes are incurred by the employer. (d) Withheld income taxes are incurred by the employee.

3. ($1,000 × 0.8%) + ($1,000 × 4%) + ($3,000 × 6.2%) + ($3,000 × 1.45%) = $277.50. $1,000 of the $3,000 March pay is subject to FUTA and SUTA—the entire $6,000 pay from January and February was subject to them.

4. (a) New businesses make monthly payroll tax deposits. (b) The company had less than $50,000 in payroll taxes in the "look-back" period (July 1, 2008, through June 30, 2009), so it makes monthly payroll tax deposits. (c) The company had more than $50,000 in payroll taxes in the "look-back" period (July 1, 2008, through June 30, 2009), so it makes semiweekly payroll tax deposits.

5. Federal payroll taxes are reported quarterly on Form 941.

6. A W-2 is an annual statement sent to each employee that reports the employee's total earnings and deductions for the year just ended. Form W-3 reports the total wage and withholding information for all of the company's employees.

7. (a) FUTA = 10 × $7,000 × 0.8% = $560. (b) SUTA = 10 × $7,000 × 2.5% = $1,750.

8. The employer files *quarterly* reports for state unemployment taxes and *annual* reports for federal unemployment taxes.

9. [($65,000 / $100) × $0.20] + [($218,000 / $100) × $3.00] = $6,670.

10.

Workers' Compensation Insurance Expense ...	6,670	
Cash		6,670

11. The company's actual workers' compensation insurance premium for 2009 is: [($66,000 / $100) × $0.20] + [($209,400 / $100) × $3.00] = $6,414. The company is entitled to a refund of $256 ($6,670 − $6,414), which is recorded as:

Workers' Compensation Insurance Refund Receivable	256	
Workers' Compensation Insurance Expense ..		256

Key Terms

Authorized depository (p. 234) A bank that can accept payroll deposits from its own checking account customers.

Employer identification number (EIN) (p. 232) A number issued by the federal government that uniquely identifies a business.

Employer's Quarterly Unemployment Tax Report (p. 241) A report filed with the state that shows an employer's unemployment taxes owed.

Federal depository bank (p. 234) Bank authorized to accept deposits of amounts payable to the federal government.

Federal Insurance Contributions Act (FICA) taxes (p. 232) Taxes assessed on both employers and employees; for Social Security and Medicare programs.

Federal Reserve Bank (p. 234) A bank that can accept payroll deposits from any business.

Federal unemployment taxes (FUTA) (p. 232) Payroll taxes on employers assessed by the federal government to support its unemployment insurance program.

Form 940 (p. 241) IRS form used to report an employer's federal unemployment taxes (FUTA) on an annual filing basis.

Form 940-EZ (p. 241) The Employer's Annual Federal Unemployment Tax Return. This shows the amount of FUTA tax the employer owes for the year.

Form 941 (p. 236) IRS form filed to report FICA taxes owed and remitted.

Form 8109 (p. 235) A preprinted Federal Tax Deposit Coupon. It is used when an employer deposits money into a federal depository bank.

Form 8109-B (p. 235) A Federal Tax Deposit Coupon used by new businesses or when the business does not have a supply of preprinted Forms 8109.

Form SS-4 (p. 232) An Internal Revenue Service form filed by a business in order to receive an employer identification number.

Form W-2 (p. 238) Annual report by an employer to each employee showing the employee's wages subject to FICA and federal income taxes along with amounts withheld.

Form W-3 (p. 239) The Transmittal of Wage and Tax Statements form. This form reports the total wages and tax withholding information for all the employer's employees for the year.

Look-back rule (p. 234) A rule used to classify business as monthly or semiweekly depositors.

Merit rating (p. 232) Rating assigned to an employer by a state based on the employer's record of employment.

State unemployment taxes (SUTA) (p. 232) State payroll taxes on employers to support its unemployment programs.

Workers' compensation insurance (p. 233) An insurance program that provides benefits to workers who are injured on the job.

Multiple Choice Quiz   Answers on p. 259   mhhe.com/wildCA2e

Additional Multiple Choice Quizzes are available at the book's Website.

1. An employee earned $50,000 during the year. FICA tax for social security is 6.2% and FICA tax for Medicare is 1.45%. The employer's share of FICA taxes is
   a. Zero, since the employee's pay exceeds the FICA limit.
   b. Zero, since FICA is not an employer tax.
   c. $3,100
   d. $725
   e. $3,825

2. Assume the FUTA tax rate is 0.8% and the SUTA tax rate is 5.4%. Both taxes are applied to the first $7,000 of an employee's pay. What is the total unemployment tax an employer must pay on an employee's annual wages of $40,000?
   a. $2,480
   b. $434
   c. $56
   d. $378
   e. Zero; the employee's wages exceed the $7,000 maximum.

3. A company estimates that its office employees will earn $70,000 next year and its construction employees will earn $145,000 next year. The company pays for workers' compensation insurance for all of its employees. The rates for this insurance are $0.40 per $100 of wages for office employees and $6.00 per $100 of wages for construction workers. The company's estimated workers' compensation insurance premium for the year is
   a. $4,780
   b. $8,980

   c. $898
   d. Zero; the company pays based on actual, not estimated, wages
   e. $13,760

4. A company's payroll register reports total employee gross pay of $16,200 for a recent pay period. A total of $14,000 of this amount is subject to Social Security tax. Only one of the company's employees has total gross pay for the year less than $7,000; this employee earned gross pay of $1,150 during the recent pay period. Assume a Social Security tax rate of 6.2%, a Medicare tax rate of 1.45%, a SUTA rate of 1.5%, and a FUTA rate of 0.8%. The employer's payroll tax expense for this pay period is
   a. $113.85
   b. $1,088.45
   c. $1,611.90
   d. $1,129.35
   e. $1,256.75

5. The Federal Insurance Contributions Act (FICA) requires that each employer file a
   a. W-4.
   b. Form 941.
   c. Form 1040.
   d. Form 1099.
   e. All of the above.

Discussion Questions

1. What is the combined amount (in percent) of the employee and employer Social Security tax rate?

2. What is the current Medicare tax rate? This rate is applied to what maximum level of salary and wages?

3. Which payroll taxes are the employee's responsibility and which are the employer's responsibility?

4. What is an employer's unemployment merit rating? How are these ratings assigned to employers?

5. What is a federal depository bank?

6. What is a Form W-2? To whom is Form W-2 sent?

7. What is a Form W-3? To whom is a Form W-3 sent?

8. How does an employer report its state and federal unemployment taxes?

9. When does an employer typically pay premiums for workers' compensation insurance?

10. How often must an employer deposit federal income tax withholdings?

11. How does an employer make federal income tax withholding deposits?

---

connect

QUICK STUDY

QS 10–1

Employer's payroll obligations

L01

Match each of the following terms A through H with the appropriate definitions 1 through 8.

A. EFTPS   **D.** FICA taxes   **G.** FUTA taxes

B. Form 941   **E.** Form 940   **H.** Federal depository bank

C. Merit rating   **F.** Form W-2

_____ **1.** A rating assigned to an employer by a state based on the employer's past record regarding stable employment.

_____ **2.** Taxes assessed on both employer and employees under the Federal Insurance Contributions Act. These taxes fund Social Security and Medicare.

_____ **3.** Payroll taxes on employers assessed by the federal government to support the federal unemployment insurance program.

_____ **4.** A bank authorized to accept deposits of amounts payable to the federal government, including payroll taxes.

_____ **5.** A system for depositing payroll taxes via computer or telephone.

_____ **6.** A statement that reports an individual employee's total earnings and deductions for the year.

_____ **7.** A form that reports an employer's federal tax withholdings for a quarter.

_____ **8.** A form that reports an employer's annual federal unemployment taxes.

Major Co. has five employees, each of whom earns $2,500 per month and has been employed since January 1. FICA Social Security taxes are 6.2% of the first $106,800 paid to each employee, and FICA Medicare taxes are 1.45% of gross pay. FUTA taxes are 0.8% and SUTA taxes are 2.8% of the first $7,000 paid to each employee. Prepare the March 31 journal entry to record the March payroll tax expense.

QS 10-2
Record employer payroll taxes
LO2   LO6

A company's employees had the following earnings records at the close of the weekly payroll period ending August 7, 2009.

QS 10-3
Employer's payroll tax expenses
LO2   LO6

Employees	Earnings through Prior Pay Period	Earnings This Pay Period
D. Adams	$11,300	$3,900
J. Hess	6,100	2,500
R. Lui	9,500	3,100
T. Morales	4,800	1,400
L. Vang	10,000	3,000

The company's payroll taxes expense on each employee's earnings includes: FICA Social Security taxes of 6.2% on the first $106,800 plus 1.45% FICA Medicare on all wages; 0.8% federal unemployment taxes on the first $7,000; and 2.5% state unemployment taxes on the first $7,000. Compute the employer's total payroll tax expense for the current pay period.

Refer to QS 10-3. Prepare the August 7, 2009, entry in the company's general journal to record the employer's payroll taxes for the current pay period.

QS 10-4
Recording employer payroll taxes
LO2   LO6

A company's employer payroll taxes are 0.8% for federal unemployment taxes, 5.4% for state unemployment taxes, 6.2% for FICA Social Security taxes on earnings up to $106,800, and 1.45% for FICA Medicare taxes on all earnings. Compute the Form W-2 Wage and Tax Statement information required below for the following employees:

QS 10-5
Preparing Form W-2   **LO5**

Employee	Gross Earnings	Federal Income Taxes Withheld
A. Baker	$84,000	$17,600
C. Dirkson	52,000	8,200

W-2 Information	A. Baker	C. Dirkson
Federal income tax withheld	_____	_____
Wages, tips, other compensation	_____	_____
Social Security tax withheld	_____	_____
Social Security wages	_____	_____
Medicare tax withheld	_____	_____
Medicare wages	_____	_____

QS 10–6
Preparing Form W-3   **LO5**

Refer to the data in QS 10-5. Compute the company's Form W-3 Transmittal of Wage and Tax Statements information required below.

W-3 Information	
Federal income tax withheld	_____
Wages, tips, other compensation	_____
Social Security tax withheld	_____
Social Security wages	_____
Medicare tax withheld	_____
Medicare wages	_____

QS 10–7
Employer's payroll taxes
LO2   LO6

A company's payroll information for the month of May follows:

Administrative salaries	$2,000
Sales salaries	3,500
Shop wages	4,000
FICA taxes withheld	700
Federal income taxes withheld	1,300
Medical insurance premiums withheld	415
Union dues withheld	205

On May 31 the company issued Check No. 335 payable to the Payroll Bank Account to pay for the May payroll. It issued payroll checks to the employees after depositing the check. (1) Prepare the journal entry to record (accrue) the employer's payroll for May. (2) Prepare the journal entry to pay the May payroll. The federal and state unemployment tax rates are 0.8% and 5.4%, respectively, on the first $7,000 paid to each employee; the wages and salaries subject to these taxes were $6,000. (3) Prepare the journal entry to record the employer's payroll taxes. (Refer to Chapter 9 if necessary in answering questions 1 and 2.)

QS 10–8
Computing employer taxes
LO1   LO2   LO6

An employee earned $62,500 during the year working for an employer. The FICA tax for Social Security is 6.2% and the FICA tax for Medicare is 1.45%. The current FUTA tax rate is 0.8%, and the SUTA tax rate is 5.4%. Both unemployment taxes are applied to the first $7,000 of an employee's pay. What is the amount of total unemployment taxes the employer will pay for this employee?

EXERCISES

Exercise 10–1
Computing payroll taxes
LO2   LO6

BMX Co. has one employee, and the company is subject to the following taxes:

Tax	Rate	Applied to
FICA—Social Security	6.20%	First $106,800
FICA—Medicare	1.45	All gross pay
FUTA	0.80	First $7,000
SUTA	2.90	First $7,000

Compute BMX's amounts for each of these four taxes as applied to the employee's gross earnings for September under each of three separate situations (*a*), (*b*), and (*c*).

Check   (a) FUTA, $1.60; SUTA, $5.80

	Gross Pay through August	Gross Pay for September
a.	$ 6,800	$ 900
b.	19,200	2,200
c.	101,800	8,000

Using the data in situation *a* of Exercise 10-1, prepare the employer's September 30 journal entries to record (1) the employer's payroll tax expense and its related liabilities and (2) its tax deposits. In preparing the tax deposit entry assume that the employer has already recorded liabilities for employee payroll taxes and withholdings. The employee's federal income taxes withheld by the employer are $150 for this pay period.

Exercise 10-2
Payroll-related journal entries
LO2   LO3

Metro Express has five sales employees, each of whom earns $4,000 per month and is paid on the last working day of the month. Each employee's wages are subject to FICA Social Security taxes of 6.2% and Medicare taxes of 1.45% on all wages. Withholding for each employee also includes federal income tax of 16%. Each employee's monthly medical insurance premium of $110 is also withheld from their paychecks. Metro Express also pays federal unemployment taxes of 0.8% of the first $7,000 paid each employee, and state unemployment taxes of 4.0% of the first $7,000 paid to each employee.

   Prepare the journal entries to record (1) the employee's wages and payroll taxes at January 31, (2) the employer's payroll taxes at January 31, and (3) payment of the employer's payroll tax liabilities at January 31 for Metro Express. Metro Express deposits taxes monthly.

Exercise 10-3
Employer's payroll taxes
LO2   LO3   LO6

Premier Landscaping reports the following in its payroll register for August. The company makes monthly tax deposits.

Exercise 10-4
Employer's tax deposits   **LO3**

Pay Period End	Employee Deductions for		
	Federal Income Tax	Social Security	Medicare
Aug. 7	$1,530.00	$632.40	$147.90
Aug. 14	1,447.50	598.30	139.93
Aug. 21	1,563.00	646.04	151.09
Aug. 28	1,620.00	669.60	156.60

Prepare the general journal entry to record Premier Landscaping's deposit of its federal income tax withholdings and FICA taxes (employee and employer portions) for August.

Ideal Systems' employees had the following earnings records at the close of the first quarter:

Exercise 10-5
Computing and reporting unemployment taxes   **LO6   LO7**

Employee	Gross Pay for First Quarter
A. Poe	$8,200
B. Rye	7,450
C. Sims	6,770

The state unemployment tax is 5.4%, but Ideal Systems pays only 2% due to its high merit rating. Ideal Systems also pays 0.8% for federal unemployment taxes. Unemployment taxes are based on the first $7,000 of each employee's earnings during the year.

1. Compute Ideal Systems' SUTA and FUTA tax liabilities for the first quarter.
2. Prepare the general journal entry to record Ideal Systems' SUTA and FUTA tax liabilities for the first quarter.
3. Prepare the general journal entry to record Ideal Systems' payment of its SUTA and FUTA tax liabilities for the first quarter.
4. Explain how Ideal Systems will report its unemployment taxes to the state and federal governments.

A1 Construction began operations on January 1, 2009. The company pays workers' compensation insurance premiums for its employees. The company's accountant assembled the data below for 2009:

Exercise 10-6
Computing workers' compensation insurance premiums   **LO8**

Classification	Estimated Wages	Rate per $100 of Wages
Office workers	$ 60,000	0.25
Construction	320,000	4.20

1. Compute A1 Construction's estimated workers' compensation insurance premium for 2009.
2. Prepare the general journal entry to record A1 Construction's payment of its 2009 workers' compensation insurance premium on January 9, 2009.

Exercise 10–7
Employer's tax deposits   **L03**

Jim Phillips Consulting reports the following in his payroll register for December 2009. The company makes monthly tax deposits.

Pay Period End	Employee Deductions for		
	Social Security	Medicare	Federal Income Tax
Dec. 6	$552.13	$129.13	$1,380.33
Dec. 13	623.87	145.91	1,559.68
Dec. 20	453.16	105.98	1,132.90
Dec. 27	527.76	123.43	1,319.40

Prepare the general journal entry to record Jim Phillips' deposit of its federal income tax withholdings and FICA taxes (employee and employer portions) for the month of December 2009.

---

connect

PROBLEM SET A

Problem 10–1A
Payroll expenses, withholdings, and taxes   **L02**   **L06**

mhhe.com/wildCA2e

Paloma Co. pays its employees each week. Its employees' gross pay is subject to these taxes:

Tax	Rate	Applied to
FICA—Social Security	6.20%	First $106,800
FICA—Medicare	1.45	All gross pay
FUTA	0.80	First $7,000
SUTA	2.15	First $7,000

The company is preparing its payroll calculations for the week ended August 25. Payroll records show the following information for the company's four employees.

		Gross Pay through 8/18	Current Week	
	Name		Gross Pay	Income Tax Withholding
3	Dahlia	$106,000	$2,800	$284
4	Trey	31,700	1,000	145
5	Kiesha	6,850	550	39
6	Chee	1,250	500	30

In addition to gross pay, the company must pay one-half of the $34 per employee weekly health insurance; each employee pays the remaining one-half. The company also contributes an extra 8% of each employee's gross pay (at no cost to employees) to a pension fund.

Required

Compute the following for the week ended August 25 (round amounts to the nearest cent):
1. Employer's FICA taxes for Social Security.
2. Employer's FICA taxes for Medicare.
3. Employer's FUTA taxes.
4. Employer's SUTA taxes.
5. Employer's total payroll-related expense for each employee.

Check   (1) $176.70
(2) $70.33
(3) $5.20

On January 8, the end of the first weekly pay period of the year, Regis Company's payroll register showed that its employees earned $22,760 of office salaries and $65,840 of sales salaries. Withholdings from the employees' salaries include FICA Social Security taxes at the rate of 6.2%, FICA Medicare taxes at the rate of 1.45%, $12,860 of federal income taxes, $1,340 of medical insurance deductions, and $840 of union dues. No employee earned more than $7,000 in this pay period. Regis Company does not pay for its employees' medical insurance premiums or union dues.

Required

1. Calculate Regis Company's FICA Social Security taxes payable and FICA Medicare taxes payable (employer portion). Prepare the journal entry to record Regis Company's January 8 (employer) payroll expenses and liabilities.

2. Prepare the journal entry to record Regis's (employer) unemployment taxes resulting from the January 8 payroll. Regis's merit rating reduces its state unemployment tax rate to 4.0% of the first $7,000 paid each employee. The federal unemployment tax rate is 0.8%.

Problem 10-2A
Entries for payroll transactions
LO2   LO6

Check (1) Cr. Social Security Taxes Payable, $5,493.20
(2) Dr. Payroll Taxes Expense, $4,252.80

Francisco Company has 10 employees, each of whom earns $2,800 per month and is paid on the last day of each month. All 10 have been employed continuously at this amount since January 1. Francisco uses a payroll bank account and special payroll checks to pay its employees. On March 1, the following accounts and balances exist in its general ledger:

a. FICA—Social Security Taxes Payable, $3,472; FICA—Medicare Taxes Payable, $812. (The balances of these accounts represent total liabilities for *both* the employer's and employees' FICA taxes for the February payroll only.)

b. Employees' Federal Income Taxes Payable, $4,000 (liability for February only).

c. Federal Unemployment Taxes Payable, $448 (liability for January and February together).

d. State Unemployment Taxes Payable, $2,240 (liability for January and February together).

During March and April, the company had the following payroll transactions.

Mar. 15 Issued check payable to Swift Bank, a federal depository bank authorized to accept employers' payments of FICA taxes and employee income tax withholdings. The $8,284 check is in payment of the February FICA and employee income taxes.

31 Recorded the March payroll and transferred funds from the regular bank account to the payroll bank account. Issued checks payable to each employee in payment of the March payroll. The payroll register shows the following summary totals for the March pay period.

Problem 10-3A
Entries for payroll transactions
LO2   LO3   LO6

Check March 31: Cr. Accrued Wages Payable, $21,858

Salaries and Wages			FICA Taxes*	Federal Income Taxes	Net Pay
Office Salaries	Shop Wages	Gross Pay			
$11,200	$16,800	$28,000	$1,736	$4,000	$21,858
			$ 406		

*FICA taxes are Social Security and Medicare, respectively.

31 Recorded the employer's payroll taxes resulting from the March payroll. The company has a merit rating that reduces its state unemployment tax rate to 4.0% of the first $7,000 paid each employee. The federal rate is 0.8%.

Apr. 15 Issued check to Swift Bank in payment of the March FICA and employee income taxes.

15 Issued check to the State Tax Commission for the January, February, and March state unemployment taxes. Mailed the check and the first quarter tax return to the Commission.

30 Issued check payable to Swift Bank in payment of the employer's FUTA taxes for the first quarter of the year.

30 Mailed Form 941 to the IRS, reporting the FICA taxes and the employees' federal income tax withholdings for the first quarter.

March 31: Dr. Payroll Taxes Expenses, $2,814

April 15: Cr. Cash, $8,284

Required

Prepare journal entries to record the transactions and events for both March and April.

Problem 10–4A
Preparing deposit coupons and
Form 941   **LO3   LO4**

Refer to Problem 10-3A. Francisco Company's tax year ends on December 31 and its Employer Identification Number is 851435867. It is located at 12 Round Rock Road, Santa Fe, New Mexico 87501.

Required

1. Prepare a Form 8109-B for Francisco Company's April 15 deposit of its March FICA and employee income taxes.
2. Prepare Francisco Company's Form 941 for the first quarter. Assume that January's and February's payroll taxes and withholdings were identical to March.

Problem 10–5A
Employer's payroll taxes,
unemployment tax returns
LO3   LO6   LO7

Warner Co. pays state unemployment tax of 2.0% of each employee's first $7,000 of annual gross pay. It also pays federal unemployment tax of 0.8% of each employee's first $7,000 of annual gross pay. Warner Co.'s Employer Identification Number is 778125398, its state taxpayer identification number is 13-458232, and it is located at 605 Main Street, Dallas, Texas 75201. Warner Co. reports the following summary information in its payroll register for 2009.

Quarter Ended	Total Gross Pay	Total Gross Pay for FUTA and SUTA
March 31	$32,310.00	31,340.70
June 30	29,675.00	24,333.50
September 30	31,274.00	7,818.50
December 31	27,420.00	1,096.80

Required

1. Compute the amounts of FUTA and SUTA taxes Warner Co. owes for each quarter in 2009.
2. Prepare the general journal entry to record Warner Co.'s FUTA and SUTA taxes for the second quarter (ending on June 30) of 2009. This journal entry is made on June 30, 2009.
3. Prepare the general journal entry to record Warner Co.'s deposit of its second quarter FUTA and SUTA taxes. This journal entry is made on June 30, 2009.
4. Prepare a Form 940-EZ for Warner Co. for the year 2009.

Problem 10–6A
Workers' compensation
insurance premiums   **LO8**

Precision Tool began operations on January 1, 2009. Precision Tool pays workers' compensation insurance premiums for its employees. The company's accountant assembled the data below for Precision Tool for 2009:

Classification	Estimated Wages	Rate per $100 of Wages
Office workers	$ 90,000	0.15
Machine operators	292,500	3.20
Warehouse workers	67,500	1.75

Classification	Actual Wages Situation A	Actual Wages Situation B
Office workers	$ 86,469	$ 99,834
Machine operators	281,024	294,748
Warehouse workers	64,852	80,818

Required

1. Prepare the general journal entry to record Precision Tool's payment of its estimated 2009 workers' compensation insurance premium on January 5, 2009.
2. For each of the two separate situations (A) and (B) prepare the general journal entry to adjust Precision Tool's 2009 workers' compensation insurance premium for its actual wages during 2009. Assume this entry is made on January 15, 2010.

Fishing Guides Co. pays its employees each week. Employees' gross pay is subject to these taxes.

Tax	Rate	Applied to
FICA—Social Security	6.20%	First $106,800
FICA—Medicare	1.45	All gross pay
FUTA	0.80	First $7,000
SUTA	1.75	First $7,000

PROBLEM SET B

Problem 10–1B
Payroll expenses, withholdings, and taxes   **LO2   LO6**

The company is preparing its payroll calculations for the week ended September 30. Payroll records show the following information for the company's four employees.

Name	Gross Pay through 9/23	Current Week	
		Gross Pay	Income Tax Withholding
Ahmed	$105,200	$2,700	$250
Carlos	58,700	1,245	190
Jun	5,350	525	51
Marie	24,300	700	64

In addition to gross pay, the company must pay one-half of the $40 per employee weekly health insurance; each employee pays the remaining one-half. The company also contributes an extra 5% of each employee's gross pay (at no cost to employees) to a pension fund.

Required

Compute the following for the week ended September 30 (round amounts to the nearest cent):

1. Employer's FICA taxes for Social Security.
2. Employer's FICA taxes for Medicare.
3. Employer's FUTA taxes.
4. Employer's SUTA taxes.
5. Employer's total payroll-related expense for each employee.

Check   (1) $252.34
(2) $74.96
(3) $4.20

Tavella Company's first weekly pay period of the year ends on January 8. On that date, the column totals in Tavella's payroll register indicate its sales employees earned $34,745, its office employees earned $21,225, and its delivery employees earned $1,030. The employees are to have withheld from their wages FICA Social Security taxes at the rate of 6.2%, FICA Medicare taxes at the rate of 1.45%, $8,625 of federal income taxes, $1,160 of medical insurance deductions, and $138 of union dues. No employee earned more than $7,000 in the first pay period. Tavella Company does not pay medical insurance premiums or union dues for its employees.

Problem 10–2B
Entries for payroll transactions
LO2   LO6

Required

1. Compute Tavella Company's FICA Social Security taxes payable and FICA Medicare taxes payable. Prepare the journal entry to record Tavella Company's January 8 (employer) payroll expenses and liabilities.
2. Prepare the journal entry to record Tavella's (employer) unemployment taxes resulting from the January 8 payroll. Tavella's merit rating reduces its state unemployment tax rate to 3.4% of the first $7,000 paid each employee. The federal unemployment tax rate is 0.8%.

Check   (1) Cr. FICA—Social Security Taxes Payable, $3,534
(2) Dr. Payroll Taxes Expense, $2,394

MLS Company has five employees, each of whom earns $1,600 per month and is paid on the last day of each month. All five have been employed continuously at this amount since January 1. MLS uses a payroll bank account and special payroll checks to pay its employees. On June 1, the following accounts and balances exist in its general ledger:

Problem 10–3B
Entries for payroll transactions
LO2   LO3   LO6

a. FICA—Social Security Taxes Payable, $992; FICA—Medicare Taxes Payable, $232. (The balances of these accounts represent total liabilities for *both* the employer's and employees' FICA taxes for the May payroll only.)

b. Employees' Federal Income Taxes Payable, $1,050 (liability for May only).

c. Federal Unemployment Taxes Payable, $88 (liability for April and May together).

d. State Unemployment Taxes Payable, $440 (liability for April and May together).

During June and July, the company had the following payroll transactions.

June 15   Issued check payable to Security Bank, a federal depository bank authorized to accept employers' payments of FICA taxes and employee income tax withholdings. The $2,274 check is in payment of the May FICA and employee income taxes.

Check June 30: Cr. Accrued Payroll Payable, $6,338

30   Recorded the June payroll and transferred funds from the regular bank account to the payroll bank account. Issued checks payable to each employee in payment of the June payroll. The payroll register shows the following summary totals for the June pay period.

Salaries and Wages		Gross Pay	FICA Taxes*	Federal Income Taxes	Net Pay
Office Salaries	Shop Wages				
$3,800	$4,200	$8,000	$496	$1,050	$6,338
			$116		

*FICA taxes are Social Security and Medicare, respectively.

Check June 30: Dr. Payroll Taxes Expenses, $612

30   Recorded the employer's payroll taxes resulting from the June payroll. The company has a merit rating that reduces its state unemployment tax rate to 4.0% of the first $7,000 paid each employee. The federal rate is 0.8%.

July 15: Cr. Cash $2,274

July 15   Issued check payable to Security Bank in payment of the June FICA and employee income taxes.

15   Issued check to the State Tax Commission for the April, May, and June state unemployment taxes. Mailed the check and the second quarter tax return to the State Tax Commission.

31   Issued check payable to Security Bank in payment of the employer's FUTA taxes for the second quarter of the year.

31   Mailed Form 941 to the IRS, reporting the FICA taxes and the employees' federal income tax withholdings for the second quarter.

Required

Prepare journal entries to record the transactions and events for both June and July.

Problem 10–4B

Preparing deposit coupons and Form 941   **LO3   LO4**

Refer to Problem 10-3B. MLS Company's tax year ends on December 31 and its federal Employer Identification Number is 548932154. It is located at 102 Grindstone Way, Columbus, Ohio 43085.

Required

1. Prepare a Form 8109 for MLS Company's July 15 deposit of its June FICA and employee income taxes.

2. Prepare MLS Company's Form 941 for the second quarter.

Problem 10–5B

Employer's payroll taxes, unemployment tax returns   **LO3   LO6   LO7**

Prestige Travel reports the following summary information in its payroll register for 2009. Prestige Travel pays state unemployment tax of 2.0% of each employee's first $7,000 of annual gross pay. Prestige Travel also pays federal unemployment tax of 0.8% of each employee's first $7,000 of annual gross pay. Prestige Travel's Employer Identification Number is 845699482. It is located at 11 Coral Lane, Miami, Florida 33101.

Quarter Ended	Total Gross Pay	Total Gross Pay for FUTA and SUTA
March 31	35,310.00	31,900.00
June 30	39,675.00	31,344.50
September 30	41,274.00	3,714.66
December 31	37,420.00	1,683.90

Required

1. Compute the amounts of FUTA and SUTA taxes Prestige Travel owes for each quarter in 2009.
2. Prepare the general journal entry to record Prestige Travel's FUTA and SUTA taxes for the third quarter (ending on September 30) of 2009. This journal entry is made on September 30, 2009.
3. Prepare the general entry to record Prestige Travel's deposit of its fourth quarter FUTA and SUTA taxes. This journal entry is made on September 30, 2009.
4. Prepare a Form 940-EZ for Prestige Travel for the year 2009.

Landmark Homes began operations on January 1, 2009. The company pays workers' compensation insurance premiums for its employees. The company's accountant assembled the data below for Landmark Homes for 2009:

Problem 10–6B
Workers' compensation insurance premiums **LO8**

Classification	Estimated Wages	Rate per $100 of Wages
Clerical office	$ 65,000	0.21
Carpentry	175,000	5.82
Electricians	100,000	3.07

Classification	Actual Wages Situation A	Actual Wages Situation B
Clerical office	$ 66,262	$ 59,834
Carpentry	186,410	171,211
Electricians	97,312	98,247

Required

1. Prepare the general journal entry to record Landmark Homes' payment of its estimated 2009 workers' compensation insurance premium on January 5, 2009.
2. For each of the two separate situations (A) and (B) prepare the general journal entry to adjust Landmark Homes' 2009 workers' compensation insurance premium for its actual wages during 2009. Assume this entry is made on January 15, 2010.

(This serial problem began in Chapter 1 and continues through most of the book. If previous chapter segments were not completed, the serial problem can begin at this point. It is helpful, but not necessary, for you to use the Working Papers that accompany the book.)

SERIAL PROBLEM

Success Systems

SP 10 Refer to the serial problem from Chapter 9. Michelle Jones' gross pay for the February 26 payroll equals $1,200.

1. Record the journal entry to reflect the employer payroll tax expenses for the February 26 payroll payment. Assume Michelle Jones has not met earnings limits for FUTA and SUTA—the FUTA rate is 0.8% and the SUTA rate is 4% for Success Systems. FICA taxes are 6.2% and 1.45% for Social Security and Medicare, respectively.

BEYOND THE NUMBERS

BTN 10–1 Refer to the financial statements of **Best Buy** in Appendix A to answer the following:

REPORTING IN ACTION
LO1

Required

1. In what income statement account(s) does Best Buy report its payroll and benefit costs?
2. Does Best Buy sponsor any retirement savings plans? (*Hint:* See footnote 7 Appendix A.) If so, what dollar amounts did Best Buy contribute to these plans during fiscal year 2008? What amounts did Best Buy's employees contribute to these plans in fiscal year 2008?

Fast Forward

3. Access Best Buy's financial statements for fiscal years ending after March 1, 2008, at its Website (www.BestBuy.com) or the SEC's EDGAR database (www.sec.gov). What dollar amounts did Best Buy and its employees contribute to retirement savings plans for years ending after March 1, 2008?

ETHICS CHALLENGE
LO3   LO4

BTN 10–2   As ZTech's accountant you make payroll tax deposits. Recently ZTech has experienced financial distress. Your boss suggests that the company skip its upcoming quarterly tax deposit, and make the amount up at the end of the year "after business improves."

Required

1. Is your boss's suggestion ethical?

2. Is it a sound business decision?

WORKPLACE COMMUNICATIONS
LO8

BTN 10–3   As the accountant for Prestige Home Construction you record your employer's workers' compensation costs. At a meeting discussing the year-end financial statements, your boss, Dusty Haynes, says, "We paid over $15,000 for workers' compensation insurance at the beginning of the year. We didn't file any workers' compensation claims this year, so we should get a refund this year. But you tell me we have to pay another $2,000 to our insurer. What is going on here?"

Required

Write a one-page memorandum to your boss explaining this situation.

TAKING IT TO THE NET
LO1

BTN 10–4   Many employers are switching to payroll cards instead of issuing paper payroll checks to employees. Go to the **American Payroll Association** Website (www.americanpayroll.org) and select "PaycardPortal" and then select "Advantages."

Required

1. Discuss at least three cost savings an employer can expect from using payroll cards instead of paper paychecks.

2. How do payroll cards help minimize the employer's risk of paycheck fraud?

3. How do payroll cards reduce employees' chances of being harmed by identity theft?

TEAMWORK IN ACTION
LO2   LO6   LO8

BTN 10–5   Form learning teams of three members each. Each team member is to become an expert on one of the types of employer payroll tax listed below:

a. FICA (Social Security and Medicare)

b. Unemployment (State and Federal)

c. Worker's Compensation

Using the following data, teams are to develop a presentation answering requirements 1 through 4.

Background

Superior Stone Company designs and installs stone walls for homes and businesses. At the beginning of the year it employed two office workers and seven stone installers. During 2009 one office worker quit and was not replaced. Due to strong demand Superior Stone's stone installers worked a lot of overtime during 2009. It reports the following data for 2009 (the state unemployment tax rate is 1%; the federal unemployment tax rate is 0.8%).

Type of Employee	Estimated 2009 Wages	Actual 2009 Wages	Workers' Compensation Rate per $100 of Wages	2009 Wages Subject to FICA, FUTA, and SUTA	
				Estimated	Actual
Office worker	$ 77,500	$ 46,500	$0.20	$14,000	$14,000
Stone installer	232,500	263,500	2.50	49,000	49,000
Total	$310,000	$310,000		$63,000	$63,000

Required

1. Each team member computes the estimated amount of one employer payroll tax for 2009.

2. Each team member computes the actual amount of one employer payroll tax for 2009.

3. Team members share their computations and compute the total estimated and actual payroll tax and workers compensation insurance amounts for 2009.

4. Team members discuss differences between estimated and actual payroll tax and workers compensation insurance amounts for 2009. Round calculations to the nearest dollar.

BTN 10-6   Review the chapter's opening feature about Brian Scudamore and **1-800-GOT-JUNK**. To build a successful business, Scudamore had to attend to payroll, employee benefits, and taxes, among other issues, in getting his company where it is today.

ENTREPRENEURS IN BUSINESS
L01

Required

Prepare a one-page memorandum that summarizes the types of employer payroll taxes and how they are reported. To the extent possible, reference the form to be filed for each tax.

---

1. e; $50,000 × (.062 + .0145) = $3,825

2. b; $7,000 × (.054 + .008) = $434

3. b; (($70,000/100) × $0.40) + (($145,000/100) × $6.00) = $8,980

4. d; ($14,000 × 0.062) + ($16,200 × 0.0145) + ($1,150 × 0.015) + ($1,150 × 0.008) = $1,129.35

5. b

ANSWERS TO MULTIPLE CHOICE QUIZ

A Look Back

Chapter 10 focused on employer payroll taxes and reporting. We showed how payroll taxes are computed and paid. We also showed how to account for workers' compensation programs.

A Look at This Chapter

This chapter emphasizes merchandise activities. We analyze merchandise sales transactions, sales discounts, and sales returns and allowances. We show how special journals, sales journals, cash receipts journals, and accounts receivable subsidiary ledgers help in accounting for merchandise activities.

A Look Ahead

Chapter 12 extends our coverage of merchandising activities, with emphasis on accounting for merchandise purchases and accounts payable. We also explain the use of a cash disbursements journal.

Chapter

Merchandise Sales and Accounts Receivable

Learning Objectives

LO 1	Analyze and record transactions for merchandise sales.
LO 2	Describe how to compute and record sales discounts.
LO 3	Explain how to record sales returns and allowances.
LO 4	Describe the use of special journals and subsidiary ledgers.
LO 5	Journalize and post transactions using a sales journal.
LO 6	Prepare and prove the accuracy of the accounts receivable subsidiary ledger.
LO 7	Journalize and post transactions using a cash receipts journal.

"Celebrate today, don't wait until tomorrow"
—Bert and John Jacobs

The Good Life!

HUDSON, NEW HAMPSHIRE—For five years, brothers Bert and John Jacobs, owners of **Life is good** (**Lifeisgood.com**), hawked tee shirts door-to-door at college dorms up and down the east coast. They lived on peanut butter and jelly and slept in their van. After heading home from a long, less-than-fruitful road trip, they brainstormed how to keep their dreams alive. The result was "Jake," a new logo with an optimistic message. They began by printing up 48 Jake tee shirts for a street fair and all 48 tee shirts sold within hours. Once Jake was introduced to local retailers, the market embraced his positive message and the company took off. In 2007, the company sold 4.2 million of its $25 T-shirts and had sales of roughly $107 million.

As a wholesaler, Life is good must ensure that its distributors have the right product mix (colors, styles and sizes), with the right volume at the right price. Bert and John use accounting and inventory systems to set the sales price, monitor costs, and establish inventory levels to avoid costs of out-of-stock and excess inventory. When told by consultants that they could make $3 more on every tee shirt by skimping on quality, John countered, "We want this to be people's favorite shirt and we want it to still be their favorite shirt 10 years from now. It won't be if it's got holes and the collar's stretched out." The inventory system captures merchandising sales information to help with these and other business decisions.

Life is good's optimism is contagious as they now sell a full range of clothing for men, women, and children, in addition to jewelry, bags and headwear. Despite the challenges from competition, copycats, and knock-off products, Life is good continues to look at the cup as half full. Bert and John Jacobs suggest that we "appreciate everything." They add, "Celebrate today, don't wait until tomorrow."

[Sources: *LifeisGood.com Website*, March 2009; *Inc.*, October 2006; *Wikipedia*, October 2006; *The New York Times*, July 2008]

Merchandising activities are a major part of modern business. Consumers expect a wealth of products, discount prices, and inventory on demand. This chapter introduces the business and accounting practices used by companies engaged in merchandising activities. We show how to account for merchandise sales, sales discounts, and sales returns. We also show how to use special journals and subsidiary ledgers to make the accounting more efficient.

Merchandise Sales and Accounts Receivable

Merchandising Sales
- Sales of merchandise
- Sales discounts
- Sales returns and allowances
- Recording and posting

Special Journals and Subsidiary Ledgers
- Sales journal
- Accounts receivable subsidiary ledger
- Cash receipts journal

Merchandising Sales

LO1 Analyze and record transactions for merchandise sales.

Previous chapters emphasized the accounting and reporting activities of service companies. The company described in Chapters 2 through 6, FastForward, is an example of a service business. A merchandising company's activities differ from those of a service company. **Merchandise** consists of products, also called *goods,* that a company acquires to resell to customers. A **merchandiser** earns net income by buying and selling merchandise. Merchandisers are often identified as either wholesalers or retailers. A **wholesaler** is an *intermediary* that buys products from manufacturers or other wholesalers and sells them to retailers or other wholesalers. Examples of wholesalers are Fleming, SUPERVALU, and SYSCO. A **retailer** is an intermediary that buys products from manufacturers or wholesalers and sells them to consumers. Many retailers sell both products and services. The Gap, Best Buy, RadioShack and Wal-Mart are examples of retailers.

In this chapter we show how to account for merchandise sales. In the next chapter, we will show how to account for merchandise purchases and accounts payable. To illustrate, we use the transactions of Z-Mart, a merchandiser. Merchandising companies must account for sales, sales discounts, and sales returns and allowances.

Sales of Merchandise

Merchandisers can have credit sales (sales on account) and cash sales. To illustrate the accounting for credit sales, the following general journal entry records Z-Mart's $2,400 sale of merchandise on credit on November 3.

Assets = Liabilities + Equity
+2,400   +2,400

Nov.	3	Accounts Receivable		2 4 0 0 00	
		Sales			2 4 0 0 00
		Sold merchandise on credit.			

This entry reflects an increase in Z-Mart's assets in the form of an account receivable. It also shows the increase in revenue (Sales). If the sale is for cash, the debit is to Cash instead of Accounts Receivable.

Sales Discounts

LO2 Describe how to compute and record sales discounts.

To encourage timely payment from its customers that buy merchandise on credit, companies often offer **sales** (or **cash**) **discounts.** Sales discounts on credit sales can benefit a seller by decreasing the delay in receiving cash and reducing future collection efforts and default.

Credit Terms   **Credit terms** for a sale include the amounts and timing of payments from a buyer to a seller. Credit terms usually reflect an industry's practices. To illustrate, when sellers require payment within 10 days after the end of the month of the invoice date, the invoice will show credit terms as "n/10 EOM," which stands for net 10 days after end of month (**EOM**). When sellers require payment within 30 days after the invoice date, the invoice shows credit terms of "n/30," which stands for *net 30 days*.

Exhibit 11.1 portrays credit terms. The amount of time allowed before full payment is due is called the **credit period.** Sellers can grant a **cash discount** to encourage buyers to pay earlier. Any cash discounts are described in the credit terms on the invoice. For example, credit terms of "2/10, n/60" mean that full payment is due within a 60-day credit period, but the buyer can deduct 2% of the invoice amount if payment is made within 10 days of the invoice date. This reduced payment applies only for the **discount period.** (Sellers sometimes charge fees if the full invoice price is not paid by the end of the credit period.)

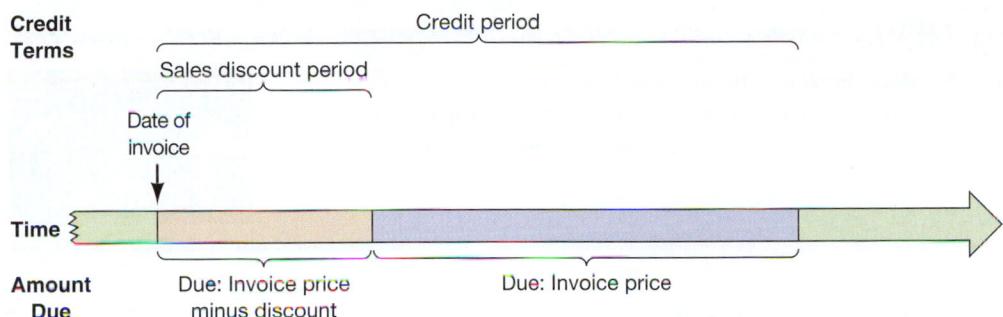

Exhibit 11.1

Credit Terms

Credit Sales Entries   At the time of a credit sale, a seller does not know whether a customer will pay within the discount period and take advantage of a purchases discount. This means the seller usually does not record a sales discount until a customer actually pays within the discount period. To illustrate, Z-Mart completes a credit sale for $1,000 on November 12 with terms of 2/10, n/60. The following entry records this sale.

Nov.	12	Accounts Receivable		1 0 0 0 00	
		Sales			1 0 0 0 00
		Sold merchandise under terms of 2/10, n/60.			

Assets = Liabilities + Equity
+1,000   +1,000

This entry records the receivable and the revenue as if the customer will pay the full amount. The customer has two options, however. One option is to wait 60 days until January 11 and pay the full $1,000. In this case, Z-Mart records that receipt as:

Jan.	11	Cash		1 0 0 0 00	
		Accounts Receivable			1 0 0 0 00
		Received payment for Nov. 12 sale			

Assets = Liabilities + Equity
+1,000
−1,000

The customer's other option is to pay within the 10-day discount period ending November 22 and receive the cash discount. The cash discount is computed by multiplying the sales price by the discount percentage. In this case, the discount is $20, computed as the $1,000 sales price multiplied by 2%. If the customer pays on (or before) November 22, Z-Mart records the receipt as:

Nov.	22	Cash		9 8 0 00	
		Sales Discounts		2 0 00	
		Accounts Receivable			1 0 0 0 00
		Received payment for Nov. 12 sale less discount.			

Assets = Liabilities + Equity
+980   −20
−1,000

Sales Discounts is a contra revenue account, meaning it is deducted from the Sales account when computing a company's net sales (see Exhibit 11.2). Management monitors Sales Discounts to assess the effectiveness and cost of its discount policy.

Exhibit 11.2

Net Sales Computation

Z-MART		
Computation of Net Sales		
For Year Ended December 31, 2010		
Sales		$321,000
Less: Sales discounts	$4,300	
Sales returns and allowances	2,000	6,300
Net sales		$314,700

IN THE NEWS

Return to Sender   Book merchandisers such as **Barnes & Noble** and **Borders Books** can return unsold books to publishers at their purchase price. Publishers say returns of new hardcover books run between 35% and 50% of sales.

Sales Returns and Allowances

LO3 Explain how to record sales returns and allowances.

Sales returns refer to merchandise that customers return to the seller after a sale. Many companies allow customers to return merchandise for a full refund. *Sales allowances* refer to reductions in the selling price of merchandise sold to customers. This can occur with damaged or defective merchandise that a customer is willing to purchase with a reduction in selling price. Sales returns and allowances usually involve dissatisfied customers, and managers need information about returns and allowances to monitor these problems.

Sales Returns   To illustrate, recall Z-Mart's sale of merchandise on November 3 for $2,400. Assume that the customer returns $800 of this merchandise on November 6. The journal entry for this transaction must reflect the decrease in sales and accounts receivable from the customer's return of merchandise as follows:

Assets = Liabilities + Equity
−800   −800

Nov.	6	Sales Returns and Allowances	800 00	
		Accounts Receivable		800 00
		Customer returns merchandise from Nov. 3 sale.		

Sales Returns and Allowances is also a contra revenue account, meaning it is deducted from the Sales account when computing net sales (see Exhibit 11.2). The Sales Returns and Allowances account is kept separate from the Sales account so the company can monitor the extent of sales returns and allowances.

Sales Allowances   To illustrate sales allowances, assume that $800 of the merchandise Z-Mart sold on November 3 is defective but the buyer decides to keep it because Z-Mart offers a $100 price reduction. Z-Mart records this transaction as:

Assets = Liabilities + Equity
−100   −100

Nov.	6	Sales Returns and Allowances	100 00	
		Accounts Receivable		100 00
		To record sales allowance on Nov. 3 sale.		

The seller usually prepares a credit memorandum to confirm a buyer's return or allowance. A seller's **credit memorandum** informs a buyer of the seller's credit to the buyer's Account Receivable (on the seller's books). The sender (maker) of a credit memorandum will *credit* the account of the receiver. The receiver of a credit memorandum will *debit* the account of the sender.

HOW YOU DOIN'?   Answers—p. 274

1. Why are sales discounts and sales returns and allowances recorded in contra revenue accounts instead of directly in the Sales account?

2. When merchandise is sold on credit and the seller notifies the buyer of a price allowance, does the seller create and send a credit memorandum or a debit memorandum?

Recording and Posting Merchandise Sales

Companies also must collect state and local government sales tax on retail sales of certain goods and services and send them to the government on a regular basis. When goods or services are sold on credit, the sales tax is recorded as sales tax payable even though the cash has not yet been collected. Sales Tax Payable is a liability account.

To illustrate the accounting (both journal entries and posting to the general ledger) for sales and sales taxes, we consider Z-Mart's following transactions during November.

Nov. 3 Sold merchandise on credit to Bradford Inc.; Sales Invoice No. 145 for $2,400 plus $144 sales tax

5 Sold merchandise on credit to Smith Inc.; Sales Invoice No. 146 for $1,050 plus $63 sales tax

8 Sold merchandise on credit to Cluff Inc.; Sales Invoice No. 147 for $250 plus $15 sales tax

11 Sold merchandise on credit to Dobson Inc.; Sales Invoice No. 148 for $550 plus $33 sales tax

The general journal entries are in Exhibit 11.3. The journal entries are then posted to the general ledger as shown in Exhibit 11.4.

GENERAL JOURNAL					Page 17
Date	**Description**	**PR**	**Debit**	**Credit**	
Nov 3	Accounts Receivable	106	2 5 4 4 00		
	Sales Tax Payable	232		1 4 4 00	
	Sales	401		2 4 0 0 00	
	Sold merchandise on credit to Bradford Inc.; Invoice No. 145				
5	Accounts Receivable	106	1 1 1 3 00		
	Sales Tax Payable	232		6 3 00	
	Sales	401		1 0 5 0 00	
	Sold merchandise on credit to Smith Inc.; Invoice No. 146				
8	Accounts Receivable	106	2 6 5 00		
	Sales Tax Payable	232		1 5 00	
	Sales	401		2 5 0 00	
	Sold merchandise on credit to Cluff Inc.; Invoice No. 147				
11	Accounts Receivable	106	5 8 3 00		
	Sales Tax Payable	232		3 3 00	
	Sales	401		5 5 0 00	
	Sold merchandise on credit to Dobson Inc.; Invoice No. 148				

Exhibit 11.3

General Journal Entries of November Sales for Z-Mart

Assets = Liabilities + Equity
+2,544   +144   +2,400

Assets = Liabilities + Equity
+1,113   +63   +1,050

Assets = Liabilities + Equity
+265   +15   +250

Assets = Liabilities + Equity
+583   +33   +550

Exhibit 11.4

Posting of Journal Entries for November Sales of Z-Mart

General Ledger

Accounts Receivable   Acct. No. 106

Date		Item	PR	Debit	Credit	Balance
Nov.	1	Balance	✓			3,152
	3		G17	2,544		5,696
	5		G17	1,113		6,809
	8		G17	265		7,074
	11		G17	583		7,657

Sales   Acct. No. 401

Date		Item	PR	Debit	Credit	Balance
Nov.	3		G17		2,400	2,400
	5		G17		1,050	3,450
	8		G17		250	3,700
	11		G17		550	4,250

Sales Tax Payable   Acct. No. 232

Date		Item	PR	Debit	Credit	Balance
Nov.	1	Balance	✓			967
	3		G17		144	1,111
	5		G17		63	1,174
	8		G17		15	1,189
	11		G17		33	1,222

Special Journals and Subsidiary Ledgers

LO4 Describe the use of special journals and subsidiary ledgers.

Exhibit 11.3 shows that entering a journal entry each time there is a credit sale is a tedious, repetitive task. Writing descriptions of each sale and posting each transaction to the general ledger takes considerable effort. To make this process more efficient, special journals are used. While a **general journal** is an all-purpose journal where we can record any transaction, a **special journal** is used to record and post transactions of a similar type. Most transactions of a merchandiser, for instance, can be categorized into the journals shown below. Special journals are efficient tools in helping journalize and post transactions. This is done by accumulating debits and credits of similar transactions.

Sales Journal	**Cash Receipts Journal**	**Purchases Journal**	**Cash Disbursement Journal**	**General Journal**
For recording credit sales	For recording cash receipts	For recording credit purchases	For recording cash payments	For transactions not in special journals

Sales Journal

A typical **sales journal** is used to record sales of inventory *on credit*. Sales of inventory for cash are not recorded in a sales journal but in a cash receipts journal. Sales of noninventory assets on credit are recorded in the general journal.

LO5 Journalize and post transactions using a sales journal.

Journalizing   Credit sale transactions are recorded with information about each sale entered separately in a sales journal. This information is often taken from a copy of the sales ticket or invoice prepared at the time of sale (as shown in Exhibit 11.5). Exhibit 11.6 shows a typical sales journal from a merchandiser. It has columns for recording the date, customer's name, invoice number, posting reference, and the amount of each credit sale. The sales journal in this exhibit is called a **columnar journal,** which is any journal with more than one column. Each transaction recorded in the sales journal yields an entry in the Accounts Receivable, Sales Tax Payable, and Sales columns. Exhibit 11.6 shows the credit sales transactions that Z-Mart experienced in November.

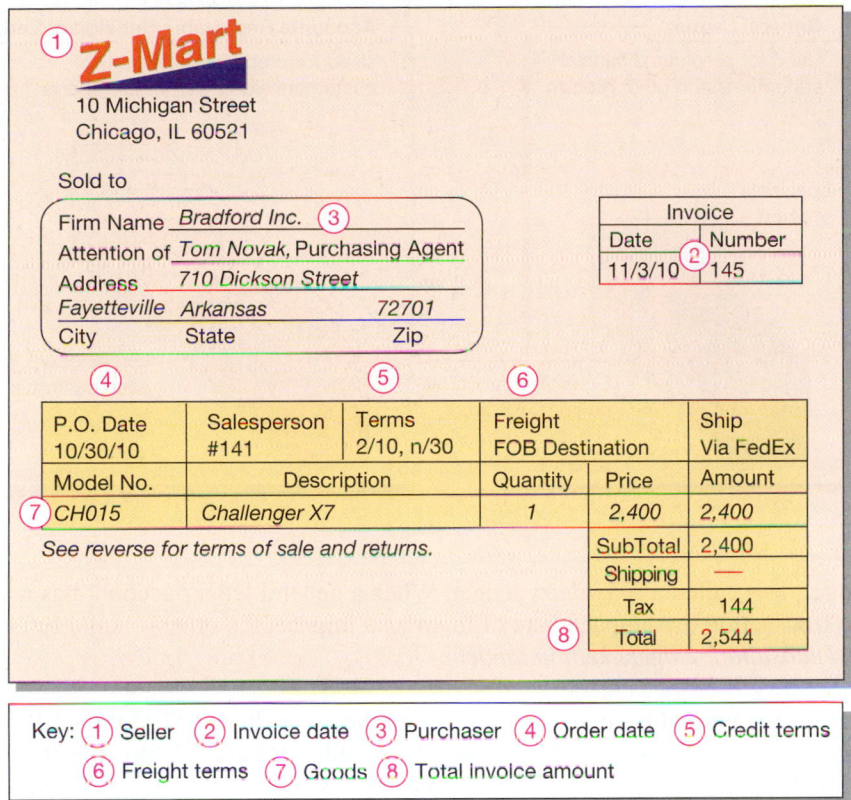

Exhibit 11.5

Sales Invoice

Sales Journal						Page 3
Date	**Account Debited**	**Invoice Number**	**PR**	**Accounts Receivable Dr.**	**Sales Tax Payable Cr.**	**Sales Cr.**
Nov. 3	Bradford Inc.	145		2,544	144	2,400
5	Smith Inc.	146		1,113	63	1,050
8	Cluff Inc.	147		265	15	250
11	Dobson Inc.	148		583	33	550
12	Taylor Inc.	149		1,431	81	1,350
15	Burns Inc.	150		636	36	600
17	Smith Inc.	151		1,484	84	1,400
23	Dobson Inc.	152		1,272	72	1,200
27	Taylor Inc.	153		318	18	300

Exhibit 11.6

Sales Journal Example

Accounts Receivable Subsidiary Ledger

A **subsidiary ledger** contains detailed information on a specific account in the general ledger. Many general ledger accounts have subsidiary ledgers. The **accounts receivable ledger** stores transaction data of individual customers. (The accounts payable ledger is presented in the next chapter.) The accounts receivable ledger shows how much each customer purchased, paid, and has yet to pay. Usually, the general ledger has a single Accounts Receivable account and the accounts receivable ledger keeps a separate account for each customer.

Controlling Account and Subsidiary Ledger Exhibit 11.7 shows the relation between the Accounts Receivable general ledger account and the individual customer accounts in the subsidiary ledger. After all items are posted, the balance in the Accounts Receivable account must equal the sum of all balances of its customers' accounts. The Accounts Receivable account is said to control the accounts receivable ledger and is called a **controlling account.** Since the accounts receivable ledger is a supplementary record controlled by an account in the

LO6 Prepare and prove the accuracy of the accounts receivable subsidiary ledger.

Exhibit 11.7

Accounts Receivable Controlling Account and Its Subsidiary Ledger

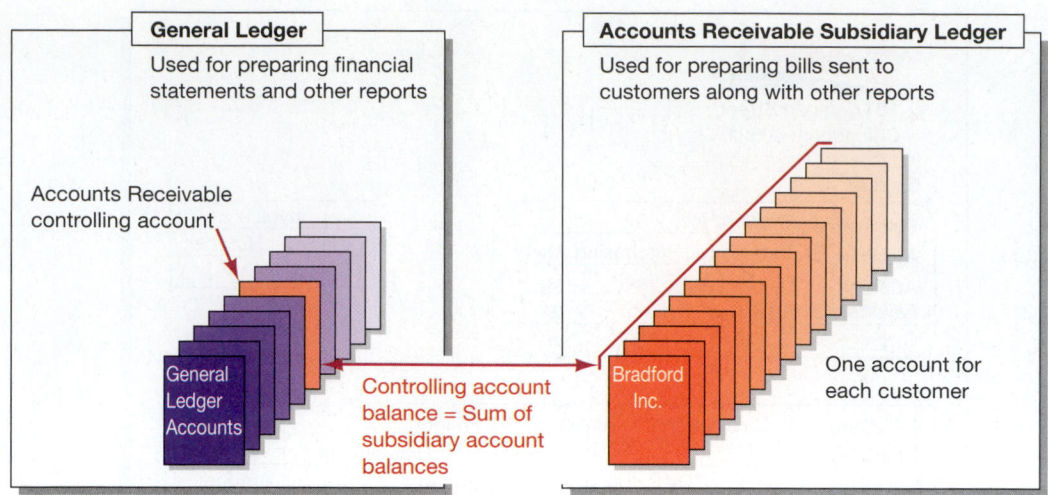

general ledger, it is called a *subsidiary* ledger. When a general ledger account has a subsidiary ledger, any transaction that impacts one of them also impacts the other—some refer to this as *general and subsidiary ledgers kept in tandem.*

Posting   A sales journal is posted as reflected in the arrow lines of Exhibit 11.8. Two types of posting are shown: (1) posting to the subsidiary ledger(s) and (2) posting to the general ledger.

Posting to subsidiary ledger.   Individual transactions in the sales journal are posted regularly to customer accounts in the accounts receivable ledger. These postings keep customer accounts up-to-date, which is important for the person granting credit to customers. When sales recorded in the sales journal are individually posted to customer accounts in the accounts receivable ledger, check marks are entered in the sales journal's PR column. Check marks are used rather than account numbers because customer accounts usually are arranged alphabetically in the accounts receivable ledger. Note that posting debits to Accounts Receivable twice—once to Accounts Receivable and once to the customer's subsidiary ledger account—does not violate the accounting equation of debits equal credits. The equality of debits and credits is always maintained in the general ledger. Postings are automatic in a computerized system, which are done when an entry is made.

Posting to general ledger.   The sales journal's account columns are totaled at the end of each period (the month of November in this case). In this example, the total accounts receivable from credit sales for the month of November of $9,646 is posted to the general ledger. The total sales tax payable for the month of $546 is also posted to the general ledger. The total sales for the month of $9,100 is posted to the general ledger. When totals are posted to accounts in the general ledger, the account numbers are entered below the column total in the sales journal for cross referencing. For example, we enter (106) below the account receivable column, (232) below the sales tax payable, and (401) below the sales column in the sales journal.

A company identifies in the PR column of its subsidiary ledgers the journal and page number from which an amount is taken. We identify a journal by using an initial. Items posted from the sales journal carry the initial *S* before their journal page numbers in a PR column. PR column is only checked *after* the amount(s) is posted.

L06 Prepare and prove the accuracy of the accounts receivable subsidiary ledger.

Proving the Ledgers   Account balances in the general ledger and subsidiary ledgers are periodically proved (or reviewed) for accuracy after posting. To do this we first prepare a trial balance of the general ledger to confirm that debits equal credits. Second, we test a subsidiary ledger by preparing a *schedule* of individual accounts and amounts. A **schedule of accounts**

Exhibit 11.8
Sales Journal with Posting

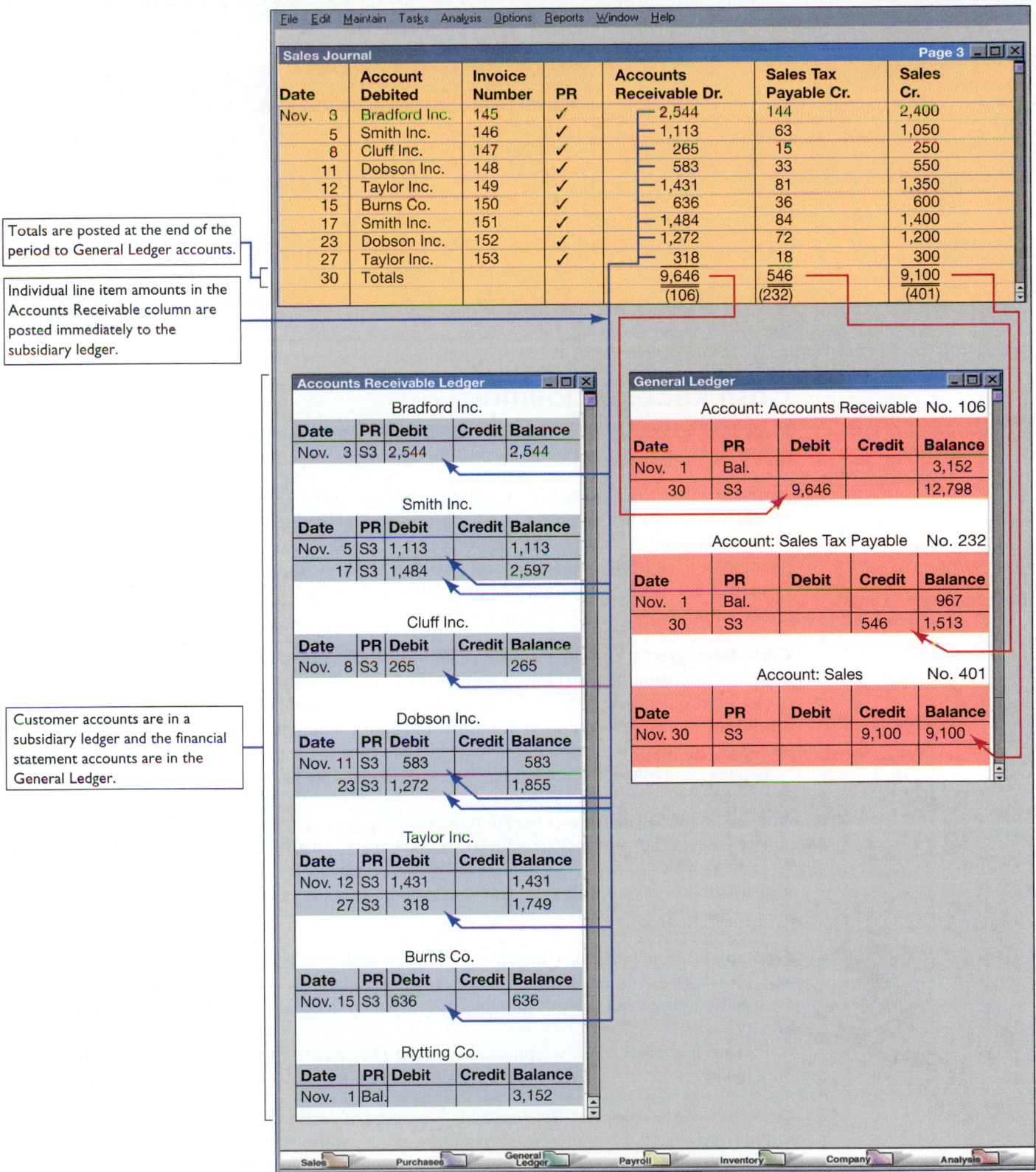

Totals are posted at the end of the period to General Ledger accounts.

Individual line item amounts in the Accounts Receivable column are posted immediately to the subsidiary ledger.

Customer accounts are in a subsidiary ledger and the financial statement accounts are in the General Ledger.

File Edit Maintain Tasks Analysis Options Reports Window Help

Sales Journal   Page 3

Date	Account Debited	Invoice Number	PR	Accounts Receivable Dr.	Sales Tax Payable Cr.	Sales Cr.
Nov. 3	Bradford Inc.	145	✓	2,544	144	2,400
5	Smith Inc.	146	✓	1,113	63	1,050
8	Cluff Inc.	147	✓	265	15	250
11	Dobson Inc.	148	✓	583	33	550
12	Taylor Inc.	149	✓	1,431	81	1,350
15	Burns Co.	150	✓	636	36	600
17	Smith Inc.	151	✓	1,484	84	1,400
23	Dobson Inc.	152	✓	1,272	72	1,200
27	Taylor Inc.	153	✓	318	18	300
30	Totals			9,646 (106)	546 (232)	9,100 (401)

Accounts Receivable Ledger

Bradford Inc.

Date	PR	Debit	Credit	Balance
Nov. 3	S3	2,544		2,544

Smith Inc.

Date	PR	Debit	Credit	Balance
Nov. 5	S3	1,113		1,113
17	S3	1,484		2,597

Cluff Inc.

Date	PR	Debit	Credit	Balance
Nov. 8	S3	265		265

Dobson Inc.

Date	PR	Debit	Credit	Balance
Nov. 11	S3	583		583
23	S3	1,272		1,855

Taylor Inc.

Date	PR	Debit	Credit	Balance
Nov. 12	S3	1,431		1,431
27	S3	318		1,749

Burns Co.

Date	PR	Debit	Credit	Balance
Nov. 15	S3	636		636

Rytting Co.

Date	PR	Debit	Credit	Balance
Nov. 1	Bal.			3,152

General Ledger

Account: Accounts Receivable No. 106

Date	PR	Debit	Credit	Balance
Nov. 1	Bal.			3,152
30	S3	9,646		12,798

Account: Sales Tax Payable   No. 232

Date	PR	Debit	Credit	Balance
Nov. 1	Bal.			967
30	S3		546	1,513

Account: Sales   No. 401

Date	PR	Debit	Credit	Balance
Nov. 30	S3		9,100	9,100

Sales   Purchases   General Ledger   Payroll   Inventory   Company   Analysis

receivable lists each customer and the balance owed. If this total equals the balance of the Accounts Receivable controlling account, the accounts in the accounts receivable ledger are assumed correct. Exhibit 11.9 shows a schedule of accounts receivable drawn from the accounts receivable ledger of Exhibit 11.8.

Exhibit 11.9

Schedule of Accounts Receivable

Schedule of Accounts Receivable November 30	
Bradford Inc.	$ 2,544
Smith Inc.	2,597
Cluff Inc.	265
Dobson Inc.	1,855
Taylor Inc.	1,749
Burns Co.	636
Rytting Co. (outstanding balance from pre-November sales)	3,152
Total accounts receivable	$12,798

Cash Receipts Journal

LO7 Journalize and post transactions using a cash receipts journal.

Many transactions involving cash are repetitive. A **cash receipts journal** is typically used to record all receipts of cash. Exhibit 11.10 shows one common form of the cash receipts journal.

Each transaction in the cash receipts journal involves a debit to Cash. Credit accounts will vary.

Journalizing and Posting   Cash receipts can be separated into one of three types: (1) cash from credit customers in payment of their accounts, (2) cash from cash sales, and (3) cash from other sources. The cash receipts journal in Exhibit 11.10 has a separate credit column for each of these three sources. We describe how to journalize transactions from each of these three sources. (An Explanation column is included in the cash receipts journal to identify the source.)

Cash from credit customers. *Journalizing.* To record cash received in payment of a customer's account, the customer's name is first entered in the Account Credited column—see transactions dated February 12, 17, 23, and 25. Then the amounts debited to both Cash and the Sales Discount (if any) are entered in their respective columns, and the amount credited to the customer's account is entered in the Accounts Receivable Cr. column.

Posting. Individual amounts in the Accounts Receivable Cr. column are posted immediately to customer accounts in the subsidiary accounts receivable ledger. These postings are identified with an "R" and the page number from the Cash Receipts journal in the PR column of the subsidiary ledger. The customer accounts in the subsidiary ledger include some postings from page three of the Sales Journal ('S3' in the PR column). The $1,500 column total is posted at the end of the period (month in this case) as a credit to the Accounts Receivable controlling account in the general ledger.

Cash sales. *Journalizing.* The amount for each cash sale is entered in the Cash Dr. column and the Sales Cr. column. The February 7, 14, 21, and 28 transactions are examples. (Cash sales are usually journalized daily or at point of sale, but are journalized weekly in Exhibit 11.10 for brevity.)

Posting. For cash sales, we place an *x* in the PR column to indicate that its amount is not individually posted. We do post the $17,300 Sales Cr. total.

Cash from other sources. *Journalizing.* Examples of cash from other sources are money borrowed from a bank, cash interest received on account, and cash sale of noninventory assets. The transactions of February 20 and 22 are illustrative. The Other Accounts Cr. column is used for these transactions.

Posting. Amounts from these transactions are immediately posted to their general ledger accounts and the PR column identifies those accounts.

Exhibit 11.10

Cash Receipts Journal
with Posting

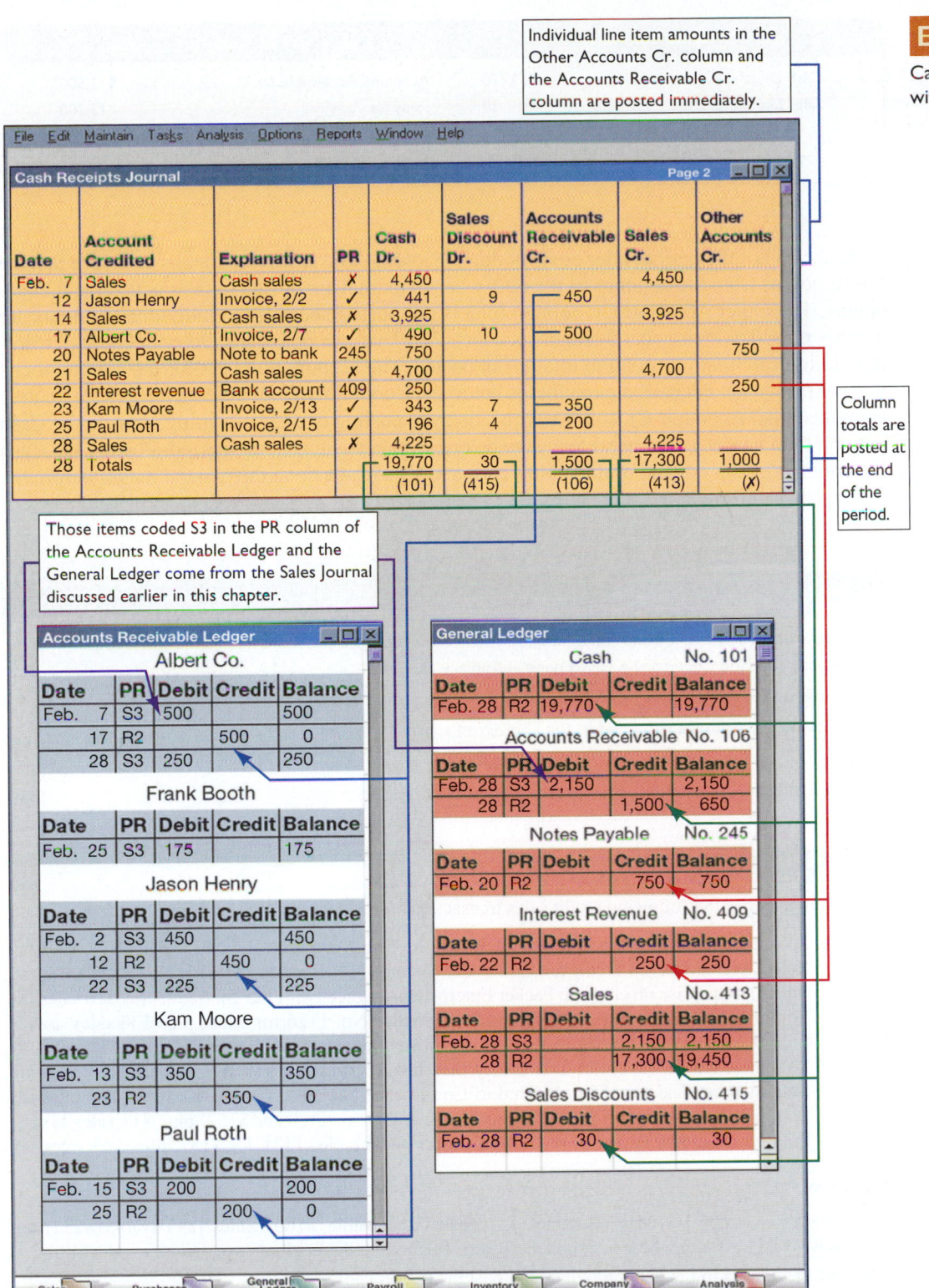

Individual line item amounts in the Other Accounts Cr. column and the Accounts Receivable Cr. column are posted immediately.

Column totals are posted at the end of the period.

Those items coded S3 in the PR column of the Accounts Receivable Ledger and the General Ledger come from the Sales Journal discussed earlier in this chapter.

Cash Receipts Journal — Page 2

Date	Account Credited	Explanation	PR	Cash Dr.	Sales Discount Dr.	Accounts Receivable Cr.	Sales Cr.	Other Accounts Cr.
Feb. 7	Sales	Cash sales	✗	4,450			4,450	
12	Jason Henry	Invoice, 2/2	✓	441	9	450		
14	Sales	Cash sales	✗	3,925			3,925	
17	Albert Co.	Invoice, 2/7	✓	490	10	500		
20	Notes Payable	Note to bank	245	750				750
21	Sales	Cash sales	✗	4,700			4,700	
22	Interest revenue	Bank account	409	250				250
23	Kam Moore	Invoice, 2/13	✓	343	7	350		
25	Paul Roth	Invoice, 2/15	✓	196	4	200		
28	Sales	Cash sales	✗	4,225			4,225	
28	Totals			19,770	30	1,500	17,300	1,000
				(101)	(415)	(106)	(413)	(X)

Accounts Receivable Ledger

Albert Co.

Date	PR	Debit	Credit	Balance
Feb. 7	S3	500		500
17	R2		500	0
28	S3	250		250

Frank Booth

Date	PR	Debit	Credit	Balance
Feb. 25	S3	175		175

Jason Henry

Date	PR	Debit	Credit	Balance
Feb. 2	S3	450		450
12	R2		450	0
22	S3	225		225

Kam Moore

Date	PR	Debit	Credit	Balance
Feb. 13	S3	350		350
23	R2		350	0

Paul Roth

Date	PR	Debit	Credit	Balance
Feb. 15	S3	200		200
25	R2		200	0

General Ledger

Cash   No. 101

Date	PR	Debit	Credit	Balance
Feb. 28	R2	19,770		19,770

Accounts Receivable   No. 106

Date	PR	Debit	Credit	Balance
Feb. 28	S3	2,150		2,150
28	R2		1,500	650

Notes Payable   No. 245

Date	PR	Debit	Credit	Balance
Feb. 20	R2		750	750

Interest Revenue   No. 409

Date	PR	Debit	Credit	Balance
Feb. 22	R2		250	250

Sales   No. 413

Date	PR	Debit	Credit	Balance
Feb. 28	S3		2,150	2,150
28	R2		17,300	19,450

Sales Discounts   No. 415

Date	PR	Debit	Credit	Balance
Feb. 28	R2	30		30

File Edit Maintain Tasks Analysis Options Reports Window Help

Sales   Purchases   General Ledger   Payroll   Inventory   Company   Analysis

Footing, Crossfooting, and Posting

To be sure that total debits and credits in a columnar journal are equal, we often crossfoot column totals before posting them. To *foot* a column of numbers is to add it. To *crossfoot* in this case is to add the Debit column totals, then add the Credit column totals, and compare the two sums for equality. Footing and crossfooting of the numbers in Exhibit 11.10 results in the report in Exhibit 11.11.

Subsidiary ledgers and their controlling accounts are *in balance* only after all posting is complete.

Exhibit 11.11

Footing and Crossfooting Journal Totals

Debit Columns		Credit Columns	
Cash Dr.	$19,770	Accounts Receivable Cr.	$ 1,500
Sales Discounts Dr.	30	Sales Cr.	17,300
		Other Accounts Cr.	1,000
Total	$19,800	Total	$19,800

At the end of the period, after crossfooting the journal to confirm that debits equal credits, the total amounts from the columns of the cash receipts journal are posted to their general ledger accounts. The Other Accounts Cr. column total is not posted because the individual amounts are directly posted to their general ledger accounts. We place an *x* below the Other Accounts Cr. column to indicate that this column total is not posted. The account numbers for the column totals that are posted are entered in parentheses below each column. (*Note:* Posting items immediately from the Other Accounts Cr. column with a delayed posting of their offsetting items in the Cash column total causes the general ledger to be out of balance during the period. Posting the Cash Dr. column total at the end of the period corrects this imbalance in the general ledger before the trial balance and financial statements are prepared.)

HOW YOU DOIN'?   Answers—p. 274

3. How do debits and credits remain equal when credit sales are posted twice (once to Accounts Receivable and once to the customer's subsidiary account)?

4. How do we identify the journal from which an amount in a ledger account was posted?

5. How are sales taxes recorded in the context of special journals?

Demonstration Problem

Perry Company has the following credit sales transactions for January.

Jan. 4   Sold merchandise on credit to Hinckley Inc., Invoice No. 1123 for $2,015, plus $161 sales tax.
Jan. 7   Sold merchandise on credit to Bednar Co., Invoice No. 1124 for $1,616, plus $129 sales tax.
Jan. 9   Sold merchandise on credit to Packer Enterprises, Invoice No. 1125 for $222, plus $18 sales tax.
Jan. 13   Sold merchandise on credit to Nelson Inc., Invoice No. 1126 for $456, plus $36 sales tax.
Jan. 14   Sold merchandise on credit to Packer Enterprises, Invoice No. 1127 for $16, plus $1 sales tax.
Jan. 19   Sold merchandise on credit to Hinckley Inc., Invoice No. 1128 for $1,732, plus $139 sales tax.
Jan. 22   Sold merchandise on credit to Uchtdorf Co., Invoice No. 1129 for $1,819, plus $145 sales tax.
Jan. 27   Sold merchandise on credit to Nelson Inc., Invoice No. 1130 for $152, plus $12 sales tax.
Jan. 30   Sold merchandise on credit to Ballard Corp., Invoice No. 1131 for $157, plus $13 sales tax.

Required

1. Record these sales in a sales journal using Accounts Receivable (#106), Sales Tax Payable (#232), and Sales (#401). Assume these accounts have zero balances at the beginning of January.
2. Post these sales to the general ledger and post the references.
3. Post these sales to the accounts receivable subsidiary ledger.

Planning the Solution

- Set up the sales journal using the template from Exhibit 11.6 or Exhibit 11.8 with a debit entry column for Accounts Receivable and credit entry columns for Sales Tax Payable and Sales.
- Record each sale, with each transaction taking one line in the sales journal.
- Post each transaction to the appropriate account in the accounts receivable subsidiary ledger. Posting to the subsidiary ledger should be done daily, not at the end of the month.
- Sum the columns in the special journal to prepare to post totals to the general ledger accounts.

Solution to Demonstration Problem

1.

				Sales Journal		Page 1 _ □ X
Date	**Account Debited**	**Invoice Number**	**PR**	**Accounts Receivable Dr.**	**Sales Tax Payable Cr.**	**Sales Cr.**
Jan. 4	Hinckley Inc.	1123		2,176	161	2,015
7	Bednar Co.	1124		1,745	129	1,616
9	Packer Enterprises	1125		240	18	222
13	Nelson Inc.	1126		492	36	456
14	Packer Enterprises	1127		17	1	16
19	Hinckley Inc.	1128		1,871	139	1,732
22	Uchtdorf Co.	1129		1,964	145	1,819
27	Nelson Inc.	1130		164	12	152
30	Ballard Corp.	1131		170	13	157

2. and **3.**

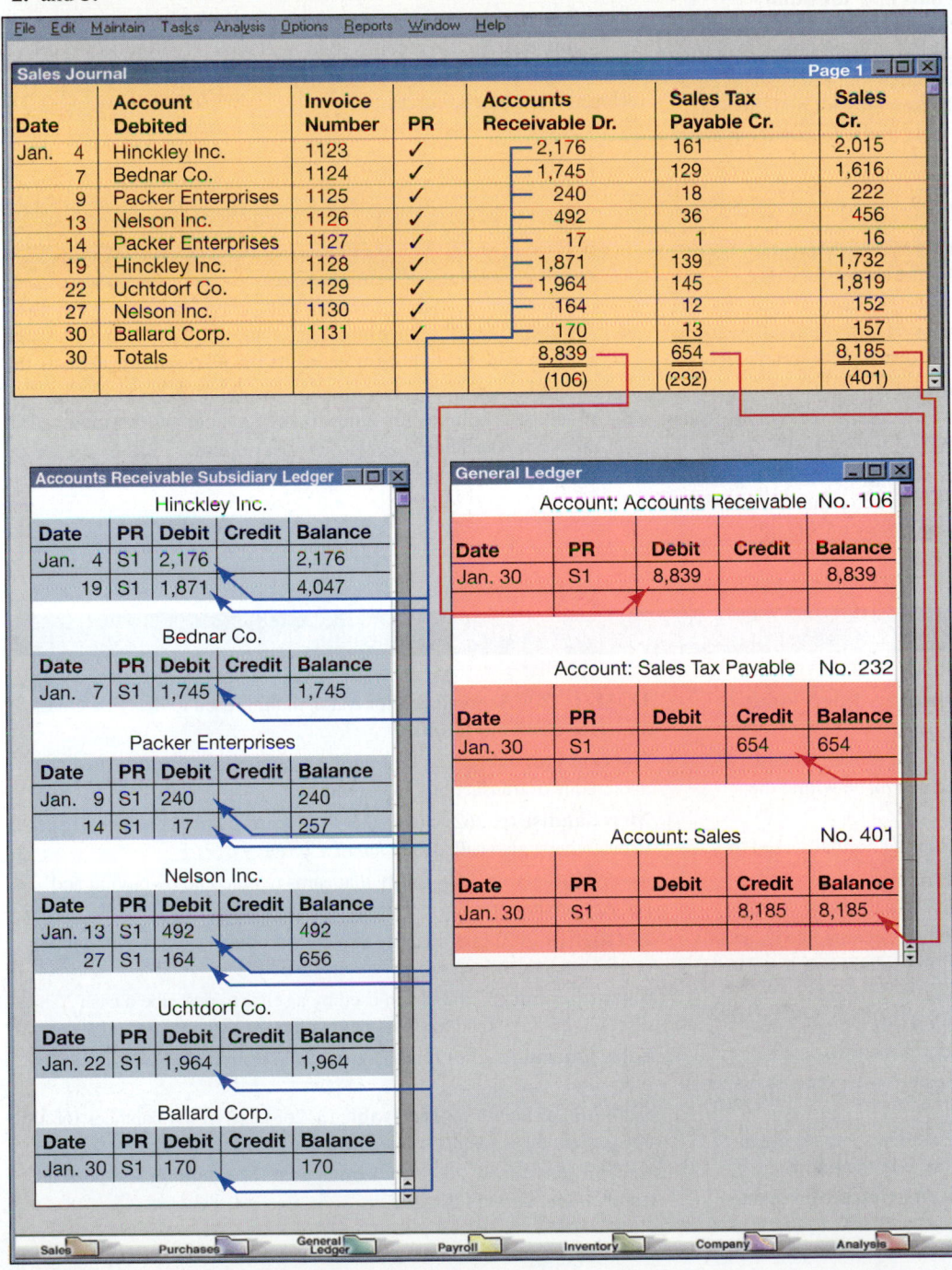

Summary

LO1 **Analyze and record transactions for merchandise sales.** A merchandiser records sales at the invoice price of the sale. The sale may be for cash or on credit.

LO2 **Describe how to compute and record sales discounts.** When cash discounts from the sales price are offered and customers pay within the discount period, the seller debits Sales Discounts, a contra account to Sales.

LO3 **Explain how to record sales returns and allowances.** Refunds or credits given to customers for unsatisfactory merchandise are recorded as debits to Sales Returns and Allowances, a contra account to Sales.

LO4 **Describe the use of special journals and subsidiary ledgers.** Special journals are used for recording transactions of similar type, each meant to cover one kind of transaction. Four of the most common special journals are the sales journal, cash receipts journal, purchases journal, and cash disbursements journal. Special journals are efficient and cost-effective tools in the journalizing and posting process.

LO5 **Journalize and post transactions using a sales journal.** The sales journal is an efficient means to record sales of inventory on credit. The sales journal will typically debit Accounts Receivable and credit Sales and Sales Tax Payable (if applicable).

LO6 **Prepare and prove the accuracy of the accounts receivable subsidiary ledger.** Account balances in the general ledger and the accounts receivable subsidiary ledger are tested for accuracy after posting is complete. This procedure is twofold: (1) prepare a trial balance of the general ledger to confirm that debits equal credits and (2) prepare a schedule of accounts receivable to confirm that the controlling account's balance equals the subsidiary ledger's balance.

LO7 **Journalize and post transactions using a cash receipts journal.** A cash receipts journal is typically used to record cash receipts from credit customers, cash from cash sales, and cash received from other sources.

Guidance Answers to **HOW YOU DOIN'?**

1. Recording sales discounts and sales returns and allowances separately from sales gives useful information to managers for internal monitoring and decision making.

2. Credit memorandum—seller credits accounts receivable from buyer.

3. The equality of debits and credits is kept within the general ledger. The subsidiary ledger keeps the customer's individual account and is used only for supplementary information.

4. An initial and the page number of the journal from which the amount was posted are entered in the PR column next to the amount.

5. A separate column for Sales Taxes Payable can be included in the sales journal.

Key Terms

Accounts receivable ledger (p. 267) Subsidiary ledger listing individual customer accounts.

Cash discount (p. 263) Reduction in the price of merchandise granted by a seller to a buyer when payment is made within the discount period.

Cash Receipts Journal (p. 270) Special journal normally used to record all receipts of cash.

Columnar journal (p. 266) Journal with more than one column.

Controlling account (p. 267) General ledger account, the balance of which (after posting) equals the sum of the balances in its related subsidiary ledger.

Credit memorandum (p. 265) Notification that the sender has credited the recipient's account in the sender's records.

Credit period (p. 263) Time period that can pass before a customer's payment is due.

Credit terms (p. 263) Description of the amounts and timing of payments that a buyer (debtor) agrees to make in the future.

Discount period (p. 263) Time period in which a cash discount is available and the buyer can make a reduced payment.

EOM (p. 263) Abbreviation for *end of month;* used to describe credit terms for credit transactions.

General journal (p. 266) All-purpose journal for recording the debits and credits of transactions and events.

Merchandise (p. 262) Goods that a company owns and expects to sell to customers; also called *merchandise inventory*.

Merchandiser (p. 262) Entity that earns net income by buying and selling merchandise.

Retailer (p. 262) Intermediary that buys products from manufacturers or wholesalers and sells them to consumers.

Sales discount (p. 262) Term used by a seller to describe a cash discount granted to buyers who pay within the discount period.

Sales journal (p. 266) Journal normally used to record sales of goods on credit.

Schedule of accounts receivable (p. 268) List of the balances for all accounts in the accounts receivable ledger and their total.

Special journal (p. 266) Any journal used for recording and posting transactions of a similar type.

Subsidiary ledger (p. 267) List of individual sub-accounts and amounts with a common characteristic; linked to a controlling account in the general ledger.

Wholesaler (p. 262) Intermediary that buys products from manufacturers or other wholesalers and sells them to retailers or other wholesalers.

Multiple Choice Quiz   Answers on p. 283   mhhe.com/wildCA2e

Additional Multiple Choice Quizzes are available at the book's Website.

1. A company has cash sales of $75,000, credit sales of $320,000, sales returns and allowances of $13,700, and sales discounts of $6,000. Its net sales equal
   a. $395,000
   b. $375,300
   c. $300,300
   d. $339,700
   e. $414,700

2. The sales journal is used to record
   a. Credit sales
   b. Cash sales
   c. Cash receipts
   d. Cash purchases
   e. Credit purchases

3. The ledger that contains the financial statement accounts of a company is the
   a. General journal
   b. Column balance journal
   c. Special ledger
   d. General ledger
   e. Special journal

4. A subsidiary ledger that contains a separate account for each customer to the company is the
   a. Controlling account
   b. Accounts payable ledger
   c. Accounts receivable ledger
   d. General ledger
   e. Special journal

5. A company sells $1,000 worth of goods to a customer on July 19 with credit terms of 2/10 net 30. If the customer pays on July 28, they would pay
   a. $1,000
   b. $1,020
   c. $983
   d. $980
   e. Cannot be determined

Discussion Questions

1. Why do companies offer cash discounts?

2. How is net sales computed?

3. What account is used to show that a company has collected sales tax but has not yet remitted it to the state or local government? Is this account an asset, a liability, or an equity account?

4. Why do businesses monitor the amount of sales returns and allowances?

5. Why would one merchandising company use a sales journal, but another merchandising company would not?

6. Why does a company maintain an accounts receivable subsidiary ledger?

7. What type of account is Sales Discounts? What is its normal balance?

8. When a company uses an accounts receivable subsidiary ledger, it must make one entry into the individual account of the subsidiary ledger and another entry into the accounts receivable account of the general ledger. If two entries are made, will the debits equal the credits in the trial balance? Why or why not?

9. Refer to the income statement for **Best Buy** in Appendix A. How does Best Buy title its net sales revenue account? Does it disclose sales returns and allowances separately?

10. Refer to the income statement for **RadioShack** in Appendix A. How does RadioShack title its net sales revenue account?

connect

Show the general journal entries for the following sales transactions for Martindale Company from June 2010. Sales tax equals 8% of sales price.

June	2	Sold merchandise on credit to A. Fullmer, $3,300 plus tax.
	9	Sold merchandise on credit to B. Olson, $2,600 plus tax.
	13	Sold merchandise on credit to P. Bleak, $1,200 plus tax.
	27	Sold merchandise on credit to B. Taysom, $4,100 plus tax.

QUICK STUDY

QS 11–1
Journalizing credit sales
LO1

QS 11–2
Interpreting credit terms **LO2**

Interpret the meaning of the following credit terms.

a. 2/10, n/60   **c.** 3/10, n/30
b. 2/EOM, n/60   **d.** 2/10, n/30

QS 11–3
Identifying special journals **LO4**

Steele Manufacturing uses special journals in its accounting system. Indicate the journal that would be used for each of the following transactions. (Use the illustration below Exhibit 11.4 as a guide.)

A. Sales Journal   **C.** Cash Receipt Journal   **E.** Purchases Journal
B. Cash Disbursement Journal   **D.** General Journal

_____ **1.** Purchased merchandise for cash.

_____ **2.** Sold merchandise for cash.

_____ **3.** Purchased merchandise on credit.

_____ **4.** Gave $700 credit for returned merchandise.

_____ **5.** Sold merchandise on credit.

_____ **6.** Paid cash for merchandise previously purchased on credit.

_____ **7.** Purchased merchandise on credit.

_____ **8.** Sold merchandise for cash.

QS 11–4
Journalizing credit sales in a sales journal **LO5**

Refer to the transactions in QS 11-1. Show how these transactions would be entered in a sales journal. (*Hint:* Use Exhibit 11.6 as a guide.)

QS 11–5
Computing net sales
LO1   LO2   LO3

Compute net sales for 2010 for Snedigar Company given the following information.

Sales (Gross)	43,251
Sales Discounts	757
Sales Returns and Allowances	2,253

QS 11–6
Journalizing cash receipts **LO7**

Show the general journal entries for the following transactions which involved cash receipts at Alan Lawson Nursing Supplies. (*Hint:* Only journalize transactions that involve a receipt of cash).

Jul.   4   Sold $4,200 of merchandise on credit from Foxworth Co., terms n/20.
      7   Sold merchandise costing $940 on credit to Cassell Co. for $1,000, subject to a $20 sales discount if paid by the end of the month.
      9   Borrowed $9,500 cash by signing a note payable to the bank.
   13   A. Lawson, the owner, contributed $5,000 cash to the company.
   20   Received $4,200 cash from Foxworth Co. on account.
   28   Received $920 cash from Cassell Co. on account within the discount period.

QS 11–7
Journalizing cash receipts in a cash receipts journal **LO7**

Refer to the transactions in QS 11-6. Show how these transactions would be entered in a cash receipts journal.

---

connect™

EXERCISES

Exercise 11–1
Recording sales returns and allowances **LO3**

Check   (c) Dr. Sales Returns and Allowances $680

Allied Parts, a wholesaler, was organized on May 1, 2010, and made its first purchase of merchandise on May 3. The purchase was for 2,000 units at a price of $10 per unit. On May 5, Allied Parts sold 1,500 of the units for $14 per unit to Baker Co. Terms of the sale were 2/10, n/60. Ignore sales taxes. Prepare entries for Allied Parts to record the May 5 sale and each of the following separate transactions *a* through *c*.

a. On May 7, Baker returns 200 units because they did not fit its customer's needs.

b. On May 8, Baker discovers that 300 units are damaged but are still of some use and, therefore, keeps the units. Allied Parts sends Baker a credit memorandum for $600 to compensate for the damage.

c. On May 15, Baker discovers that 100 units are the wrong color. Baker keeps 60 of these units because Allied sends a $120 credit memorandum to compensate. However, Baker returns the remaining 40 units to Allied.

Business decision makers desire information on sales returns and allowances. (1) Explain why a company's manager wants the accounting system to record customers' returns of unsatisfactory goods in the Sales Returns and Allowances account instead of the Sales account. (2) Explain whether this information would be useful for external decision makers.

Exercise 11-2
Sales returns and allowances
LO3

Wilcox Electronics uses a sales journal, a purchases journal, a cash receipts journal, a cash disbursements journal, and a general journal. Wilcox recently completed the following transactions *a* through *h*. Identify the journal in which each transaction should be recorded.

a. Sold merchandise on credit.
b. Purchased shop supplies on credit.
c. Paid an employee's salary in cash.
d. Borrowed cash from the bank.
e. Sold merchandise for cash.
f. Purchased merchandise on credit.
g. Purchased inventory for cash.
h. Paid cash to a creditor.

Exercise 11-3
Identifying the special journal of entry   **LO4**

At the end of May, the sales journal of Mountain View appears as follows. (There are no sales taxes on Mountain View's sales.)

Exercise 11-4
Posting to subsidiary ledger accounts; preparing a schedule of accounts receivable   **LO4**

Sales Journal

Date	Account Debited	Invoice Number	PR	Accounts Receivable Dr.	Sales Cr.
May 6	Aaron Reckers	190		3,880	3,880
10	Sara Reed	191		2,940	2,940
17	Anna Page	192		1,850	1,850
25	Sara Reed	193		1,340	1,340
31	Totals			10,010	10,010

Mountain View also recorded the return of defective merchandise with the following entry.

May	20	Sales Returns and Allowances		350 00	
		Accounts Receivable—Anna Page			350 00
		Customer returned (worthless) merchandise.			

Required

1. Open an accounts receivable subsidiary ledger that has a T-account for each customer listed in the sales journal. Post to the customer accounts the entries in the sales journal and any portion of the general journal entry that affects a customer's account. Ignore sales tax. Assume that these accounts have zero balances at the beginning of May.
2. Open a general ledger that has T-accounts for Accounts Receivable, Sales, and Sales Returns and Allowances. Assume that these accounts have zero balances at the beginning of May. Post the sales journal and any portion of the general journal entry that affects these accounts.
3. Prepare a schedule of accounts receivable as of May 31 and prove that its total equals the balance in the Accounts Receivable controlling account at May 31.

Check (3) Accounts Receivable, $9,660

Keeler Company had the following credit sales to its customers during June.

Exercise 11-5
Accounts receivable ledger; posting from sales journal   **LO4**

Date	Customer	Sales Price
June 2	Joe Mack	$ 4,600
8	Eric Horner	7,100
10	Tess Cox	14,400
14	Hong Jiang	21,500
20	Tess Cox	12,200
29	Joe Mack	8,300
	Total credit sales	$68,100

Required

1. Open an accounts receivable subsidiary ledger having a T-account for each customer. Post the invoices to the subsidiary ledger. Ignore sales tax.

2. Open an Accounts Receivable controlling T-account and a Sales T-account to reflect general ledger accounts. The Accounts Receivable controlling account has a zero balance on June 1. Post the end-of-month total from the sales journal to these accounts.

3. Prepare a schedule of accounts receivable as of June 30 and prove that its total equals the Accounts Receivable controlling account balance on June 30.

Exercise 11–6
Cash receipts journal   **LO7**

Assume the transactions in Exercise 11-5 involve cash sales instead of credit sales. Also assume that the Keeler company receives interest revenue on June 17 of $350 from the bank and receives a loan of $2,000 on June 23 from the bank. Prepare headings for a cash receipts journal like the one in Exhibit 11.10. Prepare a cash receipts journal for these cash receipts during the month of June.

Exercise 11–7
Cash receipts journal   **LO5   LO7**

Ali Co. uses a general journal and several special journals. The following transactions occur in the month of November.

Nov. 3 Purchased $3,200 of merchandise on credit from Hart Co., terms n/20.
    7 Sold merchandise costing $840 on credit to J. Than for $1,000, subject to a $20 sales discount if paid by the end of the month.
    9 Borrowed $3,750 cash by signing a note payable to the bank.
   13 J. Ali, the owner, contributed $5,000 cash to the company.
   18 Sold merchandise costing $250 to B. Cox for $330 cash.
   22 Paid Hart Co. $3,200 cash for the merchandise purchased on November 3.
   27 Received $980 cash from J. Than in payment of the November 7 purchase.
   30 Paid salaries of $1,650 in cash.

Prepare headings for a cash receipts journal like the one in Exhibit 11.10. Journalize the November transactions that should be recorded in the cash receipts journal.

Exercise 11–8
Sales and cash receipts journals
LO7

The Sun Company completed the following sales and cash receipts transactions during the first week of December. The Sun Company uses the periodic inventory system.

Dec. 1 Sold merchandise for $6,700 on credit to the Two Rivers Co., terms 2/10, n/30. Invoice Number 1455.
    1 Sold merchandise for $3,400 on credit to the Berlin Co., terms 2/10, n/30. Invoice Number 1456.
    2 Sold merchandise for $590 cash to the Ellison Co. Invoice Number 1457.
    3 Borrowed $10,000 from Custer Bank on a long-term note payable.
    3 Sold merchandise for $7,200 on credit to the Amherst Co., terms 2/10, n/30. Invoice Number 1458.
    5 Received the amount due from the Two Rivers Co. from the sale on December 1.
    6 Sold merchandise on credit for $950 to the Waupaca Co., terms 2/10, n/30. Invoice Number 1459.
    6 Received the amount due from the Berlin Co. from the sale on December 1.

Required

a. Prepare headings for a sales journal like the one in Exhibit 11.6. Prepare headings for a cash receipts journal like the one in Exhibit 11.10. Journalize the transactions that should be recorded in the sales and cash receipts journals.

b. Prepare a schedule of accounts receivable as of December 31. There were no accounts receivable as of December 1.

== connect™

PROBLEM SET A

Problem 11–1A
Sales journal and accounts receivable subsidiary ledger

LO5   LO6

Wiset Company completes the following transactions during April, its first month of operations. A tax rate of 8% applies to all sales.

Apr. 3 Sold $4,000 of merchandise on credit to Page Alistair, Invoice No. 760.
    5 Sold $8,000 of merchandise on credit to Paula Kohr, Invoice No. 761.
   11 Sold $10,500 of merchandise on credit to Nic Nelson, Invoice No. 762.
   13 Sold $5,100 of merchandise on credit to Page Alistair, Invoice No. 763.
   27 Sold $3,170 of merchandise on credit to Paula Kohr, Invoice No. 764.
   27 Sold $6,700 of merchandise on credit to Nic Nelson, Invoice No. 765.

Required

1. Prepare a sales journal like that in Exhibit 11.6. Number the sales journal page as page 3. Enter the transactions in the sales journal.
2. Open the following general ledger accounts: Accounts Receivable (#106), Sales Tax Payable (#205), and Sales (#400). Also open accounts receivable subsidiary ledger accounts for Paula Kohr, Page Alistair, and Nic Nelson. Post the transactions to the subsidiary ledger accounts. Prepare the month-end postings to the general ledger accounts.

Using your solution to Problem 11-1A, prove the accuracy of the accounts receivable subsidiary ledger by preparing a schedule of accounts receivable as of April 30.

Problem 11-2A
Schedule of Accounts Receivable
LO6

Church Company completes the following transactions during March, its first month of operations (terms for all its credit sales are 2/10, n/30).

Mar.	2	Sold merchandise on credit to Min Cho, Invoice No. 854, for $16,800 plus sales tax of $1,176.
	3	Sold merchandise on credit to Linda Witt, Invoice No. 855, for $10,200 plus sales tax of $714.
	10	Sold merchandise on credit to Jovita Albany, Invoice No. 856, for $5,600 plus sales tax of $392.
	27	Sold merchandise on credit to Jovita Albany, Invoice No. 857, for $14,910 plus sales tax of $1,044.
	28	Sold merchandise on credit to Linda Witt, Invoice No. 858, for $4,315 plus sales tax of $302.

Problem 11-3A
Sales journal, subsidiary ledger, and schedule of accounts receivable   **LO5   LO6**

mhhe.com/wildCA2e

Required

1. Open the following general ledger accounts: Accounts Receivable (#106), Sales (#400), and Sales Tax Payable (#205). Open the following accounts receivable subsidiary ledger accounts: Jovita Albany, Min Cho, and Linda Witt.
2. Enter the transactions in a sales journal like Exhibit 11.6. Number all journal pages as page 2.
3. Post all transactions to the accounts receivable subsidiary ledger and its month-end totals to the general ledger.
4. Prove the accuracy of the subsidiary ledger by preparing a schedule of accounts receivable as of March 31.

Check   (4) Total accounts receivable, $55,453

The March sales transactions of Church Company are described in Problem 11-3A. In addition to those transactions, Church has the following nonsales transactions.

Mar. 12	Received cash payment from Min Cho for the March 2 sale less the 2% cash discount.
13	Received cash payment from Linda Witt for the March 3 sale less the 2% cash discount.
20	Received cash payment from Jovita Albany for the March 10 sale less the 2% cash discount.
30	Issued a credit memorandum of $500 (plus a $35 sales tax refund) for damaged goods from the sale to Linda Witt made on March 28.

Problem 11-4A
Journal entries for cash receipts, sales discounts, and sales returns and allowances
LO1   LO2   LO3

Required

Record each cash receipt (less any cash discount) as a general journal entry. Also, record any sales return as a general journal entry.

Wiset Company completes these transactions during April of the current year (the terms of all its credit sales are 2/10, n/30).

Apr.	2	Purchased $14,300 of merchandise on credit from Noth Company, invoice dated April 2, terms 2/10, n/60.
	3	Sold merchandise on credit to Page Alistair, Invoice No. 760, for $4,000.
	3	Purchased $1,480 of office supplies on credit from Custer, Inc. Invoice dated April 2, terms n/10 EOM.
	4	Issued Check No. 587 to *World View* for advertising expense, $899.
	5	Sold merchandise on credit to Paula Kohr, Invoice No. 761, for $8,000.
	6	Received an $80 credit memorandum from Custer, Inc., for the return of some of the office supplies received on April 3.
	9	Purchased $12,125 of store equipment on credit from Hal's Supply, invoice dated April 9, terms n/10 EOM.

Problem 11-5A
Special journals, subsidiary ledgers, and schedule of accounts receivable   **LO5   LO6   LO7**

11   Sold merchandise on credit to Nic Nelson, Invoice No. 762, for $10,500.

12   Issued Check No. 588 to Noth Company in payment of its April 2 invoice, less the discount.

13   Received payment from Page Alistair for the April 3 sale, less the discount.

13   Sold $5,100 of merchandise on credit to Page Alistair, Invoice No. 763.

14   Received payment from Paula Kohr for the April 5 sale, less the discount.

16   Issued Check No. 589, payable to Payroll, in payment of sales salaries expense for the first half of the month, $10,750. Cashed the check and paid employees.

16   Cash sales for the first half of the month are $52,840. (Cash sales are recorded daily from cash register data but are recorded only twice in this problem to reduce repetitive entries.)

17   Purchased $13,750 of merchandise on credit from Grant Company, invoice dated April 17, terms 2/10, n/30.

18   Borrowed $60,000 cash from First State Bank by signing a long-term note payable.

20   Received payment from Nic Nelson for the April 11 sale, less the discount.

20   Purchased $830 of store supplies on credit from Hal's Supply, invoice dated April 19, terms n/10 EOM.

23   Received a $750 credit memorandum from Grant Company for the return of defective merchandise received on April 17.

23   Received payment from Page Alistair for the April 13 sale, less the discount.

25   Purchased $11,375 of merchandise on credit from Noth Company, invoice dated April 24, terms 2/10, n/60.

26   Issued Check No. 590 to Grant Company in payment of its April 17 invoice, less the return and the discount.

27   Sold $3,170 of merchandise on credit to Paula Kohr, Invoice No. 764.

27   Sold $6,700 of merchandise on credit to Nic Nelson, Invoice No. 765.

30   Issued Check No. 591, payable to Payroll, in payment of the sales salaries expense for the last half of the month, $10,750.

30   Cash sales for the last half of the month are $73,975.

Required

1. Prepare a sales journal like that in Exhibit 11.6 and a cash receipts journal like that in Exhibit 11.10. Number both journal pages as page 3. Then review the transactions of Wiset Company and enter those that should be journalized in the sales journal and those that should be journalized in the cash receipts journal. Ignore any transactions that should be journalized in a purchases journal, a cash disbursements journal, or a general journal.

2. Open the following general ledger accounts: Cash, Accounts Receivable, Inventory, Long-Term Notes Payable, Sales, and Sales Discounts. Enter the March 31 balances for Cash ($85,000), Inventory ($125,000), and Long-Term Notes Payable ($210,000). Also open accounts receivable subsidiary ledger accounts for Paula Kohr, Page Alistair, and Nic Nelson.

3. Verify that amounts that should be posted as individual amounts from the journals have been posted. (Such items are immediately posted.) Foot and crossfoot the journals and make the month-end postings.

Check   Trial balance totals, $434,285

4. Prepare a trial balance of the general ledger and prove the accuracy of the subsidiary ledger by preparing a schedule of accounts receivable.

PROBLEM SET B

Problem 11-1B
Sales journal and accounts receivable subsidiary ledger
LO5   LO6

Acorn Industries completes the following transactions during July, its first month of operations (the terms of all its credit sales are 2/10, n/30). A tax rate of 10% applies to all sales.

July 5   Sold merchandise on credit to Kim Nettle, Invoice No. 918, for $19,200.

6   Sold merchandise on credit to Ruth Blake, Invoice No. 919, for $7,500.

13   Sold merchandise on credit to Ashton Moore, Invoice No. 920, for $8,550.

14   Sold merchandise on credit to Kim Nettle, Invoice No. 921, for $5,100.

29   Sold merchandise on credit to Ruth Blake, Invoice No. 922, for $17,500.

30   Sold merchandise on credit to Ashton Moore, Invoice No. 923, for $16,820.

Required

1. Prepare a sales journal like that in Exhibit 11.6. Number the sales journal as page 3.

2. Open the following general ledger accounts: Accounts Receivable (#106), Sales Tax Payable (#205), and Sales (#400). Also open accounts receivable subsidiary ledger accounts for Kim Nettle, Ashton Moore, and Ruth Blake. Post the transactions to the subsidiary ledger accounts. Prepare the month-end postings to the general ledger accounts.

Using your solution to 11-1B, prove the accuracy of the accounts receivable subsidiary ledger by preparing a schedule of accounts receivable as of July 31.

Problem 11–2B

Schedule of Accounts Receivable

LO6

Grassley Company completes the following transactions during November, its first month of operations (terms for all its credit sales are 2/10, n/30).

Nov. 8   Sold merchandise on credit to Cyd Rounder, Invoice No. 439, for $6,550 plus sales tax of $524.
10   Sold merchandise on credit to Carlos Mantel, Invoice No. 440, for $13,500 plus sales tax of $1,080.
15   Sold merchandise on credit to Tori Tripp, Invoice No. 441, for $5,250 plus sales tax of $420.
22   Sold merchandise on credit to Carlos Mantel, Invoice No. 442, for $3,695 plus sales tax of $296.
24   Sold merchandise on credit to Tori Tripp, Invoice No. 443, for $4,280 plus sales tax of $342.

Problem 11–3B

Sales journal, subsidiary ledger, and schedule of accounts receivable   **LO5   LO6**

Required

1. Open the following general ledger accounts: Accounts Receivable (#106), Sales (#400), and Sales Tax Payable (#205). Open the following accounts receivable subsidiary ledger accounts: Carlos Mantel, Tori Tripp, and Cyd Rounder.
2. Enter the transactions in a sales journal like that in Exhibit 11.6. Number the journal page as page 2.
3. Post all transactions to the accounts receivable subsidiary ledger and its month-end totals to the general ledger.
4. Prove the accuracy of the subsidiary ledger by preparing a schedule of accounts receivable as of November 30.

Check   (4) Total accounts receivable, $35,937

The November sales transactions of Grassley Company are described in Problem 11-3B. In addition to those transactions, Grassley has the following nonsales transactions.

Nov. 18   Received cash payment from Cyd Rounder for the November 8 sale less the 2% cash discount.
19   Received cash payment from Carlos Mantel for the November 10 sale less the 2% cash discount.
25   Received cash payment from Tori Tripp for the November 15 sale less the 2% cash discount.
29   Issued a credit memorandum of $675 (plus a $54 sales tax refund) for damaged goods from the sale to Carlos Mantel made on November 22.

Problem 11–4B

Journal entries for sales discounts and sales returns and allowances   **LO1   LO2   LO3**

Required

Record each cash receipt (less any cash discount) as a general journal entry. Also, record any sales return as a general journal entry.

Acorn Industries completes these transactions during July of the current year (the terms of all its credit sales are 2/10, n/30).

July 1   Purchased $6,500 of merchandise on credit from Teton Company, invoice dated June 30, terms 2/10, n/30.
3   Issued Check No. 300 to *The Weekly* for advertising expense, $625.
5   Sold merchandise on credit to Kim Nettle, Invoice No. 918, for $19,200.
6   Sold merchandise on credit to Ruth Blake, Invoice No. 919, for $7,500.
7   Purchased $1,250 of store supplies on credit from Plaine, Inc., invoice dated July 7, terms n/10 EOM.
8   Received a $250 credit memorandum from Plaine, Inc., for the return of store supplies received on July 7.
9   Purchased $38,220 of store equipment on credit from Charm's Supply, invoice dated July 8, terms n/10 EOM.
10   Issued Check No. 301 to Teton Company in payment of its June 30 invoice, less the discount.

Problem 11–5B

Special journals, subsidiary ledgers, schedule of accounts receivable   **LO5   LO6   LO7**

13   Sold merchandise on credit to Ashton Moore, Invoice No. 920, for $8,550.

14   Sold merchandise on credit to Kim Nettle, Invoice No. 921, for $5,100.

15   Received payment from Kim Nettle for the July 5 sale, less the discount.

15   Issued Check No. 302, payable to Payroll, in payment of sales salaries expense for the first half of the month, $31,850. Cashed the check and paid employees.

15   Cash sales for the first half of the month are $118,350. (Cash sales are recorded daily using data from the cash registers but are recorded only twice in this problem to reduce repetitive entries.)

16   Received payment from Ruth Blake for the July 6 sale, less the discount.

17   Purchased $7,200 of merchandise on credit from Drake Company, invoice dated July 17, terms 2/10, n/30.

20   Purchased $650 of office supplies on credit from Charm's Supply, invoice dated July 19, terms n/10 EOM.

21   Borrowed $15,000 cash from College Bank by signing a long-term note payable.

23   Received payment from Ashton Moore for the July 13 sale, less the discount.

24   Received payment from Kim Nettle for the July 14 sale, less the discount.

24   Received a $2,400 credit memorandum from Drake Company for the return of defective merchandise received on July 17.

26   Purchased $9,770 of merchandise on credit from Teton Company, invoice dated July 26, terms 2/10, n/30.

27   Issued Check No. 303 to Drake Company in payment of its July 17 invoice, less the return and the discount.

29   Sold merchandise on credit to Ruth Blake, Invoice No. 922, for $17,500.

30   Sold merchandise on credit to Ashton Moore, Invoice No. 923, for $16,820.

31   Issued Check No. 304, payable to Payroll, in payment of the sales salaries expense for the last half of the month, $31,850.

31   Cash sales for the last half of the month are $80,244.

Required

1. Prepare a sales journal like that in Exhibit 11.6 and a cash receipts journal like that in Exhibit 11.10. Number both journals as page 3. Then review the transactions of Acorn Industries and enter those transactions that should be journalized in the sales journal and those that should be journalized in the cash receipts journal. Ignore any transactions that should be journalized in a purchases journal, a cash disbursements journal, or a general journal.

2. Open the following general ledger accounts: Cash, Accounts Receivable, Inventory, Long-Term Notes Payable, Sales, and Sales Discounts. Enter the June 30 balances for Cash ($100,000), Inventory ($200,000), and Long-Term Notes Payable ($300,000). Also open accounts receivable subsidiary ledger accounts for Kim Nettle, Ashton Moore, and Ruth Blake.

3. Verify that amounts that should be posted as individual amounts from the journals have been posted. (Such items are immediately posted.) Foot and crossfoot the journals and make the month-end postings.

Check   Trial balance totals, $588,264

4. Prepare a trial balance of the general ledger and prove the accuracy of the subsidiary ledger by preparing a schedule of accounts receivable.

BEYOND THE NUMBERS

REPORTING IN ACTION
LO7

BTN 11–1   Refer to **Best Buy**'s financial statements in Appendix A to answer the following.

Required

1. Identify and total the inventory assets as of March 1, 2008, and March 3, 2007, for Best Buy. Compute the percentage of inventory assets relative to current assets.

Fast Forward

2. Access Best Buy's financial statements (form 10-K) for fiscal years ending after March 1, 2008, from its Website (**BestBuy.com**) or the SEC's EDGAR database (**www.SEC.gov**). Recompute and interpret the percentage of inventory assets relative to current assets for these current fiscal years.

BTN 11-2 Amy Martin is a student who plans to attend approximately four professional events a year at her college. Each event necessitates a financial outlay of $100–$200 for a new suit and accessories. After incurring a major hit to her savings for the first event, Amy developed a different approach. She buys the suit on credit the week before the event, wears it to the event, and returns it the next week to the store for a full refund on her charge card.

Required

1. Comment on the ethics exhibited by Amy and possible consequences of her actions.
2. How does the merchandising company account for the suits that Amy returns?
3. How can an accounts receivable subsidiary ledger alert the store's manager to Amy's behavior?

ETHICS CHALLENGE
LO1 LO3 LO4

BTN 11-3 Your friend, Wendy Geiger, owns a small retail store that sells candies and nuts. Geiger acquires her goods from a few select vendors. She generally makes purchase orders by phone and on credit. Sales are primarily for cash. Geiger keeps her own manual accounting system using a general journal and a general ledger. At the end of each business day, she records one summary entry for cash sales. Geiger recently began offering items in creative gift packages. This has increased sales substantially, and she is now receiving orders from corporate and other clients who order large quantities and prefer to buy on credit. As a result of increased credit transactions in both purchases and sales, keeping the accounting records has become extremely time consuming. Geiger wants to continue to maintain her own manual system and calls you for advice. Write a memo to her advising how she might modify her current manual accounting system to accommodate the expanded business activities. Geiger is accustomed to checking her ledger by using a trial balance. Your memo should explain the advantages of what you propose and of any other verification techniques you recommend.

WORKPLACE COMMUNICATION
LO4 LO5 LO6 LO7

BTN 11-4 William Fuerst Company completes the following transactions during July of the current year. A tax rate of 8% applies to all sales.

July 3 Sold $6,000 of merchandise on credit to Susan Scholz, Invoice No. 1060.
7 Sold $4,500 of merchandise on credit to Mike Ettredge, Invoice No. 1061.
9 Sold $7,700 of merchandise on credit to Mark Hirschey, Invoice No. 1062.
13 Sold $1,600 of merchandise on credit to Susan Scholz, Invoice No. 1063.
24 Sold $5,300 of merchandise on credit to Gilbert Karuga, Invoice No. 1064.
29 Sold $7,100 of merchandise on credit to Mark Hirschey, Invoice No. 1065.

Required

Divide your team into two groups. Have one group prepare the general journal entries for each sale. Have the other group prepare a sales journal like that in Exhibit 11.6. Compare and contrast the advantages and disadvantages of each approach.

TEAMWORK IN ACTION
LO1 LO5

BTN 11-5 Refer to the opening feature about Bert and John Jacobs and their **Life is good** company.

Required

1. Identify the special journals that Life is good would likely use in its operations.
2. Identify any subsidiary ledgers that Life is good would likely use.

ENTREPRENEURS IN BUSINESS
LO4

BTN 11-6 You want to know how promptly customers are paying their bills. This information can help you plan your cash payments and decide whether to extend credit. Where do you find this information?

YOU CALL IT— ENTREPRENEUR
LO5 LO6

1. b; Net sales = $75,000 + $320,000 − $13,700 − $6,000 = $375,300
2. a
3. d
4. c
5. d; $1,000 less $20 (.02 × $1,000) discount

ANSWERS TO MULTIPLE CHOICE QUIZ

A Look Back

Chapter 11 emphasized merchandise sales transactions, sales discounts, and sales returns and allowances. We also explained the use of a sales journal, cash receipts journal, and an accounts receivable subsidiary ledger.

A Look at This Chapter

Chapter 12 extends our coverage of merchandising activities, with emphasis on accounting for merchandise purchases and accounts payable. We also explain the use of a cash disbursements journal.

A Look Ahead

Chapter 13 provides a summary of accrual accounting. We emphasize the matching of expenses with the revenues generated.

Chapter 12

Merchandise Purchases and Accounts Payable

Learning Objectives

LO 1 Analyze and record transactions for merchandise purchases.

LO 2 Journalize and post transactions using a purchases journal.

LO 3 Prepare and prove the accuracy of an accounts payable subsidiary ledger.

LO 4 Journalize and post transactions using a cash disbursements journal.

"We're selling a feeling to the consumer"
—Renee Pepys Lowe

CoCaLo Creates Sweet Dreams

COSTA MESA, CA—"I always had my mother to lean on," admits Renee Pepys Lowe. But when her mother decided to sell her small business in which Renee worked, Renee lost her job. "That was a big change," recalls Renee. "I did a lot of soul-searching."

Renee rebounded by starting an infant bedding and nursery accessories company, **CoCaLo** (**CoCaLo.com**)—named after her daughters, Courtenay and Catherine Lowe. Renee envisioned a company with fashionable, high-quality products at affordable prices. Fortunately, she says her designers have "a remarkable talent for seeing what fabrics, colors, and textures can look like in combination."

Although CoCaLo is now profiting in the infant bedding industry, the early days were not easy. "You really have to take a lot of risks," says Renee. "It's all about allowing everyone to have a bedding collection with style, without having to spend a thousand dollars to get it." Adds Renee, "The scariest part for me is that I'm responsible for . . . finances, loans [and all aspects of accounting]."

To succeed, Renee needed to make smart business decisions. She set up an accounting system to capture and communicate costs and sales information. Effectively tracking merchandising activities is needed to set prices and create policies for discounts and allowances, returns on sales, and purchases. An inventory system enabled CoCaLo to stock the right type and amount of merchandise and to avoid the costs of out-of-stock and excess inventory. And with an estimated $20 million in annual sales to stores like Babies "R" Us and J.C. Penney, keeping track of merchandise is a critical job.

Mastering accounting for merchandising is a means to an end for Renee. "I love this business," she says. "There's something about giving new parents the tools to create a room they can feel proud of." Judging by CoCaLo's sales, there are plenty of proud parents out there.

[Sources: *CoCaLo Website*, March 2009; *Orange County Business Journal*, March 2009]

Merchandising companies purchase inventory to resell to their customers. This chapter introduces the accounting for inventory purchases by merchandising companies and the use of the purchases journal and an accounts payable subsidiary ledger to further enhance this process.

Merchandise Purchases and Accounts Payable

Merchandising Purchases

- Purchasing procedures
- Trade and purchase discounts
- Purchase returns and allowances
- Transportation costs

Journals and Subsidiary Ledgers

- Purchases journal
- Accounts payable subsidiary ledger
- Cash disbursements journal

Accounting for Merchandise Purchases

A **merchandiser** buys and sells products. Merchandising companies must account for purchases, inventory, cost of goods sold, trade and purchase discounts, and purchase returns and allowances.

LO1 Analyze and record transactions for merchandise purchases.

Purchasing Procedures

Most merchandisers need inventory in their stores or warehouses to sell to customers. **Merchandise inventory,** or simply **inventory,** refers to products that a company owns and intends to sell. Inventory represents a current asset of the firm. For a large firm, a central purchasing department will locate potential suppliers and negotiate prices and credit terms and ultimately place orders for inventory. In a small retail store, the owner or manager of the store will perform all of these purchasing tasks.

When a department needs products to sell, the department (or sales) manager will prepare and sign a **purchase requisition** listing the merchandise needed (see Exhibit 12.1) and send it to the purchasing department.

Exhibit 12.1

Purchase Requisition

Purchase Requisition		No. 917
Z-Mart		

From Sporting Goods Department	**Date** October 28, 2010
To Purchasing Department	**Preferred Vendor** Trex

Request purchase of the following item(s):

Model No.	Description	Quantity
CH 015	Challenger X7	1
SD 099	SpeedDemon	1

Reason for Request Replenish inventory
Approval for Request *TZ*

For Purchasing Department use only: Order Date 10/30/10   P.O. No. P98

The purchasing department then selects a **vendor** (also called a supplier) that can supply the goods, and places a **purchase order.** A purchase order authorizes a vendor to ship ordered merchandise at the stated price and credit terms (see Exhibit 12.2). Someone with authority to approve purchases signs the purchase order (sometimes abbreviated as P.O.) and sends it to the vendor.

Exhibit 12.2

Purchase Order

Purchase Order				No. P98
Z-Mart				
10 Michigan Street				
Chicago, Illinois 60521				

To: Trex
W9797 Cherry Road
Antigo, Wisconsin 54409

Date _____ 10/30/10 _____
FOB _____ Destination _____
Ship by __ As soon as possible ____
Terms _____ 2/15, n/30 _____

Request shipment of the following item(s):

Model No.	Description	Quantity	Price	Amount
CH 015	Challenger X7	1	490	490
SD 099	SpeedDemon	1	710	710

All shipments and invoices must include purchase order number

Ordered by
T. N.

Upon receipt of the purchase order, the vendor ships the ordered merchandise to the buyer. Many companies maintain a separate department to receive all merchandise and purchased assets. When each shipment arrives, a receiving department employee counts the goods and checks them for damage and agreement with the purchase order. This person then prepares a **receiving report,** which is used within the company to notify the appropriate persons that ordered goods have been received and to describe the quantities and condition of the goods.

The seller sends an invoice when the ordered merchandise is shipped. The **invoice** is an itemized statement of goods sent by the vendor listing the customer's name, items sold, sales prices, and terms of sale. As shown in Exhibit 12.3, an invoice is also a bill sent to the buyer from the vendor. From the vendor's point of view, it is a *sales invoice.* The buyer treats it as a *purchase invoice.*

Accounting for Purchases and Freight Charges

Shortly before the invoice (or bill) is due, the accounting department will make payment. Under the periodic system of inventory accounting, the cost of merchandise purchased for resale is recorded in the Purchases account. The Purchases account is a temporary account that is closed to Cost of Goods Sold at the end of the accounting period. The normal balance for the Purchases account is a debit.

The cost of shipping the goods from the vendor to the buyer is called **transportation-in.** This freight charge is accounted for separately from the purchases account as a debit. To illustrate, Z-Mart purchases $1,200 of merchandise on credit and incurs $96 of freight charges. The journal entry to record this credit purchase is:

Nov.	2	Purchases		1 2 0 0 00	
		Transportation-In		9 6 00	
		Accounts Payable			1 2 9 6 00

Assets = Liabilities + Equity
+1,296   −1,200
           −96

Trade Discounts

When a manufacturer or wholesaler prepares a catalog of items it has for sale, it usually gives each item a **list price,** also called a *catalog price.* However, an item's intended *selling price*

Exhibit 12.3

Invoice

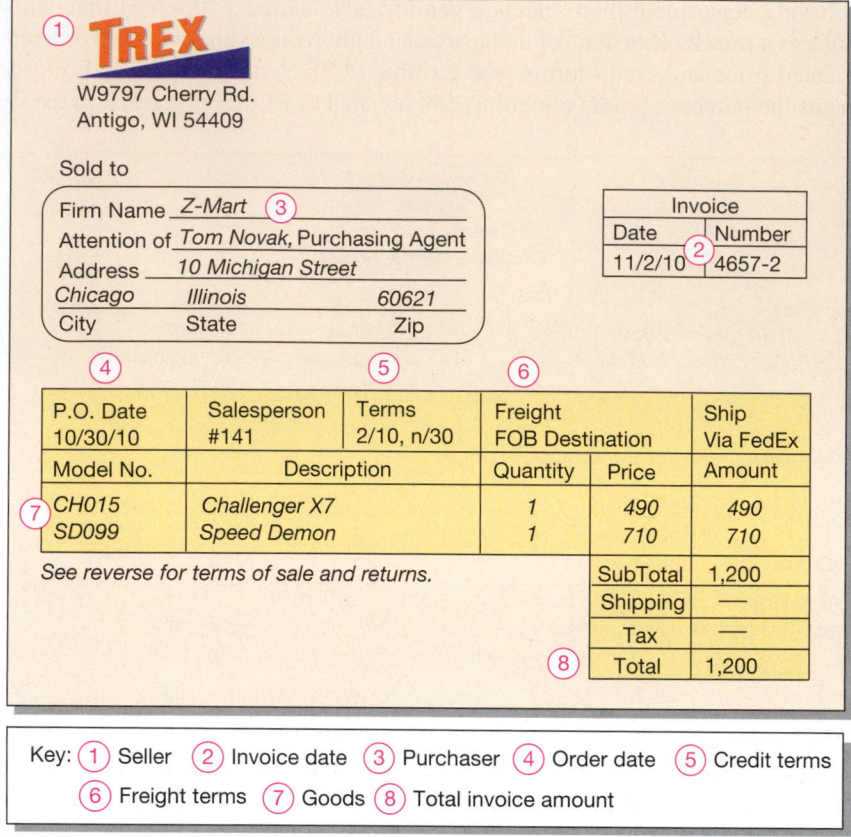

Exhibit 12.4

Credit Terms

equals list price minus a given percent called a **trade discount.** The amount of trade discount usually depends on whether a buyer is a wholesaler, retailer, or final consumer. A wholesaler buying in large quantities is often granted a larger discount than a retailer buying in smaller quantities. A buyer records the net amount of list price minus trade discount. For example, in the November 2 purchase of merchandise by Z-Mart, the merchandise was listed in the seller's catalog at $2,000 and Z-Mart received a 40% trade discount. This meant that Z-Mart's purchase price was $1,200, computed as $2,000 − (40% × $2,000).

Purchase Discounts

A buyer can receive a **purchase discount** if timely payment is made. Any purchase (cash) discount is described in the **credit terms** on the invoice. Exhibit 12.4 portrays the credit terms.

> Since both the buyer and seller know the invoice date, this date is used in determining the discount and credit periods.

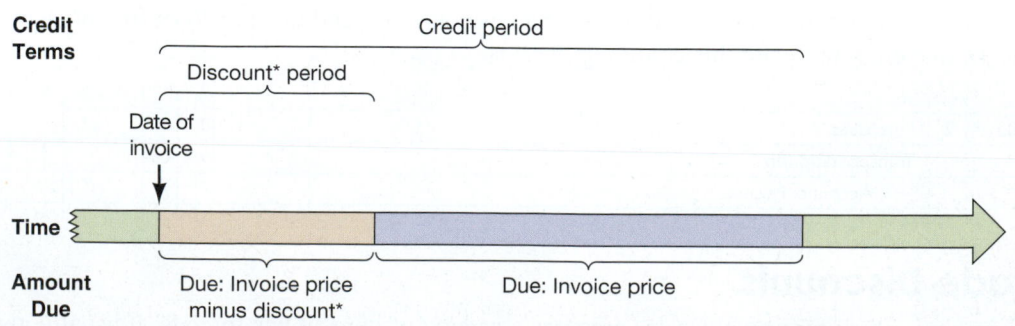

Recall from Chapter 11, credit terms of "2/10, n/30" mean that full payment is due within a 30-day **credit period,** but the buyer can deduct 2% of the invoice amount if payment is made within 10 days of the invoice date. This reduced payment applies only in the **discount period.**

Purchase discounts are recorded in a contra-purchases account that normally carries a credit balance. The entry to record the merchandise purchase under a periodic inventory system is

Nov.	2	Purchases	1 2 0 0 00	
		Accounts Payable		1 2 0 0 00
		Purchased merchandise on credit, invoice		
		dated Nov. 2, terms 2/10, n/30.		

Assets = Liabilities + Equity
        +1,200   −1,200

If Z-Mart pays the amount due on (or before) November 12, the entry is

Nov.	12	Accounts Payable	1 2 0 0 00	
		Purchase Discounts		2 4 00
		Cash		1 1 7 6 00
		Paid for the $1,200 purchase of Nov. 2 less the		
		discount of $24 (2% × $1,200).		

Assets = Liabilities + Equity
−1,176   −1,200   +24

After these entries are posted, the net cost of merchandise purchased is reflected in Purchases minus Purchase Discounts. The Accounts Payable account shows a zero balance. The ledger accounts, in T-account form, follow:

Accounts Payable				**Purchases**			**Purchase Discounts**	
Nov. 12	1,200	Nov. 2	1,200	Nov. 2	1,200		Nov. 12	24
		Balance	0	Balance	1,200		Balance	24

Purchase Returns and Allowances

Purchase returns refer to merchandise a buyer acquires but then returns to the seller. A *purchase allowance* is a reduction in the cost of defective or unacceptable merchandise that a buyer acquires. Buyers often keep defective but still marketable merchandise if the seller grants an acceptable allowance.

When a buyer returns or takes an allowance on merchandise, the buyer issues a **debit memorandum** to inform the seller of a debit made to the seller's account in the buyer's records. To illustrate, on November 15 Z-Mart (buyer) issues a $300 debit memorandum for an allowance from Trex for defective merchandise. Z-Mart's November 15 entry to record the purchase allowance is

Nov.	15	Accounts Payable	3 0 0 00	
		Purchase Returns and Allowances		3 0 0 00
		Allowance for defective merchandise.		

Assets = Liabilities + Equity
        −300   +300

If this had been a return, then the total *recorded cost* (all costs less any discounts) of the defective merchandise would be entered. The buyer's cost of returned and defective merchandise is usually offset against the buyer's current account payable balance to the seller. When cash is refunded, the Cash account is debited instead of Accounts Payable.

Transportation Costs and Ownership Transfer

The buyer and seller must agree on who is responsible for paying any freight costs and who bears the risk of loss during transit for merchandising transactions. This determines the point when ownership transfers from the seller to the buyer. The point of transfer is called the **FOB** (*free on board*) point, which determines who pays transportation costs (and often other incidental costs of transit such as insurance).

Exhibit 12.5 identifies two alternative points of transfer. (1) *FOB shipping point,* also called *FOB factory,* means the buyer accepts ownership when the goods leave the seller's place of business. The buyer is then responsible for paying shipping costs and bearing the risk of damage or loss when goods are in transit. The goods are part of the buyer's inventory when they are in transit since ownership has transferred to the buyer. **Cannondale**, a major bike manufacturer, uses FOB shipping point. (2) *FOB destination* means ownership of goods transfers to the buyer when the goods arrive at the buyer's place of business. The seller is responsible for paying shipping charges and bears the risk of damage or loss in transit. The seller does not record revenue from this sale until the goods arrive at the destination because this transaction is not complete before that point. The buyer does not record the purchase until the goods arrive at the buyer's place of business.

Exhibit 12.5

Ownership Transfer and
Transportation Costs

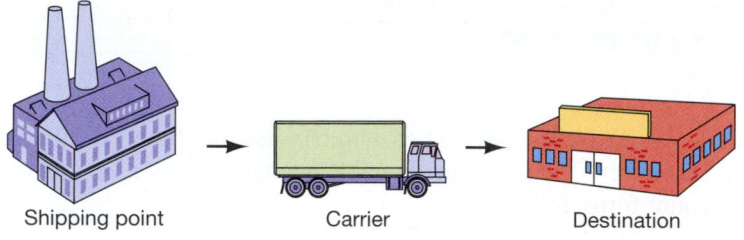

Shipping point   Carrier   Destination

	Ownership Transfers When Goods Passed to	Transportation Costs Paid by
FOB shipping point	Carrier	Buyer
FOB destination	Buyer	Seller

Z-Mart's $1,200 purchase on November 2 is on terms of FOB destination. This means Z-Mart does not pay transportation costs. When a buyer is responsible for paying transportation costs, the payment is made to a carrier or directly to the seller depending on the agreement. The cost principle requires that any necessary transportation costs of a buyer (often called *transportation-in* or *freight-in*) be included as part of the cost of purchased merchandise. To illustrate, Z-Mart's entry to record a $75 freight charge from an independent carrier for merchandise purchased FOB shipping point is

Assets = Liabilities + Equity
−75   −75

Nov.	24	Transportation-In		75 00	
		Cash			75 00
		Paid freight costs on purchased merchandise.			

A seller records the costs of shipping goods to customers in a Delivery Expense account when the seller is responsible for these costs. Delivery Expense, also called *transportation-out* or *freight-out,* is reported as a selling expense in the seller's income statement.

In sum, purchases are recorded as debits to the Purchases account. Any purchase discounts or returns and allowances are credited to the Purchase Discounts and Purchases Returns and Allowances accounts, respectively. Freight charges are debited to Transportation-In. These items are used to compute **net purchases.** Z-Mart's itemized cost of net merchandise purchases for year 2010 are shown in Exhibit 12.6.

Exhibit 12.6

Itemized Costs of Net
Merchandise Purchases

Z-MART
Itemized Costs of Net Merchandise Purchases
For Year Ended December 31, 2010

Purchases	$235,800
Less: Purchase discounts	(4,200)
Purchase returns and allowances	(1,500)
Add: Transportation-In	2,300
Net purchases	**$232,400**

HOW YOU DOIN'?
Answers—p. 302

1. How long are the credit and discount periods when credit terms are 2/10, n/60?

2. Identify which items are subtracted from the *list* amount and not recorded when computing purchase price: (*a*) transportation-in; (*b*) trade discount; (*c*) purchase discount; (*d*) purchase return.

3. What does *FOB* mean? What does *FOB destination* mean?

Purchases Journal and Accounts Payable Subsidiary Ledger

Exhibit 12.7 illustrates the accounting for several February merchandise purchases on credit by Z-Mart. The journal entries are entered in the general journal and then posted to the general ledger. As you can see from Exhibit 12.7, entering a journal entry each time there is a credit

Exhibit 12.7

General Journal Entries and
Posting of February Purchases
for Z-Mart

GENERAL JOURNAL				Page 1
Date	Description	PR	Debit	Credit
Feb. 3	Purchases	502	3 2 5 00	
	Transportation-In	503	2 5 00	
	Accounts Payable	207		3 5 0 00
	Purchased Merchandise from Horning Supply Co.,			
	Invoice 337, terms n/30			
5	Purchases	502	1 7 7 00	
	Transportation-In	503	2 3 00	
	Accounts Payable	207		2 0 0 00
	Purchased Merchandise from Ace Mfg Co.,			
	Invoice 4242, terms 2/10, n/30			
13	Purchases	502	1 3 5 00	
	Transportation-In	503	1 5 00	
	Accounts Payable	207		1 5 0 00
	Purchased Merchandise from Wynet & Co.,			
	Invoice 667, terms 2/10, n/30			
20	Purchases	502	2 8 3 00	
	Transportation-In	503	1 7 00	
	Accounts Payable	207		3 0 0 00
	Purchased Merchandise from Smite Co.,			
	Invoice 2333, terms 2/10, n/30			

[continued on next page]

[continued from previous page]

	Date	Account	PR	Debit	Credit
	25	Purchases	502	92 00	
		Transportation-In	503	8 00	
		Accounts Payable	207		100 00
		Purchased Merchandise from Ace Mfg. Co.,			
		Invoice 4295, terms 2/10, n/30			
	28	Purchases	502	207 00	
		Transportation-In	503	18 00	
		Accounts Payable	207		225 00
		Purchased Merchandise from ITT Co.,			
		Invoice 3367, terms n/30			

Account

Accounts Payable   Account No. 207

Date		Item	PR	Debit	Credit	Balance
Feb.	1	Balance				0
	3		G1		350	350
	5		G1		200	550
	13		G1		150	700
	20		G1		300	1,000
	25		G1		100	1,100
	28		G1		225	1,325

Purchases   Account No. 502

Date		Item	PR	Debit	Credit	Balance
Feb.	3		G1	325		325
	5		G1	177		502
	13		G1	135		637
	20		G1	283		920
	25		G1	92		1,012
	28		G1	207		1,219

Transportation-In   Account No. 503

Date		Item	PR	Debit	Credit	Balance
Feb.	3		G1	25		25
	5		G1	23		48
	13		G1	15		63
	20		G1	17		80
	25		G1	8		88
	28		G1	18		106

purchase is a tedious, repetitive task. Writing descriptions of each purchase and posting each transaction to the general ledger represent significant effort. To make this process more efficient, a purchases journal is used.

Purchases Journal

LO2   Journalize and post transactions using a purchases journal.

A **purchases journal** is typically used to record all credit purchases. Cash purchases are typically recorded in the cash disbursements journal or general journal. We illustrate all credit merchandise purchases for Z-Mart in the month of February in Exhibit 12.8. To record transactions in a purchases journal, use the information on the purchase invoice.

1. Enter the date of the journal entry, the invoice date, and credit terms.
2. In the Accounts Payable Credit column, enter the total owed to the supplier.
3. In the Purchases Debit column, enter the total amount of purchases bought.
4. In the Transportation-In Debit column, enter the freight charges.

Once the journal entries are entered in the purchases journal, totals are posted to the general ledger. As illustrated in Exhibit 12.8, compute totals for the Accounts Payable Credit column

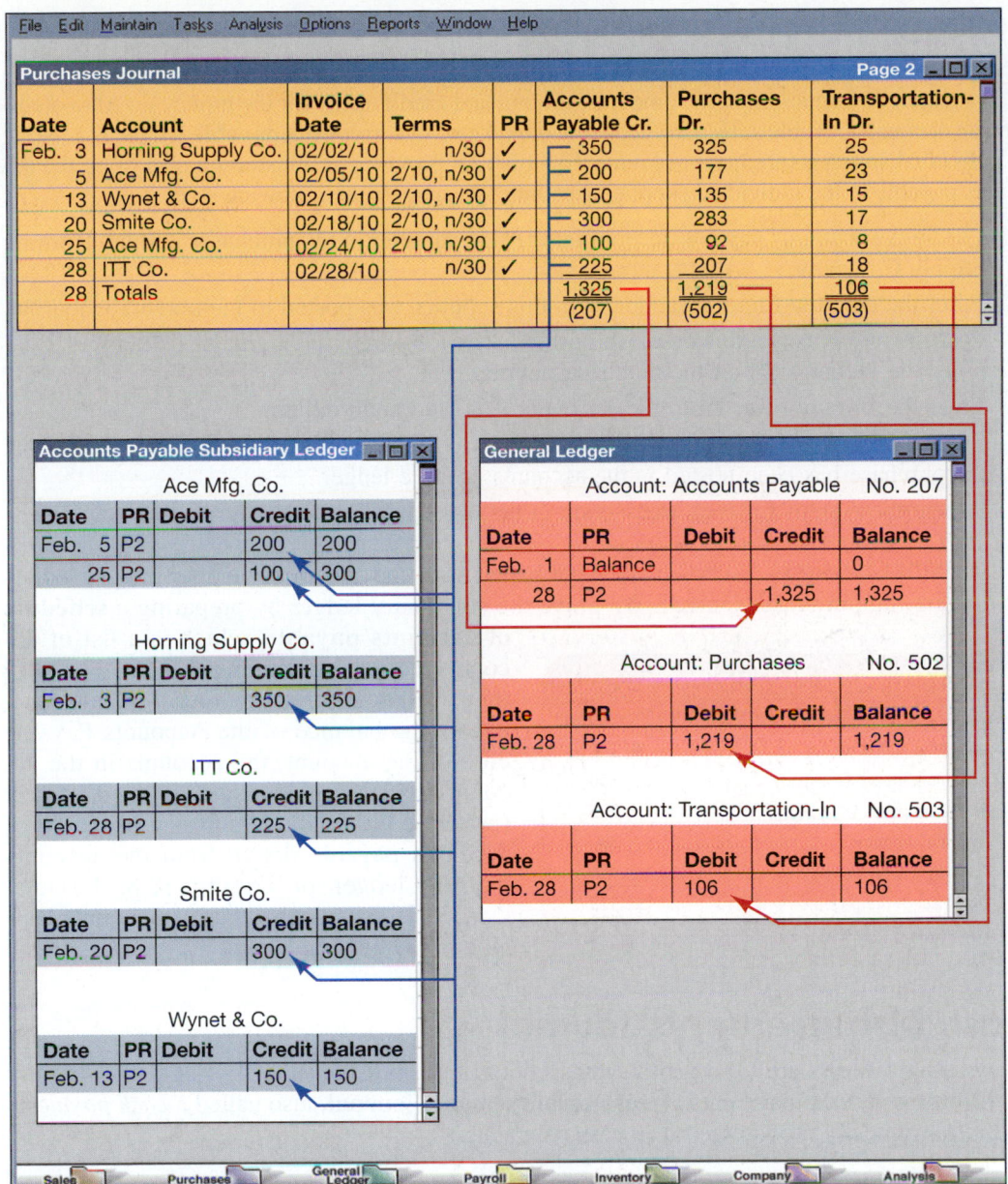

Exhibit 12.8

Purchases Journal with Posting

($1,325) and for the Purchases Debit ($1,219) and Transportation-In Debit ($106) columns. Before posting, we must ensure the debits (Purchases and Transportation-In) equal the credits (Accounts Payable). Then we post the column totals from the Purchases journal to the general ledger as follows:

1. Locate the general ledger accounts needed: Accounts Payable (207), Purchases (502), and Transportation-In (503).

2. Enter the date of the posting.

3. Post the reference. In this case, we post P2. **P** is for purchases journal. The number **2** denotes the second page of the purchases journal.

4. Post the total from the Accounts Payable Credit column. Compute the new balance.

5. Post the total from the Purchases Debit column. Compute the new balance.

6. Post the total from the Transportation-In Debit column. Compute the new balance.

Posting to the Accounts Payable Subsidiary Ledger

Once the purchases journal is posted to the general ledger, the ledger accounts are up to date. To keep accurate information on the amounts, timing, and credit terms for the money owed to creditors, an accounts payable subsidiary ledger is often kept. The **accounts payable ledger** is a listing of individual supplier (creditor) accounts. Exhibit 12.8 provides an illustration of posting the accounts payable to the individual supplier accounts. We suggest the following steps:

1. Locate the accounts payable account for the first supplier in the purchases journal, Horning Supply Company.
2. Enter the date the first transaction with this supplier was posted to the purchases journal.
3. Post the reference. In this case, we post P2. **P** is for purchases journal. The number **2** denotes the second page of the purchases journal.
4. Enter the amount owed from the Accounts Payable Credit column.
5. Enter a checkmark in the Post Reference column in the Purchases journal to indicate that the purchase has been posted in the accounts payable ledger.
6. Repeat these steps for each transaction in the purchases journal.

LO3 Prepare and prove the accuracy of an accounts payable subsidiary ledger

Proving the Ledger   Accounts payable balances in the subsidiary ledger are proved after posting the purchases journal. We prove the subsidiary ledger by preparing a **schedule of accounts payable,** which is a list of accounts from the accounts payable ledger with their balances and the total. If this total equals the balance of the Accounts Payable controlling account, the accounts in the accounts payable ledger are assumed correct (proved). Exhibit 12.9 shows a schedule of accounts payable drawn from the accounts payable ledger of Exhibit 12.8. Its total ($1,325) equals the balance of Accounts Payable in the general ledger.

Exhibit 12.9

Schedule of Accounts Payable

Schedule of Accounts Payable February 28	
Ace Mfg. Company	$ 300
Horning Supply Company	350
ITT Company	225
Smite Company	300
Wynet & Company	150
Total accounts payable	$1,325

Cash Disbursements Journal

LO4 Journalize and post transactions using a cash disbursements journal.

Many cash payments are for repetitive transactions. A cash disbursements journal can simplify the recording of cash payments. A **cash disbursements journal,** also called a *cash payments journal,* is typically used to record all cash payments.

Journalizing   The cash disbursements journal shown in Exhibit 12.10 illustrates repetitive entries to the Cash Cr. column of this journal (reflecting cash payments). Also note the frequent credits to Inventory (which reflect purchase discounts) and the debits to Accounts Payable. For example, on February 15, the company pays Ace on account (credit terms of 2/10, n/30). Since payment occurs in the discount period, the company pays $196 ($200 invoice less $4 discount). The $4 discount is credited to Purchase Discounts. Note that when this company purchases inventory for cash, it is recorded using the Other Accounts Dr. column and the Cash Cr. column as illustrated in the February 3 and 12 transactions. Generally, the Other Accounts column is used to record cash payments on items for which no column exists. For example, on February 15, the company pays salaries expense of $250. The title of the account debited (Salaries Expense) is entered in the Account Debited column.

Each transaction in the cash disbursements journal involves a credit to Cash. Debit accounts will vary.

The cash disbursements journal has a column titled Ck. No. (check number). For control over cash disbursements, all payments except for those of small amounts are made by check. Checks should be prenumbered and each check's number entered in the journal in numerical order in the column headed Ck. No. This makes it possible to scan the numbers in the column for omitted checks. When a cash disbursements journal has a column for check numbers, it is sometimes called a **check register.**

Exhibit 12.10

Cash Disbursements Journal with Posting

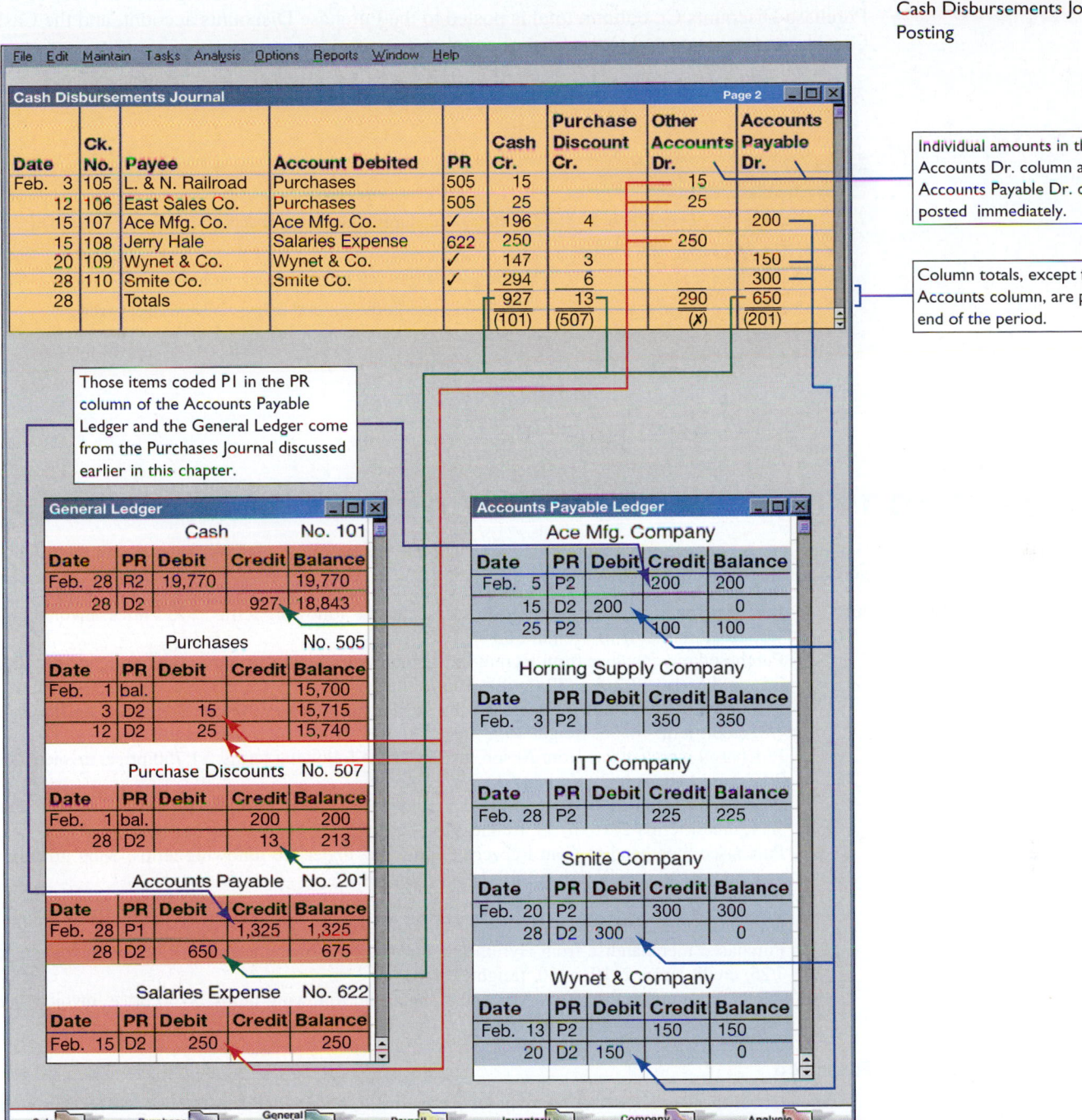

Posting Individual amounts in the Other Accounts Dr. column of a cash disbursements journal are immediately posted to their general ledger accounts. Individual amounts in the Accounts Payable Dr. column are also immediately posted to creditors' accounts in the subsidiary Accounts Payable ledger. These postings are identified with a "D" along with a page number from the cash disbursements journal in the PR column of the subsidiary ledger. The customer accounts in the subsidiary ledger include some postings from page two of the purchases journal (coded 'P2' in the PR column). At the end of the period, we crossfoot column totals and post the Accounts Payable Dr. column total to the Accounts Payable controlling account. Also, the Purchase Discounts Cr. column total is posted to the Purchase Discounts account, and the Cash Cr. column total is posted to the Cash account.

HOW YOU DOIN'?   Answers—p. 302

4. What are the normal recording and posting procedures when using special journals and controlling accounts with subsidiary ledgers?

5. What is the process for posting to a subsidiary ledger and its controlling account?

6. How do we prove the accuracy of account balances in the general ledger and subsidiary ledgers after posting?

Demonstration Problem 1

Connie Company has the following credit merchandise purchase transactions in the month of July. All goods are shipped FOB shipping point.

July 3 Purchased merchandise from Alison Inc. under the following terms: $750 price, invoice date 7/2, credit terms n/30, freight $62.

7 Purchased merchandise from Hyrum Inc. under the following terms: $1,500 price, invoice date 7/5, credit terms 2/10, n/30, freight $92.

9 Purchased merchandise from Melissa Inc. under the following terms: $75 price, invoice date 7/8, credit terms n/30, freight $5.

13 Purchased merchandise from Alison Inc. under the following terms: $1,750 price, invoice date 7/12, credit terms n/30, freight $117.

14 Purchased merchandise from Joseph Inc. under the following terms: $152 price, invoice date 7/14, credit terms 2/10, n/30, freight $23.

19 Purchased merchandise from Rebecca Supply Inc. under the following terms: $866 price, invoice date 7/19, credit terms 2/10, n/30, freight $57.

22 Purchased merchandise from Melissa Inc. under the following terms: $7,502 price, invoice date 7/19, credit terms n/30, freight $215.

27 Purchased merchandise from Hyrum Inc. under the following terms: $117 price, invoice date 7/26, credit terms 2/10, n/30, freight $14.

30 Purchased merchandise from Alison Inc. under the following terms: $750 price, invoice date 7/28, credit terms n/30, freight $62.

Required

1. Account for these purchases in a purchases journal using Accounts Payable (acct. #207), Purchases (acct. #502), and Transportation-In (acct. #503). The purchase journal page is page 3. Remember to include the invoice date and credit terms.

2. Post these accounts to the general ledger and post the references.

3. Post these transactions to the accounts payable subsidiary ledger.

Planning the Solution

1. Set up the purchases journal using the template from Exhibit 12.8 with a credit column for Accounts Payable and debit entry columns for Purchases and Transportation-In.

2. Record each credit purchase, with each transaction taking one line in the purchases journal.

3. When complete, sum the columns in the purchase journal to prepare to post totals to the general ledger accounts.

4. Post the column totals in Accounts Payable Credit, Purchases Debit, and Transportation-In Debit to their general ledger accounts.

5. Post each transaction from the purchases journal to the appropriate account in the accounts payable subsidiary ledger.

Solution to Demonstration Problem 1

1. and 2. Account for the purchases of Connie Company using a purchases journal.

Purchases Journal   Page 3

Date	Account	Invoice Date	Terms	PR	Accounts Payable Cr.	Purchases Dr.	Transportation-In Dr.
Jul. 3	Alison Inc.	July 2	n/30		812	750	62
7	Hyrum Inc.	July 5	2/10, n/30		1,592	1,500	92
9	Melissa Inc.	July 8	n/30		80	75	5
13	Alison Inc.	July 12	n/30		1,867	1,750	117
14	Joseph Inc.	July 14	2/10, n/30		175	152	23
19	Rebecca Supply Inc.	July 19	2/10, n/30		923	866	57
22	Melissa Inc.	July 19	n/30		7,717	7,502	215
27	Hyrum Inc.	July 26	2/10, n/30		131	117	14
30	Alison Inc.	July 28	n/30		812	750	62

3. and 4. Post the totals from the purchases journal to the general ledger.

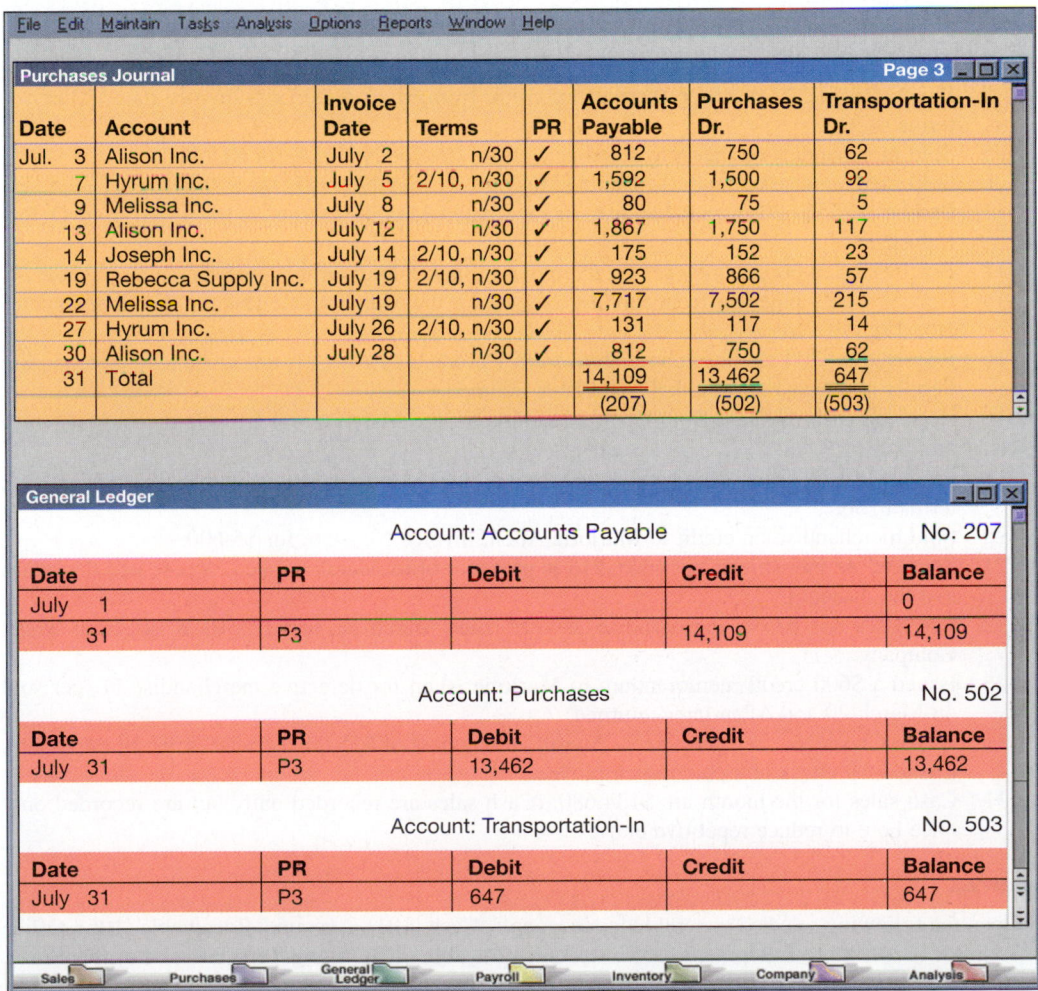

File   Edit   Maintain   Tasks   Analysis   Options   Reports   Window   Help

Purchases Journal   Page 3

Date	Account	Invoice Date	Terms	PR	Accounts Payable	Purchases Dr.	Transportation-In Dr.
Jul. 3	Alison Inc.	July 2	n/30	✓	812	750	62
7	Hyrum Inc.	July 5	2/10, n/30	✓	1,592	1,500	92
9	Melissa Inc.	July 8	n/30	✓	80	75	5
13	Alison Inc.	July 12	n/30	✓	1,867	1,750	117
14	Joseph Inc.	July 14	2/10, n/30	✓	175	152	23
19	Rebecca Supply Inc.	July 19	2/10, n/30	✓	923	866	57
22	Melissa Inc.	July 19	n/30	✓	7,717	7,502	215
27	Hyrum Inc.	July 26	2/10, n/30	✓	131	117	14
30	Alison Inc.	July 28	n/30	✓	812	750	62
31	Total				14,109	13,462	647
					(207)	(502)	(503)

General Ledger

Account: Accounts Payable   No. 207

Date	PR	Debit	Credit	Balance
July 1				0
31	P3		14,109	14,109

Account: Purchases   No. 502

Date	PR	Debit	Credit	Balance
July 31	P3	13,462		13,462

Account: Transportation-In   No. 503

Date	PR	Debit	Credit	Balance
July 31	P3	647		647

Sales   Purchases   General Ledger   Payroll   Inventory   Company   Analysis

5. Posting the accounts payable balances to the accounts payable subsidiary ledger.

Accounts Payable Subsidiary Ledger

Alison Inc.

Date	PR	Debit	Credit	Balance
Jul. 3	P3		812	812
13	P3		1,867	2,679
30	P3		812	3,491

Hyrum Inc.

Date	PR	Debit	Credit	Balance
Jul. 7	P3		1,592	1,592
27	P3		131	1,723

Melissa Inc.

Date	PR	Debit	Credit	Balance
Jul. 9	P3		80	80
22	P3		7,717	7,797

Joseph Inc.

Date	PR	Debit	Credit	Balance
Jul. 14	P3		175	175

Rebecca Supply Inc.

Date	PR	Debit	Credit	Balance
Jul. 19	P3		923	923

Demonstration Problem 2

Pepper Company completed the following selected transactions and events during March of this year. (Terms of all credit sales for the company are 2/10, n/30.)

Mar. 4   Purchased $1,220 of office supplies on credit from Mack Company. Invoice dated March 3, terms n/30.

     5   Sold merchandise on credit to Jennifer Nelson, Invoice No. 954, for $16,800.

     6   Sold merchandise on credit to Dennie Hoskins, Invoice No. 955, for $10,200.

     11   Purchased $52,600 of merchandise, invoice dated March 6, terms 2/10, n/30, from Defore Industries.

     12   Borrowed $26,000 cash by giving Commerce Bank a long-term promissory note payable.

     14   Received cash payment from Jennifer Nelson for the March 4 sale less the discount (Invoice No. 954).

     16   Received a $200 credit memorandum from Defore Industries for unsatisfactory merchandise Pepper purchased on March 11 and later returned.

     16   Received cash payment from Dennie Hoskins for the March 6 sale less the discount (Invoice No. 955).

     18   Purchased $22,850 of store equipment on credit from Schmidt Supply, invoice dated March 15, terms n/30.

     20   Sold merchandise on credit to Marjorie Allen, Invoice No. 956, for $5,600.

     21   Sent Defore Industries Check No. 516 in payment of its March 6 dated invoice less the return and the discount.

     22   Purchased $41,625 of merchandise, invoice dated March 18, terms 2/10, n/30, from Welch Company.

     26   Issued a $600 credit memorandum to Marjorie Allen for defective merchandise Pepper sold on March 20 and Allen later returned.

     31   Issued Check No. 517, payable to Payroll, in payment of $15,900 sales salaries for the month. Cashed the check and paid the employees.

     31   Cash sales for the month are $134,680. (Cash sales are recorded daily but are recorded only once here to reduce repetitive entries.)

Required

1. Open the following selected general ledger accounts: Cash (101), Accounts Receivable (106), Office Supplies (124), Store Equipment (165), Accounts Payable (201), Long-Term Notes Payable (251),

Sales (413), Sales Returns and Allowances (414), Sales Discounts (415), Purchases (505), Purchases Returns and Allowances (506), Purchases Discounts (507), and Sales Salaries Expense (621). Open the following accounts receivable ledger accounts: Marjorie Allen, Dennie Hoskins, and Jennifer Nelson. Open the following accounts payable ledger accounts: Defore Industries, Mack Company, Schmidt Supply, and Welch Company.

2. Enter the transactions using a sales journal, a purchases journal, a cash receipts journal, a cash disbursements journal, and a general journal. Regularly post to the individual customer and creditor accounts. Also, post any amounts that should be posted as individual amounts to general ledger accounts. Foot and crossfoot the journals and make the month-end postings. *Pepper Co. uses the periodic inventory system in this problem.* (Refer to Chapter 11 for an example of a sales journal and cash receipts journal and to Chapter 12 for an example of a purchases journal and cash disbursements journal.)

3. Prepare a trial balance for the selected general ledger accounts in part 1 and prove the accuracy of subsidiary ledgers by preparing schedules of accounts receivable and accounts payable.

Planning the Solution

- Set up the required general ledger, subsidiary ledger accounts, the sales journal, the cash receipts journal, the purchases journal, the cash disbursements journal, and the general journal.
- Read and analyze each transaction and decide in which special journal (or general journal) the transaction is recorded.
- Record each transaction in the proper journal (and post the appropriate individual amounts).
- Once you have recorded all transactions, total the journal columns. Post from each journal to the appropriate ledger accounts.
- Prepare a trial balance to prove the equality of the debit and credit balances in your general ledger.
- Prepare schedules of accounts receivable and accounts payable as of March 31. Compare the totals of these schedules to the Accounts Receivable and Accounts Payable controlling account balances, making sure that they agree.

Solution to Demonstration Problem 2

Sales Journal   Page 2

Date	Account Debited	Invoice Number	PR	Accounts Receivable Dr. Sales Cr.
Mar. 5	Jennifer Nelson	954	✓	16,800
6	Dennie Hoskins	955	✓	10,200
20	Marjorie Allen	956	✓	5,600
31	Totals			32,600
				(106/413)

Cash Receipts Journal   Page 3

Date	Account Credited	Explanation	PR	Cash Dr.	Sales Discount Dr.	Accounts Receivable Cr.	Sales Cr.	Other Accounts Cr.
Mar. 12	L.T. Notes Payable	Note to bank	251	26,000				26,000
14	Jennifer Nelson	Invoice 954, 3/5	✓	16,464	336	16,800		
16	Dennie Hoskins	Invoice 955, 3/6	✓	9,996	204	10,200		
31	Sales	Cash sales	x	134,680			134,680	
31	Totals			187,140	540	27,000	134,680	26,000
				(101)	(415)	(106)	(413)	(x)

Purchases Journal   Page 3

Date	Account	Date of Invoice	Terms	PR	Accounts Payable Cr.	Purchases Dr.	Office Supplies Dr.	Other Accounts Dr.
Mar. 4	Office Supplies/Mack Co.	3/3	n/30	✓	1,220		1,220	
11	Defore Industries	3/6	2/10, n/30	✓	52,600	52,600		
18	Store Equipment/Schmidt Supp.	3/15	n/30	165/✓	22,850			22,850
22	Welch Company	3/18	2/10, n/30	✓	41,625	41,625		
31	Totals				118,295	94,225	1,220	22,850
					(201)	(505)	(124)	(x)

Cash Disbursements Journal   Page 3

Date	Ck. No.	Payee	Account Debited	PR	Cash Cr.	Purch. Discount Cr.	Other Accounts Dr.	Accounts Payable Dr.
Mar. 21	516	Defore Industries	Defore Industries	✓	51,352	1,048		52,400
31	517	Payroll	Sales Salaries Expense	621	15,900		15,900	
31		Totals			67,252	1,048	15,900	52,400
					(101)	(507)	(x)	(201)

General Journal   Page 2

Mar. 16	Accounts Payable—Defore Industries	201/✓	200	
	Purchases Returns and Allowances.............	506		200
	To record credit memorandum received.			
26	Sales Returns and Allowances.....................	414	600	
	Accounts Receivable—Marjorie Allen	106/✓		600
	To record credit memorandum issued.			

Accounts Receivable Ledger

Marjorie Allen

Date	PR	Debit	Credit	Balance
Mar. 20	S2	5,600		5,600
26	G2		600	5,000

Dennie Hoskins

Date	PR	Debit	Credit	Balance
Mar. 6	S2	10,200		10,200
16	R3		10,200	0

Jennifer Nelson

Date	PR	Debit	Credit	Balance
Mar. 5	S2	16,800		16,800
14	R3		16,800	0

Accounts Payable Ledger

Defore Industries

Date	PR	Debit	Credit	Balance
Mar. 11	P3		52,600	52,600
16	G2	200		52,400
21	D3	52,400		0

Mack Company

Date	PR	Debit	Credit	Balance
Mar. 4	P3		1,220	1,220

Schmidt Supply

Date	PR	Debit	Credit	Balance
Mar. 18	P3		22,850	22,850

Welch Company

Date	PR	Debit	Credit	Balance
Mar. 22	P3		41,625	41,625

General Ledger (Partial Listing)

Cash Acct. No. 101

Date	PR	Debit	Credit	Balance
Mar. 31	R3	187,140		187,140
31	D3		67,252	119,888

Accounts Receivable Acct. No. 106

Date	PR	Debit	Credit	Balance
Mar. 26	G2		600	(600)
31	S2	32,600		32,000
31	R3		27,000	5,000

Office Supplies Acct. No. 124

Date	PR	Debit	Credit	Balance
Mar. 31	P3	1,220		1,220

Store Equipment Acct. No. 165

Date	PR	Debit	Credit	Balance
Mar. 18	P3	22,850		22,850

Accounts Payable Acct. No. 201

Date	PR	Debit	Credit	Balance
Mar. 16	G2	200		(200)
31	P3		118,295	118,095
31	D3	52,400		65,695

Long-Term Notes Payable Acct. No. 251

Date	PR	Debit	Credit	Balance
Mar. 12	R3		26,000	26,000

Sales Acct. No. 413

Date	PR	Debit	Credit	Balance
Mar. 31	S2		32,600	32,600
31	R3		134,680	167,280

Sales Returns and Allowances Acct. No. 414

Date	PR	Debit	Credit	Balance
Mar. 26	G2	600		600

Sales Discounts Acct. No. 415

Date	PR	Debit	Credit	Balance
Mar. 31	R3	540		540

Purchases Acct. No. 505

Date	PR	Debit	Credit	Balance
Mar. 31	P3	94,225		94,225

Purchases Returns and Allowances Acct. No. 506

Date	PR	Debit	Credit	Balance
Mar. 16	G2		200	200

Purchases Discounts Acct. No. 507

Date	PR	Debit	Credit	Balance
Mar. 31	D3		1,048	1,048

Sales Salaries Expense Acct. No. 621

Date	PR	Debit	Credit	Balance
Mar. 31	D3	15,900		15,900

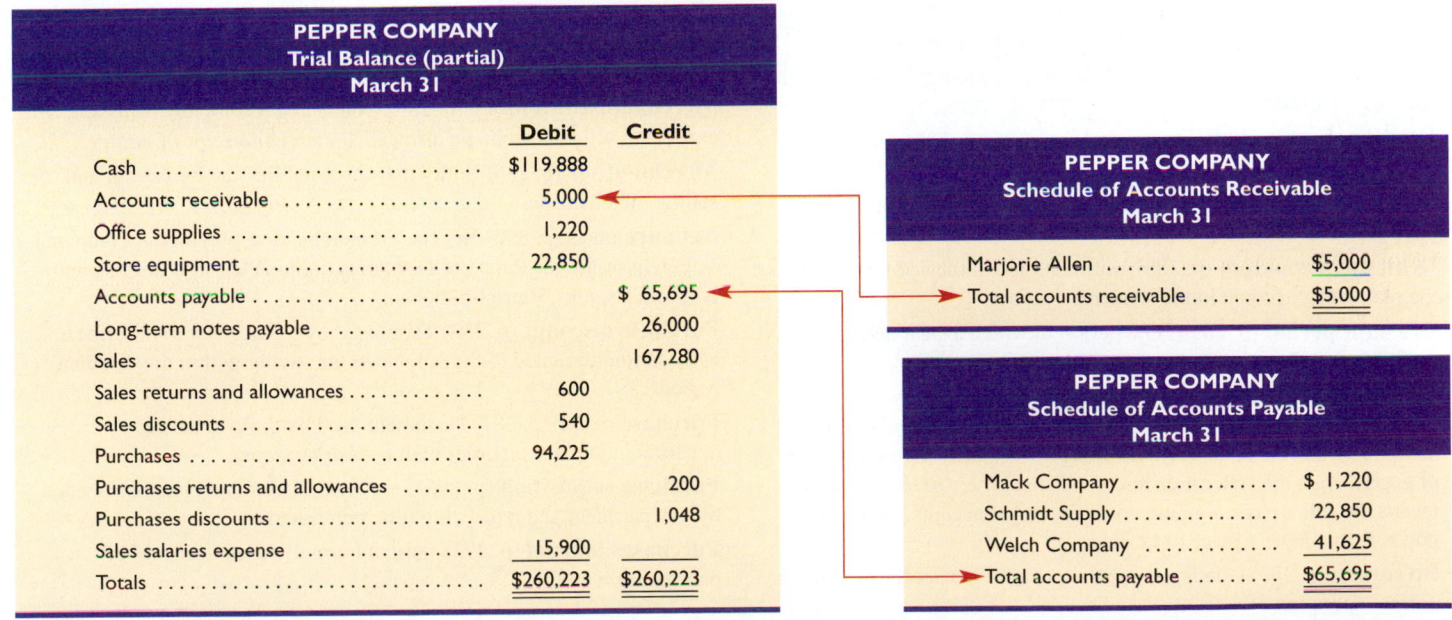

PEPPER COMPANY
Trial Balance (partial)
March 31

	Debit	Credit
Cash	$119,888	
Accounts receivable	5,000	
Office supplies	1,220	
Store equipment	22,850	
Accounts payable		$ 65,695
Long-term notes payable		26,000
Sales		167,280
Sales returns and allowances	600	
Sales discounts	540	
Purchases	94,225	
Purchases returns and allowances		200
Purchases discounts		1,048
Sales salaries expense	15,900	
Totals	$260,223	$260,223

PEPPER COMPANY
Schedule of Accounts Receivable
March 31

Marjorie Allen	$5,000
Total accounts receivable	$5,000

PEPPER COMPANY
Schedule of Accounts Payable
March 31

Mack Company	$ 1,220
Schmidt Supply	22,850
Welch Company	41,625
Total accounts payable	$65,695

Summary

LO1 **Analyze and record transactions for merchandise purchases.** A merchandiser records sales at list price less any trade discounts. The merchandiser records applicable purchase discounts for cash payment within the discount period as well as applicable purchase returns and freight charges.

LO2 **Journalize and post transactions using a purchases journal.** The purchases journal is an efficient means to record the purchase of inventory on credit. The purchases journal will typically debit merchandise inventory (and transportation-in if applicable) and credit accounts payable.

LO3 **Prepare and prove the accuracy of an accounts payable subsidiary ledger.** Account balances in the general ledger and the accounts payable subsidiary ledger are tested for accuracy after posting is complete. This procedure is twofold: (1) prepare a trial balance of the general ledger to confirm that debits equal credits and (2) prepare a schedule to confirm that the controlling account's balance equals the subsidiary ledger's balance.

LO4 **Journalize and post transactions using a cash disbursements journal.** This journal, also called a cash payments journal, is used to record cash payments for purchases, expenses, and other items.

Guidance Answers to HOW YOU DOIN'?

1. Under credit terms of 2/10, n/60, the credit period is 60 days and the discount period is 10 days.

2. (*b*) trade discount.

3. *FOB* means "free on board." It is used in identifying the point when ownership transfers from seller to buyer. *FOB destination* means that the seller transfers ownership of goods to the buyer when they arrive at the buyer's place of business. It also means that the seller is responsible for paying shipping charges and bears the risk of damage or loss during shipment.

4. The normal recording and posting procedures are threefold. First, transactions are entered in a special journal if applicable. Second, individual amounts are posted to any subsidiary ledger accounts. Third, column totals are posted to general ledger accounts if not already individually posted.

5. Individual amounts in the Accounts Payable Dr. column are posted immediately to creditor's accounts in the Accounts Payable subsidiary ledger. After crossfooting column totals at the end of the month, the Accounts Payable Dr. column is posted to the controlling account in the general ledger.

6. Tests for accuracy of account balances in the general ledger and subsidiary ledgers are twofold. First, we prepare a trial balance of the general ledger to confirm that debits equal credits. Second, we prove the subsidiary ledgers by preparing schedules of accounts receivable and accounts payable.

Key Terms

Accounts payable ledger (p. 294) Subsidiary ledger listing individual creditor (supplier) accounts.

Cash disbursements journal (p. 294) Special journal normally used to record all payments of cash; also called *cash payments journal*.

Check register (p. 294) A cash disbursements journal with a column for check numbers.

Credit period (p. 289) Time period that can pass before a customer's payment is due.

Credit terms (p. 288) Description of the amounts and timing of payments that a buyer (debtor) agrees to make in the future.

Debit memorandum (p. 289) Notification that the sender has debited the recipient's account in the sender's records.

Discount period (p. 289) Time period in which a cash discount is available and the buyer can make a reduced payment.

FOB (p. 290) Abbreviation for *free on board*; the point when ownership of goods passes to the buyer; *FOB shipping point* (or *factory*) means the buyer pays shipping costs and accepts ownership of goods when the seller transfers goods to carrier; *FOB destination* means the seller pays shipping costs and buyer accepts ownership of goods at the buyer's place of business.

Inventory (p. 286) Goods a company owns and expects to sell in its normal operations.

Invoice (p. 287) Itemized record of goods prepared by the vendor that lists the customer's name, items sold, sales prices, and terms of sale.

List price (p. 287) Catalog (full) price of an item before any trade discount is deducted.

Merchandise inventory (p. 286) Goods that a company owns and expects to sell to customers; also called *merchandise* or *inventory*.

Merchandiser (p. 286) Entity that earns net income by buying and selling merchandise.

Net purchases (p. 290) Net cost of merchandise purchased; computed as Purchases minus Purchase Discounts, minus Purchase Returns and Allowances, plus Transportation-In.

Purchase discount (p. 288) Term used by a purchaser to describe a cash discount granted to the purchaser for paying within the discount period.

Purchase order (p. 287) Document used by the purchasing department to place an order with a seller (vendor).

Purchase requisition (p. 286) Document listing merchandise needed by a department and requesting it be purchased.

Purchases journal (p. 292) Journal normally used to record all purchases on credit.

Receiving report (p. 287) Form used to report that ordered goods are received and to describe their quantity and condition.

Schedule of accounts payable (p. 294) List of the balances of all accounts in the accounts payable ledger and their total.

Trade discount (p. 288) Reduction from a list or catalog price that can vary for wholesalers, retailers, and consumers.

Transportation-In (p. 287) Freight costs paid by the buyer.

Vendor (p. 287) Seller of goods or services.

Multiple Choice Quiz   Answers on p. 313   mhhe.com/wildCA2e

Additional Multiple Choice Quizzes are available at the book's Website.

1. In the purchases journal, the _____ account is credited.
   a. Purchases
   b. Accounts Receivable
   c. Transportation-In
   d. Accounts Payable

2. A company purchased $4,500 of merchandise on May 1 with terms of 2/10, n/30. On May 6, it returned $250 of that merchandise. On May 8, it paid the balance owed for merchandise, taking any discount it is entitled to. The cash paid on May 8 is
   a. $4,500
   b. $4,250
   c. $4,160
   d. $4,165
   e. $4,410

3. Merchandise inventory
   a. Is a long-term asset account.
   b. Is a current asset account.

   c. Includes supplies.
   d. Is classified with investments on the balance sheet.
   e. Must be sold within one month.

4. Net purchases includes
   a. Any purchase discounts.
   b. Any returns and allowances.
   c. Any necessary transportation-in costs.
   d. Any trade discounts.
   e. All of the above.

5. In the cash disbursements journal, the _____ account is credited.
   a. Cash
   b. Accounts Receivable ✕
   c. Transportation-In ✕
   d. Accounts Payable ✓

Discussion Questions

1. In comparing the accounts of a merchandising company with those of a service company, what additional accounts would the merchandising company likely use?

2. What items appear in financial statements of merchandising companies but not in the statements of service companies?

3. Why do companies offer cash discounts?

4. Distinguish between cash discounts and trade discounts. Is the amount of a trade discount on purchased merchandise recorded in the accounts?

5. What is the difference between a sales discount and a purchase discount?

6. Why would a company's manager be concerned about the quantity of its purchase returns if its suppliers allow unlimited returns?

7. Refer to the balance sheet and income statement for **Best Buy** in Appendix A. What does the company title its inventory account?

8. Refer to the income statement for **RadioShack** in Appendix A. What does RadioShack title its accounts payable account?

connect

Prepare journal entries to record each of the following purchases transactions of a merchandising company.

QUICK STUDY

QS 12–1
Recording purchases   **LO1**

Mar. 5   Purchased 600 units of product with a list price of $10 per unit. The purchaser is granted a trade discount of 20%; terms of the sale are 2/10, n/60; invoice is dated March 5.

Mar. 7   Returned 25 defective units from the March 5 purchase and received full credit.

Mar. 15   Paid the amount due from the March 5 purchase, less the return on March 7.

QS 12-2
Special Journals   **LO2**   **LO4**

Wagstaff Electronics uses a sales journal, a purchases journal, a cash receipts journal, and a cash disbursements journal. Wagstaff recently completed the following transactions *a* through *d*. Identify the journal in which each transaction should be recorded.

a. Sold merchandise for cash.

b. Purchased merchandise on account.

c. Purchased inventory for cash.

d. Paid cash to a creditor.

QS 12-3
Special Journals   **LO2**   **LO4**

Beach Electronics uses a sales journal, a purchases journal, a cash receipts journal, and a cash disbursements journal. Beach recently completed the following transactions *a* through *d*. Identify the journal in which each transaction should be recorded.

a. Sold merchandise on credit.

b. Purchased shop supplies on credit.

c. Paid an employee's salary in cash.

d. Borrowed cash from a bank.

QS 12-4
Recording purchases in a purchases journal   **LO2**

Account for the following purchases in a purchases journal using Accounts Payable (acct. #207), Purchases (acct. #502), and Transportation-In (acct. #503). (*Hint:* Use the chapter demonstration problem as a guide.)

Dec.   3   Purchased $850 in merchandise from Camille Inc., credit terms n/30; invoice date 12/2, freight $72.
      7   Purchased $1,600 in merchandise from Travis Inc., credit terms 2/10, n/30; invoice date 12/5, freight $162.
      9   Purchased $65 in merchandise from Braden Inc., credit terms n/30; invoice date 12/8, freight $9.

QS 12-5
Recording purchases in a purchases journal   **LO2**

Account for the following purchases in a purchases journal using Accounts Payable (acct. #207), Purchases (acct. #502), and Transportation-In (acct. #503). (*Hint:* Use the chapter demonstration problem as a guide.)

Mar. 13   Purchased $2,750 in merchandise from Kaitlyn Supply Co., credit terms n/30; invoice date 12/12, freight $117.
     14   Purchased $162 in merchandise from Ashley Inc., credit terms 2/10, n/30; invoice date 12/14, freight $33.
     19   Purchased $966 in merchandise from Kaitlyn Supply Co., credit terms n/30; invoice date 12/19, freight $67.

QS 12-6
Cash disbursements journal   **LO4**

Ziebart uses a cash disbursements journal. Please record the following April cash payments in a cash disbursements journal.

Apr.   9   Issued check no. 520 to Muller Corp. to buy store supplies for $650.
    12   Issued check no. 521 to Hinkle Bank for note payable of $900.

QS 12-7
Cash disbursements journal   **LO4**

Sougiannis uses a cash disbursements journal. Prepare a cash disbursements journal using the following July cash payments.

July   8   Issued check no. 522 to Hammersley Corp. to pay for gardening for $1,400.
    28   Issued check no. 523 to Comprix Corp. pay for April Janitorial Services for $1,200.

connect

EXERCISES

Exercise 12-1
Recording entries for merchandise purchases   **LO1**

Prepare journal entries to record the following transactions for a retail store.

Apr.   2   Purchased merchandise from Lyon Company under the following terms: $4,600 price, invoice dated April 2, credit terms of 2/15, n/60, and FOB shipping point.
    3   Paid $300 for shipping charges on the April 2 purchase.
    4   Returned to Lyon Company unacceptable merchandise that had an invoice price of $600.

17 Sent a check to Lyon Company for the April 2 purchase, net of the discount and the returned merchandise.

18 Purchased merchandise from Frist Corp. under the following terms: $8,500 price, invoice dated April 18, credit terms of 2/10, n/30, and FOB destination.

21 After negotiations, received from Frist a $1,100 allowance on the April 18 purchase.

28 Sent check to Frist paying for the April 18 purchase, net of the discount and allowance.

Check April 28, Cr. Cash $7,252

Santa Fe Company purchased merchandise for resale from Mesa Company with an invoice price of $24,000 and credit terms of 3/10, n/60. The merchandise had cost Mesa $16,000. Santa Fe paid within the discount period. Prepare entries that Santa Fe Company should record for the merchandise purchase and the cash payment.

Exercise 12–2
Analyzing and recording merchandise transactions   **LO1**

Insert the letter for each term in the blank space beside the definition that it most closely matches.

A. Cash discount   **E.** FOB shipping point   **H.** Purchase discount

B. Credit period   **F.** Trade discount   **I.** Sales discount

C. Discount period   **G.** Merchandise inventory

D. FOB destination

Exercise 12–3
Applying merchandising terms
LO1

_____ **1.** Reduction below list or catalog price that is negotiated in setting the price of goods.

_____ **2.** Reduction in a receivable or payable if it is paid within the discount period.

_____ **3.** Time period that can pass before a customer's payment is due.

_____ **4.** Time period in which a cash discount is available.

_____ **5.** Ownership of goods is transferred when the seller delivers goods to the carrier.

_____ **6.** Ownership of goods is transferred when delivered to the buyer's place of business.

_____ **7.** Goods a company owns and expects to sell to its customers.

_____ **8.** Purchaser's description of a cash discount received from a supplier of goods.

_____ **9.** Seller's description of a cash discount granted to buyers in return for early payment.

On May 5, Baker purchases 1,500 units of merchandise from Allied Parts for $14 per unit. Baker is a retailer and purchases the units for resale. Three separate transactions *a* through *c* also occur.

a. On May 7, Baker returns 200 units because they did not fit the customer's needs.

b. On May 8, Baker discovers that 300 units are damaged but are still of some use and, therefore, keeps the units. Allied Parts sends Baker a credit memorandum for $600 to compensate for the damage.

c. On May 15, Baker discovers that 100 units are the wrong color. Baker keeps 60 of these units because Allied sends a $120 credit memorandum to compensate. However, Baker returns the remaining 40 units to Allied.

Prepare the appropriate journal entries for Baker Co. to record the May 5 purchase and each of the three separate transactions *a* through *c*.

Exercise 12–4
Recording purchase returns and allowances   **LO1**

On May 11, Sydney Co. accepts delivery of $40,000 of merchandise it purchases for resale from Troy Corporation. With the merchandise is an invoice dated May 11, with terms of 3/10, n/90, FOB shipping point. When the goods are delivered, Sydney pays $345 to Express Shipping for delivery charges on the merchandise. On May 12, Sydney returns $1,400 of goods to Troy, who receives them one day later. On May 20, Sydney mails a check to Troy Corporation for the amount owed. Troy receives it the following day.

1. Prepare journal entries that Sydney Co. records for these transactions.

2. Prepare journal entries that Troy Corporation records for these transactions.

Exercise 12–5
Analyzing and recording merchandise transactions—both buyer and seller   **LO1**

Check (1) May 20, Cr. Cash $37,442

Exercise 12–6
Preparing journal entries for inventory purchases and sales
LO1

Journalize the following merchandising transactions for Chilton Systems.

1. On November 1, Chilton Systems purchases merchandise for $1,500 on credit with terms of 2/5, n/30, FOB shipping point; invoice dated November 1.
2. On November 5, Chilton Systems pays cash for the November 1 purchase.
3. On November 7, Chilton Systems discovers and returns $200 of defective merchandise purchased on November 1 for a cash refund.
4. On November 10, Chilton Systems pays $90 cash for transportation costs for the November 1 purchase.
5. On November 13, Chilton Systems sells merchandise for $1,600 on credit. The cost of the merchandise is $800.
6. On November 16, the customer returns merchandise from the November 13 transaction. The returned items sell for $300 and cost $150.

Exercise 12–7
Cash disbursements journal
LO4

Ziegler Inc. has the following cash disbursements in April.

Apr. 2   Issued check no. 210 to Curington Corp. to buy store supplies for $650.
　　　7   Issued check no. 211 for $1,400 to pay off a note payable to First Savings Bank.
　　20   Purchased merchandise for $4,500 on credit from O'Leary-Kelly, terms 2/10, net 30.
　　28   Issued check no. 212 to O'Leary-Kelly to pay the amount due for the purchase of April 20, less the discount.

Prepare headings for a cash disbursements journal like the one in Exhibit 12.10. Journalize the April transactions that should be recorded in the cash disbursements journal.

Exercise 12–8
Cash disbursements journal   **LO4**

Marx Supply uses a sales journal, a purchases journal, a cash receipts journal, a cash disbursements journal, and a general journal. The following transactions occur in the month of April.

Apr. 3   Purchased merchandise for $2,950 on credit from Seth, Inc., terms 2/10, n/30.
　　　9   Issued check no. 210 to Kitt Corp. to buy store supplies for $650.
　　12   Sold merchandise on credit to C. Myers for $770, terms n/30.
　　17   Issued check no. 211 for $1,400 to pay off a note payable to City Bank.
　　20   Purchased merchandise for $4,500 on credit from Lite, terms 2/10, n/30.
　　28   Issued check no. 212 to Lite to pay the amount due for the purchase of April 20, less the discount.
　　29   Paid salary of $1,800 to B. Dock by issuing check no. 213.
　　30   Issued check no. 214 to Seth, Inc., to pay the amount due for the purchase of April 3.

Prepare headings for a cash disbursements journal like the one in Exhibit 12.10. Journalize the April transactions that should be recorded in the cash disbursements journal.

Exercise 12–9
Cash disbursements and purchases journal **LO2 LO4**

Williams Company began business on May 1. The following transactions involving purchases and cash disbursements occurred during the first week of May.

May 2   Purchased $25,000 of merchandise inventory on credit from the Sioux City Company, terms 2/10, n/30. Invoice dated May 1.
　　3   Purchased $12,000 of merchandise inventory on credit from the Wichita Company, terms 2/10, n/30. Invoice dated May 2.
　　3   Purchased $3,000 of office supplies for cash from Bettendorf Co. Check no. 1267.
　　4   Purchased $36,000 of office equipment on credit from Office Outfitters, terms n/60. Invoice dated May 3.
　　6   Paid the amount due for the merchandise purchased from Sioux City Company. Check no. 1268.
　　6   Purchased $14,500 of merchandise inventory for cash from the Davenport Co. Check no. 1269.

Required

a. Prepare a purchases journal like that in Exhibit 12.8 and a cash disbursements journal like that in Exhibit 12.10. Number all journal pages as page 20.
b. Prepare a schedule of accounts payable as of May 31. There were no accounts payable on May 1.

connect™

Prepare journal entries to record the following merchandising transactions of Blink Company.

July 1   Purchased merchandise from Boden Company for $6,000 under credit terms of 1/15, n/30, FOB shipping point, invoice dated July 1.
       3   Paid $125 cash for freight charges on the purchase of July 1.
       9   Purchased merchandise from Leight Co. for $2,200 under credit terms of 2/15, n/60, FOB destination, invoice dated July 9.
      11   Received a $200 credit memorandum from Leight Co. for the return of part of the merchandise purchased on July 9.
      16   Paid the balance due to Boden Company within the discount period.
      24   Paid Leight Co. the balance due within the discount period.

Prepare journal entries to record the following merchandising transactions of Sheng Company.

Aug. 1   Purchased merchandise from Arotek Company for $7,500 under credit terms of 1/10, n/30, invoice dated August 1.
       8   Purchased merchandise from Waters Corporation for $5,400 under credit terms of 1/10, n/45, FOB shipping point, invoice dated August 8. The invoice showed that at Sheng's request, Waters paid the $140 shipping charges and added that amount to the bill. (*Recall:* Discounts are not applied to freight and shipping charges.)
      12   After negotiations with Waters Corporation concerning problems with the merchandise purchased on August 8, Sheng received a credit memorandum from Waters granting a price reduction of $700.
      18   Paid the amount due Waters Corporation for the August 8 purchase less the price reduction granted.
      30   Paid Arotek Company the amount due from the August 1 purchase.

Gomez Corp. has the following credit purchase transactions in the month of October.

Oct. 4   Purchased merchandise from Benjamin Inc. under the following terms, $950 price, invoice date 10/2, credit terms n/30, freight $62.
       7   Purchased merchandise from Rachel Inc. under the following terms: $1,350, invoice date 10/5, credit terms 2/10, n/30, freight $92.
       9   Purchased merchandise from Bethany Co. under the following terms: $725, invoice date 10/8, credit terms n/30, freight $65.
      13   Purchased merchandise from Benjamin Inc. under the following terms: $1,350, invoice date 10/12, credit terms n/30, freight $117.
      14   Purchased merchandise from Matthew Inc. under the following terms: $657, invoice date 10/14, credit terms 2/10, n/30, freight $23.

Required

1. Account for these purchases in a purchases journal using Accounts Payable (acct. #207), Purchases (acct. #502) and Transportation-In (acct. #503). The purchases journal page is page 4. Include the invoice date and credit terms.
2. Post these accounts to the general ledger (including the references).
3. Post these accounts to the accounts payable subsidiary ledger.

Prepare journal entries to record the following merchandising transactions of Yarvelle Company.

May 2   Purchased merchandise from Havel Co. for $10,000 under credit terms of 1/15, n/30, FOB shipping point, invoice dated May 2.
      5   Paid $250 cash for freight charges on the purchase of May 2.
     10   Purchased merchandise from Duke Co. for $3,650 under credit terms of 2/15, n/60, FOB destination, invoice dated May 10.
     12   Received a $400 credit memorandum from Duke Co. for the return of part of the merchandise purchased on May 10.
     17   Paid the balance due to Havel Co. within the discount period.
     25   Paid Duke Co. the balance due within the discount period.

Problem 12-2B

Preparing journal entries for
merchandising activities   **LO1**

Prepare journal entries to record the following merchandising transactions of Mason Company.

July 3   Purchased merchandise from OLB Corp. for $15,000 under credit terms of 1/10, n/30, FOB
destination, invoice dated July 3.

10   Purchased merchandise from Rupert Corporation for $14,200 under credit terms of 1/10, n/45,
FOB shipping point, invoice dated July 10. The invoice showed that at Mason's request, Rupert
paid the $500 shipping charges and added that amount to the bill. (*Recall:* Discounts are not
applied to freight and shipping charges.)

14   After negotiations with Rupert Corporation concerning problems with the merchandise purchased on July 10, Mason received a credit memorandum from Rupert granting a price reduction of $2,000.

20   Paid the amount due Rupert Corporation for the July 10 purchase less the price reduction
granted.

31   Paid OLB Corp. the amount due from the July 3 purchase.

Check   July 20, Cr. Cash, $12,578
July 31, Cr. Cash, $15,000

Problem 12-3B

Purchases journal and accounts
payable subsidiary ledger
LO2   LO3

Beach Corp. has the following credit purchase transactions in the month of January.

Jan. 5   Purchased merchandise from Bethany Inc. under the following terms: $725, invoice date 1/4,
credit terms 2/10, n/30, freight $65.

9   Purchased merchandise from Daniel Inc. under the following terms: $1,650, invoice date 1/8,
credit terms n/30, freight $109.

14   Purchased merchandise from David Co. under the following terms: $673, invoice date 1/12,
credit terms n/30, freight $57.

22   Purchased merchandise from Bethany Inc. under the following terms: $675, invoice date 1/21,
credit terms 2/10, n/30, freight $123.

28   Purchased merchandise from Mason Inc. under the following terms: $553, invoice date 1/28,
credit terms 2/10, n/30, freight $52.

Required

1. Account for these purchases in a purchases journal using Accounts Payable (acct. #207), Purchases
(acct. #502), and Transportation-In (acct. #503). The purchases journal page is page 3. Include the
invoice date and credit terms.
2. Post these accounts to the general ledger (including the references).
3. Post these accounts to the accounts payable subsidiary ledger.

PRACTICE SET 1

Wiset Corp.
Special journals, subsidiary
ledgers, and schedule of
accounts receivable
LO2   LO3   LO4

connect™

Wiset Company completes these transactions during April of the current year (the terms of all its credit
sales are 2/10, n/30).

Apr. 2   Purchased $14,300 of merchandise on credit from Noth Company, invoice dated April 2, terms
2/10, n/60.

3   Sold merchandise on credit to Page Alistair, Invoice No. 760, for $4,000.

3   Purchased $1,480 of office supplies on credit from Custer, Inc., invoice dated April 2, terms
n/10 EOM.

4   Issued Check No. 587 to *World View* for advertising expense, $899.

5   Sold merchandise on credit to Paula Kohr, Invoice No. 761, for $8,000.

6   Received an $80 credit memorandum from Custer, Inc., for the return of some of the office
supplies received on April 3.

9   Purchased $12,125 of store equipment on credit from Hal's Supply, invoice dated April 9, terms
n/10 EOM.

11   Sold merchandise on credit to Nic Nelson, Invoice No. 762, for $10,500.

12   Issued Check No. 588 to Noth Company in payment of its April 2 invoice, less the discount.

13   Received payment from Page Alistair for the April 3 sale, less the discount.

13   Sold $5,100 of merchandise on credit to Page Alistair, Invoice No. 763.

14   Received payment from Paula Kohr for the April 5 sale, less the discount.

16   Issued Check No. 589, payable to Payroll, in payment of sales salaries expense for the first half of the month, $10,750. Cashed the check and paid employees.

16   Cash sales for the first half of the month are $52,840. (Cash sales are recorded daily from cash register data but are recorded only twice in this problem to reduce repetitive entries.)

17   Purchased $13,750 of merchandise on credit from Grant Company, invoice dated April 17, terms 2/10, n/30.

18   Borrowed $60,000 cash from First State Bank by signing a long-term note payable.

20   Received payment from Nic Nelson for the April 11 sale, less the discount.

20   Purchased $830 of store supplies on credit from Hal's Supply, invoice dated April 19, terms n/10 EOM.

23   Received a $750 credit memorandum from Grant Company for the return of defective merchandise received on April 17.

23   Received payment from Page Alistair for the April 13 sale, less the discount.

25   Purchased $11,375 of merchandise on credit from Noth Company, invoice dated April 24, terms 2/10, n/60.

26   Issued Check No. 590 to Grant Company in payment of its April 17 invoice, less the return and the discount.

27   Sold $3,170 of merchandise on credit to Paula Kohr, Invoice No. 764.

27   Sold $6,700 of merchandise on credit to Nic Nelson, Invoice No. 765.

30   Issued Check No. 591, payable to Payroll, in payment of the sales salaries expense for the last half of the month, $10,750.

30   Cash sales for the last half of the month are $73,975.

Required

1. Prepare a general journal, a purchases journal like that in Exhibit 12.8, and a cash disbursements journal like that in Exhibit 12.10. Number all journal pages as page 3. Review the April transactions of Wiset Company and enter those transactions that should be journalized in the general journal, the purchases journal, or the cash disbursements journal. Ignore any transactions that should be journalized in a sales journal or cash receipts journal.

2. Open the following general ledger accounts: Cash, Inventory, Office Supplies, Store Supplies, Store Equipment, Accounts Payable, Long-Term Notes Payable, Purchases, Purchases Returns and Allowances, Purchases Discounts, Sales Salaries Expense, and Advertising Expense. Enter the March 31 balances of Cash ($85,000), Inventory ($125,000), and Long-Term Notes Payable ($210,000). Also open accounts payable subsidiary ledger accounts for Hal's Supply, Noth Company, Grant Company, and Custer, Inc.

3. Verify that amounts that should be posted as individual amounts from the journals have been posted. (Such items are immediately posted.) Foot and crossfoot the journals and make the month-end postings.

4. Prepare a trial balance of the general ledger and a schedule of accounts payable as of April 30.

Check   Trial balance totals, $237,026

Acorn Industries completes these transactions during July of the current year (the terms of all its credit sales are 2/10, n/30).

July   1   Purchased $6,500 of merchandise on credit from Teton Company, invoice dated June 30, terms 2/10, n/30.

3   Issued Check No. 300 to *The Weekly* for advertising expense, $625.

5   Sold merchandise on credit to Kim Nettle, Invoice No. 918, for $19,200.

6   Sold merchandise on credit to Ruth Blake, Invoice No. 919, for $7,500.

7   Purchased $1,250 of store supplies on credit from Plaine, Inc., invoice dated July 7, terms n/10 EOM.

8   Received a $250 credit memorandum from Plaine, Inc., for the return of store supplies received on July 7.

9   Purchased $38,220 of store equipment on credit from Charm's Supply, invoice dated July 8, terms n/10 EOM.

10   Issued Check No. 301 to Teton Company in payment of its June 30 invoice, less the discount.

13   Sold merchandise on credit to Ashton Moore, Invoice No. 920, for $8,550.

14   Sold merchandise on credit to Kim Nettle, Invoice No. 921, for $5,100.

PRACTICE SET 2

Acorn Co.

Special journals, subsidiary ledgers, schedule of accounts receivable   **LO2   LO3   LO4**

15   Received payment from Kim Nettle for the July 5 sale, less the discount.

15   Issued Check No. 302, payable to Payroll, in payment of sales salaries expense for the first half of the month, $31,850. Cashed the check and paid employees.

15   Cash sales for the first half of the month are $118,350 (cost is $76,330). (Cash sales are recorded daily using data from the cash registers but are recorded only twice in this problem to reduce repetitive entries.)

16   Received payment from Ruth Blake for the July 6 sale, less the discount.

17   Purchased $7,200 of merchandise on credit from Drake Company, invoice dated July 17, terms 2/10, n/30.

20   Purchased $650 of office supplies on credit from Charm's Supply, invoice dated July 19, terms n/10 EOM.

21   Borrowed $15,000 cash from College Bank by signing a long-term note payable.

23   Received payment from Ashton Moore for the July 13 sale, less the discount.

24   Received payment from Kim Nettle for the July 14 sale, less the discount.

24   Received a $2,400 credit memorandum from Drake Company for the return of defective merchandise received on July 17.

26   Purchased $9,770 of merchandise on credit from Teton Company, invoice dated July 26, terms 2/10, n/30.

27   Issued Check No. 303 to Drake Company in payment of its July 17 invoice, less the return and the discount.

29   Sold merchandise on credit to Ruth Blake, Invoice No. 922, for $17,500.

30   Sold merchandise on credit to Ashton Moore, Invoice No. 923, for $16,820.

31   Issued Check No. 304, payable to Payroll, in payment of the sales salaries expense for the last half of the month, $31,850.

31   Cash sales for the last half of the month are $80,244.

Required

1. Prepare a general journal, a purchases journal like that in Exhibit 12.8, and a cash disbursements journal like that in Exhibit 12.10. Number all journal pages as page 3. Review the July transactions of Acorn Company and enter those transactions that should be journalized in the general journal, the purchases journal, or the cash disbursements journal. Ignore any transaction that should be journalized in a sales journal or cash receipts journal.

2. Open the following general ledger accounts: Cash, Inventory, Office Supplies, Store Supplies, Store Equipment, Accounts Payable, Long-Term Notes Payable, Purchases, Purchases Returns and Allowances, Purchases Discounts, Sales Salaries Expense, and Advertising Expense. Enter the June 30 balances of Cash ($100,000), Inventory ($200,000), and Long-Term Notes Payable ($300,000). Also open accounts payable subsidiary ledger accounts for Teton Company, Plaine, Inc., Charm's Supply, and Drake Company.

3. Verify that amounts that should be posted as individual amounts from the journals have been posted. (Such items are immediately posted.) Foot and crossfoot the journals and make the month-end postings.

Check Trial balance totals, $352,266

4. Prepare a trial balance of the general ledger and a schedule of accounts payable.

SERIAL PROBLEM

Success Systems

(This serial problem began in Chapter 1 and continues through most of the book. If previous chapter segments were not completed, the serial problem can begin at this point. It is helpful, but not necessary, that you use the Working Papers that accompany the book.)

SP 12   Adriana Lopez created Success Systems on October 1, 2010. The company has been successful, and its list of customers has grown. To accommodate the growth, the accounting system is modified to set up separate accounts for each customer. The following chart of accounts includes the account number used for each account and any balance as of December 31, 2010. These balances are taken from SP 5. Lopez decided to add a fourth digit with a decimal point to the 106 account number that had been used for the single Accounts Receivable account. This modification allows the company to continue using the existing chart of accounts. For simplicity, ignore payroll taxes and sales taxes in this problem.

No.	Account Title	Dr.	Cr.
101	Cash	$80,260	
106.1	Alex's Engineering Co.	0	
106.2	Wildcat Services	0	
106.3	Easy Leasing	0	
106.4	Clark Co.	2,300	
106.5	Chang Corp.	0	
106.6	Gomez Co.	3,500	
106.7	Delta Co.	0	
106.8	KC, Inc.	0	
106.9	Dream, Inc.	0	
106.10	Bob Building Co.	0	
119	Merchandise inventory	0	
126	Computer supplies	775	
128	Prepaid insurance	1,800	
131	Prepaid rent	875	
163	Office equipment	10,000	
164	Accumulated depreciation—Office equipment		625
167	Computer equipment	25,000	
168	Accumulated depreciation—Computer equipment		1,250
201	Accounts payable		2,100

No.	Account Title	Dr.	Cr.
210	Wages payable		600
236	Unearned computer services revenue		2,500
301	A. Lopez, Capital		117,435
302	A. Lopez, Withdrawals	0	
403	Computer services revenue		0
413	Sales		0
414	Sales returns and allowances	0	
415	Sales discounts	0	
505	Purchases	0	
506	Purchase returns and allowances		0
507	Purchase discounts		0
508	Transportation-In	0	
612	Depreciation expense—Office equipment	0	
613	Depreciation expense—Computer equipment	0	
623	Wages expense	0	
637	Insurance expense	0	
640	Rent expense	0	
652	Computer supplies expense	0	
655	Advertising expense	0	
676	Mileage expense	0	
677	Miscellaneous expenses	0	
684	Repairs expense—Computer	0	

In response to requests from customers, Lopez will begin selling computer software. The company will extend credit terms of 1/10, n/30, FOB shipping point, to all customers who purchase this merchandise. However, no cash discount is available on consulting fees. Additional accounts (Nos. 119, 413, 414, 415, 505, 506, 507, and 508) are added to its general ledger to accommodate the company's new merchandising activities. All revenue and expense accounts have zero balances as of January 1, 2011. Its transactions for January through March follow:

Jan. 4 Paid cash to Michelle Jones for five days' work at the rate of $150 per day. Four of the five days relate to wages payable that were accrued in the prior year.

5 Adriana Lopez invested an additional $10,000 cash in the business.

7 Purchased $5,700 of merchandise from Kansas Corp. with terms of 1/10, n/30, FOB shipping point, invoice dated January 7.

9 Received $3,500 cash from Gomez Co. as full payment on its account.

11 Completed a five-day project for Bob's Building Co. and billed it $6,500.

13 Sold merchandise with a retail value of $6,000 to Chang Corp., invoice dated January 13.

15 Paid $400 cash for freight charges on the merchandise purchased on January 7.

16 Received $5,600 cash from Delta Co. for computer services provided.

17 Paid Kansas Corp. for the invoice dated January 7, net of the discount.

20 Chang Corp. returned $500 of defective merchandise from its invoice dated January 13. The returned merchandise is discarded. (The policy of Success Systems is to not adjust its accounts for returned merchandise.)

22 Received the balance due from Chang Corp., net of both the discount and the credit for the returned merchandise.

24 Returned defective merchandise to Kansas Corp. and accepted a credit against future purchases. The defective merchandise invoice cost, net of the discount, was $496.

26 Purchased $9,500 of merchandise from Kansas Corp. with terms of 1/10, n/30, FOB destination, invoice dated January 26.

26 Sold merchandise for $4,700 on credit to KC, Inc., invoice dated January 26.

29 Received a $496 credit memorandum from Kansas Corp. concerning the merchandise returned on January 24.

31 Paid cash to Michelle Jones for 10 days' work at $150 per day.

Feb. 1 Paid $2,625 cash to Summit Mall for another three months' rent in advance. (Debit Prepaid Rent, an asset.)

      3 Paid Kansas Corp. for the balance due, net of the cash discount, less the $496 amount in the credit memorandum.

      5 Paid $800 cash to the local newspaper for an advertising insert in today's paper.

    11 Received the balance due from Bob's Building Co. for fees billed on January 11.

    15 Adriana Lopez withdrew $5,200 cash for personal use.

    23 Sold merchandise for $3,800 on credit to Delta Co., invoice dated February 23.

    26 Paid cash to Michelle Jones for eight days' work at $150 per day.

    27 Reimbursed Adriana Lopez for business automobile mileage (1,000 miles at $0.32 per mile).

Mar. 8 Purchased $3,250 of computer supplies from Cain Office Products on credit, invoice dated March 8.

     9 Received the balance due from Delta Co. for merchandise sold on February 23.

    11 Paid $1,200 cash for minor repairs to the company's computer.

    16 Received $6,250 cash from Dream, Inc., for computing services provided.

    19 Paid the full amount due to Cain Office Products, including amounts created on December 15 (of $2,100) and March 8.

    24 Billed Easy Leasing for $11,000 of computing services provided.

    25 Sold merchandise for $3,900 on credit to Wildcat Services, invoice dated March 25.

    30 Sold merchandise for $2,500 on credit to Clark Company, invoice dated March 30.

    31 Reimbursed Adriana Lopez for business automobile mileage (600 miles at $0.32 per mile).

Required

1. Prepare journal entries to record each of the January through March transactions.

2. Post the journal entries in part 1 to the accounts in the company's general ledger. (*Note:* Begin with the ledger's post-closing adjusted balances as of December 31, 2010.)

3. Prepare the unadjusted trial balance.

Check (2) Ending balances: Cash, $87,266; Sales, $20,900;

(3) Unadj. totals, $182,708

BEYOND THE NUMBERS

REPORTING IN ACTION
LO1

BTN 12–1   Refer to **Best Buy**'s financial statements in Appendix A to answer the following.

Best Buy includes freight costs in the merchandise inventory account. List three such costs, using information in footnote 1 for the fiscal year ended March 1, 2008.

ETHICS CHALLENGE
LO1

BTN 12–2   As the new credit manager, you are being trained by the outgoing manager. She explains that the system prepares checks for amounts net of favorable cash discounts, and the checks are dated the last day of the discount period. She also tells you that checks are not mailed until five days later, adding that "the company gets free use of cash for an extra five days, and our department looks better. When a supplier complains, we blame the computer system and the mailroom."

Required

1. In your view, is the company currently abusing its suppliers' cash discount policy? Explain.

2. Is it appropriate to indicate that the late payments are due to computer or mail problems? Explain.

3. Assume you feel uncomfortable with your company taking the suppliers' cash discounts. What steps could you take to remedy the situation?

TAKING IT TO THE NET
LO1

BTN 12–3   Access the Association of Certified Fraud Examiner's website (http://www.acfe.com/).

Required

Use the search terms "fraud and purchases" and find the discussion on fraud that can occur associated with purchases. List and explain three types of fraud associated with purchases.

BTN 12–4   Refer to the opening feature about CoCaLo. Assume that Renee Pepys Lowe considers using a purchases journal for its purchases.

In a brief memo, in your role as accountant for CoCaLo, explain the costs and benefits of using a purchases journal instead of a general journal.

ENTREPRENEURS IN BUSINESS

LO2

1. d.
2. d; ($4,500 − $250) × (100% − 2%) = $4,165
3. b.
4. e.
5. a.

ANSWERS TO MULTIPLE CHOICE QUIZ

A Look Back

Chapter 12 considered the accounting for merchandise purchases. We also explained the use of the purchases journal, the cash disbursements journal, and the accounts payable subsidiary ledger.

A Look at This Chapter

Chapter 13 shows adjusting entries for a merchandising business. We present the adjustments needed for inventory and show how a trial balance is useful in organizing information for a merchandiser. We also show the adjustments for accrued revenues and unearned revenues.

A Look Ahead

In Chapter 14 we show how to prepare classified income statements and balance sheets for a merchandiser. We also explain the closing process for the merchandiser.

Chapter 13

Merchandiser's Adjustments and Trial Balance

Learning Objectives

LO 1   Use a trial balance for a merchandiser.

LO 2   Prepare the adjusting entries for inventory.

LO 3   Prepare adjusting entries for prepaid and accrued expenses.

LO 4   Compute net sales and net purchases.

LO 5   Compute cost of goods sold.

LO 6   Compute gross profit.

LO 7   Prepare the adjusting entry for accrued revenue.

LO 8   Prepare the adjusting entry for unearned revenue.

LO 9   *Appendix* 13A—Describe the alternatives in accounting for prepayments.

"I've always been a gambler ... but we were also growing exponentially the first few years"
—Joel Boblit

New Nightmare Freddy

Toy Story

SOMERSET, WI—Joel Boblit says his first and greatest business challenge was "being teased by my friends." But now Joel is having the time of his life. His retail business, **BigBadToyStore** (**BigBadToyStore.com**), deals in new and old action figures. Launched from his parents' basement, the store now projects over $15 million in annual sales.

But the early years were not easy. "I mortgaged everything I owned for the first two years," explains Joel. The business required a merchandising accounting system that Joel says needed to account for purchases and sales transactions. Inventory was especially important to account for. "Many of the store's customers offered inventory suggestions," explains Joel.

To succeed, Joel needed to make smart business decisions. He set up an accounting system to capture and communicate costs and sales information.

Tracking merchandising activities was necessary to set prices and to manage discounts, allowances, and returns of both sales and purchases. Joel's inventory system enabled him to stock the right type and amount of merchandise and to avoid the costs of out-of-stock and excess inventory. "We're [now] able to make much more efficient use of the space we have," recounts Joel.

Mastering accounting for merchandising is a means to an end for Joel. He says he loves his business and enjoys the nostalgia of childhood toys. Joel insists, however, that he will continue to take risks. "I've always been a gambler," insists Joel, and "I've always [believed] ... that the harder you work, the more you'll be paid."

[Sources: *BigBadToyStore* Website, January 2009; *Entrepreneur,* December and October 2005; *St. Croix Chronicle,* March–April 2005; *Alma Matters,* Fall 2005; *YouMakeMillions.blogspot.com,* May 2007]

Previous chapters showed how a merchandising business records sales and purchases. In this chapter we show how the merchandiser can use a trial balance to summarize the results of sale and purchase transactions. We then show how the merchandiser adjusts its Merchandise Inventory account. The chapter also reviews the adjusting entries for prepaid and accrued expenses and shows the adjusting entries for accrued and unearned revenues.

Merchandiser's Adjustments and Trial Balance

Merchandiser's Trial Balance
- Using a trial balance
- Inventory adjustments

Expense Adjustments
- Adjusting process
- Prepaid expenses
- Accrued expenses

Partial Work Sheet
- Adjusted trial balance
- Net sales and net purchases
- Cost of goods sold
- Gross profit

Revenue Adjustments
- Accrued revenues
- Unearned revenues

Merchandiser's Trial Balance

In Chapter 11 we showed how to record individual sales transactions for Z-Mart, a merchandiser. In Chapter 12 we showed how to record Z-Mart's individual purchase transactions. After recording all of its sales and purchase transactions, and other transactions for the year ending December 31, 2010, Z-Mart reports the unadjusted trial balance shown in Exhibit 13.1.

Exhibit 13.1

Unadjusted Trial Balance for a Merchandiser

Under a periodic system, the unadjusted balance in the Merchandise Inventory account is its balance as of the end of the previous accounting period.

Chapter 11 shows how to record sales transactions.

Chapter 12 shows how to record purchase transactions.

No.	Account	Debit	Credit
	Z-MART Unadjusted Trial Balance December 31, 2010		
101	Cash	8,200	
106	Accounts receivable	11,200	
119	**Merchandise Inventory**	**19,000**	
126	Supplies	3,800	
128	Prepaid insurance	900	
167	Equipment	34,200	
168	Accumulated depr.—Equip.		3,700
201	Accounts payable		16,000
301	K. Marty, Capital		42,600
302	K. Marty, Withdrawals	4,000	
413	**Sales**		**321,000**
414	**Sales returns and allowances**	**2,000**	
415	**Sales discounts**	**4,300**	
505	**Purchases**	**235,800**	
506	**Purchases returns and allowance**		**1,500**
507	**Purchases discounts**		**4,200**
508	**Transportation-in**	**2,300**	
622	Salaries expense	43,000	
640	Rent expense	9,000	
655	Advertising expense	11,300	
	Totals	389,000	389,000

Using a Trial Balance

Z-Mart's unadjusted trial balance in Exhibit 13.1 shows several items important for a merchandiser. First, Z-Mart reports $19,000 of merchandise inventory. **Merchandise inventory,** or simply **inventory,** refers to products that a merchandiser owns and intends to sell. Since Z-Mart uses a periodic inventory system, this $19,000 is the cost of inventory as of the end of the previous accounting period. As we showed in Chapters 11 and 12, Z-Mart has made no journal entries involving the Merchandise Inventory account during the year. Second, the trial balance reports Z-Mart's total sales ($321,000), sales returns and allowances ($2,000), and sales discounts ($4,300). Third, the trial balance reports Z-Mart's total purchases of inventory ($235,800), purchases returns and allowances ($1,500), purchase discounts ($4,200), and transportation-in ($2,300). These additional accounts are not found in a service company's trial balance. We show how a merchandiser adjusts its Merchandise Inventory account next.

LO1 Use a trial balance for a merchandiser.

Adjusting Entries for Merchandise Inventory

The December 31, 2010, balance in Merchandise Inventory ($19,000) on Z-Mart's unadjusted trial balance in Exhibit 13.1 has not changed since the beginning of the year. However, a physical count shows $21,000 of inventory in Z-Mart's warehouse at the end of the year. Z-Mart now needs to prepare two adjusting entries using this account. These entries will:

LO2 Prepare the adjusting entries for inventory.

1. Replace the beginning inventory balance with its correct ending balance.
2. Aid in reflecting cost of goods sold in the Income Summary account.

As we show later in this chapter, beginning and ending inventory amounts are used in computing cost of goods sold. As part of the closing process (described in Chapter 6 and reviewed in Chapter 14), the temporary account Income Summary is used to close temporary accounts. The Income Summary account is also used to adjust the Merchandise Inventory balance under a periodic system. We show Z-Mart's inventory adjusting entries, with T-account postings, next. We label these entries with BI (for beginning inventory) or EI (for ending inventory).

Entry 1: Transfer beginning inventory balance to Income Summary

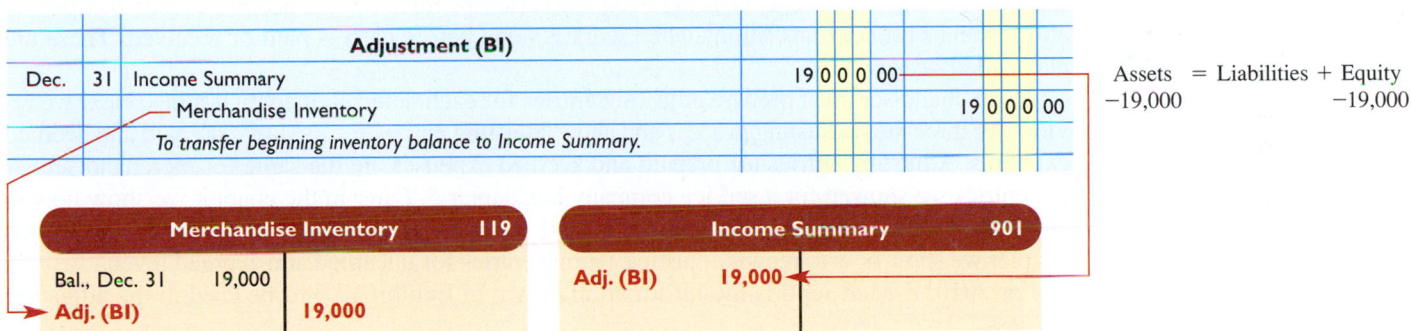

Entry 2: Record ending inventory balance

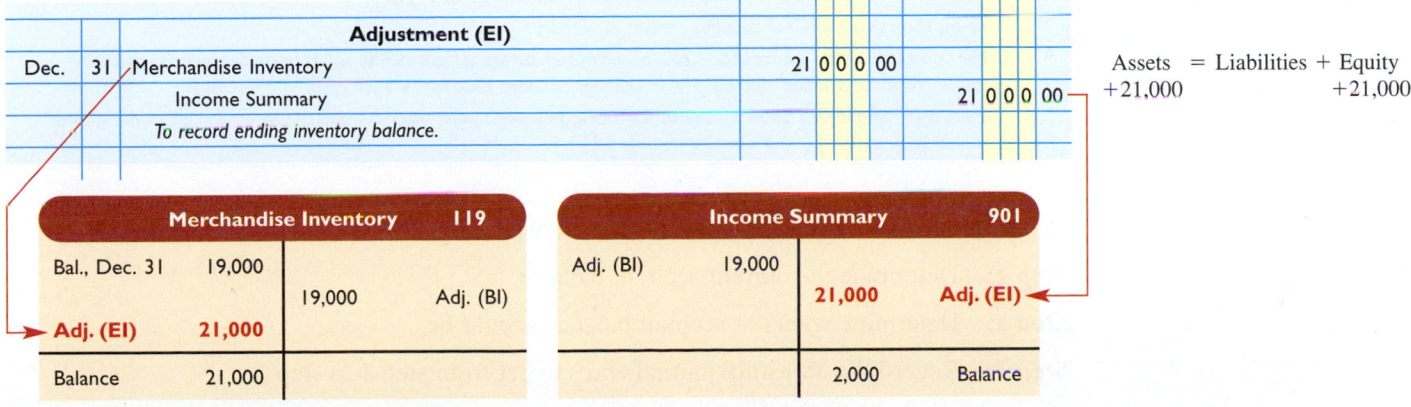

After posting entries BI and EI, the Income Summary account has a $2,000 credit balance. In Chapter 14 we illustrate the closing process for the merchandiser's Income Summary account.

Expense Adjustments

Adjusting Process

LO3 Prepare adjusting entries for prepaid and accrued expenses.

Exhibit 13.2 revisits a summary of the types of adjustments. Accrual basis accounting requires adjustments for transactions where cash receipts or payments do not occur in the same accounting period as work performed. Recall that these adjusting entries will always involve at least one income statement account and at least one balance sheet account. The cash account never appears in an adjusting entry.

Exhibit 13.2

Types of Adjustments

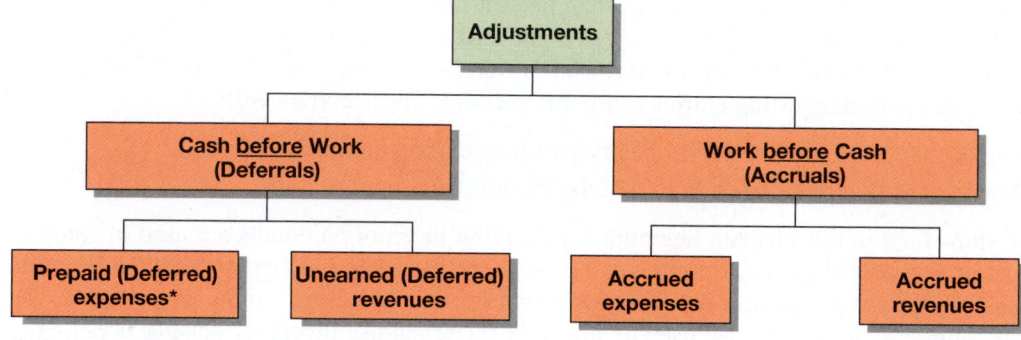

*Includes depreciation.

Prepaid expenses and unearned revenues reflect transactions where cash is paid or received before a related expense or revenue is recognized. They are also called *deferrals* because the recognition of an expense or revenue is *deferred* until after the related work is done. Accrued expenses and revenues reflect transactions when work is done before cash is paid or received. These are also called *accruals*.

A merchandiser must prepare adjusting entries for each deferral or accrual it has. Next we review our three-step adjusting process and show adjusting entries for Z-Mart's prepaid and accrued expenses. Adjusting entries for prepaid and accrued expenses are the same for merchandisers as the entries we showed for a service company in Chapter 5. Later in the chapter we show how to enter those adjusting entries on a (partial) work sheet for a merchandiser. Near the end of this chapter we show how to record adjusting journal entries for unearned and accrued revenues.

For 2010, Z-Mart reports the information shown in Exhibit 13.3 to be used in the adjusting process.

Exhibit 13.3

Information for Z-Mart's Expense Adjustments

> **a.** A review shows that $300 of insurance policies remain unexpired at year-end.
>
> **b.** A count shows that $800 of supplies remain at year-end.
>
> **c.** Z-Mart's equipment has a cost of $34,200, an estimated salvage value of $900, and is being depreciated over nine years using the straight-line method. The equipment has been used for two full years.
>
> **d.** Z-Mart owes employees $800 in salaries for work they performed near the end of December and will be paid for in early January.

Recall our three-step adjusting process from Chapter 5:

Step 1:   Determine the current account balance.

Step 2:   Determine what the account balance should be.

Step 3:   Record the adjusting journal entry to get from step 1 to step 2.

We apply this three-step process below to Z-Mart's information in Exhibit 13.3.

Adjusting Prepaid Expenses (Including Depreciation)

Prepaid Insurance

Step 1:   Z-Mart's trial balance in Exhibit 13.1 shows the Prepaid Insurance account has an unadjusted balance of $900.

Step 2:   As time passes, the benefits of the insurance gradually expire and some of the Prepaid Insurance asset becomes expense. At December 31, 2010, only $300 of the Prepaid Insurance asset has a future benefit to Z-Mart. The $600 difference ($900 − $300) should be recorded as insurance expense for the year.

Step 3:   The adjusting entry to record this expense and reduce the asset, along with postings to T-accounts, follows:

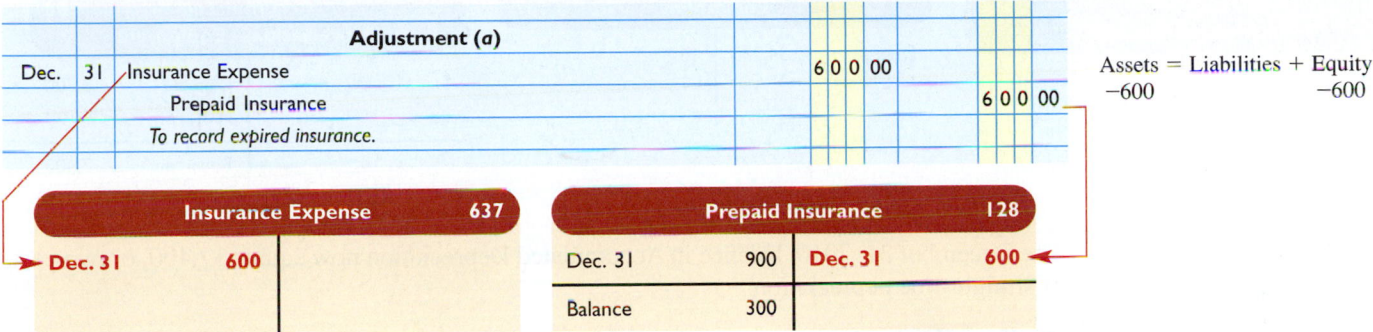

Assets = Liabilities + Equity
−600   −600

Supplies

Step 1:   Z-Mart's trial balance in Exhibit 13.1 shows the Supplies account has an unadjusted balance of $3,800.

Step 2:   On December 31, Z-Mart counts its *unused* supplies and finds $800 remaining. The $3,000 difference between these two amounts ($3,800 − $800) is the year's supplies expense.

Step 3:   The adjusting entry to record this expense and reduce the Supplies asset account, along with T-account postings, follows:

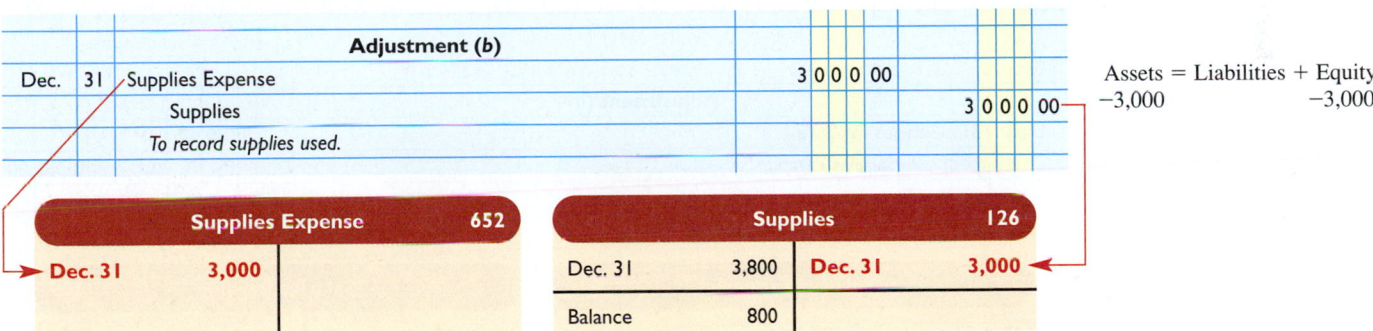

Assets = Liabilities + Equity
−3,000   −3,000

Equipment

Step 1:   From the trial balance in Exhibit 13.1, Z-Mart's equipment cost $34,200, and its related Accumulated Depreciation account has an unadjusted balance of $3,700 on December 31, 2010.

Step 2:   Since Z-Mart has used the equipment for two full years, the Accumulated Depreciation account, after adjustment, should equal two full years of depreciation. The equipment is expected to have a useful life (benefit period) of nine years. Using straight-line depreciation, Z-Mart's annual depreciation expense is:

$$\text{Annual depreciation expense} = \frac{\text{Cost} - \text{Salvage value}}{\text{Useful life}}$$

$$= \frac{(\$34,200 - 900)}{9 \text{ years}} = \$3,700 \text{ per year}$$

Thus, Z-Mart should record $3,700 of depreciation expense and increase the balance in its Accumulated Depreciation account by $3,700.

Step 3:   The adjusting entry to record depreciation expense, along with T-account postings follows:

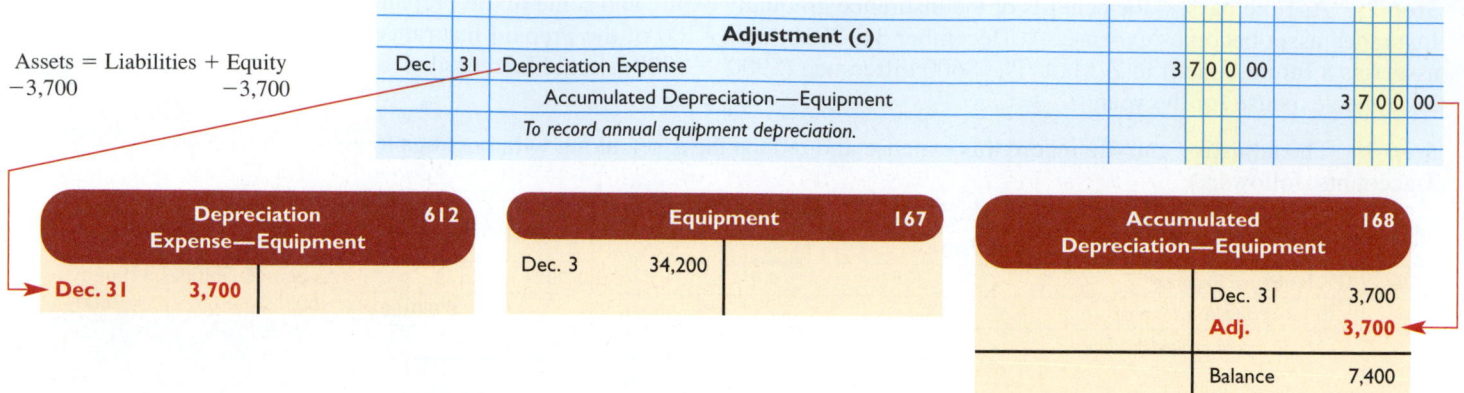

Assets = Liabilities + Equity
−3,700   −3,700

The December 31, 2010, balance in Accumulated Depreciation now equals $7,400, or two years of straight-line depreciation.

Adjusting Accrued Expenses

Accrued Salaries

Step 1:   Z-Mart owes its employees $800 for work they performed just before the end of the year. Z-Mart will pay the employees in early January of the next year. Z-Mart's balance in Salaries Payable is $0.

Step 2:   Z-Mart owes its employees $800 and thus needs to record a liability of $800 and increase its salaries expense by $800.

Step 3:   The adjusting entry to record accrued salaries, along with T-account postings, follows:

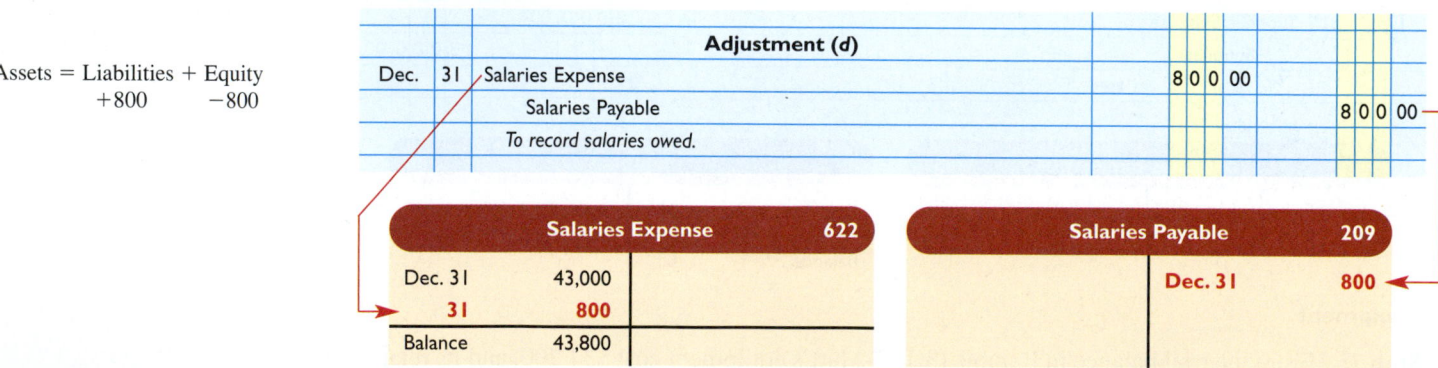

Assets = Liabilities + Equity
          +800   −800

Partial Work Sheet

Adjusted Trial Balance

After journalizing and posting the adjusting entries above, Z-Mart's partial work sheet (through the Adjusted Trial Balance columns) appears in Exhibit 13.4. As we discussed earlier, this (partial) work sheet includes accounts, such as Merchandise Inventory, Sales, and Purchases, that did not apply to the service company we studied earlier. In addition, this work sheet adds a row for

Income Summary so that we can include the adjusting entries for Merchandise Inventory. Recall from Chapter 6 that Income Summary is primarily used in the closing process (which we revisit in Chapter 14). If a business uses a periodic inventory system, like Z-Mart, then the Income Summary account is also used in the adjusting process. We also add a row for the accounts that appeared in our adjusting journal entries, including Salaries Payable, Depreciation Expense-Equipment, Insurance Expense, and Advertising Expense.

Exhibit 13.4

Z-Mart Adjusted Trial Balance and Partial Work Sheet

		Unadjusted Trial Balance		Adjustments		Adjusted Trial Balance	
No.	Account	Dr.	Cr.	Dr.	Cr.	Dr.	Cr.
101	Cash	8,200				8,200	
106	Accounts receivable	11,200				11,200	
119	Merchandise Inventory	19,000		(EI) 21,000	(BI) 19,000	21,000	
126	Supplies	3,800			(b) 3,000	800	
128	Prepaid insurance	900			(a) 600	300	
167	Equipment	34,200				34,200	
168	Accumulated depr.—Equip.		3,700		(c) 3,700		7,400
201	Accounts payable		16,000				16,000
209	Salaries payable		0		(d) 800		800
301	K. Marty, Capital		42,600				42,600
302	K. Marty, Withdrawals	4,000				4,000	
901	Income summary			(BI) 19,000	(EI) 21,000	19,000	21,000
413	Sales		321,000				321,000
414	Sales returns and allowances	2,000				2,000	
415	Sales discounts	4,300				4,300	
505	Purchases	235,800				235,800	
506	Purchases returns & allowance		1,500				1,500
507	Purchases discounts		4,200				4,200
508	Transportation-in	2,300				2,300	
612	Depreciation expense—Equip.	0		(c) 3,700		3,700	
622	Salaries expense	43,000		(d) 800		43,800	
637	Insurance expense	0		(a) 600		600	
640	Rent expense	9,000				9,000	
652	Supplies expense	0		(b) 3,000		3,000	
655	Advertising expense	11,300				11,300	
	Totals	389,000	389,000	48,100	48,100	414,500	414,500
	Net income						

Note that the debit and credit adjustment amounts for Income Summary are *both* extended into the Adjusted Trial Balance columns. This is helpful in preparing financial statements from the work sheet. In the next chapter we show how to extend this work sheet to prepare financial statements and prepare the closing entries for a merchandiser. Next we show how to use the adjusted trial balance in this partial work sheet to compute key summary measures for a merchandiser.

HOW YOU DOIN'?

Answers—p. 332

1. If the Prepaid Insurance account has an unadjusted balance of $3,200, and $2,000 of insurance policies remain unexpired at the end of the year, what is the amount of Insurance Expense for the year?

2. If the Supplies account has an unadjusted balance of $1,400 and a count shows that $620 of supplies remain at the end of the year, what is the amount of Supplies Expense for the year?

3. A machine with a four-year useful life and $2,000 salvage value was purchased for $22,000. Using the straight-line method, what is the annual depreciation expense on this machine?

Computing Net Sales and Net Purchases for a Merchandiser

LO4 Compute net sales and net purchases.

Net income to a merchandiser equals revenues from selling merchandise minus both the cost of merchandise sold during the period and the amount of other expenses for the period (see Exhibit 13.5). The usual accounting term for revenues from selling merchandise is *sales,* and the term used for the expense of buying and preparing that merchandise is **cost of goods sold** (also called *cost of sales*). Cost of goods sold is often the largest single expense on a merchandiser's income statement. **Gross profit,** also called *gross margin,* equals net sales minus the cost of goods sold, and it is used to assess a merchandiser's performance. We show how to compute net sales and net purchases next. In the next section we show to use these items to compute cost of goods sold and gross profit.

Exhibit 13.5

Computing Income for a Merchandising Company versus a Service Company

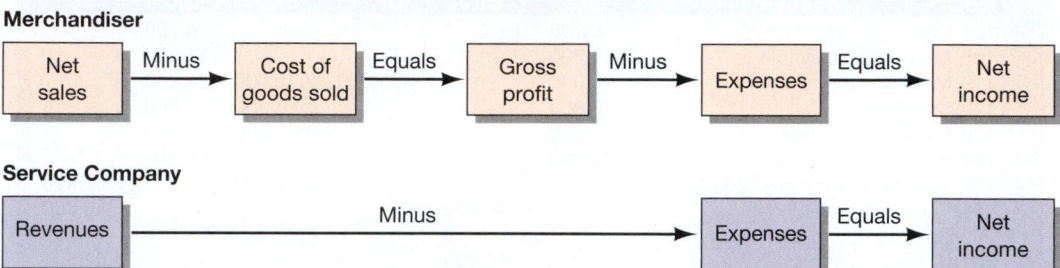

Computing Net Sales   **Net sales** is defined as sales minus sales discounts and minus sales returns and allowances. For Z-Mart for the year ending December 31, 2010, net sales is computed from its adjusted trial balance in Exhibit 13.4 as:

$$\textbf{Net sales} = \textbf{Sales} - \textbf{Sales discounts} - \textbf{Sales returns and allowances}$$

Sales		$ 321,000
Less: Sales discounts	$4,300	
Sales returns and allowances	2,000	6,300
Net sales		**$314,700**

Computing Net Purchases   We can also use Z-Mart's adjusted trial balance to compute net purchases. **Net purchases** is defined as purchases minus purchase discounts and purchase returns and allowances, plus the cost of transportation-in. For Z-Mart for the year ending December 31, 2010, net purchases is computed as:

Purchases		$235,800
Less: Purchase discounts	$4,200	
Purchase returns and allowances	1,500	(5,700)
Add: Cost of transportation-in		2,300
Net purchases		**$232,400**

Computing Cost of Goods Sold

LO5 Compute cost of goods sold.

Under a periodic inventory system, a merchandiser physically counts the number of inventory items remaining (unsold) at the end of the period, and assigns them a total cost. This information is then used along with information on beginning inventory and the net cost of purchases to compute cost of goods sold, as we show in Exhibit 13.6.

Exhibit 13.6 shows that the cost of *merchandise available for sale* equals the cost of beginning inventory plus the net purchases for the period. We obtain the cost of beginning merchandise inventory ($19,000) from the work sheet and compute net purchases ($232,400) as we showed above. So, Z-Mart had a total of $251,400 (computed as $19,000 plus $232,400) of merchandise available for sale during 2010.

As Exhibit 13.6 shows, merchandise available for sale is either sold (cost of goods sold) or not sold (ending inventory) during the period. After Z-Mart counts and assigns a cost to its ending inventory, it computes cost of goods sold for 2010 as follows:

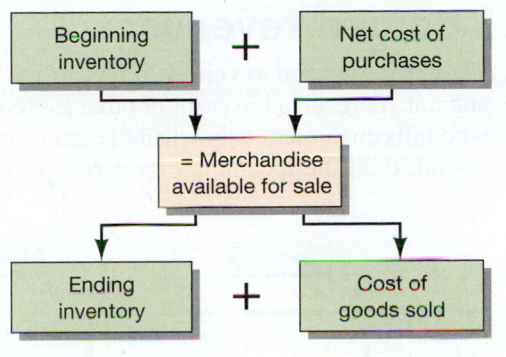

Exhibit 13.6

Merchandiser's Cost Flow for a Single Time Period

Beginning inventory	$ 19,000
Plus: Net purchases	232,400
Merchandise available for sale	$251,400
Less: Cost of ending inventory	(21,000)
Cost of goods sold	**$230,400**

Computing Gross Profit

A merchandiser is very interested in generating gross profit by selling products at prices above their costs. We compute gross profit for Z-Mart for 2010 as:

LO6 Compute gross profit.

$$\text{Gross profit} = \text{Net sales} - \text{Cost of goods sold}$$

Net sales	$314,700
Less: Cost of goods sold	230,400
Gross profit	**$84,300**

HOW YOU DOIN'?

Answers—p. 332

4. A merchandiser reports sales of $450,000, sales returns and allowances of $4,000, and sales discounts of $7,000. What is the merchandiser's net sales for the period?

5. A merchandiser reports purchases of $325,000, purchase returns and allowances of $7,000, transportation-in of $1,000, and purchase discounts of $8,000. What is the merchandiser's net purchases for the period?

6. A merchandiser reports beginning inventory of $75,000. A physical inventory count shows $42,000 of inventory remains at the end of the year. If net purchases during the year were $220,000, what is the cost of goods sold for the year? If net sales were $303,000 during the year, what is gross profit?

Revenue Adjustments

We now discuss and show how to record adjusting entries involving revenues. A business can receive cash before work is performed. As Exhibit 13.2 shows, this requires an adjustment for unearned revenue. Also, a business can have performed work for a customer, but not yet billed or received cash. As Exhibit 13.2 shows, this requires an adjustment for accrued revenue. We show each of these adjustments below for SuperSub, a sandwich shop.

LO7 Prepare the adjusting entry for accrued revenue.

Accrued Revenues

The term **accrued revenues** refers to revenues earned in a period that are both unrecorded and not yet received in cash (or other assets) at the end of the period. An example is a technician who bills customers only when the job is done. If one-third of a job is complete by the end of a period, then the technician must record one-third of the expected billing as revenue in that

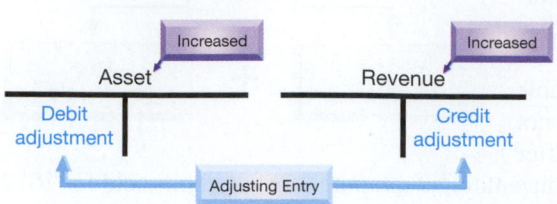

Exhibit 13.7

Adjusting for Accrued Revenues

period—even though there is no billing or collection. The adjusting entries for accrued revenues increase assets and increase revenues as shown in Exhibit 13.7. Accrued revenues commonly arise from services, products, interest, and rent. We use service fees to show how to adjust for accrued revenues.

Accrued Services Revenue   Accrued revenues are not recorded until adjusting entries are made at the end of the accounting period. These accrued revenues are earned but unrecorded because either the buyer has not yet paid for them or the seller has not yet billed the buyer. SuperSub, a submarine sandwich shop, provides an example. SuperSub has received an agreement to cater a New Year's Eve party for a group of anesthesiologists for a fixed fee of $1,800. SuperSub caters the party and then later bills for its sandwiches. The revenue recognition principle suggests that since the goods have been provided, that revenue should be recognized on SuperSub's December income statement. These $1,800 of revenues are added to the other sales SuperSub recorded during December ($9,050) as we show in the T-account below. The balance sheet also must report that the group of anesthesiologists owes SuperSub $1,800. The year-end adjusting entry to account for accrued sales revenue is

Assets = Liabilities + Equity
+1,800   +1,800

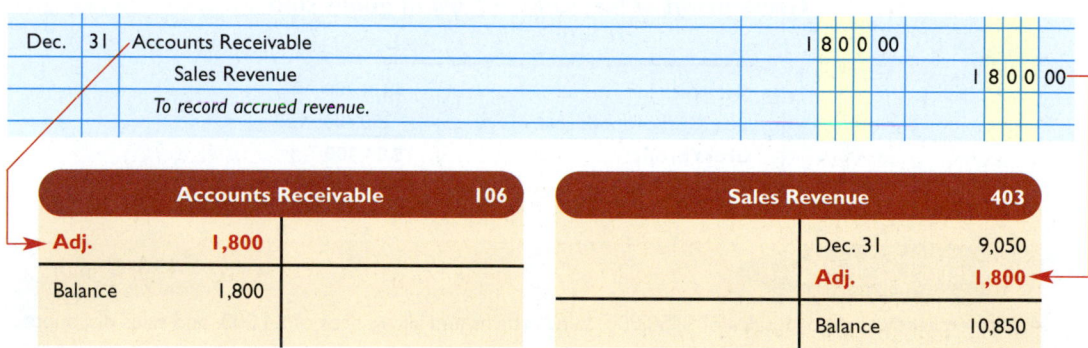

Accounts receivable are reported on the year-end balance sheet at $1,800, and an additional $1,800 of sales revenue is reported on the income statement. *Not* making the adjustment would understate (1) both sales revenue and net income by $1,800 in the December income statement and (2) both accounts receivable (assets) and equity by $1,800 on the December 31 balance sheet.

Unearned (Deferred) Revenues

LO8 Prepare the adjusting entry for unearned revenue.

The term **unearned revenues** refers to cash received in advance of providing products and services. Unearned revenues, also called *deferred revenues,* are liabilities. When cash is received in advance, an obligation to provide products or services is accepted. As products or services are provided, the unearned revenues become *earned* revenues, in line with the revenue recognition principle. Adjusting entries for unearned revenues involve increasing revenues and decreasing unearned revenues, as shown in Exhibit 13.8.

An example of unearned revenues comes from the **Boston Celtics**. When the Celtics receive cash from advance ticket sales and broadcast fees, they record it in an unearned revenue account called *Deferred Game Revenues*. The Celtics recognize this unearned revenue with adjusting entries on a game-by-game basis. Since the NBA regular season begins in October and ends in April, revenue recognition is mainly limited to this period. For a recent season, the Celtics' quarterly revenues were $0 million for July–September; $34 million for October–December; $48 million for January–March; and $17 million for April–June.

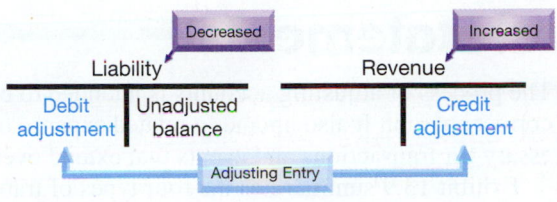

SuperSub has unearned revenues. It agreed on December 1 to provide catered lunches once a week for the local Bikers' Club for the next 10 weeks. On that same day, the Bikers' Club paid SuperSub the $3,000 fee covering the entire 10-week period. The entry to record the cash received in advance is

Exhibit 13.8
Adjusting for Unearned Revenues

Dec.	1	Cash	3 0 0 0 00	
		Unearned Sales Revenue		3 0 0 0 00
		Received advance payment for catering.		

Assets = Liabilities + Equity
+3,000   +3,000

This advance payment increases cash and creates an obligation to cater the lunches for the next 10 weeks. Unearned Sales Revenue is a liability because, if SuperSub does not provide the catered lunches, the bikers will expect their money back. As time passes, SuperSub will earn revenue by catering lunches. By December 31, it has provided four weeks of lunches and earned 4/10 of the $3,000 unearned revenue. This amounts to $1,200 ($3,000 × 4/10). The revenue recognition principle implies that $1,200 of the advance payment be reported as revenue on the December income statement. The adjusting entry to reduce the liability account and recognize earned revenue, along with T-account postings, is

		Adjustment		
Dec.	31	Unearned Sales Revenue	1 2 0 0 00	
		Sales Revenue		1 2 0 0 00
		To record earned revenue that was received in		
		advance ($3,000 × 4/10).		

Assets = Liabilities + Equity
−1,200   +1,200

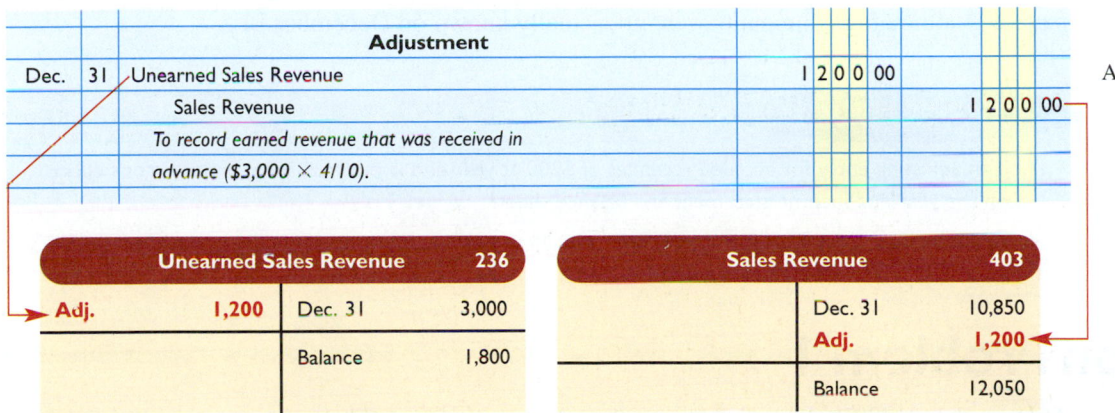

Unearned Sales Revenue		236
Adj. **1,200**	Dec. 31	3,000
	Balance	1,800

Sales Revenue		403
	Dec. 31	10,850
	Adj.	**1,200**
	Balance	12,050

The adjusting entry transfers $1,200 from unearned revenue (a liability account) to a revenue account. *Not* making the adjustment (1) understates revenue and net income by $1,200 in the December income statement and (2) overstates unearned revenue and understates equity by $1,200 on the December 31 balance sheet.

Accounting for unearned revenues is crucial to many companies. For example, the **National Retail Federation** reports that gift card sales, which are unearned revenues for sellers, are more than $20 billion annually. Gift cards are now a top-selling holiday gift. (An alternate method of accounting for unearned revenues is presented in Appendix 13A.)

Links to Financial Statements

The process of adjusting accounts is intended to bring an asset or liability account balance to its correct amount. It also updates a related expense or revenue account. These adjustments are necessary for transactions and events that extend over more than one period.

Exhibit 13.9 summarizes the four types of transactions requiring adjustment. Understanding this exhibit is important to understanding the adjusting process and its importance to financial statements. Remember that each adjusting entry affects one or more income statement accounts *and* one or more balance sheet accounts (but not cash).

Exhibit 13.9

Summary of Adjustments and Financial Statement Links

	BEFORE Adjusting Entry		
Category	**Balance Sheet**	**Income Statement**	**Adjusting Entry**
Prepaid expenses†	Asset overstated	Expense understated	**Dr. Expense**
	Equity overstated		**Cr. Asset***
Unearned revenues†	Liability overstated	Revenue understated	**Dr. Liability**
	Equity understated		**Cr. Revenue**
Accrued expenses	Liability understated	Expense understated	**Dr. Expense**
	Equity overstated		**Cr. Liability**
Accrued revenues	Asset understated	Revenue understated	**Dr. Asset**
	Equity understated		**Cr. Revenue**

* For depreciation, the credit is to Accumulated Depreciation (contra asset).

† Exhibit 13.9 assumes that Prepaid Expenses are initially recorded as assets and that Unearned Revenues are initially recorded as liabilities.

Information about some adjustments is not always available until several days or even weeks after the period-end. This means that some adjusting and closing entries are recorded later than, but dated as of, the last day of the period. One example is a company that receives a utility bill on January 10 for costs incurred for the month of December. When it receives the bill, the company records the expense and the payable as of December 31. Other examples include long-distance phone usage and costs of many service billings. The December income statement reflects these additional expenses incurred, and the December 31 balance sheet includes these payables, although the amounts were not actually known on December 31.

HOW YOU DOIN'?   Answers—p. 332

7. If an adjusting entry for accrued revenues of $200 at year-end is omitted, what is this error's effect on the year-end income statement and balance sheet?

8. Describe how an accrued revenue arises. Give an example.

Demonstration Problem 1

At December 31, 2010, SuperSub reports the following unadjusted balances as part of its unadjusted trial balance:

Merchandise inventory	$2,000
Sales	7,225
Sales returns and allowances	150
Sales discounts	200
Purchases	6,950
Purchase returns and allowances	75
Purchase discounts	175
Transportation-in	50

SuperSub uses a periodic inventory system. In addition, an inventory count shows that $3,200 of merchandise inventory remains unsold on December 31, 2010.

Required

1. Prepare the adjusting entries for SuperSub's merchandise inventory on December 31, 2010.
2. Compute net sales.
3. Compute net purchases.
4. Compute cost of goods sold.
5. Compute gross profit.

Planning the Solution

- Determine the adjustments to replace the beginning merchandise inventory balance with the amount of inventory remaining unsold at year-end.
- Recall the formulas to compute net sales and net purchases and compute these amounts.
- Use the inventory equation to compute the cost of goods sold. Subtract cost of goods sold from net sales to compute gross profit.

Solution to Demonstration Problem 1

1. Inventory adjusting entries

(BI)	Dec.	31	Income Summary	2 0 0 0 00	
			Merchandise Inventory		2 0 0 0 00
(EI)	Dec.	31	Merchandise Inventory	3 2 0 0 00	
			Income Summary		3 2 0 0 00

2. Net sales = Sales − Sales returns and allowances − Sales discounts
   = $7,225 − $150 − $200 = $6,875.

3. Net purchases = Purchases − Purchase returns and allowances − Purchase discounts
   + Transportation-in
   = $6,950 − $75 − $175 + $50 = $6,750.

4. The inventory equation is: Beginning inventory + Net purchases − Ending inventory = Cost of goods sold.
   For SuperSub, Cost of goods sold = $2,000 + $6,750 − $3,200 = $5,550.

5. Gross profit = Net sales − cost of goods sold = $6,875 − $5,550 = $1,325.

Demonstration Problem 2

The following information relates to Joel's Alarm Services on December 31, 2010. The company, which uses the calendar year as its annual reporting period, initially records prepaid and unearned items in balance sheet accounts (assets and liabilities, respectively).

a. The company's weekly payroll is $8,750, paid each Friday for a five-day workweek. Assume December 31, 2010, falls on a Monday, but the employees will not be paid their wages until Friday, January 4, 2011. (For simplicity, ignore payroll taxes for this problem).

b. Eighteen months earlier, on July 1, 2008, the company purchased equipment that cost $20,000. Its useful life is predicted to be five years, at which time the equipment is expected to be worthless (zero salvage value).

c. On October 1, 2010, the company agreed to work on a new housing development. The company is paid $120,000 on October 1 in advance of future installation of alarm systems in 24 new homes. That amount was credited to the Unearned Services Revenue account. Between October 1 and December 31, work on 20 homes was completed.

d. On September 1, 2010, the company purchased a 12-month insurance policy for $2,400. The transaction was recorded with a $2,400 debit to Prepaid Insurance.

e. On December 29, 2010, the company completed a $7,000 alarm installation service that has not been billed and not recorded as of December 31, 2010.

Required

1. Prepare any necessary adjusting entries on December 31, 2010, in relation to transactions and events *a* through *e*.

2. Prepare T-accounts for the accounts affected by adjusting entries, and post the adjusting entries. Determine the adjusted balances for the Unearned Revenue and the Prepaid Insurance accounts.

3. Complete the following table and determine the amounts and effects of your adjusting entries on the year 2010 income statement and the December 31, 2010, balance sheet. Use up (down) arrows to indicate an increase (decrease) in the Effect columns.

Entry	Amount in the Entry	Effect on Net Income	Effect on Total Assets	Effect on Total Liabilities	Effect on Total Equity

Planning the Solution

- Analyze each situation to determine which accounts need to be updated with an adjustment.
- Calculate the amount of each adjustment and prepare the necessary journal entries.
- Show the amount of each adjustment in the designated accounts, determine the adjusted balance, and identify the balance sheet classification of the account.
- Determine each entry's effect on net income for the year and on total assets, total liabilities, and total equity at the end of the year.

Solution to Demonstration Problem 2

1. Adjusting journal entries.

				Debit	Credit
(a)	Dec.	31	Wages Expense	1 7 5 0 00	
			Wages Payable		1 7 5 0 00
			To accrue wages for the last day of the year		
			($8,750 × 1/5).		
(b)	Dec.	31	Depreciation Expense—Equipment	4 0 0 0 00	
			Accumulated Depreciation—Equipment		4 0 0 0 00
			To record depreciation expense for the year		
			($20,000/5 years = $4,000 per year).		
(c)	Dec.	31	Unearned Services Revenue	100 0 0 0 00	
			Services Revenue		100 0 0 0 00
			To recognize services revenue earned		
			($120,000 × 20/24).		
(d)	Dec.	31	Insurance Expense	8 0 0 00	
			Prepaid Insurance		8 0 0 00
			To adjust for expired portion of insurance		
			($2,400 × 4/12).		
(e)	Dec.	31	Accounts Receivable	7 0 0 0 00	
			Services Revenue		7 0 0 0 00
			To record services revenue earned.		

2. T-accounts for adjusting journal entries *a* through *e*.

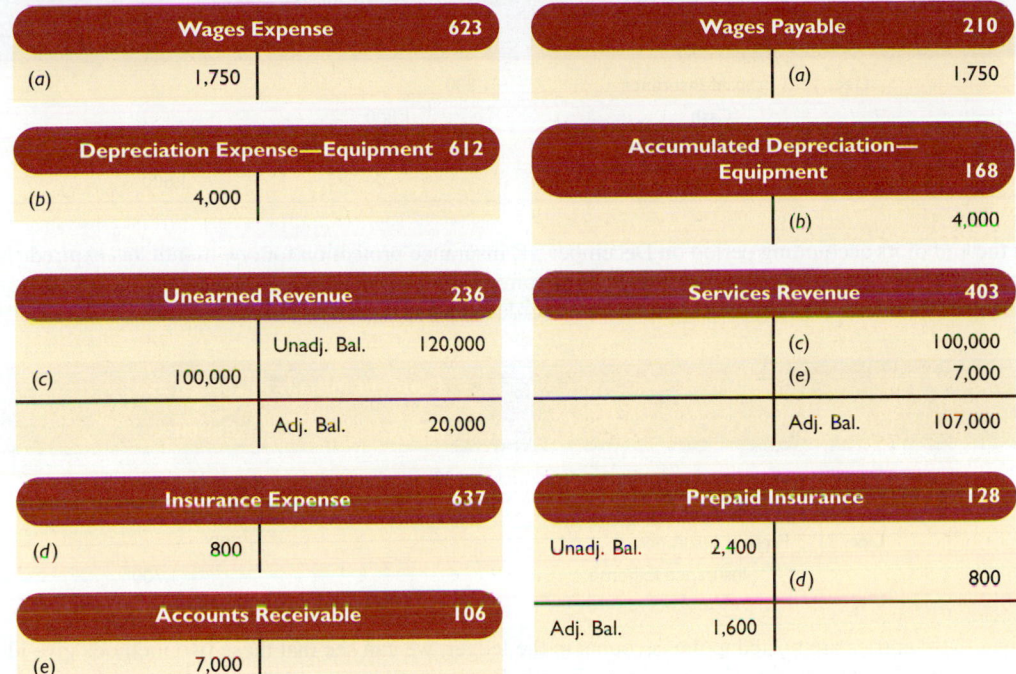

Wages Expense	623
(a) 1,750	

Wages Payable	210
	(a) 1,750

Depreciation Expense—Equipment	612
(b) 4,000	

Accumulated Depreciation—Equipment	168
	(b) 4,000

Unearned Revenue		236
	Unadj. Bal.	120,000
(c) 100,000		
	Adj. Bal.	20,000

Services Revenue		403
	(c)	100,000
	(e)	7,000
	Adj. Bal.	107,000

Insurance Expense	637
(d) 800	

Prepaid Insurance		128
Unadj. Bal.	2,400	
	(d)	800
Adj. Bal.	1,600	

Accounts Receivable	106
(e) 7,000	

3. Financial statement effects of adjusting journal entries.

Entry	Amount in the Entry	Effect on Net Income	Effect on Total Assets	Effect on Total Liabilities	Effect on Total Equity
a	$ 1,750	$ 1,750 ↓	No effect	$ 1,750 ↑	$ 1,750 ↓
b	4,000	4,000 ↓	$4,000 ↓	No effect	4,000 ↓
c	100,000	100,000 ↑	No effect	$100,000 ↓	100,000 ↑
d	800	800 ↓	$ 800 ↓	No effect	800 ↓
e	7,000	7,000 ↑	$7,000 ↑	No effect	7,000 ↑

Alternative Accounting for Prepayments

APPENDIX

13A

This appendix explains an alternative in accounting for prepaid expenses and unearned revenues.

Recording the Prepayment of Expenses in Expense Accounts

An alternative method is to record *all* prepaid expenses with debits to expense accounts. If any prepaids remain unused or unexpired at the end of an accounting period, then adjusting entries must transfer the cost of the unused portions from expense accounts to prepaid expense (asset) accounts. This alternative method is acceptable. The financial statements are identical under either method, but the adjusting entries are different. To illustrate the differences between these two methods, let's look at SuperSub's cash payment of $1,800 on December 1 for 18 months of insurance coverage beginning on December 1. SuperSub recorded that payment with a debit to an asset account, but it could have recorded a debit to an expense account. These alternatives are shown in Exhibit 13A.1.

LO9 Describe the alternatives in accounting for prepayments.

Exhibit 13A.1

Alternative Initial Entries for Prepaid Expenses

			Payment Initially Recorded as	
			Asset	**Expense**
Dec. 1	Prepaid Insurance	1,800		
	Cash		1,800	
Dec. 1	Insurance Expense			1,800
	Cash			1,800

At the end of its accounting period on December 31, insurance protection for one month has expired. This means $100 ($1,800/18) of insurance coverage expired and is an expense for December. The adjusting entry depends on how the original payment was recorded. This is shown in Exhibit 13A.2.

Exhibit 13A.2

Adjusting Entry for Prepaid Expenses for the Two Alternatives

			Payment Initially Recorded as	
			Asset	**Expense**
Dec. 31	Insurance Expense	100		
	Prepaid Insurance		100	
Dec. 31	Prepaid Insurance			1,700
	Insurance Expense			1,700

When these entries are posted to the accounts in the ledger, we can see that these two methods give identical results. The December 31 adjusted account balances in Exhibit 13A.3 show Prepaid Insurance of $1,700 and Insurance Expense of $100 for both methods.

Exhibit 13A.3

Account Balances under Two Alternatives for Recording Prepaid Expenses

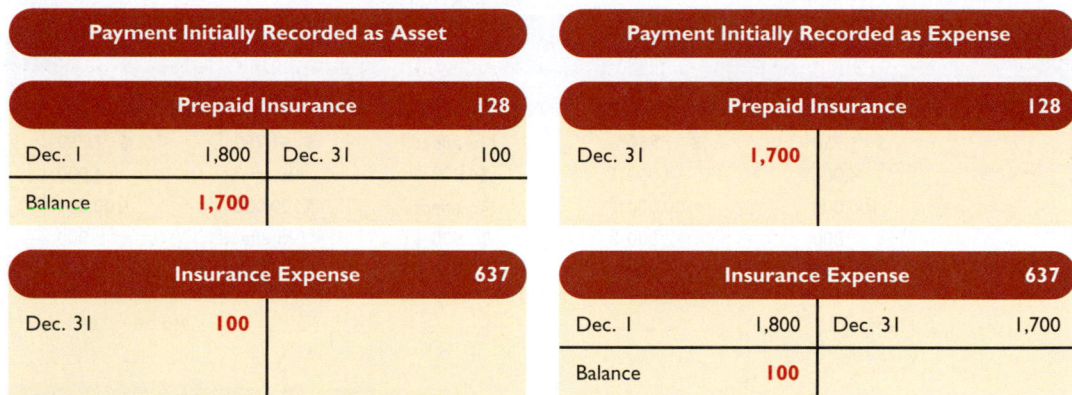

Payment Initially Recorded as Asset			
Prepaid Insurance			**128**
Dec. 1	1,800	Dec. 31	100
Balance	**1,700**		

Insurance Expense			**637**
Dec. 31	**100**		

Payment Initially Recorded as Expense			
Prepaid Insurance			**128**
Dec. 31	**1,700**		

Insurance Expense			**637**
Dec. 1	1,800	Dec. 31	1,700
Balance	**100**		

Recording the Prepayment of Revenues in Revenue Accounts

As with prepaid expenses, an alternative method is to record *all* unearned revenues with credits to revenue accounts. If any revenues are unearned at the end of an accounting period, then adjusting entries must transfer the unearned portions from revenue accounts to unearned revenue (liability) accounts. The adjusting entries are different for these two alternatives, but the financial statements are identical. To illustrate the accounting differences between these two methods, let's look at SuperSub's December 1 receipt of $3,000 for services covering 10 weekly lunches. SuperSub recorded this transaction with a credit to a liability account. The alternative is to record it with a credit to a revenue account, as shown in Exhibit 13A.4.

Exhibit 13A.4

Alternative Initial Entries for Unearned Revenues

			Receipt Initially Recorded as	
			Liability	**Revenue**
Dec. 1	Cash	3,000		
	Unearned Sales Revenue		3,000	
Dec. 1	Cash			3,000
	Sales Revenue			3,000

By the end of its accounting period on December 31, SuperSub has earned $1,200 of this revenue. This means $1,200 of the liability has been satisfied. Depending on how the initial receipt is recorded, the adjusting entry is as shown in Exhibit 13A.5.

		Receipt Initially Recorded as	
		Liability	Revenue
Dec. 31	Unearned Sales Revenue	1,200	
	Sales Revenue		1,200
Dec. 31	Sales Revenue	1,800	
	Unearned Sales Revenue		1,800

Exhibit 13A.5

Adjusting Entry for Unearned Revenues for the Two Alternatives

After adjusting entries are posted, the two alternatives give identical results. The December 31 adjusted account balances in Exhibit 13A.6 show unearned revenue of $1,800 and sales revenue of $1,200 for both methods.

Receipt Initially Recorded as Liability

Unearned Consulting Revenue			236
Dec. 31	1,200	Dec. 1	3,000
		Balance	1,800

Consulting Revenue			403
		Dec. 31	1,800

Receipt Initially Recorded as Revenue

Unearned Consulting Revenue		236
	Dec. 31	1,800

Consulting Revenue			403
Dec. 31	1,800	Dec. 1	3,000
		Balance	1,200

Exhibit 13A.6

Account Balances under Two Alternatives for Recording Unearned Revenues

Summary

LO1 Use a trial balance for a merchandiser. The merchandiser's trial balance includes accounts for merchandise inventory, sales, and purchases. Under a periodic inventory system the unadjusted merchandise inventory balance is its balance as of the beginning of the period.

LO2 Prepare the adjusting entries for inventory. Two entries are needed to adjust inventory. First, debit Income Summary and credit Merchandise Inventory for the beginning balance of merchandise inventory from the unadjusted trial balance. Second, debit Merchandise Inventory and credit Income Summary for the ending balance of inventory, determined by a physical count.

LO3 Prepare adjusting entries for prepaid and accrued expenses. Prepaid assets, like prepaid insurance or supplies, are used during a period. An adjusting entry records the amount used as expense and reduces the related asset to the amount that remains for future use. Depreciation is a special case of prepaid expenses. Accrued expenses are costs, like employee salaries, that occur before the end of an accounting period but that won't be paid until the next

period. An adjusting entry records these expenses and creates a liability for the amount owed.

LO4 Compute net sales and net purchases. Net sales is computed as: sales minus sales returns and allowances minus sales discounts. Net purchases is computed as purchases plus transportation-in minus purchase returns and allowances minus purchase discounts. Balances for each of these accounts come from the ending unadjusted trial balance.

LO5 Compute cost of goods sold. The inventory equation is used to compute cost of goods sold: Beginning inventory plus net purchases minus ending inventory equals cost of goods sold. Ending inventory is determined from a physical count of the inventory that remains unsold at the end of the period.

LO6 Compute gross profit. Gross profit is computed as net sales minus cost of goods sold. It is an important measure of performance for a merchandiser.

LO7 Prepare the adjusting entry for accrued revenue. Accrued revenue is revenue earned for work performed before the end of a period, but amounts won't be collected until the next period. An adjusting entry is recorded with a debit to Accounts Receivable and a credit to Sales (or Revenue).

LO8 **Prepare the adjusting entry for unearned revenue.** When a business receives cash before it performs work, it has a liability to perform that future work. When the work is performed, Unearned Revenue (a liability) is reduced with a debit and Revenue is increased with a credit.

LO9 **Appendix 13A—Describe the alternatives in accounting for prepayments.** Debiting all prepaid expenses to expense accounts when they are purchased is acceptable. When this is done, adjusting entries must transfer any unexpired amounts from expense accounts to asset accounts. Crediting all unearned revenues to revenue accounts when cash is received is also acceptable. In this case, the adjusting entries must transfer any unearned amounts from revenue accounts to unearned revenue accounts.

Guidance Answers to   HOW YOU DOIN'?

1. Insurance expense = $3,200 − $2,000 = $1,200.

2. Supplies expense = $1,400 − $620 = $780.

3. Annual depreciation expense = ($22,000 − $2,000)/4 = $5,000.

4. Net sales = Sales − Sales returns and allowances − Sales discounts, or, $450,000 − $4,000 − $7,000 = $439,000.

5. Net purchases = Purchases − Purchase returns and allowances − Purchase discounts + Transportation-in, or $325,000 − $7,000 − $8,000 + $1,000 = $311,000.

6. Cost of goods sold = Beginning inventory + Net purchases − Ending inventory, or $75,000 + $220,000 − $42,000 =

$253,000. Gross profit = Net sales − Cost of goods sold, or $303,000 − $253,000 = $50,000.

7. If the accrued revenues adjustment of $200 is not made, then both revenues and net income are understated by $200 on the current year's income statement, and both assets and equity are understated by $200 on the balance sheet.

8. An accrued revenue arises when revenue is earned but not yet received in cash nor recorded in the books. An example would be consulting work that has been performed for which payment has not yet been received.

Key Terms

Accrued revenues (p. 324) Revenues earned in a period that are both unrecorded and not yet received in cash (or other assets); adjusting entries for recording accrued revenues involve increasing assets and increasing revenues.

Cost of goods sold (p. 322) Cost of inventory sold to customers during a period; also called *cost of sales*.

Gross profit (p. 322) Net sales minus cost of goods sold; also called *gross margin*.

Merchandise inventory (p. 317) Goods that a company owns and expects to sell to customers; also called *merchandise* or *inventory*.

Net purchases (p. 322) Net cost of merchandise purchased; computed as purchases minus purchase discounts, minus purchase returns and allowances, plus transportation-in.

Net sales (p. 322) Net amount of merchandise sold; computed as sales minus sales returns and allowances minus sales discounts.

Unearned revenues (p. 324) Liability created when customers pay in advance for products or services; earned when the products or services are later delivered.

Multiple Choice Quiz   Answers on p. 343   mhhe.com/wildCA2e

Additional Multiple Choice Quizzes are available at the book's Website.

1. The accounting principle that requires revenue to be reported when earned is the
   a. Matching principle.
   b. Revenue recognition principle.
   c. Time period principle.
   d. Accrual reporting principle.
   e. Going-concern principle.

2. Adjusting entries
   a. Affect only income statement accounts.
   b. Affect only balance sheet accounts.
   c. Affect both income statement and balance sheet accounts.

   d. Affect only cash flow statement accounts.
   e. Affect only equity accounts.

3. On May 1, 2010, a two-year insurance policy was purchased for $12,000 with coverage to begin immediately. What is the amount of insurance expense that appears on the company's income statement for the year ended December 31, 2010?
   a. $2,000
   b. $4,000
   c. $6,000
   d. $10,000
   e. $12,000

4. On November 1, 2010, Stockton Co. receives $3,600 cash from Hans Co. for consulting services to be provided evenly over the period November 1, 2010, to April 30, 2011—at which time Stockton credited $3,600 to Unearned Consulting Fees. The adjusting entry on December 31, 2010 (Stockton's year-end) would include a

  a. Debit to Unearned Consulting Fees for $1,200.
  b. Debit to Unearned Consulting Fees for $2,400.
  c. Credit to Consulting Fees Earned for $2,400.
  d. Debit to Consulting Fees Earned for $1,200.
  e. Credit to Cash for $3,600.

5. Employees at Guthrie Co. worked three days at the end of 2010 and earned $5,400. They will be paid for this work at the next payroll date on January 9, 2011. What is the adjusting entry that Guthrie must make for the year ending December 31, 2010?

  a. Debit Wages Expense $5,400, Credit Prepaid Wages $5,400.
  b. Debit Wages Payable $5,400, Credit Wages Expense $5,400.
  c. Debit Prepaid Wages $5,400, Credit Wages Payable $5,400.
  d. Debit Wages Expense $5,400, Credit Wages Payable $5,400.

Superscript letter ^A *denotes assignments based on Appendix 13A.*

Discussion Questions

1. How does a merchandiser compute net sales?

2. How does a merchandiser compute cost of goods sold?

3. What is an accrued expense and where is it reported in the financial statements?

4. What is unearned revenue and where is it reported in financial statements?

5. What is an accrued revenue? Give an example.

6. ^AIf a company initially records prepaid expenses with debits to expense accounts, what type of account is debited in the adjusting entries for those prepaid expenses?

7. Review the balance sheet of **Best Buy** in Appendix A. Identify the liability accounts that require adjustment before annual financial statements can be prepared. What would be the effect on the income statement if these liability accounts were not adjusted?

8. Review the balance sheet of Best Buy in Appendix A. What amount does Best Buy report for Merchandise Inventories on its most recent balance sheet?

---

connect

Compute net sales and gross profit from the adjusted trial balance information below.

Sales	$150,000
Sales discounts	5,200
Sales returns and allowances	20,000
Cost of goods sold	79,600

QUICK STUDY

QS 13-1
Computing net sales and gross profit   LO4   LO6

Compute net purchases and cost of goods sold from the adjusted trial balance information below.

Beginning inventory	50,000
Ending inventory	42,000
Purchases	143,000
Purchase discounts	18,000
Purchase returns	16,000
Net sales	200,000

QS 13-2
Computing net purchases and cost of goods sold   LO4   LO5

Refer to the data in QS 13-2. Prepare the necessary adjusting entries for merchandise inventory at the end of the year. The company uses a periodic inventory system. Use December 31 for the date of the entries.

QS 13-3
Adjusting entries for inventory
LO2

QS 13–4

Identifying accounting adjustments

LO5   LO7   LO8

Classify the following adjusting entries as involving prepaid expenses (PE), unearned revenues (UR), accrued expenses (AE), or accrued revenues (AR).

a. _____ To record revenue earned that was previously received as cash in advance.

b. _____ To record wages expense incurred but not yet paid (nor recorded).

c. _____ To record revenue earned but not yet billed (nor recorded).

d. _____ To record expiration of prepaid insurance.

e. _____ To record annual depreciation expense.

QS 13–5

Preparing adjusting entries for prepaid and accrued expenses

LO3

Check (b) Dr. Insurance Expense, $2,100

Prepare adjusting journal entries for the year ended December 31, 2010, for each of these separate situations. Assume that prepaid expenses are initially recorded in asset accounts.

a. Depreciation on the company's equipment for 2010 is computed to be $23,000.

b. The Prepaid Insurance account had a $2,600 debit balance at December 31, 2010, before adjusting for the costs of any expired coverage. An analysis of insurance policies showed that $2,100 of coverage had expired as of December 31, 2010.

c. Wage expenses of $6,700 have been incurred but are not paid as of December 31, 2010.

QS 13–6

Preparing adjusting entries for unearned revenues   **LO8**

One-third of the work related to $15,000 cash received in advance is performed this period. Prepare the adjusting entry needed at year-end, assuming fees collected in advance of work are initially recorded as liabilities.

QS 13–7

Adjusting entry for accrued revenue   **LO7**

Premier Lawn has earned but unbilled (and unrecorded) mowing fees of $1,200 at the end of its first accounting period. What journal entry is needed?

QS 13–8

Adjusting for unearned revenues

LO8

Tao receives $10,000 cash in advance for four months of legal services on October 1, 2010, and records it by debiting Cash and crediting Unearned Revenue both for $10,000. It is now December 31, 2010, and Tao has provided legal services as planned. What adjusting entry should Tao make to account for the work performed from October 1 through December 31, 2010?

QS 13–9

Preparing adjusting entries

LO3   LO7   LO8

During the year, Sereno Co. recorded prepayments of expenses in asset accounts, and cash receipts of unearned revenues in liability accounts. At the end of its annual accounting period, the company must make three adjusting entries: (1) accrue salaries expense, (2) adjust the Unearned Services Revenue account to recognize earned revenue, and (3) record services revenue earned for which cash will be received the following period. For each of these adjusting entries (1), (2), and (3), indicate the account from _a_ through _i_ to be debited and the account to be credited.

a. Prepaid Salaries   **d.** Unearned Services Revenue   **g.** Accounts Receivable

b. Cash   **e.** Salaries Expense   **h.** Accounts Payable

c. Salaries Payable   **f.** Services Revenue   **i.** Equipment

---

QS 13–10

Interpreting adjusting entries

LO3

The following information is taken from Brooke Company's unadjusted and adjusted trial balances.

	Unadjusted		Adjusted	
	Debit	Credit	Debit	Credit
Prepaid insurance	$4,100		$3,700	
Wages payable		$ 0		$800

Given this information, which of the following is likely included among its adjusting entries?

a. A $400 debit to Insurance Expense and an $800 debit to Wages Payable.

b. A $400 debit to Insurance Expense and an $800 debit to Wages Expense.

c. A $400 credit to Prepaid Insurance and an $800 debit to Wages Payable.

In making adjusting entries at the end of its accounting period, Chao Consulting failed to record $1,600 of insurance coverage that had expired. This $1,600 cost had been initially debited to the Prepaid Insurance account. The company also failed to record accrued salaries expense of $1,000. As a result of these two oversights, the financial statements for the reporting period will [choose one] (1) understate assets by $1,600; (2) understate expenses by $2,600; (3) understate net income by $1,000; or (4) overstate liabilities by $1,000.

QS 13-11
Determining effects of adjusting entries   **LO3**

Calvin Consulting initially records prepaid and unearned items in income statement accounts. Given Calvin Consulting's accounting practices, which of the following applies to the preparation of adjusting entries at the end of its first accounting period?

a. Earned but unbilled (and unrecorded) consulting fees are recorded with a debit to Unearned Consulting Fees and a credit to Consulting Fees Earned.

b. Unpaid salaries are recorded with a debit to Prepaid Salaries and a credit to Salaries Expense.

c. The cost of unused office supplies is recorded with a debit to Supplies Expense and a credit to Office Supplies.

d. Unearned fees (on which cash was received in advance earlier in the period) are recorded with a debit to Consulting Fees Earned and a credit to Unearned Consulting Fees.

QS 13-12^A
Preparing adjusting entries
LO9

connect™

Compute net sales and gross profit for each separate case *a* through *c*.

EXERCISES

	a	b	c
Sales	$550,000	$38,700	$255,700
Sales discounts	17,500	600	4,200
Sales returns and allowances	6,000	5,300	900
Cost of goods sold	329,700	24,300	126,900

Exercise 13-1
Computing net sales and gross profit   **LO3   LO6**

Following are financial figures for three companies. Compute net purchases, cost of goods sold, and gross profit for each company.

	Company a	Company b	Company c
Beginning inventory	$ 75,000	$ 18,000	$ 25,000
Ending inventory	98,000	16,000	28,000
Purchases	177,000	86,000	110,000
Purchase discounts	23,000	16,000	0
Purchase returns	12,000	7,000	8,000
Net sales	188,000	119,000	152,000

Exercise 13-2
Computing net purchases, cost of goods sold, and gross profit
LO4   LO5   LO6

Refer to Exercise 13-2. For each of the three companies, prepare the necessary adjusting entries for merchandise inventory at the end of the accounting period. Each company uses the periodic inventory method.

Exercise 13-3
Adjusting entries for inventory
LO2

In the blank space beside each adjusting entry that follows, enter the letter of the explanation A through E that most closely describes the entry.

A. To record this period's depreciation expense.

B. To record accrued salaries expense.

C. To record this period's use of a prepaid expense.

D. To record accrued consulting fee revenue.

E. To record the earning of previously unearned income.

Exercise 13-4
Classifying adjusting entries
LO3   LO7   LO8

_____	1.	Insurance Expense	1,653	
		Prepaid Insurance		1,653
_____	2.	Unearned Professional Fees	19,250	
		Professional Fees Earned		19,250
_____	3.	Consulting Fee Receivable	3,300	
		Consulting Fee Revenue		3,300
_____	4.	Depreciation Expense	12,413	
		Accumulated Depreciation		12,413
_____	5.	Salaries Expense	6,250	
		Salaries Payable		6,250

Exercise 13–5
Adjusting and paying accrued wages **LO3**

Reese Management has four part-time employees, each of whom earns $300 per day. They are normally paid on Fridays for work completed Monday through Friday of the same week. They were paid in full on Friday, December 28, 2010. The next week, the five employees worked only four days because New Year's Day was an unpaid holiday. Show (*a*) the adjusting entry that would be recorded on Monday, December 31, 2010, and (*b*) the journal entry that would be made to record payment of the employees' wages on Friday, January 4, 2011. (For simplicity, ignore payroll taxes.)

Exercise 13–6
Adjusting for accrued expenses and accrued revenues
LO3   LO7

The following two separate situations require adjusting journal entries to prepare financial statements as of April 30. For each situation, present both the April 30 adjusting entry and the subsequent entry during May to record the payment of the accrued expenses or collection of the accrued revenue.

a. On April 1, the company retained an attorney at a flat monthly fee of $3,500. This amount is payable on the 12th of May.

b. On April 30 the company has earned $7,500 of design fees, which it has yet to bill or record. This amount is collected on May 28.

Exercise 13–7
Computing cost of goods sold and gross profit **LO5   LO6**

Following are financial figures for five companies. Solve for the missing items a through e.

	Company 1	Company 2	Company 3	Company 4	Company 5
Beginning inventory	$ 57,000	$ 63,000	$ 97,000	$ 30,000	$ e
Purchases	150,000	173,000	92,000	115,000	255,000
Purchase discounts	17,000	21,000	15,000	12,000	23,000
Purchase returns	17,000	13,000	8,000	7,000	15,000
Cost of goods available for sale	a	202,000	166,000	126,000	329,000
Ending inventory	56,000	69,000	72,000	d	130,000
Cost of goods sold	117,000	133,000	c	110,000	199,000
Sales..............................	200,000	b	119,000	152,000	313,000
Gross profit........................	83,000	55,000	25,000	42,000	114,000

Exercise 13–8
Preparing adjusting entries
LO3   LO8

The following information is available for Goode Company. Assume that December 31 is the end of its annual accounting period.

a. The Prepaid Insurance account shows a debit balance of $2,340, representing the cost of a three-year fire insurance policy that was purchased on October 1 of the current year.

b. The Office Supplies account has a debit balance of $400; a year-end count reveals $80 of supplies still available.

c. On November 1 of the current year, Unearned Rent was credited for $1,500. This amount represented a prepayment received for a three-month period beginning November 1.

d. Depreciation on office equipment is $600.

Required

Record the December 31 adjusting entries for the transactions and events *a* through *d*.

The following information is available for Blassie Company. Assume that December 31 is the end of the annual accounting period.

a. The Prepaid Insurance account shows a debit balance of $3,600, representing the cost of a three-year fire insurance policy that was purchased on October 1 of the current year.

b. The Office Supplies account has a debit balance of $800; a year-end count reveals $90 of supplies still available.

c. On November 1 of the current year, Unearned Rent was credited for $3,300. This amount represented a prepayment received for a three-month period beginning November 1.

d. Depreciation on office equipment is $900.

Exercise 13-9
Preparing adjusting entries
LO3   LO8

Required

Record the December 31 adjusting entries for the transactions and events *a* through *d*.

Following are two income statements for Alexis Co. for the year ended December 31. The left column is prepared before any adjusting entries are recorded, and the right column includes the effects of adjusting entries. The company records cash receipts and payments related to unearned and prepaid items in balance sheet accounts. Analyze the statements and prepare the eight adjusting entries that likely were recorded. (*Note:* 30% of the $7,000 adjustment for Fees Earned has been earned but not billed, and the other 70% has been earned by performing services that were paid for in advance.)

Exercise 13-10
Analyzing and preparing adjusting entries   LO3   LO7

ALEXIS CO. Income Statements For Year Ended December 31		
	Unadjusted	**Adjusted**
Revenues		
Fees earned	$18,000	$25,000
Commissions earned	36,500	36,500
Total revenues	$54,500	$61,500
Expenses		
Depreciation expense—Computers	0	1,600
Depreciation expense—Office furniture	0	1,850
Salaries expense	13,500	15,750
Insurance expense	0	1,400
Rent expense	3,800	3,800
Office supplies expense	0	580
Advertising expense	2,500	2,500
Utilities expense	1,245	1,335
Total expenses	21,045	28,815
Net income	$33,455	$32,685

Ricardo Construction began operations on December 1. In setting up its accounting procedures, the company decided to debit expense accounts when it prepays its expenses and to credit revenue accounts when customers pay for services in advance. Prepare journal entries for items *a* through *d* and the adjusting entries as of its December 31 period-end for items *e* through *g*.

Exercise 13-11ᴬ
Adjusting for prepaids recorded as expenses and unearned revenues recorded as revenues   LO9

a. Supplies are purchased on December 1 for $2,000 cash.

b. The company prepaid its insurance premiums for $1,540 cash on December 2.

c. On December 15, the company receives an advance payment of $13,000 cash from customers for remodeling work.

d. On December 28, the company receives $3,700 cash from another customer for remodeling work to be performed in January.

e. A physical count on December 31 indicates that Ricardo has $1,840 of supplies available.

f. An analysis of the insurance policies in effect on December 31 shows that $340 of insurance coverage had expired.

g. As of December 31, one remodeling project has been worked on and completed. The $5,570 fee for this project had been received in advance.

PROBLEM SET A

Problem 13–1A
Merchandiser's partial work sheet, adjusting entries, and gross profit

LO1   LO2   LO3   LO4
LO5   LO6   LO7

The following unadjusted trial balance is prepared at fiscal year-end for Helix Company.

HELIX COMPANY
Unadjusted Trial Balance
January 31, 2010

	Debit	Credit
Cash	$ 28,750	
Merchandise inventory	13,000	
Store supplies	5,500	
Prepaid insurance	2,400	
Store equipment	42,600	
Accumulated depreciation—Store equipment		$ 19,750
Accounts payable		14,000
A. Helix, Capital		39,000
A. Helix, Withdrawals	2,000	
Income summary	0	0
Sales		115,800
Sales discounts	1,900	
Sales returns and allowances	2,300	
Purchases	37,750	
Purchase discounts		400
Purchase returns and allowances		350
Transportation-in	1,000	
Depreciation expense—Store equipment	0	
Salaries expense	27,400	
Insurance expense	0	
Rent expense	15,000	
Store supplies expense	0	
Advertising expense	9,700	
Totals	$ 189,300	$ 189,300

Helix Company uses a periodic inventory system.

Required

1. Prepare adjusting journal entries to reflect each of the items below. Record your entries on a (partial) work sheet, using Exhibit 13.4 as a guide.
   a. Store supplies still available at year-end amount to $2,550.
   b. Expired insurance for the year is $1,450.
   c. Depreciation expense on store equipment is $1,975 for the year.
   d. $10,300 of inventory is still available at fiscal year-end.

2. Complete the (partial) worksheet through the Adjusted Trial Balance columns.

3. Compute net sales.

4. Compute net purchases.

5. Compute cost of goods sold.

6. Compute gross profit.

For each of the following entries, enter the letter of the explanation that most closely describes it in the space beside each entry. (You can use letters more than once.)

Problem 13-2A

Identifying adjusting entries with explanations LO3 LO7

A. To record receipt of unearned revenue.

B. To record this period's earning of prior unearned revenue.

C. To record payment of an accrued expense.

D. To record receipt of an accrued revenue.

E. To record an accrued expense.

F. To record an accrued revenue.

G. To record this period's use of a prepaid expense.

H. To record payment of a prepaid expense.

I. To record this period's depreciation expense.

_____	**1.**	Salaries Expense	1,000
		Salaries Payable	1,000
_____	**2.**	Depreciation Expense	4,000
		Accumulated Depreciation	4,000
_____	**3.**	Unearned Professional Fees	3,000
		Professional Fees Earned	3,000
_____	**4.**	Insurance Expense	4,200
		Prepaid Insurance	4,200
_____	**5.**	Salaries Payable	1,400
		Cash	1,400
_____	**6.**	Prepaid Rent	4,500
		Cash	4,500
_____	**7.**	Salaries Expense	6,000
		Salaries Payable	6,000
_____	**8.**	Accounts Receivable	5,000
		Sales	5,000
_____	**9.**	Cash	9,000
		Accounts Receivable	9,000
_____	**10.**	Cash	7,500
		Unearned Professional Fees	7,500
_____	**11.**	Rent Expense	2,000
		Prepaid Rent	2,000

Gomez Co. had the following transactions in the last two months of its year ended December 31.

Problem 13-3A[A]

Recording prepaid expenses and unearned revenues

LO6 LO8 LO9

Nov. 1 Paid $1,800 cash for future newspaper advertising.
  1 Paid $2,460 cash for 12 months of insurance through October 31 of the next year.
  30 Received $3,600 cash for future services to be provided to a customer.
Dec. 1 Paid $3,000 cash for a consultant's services to be received over the next three months.
  15 Received $7,950 cash for future services to be provided to a customer.
  31 Of the advertising paid for on November 1, $1,200 worth is not yet used.
  31 A portion of the insurance paid for on November 1 has expired. No adjustment was made in November to Prepaid Insurance.
  31 Services worth $1,500 are not yet provided to the customer who paid on November 30.
  31 One-third of the consulting services paid for on December 1 have been received.
  31 The company has performed $3,300 of services that the customer paid for on December 15.

Required

1. Prepare entries for these transactions under the method that records prepaid expenses as assets and records unearned revenues as liabilities. Also prepare adjusting entries at the end of the year.

2. Prepare entries for these transactions under the method that records prepaid expenses as expenses and records unearned revenues as revenues. Also prepare adjusting entries at the end of the year. (*Hint:* Refer to Appendix 13A).

PROBLEM SET B

Problem 13-1B
Merchandiser's partial work sheet, adjusting entries, and gross profit
LO1   LO2   LO3   LO4
LO5   LO6   LO7

The following unadjusted trial balance is prepared at fiscal year-end for Giaccio Products Company.

	File Edit View Insert Format Tools Data Accounting Window Help		
	GIACCIO PRODUCTS COMPANY **Unadjusted Trial Balance** **October 31, 2010**	**Debit**	**Credit**
2	Cash	$ 30,150	
3	Merchandise inventory	13,000	
4	Store supplies	5,300	
5	Prepaid insurance	2,700	
6	Store equipment	42,900	
7	Accumulated depreciation—Store equipment		$ 19,900
8	Accounts payable		15,000
9	G. Giaccio, Capital		38,000
10	G. Giaccio, Withdrawals	2,050	
11	Income summary	0	0
12	Sales		116,250
13	Sales discounts	1,950	
14	Sales returns and allowances	2,300	
15	Purchases	38,000	
16	Purchase returns and allowances		1,200
17	Purchase discounts		800
18	Transportation-in	3,000	
19	Depreciation expense—Store equipment	0	
20	Salaries expense	26,000	
21	Insurance expense	0	
22	Rent expense	14,000	
23	Store supplies expense	0	
24	Advertising expense	9,800	
25	Totals	$ 191,150	$ 191,150
26			

Sheet1 / Sheet2 / Sheet3 /

Giaccio Products Company uses a periodic inventory system.

Required

1. Prepare adjusting journal entries to reflect each of the items below. Record your entries on a (partial) work sheet, using Exhibit 13.4 as a guide.
   a. Store supplies still available at year-end amount to $1,650.
   b. Expired insurance for the year is $1,300.
   c. Depreciation expense on store equipment is $1,990 for the year.
   d. $11,600 of inventory is still available at fiscal year-end.

2. Complete the (partial) worksheet through the Adjusted Trial Balance columns.

3. Compute net sales.

4. Compute net purchases.

5. Compute cost of goods sold.

6. Compute gross profit.

For each of the following entries, enter the letter of the explanation that most closely describes it in the space beside each entry. (You can use letters more than once.)

Problem 13–2B
Identifying adjusting entries with explanations   **LO7   LO8**

A. To record payment of a prepaid expense.

B. To record this period's use of a prepaid expense.

C. To record this period's depreciation expense.

D. To record receipt of unearned revenue.

E. To record this period's earning of prior unearned revenue.

F. To record an accrued expense.

G. To record payment of an accrued expense.

H. To record an accrued revenue.

I. To record receipt of accrued revenue.

_____ 1.	Accounts Receivable	3,500	
	Sales		3,500
_____ 2.	Salaries Payable	9,000	
	Cash		9,000
_____ 3.	Depreciation Expense	8,000	
	Accumulated Depreciation		8,000
_____ 4.	Cash	9,000	
	Unearned Professional Fees		9,000
_____ 5.	Insurance Expense	4,000	
	Prepaid Insurance		4,000
_____ 6.	Salaries Expense	5,000	
	Salaries Payable		5,000
_____ 7.	Cash	1,500	
	Accounts Receivable		1,500
_____ 8.	Salaries Expense	7,000	
	Salaries Payable		7,000
_____ 9.	Prepaid Rent	3,000	
	Cash		3,000
_____ 10.	Rent Expense	7,500	
	Prepaid Rent		7,500
_____ 11.	Unearned Professional Fees	6,000	
	Professional Fees Earned		6,000

Tremor Co. had the following transactions in the last two months of its fiscal year ended May 31.

Problem 13–3B[A]
Recording prepaid expenses and unearned revenues   **LO9**

Apr. 1   Paid $2,450 cash to an accounting firm for future consulting services.

1   Paid $3,600 cash for 12 months of insurance through March 31 of the next year.

30   Received $8,500 cash for future services to be provided to a customer.

May 1   Paid $4,450 cash for future newspaper advertising.

23   Received $10,450 cash for future services to be provided to a customer.

31   Of the consulting services paid for on April 1, $2,000 worth has been received.

31   A portion of the insurance paid for on April 1 has expired. No adjustment was made in April to Prepaid Insurance.

31   Services worth $4,600 are not yet provided to the customer who paid on April 30.

31   Of the advertising paid for on May 1, $2,050 worth is not yet used.

31   The company has performed $5,500 of services that the customer paid for on May 23.

Required

1. Prepare entries for these transactions under the method that records prepaid expenses and unearned revenues in balance sheet accounts. Also prepare adjusting entries at the end of the year.

2. Prepare entries for these transactions under the method that records prepaid expenses and unearned revenues in income statement accounts. Also prepare adjusting entries at the end of the year. (*Hint:* Refer to Appendix 13A).

(This serial problem began in Chapter 1 and continues through most of the book. If previous chapter segments were not completed, the serial problem can begin at this point. It is helpful, but not necessary, that you use the Working Papers that accompany the book.)

SERIAL PROBLEM

Success Systems

SP 13   Adriana Lopez created Success Systems on October 1, 2010. Below is a list of the company's (unadjusted) general ledger account balances as of March 31, 2011 and additional facts needed to prepare adjusting entries on March 31, 2011.

No.	Account Title	Dr.	Cr.
101	Cash	$87,266	
106.1	Alex's Engineering Co.	0	
106.2	Wildcat Services	3,900	
106.3	Easy Leasing	11,000	
106.4	Clark Co.	4,800	
106.5	Chang Corp.	0	
106.6	Gomez Co.	0	
106.7	Delta Co.	0	
106.8	KC, Inc.	4,700	
106.9	Dream, Inc.	0	
106.10	Bob's Building Co.	0	
119	Merchandise inventory	0	
126	Computer supplies	4,025	
128	Prepaid insurance	1,800	
131	Prepaid rent	3,500	
163	Office equipment	10,000	
164	Accumulated depreciation— Office equipment		625
167	Computer equipment	25,000	
168	Accumulated depreciation— Computer equipment		1,250
201	Accounts payable		0

No.	Account Title	Dr.	Cr.
210	Wages payable		0
236	Unearned computer services revenue		2,500
301	A. Lopez, Capital		127,435
302	A. Lopez, Withdrawals	5,200	
403	Computer services revenue		29,350
413	Sales		20,900
414	Sales returns and allowances	500	
415	Sales discounts	55	
505	Purchases	15,200	
506	Purchase returns and allowances		496
507	Purchase discounts		152
508	Transportation-In	400	
612	Depreciation expense—Office equipment	0	
613	Depreciation expense—Computer equipment	0	
623	Wages expense	2,850	
637	Insurance expense	0	
640	Rent expense	0	
652	Computer supplies expense	0	
655	Advertising expense	800	
676	Mileage expense	512	
677	Miscellaneous expenses	0	
684	Repairs expense—Computer	1,200	

The following additional facts are available for preparing adjustments on March 31:

a. The March 31 amount of computer supplies still available totals $1,950.

b. Three more months have expired since the company purchased its annual insurance policy at a $2,400 cost for 12 months of coverage.

c. Michelle Jones has not been paid for seven days of work at the rate of $150 per day.

d. Three months have passed since any prepaid rent has been transferred to expense. The monthly rent expense is $875.

e. Depreciation on the computer equipment for January 1 through March 31 is $1,250.

f. Depreciation on the office equipment for January 1 through March 31 is $625.

g. An inventory count shows that $680 of merchandise remains unsold on March 31.

h. Success Systems completed a project for Alex's Engineering Co., thereby earning the $2,500 advance cash payment previously paid by Alex.

Required

1. Using Exhibit 13.4 as a guide, enter the account numbers, account titles, and unadjusted balances in a partial worksheet. Include a row for the Income Summary account directly after the A. Lopez, Withdrawals account.

2. Enter the necessary adjusting journal entries for March 31 in the adjustments columns of your partial worksheet. *Hint:* No entry "BI" is needed since the beginning inventory balance is zero.

3. Prepare an adjusted trial balance.

4. From the adjusted trial balance, compute the following for the quarter ended March 31:
(*a*) Net sales, (*b*) Net purchases, (*c*) Cost of goods sold, and (*d*) Gross profit.

BEYOND THE NUMBERS

REPORTING IN ACTION

LO4 LO5 LO6

BTN 13-1   Refer to **Best Buy**'s financial statements in Appendix A to answer the following.

1. What were the amounts of Best Buy's cost of goods sold and gross profit for the year ended March 1, 2008?

2. Assume that the amounts for inventories and cost of sales reflect items purchased in a form ready for resale. Compute the net cost of goods purchased for the year ended March 1, 2008.

BTN 13-2   At year-end, the president instructs you, the financial officer, not to record accrued expenses until next year because they will not be paid until then. The president also directs you to record in current-year sales a recent purchase order from a customer that requires merchandise to be delivered two weeks after the year-end. Your company would report a net income instead of a net loss if you carry out these instructions.

ETHICS CHALLENGE
LO3   LO7

Required

1. Relying on the matching principle, discuss the rationale for revenue recognition. Explain why the delayed recognition of accrued expense and the early recognition of revenue would violate GAAP.
2. If the president insists on such accounting treatment, what would you do to remedy this ethical situation?

BTN 13-3   Best Buy sells gift cards to generate future revenues.

TAKING IT TO THE NET
LO8

Required

Obtain Best Buy's 2008 financial statements from its website (**BestBuy.com**) or the SEC (**sec.gov**) and answer the following questions:

1. When does Best Buy recognize revenue from gift cards? (*Hint:* Refer to footnote 1).
2. Explain what Best Buy means by "gift card breakage."
3. What is the amount of Best Buy's gift card breakage revenue for the year ending March 1, 2008?

BTN 13-4   Official Brands' general ledger and supplementary records at the end of its current period reveal the following.

TEAMWORK IN ACTION
LO4   LO5   LO6

Sales	$600,000	Merchandise inventory (beginning of period)	$ 98,000
Sales returns	20,000	Invoice cost of merchandise purchases	360,000
Sales discounts	13,000	Purchase discounts	9,000
Cost of transportation-in	22,000	Purchase returns and allowances	11,000
		Merchandise inventory (end of period)	84,000

Required

1. *Each* member of the team is to assume responsibility for computing *one* of the following items. You are not to duplicate your teammates' work. Get any necessary amounts to compute your item from the appropriate teammate. Each member is to explain his or her computation to the team in preparation for reporting to the class.

   a. Net sales   **c.** Cost of goods sold

   b. Total cost of merchandise purchases   **d.** Gross profit

BTN 13-5   Refer to the chapter's opening feature about Joel Boblit and his **BigBadToyStore** company. Assume that Joel's business currently pays for costs of delivery of goods to customers, and that customers can receive a 1% discount for quick payment. Joel is considering offering customers a 3% discount for quick payment but also having customers pay for the costs of delivery. If Joel implements this proposal, he expects his net income to increase by more than 10%.

ENTREPRENEURS IN BUSINESS

Required

1. Based on the predicted change in net income alone, should Joel implement the proposal?
2. What other factors (beside the predicted change in net income) should Joel consider before he implements the proposal? Explain.

BTN 13-6   The owner of an electronics store applies for a business loan. The store's financial statements reveal large increases in current-year revenues and income. Analysis shows that these increases are due to a promotion that lets consumers buy now and pay nothing until January 1 of next year. The store recorded these sales as accrued revenue. Does your analysis raise any concerns?

YOU CALL IT
LO7

ANSWERS TO MULTIPLE CHOICE QUIZ

1. b
2. c
3. b; Insurance expense = $12,000 × (8/24) = $4,000; adjusting entry is: *dr.* Insurance Expense for $4,000, *cr.* Prepaid Insurance for $4,000.
4. a; Consulting fees earned = $3,600 × (2/6) = $1,200; adjusting entry is: *dr.* Unearned Consulting Fee for $1,200, *cr.* Consulting Fees Earned for $1,200.
5. d

A Look Back

Chapter 13 showed how to compute net sales, net purchases, and cost of goods sold for a merchandiser. It also showed common adjusting entries for a merchandiser.

A Look at This Chapter

This chapter shows how to prepare financial statements for a merchandiser. These financial statements include multiple-step and single-step income statements, the statement of owner's equity, and a classified balance sheet. The chapter also illustrates the closing process for a merchandiser.

A Look Ahead

Chapter 15 describes how companies account for and report accounts receivable. It also explains how to account for receivables that are uncollectible.

Chapter 14

Merchandiser's Financial Statements and the Closing Process

Learning Objectives

LO 1	Prepare a work sheet for a merchandising business.
LO 2	Define and prepare multiple-step and single-step income statements.
LO 3	Prepare a statement of owner's equity.
LO 4	Explain and prepare a classified balance sheet.
LO 5	Prepare journal entries to close temporary accounts.
LO 6	Prepare a post-closing trial balance.
LO 7	Prepare reversing entries and explain their purpose.

"The more clicks we can get, the better our future"
—Todd Rath

On the Green

ROCHESTER, NY—Brothers Tom and Todd Rath paid their college tuition by diving for lost golf balls and then reselling them. Today, their company RockBottomGolf.com applies a similar strategy of buying leftover products and reselling them. "Some of our critics refer to us as the 'graveyard of golf,'" explains Tom. "Oftentimes, we may be selling the last 3,000 drivers a manufacturer has ever made. If anyone can find a home for it, we can." The company boasts over 500,000 customers, affectionately referred to as "Rock Heads."

RockBottom's warehouse sports signs with "Scratch," the company's cartoonish, red-bearded caveman mascot. Scratch is surrounded with slogans such as: "A Clean Cave Is a Happy Cave" and "A Happy Rock Head Stays a Rock Head." Though Scratch is goofy, the company is all business. Offering a wide inventory of well-known brands of golf clubs, bags, balls, apparel, and accessories, this merchandising company buys in large lots and strives to keep costs low. For example, they located their distribution center in Virginia—enabling them to ship to over 60% of the U.S. population within two days. Also, they pack items in small, uniformly-sized boxes to lower costs.

Multiple-step income statements allow the company's managers to tell if sales are high enough above costs of goods sold, or if the company is paying too much for the items it sells. These income statements also give details on the company's other costs, for example shipping costs, to help managers make decisions. Classified balance sheets help company managers assess financial position.

In addition to financial statements, the company tracks "checkout flow," providing details on the point at which potential customers drop out of the checkout process and how many drop out. "If I had a 50% checkout success rate one day and 23% the next day, this lets me see that," explains Todd. This helps Todd steer more customers through the checkout process. He also tracks customer approval ratings, currently above 99%, as a performance measure.

As Todd says, the company plans to expand "as long as there are customers to win." Their expansion plans do not stop with golf. RockBottomGolf wants to become RockBottomSports, with many other sporting goods products available. With its fast-paced growth and position as the top golf retailer on the Internet, RockBottomGolf is "on the green."

[Sources: *RockBottomGolf.com Website,* January 2009; *Internet Retailer,* July 2007; *Inside Business-Hampton Roads,* October 2006.]

Once we make all necessary adjustments to the trial balance, we are ready to produce financial statements. Different financial statement formats can provide useful information to different financial statement users. We describe alternative formats for both income statements and balance sheets. We also describe the closing processes necessary to prepare for the next period's transactions.

Merchandiser's Financial Statements and the Closing Process

Work Sheet
- Preparing the work sheet for a merchandising business

Financial Statement Formats
- Multiple-step income statement
- Single-step income statement
- Statement of owner's equity
- Classified balance sheet

Completing the Accounting Cycle
- Closing entries
- Post-closing trial balance
- Reversing entries

The Work Sheet

Preparing the Work Sheet

LO1 Prepare a work sheet for a merchandising business.

Preparing the work sheet for a merchandiser follows the steps we showed for a service business in Chapter 6. Below we list the five steps in preparing the work sheet.

Step 1: Enter unadjusted trial balance.

Step 2: Enter adjustments.

Step 3: Prepare adjusted trial balance.

Step 4: Sort adjusted trial balance amounts to financial statement columns.

Step 5: Total statement columns, compute income or loss, and balance columns.

Exhibit 14.1 presents a completed work sheet for Z-Mart as of December 31, 2010. Steps 1 through 3 were completed in Chapter 13. In completing step 4, note that we extend the ending balance of merchandise inventory, obtained from a count of the items remaining unsold, to the balance sheet debit column. In addition, a merchandiser typically uses several detailed accounts to record sales and purchases. All of these accounts are temporary accounts, and thus they are extended into the income statement columns.

In completing step 5, we compute the total of each financial statement column. Z-Mart's income statement debit column totals $334,800, and its income statement credit column totals $347,700. The difference between these two totals ($12,900) is Z-Mart's net income for the period. This amount is added to the income statement debit column. Likewise, this $12,900 is added to the balance sheet credit column so that the two balance sheet column totals equal.

In the next section we show how to prepare the merchandiser's financial statements from work sheet information.

Exhibit 14.1

10-Column Work Sheet

No.	Account	Unadjusted Trial Balance Dr.	Cr.	Adjustments Dr.	Cr.	Adjusted Trial Balance Dr.	Cr.	Income Statement Dr.	Cr.	Balance Sheet Dr.	Cr.
101	Cash	8,200				8,200				8,200	
106	Accounts receivable	11,200				11,200				11,200	
119	Merchandise Inventory	19,000		(EI) 21,000	(BI) 19,000	21,000				21,000	
126	Supplies	3,800			(b) 3,000	800				800	
128	Prepaid insurance	900			(a) 600	300				300	
167	Equipment	34,200				34,200				34,200	
168	Accumulated depr.—Equip.		3,700		(c) 3,700		7,400				7,400
201	Accounts payable		16,000				16,000				16,000
209	Salaries payable				(d) 800		800				800
301	K. Marty, Capital		42,600				42,600				42,600
302	K. Marty, Withdrawals	4,000				4,000				4,000	
901	Income Summary			(BI) 19,000	(EI) 21,000	19,000	21,000	19,000	21,000		
413	Sales		321,000				321,000		321,000		
414	Sales returns and allowances	2,000				2,000		2,000			
415	Sales discounts	4,300				4,300		4,300			
505	Purchases	235,800				235,800		235,800			
506	Purchases returns & allowance		1,500				1,500		1,500		
507	Purchases discounts		4,200				4,200		4,200		
508	Transportation-in	2,300				2,300		2,300			
612	Depreciation expense—Equip.			(c) 3,700		3,700		3,700			
622	Salaries expense	43,000		(d) 800		43,800		43,800			
637	Insurance expense			(a) 600		600		600			
640	Rent expense	9,000				9,000		9,000			
652	Supplies expense			(b) 3,000		3,000		3,000			
655	Advertising expense	11,300				11,300		11,300			
	Totals	389,000	389,000	48,100	48,100	414,500	414,500	334,800	347,700	79,700	66,800
	Net income							12,900			12,900
	Totals							347,700	347,700	79,700	79,700

Financial Statement Formats

Generally accepted accounting principles do not require companies to use any one presentation format for financial statements. This section describes formats for multiple-step and single-step income statements, a statement of owner's equity, and a classified balance sheet.

Multiple-Step Income Statement

A **multiple-step income statement** format shows detailed computations of net sales and other costs and expenses, and reports subtotals for various classes of items. Exhibit 14.2 shows a multiple-step income statement for Z-Mart. The statement has three main parts: (1) *gross profit*, determined by net sales less cost of goods sold, (2) *income from operations*, determined by gross profit less operating expenses, and (3) *net income*, determined by income from operations adjusted for nonoperating items. The gross profit section includes a detailed cost of goods computation. Also, Z-Mart does not report any nonoperating items.

Some companies further classify operating expenses into two sections. **Selling expenses** include the expenses of promoting sales by displaying and advertising merchandise, making sales, and delivering goods to customers. Depreciation expense on store equipment is included since

LO2 Define and prepare multiple-step and single-step income statements.

Exhibit 14.2

Multiple-Step Income Statement

Z-MART Income Statement For Year Ended December 31, 2010			
Sales			$321,000
Less: Sales discounts		$ 4,300	
Sales returns and allowances		2,000	6,300
Net sales			$314,700
Cost of goods sold:			
Merchandise inventory, January 1, 2010			$19,000
Purchases		$235,800	
Less: Purchase returns and allowances	($1,500)		
Purchase discounts	(4,200)		
Plus: Transportation-in	2,300	($3,400)	
Net purchases		$232,400	
Goods available for sale		$251,400	
Less: Merchandise inventory, December 31, 2010		21,000	
Cost of goods sold			$230,400
Gross profit			$ 84,300
Operating expenses			
Depreciation expense-Equipment		$ 3,700	
Salaries expense		43,800	
Insurance expense		600	
Rent expense		9,000	
Supplies expense		3,000	
Advertising expense		11,300	
Total operating expenses			71,400
Net income			$ 12,900

Gross profit computation brackets the section from Sales through Gross profit.

Income from operations computation brackets the section from Operating expenses through Net income.

this equipment is used to generate sales. **General and administrative expenses** support a company's overall operations and include expenses related to accounting, human resource management, and financial management. These expenses are not directly related to the sales function of the business. If a company further classifies its operating expenses this way, the multiple-step income statement will include subtotals for the total selling expenses and the total general and administrative expenses.

Nonoperating activities consist of other expenses, revenues, losses, and gains that are unrelated to a company's operations. They are reported in two sections: (1) *other revenues and gains,* which often include interest revenue, dividend revenue, rent revenue, and gains from asset disposals, and (2) *other expenses and losses,* which often include interest expense, losses from asset disposals, and casualty losses. When a company has no reportable nonoperating activities, its income from operations is simply labeled net income. A partial income statement for a company with nonoperating activities might look like the following:

Income from operations		12,900
Other revenues and gains (expenses and losses)		
Interest revenue	1,000	
Gain on sale of building	2,500	
Interest expense	(1,500)	
Total other revenue and gains (expenses and losses)		2,000
Net income		$14,900

Nonoperating activities computation brackets the section from Other revenues and gains through Net income.

Single-Step Income Statement

A **single-step income statement** is another widely used format. An example is shown in Exhibit 14.3 for Z-Mart. It lists cost of goods sold as another expense and shows only one subtotal for total expenses. Expenses are grouped into very few, if any, categories. Many companies use formats that combine features of both the single- and multiple-step statements. Provided that income statement items are shown sensibly, management can choose the format. (In later chapters, we describe some items, such as extraordinary gains and losses, that must be reported in certain locations on the income statement.)

Z-MART Income Statement For Year Ended December 31, 2010		
Revenues		
Net sales		$314,700
Expenses		
Cost of goods sold	$230,400	
Operating expenses	71,400	
Total expenses		301,800
Net income		$ 12,900

Exhibit 14.3

Single-Step Income Statement

Statement of Owner's Equity

The statement of owner's equity summarizes changes in the owner's equity account during the year due to:

LO3 Prepare a statement of owner's equity.

Item	Source of information
Net income or loss for the year	Income statement
Owner investments during the year	Owner, Capital, general ledger account
Owner withdrawals during the year	Work sheet

The Owner, Capital, account is updated during the year only for additional owner investments. Thus, for Z-Mart, the ending balance in K. Marty, Capital, on the work sheet ($42,600) must be increased for 2010's net income of $12,900 and decreased by K. Marty's withdrawals ($4,000) during the year. If K. Marty made no additional investments in Z-Mart during the year, Z-Mart's statement of owner's equity for 2010 would appear as in Exhibit 14.4 below.

Z-MART Statement of Owner's Equity For Year Ended December 31, 2010	
K. Marty, Capital, January 1, 2010	$42,600
Add: Net income	12,900
	55,500
Less: Withdrawals by owner	4,000
K. Marty, Capital, December 31, 2010	$51,500

Exhibit 14.4

Statement of Owner's Equity

Classified Balance Sheet

This section describes a classified balance sheet. An **unclassified balance sheet** is one whose items are broadly grouped into assets, liabilities, and equity. A **classified balance sheet** organizes assets and liabilities into important subgroups that provide more information to decision makers.

LO4 Explain and prepare a classified balance sheet.

Exhibit 14.5

Typical Categories in a Classified Balance Sheet

Assets	Liabilities and Equity
Current assets	Current liabilities
Noncurrent assets	Noncurrent liabilities
Long-term investments	Equity
Plant assets	
Intangible assets	

Current is also called *short-term,* and noncurrent is also called *long-term.*

Classification Structure A classified balance sheet has no required layout, but it usually contains the categories in Exhibit 14.5. One of the more important classifications is the separation between current and noncurrent items for both assets and liabilities. Current items are those expected to come due (either collected or owed) within one year or the company's operating cycle, whichever is longer. The **operating cycle** is the time span from when *cash is used* to acquire goods and services until *cash is received* from the sale of goods and services. "Operating" refers to company operations and "cycle" refers to the circular flow of cash used for company inputs and then cash received from its outputs. The length of a company's operating cycle depends on its activities. For a service company, the operating cycle is the time span between (1) paying employees who perform the services and (2) receiving cash from customers. For a merchandiser selling products, the operating cycle is the time span between (1) paying suppliers for merchandise and (2) receiving cash from customers.

Most operating cycles are less than one year. This means most companies use a one-year period in deciding which assets and liabilities are current. A few companies have an operating cycle longer than one year. For instance, producers of certain beverages (wine) and products (ginseng) that require aging for several years have operating cycles longer than one year. A classified balance sheet lists current assets before noncurrent assets and current liabilities before noncurrent liabilities. This consistency in presentation allows users to quickly identify current assets that are most easily converted to cash and current liabilities that are shortly coming due. Items in current assets and current liabilities are listed in the order of how quickly they will be converted to, or paid in, cash.

Classification Categories This section describes the most common categories in a classified balance sheet. The balance sheet for Z-Mart in Exhibit 14.6 shows some of these typical categories. Its assets are classified as either current or noncurrent. Its liabilities are all classified as current. Not all companies use the same categories of assets and liabilities for their balance

Exhibit 14.6

Example of a Classified Balance Sheet

Z-MART Balance Sheet December 31, 2010		
Assets		
Current assets		
Cash		$ 8,200
Accounts receivable		11,200
Merchandise inventory		21,000
Prepaid expenses		
Prepaid insurance	$ 300	
Supplies	800	1,100
Total current assets		41,500
Noncurrent assets		
Equipment	34,200	
Less: Accumulated depreciation	7,400	26,800
Total assets		$68,300
Liabilities and Owner's Equity		
Current liabilities		
Accounts payable		$16,000
Salaries payable		800
Total current liabilities		$16,800
Owner's equity		
K. Marty, Capital		51,500
Total liabilities and owner's equity		$68,300

sheets. **K2 Inc.**'s balance sheet lists only three asset classes: current assets; property, plant, and equipment; and other assets.

Current assets   **Current assets** are cash and other resources that are expected to be sold, collected, or used within one year or the company's operating cycle, whichever is longer. Examples are cash, short-term investments, accounts receivable, short-term notes receivable, merchandise inventory, and prepaid expenses. Current assets are usually listed according to the ease with which they can be converted to cash. Contra-assets, like Accumulated Depreciation, are listed in the assets section, even though they have credit balances. Prepaid expenses are usually listed last because they will not be converted to cash (instead, they are used).

Long-term investments   A second major balance sheet classification is **long-term** (or *noncurrent*) **investments.** Notes receivable and investments in stocks and bonds are long-term assets when they are expected to be held for more than the longer of one year or the operating cycle. Land held for future expansion is a long-term investment because it is *not* used in operations.

Plant assets   Plant assets are tangible assets that are both *long lived* and *used to produce* or *sell products and services.* Examples are equipment, machinery, buildings, and land used to produce or sell products and services. Plant assets are also called *fixed assets; property, plant, and equipment; or long-lived assets.*

Intangible assets   **Intangible assets** are long-term resources that benefit business operations. They usually lack physical form and have uncertain benefits. Examples are patents, trademarks, copyrights, franchises, and goodwill. Their value comes from the privileges or rights granted to or held by the owner. **K2, Inc.,** reports intangible assets of $228 million, which is nearly 20 percent of its total assets. Its intangibles include trademarks, patents, and licensing agreements.

Current liabilities   **Current liabilities** are obligations due to be paid or settled within one year or the operating cycle, whichever is longer. They are usually settled by paying out current assets such as cash. Current liabilities often include accounts payable, notes payable, wages payable, taxes payable, interest payable, and unearned revenues. Also, any portion of a long-term liability due to be paid within one year or the operating cycle, whichever is longer, is a current liability. Unearned revenues are current liabilities when they will be settled by delivering products or services within one year or the operating cycle, whichever is longer. Current liabilities are reported in the order of those to be settled first.

Long-term liabilities   **Long-term liabilities** are obligations *not* due within one year or the operating cycle, whichever is longer. Notes payable, mortgages payable, bonds payable, and lease obligations are common long-term liabilities. If a company has both short- and long-term items in any of these categories, they are commonly reported in both sections of the classified balance sheet. For example, assume a company owes $20,000 on a note payable, $2,000 of which is due next year. The company would include $2,000 for notes payable in the current liabilities section and $18,000 for notes payable in the noncurrent liabilities section.

Equity   Equity is the owner's claim on assets. For a proprietorship, this claim is reported in the equity section with an owner's capital account. (For a partnership, the equity section reports a capital account for each partner. For a corporation, the equity section is divided into two main subsections, common stock and retained earnings. We discuss accounting for partnerships and corporations in later chapters.)

HOW YOU DOIN'?   Answers—p. 358

  1. Classify the following assets as (1) current assets, (2) plant assets, or (3) intangible assets:
   (a) land used in operations, (b) office supplies, (c) receivables from customers due in 10 months,
   (d) insurance protection for the next nine months, (e) trucks used to provide services to customers,
   (f) trademarks.
  2. Cite two examples of assets classified as investments on the balance sheet.
  3. Explain the operating cycle for a service company.

Completing the Accounting Cycle

After journalizing and posting the adjusting entries and preparing financial statements, the accountant completes the accounting cycle by journalizing and posting closing entries and preparing a post-closing trial balance. We illustrate these steps next.

Closing Entries

LO5 Prepare journal entries to close temporary accounts.

There are four necessary steps to record and post the closing entries for a merchandiser.

Step 1: Close revenue accounts and those accounts used in computing cost of goods sold having credit balances to Income Summary.

Step 2: Close expense accounts and those accounts used in computing cost of goods sold having debit balances to Income Summary.

Step 3: Close the Income Summary account to the owner's capital account.

Step 4: Close the Withdrawals account to the owner's capital account.

Like service companies, merchandisers follow these four steps in closing temporary accounts. However, merchandisers typically have additional temporary accounts related to the recording of sales and purchases.

We illustrate the closing entries for Z-Mart, using information from Z-Mart's partial work sheet (from Exhibit 14.1) in Exhibit 14.7. The dollar amount for step 3 is obtained from a review of the postings to the Income Summary account, shown in Exhibit 14.8.

Exhibit 14.7

Closing Journal Entries for a Merchandiser

No.	Account	Income Statement Dr.	Income Statement Cr.	Balance Sheet Dr.	Balance Sheet Cr.
101	Cash			8,200	
106	Accounts receivable			11,200	
119	Merchandise Inventory			21,000	
126	Supplies			800	
128	Prepaid insurance			300	
167	Equipment			34,200	
168	Accumulated depr.—Equip.				7,400
201	Accounts payable				16,000
209	Salaries payable				800
301	K. Marty, Capital				42,600
302	K. Marty, Withdrawals			4,000	
901	Income Summary	19,000	21,000		
413	Sales		321,000		
414	Sales returns and allowances	2,000			
415	Sales discounts	4,300			
505	Purchases	235,800			
506	Purchases returns & allowance		1,500		
507	Purchases discounts		4,200		
508	Transportation-in	2,300			
612	Depreciation expense—Equip.	3,700			
622	Salaries expense	43,800			
637	Insurance expense	600			
640	Rent expense	9,000			
652	Supplies expense	3,000			
655	Advertising expense	11,300			
	Totals	334,800	347,700	79,700	66,800
	Net income	12,900			12,900
	Totals	347,700	347,700	79,700	79,700

Closing entries	Debit	Credit
Step 1		
Sales	321 0 0 0 00	
Purchase Returns and Allowances	1 5 0 0 00	
Purchase Discounts	4 2 0 0 00	
Income Summary		326 7 0 0 00
Step 2		
Income Summary	315 8 0 0 00	
Purchases		235 8 0 0 00
Sales Returns and Allowances		2 0 0 0 00
Sales Discounts		4 3 0 0 00
Transportation-in		2 3 0 0 00
Depreciation expense—Equip.		3 7 0 0 00
Salaries Expense		43 8 0 0 00
Insurance Expense		6 0 0 00
Rent Expense		9 0 0 0 00
Supplies Expense		3 0 0 0 00
Advertising Expense		11 3 0 0 00
Step 3		
Income Summary	12 9 0 0 00	
K. Marty, Capital		12 9 0 0 00
Step 4		
K. Marty, Capital	4 0 0 0 00	
K. Marty, Withdrawals		4 0 0 0 00

The closing entries are all posted to general ledger accounts as we showed in Chapter 6. In Exhibit 14.8 below we show the posting of closing entries to just the Income Summary account. In addition, we post the adjusting entries to Income Summary for the beginning and ending merchandise inventory balances (from Chapter 13). After posting these adjusting and closing entries, the Income Summary account should have a zero balance, as we show in Exhibit 14.8.

Income Summary				Account No. 901
Date	Explanation	Debit	Credit	Balance
2010 Dec. 31	Adjusting (BI)	19,000		19,000
Dec. 31	Adjusting (EI)		21,000	(2,000)
Dec. 31	Closing (Step 1)		326,700	(328,700)
Dec. 31	Closing (Step 2)	315,800		(12,900)
Dec. 31	Closing (Step 3)	12,900		-0-

Exhibit 14.8

Postings to Income Summary Account

Post-Closing Trial Balance

After journalizing and posting the closing entries a post-closing trial balance is prepared using the balances in the *permanent* accounts from the work sheet. Since all the temporary accounts have been closed, they have zero balances and do not appear on the post-closing trial balance. Recall that the work sheet does not have an updated balance for the owner's capital account; this can be obtained from the statement of owner's equity (see Exhibit 14.4) or from the general ledger.

The post-closing trial balance is used to prove that total debits equal total credits in the permanent accounts in the general ledger. Exhibit 14.9 presents Z-Mart's post-closing trial balance at December 31, 2010.

LO6 Prepare a post-closing trial balance.

Z-MART
Post-Closing Trial Balance
December 31, 2010

Account	Debit	Credit
Cash	$ 8,200	
Accounts receivable	11,200	
Merchandise inventory	21,000	
Supplies	800	
Prepaid insurance	300	
Equipment	34,200	
Accumulated depreciation—Equipment		$ 7,400
Accounts payable		16,000
Salaries payable		800
K. Marty, Capital		51,500
Totals	$75,700	$75,700

Exhibit 14.9

Z-Mart Post-Closing Trial Balance

The final optional step in the accounting cycle is to prepare reversing entries. Some companies use reversing entries in preparation for the next accounting period. Reversing entries are discussed in the appendix to this chapter.

Demonstration Problem

Presented below is the adjusted trial balance for Worker Products Company as of December 31, 2010. The company started the year with a balance of $24,000 in Merchandise Inventory.

WORKER PRODUCTS COMPANY Adjusted Trial Balance December 31, 2010		
	Debit	**Credit**
Cash	$ 9,400	
Accounts receivable	25,000	
Merchandise inventory	36,000	
Office supplies	900	
Store equipment	75,000	
Accumulated depreciation—store equipment		$ 22,000
Office equipment	60,000	
Accumulated depreciation—office equipment		15,000
Accounts payable		42,000
Notes payable		10,000
F. Worker, Capital		110,700
F. Worker, Withdrawals	48,000	
Income Summary		12,000
Sales		325,000
Sales discounts	6,000	
Sales returns and allowances	16,500	
Purchases	210,000	
Purchase discounts		2,500
Purchase returns and allowances		1,500
Transportation-in	1,000	
Sales salaries expense	32,500	
Depreciation expense—store equipment	11,000	
Depreciation expense—office equipment	7,500	
Office supplies expense	1,300	
Interest expense	600	
Totals	$540,700	$540,700

Required

1. Prepare a multiple-step income statement in good form.
2. Prepare the necessary closing entries.

Planning the Solution

- Classify each income statement item as either a component of (1) gross profit, (2) income from operations, or (3) net income.
- Classify operating expenses into either selling or general and administrative.
- Use Exhibit 14.2 as a guide for the format of a multiple-step income statement.
- Follow the four steps for recording the closing entries.

Solution to Demonstration Problem

1. Multiple-step income statement

WORKER PRODUCTS COMPANY
Income Statement
For the Year Ended December 31, 2010

Sales			$325,000
Less: Sales discounts		$ 6,000	
Sales returns and allowances		16,500	22,500
Net sales			$302,500
Merchandise inventory, 12/31/09		24,000	
Purchases	210,000		
Transportation-in	1,000		
Less: Purchase discounts	(2,500)		
Purchase returns and allowances	(1,500)		
Net purchases		207,000	
Goods available for sale		231,000	
Less: Merchandise inventory, 12/31/10		(36,000)	
Cost of goods sold			195,000
Gross profit			107,500
Operating expenses			
Selling expenses			
Sales salaries expense		32,500	
Depreciation expense—store equipment		11,000	
Total selling expenses		43,500	
General and administrative expenses			
Depreciation expense—office equipment		7,500	
Office supplies expense		1,300	
Total general and administrative expenses		8,800	
Total operating expenses			52,300
Income from operations			55,200
Other expenses			
Interest expense			600
Net income			$ 54,600

2. Closing journal entries

	Debit	Credit
Sales	325 0 0 0 00	
Purchase Returns and Allowances	1 5 0 0 00	
Purchase Discounts	2 5 0 0 00	
Income Summary		329 0 0 0 00
To close temporary accounts having credit balances		
Income Summary	286 4 0 0 00	
Purchases		210 0 0 0 00
Sales Returns and Allowances		16 5 0 0 00
Sales Discounts		6 0 0 0 00
Transportation-In		1 0 0 0 00
Depreciation Expense—Store Equipment		11 0 0 0 00
Depreciation Expense—Office Equipment		7 5 0 0 00
Sales Salaries Expense		32 5 0 0 00
Office Supplies Expense		1 3 0 0 00
Interest Expense		6 0 0 00
To close temporary accounts having debit balances		
Income Summary	54 6 0 0 00	
F. Worker, Capital		54 6 0 0 00
To close Income Summary		
F. Worker, Capital	48 0 0 0 00	
F. Worker, Withdrawals		48 0 0 0 00
To close owner withdrawals		

Reversing Entries

Reversing entries are optional. They are recorded in response to accrued assets and accrued liabilities that were created by adjusting entries at the end of a reporting period. The purpose of reversing entries is to simplify a company's recordkeeping. Exhibit 14A.1 shows an example of FastForward's (a company

Exhibit 14A.1

Reversing Entries for an
Accrued Expense

Accrue salaries expense on December 31, 2010

Salaries Expense 210
    Salaries Payable 210

Salaries Expense

Date	Expl.	Debit	Credit	Balance
2010				
Dec. 12		700		700
26		700		1,400
31		210		1,610

Salaries Payable

Date	Expl.	Debit	Credit	Balance
2010				
Dec. 31			210	210

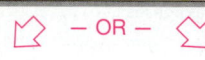
— OR —

No reversing entry recorded on January 1, 2011

NO ENTRY

Salaries Expense

Date	Expl.	Debit	Credit	Balance
2011				

Salaries Payable

Date	Expl.	Debit	Credit	Balance
2010				
Dec. 31			210	210
2011				

Reversing entry recorded on January 1, 2011

Salaries Payable 210
    Salaries Expense 210

Salaries Expense*

Date	Expl.	Debit	Credit	Balance
2011				
Jan. 1			210	(210)

Salaries Payable

Date	Expl.	Debit	Credit	Balance
2010				
Dec. 31			210	210
2011				
Jan. 1		210		0

Pay the accrued and current salaries on January 9, the first payday in 2011

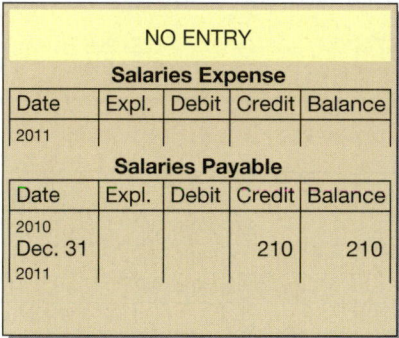

Salaries Expense 490
Salaries Payable 210
    Cash 700

Salaries Expense

Date	Expl.	Debit	Credit	Balance
2011				
Jan. 9		490		**490**

Salaries Payable

Date	Expl.	Debit	Credit	Balance
2010				
Dec. 31			210	210
2011				
Jan. 9		210		**0**

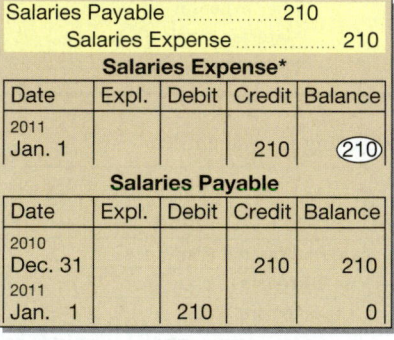

Salaries Expense 700
    Cash 700

Salaries Expense*

Date	Expl.	Debit	Credit	Balance
2011				
Jan. 1			210	(210)
Jan. 9		700		**490**

Salaries Payable

Date	Expl.	Debit	Credit	Balance
2010				
Dec. 31			210	210
2011				
Jan. 1		210		**0**

Under both approaches, the expense and liability accounts have
identical balances after the cash payment on January 9.

Salaries Expense $490
Salaries Payable .... $ 0

*Circled numbers in the *Balance* column indicate abnormal balances.

whose transactions we examined in detail in Chapters 2 through 6) reversing entries. The top of the exhibit shows the adjusting entry FastForward recorded on December 31 for its employee's earned but unpaid salary. We explained this entry in Chapter 5. The entry recorded three days' salary of $210, which increased December's total salary expense to $1,610. The entry also recognized a liability of $210. The expense is reported on December's income statement. The expense account is then closed. The ledger on January 1, 2010, shows a $210 liability and a zero balance in the Salaries Expense account. At this point, the choice is made between using or not using reversing entries.

> As a general rule, adjusting entries that create new asset or liability accounts are likely candidates for reversing.

Accounting *without* Reversing Entries

The path down the left side of Exhibit 14A.1 is described in the chapter. To summarize here, when the next payday occurs on January 9, we record payment with a compound entry that debits both the expense and liability accounts and credits Cash. Posting that entry creates a $490 balance in the expense account and reduces the liability account balance to zero because the payable has been settled. The disadvantage of this approach is the slightly more complex entry required on January 9. Paying the accrued liability means that this entry differs from the routine entries made on all other paydays. To construct the proper entry on January 9, we must recall the effect of the December 31 adjusting entry. Reversing entries overcome this disadvantage.

Accounting *with* Reversing Entries

The right side of Exhibit 14A.1 shows how reversing entries can be helpful. *A reversing entry is the exact opposite of an adjusting entry*. For FastForward, the Salaries Payable liability account is debited for $210, meaning that this account now has a zero balance after the entry is posted. The Salaries Payable account temporarily understates the liability, but this is not a problem since financial statements are not prepared before the liability is settled on January 9. The credit to the Salaries Expense account is unusual because it gives the account an *abnormal credit balance*. We highlight an abnormal balance by circling it. Because of the reversing entry, the January 9 entry to record payment is straightforward. This entry debits the Salaries Expense account and credits Cash for the full $700 paid. It is the same as all other entries made to record 10 days' salary for the employee. Notice that after the payment entry is posted, the Salaries Expense account has a $490 balance that reflects seven days' salary of $70 per day (see the lower right side of Exhibit 14A.1). The zero balance in the Salaries Payable account is now correct. The lower section of Exhibit 14A.1 shows that the expense and liability accounts have exactly the same balances whether reversing entries are used or not. This means that both approaches yield identical results.

LO7 Prepare reversing entries and explain their purpose.

Summary

LO1 Prepare a work sheet for a merchandising business. A work sheet can be useful in organizing data, preparing financial statements, and preparing closing entries. The work sheet includes columns for the unadjusted trial balance, the adjusting entries, and the adjusted trial balance. Balances in the adjusted trial balance columns are then extended into either income statement or balance sheet columns.

LO2 Define and prepare multiple-step and single-step income statements. Multiple-step income statements include greater detail for sales, purchases, and expenses than do single-step income statements. Multiple-step income statements often report expenses in categories reflecting different activities.

LO3 Prepare a statement of owner's equity. The statement of owner's equity is used to summarize changes in the owner's capital account during the year. The beginning balance of owner's capital is updated for the net income or loss for the period, additional owner investments during the period, and any owner withdrawals during the period. The ending balance of owner's capital is included on the end of period balance sheet.

LO4 Explain and prepare a classified balance sheet. Classified balance sheets report assets and liabilities in two categories: current and noncurrent. Current assets often include cash, accounts receivable, and merchandise inventory. Noncurrent assets often include long-term investments, plant assets, and intangible assets. Current liabilities often include accounts payable and wages payable. Noncurrent liabilities often include notes payable, bonds payable, and leases.

LO5 Prepare journal entries to close temporary accounts. Closing entries involve four steps: (1) close temporary accounts having credit balances to Income Summary, (2) close temporary accounts having debit balances to Income Summary, (3) close Income Summary to the owner's capital account, and (4) close the owner withdrawals account to the owner's capital account.

LO6 Prepare a post-closing trial balance. After journalizing and posting the closing entries, a trial balance is prepared using the ending balances in the permanent accounts. This post-closing trial balance proves the equality of debits and credits in the general ledger.

LO7 Prepare reversing entries and explain their purpose. Reversing entries are an optional step in the accounting cycle. They are applied to accrued expenses and revenues. The purpose of reversing entries is to simplify subsequent journal entries. Financial statements are not affected by the choice to use or not use reversing entries.

1. Current assets: (*b*), (*c*), (*d*). Plant assets: (*a*), (*e*). Item (*f*) is an intangible asset.

2. Investment in common stock, investment in bonds, and land held for future expansion.

3. For a service company, the operating cycle is the usual time between (1) paying employees who do the services and (2) receiving cash from customers for services provided.

4. Purchase Discounts, Purchase Returns and Allowances, Transportation-in, Sales, Sales Returns and Allowances, and Sales Discounts.

5. Four closing entries: (1) close temporary accounts with credit balances to Income Summary, (2) close temporary accounts with debit balances to Income Summary, (3) close Income Summary to owner's capital, and (4) close withdrawals account to owner's capital.

Key Terms

Classified balance sheet (p. 349) Balance sheet that presents assets and liabilities in relevant subgroups, including current and noncurrent classifications.

Current assets (p. 351) Cash and other assets expected to be sold, collected, or used within one year or the company's operating cycle, whichever is longer.

Current liabilities (p. 351) Obligations due to be paid or settled within one year or the company's operating cycle, whichever is longer.

General and administrative expenses (p. 348) Expenses that support the operating activities of a business.

Intangible assets (p. 351) Long-term assets (resources) used to produce or sell products or services; usually lack physical form and have uncertain benefits.

Long-term investments (p. 351) Long-term assets not used in operating activities such as notes receivable and investments in stocks and bonds.

Long-term liabilities (p. 351) Obligations not due to be paid within one year or the operating cycle, whichever is longer.

Multiple-step income statement (p. 347) Income statement format that shows subtotals between sales and net income, categorizes expenses, and often reports the details of net sales and expenses.

Operating cycle (p. 350) Normal time between paying cash for merchandise or employee services and receiving cash from customers.

Reversing entries (p. 356) Optional entries recorded at the beginning of a period that prepare the accounts for the usual journal entries as if adjusting entries had not occurred in the prior period.

Selling expenses (p. 347) Expenses of promoting sales, such as displaying and advertising merchandise, making sales, and delivering goods to customers.

Single-step income statement (p. 349) Income statement format that includes cost of goods sold as an expense and shows only one subtotal for total expenses.

Unclassified balance sheet (p. 349) Balance sheet that broadly groups assets, liabilities, and equity accounts.

Multiple Choice Quiz
Answers on p. 367
mhhe.com/wildCA2e

Additional Multiple Choice Quizzes are available at the book's Website.

1. A company has $550,000 in net sales and $123,000 in gross profit. Its cost of goods sold equals
   a. $427,000
   b. $673,000
   c. $550,000
   d. $123,000
   e. ($123,000)

2. J. Awn, the proprietor of Awn Services, withdrew $8,700 from the business during the current year. The entry to close the withdrawals account at the end of the year is

a.	J. Awn, Withdrawals	8,700	
	Cash		8,700
b.	J. Awn, Capital	8,700	
	J. Awn, Withdrawals		8,700
c.	J. Awn, Withdrawals	8,700	
	J. Awn, Capital		8,700
d.	J. Awn, Capital	8,700	
	Salary Expense		8,700
e.	Income Summary	8,700	
	J. Awn, Capital		8,700

3. An income statement that includes cost of goods sold as another expense and shows only one subtotal for total expenses is a

   a. Balanced income statement.
   b. Single-step income statement.
   c. Multiple-step income statement.
   d. Combined income statement.
   e. Simplified income statement.

4. A classified balance sheet
   a. Measures a company's ability to pay its bills on time.
   b. Organizes assets and liabilities into important subgroups.
   c. Presents revenues, expenses, and net income.
   d. Reports operating, investing, and financing activities.
   e. Reports the effect of profit and withdrawals on owner's capital.

5. A company shows a $60,000 debit balance in Merchandise Inventory in the Unadjusted Trial Balance columns of the work sheet. The company uses a periodic inventory system. This $60,000 balance represents
   a. The amount of inventory at the beginning of the year.
   b. Cost of goods sold for the year.
   c. The cost of merchandise purchased during the year.
   d. The amount of inventory at the end of the year.
   e. Sales returns and allowances.

Superscript letter ^A denotes assignments based on Appendix 14A.

Discussion Questions

1. What is a company's operating cycle?

2. What classes of assets and liabilities are shown on a typical classified balance sheet?

3. How is unearned revenue classified on the balance sheet?

4. What are the characteristics of plant assets?

5. What is the difference between the single-step and multiple-step income statement formats?

6.^AHow do reversing entries simplify recordkeeping?

7.^AIf a company recorded accrued salaries expense of $500 at the end of its fiscal year, what reversing entry could be made? When would it be made?

8. Refer to the balance sheet for **Best Buy** in Appendix A. What five noncurrent asset categories are used on its classified balance sheet?

9. Refer to Best Buy's balance sheet in Appendix A. Identify the accounts listed as current liabilities.

---

connect

The following are common categories on a classified balance sheet.

A. Current assets   **D.** Intangible assets

B. Long-term investments   **E.** Current liabilities

C. Plant assets   **F.** Long-term liabilities

For each of the following items, select the letter that identifies the balance sheet category where the item typically would appear. Some letters are used more than once.

_____ **1.** Land not currently used in operations

_____ **2.** Notes payable (due in three years)

_____ **3.** Accounts receivable

_____ **4.** Trademarks

_____ **5.** Accounts payable

_____ **6.** Store equipment

_____ **7.** Wages payable

_____ **8.** Cash

QUICK STUDY

QS 14–1
Classifying balance sheet items
LO4

List the following steps in preparing a work sheet in their proper order by writing numbers 1–5 in the blank spaces provided.

a. _____ Total the statement columns, compute net income (loss), and complete work sheet.

b. _____ Extend adjusted balances to appropriate financial statement columns.

c. _____ Prepare an unadjusted trial balance on the work sheet.

d. _____ Prepare an adjusted trial balance on the work sheet.

e. _____ Enter adjustments data on the work sheet.

QS 14–2
Ordering work sheet steps
LO1

Match the following terms **A** through **J** with the appropriate definitions 1 through 10.

A. Plant assets   **F.** Closing entries

B. Owner's capital   **G.** Current liabilities

C. Classified balance sheet   **H.** Long-term investments

D. Intangible assets   **I.** Current assets

E. Operating cycle   **J.** Unclassified balance sheet

_____ **1.** The owner's claim on the assets of a company.

_____ **2.** Tangible long-lived assets used to produce or sell products or services.

_____ **3.** Cash or other assets that are expected to be sold, collected, or used within one year or the company's operating cycle, whichever is longer.

_____ **4.** Entries recorded at the end of each accounting period to transfer end-of-period balances in revenue, expense, and withdrawals accounts to the permanent owner's capital account.

_____ **5.** Long-term assets used to produce or sell products or services; these assets usually lack physical form and their benefits are uncertain.

_____ **6.** Assets such as notes receivable or investments in stocks which are held for the longer of one year or the operating cycle of the company.

_____ **7.** A balance sheet that organizes the assets and liabilities into important subgroups.

_____ **8.** Obligations that are due to be paid or settled within one year or the operating cycle of a business, whichever is longer.

QS 14–3
Balance sheet classifications
LO4

_____ **9.** A balance sheet that broadly groups assets, liabilities, and equity items.

_____ **10.** The time it takes a merchandiser to go from paying cash to buy goods to receiving cash from selling those goods.

QS 14–4

Income statement terms   **LO2**

Match the following terms **A** through **E** with the appropriate definitions 1 through 5.

A. Merchandise inventory   **D.** Multiple-step income statement

B. Single-step income statement   **E.** General and administrative expenses

C. Selling expenses

_____ **1.** An income statement format that shows only one subtotal for total expenses.

_____ **2.** Products a company owns and intends to sell.

_____ **3.** Expenses that support overall operations and includes expenses related to accounting, human resource management, and financial management.

_____ **4.** An income statement format that shows detailed computations of net sales and other costs and expenses, and reports subtotals for various classes of items.

_____ **5.** The expenses of promoting sales by displaying and advertising merchandise, making sales, and delivering goods to customers.

QS 14–5

Net sales section of the income statement   **LO2**

EL Merchandising reports the (partial) adjusted trial balance information below for the year ending December 31, 2010. Prepare the net sales section of a multiple-step income statement for EL Merchandising for 2010.

Merchandise inventory	$ 25,000
E. Lynn, Capital, ...	70,000
E. Lynn, Withdrawals	33,000
Operating expenses	150,000
Purchases	208,500
Purchase discounts	4,250
Purchase returns and allowances	6,250
Sales	384,250
Sales discounts	7,750
Sales returns and allowances	1,500
Transportation-in	2,000

QS 14–6

Cost of goods sold section of the income statement   **LO2**

Refer to the data in Quick Study 14-5. In addition, EL Merchandising reports an inventory balance of $30,000 on January 1, 2010. Prepare the cost of goods sold section of a multiple-step income statement for EL Merchandising for 2010.

QS 14–7

Statement of owner's equity

LO3

Refer to the data in Quick Study 14-5. EL Merchandising reports net income of $120,000 for 2010. Prepare the statement of owner's equity for 2010.

QS 14–8

Post-closing trial balance   **LO6**

Refer to the data in Quick Study 14-5. What accounts would appear on EL Merchandising's December 31, 2010, post-closing trial balance?

QS 14–9

Closing entries   **LO5**

Refer to the data in Quick Study 14-5. Prepare the journal entries to close EL Merchandising's temporary accounts on December 31, 2010.

QS 14–10[A]

Reversing entries   **LO7**

On December 31, 2010, Yates Co. prepared an adjusting entry for $12,000 of earned but unrecorded management fees. On January 16, 2011, Yates received $26,700 cash in management fees, which included the accrued fees earned in 2010. Assuming the company uses reversing entries, prepare the January 1, 2011, reversing entry and the January 16, 2011, cash receipt entry.

connect™

Use the following post-closing trial balance of Jones Merchandising Company to prepare a statement of owner's equity for 2010. Net income for 2010 was $25,500. K. Jones withdrew $20,000 during the year. (*Hint:* Solve for beginning K. Jones, Capital).

EXERCISES

Exercise 14-1
Preparing a statement of owner's equity   **LO3**

Account Title	Debit	Credit
Cash	$ 18,000	
Accounts receivable	17,500	
Merchandise inventory	85,000	
Office supplies	3,000	
Trucks	172,000	
Accumulated depreciation—Trucks		$ 36,000
Accounts payable		37,500
Interest payable		4,000
Long-term notes payable (all due in 2014)		53,000
K. Jones, Capital		165,000
Totals.....................................	$295,500	$295,500

Use the information in the post-closing trial balance reported in Exercise 14-1 to prepare Jones Merchandising Company's classified balance sheet as of December 31, 2010.

Exercise 14-2
Preparing a classified balance sheet
LO4

Check   Total assets, $259,500; K. Jones, Capital, $165,000

Listed below are a number of accounts. Use the table to classify each account. Indicate whether it is a temporary or permanent account (T or P), whether it is included in the income statement or balance sheet (IS or BS), whether it is closed at the end of the accounting period, and if so, how it is closed (Dr. or Cr. entry). The first one is done as an example.

Exercise 14-3
LO1   LO5

Account	Permanent (P) or Temporary (T)	Income Statement (IS) or Balance Sheet (BS)	Closed (C) or Not Closed (NC)	Closed with a Debit (Dr) or Credit (CR)
a. Accounts payable	P	BS	NC	—
b. Accounts receivable				
c. Accumulated depreciation—equipment				
d. Advertising expense				
e. Cash				
f. Depreciation expense—equipment				
g. Equipment				
h. Insurance expense				
i. Interest expense				
j. Merchandise inventory (ending balance)				
k. Notes payable				
l. Office supplies				
m. Office supplies expense				
n. Purchases				
o. Purchase returns				
p. Owner, capital				
q. Owner, withdrawals				
r. Salaries expense				
s. Sales				
t. Sales discounts				
u. Transportation-in				

Exercise 14-4
Preparing classified balance sheets
LO4

Based on the post-closing trial balance shown below, prepare a classified balance sheet for J-Mart as of December 31. Net income for 2010 was $63,700.

J-MART Post-Closing Trial Balance December 31		
	Debit	**Credit**
Cash	$ 18,200	
Accounts receivable	34,200	
Supplies	2,100	
Merchandise inventory	25,000	
Delivery equipment	45,000	
Accumulated depreciation—delivery equipment		$ 11,080
Intangible assets	16,000	
Accounts payable		16,200
Wages payable		4,120
Long-term notes payable*		20,000
Emily Jacobs, Capital		89,100
Totals	$140,500	$140,500

* $2,000 of the long-term note payable is due during the next year.

Exercise 14-5
Preparing the multiple-step income statement   **LO2**

JK Products reports the following adjusted trial balance at December 31, 2010, the end of its first year of operations. Prepare a multiple-step income statement for the year ending December 31, 2010.

JK PRODUCTS Adjusted Trial Balance December 31, 2010		
Account	**Debit**	**Credit**
Cash	$ 8,250	
Accounts receivable	12,400	
Merchandise inventory	17,650	
Office equipment	90,000	
Less: Accumulated depreciation		$ 22,500
Accounts payable		8,500
Salaries payable		4,250
Notes payable (long-term)		60,000
J. Kwon, Capital		59,250
J. Kwon, Withdrawals	30,000	
Income summary	40,000	17,650
Sales		433,500
Sales discounts	41,250	
Sales returns and allowances	12,250	
Purchases	285,000	
Purchase discounts		32,500
Purchase returns and allowances		15,250
Transportation-in	22,750	
Advertising expense	21,000	
Depreciation expense—office equipment	22,500	
Interest expense	8,000	
Rent expense	12,000	
Sales salaries expense	30,350	
Total	$653,400	$653,400

Check Net income, $3,800

Refer to the data in Exercise 14-5. JK Products' cost of goods sold was $282,350 for 2010. Prepare a single-step income statement for the year ending December 31, 2010.

Exercise 14-6
Preparing the single-step income statement LO2

Refer to the data in Exercise 14-5. JK's net income for 2010 was $3,800. Prepare the statement of owner's equity for 2010.

Exercise 14-7
Preparing the statement of owner's equity LO3

Refer to the data in Exercise 14-5. The December 31, 2010, ending balance in the J. Kwon capital account after closing entries have been posted is $33,050. Prepare a classified balance sheet as of December 31, 2010.

Exercise 14-8
Preparing the classified balance sheet LO4

Check Total assets, $105,800

Refer to the data in Exercise 14-5. The December 31, 2010, ending balance in the J. Kwon capital account after closing entries have been posted is $33,050. Prepare a post-closing trial balance as of December 31, 2010.

Exercise 14-9
Post-closing trial balance LO6

Check T.B. totals $128,300

Hawk Company records prepaid assets and unearned revenues in balance sheet accounts. The following information was used to prepare adjusting entries for Hawk Company as of August 31, the end of the company's fiscal year.

a. The company has earned $6,000 in unrecorded service fees.

b. The expired portion of prepaid insurance is $3,700.

c. The company has earned $2,900 of its Unearned Service Fees account balance.

d. Depreciation expense for office equipment is $3,300.

e. Employees have earned but have not been paid salaries of $3,400.

Prepare any necessary reversing entries for the accounting adjustments *a* through *e* assuming that Hawk uses reversing entries in its accounting system.

Exercise 14-10^A
Preparing reversing entries LO7

connect

In the blank space beside each numbered balance sheet item, enter the letter of its balance sheet classification. If the item should not appear on the balance sheet, enter a Z in the blank.

A. Current assets   **D.** Intangible assets   **F.** Long-term liabilities

B. Long-term investments   **E.** Current liabilities   **G.** Equity

C. Plant assets

_____ **1.** Long-term investment in stock

_____ **2.** Sales

_____ **3.** Merchandise inventory

_____ **4.** Interest receivable

_____ **5.** Sales discounts

_____ **6.** Automobiles

_____ **7.** Notes payable (due in 3 years)

_____ **8.** Accounts payable

_____ **9.** Prepaid insurance

_____ **10.** Owner, Capital

_____ **11.** Unearned revenue

PROBLEM SET A

Problem 14-1A
Determining balance sheet classifications LO4

_____ **12.** Accumulated depreciation—Trucks
_____ **13.** Cash
_____ **14.** Buildings
_____ **15.** Store supplies
_____ **16.** Office equipment
_____ **17.** Land (used in operations)
_____ **18.** Purchases
_____ **19.** Office supplies
_____ **20.** Current portion of long-term note payable

Problem 14-2A
Computing merchandising amounts and formatting income statements
LO1   LO2

Cacuango Company's adjusted trial balance on August 31, 2010, its fiscal year-end, follows.

	Debit	Credit
Merchandise inventory	$ 41,000	
Other (noninventory) assets	130,400	
Total liabilities		$ 25,000
C. Cacuango, Capital		104,550
C. Cacuango, Withdrawals	8,000	
Income summary	25,400	41,000
Sales		225,600
Sales discounts	2,250	
Sales returns and allowances	12,000	
Purchases	92,000	
Purchase discounts		2,000
Purchase returns and allowances		4,500
Transportation-in	4,600	
Sales salaries expense	32,000	
Rent expense—Selling space	8,000	
Store supplies expense	1,500	
Advertising expense	13,000	
Office salaries expense	28,500	
Rent expense—Office space	3,600	
Office supplies expense	400	
Totals	$402,650	$402,650

On August 31, 2009, merchandise inventory was $25,400.

Required

1. Compute the company's net sales for the year.

2. Compute the company's total cost of net purchases for the year.

3. Prepare a multiple-step income statement that includes separate categories for selling expenses and for general and administrative expenses.

4. Prepare a single-step income statement that includes these expense categories: cost of goods sold, selling expenses, and general and administrative expenses.

Check   (2) $90,100

(3) Gross profit, $136,850; Net income, $49,850

(4) Total expenses, $161,500

Problem 14-3A
Preparing closing entries
LO5

Use the data for Cacuango Company in Problem 14-2A to complete the following requirements.

Required

Prepare closing entries as of August 31, 2010.

Check $49,850 Dr. to close Income Summary

In the blank space beside each numbered balance sheet item, enter the letter of its balance sheet classification. If the item should not appear on the balance sheet, enter a Z in the blank.

A. Current assets

E. Current liabilities

B. Long-term investments

F. Long-term liabilities

C. Plant assets

G. Equity

D. Intangible assets

_____ **1.** Sales

_____ **2.** Interest receivable

_____ **3.** Long-term investment in stock

_____ **4.** Merchandise inventory

_____ **5.** Machinery

_____ **6.** Notes payable (due in 15 years)

_____ **7.** Copyrights

_____ **8.** Current portion of long-term note payable

_____ **9.** Accumulated depreciation—Trucks

_____ **10.** Office equipment

_____ **11.** Rent receivable

_____ **12.** Salaries payable

_____ **13.** Purchase discounts

_____ **14.** Owner, Capital

_____ **15.** Office supplies

_____ **16.** Interest payable

_____ **17.** Rent expense

_____ **18.** Notes receivable (due in 120 days)

_____ **19.** Land (used in operations)

_____ **20.** Transportation-in

White Company's adjusted trial balance on March 31, 2010, its fiscal year-end, follows.

	Debit	Credit
Merchandise inventory	$ 56,500	
Other (noninventory) assets	202,600	
Total liabilities		$ 42,500
J. White, Capital		164,425
J. White, Withdrawals	3,000	
Income summary	37,500	56,500
Sales		332,650
Sales discounts	5,875	
Sales returns and allowances	20,000	
Purchases	138,500	
Purchase discounts		2,950
Purchase returns and allowances		6,700
Transportation-in	5,750	
Sales salaries expense	44,500	
Rent expense—Selling space	16,000	
Store supplies expense	3,850	
Advertising expense	26,000	
Office salaries expense	40,750	
Rent expense—Office space	3,800	
Office supplies expense	1,100	
Totals	$605,725	$605,725

On March 31, 2009, merchandise inventory was $37,500.

Required

1. Calculate the company's net sales for the year.
2. Calculate the company's total cost of net purchases for the year.
3. Prepare a multiple-step income statement that includes separate categories for selling expenses and for general and administrative expenses.
4. Prepare a single-step income statement that includes these expense categories: cost of goods sold, selling expenses, and general and administrative expenses.

Problem 14–3B
Preparing closing entries
L05

Use the data for White Company in Problem 14-2B to complete the following requirements:

Required

Prepare closing entries as of March 31, 2010.

SERIAL PROBLEM

Success Systems

(This serial problem began in Chapter 1 and continues through most of the book. If previous chapter segments were not completed, the serial problem can begin at this point. It is helpful, but not necessary, that you use the Working Papers that accompany the book.)

SP 14   The March 31, 2011, adjusted trial balance of Success Systems (reflecting its transactions from October 2010 through March of 2011) follows.

No.	Account Title	Dr.	Cr.
101	Cash	$ 87,266	
106.1	Alex's Engineering Co.	0	
106.2	Wildcat Services	3,900	
106.3	Easy Leasing	11,000	
106.4	Clark Co.	4,800	
106.5	Chang Corporation	0	
106.6	Gomez Co.	0	
106.7	Delta Co.	0	
106.8	KC, Inc.	4,700	
106.9	Dream, Inc.	0	
106.10	Bob's Building Co.	0	
119	Merchandise inventory	680	
126	Computer supplies	1,950	
128	Prepaid insurance	1,200	
131	Prepaid rent	875	
163	Office equipment	10,000	
164	Accumulated depreciation—Office equipment		$ 1,250
167	Computer equipment	25,000	
168	Accumulated depreciation—Computer equip.		2,500
201	Accounts payable		0
210	Wages payable		1,050

No.	Account Title	Dr.	Cr.
236	Unearned computer services revenue		$ 0
301	A. Lopez, Capital		127,435
302	A. Lopez, Withdrawals	$ 5,200	
901	Income Summary		680
403	Computer services revenue		31,850
413	Sales		20,900
414	Sales returns and allowances	500	
415	Sales discounts	55	
505	Purchases	15,200	
506	Purchase returns and allowances		496
507	Purchase discounts		152
508	Transportation-in	400	
612	Depreciation expense—Office equipment	625	
613	Depreciation expense—Computer equipment	1,250	
623	Wages expense	3,900	
637	Insurance expense	600	
640	Rent expense	2,625	
652	Computer supplies expense	2,075	
655	Advertising expense	800	
676	Mileage expense	512	
677	Miscellaneous expenses	0	
684	Repairs expense—Computer	1,200	
	Totals	$186,313	$186,313

Required

1. Record the necessary closing entries at March 31, 2011.
2. Prepare a single-step income statement for the three months ended March 31, 2011.
3. Prepare a statement of owner's equity for the three months ended March 31, 2011.
4. Prepare a classified balance sheet as of March 31, 2011.

BTN 14–1 Refer to **Best Buy**'s financial statements in Appendix A to answer the following.

REPORTING IN ACTION
LO2

Required

1. In its first footnote, Best Buy lists the primary costs classified in both costs of goods sold and selling, general, and administrative expenses. Give some examples of the primary costs included in each category.

BTN 14–2 Access the SEC's EDGAR database (www.SEC.gov) and obtain the March 23, 2009, filing of its fiscal 2008 10-K report (for year ended January 31, 2009) for **J. Crew Group, Inc**.

TAKING IT TO THE NET
LO4

Required

Prepare a table that reports the gross profit amounts for J. Crew using the revenues and cost of goods sold data from J. Crew's income statement for each of its most recent three years. Analyze and comment on the trend in its gross profit amounts.

BTN 14–3 Review this chapter's opening feature involving **RockBottomGolf.com**. Assume that Todd and Tom Rath want to expand their business to sell apparel for high-altitude camping. They plan on meeting with a bank for potential funding and have been asked by its loan officers for their financial statements.

ENTREPRENEURS IN BUSINESS
LO4

Required

1. What type of financial statement information will the loan officers consider?

2. What information on the classified balance sheet would help the loan officers assess whether RockBottomGolf.com will be able to repay its loans?

BTN 14–4 The controller of Orvil Corporation is contemplating a balance sheet which offers few details. He reasons that this will cause less questions from the company's shareholders. Does your analysis of this situation raise any concerns?

YOU CALL IT
LO4

---

1. a; $550,000 − $123,000 = $427,000
2. b
3. b

4. b
5. a

ANSWERS TO MULTIPLE CHOICE QUIZ

A Look Back

Chapter 14 showed how to prepare financial statements for a merchandiser. We also illustrate the closing process for a merchandiser.

A Look at This Chapter

This chapter emphasizes accounts receivable. We explain that they are liquid assets and describe how companies account for and report them. We also discuss the importance of estimating uncollectibles.

A Look Ahead

Chapter 16 focuses on notes receivable and notes payable. We explain how to account for and report these notes. We also describe how companies compute interest.

Chapter **15**

Accounts Receivable and Uncollectibles

Learning Objectives

LO 1	Describe accounts receivable and how they occur and are recorded.
LO 2	Apply the direct write-off method to account for bad debts.
LO 3	Apply the allowance method to account for bad debts.
LO 4	Estimate uncollectibles using the percent of sales method.
LO 5	Estimate uncollectibles using the percent of accounts receivable method.
LO 6	Estimate uncollectibles using the aging of accounts receivable method.
LO 7	Compute accounts receivable turnover and use it to help assess financial condition.

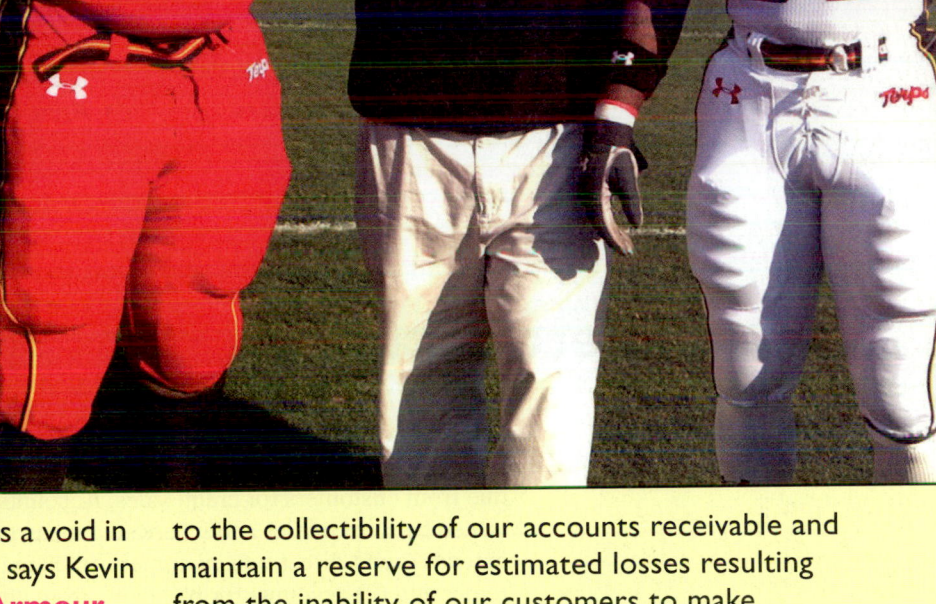

"Create what the industry is missing . . . it is worth the hardships"
—Kevin Plank (center)

Sweat Equity

BALTIMORE, MD—"There was a void in apparel and I decided to fill it," says Kevin Plank, the founder of **Under Armour (UnderArmour.com),** a manufacturer of athletic apparel using a polyester fabric that whisks perspiration away. He invested his life savings of $20,000 and began by working out of his grandma's basement.

As sales grew, Kevin partnered with a factory in Ohio and hit it off with the factory manager, Sal Fasciana. Sal spent many evenings and weekends teaching Kevin about accounting and costs. "I said, 'OK, kid. This is the way it's going to be done,'" recalls Sal. Attention to details carried over to where Kevin learned to monitor receivables. Decisions on credit sales and policies for extending credit can make or break a start-up.

Kevin applied well what Sal taught him. He ensured that credit sales were extended to customers in good credit standing. Kevin knows his customers, including who pays and when. Says Kevin, we understand our customers—inside and out—including cash payment patterns that allow us to estimate uncollectibles and minimize bad debts. His financial report says, "We make ongoing estimates relating to the collectibility of our accounts receivable and maintain a reserve for estimated losses resulting from the inability of our customers to make required payments."

A commitment to quality customers is propelling Under Armour's sales and shattering Kevin's most optimistic goals. "It's about educating consumers . . . investing in the product." Kevin has also issued notes receivable to select employees. Both accounts and notes receivables receive his attention. His financial report states that they "review the allowance for doubtful accounts monthly."

"When I first started . . . I was a young punk who thought he knew everything," explains Kevin. Although he admits that insight and ingenuity are vital, he knows accounting reports must show profits for long-term success. "Most people out there are saying we're going to trip up at some point," says Kevin. "Our job is to prove them wrong." He might also prove Thomas Edison right: genius is 99 percent perspiration and 1 percent inspiration.

[Sources: *Under Armour Website*, January 2009; *Under Armour 10-K Report*, Filed February 2007; *Entrepreneur*, November 2003; *FastCompany*, 2005 and 2002; *USA Today*, December 2004; *Inc.com*, 2003 and 2004; *All Headline News*, August 2005; *Entrepreneur's Journey*, November 2007]

This chapter focuses on accounts receivable. We describe how accounts receivable are accounted for and reported in financial statements. We also explain methods to estimate future losses from uncollectible accounts. This information can help in predicting future company performance and financial condition as well as in managing one's own business.

Accounts Receivable and Uncollectibles

Accounts Receivable	Estimating Bad Debts
• Recognizing accounts receivable • Credit card sales • Valuing accounts receivable	• Percent of sales • Percent of accounts receivable balance • Aging of accounts

Accounts Receivable

A *receivable* is an amount due from another party. The two most common receivables are accounts receivable and notes receivable. Other receivables include interest receivable, rent receivable, tax refund receivable, and receivables from employees. **Accounts receivable** are amounts due from customers for credit sales. Accounts receivable occur when customers use credit cards issued by third parties and when a company gives credit directly to customers. When a company extends credit directly to customers, it (1) maintains a separate account receivable for each customer and (2) accounts for bad debts from credit sales.

Recognizing Accounts Receivable

LO1 Describe accounts receivable and how they occur and are recorded.

Accounts receivable occur from credit sales to customers. The amount of credit sales has increased in recent years, reflecting several factors including an efficient financial system. Retailers such as **Limited Brands** and **Best Buy** hold millions of dollars in accounts receivable. Similar amounts are held by wholesalers such as **SUPERVALU** and **SYSCO**. Exhibit 15.1 shows recent dollar amounts of accounts receivable and their percent of total assets for four well-known companies.

Sales on Credit   Credit sales are recorded by increasing (debiting) Accounts Receivable. A company also maintains a separate account for each customer that tracks how much that customer purchases, has already paid, and still owes. This information provides the basis for sending bills to customers. Companies that extend credit directly to their customers keep a separate account receivable for each one of them. The general ledger has a single Accounts Receivable account. Then a supplementary *accounts receivable ledger* contains separate accounts for each customer.

Exhibit 15.2 shows the relation between the Accounts Receivable account in the general ledger and its individual customer accounts in the accounts receivable ledger

Exhibit 15.1

Accounts Receivable for Selected Companies

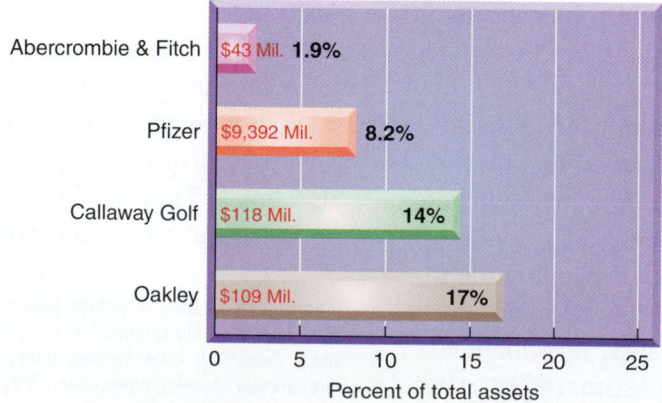

Company	Amount	Percent of total assets
Abercrombie & Fitch	$43 Mil.	1.9%
Pfizer	$9,392 Mil.	8.2%
Callaway Golf	$118 Mil.	14%
Oakley	$109 Mil.	17%

Percent of total assets

for TechCom, a small electronics wholesaler. This exhibit reports a $3,000 ending balance of TechCom's accounts receivable for June 30. TechCom's transactions are mainly in cash, but it has two major credit customers: CompStore and RDA Electronics. Its *schedule of accounts receivable* shows that the $3,000 balance of the Accounts Receivable account in the general ledger equals the total of its two customers' balances in the accounts receivable ledger.

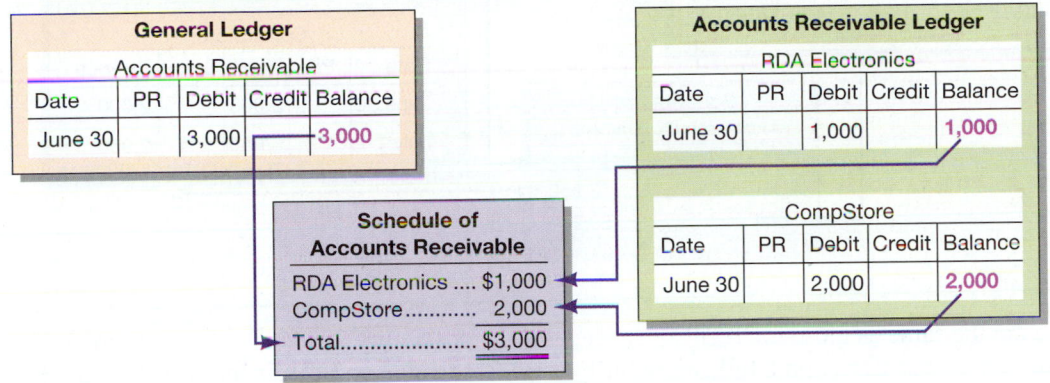

Exhibit 15.2

General Ledger and the Accounts Receivable Ledger (before July 1 transactions)

To see how accounts receivable from credit sales are recognized in the accounting records, we look at two transactions on July 1 between TechCom and its credit customers—see Exhibit 15.3.

1. The first is a credit sale of $950 to CompStore. A credit sale is posted with both a debit to the Accounts Receivable account in the general ledger and a debit to the customer account in the accounts receivable ledger.

2. The second transaction is a collection of $720 from RDA Electronics from a prior credit sale. Cash receipts from a credit customer are posted with a debit to cash in the general ledger, a credit to the Accounts Receivable account in the general ledger, and a credit to the customer account in the accounts receivable ledger.

July	1	Accounts Receivable—CompStore	9 5 0 00	
		Sales		9 5 0 00
		*To record credit sales**		
July	1	Cash	7 2 0 00	
		Accounts Receivable—RDA Electronics		7 2 0 00
		To record collection of credit sales.		

Exhibit 15.3

Accounts Receivable Transactions

Assets = Liabilities + Equity
+950   +950
Assets = Liabilities + Equity
+720
−720

* In this chapter we assume the seller uses a **periodic inventory system.** Under a periodic inventory system the Cost of Goods Sold and Merchandise Inventory accounts are updated only at the end of an accounting period. We omit these entries in our examples to focus on sales and receivables.

Exhibit 15.4 shows the general ledger and the accounts receivable ledger after recording the two July 1 transactions. The general ledger shows the effects of the sale, the collection, and the resulting balance of $3,230. These events are also reflected in the individual customer accounts: RDA Electronics has an ending balance of $280, and CompStore's ending balance is $2,950. The $3,230 sum of the individual accounts equals the debit balance of the Accounts Receivable account in the general ledger.

Credit Card Sales

Retail Credit Cards   Like TechCom, many large retailers such as **Sears** and **JCPenney** sell on credit. Many also maintain their own credit cards to grant credit to approved customers and to earn interest on any balance not paid within a specified period of time. The entries in this

Software helps merchants build Web storefronts quickly and easily. Merchants simply enter product details such as names and prices, and out comes a respectable-looking Website complete with order forms. They also offer security with credit card orders and can track sales and site visits.

Exhibit 15.4

General Ledger and the
Accounts Receivable Ledger
(after July 1 transactions)

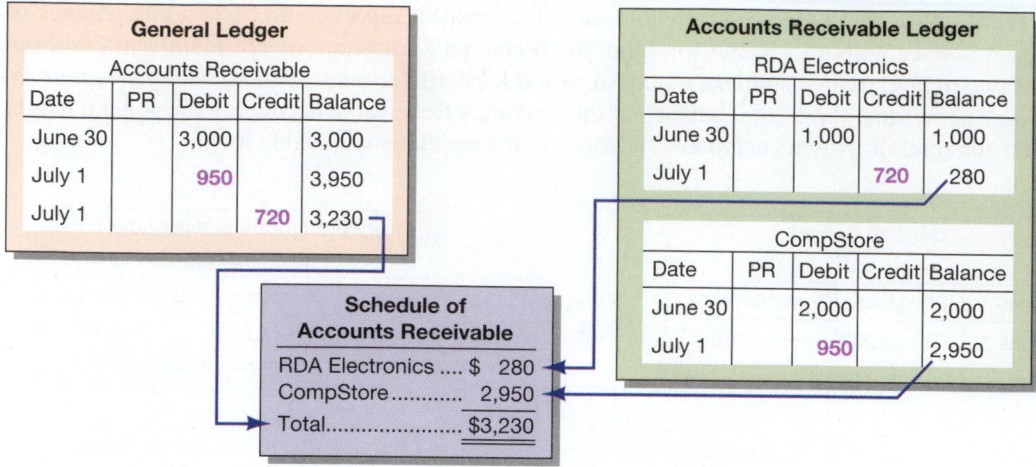

General Ledger

Accounts Receivable

Date	PR	Debit	Credit	Balance
June 30		3,000		3,000
July 1		950		3,950
July 1			720	3,230

Accounts Receivable Ledger

RDA Electronics

Date	PR	Debit	Credit	Balance
June 30		1,000		1,000
July 1			720	280

CompStore

Date	PR	Debit	Credit	Balance
June 30		2,000		2,000
July 1		950		2,950

Schedule of Accounts Receivable

RDA Electronics	$ 280
CompStore.............	2,950
Total......................	$3,230

case are the same as those for TechCom except for the possibility of added interest revenue. If a customer owes interest on a bill, we debit Interest Receivable and credit Interest Revenue for that amount.

Third-Party Credit Cards   Many companies allow their customers to pay for products and services using third-party credit cards such as **Visa**, **MasterCard**, or **American Express**, and debit cards (also called ATM or bank cards). This allows customers to make purchases without cash or checks. Once credit is established with a credit card company or bank, the customer does not have to open an account with each store. Customers using these cards can make single monthly payments instead of several payments to different creditors and can defer their payments.

Benefits of third-party credit cards.   Sellers allow customers to use third-party credit cards and debit cards instead of granting credit directly for several reasons. First, the seller does not have to evaluate each customer's credit standing or make decisions about who gets credit and how much. Second, the seller avoids the risk of extending credit to customers who cannot or do not pay. This risk is transferred to the card company. Third, the seller typically receives cash from the card company sooner than had it granted credit directly to customers. Fourth, offering a variety of credit options can increase sales volume.

IN THE NEWS

Debit Card vs. Credit Card   A buyer's debit card purchase reduces the buyer's cash account balance at the card company, which is often a bank. Since the buyer's cash account balance is a liability (with a credit balance) for the card company to the buyer, the card company would debit that account for a buyer's purchase—hence, the term *debit card*. A credit card reflects authorization by the card company of a line of credit for the buyer with preset interest rates and payment terms—hence, the term *credit card*. Most card companies waive interest charges if the buyer pays its balance each month.

Visa USA transacted more than $1 trillion in 2008 from its credit, debit, and prepaid cards.

Accounting for Third-Party Credit Card Sales   Businesses that use third-party credit cards must pay fees to the card company. These fees range from 1% to 5% of the credit card sales. These fees are recorded with a debit to Credit Card Expense. The remaining procedures in accounting for third-party credit card sales depend on whether cash is received immediately on deposit or delayed until the credit card company makes the payment.

Cash received immediately.   Debit cards, and some credit cards, credit the seller's Cash account immediately upon deposit. In this case the seller deposits a copy of each card sales receipt in its bank account. To illustrate, if TechCom has $100 of credit card sales with a 4% fee, and its $96 is received immediately upon deposit, the entry is

July	15	Cash		9 6 00	
		Credit Card Expense		4 00	
		Sales			1 0 0 00
		To record credit card sales less a 4% credit card expense.			

Assets = Liabilities + Equity
+96   +100
                    −4

Cash received later. Some credit card companies require sellers to send copies (often electronically) of each sales receipt to the card company. Until the credit card company sends cash, the seller has an account receivable from the credit card company. To illustrate, if TechCom has $100 of credit card sales with a 4% fee and must send credit card sales receipts to the credit card company and wait for cash payment, the entry on the date of sale is

July	15	**Accounts Receivable—Credit Card Co.**		9 6 00	
		Credit Card Expense		4 00	
		Sales			1 0 0 00
		To record credit card sales less 4% credit card expense.			

Assets = Liabilities + Equity
+96   +100
                    −4

> Third-party credit card costs can be large. JCPenney recently reported third-party credit card costs exceeding $10 million.

When cash is later received from the credit card company, usually through electronic funds transfer, the entry is

July	20	Cash		9 6 00	
		Accounts Receivable—Credit Card Co.			9 6 00
		To record cash receipt.			

Assets = Liabilities + Equity
+96
−96

HOW YOU DOIN'?

Answers—p. 383

1. In recording credit card sales, when do you debit Accounts Receivable and when do you debit Cash?

2. A company accumulates sales receipts and remits them to the credit card company for payment. When are the credit card expenses recorded? When are these expenses incurred?

Valuing Accounts Receivable

When a company directly grants credit to its customers, it expects that some customers will not pay what they promised. The accounts of these customers are *uncollectible accounts,* commonly called **bad debts.** The total amount of uncollectible accounts is an expense of selling on credit. Why do companies sell on credit if they expect some accounts to be uncollectible? Companies must believe that granting credit will increase total sales and net income enough to offset bad debts. Companies use two methods to account for uncollectible accounts: (1) direct write-off method and (2) allowance method. The direct write-off method is commonly used for tax reporting, whereas the allowance method is commonly used for financial reporting. We describe both.

IN THE NEWS

PayPal PayPal is legally just a money transfer agent, but it is increasingly challenging big credit card brands—see chart. PayPal is successful for two reasons. (1) Online credit card processing fees often exceed $0.15 per dollar, but PayPal's fees are under $0.10 per dollar. (2) PayPal estimates its merchant fraud losses at under 0.2% of revenues, which compares to 1.8% for online merchants using credit cards.

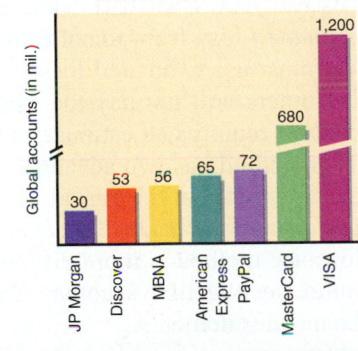

LO2 Apply the direct write-off method to account for bad debts.

Direct Write–Off Method

The **direct write-off method** of accounting for bad debts records the loss from an uncollectible account receivable when it is determined to be uncollectible. No attempt is made to predict bad debts expense. To illustrate, if TechCom determines on January 23 that it cannot collect $520 owed to it by its customer J. Kent, it recognizes the loss using the direct write-off method as follows:

Assets = Liabilities + Equity
−520   −520

Jan.	23	Bad Debts Expense	5 2 0 00	
		Accounts Receivable—J. Kent		5 2 0 00
		To write off an uncollectible account.		

The debit in this entry charges the uncollectible amount directly to the current period's Bad Debts Expense account. The credit removes its balance from the Accounts Receivable account in the general ledger (and in J. Kent's account in the accounts receivable ledger.)

> Managers realize that some portion of credit sales will be uncollectible, but which credit sales are uncollectible is unknown at the time of sale.

Recovering a bad debt. Sometimes an account written off is later collected. This can be due to factors such as continual collection efforts or a customer's good fortune. A customer might also pay up to improve his credit rating. If the account of J. Kent that was written off directly to Bad Debts Expense is later collected in full, the following two entries record this recovery.

Assets = Liabilities + Equity
+520   +520

Assets = Liabilities + Equity
+520
−520

Mar.	11	Accounts Receivable—J. Kent	5 2 0 00	
		Bad Debts Expense		5 2 0 00
		To reinstate account previously written off.		
Mar.	11	Cash	5 2 0 00	
		Accounts Receivable—J. Kent		5 2 0 00
		To record full payment of account.		

The first entry reverses the write-off and reinstates the customer's account. The second entry records the collection of the reinstated account.

Companies must weigh at least two accounting concepts when considering the use of the direct write-off method: the matching principle and materiality constraint.

> If a customer fails to pay within the credit period, most companies send out repeated billings and make other efforts to collect.

Analysis of direct write-off method. The direct write-off method is typically used by small companies. It is also required for federal income tax purposes. However, the direct write-off method has two major problems. First, it usually does not match bad debt expense with the related credit sales in the same income statement period. The **matching principle** requires expenses to be reported in the same accounting period as the sales they helped produce. The direct write-off method often records bad debt expense in a period after that of the credit sale. This poor matching means that each year's income is a less accurate measure of that year's financial performance. Second, the direct write-off method overstates the Accounts Receivable balance on the balance sheet. As a result, many companies use the allowance method. If the results of the two methods are not different (or material) enough to make an impact on business decisions, the **materiality constraint** suggests indifference as to which method is chosen.

LO3 Apply the allowance method to account for bad debts.

Allowance Method

The **allowance method** of accounting for bad debts matches the *estimated* loss from uncollectible accounts receivable against the sales they helped produce. We must use estimated losses because when sales occur, management does not know which customers will not pay their bills. This means that at the end of each period, the allowance method requires an estimate of the total bad debts expected to result from that period's sales. This method has two advantages over the direct write-off method: (1) it records estimated bad debts expense in the period when the related sales are recorded and (2) it reports accounts receivable on the balance sheet at the estimated amount of cash to be collected. However, the allowance method is more difficult to use and requires management to make good estimates of future uncollectible accounts. The allowance method is required for companies that issue public financial statements.

> Under the direct write-off method, expense is recorded each time an account is written off. Under the allowance method, expense is recorded with an adjusting entry equal to the total estimated uncollectibles for that period's sales.

Recording bad debts expense.   The allowance method estimates bad debts expense at the end of each accounting period and records it with an adjusting journal entry. TechCom, for instance, had credit sales of $300,000 during its first year of operations. At the end of the first year, $20,000 of credit sales remained uncollected. Based on the experience of similar businesses, TechCom estimated that $1,500 of its accounts receivable would be uncollectible. This estimated expense is recorded with the following adjusting journal entry.

Dec.	31	Bad Debts Expense	1 5 0 0 00	
		Allowance for Doubtful Accounts		1 5 0 0 00
		To record estimated bad debts.		

Assets = Liabilities + Equity
−1,500   −1,500

The estimated Bad Debts Expense of $1,500 is reported on the income statement. The **Allowance for Doubtful Accounts** is a contra asset account. A contra account is used instead of reducing accounts receivable directly because at the time of the adjusting entry, the company does not know which customers will not pay. After the bad debts adjusting entry is posted, TechCom's general ledger account balances (in T-account form) for Accounts Receivable and its Allowance for Doubtful Accounts are as shown in Exhibit 15.5.

Accounts Receivable	
Dec. 31 20,000	

	Allowance for Doubtful Accounts
	Dec. 31 1,500

Exhibit 15.5

General Ledger Balances after Bad Debts Adjusting Entry

The Allowance for Doubtful Accounts credit balance of $1,500 reduces accounts receivable to its estimated realizable value. **Realizable value** is the expected proceeds from converting an asset into cash. Although credit customers owe $20,000 to TechCom, only $18,500 is expected to be collected from these customers. In the balance sheet, the Allowance for Doubtful Accounts is subtracted from Accounts Receivable and is often reported as shown in Exhibit 15.6.

Bad Debts Expense is also called *Uncollectible Accounts Expense.* The Allowance for Doubtful Accounts is also called *Allowance for Uncollectible Accounts.*

Current assets		
Accounts receivable	$20,000	
Less allowance for doubtful accounts	1,500	$18,500

Exhibit 15.6

Balance Sheet Presentation of the Allowance for Doubtful Accounts

Sometimes the Allowance for Doubtful Accounts is not reported separately on the balance sheet. This alternative presentation is shown in Exhibit 15.7.

Current assets	
Accounts receivable (net of $1,500 doubtful accounts)	$18,500

Exhibit 15.7

Alternative Balance Sheet Presentation of the Allowance for Doubtful Accounts

In summary, Exhibit 15.8 details the differences between the methods used to account for uncollectible accounts.

	Period When Expense Is Recognized	Amount Written Off	Type of Reporting in Which Method Is Commonly Used
Direct Write-Off Method	In period when the account receivable is determined not to be collectible	Actual amount not collected	Tax reporting
Allowance Method	In period when the credit is granted and sales are recognized	Estimated amount not collected	Financial reporting

Exhibit 15.8

Differences in Methods to Account for Uncollectible Accounts

Writing off a bad debt.   When specific accounts are identified as uncollectible, they are written off against the Allowance for Doubtful Accounts. To illustrate, TechCom decides that J. Kent's $520 account is uncollectible and makes the following entry to write it off.

Assets = Liabilities + Equity
+520
−520

Jan.	23	Allowance for Doubtful Accounts	5 2 0 00	
		Accounts Receivable—J. Kent		5 2 0 00
		To write off an uncollectible account.		

> The Bad Debts Expense account is not debited in the write-off entry because it was recorded in the period when sales occurred.

Posting this write-off entry to the Accounts Receivable account removes the amount of the bad debt from the general ledger (it is also posted to J. Kent's account in the accounts receivable subsidiary ledger). The general ledger accounts now appear as in Exhibit 15.9 (assuming no other transactions affecting these accounts).

Exhibit 15.9

General Ledger Balances after Bad Debt Write-Off

Accounts Receivable			Allowance for Doubtful Accounts		
Dec. 31	20,000			Dec. 31	1,500
		Jan. 23 **520**	Jan. 23 **520**		

> In posting a write-off, the ledger's Explanation column indicates the reason for this credit so it is not misinterpreted as payment in full.

The write-off does not affect the realizable value of accounts receivable, as shown in Exhibit 15.10. Neither total assets nor net income is affected by the write-off of a specific account when using the allowance method. Instead, both assets and net income are affected in the period when bad debts expense is predicted and recorded with an adjusting entry.

Exhibit 15.10

Realizable Value before and after Write-Off of a Bad Debt

	Before Write-Off	After Write-Off
Accounts receivable	$ 20,000	$ 19,480
Less allowance for doubtful accounts	1,500	980
Estimated realizable accounts receivable	**$18,500**	**$18,500**

> If TechCom used a collection agency and paid a 35% commission on $520 collected from Kent, how is this recorded? *Answer:*
> Cash 338
> Collection Expense . . 182
>   Accts. Recble.—
>   J. Kent 520

Recovering a bad debt.   When a customer fails to pay and the account is written off as uncollectible, his or her credit standing is jeopardized. To help restore credit standing, a customer sometimes volunteers to pay all or part of the amount owed. A company makes two entries when collecting an account previously written off by the allowance method. The first is to reverse the write-off and reinstate the customer's account. The second entry records the collection of the reinstated account. To illustrate, if on March 11 J. Kent pays in full his account previously written off, the entries are

Assets = Liabilities + Equity
+520
−520

Mar.	11	Accounts Receivable—J. Kent	5 2 0 00	
		Allowance for Doubtful Accounts		5 2 0 00
		To reinstate account previously written off.		

Assets = Liabilities + Equity
+520
−520

Mar.	11	Cash	5 2 0 00	
		Accounts Receivable—J. Kent		5 2 0 00
		To record full payment of account.		

In this illustration, J. Kent paid the entire amount previously written off, but sometimes a customer pays only a portion of the amount owed. A question then arises as to whether the entire balance of the account or just the amount paid is returned to accounts receivable. This is a matter of judgment. If we believe this customer will later pay in full, we return the entire amount owed to accounts receivable. If we expect no further collection, we return only the amount paid.

IN THE NEWS

Aging Pains   Experience shows that the longer a receivable is past due, the lower is the likelihood of its collection. An *aging schedule* uses this knowledge to estimate bad debts. The chart here is from a survey that reported estimates of bad debts for receivables grouped by how long they are past their due dates. Each company sets its own estimates based on its customers' attributes.

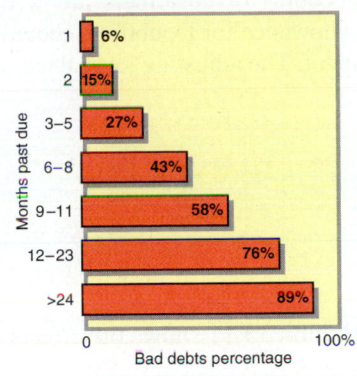

Estimating Bad Debts Expense

Companies with direct credit sales must estimate bad debts expense to both manage their receivables and set credit policies. The allowance method also requires an estimate of bad debts expense to prepare an adjusting entry at the end of each accounting period. There are two common methods. One is based on the income statement relation between bad debts expense and sales. The second is based on the balance sheet relation between accounts receivable and the allowance for doubtful accounts.

LO4 Estimate uncollectibles using the percent of sales method.

Percent of Sales Method

The *percent of sales method* is based on the idea that a given percent of a company's credit sales for the period are uncollectible. To illustrate, assume that Musicland has credit sales of $400,000 in year 2010. From past experience, Musicland estimates 0.6% of credit sales to be uncollectible. Musicland expects $2,400 of bad debts expense from its sales (computed as $400,000 \times 0.006 = \$2,400$). The adjusting journal entry to record this estimated expense is

> The focus is on *credit* sales because cash sales do not produce bad debts. If cash sales are a small or stable percent of credit sales, total sales can be used.

Dec.	31	Bad Debts Expense	2 4 0 0 00	
		Allowance for Doubtful Accounts		2 4 0 0 00
		To record estimated bad debts.		

Assets = Liabilities + Equity
−2,400   −2,400

> When using the *percent of sales method* for estimating uncollectibles, the estimate of bad debts is the number used in the adjusting entry.

Accounts Receivable Methods

Accounts receivable methods use balance sheet relations to estimate bad debts—mainly the relation between accounts receivable and the allowance amount. These methods set the Allowance for Doubtful Accounts balance equal to the portion of accounts receivable that is estimated to be uncollectible. The estimated balance for the allowance account is obtained in one of two ways: (1) computing the percent uncollectible from the total accounts receivable or (2) aging accounts receivable.

Percent of Accounts Receivable Method   The *percent of accounts receivable method* assumes that a given percent of a company's receivables is uncollectible. This percent is based on past experience and is impacted by current conditions such as economic trends and customer difficulties. The total dollar amount of all receivables is multiplied by this percent to get the estimated dollar amount of uncollectible accounts—reported in the balance sheet as the Allowance for Doubtful Accounts.

LO5 Estimate uncollectibles using the percent of accounts receivable method.

When using an accounts receivable method for estimating uncollectibles, the allowance account balance is adjusted to equal the estimate of uncollectibles.

To illustrate, assume that Musicland has $50,000 of accounts receivable on December 31, 2010. Experience suggests 5% of its receivables are uncollectible. This means that after the adjusting entry is posted, the Allowance for Doubtful Accounts on December 31, 2010, must show a $2,500 credit balance (5% of $50,000). (*Note:* Its beginning (credit) balance is $2,200, which is 5% of the $44,000 accounts receivable on December 31, 2009—see Exhibit 15.11) Also during 2010, accounts of customers are written off on February 6, July 10, and November 20. Thus, the Allowance for Doubtful Accounts has a $200 credit balance before the December 31, 2010, adjustment. The adjusting journal entry to give the allowance account the estimated $2,500 balance is

Assets = Liabilities + Equity
−2,300   −2,300

Dec.	31	Bad Debts Expense	2 3 0 0 00	
		Allowance for Doubtful Accounts		2 3 0 0 00
		To record estimated bad debts.		

Exhibit 15.11 shows the effects of these transactions and adjustments on the allowance amount.

Exhibit 15.11

Allowance for Doubtful Accounts after Bad Debts Adjusting Entry

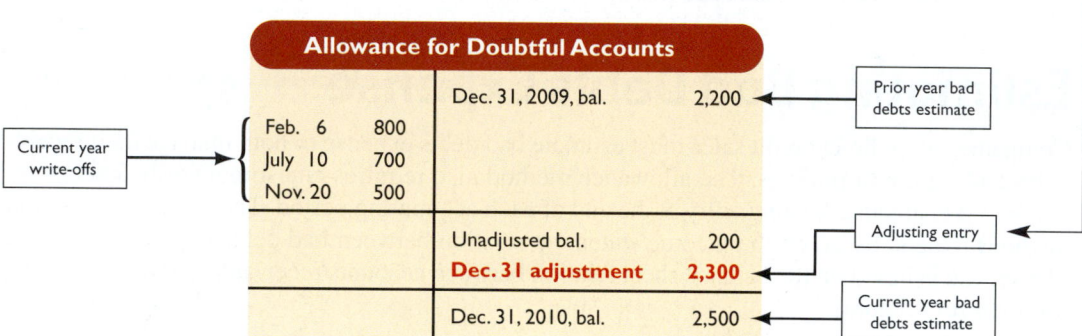

LO6 Estimate uncollectibles using the aging of accounts receivable method.

Aging of Accounts Receivable Method   The **aging of accounts receivable** method uses both past and current receivables information to estimate the allowance amount. Specifically, each receivable is classified by how long it is past its due date. The longer an amount is past due, the more likely it is to be uncollectible. Classifications are often based on 30-day periods. After the accounts are classified (or aged), experience is used to estimate the percent uncollectible of each class. These percents are applied to the amounts in each class and then totaled to get the estimated balance of the Allowance for Doubtful Accounts. Exhibit 15.12 shows this computation.

Exhibit 15.12

Aging of Accounts Receivable

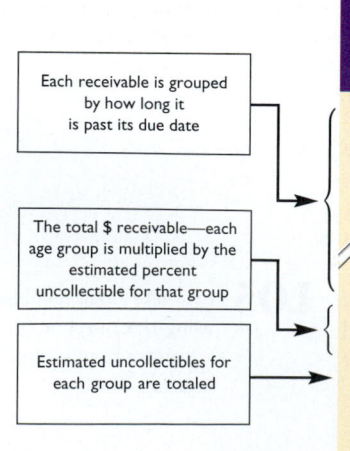

MUSICLAND
Schedule of Accounts Receivable by Age
December 31, 2010

Customer	Totals	Not Yet Due	1 to 30 Days Past Due	31 to 60 Days Past Due	61 to 90 Days Past Due	Over 90 Days Past Due
Carlie Abbott	$ 450	$ 450				
Jamie Allen	710			$ 710		
Chavez Andres	500	300	$ 200			
Belicia Company	740				$ 100	$ 640
Zamora Services	1,000	810	190			
Total receivables	$ 50,000	$37,000	$6,500	$3,700	$1,900	$ 900
Percent uncollectible		× 2%	× 5%	× 10%	× 25%	× 40%
Estimated uncollectible	$ 2,270	$ 740	$ 325	$ 370	$ 475	$ 360

Each receivable is grouped by how long it is past its due date

The total $ receivable—each age group is multiplied by the estimated percent uncollectible for that group

Estimated uncollectibles for each group are totaled

Exhibit 15.12 lists each customer's individual balances assigned to one of five classes based on its days past due. The amounts in each class are totaled and multiplied by the estimated percent of uncollectible accounts for each class. The percentages used are regularly reviewed to reflect changes in the company and economy.

To explain, Musicland has $3,700 in accounts receivable that are 31 to 60 days past due. Its management estimates 10% of the amounts in this age class are uncollectible, or a total of $370 (computed as $3,700 × 10%).

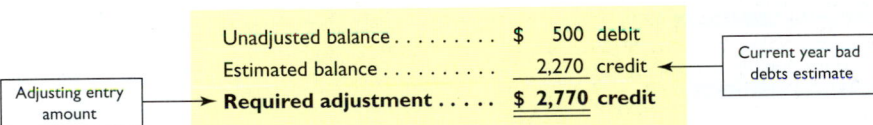

Unadjusted balance	$ 200 credit
Estimated balance	2,270 credit
Required adjustment	**$2,070 credit**

Exhibit 15.13

Computation of the Required Adjustment for the Aging of Accounts Receivable Method

Similar analysis is done for each of the other four classes. The final total of $2,270 ($740 + $325 + 370 + $475 + $360) shown in the first column is the estimated balance for the Allowance for Doubtful Accounts. Exhibit 15.13 shows that since the allowance account has an unadjusted credit balance of $200, the required adjustment to the Allowance for Doubtful Accounts is $2,070. This yields the following end-of-period adjusting entry.

Dec.	31	Bad Debts Expense		2 0 7 0 00	
		Allowance for Doubtful Accounts			2 0 7 0 00
		To record estimated bad debts.			

Assets = Liabilities + Equity
−2,070   −2,070

Alternatively, if the allowance account had an unadjusted *debit* balance of $500 (instead of the $200 credit balance), its required adjustment would be computed as follows.

Adjusting entry amount →

Unadjusted balance	$ 500 debit
Estimated balance	2,270 credit	← Current year bad debts estimate
Required adjustment	**$ 2,770 credit**

The entry to record the end-of-period adjustment for this alternative case is

Dec.	31	Bad Debts Expense		2 7 7 0 00	
		Allowance for Doubtful Accounts			2 7 7 0 00
		To record estimated bad debts.			

Assets = Liabilities + Equity
−2,770   −2,770

The aging of accounts receivable method is a more detailed examination of specific accounts and is usually the most reliable of the estimation methods.

Exhibit 15.14 summarizes the principles guiding all three estimation methods and their focus of analysis. Percent of sales, with its income statement focus, does a good job at matching bad debts expense with sales. The accounts receivable methods, with their balance sheet focus, do a better job at reporting accounts receivable at realizable value.

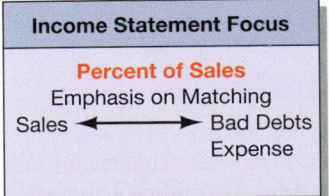
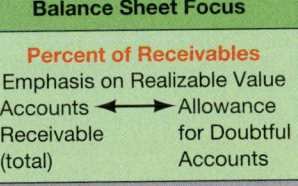
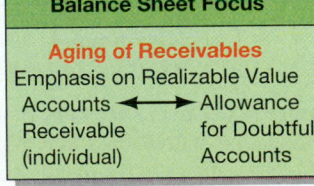

Exhibit 15.14

Methods to Estimate Bad Debts

HOW YOU DOIN'?

Answers—p. 383

3. Why must bad debts expense be estimated if such an estimate is possible?

4. What term describes the balance sheet valuation of Accounts Receivable less the Allowance for Doubtful Accounts?

5. Why is estimated bad debts expense credited to a contra account (Allowance for Doubtful Accounts) rather than to the Accounts Receivable account?

6. SnoBoard Company's year-end balance in its Allowance for Doubtful Accounts is a credit of $440. By aging accounts receivable, it estimates that $6,142 is uncollectible. Prepare SnoBoard's year-end adjusting entry for bad debts.

7. Record entries for these transactions assuming the allowance method is used:

Jan.   10   The $300 account of customer Cool Jam is determined uncollectible.

April 12   Cool Jam unexpectedly pays in full the account deemed uncollectible on Jan. 10.

IN THE NEWS

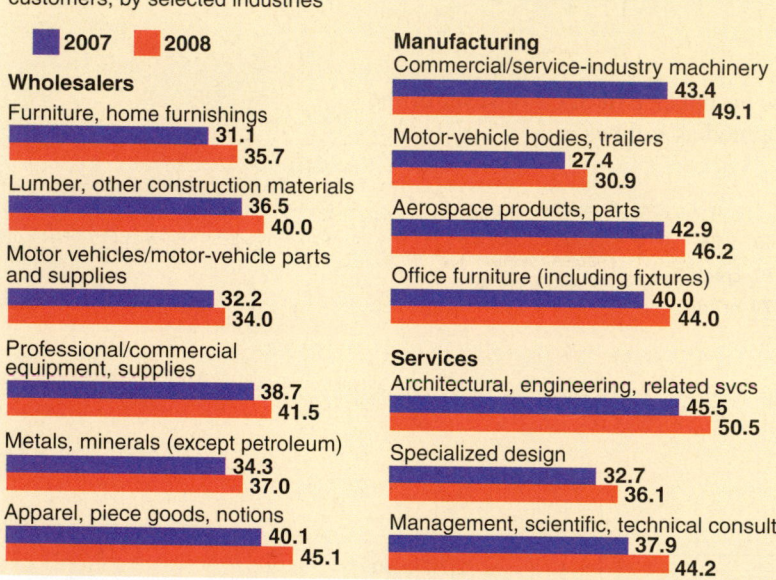

The Check is in the Mail

Average number of days it takes private companies to collect money owed by customers, by selected industries

█ 2007   █ 2008

Wholesalers

Furniture, home furnishings   31.1 / 35.7

Lumber, other construction materials   36.5 / 40.0

Motor vehicles/motor-vehicle parts and supplies   32.2 / 34.0

Professional/commercial equipment, supplies   38.7 / 41.5

Metals, minerals (except petroleum)   34.3 / 37.0

Apparel, piece goods, notions   40.1 / 45.1

Manufacturing

Commercial/service-industry machinery   43.4 / 49.1

Motor-vehicle bodies, trailers   27.4 / 30.9

Aerospace products, parts   42.9 / 46.2

Office furniture (including fixtures)   40.0 / 44.0

Services

Architectural, engineering, related svcs   45.5 / 50.5

Specialized design   32.7 / 36.1

Management, scientific, technical consulting   37.9 / 44.2

Depending on the industry, customers pay their accounts receivable balances at different frequencies. The graphic below shows the average number of days it takes private companies to collect money owed by customers, by selected industries (*Wall Street Journal*, R8, May 11, 2009).

ACCOUNTS RECEIVABLE TURNOVER

LO7 Compute accounts receivable turnover and use it to help assess financial condition.

For a company selling on credit, we want to assess both the quality and liquidity of its accounts receivable. *Quality* of receivables refers to the likelihood of collection without loss. Experience shows that the longer receivables are outstanding beyond their due date, the lower the likelihood of collection. *Liquidity* of receivables refers to the speed of collection. **Accounts receivable turnover** is a measure of both the quality and liquidity of accounts receivable. It indicates how often, on average, receivables are received and collected during the period. The formula for this ratio is shown in Exhibit 15.15.

Exhibit 15.15

Accounts Receivable Turnover

$$\text{Accounts receivable turnover} = \frac{\text{Net sales}}{\text{Average accounts receivable}}$$

We prefer to use net *credit* sales in the numerator because cash sales do not create receivables. However, since financial statements rarely report net credit sales, our analysis uses net sales. The denominator is the *average* accounts receivable balance, computed as (Beginning balance + Ending balance) ÷ 2.

TechCom has an accounts receivable turnover of 5.1. This indicates its average accounts receivable balance is converted into cash 5.1 times during the period. Exhibit 15.16 shows graphically this turnover activity for TechCom.

5.1 times per year

Jan. Feb. March Apr. May June July Aug. Sept. Oct. Nov. Dec.

Exhibit 15.16

Rate of Accounts Receivable Turnover for TechCom

Accounts receivable turnover also reflects how well management is doing in granting credit to customers in a desire to increase sales. A high turnover in comparison with competitors suggests that management should consider using more liberal credit terms to increase sales. A low turnover suggests management should consider stricter credit terms and more aggressive collection efforts to avoid having its resources tied up in accounts receivable.

To illustrate, we take data from two competitors: **Dell Inc.** and **Apple Computer**. Exhibit 15.17 shows accounts receivable turnover for both companies.

Credit risk ratio is computed by dividing the Allowance for Doubtful Accounts by Accounts Receivable. The higher this ratio, the higher is credit risk.

Company	Figure ($ millions)	2008	2007	2006
Dell	Net sales	$61,101	$61,133	$57,420
	Average accounts receivable	$ 6,433	$ 7,693	$ 6,152
	Accounts receivable turnover	**9.50**	**7.95**	**9.33**
Apple	Net sales	$32,479	$24,006	$19,315
	Average accounts receivable	$ 4,704	$ 4,029	$ 2,845
	Accounts receivable turnover	**6.90**	**5.96**	**6.79**

Exhibit 15.17

Analysis Using Accounts Receivable Turnover

Demonstration Problem

Clayco Company completes the following selected transactions during year 2010.

July 14 Writes off a $750 account receivable arising from a sale to Briggs Company 10 months earlier. (Clayco Company uses the allowance method.)

Nov. 1 Completed a $200 credit card sale with a 4% fee. The cash is received immediately from the credit card company.

5 Completed a $500 credit card sale with a 5% fee. The payment from the credit card company is received on Nov. 9.

15 Received the full amount of $750 from Briggs Company that was previously written off on July 14.

Required

1. Prepare journal entries to record these transactions on Clayco Company's books.
2. Prepare an adjusting journal entry as of December 31, 2010, assuming the following:
   a. Clayco estimates its ending Allowance for Doubtful Accounts should be $20,400 by aging accounts receivable. The unadjusted balance of the Allowance for Doubtful Accounts is $1,000 debit.
   b. Alternatively, assume that bad debts expense is estimated using the percent of sales method. The Allowance for Doubtful Accounts had a $1,000 debit balance before adjustment, and the company estimates bad debts to be 1% of its credit sales of $2,000,000.

Planning the Solution

- Examine each transaction to determine the accounts affected, and then record the entries.
- For the year-end adjustment, record the bad debts expense for the two approaches.

Solution to Demonstration Problem

I.

July	14	Allowance for Doubtful Accounts		7 5 0 00		
		Accounts Receivable—Briggs Co.			7 5 0 00	
		Wrote off an uncollectible account.				
Nov.	1	Cash		1 9 2 00		
		Credit Card Expense		8 00		
		Sales			2 0 0 00	
		To record credit card sale less a 4% credit card expense.				
Nov.	5	Accounts Receivable—Credit Card Co.		4 7 5 00		
		Credit Card Expense		2 5 00		
		Sales			5 0 0 00	
		To record credit card sale less a 5% credit card expense.				
Nov.	9	Cash		4 7 5 00		
		Accounts Receivable—Credit Card Co.			4 7 5 00	
		To record cash receipt from Nov. 5 sale.				
Nov.	15	Accounts Receivable—Briggs Co.		7 5 0 00		
		Allowance for Doubtful Accounts			7 5 0 00	
		To reinstate the account of Briggs Company previously written off.				
Nov.	15	Cash		7 5 0 00		
		Accounts Receivable—Briggs Co.			7 5 0 00	
		Cash received in full payment of account.				

2a. Aging of accounts receivable method.

Dec.	31	Bad Debts Expense		21 4 0 0 00		
		Allowance for Doubtful Accounts			21 4 0 0 00	
		To adjust allowance account from a $1,000 debit balance				
		to a $20,400 credit balance.				

2b. Percent of sales method.*

Dec.	31	Bad Debts Expense		20 0 0 0 00		
		Allowance for Doubtful Accounts			20 0 0 0 00	
		To provide for bad debts as 1% × $2,000,000 in credit sales.				

* For the income statement approach, which requires estimating bad debts as a percent of sales or credit sales, the Allowance account balance is *not* considered when making the adjusting entry.

Summary

LO1 Describe accounts receivable and how they occur and are recorded. Accounts receivable are amounts due from customers for credit sales. A subsidiary accounts receivable ledger lists amounts owed by each customer. Credit sales arise from at least two sources: (1) sales on credit and (2) credit card sales. *Sales on credit* refers to a company's granting credit directly to customers. Credit card sales involve customers' use of credit cards.

LO2 Apply the direct write-off method to account for bad debts. The direct write-off method charges Bad Debts

Expense when accounts are written off as uncollectible. This method is required for federal income tax purposes and is sometimes used for financial accounting purposes.

LO3 Apply the allowance method to account for bad debts. Under the allowance method, bad debt expense is recorded with an adjusting journal entry at the end of each accounting period that debits Bad Debts Expense and credits the Allowance for Doubtful Accounts.

LO4 Estimate uncollectibles using the percent of sales method. The percent of sales method assumes a given percentage of a company's credit sales for the period are uncollectible. Bad Debts Expense is computed by multiplying the credit sales for the period by an estimated percent uncollectible.

LO5 Estimate uncollectibles using the percent of accounts receivable method. The percent of accounts receivable method assumes that a given percentage of a company's ending accounts receivable is uncollectible. The ending Allowance for Doubtful Accounts is computed by multiplying the ending Accounts Receivable by an estimated percent uncollectible. The Bad Debts Expense for the period is the adjusting journal entry amount that will produce the desired ending Allowance for Doubtful Accounts.

LO6 Estimate uncollectibles using the aging of accounts receivable method. Under this method each account receivable is classified by how many days it is past due. The longer an account is past due, the more likely the company will not collect it. The company estimates the percentage uncollectible for each age category of receivables and computes an ending Allowance for Doubtful Accounts by multiplying these percentages by the dollars receivable in each age category. The Bad Debts Expense for the period is the adjusting journal entry amount that will produce the desired ending Allowance for Doubtful Accounts.

LO7 Compute accounts receivable turnover and use it to help assess financial condition. Accounts receivable turnover is a measure of both the quality and liquidity of accounts receivable. The accounts receivable turnover measure indicates how often, on average, receivables are received and collected during the period. Accounts receivable turnover is computed as net sales divided by average accounts receivable.

Guidance Answers to HOW YOU DOIN'?

1. If cash is immediately received when credit card sales receipts are deposited, the company debits Cash at the time of sale. If the company does not receive payment until after it submits receipts to the credit card company, it debits Accounts Receivable at the time of sale. (Cash is later debited when payment is received from the credit card company.)

2. Credit card expenses are usually *recorded* and *incurred* at the time of their related sales, not when cash is received from the credit card company.

3. If possible, bad debts expense must be matched with the sales that gave rise to the accounts receivable. This requires that companies estimate future bad debts at the end of each period before they learn which accounts are uncollectible.

4. Realizable value (also called *net realizable value*).

5. The estimated amount of bad debts expense cannot be credited to the Accounts Receivable account because the specific customer accounts that will prove uncollectible cannot yet be identified and removed from the accounts receivable subsidiary ledger. Moreover, if only the Accounts Receivable account is credited, its balance would not equal the sum of its subsidiary account balances.

6.

| Dec. 31 | Bad Debts Expense | 5,702 | |
| | Allowance for Doubtful Accounts | | 5,702 |

7.

Jan. 10	Allowance for Doubtful Accounts	300	
	Accounts Receivable—Cool Jam		300
Apr. 12	Accounts Receivable—Cool Jam	300	
	Allowance for Doubtful Accounts		300
Apr. 12	Cash	300	
	Accounts Receivable—Cool Jam		300

Key Terms

Accounts receivable (p. 370) Amounts due from customers for credit sales; backed by the customer's general credit standing.

Accounts receivable turnover (p. 380) Measure of both the quality and liquidity of accounts receivable; indicates how often receivables are received and collected during the period; computed by dividing net sales by average accounts receivable.

Aging of accounts receivable (p. 378) Process of classifying accounts receivable by how long they are past due for purposes of estimating uncollectible accounts.

Allowance for Doubtful Accounts (p. 375) Contra asset account with a balance approximating uncollectible accounts receivable; also called *Allowance for Uncollectible Accounts*.

Allowance method (p. 374) Procedure that (a) estimates and matches bad debts expense with its sales for the period and/or (b) reports accounts receivable at estimated realizable value.

Bad debts (p. 373) Accounts of customers who do not pay what they have promised to pay; an expense of selling on credit; also called *uncollectible accounts*.

Direct write-off method (p. 374) Method that records the loss from an uncollectible account receivable at the time it is determined to be uncollectible; no attempt is made to estimate bad debts.

Matching principle (p. 374) Prescribes expenses to be reported in the same period as the revenues that were earned as a result of the expenses.

Materiality constraint (p. 374) Prescribes that accounting for items that significantly impact financial statement and any inferences from them strictly adhere to GAAP.

Periodic inventory system (p. 371) Method that records the cost of inventory purchased but does not continuously track the quantity available or sold to customers; records are updated at the end of each period to reflect the physical count and costs of goods available.

Realizable value (p. 375) Expected proceeds from converting an asset into cash.

Multiple Choice Quiz

Answers on p. 393   **mhhe.com/wildCA2e**

Additional Multiple Choice Quizzes are available at the book's Website.

1. A company's Accounts Receivable balance at its December 31 year-end is $125,650, and its Allowance for Doubtful Accounts has a credit balance of $328 before year-end adjustment. Its net sales are $572,300. It estimates that 4% of outstanding accounts receivable are uncollectible. What amount of Bad Debts Expense is recorded at December 31?
 a. $5,354
 b. $328
 c. $5,026
 d. $4,698
 e. $34,338

2. A company's Accounts Receivable balance at its December 31 year-end is $489,300, and its Allowance for Doubtful Accounts has a debit balance of $554 before year-end adjustment. Its net sales are $1,300,000. It estimates that 6% of outstanding accounts receivable are uncollectible. What amount of Bad Debts Expense is recorded at December 31?
 a. $29,912
 b. $28,804
 c. $78,000
 d. $29,358
 e. $554

3. A company completed a $200 credit card sale with a 4% fee. The credit card company sends cash only after receiving credit card sales receipts from the seller. The entry to record this sale will include a
 a. Debit of $200 to Accounts Receivable.
 b. Debit of $192 to Accounts Receivable.

 c. Debit of $192 to Cash.
 d. Credit of $192 to Sales Revenue.
 e. Credit of $192 to Cash.

4. A company uses the allowance method of accounting for bad debts. On December 15, 2010, it collects $750 from a customer whose account was previously written off. The journal entries to record this collection will include a
 a. Debit of $750 to the Allowance for Doubtful Accounts.
 b. Credit of $750 to Bad Debts Expense.
 c. Credit of $750 to Sales Revenue.
 d. Debit of $750 to Accounts Receivable.
 e. No entry is needed.

5. On December 31 of the current year, a company's unadjusted trial balance included the following: Accounts Receivable, debit balance of $97,250; and Allowance for Doubtful Accounts, credit balance of $951. What amount should be debited to Bad Debts Expense, assuming 6% of outstanding accounts receivable at the end of the current year will be uncollectible?
 a. $951
 b. $3,992
 c. $4,884
 d. $5,835
 e. $6,786

Discussion Questions

1. How do sellers benefit from allowing their customers to use credit cards?

2. Why does the direct write-off method of accounting for bad debts usually fail to match revenues and expenses?

3. What are the two methods of accounting for uncollectible accounts? How is bad debt expense computed under each of these alternative methods?

4. Explain why writing off a bad debt against the Allowance for Doubtful Accounts does not reduce the estimated realizable value of a company's accounts receivable.

5. Why does the Bad Debts Expense account usually not have the same adjusted balance as the Allowance for Doubtful Accounts?

6. What is the purpose of a *subsidiary accounts receivable ledger*?

7. What are the three primary methods of estimating uncollectible accounts?

8. Explain how a business might end an accounting period with a debit balance in its *unadjusted* Allowance for Doubtful Accounts?

9. Refer to the financial statements of **Best Buy** in  Appendix A. In its presentation of accounts receivable, Best Buy does not mention uncollectible accounts, nor does it list its receivables as "net." Why do you believe that Best Buy does not include information about uncollectible accounts?

---

connect

QUICK STUDY

QS 15–1

Credit card sales   **LO1**

Prepare journal entries for the following credit transactions.

1. Sold $20,000 of merchandise on MasterCard credit cards. The net cash receipts from sales are immediately deposited in the seller's bank account. MasterCard charges a 5% fee.

2. Sold $5,000 of merchandise on an assortment of credit cards. Net cash receipts are received 5 days later, and a 4% fee is charged.

Gomez Corp. uses the allowance method to account for uncollectibles. On October 31, it wrote off an $800 account of a customer, C. Green. On December 9, it receives a $300 payment from Green.

1. Prepare the journal entry or entries for October 31.

2. Prepare the journal entry or entries for December 9; assume no additional money is expected from Green.

QS 15-2
Allowance method for bad debts
LO3

Warner Company's year-end unadjusted trial balance shows accounts receivable of $99,000, allowance for doubtful accounts of $600 (credit), and sales of $280,000. Uncollectibles are estimated to be 1.5% of accounts receivable.

1. Prepare the December 31 year-end adjusting entry for uncollectibles.

2. What amount would have been used in the year-end adjusting entry if the allowance account had a year-end unadjusted debit balance of $300?

QS 15-3
Percent of accounts receivable method   **LO5**

Assume the same facts as in QS 15-3, except that Warner estimates uncollectibles as 0.5% of sales. Prepare the December 31 year-end adjusting entry for uncollectibles.

QS 15-4
Percent of sales method   **LO4**

A company ages its accounts receivables to determine its end of period adjustment for bad debts. At the end of the current year, management estimated that $14,570 of the accounts receivable balance would be uncollectible. Prior to any year-end adjustments, the Allowance for Doubtful Accounts had a debit balance of $225. What adjusting entry should the company make at the end of the current year to record its estimated bad debts expense?

QS 15-5
Aging of accounts receivable method   **LO6**

Griggs Company uses the direct write-off method of accounting for uncollectible accounts receivable. On December 6, 2009, Griggs sold $6,300 of merchandise to the Hillman Company. On August 8, 2010, after numerous attempts to collect the account, Griggs determined that the $6,300 account of the Hillman Company was uncollectible.

QS 15-6
Direct write-off method   **LO2**

Required

1. Prepare the general journal entry required to record the write-off on August 8.

2. Explain how the direct write-off method violates the matching principle in this case.

The following data are taken from the comparative balance sheets of Rodriguez Company. Compute and interpret its accounts receivable turnover for year 2010 (competitors average a turnover of 7.5).

QS 15-7
Accounts receivable turnover
LO7

	2010	2009
Accounts receivable	$153,400	$138,500
Net sales	854,200	910,600

---

connect

Levine Company allows customers to use two credit cards in charging purchases. With the Omni Bank Card, Levine receives an immediate credit to its account when it deposits sales receipts. Omni assesses a 4% service charge for credit card sales. The second credit card that Levine accepts is the Continental Card. Levine sends its accumulated receipts to Continental on a weekly basis and is paid by Continental about a week later. Continental assesses a 2.5% charge on sales for using its card. Prepare journal entries to record the following selected credit card transactions of Levine Company:

EXERCISES

Exercise 15-1
Accounting for credit card sales
LO1

Apr. 8   Sold merchandise for $8,400 and accepted the customer's Omni Bank Card. The Omni receipts are immediately deposited in Levine's bank account.

12   Sold merchandise for $5,600 and accepted the customer's Continental Card. Transferred $5,600 of credit card receipts to Continental, requesting payment.

20   Received Continental's check for the April 12 billing, less the service charge.

Exercise 15-2
Accounts receivable subsidiary ledger; schedule of accounts receivable   **LO1**

Morales Company recorded the following selected transactions during November 2010.

Nov.	5	Accounts Receivable—Ski Shop	4 6 1 5 00	
		Sales		4 6 1 5 00
	10	Accounts Receivable—Welcome Enterprises	1 3 5 0 00	
		Sales		1 3 5 0 00
	13	Accounts Receivable—Zia Natara	8 3 2 00	
		Sales		8 3 2 00
	21	Sales Returns and Allowances	2 0 9 00	
		Accounts Receivable—Zia Natara		2 0 9 00
	30	Accounts Receivable—Ski Shop	2 7 1 3 00	
		Sales		2 7 1 3 00

1. Open a general ledger having T-accounts for Accounts Receivable, Sales, and Sales Returns and Allowances. Also open an accounts receivable subsidiary ledger having a T-account for each customer. Post these entries to both the general ledger and the accounts receivable ledger.

Check Accounts Receivable ending balance, $9,301

2. Prepare a schedule of accounts receivable (see Exhibit 15.4) and compare its total with the balance of the Accounts Receivable controlling account as of November 30.

Exercise 15-3
Percent of sales method; write-off   **LO4**

At year-end (December 31), Chan Company estimates its bad debts as 0.5% of its annual credit sales of $975,000. Chan records its Bad Debts Expense for that estimate. On the following February 1, Chan decides that the $580 account of P. Park is uncollectible and writes it off as a bad debt. On June 5, Park unexpectedly pays the amount previously written off. Prepare the journal entries of Chan to record these transactions and events of December 31, February 1, and June 5.

Exercise 15-4
Percent of accounts receivable method   **LO1   LO5**

At each calendar year-end, Booyah Supply Co. uses the percent of accounts receivable method to estimate bad debts. On December 31, 2010, it has outstanding accounts receivable of $55,000, and it estimates that 2% will be uncollectible. Prepare the adjusting entry to record bad debts expense for year 2010 under the assumption that the Allowance for Doubtful Accounts has (*a*) a $415 credit balance before the adjustment and (*b*) a $291 debit balance before the adjustment.

Exercise 15-5
Accounts receivable terms   **LO1   LO3**

Match each of the following terms *a* through *g* with the appropriate definitions 1 through 7.

A. Bad debts

B. Aging of accounts receivable

C. Interest

D. Accounts receivable

E. Allowance for doubtful accounts

F. Realizable value

G. Matching principle

_____ **1.** Amounts due from customers arising from credit sales.

_____ **2.** A process of classifying accounts receivable by how long it is past its due date for the purpose of estimating the amount of uncollectible accounts.

_____ **3.** The expected proceeds from converting an asset into cash.

_____ **4.** The accounts of customers who do not pay what they have promised to pay a company.

_____ **5.** The accounting principle that requires expenses to be reported in the same period as the sales they helped to produce.

_____ **6.** A contra asset account with a balance approximating the amount of accounts receivable expected to be uncollectible.

_____ **7.** The cost of borrowing money for a borrower; alternatively, the profit from lending money for a lender.

Exercise 15-6
Recoveries of previously written off accounts   **LO3**

Newton Company uses the allowance method of accounting for uncollectible accounts. On May 3, the Newton Company wrote off the $3,000 uncollectible account of its customer, P. Best. On July 10, Newton received a check for the full amount of $3,000 from P. Best. Prepare the (*a*) May 3 journal entry Newton makes to write off the debt and the (*b*) July 10 journal entry or entries Newton makes to record the recovery of the bad debt.

Refer to the data in Exercise 15-6. Assume instead that Newton Company uses the direct write-off method of accounting for uncollectible accounts. On May 3, the Newton Company wrote off the $3,000 uncollectible account of its customer, P. Best. On July 10, Newton received a check for the full amount of $3,000 from P. Best. Prepare the (a) May 3 journal entry Newton makes to write off the debt and (b) the July 10 journal entry or entries Newton makes to record the recovery of the bad debt.

Exercise 15–7
Recoveries of previously written off accounts   **LO2**

Zamora, Inc., reports the following (partial) aging of accounts receivable at its December 31, 2010, year-end:

Exercise 15–8
Estimating the allowance for doubtful accounts   **LO6**

	Number of Days Past Due		
	1–30 Days	31–60 Days	61–90 Days
Total receivable	$103,246	$64,930	$18,325
Percent uncollectible	1.2%	11%	35%

Required

1. Compute the desired ending balance (after adjustment) in Zamora's Allowance for Doubtful Accounts at December 31, 2010.
2. Compute Zamora's Bad Debt Expense for the year 2010 under each of the following separate scenarios a through c.

	Scenario		
	(a)	(b)	(c)
Allowance for Doubtful Accounts, January 1, 2010 (credit balances)	$ 8,200	$12,614	$16,277
Accounts written off during 2010	10,000	10,000	10,000

Read the article "How to Beat the Deadbeats" in the February 24, 2005, issue of *BusinessWeek*. (The book's Website provides a free link.)

Exercise 15–9
Collecting receivables from customers   **LO3**

Required

1. What does Carol Frischer say is the reason that small businesses have problems collecting on their receivables?
2. What does Frischer recommend businesses do to collect their receivables?

The following information is from the annual financial statements of Raheem Company. Compute its accounts receivable turnover for 2009 and 2010. Compare the two years' results and give a possible explanation for any change (assume that competitors' average accounts receivable turnover is 7).

Exercise 15–10
Accounts receivable turnover   **LO7**

	2010	2009	2008
Net sales	$405,000	$336,000	$388,000
Accounts receivable (year-end)	44,800	41,400	34,800

connect

Mayfair Co. allows select customers to make purchases on credit. Its other customers can use either of two credit cards: Zisa or Access. Zisa deducts a 3% service charge for sales on its credit card and credits the bank account of Mayfair immediately when credit card receipts are deposited. Mayfair deposits the Zisa credit card receipts each business day. When customers use Access credit cards, Mayfair accumulates the receipts for several days before submitting them to Access for payment. Access deducts a 2% service charge and usually pays within one week of being billed. Mayfair completes the following transactions in June. (The terms of all credit sales are 2/15, n/30, and all sales are recorded at the gross price.)

PROBLEM SET A

Problem 15–1A
Sales on account and credit card sales   **LO1   LO3**

June 4   Sold $650 of merchandise on credit to Natara Morris.
     5   Sold $6,900 of merchandise to customers who used their Zisa cards.
     6   Sold $5,872 of merchandise to customers who used their Access cards.
     8   Sold $4,335 of merchandise to customers who used their Access cards.
    10   Submitted Access card receipts accumulated since June 6 to the credit card company for payment.
    13   Wrote off the account of Abigail McKee against the Allowance for Doubtful Accounts. The
           $429 balance in McKee's account stemmed from a credit sale in October of last year.
    17   Received the amount due from Access.
    18   Received Morris's check in full payment for the purchase of June 4.

Check June 17, Dr. Cash $10,003

Required

Prepare journal entries to record the preceding transactions and events. (Round amounts to the nearest dollar.)

Problem 15–2A
Accounts receivable transactions and bad debts adjustments
LO1 LO3 LO5

Liang Company began operations on January 1, 2009. During its first two years, the company completed a number of transactions involving sales on credit, accounts receivable collections, and bad debts. These transactions are summarized as follows.

2009

a. Sold $1,345,400 of merchandise on credit, terms n/30.

b. Wrote off $18,300 of uncollectible accounts receivable.

c. Received $669,200 cash in payment of accounts receivable.

Check (d) Dr. Bad Debts Expense
$28,169

d. In adjusting the accounts on December 31, the company estimated that 1.5% of accounts receivable will be uncollectible.

2010

e. Sold $1,525,600 of merchandise on credit, terms n/30.

f. Wrote off $27,800 of uncollectible accounts receivable.

g. Received $1,204,600 cash in payment of accounts receivable.

(h) Dr. Bad Debts Expense
$32,198

h. In adjusting the accounts on December 31, the company estimated that 1.5% of accounts receivable will be uncollectible.

Required

Prepare journal entries to record Liang's 2009 and 2010 summarized transactions and its year-end adjustments to record bad debts expense. (Round amounts to the nearest dollar.)

Problem 15–3A
Estimating and reporting bad debts **LO1 LO3 LO4 LO6**

At December 31, 2010, Aaliyah Company reports the following results for its calendar year.

Cash sales	$1,905,000
Credit sales	5,682,000

In addition, its unadjusted trial balance includes the following items.

Accounts receivable	$1,270,100 debit
Allowance for doubtful accounts	16,580 debit

Required

1. Prepare the adjusting entry for Aaliyah Co. to recognize bad debts under each of the following independent assumptions:
    a. Bad debts are estimated to be 1.5% of credit sales.
    b. Bad debts are estimated to be 1% of total sales.
    c. An aging analysis estimates that 5% of year-end accounts receivable are uncollectible.

Check Bad Debts Expense:
(1a) $85,230, (1c) $80,085

2. Show how Accounts Receivable and the Allowance for Doubtful Accounts appear on its December 31, 2010, balance sheet given the facts in part 1a.

3. Show how Accounts Receivable and the Allowance for Doubtful Accounts appear on its December 31, 2010, balance sheet given the facts in part 1c.

Jarden Company has credit sales of $3.6 million for year 2010. On December 31, 2010, the company's Allowance for Doubtful Accounts has an unadjusted credit balance of $14,500. Jarden prepares a schedule of its December 31, 2010, accounts receivable by age. On the basis of past experience, it estimates the percent of receivables in each age category that will become uncollectible. This information is summarized here.

Problem 15–4A

Aging accounts receivable and accounting for bad debts

LO3   LO6

File Edit View Insert Format Tools Data Accounting Window Help		
December 31, 2010 Accounts Receivable	**Age of Accounts Receivable**	**Expected Percent Uncollectible**
$830,000	Not yet due	1.25%
254,000	1 to 30 days past due	2.00
86,000	31 to 60 days past due	6.50
38,000	61 to 90 days past due	32.75
12,000	Over 90 days past due	68.00

Required

1. Estimate the required balance of the Allowance for Doubtful Accounts at December 31, 2010, using the aging of accounts receivable method.

2. Prepare the adjusting entry to record bad debts expense at December 31, 2010.

Check   (2) Dr. Bad Debts Expense $27,150

Analysis Component

3. On June 30, 2011, Jarden Company concludes that a customer's $4,750 receivable (created in 2010) is uncollectible and that the account should be written off. What effect will this action have on Jarden's 2011 net income? Explain.

Archer Co. allows select customers to make purchases on credit. Its other customers can use either of two credit cards: Commerce Bank or Aztec. Commerce Bank deducts a 3% service charge for sales on its credit card and immediately credits the bank account of Archer when credit card receipts are deposited. Archer deposits the Commerce Bank credit card receipts each business day. When customers use the Aztec card, Archer accumulates the receipts for several days and then submits them to Aztec for payment. Aztec deducts a 2% service charge and usually pays within one week of being billed. Archer completed the following transactions in August (terms of all credit sales are 2/10, n/30; and all sales are recorded at the gross price).

PROBLEM SET B

Problem 15–1B

Sales on account and credit card sales   **LO1   LO3**

Aug. 4   Sold $3,700 of merchandise on credit to MacKenzie Carpenter.
10   Sold $5,200 of merchandise to customers who used their Commerce Bank credit cards.
11   Sold $1,250 of merchandise to customers who used their Aztec cards.
14   Received Carpenter's check in full payment for the purchase of August 4.
15   Sold $3,240 of merchandise to customers who used their Aztec cards.
18   Submitted Aztec card receipts accumulated since August 11 to the credit card company for payment.
22   Wrote off the account of Craw Co. against the Allowance for Doubtful Accounts. The $498 balance in Craw's account stemmed from a credit sale in November of last year.
25   Received the amount due from Aztec.

Check   Aug. 25, Dr. Cash $4,400

Required

Prepare journal entries to record the preceding transactions and events. (Round amounts to the nearest dollar.)

Problem 15-2B
Accounts receivable transactions and bad debts adjustments
LO1   LO3   LO5

Sherman Co. began operations on January 1, 2009, and completed several transactions during 2009 and 2010 that involved sales on credit, accounts receivable collections, and bad debts. These transactions are summarized as follows.

2009

a. Sold $685,320 of merchandise on credit, terms n/30.

b. Received $482,300 cash in payment of accounts receivable.

c. Wrote off $9,350 of uncollectible accounts receivable.

Check *(d)* Dr. Bad Debts Expense $11,287

d. In adjusting the accounts on December 31, the company estimated that 1% of accounts receivable will be uncollectible.

2010

e. Sold $870,200 of merchandise on credit, terms n/30.

f. Received $990,800 cash in payment of accounts receivable.

g. Wrote off $11,090 of uncollectible accounts receivable.

(h) Dr. Bad Debts Expense $9,773

h. In adjusting the accounts on December 31, the company estimated that 1% of accounts receivable will be uncollectible.

Required

Prepare journal entries to record Sherman's 2009 and 2010 summarized transactions and its year-end adjusting entry to record bad debts expense. (Round amounts to the nearest dollar.)

Problem 15-3B
Estimating and reporting bad debts   **LO3   LO4   LO6**

At December 31, 2010, Ingleton Company reports the following results for the year.

Cash sales	$1,025,000
Credit sales	1,342,000

In addition, its unadjusted trial balance includes the following items.

Accounts receivable	$575,000 debit
Allowance for doubtful accounts	7,500 credit

Required

1. Prepare the adjusting entry for Ingleton Co. to recognize bad debts under each of the following independent assumptions:

   a. Bad debts are estimated to be 2.5% of credit sales.

   b. Bad debts are estimated to be 1.5% of total sales.

   Check Bad debts expense: *(1b)* $35,505, *(1c)* $27,000

   c. An aging analysis estimates that 6% of year-end accounts receivable are uncollectible.

2. Show how Accounts Receivable and the Allowance for Doubtful Accounts appear on its December 31, 2010, balance sheet given the facts in part 1*a*.

3. Show how Accounts Receivable and the Allowance for Doubtful Accounts appear on its December 31, 2010, balance sheet given the facts in part 1*c*.

Problem 15-4B
Aging accounts receivable and accounting for bad debts
LO3   LO6

Hovak Company has credit sales of $4.5 million for year 2010. At December 31, 2010, the company's Allowance for Doubtful Accounts has an unadjusted debit balance of $3,400. Hovak prepares a schedule of its December 31, 2010, accounts receivable by age. On the basis of past experience, it estimates the percent of receivables in each age category that will become uncollectible. This information is summarized here:

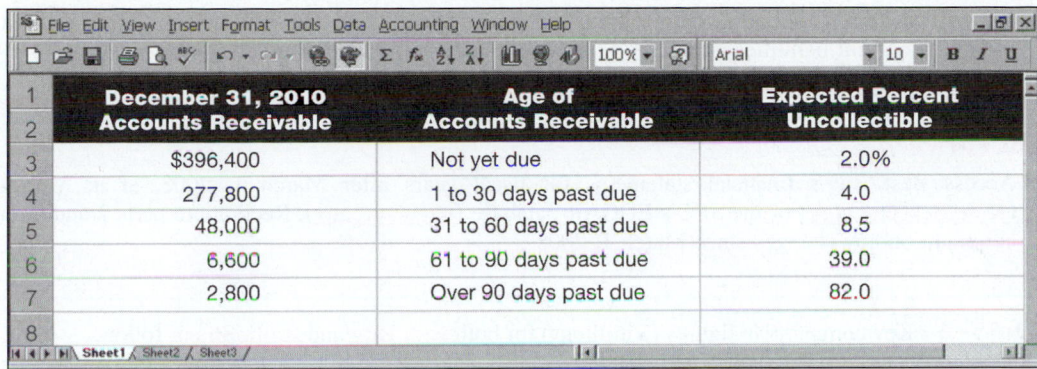

December 31, 2010 Accounts Receivable	Age of Accounts Receivable	Expected Percent Uncollectible
$396,400	Not yet due	2.0%
277,800	1 to 30 days past due	4.0
48,000	31 to 60 days past due	8.5
6,600	61 to 90 days past due	39.0
2,800	Over 90 days past due	82.0

Required

1. Compute the required balance of the Allowance for Doubtful Accounts at December 31, 2010, using the aging of accounts receivable method.

2. Prepare the adjusting entry to record bad debts expense at December 31, 2010.

Check   (2) Dr. Bad Debts Expense
$31,390

Analysis Component

3. On July 31, 2011, Hovak concludes that a customer's $3,455 receivable (created in 2010) is uncollectible and that the account should be written off. What effect will this action have on Hovak's 2011 net income? Explain.

(This serial problem began in Chapter 1 and continues through most of the book. If previous chapter segments were not completed, the serial problem can begin at this point. It is helpful, but not necessary, that you use the Working Papers that accompany the book.)

SERIAL PROBLEM

Success Systems

SP 15   Adriana Lopez, owner of Success Systems, realizes that she needs to begin accounting for bad debts expense. Assume that Success Systems has total revenues of $52,195 during the first three months of 2011, and that the Accounts Receivable balance on March 31, 2011, is $24,400.

Required

1. Prepare the adjusting entry needed for Success Systems to recognize bad debts expense on March 31, 2011, under each of the following independent assumptions (assume a zero unadjusted balance in the Allowance for Doubtful Accounts at March 31).

  a. Bad debts are estimated to be 1% of total revenues.

  b. Bad debts are estimated to be 2% of accounts receivable.

2. Assume that Success Systems's Accounts Receivable balance at June 30, 2011, is $26,500 and that one account of $100 has been written off against the Allowance for Doubtful Accounts since March 31, 2011. If Lopez uses the method prescribed in Part 1b, what adjusting journal entry must be made to recognize bad debts expense on June 30, 2011?

3. Should Lopez consider adopting the direct write-off method of accounting for bad debts expense rather than one of the allowance methods considered in part 1? Explain.

BEYOND THE NUMBERS

BTN 15-1   Refer to **Best Buy**'s financial statements in Appendix A to answer the following.

1. What is the amount of Best Buy's accounts receivable as of March 1, 2008?

2. Compute Best Buy's accounts receivable turnover as of March 1, 2008.

3. How long does it take, *on average,* for Best Buy to collect receivables? Why is this period so short? Do you believe that customers actually pay the amounts due within this short period? Explain.

4. Best Buy's most liquid assets include (*a*) cash and cash equivalents, (*b*) short-term investments, and (*c*) receivables. Compute the percentage that these liquid assets make up of current liabilities as of

REPORTING IN ACTION

L07

March 1, 2008. Do the same computations for March 3, 2007. Comment on the company's ability to satisfy its current liabilities at the 2008 fiscal year-end compared to the 2007 fiscal year.

5. What criteria did Best Buy use to classify items as cash equivalents?

Fast Forward

6. Access Best Buy's financial statements for fiscal years after March 1, 2008, at its Website (www.BestBuy.com) or the SEC's EDGAR database (www.SEC.gov). Recompute parts 2 and 4 and comment on any changes since March 1, 2008.

> Average collection period equals 365 divided by the accounts receivable turnover.

COMPARATIVE ANALYSIS
LO7

BTN 15-2   Key comparative figures ($ millions) for both **Best Buy** and **RadioShack** follow.

Figures	Best Buy			RadioShack		
	Current Year	One-Year Prior	Two-Years Prior	Current Year	One-Year Prior	Two-Years Prior
Accounts receivable, net ...	$ 549	$ 548	$ 449	$ 256	$ 248	$ 309
Net sales	45,015	40,023	35,934	4,252	4,778	5,082

Required

1. Compute the accounts receivable turnover for both Best Buy and RadioShack for each of the two most recent years using the data shown.

2. Using results from part 1, compute how many days it takes each company, *on average,* to collect receivables. Why are these periods so short? Do you believe that receivables are actually collected this quickly? Explain.

3. Which company is more efficient in collecting its accounts receivable? Explain.

> Average collection period equals 365 divided by the accounts receivable turnover.

ETHICS CHALLENGE
LO3

BTN 15-3   Anton Blair is the manager of a medium-size company. A few years ago, Blair persuaded the owner to base a part of his compensation on the net income the company earns each year. Each December he estimates year-end financial figures in anticipation of the bonus he will receive. If the bonus is not as high as he would like, he offers several recommendations to the accountant for year-end adjustments. One of his favorite recommendations is for the controller to reduce the estimate of doubtful accounts.

Required

1. What effect does lowering the estimate for doubtful accounts have on the income statement and balance sheet?

2. Do you believe Blair's recommendation to adjust the allowance for doubtful accounts is within his right as manager, or do you believe this action is an ethics violation? Justify your response.

3. What type of internal control(s) might be useful for this company in overseeing the manager's recommendations for accounting changes?

WORKPLACE COMMUNICATION
LO1   LO3   LO4

BTN 15-4   As the accountant for Pure-Air Distributing, you attend a sales managers' meeting devoted to a discussion of credit policies. At the meeting, you report that bad debts expense is estimated to be $59,000 and accounts receivable at year-end amount to $1,750,000 less a $43,000 allowance for doubtful accounts. Sid Omar, a sales manager, expresses confusion over why bad debts expense and the allowance for doubtful accounts are different amounts. Write a one-page memorandum to him explaining why a difference in bad debts expense and the allowance for doubtful accounts is not unusual. The company estimates bad debts expense as 2% of sales.

TAKING IT TO THE NET
LO1

BTN 15-5   Access **eBay**'s February 20, 2009, filing of its 10-K report for the year ended December 31, 2008, at www.SEC.gov.

Required

1. What is the amount of eBay's net accounts receivable at December 31, 2008, and at December 31, 2007?

BTN 15-6 Each member of a team is to participate in estimating uncollectibles using the aging schedule and percents shown in Problem 15-4A. The division of labor is up to the team. Your goal is to accurately complete this task as soon as possible. After estimating uncollectibles, check your estimate with the instructor. If the estimate is correct, the team then should prepare the adjusting entry and the presentation of accounts receivable (net) for the December 31, 2010, balance sheet.

TEAMWORK IN ACTION
L06

BTN 15-7 Kevin Plank of **Under Armour** is introduced in the chapter's opening feature. Kevin currently sells his products through multiple outlets. Assume that he is considering two new selling options.

ENTREPRENEURS IN BUSINESS
L01 L03

Plan A. Under Armour would begin selling products online directly to customers. Online customers would use their credit cards. It currently has the capability of selling through its Website with no additional investment in hardware or software. Credit sales are expected to increase by $250,000 per year. Costs associated with this plan are: cost of these sales will be $135,500, credit card fees will be 4.75% of sales, and additional recordkeeping and shipping costs will be 6% of sales. These online sales will reduce the sales to stores by $35,000 because some customers will now purchase items online. Sales to stores have a 25% gross margin percentage.

Plan B. Under Armour would expand its market to more stores. It would make additional credit sales of $500,000 to those stores. Costs associated with those sales are: cost of sales will be $375,000, additional recordkeeping and shipping will be 4% of sales, and uncollectible accounts will be 6.2% of sales.

Required

1. Compute the additional annual net income or loss expected under (a) Plan A and (b) Plan B.

Check (1b) Net income, $74,000

2. Should Under Armour pursue either plan? Discuss both the financial and nonfinancial factors relevant to this decision.

---

1. d; Desired balance in Allowance
   for Doubtful Accounts   = $ 5,026 cr.
   ($125,650 × 0.04)
   Current balance in Allowance
   for Doubtful Accounts   =   (328) cr.
   Bad Debts Expense to be
   recorded   = $ 4,698

2. a; Desired balance in Allowance
   for Doubtful Accounts   = $29,358 cr.
   ($489,300 × 0.06)
   Current balance in Allowance
   for Doubtful Accounts   =   554 dr.
   Bad Debts Expense to
   be recorded   = $29,912

3. b

4. d

5. c; Desired balance in Allowance
   for Doubtful Accounts   = $ 5,835 cr.
   ($97,250 × 0.06)
   Current balance in Allowance
   for Doubtful Accounts   =   (951) cr.
   Bad Debts Expense to
   be recorded   = $ 4,884 cr.

ANSWERS TO MULTIPLE CHOICE QUIZ

Chapter 16

A Look Back

Chapter 15 described how companies account for and report accounts receivable. We also describe how to value accounts receivable.

A Look at This Chapter

This chapter focuses on how companies account for and report notes receivable and notes payable. We also describe how companies compute interest on notes.

A Look Ahead

Chapter 17 emphasizes accounting for inventory. We describe methods for assigning costs to inventory. We also describe methods of estimating and measuring inventory.

Notes Receivable and Notes Payable

Learning Objectives

LO 1	Describe a promissory note.
LO 2	Compute the maturity date and interest due on a promissory note.
LO 3	Record the receipt of a note receivable.
LO 4	Record the honoring, discounting, and dishonoring of a note and the adjustment for interest.
LO 5	Prepare entries to account for notes payable.
LO 6	Explain the types and payment patterns of notes.
LO 7	Compute the times interest earned ratio and use it to analyze liabilities.

"Stay focused on your goal and not be swayed either way by people giving you too much props or too many insults"—Stu Levy

Manga-nificent Entertainment

LOS ANGELES, CA—"I fell in love with the combination of old and new, East and West—sort of a neo-Buddhist modernism—that hooked me the most," says Stu Levy, founder of **TOKYOPOP** (**Tokyopop.com**). The object of Stu's desire is manga (pronounced MAHN-gah), a form of graphic entertainment native to Japan. TOKYOPOP is a leading multimedia company that specializes in publishing manga in English. Manga is described as the Japanese counterpart to comic books, though quicker to read and with a wider range of genres, characters, and layouts.

"The art [of manga] really resonates with this generation of young people, teenagers, and children," explains Stu. "We are putting a lot of time and energy into getting it out there into the hands of the potential audience. I love the ability to merge the visual medium with lyrical storytelling."

The art of running a company that publishes manga involves the business of acquiring and developing material. Stu likens himself to a producer. As he puts it, "A producer gets the team together, handles the finances, but is also totally involved in the creative side. I also handle our capital-raising activities."

TOKYOPOP's capital-raising activities involve considerable investment in manga. Accordingly, Stu's job requires making and accepting notes for loans to finance its business. This demands that he know the accounting for notes payable and notes receivable. He must also deal with the accounting for issuance, valuation, and settlement of both its notes receivable and payable.

"The publishing part of our business is kind of like a platform . . . we are a delivering mechanism," says Stu. "Most people who read manga . . . get hooked. It's addictive," he adds. Revenues should continue to look *manga-nificent* for years to come because the more people experience manga, the larger the market grows. "Our goal at TOKYOPOP is to deliver the most exciting entertainment possible and merging the best cultures in the world to do so," says Stu. "I dove into the Japanese culture and Asian culture . . . but I fell in love with manga."

[Sources: *TOKYOPOP Website*, May 2009, *Entrepreneur*, November 2004; *Japan Today*, February 2004]

Promissory notes are used in many transactions to pay for products and services and to lend and borrow money. This chapter explains the accounting for the issuance, valuation, and settlement of both notes receivable and notes payable. We also explain how to compute the interest that applies to these notes.

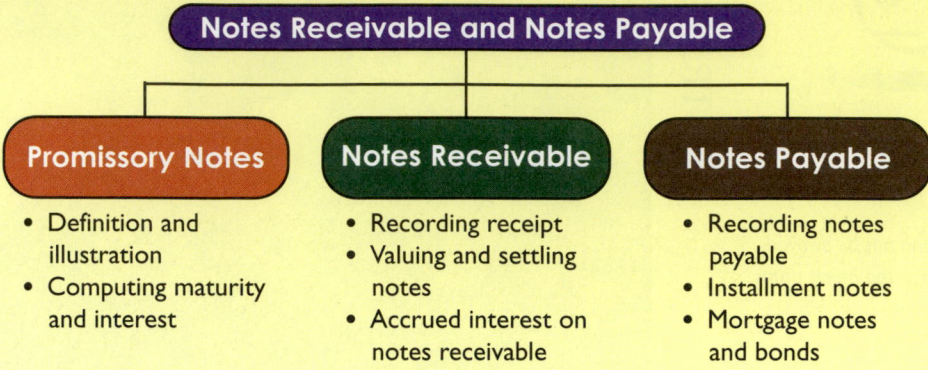

Notes Receivable and Notes Payable

Promissory Notes
- Definition and illustration
- Computing maturity and interest

Notes Receivable
- Recording receipt
- Valuing and settling notes
- Accrued interest on notes receivable

Notes Payable
- Recording notes payable
- Installment notes
- Mortgage notes and bonds

Promissory Notes

LO1 Describe a promissory note.

A **promissory note** is a written promise to pay a specified amount of money, usually with interest, either on demand or at a definite future date. Promissory notes are used in many transactions, including paying for products and services, and lending and borrowing money. Sellers sometimes ask for a note to replace an account receivable when a customer requests additional time to pay a past-due account. For legal reasons, sellers generally prefer to receive notes when the credit period is long and when the receivable is for a large amount. If a lawsuit is needed to collect from a customer, a note is the buyer's written acknowledgment of the debt, its amount, and its terms.

An Example of a Promissory Note

Exhibit 16.1 shows a simple promissory note dated July 10, 2010. For this note, Julia Browne promises to pay TechCom or to its order (according to TechCom's instructions) a specified amount of money ($1,000), called the **principal of a note,** at a definite future date 90 days later (October 8, 2010). As the one who signed the note and promised to pay it at maturity, Browne is the **maker of the note.** As the entity to whom the note is payable, TechCom is the **payee of the note.** To Browne, the note is a liability called a *note payable*. To TechCom, the same note is an asset called a *note receivable*. This note bears interest at 12%, as written on the note. **Interest** is the charge for using (not paying) the money until a later date. To a borrower, interest is an expense. To a lender, it is revenue.

Exhibit 16.1

Promissory Note

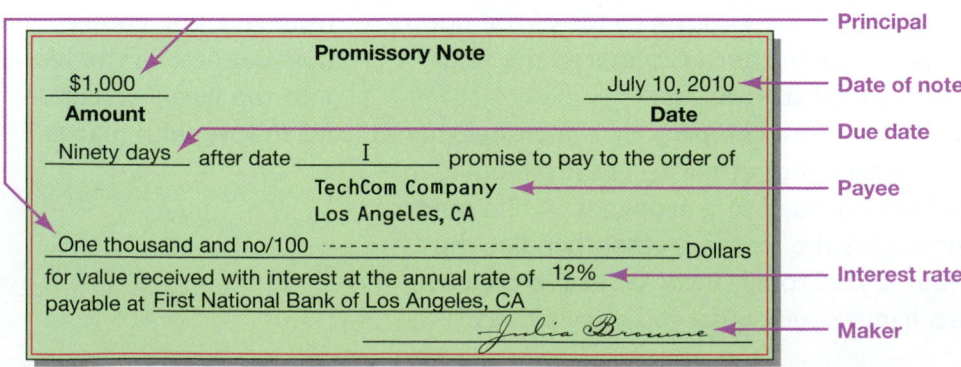

Principal

Promissory Note

$1,000   July 10, 2010   — Date of note
Amount   **Date**

Ninety days after date _____I_____ promise to pay to the order of   — Due date

TechCom Company   — Payee
Los Angeles, CA

One thousand and no/100 - Dollars

for value received with interest at the annual rate of 12%   — Interest rate
payable at First National Bank of Los Angeles, CA

Julia Browne   — Maker

Computing Maturity and Interest

This section describes key computations for notes, including the determination of maturity date, period covered, and interest.

Maturity Date and Period The **maturity date of a note** is the day the note (principal and interest) must be repaid. The *period* of a note is the time from the note's (contract) date to its maturity date. Many notes mature in less than a full year, and the period they cover is often expressed in days. When the time of a note is expressed in days, its maturity date is the specified number of days after the note's date. As an example, a five-day note dated June 15 matures and is due on June 20. A 90-day note dated July 10 matures on October 8. This October 8 due date is computed as shown in Exhibit 16.2. The period of a note is sometimes expressed in months or years. When months are used, the note matures and is payable in the month of its maturity on the *same day of the month* as its original date. A nine-month note dated July 10, for instance, is payable on April 10. The same analysis applies when years are used.

Days in July	31
Minus the date of the note	10
Days remaining in July	21 ← July 11–31
Add days in August	31 ← Aug. 1–31
Add days in September	30 ← Sept. 1–30
Days to equal 90 days, or **maturity date of October 8**	8 ← Oct. 1–8
Period of the note in days	90

Exhibit 16.2

Maturity Date Computation

Interest Computation *Interest* is the cost of borrowing money for the borrower or, alternatively, the profit from lending money for the lender. Unless otherwise stated, the rate of interest on a note is the rate charged for the use of the principal for one year. The formula for computing interest on a note is shown in Exhibit 16.3.

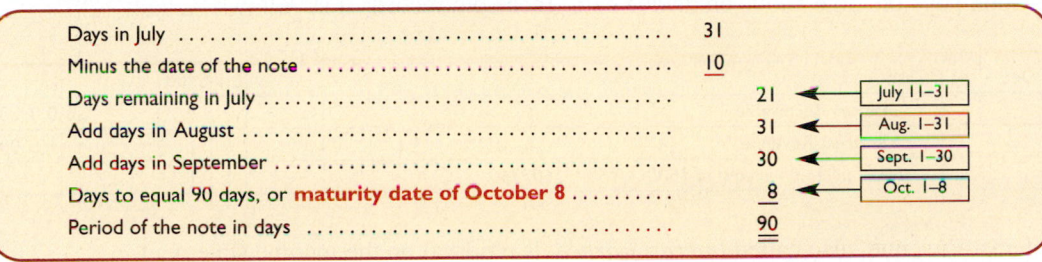

$$\text{Interest} = \frac{\text{Principal}}{\text{of the note}} \times \frac{\text{Annual}}{\text{interest rate}} \times \frac{\text{Time expressed}}{\text{in years}}$$

Exhibit 16.3

Formula for Computing Interest

To simplify interest computations, a year is commonly treated as having 360 days (called the *banker's rule* in the business world). **We treat a year as having 360 days for interest computations in the examples and assignments.** Using the promissory note in Exhibit 16.1 where we have a 90-day, 12%, $1,000 note, the total interest is computed as follows.

$$\$1,000 \times 12\% \times \frac{90}{360} = \$1,000 \times 0.12 \times 0.25 = \$30$$

Notes Receivable

Notes receivable are usually recorded in a single Notes Receivable account to simplify record-keeping. The original notes are kept on file, including information on the maker, rate of interest, and due date. (When a company holds a large number of notes, it sometimes sets up a controlling account and a subsidiary ledger for notes. This is similar to the handling of accounts receivable.) To illustrate the recording for the receipt of a note, we use the $1,000, 90-day, 12% promissory note in Exhibit 16.1. TechCom received this note at the time of a product sale to Julia Browne. This transaction is recorded as follows.

LO3 Record the receipt of a note receivable.

July	10	Notes Receivable	1 0 0 0 00		
		Sales		1 0 0 0 00	
		Sold goods in exchange for a 90-day, 12% note.			

Assets = Liabilities + Equity
+1,000   +1,000

When a seller accepts a note from an overdue customer as a way to grant a time extension on a past-due account receivable, it will often collect part of the past-due balance in cash. This partial

Notes receivable often are a major part of a company's assets. Likewise, notes payable often are a large part of a company's liabilities.

payment forces a concession from the customer, reduces the customer's debt (and the seller's risk), and produces a note for a smaller amount. To illustrate, assume that TechCom agreed to accept $232 in cash along with a $600, 60-day, 15% note from Jo Cook to settle her $832 past-due account. TechCom made the following entry to record receipt of this cash and note.

Assets = Liabilities + Equity
+232
+600
−832

Oct.	5	Cash		2 3 2 00	
		Notes Receivable		6 0 0 00	
		Accounts Receivable—J. Cook			8 3 2 00
		Received cash and note to settle account.			

Valuing and Settling Notes Receivable

LO4 Record the honoring, discounting, and dishonoring of a note and the adjustment for interest.

Recording an Honored Note The principal and interest of a note are due on its maturity date. The maker of the note usually *honors* the note and pays it in full. To illustrate, when J. Cook pays the note above on its due date, TechCom records it as follows.

Assets = Liabilities + Equity
+615   +15
−600

Dec.	4	Cash		6 1 5 00	
		Notes Receivable			6 0 0 00
		Interest Revenue			1 5 00
		Collect note with interest of $600 × 15% × 60/360.			

Interest Revenue, also called *Interest Earned,* is reported on the income statement.

Renewal of Note at Maturity If the note's maker is unable to pay at maturity, the payee can allow the note to be renewed. The payee adds the accrued interest revenue to the principal balance of the new note. The journal entry to record the renewed note is

Assets = Liabilities + Equity
+615   +15
−600

Dec.	4	Notes Receivable (new note)		6 1 5 00	
		Notes Receivable (old note)			6 0 0 00
		Interest Revenue			1 5 00
		To renew note with interest ($600 × 15% × 60/360).			

Note Discounted before Maturity A note receivable is an asset. The holder can either wait for the maturity date to receive cash, or it may sell the note to a bank before the maturity date. This is sometimes called *discounting a note.* The bank will pay the note's holder the principal and interest (maturity value) less a discounting charge.

Assume that TechCom holds a $2,000, 12%, 60-day note from H. Potter dated November 15. On December 15, TechCom discounts H. Potter's note at the bank at 15%. To calculate TechCom's proceeds (maturity value less discount charges), follow these four steps:

Step 1: **Calculate the maturity value of the note.** Maturity value is the principal plus the interest due at maturity.

Interest = Principal of the note × Annual interest rate × Time expressed in years

Interest = $2,000   × 12%   × 60/360 = $40

Maturity value = Principal + Interest = $2,000 + $40 = $2,040

Step 2: **Determine the number of days in the discount period.** Count the number of days from the discount date to the maturity date.

The discount date is December 15, and the maturity date is January 14.

Days discounted in December (December 15 to December 31)	= 16 days
Days discounted in January (January 1 to January 14)	= 14 days
Days in discount period	= 30 days

Step 3: Compute the bank discount charges. The bank charges the discount rate of 15% for the 30 days in the discount period, or $25.50 ($2,040 maturity value $\times$ 15% $\times$ 30/360).

Step 4: Compute the cash proceeds of the note at the discount date. The proceeds are $2,014.50, computed as

$$\text{Proceeds} = \text{Maturity value} - \text{Discount charges}$$

$$\$2,014.50 = \$2,040.00 - \$25.50$$

To record the discounting of H. Potter's note, TechCom needs to compute the amount of interest earned on the H. Potter note. This amount is the interest calculated in step 1 to compute maturity value less the discount charged by the bank (step 4), or $40 − $25.50 = $14.50 in interest revenue. The journal entry to record the discounting of H. Potter's note is

Dec.	15	Cash		2 0 1 4 50	
		Notes Receivable (Discounted)			2 0 0 0 00
		Interest Revenue			1 4 50
		To record discounting of H. Potter's note.			

Assets = Liabilities + Equity
+2,014.50   +14.50
−2,000.00

Recording a Dishonored Note When a note's maker is unable or refuses to pay at maturity, the note is *dishonored*. The act of dishonoring a note does not relieve the maker of the obligation to pay. The payee should use every legitimate means to collect. How do companies report this event? The balance of the Notes Receivable account should include only those notes that have not matured. Thus, when a note is dishonored, we remove the amount of this note from the Notes Receivable account and charge it back to an account receivable from its maker. The payee adds accrued interest to the account. To illustrate, TechCom holds an $800, 12%, 60-day note from Greg Hart. At maturity, Hart dishonors the note. TechCom records this dishonoring of the note as follows.

When posting a dishonored note to a customer's account, an explanation is included so as not to misinterpret the debit as a sale on account.

Oct.	14	Accounts Receivable—G. Hart		8 1 6 00	
		Interest Revenue			1 6 00
		Notes Receivable			8 0 0 00
		To charge account of G. Hart for a dishonored note			
		and interest of $800 $\times$ 12% $\times$ 60/360.			

Assets = Liabilities + Equity
+816   +16
−800

Charging a dishonored note back to the account of its maker serves two purposes. First, it removes the amount of the note from the Notes Receivable account and records the dishonored note in the maker's account. Second, and more important, if the maker of the dishonored note applies for credit in the future, his or her account will reveal all past dealings, including the dishonored note. Restoring the account also reminds the company to continue collection efforts from Hart for both principal and interest. The entry records the full amount, including interest, to ensure that it is included in collection efforts. If TechCom is unable to collect Hart's account receivable, it writes off his account as we showed in Chapter 15.

Reporting the details of notes is consistent with the **full disclosure principle,** which requires financial statements (including footnotes) to report all relevant information.

Accrued Interest on Notes Receivable

When notes receivable are outstanding at the end of an accounting period, any accrued interest earned is computed and recorded. To illustrate, on December 16, TechCom accepts a $3,000, 60-day, 12% note from a customer for granting an extension on a past-due account. When TechCom's accounting period ends on December 31, $15 of interest has accrued on this note ($3,000 $\times$ 12% $\times$ 15/360). The following adjusting entry records this revenue.

Dec.	31	Interest Receivable		1 5 00	
		Interest Revenue			1 5 00
		To record accrued interest earned.			

Assets = Liabilities + Equity
+15   +15

Interest Revenue appears on the income statement, and Interest Receivable appears on the balance sheet as a current asset. When the December 16 note is collected on February 14 of the next year, TechCom's entry to record the cash receipt is

Assets = Liabilities + Equity
+3,060   +45
  −15
−3,000

Feb.	14	Cash		3 0 6 0 00	
		Interest Revenue			4 5 00
		Interest Receivable			1 5 00
		Notes Receivable			3 0 0 0 00
		Received payment of note and its interest.			

Total interest earned on the 60-day note is $60. The $15 credit to Interest Receivable on February 14 reflects the collection of the interest accrued from the December 31 adjusting entry. The $45 interest earned reflects TechCom's revenue from holding the note from January 1 to February 14 of the current period. This is computed as $3,000 × 12% × 45/360.

HOW YOU DOIN'?
Answers—p. 405

1. Irwin purchases $7,000 of merchandise from Stamford on December 16, 2010. Stamford accepts Irwin's $7,000, 90-day, 12% note as payment. Stamford's accounting period ends on December 31, and it does not make reversing entries. Prepare entries for Stamford on December 16, 2010, and December 31, 2010.

2. Using the information in question 1 above, prepare Stamford's March 16, 2011, entry if Irwin dishonors the note.

Notes Payable

Notes payable are issued to obtain liquid assets such as cash or long-term assets such as equipment. Notes payable are typically transacted with a *single* lender such as a bank.

Recording Notes Payable Transactions

LO5 Prepare entries to account for notes payable.

Recording the Issuance of a Note   A **note payable** is a written promise to pay a specified sum on a specified date. For example, on July 28, Greg's Garage issues a 90-day, $30,000 note payable at 10% annual interest to purchase new auto mechanic equipment. The entry to record this issuance is

Assets = Liabilities + Equity
+30,000   +30,000

Jul.	28	Equipment		30 0 0 0 00	
		Notes Payable			30 0 0 0 00
		To record issuance of note to purchase equipment.			

Recording the Payment of the Note at Maturity   On October 26, the maturity date, Greg pays the $30,000 note principal plus the interest. The interest is computed as:

Interest = Principal of the note × Annual interest rate × Time expressed in years

Interest = $30,000   × 10%   × 90/360 = $750

The entry to record the payment of the note follows (Interest Expense is reported on the income statement)

Assets = Liabilities + Equity
−30,750   −30,000   −750

Oct.	26	Notes Payable		30 0 0 0 00	
		Interest Expense		7 5 0 00	
		Cash			30 7 5 0 00
		To record payment of July 28 note.			

Recording the Issuance and Payment of a Discounted Note Payable   Rather than collecting interest when the note comes due, banks sometimes will deduct the interest charges from the initial proceeds of the note. We illustrate by considering Greg's Garage's 60-day, $20,000 note payable at 12% annual interest on Oct. 9. We calculate the total interest as

Interest = Principal of the note × Annual interest rate × Time expressed in years

Interest = $20,000   × 12%   × 60/360 = $400

The bank deducts this interest from the proceeds and Greg's Garage records it as follows:

Oct.	9	Cash	19 6 0 0 00	
		Interest Expense	4 0 0 00	
		Notes Payable		20 0 0 0 00
		To record issuance of a discounted note.		

Assets = Liabilities + Equity
+19,600   +20,000   −400

On December 8, Greg's Garage pays the principal on the note payable. Since the interest expense has already been recorded, the journal entry is

Dec.	8	Notes Payable	20 0 0 0 00	
		Cash		20 0 0 0 00
		To record payment of Oct. 9 discounted note.		

Assets = Liabilities + Equity
−20,000   −20,000

Installment Notes

An **installment note** is an obligation requiring a series of payments to the lender. Installment notes are common for franchises and other businesses when lenders and borrowers agree to spread payments over several periods. To illustrate, assume that Foghog borrows $60,000 from a bank to purchase equipment. It signs an 8% installment note requiring six annual payments of principal plus interest. Foghog records the note's issuance at January 1, 2010, as follows.

LO6 Explain the types and payment patterns of notes.

Jan.	1	Cash	60 0 0 0 00	
		Notes Payable		60 0 0 0 00
		Borrowed $60,000 by signing an 8%, six-year		
		installment note.		

Assets = Liabilities + Equity
+60,000   +60,000

Payments on an installment note normally include the accrued interest expense plus a portion of the amount borrowed (the *principal*). This section describes an installment note with equal payments.

The equal total payments pattern consists of changing amounts of both interest and principal. To illustrate, assume that Foghog's $60,000 note requires six *equal payments* of $12,979 at the end of each year. The $12,979 includes both interest and principal, the amounts of which change with each payment. Exhibit 16.4 shows the pattern of equal total payments and its two parts, interest and principal. Column A shows the note's beginning of year balance. Column B shows accrued interest for each year at 8% of the beginning note balance. Column C shows the impact on the note's principal, which equals the difference between the total payment in column D and the interest expense in column B. Column E shows the note's year-end balance. Foghog will repay a total of $77,874 ($12,979 × 6) for this note. Since $60,000 of this total is for principal, $17,874 ($77,874 − $60,000) is for interest.

Although the six cash payments are equal, interest expense decreases each year because the principal balance of the note declines. As the amount of interest decreases each year, the portion of each payment applied to principal increases. This pattern is graphed in the lower part of

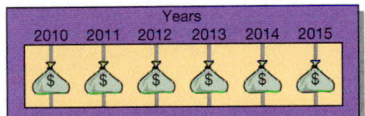

Most consumer notes are installment notes that require equal total payments.

Exhibit 16.4

Installment Note with Equal Payments

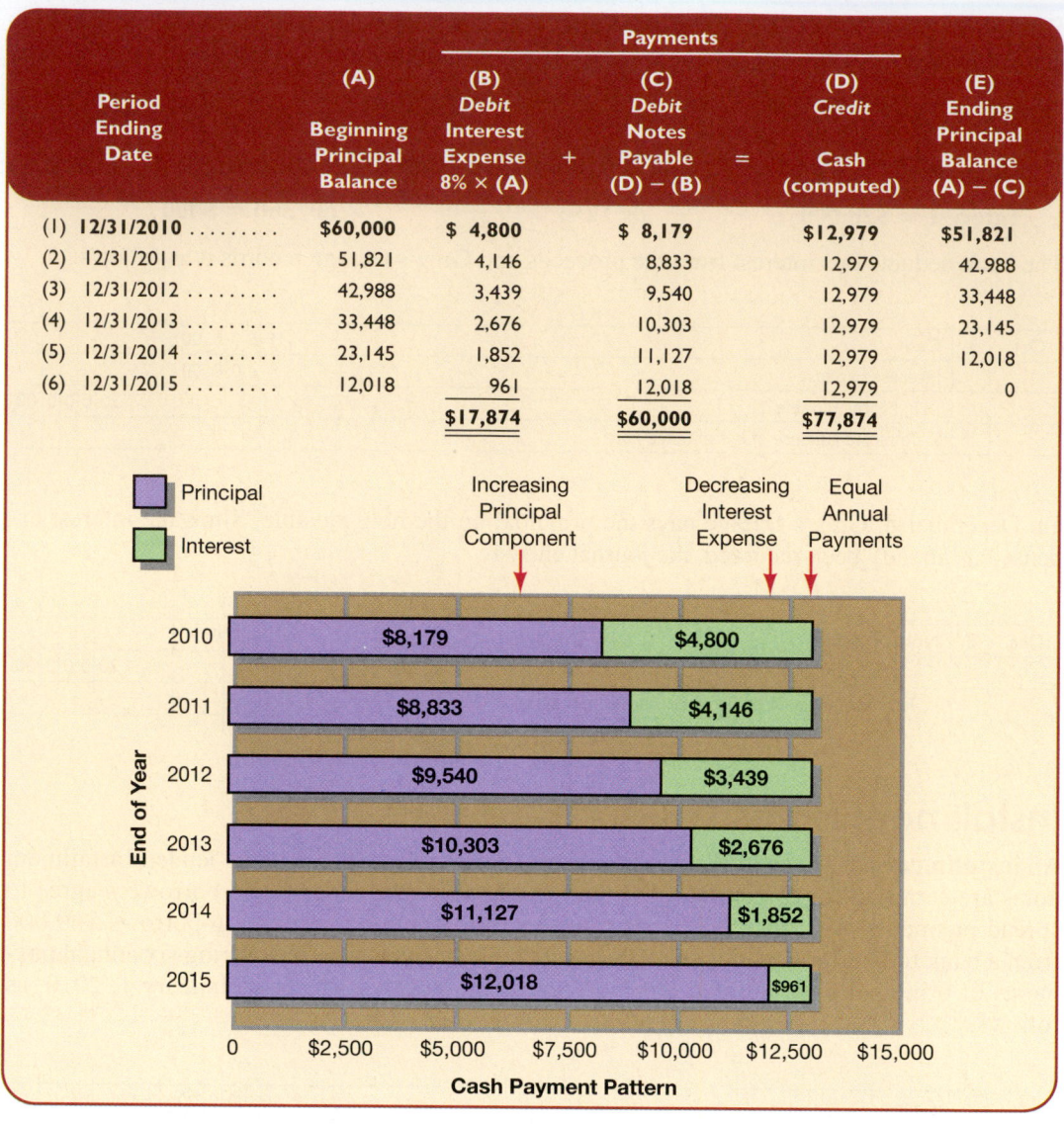

	Period Ending Date	(A) Beginning Principal Balance	(B) Debit Interest Expense 8% × (A)	+	(C) Debit Notes Payable (D) − (B)	=	(D) Credit Cash (computed)	(E) Ending Principal Balance (A) − (C)
(1)	12/31/2010	$60,000	$ 4,800		$ 8,179		$12,979	$51,821
(2)	12/31/2011	51,821	4,146		8,833		12,979	42,988
(3)	12/31/2012	42,988	3,439		9,540		12,979	33,448
(4)	12/31/2013	33,448	2,676		10,303		12,979	23,145
(5)	12/31/2014	23,145	1,852		11,127		12,979	12,018
(6)	12/31/2015	12,018	961		12,018		12,979	0
			$17,874		$60,000		$77,874	

Payments

Principal
Interest

Increasing Principal Component

Decreasing Interest Expense

Equal Annual Payments

End of Year		
2010	$8,179	$4,800
2011	$8,833	$4,146
2012	$9,540	$3,439
2013	$10,303	$2,676
2014	$11,127	$1,852
2015	$12,018	$961

0   $2,500 $5,000 $7,500 $10,000 $12,500 $15,000

Cash Payment Pattern

Exhibit 16.4. Foghog uses the amounts in Exhibit 16.4 to record its first two payments (for years 2010 and 2011) as follows:

Assets   = Liabilities + Equity
−12,979   −8,179   −4,800

2010 Dec.	31	Interest Expense	4 8 0 0 00	
		Notes Payable	8 1 7 9 00	
		Cash		12 9 7 9 00
		To record first installment payment.		

Assets   = Liabilities + Equity
−12,979   −8,833   −4,146

2011 Dec.	31	Interest Expense	4 1 4 6 00	
		Notes Payable	8 8 3 3 00	
		Cash		12 9 7 9 00
		To record second installment payment.		

Foghog records similar entries but with different amounts for each of the remaining four payments. On December 31, 2015, Foghog makes its sixth $12,979 payment, and the Notes Payable account balance is zero.

Mortgage Notes and Bonds

A **mortgage** is a legal agreement that helps protect a lender if a borrower fails to make required payments on notes or bonds. A mortgage gives the lender a right to be paid from the cash proceeds of the sale of a borrower's assets identified in the mortgage. A legal document, called a *mortgage contract,* describes the mortgage terms.

Mortgage notes carry a mortgage contract pledging title to specific assets as security for the note. Mortgage notes are especially popular in the purchase of homes and the acquisition of plant assets. Less common *mortgage bonds* are backed by the issuer's assets. Accounting for mortgage notes and bonds is similar to that for unsecured notes and bonds, except that the mortgage agreement must be disclosed.

HOW YOU DOIN'?
Answers—p. 405

3. Which of the following is true for an installment note requiring a series of equal total cash payments? (a) Payments consist of increasing interest and decreasing principal; (b) Payments consist of changing amounts of principal but constant interest; or (c) Payments consist of decreasing interest and increasing principal.
4. How is the interest portion of an installment note payment computed?
5. When a borrower records an interest payment on an installment note, how are the balance sheet and income statement affected?

TIMES INTEREST EARNED RATIO

A company incurs interest expense on many of its current and long-term liabilities. When a company has long-term liabilities, lenders want to know if there will be sufficient earnings to pay interest as it comes due. This is numerically reflected in the **times interest earned ratio** in Exhibit 16.5.

LO7 Compute the times interest earned ratio and use it to analyze liabilities.

$$\text{Times interest earned} = \frac{\text{Income before interest expense and income taxes}}{\text{Interest expense}}$$

Exhibit 16.5

Times Interest Earned

The times interest earned ratio reflects a company's ability to pay interest obligations. To illustrate, consider Diego Co.'s results for 2010 and 2011 in Exhibit 16.6.

($ thousands)	2010	2011
Sales	$600	$900
Expenses (75% of sales)	450	675
Income before interest	150	225
Interest expense (fixed)	60	60
Net income	$ 90	$165

Exhibit 16.6

Diego Company Results

For 2010, Diego's times interest earned is computed as $150,000/$60,000, or 2.5 times. For 2011, Diego's times interest earned ratio is computed as $225,000/$60,000, or 3.75 times, which would be satisfactory to Diego's lenders. In most companies, a ratio of 2.0 to 3.0 is considered adequate.

Experience shows that when times interest earned falls below 1.5 to 2.0 and remains at that level or lower for several periods, the default rate on liabilities increases sharply.

Demonstration Problem

Salads & Such (S&S) has successfully opened its first restaurant in Tempe, Arizona. To finance its planned expansion to more locations, S&S signs a $400,000, 10% note on January 1, 2010, to be repaid with five equal annual installment payments of $105,519 to be made on December 31 each year from 2010 through 2014.

Required

1. Prepare an amortization table for the installment note such as shown in Exhibit 16.4 (round amounts to the nearest dollar).
2. Prepare the journal entry for the first installment payment on December 31, 2010.

Planning the Solution

- Prepare a table similar to Exhibit 16.4 and use the numbers in the table's first line for the journal entry.

Solution to Demonstration Problem

1. Amortization table follows.

Period Ending Date	(A) Beginning Principal Balance	Payments (B) Debit Interest Expense 10% × (A)	+	(C) Debit Notes Payable (D) − (B)	=	(D) Credit Cash (computed)	(E) Ending Principal Balance (A) − (C)
(1) 12/31/2010	$400,000	$ 40,000		$ 65,519		$105,519	$334,481
(2) 12/31/2011	334,481	33,448		72,071		105,519	262,410
(3) 12/31/2012	262,410	26,241		79,278		105,519	183,132
(4) 12/31/2013	183,132	18,313		87,206		105,519	95,926
(5) 12/31/2014	95,926	9,593		95,926		105,519	0
		$127,595		$400,000		$527,595	

2. Journal entry for December 31, 2010, payment.

Assets	= Liabilities +	Equity
−105,519	−65,519	−40,000

Dec.	31	Interest Expense		40 0 0 0 00	
		Notes Payable		65 5 1 9 00	
		Cash			105 5 1 9 00
		To record first installment payment.			

Summary

LO1 **Describe a promissory note.** A promissory note is a written promise to pay a specified amount of money, usually with interest, either on demand or at a definite future date.

LO2 **Compute the maturity date and interest due on a promissory note.** The maturity date is the day the note (principal and interest) must be repaid. Interest rates are normally stated in annual terms. The amount of interest on the note is computed by expressing time as a fraction of one year and multiplying the note's principal by this fraction and the annual interest rate.

LO3 **Record the receipt of a note receivable.** A note received is recorded at its principal amount by debiting the Notes Receivable account. The credit amount is to the asset, product, or service provided in return for the note.

LO4 **Record the honoring, discounting, and dishonoring of a note and the adjustment for interest.** When a note is honored, the payee debits the money received and credits both Notes Receivable and

Interest Revenue. If the payee (holder) sells the note to another party before the maturity date, this is called discounting. Dishonored notes are credited to Notes Receivable and debited to Accounts Receivable (to the account of the maker in an attempt to collect), and Interest Revenue is recorded for interest earned for the time the note is held.

LO5 **Prepare entries to account for notes payable.** Interest is allocated to each period in a note's life by multiplying its beginning-period carrying value by its market rate at issuance.

LO6 **Explain the types and payment patterns of notes.** Notes repaid over a period of time are called *installment notes* and often involve equal total payments. Mortgage notes also are common.

LO7 **Compute the times interest earned ratio and use it to analyze liabilities.** Times interest earned is computed by dividing a company's net income before interest expense and income taxes by the amount of interest expense. The times interest earned ratio reflects a company's ability to pay interest obligations.

1.

Dec. 16	Note Receivable—Irwin.	7,000	
	Sales.		7,000
Dec. 31	Interest Receivable	35	
	Interest Revenue.		35
	($7,000 × 12% × 15/360)		

2.

Mar. 16	Accounts Receivable—Irwin	7,210	
	Interest Revenue.		175
	Interest Receivable		35
	Notes Receivable—Irwin.		7,000

3. (*c*)

4. The interest portion of an installment payment equals the period's beginning loan balance multiplied by the market interest rate at the time of the note's issuance.

5. On the balance sheet, the account balances of the related liability (note payable) and asset (cash) accounts are decreased. On the income statement, interest expense is recorded.

Key Terms

Full disclosure principle (p. 399) Principle that prescribes financial statements (including notes) to report all relevant information about an entity's operations and financial condition.

Installment note (p. 401) Liability requiring a series of periodic payments to the lender.

Interest (p. 396) Charge for using money (or other assets) loaned from one entity to another.

Maker of the note (p. 396) Entity who signs a note and promises to pay it at maturity.

Maturity date of a note (p. 397) Date when a note's principal and interest are due.

Mortgage (p. 403) Legal loan agreement that protects a lender by giving the lender the right to be paid from the cash proceeds from the sale of a borrower's assets identified in the mortgage.

Note payable (p. 400) Liability expressed by a written promise to pay a definite sum of money on demand or on a specific future date(s).

Payee of the note (p. 396) Entity to whom a note is made payable.

Principal of a note (p. 396) Amount that the signer of a note agrees to pay back when it matures, not including interest.

Promissory note (or note) (p. 396) Written promise to pay a specified amount either on demand or at a definite future date; is a *note receivable* for the lender but a *note payable* for the lendee.

Times interest earned ratio (p. 403) Ratio of income before interest expense (and any income taxes) divided by interest expense; reflects risk of covering interest commitments when income varies.

Multiple Choice Quiz   Answers on p. 411   mhhe.com/wildCA2e

Additional Multiple Choice Quizzes are available at the book's Website.

1. Total interest accrued on a $7,500, 5%, 90-day note is
  a. $93.75
  b. $375.00
  c. $1,125.00
  d. $31.25
  e. $125.00

2. A company receives a $9,000, 8%, 60-day note. The maturity value of the note is
  a. $120
  b. $9,000
  c. $9,120
  d. $720
  e. $9,720

3. The amount due on the maturity date of a $6,000, 60-day, 8% note receivable is:
  a. $6,000
  b. $6,480
  c. $5,520

  d. $6,080
  e. $5,920

4. MixRecording Studios purchased $7,800 in electronic components from TechCom. MixRecording Studios signed a 60-day, 10% promissory note for $7,800. TechCom's journal entry to record the sales portion of this transaction is

a.	Accounts Receivable	7,800	
	Sales		7,800
b.	Accounts Receivable	7,930	
	Sales		7,930
c.	Notes Receivable	7,800	
	Sales		7,800
d.	Notes Receivable	7,930	
	Sales		7,930
e.	Notes Receivable	7,800	
	Interest Receivable	130	
	Sales		7,930

5. Promissory notes that require the issuer to make a series of payments consisting of both interest and principal are
   a. Debentures
   b. Discounted notes
   c. Installment notes
   d. Indentures
   e. Investment notes

Discussion Questions

1. Define a note receivable and explain how to calculate the interest due on a short-term note receivable.

2. Explain how to record the receipt of a note receivable.

3. Explain the difference between honoring and dishonoring a note receivable.

4. What are the four steps for calculating the proceeds from a discounted note receivable?

5. What is the formula for computing interest on a note?

6. What is the entry to record a renewal of a note at maturity?

7. Describe the journal entries required to record the issuance of a note payable.

8. Refer to the debt footnote for **Best Buy** in Appendix A. What is the range of interest rates for mortgage and other debt (notes payable)?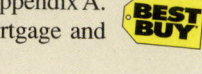

9. Refer to the balance sheet for **RadioShack** in Appendix A. Where would a long-term note payable (like an installment note) be reported on the balance sheet?

---

connect

QUICK STUDY

QS 16–1
Computation of due dates   **LO2**

Determine the due dates for the following notes:

	Date of Note	Term	Due Date
a.	2/21/2010	60 days	_____
b.	6/17/2010	90 days	_____
c.	8/4/2010	2 years	_____
d.	10/9/2010	30 days	_____
e.	12/24/2010	45 days	_____

QS 16–2
Computation of interest   **LO2**

Compute interest on the following notes *a* through *d*, using Exhibit 16.3 as a guide. Treat a year as having 360 days for interest computation in this assignment.

	Principal	Interest Rate	Length of Time
a.	$ 8,000	10%	90 days
b.	12,000	8%	120 days
c.	15,000	12%	30 days
d.	25,000	15%	300 days

QS 16–3
Calculation of maturity value
LO4

Calculate the maturity value for the following notes:

	Principal	Interest Rate	Length of Time
a.	$ 9,000	12%	90 days
b.	11,000	10%	60 days
c.	14,000	8%	30 days

QS 16–4
Calculation of maturity value
LO4

Calculate the maturity value for the following notes:

	Principal	Interest Rate	Length of Time
a.	$12,000	11%	45 days
b.	15,000	9%	30 days
c.	6,000	15%	90 days

On August 2, Jun Co. receives a $6,000, 90-day, 12% note from customer Ryan Albany as payment on his $6,000 account. Prepare Jun's journal entries for August 2 and for the note's maturity date, assuming the note is honored by Albany.

QS 16–5
Note receivable
LO2 LO3 LO4

Dominika Company's December 31 year-end unadjusted trial balance shows a $10,000 balance in Notes Receivable. This balance is from one 6% note dated December 1, with a period of 45 days. Prepare journal entries for December 31 and for the note's maturity date, assuming it is honored.

QS 16–6
Note receivable LO4

Compute times interest earned for Park Company, which reports income before interest expense and income taxes of $1,885,000, and interest expense of $145,000. Interpret its times interest earned (assume that its competitors average a times interest earned of 4.0).

QS 16–7
Times interest earned LO7

Compute times interest earned for Rodney Smith Company, which reports income before interest expense and income taxes of $619,500, and interest expense of $177,000. Interpret its times interest earned (assume that its competitors average a times interest earned of 5.0).

QS 16–8
Times interest earned LO7

connect™

Match each of the following terms A through F with the appropriate definitions 1 through 6.

EXERCISES

A. Maker of a note
D. Payee of a note
B. Interest
E. Principal of a note
C. Promissory note
F. Dishonoring a note

Exercise 16–1
Defining promissory notes
LO1 LO3

_____ **1.** A written promise to pay a specified amount either on demand or at a definite future date.

_____ **2.** The cost of borrowing money for a borrower; alternatively the profit from lending money for a lender.

_____ **3.** One who signs a note and promises to pay it at maturity.

_____ **4.** The one to whom the promissory note is made payable.

_____ **5.** Refers to a note maker's inability or refusal to pay the note at maturity.

_____ **6.** The amount that the signer of a note agrees to pay back when the note matures, not including interest.

Prepare journal entries to record these selected transactions for Phillip Bleak Corp.

Mar 1 Phillip Bleak Corp. accepted a $5,000, 90-day, 9% note from Taysom Inc. in exchange for the purchase of equipment.

May 30 Taysom honors the note when it is presented for payment.

Exercise 16–2
Honoring a note
LO2 LO3 LO4

Prepare journal entries to record these selected transactions for Vitalo Company.

Nov. 1 Accepted a $6,000, 180-day, 8% note dated November 1 from Kelly White in granting a time extension on her past-due account receivable.

Dec. 31 Adjusted the year-end accounts for the accrued interest earned on the White note.

Apr. 30 White honors her note when presented for payment.

Exercise 16–3
Honoring a note
LO2 LO3 LO4

Prepare journal entries to record the following selected transactions of Ridge Company.

Mar. 21 Accepted a $9,500, 180-day, 8% note dated March 21 from Taurean Jackson in granting a time extension on his past-due account receivable.

Sept. 17 Jackson dishonors his note when it is presented for payment.

Dec. 31 After exhausting all legal means of collection, Ridge Company writes off Jackson account against the Allowance for Doubtful Accounts.

Exercise 16–4
Dishonoring a note
LO2 LO3 LO4

On January 1, Fullmer Co. accepted a $10,000, 60-day, 8% note from Olson Inc. given for a purchase of equipment. On January 30, Fullmer discounts the note receivable at First Federal Savings. The bank charges a discount rate of 10%.

1. Record the journal entry for receipt of the note on January 1.

2. Record the journal entry for the discounted note receivable on January 30.

Exercise 16–5
Recording discounted note LO4

Exercise 16-6

Analyzing and journalizing notes
receivable transactions

LO2   LO3   LO4

Check   Feb. 14, Cr. Interest
Revenue $108

The following selected transactions are from Ohlmeyer Company.

2010

Dec. 16   Accepted a $10,800, 60-day, 8% note dated this day in granting Danny Todd a time extension
on his past-due account receivable.

    31   Made an adjusting entry to record the accrued interest on the Todd note.

2011

Feb. 14   Received Todd's payment of principal and interest on the note dated December 16.

Required

Prepare journal entries to record these transactions and events. (Round amounts to the nearest dollar.)

Exercise 16-7

Installment note with equal annual
payments   **LO6**

On January 1, 2010, Eagle borrows $100,000 cash by signing a four-year, 7% installment note. The note re-
quires four equal annual payments of $29,523 for accrued interest and principal on December 31 of each year
from 2010 through 2013. Prepare an amortization table for this installment note like the one in Exhibit 16.4.

Exercise 16-8

Installment note entries   **LO6**

Use the information in Exercise 16-7 to prepare the journal entries for Eagle to record the loan on
January 1, 2010, and the four payments from December 31, 2010, through December 31, 2013.

Exercise 16-9

Computing and interpreting times
interest earned   **LO7**

Check   (b) 11.00

Use the following information from separate companies *a* through *f* to compute times interest earned.
Which company indicates the strongest ability to pay interest expense as it comes due?

	Net Income (Loss)	Interest Expense	Income Taxes
a.	$115,000	$44,000	$ 35,000
b.	110,000	16,000	50,000
c.	100,000	12,000	70,000
d.	235,000	14,000	130,000
e.	59,000	14,000	30,000
f.	(5,000)	10,000	0

connect

PROBLEM SET A

Problem 16-1A

Notes receivable transactions and
entries   **LO2   LO3   LO4**

Check   Dec. 31, Cr. Interest
Revenue $38

Feb. 11, Dr. Cash $9,627

June 1, Dr. Cash $5,125

Prepare journal entries for the following selected transactions of Dulcinea Company.

2010

Dec. 13   Accepted a $9,500, 60-day, 8% note dated December 13 in granting Miranda Lee a time exten-
sion on her past-due account receivable.

    31   Prepared an adjusting entry to record the accrued interest on the Lee note.

2011

Feb. 11   Received Lee's payment for principal and interest on the note dated December 13.

Mar. 3   Accepted a $5,000, 10%, 90-day note dated March 3 in granting a time extension on the past-
due account receivable of Tomas Company.

    17   Accepted a $2,000, 30-day, 9% note dated March 17 in granting Hiroshi Cheng a time exten-
sion on his past-due account receivable.

Apr. 16   Cheng dishonors his note when presented for payment.

June 1   Received the Tomas payment for principal and interest on the note dated March 3.

Problem 16-2A

Analyzing and journalizing notes
receivable transactions

LO2   LO3   LO4

The following selected transactions are from Neil Martin Inc.

2010

Mar. 2   Accepted a $6,120, 8%, 90-day note dated this day in granting a time extension on the past-
due account receivable from Midnight Co.

    17   Accepted a $2,400, 30-day, 7% note dated this day in granting Ava Privet a time extension on
her past-due account receivable.

Apr. 16   Privet dishonored her note when presented for payment.

June   2   Midnight Co. refuses to pay the note that was due to Neil Martin, Inc. on May 31. Prepare the journal entry to charge the dishonored note plus accrued interest to Midnight Co.'s accounts receivable.

July 17   Received payment from Midnight Co. for the maturity value of its dishonored note plus interest for 46 days beyond maturity at 8%.

Dec.   1   Wrote off the Ava Privet account against Allowance for Doubtful Accounts.

Required

Prepare journal entries to record these transactions and events. (Round amounts to the nearest dollar.)

Check   June 2, Cr. Interest Revenue $122

On July 1, Whyte Co. accepted a $20,000, 90-day, 12% note from Olson Inc. for the purchase of equipment. On July 31, Whyte discounts the note receivable at First Federal Savings. The bank charges a discount rate of 15%.

Required

1. Record the journal entry for receipt of the note on July 1.

2. Record the journal entry for the discounted note receivable on July 31.

Problem 16–3A
Recording discounted note
LO3   LO4

On November 1, 2010, Norwood borrows $200,000 cash from a bank by signing a five-year installment note bearing 8% interest. The note requires equal annual payments of $50,091 each year on October 31. (*Hint:* Use the demonstration problem as a guide.)

Required

1. Complete an amortization table for this installment note similar to the one in Exhibit 16.4.

2. Prepare the journal entries in which Norwood (*a*) records accrued interest as of December 31, 2010 (the end of its annual reporting period), and (*b*) the first annual payment on the note.

Problem 16–4A
Installment notes   **LO6**

Check   (1) 10/31/2014 ending balance, $46,382

The following selected transactions are from Springer Company.

PROBLEM SET B

2010

Nov.   1   Accepted a $4,800, 90-day, 8% note dated this day in granting Steve Julian a time extension on his past-due account receivable.

Dec. 31   Made an adjusting entry to record the accrued interest on the Julian note.

Problem 16–1B
Analyzing and journalizing notes receivable transactions
LO2   LO3   LO4

2011

Jan. 30   Received Julian's payment for principal and interest on the note dated November 1.

Feb. 28   Accepted a $12,600, 8%, 30-day note dated this day in granting a time extension on the past-due account receivable from King Co.

Mar.   1   Accepted a $6,200, 60-day, 12% note dated this day in granting Myron Shelley a time extension on his past-due account receivable.

        30   The King Co. dishonored its note when presented for payment.

April 30   Received payment of principal plus interest from M. Shelley for the March 1 note.

Nov. 30   Wrote off King Co.'s account against Allowance for Doubtful Accounts.

Check   Jan. 30, Cr. Interest Revenue $32

April 30, Cr. Interest Revenue $124

Required

Prepare journal entries to record these transactions and events. (Round amounts to the nearest dollar.)

The following selected transactions are from Zucco Enterprises.

Problem 16–2B
Journalizing notes receivable transactions
LO2   LO3   LO4

2010

Aug.   7   Accepted a $7,450, 90-day, 10% note dated this day in granting a time extension on the past-due account receivable of Mulan Co.

Sept. 3   Accepted a $2,120, 60-day, 10% note dated this day in granting Noah Carson a time extension on his past-due account receivable.

Nov.   2   Received payment of principal plus interest from Carson for the September 3 note.

Nov.   5   Received payment of principal plus interest from Mulan for the August 7 note.

Check   Nov. 2, Cr. Interest Revenue $35

Required

Prepare journal entries to record these transactions and events. (Round amounts to the nearest dollar.)

Problem 16-3B
Recording discounted note

LO3 LO4

On December 1, Greer Co. accepted a $25,000, 60-day, 10% note from Olson Inc. for the purchase of equipment. On December 31, Greer discounts the note receivable at First Federal Savings. The bank charges a discount rate of 12%.

Required

1. Record the journal entry for receipt of the note on December 1.

2. Record the journal entry for the discounted note receivable on December 31.

Problem 16-4B
Installment notes   **LO6**

On October 1, 2010, Gordon Enterprises borrows $150,000 cash from a bank by signing a three-year installment note bearing 10% interest. The note requires equal total payments of $60,316 each year on September 30. (*Hint:* Use the demonstration problem as a guide)

Required

Check   (1) 9/30/2012 ending balance, $54,836

1. Complete an amortization table for this installment note similar to the one in Exhibit 16.4.

2. Prepare the journal entries in which Gordon records (*a*) accrued interest as of December 31, 2010 (the end of its annual reporting period), and (*b*) the first annual payment on the note.

SERIAL PROBLEM

Success Systems

(This serial problem began in Chapter 1 and continues through most of the book. If previous chapter segments were not completed, the serial problem can begin at this point. It is helpful, but not necessary, that you use the Working Papers that accompany the book.)

SP 16   Adriana Lopez, owner of Success Systems, needs to account for the company's installment notes payable. On January 1, 2010, Success Systems borrows $60,000 cash from a bank by signing a four-year installment note bearing 9% interest. The note requires equal total payments of $18,520 on December 31 of each year.

Required

1. Complete an amortization table for this installment note similar to the one in Exhibit 16.4.

2. Prepare the journal entries for the first December 31 payment on the note.

BEYOND THE NUMBERS

REPORTING IN ACTION
LO1 LO7

BTN 16-1   Refer to **Best Buy**'s financial statements in Appendix A to answer the following. Best Buy reports its interest income and interest expense in footnote 6 to its financial statements.

Required

1. Compute times interest earned for the fiscal years ended 2008, 2007, and 2006. Comment on Best Buy's ability to cover interest expense for this period. Assume an industry average times interest earned of 19.9.

2. How did Best Buy's net interest income change between fiscal years 2007 and 2008? What does that suggest about the overall notes receivable and notes payable that Best Buy has?

Fast Forward

3. Access Best Buy's financial statements for fiscal years after March 1, 2008, at its Website (**www.BestBuy.com**) or the SEC's EDGAR database (**www.SEC.gov**). Recompute parts *1* and *2*, and comment on any changes since March 1, 2008.

ETHICS CHALLENGE
LO4 LO6

BTN 16-2   Reporting the details of notes receivable and notes payable is consistent with the *full disclosure principle,* which requires financial statements (including footnotes) to report all relevant information. Assume that you are a financial manager for a medium-sized company and the owner believes that information on notes receivable and notes payable is too complicated for the normal investor. The owner asks that you stop disclosing the details of its loans outstanding. What action, if any, do you take?

BTN 16-3   You are an electronics retailer planning a holiday sale on a custom stereo system that requires no payments for two years. At the end of two years, buyers must pay the full amount. The system's suggested retail price is $4,100, but you are willing to sell it today for $3,000 cash.

ETHICS CHALLENGE
LO6

Required

What is your holiday sale price if payment will not occur for two years and the market interest rate is 10%?

BTN 16-4   An owner of a small but growing business has financed a large part of his operations with installment notes. He comes to you, as the company's accountant, and asks "If the interest expense decreases each year, why don't our cash payments also decrease?" Prepare a one-half page memorandum addressed to the owner that explains how an installment loan impacts cash payments and interest expense.

WORKPLACE COMMUNICATION
LO6

BTN 16-5   Access the March 13, 2008, filing of the 10-K report of **Target** for the year ended February 2, 2008, from www.SEC.gov (Ticker: TGT). Refer to Target's balance sheet, including its Note 18 (on notes payable and long-term debt).

TAKING IT TO THE NET
LO1   LO2   LO5

Required

1. Identify Target's long-term liabilities and the amounts for those liabilities from Target's balance sheet at February 2, 2008.
2. Review Target's Note 18. Notes payable provide what type of financing for Target?
3. What is the average amount of short-term notes payable outstanding for fiscal year 2007? 2006?
4. What is the weighted average interest rate on Target's short-term notes payable for 2007 and 2006?

BTN 16-6   Each member of a team is to participate in recording a transaction. On November 1, 2010, Gomez Inc. accepts a $20,000, 90-day, 12% promissory note from Larson Inc. in exchange for the purchase of equipment. The note is honored on January 30, 2011. Choose one-half of the team to record all necessary journal entries for the note receivable for Gomez Inc. The other half of the team records all necessary journal entries for the note payable for Larson Inc.

Gomez Inc. and Larson Inc. both have calendar year-ends. Record the accrued interest as of December 31, 2010 for both companies.

TEAMWORK IN ACTION
LO3   LO4   LO5

BTN 16-7   Refer to the opening feature in this chapter about Stu Levy and **TOKYOPOP**. Stu must acquire the Japanese rights to material that is then translated for the U.S. audience. Assume that on January 1, 2010, Stu gets financing to acquire the Japanese rights by borrowing $90,000 cash from a bank by signing a four-year installment note bearing 10% interest. The note requires equal payments of $28,392 each year on December 30.

ENTREPRENEURS IN BUSINESS
LO5

Required

1. Complete an amortization table for this installment note similar to the one in Exhibit 16.4.
2. Prepare the journal entries for the first annual payment on the note.

A Look Back

Chapter 16 focused on how notes receivable and notes payable are accounted for and reported. We also described how companies compute interest on notes.

A Look at This Chapter

This chapter emphasizes accounting for inventory. We describe methods for assigning costs to inventory and we explain the items and costs making up merchandise inventory. We also discuss methods of estimating and measuring inventory.

A Look Ahead

Chapter 18 focuses on plant assets, natural resources, and intangible assets. We explain how to account for and report these long-term assets.

Chapter 17

Inventories and Cost of Sales

Learning Objectives

LO 1   Identify the items making up merchandise inventory.

LO 2   Identify the costs of merchandise inventory.

LO 3   Compute inventory in a periodic system using the methods of specific identification, FIFO, LIFO, and weighted average.

LO 4   Analyze the effects of inventory methods for both financial and tax reporting.

LO 5   Apply the lower of cost or market valuation.

LO 6   Assess inventory management using both inventory turnover and days' sales in inventory.

LO 7   *Appendix 17A*—Compute inventory in a perpetual system using the methods of FIFO, LIFO, and weighted average.

LO 8   *Appendix 17B*—Apply the gross profit method to estimate inventory.

"Believe in yourself, your product and services"
—Jacquelyn Tran

Scent of Success

HUNTINGTON BEACH, CA—As U.S. immigrants, Jacquelyn Tran and her family had no money and did not speak English. "They [her family] took the risk," explains Jacquelyn, in the hope of opportunity. A few years passed and Jacquelyn caught a glimpse of her future. "I saw an opportunity to take . . . the retail perfume business to the next level." She launched **Beauty Encounter (BeautyEncounter.com)** to provide perfume and beauty products to consumers.

The entrepreneurial road was rough at times. Jacquelyn struggled with inventory and sales, and had to deal with discounts, returns, and allowances. A major challenge was maintaining appropriate inventories while controlling costs. "I made plenty of mistakes," admits Jacquelyn. "I just had to throw myself in there and learn."

Learn she did. Applying modern inventory management, and trial and error, Jacquelyn learned to fill orders, collect money, and stock the right inventory. "We have something for everyone," explains Jacquelyn, and her perpetual inventory system accounts for inventory sales and purchases in real time. "It's really important for customers to be able to find products . . . [and for me] to give them what they want."

But business success requires more than good products and inventory management, insists Jacquelyn. "[It] requires a lot of patience, energy and faith. We focus on customer satisfaction," says Jacquelyn. As a result, "we have very loyal customers."

Although Jacquelyn continues to measure, monitor, and manage inventories and costs, her success and growth are pushing her to a more managerial role. "We are moving into a larger warehouse, allowing us to expand our selection," explains Jacquelyn. Her inventory procedures contribute to her success and allow her customers to know which products are hot. "I never imagined I would be where I am today," says Jacquelyn. "It is really cool."

[Sources: *Beauty Encounter Website,* January 2009; *USA Today,* April 2008; *CNN Money,* June 2005; *Inc.com,* July 2007; *Entrepreneur,* December 2007; *MyWomanOwnedBusiness.com,* August 2007]

Merchandisers' activities include the purchasing and reselling of merchandise. In this chapter, we explain the methods used to assign costs to merchandise inventory *and* to cost of goods sold. Retailers, wholesalers, and other merchandising companies that purchase products for resale use the principles and methods described here. Understanding inventory accounting helps in the analysis and interpretation of financial statements, and helps people run their own businesses.

Inventories and Cost of Sales

Inventory Basics
- Determining inventory items
- Inventory costing methods
- Perpetual vs. periodic
- Internal controls and taking a physical count

Inventory Costing
- Inventory cost flow assumptions
- Specific identification
- First-in, first-out
- Last-in, first-out
- Weighted average
- Financial statement effects

Inventory Valuation
- Inventory valuation at lower of cost or market
- Computing the lower of cost or market

Inventory Basics

Inventories are a large portion of current assets for most wholesalers, retailers, and manufacturers. Accounting for inventory affects both the balance sheet and the income statement. A major goal in accounting for inventory is to properly match costs with sales.

Management decisions in accounting for inventory involve the following:

■ Items included in inventory and their costs.
■ Costing method (specific identification, FIFO, LIFO, or weighted average).
■ Inventory system (perpetual or periodic).
■ Use of market values or other estimates.

Decisions on these points affect the reported amounts for inventory, cost of goods sold, gross profit, income, current assets, and other accounts.

Determining Inventory Items

LO1 Identify the items making up merchandise inventory.

Merchandise inventory includes all goods that a company owns and holds for sale. This rule holds regardless of where the goods are located when inventory is counted. Goods in transit and goods that are damaged or obsolete need special attention.

Goods in Transit   If the purchaser is responsible for freight costs on goods in transit from a supplier, ownership passes to the buyer when goods are loaded on the transport vehicle. If the seller is responsible for freight, ownership passes to the buyer when goods arrive at their destination.

Goods Damaged or Obsolete   Damaged and obsolete goods are not counted in inventory if they cannot be sold. If these goods can be sold at a reduced price, they are included in inventory at their sales price minus the cost of making the sale. This is called **net realizable value.**

Inventory Costing Methods

One of the most important issues in accounting for inventory is determining the per unit costs of inventory items. When all units are purchased at the same unit cost, this process is simple. When identical items are purchased at different costs, however, a question arises as to which amounts to record in cost of goods sold and which amounts remain in inventory.

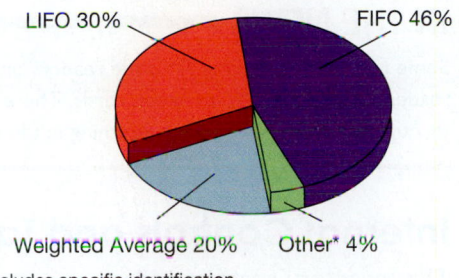

LIFO 30%   FIFO 46%

Weighted Average 20%   Other* 4%

*Includes specific identification.

Exhibit 17.1

Frequency in Use of Inventory Methods

Four methods are commonly used to assign costs to inventory and to cost of goods sold: (1) specific identification; (2) first-in, first-out (FIFO); (3) last-in, first-out (LIFO); and (4) weighted average. Exhibit 17.1 shows the frequency of use of these methods.

Each method assumes a particular pattern for how costs flow through inventory. FIFO assumes costs flow in the order incurred. The *first* units purchased are assumed to be the first units sold. LIFO assumes costs flow in the reverse order incurred. The *last* units purchased are assumed to be the first units sold. Weighted average assumes costs flow at an average of the costs available. Cost flow assumptions can markedly impact reported cost of goods sold and ending inventory numbers. We illustrate each of these costing assumptions and compare their effects on cost of goods sold and ending inventory.

Each of these four methods is acceptable whether or not the actual physical flow of goods follows the cost flow assumption. Physical flow of goods depends on the type of product and the way it is stored. (Perishable goods such as fresh fruit demand that a business attempt to sell them in a first-in, first-out physical flow. Other products such as crude oil and minerals such as coal, gold, and decorative stone can be sold in a last-in, first-out physical flow.) **Physical flow and cost flow need not be the same.**

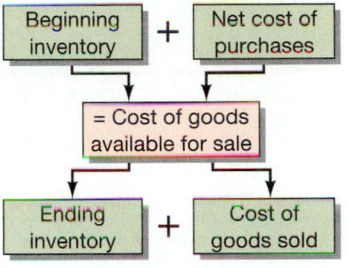

IN THE NEWS

A wireless portable computer with a two-way radio allows clerks to quickly record inventory by scanning bar codes and to instantly send and receive inventory data. It gives managers access to up-to-date information on inventory and its location.

Determining Inventory Costs

Merchandise inventory includes all costs necessary to bring an item to a salable condition and location. So, the cost of an inventory item includes its invoice cost minus any discount, and plus any other costs necessary to put it in a place and condition for sale. Other costs can include import duties, freight, storage, and insurance.

LO2 Identify the costs of merchandise inventory.

Inventory Systems: Perpetual versus Periodic

Management chooses between the *perpetual* system and the *periodic* system in collecting information about cost of goods sold and cost of inventory. The **perpetual inventory system** continually updates inventory accounts as purchases and sales of merchandise occur. The **periodic inventory system** updates inventory accounts for merchandise transactions only at the *end of a period*. Under a periodic system, purchases, purchase returns and allowances, purchase discounts, and transportation-in transactions are recorded in separate temporary accounts. We illustrated these procedures in detail in Chapter 12. At period-end, each of these temporary accounts is closed and the Merchandise Inventory account is updated. We showed this closing process in detail in Chapter 14.

The perpetual inventory system provides management with more up-to-date information. Under a perpetual inventory system, management knows the number of units of inventory available and their unit cost at all times. Under a periodic inventory system, inventory records are updated only at the end of the period. While a perpetual inventory system requires more extensive recordkeeping than a periodic inventory system, technological advances and competitive pressures have greatly increased the use of perpetual inventory systems.

IN THE NEWS

Some retailers are adding bar code readers on shopping carts for customers to swipe products over the reader, charging it to their credit cards. There is no need to stand in a checkout line. Customers simply pass through a gate to verify that everything in the cart is scanned.

Internal Controls and Taking a Physical Count

The Inventory account under a perpetual system is updated for each purchase and sale, but events can cause the account balance to differ from the actual inventory available. Such events include theft, loss, damage, and errors. Under a periodic system, the Inventory account is not updated until the end of the accounting period, so management does not know the number of units available during the period. Thus, nearly all companies take a *physical count of inventory* at least once each year—informally called *taking an inventory*. This often occurs at the end of a fiscal year or when inventory amounts are low. This physical count is used to adjust the Inventory account balance to the actual inventory available.

A business must apply internal controls when taking a physical count of inventory. These would usually include the following:

- *Prenumbered inventory tickets* are prepared and distributed to *counters*—each ticket must be accounted for.
- Counters of inventory are assigned that do not include persons responsible for inventory.
- Counters confirm the validity of inventory, including its existence, amount, and quality.
- A second count should be performed by a different counter.
- A manager confirms that all inventories are ticketed once, and only once.

HOW YOU DOIN'?   Answers—p. 431

1. Which inventory system (periodic or perpetual) provides up-to-date inventory cost information?
2. If **Skechers** sells goods to **Target**, and Target pays shipping costs, which company reports these goods in its inventory while they are in transit?
3. An art gallery purchases a painting for $11,400. Additional costs in obtaining and offering the artwork for sale include $130 for transportation-in, $150 for import duties, $100 for insurance during shipment, $180 for advertising, $400 for framing, and $800 for office salaries. For computing inventory, what cost is assigned to the painting?

The following sections on inventory costing methods use the periodic system. Appendix 17A uses the perpetual system. An instructor can choose to cover either one or both inventory systems.

Inventory Costing under a Periodic System

LO3 Compute inventory in a periodic system using the methods of specific identification, FIFO, LIFO, and weighted average.

Inventory Costing Illustration

This section provides a comprehensive illustration of inventory costing methods. We use information from Trekking, a sporting goods store. Among its many products, Trekking carries one type of mountain bike whose sales are directed at resorts that provide inexpensive mountain bikes for complimentary guest use. Its customers usually purchase in amounts of 10 or more bikes. We use Trekking's data from August 2010. Its mountain bike (unit) inventory at the beginning of August and its purchases and sales during August are shown in Exhibit 17.2. It ends August with 12 bikes remaining in inventory.

Trekking uses the periodic inventory system, which means that its merchandise inventory account is updated only at the end of a period. (**Appendix 17A describes the assignment of**

> Accounting for inventories is key to determining cost of goods sold and gross profit.

Date	Activity	Units Acquired at Cost	Units Sold at Retail	Unit Inventory
Aug. 1	Beginning inventory	10 units @ $ 91 = $ 910		10 units
Aug. 3	Purchases	15 units @ $106 = $ 1,590		25 units
Aug. 14	Sales		20 units @ $130	5 units
Aug. 17	Purchases	20 units @ $115 = $ 2,300		25 units
Aug. 28	Purchases	10 units @ $119 = $ 1,190		35 units
Aug. 31	Sales		23 units @ $150	**12 units**
	Totals	**55 units** **$5,990**	**43 units**	

Exhibit 17.2

Purchases and Sales of Goods

> Cost of goods sold plus ending inventory equals cost of goods available for sale.

costs to inventory using a perpetual system.) Regardless of what inventory method or system is used, cost of goods available for sale must be allocated between cost of goods sold and ending inventory.

Specific Identification

When each item in inventory can be identified with a specific purchase and invoice, we can use **specific identification** (also called *specific invoice inventory pricing*) to assign costs. We also need sales records that identify exactly which items were sold and when. Trekking's internal documents reveal that 7 of the 12 unsold units in ending inventory were from the August 28 purchase and 5 were from the August 17 purchase. We use this information and the specific identification method to assign costs to the 12 units in ending inventory and to the 43 units sold as shown in Exhibit 17.3. Carefully study this exhibit and the boxed explanations to see the flow of costs both in and out of inventory. Each unit, whether sold or remaining in inventory, has its own specific cost attached to it.

> Three key variables determine the dollar value of ending inventory: (1) inventory quantity, (2) costs of inventory, and (3) cost flow assumption.

When using specific identification, Trekking's cost of goods sold reported on the income statement totals **$4,582**, the sum of $2,000 and $2,582 from the third column of Exhibit 17.3. Trekking's ending inventory reported on the balance sheet is **$1,408**, which is the final inventory balance from the right-most column of Exhibit 17.3. Under specific identification, a company

> Data in the "Goods Purchased" column are taken from Exhibit 17.2.

Date	Goods Purchased	Cost of Goods Sold	Inventory Balance
	"goods in"	"goods out"	"what's left"
Aug. 1	Beginning balance		10 @ $ 91 = $ 910
Aug. 3	15 @ $106 = $1,590		10 @ $ 91 ⎫ 15 @ $106 ⎬ = $2,500
Aug. 14		8 @ $ 91 = $ 728 ⎫ 12 @ $106 = $1,272 ⎬ = **$2,000***	2 @ $ 91 ⎫ 3 @ $106 ⎬ = $ 500
Aug. 17	20 @ $115 = $2,300		2 @ $ 91 ⎫ 3 @ $106 ⎬ = $2,800 20 @ $115
Aug. 28	10 @ $119 = $1,190		2 @ $ 91 ⎫ 3 @ $106 ⎪ 20 @ $115 ⎬ = $3,990 10 @ $119 ⎭
Aug. 31		2 @ $ 91 = $ 182 ⎫ 3 @ $106 = $ 318 ⎪ 15 @ $115 = $1,725 ⎬ = **$2,582*** 3 @ $119 = $ 357 ⎭	5 @ $115 ⎫ 7 @ $119 ⎬ = **$1,408**
		$4,582	

For the 20 units sold on Aug. 14, the company specifically identified that 8 of those had cost $91 and 12 had cost $106.

For the 23 units sold on Aug. 31, the company specifically identified each bike sold and its acquisition cost from prior purchases.

Exhibit 17.3

Specific Identification Computations

* Identification of items sold (and their costs) is obtained from internal documents that track each unit from its purchase to its sale.

reports the same amounts for cost of goods sold and ending inventory regardless of whether it uses a periodic or perpetual inventory system.

The purchases and sales entries for Exhibit 17.3 follow (the colored boldface numbers are those determined by the cost flow assumption).

Purchases		
Aug. 3 Purchases	1,590	
Accounts Payable		1,590
17 Purchases	2,300	
Accounts Payable		2,300
28 Purchases	1,190	
Accounts Payable		1,190

Sales		
Aug. 14 Accounts Receivable	2,600	
Sales		2,600
31 Accounts Receivable	3,450	
Sales		3,450
Inventory Closing Entry		
31 Merchandise Inventory (ending)....	**1,408**	
Income Summary	4,582	
Merchandise Inventory (beg.)..		**910**
Purchases.................		5,080

Trekking debits Purchases for the cost of its Purchases, and records Sales, but not Cost of Goods Sold, as they occur. At period-end Trekking updates its Merchandise Inventory account by closing its beginning balance (credit entry of $910) and recording its ending balance (debit of $1,408). Trekking also closes its Purchases account. The debit to Income Summary is the cost of goods sold for the month.

First-In, First-Out

The **first-in, first-out (FIFO)** method of assigning costs to both inventory and cost of goods sold assumes that inventory items are sold in the order acquired. Ending inventory is assumed to contain the most recent items acquired. We work backward through the Purchases in Exhibit 17.2 until we reach 12 units. The FIFO method using the periodic system is shown in Exhibit 17.4.

Exhibit 17.4

FIFO Computations—Periodic System

Exhibit 17.2 shows that the 12 units in ending inventory consist of 10 units from the latest purchase on Aug. 28 and 2 units from the next latest purchase on Aug. 17.

Total cost of 55 units available for sale (from Exhibit 17.2)		$5,990
Less ending inventory priced using FIFO		
10 units from August 28 purchase at $119 each	$1,190	
2 units from August 17 purchase at $115 each	230	
Ending inventory		**1,420**
Cost of goods sold		**$4,570**

Trekking's FIFO cost of goods sold reported on its income statement (reflecting the 43 units sold) is **$4,570** ($1,970 + $2,600), and its ending inventory reported on the balance sheet (reflecting the 12 units unsold) is **$1,420**. Trekking would also report FIFO cost of goods sold of $4,570 and ending inventory of $1,420 if it used a periodic system. (We show these calculations and the journal entries under the FIFO perpetual method in Appendix 17A.)

The purchases and sales entries for Exhibit 17.4 follow (the colored boldface numbers are those affected by the cost flow assumption).

Purchases		
Aug. 3 Purchases....................	1,590	
Accounts Payable..........		1,590
17 Purchases....................	2,300	
Accounts Payable..........		2,300
28 Purchases....................	1,190	
Accounts Payable..........		1,190

Sales		
Aug. 14 Accounts Receivable	2,600	
Sales		2,600
31 Accounts Receivable	3,450	
Sales		3,450
Inventory Closing Entry		
31 Merchandise Inventory (ending)	**1,420**	
Income Summary...............	4,570	
Merchandise Inventory (beg.)...		**910**
Purchases		5,080

Last-In, First-Out

The **last-in, first-out (LIFO)** method of assigning costs assumes that the most recent purchases are sold first. These more recent costs are charged to the goods sold, and the costs of the earliest purchases are assigned to inventory. As with other methods, LIFO is acceptable even when the physical flow of goods does not follow a last-in, first-out pattern. One appeal of LIFO is that by assigning costs from the most recent purchases to cost of goods sold, LIFO comes closest to matching current costs of goods sold with revenues (compared to FIFO or weighted average). Exhibit 17.5 shows how LIFO assigns the costs of mountain bikes to the 12 units in ending inventory and to the 43 units sold. To determine ending inventory, we work forward through the Purchases in Exhibit 17.2 until we reach 12 units.

> Under LIFO, a unit sold is assigned the most recent (latest) cost from inventory. This leaves the oldest costs in inventory.

Total cost of 55 units available for sale (from Exhibit 17.2)		$5,990
Less ending inventory priced using LIFO		
10 units in beginning inventory at $91 each	$910	
2 units from August 3 purchase at $106 each	212	
Ending inventory		1,122
Cost of goods sold		$4,868

Exhibit 17.5

LIFO Computations—
Periodic System

Exhibit 17.2 shows that the 12 units in ending inventory consist of 10 units from the earliest purchase (beg. inv.) and 2 units from the next earliest purchase on Aug. 3.

Trekking's ending inventory reported on the balance sheet is **$1,122**, and its cost of goods sold reported on the income statement is **$4,868**. When LIFO is used with the periodic system, cost of goods sold is assigned costs from the most recent purchases for the period. The purchases and sales entries for Exhibit 17.5 follow (the colored boldface numbers are those affected by the cost flow assumption).

Purchases				**Sales**		
Aug. 3	Purchases	1,590		Aug. 14	Accounts Receivable	2,600
	Accounts Payable		1,590		Sales	2,600
17	Purchases	2,300		31	Accounts Receivable	3,450
	Accounts Payable		2,300		Sales	3,450
28	Purchases	1,190				
	Accounts Payable		1,190		**Inventory Closing Entry**	
				31	Merchandise Inventory (ending)	**1,122**
					Income Summary	4,868
					Merchandise Inventory (beg.) ..	**910**
					Purchases	5,080

Weighted Average

The weighted average method of assigning cost involves three important steps. The first two steps are shown in Exhibit 17.6. First, multiply the per unit cost for beginning inventory and each purchase by the corresponding number of units (from Exhibit 17.2). Second, add these amounts and divide by the total number of units available for sale to find the weighted average cost per unit.

Step 1:	10 units @ $ 91 = $ 910	
	15 units @ $106 = 1,590	
	20 units @ $115 = 2,300	
	10 units @ $119 = 1,190	
	55 **$5,990**	
Step 2:	$5,990/55 units = **$108.91** weighted average cost per unit	

Exhibit 17.6

Weighted Average Cost per Unit

The third step is to use the weighted average cost per unit to assign costs to inventory and to the units sold as shown in Exhibit 17.7. (The cost of ending inventory is rounded to the nearest dollar.)

Exhibit 17.7

Weighted Average
Computations—Periodic

Step 3:	Total cost of 55 units available for sale (from Exhibit 17.2)	$ 5,990
	Less **ending inventory** priced on a weighted average cost basis: 12 units at $108.91 each (from Exhibit 17.6)	**1,307**
	Cost of goods sold	**$4,683**

Trekking's ending inventory reported on the balance sheet is **$1,307**, and its cost of goods sold reported on the income statement is **$4,683** when using the weighted average (periodic) method. The purchases and sales entries for Exhibit 17.7 follow (the colored boldface numbers are those affected by the cost flow assumption).

Purchases

Aug.	3	Purchases....................	1,590	
		Accounts Payable..........		1,590
	17	Purchases....................	2,300	
		Accounts Payable..........		2,300
	28	Purchases....................	1,190	
		Accounts Payable..........		1,190

Sales

Aug.	14	Accounts Receivable	2,600	
		Sales		2,600
	31	Accounts Receivable	3,450	
		Sales		3,450

Inventory Closing Entry

	31	Merchandise Inventory (ending) ...	**1,307**	
		Income Summary................	4,683	
		Merchandise Inventory (beg.) ..		**910**
		Purchases..................		5,080

4. A company reports the following beginning inventory and purchases, and it ends the period with 30 units in inventory.

Beginning Inventory	....	100 units at $10 cost per unit
Purchase 1	....	40 units at $12 cost per unit
Purchase 2	....	20 units at $14 cost per unit

   a. Compute ending inventory using the FIFO periodic system.

   b. Compute cost of goods sold using the LIFO periodic system.

Financial Statement Effects

When purchase prices do not change, each inventory costing method assigns the same cost amounts to inventory and to cost of goods sold. When purchase prices differ, however, the methods nearly always assign different cost amounts. We show these differences in Exhibit 17.8 using Trekking's data.

When purchase costs *regularly rise,* as in Trekking's case, observe the following from Exhibit 17.8:

■ FIFO assigns the lowest amount to cost of goods sold—yielding the highest gross profit and net income.

■ LIFO assigns the highest amount to cost of goods sold—yielding the lowest gross profit and net income; this yields a temporary tax advantage by postponing payment of some income tax.

■ Weighted average yields results between FIFO and LIFO.

■ Specific identification always yields results that depend on which units are sold.

When costs *regularly decline,* the reverse occurs for FIFO and LIFO. Some industries, for example computers, have seen falling costs in recent years.

LIFO inventory is often less than the inventory's replacement cost because LIFO inventory is valued using the oldest inventory purchase costs.

	Specific Identification	FIFO	LIFO	Weighted Average
TREKKING COMPANY For Month Ended August 31				
Income Statement				
Sales	$ 6,050	$ 6,050	$ 6,050	$ 6,050
Cost of goods sold	4,582	4,570	4,868	4,683
Gross profit	1,468	1,480	1,182	1,367
Expenses	450	450	450	450
Income before taxes	1,018	1,030	732	917
Income tax expense (30%)	305.40	309	219.60	275.10
Net income	$ 712.60	$ 721	$ 512.40	$ 641.90
Balance Sheet				
Inventory	$1,408	$1,420	$1,122	$1,307

Exhibit 17.8

Financial Statement Effects of Inventory Costing Methods

All four inventory costing methods are acceptable in practice. A company must disclose the inventory method it uses. Each method offers certain advantages as follows:

- FIFO assigns an amount to inventory on the balance sheet that approximates its current cost; it also mimics the actual flow of goods for most businesses.
- LIFO assigns an amount to cost of goods sold on the income statement that approximates its current cost; it also better matches current costs with revenues in computing gross profit.
- Weighted average tends to smooth out erratic changes in costs.
- Specific identification exactly matches the costs of items with the revenues they generate.

Tax Effects of Costing Methods   Trekking's segment income statement in Exhibit 17.8 includes income tax expense (at a rate of 30%) because it was formed as a corporation. Since inventory costs affect net income, they have potential tax effects. Trekking gains a temporary tax advantage by using LIFO. Many companies that have rising costs use LIFO for this reason.

Companies can and often do use different costing methods for financial reporting and tax reporting. *The only exception is when LIFO is used for tax reporting; in this case, the IRS requires that it also be used in financial statements*—called the **LIFO conformity rule.**

Consistency in Using Costing Methods

The **consistency concept** prescribes that a company use the same accounting methods period after period so that financial statements are comparable across periods—the only exception is when a change from one method to another will improve its financial reporting. The *full disclosure principle* prescribes that the notes to the statements report this type of change, its justification, and its effect on income.

The consistency concept does *not* require a company to use one method exclusively. For example, it can use different methods to value different categories of inventory.

HOW YOU DOIN'?   Answers—p. 431

5. Describe one advantage for each of the inventory costing methods: specific identification, FIFO, LIFO, and weighted average.

6. When costs are rising, which method reports higher net income—LIFO or FIFO?

7. When costs are rising, what effect does LIFO have on a balance sheet compared to FIFO?

Valuing Inventory at Lower of Cost or Market

This section examines the role of market costs in determining inventory on the balance sheet.

Lower of Cost or Market

LO5 Apply the lower of cost or market valuation.

We explained how to assign costs to ending inventory and cost of goods sold using FIFO, LIFO, weighted average, and specific identification. However, *accounting principles require that inventory be reported at the market value (cost) of replacing inventory when market value is lower than cost.* Merchandise inventory is then said to be reported on the balance sheet at the **lower of cost or market (LCM).**

Computing the Lower of Cost or Market   *Market* in the term *LCM* is defined as the current replacement cost of purchasing the same inventory items in the usual manner. A decline in replacement cost reflects a loss of value in inventory. When the recorded cost of inventory is higher than the replacement cost, a loss is recognized. When the recorded cost is lower, no adjustment is made.

LCM is applied in one of three ways: (1) to each individual item separately, (2) to major categories of items, or (3) to the entire inventory. The less similar the items that make up inventory, the more likely companies are to apply LCM to individual items. To illustrate, we apply LCM to the ending inventory of a motorsports retailer in Exhibit 17.9.

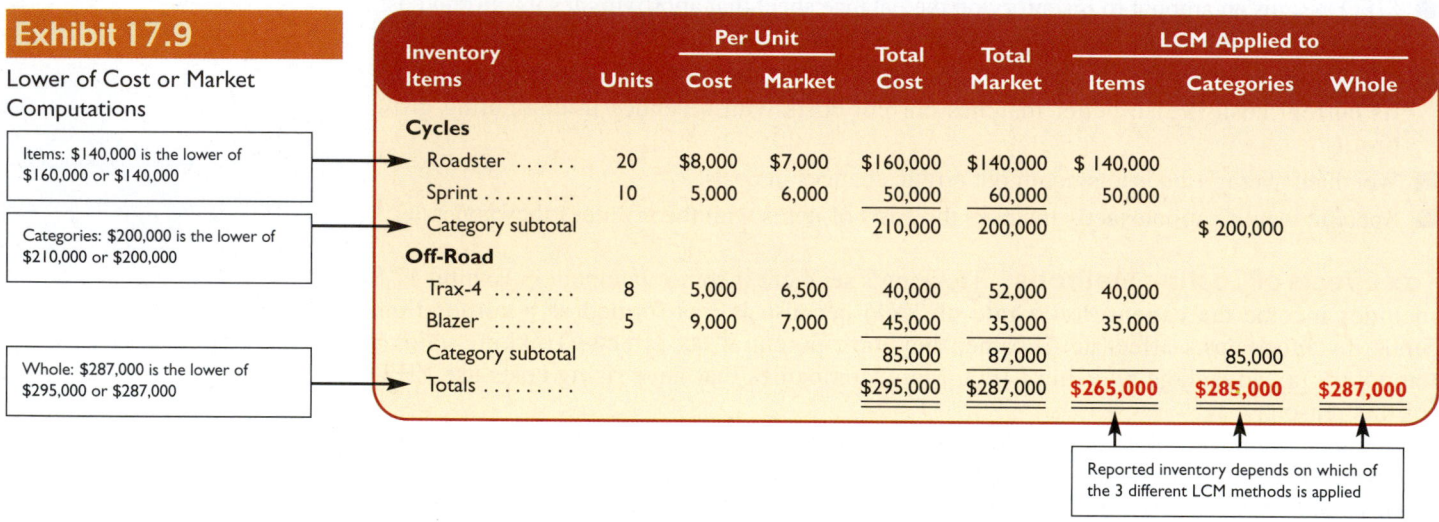

Exhibit 17.9

Lower of Cost or Market Computations

Items: $140,000 is the lower of $160,000 or $140,000

Categories: $200,000 is the lower of $210,000 or $200,000

Whole: $287,000 is the lower of $295,000 or $287,000

Inventory Items	Units	Per Unit Cost	Per Unit Market	Total Cost	Total Market	LCM Applied to Items	LCM Applied to Categories	LCM Applied to Whole
Cycles								
Roadster	20	$8,000	$7,000	$160,000	$140,000	$ 140,000		
Sprint	10	5,000	6,000	50,000	60,000	50,000		
Category subtotal				210,000	200,000		$ 200,000	
Off-Road								
Trax-4	8	5,000	6,500	40,000	52,000	40,000		
Blazer	5	9,000	7,000	45,000	35,000	35,000		
Category subtotal				85,000	87,000		85,000	
Totals				$295,000	$287,000	**$265,000**	**$285,000**	**$287,000**

Reported inventory depends on which of the 3 different LCM methods is applied

When LCM is applied to the *entire* inventory, the market amount is $287,000. Since this market amount is $8,000 lower than the $295,000 recorded cost, the $287,000 amount is reported for inventory on the balance sheet. When LCM is applied to the major *categories* of inventory, the market is $285,000. When LCM is applied to individual *items* of inventory, the market is $265,000. Since market amounts for these cases is less than the $295,000 recorded cost, the market amount is reported for inventory. Any one of these three applications of LCM is acceptable. The retailer **Best Buy** applies LCM and reports that its "merchandise inventories are recorded at the lower of average cost or market."

Recording the Lower of Cost or Market   Inventory must be adjusted downward when market is less than cost. To illustrate, if LCM is applied to the individual items of inventory in Exhibit 17.9, the Merchandise Inventory account must be adjusted from the $295,000 recorded cost down to the $265,000 market amount. The decline in inventory value (of $30,000) is included on the income statement. This related entry is

Loss from Decline in Inventory Value	30,000	
Merchandise Inventory		30,000
To adjust inventory cost to market.		

Accounting rules require that inventory be adjusted to market when market is less than cost, but inventory usually cannot be written up to market when market exceeds cost. If recording inventory down to market is acceptable, why are companies not allowed to record inventory up to market? One view is that a gain from a market increase should not be realized until a sales transaction verifies the gain. However, this problem also applies when market is less than cost. A second and primary reason is the **conservatism concept,** which prescribes the use of the less optimistic amount when more than one estimate of the amount to be received or paid exist and these estimates are about equally likely.

HOW YOU DOIN'?   Answer—p. 431

8. Use LCM applied separately to the following individual items to compute ending inventory.

Product	Units	Unit Recorded Cost	Unit Market Cost
A	20	$ 6	$ 5
B	40	9	8
C	10	12	15

INVENTORY TURNOVER AND DAYS' SALES IN INVENTORY

Inventory Turnover

A merchandiser's ability to pay its short-term obligations also depends on how quickly it sells its merchandise inventory. **Inventory turnover,** also called *merchandise inventory turnover,* is one ratio used to assess this. It is defined in Exhibit 17.10.

$$\text{Inventory turnover} = \frac{\text{Cost of goods sold}}{\text{Average inventory}}$$

LO6 Assess inventory management using both inventory turnover and days' sales in inventory.

Exhibit 17.10

Inventory Turnover

This ratio reveals how many *times* a company turns over (sells) its inventory during a period. If a company's inventory greatly varies within a year, average inventory amounts can be computed from interim periods such as quarters or months.

Users apply inventory turnover to help analyze short-term liquidity and to assess whether management is doing a good job controlling the amount of inventory available. A low ratio compared to that of competitors suggests inefficient use of assets. The company may be holding more inventory than it needs to support its sales volume. Simiiarly, a very high ratio compared to that of competitors suggests inventory might be too low. This can cause lost sales if customers must back-order merchandise. Inventory turnover has no simple rule except to say *a high ratio is preferable provided inventory is adequate to meet demand.*

IN THE NEWS

Dell-ocity From its roots in a college dorm room, **Dell** now sells over 50 million dollars' worth of computers each day from its Website. The speed of Web technology has allowed Dell to slash inventories. Dell's inventory turnover is 102 and its days' sales in inventory is 4 days. Michael Dell asserts, "Speed is everything in this business."

Days' Sales in Inventory

To better interpret inventory turnover, many users measure the adequacy of inventory to meet sales demand. **Days' sales in inventory,** also called *days' stock on hand,* is a ratio that reveals how much inventory is available in terms of the number of days' sales. It can be interpreted as the number of days one can sell from inventory if no new items are purchased. This ratio is often viewed as a measure of the buffer against out-of-stock inventory and is useful in evaluating liquidity of inventory. It is defined in Exhibit 17.11.

$$\text{Days' sales in inventory} = \frac{\text{Ending inventory}}{\text{Cost of goods sold}} \times 365$$

Exhibit 17.11

Days' Sales in Inventory

Days' sales in inventory focuses on ending inventory and it estimates how many days it will take to convert inventory at the end of a period into accounts receivable or cash. Notice that days' sales in inventory focuses on *ending* inventory whereas inventory turnover focuses on *average* inventory.

Analysis of Inventory Management

Inventory management is a major emphasis for merchandisers. They must both plan and control inventory purchases and sales. **Toys "R" Us** is one of those merchandisers. Its inventory in fiscal year 2007 was $1,690 million. This inventory constituted 59% of its current assets and 20% of its total assets. We apply the analysis tools in this section to Toys "R" Us, as shown in Exhibit 17.12—also see margin graph.

Exhibit 17.12

Inventory Turnover and Days' Sales in Inventory for Toys "R" Us

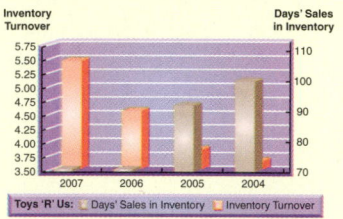

($ millions)	2007	2006	2005	2004
Cost of goods sold	$8,638	$7,652	$7,506	$7,646
Ending inventory	$1,690	$1,488	$1,884	$2,094
Inventory turnover	**5.4** times	**4.5** times	**3.8** times	**3.6** times
Industry inventory turnover	3.0 times	2.8 times	2.6 times	2.6 times
Days' sales in inventory	**71** days	**71** days	**92** days	**100** days
Industry days' sales in inventory	129 days	135 days	139 days	141 days

Its 2007 inventory turnover of 5.4 times means that Toys "R" Us turned over its inventory 5.4 times per year, or once every 68 days (365 days ÷ 5.4). We prefer inventory turnover to be high provided inventory is not out of stock and the company is not losing customers. The 2007 days' sales in inventory of 71 days reveals that it was carrying 71 days of sales in inventory. This inventory buffer seems more than adequate. Toys "R" Us would benefit from further management efforts to increase inventory turnover and reduce inventory levels.

DILBERT reprinted by permission of United Feature Syndicate, Inc.

Demonstration Problem

Craig Company uses a periodic inventory system for its one product. Its beginning inventory, purchases, and sales during calendar year 2010 follow.

Date	Activity	Units Acquired at Cost	Units Sold at Retail	Unit Inventory
Jan. 1	Beg. Inventory ..	400 units @ $14 = $ 5,600		400 units
Jan. 15	Sale		200 units @ $30	200 units
March 10	Purchase	200 units @ $15 = $ 3,000		400 units
April 1	Sale		200 units @ $30	200 units
May 9	Purchase	300 units @ $16 = $ 4,800		500 units
Sept. 22	Purchase	250 units @ $20 = $ 5,000		750 units
Nov. 1	Sale		300 units @ $35	450 units
Nov. 28	Purchase	100 units @ $21 = $ 2,100		550 units
	Totals	1,250 units $20,500	700 units	

Additional tracking data for specific identification: (1) January 15 sale—200 units @ $14, (2) April 1 sale—200 units @ $15, and (3) November 1 sale—200 units @ $14 and 100 units @ $20.

Required

1. Calculate the cost of goods available for sale.
2. Apply the four different methods of inventory costing (FIFO, LIFO, weighted average, and specific identification) to calculate ending inventory and cost of goods sold under each method.
3. Management wants a report that shows how changing from FIFO to another method would change income before taxes. Prepare a table showing (1) the cost of goods sold amount under each of the four methods, (2) the amount by which each cost of goods sold total is different from the FIFO cost of goods sold, and (3) the effect on income before taxes if another method is used instead of FIFO.

Planning the Solution

- Compute cost of goods available for sale by multiplying the units of beginning inventory and each purchase by their unit costs to determine the total cost of goods available for sale.
- Prepare a periodic FIFO table starting with the total cost of goods available and compute ending inventory using the most recent purchases (see Exhibit 17.4).
- Prepare a periodic LIFO table starting with the total cost of goods available and compute ending inventory using the earliest purchases (see Exhibit 17.5).
- Make a table of beginning inventory and purchases and compute the weighted average cost of ending inventory and goods sold (see Exhibit 17.6).
- Prepare a table showing the computation of cost of goods sold and ending inventory using the specific identification method (see Exhibit 17.3).
- Create a table showing cost of goods sold under each method and how net income would differ from FIFO net income if an alternate method is adopted.

Solution to Demonstration Problem

1. Cost of goods available for sale (this amount is the same for all methods).

Date			Units	Unit Cost	Cost
Jan.	1	Beg. Inventory	400	$14	$ 5,600
March 10		Purchase	200	15	3,000
May	9	Purchase	300	16	4,800
Sept. 22		Purchase	250	20	5,000
Nov. 28		Purchase	100	21	2,100
Total goods available for sale			1,250		$20,500

2a. FIFO periodic method.

Total cost of 1,250 units available for sale..............	$20,500
Less ending inventory using FIFO	
100 units from Nov. 28 purchase at $21 each	$2,100
250 units from Sept. 22 purchase at $20 each	5,000
200 units from May 9 purchase at $16 each	3,200
Ending inventory	10,300
Cost of goods sold......................................	$10,200

2b. LIFO periodic method

Total cost of 1,250 units available for sale	$20,500
Less ending inventory using LIFO	
400 units from beginning inventory at $14 each $5,600	
150 units from March 10 purchase at $15 each 2,250	
Ending inventory	7,850
Cost of goods sold	$12,650

2c. Weighted average periodic method

The weighted average cost per unit, for 1,250 units with a cost available for sale of $20,500, is:

$$\$20,500/1,250 \text{ units} = \$16.40 \text{ weighted average cost per unit}$$

Total cost of 1,250 units available for sale	$20,500
Less ending inventory on a weighted	
average cost basis: 550 units at $16.40 each	9,020
Cost of goods sold	$11,480

2d. Specific identification method.

Date	Goods Purchased	Cost of Goods Sold	Inventory Balance	
Jan. 1	Beginning balance		400 @ $14	= $ 5,600
Jan. 15		200 @ $14 = $2,800	200 @ $14	= $ 2,800
Mar. 10	200 @ $15 = $3,000		200 @ $14 200 @ $15	= $ 5,800
April 1		200 @ $15 = $3,000	200 @ $14	= $ 2,800
May 9	300 @ $16 = $4,800		200 @ $14 300 @ $16	= $ 7,600
Sept. 22	250 @ $20 = $5,000		200 @ $14 300 @ $16 250 @ $20	= $12,600
Nov. 1		200 @ $14 = $2,800 100 @ $20 = $2,000	300 @ $16 150 @ $20	= $ 7,800
Nov. 28	100 @ $21 = $2,100		300 @ $16 150 @ $20 100 @ $21	= **$ 9,900**
Total cost of goods sold		**$10,600**		

3. Analysis of the effects of alternative inventory methods.

	Cost of Goods Sold	Difference from FIFO Cost of Goods Sold	Effect on Income before Taxes If Adopted Instead of FIFO
FIFO	$10,200	—	—
LIFO	12,650	+2,450	$2,450 lower
Weighted average	11,480	+1,280	1,280 lower
Specific identification	10,600	+ 400	400 lower

Inventory Costing under a Perpetual System

The basic aim of the periodic system and the perpetual system is the same: to assign costs to inventory and cost of goods sold. The same four methods are used to assign costs under both systems: specific identification; first-in, first-out; last-in, first-out; and weighted average. Under a perpetual system, the Merchandise Inventory account is continually updated to reflect purchases and sales. We use information from Trekking to show how to assign costs using these four methods with a perpetual system. Data for sales and purchases are reported in the chapter (see Exhibit 17.2).

LO7 Compute inventory in a perpetual system using the methods of FIFO, LIFO, and weighted average.

> The "Goods Purchased" column is identical for all methods. Data are taken from Exhibit 17.2.

First-In, First-Out

Use of FIFO for computing the cost of inventory and cost of goods sold is shown in Exhibit 17A.1.

Date	Goods Purchased	Cost of Goods Sold	Inventory Balance
Aug. 1	Beginning balance		10 @ $ 91 = $ 910
Aug. 3	15 @ $106 = $1,590		10 @ $ 91 ⎫ 15 @ $106 ⎭ = $2,500
Aug. 14		10 @ $ 91 = $ 910 ⎫ 10 @ $106 = $1,060 ⎭ = **$1,970**	5 @ $106 = $ 530
Aug. 17	20 @ $115 = $2,300		5 @ $106 ⎫ 20 @ $115 ⎭ = $2,830
Aug. 28	10 @ $119 = $1,190		5 @ $106 ⎫ 20 @ $115 ⎬ = $4,020 10 @ $119 ⎭
Aug. 31		5 @ $106 = $ 530 ⎫ 18 @ $115 = $2,070 ⎭ = **$2,600** **$4,570**	2 @ $115 ⎫ 10 @ $119 ⎭ = **$1,420**

Exhibit 17A.1

FIFO Computations— Perpetual System

> For the 20 units sold on Aug. 14, the first 10 sold are assigned the earliest cost of $91 (from beg. bal.). The next 10 sold are assigned the next earliest cost of $106.

> For the 23 units sold on Aug. 31, the first 5 sold are assigned the earliest available cost of $106 (from Aug. 3 purchase). The next 18 sold are assigned the next earliest cost of $115 (from Aug. 17 purchase).

Trekking's FIFO cost of goods sold reported on its income statement (reflecting the 43 units sold) is **$4,570** ($1,970 + $2,600), and its ending inventory reported on the balance sheet (reflecting the 12 units unsold) is **$1,420**.

The purchases and sales entries for Exhibit 17A.1 follow (the colored boldface numbers are those affected by the cost flow assumption). We see that the Merchandise Inventory account is updated each time an inventory purchase or sale is made.

Purchases

Aug. 3	Merchandise Inventory	1,590	
	Accounts Payable		1,590
17	Merchandise Inventory	2,300	
	Accounts Payable		2,300
28	Merchandise Inventory	1,190	
	Accounts Payable		1,190

Sales

Aug. 14	Accounts Receivable	2,600	
	Sales		2,600
14	Cost of Goods Sold	**1,970**	
	Merchandise Inventory		**1,970**
31	Accounts Receivable	3,450	
	Sales		3,450
31	Cost of Goods Sold	**2,600**	
	Merchandise Inventory		**2,600**

> Sales and costs of goods sold are closed to Income Summary at the end of each period.

Last-In, First-Out

Exhibit 17A.2 shows how LIFO assigns the costs of mountain bikes to the 12 units in ending inventory and to the 43 units sold.

Exhibit 17A.2

LIFO Computations—
Perpetual System

For the 20 units sold on Aug. 14, the first 15 sold are assigned the most recent cost of $106. The next 5 sold are assigned the next most recent cost of $91.

For the 23 units sold on Aug. 31, the first 10 sold are assigned the most recent cost of $119. The next 13 sold are assigned the next most recent cost of $115.

Date	Goods Purchased	Cost of Goods Sold	Inventory Balance
Aug. 1	Beginning balance		10 @ $ 91 = $ 910
Aug. 3	15 @ $106 = $1,590		10 @ $ 91 ⎫ = $ 2,500 15 @ $106 ⎭
Aug. 14		15 @ $106 = $1,590 ⎫ = **$2,045** 5 @ $ 91 = $ 455 ⎭	5 @ $ 91 = $ 455
Aug. 17	20 @ $115 = $2,300		5 @ $ 91 ⎫ = $ 2,755 20 @ $115 ⎭
Aug. 28	10 @ $119 = $1,190		5 @ $ 91 ⎫ 20 @ $115 ⎬ = $ 3,945 10 @ $119 ⎭
Aug. 31		10 @ $119 = $1,190 ⎫ = **$2,685** 13 @ $115 = $1,495 ⎭	5 @ $ 91 ⎫ = **$1,260** 7 @ $115 ⎭
		$4,730	

Trekking's LIFO cost of goods sold reported on the income statement is **$4,730** ($2,045 + $2,685), and its ending inventory reported on the balance sheet is **$1,260**.

The purchases and sales entries for Exhibit 17A.2 follow (the colored boldface numbers are those affected by the cost flow assumption).

	Purchases				**Sales**		
Aug. 3	Merchandise Inventory	1,590		Aug. 14	Accounts Receivable	2,600	
	Accounts Payable		1,590		Sales		2,600
17	Merchandise Inventory	2,300		14	Cost of Goods Sold	**2,045**	
	Accounts Payable		2,300		Merchandise Inventory		**2,045**
28	Merchandise Inventory	1,190		31	Accounts Receivable	3,450	
	Accounts Payable		1,190		Sales		3,450
				31	Cost of Goods Sold	**2,685**	
					Merchandise Inventory		**2,685**

Weighted Average

The **weighted average** (also called **average cost**) method of assigning cost requires that we use the weighted average cost per unit of inventory at the time of each sale. Weighted average cost per unit at the time of each sale equals the cost of goods available for sale divided by the units available. The results using weighted average for Trekking are shown in Exhibit 17A.3.

Under weighted average, a unit sold is assigned the average cost of all items currently available for sale at the date of each sale.

Trekking's cost of goods sold reported on the income statement (reflecting the 43 units sold) is **$4,622** ($2,000 + $2,622), and its ending inventory reported on the balance sheet (reflecting the 12 units unsold) is **$1,368**.

Date	Goods Purchased	Cost of Goods Sold	Inventory Balance
Aug. 1	Beginning balance		10 @ $ 91 = $ 910
Aug. 3	15 @ $106 = $1,590		10 @ $ 91 ⎫ = $2,500 (or $100 per unit)ᵃ 15 @ $106 ⎭
Aug. 14		20 @ $100 = **$2,000**	5 @ $100 = $ 500 (or $100 per unit)ᵇ
Aug. 17	20 @ $115 = $2,300		5 @ $100 ⎫ = $2,800 (or $112 per unit)ᶜ 20 @ $115 ⎭
Aug. 28	10 @ $119 = $1,190		5 @ $100 ⎫ 20 @ $115 ⎬ = $3,990 (or $114 per unit)ᵈ 10 @ $119 ⎭
Aug. 31		23 @ $114 = **$2,622**	12 @ $114 = **$1,368** (or $114 per unit)ᵉ
		$4,622	

Exhibit 17A.3

Weighted Average Computations—Perpetual System

> For the 20 units sold on Aug. 14, the cost assigned is the $100 *average cost* per unit from the inventory balance column at the time of sale.

> For the 23 units sold on Aug. 31, the cost assigned is the $114 *average cost* per unit from the inventory balance column at the time of sale.

ᵃ $100 per unit = ($2,500 inventory balance ÷ 25 units in inventory).
ᵇ $100 per unit = ($500 inventory balance ÷ 5 units in inventory).
ᶜ $112 per unit = ($2,800 inventory balance ÷ 25 units in inventory).
ᵈ $114 per unit = ($3,990 inventory balance ÷ 35 units in inventory).
ᵉ $114 per unit = ($1,368 inventory balance ÷ 12 units in inventory).

The purchases and sales entries for Exhibit 17A.3 follow (the colored boldface numbers are those affected by the cost flow assumption).

Purchases		
Aug. 3	Merchandise Inventory	1,590	
	Accounts Payable.		1,590
17	Merchandise Inventory	2,300	
	Accounts Payable.		2,300
28	Merchandise Inventory	1,190	
	Accounts Payable.		1,190

Sales		
Aug. 14	Accounts Receivable	2,600	
	Sales.		2,600
14	Cost of Goods Sold.	**2,000**	
	Merchandise Inventory		**2,000**
31	Accounts Receivable	3,450	
	Sales.		3,450
31	Cost of Goods Sold.	**2,622**	
	Merchandise Inventory		**2,622**

Financial Statement Effects of Costing Methods

When purchase prices do not change, each inventory costing method assigns the same cost amounts to inventory and to cost of goods sold. When purchase prices are different, however, the methods nearly always assign different cost amounts. We show these differences in Exhibit 17A.4 using Trekking's data. We see that the amounts for specific identification and FIFO are the same as those in Exhibit 17.8.

TREKKING COMPANY For Month Ended August 31	Specific Identification	FIFO	LIFO	Weighted Average
Income Statement				
Sales	$ 6,050	$ 6,050	$ 6,050	$ 6,050
Cost of goods sold	4,582	4,570	4,730	4,622
Gross profit	1,468	1,480	1,320	1,428
Expenses.	450	450	450	450
Income before taxes	1,018	1,030	870	978
Income tax expense (30%)	305.40	309	261	293.40
Net income	$ 712.60	$ 721	$ 609	$ 684.60
Balance Sheet				
Inventory	$1,408	$1,420	$1,260	$1,368

Exhibit 17A.4

Financial Statement Effects of Inventory Costing Methods

APPENDIX 17B Inventory Estimation Methods

LO8 Apply the gross profit method to estimate inventory.

Inventory sometimes requires estimation for two reasons. First, companies often require **interim financial statements** (financial statements prepared for periods of less than one year), but they only annually take a physical count of inventory. Second, companies may require an inventory estimate if some casualty such as fire or flood makes taking a physical count impossible. Estimates are usually only required for companies that use the periodic system. Companies using a perpetual system would presumably have updated inventory data.

This appendix describes the gross profit method to estimate inventory.

Gross Profit Method

The **gross profit method** estimates the cost of ending inventory by applying the gross profit ratio to net sales (at retail). This type of estimate often is needed when inventory is destroyed, lost, or stolen. These cases require an inventory estimate so that a company can file a claim with its insurer. Users also apply this method to see whether inventory amounts from a physical count are reasonable. This method uses the historical relation between cost of goods sold and net sales to estimate the proportion of cost of goods sold making up current sales. This cost of goods sold estimate is then subtracted from cost of goods available for sale to estimate the ending inventory at cost. These two steps are shown in Exhibit 17B.1.

Exhibit 17B.1

Gross Profit Method of Inventory Estimation

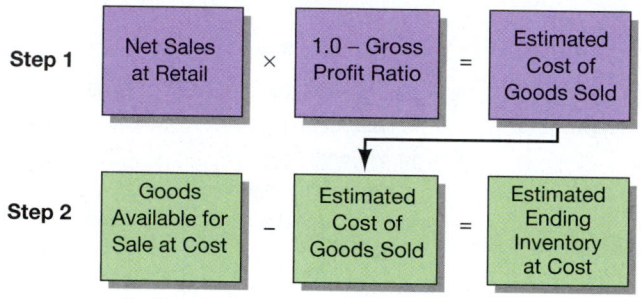

To illustrate, assume that a company's inventory is destroyed by fire in March 2010. When the fire occurs, the company's accounts show the following balances for January through March: sales, $31,500; sales returns, $1,500; inventory (January 1, 2010), $12,000; and cost of goods purchased, $20,500. If this company's gross profit ratio is 30%, then 30% of each net sales dollar is gross profit and 70% is cost of goods sold. We show in Exhibit 17B.2 how this 70% is used to estimate lost inventory of $11,500. To understand this exhibit, think of subtracting cost of goods sold from the goods available for sale to get ending inventory.

> Reliability of the gross profit method depends on a good estimate of the gross profit ratio.

Exhibit 17B.2

Estimated Inventory Using the Gross Profit Method

Goods available for sale		
Inventory, January 1, 2010		$12,000
Cost of goods purchased		20,500
Goods available for sale (at cost)		32,500
Net sales at retail ($31,500 − $1,500)		$30,000
Step 1:	**Estimated cost of goods sold ($30,000 × 70%)**	**(21,000)** ← × 0.70
Step 2:	**Estimated March inventory at cost**	**$11,500**

Summary

LO1 Identify the items making up merchandise inventory.
Merchandise inventory refers to goods owned by a company and held for resale. Two special cases merit our attention. Goods in transit are reported in inventory of the company that holds ownership rights. Goods damaged or obsolete are reported in inventory at their net realizable value.

LO2 Identify the costs of merchandise inventory. Costs of merchandise inventory include expenditures necessary to bring an item to a salable condition and location. This includes its invoice cost minus any discount plus any added or incidental costs necessary to put it in a place and condition for sale.

LO3 Compute inventory in a periodic system using the methods of specific identification, FIFO, LIFO, and weighted average. Periodic inventory systems allocate the cost of goods available for sale between cost of goods sold and ending inventory *at the end of a period*. Specific identification and FIFO give identical results whether the periodic or perpetual system is used. LIFO assigns costs to cost of goods sold assuming the last units purchased for the period are the first units sold. The weighted average cost per unit is computed by dividing the total cost of beginning inventory and net purchases for the period by the total number of units available. Then, it multiplies cost per unit by the number of units sold to give cost of goods sold.

LO4 Analyze the effects of inventory methods for both financial and tax reporting. When purchase costs are rising or falling, the inventory costing methods are likely to assign different costs to inventory. Specific identification exactly matches costs and revenues. Weighted average smooths out cost changes. FIFO assigns an amount to inventory closely approximating current replacement cost. LIFO assigns the most recent costs incurred to cost of goods sold and likely better matches current costs with revenues.

LO5 Apply the lower of cost or market valuation. Inventory is reported at market cost when market is *lower* than recorded cost, called the *lower of cost or market (LCM) inventory*. Market is typically measured as replacement cost. Lower of cost or market can be applied separately to each item, to major categories of items, or to the entire inventory.

LO6 Assess inventory management using both inventory turnover and days' sales in inventory. We prefer a high inventory turnover, provided that goods are not out of stock and customers are not turned away. We use days' sales in inventory to assess the likelihood of goods being out of stock. We prefer a small number of days' sales in inventory if we can serve customer needs and provide a buffer for uncertainties.

LO7^A Compute inventory in a perpetual system using the methods of FIFO, LIFO, and weighted average. Costs are assigned to the cost of goods sold account *each time* a sale occurs in a perpetual system. Weighted average assigns a cost to items sold by dividing the current balance in the inventory account by the total items available for sale to determine cost per unit. We then multiply the number of units sold by this cost per unit to get the cost of each sale. FIFO assigns cost to items sold assuming that the earliest units purchased are the first units sold. LIFO assigns cost to items sold assuming that the most recent units purchased are the first units sold.

LO8^B Apply the gross profit method to estimate inventory. The gross profit method involves two steps: (1) net sales at retail multiplied by 1 minus the gross profit ratio equals estimated cost of goods sold and (2) goods available at cost minus estimated cost of goods sold equals estimated ending inventory at cost.

Guidance Answers to HOW YOU DOIN'?

1. A perpetual inventory system.

2. Target reports these goods in its inventory.

3. Total cost assigned to the painting is $12,180, computed as $11,400 + $130 + $150 + $100 + $400.

4. **a.** FIFO periodic inventory = $(20 \times \$14) + (10 \times \$12)$
       = $400

   b. LIFO periodic cost of goods sold = $(100 \times \$10) + (40 \times \$12) + (20 \times \$14) - (30 \times \$10) = \$1,460$

5. Specific identification exactly matches costs and revenues. Weighted average tends to smooth out cost changes. FIFO assigns an amount to inventory that closely approximates current replacement cost. LIFO assigns the most recent costs incurred to cost of goods sold and likely better matches current costs with revenues.

6. FIFO—it gives a lower cost of goods sold, a higher gross profit, and a higher net income when costs are rising.

7. When costs are rising, LIFO gives a lower inventory figure on the balance sheet as compared to FIFO. FIFO's inventory amount approximates current replacement costs.

8. The reported LCM inventory amount (using items) is $540, computed as $[(20 \times \$5) + (40 \times \$8) + (10 \times \$12)]$.

Key Terms

Average cost (p. 428) See *weighted average*.

Conservatism concept (p. 423) Concept that prescribes the less optimistic estimate when two estimates are about equally likely.

Consistency concept (p. 421) Concept that prescribes use of the same accounting method(s) over time so that financial statements are comparable across periods.

Days' sales in inventory (p. 423) Estimate of number of days needed to convert inventory into receivables or cash; equals ending inventory divided by cost of goods sold and then multiplied by 365; also called *days' stock on hand*.

First-in, first-out (FIFO) (p. 418) Method to assign cost to inventory that assumes items are sold in the order acquired; earliest items purchased are the first sold.

Gross profit method (p. 430) Procedure to estimate inventory when the past gross profit rate is used to estimate cost of goods sold, which is then subtracted from the cost of goods available for sale.

Interim financial statements (p. 430) Financial statements covering periods of less than one year; usually based on one-, three-, or six-month periods.

Inventory turnover (p. 423) Number of times a company's average inventory is sold during a period; computed by dividing cost of goods sold by average inventory; also called *merchandise turnover*.

Last-in, first-out (LIFO) (p. 419) Method to assign cost to inventory that assumes costs for the most recent items purchased are sold first and charged to cost of goods sold.

LIFO conformity rule (p. 421) If LIFO is used for tax reporting, it must also be used for financial reporting.

Lower of cost or market (LCM) (p. 422) Required method to report inventory at market replacement cost when that market cost is lower than recorded cost.

Net realizable value (p. 414) Expected selling price (value) of an item minus the cost of making the sale.

Periodic inventory system (p. 415) Method that records the cost of inventory purchased but does not continuously track the quantity available or sold to customers; records are updated at the end of each period to reflect the physical count and costs of goods available.

Perpetual inventory system (p. 415) Method that maintains continuous records of the cost of inventory available and the cost of goods sold.

Specific identification (p. 417) Method to assign cost to inventory when the purchase cost of each item in inventory is identified and used to compute cost of inventory.

Weighted average (p. 428) Method to assign inventory cost to sales; the cost of available-for-sale units is divided by the number of units available to determine per unit cost prior to each sale that is then multiplied by the units sold to yield the cost of that sale.

Multiple Choice Quiz   Answers on p. 443   mhhe.com/wildCA2e

Additional Multiple Choice Quizzes are available at the book's Website.

Use the following information from Marvel Company for the month of July to answer questions 1 through 4.

July 1	Beginning inventory	75 units @ $25 each
July 3	Purchase	348 units @ $27 each
July 8	Sale	300 units
July 15	Purchase	257 units @ $28 each
July 23	Sale	275 units

1. Assume that Marvel uses a periodic FIFO inventory system. What is the dollar value of its ending inventory?
   a. $2,940   **d.** $2,852
   b. $2,685   **e.** $2,705
   c. $2,625

2. Assume that Marvel uses a perpetual LIFO inventory system. What is the dollar value of its ending inventory?
   a. $2,940   **d.** $2,852
   b. $2,685   **e.** $2,705
   c. $2,625

3. Assume that Marvel uses a specific identification inventory system. Its ending inventory consists of 20 units from beginning inventory, 40 units from the July 3 purchase, and 45 units from the July 15 purchase. What is the dollar value of its ending inventory?
   a. $2,940   **d.** $2,852
   b. $2,685   **e.** $2,840
   c. $2,625

4. Assume that Marvel uses a *periodic* weighted average inventory system. What is the dollar value of its cost of goods sold?
   a. $2,850   **d.** $14,375
   b. $15,813   **e.** $15,617
   c. $15,333

5. A company has cost of goods sold of $85,000 and ending inventory of $18,000. Its days' sales in inventory equals:
   a. 49.32 days   **d.** 77.29 days
   b. 0.21 day   **e.** 1,723.61 days
   c. 4.72 days

Superscript letter ^A (^B) denotes assignments based on Appendix 17A (17B).

Discussion Questions

1. Describe how costs flow from inventory to cost of goods sold for the following methods: (*a*) FIFO and (*b*) LIFO.

2. Where is the amount of merchandise inventory disclosed in the financial statements?

3. If costs are declining, will the LIFO or FIFO method of inventory valuation yield the lower cost of goods sold? Why?

4. What does the full-disclosure principle prescribe if a company changes from one acceptable accounting method to another?

5. Can a company change its inventory method each accounting period? Explain.

6. Does the accounting principle of consistency preclude any changes from one accounting method to another?

7. What is the meaning of *market* as it is used in determining the lower of cost or market for inventory?

8. What guidance does the principle of conservatism offer?

9. What factors contribute to (or cause) inventory shrinkage?

10.^A What accounts are used in a periodic inventory system but not in a perpetual inventory system?

11.^B When preparing interim financial statements, what method can companies utilize to estimate cost of goods sold and ending inventory?

12. Refer to **Best Buy**'s financial statements in Appendix A. On March 1, 2008, what percent of current assets are represented by inventory?

13. Refer to **RadioShack**'s financial statements in Appendix A. Compute its cost of goods available for sale for the year ended December 31, 2007.

connect

A company reports the following beginning inventory and purchases for the month of January. On January 26, 355 units were sold. What is the cost of the 160 units that remain in ending inventory at January 31, assuming costs are assigned based on a periodic inventory system and use of FIFO? What are the cost of goods sold?

QUICK STUDY

QS 17-1
Inventory costing methods   **LO3**

	Units	Unit Cost
Beginning inventory on January 1	320	$3.00
Purchase on January 9	85	3.20
Purchase on January 25	110	3.30

Using the information from QS 17-1, what is the cost of the 160 units that remain in ending inventory at January 31, assuming costs are assigned based on a periodic inventory system and use of LIFO?

QS 17-2
Inventory costing methods—LIFO
LO3

Using the information from QS 17-1, what is the cost of the 160 units that remain in ending inventory at January 31, assuming costs are assigned based on a periodic inventory system and use of weighted average? (Round per unit costs to three decimals, but inventory balances to the dollar.)

QS 17-3
Inventory costing methods—LIFO
LO3

Check $496

Wattan Company reports beginning inventory of 10 units at $60 each. Every week for four weeks it purchases an additional 10 units at respective costs of $61, $62, $65, and $70 per unit for weeks 1 through 4. Calculate the cost of goods available for sale and the units available for sale for this four-week period.

QS 17-4
Computing goods available for sale
LO3

Trey Monson starts a merchandising business on December 1 and enters into three inventory purchases:

QS 17-5
Assigning costs to inventory—
periodic systems   **LO3**

December 7	10 units @ $ 7 cost
December 14	20 units @ $ 8 cost
December 21	15 units @ $10 cost

Monson sells 15 units for $20 each on December 15. Eight of the sold units are from the December 7 purchase and seven are from the December 14 purchase. Monson uses a periodic inventory system. Determine the costs assigned to the December 31 ending inventory based on (a) FIFO, (b) LIFO, (c) weighted average, and (d) specific identification. (Round per unit costs to three decimals, but inventory balances to the dollar.)

Check   (a) $270

Identify the inventory costing method best described by each of the following separate statements. Assume a period of increasing costs.

QS 17-6
Contrasting inventory
costing methods   **LO4**

1. Yields a balance sheet inventory amount often markedly less than its replacement cost.
2. Matches recent costs against current sales.
3. Results in a balance sheet inventory amount approximating replacement cost.
4. Provides a tax advantage (deferral) to a corporation when costs are rising.
5. The preferred method when each unit of product has unique features that markedly affect cost.

1. At year-end, Liu Co. had shipped $750 of merchandise to Kwon Co. Liu Co. pays the cost of shipping. Which company should include the $750 of merchandise in transit as part of its year-end inventory?
2. Jabar Company has $600 of damaged goods in its warehouse. Jabar estimates it can sell these goods for $550, after paying $75 to fix the goods. What dollar amount should Jabar Co. include for these goods in its inventory?

QS 17-7
Inventory ownership   **LO1**

Homestead Crafts, a distributor of handmade gifts, operates out of owner Emma Flynn's house. At the end of the current period, Emma reports she has 1,300 units (products) in her basement, 20 of which were damaged by water and cannot be sold. She also has another 350 units in her van, ready to deliver per a customer order. Homestead Crafts pays shipping. How many units should Emma include in her company's period-end inventory?

QS 17-8
Inventory ownership   **LO1**

QS 17–9
Inventory costs   **LO2**

A car dealer acquires a used car for $14,000. Additional costs in obtaining and offering the car for sale include $250 for transportation-in (paid by the dealer), $900 for import duties, $300 for insurance during shipment, $150 for advertising, and $1,250 for sales staff salaries. For computing inventory, what cost is assigned to the used car?

QS 17–10
Inventory costs   **LO2**

Majors & Son, antique dealers, purchased the contents of an estate for $38,500. The cost of transporting the goods to Majors & Son's warehouse was $2,100. Majors & Son paid these shipping costs and also insured the shipment at a cost of $250. Before putting the antiques up for sale, Majors & Son cleaned and refurbished them at a cost of $800. Determine the cost of the inventory acquired from the estate.

QS 17–11
Applying LCM to inventories
LO5

Amulet Trading Co. has the following products in its ending inventory. Compute lower of cost or market for inventory (a) as a whole and (b) applied separately to each product.

Product	Quantity	Cost per Unit	Market per Unit
Mountain bikes	11	$600	$550
Skateboards	13	350	425
Gliders	26	800	700

QS 17–12
Analyzing inventory   **LO6**

Endor Company begins the year with $150,000 of goods in inventory. At year-end, the amount in inventory has increased to $180,000. Cost of goods sold for the year is $1,200,000. Compute Endor's inventory turnover and days' sales in inventory. Assume that there are 365 days in the year.

QS 17–13ᴬ
Costing methods—
perpetual system   **LO7**

Refer to QS 17-1 and assume the perpetual inventory system is used. Determine the costs assigned to the ending inventory when costs are assigned based on (a) FIFO, (b) LIFO, and (c) weighted average. (Round per unit costs to three decimals, but inventory balances to the dollar.)

QS 17–14ᴬ
Costing methods—
perpetual system   **LO7**

Refer to QS 17-5 and assume the perpetual inventory system is used. Determine the costs assigned to the December 31 ending inventory when costs are assigned based on (a) FIFO, (b) LIFO, (c) weighted average, and (d) specific identification. (Round per unit costs to three decimals, but inventory balances to the dollar.)

QS 17–15ᴮ
Estimating inventories—gross
profit method   **LO8**

Kauai Store's inventory is destroyed by a fire on September 5, 2010. The following data for year 2010 are available from the accounting records. Estimate the cost of the inventory destroyed.

Jan. 1 inventory	$190,000
Jan. 1 through Sept. 5 purchases (net)	$352,000
Jan. 1 through Sept. 5 sales (net)	$685,000
Year 2010 estimated gross profit rate	44%

EXERCISES

connect

Exercise 17–1
Inventory costing
methods—periodic   **LO3**

Laker Company reported the following January purchases and sales data for its only product.

Date	Activities	Units Acquired at Cost	Units Sold at Retail
Jan. 1	Beginning inventory	140 units @ $6.00 = $ 840	
Jan. 10	Sales		100 units @ $15
Jan. 20	Purchase	300 units @ $5.60 = 1,680	
Jan. 25	Sales		250 units @ $15
Jan. 30	Purchase	100 units @ $5.00 = 500	
	Totals	540 units $3,020	350 units

Laker uses a periodic inventory system. Ending inventory consists of 190 units, 100 from the January 30 purchase, 70 from the January 20 purchase, and 20 from beginning inventory. Determine the cost assigned to ending inventory and to cost of goods sold using (a) specific identification, (b) weighted average, (c) FIFO, and (d) LIFO. (Round per unit costs to three decimals, but inventory balances to the dollar.)

Check   Ending inventory: WA, $1,063
(rounded); LIFO, $1,120

Use the data in Exercise 17-1 to prepare comparative income statements for the month of January for Laker Company similar to those shown in Exhibit 17.8 for the four inventory methods. Assume that expenses other than cost of goods sold are $1,250, and that the applicable income tax rate is 30%.

1. Which method yields the highest net income?

2. Does net income using weighted average fall between that using FIFO and LIFO?

3. If costs were rising instead of falling, which method would yield the highest net income?

Exercise 17-2
Income effects of
inventory methods **LO4**

Hemming Co. reported the following current-year purchases and sales data for its only product.

Date	Activities	Units Acquired at Cost	Units Sold at Retail
Jan. 1	Beginning inventory	200 units @ $10 = $ 2,000	
Jan. 10	Sales		150 units @ $40
Mar. 14	Purchase	350 units @ $15 = 5,250	
Mar. 15	Sales		300 units @ $40
July 30	Purchase	450 units @ $20 = 9,000	
Oct. 5	Sales		430 units @ $40
Oct. 26	Purchase	100 units @ $25 = 2,500	
	Totals	1,100 units $18,750	880 units

Exercise 17-3
Inventory costing methods
(periodic)—FIFO and LIFO **LO3**

Hemming uses a periodic inventory system. Determine the costs assigned to ending inventory and to cost of goods sold using (a) FIFO and (b) LIFO. Compute the gross profit for each method.

Check Ending inventory: LIFO, $2,300

Martinez Co. reported the following current-year data for its only product. The company uses a periodic inventory system, and its ending inventory consists of 150 units—50 from each of the last three purchases. Determine the cost assigned to ending inventory and to cost of goods sold using (a) specific identification, (b) weighted average, (c) FIFO, and (d) LIFO. (Round per unit costs to three decimals, but inventory balances to the dollar.) Which method yields the highest net income?

Exercise 17-4
Inventory costing
methods—periodic **LO3**

Jan. 1	Beginning inventory	100 units @ $2.00 = $ 200
Mar. 7	Purchase	220 units @ $2.25 = 495
July 28	Purchase	540 units @ $2.50 = 1,350
Oct. 3	Purchase	480 units @ $2.80 = 1,344
Dec. 19	Purchase	160 units @ $2.90 = 464
	Totals	1,500 units $3,853

Check Inventory: FIFO, $435; LIFO, $313

Flora's Gifts reported the following current-year data for its only product. The company uses a periodic inventory system, and its ending inventory consists of 150 units—50 from each of the last three purchases. Determine the cost assigned to ending inventory and to cost of goods sold using (a) specific identification, (b) weighted average, (c) FIFO, and (d) LIFO. (Round per unit costs to three decimals, but inventory balances to the dollar.) Which method yields the lowest net income?

Exercise 17-5
Assigning costs to inventory—
periodic systems **LO3**

Jan. 1	Beginning inventory	140 units @ $3.00 = $ 420
Mar. 7	Purchase	300 units @ $2.80 = 840
July 28	Purchase	400 units @ $2.50 = 1,000
Oct. 3	Purchase	550 units @ $2.30 = 1,265
Dec. 19	Purchase	125 units @ $2.00 = 250
	Totals	1,515 units $3,775

Check Inventory: FIFO, $308;
LIFO, $448

Refer to the data in Exercise 17-3. Assume that ending inventory is made up of 45 units from the March 14 purchase, 75 units from the July 30 purchase, and all the units of the October 26 purchase. Using the specific identification method, calculate (a) the cost of goods sold and (b) the gross profit.

Exercise 17-6
Specific identification **LO3**

Exercise 17-7

Lower of cost or market   **L05**

Martinez Company's ending inventory includes the following items. Compute the lower of cost or market for ending inventory (*a*) as a whole and (*b*) applied separately to each product.

Product	Units	Per Unit	
		Cost	Market
Helmets	24	$50	$54
Bats	17	78	72
Shoes	38	95	91
Uniforms	42	36	36

Check   (*b*) $7,394

Exercise 17-8

Inventory turnover and days' sales in inventory   **L06**

Use the following information for Palmer Co. to compute inventory turnover for 2010 and 2009, and its days' sales in inventory at December 31, 2010 and 2009. (Round answers to the tenth place.) Comment on Palmer's efficiency in using its assets to increase sales from 2009 to 2010.

	2010	2009	2008
Cost of goods sold	$643,825	$426,650	$391,300
Ending inventory	97,400	87,750	92,500

Exercise 17-9

Comparing LIFO numbers to FIFO numbers; ratio analysis **L04**   **L06**

Cruz Company uses LIFO for inventory costing and reports the following financial data. It also recomputed inventory and cost of goods sold using FIFO for comparison purposes.

	2010	2009
LIFO inventory	$160	$110
LIFO cost of goods sold	740	680
FIFO inventory	240	145
FIFO cost of goods sold	660	645
Current assets (using LIFO)	220	180
Current liabilities	200	170

Check   (1) FIFO: Inventory turnover, 3.4 times

1. Compute its inventory turnover and days' sales in inventory for 2010 using (*a*) LIFO numbers and (*b*) FIFO numbers. (Round answers to the tenth place.)

2. Comment on and interpret the results of part 1.

Exercise 17-10ᴬ

Inventory costing— perpetual system   **L07**

Refer to Exercise 17-1 and assume the perpetual inventory system is used. Determine the costs assigned to ending inventory and to cost of goods sold using (*a*) specific identification, (*b*) weighted average, (*c*) FIFO, and (*d*) LIFO. (Round per unit costs to three decimals, but inventory balances to the dollar.)

Check   Ending inventory: LIFO, $1,020; WA, $1,008

Exercise 17-11ᴬ

Inventory costing— perpetual system   **L07**

Refer to Exercise 17-3 and assume the perpetual inventory system is used. Determine the costs assigned to ending inventory and to cost of goods sold using (*a*) FIFO and (*b*) LIFO. Compute the gross profit for each method.

Exercise 17-12ᴮ

Estimating ending inventory— gross profit method   **L08**

On January 1, JKR Store had $225,000 of inventory at cost. In the first quarter of the year, it purchased $795,000 of merchandise, returned $11,550, and paid freight charges of $18,800 on purchased merchandise. The store's gross profit averages 30%. The store had $1,000,000 of net sales (at retail) in the first quarter of the year. Use the gross profit method to estimate its cost of inventory at the end of the first quarter.

connect

Seminole Company began year 2010 with 25,000 units of product in its January 1 inventory costing $15 each. It made successive purchases of its product in year 2010 as follows. The company uses a periodic inventory system. On December 31, 2010, a physical count reveals that 40,000 units of its product remain in inventory.

Problem 17–1A

Alternative cost flows—periodic

LO3

Mar. 7	30,000 units @ $18 each
May 25	32,000 units @ $22 each
Aug. 1	22,000 units @ $24 each
Nov. 10	35,000 units @ $27 each

Required

1. Compute the number and total cost of the units available for sale in year 2010.

2. Compute the amounts assigned to the 2010 ending inventory and the cost of goods sold using (*a*) FIFO, (*b*) LIFO, and (*c*) weighted average. (Round per unit costs to three decimals, but inventory balances to the dollar.)

Check   (2) Cost of goods sold: FIFO, $2,027,000; LIFO, $2,447,000; WA, $2,233,120

QP Corp. sold 6,500 units of its product at $50 per unit in year 2010 and incurred operating expenses of $5 per unit in selling the units. It began the year with 700 units in inventory and made successive purchases of its product as follows.

Problem 17–2A

Income comparisons and cost flows—periodic   **LO3   LO4**

Jan. 1	Beginning inventory	700 units @ $18 per unit
Feb. 20	Purchase	1,600 units @ $19 per unit
May 16	Purchase	800 units @ $20 per unit
Oct. 3	Purchase	500 units @ $21 per unit
Dec. 11	Purchase	3,500 units @ $22 per unit
	Total	7,100 units

Required

1. Prepare comparative income statements similar to Exhibit 17.8 for the three inventory costing methods of FIFO, LIFO, and weighted average. Include a detailed cost of goods sold section as part of each statement. The company uses a periodic inventory system, and its income tax rate is 30%. (Round per unit costs to three decimals, but inventory balances to the dollar.)

2. How would the financial results from using the three alternative inventory costing methods change if QP had been experiencing declining costs in its purchases of inventory?

3. What advantages and disadvantages are offered by using (*a*) LIFO and (*b*) FIFO? Assume the continuing trend of increasing costs.

Check   (1) Net income: LIFO, $109,760; FIFO, $111,440; WA, $110,866

A physical inventory of Liverpool Unlimited taken at December 31 reveals the following.

Problem 17–3A

Lower of cost or market   **LO5**

		Per Unit	
Item	**Units**	**Cost**	**Market**
Audio equipment			
Receivers	345	$ 90	$ 98
CD players	260	111	100
MP3 players	326	86	95
Speakers	204	52	41
Video equipment			
Handheld LCDs	480	150	125
VCRs	291	93	84
Camcorders	212	310	322
Car audio equipment			
Satellite radios	185	70	84
CD/MP3 radios	170	97	105

Required

Calculate the lower of cost or market for the inventory (*a*) as a whole, (*b*) by major category, and (*c*) applied separately to each item.

Check   (b) $280,702; (c) $273,054

Problem 17-4A^A

Alternative cost flows—perpetual

LO7

Montoure Company uses a perpetual inventory system. It entered into the following calendar-year 2010 purchases and sales transactions.

Date	Activities	Units Acquired at Cost	Units Sold at Retail
Jan. 1	Beginning inventory	600 units @ $45/unit	
Feb. 10	Purchase	350 units @ $42/unit	
Mar. 13	Purchase	200 units @ $29/unit	
Mar. 15	Sales		600 units @ $75/unit
Aug. 21	Purchase	150 units @ $50/unit	
Sept. 5	Purchase	545 units @ $46/unit	
Sept. 10	Sales		650 units @ $75/unit
	Totals	1,845 units	1,250 units

Required

1. Compute cost of goods available for sale and the number of units available for sale.
2. Compute the number of units in ending inventory.

Check   (3) Ending inventory: FIFO, $27,570; LIFO, $27,000; WA, $26,422;

3. Compute the cost assigned to ending inventory using (*a*) FIFO, (*b*) LIFO, (*c*) specific identification— units sold consist of 500 units from beginning inventory, 300 from the February 10 purchase, 200 from the March 13 purchase, 50 from the August 21 purchase, and 200 from the September 5 purchase, and (*d*) weighted average. (Round per unit costs to three decimals, but inventory balances to the dollar.)

(4) LIFO gross profit, $40,680

4. Compute gross profit earned by the company for each of the four costing methods in part 3.
5. If the company's manager earns a bonus based on a percent of gross profit, which method of inventory costing will the manager likely prefer?

Problem 17-5A^B

Gross profit method   **LO8**

Wayward Company wants to prepare interim financial statements for the first quarter. The company wishes to avoid making a physical count of inventory. Wayward's gross profit rate averages 34%. The following information for the first quarter is available from its records.

January 1 beginning inventory	$ 302,580
Cost of goods purchased	941,040
Sales	1,211,160
Sales returns	8,398

Check   Estimated ending inventory, $449,797

Required

Use the gross profit method to estimate the company's first-quarter ending inventory.

PROBLEM SET B

Problem 17-1B

Alternative cost flows—periodic

LO3

Seneca Co. began year 2010 with 6,500 units of product in its January 1 inventory costing $35 each. It made successive purchases of its product in year 2010 as follows. The company uses a periodic inventory system. On December 31, 2010, a physical count reveals that 18,500 units of its product remain in inventory.

Jan. 4	11,500 units @ $33 each
May 18	13,400 units @ $32 each
July 9	11,000 units @ $29 each
Nov. 21	16,500 units @ $26 each

Required

1. Compute the number and total cost of the units available for sale in year 2010.

Check   (2) Cost of goods sold: FIFO, $1,296,800; LIFO, $1,160,800; WA, $1,223,527

2. Compute the amounts assigned to the 2010 ending inventory and the cost of goods sold using (*a*) FIFO, (*b*) LIFO, and (*c*) weighted average. (Round per unit costs to three decimals, but inventory balances to the dollar.)

Shepard Company sold 2,000 units of its product at $108 per unit in year 2010 and incurred operating expenses of $14 per unit in selling the units. It began the year with 840 units in inventory and made successive purchases of its product as follows.

Jan. 1	Beginning inventory	840 units @ $58 per unit
April 2	Purchase	600 units @ $59 per unit
June 14	Purchase	500 units @ $61 per unit
Aug. 29	Purchase	700 units @ $64 per unit
Nov. 18	Purchase	900 units @ $65 per unit
	Total	3,540 units

Problem 17–2B

Income comparisons and cost flows—periodic   LO3   LO4

Required

1. Prepare comparative income statements similar to Exhibit 17.8 for the three inventory costing methods of FIFO, LIFO, and weighted average. Include a detailed cost of goods sold section as part of each statement. The company uses a periodic inventory system, and its income tax rate is 30%. (Round per unit costs to three decimals, but inventory balances to the dollar.)

2. How would the financial results from using the three alternative inventory costing methods change if Shepard had been experiencing decreasing prices in its purchases of inventory?

3. What advantages and disadvantages are offered by using (a) LIFO and (b) FIFO? Assume the continuing trend of increasing costs.

Check   (1) Net income: LIFO, $42,210; FIFO, $48,678; WA, $45,417

A physical inventory of Office Necessities taken at December 31 reveals the following.

Problem 17–3B

Lower of cost or market   LO5

File Edit View Insert Format Tools Data Accounting Window Help

		Per Unit	
Item	**Units**	**Cost**	**Market**
Office furniture			
Desks	536	$261	$305
Credenzas	395	227	256
Chairs	687	49	43
Bookshelves	421	93	82
Filing cabinets			
Two-drawer	114	81	70
Four-drawer	298	135	122
Lateral	75	104	118
Office equipment			
Fax machines	370	168	200
Copiers	475	317	288
Telephones	302	125	117

Sheet1 / Sheet2 / Sheet3

Required

Compute the lower of cost or market for the inventory (a) as a whole, (b) by major category, and (c) applied separately to each item.

Check   (b) $601,697; (c) $580,054

Aloha Company uses a perpetual inventory system. It entered into the following calendar-year 2010 purchases and sales transactions.

Problem 17–4B[A]

Alternative cost flows—perpetual

LO7

Date	Activities	Units Acquired at Cost	Units Sold at Retail
Jan. 1	Beginning inventory	700 units @ $55/unit	
Jan. 10	Purchase	550 units @ $56/unit	
Feb. 13	Purchase	220 units @ $57/unit	
Feb. 15	Sales		900 units @ $90/unit
July 21	Purchase	270 units @ $58/unit	
Aug. 5	Purchase	445 units @ $59/unit	
Aug. 10	Sales		750 units @ $90/unit
	Total	2,185 units	1,650 units

Required

1. Compute cost of goods available for sale and the number of units available for sale.
2. Compute the number of units in ending inventory.

Check (3) Ending inventory: FIFO, $31,475; LIFO, $29,425; WA, $30,663;

3. Compute the cost assigned to ending inventory using (*a*) FIFO, (*b*) LIFO, (*c*) specific identification—units sold consist of 700 units from beginning inventory, 500 units from the January 10 purchase, 220 units from the February 13 purchase, 200 units from the July 21 purchase, and 30 units from the August 5 purchase, and (*d*) weighted average. (Round per unit costs to three decimals, but inventory balances to the dollar.)

(4) LIFO gross profit, $54,170

4. Compute gross profit earned by the company for each of the four costing methods in part 3.
5. If the company's manager earns a bonus based on a percent of gross profit, which method of inventory costing will the manager likely prefer?

Problem 17–5B[B]
Gross profit method   L08

Otingo Equipment Co. wants to prepare interim financial statements for the first quarter. The company wishes to avoid making a physical count of inventory. Otingo's gross profit rate averages 35%. The following information for the first quarter is available from its records.

January 1 beginning inventory	$ 802,880
Cost of goods purchased	2,209,630
Sales	3,760,250
Sales returns	79,300

Required

Check Estim. ending inventory, $619,892

Use the gross profit method to estimate the company's first quarter ending inventory.

SERIAL PROBLEM

Success Systems

(This serial problem began in Chapter 1 and continues through most of the book. If previous chapter segments were not completed, the serial problem can begin at this point.)

SP 17
Part A

Adriana Lopez of Success Systems is evaluating her inventory to determine whether it must be adjusted based on lower of cost or market rules. Lopez has three different types of software in her inventory and the following information is available for each.

		Per Unit	
Inventory Items	**Units**	**Cost**	**Market**
Office productivity	3	$ 75	$73
Desktop publishing	2	100	98
Accounting	3	85	90

Required

1. Compute the lower of cost or market for ending inventory assuming Lopez applies the lower of cost or market rule to inventory as a whole. Must Lopez adjust the reported inventory value? Explain.
2. Assume that Lopez had instead applied the lower of cost or market rule to each product in inventory. Under this assumption, must Lopez adjust the reported inventory value? Explain.

Part B

Selected accounts and balances for the three months ended March 31, 2010, for Success Systems follow.

January 1 beginning inventory	$	0
Cost of goods sold		14,272
March 31 ending inventory		680

Required

1. Compute inventory turnover and days' sales in inventory for the three months ended March 31, 2010.

2. Assess its performance if competitors average 10 times for inventory turnover and 29 days for days' sales in inventory.

BEYOND THE NUMBERS

BTN 17-1   Refer to **Best Buy**'s financial statements in Appendix A to answer the following.

REPORTING IN ACTION

LO2

Required

1. What amount of inventories did Best Buy hold as a current asset on March 1, 2008? On March 3, 2007?

2. Inventories represent what percent of total assets on March 1, 2008? On March 3, 2007?

3. Comment on the relative size of Best Buy's inventories compared to its other types of assets.

4. What accounting method did Best Buy use to compute inventory amounts on its balance sheet?

5. Compute inventory turnover for fiscal year ended March 1, 2008, and days' sales in inventory as of March 1, 2008.

Fast Forward

6. Access Best Buy's financial statements for fiscal years ended after March 1, 2008, from its Website (BestBuy.com) or the SEC's EDGAR database (www.SEC.gov). Answer questions 1 through 5 using the current Best Buy information and compare results to those prior years.

BTN 17-2   Key comparative figures ($ millions) for both **Best Buy** and **RadioShack** follow.

COMPARATIVE ANALYSIS

LO6

R RadioShack®

Key Figures	Best Buy			RadioShack		
	Current Year	One Year Prior	Two Years Prior	Current Year	One Year Prior	Two Years Prior
Inventory	$ 4,708	4,028	3,338	$ 705	752	965
Cost of sales	30,477	27,165	23,122	2,225	2,648	2,815

Required

1. Compute inventory turnover for both companies for the most recent two years shown.

2. Compute days' sales in inventory for both companies for the three years shown.

3. Comment on and interpret your findings from parts 1 and 2. Assume an industry average for inventory turnover of 5.5.

BTN 17-3   Golf Challenge Corp. is a retail sports store carrying golf apparel and equipment. The store is at the end of its second year of operation and is struggling. A major problem is that its cost of inventory has continually increased in the past two years. In the first year of operations, the store assigned inventory costs using LIFO. A loan agreement the store has with its bank, its prime source of financing, requires the store to maintain a certain profit margin and current ratio. The store's owner is currently looking over Golf Challenge's preliminary financial statements for its second year. The numbers are not favorable. The only way the store can meet the required financial ratios agreed on with the bank is to change from LIFO to FIFO. The store originally decided on LIFO because of its tax advantages. The owner recalculates ending inventory using FIFO and submits those numbers and statements to the loan officer at the bank for the required bank review. The owner thankfully reflects on the available latitude in choosing the inventory costing method.

ETHICS CHALLENGE

LO4

Required

1. How does Golf Challenge's use of FIFO improve its net profit margin and current ratio?

2. Is the action by Golf Challenge's owner ethical? Explain.

WORKPLACE COMMUNICATION
LO4

BTN 17–4   You are a financial adviser with a client in the wholesale produce business that just completed its first year of operations. Due to weather conditions, the cost of acquiring produce to resell has escalated during the later part of this period. Your client, Javonte Gish, mentions that because her business sells perishable goods, she has striven to maintain a FIFO flow of goods. Although sales are good, the increasing cost of inventory has put the business in a tight cash position. Gish has expressed concern regarding the ability of the business to meet income tax obligations.

Required

Prepare a memorandum that identifies, explains, and justifies the inventory method you recommend your client, Ms. Gish, adopt.

TAKING IT TO THE NET
LO6

BTN 17–5   Access the 2008 annual 10-K report for **Wal-Mart**. (Ticker WMT), filed on April 1, 2009, from the EDGAR filings at **www.SEC.gov** for the year ended January 31, 2009.

Required

1. What inventory method does Wal-Mart use? (*Hint:* See the notes to its financial statements.)
2. Compute Wal-Mart's inventory turnover and days' sales in inventory for the year ended January 31, 2009.
3. Wal-Mart is well known for its quick inventory turnover. If the industry average inventory turnover is 3.9, does Wal-Mart live up to its reputation?

TEAMWORK IN ACTION
LO3   LO4

> Step 1 allows four choices or areas for expertise. Larger teams will have some duplication of choice, but the specific identification method should not be duplicated.

BTN 17–6   Each team member has the responsibility to become an expert on an inventory method. This expertise will be used to facilitate teammates' understanding of the concepts relevant to that method.

1. Each learning team member should select an area for expertise by choosing one of the following inventory methods: specific identification, LIFO, FIFO, or weighted average.
2. Form expert teams made up of students who have selected the same area of expertise. The instructor will identify where each expert team will meet.
3. Using the following data, each expert team must collaborate to develop a presentation that illustrates the relevant concepts and procedures for its inventory method. Each team member must write the presentation in a format that can be shown to the learning team.

Data

Wiseman Company uses a perpetual inventory system. It had the following beginning inventory and current year purchases of its product.

Jan. 1	Beginning inventory	50 units @ $100 = $ 5,000
Jan. 14	Purchase	150 units @ $120 = 18,000
Apr. 30	Purchase	200 units @ $150 = 30,000
Sept. 26	Purchase	300 units @ $200 = 60,000

Wiseman Company transacted sales on the following dates at a $350 per unit sales price.

Jan. 10	30 units	(specific cost: 30 @ $100)
Feb. 15	100 units	(specific cost: 100 @ $120)
Oct. 5	350 units	(specific cost: 100 @ $150 and 250 @ $200)

Concepts and Procedures to Illustrate in Expert Presentation

a. Identify and compute the costs to assign to the units sold. (Round per unit costs to three decimals, but inventory balances to the dollar.)
b. Identify and compute the costs to assign to the units in ending inventory.
c. How likely is it that this inventory costing method will reflect the actual physical flow of goods? How relevant is that factor in determining whether this is an acceptable method to use?

d. What is the impact of this method versus others in determining net income and income taxes?

e. How closely does the ending inventory amount reflect replacement cost?

4. Re-form learning teams. In rotation, each expert is to present to the team the presentation developed in part 3. Experts are to encourage and respond to questions.

BTN 17-7 Review the chapter's opening feature highlighting Jacquelyn Tran and their company, **Beauty Encounter**. Assume that Beauty Encounter consistently maintains an inventory level of $300,000, meaning that its average and ending inventory levels are the same. Also assume its annual cost of sales is $1,200,000. To cut costs, Jacquelyn proposes to slash inventory to a constant level of $150,000 with no impact on cost of sales. They plan to work with suppliers to get quicker deliveries and to order smaller quantities more often.

ENTREPRENEURS IN BUSINESS
LO6

Required

1. Compute the company's inventory turnover and its days' sales in inventory under (*a*) current conditions and (*b*) proposed conditions.

2. Evaluate and comment on the merits of Jacquelyn's proposal given your analysis in part 1. Identify any concerns you might have about the proposal.

ANSWERS TO MULTIPLE CHOICE QUIZ

1. a; FIFO periodic—Ending inventory computation.
   105 units @ $28 each = $2,940; These units are from the July 15 purchase.

2. b; LIFO perpetual

Date	Goods Purchased	Cost of Goods Sold	Inventory Balance
July 1			75 units @ $25 = $ 1,875
July 3	348 units @ $27 = $9,396		75 units @ $25 348 units @ $27 } = $11,271
July 8		300 units @ $27 = $ 8,100	75 units @ $25 48 units @ $27 } = $ 3,171
July 15	257 units @ $28 = $7,196		75 units @ $25 48 units @ $27 257 units @ $28 } = $ 10,367
July 23		257 units @ $28 18 units @ $27 } = $ 7,682 $15,782	75 units @ $25 30 units @ $27 } = **$ 2,685**

3. e; Specific identification perpetual—Ending inventory computation.

20 units @ $25	$ 500
40 units @ $27	1,080
45 units @ $28	1,260
105 units	$2,840

4. e; Weighted average cost per unit = $27.16 (rounded).
   575 units sold × $27.16 = $15,617.

5. d; Days' sales in inventory = (Ending inventory/ Cost of goods sold × 365) = ($18,000/$85,000) × 365 = 77.29 days

Chapter 18

Plant Assets, Natural Resources, and Intangibles

Learning Objectives

LO 1   Describe plant assets and factors in accounting for them.

LO 2   Compute the reported cost of plant assets.

LO 3   Explain the factors that determine depreciation.

LO 4   Compute and record depreciation using the straight-line, units-of-production, declining-balance, and MACRS methods.

LO 5   Distinguish between and account for revenue expenditures and capital expenditures.

LO 6   Account for asset disposals and exchanges.

LO 7   Account for natural resources and their depletion.

LO 8   Account for intangible assets and their amortization.

LO 9   Compute total asset turnover and apply it for analysis.

"The best way to predict the future is to create it"
—Jeremy Black (from left: E. Nichols, R. Black, T. Baumgardner, J. Black)

Fruitful Assets

SAN CLEMENTE, CA—Surfing is the common bond for Ryan Black, Ed Nichols, and Jeremy Black. It also was the driving force for an excursion to ride the waves of Brazil. But what they encountered would change their lives forever.

The three surfers discovered beachgoers eating a purple berry called *acai* (ah-sigh-ee). "We too fell in love with it," says Ed. "We didn't want to leave Brazil without it." Adds Jeremy, "When people start eating acai, they want it . . . every day."

The three decided to become business missionaries and introduce acai to the masses. They launched **Sambazon (Sambazon.com),** short for Sustainable Management of the Brazilian Amazon, to manufacture and distribute acai. Scraping up just enough money, they started operations. Says Jeremy, "Financing our equipment, machinery, and other assets was a struggle as our operating cycle is long. We must pay cash to Brazilian acai growers, then pay for processing and shipping, and finally package and distribute acai products to buyers."

The power of the wave was with them. Sambazon now employs 120 workers, churns out numerous acai products, and generates nearly $20 million in annual sales. A continuing challenge is maintaining the right kind and amount of plant assets to meet demand and be profitable. Explains Jeremy, "Sambazon's success depends on monitoring and controlling plant asset costs, which range from bottling and packaging equipment to delivery vehicles, plant facilities, and land."

Sambazon must account for, manage, and recover all costs of long-term assets. "We built Sambazon on a triple bottom line business model . . . economic, environmental, and social," says Ryan. "[And we] recognize some things that are not just on our balance sheet."

Their success in asset management permits them to pursue other passions. "We've been given this incredible opportunity to make a lot of positive change with this berry," declares Jeremy. "It's not just a job . . . it's a mission!"

[Sources: *Sambazon Website,* January 2009; *The Wall Street Journal,* March 2007; *San Clemente Times,* March 2006; *CU Business Portfolio,* Spring 2007; *Entrepreneur,* November 2007]

This chapter focuses on long-term assets used to operate a company. These assets can be grouped into plant assets, natural resource assets, and intangible assets. Plant assets are a major investment for most companies. They make up a large part of assets on most balance sheets, and they yield depreciation, often one of the largest expenses on income statements. The acquisition or building of a plant asset is often referred to as a *capital expenditure*. Capital expenditures are important events because they impact both the short- and long-term success of a company. Natural resource assets and intangible assets have similar impacts. This chapter describes the purchase and use of these assets. We also explain what distinguishes these assets from other types of assets, how to determine their cost, how to allocate their costs to periods benefiting from their use, and how to dispose of them.

Plant Assets, Natural Resources, and Intangibles

Plant Assets
- Cost determination
- Depreciation
- Additional expenditures
- Disposals

Natural Resources
- Cost determination and depletion
- Plant assets used in extracting resources

Intangible Assets
- Cost determination and amortization
- Types of intangibles

Section 1—Plant Assets

Plant assets are tangible assets used in a company's operations that have a useful life of more than one accounting period. Plant assets are also called *plant and equipment; property, plant, and equipment;* or *fixed assets.* For many companies, plant assets make up the single largest class of assets they own. Exhibit 18.1 shows plant assets as a percent of total assets for several companies. Not only do they make up a large percent of these companies' assets, but their dollar values are large. **McDonald's** plant assets, for instance, are reported at more than $20 billion, and **Wal-Mart** reports plant assets of more than $85 billion.

Exhibit 18.1

Plant Assets of Selected Companies

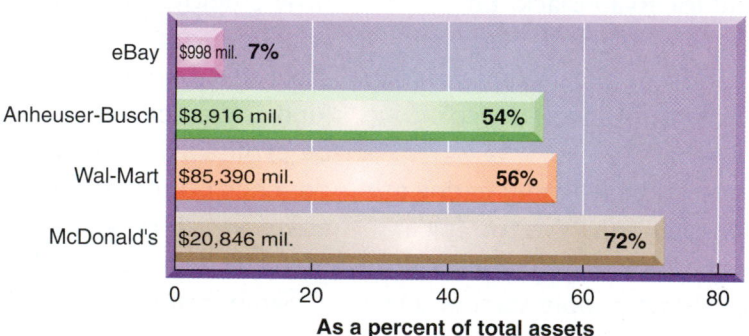

As a percent of total assets

LO1 Describe plant assets and factors in accounting for them.

Plant assets differ from other assets in two key ways. First, *plant assets are used in operations*. This makes them different from, for instance, inventory that is held for sale and not used in operations. The distinctive feature here is use, not type of asset. A company that purchases a computer to resell it reports it on the balance sheet as inventory. If the same company purchases this computer to use in operations, it is a plant asset.

Second, *plant assets have useful lives extending over more than one accounting period.* This makes plant assets different from current assets such as supplies that are normally consumed in a short time period after they are placed in use.

The accounting for plant assets reflects these two features. Since plant assets are used in operations, we try to match their costs against the revenues they generate. Also, since their useful lives extend over more than one period, this matching extends over several periods. Specifically, we value plant assets (balance sheet effect) and then allocate their costs to periods benefiting from their use (income statement effect). Allocation means spreading the initial cost of a plant asset over several future accounting periods.

It can help to view plant assets as prepaid expenses that benefit several future accounting periods.

Exhibit 18.2 shows four main issues in accounting for plant assets: (1) computing the costs of plant assets, (2) allocating the costs of plant assets (less any salvage amounts) against revenues for the periods they benefit, (3) accounting for expenditures such as repairs and improvements to plant assets, and (4) recording the disposal of plant assets. The following sections discuss these issues.

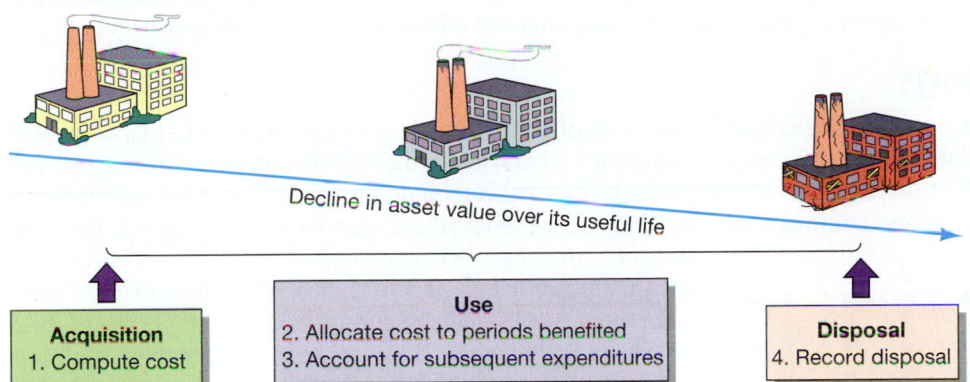

Decline in asset value over its useful life

Acquisition	**Use**	**Disposal**
1. Compute cost	2. Allocate cost to periods benefited 3. Account for subsequent expenditures	4. Record disposal

Exhibit 18.2

Issues in Accounting for Plant Assets

Cost Determination

Plant assets are recorded at cost when acquired. **Cost** includes all normal and reasonable expenditures necessary to get the asset in place and ready for its intended use. The cost of a factory machine, for instance, includes its invoice cost less any cash discount for early payment, plus any necessary freight, unpacking, assembling, installing, and testing costs. Examples are the costs of building a base or foundation for a machine, providing electrical hook-ups, and testing the machine before using it in operations. Only necessary expenditures are included in an asset's cost.

If an asset is damaged during unpacking, the repairs are not added to its cost. Instead, they are expensed. A paid traffic fine for moving heavy machinery on city streets without a proper permit is expensed; payment for a proper permit is included in the cost of machinery. Costs are sometimes incurred to modify or customize a new plant asset. These amounts are added to the asset's cost. We explain in this section how to determine the cost of plant assets for each of its four major classes: land, land improvements, buildings, and machinery and equipment.

Land

The cost of land includes the total amount paid for the land. This includes any real estate commissions, title insurance fees, legal fees, and any accrued property taxes paid by the purchaser. Payments for surveying, clearing, grading, and draining also are included in the cost of land. Other costs include government assessments for items such as public roadways, sewers, and sidewalks. These assessments are included because they permanently add to the land's value.

LO2 Compute the reported cost of plant assets.

Land Purchased with Structures Land purchased as a building site sometimes includes structures that must be removed. In such cases, the total purchase price is charged to the Land account. The cost of removing the structures, less any amounts recovered through sale of salvaged materials, is also added to the cost of Land. To illustrate, assume that **Starbucks** paid $167,000 cash to acquire land for a retail store. This land had an old service garage that was removed at a net cost of $13,000 ($15,000 in costs less $2,000 proceeds from salvaged materials). Closing costs included brokerage fees ($8,000), legal fees ($1,500), and title costs ($500). All of these costs are normal, reasonable, and necessary to get the land ready to hold a retail store. The cost of this land to Starbucks is $190,000 and is computed as shown in Exhibit 18.3.

Exhibit 18.3

Computing Cost of Land

Cash price of land	$ 167,000
Net cost of garage removal	13,000
Closing costs	10,000
Cost of land	**$190,000**

Land Improvements

Land has an unlimited life and is not usually used up over time. **Land improvements** such as parking lot surfaces, driveways, fences, shrubs, and lighting systems, however, have limited useful lives and are used up. While these improvements increase the usefulness of the land, their costs are added to a separate Land Improvement account and allocated to the periods they benefit.

Buildings

A Building account is charged for the costs of purchasing or constructing a building that is used in operations. When purchased, a building's costs usually include its purchase price, brokerage fees, taxes, title fees, and attorney fees. Its costs also include all expenditures to ready it for its intended use, including any necessary repairs or renovations such as wiring, lighting, flooring,

and wall coverings. When a company constructs a building or any plant asset for its own use, its costs include materials and labor plus a reasonable amount of indirect *overhead cost*. Overhead includes the costs of items such as heat, lighting, power, and depreciation on machinery used to construct the asset. Costs of construction also include design fees, building permits, and insurance *during* construction. However, costs such as insurance to cover the asset *after* it is placed in use are operating expenses.

Machinery and Equipment

The costs of machinery and equipment consist of all costs normal and necessary to purchase them and prepare them for their intended use. These include the purchase price, taxes, transportation charges, insurance while in transit, and the installing, assembling, and testing of the machinery and equipment.

Assigning Cost in a Lump-Sum Purchase

Plant assets sometimes are purchased as a group in a single transaction for a lump-sum price. This is called a *lump-sum purchase,* or *group, bulk,* or *basket purchase.* Here we do not have an individual cost for each asset. We allocate the cost of the purchase among the different types of assets acquired based on their *relative market values*. Market values can be estimated by an appraiser or the tax-assessed valuations can be used. To illustrate, assume Honeywell paid $90,000 cash on January 1 to acquire a group of assets consisting of land appraised at $30,000, land improvements appraised at $10,000, and a building appraised at $60,000. The total appraised value of the assets is $100,000, but the cost of the basket purchase is only $90,000. The $90,000 cost is allocated on the basis of these appraised values as shown in Exhibit 18.4.

Exhibit 18.4

Computing Costs in a Lump-Sum Purchase

	Appraised Value	Percent of Total	Allocated Cost
Land	$ 30,000	30% ($30,000/$100,000)	**$27,000** ($90,000 × 30%)
Land improvements	10,000	10 ($10,000/$100,000)	9,000 ($90,000 × 10%)
Building	60,000	60 ($60,000/$100,000)	**54,000** ($90,000 × 60%)
Totals	$100,000	100%	$ 90,000

The journal entry to record this lump-sum purchase is

Assets = Liabilities + Equity
+27,000
 +9,000
+54,000
−90,000

Jan.	1	Land		27 0 0 0 00	
		Land Improvements		9 0 0 0 00	
		Building		54 0 0 0 00	
		Cash			90 0 0 0 00
		To record cost of assets purchased as a lump sum.			

Answers—p. 469

HOW YOU DOIN'?

1. Identify the asset class for each of the following: (*a*) supplies, (*b*) office equipment, (*c*) inventory, (*d*) land for future expansion, and (*e*) trucks used in operations. Classify each asset as either a current asset, plant asset, or long-term investment.

2. Identify the asset account debited for each of the following: (*a*) purchase price of a vacant lot to be used in operations and (*b*) cost of paving that same vacant lot.

3. Compute the amount recorded as the cost of a new machine given the following payments related to its purchase: gross purchase price, $700,000; sales tax, $49,000; purchase discount taken, $21,000; freight cost paid by buyer—terms FOB shipping point, $3,500; normal assembly costs, $3,000; cost of necessary machine platform, $2,500; cost of parts used in maintaining machine, $4,200.

Depreciation

Depreciation is the process of allocating the cost of a plant asset to expense in the accounting periods benefiting from its use. Depreciation does not measure the actual decline in the asset's market value each period, nor does it measure the asset's physical deterioration. Depreciation is the attempt to allocate a plant asset's cost to the income statement in a reasonable way. Depreciation charges are recorded only when the asset is actually in service. This section describes the factors that determine depreciation.

Factors in Computing Depreciation

Factors that determine depreciation are (1) cost, (2) salvage value, and (3) useful life.

LO3 Explain the factors that determine depreciation.

Cost   The **cost** of a plant asset includes all necessary and reasonable expenditures to acquire it and to prepare it for its intended use.

Salvage Value   The total amount of depreciation to be allocated over an asset's benefit period equals the asset's cost minus its salvage value. **Salvage value,** also called *residual value* or *scrap value*, is an estimate of the asset's value at the end of its benefit period. This is the amount the owner expects to receive from disposing of the asset at the end of its benefit period. If the asset is expected to be traded in on a new asset, its salvage value is the expected trade-in value.

> If we expect additional costs in preparing a plant asset for disposal, the salvage value equals the expected amount from disposal less any disposal costs.

Useful Life   The **useful life** of a plant asset is the length of time it is productively used in a company's operations. Useful life, also called *service life*, might not be as long as the asset's total productive life. For example, the productive life of a computer can be eight years or more. Some companies, however, trade in old computers for new ones every two years. In this case, these computers have a two-year useful life for depreciation purposes. The cost of these computers (less their expected trade-in values) is charged to depreciation expense over a two-year period.

A company is best able to predict a new asset's useful life when it has past experience with a similar asset. When it has no such experience, a company relies on the experience of others or on engineering studies and judgment.

IN THE NEWS

Life Line   Life expectancy of plant assets is often in the eye of the beholder. For instance, **Hershey Foods** and **Tootsie Roll** are competitors, yet their equipment's life expectancies are different. Hershey depreciates equipment over 3 to 15 years, but Tootsie Roll depreciates them over 5 to 20 years. Such differences markedly impact financial statements.

Depreciation Methods

Depreciation methods allocate a plant asset's cost to expense over its useful life. The most frequently used method of depreciation is the straight-line method. Another common depreciation method is the units-of-production method. We explain both of these methods in this section. This section also describes accelerated depreciation methods, with a focus on the declining-balance method.

The computations in this section use information about a machine that inspects athletic shoes before packaging. Manufacturers such as **Converse**, **Reebok**, **Adidas**, and **Fila** use this machine. Data for this machine are in Exhibit 18.5.

Cost	$10,000
Salvage value	1,000
Depreciable cost	$ 9,000
Useful life	
Accounting periods	5 years
Units inspected	36,000 shoes

LO4 Compute and record depreciation using the straight-line, units-of-production, declining-balance, and MACRS methods.

Straight-Line Method   **Straight-line depreciation** charges the same amount of expense to each period of the asset's useful life. A two-step process is used. We first compute the *depreciable cost* of the asset; this amount is also called the *cost to be depreciated*. It equals the asset's cost minus its salvage value. Second, depreciable cost is divided by the number of accounting periods in the asset's useful life. The formula for straight-line depreciation, along with its computation for the inspection machine described above, is shown in Exhibit 18.6.

$$\frac{\text{Cost} - \text{Salvage value}}{\text{Useful life in periods}} = \frac{\$10,000 - \$1,000}{5 \text{ years}} = \$1,800 \text{ per year}$$

If this machine is purchased on December 31, 2009, and used throughout its predicted useful life of five years, the straight-line method allocates $1,800 of depreciation expense to each of the years 2010 through 2014. We make the following adjusting entry at the end of each of the five years to record straight-line depreciation of this machine:

Assets = Liabilities + Equity
−1,800   −1,800

Dec.	31	Depreciation Expense	1 8 0 0 00	
		Accumulated Depreciation—Machinery		1 8 0 0 00
		To record annual depreciation.		

The $1,800 Depreciation Expense is reported on the income statement among operating expenses. The $1,800 Accumulated Depreciation is a contra asset account to the Machinery account in the balance sheet. The graph on the left in Exhibit 18.7 shows the $1,800 per year of depreciation expense reported in each of the five years. The graph on the right shows the amounts reported on each of the six December 31 balance sheets while the company owns the asset.

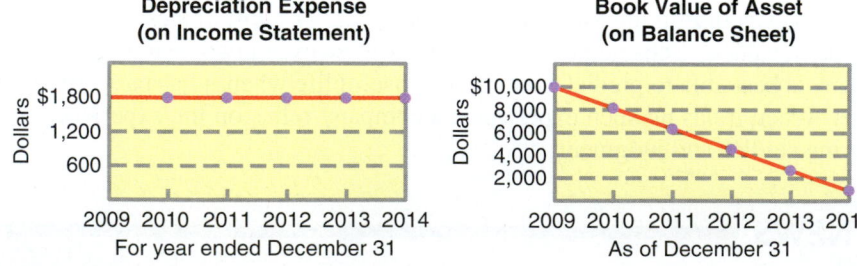

The net balance sheet amount is the asset's **book value.** It equals the plant asset's total cost less its accumulated depreciation. For example, at the end of year 2 (December 31, 2011), the asset's book value is $6,400, and it is reported in the balance sheet as follows:

Machinery	$10,000	
Less accumulated depreciation	3,600	$6,400

The book value of this machine declines by $1,800 each year due to depreciation. At the end of this asset's useful life its book value ($1,000) equals its salvage value. From the graphs in Exhibit 18.7 we see why this method is called straight line.

Units–of–Production Method The straight-line method charges an equal amount of an asset's cost to expense in each period. If plant assets are used up in about equal amounts each accounting period, this method produces a reasonable matching of expenses with revenues. However, the use of some plant assets varies greatly from one period to the next. A builder, for instance, might use a piece of construction equipment for a month and then not use it again for several months. When equipment use varies from period to period, the units-of-production depreciation method can better match expenses with revenues. **Units-of-production depreciation** charges a different amount to expense for each period of an asset's useful life depending on its usage.

A two-step process is used to compute units-of-production depreciation. We first compute *depreciation per unit* by subtracting the asset's salvage value from its total cost and then dividing by the total number of units expected to be produced during its useful life. Units of production can be expressed in product or other units such as hours used or miles driven. The second step is to compute depreciation expense for the period by multiplying the units produced in the period by the depreciation per unit. The formula for units-of-production depreciation, along with its computation for the machine described in Exhibit 18.5, is shown in Exhibit 18.8. (7,000 shoes are inspected and sold in its first year.)

> **Accumulated Depreciation is a permanent account. It is not closed at the end of an accounting period.**

> **Exhibit 18.8**
>
> Units-of-Production Depreciation Formula and Example

Step 1

$$\text{Depreciation per unit} = \frac{\text{Cost} - \text{Salvage value}}{\text{Total units of production}} = \frac{\$10,000 - \$1,000}{36,000 \text{ shoes}} = \$0.25 \text{ per shoe}$$

Step 2

$$\text{Depreciation expense} = \text{Depreciation per unit} \times \text{Units produced in period}$$
$$\$0.25 \text{ per shoe} \times 7,000 \text{ shoes} = \$1,750$$

Assume that the following numbers of shoes are made from 2009 through 2014: 2009, 0; 2010, 7,000; 2011, 8,000; 2012, 9,000; 2013, 7,000; and 2014, 5,000. Depreciation expense for 2011 is $2,000 (8,000 shoes at $0.25 per shoe). Book value at the end of 2011 is $6,250 ($10,000 − $1,750 − $2,000). Amounts for the other years are computed similarly. Exhibit 18.9 graphs the depreciation expense and book value amounts reported in the financial statements in each of the six years the company owns the asset.

> **Refer to Exhibit 18.9. If the number of shoes inspected in 2014 is 5,500, what is depreciation expense for that year?** *Answer:* $1,250 (never depreciate below salvage value)

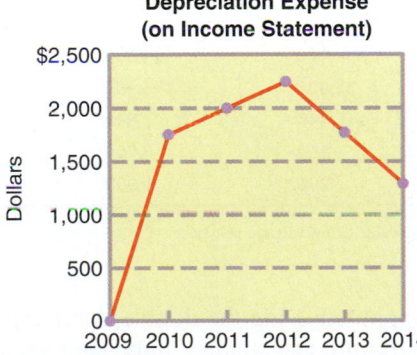

Depreciation Expense (on Income Statement)

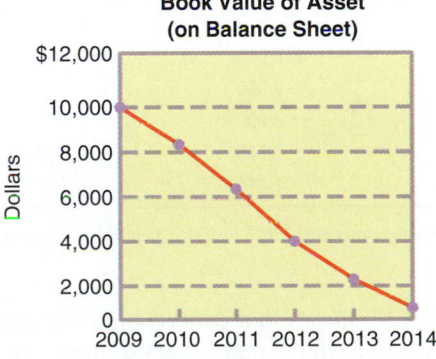

Book Value of Asset (on Balance Sheet)

> **Exhibit 18.9**
>
> Financial Statement Effects of Units-of-Production Depreciation

Exhibit 18.9 shows that (1) depreciation expense depends on unit output, and (2) book value declines in each period until it equals salvage value at the end of the asset's useful life.

Do not subtract salvage value in computing depreciation expense with declining-balance methods.

Declining–Balance Method

An **accelerated depreciation method** yields larger depreciation expenses in the early years of an asset's life and less depreciation in later years. The most common is the **declining-balance method** which uses a depreciation rate that is a multiple of the straight-line rate. This rate is multiplied by the asset's beginning-of-period book value. The amount of depreciation declines each period because book value declines each period to compute depreciation expense.

A common method is the *double-declining-balance (DDB)* method. It is applied in three steps: (1) compute the asset's straight-line depreciation rate (100% divided by the number of periods in the asset's useful life), (2) double the straight-line rate, and (3) compute depreciation expense by multiplying this rate by the asset's beginning-of-period book value. To illustrate, let's return to the machine in Exhibit 18.5 and apply the double-declining-balance method to compute depreciation expense. Exhibit 18.10 shows the first-year depreciation computation for the machine. The three-step process is to (1) divide 100% by five years to determine the straight-line depreciation rate of 20% per year, (2) double this 20% rate to get the double-declining-balance rate of 40% per year, and (3) compute depreciation expense as 40% multiplied by the beginning-of-period book value.

Exhibit 18.10

Double-Declining-Balance Depreciation Method

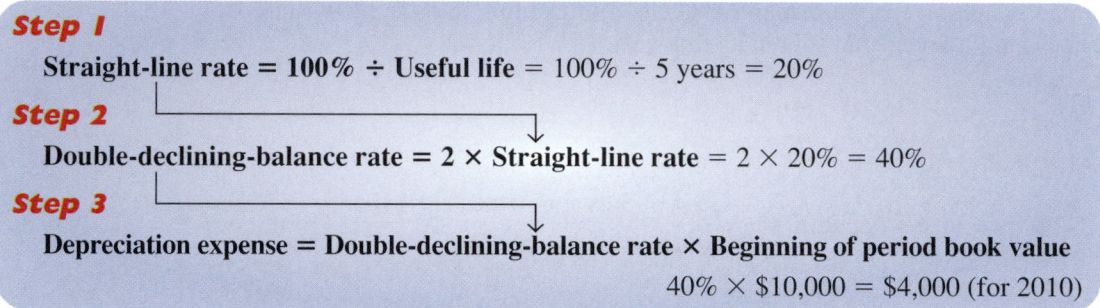

Step 1

Straight-line rate = 100% ÷ Useful life = 100% ÷ 5 years = 20%

Step 2

Double-declining-balance rate = 2 × Straight-line rate = 2 × 20% = 40%

Step 3

Depreciation expense = Double-declining-balance rate × Beginning of period book value

40% × $10,000 = $4,000 (for 2010)

The *double-declining-balance depreciation schedule* is shown in Exhibit 18.11. The schedule follows the formula except for year 2014, when depreciation expense is $296. This $296 is not equal to 40% × $1,296, or $518.40. If we had used the $518.40 for depreciation expense in 2014, ending book value would equal $777.60, which is less than the $1,000 salvage value. Instead, the $296 is computed by subtracting the $1,000 salvage value from the $1,296 book value at the beginning of the fifth year (the year when DDB depreciation cuts into salvage value).

Exhibit 18.11

Double-Declining-Balance Depreciation Schedule

Annual Period	Depreciation for the Period			End of Period	
	Beginning of Period Book Value	Depreciation Rate	Depreciation Expense	Accumulated Depreciation	Book Value
2009	—	—	—	—	$10,000
2010	$10,000	40%	**$4,000**	$4,000	6,000
2011	6,000	40	**2,400**	6,400	3,600
2012	3,600	40	**1,440**	7,840	2,160
2013	2,160	40	**864**	8,704	1,296
2014	1,296	40	**296***	9,000	**1,000**

* Year 2014 depreciation is $1,296 − $1,000 = $296 (never depreciate book value below salvage value).

Exhibit 18.11 shows that depreciation expense computed using the double-declining balance method is larger in the early years of the asset's useful life and smaller in the later years.

Comparing Depreciation Methods

Exhibit 18.12 shows depreciation expense for each year of the machine's useful life under each of the three depreciation methods. While the amount of depreciation expense per period differs for different methods, *total depreciation expense is the same over the machine's useful life.* The straight-line method yields a steady pattern of depreciation

Period	Straight-Line	Units-of-Production	Double-Declining-Balance
2010	$1,800	$1,750	$4,000
2011	1,800	2,000	2,400
2012	1,800	2,250	1,440
2013	1,800	1,750	864
2014	1,800	1,250	296
Totals	**$9,000**	**$9,000**	**$9,000**

Exhibit 18.12

Depreciation Expense for the Different Methods

expense while the units-of-production depreciation depends on the number of units produced. Each of these methods is acceptable because it allocates cost in a systematic and rational manner.

Each method starts with a total cost of $10,000 and ends with a book value of $1,000. The book value at the end of the asset's useful life equals its salvage value.

IN THE NEWS

In Vogue   About 85% of companies use straight-line depreciation for plant assets, 4% use units-of-production, and 4% use declining-balance. Another 7% use an unspecified accelerated method—most likely declining-balance.

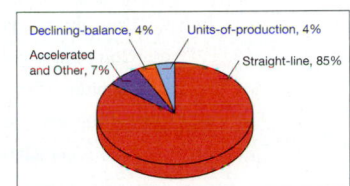

Partial-Year Depreciation

When an asset is purchased (or disposed of) at a time other than the beginning or end of an accounting period, depreciation is recorded for part of a year.

To illustrate, assume that the machine in Exhibit 18.5 is purchased and placed in service on October 8, 2009, and the annual accounting period ends on December 31. Since this machine is purchased and used for nearly three months in 2009, the calendar-year income statement should report depreciation expense on the machine for three months. Normally, depreciation assumes that the asset is purchased on the first day of the month nearest the actual date of purchase. In this case, since the purchase occurred on October 8, we assume an October 1 purchase date. This means that three months' depreciation is recorded in 2009. Using straight-line depreciation, we compute three months' depreciation of $450 as follows.

$$\frac{\$10,000 - \$1,000}{5 \text{ years}} \times \frac{3}{12} = \$450$$

Change in Estimates for Depreciation

Depreciation is based on estimates of salvage value and useful life. During the useful life of an asset, new information may indicate that these estimates are inaccurate. If our estimate of an asset's useful life and/or salvage value changes, what should we do? Use the new estimate to compute depreciation for current and future periods. This approach is used for all depreciation methods.

Let's return to the machine described in Exhibit 18.5 using straight-line depreciation. At the beginning of this asset's third year, its book value is $6,400, computed as $10,000 minus $3,600. Assume that at the beginning of its third year, the estimated number of years remaining in its useful life changes from three to four years *and* its estimate of salvage value changes from $1,000 to $400. Straight-line depreciation for each of the four remaining years is computed as shown in Exhibit 18.13.

> Remaining depreciable cost equals book value less revised salvage value at the point of revision.

> Income is overstated (and depreciation understated) when useful life is too high; a useful life that is too low yields opposite results.

$$\frac{\text{Book value} - \text{Revised salvage value}}{\text{Revised remaining useful life}} = \frac{\$6,400 - \$400}{4 \text{ years}} = \$1,500 \text{ per year}$$

Exhibit 18.13

Computing Revised Straight-Line Depreciation

Thus, $1,500 of depreciation expense is recorded for the machine at the end of the third through sixth years—each year of its remaining useful life. We do not go back and restate prior years' financial statements for this type of new information. Revising an estimate of the useful life or salvage value of a plant asset is referred to as a **change in an accounting estimate.** These changes are reflected in current and future financial statements, not in prior statements.

Impairment of Property, Plant, and Equipment

Sometimes new information indicates that a plant asset's book value exceeds its *fair value,* an estimate of the asset's current worth. This asset is said to be **impaired.** The company must record a loss from impairment to reduce the book value of its plant assets. The procedures for measuring and recording impairment losses are discussed in advanced courses.

Reporting Depreciation

Both the cost and accumulated depreciation of plant assets are reported on the balance sheet or in its notes. **Yahoo!**, for instance, reports the following.

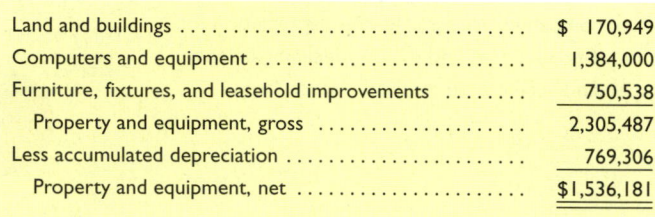

Land and buildings	$ 170,949
Computers and equipment	1,384,000
Furniture, fixtures, and leasehold improvements	750,538
Property and equipment, gross	2,305,487
Less accumulated depreciation	769,306
Property and equipment, net	$1,536,181

> A company usually keeps records for each asset showing its cost and depreciation to date. The combined records for individual assets are a type of *plant asset subsidiary ledger.*

Many companies also show plant assets on one line with the net amount of cost less accumulated depreciation. For example, Yahoo! could report $1,536,181 of net property and equipment in its balance sheet. When this is done, the amount of accumulated depreciation is disclosed in a footnote.

Reporting both the cost and accumulated depreciation of plant assets helps users compare the assets of different companies. For example, a company holding assets costing $50,000 and accumulated depreciation of $40,000 is likely different from a company with new assets costing $10,000. While the net undepreciated cost of $10,000 is the same in both cases, the first company likely is facing the need to replace older assets.

Depreciation for Tax Purposes

> Companies often use different accounting methods for financial accounting versus tax purposes.

The records a company keeps for financial accounting purposes are usually separate from those it keeps for tax purposes. Financial accounting aims to report useful information on financial performance and position. Tax accounting reflects government objectives in raising revenues and encouraging certain behaviors. Differences between these two accounting systems are normal and expected.

Depreciation is a common example of where accounting records differ. Many companies use accelerated depreciation for tax purposes. This reduces the company's taxable income in the early years of the asset's life, lowering the company's tax payments in those years. The company thus *postpones* tax payments and uses the extra resources now to earn more income. The same company often uses straight-line depreciation for financial reporting purposes.

> Companies prefer to pay taxes later rather than sooner, whenever legal and possible.

Modified Accelerated Cost Recovery System (MACRS) For assets purchased after December 31, 1986, depreciation for U.S. federal income tax purposes follows the **Modified Accelerated Cost Recovery System (MACRS).** This system separates assets into classes, based on their useful lives. A depreciation rate is then defined for each class. These rates use accelerated depreciation methods for many assets.

Exhibit 18.14 presents a table of depreciation rates for several common MACRS asset classes. The depreciation expense for tax purposes (also called *cost recovery*) for a given year is the depreciation rate for that year multiplied by the asset's cost. MACRS ignores salvage values. MACRS also uses a half-year convention. This means that a half-year of depreciation is taken in

Class	5-Year Class	7-Year Class	15-Year Class	27.5-Year Class	39-Year Class
Example	Autos, taxis, computers, office	Office furniture and fixtures	Land improvements (fences)	Residential rental property	Office buildings, warehouses
Method	200% declining balance	200% declining balance	150% declining balance	Straight-line	Straight-line
Year	Rate Used to Compute Annual Depreciation Expense				
1	20.00	14.28	5.00	3.64	2.56
2	32.00	24.49	9.50	3.64	2.56
3	19.20	17.49	8.55	3.64	2.56
4	11.52*	12.49	7.69	3.64	2.56
5	11.52	8.93*	6.93	3.64	2.56
6	5.76	8.93	6.23	3.64	2.56
7		8.93	5.90*	3.64	2.56
8		4.46	5.90	3.64	2.56
9			5.90	3.64	2.56
10			5.90	3.64	2.56
11			5.90	3.64	2.56
12			5.90	3.64	2.56
13			5.90	3.64	2.56
14			5.90	3.64	2.56
15			5.90	3.64	2.56
28				1.72	2.56
39					2.56

* The company switches to straight-line when it yields a depreciation expense higher than the declining-balance method.

Exhibit 18.14

MACRS Cost Recovery Rates for Certain Asset Classes

the first year of the asset's life, no matter when it was purchased during that year. The remaining half-year of depreciation is taken in the year after the last year of the asset's life. Finally, the MACRS tables assume a switch to the straight-line method at some point in the asset's life. MACRS is not acceptable for financial reporting because it often allocates costs over an arbitrary period that is less than the asset's useful life.

Return to our example of a $10,000 shoe inspection machine with a five-year useful life. This asset is assigned to the five-year class for tax purposes. Depreciation in the year of purchase is $2,000 ($10,000 × 0.20). This is true even though the asset was purchased on the last day of 2009. Exhibit 18.15 shows the depreciation for each of the years 2009 through 2014. We see that MACRS ignores salvage value, and the sum of the annual depreciation equals the cost of the asset ($10,000).

Year	Original Cost		MACRS Percentage		Cost Recovery
2009	$10,000	×	20.00	=	$ 2,000
2010	10,000	×	32.00	=	3,200
2011	10,000	×	19.20	=	1,920
2012	10,000	×	11.52	=	1,152
2013	10,000	×	11.52	=	1,152
2014	10,000	×	5.76	=	576
					$10,000

Exhibit 18.15

MACRS Cost Recovery Schedule

Answers—p. 469

HOW YOU DOIN'?

4. On January 1, 2011, a company pays $77,000 to purchase office furniture with a zero salvage value. The furniture's useful life is somewhere between 7 and 10 years. What is the year 2011 straight-line depreciation on the furniture using (a) a 7-year useful life and (b) a 10-year useful life? What is the 2011 depreciation under MACRS if the asset is assigned to the 7-year asset class?

5. What does the term *depreciation* mean in accounting?

6. A company purchases a machine for $96,000 on January 1, 2011. Its useful life is five years or 100,000 units of product, and its salvage value is $8,000. During 2011, 10,000 units of product are produced. Compute the book value of this machine on December 31, 2011, assuming (a) straight-line depreciation and (b) units-of-production depreciation.

7. In early January 2011, a company acquires equipment for $3,800. The company estimates this equipment to have a useful life of three years and a salvage value of $200. Early in 2013, the company changes its estimates to a total four-year useful life and zero salvage value. Using the straight-line method, what is depreciation for the year ended 2013?

Section 2—Additional Expenditures and Asset Disposals

Additional Expenditures

LO5 Distinguish between and account for revenue expenditures and capital expenditures.

Plant assets require additional expenditures for their operation, maintenance, repair, and improvement. The company must decide whether to capitalize or expense these expenditures. To capitalize an expenditure is to debit an asset account. The issue is whether more useful information is provided by reporting these expenditures as current period expenses or by adding them to the plant asset's cost and depreciating them over its remaining useful life.

Revenue expenditures, also called *income statement expenditures,* are additional costs of plant assets that do not materially increase the asset's life or productive capabilities. They are recorded as expenses and deducted from revenues in the current period's income statement. Examples of revenue expenditures are cleaning, repainting, adjustments, and lubricants. **Capital expenditures,** also called *balance sheet expenditures,* are additional costs of plant assets that provide benefits extending beyond the current period. They are debited to asset accounts and reported on the balance sheet. Capital expenditures increase or improve the type or amount of service an asset provides. Examples are roofing replacement, plant expansion, and major overhauls of machinery and equipment.

Financial statements are affected for several years by the accounting choice of recording costs as either revenue expenditures or capital expenditures. Managers must be careful in classifying them. This classification decision is based on whether these expenditures are identified as either ordinary repairs or as betterments and extraordinary repairs.

> When an amount is said to be *capitalized* to an account, the amount is added to the account's normal balance.

Financial Statement Effect			
Cost Category	Accounting	Expense Timing	Current Income
Revenue expenditure	Income stmt. account debited	Expensed currently	Lower
Capital expenditure	Balance sheet account debited	Expensed in future	Higher

> Many companies apply the *materiality principle* to treat *low-cost plant assets* (say, less than $500) as revenue expenditures.

Ordinary Repairs

Ordinary repairs are expenditures to keep an asset in normal, good operating condition. They are necessary if an asset is to perform to expectations over its useful life. Ordinary repairs do not extend an asset's useful life beyond its original estimate or increase its productivity beyond original expectations. Examples are normal costs of cleaning, lubricating, adjusting, and replacing small parts of a machine. Ordinary repairs are treated as *revenue expenditures.*

Betterments and Extraordinary Repairs

Accounting for betterments and extraordinary repairs is similar. **Betterments,** also called *improvements,* are expenditures that make a plant asset more efficient or productive. A betterment often involves adding a component to an asset or replacing one of its old components with a better one. A betterment does not always increase an asset's useful life. An example is replacing manual controls on a machine with automatic controls. One special type of betterment is an *addition,* such as adding a new wing or dock to a warehouse. Since a betterment benefits future periods, it is debited to the asset account as a capital expenditure. The new book value (less salvage value) is then depreciated over the asset's remaining useful life. To illustrate, suppose a company pays $8,000 for a machine with an eight-year useful life and no salvage value. After three years and $3,000 of straight-line depreciation, it adds an automated control system to the machine at a cost of $1,800. This results in reduced labor costs in future periods. The cost of the betterment is added to the Machinery account with this entry.

> Assume a company owns a Web server. Identify each item as a revenue or capital expenditure: (1) purchase price, (2) necessary wiring, (3) platform for operation, (4) circuits to increase capacity, (5) cleaning after each three months of use, (6) repair of a faulty connection, and (7) replaced a worn cooling fan. *Answer:* Capital expenditures: 1, 2, 3, 4; Revenue expenditures: 5, 6, 7.

Jan.	2	Machinery		1 8 0 0 00	
		Cash			1 8 0 0 00
		To record installation of automated system.			

Assets = Liabilities + Equity
+1,800
−1,800

After the betterment, the remaining cost to be depreciated is $6,800, computed as $8,000 − $3,000 + $1,800. Depreciation expense for the remaining five years is $1,360 per year, computed as $6,800/5 years.

Extraordinary repairs are expenditures extending the asset's useful life beyond its original estimate. Extraordinary repairs are *capital expenditures* because they benefit future periods. Their costs are debited to the asset account. For example, **America West Airlines** reports: "cost of major scheduled airframe, engine and certain component overhauls are capitalized (and expensed) . . . over the periods benefited."

> Both extraordinary repairs and betterments demand revised depreciation schedules.

Disposals of Plant Assets

Plant assets are disposed of for several reasons. Some are discarded because they wear out or become obsolete. Others are sold because of changing business plans. Regardless of the reason, disposals of plant assets occur in one of three basic ways: discarding, sale, or exchange. The general steps in accounting for a disposal of plant assets are described in Exhibit 18.16.

> 1. Record depreciation up to the date of disposal—this also updates Accumulated Depreciation.
> 2. Record the removal of the disposed asset's account balances—including its Accumulated Depreciation.
> 3. Record any cash (and/or other assets) received or paid in the disposal.
> 4. Record any gain or loss—computed by comparing the disposed asset's book value with the market value of any assets received.*

Exhibit 18.16

Accounting for Disposals of Plant Assets

* An exception to step 4 is the case of an exchange that lacks *commercial substance*—see Appendix 18A.

Discarding Plant Assets

Plant Asset Fully Depreciated   A plant asset is *discarded* when it is no longer useful to the company and it has no market value. To illustrate, assume that a machine costing $9,000 with accumulated depreciation of $9,000 is discarded. When accumulated depreciation equals the asset's cost, it is said to be *fully depreciated* (zero book value). The entry to record the discarding of this asset is

LO6 Account for asset disposals and exchanges.

June	5	Accumulated Depreciation—Machinery		9 0 0 0 00	
		Machinery			9 0 0 0 00
		To discard fully depreciated machinery.			

Assets = Liabilities + Equity
+9,000
−9,000

> Bringing depreciation expense up-to-date gives a current book value for determining gain or loss.

Plant Asset Not Fully Depreciated

How do we account for discarding an asset that is not fully depreciated or one whose depreciation is not up-to-date? To answer this, consider equipment costing $8,000 with accumulated depreciation of $6,000 on December 31 of the prior fiscal year-end. This equipment is being depreciated using the straight-line method over eight years with zero salvage. On July 1 of the current year it is discarded. Step 1 is to bring depreciation up-to-date.

Assets = Liabilities + Equity
−500　　　　　　　　−500

July	1	Depreciation Expense	500 00	
		Accumulated Depreciation—Equipment		500 00
		To record 6 months' depreciation ($1,000 × 6/12).		

Steps 2 through 4 of Exhibit 18.16 are reflected in the second (and final) entry.

Assets = Liabilities + Equity
+6,500　　　　　　　−1,500
−8,000

July	1	Accumulated Depreciation—Equipment	6500 00	
		Loss on Disposal of Equipment	1500 00	
		Equipment		8000 00
		To discard equipment with a $1,500 book value.		

> Gain or loss is determined by comparing "value given" (book value) to "value received."

The loss is computed by comparing the equipment's $1,500 book value ($8,000 − $6,000 − $500) with the zero net cash proceeds. This loss is reported in the Other Expenses and Losses section of the income statement. Discarding an asset can sometimes require a cash payment that would increase the loss. The income statement reports any loss from discarding an asset, and the balance sheet reflects the changes in the asset and accumulated depreciation accounts.

Selling Plant Assets

Companies often sell plant assets when they restructure or downsize operations. To illustrate the accounting for the sale of plant assets, we consider BTO's March 31 sale of equipment that cost $16,000 and has accumulated depreciation of $12,000 at December 31 of the prior calendar year-end. Annual depreciation on this equipment is $4,000 computed using straight-line depreciation. Step 1 of this sale is to record depreciation expense and update accumulated depreciation to March 31 of the current year.

Assets = Liabilities + Equity
−1,000　　　　　　　−1,000

March	31	Depreciation Expense	1000 00	
		Accumulated Depreciation—Equipment		1000 00
		To record 3 months' depreciation ($4,000 × 3/12).		

After this entry, the equipment has a book value of $3,000. Steps 2 through 4 of Exhibit 18.16 can be reflected in one final entry that depends on the amount received from the asset's sale. We consider three different possibilities.

Sale at Book Value

If BTO receives $3,000, an amount equal to the equipment's book value as of March 31, no gain or loss occurs on disposal. The entry is

Assets = Liabilities + Equity
+3,000
+13,000
−16,000

March	31	Cash	3000 00	
		Accumulated Depreciation—Equipment	13000 00	
		Equipment		16000 00
		To record sale of equipment for no gain or loss.		

Sale above Book Value   If BTO receives $7,000, an amount that is $4,000 above the equipment's book value as of March 31, a gain on disposal occurs. The entry is

March	31	Cash	7 0 0 0 00		
		Accumulated Depreciation—Equipment	13 0 0 0 00		
		Gain on Disposal of Equipment			4 0 0 0 00
		Equipment			16 0 0 0 00
		To record sale of equipment for a $4,000 gain.			

Assets = Liabilities + Equity
+7,000   +4,000
+13,000
−16,000

Sale below Book Value   If BTO receives $2,500, an amount that is $500 below the equipment's book value as of March 31, a loss on disposal occurs. The entry is

March	31	Cash	2 5 0 0 00		
		Loss on Disposal of Equipment	5 0 0 00		
		Accumulated Depreciation—Equipment	13 0 0 0 00		
		Equipment			16 0 0 0 00
		To record sale of equipment for a $500 loss.			

Assets = Liabilities + Equity
+2,500   −500
+13,000
−16,000

HOW YOU DOIN'?   Answers—p. 469

8. Early in the fifth year of a machine's six-year useful life, it is overhauled, and its useful life is extended to nine years. This machine originally cost $108,000 and the overhaul cost is $12,000. Prepare the entry to record the overhaul cost.

9. Explain the difference between revenue expenditures and capital expenditures and how both are recorded.

10. What is a betterment? How is a betterment recorded?

11. A company acquires equipment on January 10, 2011, at a cost of $42,000. Straight-line depreciation is used with a five-year life and $7,000 salvage value. On June 27, 2012, the company sells this equipment for $32,000. Prepare the entry(ies) for June 27, 2012.

Section 3—Depletion of Natural Resources

Natural resources are assets that are physically consumed when used. Examples are standing timber, mineral deposits, and oil and gas fields. They are often called *wasting assets*. These assets represent soon-to-be inventories of raw materials that will be converted into one or more products by cutting, mining, or pumping. Natural resources are reported under either plant assets or their own separate category. The following section discusses the accounting for natural resources.

Natural resources are recorded at cost, which includes all expenditures necessary to acquire the resource and prepare it for its intended use. **Depletion** is the process of allocating the cost of a natural resource to the period when it is consumed. Natural resources are reported on the balance sheet at cost less *accumulated depletion*. The depletion expense per period is usually based on the units-of-production approach. **Exxon Mobil** uses this approach to amortize the costs of discovering and operating its oil wells.

L07 Account for natural resources and their depletion.

To illustrate depletion, let's consider a mineral deposit with an estimated 250,000 tons of available ore. It is purchased for $500,000, and we expect zero salvage value. The depletion charge per ton of ore mined is $2, computed as $500,000 ÷ 250,000 tons. If 85,000 tons are mined and sold in the first year, the depletion charge for that year is $170,000 (85,000 × $2). These computations are detailed in Exhibit 18.17.

Exhibit 18.17

Depletion Formula and Example

> **Step 1**
>
> $$\text{Depletion per unit} = \frac{\text{Cost} - \text{Salvage value}}{\text{Total units of capacity}} = \frac{\$500,000 - \$0}{250,000 \text{ tons}} = \$2 \text{ per ton}$$
>
> **Step 2**
>
> $$\text{Depletion expense} = \text{Depletion per unit} \times \text{Units extracted and sold in period}$$
> $$= \$2 \times 85,000 = \$170,000$$

Depletion expense for the first year is recorded as follows.

Assets	= Liabilities +	Equity			
−170,000		−170,000			

Dec.	31	Depletion Expense—Mineral Deposit	170 0 0 0 00	
		Accumulated Depletion—Mineral Deposit		170 0 0 0 00
		To record depletion of the mineral deposit.		

The period-end balance sheet reports the mineral deposit as shown in Exhibit 18.18.

Exhibit 18.18

Balance Sheet Presentation of Natural Resources

> Mineral deposit $500,000
> **Less accumulated depletion** **170,000** $330,000

Since all 85,000 tons of the mined ore are sold during the year, the entire $170,000 of depletion is reported as an expense on the income statement. If some of the ore remains unsold at year-end, however, the depletion related to the unsold ore is reported on the balance sheet as Ore Inventory, a current asset.

Section 4—Intangible Assets

LO8   Account for intangible assets and their amortization.

Intangible assets are nonphysical assets (used in operations) that give their owners long-term rights, privileges, or competitive advantages. Examples are patents, copyrights, licenses, leaseholds, franchises, goodwill, and trademarks. Lack of physical substance does not necessarily make an asset intangible. Accounts receivable, for instance, lack physical substance, but are not intangibles. This section identifies common intangible assets and explains their accounting.

Cost Determination and Amortization

An intangible asset is recorded at cost when purchased. Its cost is allocated to expense over its estimated useful life through the process of **amortization.** If an intangible asset has an **indefinite useful life**—meaning that no legal, regulatory, contractual, competitive, economic, or other factors limit its useful life—it should not be amortized. Amortization of intangible assets is like depreciation of plant assets and the depletion of natural resources in that it is a process of cost allocation. However, only the straight-line method is used for amortizing intangibles *unless* the company can show that another method is preferred. The effects of amortization are recorded in a contra account (Accumulated Amortization). The gross acquisition cost of intangible assets is disclosed in the balance sheet along with their accumulated amortization. The eventual disposal of an intangible asset involves removing its book value, recording any other asset(s) received or given up, and recognizing gain or loss.

Many intangibles have limited useful lives due to laws, contracts, or other asset characteristics. Examples are patents, copyrights, and leaseholds. Other intangibles such as goodwill, trademarks, and trade names have useful lives that cannot be easily determined. The cost of intangible assets is amortized over the periods expected to benefit by their use, but in no case can this period be longer than the asset's legal existence. The values of some intangible assets such as goodwill continue indefinitely into the future and are not amortized. (An intangible asset that is not amortized is tested annually for impairment—if necessary, an impairment loss is recorded. Details for this test are in advanced courses.)

Intangible assets are often shown in a separate section of the balance sheet immediately after plant assets. **Callaway Golf**, for instance, follows this approach in reporting nearly $150 million of intangible assets in its balance sheet. Companies usually disclose their amortization periods for intangibles. The remainder of our discussion focuses on accounting for specific types of intangible assets.

> The cost to acquire a Website address is an intangible asset.

> Goodwill is not amortized; instead, it is annually tested for impairment.

Types of Intangibles

Patents

The federal government grants patents to encourage the invention of new technology, mechanical devices, and production processes. A **patent** is an exclusive right granted to its owner to manufacture and sell a patented item or to use a process for 20 years. When patent rights are purchased, the cost to acquire the rights is debited to an asset account called Patents. If the owner engages in lawsuits to successfully defend a patent, the cost of lawsuits is debited to the Patents asset account. However, the costs of research and development leading to a new patent are expensed when incurred.

IN THE NEWS

Drug War   Mention "drug war" and most people think of illegal drug trade. But another drug war is under way: Brand-name drugmakers are fighting to stop generic copies of their products from hitting the market once patents expire. Delaying a generic rival can yield millions in extra sales.

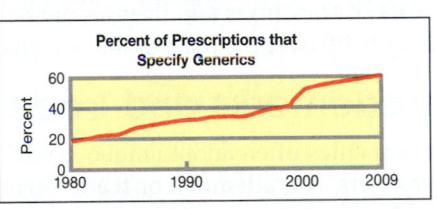

A patent's cost is amortized over its estimated useful life (not to exceed 20 years). If we purchase a patent costing $25,000 with a useful life of 10 years, we make the following adjusting entry at the end of each of the 10 years to amortize one-tenth of its cost:

Dec.	31	Amortization Expense—Patents	2 5 0 0 00		
		Accumulated Amortization—Patents		2 5 0 0 00	
		To amortize patent costs over its useful life.			

Assets = Liabilities + Equity
−2,500   −2,500

The $2,500 debit to Amortization Expense appears on the income statement as a cost of the product or service provided under protection of the patent. The Accumulated Amortization—Patents account is a contra asset account to Patents.

Copyrights

A **copyright** gives its owner the exclusive right to publish and sell a musical, literary, or artistic work during the life of the creator plus 70 years. The useful life of most copyrights is much shorter. The costs of a copyright are amortized over its useful life. The only identifiable cost of many copyrights is the fee paid to the Copyright Office of the federal government or international agency granting the copyright. If this fee is immaterial, it is debited directly to an expense account, but if the identifiable costs of a copyright are material, they are capitalized (recorded in an asset account) and periodically amortized by debiting an account called Amortization Expense—Copyrights.

Leaseholds

Property is rented under a contract called a **lease.** The property's owner, called the **lessor,** grants the lease. The one who secures the right to possess and use the property is called the **lessee.** A **leasehold** refers to the rights the lessor grants to the lessee under the terms of the lease. A leasehold is an intangible asset for the lessee.

   If a long-term lease requires the lessee to pay the final period's rent in advance when the lease is signed, the lessee records this advance payment with a debit to the Leasehold account. Since the advance payment is not used until the final period, the Leasehold account balance remains intact until that final period when its balance is transferred to Rent Expense. If a lease does not require advance payments, each monthly payment is debited directly to Rent Expense.

Leasehold Improvements

A lessee sometimes pays for changes or improvements to the leased property such as partitions, painting, and storefronts. These items are **leasehold improvements.** The lessee debits these costs to a Leasehold Improvements account. Since the lessor owns the leasehold improvements at the end of the lease, the lessee amortizes these costs over the life of the lease or the life of the improvements, whichever is shorter. The amortization entry debits Amortization Expense—Leasehold Improvements and credits Accumulated Amortization—Leasehold Improvements.

Franchises and Licenses

Franchises and **licenses** are rights that a company or government grants an entity to deliver a product or service under specified conditions. Many organizations grant franchise and license rights—**McDonald's**, **Pizza Hut**, and **Major League Baseball** are just a few examples. The costs of franchises and licenses are debited to a Franchises and Licenses asset account and are amortized over the lives of the agreements.

Trademarks and Trade Names

Companies often adopt unique symbols or select unique names and brands in marketing their products. A **trademark** or **trade (brand) name** is a symbol, name, phrase, or jingle identified with a company, product, or service. Examples are Nike swoosh, Marlboro Man, Big Mac, Coca-Cola, and Corvette. Ownership and exclusive right to use a trademark or trade name is often established by showing that one company used it before another. Ownership is best established by registering a trademark or trade name with the government's Patent Office. The cost of developing, maintaining, or enhancing the value of a trademark or trade name (such as advertising) is expensed when incurred. If a trademark or trade name is purchased, however, its cost is debited to an asset account and then amortized over its expected useful life.

McDonald's "golden arches" is one of the world's most valuable trademarks, yet this asset is not shown on McDonald's balance sheet.

IBM's balance sheet reports more than $9 billion of goodwill.

Goodwill

Goodwill has a specific meaning in accounting. Goodwill is the amount by which a company's value exceeds the value of its individual assets and liabilities. This usually implies that the company as a whole has certain valuable attributes not measured among its individual assets and liabilities. These can include superior management, skilled workforce, good supplier or customer relations, quality products or services, good location, or other competitive advantages.

To keep accounting information from being too subjective, *goodwill is recorded only when an entire company or business segment is purchased.* Purchased goodwill is measured by taking the purchase price of the company and subtracting the market value of its individual net assets (excluding goodwill). For instance, **Yahoo!** paid nearly $3.0 billion to acquire **GeoCities**; about $2.8 of the $3.0 billion was for goodwill and other intangibles.

Goodwill is recorded as an asset, and it is *not* amortized. Instead, goodwill is annually tested for impairment. If the book value of goodwill does not exceed its fair (market) value, goodwill is not impaired. However, if the book value of goodwill does exceed its fair value, an impairment loss is recorded. (Details of this test are in advanced courses.)

> Accounting for goodwill is different for financial accounting and tax accounting. The IRS requires the amortization of goodwill over 15 years.

HOW YOU DOIN'?

Answers—p. 469

12. Give an example of a natural resource and of an intangible asset.

13. A company pays $650,000 for an ore deposit. The deposit is estimated to have 325,000 tons of ore that will be mined over the next 10 years. During the first year, it mined, processed, and sold 91,000 tons. What is that year's depletion expense?

14. On January 6, 2011, a company pays $120,000 for a patent with a remaining 17-year legal life to produce a toy expected to be marketable for three years. Prepare entries to record its acquisition and the December 31, 2011, amortization entry.

TOTAL ASSET TURNOVER

A company's assets are important in determining its ability to generate sales and earn income. Managers devote much attention to deciding what assets a company acquires, how much it invests in assets, and how to use assets most efficiently and effectively. One important measure of a company's ability to use its assets is **total asset turnover,** defined in Exhibit 18.19.

LO9 Compute total asset turnover and apply it for analysis.

$$\text{Total asset turnover} = \frac{\text{Net sales}}{\text{Average total assets}}$$

Exhibit 18.19

Total Asset Turnover

The numerator reflects the net amounts earned from the sale of products and services. The denominator reflects the average total resources devoted to operating the company and generating sales.

To illustrate, let's look at total asset turnover in Exhibit 18.20 for two competing companies: **Molson Coors** and **Anheuser-Busch**.

Company	Figure ($ millions)	2007	2006	2005	2004
Molson Coors	Net sales	$ 6,191	$ 5,845	$ 5,507	$ 4,306
	Average total assets	$13,451	$11,701	$ 8,228	$ 4,551
	Total asset turnover	**0.46**	**0.50**	**0.67**	**0.95**
Anheuser-Busch	Net sales	$16,686	$15,717	$15,036	$14,934
	Average total assets	$17,155	$16,466	$16,362	$15,431
	Total asset turnover	**0.97**	**0.95**	**0.92**	**0.97**

Exhibit 18.20

Analysis Using Total Asset Turnover

To show how we use total asset turnover, let's look at Molson Coors. We express Molson Coors's use of assets in generating net sales by saying "it turned its assets over 0.46 times during 2007." This means that each $1.00 of assets produced $0.46 of net sales. Is a total asset turnover of 0.46 good or bad? All companies desire a high total asset turnover. Like many ratio analyses, however, a company's total asset turnover

> An estimate of **plant asset useful life** equals the plant asset cost divided by depreciation expense.

must be compared to that of prior years and of its competitors. Interpreting the total asset turnover also requires an understanding of the company's operations. Some operations are *capital intensive,* meaning that a relatively large amount is invested in assets to generate sales. This suggests a relatively lower total asset turnover. Other companies' operations are labor intensive, meaning that they generate sales more by the efforts of people than the use of assets. In that case, we expect a higher total asset turnover. Companies with low total asset turnover require higher profit margins (examples are hotels and real estate); companies with high total asset turnover can succeed with lower profit margins; examples are food stores and toy merchandisers. Molson Coors's turnover recently declined, but it is similar to that for Anheuser-Busch. Total asset turnover for Molson Coors's competitors, available in industry publications such as Dun & Bradstreet, is generally in the range of 0.7 to 1.0 over this same period. Overall, Molson Coors must improve relative to its competitors on total asset turnover.

> The **plant asset age** is estimated by dividing accumulated depreciation by depreciation expense. Older plant assets can signal needed asset replacements; it may also signal less efficient assets.

Demonstration Problem

On July 14, 2010, Tulsa Company pays $600,000 to acquire a fully equipped factory. The purchase involves the following assets.

Asset	Appraised Value	Salvage Value	Useful Life	Depreciation Method
Land	$160,000			Not depreciated
Land improvements	80,000	$ 0	10 years	Straight-line
Building	320,000	100,000	10 years	Double-declining-balance
Machinery	240,000	20,000	10,000 units	Units-of-production*
Total	$800,000			

* The machinery is used to produce 700 units in 2010 and 1,800 units in 2011.

Required

1. Allocate the total $600,000 purchase cost among the separate assets.

2. Compute the 2010 (six months) and 2011 depreciation expense for each asset and compute total depreciation expense for both years.

3.^A On the first day of 2012, Tulsa exchanged machinery that was acquired on July 14, 2010, and $5,000 cash for machinery with a $210,000 market value. Journalize the exchange of these assets assuming the exchange lacked commercial substance.

4. On the last day of calendar year 2012, Tulsa discarded machinery that had been on its books for five years. The machinery's original cost was $12,000 (estimated life of five years) and its salvage value was $2,000. No depreciation had been recorded for the fifth year when the disposal occurred. Journalize the fifth year of depreciation (straight-line method) and the asset's disposal.

5. At the beginning of year 2012, Tulsa purchased a patent for $100,000 cash. The company estimated the patent's useful life to be 10 years. Journalize the patent acquisition and its amortization for the year 2012.

6. Late in the year 2012, Tulsa acquired an ore deposit for $600,000 cash. It added roads and built mine shafts for an additional cost of $80,000. Salvage value of the mine is estimated to be $20,000. The company estimated 330,000 tons of available ore. In year 2012, Tulsa mined and sold 10,000 tons of ore. Journalize the mine's acquisition and its first year's depletion.

Planning the Solution

- Complete a three-column table showing the following amounts for each asset: appraised value, percent of total value, and allocated cost.
- Using allocated costs, compute depreciation for 2010 (only one-half year) and 2011 (full year) for each asset. Summarize those computations in a table showing total depreciation for each year.
- Remember that gains and losses on asset exchanges that lack commercial substance are not recognized. Make a journal entry to add the acquired machinery to the books and to remove the old machinery, along with its accumulated depreciation, and to record the cash given in the exchange.

- Remember that depreciation must be recorded up-to-date before discarding an asset. Calculate and record depreciation expense for the fifth year using the straight-line method. Since salvage value is not received at the end of a discarded asset's life, the amount of any salvage value becomes a loss on disposal. Record the loss on the disposal as well as the removal of the discarded asset and its related accumulated depreciation.
- Record the patent (an intangible asset) at its purchase price. Use straight-line amortization over its useful life to calculate amortization expense.
- Record the ore deposit (a natural resource asset) at its cost, including any added costs to ready the mine for use. Calculate depletion per ton using the depletion formula. Multiply the depletion per ton by the amount of tons mined and sold to calculate depletion expense for the year.

Solution to Demonstration Problem

1. Allocation of the total cost of $600,000 among the separate assets.

Asset	Appraised Value	Percent of Total Value	Allocated Cost
Land	$160,000	20%	**$120,000** ($600,000 × 20%)
Land improvements	80,000	10	**60,000** ($600,000 × 10%)
Building	320,000	40	**240,000** ($600,000 × 40%)
Machinery	240,000	30	**180,000** ($600,000 × 30%)
Total	$800,000	100%	$ 600,000

2. Depreciation for each asset. (*Note:* Land is not depreciated.)

Land Improvements

Cost	$ 60,000
Salvage value	0
Depreciable cost	$ 60,000
Useful life	10 years
Annual depreciation expense ($60,000/10 years)	$ 6,000
2010 depreciation ($6,000 × 6/12)	**$ 3,000**
2011 depreciation	**$ 6,000**

Building

Straight-line rate = 100%/10 years = 10%
Double-declining-balance rate = 10% × 2 = 20%

2010 depreciation ($240,000 × 20% × 6/12)	**$ 24,000**
2011 depreciation [($240,000 − $24,000) × 20%]	**$ 43,200**

Machinery

Cost	$180,000
Salvage value	20,000
Depreciable cost	$160,000
Total expected units of production	10,000 units
Depreciation per unit ($160,000/10,000 units)	$ 16
2010 depreciation ($16 × 700 units)	**$ 11,200**
2011 depreciation ($16 × 1,800 units)	**$ 28,800**

Total depreciation expense:

	2010	2011
Land improvements	$ 3,000	$ 6,000
Building	24,000	43,200
Machinery	11,200	28,800
Total	$38,200	$78,000

3. Record the asset exchange: The book value on the exchange date is $180,000 (cost) − $40,000 (accumulated depreciation). The book value of the machinery given up in the exchange ($140,000) plus the $5,000 cash paid is less than the $210,000 value of the machine acquired. The entry to record this exchange of assets that lacks commercial substance does not recognize the $65,000 "gain":

Machinery (new)	145,000*	
Accumulated Depreciation—Machinery (old)	40,000	
Machinery (old)		180,000
Cash		5,000
To record asset exchange that lacks commercial substance.		

* Market value of the acquired asset of $210,000 minus $65,000 "gain."

4. Record the depreciation up to date on the discarded asset.

Depreciation Expense—Machinery	2,000	
Accumulated Depreciation—Machinery		2,000
To record depreciation up to date of disposal: ($12,000 − $2,000)/5		

Record the removal of the discarded asset and its loss on disposal.

Accumulated Depreciation—Machinery	10,000	
Loss on Disposal of Machinery	2,000	
Machinery		12,000
To record the discarding of machinery with a $2,000 book value.		

5.

Patent	100,000	
Cash		100,000
To record patent acquisition.		

Amortization Expense—Patent	10,000	
Accumulated Amortization—Patent		10,000
To record amortization expense: $100,000/10 years = $10,000.		

6.

Ore Deposit	680,000	
Cash		680,000
To record ore deposit acquisition and its related costs.		

Depletion Expense—Ore Deposit	20,000	
Accumulated Depletion—Ore Deposit		20,000
To record depletion expense: ($680,000 − $20,000)/330,000 tons =		
$2 per ton. 10,000 tons mined and sold × $2 = $20,000 depletion.		

Exchanging Plant Assets

Many plant assets such as machinery, automobiles, and office equipment are disposed of by exchanging them for newer assets. In a typical exchange of plant assets, a *trade-in allowance* is received on the old asset and the balance is paid in cash. Accounting for the exchange of assets depends on whether the transaction has *commercial substance*. If an asset exchange has commercial substance, a gain or loss is recorded based on the difference between the book value of the asset(s) given up and the market value of the asset(s) received. If an asset exchange lacks commercial substance, no gain or loss is recorded, and the asset(s) received is recorded based on the book value of the asset(s) given up. An exchange has commercial substance if the company's expected future cash flows change as a result of the transaction. This section describes the accounting for the exchange of assets.

Exchange with Commercial Substance: A Loss

Let's assume that a company exchanges both old equipment and $33,000 in cash for new equipment; assume this transaction has commercial substance. The old equipment originally cost $36,000 and has accumulated depreciation of $20,000 at the time of exchange. The new equipment has a market value of $42,000. These details are reflected in the middle (Loss) columns of Exhibit 18A.1.

> Trade-in allowance minus book value equals the gain (or loss if negative) on exchange.

> **Exhibit 18A.1**
>
> Computing Gain or Loss on Asset Exchange with Commercial Substance

Asset Exchange Has Commercial Substance	Loss		Gain	
Market value of asset received		$ 42,000		$ 52,000
Book value of assets given up:				
Equipment ($36,000 − $20,000)	$16,000		$16,000	
Cash	33,000	49,000	33,000	49,000
Gain (loss) on exchange		$(7,000)		$ 3,000

The entry to record this asset exchange is

Jan.	3	Equipment (**new**)	42 0 0 0 00	
		Loss on Exchange of Assets	7 0 0 0 00	
		Accumulated Depreciation—Equipment (**old**)	20 0 0 0 00	
		Equipment (**old**)		36 0 0 0 00
		Cash		33 0 0 0 00
		To record exchange (with commercial substance) of		
		old equipment and cash for new equipment.		

Assets = Liabilities + Equity
+42,000   −7,000
+20,000
−36,000
−33,000

The book value of the assets given up consists of the $33,000 cash and the $16,000 ($36,000 − $20,000) book value of the old equipment. The total $49,000 book value of assets given up is compared to the $42,000 market value of the new equipment received. This yields a loss of $7,000 ($42,000 − $49,000).

> Parenthetical journal entry notes to "new" and "old" equipment are for illustration only. Both the debit and credit are to the same Equipment account in the general ledger.

Exchange with Commercial Substance: A Gain

Let's assume the same facts as in the preceding asset exchange *except* that the new equipment received has a market value of $52,000 instead of $42,000. The entry to record this asset exchange is

Jan.	3	Equipment (**new**)	52 0 0 0 00	
		Accumulated Depreciation—Equipment (**old**)	20 0 0 0 00	
		Equipment (**old**)		36 0 0 0 00
		Cash		33 0 0 0 00
		Gain on Exchange of Assets		3 0 0 0 00
		To record exchange (with commercial substance)		
		of old equipment and cash for new equipment.		

Assets = Liabilities + Equity
+52,000   +3,000
+20,000
−36,000
−33,000

Exchanges without Commercial Substance

Let's assume the same facts as in the preceding asset exchange involving new equipment received with a market value of $52,000, but let's instead assume the transaction *lacks commercial substance*. The entry to record this asset exchange is

Jan.	3	Equipment (**new**)	49 0 0 0 00		
		Accumulated Depreciation—Equipment (**old**)	20 0 0 0 00		
		Equipment (**old**)		36 0 0 0 00
		Cash		33 0 0 0 00
		To record exchange (without commercial substance)		
		of old equipment and cash for new equipment.		

Assets = Liabilities + Equity
+49,000
+20,000
−36,000
−33,000

No gain or loss is recognized for asset exchanges without commercial substance.

Exhibit 18A.2

Cost Basis of New Asset when Gain Not Recorded on Asset Exchange without Commercial Substance

Cost of old equipment	$ 36,000
Less accumulated depreciation	20,000
Book value of old equipment	16,000
Cash paid in the exchange	33,000
Cost recorded for new equipment	**$49,000**

The $3,000 gain recorded when the transaction has commercial substance is *not* recognized in this entry because of the rule prohibiting recording a gain or loss on asset exchanges without commercial substance. The $49,000 recorded for the new equipment equals its cash price ($52,000) less the unrecognized gain ($3,000) on the exchange. The $49,000 cost recorded is called the *cost basis* of the new machine. This cost basis is the amount we use to compute depreciation and book value. The cost basis of the new asset also can be computed by summing the book values of the assets given up as shown in Exhibit 18A.2.

HOW YOU DOIN'?

Answer—p. 469

15. A company trades an old Web server for a new one. The cost of the old server is $30,000, and its accumulated depreciation at the time of the trade is $23,400. The new server has a cash price of $45,000. Prepare entries to record the trade under two different assumptions where the company receives a trade-in allowance of (*a*) $3,000 and the exchange has commercial substance, and (*b*) $7,000 and the exchange lacks commercial substance.

Summary

LO1 Describe plant assets and factors in accounting for them.
Plant assets are tangible assets used in the operations of a company and have a useful life of more than one accounting period. Plant assets are set apart from other tangible assets by two important features: use in operations and useful lives longer than one period. The four main accounting issues with plant assets are (1) computing their costs, (2) allocating their costs to the periods they benefit, (3) accounting for subsequent expenditures, and (4) recording their disposal.

LO2 Compute the reported cost of plant assets. Plant assets are recorded at cost when purchased. Cost includes all normal and reasonable expenditures necessary to get the asset in place and ready for its intended use. The cost of a lump-sum purchase is allocated among its individual assets. In a lump-sum purchase a company pays one price for a group of plant assets. Costs are allocated to each of the individual plant assets purchased based on their relative market values.

LO3 Explain the factors that determine depreciation.
Depreciation is the process of allocating to expense the cost of a plant asset over the accounting periods that benefit from its use. Depreciation does not measure the decline in a plant asset's market value or its physical deterioration. Three factors determine depreciation: cost, salvage value, and useful life. Salvage value is an estimate of the asset's value at the end of its benefit period. Useful (service) life is the length of time an asset is productively used.

LO4 Compute and record depreciation using the straight-line, units-of-production, declining-balance, and MACRS methods. The straight-line method divides cost less salvage value by the asset's useful life to determine depreciation expense per period. The units-of-production method divides cost less salvage value by the estimated number of units the asset will produce over its life to determine depreciation per unit. The declining-balance method multiplies the asset's beginning-of-period book value by a factor that is often double the straight-line rate. Partial-year depreciation is often required because assets are bought and sold throughout the year. Depreciation is revised when changes in estimates such as salvage value and useful life occur. If the useful life of a plant asset changes, for instance, the remaining cost to be depreciated is spread over the remaining (revised) useful life of the asset. The MACRS system assigns plant assets to classes, based on useful lives. Cost recovery rates are developed for each year for each asset class. Depreciation is computed by multiplying the cost recovery percentage for a year for an asset class by the original cost of the asset.

LO5 **Distinguish between and account for revenue expenditures and capital expenditures.** Revenue expenditures expire in the current period and are debited to expense accounts and matched with current revenues. Ordinary repairs are an example of revenue expenditures. Capital expenditures benefit future periods and are debited to asset accounts. Examples of capital expenditures are extraordinary repairs and betterments.

LO6 **Account for asset disposals and exchanges.** When a plant asset is discarded or sold, its cost and accumulated depreciation are removed from the accounts. Any cash proceeds from discarding or selling an asset are recorded and compared to the asset's book value to determine gain or loss. For an asset exchange with commercial substance, a gain or loss is recorded based on the difference between the book value of the asset given up and the market value of the asset received. For an asset exchange without commercial substance, no gain or loss is recorded, and the asset received is recorded based on book value of the asset given up.

LO7 **Account for natural resources and their depletion.** The cost of a natural resource is recorded in a noncurrent asset account. Depletion of a natural resource is recorded by allocating its cost to depletion expense using the units-of-production method. Depletion is credited to an Accumulated Depletion account.

LO8 **Account for intangible assets and their amortization.** An intangible asset is recorded at the cost incurred to purchase it. The cost of an intangible asset with a definite useful life is allocated to expense using the straight-line method, and is called *amortization*. Goodwill and intangible assets with an indefinite useful life are not amortized—they are annually tested for impairment. Intangible assets include patents, copyrights, leaseholds, goodwill, and trademarks.

LO9 **Compute total asset turnover and apply it for analysis.** Total asset turnover measures a company's ability to use its assets to generate sales. It is defined as net sales divided by average total assets. While all companies desire a high total asset turnover, it must be interpreted in comparison with that for prior years and its competitors.

Guidance Answers to HOW YOU DOIN'?

1. a. Supplies—current assets

   b. Office equipment—plant assets

   c. Inventory—current assets

   d. Land for future expansion—long-term investments

   e. Trucks used in operations—plant assets

2. a. Land   **b.** Land Improvements

3. $700,000 + $49,000 − $21,000 + $3,500 + $3,000 + $2,500 = $737,000

4. a. Straight-line with 7-year life: ($77,000/7) = $11,000

   b. Straight-line with 10-year life: ($77,000/10) = $7,700

   MACRS, 7-year asset class: ($77,000 × 14.28%) = $10,996

5. Depreciation is a process of allocating the cost of plant assets to the accounting periods that benefit from the assets' use.

6. a. Book value using straight-line depreciation: $96,000 − [($96,000 − $8,000)/5] = $78,400

   b. Book value using units of production: $96,000 − [($96,000 − $8,000) × (10,000/100,000)] = $87,200

7. ($3,800 − $200)/3 = $1,200 (original depreciation per year)

$1,200 × 2 = $2,400 (accumulated depreciation)

($3,800 − $2,400)/2 = $700 (revised depreciation)

8.

Machinery	12,000	
Cash..................................		12,000

9. A revenue expenditure benefits only the current period and should be charged to expense in the current period. A capital expenditure yields benefits that extend beyond the end of the current period and should be charged to an asset.

10. A betterment involves modifying an existing plant asset to make it more efficient, usually by replacing part of the asset with an improved or superior part. The cost of a betterment is debited to the asset account.

11.

Depreciation Expense.......................	3,500	
Accumulated Depreciation................		3,500
Cash	32,000	
Accumulated Depreciation.....................	10,500	
Gain on Sale of Equipment................		500
Equipment...........................		42,000

12. Examples of natural resources are timberlands, mineral deposits, and oil reserves. Examples of intangible assets are patents, copyrights, leaseholds, leasehold improvements, goodwill, trademarks, and licenses.

13. ($650,000/325,000 tons) × 91,000 tons = $182,000

14.

Jan.	6	Patents..........................	120,000	
		Cash		120,000
Dec. 31		Amortization Expense	40,000*	
		Accumulated		
		Amortization—Patents		40,000

* $120,000/3 years = $40,000.

15.

(a) Equipment (new)	45,000	
Loss on Exchange of Assets...............	3,600	
Accumulated Depreciation—Equipment (old) ..	23,400	
Equipment (old)		30,000
Cash ($45,000 − $3,000)		42,000

(b) Equipment (new)*	44,600	
Accumulated Depreciation—Equipment (old) ..	23,400	
Equipment (old)		30,000
Cash ($45,000 − $7,000)		38,000

* Includes $400 unrecognized gain.

Key Terms

Accelerated depreciation method (p. 452) Method that produces larger depreciation charges in the early years of an asset's life and smaller charges in its later years.

Amortization (p. 460) Process of allocating the cost of an intangible asset to expense over its estimated useful life.

Betterments (p. 456) Expenditures to make a plant asset more efficient or productive; also called *improvements*.

Book value (p. 450) Asset's acquisition costs less its accumulated depreciation (or depletion, or amortization); also sometimes used synonymously as the *carrying value* of an account.

Capital expenditures (p. 456) Additional costs of plant assets that provide material benefits extending beyond the current period; also called *balance sheet expenditures*.

Change in an accounting estimate (p. 454) Change in an accounting estimate that results from new information, subsequent developments, or improved judgment that impacts current and future periods.

Copyright (p. 462) Right giving the owner the exclusive privilege to publish and sell musical, literary, or artistic work during the creator's life plus 70 years.

Cost (p. 449) All normal and reasonable expenditures necessary to get an asset in place and ready for its intended use.

Declining-balance method (p. 452) Method that determines depreciation charge for the period by multiplying a depreciation rate (often twice the straight-line rate) by the asset's beginning-period book value.

Depletion (p. 459) Process of allocating the cost of natural resources to periods when they are consumed and sold.

Depreciation (p. 449) Expense created by allocating the cost of plant and equipment to periods in which they are used; represents the expense of using the asset.

Extraordinary repairs (p. 457) Major repairs that extend the useful life of a plant asset beyond prior expectations; treated as a capital expenditure.

Franchises (p. 462) Privileges granted by a company or government to sell a product or service under specified conditions.

Goodwill (p. 462) Amount by which a company's (or a segment's) value exceeds the value of its individual assets less its liabilities.

Impairment (p. 454) Diminishment of an asset value.

Indefinite useful life (p. 460) Asset life that is not limited by legal, regulatory, contractual, competitive, economic, or other factors.

Intangible assets (p. 460) Long-term assets (resources) used to produce or sell products or services; usually lack physical form and have uncertain benefits.

Land improvements (p. 448) Assets that increase the benefits of land, have a limited useful life, and are depreciated.

Lease (p. 462) Contract specifying the rental of property.

Leasehold (p. 462) Rights the lessor grants to the lessee under the terms of a lease.

Leasehold improvements (p. 462) Alterations or improvements to leased property such as partitions and storefronts.

Lessee (p. 462) Party to a lease who secures the right to possess and use the property from another party (the lessor).

Lessor (p. 462) Party to a lease who grants another party (the lessee) the right to possess and use its property.

Licenses (p. 462) (See *franchises*.)

Modified Accelerated Cost Recovery System (MACRS) (p. 454) Depreciation system required by federal income tax law.

Natural resources (p. 459) Assets physically consumed when used; examples are timber, mineral deposits, and oil and gas fields; also called *wasting assets*.

Ordinary repairs (p. 456) Repairs to keep a plant asset in normal, good operating condition; treated as a revenue expenditure and immediately expensed.

Patent (p. 461) Exclusive right granted to its owner to produce and sell an item or to use a process for 17 years.

Plant assets (p. 446) Tangible long-lived assets used to produce or sell products and services; also called *property, plant and equipment (PP&E)* or *fixed assets*.

Plant asset age (p. 464) Estimated by dividing accumulated depreciation by depreciation expense.

Plant asset useful life (p. 463) Equals the plant asset cost divided by depreciation expense. It is the length of time an asset will be productively used in the operations of a business.

Revenue expenditures (p. 456) Expenditures reported on the current income statement as an expense because they do not provide benefits in future periods.

Salvage value (p. 449) Estimate of amount to be recovered at the end of an asset's useful life; also called *residual value* or *scrap value*.

Straight-line depreciation (p. 450) Method that allocates an equal portion of the depreciable cost of plant asset (cost minus salvage) to each accounting period in its useful life.

Total asset turnover (p. 463) Measure of a company's ability to use its assets to generate sales; computed by dividing net sales by average total assets.

Trademark or **trade (brand) name** (p. 462) Symbol, name, phrase, or jingle identified with a company, product, or service.

Units-of-production depreciation (p. 451) Method that charges a varying amount to depreciation expense for each period of an asset's useful life depending on its usage.

Useful life (p. 449) Length of time an asset will be productively used in the operations of a business; also called *service life*.

Multiple Choice Quiz

Answers on p. 483

mhhe.com/wildCA2e

Additional Multiple Choice Quizzes are available at the book's Website.

1. A company paid $326,000 for property that included land, land improvements, and a building. The land was appraised at $175,000, the land improvements were appraised at $70,000, and the building was appraised at $105,000. What is the allocation of property costs to the three assets purchased?
  a. Land, $150,000; Land Improvements, $60,000; Building, $90,000
  b. Land, $163,000; Land Improvements, $65,200; Building, $97,800
  c. Land, $150,000; Land Improvements, $61,600; Building, $92,400
  d. Land, $159,000; Land Improvements, $65,200; Building, $95,400
  e. Land, $175,000; Land Improvements, $70,000; Building, $105,000

2. A company purchased a truck for $35,000 on January 1, 2010. The truck is estimated to have a useful life of four years and an estimated salvage value of $1,000. Assuming that the company uses straight-line depreciation, what is depreciation expense on the truck for the year ended December 31, 2011?
  a. $8,750
  b. $17,500
  c. $8,500
  d. $17,000
  e. $25,500

3. A company purchased machinery for $10,800,000 on January 1, 2010. The machinery has a useful life of 10 years and an estimated salvage value of $800,000. What is depreciation expense on the machinery for the year ended December 31, 2011, assuming that the double-declining-balance method is used?
  a. $2,160,000
  b. $3,888,000
  c. $1,728,000
  d. $2,000,000
  e. $1,600,000

4. A company sold a machine that originally cost $250,000 for $120,000 when accumulated depreciation on the machine was $100,000. The gain or loss recorded on the sale of this machine is
  a. $0 gain or loss.
  b. $120,000 gain.
  c. $30,000 loss.
  d. $30,000 gain.
  e. $150,000 loss.

5. A company had average total assets of $500,000, gross sales of $575,000, and net sales of $550,000. The company's total asset turnover is
  a. 1.15
  b. 1.10
  c. 0.91
  d. 0.87
  e. 1.05

Superscript letter [A] *denotes assignments based on Appendix 18A.*

Discussion Questions

1. What characteristics of a plant asset make it different from other assets?

2. What is the general rule for costs inclusion for plant assets?

3. What is different between land and land improvements?

4. Why is the cost of a lump sum purchase allocated to the individual assets acquired?

5. Does the balance in the Accumulated Depreciation—Machinery account represent funds to replace the machinery when it wears out? If not, what does it represent?

6. Why is the Modified Accelerated Cost Recovery System not generally accepted for financial accounting purposes?

7. What accounting principle justifies charging low-cost plant asset purchases immediately to an expense account?

8. What is the difference between ordinary repairs and extraordinary repairs? How should each be recorded?

9. Identify events that might lead to disposal of a plant asset.

10. What is the process of allocating the cost of natural resources to expense as they are used?

11. Is the declining-balance method an acceptable way to compute depletion of natural resources? Explain.

12. What are the characteristics of an intangible asset?

13. What general procedures are applied in accounting for the acquisition and potential cost allocation of intangible assets?

14. When do we know that a company has goodwill? When can goodwill appear in a company's balance sheet?

15. Assume that a company buys another business and pays for its goodwill. If the company plans to incur costs each year to maintain the value of the goodwill, must it also amortize this goodwill?

16. How is total asset turnover computed? Why would a financial statement user or business owner be interested in total asset turnover?

17. Refer to **Best Buy**'s balance sheet in Appendix A. What plant and equipment assets does Best Buy list on its balance sheet? What is the book value of its total plant and equipment assets at March 1, 2008?

18. Refer to **RadioShack**'s balance sheet in Appendix A. What does it title its plant assets? What is the book value of its plant assets at December 31, 2007?

connect

QUICK STUDY

QS 18-1
Cost of plant assets **LO2**

Kegler Bowling installs automatic scorekeeping equipment with an invoice cost of $190,000. The electrical work required for the installation costs $20,000. Additional costs are $4,000 for delivery and $13,700 for sales tax. During the installation, a component of the equipment is carelessly left on a lane and hit by the automatic lane-cleaning machine. The cost of repairing the component is $1,850. What is the total recorded cost of the automatic scorekeeping equipment?

QS 18-2
Defining assets **LO1**

Identify the main difference between (1) plant assets and current assets, (2) plant assets and inventory, and (3) plant assets and long-term investments.

QS 18-3
Depreciation methods **LO4**

On January 2, 2010, the Cerritos Band acquires sound equipment for concert performances at a cost of $65,800. The band estimates it will use this equipment for four years, during which time it anticipates performing about 200 concerts. It estimates that after four years it can sell the equipment for $2,000. During year 2010, the band performs 45 concerts. Compute the year 2010 depreciation using the (1) straight-line method and (2) units-of-production method.

QS 18-4
Computing revised depreciation
LO4

Refer to the facts in QS 18-3. Assume that Cerritos Band chose straight-line depreciation but realizes early in the second year that due to concert bookings beyond expectations, this equipment will last only a total of three years. The salvage value remains unchanged. Compute the revised depreciation for both the second and third years.

QS 18-5
Double-declining-balance method
LO4

A fleet of refrigerated delivery trucks is acquired on January 5, 2010, at a cost of $830,000 with an estimated useful life of eight years and an estimated salvage value of $75,000. Compute the depreciation expense for each of the first three years using the double-declining-balance method.

QS 18-6
Revenue and capital expenditures
LO5

1. Classify the following as either a revenue or a capital expenditure.
   a. Paid $40,000 cash to replace a compressor on a refrigeration system that extends its useful life by four years.
   b. Paid $200 cash per truck for the cost of their annual tune-ups.
   c. Paid $175 for the monthly cost of replacement filters on an air-conditioning system.
   d. Completed an addition to an office building for $225,000 cash.
2. Prepare the journal entries to record transactions *a* and *d* of part 1.

QS 18-7
Disposal of assets **LO6**

Hortez Co. owns equipment that cost $76,800, with accumulated depreciation of $40,800. Hortez sells the equipment for cash. Record the sale of the equipment assuming Hortez sells the equipment for (1) $47,000 cash, (2) $36,000 cash, and (3) $31,000 cash.

QS 18-8
Computing total asset turnover
LO9

Aneko Company reports the following ($ millions): net sales of $14,880 for 2011 and $13,990 for 2010; end-of-year total assets of $15,869 for 2011 and $17,819 for 2010. Compute its total asset turnover for 2011, and assess its level if competitors average a total asset turnover of 2.0 times.

QS 18-9[A]
Asset exchange **LO9**

Caleb Co. owns a machine that costs $42,400 with accumulated depreciation of $18,400. Caleb exchanges the machine for a newer model that has a market value of $52,000. Record the exchange assuming Caleb also paid cash of (1) $30,000 and the exchange has commercial substance, and (2) $22,000 and the exchange lacks commercial substance.

QS 18-10
MACRS depreciation **LO4**

Refer to the data in QS 18-5. Assume this asset is placed in the five-year asset class for depreciation purposes for federal income tax reporting. Compute depreciation for each of the first three years of the asset's life using the MACRS table provided in Exhibit 18.14.

Corentine Company acquires an ore mine at a cost of $1,400,000. It incurs additional costs of $400,000 to access the mine, which is estimated to hold 1,000,000 tons of ore. The estimated value of the land after the ore is removed is $200,000.

1. Prepare the entry(ies) to record the cost of the ore mine.

2. Prepare the year-end depletion adjusting entry if 180,000 tons of ore are mined and sold the first year.

QS 18-11
Natural resources and depletion
L07

Which of the following assets are reported on the balance sheet as intangible assets? Which are reported as natural resources? (*a*) Oil well, (*b*) Trademark, (*c*) Leasehold, (*d*) Gold mine, (*e*) Building, (*f*) Copyright, (*g*) Franchise, (*h*) Timberland.

QS 18-12
Classify assets   **L07   L08**

On January 4 of this year, Bibiana Boutique incurs a $105,000 cost to modernize its store. Improvements include new floors, ceilings, wiring, and wall coverings. These improvements are estimated to yield benefits for 10 years. Bibiana leases its store and has eight years remaining on the lease. Prepare the entry to record (1) the cost of modernization and (2) amortization at the end of this current year.

QS 18-13
Intangible assets and amortization
L08

Compare and contrast intangible assets and plant assets.

QS 18-14
Intangible assets and plant assets
L01   L08

---

connect™

Rizio Co. purchases a machine for $12,500, terms 2/10, n/60, FOB shipping point. The seller prepaid the $360 freight charges, adding the amount to the invoice and bringing its total to $12,860. The machine requires special steel mounting and power connections costing $895. Another $475 is paid to assemble the machine and get it into operation. In moving the machine to its steel mounting, $180 in damages occurred. Also, $40 of materials is used in adjusting the machine to produce a satisfactory product. The adjustments are normal for this machine and are not the result of the damages. Compute the cost recorded for this machine. (Rizio pays for this machine within the cash discount period.)

EXERCISES

Exercise 18-1
Cost of plant assets   **L02**

Cala Manufacturing purchases a large lot on which an old building is located as part of its plans to build a new plant. The negotiated purchase price is $280,000 for the lot plus $110,000 for the old building. The company pays $33,500 to tear down the old building and $47,000 to fill and level the lot. It also pays a total of $1,540,000 in construction costs—this amount consists of $1,452,200 for the new building and $87,800 for lighting and paving a parking area next to the building. Prepare a single journal entry to record these costs incurred by Cala, all of which are paid in cash.

Exercise 18-2
Recording costs of plant assets
L01   L02

Liltua Company pays $355,280 for real estate plus $20,100 in closing costs. The real estate consists of land appraised at $157,040; land improvements appraised at $58,890; and a building appraised at $176,670. Allocate the total cost among the three purchased assets and prepare the journal entry to record the purchase.

Exercise 18-3
Lump-sum purchase
of plant assets   **L02**

In early January 2010, NewTech purchases computer equipment for $154,000 to use in operating activities for the next four years. It estimates the equipment's salvage value at $25,000. Prepare tables showing depreciation and book value for each of the four years assuming (1) straight-line and (2) double-declining-balance depreciation.

Exercise 18-4
Depreciation methods   **L04**

Ramirez Company installs a computerized manufacturing machine in its factory at the beginning of the year at a cost of $43,500. The machine's useful life is estimated at 10 years, or 385,000 units of product, with a $5,000 salvage value. During its second year, the machine produces 32,500 units of product. Determine the machine's second-year depreciation under the (1) straight-line, (2) units-of-production, and (3) double-declining-balance methods.

Exercise 18-5
Depreciation methods   **L04**

Check   (3) $6,960

On April 1, 2010, Cyclone Backhoe Co. purchases a trencher for $280,000. The machine is expected to last five years and have a salvage value of $40,000. Compute depreciation expense for year 2011 using the (1) straight-line, (2) double-declining-balance, and (3) MACRS methods (using five-year class).

Exercise 18-6
Depreciation methods;
partial year depreciation   **L04**

Exercise 18-7
Revising depreciation   **LO4**

Check   (2) $3,710

Apex Fitness Club uses straight-line depreciation for a machine costing $23,860, with an estimated four-year life and a $2,400 salvage value. At the beginning of the third year, Apex determines that the machine has three more years of remaining useful life, after which it will have an estimated $2,000 salvage value. Compute (1) the machine's book value at the end of its second year and (2) the amount of depreciation for each of the final three years given the revised estimates.

Exercise 18-8
Income effects of depreciation methods   **LO4**

Check   (2) Year 3 NI, $54,170

Tory Enterprises pays $238,400 for equipment that will last five years and have a $43,600 salvage value. By using the machine in its operations for five years, the company expects to earn $88,500 annually, after deducting all expenses except depreciation. Prepare a table showing income before depreciation, depreciation expense, and net (pretax) income for each year and for the total five-year period, assuming (1) straight-line depreciation and (2) double-declining-balance depreciation.

Exercise 18-9
Extraordinary repairs; plant asset age   **LO4 LO5**

Veradis Company owns a building that appears on its prior year-end balance sheet at its original $572,000 cost less $429,000 accumulated depreciation. The building is depreciated on a straight-line basis assuming a 20-year life and no salvage value. During the first week in January of the current calendar year, major structural repairs are completed on the building at a $68,350 cost. The repairs extend the building's useful life for 7 years beyond the 20 years originally estimated.

1. Determine the building's age (plant asset age) as of the prior year-end balance sheet date.

2. Prepare the entry to record the cost of the structural repairs that are paid in cash.

Check   (3) $211,350

3. Determine the book value of the building immediately after the repairs are recorded.

4. Prepare the entry to record the current calendar year's depreciation.

Exercise 18-10
Ordinary repairs, extraordinary repairs and betterments   **LO5**

Oki Company pays $264,000 for equipment expected to last four years and have a $29,000 salvage value. Prepare journal entries to record the following costs related to the equipment.

1. During the second year of the equipment's life, $22,000 cash is paid for a new component expected to increase the equipment's productivity by 10% a year.

2. During the third year, $6,250 cash is paid for normal repairs necessary to keep the equipment in good working order.

3. During the fourth year, $14,870 is paid for repairs expected to increase the useful life of the equipment from four to five years.

Exercise 18-11
Disposal of assets   **LO6**

Diaz Company owns a milling machine that cost $250,000 and has accumulated depreciation of $182,000. Prepare the entry to record the disposal of the milling machine on January 3 under each of the following independent situations.

1. The machine needed extensive repairs, and it was not worth repairing. Diaz disposed of the machine, receiving nothing in return.

2. Diaz sold the machine for $35,000 cash.

3. Diaz sold the machine for $68,000 cash.

4. Diaz sold the machine for $80,000 cash.

Exercise 18-12
Partial year depreciation; disposal of plant asset   **LO4 LO6**

Rayya Co. purchases and installs a machine on January 1, 2010, at a total cost of $105,000. Straight-line depreciation is taken each year for four years assuming a seven-year life and no salvage value. The machine is disposed of on July 1, 2014, during its fifth year of service. Prepare entries to record the partial year's depreciation on July 1, 2014, and to record the disposal under the following separate assumptions: (1) the machine is sold for $45,500 cash and (2) Rayya receives an insurance settlement of $25,000 resulting from the total destruction of the machine in a fire.

Exercise 18-13
Depletion of natural resources   **LO4 LO7**

On April 2, 2010, Montana Mining Co. pays $3,721,000 for an ore deposit containing 1,525,000 tons. The company installs machinery in the mine costing $213,500, with an estimated seven-year life and no salvage value. The machinery will be abandoned when the ore is completely mined. Montana began mining on May 1, 2010, and mined and sold 166,200 tons of ore during the remaining eight months of 2010. Prepare the December 31, 2010, entries to record both the ore deposit depletion and the mining machinery depreciation. Mining machinery depreciation should be figured using the units of production method.

Exercise 18-14
Amortization of intangible assets   **LO8**

Milano Gallery purchases the copyright on an oil painting for $418,000 on January 1, 2010. The copyright legally protects its owner for 19 more years. However, the company plans to market and sell prints of the original for only 10 years. Prepare entries to record the purchase of the copyright on January 1, 2010, and its annual amortization on December 31, 2010.

On January 1, 2010, Robinson Company purchased Franklin Company at a price of $2,500,000. The fair market value of the net assets purchased equals $1,800,000.

Exercise 18-15
Goodwill   **LO8**

1. What is the amount of goodwill that Robinson records at the purchase date?

2. Explain how Robinson would determine the amount of goodwill amortization for the year ended December 31, 2010.

3. Robinson Company believes that its employees provide superior customer services, and through their efforts, Robinson Company believes it has created $900,000 of goodwill. Should Robinson Company record this goodwill?

Refer to the statement of cash flows for **RadioShack** in Appendix A for the fiscal year ended December 31, 2007, to answer the following:

Exercise 18-16
Cash flows related to assets

LO1

1. What amount of cash is used to purchase property and equipment?

2. How much depreciation and amortization are recorded?

3. What total amount of net cash is used in investing activities?

Lok Co. reports net sales of $5,865,000 for 2010 and $8,689,000 for 2011. End-of-year balances for total assets are: 2009, $1,686,000; 2010, $1,800,000; and 2011, $1,982,000. (*a*) Compute Lok's total asset turnover for 2010 and 2011. (*b*) Comment on Lok's efficiency in using its assets if its competitors average a total asset turnover of 3.0.

Exercise 18-17
Evaluating efficient use of assets

LO9

Gilly Construction trades in an old tractor for a new tractor, receiving a $29,000 trade-in allowance and paying the remaining $83,000 in cash. The old tractor had cost $96,000, and straight-line accumulated depreciation of $52,500 had been recorded to date under the assumption that it would last eight years and have a $12,000 salvage value. Answer the following questions assuming the exchange has commercial substance.

Exercise 18-18ᴬ
Exchanging assets   **LO6**

1. What is the book value of the old tractor at the time of exchange?

2. What is the loss on this asset exchange?

Check   (2) $14,500

3. What amount should be recorded (debited) in the asset account for the new tractor?

On January 2, 2011, Bering Co. disposes of a machine costing $44,000 with accumulated depreciation of $24,625. Prepare the entries to record the disposal under each of the following separate assumptions.

Exercise 18-19ᴬ
Recording plant asset disposals

LO6

1. Machine is sold for $18,250 cash.

2. Machine is traded in on a newer machine having a $60,200 cash price. A $25,000 trade-in allowance is received, and the balance is paid in cash. Assume the asset exchange lacks commercial substance.

Check   (2) Dr. Machinery, $54,575

3. Machine is traded in on a newer machine having a $60,200 cash price. A $15,000 trade-in allowance is received, and the balance is paid in cash. Assume the asset exchange has commercial substance.

---

connect

Timberly Construction negotiates a lump-sum purchase of several assets from a company that is going out of business. The purchase is completed on January 1, 2010, at a total cash price of $900,000 for a building, land, land improvements, and four vehicles. The estimated market values of the assets are building, $508,800; land, $297,600; land improvements, $28,800; and four vehicles, $124,800. The company's fiscal year ends on December 31.

PROBLEM SET A

Problem 18-1A
Plant asset costs; depreciation methods   **LO2 LO4**

mhhe.com/wildCA2e

Required

1. Prepare a table to allocate the lump-sum purchase price to the separate assets purchased. Prepare the journal entry to record the purchase.

Check   (2) $30,000

2. Compute the depreciation expense for year 2010 on the building using the straight-line method, assuming a 15-year life and a $27,000 salvage value.

3. Compute the depreciation expense for year 2010 on the land improvements assuming a five-year life and double-declining-balance depreciation.

(3) $10,800

4. Defend or refute this statement: Accelerated depreciation results in payment of less taxes over the asset's life.

Problem 18-2A
Asset cost allocation; straight-line depreciation
LO2   LO4

mhhe.com/wildCA2e

In January 2010, Mitzu Co. pays $2,600,000 for a tract of land with two buildings on it. It plans to demolish Building 1 and build a new store in its place. Building 2 will be a company office; it is appraised at $644,000, with a useful life of 20 years and a $60,000 salvage value. A lighted parking lot near Building 1 has improvements (Land Improvements 1) valued at $420,000 that are expected to last another 12 years with no salvage value. Without the buildings and improvements, the tract of land is valued at $1,736,000. Mitzu also incurs the following additional costs:

Cost to demolish Building 1	$ 328,400
Cost of additional land grading	175,400
Cost to construct new building (Building 3), having a useful life of 25 years and a $392,000 salvage value	2,202,000
Cost of new land improvements (Land Improvements 2) near Building 2 having a 20-year useful life and no salvage value	164,000

Required

Check (1) Land costs, $2,115,800; Building 2 costs, $598,000

1. Prepare a table with the following column headings: Land, Building 2, Building 3, Land Improvements 1, and Land Improvements 2. Allocate the costs incurred by Mitzu to the appropriate columns and total each column.

2. Prepare a single journal entry to record the original purchase and all the incurred costs assuming they are paid in cash on January 1, 2010.

(3) Depr.—Land Improv. 1 and 2, $32,500 and $8,200

3. Using the straight-line method, prepare the December 31 adjusting entries to record depreciation for the 12 months of 2010 when these assets were in use.

Problem 18-3A
Computing and revising depreciation; revenue and capital expenditures
LO2   LO4   LO5

Champion Contractors completed the following transactions and events involving the purchase and operation of equipment in its business.

2009

Jan. 1   Paid $287,600 cash plus $11,500 of sales tax and $1,500 of transportation-in (FOB shipping point) for a new loader. The loader is estimated to have a four-year life and a $20,600 salvage value. Loader costs are recorded in the Equipment account.

Jan. 3   Paid $4,800 to enclose the cab and install air conditioning in the loader to enable operations under harsher conditions. This increased the estimated salvage value of the loader by another $1,400.

Check Dec. 31, 2009, Dr. Depr. Expense—Equip., $70,850

Dec. 31   Recorded annual straight-line depreciation on the loader.

2010

Jan. 1   Paid $5,400 to overhaul the loader's engine, which increased the loader's estimated useful life by two years.

Feb. 17   Paid $820 to repair the loader after the operator backs it into a tree.

Dec. 31, 2010, Dr. Depr. Expense—Equip., $43,590

Dec. 31   Recorded annual straight-line depreciation on the loader.

Required

Prepare journal entries to record these transactions and events.

Problem 18-4A
Computing and revising depreciation; selling plant assets
LO2   LO4   LO6

Yoshi Company completed the following transactions and events involving its delivery trucks.

2009

Jan. 1   Paid $20,515 cash plus $1,485 in sales tax for a new delivery truck estimated to have a five-year life and a $2,000 salvage value. Delivery truck costs are recorded in the Trucks account.

Dec. 31   Recorded annual straight-line depreciation on the truck.

2010

Check Dec. 31, 2010, Dr. Depr. Expense—Trucks, $5,200

Dec. 31   Due to new information obtained at the beginning of the year, the truck's estimated useful life was changed from five to four years, and the estimated salvage value was increased to $2,400. Recorded annual straight-line depreciation on the truck.

2011

Dec. 31   Recorded annual straight-line depreciation on the truck.

Dec. 31   Sold the truck for $5,300 cash.

Dec. 31, 2011, Dr. Loss on Disposal of Trucks, $2,300

Required

Prepare journal entries to record these transactions and events.

A machine costing $257,500 with a four-year life and an estimated $20,000 salvage value is installed in Luther Company's factory on January 1. The factory manager estimates the machine will produce 475,000 units of product during its life. It actually produces the following units: year 1, 220,000; year 2, 124,600; year 3, 121,800; and year 4, 15,200. The total number of units produced by the end of year 4 exceeds the original estimate—this difference was not predicted. (The machine must not be depreciated below its estimated salvage value.)

Problem 18–5A
Depreciation methods   **LO4**

Required

Prepare a table with the following column headings and compute depreciation for each year (and total depreciation of all years combined) for the machine under each depreciation method.

Year	Straight-Line	Units-of-Production	Double-Declining-Balance

Check Year 4: Units-of-Production Depreciation, $4,300; DDB Depreciation, $12,187

Onslow Co. purchases a used machine for $178,000 cash on January 2 and readies it for use the next day at a $2,840 cost. On January 3, it is installed on a required operating platform costing $1,160, and it is further readied for operations. The company predicts the machine will be used for six years and have a $14,000 salvage value. Depreciation is to be charged on a straight-line basis. On December 31, at the end of its fifth year in operations, it is disposed of.

Problem 18–6A
Disposal of plant assets
LO2   LO4   LO6

Required

1. Prepare journal entries to record the machine's purchase and the costs to ready and install it. Cash is paid for all costs incurred.

2. Prepare journal entries to record depreciation of the machine at December 31 of (*a*) its first year in operations and (*b*) the year of its disposal.

Check (2*b*) Depr. Exp., $28,000

3. Prepare journal entries to record the machine's disposal under each of the following separate assumptions: (*a*) it is sold for $15,000 cash; (*b*) it is sold for $50,000 cash; and (*c*) it is destroyed in a fire and the insurance company pays $30,000 cash to settle the loss claim.

(3*c*) Dr. Loss from Fire, $12,000

On July 23 of the current year, Dakota Mining Co. pays $4,715,000 for land estimated to contain 5,125,000 tons of recoverable ore. It installs machinery costing $410,000 that has a 10-year life and no salvage value and is capable of mining the ore deposit in eight years. The machinery is paid for on July 25, seven days before mining operations begin. The company removes and sells 480,000 tons of ore during its first five months of operations. Depreciation of the machinery is based on the units of production method as the machinery will be abandoned after the ore is mined.

Problem 18–7A
Natural resources   **LO7**

Required

1. Prepare entries to record (*a*) the purchase of the land, (*b*) the cost and installation of machinery, (*c*) the first five months' depletion assuming the land has a net salvage value of zero after the ore is mined, and (*d*) the first five months' depreciation on machinery.

Check (*c*) Depletion, $441,600
(*d*) Depreciation, $38,400

2. Describe both the similarities and differences in amortization, depletion, and depreciation.

On July 1, 2010, Ryan and Associates signed a contract to lease space in a building for 10 years. The lease contract calls for annual (prepaid) rental payments of $80,000 on each July 1 throughout the life of the lease and for the lessee to pay for all additions and improvements to the leased property. After taking possession of the leased space, Ryan pays for improving the office portion of the leased space at a $130,000 cost. The improvements are paid for on July 5, 2010, and are estimated to have a useful life equal to the 16 years remaining in the life of the building.

Problem 18–8A
Intangible assets   **LO8**

Problem 18-7B
Natural resources   **LO7**

On February 19 of the current year, Quartzite Co. pays $5,400,000 for land estimated to contain 4 million tons of recoverable ore. It installs machinery costing $400,000 that has a 16-year life and no salvage value and is capable of mining the ore deposit in 12 years. The machinery is paid for on March 21, eleven days before mining operations begin. The company removes and sells 254,000 tons of ore during its first nine months of operations. Depreciation of the machinery is figured using the units of production method as the machinery will be abandoned after the ore is mined.

Required

Check   (c) Depletion, $342,900;   (d) Depreciation, $25,400

1. Prepare entries to record (*a*) the purchase of the land, (*b*) the cost and installation of machinery, (*c*) the first nine months' depletion assuming the land has a net salvage value of zero after the ore is mined, and (*d*) the first nine months' depreciation on machinery.

2. Describe both the similarities and differences in amortization, depletion, and depreciation.

Problem 18-8B
Intangible assets   **LO8**

On January 1, 2010, Stewart Co. entered into a 5-year lease on a building. The lease contract requires (1) annual (prepaid) rental payments of $36,000 each January 1 throughout the life of the lease and (2) for the lessee to pay for all additions and improvements to the leased property. After taking possession of the leased space, Stewart pays for improving the office portion of the leased space at a $20,000 cost. The improvements are paid for on January 3, 2010, and are estimated to have a useful life equal to the 13 years remaining in the life of the building.

Required

Check   Dr. Rent Expense: (2b) $36,000

1. Prepare entries for Stewart to record (*a*) its payment of the 2010 annual rent to the building owner, and (*b*) its payment for the office improvements.

2. Prepare Stewart's year-end adjusting entries required on December 31, 2010, to (*a*) amortize the office improvements, and (*b*) record rent expense.

SERIAL PROBLEM

Success Systems

(This serial problem began in Chapter 1 and continues through most of the book. If previous chapter segments were not completed, the serial problem can begin at this point. It is helpful, but not necessary, for you to use the Working Papers that accompany the book.)

SP 18   Selected ledger account balances for Success Systems follow.

	For Three Months Ended December 31, 2010	For Three Months Ended March 31, 2011
Office equipment	$ 10,000	$ 10,000
Accumulated depreciation—		
Office equipment	625	1,250
Computer equipment	25,000	25,000
Accumulated depreciation—		
Computer equipment	1,250	2,500
Total revenue	36,170	51,195
Total assets	122,635	147,621

Required

1. Assume that Success Systems does not acquire additional office equipment or computer equipment in 2011. Compute the amounts for the year ended December 31, 2011, for Depreciation Expense—Office Equipment and for Depreciation Expense—Computer Equipment (assume use of the straight-line method).

2. Given the assumptions in part 1, what is the book value of both the Office Equipment account and the Computer Equipment account as of December 31, 2011?

3. Compute the 3-month total asset turnover for Success Systems as of March 31, 2011. Use total revenue for the numerator and average the December 31, 2010, total assets and the March 31, 2011, total assets for the denominator. Interpret its total asset turnover if competitors average 2.5 for annual periods.

BTN 18-1   Refer to the financial statements of **Best Buy** in Appendix A to answer the following.

1. What percent of the original cost of Best Buy's property and equipment remains to be depreciated as of March 1, 2008, and at March 3, 2007? Assume these assets have no salvage value.
2. Over what length(s) of time is Best Buy amortizing its intangible assets?
3. What is the change in total property and equipment (before accumulated depreciation) for the year ended March 1, 2008? What is the amount of cash provided (used) by investing activities for property and equipment for the year ended March 1, 2008? What is one possible explanation for the difference between these two amounts?
4. Compute its total asset turnover for the year ended March 1, 2008, and the year ended March 3, 2007. Assume total assets at February 25, 2006 are $11,864 ($ millions).

Fast Forward

5. Access Best Buy's financial statements for fiscal years ending after March 1, 2008, at its Website (BestBuy.com) or the SEC's EDGAR database (www.SEC.gov). Recompute Best Buy's total asset turnover for the additional years' data you collect. Comment on any differences relative to the turnover computed in part 4.

REPORTING IN ACTION
LO1   LO9

BTN 18-2   Key comparative figures ($ millions) for **Best Buy** and **RadioShack** follow.

COMPARATIVE ANALYSIS
LO9

 RadioShack.

Key Figures	Best Buy Current Year	One Year Prior	Two Years Prior	RadioShack Current Year	One Year Prior	Two Years Prior
Total assets	$12,758	$13,570	$11,864	$1,990	$2,070	$2,205
Net sales	40,023	35,934	30,848	4,251	4,778	5,082

Required

1. Compute total asset turnover for the most recent three years for both Best Buy and RadioShack using the data shown.
2. Which company is more efficient in generating net sales given the total assets it employs? Assume an industry average of 2.4.

BTN 18-3   Flo Choi owns a small business and manages its accounting. Her company just finished a year in which a large amount of borrowed funds was invested in a new building addition as well as in equipment and fixture additions. Choi's banker requires her to submit semiannual financial statements so he can monitor the financial health of her business. He has warned her that if profit margins erode, he might raise the interest rate on the borrowed funds to reflect the increased loan risk from the bank's point of view. Choi knows profit margin is likely to decline this year. As she prepares year-end adjusting entries, she decides to apply the following depreciation rule: All asset additions are considered to be in use on the first day of the following month. (The previous rule assumed assets are in use on the first day of the month nearest to the purchase date.)

ETHICS CHALLENGE
LO1   LO4

Required

1. Identify decisions that managers like Choi must make in applying depreciation methods.
2. Is Choi's rule an ethical violation, or is it a legitimate decision in computing depreciation?
3. How will Choi's new depreciation rule affect the profit margin of her business?

BTN 18-4   Your start-up Internet services company needs cash, and as the company's accountant you are preparing financial statements to apply for a short-term loan. The owner of your company suggests that you treat as many expenses as possible as capital expenditures.

Prepare a memorandum that (a) summarizes the financial statement impacts of this suggestion and (b) gives your recommendation as to whether the company should follow the owner's recommendation.

WORKPLACE COMMUNICATION
LO5

**TAKING IT TO
THE NET**
LO8

BTN 18-5   Access the **Yahoo!** (ticker: YHOO) 10-K report for the year ended December 31, 2008, filed on February 27, 2009, at **www.SEC.gov**.

Required

1. What amount of goodwill is reported on Yahoo!'s balance sheet? What percentage of total assets does its goodwill represent? Is goodwill a major asset for Yahoo! Explain.

2. Locate Note 5 to its financial statements. Identify the change in goodwill from January 1, 2007, to December 31, 2008. Comment on the change in goodwill over this period.

3. Locate Note 6 to its financial statements. What other intangible assets does Yahoo! report at December 31, 2008? What proportion of total assets do the other intangibles represent?

4. What does Yahoo! indicate is the life of "Trademark, trade name, and domain name" according to its Note 6? Comment on the difference between the estimated economic life and the legal life of Yahoo!'s trademark.

**TEAMWORK IN
ACTION**
LO1   LO4

> This activity can follow an overview of each method. Step 1 allows for three areas of expertise. Larger teams will have some duplication of areas, but the straight-line choice should not be duplicated. Expert teams can use the book and consult with the instructor.

BTN 18-6   Each team member is to become an expert on one depreciation method to facilitate team-mates' understanding of that method. Follow these procedures:

a. Each team member is to select an area for expertise from one of the following depreciation methods: straight-line, units-of-production, or double-declining-balance.

b. Expert teams are to be formed from those who have selected the same area of expertise. The instructor will identify the location where each expert team meets.

c. Using the following data, expert teams are to collaborate and develop a presentation answering the requirements. Expert team members must write the presentation in a format they can show to their learning teams.

Data and Requirements On January 8, 2010, Whitewater Riders purchases a van to transport rafters back to the point of departure at the conclusion of the rafting adventures they operate. The cost of the van is $44,000. It has an estimated salvage value of $2,000 and is expected to be used for four years and driven 60,000 miles. The van is driven 12,000 miles in 2010, 18,000 miles in 2011, 21,000 in 2012, and 10,000 in 2013.

1. Compute annual depreciation expense for each year of the van's estimated useful life.
2. Explain when and how annual depreciation is recorded.
3. Explain the impact on income of this depreciation method versus others over the van's life.
4. Identify the van's book value for each year of its life and illustrate the reporting of this amount for any one year.

d. Re-form original learning teams. In rotation, experts are to present to their teams the results from part *c*. Experts are to encourage and respond to questions.

**ENTREPRENEURS
IN BUSINESS**
LO9

BTN 18-7   Review the chapter's opening feature involving **Sambazon**. Assume that the company currently has net sales of $8,000,000. Assume that it is planning an expansion that will increase net sales by $4,000,000. To accomplish this expansion, Sambazon must increase its average total assets from $2,500,000 to $3,000,000.

Required

1. Compute the company's total asset turnover under (*a*) current conditions and (*b*) proposed conditions.

2. Evaluate and comment on the merits of the proposal given your analysis in part 1. Identify any concerns you would express about the proposal.

ETHICS CHALLENGE
LO4

BTN 18-8   You are the controller for a struggling company. Its operations require regular investments in equipment, and depreciation is its largest expense. Its competitors frequently replace equipment—often depreciated over three years. The company president instructs you to revise useful lives of equipment from three to six years and to use a six-year life on all new equipment. What actions do you take?

1. b;

	Appraisal Value	%	Total Cost	Allocated
Land	$175,000	50%	$326,000	$163,000
Land improvements	70,000	20	326,000	65,200
Building	105,000	30	326,000	97,800
Totals	$350,000			$326,000

2. c; ($35,000 − $1,000)/4 years = $8,500 per year.

3. c; 2010: $10,800,000 × (2 × 10%) = $2,160,000
   2011: ($10,800,000 − $2,160,000) × (2 × 10%)
   = $1,728,000

4. c;

Cost of machine	$250,000
Accumulated depreciation	100,000
Book value	150,000
Cash received	120,000
Loss on sale	$ 30,000

5. b; $550,000/$500,000 = 1.10

Chapter 19

Accounting for Partnerships

A Look Back

Chapter 18 focused on accounting for long-term assets, including plant assets and intangibles.

A Look at This Chapter

This chapter explains the partnership form of organization. Important partnership characteristics are described along with the accounting concepts and procedures for its most fundamental transactions.

A Look Ahead

Chapter 20 extends our discussion to the corporate form of organization. We describe the accounting and reporting for stock issuances and other equity transactions.

Learning Objectives

LO 1	Identify characteristics of partnerships.
LO 2	Identify common types of organizations with partnership characteristics.
LO 3	Prepare entries for partnership formation.
LO 4	Allocate and record income and loss among partners.
LO 5	Prepare a statement of partners' equity.
LO 6	Account for the admission and withdrawal of partners.
LO 7	Prepare entries for partnership liquidation.
LO 8	Compute partner return on equity and use it to evaluate partnership performance.

"Be your best, make a difference, and live with passion"—Samanta and Kelvin Joseph

A Fitting Pair

NEW YORK—Business recipe: Take one information systems graduate, mix a bit of international flair, add an accountant, and stir. The result is **Samanta Shoes (SamantaShoes.com),** a start-up shoe manufacturer. Founded by Samanta and Kelvin Joseph, their partnership is aimed at providing "stylish, comfortable, and affordable" shoes, explains Samanta. "I design every shoe, and nothing less than the best material is used."

Kelvin's focus is on the accounting and financial side of Samanta Shoes. "The knowledge gained from my years at Ernst & Young LLP [a major accounting firm]," explains Kelvin, "has enabled me to be more helpful." Kelvin's knowledge of partnerships and their financial implications are important to Samanta's success. Both partners stress the importance of attending to partnership formation, partnership agreements, and financial reports to stay afloat. They refer to the partners' return on equity and the organizational form as key inputs to partnership success.

Success is causing their partnership to evolve, but the partners adhere to a quality first mentality. "It's all in the design," insists Samanta. "[A quality design] allows for more comfort and support." But quality also extends to style and uniqueness. "Women don't like other women having their shoe," explains Samanta. "We don't want to dilute our brand by being too mass market." Kelvin explains that the smallest manufacturing run they can have is 18 pairs of a special line. In a world of 6 billion people, that is unique.

The partners also continue to apply strict accounting fundamentals. "The partnership cannot survive," says Kelvin, "unless our business is profitable." They regularly review the accounting results and assess the partnership's costs and revenues. Although he adds, "money does not equal happiness." Samanta explains, "Live your dreams . . . make a difference . . . give back to your community"—advice that we can all live by. "If you're not enjoying it," continues Samanta, "there's no point to doing it."

[Sources: *Samanta Shoes Website,* January 2009; *New York Resident,* August 2004; *Caribbean Vibe,* August 2004; *Black Enterprise,* June 2006; *Regine Magazine,* Spring 2004; *Inc.com,* July 2007]

The three basic types of business organizations are proprietorships, partnerships, and corporations. Partnerships are like proprietorships, except they have more than one owner. This chapter explains partnerships and looks at several variations of them such as limited partnerships, limited liability partnerships, S corporations, and limited liability companies. Understanding the advantages and disadvantages of the partnership form of business organization is important in choosing the right business form.

Accounting for Partnerships

Partnership Organization
- Characteristics
- Organizations with partnership characteristics
- Choosing a business form

Basic Partnership Accounting
- Organizing a partnership
- Dividing income or loss
- Partnership financial statements

Partner Admission and Withdrawal
- Admission of partner
- Withdrawal of partner
- Death of partner

Partnership Liquidation
- No capital deficiency
- Capital deficiency

Partnership Form of Organization

LO1 Identify characteristics of partnerships.

A **partnership** is an unincorporated association of two or more people to pursue a business for profit as co-owners. Partnerships are especially common in small retail and service businesses. Physicians, lawyers, investors, and accountants also often organize their practices as partnerships.

Characteristics of Partnerships

We describe the unique characteristics of partnerships in this section.

Voluntary Association   A partnership is a voluntary association between partners. Joining a partnership increases the risk to one's personal financial position.

Partnership Agreement   Forming a partnership requires that two or more legally competent people (who are of age and of sound mental capacity) agree to be partners. Their agreement becomes a **partnership contract,** also called *articles of copartnership* (if written). This should be in writing, but the contract is binding even if it is only expressed verbally. Partnership agreements normally include details of the partners' (1) names and contributions, (2) rights and duties, (3) sharing of income and losses, (4) withdrawal arrangement, (5) dispute procedures, (6) admission and withdrawal of partners, and (7) rights and duties in the event a partner dies. When a new partner is admitted, all parties usually must agree to the admission.

Taxation   A partnership is not taxed on its income. The income or loss of a partnership is allocated to the partners according to the partnership agreement, and it is included in determining the taxable income for each partner's tax return. Partnership income or loss is allocated each year whether or not cash is distributed to partners.

Co-Ownership of Property   Partnership assets are owned jointly by all partners. Any investment by a partner becomes the joint property of all partners. Partners have a claim on partnership assets based on their capital account and the partnership contract.

Limited Life   The life of a partnership is limited. Death, bankruptcy, or any event taking away the ability of a partner to enter into or fulfill a contract ends a partnership. Any one of the partners can also terminate a partnership at will. The end of a partnership is referred to as its *dissolution*.

Mutual Agency   **Mutual agency** implies that each partner is a fully authorized agent of the partnership. As its agent, a partner can commit or bind the partnership to any contract within the scope of the partnership business. For instance, a partner in a merchandising business can sign contracts binding the partnership to buy merchandise, lease a store building, borrow money, or hire employees. These activities are all within the scope of a merchandising firm. A partner in a law firm, acting alone, however, cannot bind the other partners to a contract to buy snowboards for resale or rent an apartment for parties. These actions are outside the normal scope of a law firm's business. Partners also can agree to limit the power of any one or more of the partners to negotiate contracts for the partnership. Such a restriction might not hold up if challenged by an injured party who was unaware of the restriction. Mutual agency exposes partners to the risk of unwise actions by any one partner.

Unlimited Liability   **Unlimited liability** implies that each partner can be called on to pay a partnership's debts. When a partnership cannot pay its debts, creditors usually can apply their claims to partners' *personal* assets. If a partner does not have enough personal assets to meet his or her share of the partnership debt, the creditors can apply their claims to the assets of the other partners. A partnership in which all partners have *mutual agency* and *unlimited liability* is called a **general partnership.** Mutual agency and unlimited liability are two main reasons that most general partnerships have only a few members.

   The partnership form has three major advantages. First, partnership income is not taxed. Second, partnerships allow for the combining of talents and skills of two or more individuals. Third, partnerships are easy to form. The major disadvantage of the partnership is that each partner is personally liable for all the partnership's debt.

Organizations with Partnership Characteristics

Organizations exist that combine certain characteristics of partnerships with other forms of organization. We discuss several of these forms in this section.

Limited Partnerships   Some individuals who want to invest in a partnership are unwilling to accept the risk of unlimited liability. Their needs can be met with a **limited partnership.** This type of organization is identified in its name with the words "Limited Partnership," or "Ltd.," or "LP." A limited partnership has two classes of partners, general and limited. At least one partner must be a **general partner,** who assumes management duties and unlimited liability for the debts of the partnership. The **limited partners** have no personal liability beyond the amounts they invest in the partnership. Limited partners typically have no active management role. A limited partnership agreement often specifies unique procedures for allocating income and losses between general and limited partners. The accounting procedures are similar for both limited and general partnerships.

LO2 Identify common types of organizations with partnership characteristics.

IN THE NEWS

Nutty Partners   The Hawaii-based **ML Macadamia Orchards LP** is one of the world's largest growers of macadamia nuts. It reported the following partners' capital balances ($ 000s) in its balance sheet:

General Partner	$ 81
Limited Partners	$43,365

Limited Liability Partnerships   Most states allow individuals to form a **limited liability partnership.** This is identified in its name with the words "Limited Liability Partnership" or by "LLP." This type of partnership is designed to protect innocent partners from malpractice or negligence claims resulting from the acts of another partner. When a partner provides service resulting in a malpractice claim, only that partner has personal liability for the claim. The remaining partners who were not responsible for the actions resulting in the claim are not personally liable for it. However, most states hold all partners personally liable for other partnership debts, as in a general partnership. Accounting for a limited liability partnership is the same as for a general partnership. Many accounting services firms are set up as LLPs.

S Corporations   Certain corporations with 75 or fewer stockholders can elect to be treated as a partnership for income tax purposes. These corporations are called *Subchapter S* or simply **S corporations.** S corporations provide stockholders limited personal liability. The S corporation also does not pay income taxes. If stockholders work for an S corporation, their salaries are treated as expenses of the corporation. The remaining income or loss of the corporation is allocated to stockholders for inclusion on their personal tax returns.

Limited Liability Companies   A relatively new form of business organization is the **limited liability company.** The names of these businesses usually include the words "Limited Liability Company" or an abbreviation such as "LLC" or "LC." This form of business has certain features similar to a corporation and others similar to a limited partnership. The owners, who are called *members,* are protected with the same limited liability feature as owners of corporations. While limited partners cannot actively participate in the management of a limited partnership, the members of a limited liability company can assume an active management role. A limited liability company usually has a limited life. For income tax purposes, a limited liability company is typically treated as a partnership.

The majority of proprietorships and partnerships that are being organized today are being set up as LLCs. Accounting for LLCs is similar to that for partnerships (and proprietorships). One difference is that Owner (Partner), Capital is usually called *Members, Capital* for LLCs.

Choosing a Business Form

Choosing the proper business form is crucial. Many factors should be considered, including taxes, liability risk, tax and fiscal year-end, ownership structure, estate planning, business risks, and earnings and property distributions. The following table summarizes several important characteristics of business organizations:

	Proprietorship	Partnership	LLP	LLC	S Corp.	Corporation
Business entity	yes	yes	yes	yes	yes	yes
Legal entity	no	no	no	yes	yes	yes
Limited liability	no	no	limited*	yes	yes	yes
Business taxed	no	no	no	no	no	yes
One owner allowed	yes	no	no	yes	yes	yes

* A partner's personal liability for LLP debts is limited. Most LLPs carry insurance to protect against malpractice.

We must remember that this table is a summary, not a detailed list. Many details underlie each of these business forms, and several details differ across states. Also, state and federal laws change, and a body of law is still developing around LLCs. Business owners should look at these details and consider unique business arrangements such as organizing various parts of their businesses in different forms. The Small Business Administration provides suggestions and information on setting up the proper form for your organization—see **SBA.gov**.

HOW YOU DOIN'?   Answers—p. 503

1. A partnership ends when (*a*) a partnership agreement is not in writing, (*b*) a partner dies, (*c*) a partner exercises mutual agency.
2. What does the term *unlimited liability* mean when applied to a general partnership?
3. Which of the following forms of organization does not provide limited liability to *all* of its owners: (*a*) S corporation, (*b*) limited liability company, (*c*) limited partnership?

Basic Partnership Accounting

Since ownership rights in a partnership are divided among partners, partnership accounting

- Uses a capital account for each partner.
- Uses a withdrawals account for each partner.
- Allocates net income or loss to partners according to the partnership agreement.

This section describes partnership accounting for organizing a partnership, distributing income and loss, and preparing financial statements.

Organizing a Partnership

When partners invest in a partnership, their capital accounts are credited for the invested amounts. Partners can invest both assets and liabilities. Each partner's investment is recorded at an agreed-on value, normally the market values of the contributed assets and liabilities at the date of contribution. To illustrate, Kayla Zayn and Hector Perez organize a partnership on January 11 called BOARDS that offers year-round facilities for skateboarding and snowboarding. Zayn's initial net investment in BOARDS is $30,000, made up of cash ($7,000), boarding facilities ($33,000), and a note payable reflecting a bank loan for the new business ($10,000). Perez's initial investment is cash of $10,000. These amounts are the values agreed on by both partners. The entries to record these investments follow.

LO3 Prepare entries for partnership formation.

		Zayn's Investment		
Jan.	11	Cash	7 0 0 0 00	
		Boarding facilities	33 0 0 0 00	
		Note payable		10 0 0 0 00
		K. Zayn, Capital		30 0 0 0 00
		To record the investment of Zayn.		

Assets = Liabilities + Equity
+7,000   +10,000   +30,000
+33,000

		Perez's Investment		
Jan.	11	Cash	10 0 0 0 00	
		H. Perez, Capital		10 0 0 0 00
		To record the investment of Perez.		

Assets = Liabilities + Equity
+10,000   +10,000

In accounting for a partnership, the following additional relations hold true: (1) Partners' withdrawals are debited to their own separate withdrawals accounts. (2) Partners' capital accounts are credited (or debited) for their shares of net income (or net loss) when closing the accounts at the end of a period. (3) Each partner's withdrawals account is closed to that partner's capital account. Separate capital and withdrawals accounts are kept for each partner.

IN THE NEWS

Broadway Partners   **Big River Productions** is a partnership that owns the rights to the play *Big River*. The play is performed on tour and periodically on Broadway. For 2006, its ending Partners' Capital was $288,640 and it was distributed in its entirety to its partners.

LO4 Allocate and record income and loss among partners.

Income or Loss Division among Partners

Partners are not employees of the partnership but are its owners. If partners work for their partnership, they do so for profit, not for salary. This means there are no salaries to partners that are reported as expenses on the partnership income statement. However, when net income or loss of a partnership is divided among partners, the partners can agree to allocate "salary allowances" reflecting the relative value of services provided. Partners also can agree to allocate "interest allowances" based on the amount invested. For instance, since Zayn contributes three times the investment of Perez, it is only fair that this be considered when allocating income between them. Like salary allowances, these interest allowances are not expenses on the partnership's income statement.

Partners can agree to any method of dividing income or loss. In the absence of an agreement, the law says that the partners share income or loss of a partnership equally. If partners agree on how to share income but say nothing about losses, they share losses the same way they share income. Three common methods to divide income or loss use (1) a stated ratio basis, (2) the ratio of capital balances, or (3) salary and interest allowances and any remainder according to a fixed ratio. We explain each of these methods in this section.

> Partners can agree on one ratio to divide income and another ratio to divide a loss.

Allocation Based on Stated Ratios   The *stated ratio* (also called the *income-and-loss-sharing ratio*, the *profit and loss ratio*, or the *P&L ratio*) method of allocating partnership income or loss gives each partner a fraction of the total. Partners must agree on the fractional share each receives. The fractional basis can be stated as a proportion, ratio, or percent. For example, a 3:2 basis is the same as $\frac{3}{5}$ and $\frac{2}{5}$, or 60% and 40%. To illustrate, assume the partnership agreement of K. Zayn and H. Perez says Zayn receives two-thirds and Perez one-third of partnership income and loss. If their partnership's net income is $60,000, it is allocated to the partners as follows.

Zayn $60,000 × $\frac{2}{3}$ = $40,000

Perez $60,000 × $\frac{1}{3}$ = $20,000

The entry to update the partners' capital accounts and close Income Summary is as follows.

Assets = Liabilities + Equity				
−60,000				
+40,000				
+20,000				

Dec.	31	Income Summary	60 0 0 0 00	
		K. Zayn, Capital		40 0 0 0 00
		H. Perez, Capital		20 0 0 0 00
		To allocate income and close Income Summary.		

Allocation Based on Capital Balances   The *capital balances* method of allocating partnership income or loss assigns an amount based on the ratio of each partner's relative capital balance. If Zayn and Perez agree to share income and loss on the ratio of their beginning capital balances—Zayn's $30,000 and Perez's $10,000—Zayn receives three-fourths of any income or loss ($30,000/$40,000) and Perez receives one-fourth ($10,000/$40,000). In this case the partnership's net income of $60,000 is allocated to the partners as follows.

Zayn $60,000 × $\frac{3}{4}$ = $45,000

Perez $60,000 × $\frac{1}{4}$ = $15,000

The entry to update the partner's capital accounts follows the format of the entry above.

Allocation Based on Services, Capital, and Stated Ratios   The *services, capital, and stated ratio* method of allocating partnership income or loss recognizes that service and capital contributions of partners often are not equal. Salary allowances can make up for differences in service contributions. Interest allowances can make up for unequal capital contributions. Also, the allocation of income and loss can include *both* salary and interest allowances. To illustrate, assume that the partnership agreement of K. Zayn and H. Perez reflects differences in service and capital contributions as follows: (1) annual salary allowances of $36,000 to Zayn and $24,000 to Perez, (2) annual interest allowances of 10% of a partner's beginning-year capital balance, and (3) equal share of any remaining balance of income or loss. These salaries and interest allowances are *not* reported as expenses on the partnership's income statement. They are simply a means of dividing partnership income or loss. The remainder of this section provides three illustrations using this three-point allocation agreement.

Illustration when income exceeds allowance. If BOARDS has first-year net income of $70,000, and Zayn and Perez apply the three-point partnership agreement described in the prior paragraph, income is allocated as shown in Exhibit 19.1. First, a salary allowance of $36,000 is allocated to Zayn and a salary allowance of $24,000 is allocated to Perez. Interest allowances, based on beginning-year capital balances, are allocated as

Zayn	$30,000 × 10% = $3,000
Perez	$10,000 × 10% = $1,000

	Zayn	Perez	Total
Net income			**$70,000**
Salary allowances			
Zayn	$ 36,000		
Perez		$ 24,000	
Interest allowances			
Zayn (10% × $30,000)	3,000		
Perez (10% × $10,000)		1,000	
Total salaries and interest	39,000	25,000	64,000
Balance of income			6,000
Balance allocated equally			
Zayn	3,000 ←		
Perez		3,000 ←	
Total allocated			6,000
Balance of income			$ 0
Income of each partner	**$42,000**	**$28,000**	

Exhibit 19.1

Dividing Income When Income Exceeds Allowances

At this point there is $6,000 of partnership net income remaining to allocate to the partners ($70,000 − $36,000 − $24,000 − $3,000 − $1,000). Each partner shares equally in this remaining amount and receives another $3,000. Zayn gets $42,000 and Perez gets $28,000 of the partnership's $70,000 total net income.

Illustration when allowances exceed income. The sharing agreement between Zayn and Perez must be followed even if net income is less than the total of the allowances. When allowances exceed income, the amount of this negative balance often is referred to as a *sharing agreement loss* or *deficit*. For example, if BOARDS' first-year net income is $50,000 instead of $70,000, it is allocated to the partners as shown in Exhibit 19.2. Computations for salaries and interest are identical to those in Exhibit 19.1. However, when we apply the total allowances against income, the balance of income is negative. This $(14,000) negative balance is allocated equally to the partners per their sharing agreement. This means that a negative $(7,000) is allocated to each partner. In this case, Zayn ends up with $32,000 and Perez with $18,000 of the partnership's $50,000 total net income.

Exhibit 19.2

Dividing Income When
Allowances Exceed Income

	Zayn	Perez	Total
Net income			**$50,000**
Salary allowances			
Zayn	$ 36,000		
Perez		$ 24,000	
Interest allowances			
Zayn (10% × $30,000)	3,000		
Perez (10% × $10,000)		1,000	
Total salaries and interest	39,000	25,000	64,000
Balance of income			**(14,000)**
Balance allocated equally			
Zayn	(7,000) ←		
Perez		(7,000) ←	
Total allocated			(14,000)
Balance of income			$ 0
Income of each partner	**$32,000**	**$18,000**	

Illustration when allowances exceed income and partnership reports loss.   If BOARDS had experienced a net loss, Zayn and Perez would share it in the same manner as the $50,000 income. For example, if BOARDS reported a first-year net loss of $20,000, it is allocated to the partners as shown in Exhibit 19.3. After applying the total allowances against the net loss of $20,000, the balance of income is negative. This $(84,000) balance is allocated evenly to the partners. In this case, a negative $(42,000) is allocated to each partner. Zayn ends up with $(3,000) and Perez with $(17,000) of the partnership's $(20,000) total net loss.

Exhibit 19.3

Dividing Income When
Allowances Exceed Income and
Partnership Reports Loss

	Zayn	Perez	Total
Net income			**$(20,000)**
Salary allowances			
Zayn	$ 36,000		
Perez		$ 24,000	
Interest allowances			
Zayn (10% × $30,000)	3,000		
Perez (10% × $10,000)		1,000	
Total salaries and interest	39,000	25,000	64,000
Balance of income			**(84,000)**
Balance allocated equally			
Zayn	(42,000) ←		
Perez		(42,000) ←	
Total allocated			(84,000)
Balance of income			$ 0
Income of each partner	**$(3,000)**	**$(17,000)**	

HOW YOU DOIN'?   Answer—p. 503

4. Denzel and Shantell form a partnership by contributing $70,000 and $35,000 cash, respectively. They agree to an interest allowance equal to 10% of each partner's capital balance at the beginning of the year, with the remaining income shared equally. Allocate first-year income of $40,000 to the partners.

Partnership Financial Statements

Partnership financial statements are like those of other organizations. The **statement of partners' equity,** also called *statement of partners' capital,* is one exception. It shows *each* partner's beginning capital balance, additional investments, allocated income or loss, withdrawals, and ending capital balance. To illustrate, Exhibit 19.4 shows the statement of partners' equity for BOARDS prepared using the sharing agreement of Exhibit 19.1. Recall that BOARDS' income was $70,000; also, assume that Zayn withdrew $20,000 and Perez $12,000 at year-end.

L05 Prepare a statement of partners' equity.

Exhibit 19.4

Statement of Partners' Equity

BOARDS Statement of Partners' Equity For Year Ended December 31, 2010					
	Zayn		**Perez**		**Total**
Beginning capital balances		$ 0		$ 0	$ 0
Plus					
Investments by partners		30,000		10,000	40,000
Net income					
Salary allowances	$36,000		$24,000		
Interest allowances	3,000		1,000		
Balance allocated	3,000		3,000		
Total net income		42,000		28,000	70,000
		72,000		38,000	110,000
Less partners' withdrawals		(20,000)		(12,000)	(32,000)
Ending capital balances		**$52,000**		**$26,000**	**$78,000**

IN THE NEWS

Gambling Partners **Trump Entertainment Resorts LP** and subsidiaries operate three casino hotel properties in Atlantic City: Trump Taj Mahal Casino Resort ("Trump Taj Mahal"), Trump Plaza Hotel and Casino ("Trump Plaza"), and Trump Marina Hotel Casino ("Trump Marina"). Its recent statement of partners' equity reports $979,000 in partners' withdrawals, leaving $594,230,000 in partners' capital balances.

Recording Partner Withdrawals These withdrawals were recorded as follows.

Dec.	31	K. Zayn, Withdrawals	20 0 0 0 00	
		H. Perez, Withdrawals	12 0 0 0 00	
		Cash		32 0 0 0 00
		To record partner withdrawals.		

Assets = Liabilities + Equity
−32,000   −20,000
                          −12,000

The partners' Withdrawals accounts are contra accounts to the partners' Capital accounts. Partners' withdrawals are not constrained by the partnership's annual income or loss. These Withdrawals accounts are closed to the partners' Capital accounts with the following entry.

Dec.	31	K. Zayn, Capital	20 0 0 0 00	
		K. Zayn, Withdrawals		20 0 0 0 00
		To reduce K. Zayn's capital account for withdrawals.		

Assets = Liabilities + Equity
                          −20,000
                          +20,000

		H. Perez, Capital	12 0 0 0 00	
		H. Perez, Withdrawals		12 0 0 0 00
		To reduce H. Perez's capital account for withdrawals.		

Assets = Liabilities + Equity
                          −12,000
                          +12,000

The equity section of the balance sheet of a partnership usually shows the separate capital account balance of each partner. In the case of BOARDS' December 31, 2010, balance sheet, both K. Zayn, Capital, and H. Perez, Capital, are listed in the equity section along with their balances of $52,000 and $26,000, respectively.

Admission and Withdrawal of Partners

LO6 Account for the admission and withdrawal of partners.

A partnership is based on a contract between individuals. When a new partner is admitted or a current partner withdraws, the present partnership ends. Still, the business can continue to operate as a new partnership consisting of the remaining partners. This section shows how to account for the admission and withdrawal of partners.

Admission of a Partner

A new partner either purchases an interest from one or more current partners or invests cash or other assets in the partnership.

Purchase of Partnership Interest The purchase of partnership interest is a *personal transaction between one or more current partners and the new partner*. To become a partner, the current partners must accept the purchaser. Accounting for the purchase of partnership interest involves reallocating current partners' capital to the new partner to reflect the transaction. To illustrate, at the end of BOARDS' first year, H. Perez sells one-half of his partnership interest to Tyrell Rasheed for $18,000. This means that Perez gives up a $13,000 recorded interest ($26,000 × ½) in the partnership (see H. Perez's ending capital balance in Exhibit 19.4). The partnership records this January 4, 2011, transaction as follows.

Assets = Liabilities + Equity
−13,000
+13,000

Jan.	4	H. Perez, Capital	13 0 0 0 00	
		T. Rasheed, Capital		13 0 0 0 00
		To record admission of Rasheed by purchase.		

After this entry is posted, BOARDS' equity shows K. Zayn, Capital; H. Perez, Capital; and T. Rasheed, Capital, and their respective balances of $52,000, $13,000, and $13,000.

Two aspects of this transaction are important. First, the partnership does *not* record the $18,000 Rasheed paid Perez. The partnership's assets, liabilities, and *total equity* are unaffected by this transaction among partners. Second, Zayn and Perez must agree that Rasheed is to become a partner. If they agree to accept Rasheed, a new partnership is formed and a new contract with a new income-and-loss-sharing agreement is prepared.

Investing Assets in a Partnership Admitting a partner by accepting assets is a *transaction between the new partner and the partnership*. The invested assets become partnership property. To illustrate, if Zayn (with a $52,000 interest) and Perez (with a $26,000 interest) agree to accept Rasheed as a partner in BOARDS after an investment of $22,000 cash, this is recorded as follows.

Assets = Liabilities + Equity
+22,000   +22,000

Jan.	4	Cash	22 0 0 0 00	
		T. Rasheed, Capital		22 0 0 0 00
		To record admission of Rasheed by investment.		

After this entry is posted, both assets (cash) and equity (T. Rasheed, Capital) increase by $22,000. Rasheed now has a 22% equity in the assets of the business, computed as $22,000 divided by the entire partnership equity ($52,000 + $26,000 + $22,000). Rasheed does not necessarily have a right to 22% of income. Dividing income and loss is a separate matter on which partners must agree. Without an explicit agreement, partners share income and loss equally.

Bonus to old partners.   When the current value of a partnership is greater than the recorded amounts of equity, the partners usually require a new partner to pay a bonus for the privilege of joining. To illustrate, assume that Zayn and Perez agree to accept Rasheed as a partner with a 25% interest in BOARDS if Rasheed invests $42,000. Recall the partnership's accounting records show Zayn's recorded equity in the business is $52,000 and Perez's recorded equity is $26,000 (see Exhibit 19.4). Rasheed's equity is determined as follows.

Equities of existing partners ($52,000 + $26,000)	$ 78,000
Investment of new partner	42,000
Total partnership equity	$120,000
Equity of Rasheed (25% × $120,000)	$ 30,000

Although Rasheed invests $42,000, the equity attributed to Rasheed in the new partnership is only $30,000. The $12,000 difference is called a *bonus* and is allocated to existing partners (Zayn and Perez) according to their income-and-loss-sharing agreement. A bonus is shared in this way because it is viewed as reflecting a higher value of the partnership that is not yet reflected in income. The entry to record this transaction follows.

Jan.	4	Cash	42 0 0 0 00	
		T. Rasheed, Capital		30 0 0 0 00
		K. Zayn, Capital ($12,000 × ½)		6 0 0 0 00
		H. Perez, Capital ($12,000 × ½)		6 0 0 0 00
		To record admission of Rasheed and bonus.		

Assets = Liabilities + Equity
+42,000   +30,000
                   +6,000
                   +6,000

Bonus to new partner.   Alternatively, existing partners can grant a bonus to a new partner. This usually occurs when the partnership needs additional cash or the new partner has exceptional talents. The bonus to the new partner is in the form of a larger share of equity than the amount invested. To illustrate, assume that Zayn (with a $52,000 interest) and Perez (with a $26,000 interest) agree to accept Rasheed as a partner with a 25% interest in the partnership, but they require Rasheed to invest only $18,000. Rasheed's equity is determined as follows.

Equities of existing partners ($52,000 + $26,000)	$78,000
Investment of new partner	18,000
Total partnership equity	$96,000
Equity of Rasheed (25% × $96,000)	$24,000

The old partners contribute the $6,000 bonus (computed as $24,000 minus $18,000) to Rasheed according to their income-and-loss-sharing ratio. Moreover, Rasheed's 25% equity does not necessarily entitle Rasheed to 25% of future income or loss. This is a separate matter for agreement by the partners. The entry to record the admission and investment of Rasheed is

Jan.	4	Cash	18 0 0 0 00	
		K. Zayn, Capital ($6,000 × ½)	3 0 0 0 00	
		H. Perez, Capital ($6,000 × ½)	3 0 0 0 00	
		T. Rasheed, Capital		24 0 0 0 00
		To record Rasheed's admission and bonus.		

Assets = Liabilities + Equity
+18,000   −3,000
                   −3,000
                   +24,000

Withdrawal of a Partner

A partner generally withdraws from a partnership in one of two ways. (1) First, the withdrawing partner can sell his or her interest to another person who pays for it in cash or other assets. For this, we need only debit the withdrawing partner's capital account and credit the new partner's capital account. (2) The second case is when cash or other assets of the partnership are distributed to the withdrawing partner in settlement of his or her interest. To illustrate these cases, assume that Perez withdraws from the partnership of BOARDS in some future period. The partnership shows the following capital balances at the date of Perez's withdrawal: K. Zayn, $84,000; H. Perez, $38,000; and T. Rasheed, $38,000. The partners (Zayn, Perez, and Rasheed) share income and loss equally. Accounting for Perez's withdrawal depends on whether a bonus is paid. We describe three possibilities.

No Bonus   If Perez withdraws and takes cash equal to Perez's capital balance, the entry is

Assets = Liabilities + Equity
−38,000   −38,000

Oct.	31	H. Perez, Capital	38 0 0 0 00	
		Cash		38 0 0 0 00
		To record withdrawal of Perez from partnership with no bonus.		

Perez can take any combination of assets to which the partners agree to settle Perez's equity. Perez's withdrawal creates a new partnership between the remaining partners. A new partnership contract and a new income-and-loss-sharing agreement are required.

Bonus to Remaining Partners   A withdrawing partner is sometimes willing to take less than the recorded value of his or her equity to get out of the partnership or because the recorded value is overstated. When this occurs the withdrawing partner in effect gives the remaining partners a bonus equal to the equity left behind. The remaining partners share this bonus according to their income-and-loss-sharing ratio. To illustrate, if Perez withdraws and agrees to take $34,000 cash in settlement of Perez's capital balance, the entry is

Assets = Liabilities + Equity
−34,000   −38,000
                           +2,000
                           +2,000

Oct.	31	H. Perez, Capital	38 0 0 0 00	
		Cash		34 0 0 0 00
		K. Zayn, Capital		2 0 0 0 00
		T. Rasheed, Capital		2 0 0 0 00
		To record withdrawal of Perez and bonus to remaining partners.		

Perez withdrew $4,000 less than Perez's recorded equity of $38,000. This $4,000 is divided between Zayn and Rasheed according to their income-and-loss-sharing ratio.

Bonus to Withdrawing Partner   A withdrawing partner may be able to receive more than his or her recorded equity for at least two reasons. First, the recorded equity may be understated. Second, the remaining partners may agree to remove this partner by giving assets of greater value than this partner's recorded equity. In either case, the withdrawing partner receives a bonus. The remaining partners reduce their equity by the amount of this bonus according to their income-and-loss-sharing ratio. To illustrate, if Perez withdraws and receives $40,000 cash in settlement of Perez's capital balance, the entry is

Assets = Liabilities + Equity
−40,000   −38,000
                           −1,000
                           −1,000

Oct.	31	H. Perez, Capital	38 0 0 0 00	
		K. Zayn, Capital	1 0 0 0 00	
		T. Rasheed, Capital	1 0 0 0 00	
		Cash		40 0 0 0 00
		To record Perez's withdrawal from partnership with		
		a bonus to Perez.		

Falcon Cable Communications LLC set up a partnership withdrawal agreement. Falcon owns and operates cable television systems and had two managing general partners. The partnership agreement stated that either partner "can offer to sell to the other partner the offering partner's entire partnership interest . . . for a negotiated price. If the partner receiving such an offer rejects it, the offering partner may elect to cause [the partnership] . . . to be liquidated and dissolved."

Death of a Partner

A partner's death ends a partnership. A deceased partner's estate is entitled to receive his or her equity. The partnership contract should contain provisions for settlement in this case. These provisions usually require (1) closing the books to determine income or loss since the end of the previous period and (2) determining and recording current market values for both assets and liabilities. The remaining partners and the deceased partner's estate then must agree to a settlement of the deceased partner's equity. This can involve selling the equity to remaining partners or to an outsider, or it can involve withdrawing assets.

Liquidation of a Partnership

When a partnership is liquidated, its business ends and four concluding steps are required.

1. Record the sale of noncash assets for cash and any gain or loss from their liquidation.
2. Allocate any gain or loss from liquidation of the assets in step 1 to the partners using their income-and-loss-sharing ratio.
3. Pay or settle all partner liabilities.
4. Distribute any remaining cash to partners based on their capital balances.

Partnership liquidation usually falls into one of two cases, as described in this section.

No Capital Deficiency

No capital deficiency means that all partners have a zero or credit balance in their capital accounts for final distribution of cash. To illustrate, assume that Zayn, Perez, and Rasheed operate their partnership in BOARDS for several years, sharing income and loss equally. The partners then decide to liquidate. On the liquidation date, the current period's income or loss is transferred to the partners' capital accounts according to the sharing agreement. After that transfer, the partnership reports the balance sheet in Exhibit 19.5 (immediately before liquidation):

LO7 Prepare entries for partnership liquidation.

Assets		Liabilities	
Cash	$178,000	Accounts Payable	$ 20,000
Boarding facilities	15,000	Partners' Equity	
Land	25,000	K. Zayn, Capital	70,000
		H. Perez, Capital	66,000
		T. Rasheed, Capital	62,000
Total assets	$218,000	Total Liabilities and Partners' Equity	$218,000

Exhibit 19.5

Partnership Balance Sheet before Liquidation

Next, assume that BOARDS sells its boarding facilities and land for $46,000, for a net gain of $6,000. In a liquidation, gains or losses usually result from the sale of noncash assets, which are called *losses and gains from liquidation*. Partners share losses and gains from liquidation according to their income-and-loss-sharing agreement (equal for these partners) yielding the partners' revised equity balances of Zayn, $72,000; Perez, $68,000; and

Rasheed, $64,000.[1] BOARDS then pays $20,000 to settle its accounts payable. After creditors are paid, BOARDS' remaining cash of $204,000 (computed as $178,000 + $46,000 − $20,000) is divided among partners according to their capital account balances. The total partners' capital account balances of $204,000 (computed as $72,000 + $68,000 + $64,000) exactly equal the partnership's cash. This will always be the case when the partnership has positive equity after selling assets and paying liabilities.

Assets = Liabilities + Equity
−20,000   −20,000

Jan.	15	Accounts Payable	20 0 0 0 00	
		Cash		20 0 0 0 00
		To pay claims of creditors.		

Assets = Liabilities + Equity
−204,000   −72,000
                              −68,000
                              −64,000

Jan.	15	K. Zayn, Capital	72 0 0 0 00	
		H. Perez, Capital	68 0 0 0 00	
		T. Rasheed, Capital	64 0 0 0 00	
		Cash		204 0 0 0 00
		To distribute remaining cash to partners.		

It is important to remember that the final cash payment is distributed to partners according to their capital account balances, whereas gains and losses from liquidation are allocated according to the income-and-loss-sharing ratio.

Capital Deficiency

Capital deficiency means that at least one partner has a debit (abnormal) balance in his or her capital account at the point of final cash distribution. This can arise from liquidation losses, excessive withdrawals before liquidation, or recurring losses in prior periods. A partner with a capital deficiency must, if possible, cover the deficit by paying cash into the partnership.

To illustrate, assume that Zayn, Perez, and Rasheed operate their partnership in BOARDS for several years, sharing income and losses equally. The partners then decide to liquidate. Immediately prior to the final distribution of cash, the partners' recorded capital balances are Zayn, $19,000; Perez, $8,000; and Rasheed, $(3,000). The partnership also has $24,000 cash, no other assets, and no liabilities. Rasheed owes the partnership $3,000. Both Zayn and Perez have a legal claim against Rasheed's personal assets for $3,000. The final distribution of cash in this case depends on how this capital deficiency is handled. Two possibilities exist.

Partner Pays Deficiency   Rasheed is obligated to pay $3,000 into the partnership to cover the deficiency. If Rasheed is willing and able to pay, the entry to record receipt of payment from Rasheed follows.

Assets = Liabilities + Equity
+3,000   +3,000

Jan.	15	Cash	3 0 0 0 00	
		T. Rasheed, Capital		3 0 0 0 00
		To record payment of deficiency by Rasheed.		

---

[1] The concepts behind these entries are not new. The entry to sell BOARDS' noncash assets for $46,000 is

Jan. 15	Cash	46,000	
	Boarding facilities		15,000
	Land		25,000
	Gain from liquidation		6,000
	Sold noncash assets at a gain.		

We then record the allocation of any loss or gain (a $6,000 gain in this case) from liquidation according to the partners' income-and-loss-sharing agreement as follows.

Jan. 15	Gain from Liquidation	6,000	
	K. Zayn, Capital		2,000
	H. Perez, Capital		2,000
	T. Rasheed, Capital		2,000
	To allocate liquidation gain to partners.		

After the $3,000 payment, the partners' capital balances are Zayn, $19,000; Perez, $8,000; and Rasheed, $0. The entry to record the final cash distributions to partners is

Jan.	15	K. Zayn, Capital	19 0 0 0 00	
		H. Perez, Capital	8 0 0 0 00	
		Cash		27 0 0 0 00
		To distribute remaining cash to partners.		

Assets = Liabilities + Equity
−27,000   −19,000
                         −8,000

Partner Cannot Pay Deficiency   The remaining partners with credit balances absorb any partner's unpaid deficiency according to their income-and-loss-sharing ratio. To illustrate, if Rasheed is unable to pay the $3,000 deficiency, Zayn and Perez absorb it. Since they share income and loss equally, Zayn and Perez each absorbs $1,500 of the deficiency. This is recorded as follows.

Jan.	15	K. Zayn, Capital	1 5 0 0 00	
		H. Perez, Capital	1 5 0 0 00	
		T. Rasheed, Capital		3 0 0 0 00
		To transfer Rasheed deficiency to Zayn and Perez.		

Assets = Liabilities + Equity
                         −1,500
                         −1,500
                         +3,000

After Zayn and Perez absorb Rasheed's deficiency, the capital accounts of the partners are Zayn, $17,500; Perez, $6,500; and Rasheed, $0. The entry to record the final cash distribution to the partners is

Jan.	15	K. Zayn, Capital	17 5 0 0 00	
		H. Perez, Capital	6 5 0 0 00	
		Cash		24 0 0 0 00
		To distribute remaining cash to partners.		

Assets = Liabilities + Equity
−24,000   −17,500
                         −6,500

Rasheed's inability to cover this deficiency does not relieve Rasheed of the liability. If Rasheed becomes able to pay at a future date, Zayn and Perez can each collect $1,500 from Rasheed.

PARTNER RETURN ON EQUITY

An important role of partnership financial statements is to aid current and potential partners in evaluating partnership success compared with other opportunities. One measure of this success is the **partner return on equity** ratio:

LO8 Compute partner return on equity and use it to evaluate partnership performance.

$$\text{Partner return on equity} = \frac{\text{Partner net income}}{\text{Average partner equity}}$$

This measure is separately computed for each partner. To illustrate, Exhibit 19.6 reports selected data from the **Boston Celtics LP**. The return on equity for the *total* partnership (stated as a percent with one decimal place) is computed as $216/[($84 + $252)/2] = 128.6\%$. However, return on equity is quite different across the partners. For example, the **Boston Celtics LP I** partner return on equity is computed as $44/[($122 + $166)/2] = 30.6\%$, whereas the **Celtics LP** partner return on equity is computed as $111/[($270 + $333)/2] = 36.8\%$. Partner return on equity provides *each* partner an assessment of its return on its equity invested in the partnership. A specific partner often uses this return to decide whether additional investment or withdrawal of resources is best for that partner. Exhibit 19.6 reveals that the year shown produced good returns for all partners (the **Boston Celtics LP II** return is not computed because its average equity is negative due to an unusual and large distribution in the prior year).

Exhibit 19.6

Selected Data from Boston
Celtics LP

($ thousands)	Total*	Boston Celtics LP I	Boston Celtics LP II	Celtics LP
Beginning-year balance	$ 84	$122	$(307)	$270
Net income (loss) for year	216	44	61	111
Cash distribution	(48)	—	—	(48)
Ending-year balance	$252	$166	$(246)	$333
Partner return on equity	**128.6%**	**30.6%**	**n.a.**	**36.8%**

* Totals may not add up due to rounding.

Demonstration Problem

The following transactions and events affect the partners' capital accounts in several successive partnerships. Prepare a table with six columns, one for each of the five partners along with a total column to show the effects of the following events on the five partners' capital accounts.

Part 1

4/13/2007	Ries and Bax create R&B Company. Each invests $10,000, and they agree to share income and losses equally.
12/31/2007	R&B Co. earns $15,000 in income for its first year. Ries withdraws $4,000 from the partnership, and Bax withdraws $7,000.
1/1/2008	Royce is made a partner in RB&R Company after contributing $12,000 cash. The partners agree that a 10% interest allowance will be given on each partner's beginning-year capital balance. In addition, Bax and Royce are to receive $5,000 salary allowances. The remainder of the income or loss is to be divided evenly.
12/31/2008	The partnership's income for the year is $40,000, and withdrawals at year-end are Ries, $5,000; Bax, $12,500; and Royce, $11,000.
1/1/2009	Ries sells her interest for $20,000 to Murdock, whom Bax and Royce accept as a partner in the new BR&M Co. Income or loss is to be shared equally after Bax and Royce each receives a $25,000 salary allowance.
12/31/2009	The partnership's income for the year is $35,000, and year-end withdrawals are Bax, $2,500, and Royce, $2,000.
1/1/2010	Elway is admitted as a partner after investing $60,000 cash in the new Elway & Associates partnership. He is given a 50% interest in capital after the other partners transfer $3,000 to his account from each of theirs. A 20% interest allowance (on the beginning-year capital balances) will be used in sharing any income or loss, there will be no salary allowances, and Elway will receive 40% of the remaining balance—the other three partners will each get 20%.
12/31/2010	Elway & Associates earns $127,600 in income for the year, and year-end withdrawals are Bax, $25,000; Royce, $27,000; Murdock, $15,000; and Elway, $40,000.
1/1/2011	Elway buys out Bax and Royce for the balances of their capital accounts after a revaluation of the partnership assets. The revaluation gain is $50,000, which is divided in using a 1:1:1:2 ratio (Bax:Royce:Murdock:Elway). Elway pays the others from personal funds. Murdock and Elway will share income on a 1:9 ratio.
2/29/2011	The partnership earns $10,000 of income since the beginning of the year. Murdock retires and receives partnership cash equal to her capital balance. Elway takes possession of the partnership assets in his own name, and the company is dissolved.

Part 2

Journalize the events affecting the partnership for the year ended December 31, 2008.

Planning the Solution

- Evaluate each transaction's effects on the capital accounts of the partners.
- Each time a new partner is admitted or a partner withdraws, allocate any bonus based on the income-or-loss-sharing agreement.
- Each time a new partner is admitted or a partner withdraws, allocate subsequent net income or loss in accordance with the new partnership agreement.

- Prepare entries to (1) record Royce's initial investment; (2) record the allocation of interest, salaries, and remainder; (3) show the cash withdrawals from the partnership; and (4) close the withdrawal accounts on December 31, 2008.

Solution to Demonstration Problem

Part 1

Event	Ries	Bax	Royce	Murdock	Elway	Total
4/13/2007						
Initial Investment	$10,000	$10,000				$ 20,000
12/31/2007						
Income (equal)	7,500	7,500				15,000
Withdrawals	(4,000)	(7,000)				(11,000)
Ending balance	$13,500	$10,500				$ 24,000
1/1/2008						
New investment			$12,000			12,000
12/31/2008						
10% interest	1,350	1,050	1,200			3,600
Salaries		5,000	5,000			10,000
Remainder (equal)	8,800	8,800	8,800			26,400
Withdrawals	(5,000)	(12,500)	(11,000)			(28,500)
Ending balance	$18,650	$12,850	$16,000			$ 47,500
1/1/2009						
Transfer interest	(18,650)			$18,650		$ 0
12/31/2009						
Salaries		25,000	25,000			50,000
Remainder (equal)		(5,000)	(5,000)	(5,000)		(15,000)
Withdrawals		(2,500)	(2,000)			(4,500)
Ending balance	$ 0	$30,350	$34,000	$13,650		$ 78,000
1/1/2010						
New investment					$ 60,000	60,000
Bonuses to Elway		(3,000)	(3,000)	(3,000)	9,000	0
Adjusted balance		$27,350	$31,000	$10,650	$ 69,000	$138,000
12/31/2010						
20% interest		5,470	6,200	2,130	13,800	27,600
Remainder (1:1:1:2)		20,000	20,000	20,000	40,000	100,000
Withdrawals		(25,000)	(27,000)	(15,000)	(40,000)	(107,000)
Ending Balance		$27,820	$30,200	$17,780	$ 82,800	$158,600
1/1/2011						
Gain (1:1:1:2)		10,000	10,000	10,000	20,000	50,000
Adjusted balance		$37,820	$40,200	$27,780	$102,800	$208,600
Transfer interests		(37,820)	(40,200)		78,020	0
Adjusted balance		$ 0	$ 0	$27,780	$180,820	$208,600
2/29/2011						
Income (1:9)				1,000	9,000	10,000
Adjusted balance				$28,780	$189,820	$218,600
Final distributions				(28,780)	(189,820)	(218,600)
Final balance				$ 0	$ 0	$ 0

Part 2

2008				Debit	Credit
Jan.	1	Cash		12 000 00	
		Royce, Capital			12 000 00
		To record investment of Royce.			
Dec.	31	Income Summary		40 000 00	
		Ries, Capital			10 150 00
		Bax, Capital			14 850 00
		Royce, Capital			15 000 00
		To allocate interest, salaries, and remainders.			
Dec.	31	Ries, Withdrawals		5 000 00	
		Bax, Withdrawals		12 500 00	
		Royce, Withdrawals		11 000 00	
		Cash			28 500 00
		To record cash withdrawals by partners.			
Dec.	31	Ries, Capital		5 000 00	
		Bax, Capital		12 500 00	
		Royce, Capital		11 000 00	
		Ries, Withdrawals			5 000 00
		Bax, Withdrawals			12 500 00
		Royce, Withdrawals			11 000 00
		To close withdrawal accounts.			

Summary

LO1 **Identify characteristics of partnerships.** Partnerships are voluntary associations, involve partnership agreements, have limited life, are not subject to income tax, include mutual agency, and have unlimited liability.

LO2 **Identify common types of organizations with partnership characteristics.** Organizations that combine selected characteristics of partnerships and corporations include limited partnerships, limited liability partnerships, S corporations, and limited liability companies.

LO3 **Prepare entries for partnership formation.** A partner's initial investment is recorded at the market value of the assets contributed to the partnership.

LO4 **Allocate and record income and loss among partners.** A partnership agreement should specify how to allocate partnership income or loss among partners. Allocation can be based on a stated ratio, capital balances, or salary and interest allowances to compensate partners for differences in their service and capital contributions.

LO5 **Prepare a statement of partners' equity.** The statement of partners' equity shows each partner's beginning and ending capital balances, additional investments and withdrawals, and allocated income or loss.

LO6 **Account for the admission and withdrawal of partners.** When a new partner buys a partnership interest directly from one or more existing partners, the amount of cash paid from one partner to another does not affect the partnership total recorded equity. When a new partner purchases equity by investing additional assets in the partnership, the new partner's investment can yield a bonus either to existing partners or to the new partner. The entry to record a withdrawal can involve payment from either (1) the existing partners' personal assets or (2) partnership assets. The latter can yield a bonus to either the withdrawing or remaining partners.

LO7 **Prepare entries for partnership liquidation.** When a partnership is liquidated, losses and gains from selling partnership assets are allocated to the partners according to their income-and-loss-sharing ratio. If a partner's capital account has a deficiency that the partner cannot pay, the other partners share the deficit according to their relative income-and-loss-sharing ratio.

LO8 **Compute partner return on equity and use it to evaluate partnership performance.** Partner return on equity provides each partner an assessment of his or her return on equity invested in the partnership.

1. (*b*)

2. *Unlimited liability* means that the creditors of a partnership require each partner to be personally responsible for all partnership debts.

3. (*c*)

4.

	Denzel	Shantell	Total
Net Income			$ 40,000
Interest allowance (10%)	$ 7,000	$ 3,500	10,500
Balance of income			29,500
Balance allocated equally	14,750	14,750	29,500
Balance of income			$ 0
Income of partners	**$21,750**	**$18,250**	

Key Terms

General partner (p. 487) Partner who assumes unlimited liability for the debts of the partnership; responsible for partnership management.

General partnership (p. 487) Partnership in which all partners have mutual agency and unlimited liability for partnership debts.

Limited liability company (LLC) (p. 488) Organization form that combines select features of a corporation and a limited partnership; provides limited liability to its members (owners), is free of business tax, and allows members to actively participate in management.

Limited liability partnership (p. 487) Partnership in which a partner is not personally liable for malpractice or negligence unless that partner is responsible for providing the service that resulted in the claim.

Limited partners (p. 487) Partners who have no personal liability for partnership debts beyond the amounts they invested in the partnership.

Limited partnership (p. 487) Partnership that has two classes of partners: limited partners and general partners.

Mutual agency (p. 487) Legal relationship among partners whereby each partner is an agent of the partnership and is able to bind the partnership to contracts within the scope of the partnership's business.

Partner return on equity (p. 499) Partner net income divided by average partner equity for the period.

Partnership (p. 486) Unincorporated association of two or more persons to pursue a business for profit as co-owners.

Partnership contract (p. 486) Agreement among partners that sets terms under which the affairs of the partnership are conducted; also called *articles of partnership* if in writing.

Partnership liquidation (p. 497) Dissolution of a partnership by (1) selling noncash assets and allocating any gain or loss according to partners' income-and-loss ratio, (2) paying liabilities, and (3) distributing any remaining cash according to partners' capital balances.

S corporation (p. 488) Corporation that meets special tax qualifications so as to be treated like a partnership for income tax purposes.

Statement of partners' equity (p. 493) Financial statement that shows total capital balances at the beginning of the period, any additional investment by partners, the income or loss of the period, the partners' withdrawals, and the partners' ending capital balances; also called *statement of partners' capital*.

Unlimited liability (p. 487) Legal relationship among general partners that makes each of them responsible for partnership debts if the other partners are unable to pay their shares.

Multiple Choice Quiz   Answers on p. 513   mhhe.com/wildCA2e

Additional Multiple Choice Quizzes are available at the book's Website.

1. Stokely and Leder are forming a partnership. Stokely invests a building that has a market value of $250,000; and the partnership assumes responsibility for a $50,000 note secured by a mortgage on that building. Leder invests $100,000 cash. For the partnership, the amounts recorded for the building and for Stokely's Capital account are:
   a. Building, $250,000; Stokely, Capital, $250,000.
   b. Building, $200,000; Stokely, Capital, $200,000.
   c. Building, $200,000; Stokely, Capital, $100,000.
   d. Building, $200,000; Stokely, Capital, $250,000.
   e. Building, $250,000; Stokely, Capital, $200,000.

2. Katherine, Alliah, and Paulina form a partnership. Katherine contributes $150,000, Alliah contributes $150,000, and Paulina

contributes $100,000. Their partnership agreement calls for the income or loss division to be based on the ratio of capital invested. If the partnership reports income of $90,000 for its first year of operations, what amount of income is credited to Paulina's capital account?
   a. $22,500
   b. $25,000
   c. $45,000
   d. $30,000
   e. $90,000

3. Jamison and Blue form a partnership with capital contributions of $600,000 and $800,000, respectively. Their partnership agreement calls for Jamison to receive $120,000 per year in salary. Also, each partner is to receive an interest allowance equal to 10% of the partner's beginning capital contributions, with any remaining income or loss divided equally. If net income for its initial year is $270,000, then Jamison's and Blue's respective shares are:

a. $135,000; $135,000
b. $154,286; $115,714
c. $120,000; $150,000
d. $185,000; $85,000
e. $85,000; $185,000

4. Hansen and Fleming are partners and share equally in income or loss. Hansen's current capital balance in the partnership is $125,000 and Fleming's is $124,000. Hansen and Fleming agree to accept Black with a 20% interest. Black invests $75,000 in the partnership. The bonus granted to Hansen and Fleming equals:

a. $13,000 each.
b. $5,100 each.
c. $4,000 each.
d. $5,285 to Hansen; $4,915 to Fleming.
e. $0; Hansen and Fleming grant a bonus to Black.

5. Mee Su is a partner in Hartford Partners, LLC. Her partnership capital balance at the beginning of the current year was $110,000, and her ending balance was $124,000. Her share of the partnership income is $10,500. What is her partner return on equity?

a. 8.97%
b. 1060.00%
c. 9.54%
d. 1047.00%
e. 8.47%

Discussion Questions

1. If a partnership contract does not state the period of time the partnership is to exist, when does the partnership end?

2. What does the term *mutual agency* mean when applied to a partnership?

3. Can partners limit the right of a partner to commit their partnership to contracts? Would such an agreement be binding (*a*) on the partners and (*b*) on outsiders?

4. Assume that Amey and Lacey are partners. Lacey dies, and her son claims the right to take his mother's place in the partnership. Does he have this right? Why or why not?

5. Assume that the Barnes and Ardmore partnership agreement provides for a two-third/one-third sharing of income but says nothing about losses. The first year of partnership operation resulted in a loss, and Barnes argues that the loss should be shared equally because the partnership agreement said nothing about sharing losses. Is Barnes correct? Explain.

6. Allocation of partnership income among the partners appears on what financial statement?

7. What does the term *unlimited liability* mean when it is applied to partnership members?

8. How does a general partnership differ from a limited partnership?

9. George, Burton, and Dillman have been partners for three years. The partnership is being dissolved. George is leaving the firm, but Burton and Dillman plan to carry on the business. In the final settlement, George places a $75,000 salary claim against the partnership. He contends that he has a claim for a salary of $25,000 for each year because he devoted all of his time for three years to the affairs of the partnership. Is his claim valid? Why or why not?

10. Kay, Kat, and Kim are partners. In a liquidation, Kay's share of partnership losses exceeds her capital account balance. Moreover, she is unable to meet the deficit from her personal assets, and her partners shared the excess losses. Does this relieve Kay of liability?

11. After all partnership assets have been converted to cash and all liabilities paid, the remaining cash should equal the sum of the balances of the partners' capital accounts. Why?

12. Assume a partner withdraws from a partnership and receives assets of greater value than the book value of his equity. Should the remaining partners share the resulting reduction in their equities in the ratio of their relative capital balances or according to their income-and-loss-sharing ratio?

---

connect

QUICK STUDY

QS 19–1
Partnership liability   **LO1**

Amaya and Leon are partners in operating a store. Without consulting Amaya, Leon enters into a contract to purchase merchandise for the store. Amaya contends that she did not authorize the order and refuses to pay for it. The vendor sues the partners for the contract price of the merchandise. (*a*) Must the partnership pay for the merchandise? Why? (*b*) Does your answer differ if Amaya and Leon are partners in a public accounting firm? Explain.

QS 19–2
Partnership income allocation
LO4

Ann Stolton and Susie Bright are partners in a business they started two years ago. The partnership agreement states that Stolton should receive a salary allowance of $15,000 and that Bright should receive a $20,000 salary allowance. Any remaining income or loss is to be shared equally. Determine each partner's share of the current year's net income of $52,000.

Blake and Matthai are partners who agree that Blake will receive a $100,000 salary allowance and that any remaining income or loss will be shared equally. If Matthai's capital account is credited for $2,000 as her share of the net income in a given period, how much net income did the partnership earn in that period?

QS 19–3
Partnership income allocation
LO4

Frain organized a limited partnership and is the only general partner. Mourlan invested $20,000 in the partnership and was admitted as a limited partner with the understanding that he would receive 10% of the profits. After two unprofitable years, the partnership ceased doing business. At that point, partnership liabilities were $85,000 larger than partnership assets. How much money can the partnership's creditors obtain from Mourlan's personal assets to satisfy the unpaid partnership debts?

QS 19–4
Liability in limited partnerships
LO2

Stein agrees to pay Choi and Amal $10,000 each for a one-third (33⅓%) interest in the Choi and Amal partnership. Immediately prior to Stein's admission, each partner had a $30,000 capital balance. Make the journal entry to record Stein's purchase of the partners' interest.

QS 19–5
Partner admission through purchase of interest **LO6**

Jules and Johnson are partners, each with $40,000 in their partnership capital accounts. Kwon is admitted to the partnership by investing $40,000 cash. Make the entry to show Kwon's admission to the partnership.

QS 19–6
Admission of a partner **LO6**

Howe and Duley's company is organized as a partnership. At the prior year-end, partnership equity totaled $150,000 ($100,000 from Howe and $50,000 from Duley). For the current year, partnership net income is $25,000 ($20,000 allocated to Howe and $5,000 allocated to Duley), and year-end total partnership equity is $200,000 ($140,000 from Howe and $60,000 from Duley). Compute the total partnership return on equity *and* the individual partner return on equity ratios. State your answers as percentages rounded to one decimal place.

QS 19–7
Partner return on equity **LO8**

Refer to QS 19-7. Assume that neither Howe nor Duley made any withdrawals during the year. Prepare a statement of partners' equity for the current year. Assume the partnership is called the HD Partnership and the current year ends on December 31, 2010.

QS 19–8
Statement of partners' equity
LO5

---

connect

Next to the following list of eight characteristics of business organizations, write a brief description of how each characteristic applies to general partnerships.

EXERCISES

Exercise 19–1
Characteristics of partnerships
LO1

Characteristic	Application to General Partnerships
1. Life	
2. Owners' liability	
3. Legal status	
4. Tax status of income	
5. Owners' authority	
6. Ease of formation	
7. Transferability of ownership	
8. Ability to raise large amounts of capital	

For each of the following separate cases, recommend a form of business organization. With each recommendation, explain how business income would be taxed if the owners adopt the form of organization recommended. Also list several advantages that the owners will enjoy from the form of business organization that you recommend.

a. Sharif, Henry, and Korb are recent college graduates in computer science. They want to start a Website development company. They all have college debts and currently do not own any substantial computer equipment needed to get the company started.

Exercise 19–2
Forms of organization
LO1 LO2

b. Dr. Ward and Dr. Liu are recent graduates from medical residency programs. Both are family practice physicians and would like to open a clinic in an underserved rural area. Although neither has any funds to bring to the new venture, a banker has expressed interest in making a loan to provide start-up funds for their practice.

c. Munson has been out of school for about five years and has become quite knowledgeable about the commercial real estate market. He would like to organize a company that buys and sells real estate. Munson believes he has the expertise to manage the company but needs funds to invest in commercial property.

Exercise 19-3
Journalizing partnership
transactions   **LO3   LO4**

On March 1, 2010, Eckert and Kelley formed a partnership. Eckert contributed $82,500 cash and Kelley contributed land valued at $60,000 and a building valued at $100,000. The partnership also assumed responsibility for Kelley's $92,500 long-term note payable associated with the land and building. The partners agreed to share income as follows: Eckert is to receive an annual salary allowance of $25,000, both are to receive an annual interest allowance of 10% of their beginning-year capital investment, and any remaining income or loss is to be shared equally. On October 20, 2010, Eckert withdrew $34,000 cash and Kelley withdrew $20,000 cash. After the adjusting and closing entries are made to the revenue and expense accounts at December 31, 2010, the Income Summary account had a credit balance of $90,000.

1. Prepare journal entries to record (*a*) the partners' initial capital investments, (*b*) their cash withdrawals, and (*c*) the December 31 closing of both the Withdrawals and Income Summary accounts.

Check   (2) Kelley, $79,250

2. Determine the balances of the partners' capital accounts as of December 31, 2010.

Exercise 19-4
Income allocation in a
partnership   **LO4**

Kramer and Knox began a partnership by investing $60,000 and $80,000, respectively. During its first year, the partnership earned $160,000. Prepare calculations showing how the $160,000 income should be allocated to the partners under each of the following three separate plans for sharing income and loss: (1) the partners failed to agree on a method to share income; (2) the partners agreed to share income and loss in proportion to their initial investments (round amounts to the nearest dollar); and (3) the partners agreed to share income by granting a $50,000 per year salary allowance to Kramer, a $40,000 per year salary allowance to Knox, 10% interest on their initial capital investments, and the remaining balance shared equally.

Check   Plan 3, Kramer, $84,000

Exercise 19-5
Income allocation in a partnership
LO4

Assume that the partners of Exercise 19-4 agreed to share net income and loss by granting annual salary allowances of $50,000 to Kramer and $40,000 to Knox, 10% interest allowances on their investments, and any remaining balance shared equally.

1. Determine the partners' shares of Kramer and Knox given a first-year net income of $98,800.

Check   (2) Kramer, $(4,400)

2. Determine the partners' shares of Kramer and Knox given a first-year net loss of $16,800.

Exercise 19-6
Sale of partnership interest
LO6

The partners in the Biz Partnership have agreed that partner Mandy may sell her $100,000 equity in the partnership to Brittney, for which Brittney will pay Mandy $85,000. Present the partnership's journal entry to record the sale of Mandy's interest to Brittney on September 30.

Exercise 19-7
Admission of new partner   **LO6**

The Struter Partnership has total partners' equity of $510,000, which is made up of Main, Capital, $400,000, and Frist, Capital, $110,000. The partners share net income and loss in a ratio of 80% to Main and 20% to Frist. On November 1, Madison is admitted to the partnership and given a 15% interest in equity and a 15% share in any income and loss. Prepare the journal entry to record the admission of Madison under each of the following separate assumptions: Madison invests cash of (1) $90,000; (2) $120,000; and (3) $80,000.

Exercise 19-8
Retirement of partner   **LO6**

Holland, Flowers, and Tulip have been partners while sharing net income and loss in a 5:3:2 ratio. On January 31, the date Tulip retires from the partnership, the equities of the partners are Holland, $150,000; Flowers, $90,000; and Tulip, $60,000. Present journal entries to record Tulip's retirement under each of the following separate assumptions: Tulip is paid for her equity using partnership cash of (1) $60,000; (2) $80,000; and (3) $30,000.

The Red, White & Blue partnership was begun with investments by the partners as follows: Red, $180,000; White, $240,000; and Blue, $210,000. The operations did not go well, and the partners eventually decided to liquidate the partnership, sharing all losses equally. On August 31, after all assets were converted to cash and all creditors were paid, only $60,000 in partnership cash remained.

1. Compute the capital account balance of each partner after the liquidation of assets and the payment of creditors.

2. Assume that any partner with a deficit agrees to pay cash to the partnership to cover the deficit. Present the journal entries on August 31 to record (*a*) the cash receipt from the deficient partner(s) and (*b*) the final disbursement of cash to the partners.

3. Assume that any partner with a deficit is not able to reimburse the partnership. Present journal entries (*a*) to transfer the deficit of any deficient partners to the other partners and (*b*) to record the final disbursement of cash to the partners.

Exercise 19-9
Liquidation of partnership   **LO6**

Check   (1) Red, $(10,000)

Turner, Roth, and Lowe are partners who share income and loss in a 1:4:5 ratio. After lengthy disagreements among the partners and several unprofitable periods, the partners decided to liquidate the partnership. Immediately before liquidation, the partnership balance sheet shows: total assets, $126,000; total liabilities, $78,000; Turner, Capital, $2,500; Roth, Capital, $14,000; and Lowe, Capital, $31,500. The cash proceeds from selling the assets were sufficient to repay all but $28,000 to the creditors. (*a*) Calculate the loss from selling the assets. (*b*) Allocate the loss to the partners. (*c*) Determine how much of the remaining liability should be paid by each partner.

Exercise 19-10
Liquidation of partnership   **LO6**

Check   (b) Lowe, Capital after allocation, $(6,500)

Assume that the Turner, Roth, and Lowe partnership of Exercise 19-10 is a limited partnership. Turner and Roth are general partners and Lowe is a limited partner. How much of the remaining $28,000 liability should be paid by each partner?

Exercise 19-11
Liquidation of limited partnership
LO7

Hart Sports Enterprises LP is organized as a limited partnership consisting of two individual partners: Soccer LP and Football LP. Both partners separately operate a minor league soccer team and a semipro football team. Compute partner return on equity for each limited partnership (and the total) for the year ended June 30, 2010, using the following selected data on partner capital balances from Hart Sports Enterprises LP. Express your answers as percents, rounded to one decimal.

Exercise 19-12
Partner return on equity   **LO8**

	Soccer LP	Football LP	Total
Balance at 6/30/2009	$189,000	$ 758,000	$ 947,000
Annual net income	22,134	445,898	468,032
Cash distribution	—	(50,000)	(50,000)
Balance at 6/30/2010	$211,134	$1,153,898	$1,365,032

Refer to information in Exercise 19-3. Prepare a statement of partners' equity for the year ended December 31, 2010. Assume that the partnership is named EK Partners.

Exercise 19-13
Statement of partners' equity
LO5

connect

Kim Ries, Tere Bax, and Josh Thomas invested $80,000, $112,000, and $128,000, respectively, in a partnership. During its first calendar-year, the firm earned $249,000.

Required

Prepare the entry to close the firm's Income Summary account as of its December 31 year-end and to allocate the $249,000 net income to the partners under each of the following separate assumptions: The partners (1) have no agreement on the method of sharing income and loss; (2) agreed to share income and loss in the ratio of their beginning capital investments; and (3) agreed to share income and loss by providing annual salary allowances of $66,000 to Ries, $56,000 to Bax, and $80,000 to Thomas; granting 10% interest on the partners' beginning capital investments; and sharing the remainder equally.

PROBLEM SET A

Problem 19-1A
Allocating partnership income
LO4

Check   (3) Thomas, Capital, $97,800

Problem 19-2A
Allocating partnership income
and loss; sequential years   **LO4**

Irma Watts and John Lyon are forming a partnership to which Watts will devote one-half time and Lyon will devote full time. They have discussed the following alternative plans for sharing income and loss: (*a*) in the ratio of their initial capital investments, which they have agreed will be $42,000 for Watts and $63,000 for Lyon; (*b*) in proportion to the time devoted to the business; (*c*) a salary allowance of $6,000 per month to Lyon and the balance in accordance with the ratio of their initial capital investments; or (*d*) a salary allowance of $6,000 per month to Lyon, 10% interest on their initial capital investments, and the balance shared equally. The partners expect the business to perform as follows: Year 1, $36,000 net loss; Year 2, $90,000 net income; and Year 3, $150,000 net income.

Required

Check   Plan *d*, Year 1, Lyon's share,
$19,050

Prepare three tables with the following column headings. Complete the tables, one for each of the first three years, by showing how to allocate partnership income or loss to the partners under each of the four plans being considered. (Round answers to the nearest whole dollar.)

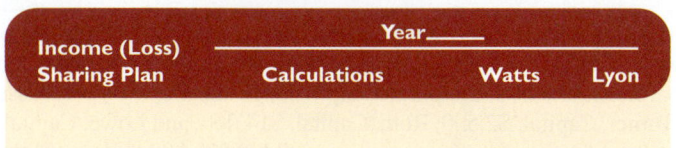

Income (Loss) Sharing Plan	Year_____		
	Calculations	Watts	Lyon

Problem 19-3A
Partnership income allocation,
statement of partners' equity, and
closing entries   **LO4**

Bill Beck, Bruce Beck, and Barb Beck formed the BBB Partnership by making capital contributions of $67,500, $262,500, and $420,000, respectively. They predict annual partnership net income of $450,000 and are considering the following alternative plans of sharing income and loss: (*a*) equally; (*b*) in the ratio of their initial capital investments; or (*c*) salary allowances of $80,000 to Bill, $60,000 to Bruce, and $90,000 to Barb; interest allowances of 10% on their initial capital investments; and the balance shared equally.

Required

1. Prepare a table with the following column headings. Use the table to show how to distribute net income of $450,000 for the calendar year under each of the alternative plans being considered. (Round answers to the nearest whole dollar.)

Income (Loss) Sharing Plan	Calculations	Bill	Bruce	Barb	Total

Check   (2) Barb, Ending Capital,
$456,000

2. Prepare a statement of partners' equity showing the allocation of income to the partners assuming they agree to use plan (*c*), that income earned is $209,000, and that Bill, Bruce, and Barb withdraw $34,000, $48,000, and $64,000, respectively, at year-end.

3. Prepare the December 31 journal entry to close Income Summary assuming they agree to use plan (*c*) and that net income is $209,000. Also close the withdrawals accounts.

Problem 19-4A
Partner withdrawal
and admission   **LO6**

Part 1. Meir, Benson, and Lau are partners and share income and loss in a 3:2:5 ratio. The partnership's capital balances are as follows: Meir, $168,000; Benson, $138,000; and Lau, $294,000. Benson decides to withdraw from the partnership, and the partners agree to not have the assets revalued upon Benson's retirement. Prepare journal entries to record Benson's February 1 withdrawal from the partnership under each of the following separate assumptions: Benson (*a*) sells his interest to North for $160,000 after Meir and Lau approve the entry of North as a partner; (*b*) gives his interest to a son-in-law, Schmidt, and thereafter Meir and Lau accept Schmidt as a partner; (*c*) is paid $138,000 in partnership cash for his equity; (*d*) is paid $214,000 in partnership cash for his equity; and (*e*) is paid $30,000 in partnership cash plus equipment recorded on the partnership books at $70,000 less its accumulated depreciation of $23,200.

Check   (1e) Cr. Lau, Capital, $38,250

Part 2. Assume that Benson does not retire from the partnership described in Part 1. Instead, Rhodes is admitted to the partnership on February 1 with a 25% equity. Prepare journal entries to record Rhodes's entry into the partnership under each of the following separate assumptions: Rhodes invests (*a*) $200,000; (*b*) $145,000; and (*c*) $262,000.

(2c) Cr. Benson, Capital,
$9,300

Kendra, Cogley, and Mei share income and loss in a 3:2:1 ratio. The partners have decided to liquidate their partnership. On the day of liquidation their balance sheet appears as follows.

KENDRA, COGLEY, AND MEI Balance Sheet May 31			
Assets		**Liabilities and Equity**	
Cash	$180,800	Accounts payable	$245,500
Inventory	537,200	Kendra, Capital	93,000
		Cogley, Capital	212,500
		Mei, Capital	167,000
Total assets	$718,000	Total liabilities and equity	$718,000

Required

Prepare journal entries for (a) the sale of inventory, (b) the allocation of its gain or loss, (c) the payment of liabilities at book value, and (d) the distribution of cash in each of the following separate cases: Inventory is sold for (1) $600,000; (2) $500,000; (3) $320,000 and any partners with capital deficits pay in the amount of their deficits; and (4) $250,000 and the partners have no assets other than those invested in the partnership. (Round to the nearest dollar.)

Matt Albin, Ryan Peters, and Seth Ramsey invested $164,000, $98,400, and $65,600, respectively, in a partnership. During its first calendar year, the firm earned $270,000.

Required

Prepare the entry to close the firm's Income Summary account as of its December 31 year-end and to allocate the $270,000 net income to the partners under each of the following separate assumptions. (Round answers to whole dollars.) The partners (1) have no agreement on the method of sharing income and loss; (2) agreed to share income and loss in the ratio of their beginning capital investments; and (3) agreed to share income and loss by providing annual salary allowances of $96,000 to Albin, $72,000 to Peters, and $50,000 to Ramsey; granting 10% interest on the partners' beginning capital investments; and sharing the remainder equally.

Maria Bell and J. R. Green are forming a partnership to which Bell will devote one-third time and Green will devote full time. They have discussed the following alternative plans for sharing income and loss: (a) in the ratio of their initial capital investments, which they have agreed will be $104,000 for Bell and $156,000 for Green; (b) in proportion to the time devoted to the business; (c) a salary allowance of $4,000 per month to Green and the balance in accordance with the ratio of their initial capital investments; or (d) a salary allowance of $4,000 per month to Green, 10% interest on their initial capital investments, and the balance shared equally. The partners expect the business to perform as follows: Year 1, $36,000 net loss; Year 2, $76,000 net income; and Year 3, $188,000 net income.

Problem 19–2B
Allocating partnership income
and loss; sequential years   LO4

Required

Prepare three tables with the following column headings. Complete the tables, one for each of the first three years, by showing how to allocate partnership income or loss to the partners under each of the four plans being considered. (Round answers to the nearest whole dollar.)

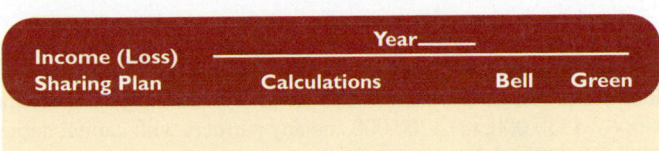

Income (Loss) Sharing Plan	Year_____		
	Calculations	Bell	Green

Problem 19–3B

Partnership income allocation, statement of partners' equity, and closing entries   **LO4**

Sally Cook, Lin Xi, and Ken Schwartz formed the CXS Partnership by making capital contributions of $144,000, $216,000, and $120,000, respectively. They predict annual partnership net income of $240,000 and are considering the following alternative plans of sharing income and loss: (a) equally; (b) in the ratio of their initial capital investments; or (c) salary allowances of $40,000 to Cook, $30,000 to Xi, and $80,000 to Schwartz; interest allowances of 12% on their initial capital investments; and the balance shared equally.

Required

1. Prepare a table with the following column headings. Use the table to show how to distribute net income of $240,000 for the calendar year under each of the alternative plans being considered. (Round answers to the nearest whole dollar.)

Income (Loss) Sharing Plan	Calculations	Cook	Xi	Schwartz	Total

Check   (2) Schwartz, Ending Capital, $150,400

2. Prepare a statement of partners' equity showing the allocation of income to the partners assuming they agree to use plan (c), that income earned is $87,600, and that Cook, Xi, and Schwartz withdraw $18,000, $38,000, and $24,000, respectively, at year-end.

3. Prepare the December 31 journal entry to close Income Summary assuming they agree to use plan (c) and that net income is $87,600. Also close the withdrawals accounts.

Problem 19–4B

Partner withdrawal and admission   **LO6**

Part 1. Craig, Cook, and Chan are partners and share income and loss in a 5:1:4 ratio. The partnership's capital balances are as follows: Craig, $606,000; Cook, $148,000; and Chan, $446,000. Craig decides to withdraw from the partnership, and the partners agree not to have the assets revalued upon Craig's retirement. Prepare journal entries to record Craig's April 30 withdrawal from the partnership under each of the following separate assumptions: Craig (a) sells her interest to Collin for $250,000 after Cook and Chan approve the entry of Collin as a partner; (b) gives her interest to a daughter-in-law, Cam, and thereafter Cook and Chan accept Cam as a partner; (c) is paid $606,000 in partnership cash for her equity; (d) is paid $350,000 in partnership cash for her equity; and (e) is paid $200,000 in partnership cash plus manufacturing equipment recorded on the partnership books at $538,000 less its accumulated depreciation of $336,000.

Check   (1e) Cr. Chan, Capital, $163,200

Part 2. Assume that Craig does not retire from the partnership described in Part 1. Instead, Chip is admitted to the partnership on April 30 with a 20% equity. Prepare journal entries to record the entry of Chip under each of the following separate assumptions: Chip invests (a) $300,000; (b) $196,000; and (c) $426,000.

Check   (2c) Cr. Cook, Capital, $10,080

Problem 19–5B

Liquidation of a partnership   **LO7**

Lasure, Ramirez, and Toney, who share income and loss in a 2:1:2 ratio, plan to liquidate their partnership. At liquidation, their balance sheet appears as follows.

LASURE, RAMIREZ, AND TONEY Balance Sheet January 18			
Assets		**Liabilities and Equity**	
Cash	$348,600	Accounts payable	$342,600
Equipment	617,200	Lasure, Capital	300,400
		Ramirez, Capital	195,800
		Toney, Capital	127,000
Total assets	$965,800	Total liabilities and equity	$965,800

Required

Prepare journal entries for (a) the sale of equipment, (b) the allocation of its gain or loss, (c) the payment of liabilities at book value, and (d) the distribution of cash in each of the following separate cases: Equipment is sold for (1) $650,000; (2) $530,000; (3) $200,000 and any partners with capital deficits pay in the amount of their deficits; and (4) $150,000 and the partners have no assets other than those invested in the partnership.

Check   (4) Cash distribution, Lasure, $73,600

(This serial problem began in Chapter 1 and continues through most of the book. If previous chapter segments were not completed, the serial problem can begin at this point. It is helpful, but not necessary, for you to use the Working Papers that accompany the book.)

SP 19   At the start of 2011, Adriana Lopez is considering adding a partner to her business. She envisions the new partner taking the lead in generating sales of both services and merchandise for Success Systems. Lopez's equity in Success Systems as of January 1, 2011, is reflected in the following capital balance.

> A. Lopez, Capital $117,435

Required

1. Lopez is evaluating whether the prospective partner should be an equal partner with respect to capital investment and profit sharing (1:1) or whether the agreement should be 3:1 with Lopez retaining three-fourths interest with rights to three-fourths of the net income or loss. What factors should she consider in deciding which partnership agreement to offer?

2. Prepare the January 1, 2011, journal entry(ies) necessary to admit a new partner to Success Systems through the purchase of a partnership interest for each of the following two separate cases (*a*) 1:1 sharing agreement and (*b*) 3:1 sharing agreement.

3. Prepare the January 1, 2011, journal entry(ies) required to admit a new partner if the new partner invests cash of $39,145.

4. After posting the entry in part 3, what would be the new partner's equity percentage?

BTN 19-1   Take a step back in time and imagine **Best Buy** in its infancy as a company. The year is 1966.

Required

1. Read the history of Best Buy at http://www.bestbuyinc.com/about/history.htm. Can you determine from the history whether Best Buy was originally organized as a sole proprietorship, partnership, or corporation?

2. Assume that Best Buy was originally organized as a partnership. Best Buy's income statement in Appendix A varies in several key ways from what it would look like for a partnership. Explain how a corporate income statement differs from a partnership income statement.

3. Compare the Best Buy balance sheet in Appendix A to what a partnership balance sheet would have shown. Identify and explain any account differences you would anticipate.

BTN 19-2   Doctors Maben, Orlando, and Clark have been in a group practice for several years. Maben and Orlando are family practice physicians, and Clark is a general surgeon. Clark receives many referrals for surgery from his family practice partners. Upon the partnership's original formation, the three doctors agreed to a two-part formula to share income. Every month each doctor receives a salary allowance of $3,000. Additional income is divided according to a percent of patient charges the doctors generate for the month. In the current month, Maben generated 10% of the billings, Orlando 30%, and Clark 60%. The group's income for this month is $50,000. Clark has expressed dissatisfaction with the income-sharing formula and asks that income be split entirely on percent of patient charges.

Required

1. Compute the income allocation for the current month using the original agreement.

2. Compute the income allocation for the current month using Clark's proposed agreement.

3. Identify the ethical components of this partnership decision for the doctors.

WORKPLACE COMMUNICATION
LO1   LO2

BTN 19-3   Assume that you are studying for an upcoming accounting exam with a good friend. Your friend says that she has a solid understanding of general partnerships but is less sure that she understands organizations that combine certain characteristics of partnerships with other forms of business organization. You offer to make some study notes for your friend to help her learn about limited partnerships, limited liability partnerships, S corporations, and limited liability companies. Prepare a one-page set of well-organized, complete study notes on these four forms of business organization.

TAKING IT TO THE NET
LO3   LO4

BTN 19-4   Access the March 4, 2009, filing of the December 31, 2008, 10-K of **America First Tax Exempt Investors LP**. This company deals with tax-exempt mortgage revenue bonds that, among other things, finance student housing properties.

Required

1. Locate its December 31, 2008, balance sheet and list the account titles reported in the equity section of the balance sheet.
2. Locate its statement of partners' capital and comprehensive income (loss). How many units of limited partnership (known as "beneficial unit certificate holders") are outstanding at December 31, 2008?
3. What is the partnership's largest asset and its amount at December 31, 2008?

TEAMWORK IN ACTION
LO4

BTN 19-5   This activity requires teamwork to reinforce understanding of accounting for partnerships.

Required

1. Assume that Baker, Warner, and Rice form the BWR Partnership by making capital contributions of $200,000, $300,000, and $500,000, respectively. BWR predicts annual partnership net income of $600,000. The partners are considering various plans for sharing income and loss. Assign a different team member to compute how the projected $600,000 income would be shared under each of the following separate plans:
   a. Shared equally.
   b. In the ratio of the partners' initial capital investments.
   c. Salary allowances of $50,000 to Baker, $60,000 to Warner, and $70,000 to Rice, with the remaining balance shared equally.
   d. Interest allowances of 10% on the partners' initial capital investments, with the remaining balance shared equally.
2. In sequence, each member is to present his or her income-sharing calculations with the team.
3. As a team, identify and discuss at least one other possible way that income could be shared.

ENTREPRENEURS IN BUSINESS
LO1

BTN 19-6   Revisit the chapter's opening feature involving Samanta and Kelvin Joseph and their company **Samanta Shoes**. Assume that Samanta and Kelvin, partners in Samanta Shoes, have decided to expand with the help of general partners.

Required

1. What details should Samanta, Kelvin, and their future partners specify in their general partnership agreement?
2. What advantages should Samanta, Kelvin, and their future partners be aware of with respect to organizing as a general partnership?
3. What disadvantages should Samanta, Kelvin, and their future partners be aware of with respect to organizing as a general partnership?

1. e; Capital = $250,000 − $50,000

2. a; $90,000 × [$100,000/($150,000 + $150,000 +
$100,000)] = $22,500

3. d;

	Jamison	Blue	Total
Net income.			$ 270,000
Salary allowance	$120,000		(120,000)
Interest allowance	60,000	$80,000	(140,000)
Balance of income			10,000
Balance divided equally	5,000	5,000	(10,000)
Totals	$185,000	$85,000	$ 0

4. b; Total partnership equity = $125,000 + $124,000
+ $75,000 = $324,000

Equity of Black = $324,000 × 20% = $64,800

Bonus to old partners = $75,000 − $64,800
= $10,200, split equally

5. a; $10,500/[($110,000 + $124,000)/2] = 8.97%

A Look Back

Chapter 19 focused on the partnership form of organization. We described crucial characteristics of partnerships and the accounting and reporting of their transactions.

A Look at This Chapter

This chapter emphasizes details of the corporate form of organization. The accounting concepts and procedures for stock issuances are explained. We also describe components of stockholders' equity and how to compute book value.

A Look Ahead

Chapter 21 focuses on corporate dividends and stock repurchases. We explain how to value and record these transactions. We also show how to report changes in stockholders' equity.

Chapter 20

Corporate Formation and Stock Transactions

Learning Objectives

LO 1	Identify characteristics of corporations and their organization.
LO 2	Define capital stock terminology.
LO 3	Describe the components of stockholders' equity.
LO 4	Record the issuance of common stock for cash.
LO 5	Record the issuance of common stock for noncash assets or services.
LO 6	Explain characteristics of preferred stock.
LO 7	Record the issuance of preferred stock.
LO 8	Compute book value and explain its use in analysis.

"We weren't planning on starting a company"
—Ali Perry

Breathing New Life

SANTA BARBARA, CA—"My grandma has COPD [chronic obstructive pulmonary disease] and she got put on oxygen," explains Ali Perry. "Her quality of life got destroyed because she couldn't go anywhere, she couldn't do anything. Everything was limited by how much she had in her bottles of compressed oxygen." Ali dreamed to help her grandma. She explains that COPD is the fourth leading cause of death, and is predicted to soon be third on that list. COPD is a disease where the airways of the lungs narrow, which limits the flow of air and causes shortness of breath.

To make her dream a reality, Ali enlisted the aid of two college classmates, Byron Myers and Brenton Taylor. The three of them designed a portable oxygen system, wrote a business plan, and set off to secure financing. Their company, named **Inogen**, which is a combination of the words innovation and oxygen (**Inogen.net**), soon had a portable oxygen supply unit whose sales exceed 10,000 units to date. "We worked really hard at the technology," explains Ali. "We saw the value of the company was in creating technology that was thought impossible in the marketplace."

The three founders insist that proper financing was a key to their success. To make it happen, says Ali, they needed equity (stock) financing. With their business plan and prototype, the three raised a whopping $4 million from a venture capital firm. Still, explains Ali, the focus is on helping folks, including her grandma. Adds Byron, "Oxygen users can now take off on a moment's notice, without having to watch the clock or guess at how long their oxygen will last."

Their equity financing "brings both opportunities and challenges," explains Byron. "New patients do not know anything about oxygen therapy. All they know is that their life has changed and they now need to have a supply of oxygen with them whenever and wherever." Inogen answers that call. Their focus on people continues to reap rewards as they recently secured another $22 million in equity financing. As Byron put it: "[Inogen] makes old ways of thinking and operating inadequate."

[Sources: *Inogen Website,* January 2009; *HME Business,* January 2006; *Daily Nexus,* January 2004; *Goleta Valley Voice,* December 2003; *Inc.com,* July 2007]

This chapter focuses on the corporate form of organization. We explain the characteristics of a corporation's common stock and preferred stock. We show how to record common and preferred stock issuances, and compute book value.

Corporate Formation and Stock Transactions

Corporations
- Characteristics
- Organization and management
- Stockholders
- Stock basics

Common Stock
- Par value
- No-par value
- Stated value
- Stock for noncash assets or services

Preferred Stock
- Issuance of preferred
- Convertible preferred
- Callable preferred

Corporate Form of Organization

A **corporation** is an entity created by law that is separate from its owners. It has most of the rights and privileges granted to individuals. Owners of corporations are called *stockholders* or *shareholders*. Corporations can be separated into two types. A *privately held* (or *closely held*) corporation does not offer its stock for public sale and usually has few stockholders. A *publicly held* corporation offers its stock for public sale and can have thousands of stockholders. *Public sale* usually refers to issuance and trading on an organized stock market such as the New York Stock Exchange.

Characteristics of Corporations

L01 Identify characteristics of corporations and their organization.

Corporations offer unique advantages and disadvantages.

Advantages of Corporate Form

- ■ **Separate legal entity:** A corporation has the same rights, duties, and responsibilities of a person. It takes actions through its officers and managers.
- ■ **Limited liability of stockholders:** Stockholders are neither liable for corporate acts nor corporate debt.
- ■ **Transferable ownership rights:** The transfer of shares from one stockholder to another usually has no effect on the corporation or its operations.
- ■ **Continuous life:** A corporation's life continues indefinitely because it is not tied to the physical lives of its owners.
- ■ **Lack of mutual agency for stockholders:** Stockholders who are not also officers or managers cannot bind the corporation to contracts—referred to as *lack of mutual agency.*
- ■ **Ease of capital accumulation:** Investors like the advantages of the corporate form. This enables corporations to accumulate large amounts of capital from the combined investments of many stockholders.

IN THE NEWS

Stock Financing Marc Andreessen cofounded **Netscape** at age 22, only four months after earning his college degree. One year later, he and friends issued Netscape shares to the public. The stock soared, making Andreessen a multimillionaire.

Disadvantages of Corporate Form

■ **Government regulation:** A corporation must meet requirements of a state's incorporation laws, which subject the corporation to state regulation and control. Proprietorships and partnerships avoid many of these regulations and governmental reports.

■ **Corporate taxation:** Corporations pay the same property and payroll taxes as proprietorships and partnerships, plus *additional* taxes. These federal and state income taxes together can take 40% or more of corporate pretax income. Moreover, corporate income is usually taxed a second time as part of stockholders' personal income when stockholders receive cash distributed as dividends. This is called *double taxation*.

> Double taxation is less severe when a corporation's owner-manager collects a salary that is taxed only once as part of his or her personal income.

IN THE NEWS

Seed Money   Sources for start-up money include (1) "angel" investors such as family, friends, or anyone who believes in a company, (2) employees, investors, and even suppliers who can be paid with stock, and (3) venture capitalists (investors) who have a record of entrepreneurial success. See the National Venture Capital Association (**NVCA.org**) for information.

Corporate Organization and Management

This section describes the incorporation, costs, and management of corporate organizations.

Incorporation   A corporation is created by obtaining a charter from a state government. A charter application usually must be signed by the prospective stockholders, called *incorporators* or *promoters,* and then filed with the proper state official. When the application process is complete and fees paid, the charter is issued and the corporation is formed. Investors then purchase the corporation's stock, meet as stockholders, and elect a board of directors. Directors oversee a corporation's affairs.

Organization Expenses   **Organization expenses** (also called *organization costs*) are the costs to organize a corporation; they include legal fees, promoters' fees, and amounts paid to obtain a charter. The corporation debits these costs to *Organization Expenses*. Organization costs are expensed as incurred because it is hard to determine the amount and timing of their future benefits.

Management of a Corporation   The ultimate control of a corporation rests with stockholders who control a corporation by electing its *board of directors,* or simply, *directors.* Each stockholder usually has one vote for each share of stock owned. This control relation is shown in Exhibit 20.1. Directors are responsible for and have final authority for managing corporate activities. A board can act only as a collective body and usually limits its actions to setting general policy.

A corporation usually holds a stockholder meeting at least once a year to elect directors and transact business as its bylaws require. A group of stockholders owning or controlling votes of more than a 50% share of a corporation's stock can elect the board and control the corporation. Stockholders who do not attend stockholders' meetings must have an opportunity to delegate their voting rights to an agent by signing a **proxy,** a document that gives a designated agent the right to vote the stock.

Exhibit 20.1

Stockholders and the Management of a Corporation

Day-to-day direction of corporate business is delegated to executive officers appointed by the board. A corporation's chief executive officer (CEO) is often its president. Several vice presidents, who report to the president, are commonly assigned specific areas of management responsibility such as finance, production, and marketing. One person often has the dual role of chairperson of the board of directors and CEO.

Stockholders of Corporations

This section explains stockholder rights, stock purchases and sales, and the role of registrar and transfer agents.

Rights of Stockholders   When investors buy stock, they acquire all *specific* rights the corporation's charter grants to stockholders. They also acquire *general* rights granted stockholders by the laws of the state in which the company is incorporated. When a corporation has only one class of stock, it is **common stock.** State laws vary, but common stockholders usually have the general right to:

1. Vote at stockholders' meetings.
2. Sell or otherwise dispose of their stock.
3. Purchase their proportional share of any common stock later issued by the corporation. This **preemptive right** protects stockholders' proportionate interest in the corporation. For example, a stockholder who owns 25% of a corporation's common stock has the first opportunity to buy 25% of any new common stock issued.
4. Receive the same dividend, if any, on each common share of the corporation.
5. Share in any assets remaining after creditors are paid when, and if, the corporation is liquidated. Each share receives the same amount of remaining liquidated assets.

Stockholders also have the right to receive timely financial reports.

Basics of Capital Stock

Capital stock is a general term that refers to any shares issued to obtain capital (owner financing). This section introduces terminology and accounting for capital stock.

LO2 Define capital stock terminology.

Authorized Stock   **Authorized stock** is the maximum number of shares that a corporation can sell. The number of authorized shares is usually more than the number of shares issued (and outstanding). (*Outstanding stock* refers to issued stock held by stockholders.) No formal journal entry is required for stock authorization. A corporation must apply to the state for a change in its charter if it wishes to issue more shares than previously authorized. A corporation discloses the number of shares authorized in the equity section of its balance sheet or notes. **Best Buy**'s balance sheet in Appendix A reports 1 billion shares authorized as of 2008.

Selling (Issuing) Stock   A corporation can sell stock directly or indirectly. To *sell directly,* it advertises its stock issuance to potential buyers. This type of issuance is most common with privately held corporations. To *sell indirectly,* a corporation pays a brokerage house (investment banker) to issue its stock. Some brokerage houses *underwrite* an indirect issuance of stock; that is, they buy the stock from the corporation and take all gains or losses from its resale.

Market Value of Stock   **Market value per share** is the price at which a stock is bought and sold. Expected future earnings, dividends, growth, and other company and economic factors influence market value. Traded stocks' market values are available daily in newspapers such as *The Wall Street Journal* and online at Websites like **http://finance.yahoo.com**. The current market value of previously issued shares (for example, the price of stock in trades between investors) does not impact the issuing corporation's stockholders' equity.

Classes of Stock   A corporation sometimes issues more than one class of stock. This could include preferred stock and different classes of common stock. **American Greetings**, for instance, has two types of common stock: Class A stock has 1 vote per share and Class B stock has 10 votes per share. Therefore, American Greetings' Class B shareholders control company decisions.

IN THE NEWS

Stock Quote   The **Best Buy** stock quote is interpreted as (left to right): **Hi,** highest price in past 52 weeks; **Lo,** lowest price in past 52 weeks; **Sym,** company exchange symbol;

52 Weeks				Yld		Vol				Net
Hi	Lo	Sym	Div	%	PE	100s	Hi	Lo	Close	Chg
53.17	31.85	BBY	0.32	0.7	22	220	47.26	46.48	46.61	−0.37

Div, dividends paid per share in past year; **Yld %,** dividend divided by closing price; **PE,** stock price per share divided by earnings per share; **Vol 100s,** number (in 100s) of shares traded; **Hi,** highest price for the day; **Lo,** lowest price for the day; **Close,** closing price for the day; **Net Chg,** change in closing price from prior day.

Par Value Stock   **Par value stock** is assigned a **par value** per share by the corporation in its charter. For example, Best Buy's common stock has a par value of $0.10. Other commonly assigned par values are $10, $5, $1 and $0.01. There is no restriction on the assigned par value. In many states, the par value of a common stock establishes **minimum legal capital,** which is the least amount that the buyers of stock must pay to the corporation. For example, if a corporation issues 1,000 shares of $10 par value stock, the corporation's minimum legal capital in these states would be $10,000. Minimum legal capital is intended to protect a corporation's creditors. Since creditors cannot demand payment from stockholders' personal assets, their claims are limited to the corporation's assets and any minimum legal capital. At liquidation, creditor claims are paid before any amounts are distributed to stockholders.

Par, no-par, and stated value do not set the stock's market value.

No–Par Value Stock   **No-par value stock,** or simply *no-par stock,* is *not* assigned a value per share by the corporate charter. Its advantage is that it can be issued at any price without the possibility of a minimum legal capital deficiency.

L03 Describe the components of stockholders' equity.

Stated Value Stock   **Stated value stock** is no-par stock to which the directors assign a "stated" value per share. Stated value per share becomes the minimum legal capital per share in this case.

Stockholders' Equity   A corporation's equity is known as **stockholders' equity,** also called *shareholders' equity* or *corporate capital.* Stockholders' equity consists of (1) paid-in (or contributed) capital and (2) retained earnings; see Exhibit 20.2. **Paid-in capital** is the total amount of cash and other assets the corporation receives from its stockholders in exchange for stock. **Retained earnings** is the cumulative net income (and loss) retained (not paid out in dividends) by a corporation.

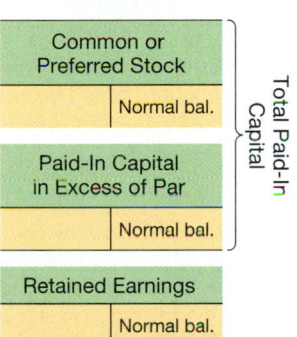

Exhibit 20.2

Stockholders' Equity Composition

Paid-in capital comes from stock-related transactions, whereas retained earnings comes from operations.

Retained earnings can be negative, reflecting accumulated losses. Amazon.com had an accumulated deficit of $730 million at the start of 2009.

HOW YOU DOIN'?   Answers—p. 526

1. Which of the following is *not* a characteristic of the corporate form of business? (*a*) Ease of capital accumulation, (*b*) Stockholder responsibility for corporate debts, (*c*) Ease in transferability of ownership rights, or (*d*) Double taxation.
2. Why is a corporation's income said to be taxed twice?
3. What is a proxy?

Common Stock

Accounting for the issuance of common stock for cash affects only cash and paid-in (contributed) capital accounts. No income or retained earnings accounts are affected.

L04 Record the issuance of common stock for cash.

Issuing Par Value Stock

Par value stock can be issued at par, at a premium (above par), or at a discount (below par). In each case, stock can be exchanged for either cash or noncash assets.

Issuing Par Value Stock at Par

When common stock is issued at par value, we record amounts for both the asset(s) received and the par value stock issued. To illustrate, the entry to record Dillon Snowboards' issuance of 30,000 shares of $10 par value stock for $300,000 cash on June 5, 2010, is

Assets = Liabilities + Equity
+300,000   +300,000

June	5	Cash	300 0 0 0 00	
		Common Stock, $10 Par Value		300 0 0 0 00
		Issued 30,000 shares of $10 par value common stock at par.		

Exhibit 20.3 shows the stockholders' equity of Dillon Snowboards at year-end 2010 (its first year of operations) after income of $65,000 and no dividend payments.

Exhibit 20.3

Stockholders' Equity for Stock Issued at Par

Stockholders' Equity	
Common Stock—$10 par value; 50,000 shares authorized;	
30,000 shares issued and outstanding	$300,000
Retained earnings	65,000
Total stockholders' equity	$365,000

Issuing Par Value Stock at a Premium

A **premium on stock** occurs when a corporation sells its stock for more than par (or stated) value. To illustrate, if Dillon Snowboards issues its $10 par value common stock at $12 per share, its stock is sold at a $2 per share premium. The premium, known as **paid-in capital in excess of par value,** is reported as part of equity. The "Paid-In Capital in Excess of Par Value, Common Stock" account is also called "Additional Paid-In Capital, Common Stock." It is not revenue nor gain and is not listed on the income statement. The entry to record Dillon Snowboards' issuance of 30,000 shares of $10 par value stock for $12 per share on June 5, 2010, is

Assets = Liabilities + Equity
+360,000   +300,000
                            +60,000

June	5	Cash	360 0 0 0 00	
		Common Stock, $10 Par Value		300 0 0 0 00
		Paid-In Capital in Excess of Par Value, Common Stock		60 0 0 0 00
		Sold and issued 30,000 shares of $10 par value common		
		stock at $12 per share.		

The Paid-In Capital in Excess of Par Value, Common Stock account is added to the par value of the stock in the equity section of the balance sheet as shown in Exhibit 20.4.

Exhibit 20.4

Stockholders' Equity for Stock Issued at a Premium

Stockholders' Equity	
Common Stock—$10 par value; 50,000 shares authorized;	
30,000 shares issued and outstanding	$300,000
Paid-in capital in excess of par value, common stock	**60,000**
Retained earnings	65,000
Total stockholders' equity	$425,000

Frequency of Stock Types

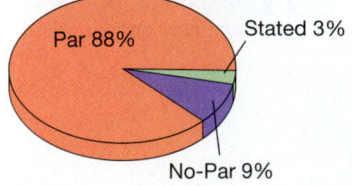

Par 88% Stated 3% No-Par 9%

Issuing No-Par Value Stock

When no-par stock is issued and is not assigned a stated value, the amount the corporation receives becomes the minimum legal capital and is recorded as Common Stock. This means that the entire proceeds are credited to a no-par stock account. To illustrate, a corporation records its October 20 issuance of 1,000 shares of no-par stock for $40 cash per share as follows.

Oct.	20	Cash	40 0 0 0 00		
		Common Stock, No-Par Value		40 0 0 0 00	
		Issued 1,000 shares of no-par value common stock			
		at $40 per share.			

Assets = Liabilities +   Equity
+40,000   +40,000

Issuing Stated Value Stock

When no-par stock is issued and assigned a stated value, its stated value becomes legal capital and is credited to a stated value stock account. Assuming that stated value stock is issued at a price above stated value (the usual case), the excess is credited to Paid-In Capital in Excess of Stated Value, Common Stock, which is reported in the stockholders' equity section. The entry would be similar to that for the issuance of par value stock at a premium.

Issuing Stock for Noncash Assets

A corporation can receive assets other than cash in exchange for its stock. (It can also assume liabilities on the assets received such as a mortgage on property received.) The corporation records the assets received at their market values as of the date of the transaction. The stock given in exchange is recorded at its par (or stated) value with any excess recorded in the Paid-In Capital in Excess of Par (or Stated) Value account. (If no-par stock is issued, the stock is recorded at the assets' market value.) To illustrate, the entry to record receipt of land valued at $105,000 in return for issuance of 4,000 shares of $20 par value common stock on June 10 is

L05 Record the issuance of common stock for noncash assets or services.

Stock issued for noncash assets should be recorded at the market value of either the stock or the noncash asset, whichever is more clearly determinable.

June	10	Land	105 0 0 0 00		
		Common Stock, $20 Par Value		80 0 0 0 00	
		Paid-In Capital in Excess of Par Value, Common Stock		25 0 0 0 00	
		Exchanged 4,000 shares of $20 par value			
		common stock for land.			

Assets   = Liabilities +   Equity
+105,000   +80,000
                                         +25,000

Issuing Stock for Services

A corporation sometimes gives shares of its stock to promoters in exchange for their services in organizing the corporation. The entry to record receipt of services valued at $12,000 in organizing the corporation in return for 600 shares of $15 par value common stock on June 5 is

Any type of stock can be issued for noncash assets.

June	5	Organization Expenses	12 0 0 0 00		
		Common Stock, $15 Par Value		9 0 0 0 00	
		Paid-In Capital in Excess of Par Value, Common Stock		3 0 0 0 00	
		Gave promoters 600 shares of $15 par value common stock			
		in exchange for their services.			

Assets = Liabilities +   Equity
                                       −12,000
                                        +9,000
                                        +3,000

HOW YOU DOIN'?   Answers—p. 526

4. A company issues 7,000 shares of its $10 par value common stock in exchange for equipment valued at $105,000. The entry to record this transaction includes a credit to (*a*) Paid-In Capital in Excess of Par Value, Common Stock, for $35,000. (*b*) Retained Earnings for $35,000. (*c*) Common Stock, $10 Par Value, for $105,000.

5. What is a premium on stock?

6. Who is intended to be protected by minimum legal capital?

Preferred Stock

LO6 Explain characteristics of preferred stock.

Preferred stock has special rights that give it priority (or senior status) over common stock in one or more areas. Special rights typically include a preference for receiving dividends and for the distribution of assets if the corporation is liquidated. Preferred stock carries all rights of common stock unless the corporate charter nullifies them. Most preferred stock, for instance, does not have the right to vote. Exhibit 20.5 shows that preferred stock is issued by about one-fourth of large corporations. All corporations issue common stock.

Exhibit 20.5

Corporations and Preferred Stock

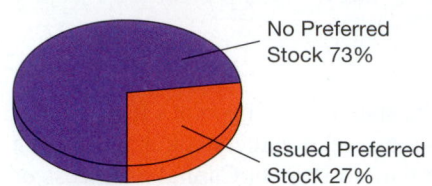

No Preferred Stock 73%

Issued Preferred Stock 27%

Issuance of Preferred Stock

LO7 Record the issuance of preferred stock.

Preferred stock usually has a par value. Like common stock, it can be sold at a price different from par. Preferred stock is recorded in its own separate capital accounts. To illustrate, if Dillon Snowboards issues 50 shares of $100 par value preferred stock for $6,000 cash on July 1, 2010, the entry is

Assets = Liabilities + Equity
+6,000   +5,000
                        +1,000

July	1	Cash	6 0 0 0 00	
		Preferred Stock, $100 Par Value		5 0 0 0 00
		Paid-In Capital in Excess of Par Value, Preferred Stock		1 0 0 0 00
		Issued preferred stock for cash.		

The equity section of the year-end 2010 balance sheet for Dillon Snowboards, including preferred stock, is shown in Exhibit 20.6. (This exhibit assumes that common stock was issued at par.) Issuing no-par preferred stock is similar to issuing no-par common stock. Also, the entries for issuing preferred stock for noncash assets are similar to those for common stock.

Exhibit 20.6

Stockholders' Equity with Common and Preferred Stock

Stockholders' Equity	
Preferred stock—$100 par value; 1,000 shares authorized;	
** 50 shares issued and outstanding**	**$ 5,000**
Paid-in capital in excess of par value, preferred stock	**1,000**
Common stock—$10 par value; 50,000 shares authorized;	
30,000 shares issued and outstanding	300,000
Retained earnings	65,000
Total stockholders' equity	$371,000

Dividend Preference of Preferred Stock   Preferred stockholders are usually allocated their dividends before any dividends are allocated to common stockholders. The dividends allocated to preferred stockholders are usually expressed as a dollar amount per share or a percent applied to par value. This preference for dividends does *not* ensure dividends. If the directors do not declare a dividend, neither the preferred nor the common stockholders receive one. Dividend preference does not imply that preferred stockholders receive more dividends than common stockholders, nor does it guarantee a dividend. We study the accounting for dividends in detail in the next chapter.

Convertible Preferred Stock

Preferred stock is more attractive to investors if it can be converted into common shares. **Convertible preferred stock** gives holders the option to exchange their preferred shares for common shares at a specified rate. When a company's common stock increases in value, convertible preferred stockholders can share in this success by converting their preferred stock into more valuable common stock.

Callable Preferred Stock

Callable preferred stock gives the issuing corporation the right to purchase (retire) this stock from its holders at specified future prices and dates. Many issues of preferred stock are callable. The amount paid to call and retire a preferred share is its **call price,** or *redemption value,* and is set when the stock is issued. The call price normally includes the stock's par value plus a premium giving holders additional return on their investment. When the issuing corporation calls and retires a preferred stock, the terms of the agreement often require it to pay the call price *and* any dividends owed to the preferred shareholders.

> The issuing corporation has the right, or option, to retire its callable preferred stock.

Reasons for Issuing Preferred Stock

Corporations issue preferred stock for several reasons. One is to raise capital without sacrificing control. Preferred stock typically has no voting rights.

Other reasons for issuing preferred stock include its appeal to some investors who believe that the corporation's common stock is too risky or that the expected return on common stock is too low.

HOW YOU DOIN'? Answer—p. 526

7. In what ways does preferred stock often have priority over common stock?

BOOK VALUE PER SHARE

Case 1: Common Stock (Only) Outstanding. **Book value per common share,** defined in Exhibit 20.7, is the recorded amount of stockholders' equity applicable to *common* shares on a per share basis. To illustrate, we use Dillon Snowboards' data from Exhibit 20.3. Dillon has 30,000 outstanding common shares, and the stockholders' equity applicable to common shares is $365,000. Dillon's book value per common share is $12.17, computed as $365,000 divided by 30,000 shares.

LO8 Compute book value and explain its use in analysis.

$$\text{Book value per common share} = \frac{\text{Stockholders' equity applicable to common shares}}{\text{Number of common shares outstanding}}$$

Exhibit 20.7

Book Value per Common Share

Case 2: Common and Preferred Stock Outstanding. To compute book value when both common and preferred shares are outstanding, we allocate total stockholders' equity between the two types of shares. The **book value per preferred share** is computed first; its computation is shown in Exhibit 20.8.

$$\text{Book value per preferred share} = \frac{\text{Stockholders' equity applicable to preferred shares}}{\text{Number of preferred shares outstanding}}$$

Exhibit 20.8

Book Value per Preferred Share

The stockholders' equity applicable to preferred shares equals the preferred shares' call price (or par value if the preferred is not callable) plus any cumulative dividends owed to preferred shareholders (called *dividends in arrears*). The remaining stockholders' equity is the portion applicable to common shares. To illustrate, consider LTD's stockholders' equity in Exhibit 20.9. Its preferred stock is callable at $108 per share, and $14,000 of preferred dividends are in arrears.

Stockholders' Equity	
Preferred stock—$100 par value, 2,000 shares authorized, 1,000 shares issued and outstanding	$100,000
Common stock—$25 par value, 12,000 shares authorized, 10,000 shares issued and outstanding	250,000
Paid-in capital in excess of par value, common stock	15,000
Retained earnings	82,000
Total stockholders' equity	$447,000

Exhibit 20.9

Stockholders' Equity with Preferred and Common Stock

The book value computations are in Exhibit 20.10. Equity is first allocated to preferred shares before the book value of common shares is computed.

Exhibit 20.10

Computing Book Value per Preferred and Common Share

Total stockholders' equity		$447,000
Less equity applicable to preferred shares		
Call price (1,000 shares × $108)	$108,000	
Dividends in arrears	14,000	(122,000)
Equity applicable to common shares		$325,000
Book value per preferred share ($122,000/1,000 shares)		**$122.00**
Book value per common share ($325,000/10,000 shares)		**$ 32.50**

Book value per share reflects the value per share if a company is liquidated at balance sheet amounts and represents the cumulation of all transactions in the company that have affected stockholders' equity. Book value is also the starting point in many stock valuation models, merger negotiations, price setting for public utilities, and loan contracts. The main limitation in using book value is the potential difference between recorded value and market value for assets and liabilities. Investors often adjust their analysis for estimates of these differences.

Demonstration Problem

Barton Corporation began operations on January 1, 2010. The following transactions relating to stockholders' equity occurred in the first two years of the company's operations.

2010

Jan. 1 Authorized the issuance of 2 million shares of $5 par value common stock and 100,000 shares of $100 par value, preferred stock.

Jan. 2 Issued 200,000 shares of common stock for $12 cash per share.

Jan. 3 Issued 100,000 shares of common stock in exchange for a building valued at $820,000 and merchandise inventory valued at $380,000.

Jan. 4 Paid $10,000 cash to the company's founders for organization activities.

Jan. 5 Issued 12,000 shares of preferred stock for $110 cash per share.

2011

June 4 Issued 100,000 shares of common stock for $15 cash per share.

Required

1. Prepare journal entries to record these transactions.

2. Prepare the contributed capital portion of the stockholders' equity section of the balance sheet as of December 31, 2010, and December 31, 2011, based on these transactions.

3. Prepare the January 2, 2010, journal entry for Barton's issuance of 200,000 shares of common stock for $12 cash per share assuming

   a. Common stock is no-par stock without a stated value.

   b. Common stock is no-par stock with a stated value of $10 per share.

Planning the Solution

- Record journal entries for the transactions for 2010 and 2011.
- Determine the balances for the 2010 and 2011 equity accounts for the balance sheet.
- Prepare the contributed capital portion of the 2010 and 2011 balance sheets.
- Record the issuance of common stock under both specifications of no-par stock.

Solution to Demonstration Problem

1. Journal entries.

2010						
Jan.	2	Cash	2400 0 0 0 00			
		Common Stock, $5 Par Value			1000 0 0 0 00	
		Paid-In Capital in Excess of Par Value, Common Stock			1400 0 0 0 00	
		Issued 200,000 shares of common stock.				
Jan.	3	Building	820 0 0 0 00			
		Merchandise Inventory	380 0 0 0 00			
		Common Stock, $5 Par Value			500 0 0 0 00	
		Paid-In Capital in Excess of Par Value, Common Stock			700 0 0 0 00	
		Issued 100,000 shares of common stock.				
Jan.	4	Organization Expenses	10 0 0 0 00			
		Cash			10 0 0 0 00	
		Paid founders for organization costs.				
Jan.	5	Cash	1320 0 0 0 00			
		Preferred Stock, $100 Par Value			1200 0 0 0 00	
		Paid-In Capital in Excess of Par Value, Preferred Stock			120 0 0 0 00	
		Issued 12,000 shares of preferred stock.				
2011 June	4	Cash	1500 0 0 0 00			
		Common Stock, $5 Par Value			500 0 0 0 00	
		Paid-In Capital in Excess of Par Value, Common Stock			1000 0 0 0 00	
		Issued 100,000 shares of common stock.				

2. Balance sheet presentations (at December 31 year-end).

	2010	2011
Stockholders' Equity		
Preferred stock—$100 par value, 100,000 shares authorized, 12,000 shares issued and outstanding	$1,200,000	$1,200,000
Paid-in capital in excess of par value, preferred stock	120,000	120,000
Total paid-in capital by preferred stockholders	1,320,000	1,320,000
Common stock—$5 par value, 2,000,000 shares authorized, 300,000 shares issued and outstanding in 2010, and 400,000 shares issued and outstanding in 2011	1,500,000	2,000,000
Paid-in capital in excess of par value, common stock	2,100,000	3,100,000
Total paid-in capital by common stockholders	3,600,000	5,100,000
Total paid-in capital	$4,920,000	$6,420,000

3. Journal entries.

   a. No-par stock without a stated value.

Jan.	2	Cash	2400 0 0 0 00			
		Common Stock, No-Par Value			2400 0 0 0 00	
		Issued 200,000 shares of no-par common				
		stock at $12 per share.				

b. No-par stock with a $10 stated value per share.

Jan.	2	Cash		2400 0 0 0 00	
		Common Stock $10 Stated Value			2000 0 0 0 00
		Paid-in Capital in Excess of Stated Value, Common Stock			400 0 0 0 00
		Issued 200,000 shares of $10 stated value			
		common stock at $12 per share.			

Summary

LO1 Identify characteristics of corporations and their organization. Corporations are legal entities whose stockholders are not liable for its debts. Stock is easily transferred, and the life of a corporation does not end with the incapacity of a stockholder. A corporation acts through its agents, who are its officers and managers. Corporations are regulated and subject to income taxes.

LO2 Define capital stock terminology. Authorized stock is stock that a corporation's charter authorizes it to sell. Issued stock is the portion of authorized shares sold. Par value stock is a value per share assigned by the charter. No-par value stock is not assigned a value per share by the charter. Stated value stock is no-par stock to which the corporation's directors assign a value per share.

LO3 Describe the components of stockholders' equity. Stockholders' equity is made up of (1) paid-in capital and (2) retained earnings. Paid-in capital consists of funds raised by stock issuances. Retained earnings consists of cumulative net income (losses) not distributed as dividends.

LO4 Record the issuance of common stock for cash. When stock is issued, its par or stated value is credited to the stock account and any excess is credited to a separate contributed capital account. If a stock has neither par nor stated value, the entire proceeds are credited to the stock account. Stockholders must contribute assets equal to minimum legal capital or be potentially liable for the deficiency.

LO5 Record the issuance of common stock for noncash assets or services. When stock is issued in exchange for something other than cash, the stock is recorded at the market value of either the stock or the noncash assets or services, whichever is more clearly determinable.

LO6 Explain characteristics of preferred stock. Preferred stock has special rights over common stock. These rights usually include a preference for receiving dividends and for the distribution of assets if the corporation is liquidated. Preferred stock usually does not have voting rights. Some preferred stock is convertible at the option of the holder or callable at the option of the issuing corporation.

LO7 Record the issuance of preferred stock. When preferred stock is issued, its par value is credited to the stock account and excess is credited to a separate contributed capital account.

LO8 Compute book value and explain its use in analysis. Book value per common share is equity applicable to common shares divided by the number of outstanding common shares. Book value per preferred share is equity applicable to preferred shares divided by the number of outstanding preferred shares.

1. (*b*)

2. A corporation pays taxes on its income, and its stockholders normally pay personal income taxes on any cash dividends received from the corporation.

3. A proxy is a legal document used to transfer a stockholder's right to vote to another person.

4. (*a*)

5. A stock premium is an amount in excess of par (or stated) value paid by purchasers of newly issued stock.

6. Minimum legal capital intends to protect creditors of a corporation by obligating stockholders to some minimum level of equity financing and by constraining a corporation from excessive payments to stockholders.

7. Typically, preferred stock has a preference in receipt of dividends and in distribution of assets.

Key Terms

Authorized stock (p. 518) Total amount of stock that a corporation's charter authorizes it to issue.

Book value per common share (p. 523) Recorded amount of equity applicable to common shares divided by the number of common shares outstanding.

Book value per preferred share (p. 523) Equity applicable to preferred shares (equals its call price [or par value if it is not callable] plus any cumulative dividends in arrears) divided by the number of preferred shares outstanding.

Call price (p. 523) Amount that must be paid to call and retire a callable preferred stock or a callable bond.

Callable preferred stock (p. 523) Preferred stock that the issuing corporation, at its option, may retire by paying the call price plus any dividends in arrears.

Capital stock (p. 518) General term referring to a corporation's stock used in obtaining capital (owner financing).

Common stock (p. 518) Corporation's basic ownership share; also called *capital stock* or *contributed capital* (see *paid-in capital*).

Convertible preferred stock (p. 522) Preferred stock with an option to exchange it for common stock at a specified rate.

Corporation (p. 516) Business that is a separate legal entity under state or federal laws with owners called *shareholders* or *stockholders*.

Market value per share (p. 518) Price at which stock is bought or sold.

Minimum legal capital (p. 519) Amount of assets defined by law that stockholders must (potentially) invest in a corporation; usually defined as par value of the stock; intended to protect creditors.

No-par value stock (p. 519) Stock class that has not been assigned a par (or stated) value by the corporate charter.

Organization expenses (costs) (p. 517) Costs such as legal fees and promoter fees to bring an entity into existence.

Paid-in capital (p. 519) Total amount of cash and other assets a corporation receives from its stockholders in exchange for its stock.

Paid-in capital in excess of par value (p. 520) Amount received from issuance of stock that is in excess of the stock's par value.

Par value (p. 519) Value assigned a share of stock by the corporate charter when the stock is authorized.

Par value stock (p. 519) Class of stock assigned a par value by the corporate charter.

Preemptive right (p. 518) Stockholders' right to maintain their proportionate interest in a corporation with any additional shares issued.

Preferred stock (p. 522) Stock with a priority status over common stockholders in one or more ways, such as paying dividends or distributing assets.

Premium on stock (p. 520) (See *paid-in capital in excess of par value*.)

Proxy (p. 517) Legal document giving a stockholder's agent the power to exercise the stockholder's voting rights.

Retained earnings (p. 519) Cumulative income less cumulative losses and dividends.

Stated value stock (p. 519) No-par stock assigned a stated value per share; this amount is recorded in the stock account when the stock is issued.

Stockholders' equity (p. 519) A corporation's equity; also called *shareholders' equity* or *corporate capital*.

Multiple Choice Quiz   Answers on p. 535   mhhe.com/wildCA2e

Additional Multiple Choice Quizzes are available at the book's Website.

1. A corporation issues 6,000 shares of $5 par value common stock for $8 cash per share. The entry to record this transaction includes:
   a. A debit to Paid-In Capital in Excess of Par Value for $18,000.
   b. A credit to Common Stock for $48,000.
   c. A credit to Paid-In Capital in Excess of Par Value for $30,000.
   d. A credit to Cash for $48,000.
   e. A credit to Common Stock for $30,000.

2. A corporation was formed on January 1. The corporate charter authorized 100,000 shares of $10 par value common stock. During the first month of operation, the corporation issued 300 shares to its attorneys in payment of a $5,000 bill for writing the articles of incorporation. The entry to record this transaction would include
   a. A debit to Organization Expenses for $3,000.
   b. A debit to Organization Expenses for $5,000.
   c. A credit to Common Stock for $5,000.

   d. A credit to Contributed Capital in Excess of Par Value, Common Stock for $5,000.
   e. A debit to Contributed Capital in Excess of Par Value, Common Stock for $2,000.

3. A company has 5,000 shares of $100 par preferred stock and 50,000 shares of $10 par common stock outstanding. Its total stockholders' equity is $2,000,000. Its book value per common share is:
   a. $100.00
   b. $10.00
   c. $40.00
   d. $30.00
   e. $36.36

4. A premium on common stock
   a. Is the amount paid in excess of par by purchasers of newly issued stock.
   b. Is the difference between par value and issue price when the amount paid is below par.

c. Represents profit from issuing stock.
d. Represents capital gain on sale of stock.
e. Is prohibited in most states.

5. A corporation issues 10,000 shares of its $1 par value per share common stock in exchange for equipment. The stock is worth $75,000 based on its price on the Exchange. The equipment originally cost $100,000, and $60,000 of accumulated depreciation has been recorded on it at the date of the exchange. The equipment has an estimated market value of $50,000. At what amount should the equipment appear in the corporation's balance sheet after the exchange?

a. $10,000
b. $40,000
c. $50,000
d. $75,000
e. $100,000

Discussion Questions

1. What are organization expenses? Provide examples.
2. How are organization expenses reported?
3. Who is responsible for directing a corporation's affairs?
4. What is the preemptive right of common stockholders?
5. List the general rights of common stockholders.
6. What is the difference between authorized shares and outstanding shares?
7. Why would an investor find convertible preferred stock attractive?
8. What is the difference between a stock's market value per share and the par value per share?

9. What is the difference between the par value and the call price of a share of preferred stock?
10. How is book value per share computed for a corporation with no preferred stock? What is the main limitation of using book value per share to value a corporation?
11. Review the balance sheet for **Best Buy** in Appendix A and list the classes of stock that it has issued.
12. Refer to the balance sheet for **RadioShack** in Appendix A. What is the par value per share of its common stock? Suggest a rationale for the amount of par value it assigned.

QUICK STUDY

QS 20-1
Characteristics of corporations
LO1

Which of the following statements are true for the corporate form of organization?
1. Ownership rights cannot be easily transferred.
2. Owners have unlimited liability for corporate debts.
3. Capital is more easily accumulated than with most other forms of organization.
4. Corporate income that is distributed to shareholders is usually taxed twice.
5. It is a separate legal entity.
6. It has a limited life.
7. Owners are not agents of the corporation.

QS 20-2
Issuance of common stock
for cash   **LO4**

Prepare the journal entry to record Zende Company's issuance of 75,000 shares of $5 par value common stock assuming the shares sell for:
a. $5 cash per share.
b. $6 cash per share.

QS 20-3
Issuance of par and stated value
common stock for cash   **LO4**

Prepare the journal entry to record Jevonte Company's issuance of 36,000 shares of its common stock assuming the shares have a:
a. $2 par value and sell for $18 cash per share.
b. $2 stated value and sell for $18 cash per share.

QS 20-4
Issuance of no-par common stock
LO4   LO5

Prepare the journal entry to record Autumn Company's issuance of 63,000 shares of no-par value common stock assuming the shares:
a. Sell for $29 cash per share.
b. Are exchanged for land valued at $1,827,000.

QS 20-5
Issuance of common stock
LO4   LO5

Prepare the issuer's journal entry for each separate transaction. (*a*) On March 1, Atlantic Co. issues 42,500 shares of $4 par value common stock for $297,500 cash. (*b*) On April 1, OP Co. issues no-par value common stock for $70,000 cash. (*c*) On April 6, MPG issues 2,000 shares of $25 par value common stock for $45,000 of inventory, $145,000 of machinery, and acceptance of a $94,000 note payable.

Prepare the journal entry to record Tamasine Company's issuance of 5,000 shares of $100 par value preferred stock for $102 cash per share.

QS 20-6
Issuance of preferred stock   **L07**

The stockholders' equity section of Jun Company's balance sheet as of April 1 follows. The stock's per share market value on April 1 is $20.

1. Compute Jun Company's book value per share.

2. Why might Jun Company's market value per share be greater than its book value per share?

QS 20-7
Compute book value per share
L08

Common stock—$5 par value, 375,000 shares authorized, 200,000 shares issued and outstanding	$1,000,000
Paid-in capital in excess of par value, common stock	600,000
Retained earnings	833,000
Total stockholders' equity	$2,433,000

The stockholders' equity section of Montaigne Company's balance sheet follows. The preferred stock's call price is $40. Determine the book value per share of the common stock.

QS 20-8
Book value per common share
L08

Preferred stock—$10 par value, 20,000 shares authorized, issued, and outstanding	$ 200,000
Common stock—$5 par value, 200,000 shares authorized, 150,000 shares issued and outstanding	750,000
Retained earnings	890,000
Total stockholders' equity	$1,840,000

James Myers Co. is authorized to issue 50,000 shares of $50 par preferred stock and 500,000 shares of no-par common stock. Prepare journal entries to record the following selected transactions that occurred during this year:

Mar. 1   Issued 1,000 shares of common stock for $30 cash per share.
      15   Exchanged 2,000 shares of preferred stock for equipment and merchandise inventory with market values of $90,000 and $20,000, respectively.

QS 20-9
Issuances of common and preferred stock
L04   L05   L07

---

connect

Describe how each of the following characteristics of organizations applies to corporations.

EXERCISES

1. Owner authority and control	5. Duration of life
2. Ease of formation	6. Owner liability
3. Transferability of ownership	7. Legal status
4. Ability to raise large capital amounts	8. Tax status of income

Exercise 20-1
Characteristics of corporations
L01

Rodriguez Corporation issues 19,000 shares of its common stock for $152,000 cash on February 20. Prepare journal entries to record this event under each of the following separate situations.

1. The stock has neither par nor stated value.

2. The stock has a $2 par value.

3. The stock has a $5 stated value.

Exercise 20-2
Accounting for par, stated, and no-par stock issuances   **L04**

Prepare journal entries to record the following four separate issuances of stock.

1. Two thousand shares of no-par common stock are issued to the corporation's promoters in exchange for their efforts, estimated to be worth $40,000. The stock has no stated value.

2. Two thousand shares of no-par common stock are issued to the corporation's promoters in exchange for their efforts, estimated to be worth $40,000. The stock has a $1 per share stated value.

3. Four thousand shares of $5 par value common stock are issued for $35,000 cash.

4. One thousand shares of $50 par value preferred stock are issued for $60,000 cash.

Exercise 20-3
Recording stock issuances
L04   L05

Exercise 20-4
Stock issuance for noncash assets
LO5

Sudoku Company issues 7,000 shares of $7 par value common stock in exchange for land and a building. The land is valued at $45,000 and the building at $85,000. Prepare the journal entry to record issuance of the stock in exchange for the land and building.

Exercise 20-5
Stock terminology
LO2   LO3   LO6

Match each of the following terms A through H with the appropriate definitions 1 through 8.

A. No-par value stock   **E.** Preemptive right
B. Convertible preferred stock   **F.** Common stock
C. Minimum legal capital   **G.** Callable preferred stock
D. Authorized stock   **H.** Organization expenses

_____ **1.** The number of shares of stock that a corporation's charter allows it to sell.

_____ **2.** A class of stock that has not been assigned a par value by the corporate charter.

_____ **3.** The basic stock of a corporation that usually carries voting rights for controlling the corporation.

_____ **4.** The right of common stockholders to maintain their proportionate interest in a corporation by having the first opportunity to buy additional proportionate shares of stock issued.

_____ **5.** The least amount that buyers of stock must contribute to the corporation or be subject to paying at a future date.

_____ **6.** Preferred stock that gives the issuing corporation the right to purchase or retire it at specified future prices and dates.

_____ **7.** Preferred stock giving the holder the option of exchanging it for common stock at a specified rate.

_____ **8.** The costs of bringing a corporation into existence that include legal fees, promoters' fees, and amounts paid to obtain a charter.

Exercise 20-6
Issuance of common and preferred stock
LO4   LO5   LO7

Linda Myers Co. is authorized to issue 50,000 shares of $50 par preferred stock and 500,000 shares of no-par common stock. Prepare journal entries to record the following selected transactions that occurred during this year:

July   4   Issued 1,000 shares of common stock for $40 cash per share.
      28   Exchanged 2,000 shares of preferred stock for equipment and merchandise inventory with market values of $70,000 and $40,000, respectively.

connect

PROBLEM SET A

Problem 20-1A
Stockholders' equity transactions and analysis
LO3   LO4   LO5   LO8

Kinkaid Co. is incorporated at the beginning of this year and engages in a number of transactions. The following journal entries impacted its stockholders' equity during its first year of operations.

a.	Cash	300,000	
	Common Stock, $25 Par Value		250,000
	Paid-In Capital in Excess of Par Value, Common Stock..................		50,000
b.	Organization Expenses........................	150,000	
	Common Stock, $25 Par Value		125,000
	Paid-In Capital in Excess of Par Value, Common Stock..................		25,000
c.	Cash	43,000	
	Accounts Receivable	15,000	
	Building......................................	81,500	
	Notes Payable		59,500
	Common Stock, $25 Par Value		50,000
	Paid-In Capital in Excess of Par Value, Common Stock..................		30,000
d.	Cash	120,000	
	Common Stock, $25 Par Value		75,000
	Paid-In Capital in Excess of Par Value, Common Stock..................		45,000

Required

1. Explain each journal entry (*a*) through (*d*).
2. How many shares of common stock are outstanding at year-end?
3. What is the amount of minimum legal capital (based on par value) at year-end?
4. What is the total paid-in capital at year-end?
5. What is the book value per share of the common stock at year-end if total paid-in capital plus retained earnings equals $695,000?

Check   (2) 20,000 shares

(3) $500,000

(4) $650,000

Saki Corporation began operations on January 1, 2010. The following transactions relating to stockholders' equity occurred in the first two years of the company's operations.

Problem 20-2A
Stock issuances
LO3   LO4   LO5   LO7

2010

Jan. 1   Authorized the issuance of 4 million shares of $1 par value common stock and 25,000 shares of $100 par value preferred stock.
Jan. 2   Issued 700,000 shares of common stock for $15 per share.
Jan. 3   Issued 20,000 common shares in exchange for merchandise inventory valued at $100,000 and a building valued at $260,000.
Jan. 4   Issued 1,000 common shares to the company's founders for organization activities. The stock's market price is $16 on this date.
Jan. 5   Issued 14,000 shares of preferred stock for $125 per share.

2011

June 3   Issued 60,000 shares of common stock for $19 per share.

Other Information:

Saki Corporation reported a net loss of $32,240 in 2010 and net income of $16,735 in 2011. Saki paid no dividends in either year.

Required

1. Prepare journal entries to record these transactions.
2. Prepare the stockholders' equity section of the balance sheet as of December 31, 2010, and December 31, 2011, based on these transactions.

Raphael Corporation's common stock is currently selling on a stock exchange at $85 per share, and its current balance sheet shows the following stockholders' equity section.

Problem 20-3A
Computation of book values
LO2   LO8

Preferred stock—$___ par value, 1,000 shares authorized, issued, and outstanding	$ 50,000
Common stock—$___ par value, 4,000 shares authorized, issued, and outstanding	80,000
Retained earnings	150,000
Total stockholders' equity	$280,000

Required

1. What is the current market value (price per share) of this corporation's common stock?
2. What are the par values per share of the corporation's preferred stock and its common stock?
3. What are the book values per share of the preferred stock and the common stock?
4. Assume Raphael Corporation's preferred stock has a call price of $53 per share. What are the book values per share of the preferred stock and common stock?

Analysis Component

5. What are some factors that can contribute to a difference between the book value of common stock and its market value (price)?

Problem 20–4A

Stockholders' equity transactions

LO4   LO5

Geddy Corporation began operations on January 1, 2010. The following transactions relating to stockholders' equity occurred in the first month of operations.

2010

Jan. 1   Authorized the issuance of 5 million shares of no-par value common stock.
Jan. 2   Issued 350,000 shares of common stock for $14 cash per share.
Jan. 3   Issued 2,000 shares to the company's founders for organization activities valued at $28,000.
Jan. 14   Issued 6,000 shares in exchange for land valued at $84,000.

Required

1. Prepare journal entries to record each of these transactions for January 2010.

2. Prepare the stockholders' equity section of the company's balance sheet as of January 31, 2010.

PROBLEM SET B

Problem 20–1B

Stockholders' equity transactions and analysis

LO3   LO4   LO5   LO8

Weiss Company is incorporated at the beginning of this year and engages in a number of transactions. The following journal entries impacted its stockholders' equity during its first year of operations.

a.	Cash	120,000	
	Common Stock, $1 Par Value		3,000
	Paid-In Capital in Excess of Par Value, Common Stock		117,000
b.	Organization Expenses.	40,000	
	Common Stock, $1 Par Value		1,000
	Paid-In Capital in Excess of Par Value, Common Stock		39,000
c.	Cash	13,300	
	Accounts Receivable	8,000	
	Building.	37,000	
	Notes Payable		18,300
	Common Stock, $1 Par Value		800
	Paid-In Capital in Excess of Par Value, Common Stock		39,200
d.	Cash	60,000	
	Common Stock, $1 Par Value		1,200
	Paid-In Capital in Excess of Par Value, Common Stock		58,800

Required

1. Explain each journal entry (*a*) through (*d*).

2. How many shares of common stock are outstanding at year-end?

3. What is the amount of minimum legal capital (based on par value) at year-end?

4. What is the total paid-in capital at year-end?

5. What is the book value per share of the common stock at year-end if total paid-in capital plus retained earnings equals $283,000?

Check   (2) 6,000 shares

  (3) $6,000

  (4) $260,000

Problem 20–2B

Stock issuances

LO3   LO4   LO5   LO7

Harrison Corporation began operations on January 1, 2010. The following transactions relating to stockholders' equity occurred in the first two years of the company's operations.

2010

Jan. 1   Authorized the issuance of 3 million shares of $10 stated value common stock and 50,000 shares of $100 par value preferred stock.
Jan. 2   Issued 400,000 shares of common stock for $18 per share.
Jan. 3   Issued 20,000 common shares in exchange for land valued at $100,000 and a building valued at $260,000.
Jan. 4   Paid $15,000 cash to the company's founders for organization activities.
Jan. 5   Issued 14,000 shares of preferred stock for $125 per share.

2011

June 3   Issued 60,000 shares of common stock for $19 per share.

Other Information:

Harrison Corporation reported net income of $11,500 in 2010 and $6,250 in 2011. Harrison paid no dividends in either year.

Required

1. Prepare journal entries to record these transactions.
2. Prepare the stockholders' equity section of the balance sheet as of December 31, 2010, and December 31, 2011, based on these transactions.

Soltech Company's common stock is currently selling on a stock exchange at $90 per share, and its current balance sheet shows the following stockholders' equity section.

Problem 20-3B
Computation of book values
LO3 LO8

Preferred stock—$___ par value, 1,500 shares authorized, issued, and outstanding	$ 375,000
Common stock—$___ par value, 18,000 shares authorized, issued, and outstanding	900,000
Retained earnings	1,125,000
Total stockholders' equity	$2,400,000

Required

1. What is the current market value (price per share) of this corporation's common stock?
2. What are the par values per share of the corporation's preferred stock and its common stock?
3. What are the book values per share of the preferred stock and the common stock?
4. Assume Soltech Company's preferred stock has a call price of $280 per share. What are the book values per share of the preferred stock and the common stock?

Analysis Component

5. Discuss why the book value of common stock is not always a good estimate of its market value.

Pearl Corporation began operations on January 1, 2010. The following transactions relating to stockholders' equity occurred in the first month of operations.

Problem 20-4B
Stockholders' equity transactions
LO4 LO5

2010

Jan.	1	Authorized the issuance of 10 million shares of no-par value common stock.
Jan.	2	Issued 150,000 shares of common stock for $24 cash per share.
Jan.	3	Issued 1,000 shares to the company's founders for organization activities for services valued at $24,000.
Jan.	14	Issued 6,000 shares in exchange for equipment valued at $122,000.

Required

1. Prepare journal entries to record each of these transactions for January 2010.
2. Prepare the stockholders' equity section of the company's balance sheet as of January 31, 2010.

(This serial problem began in Chapter 1 and continues through most of the book. If previous chapter segments were not completed, the serial problem can begin at this point. It is helpful, but not necessary, for you to use the Working Papers that accompany the book.)

SERIAL PROBLEM

Success Systems

SP 20 Adriana Lopez created Success Systems on October 1, 2010. The company has been successful, and Adriana plans to expand her business. She believes that an additional $100,000 is needed and is investigating three funding sources.

a. Adriana's sister Cicely is willing to invest $100,000 in the business as a common shareholder. Since Adriana currently has $120,000 invested in the business, Cicely's investment will mean that Adriana will maintain about 55% ownership, and Cicely will have 45% ownership of Success Systems.

b. Adriana's uncle Marcello is willing to invest $100,000 in the business as a preferred shareholder. Marcello would purchase 1,000 shares of $100 par value preferred stock.

c. Adriana's banker is willing to lend her $100,000 on a 7%, 10-year note payable. Adriana would make monthly payments of $1,160.00 per month for 10 years.

Required

1. Prepare the journal entry to reflect the initial $100,000 in investment under each of the options (*a*), (*b*), and (*c*). Assume that the common stock is no-par or stated value.
2. Evaluate the three proposals for expansion, providing the pros and cons of each option.
3. Which option do you recommend Adriana adopt? Explain.

REPORTING IN ACTION
LO3   LO8

BTN 20-1   Refer to **Best Buy**'s financial statements in Appendix A to answer the following.

1. How many shares of common stock are issued and outstanding at March 1, 2008, and March 3, 2007?
2. What is its par value per common share?
3. What is the book value of its entire common stock at March 1, 2008?

Fast Forward

4. Access Best Buy's financial statements for fiscal years ending after March 1, 2008, from its Website (**BestBuy.com**) or the SEC's EDGAR database (**www.SEC.gov**). Has the number of common shares outstanding increased since March 1, 2008? Has Best Buy issued any preferred stock? Explain.

COMPARATIVE ANALYSIS
LO8

R RadioShack.

BTN 20-2   Key comparative figures for both **Best Buy** and **RadioShack** follow.

Key Figures	Best Buy	RadioShack
Net income (in millions)	$1,407	$ 236
Common shares outstanding (in millions)	484	191
Market value (price) per share	$38.16	$13.24
Equity applicable to common shares (in millions)	$4,484	$1,990

Required

1. Compute the book value per common share for each company using these data.
2. Are the companies' market values per share higher or lower than their book values per share?
3. For which company is the difference between the recorded value and the market value of assets largest? Explain.

ETHICS CHALLENGE
LO1

BTN 20-3   Harriet Moore is an accountant for New World Pharmaceuticals. Her duties include tracking research and development spending in the new product development division. Over the course of the past six months, Harriet notices that a great deal of funds have been spent on a particular project for a new drug. She hears "through the grapevine" that the company is about to patent the drug and expects it to be a major advance in antibiotics. Harriet believes that this new drug will greatly improve company performance and will cause the company's stock to increase in value. Harriet decides to purchase shares of New World in order to benefit from this expected increase.

Required

What are Harriet's ethical responsibilities, if any, with respect to the information she has learned through her duties as an accountant for New World Pharmaceuticals? What are the implications to her planned purchase of New World shares?

WORKPLACE COMMUNICATION
LO1   LO8

BTN 20-4   Teams are to select an industry, and each team member is to select a different company in that industry. Each team member then is to acquire the selected company's financial statements (or Form 10-K) from the SEC EDGAR site (**www.SEC.gov**). Use these data to identify the par value of the company's common stock, and compute the book value per share of the company's common stock. Use the financial press (or **finance.yahoo.com**) to determine the market price of this stock. Communicate with teammates via a meeting, e-mail, or telephone to discuss the significance of the company's par value, to compare the par and book values per share with the market price per share, and to compare companies and industry norms. The team must prepare a single memorandum reporting the ratio for each company and identify the team conclusions or consensus of opinion. The memorandum is to be duplicated and distributed to the instructor and teammates.

Make a transparency of each team's memo for a class discussion.

BTN 20-5 Access the February 25, 2009, filing of the 2008 calendar-year 10-K report of **McDonald's** (ticker MCD) from **www.SEC.gov**.

Required

1. How many classes of stock has McDonald's issued?
2. What are the par values, number of authorized shares, and issued shares of the classes of stock you identified in part 1?

TAKING IT TO THE NET

LO2

BTN 20-6 Assume that you are a concert organizer. In the past you have organized concerts targeted at drawing attendance of 1,000 people or less. You now want to change your business strategy to focus on concerts that will draw between 5,000 and 20,000 people. You are concerned however that larger concerts have an increased risk of lawsuits.

TEAMWORK IN ACTION

LO1 LO2

Required

Write a brief team statement to answer the following.

1. Discuss the advantages and disadvantages of incorporating your business, as it pertains to the new business strategy.
2. Assume that you decide to incorporate your business. It is important that you control the company for decisions on which acts to schedule. Discuss the types of stock you can offer to maintain control of the company's decisions.

BTN 20-7 Assume that the owners' launch of **Inogen** requires $500,000 of start-up capital. The original owners contribute $375,000 of personal assets in return for 15,000 shares of common stock but need to raise another $125,000 in cash. There are two alternative plans for raising the additional cash. Plan A is to sell 3,750 shares of common stock to one or more investors for $125,000 cash. Plan B is to sell 1,250 shares of preferred stock to one or more investors for $125,000 cash (this preferred stock would have a $100 par value, be issued at par and require dividend payments of $10,000 per year). (*Hint:* Return on equity represents the net income return for its owner(s). It is defined as (Net income − Preferred dividends)/ Stockholders' equity).

ENTREPRENEURS IN BUSINESS

LO3 LO6

1. If the business is expected to earn $72,000 of after-tax net income in the first year, what rate of return on beginning equity (the original owners' share of income divided by their beginning equity) will the owners personally earn under each alternative? Which plan will provide the higher expected return to the owners?
2. If the business is expected to earn $16,800 of after-tax net income in the first year, what rate of return on beginning equity will the original owners personally earn under each alternative? Which plan will provide the higher expected return to the original owners?
3. Analyze and interpret the differences between the results for parts 1 and 2.

---

1. e; Entry to record this stock issuance is:

Cash (6,000 × $8)	48,000	
Common Stock (6,000 × $5)		30,000
Paid-In Capital in Excess of Par Value, Common Stock		18,000

2. b; The entry to record this stock issuance is

Organization Expenses	5,000	
Common Stock (300 × $10)		3,000
Paid-In Capital in Excess of Par Value, Common Stock		2,000

3. d; Preferred stock = 5,000 × $100 = $500,000
   Book value per share = ($2,000,000 − $500,000)/50,000 shares = $30 per common share

4. a

5. d; The market price of the stock is more reliable in this case.

ANSWERS TO MULTIPLE CHOICE QUIZ

A Look Back

Chapter 20 focused on the corporate form of organization. We described characteristics of corporations and the accounting and reporting of stock issuances.

A Look at This Chapter

This chapter continues our study of the corporate form of organization. Accounting for dividend transactions is explained. We also describe how to compute corporate income taxes and how to report retained earnings and shareholders' equity.

A Look Ahead

Chapter 22 focuses on accounting for bonds. We explain how to value, record, amortize, and report these liabilities in financial statements.

Chapter 21

Corporate Earnings, Taxes, and Distributions

Learning Objectives

LO 1	Compute and record corporate income tax.
LO 2	Record transactions involving cash dividends.
LO 3	Account for stock dividends and stock splits.
LO 4	Distribute dividends between common stock and preferred stock.
LO 5	Record purchases and sales of treasury stock.
LO 6	Describe events that can affect retained earnings.
LO 7	Prepare a statement of retained earnings.
LO 8	Prepare a statement of stockholders' equity.
LO 9	Compute earnings per share and describe its use.
LO 10	Compute price-earnings ratio and describe its use.
LO 11	Compute dividend yield and explain its use.

"Think bigger than you are"
—Ron Snyder, CEO and founder

Ugly Profits

The founders of **Crocs, Inc.** (**Crocs.com**) knew they were on to something big when a fire marshal at a Florida boat show complained about the size of the crowd gathered around the Crocs' shoe booth. Founder Lyndon "Duke" Hanson explains, "People would say, 'Man, those are ugly,' and we'd say, 'Just try them on.'" Since then, millions of people have done so, resulting in sales of over 6 million pairs annually.

Crocs were originally designed as a boating and outdoor shoe because of their slip-resistant, non-marking sole. But their comfort, affordability, and, well, ugliness, appealed to doctors, chefs, athletes, outdoor enthusiasts, celebrities, families, and, yes, boaters. "They give people a sense of cool for being brave enough to wear them in public," insists Hanson.

With such rapid growth comes the need for financing. In February 2006, the company's founders sold over 11 million shares of company stock, raising almost $97 million. While the company must now contend with the realities of stock financing, such as dividends, stock distributions, and equity reporting, the cash inflow enabled the company to pay off outstanding debt and invest in further expansion. For example, in June 2007, the company declared a 2-for-1 stock split to its shareholders. In addition, while the company has yet to pay a cash dividend on its common stock, its board of directors must continue to monitor its company performance to assess whether a cash dividend is appropriate.

The realities of being a public company have not changed its consumer focus. Says Crocs CEO Ron Snyder, "The most important thing for us is to continue making great shoes that people love and can't live without."

[Sources: *Crocs.com* Website, May 2009; *Rocky Mountain News.com*, February 2006]

This chapter focuses on corporate taxes and special equity transactions. We explain the accounting for cash and stock dividends, stock splits, and treasury stock. We also explain accounting for retained earnings, including prior period adjustments, retained earnings restrictions, and reporting guidelines.

Corporate Earnings, Taxes, and Distributions

Corporate Taxes	Dividends	Treasury Stock	Reporting on Equity
• Taxable income • Tax liability • Corporate income statement	• Cash dividends • Stock dividends • Stock splits • Preferred stock	• Purchasing treasury stock • Reissuing treasury stock	• Statement of retained earnings • Statement of stockholders' equity

Corporate Taxes

LO1 Compute and record corporate income tax.

Corporations must pay federal, state, and local taxes. We illustrate procedures for computing and paying federal income taxes. Procedures to compute and pay other taxes are similar but are left to advanced courses.

Taxable Income

Corporations pay taxes based on their **taxable income.** Taxable income equals the corporation's total revenues under tax laws minus its total expenses under tax laws. *Taxable income rarely equals financial income.* This is because the rules to compute revenues and expenses are not exactly the same for tax and financial accounting purposes. For our purposes we ignore these differences and assume that taxable income and financial income are the same.

Exhibit 21.1

Corporate 2009 Tax Rates

Taxable Income Over	Not Over	Tax Rate
$ 0	$ 50,000	15%
50,000	75,000	25%
75,000	100,000	34%
100,000	335,000	39%
335,000	10,000,000	34%
10,000,000	15,000,000	35%
15,000,000	18,333,333	38%
18,333,333	....	35%

Corporate Tax Rates   Corporate tax rates vary with taxable income. Exhibit 21.1 shows the 2009 corporate tax rates.

Estimated Tax Payments   Corporations make estimated tax payments after the end of each quarter. A corporation with a calendar year-end makes estimated tax payments each April 15, June 15, September 15, and January 15. These payments are based on the corporation's estimated taxable income for that year and the appropriate tax rates as shown in Exhibit 21.1.

Computing Estimated Tax Payments   To illustrate, assume that Surf Outlet expects taxable income of $210,000 for 2010. Its **estimated tax liability,** the amount it expects to pay in taxes, is computed as follows:

	Expected Taxable Income	×	Tax Rate	=	Estimated Tax Liability
First	$ 50,000		15%		$ 7,500
Next	25,000		25		6,250
Next	25,000		34		8,500
Remainder	110,000		39		42,900
Total	$210,000				$65,150

Journal Entry to Record Quarterly Tax Payment Surf Outlet's quarterly tax payments are $16,287.50 ($65,150/4 quarters). The journal entry to record the first quarterly payment on April 15 is

Apr.	15	Income Tax Expense	16 2 8 7 50		
		Cash		16 2 8 7 50	
		Paid estimated quarterly tax due.			

Assets = Liabilities + Equity
−16,287.50   −16,287.50

Adjusting Tax Liability to Amount Owed

At the end of the year the corporation computes its actual taxable income and actual tax liability. These amounts likely differ from the amounts the corporation estimated at the beginning of the year. The corporation then records either (a) a tax refund receivable (if it overpaid) or (b) an additional tax payable (if it underpaid).

Journal Entry to Record Income Tax Refund Receivable Assume that Surf Outlet has paid its three remaining estimated tax payments of $16,287.50 each by December 31, 2010, and made the necessary journal entries. Next, assume Surf Outlet reports actual taxable income of $194,273 for 2010. It computes its tax overpayment, and its receivable, as follows:

Tax payments made, 2010	$ 65,150.00
Tax liability, 2010	$(59,016.47)*
Tax refund receivable	$ 6,133.53

* ($50,000 × 15%) + ($25,000 × 25%) + ($25,000 × 34%) + ($94,273 × 39%)

Surf Outlet then makes the following journal entry to reflect its expected tax refund of $6,133.53.

Dec.	31	Income Tax Refund Receivable	6 1 3 3 53		
		Income Tax Expense		6 1 3 3 53	
		Record tax refund receivable.			

Assets = Liabilities + Equity
+6,133.53   +6,133.53

In this example Surf Outlet reports corporate net income of $135,256.53, computed as income before tax ($194,273) minus tax expense ($59,016.47) on its 2010 income statement.

Journal Entry to Record Additional Income Tax Payable Assume instead that Surf Outlet reported actual taxable income of $213,683 for 2010. It computes its additional taxes owed as follows:

Tax payments made, 2010	$ 65,150.00
Tax liability, 2010	(66,586.37)*
Additional taxes owed	$ (1,436.37)

* ($50,000 × 15%) + ($25,000 × 25%) + ($25,000 × 34%) + ($113,683 × 39%)

Surf Outlet then makes the following journal entry to reflect its additional taxes owed of $1,436.37.

Dec.	31	Income Tax Expense	1 4 3 6 37		
		Income Tax Payable		1 4 3 6 37	
		Record additional taxes owed.			

Assets = Liabilities + Equity
           +1,436.37   −1,436.37

In this example Surf Outlet reports corporate net income of $147,096.63, computed as income before tax ($213,683) minus income tax expense ($66,586.37) on its 2010 income statement.

Corporate Income Statement

In Chapter 14 we showed the closing process and an income statement for a sole proprietorship. The closing process for a corporation is like that for a sole proprietorship. Revenues and expenses are closed to Income Summary, and Income Summary is closed to Retained Earnings. However, since a corporation is taxed on its earnings, income tax expense must also appear in a corporation's closing entries.

On its income statement the corporation typically reports income tax expense after a line titled "Income Before Income Taxes." Income tax expense is sometimes called "Provision for income taxes" on corporate income statements. Exhibit 21.2 shows a corporate income statement for **Crocs, Inc.**

Exhibit 21.2

Corporate Income Statement

CROCS, INC. Consolidated Statement of Operations For Year Ended December 31, 2007 (in thousands)	
Revenues	$847,350
Cost of sales	349,701
Gross profit	497,649
Selling, general, and administrative expenses	259,882
Income from operations	237,767
Interest expense	438
Other income	(2,997)
Income before income taxes	240,326
Income tax expense	72,098
Net income	$168,228

Dividends on Common Stock

LO2 Record transactions involving cash dividends.

This section describes both cash and stock dividend transactions. A company's board of directors makes dividend decisions. Retained earnings are part of stockholders' claims on the company's net assets, but this does *not* imply that a certain amount of cash or other assets is available to pay stockholders. For example, at the end of 2007, **RadioShack** had $1,992 million in retained earnings but only $509 million in cash.

Cash Dividends

The decision to pay cash dividends involves more than evaluating the amounts of retained earnings and cash. The directors, for instance, may decide to keep the cash to invest in the corporation's growth, to meet emergencies, to take advantage of unexpected opportunities, or to pay off debt. Alternatively, many corporations pay cash dividends to their stockholders at regular dates.

Accounting for Cash Dividends   Cash dividends involve three important dates: declaration, record, and payment. **Date of declaration** is the date the directors vote to declare and pay a dividend. This creates a legal liability of the corporation to its stockholders. **Date of record** is the future date specified by the directors for identifying those stockholders listed in the corporation's records to receive dividends. The date of record usually follows the date of declaration by at least two weeks. Persons who own stock on the date of record receive dividends. **Date of payment** is the date when the corporation makes payment; it follows the date of record by enough time to allow the corporation to arrange checks, money transfers, or other means to pay dividends.

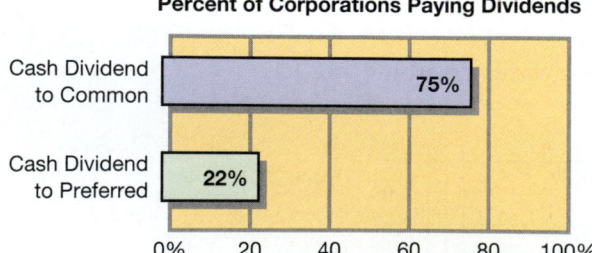

To illustrate, the entry to record a January 9 declaration of a $1 per share cash dividend by the directors of Z-Tech, Inc., with 5,000 outstanding shares is

		Date of Declaration			
Jan.	9	Retained Earnings	5 0 0 0 00		
		Common Dividend Payable		5 0 0 0 00	
		Declared $1 per common share cash dividend.			

Assets = Liabilities + Equity
+5,000   −5,000

Common Dividend Payable is a current liability. The date of record for the Z-Tech dividend is January 22. *No formal journal entry is needed on the date of record*. The February 1 date of payment requires an entry to record both the settlement of the liability and the reduction of the cash balance, as follows:

		Date of Payment			
Feb.	1	Common Dividend Payable	5 0 0 0 00		
		Cash		5 0 0 0 00	
		Paid $1 per common share cash dividend.			

Assets = Liabilities + Equity
−5,000   −5,000

HOW YOU DOIN'?

Answers—p. 552

1. What type of an account is the Common Dividend Payable account?
2. What three crucial dates are involved in the process of paying a cash dividend?
3. When does a dividend become a company's legal obligation?

Stock Dividends

A **stock dividend** is a distribution of additional shares of the corporation's own stock to its stockholders without the receipt of any payment in return. Stock dividends and cash dividends are different. A stock dividend does not reduce assets and equity. Instead, a stock dividend transfers a portion of equity from retained earnings to contributed capital.

LO3 Account for stock dividends and stock splits.

Reasons for Stock Dividends   Stock dividends exist for at least two reasons. First, directors are said to use stock dividends to keep the market price of the stock affordable. For example, if a corporation continues to earn income but does not issue cash dividends, the price of its common stock likely increases. The price of such a stock may become so high that it discourages some investors from buying the stock. When a corporation has a stock dividend, it increases the number of outstanding shares, which lowers the per share stock price. Stock dividends also provide evidence of management's confidence that the company is doing well and will continue to do well.

Accounting for Stock Dividends   Accounting for a stock dividend depends on its size. A **small stock dividend** is a distribution of 25% or less of previously outstanding shares. It is recorded by debiting retained earnings for an amount equal to the market value of the shares to be distributed. A **large stock dividend** is a distribution of more than 25% of previously outstanding shares. A large stock dividend is recorded by debiting retained earnings for the minimum amount required by state law governing the corporation. Most states require debiting retained earnings for the par or stated value of the stock.

To illustrate stock dividends, we use the equity section of X-Quest's balance sheet shown in Exhibit 21.3 just *before* its declaration of a stock dividend on December 31.

Stockholders' Equity (before stock dividend declaration)	
Common stock—$10 par value, 15,000 shares authorized, 10,000 shares issued and outstanding	$100,000
Paid-in capital in excess of par value, common stock	8,000
Retained earnings	35,000
Total stockholders' equity	$143,000

Exhibit 21.3

Stockholders' Equity *before* Declaring a Stock Dividend

Recording a small stock dividend.   Assume that X-Quest's directors declare a 10% stock dividend on December 31. This stock dividend of 1,000 shares, computed as 10% of its 10,000 issued and outstanding shares, is to be distributed on January 20 to the stockholders of record on January 15. Since the market price of X-Quest's stock on December 31 is $15 per share, this small stock dividend declaration is recorded as follows:

> Small stock dividends are recorded at market value.

Date of Declaration				
Dec.	31	Retained Earnings	15 000 00	
		Common Stock Dividend Distributable		10 000 00
		Paid-In Capital in Excess of Par Value, Common Stock		5 000 00
		Declared a 1,000-share (10%) stock dividend.		

Assets = Liabilities + Equity
                  −15,000
                  +10,000
                  +5,000

The $10,000 credit in the dividend declaration entry equals the total par value of the shares, and is recorded in *Common Stock Dividend Distributable*. Its balance exists only until the shares are issued. The $5,000 credit to Paid-In Capital in Excess of Par Value equals the amount by which market value exceeds par value. In general, the balance sheet changes in three ways when a stock dividend is declared. First, the amount of equity attributed to common stock increases; for X-Quest, from $100,000 to $110,000 for 1,000 additional declared shares. Second, paid-in capital in excess of par increases by the excess of market value over par value for the declared shares. Third, retained earnings decreases, reflecting the transfer of amounts to both common stock and paid-in capital in excess of par. The stockholders' equity of X-Quest is shown in Exhibit 21.4 *after* its 10% stock dividend is declared on December 31. While the components of stockholders' equity change, the total dollar amount of stockholders' equity does not.

> The term *Distributable* (not *Payable*) is used for stock dividends. A stock dividend is never a liability on a balance sheet because it never reduces assets.

> The credit to Paid-In Capital in Excess of Par Value is recorded when the stock dividend is declared. This account is not affected when stock is later distributed.

Exhibit 21.4

Stockholders' Equity *after* Declaring a Stock Dividend

Stockholders' Equity (after stock dividend declaration)	
Common stock—$10 par value, 15,000 shares authorized, 10,000 shares issued and outstanding	$100,000
Common stock dividend distributable—1,000 shares	**10,000**
Paid-in capital in excess of par value, common stock	**13,000**
Retained earnings	**20,000**
Total stockholders' equity	$143,000

No entry is made on the date of record for a stock dividend. On January 20, the date of payment, X-Quest distributes the new shares to stockholders and records this entry:

Assets = Liabilities + Equity
                  −10,000
                  +10,000

Date of Payment				
Jan.	20	Common Stock Dividend Distributable	10 000 00	
		Common Stock, $10 Par Value		10 000 00
		To record issuance of common stock dividend.		

The combined effect of these stock dividend entries is to transfer (or capitalize) $15,000 of retained earnings to paid-in capital accounts. The amount transferred equals the market value of the 1,000 issued shares ($15 × 1,000 shares). A stock dividend has no effect on the ownership percent of individual stockholders. Each shareholder owns the same percentage of the corporation, both before and after the stock dividend.

Recording a large stock dividend.   A corporation capitalizes retained earnings equal to the minimum amount required by state law for a large stock dividend. For most states, this amount is the par or stated value of the newly issued shares. To illustrate, suppose X-Quest's board declares a stock dividend of 30% instead of 10% on December 31. Since this dividend is more than 25%, it is a large stock dividend. Thus, the par value of the 3,000 (10,000 × 30%) dividend shares is capitalized for $30,000 (3,000 shares × $10 par value) at the date of declaration with this entry:

Large stock dividends are recorded at par or stated value.

Date of Declaration			
Dec.	31	Retained Earnings	30 0 0 0 00	
		Common Stock Dividend Distributable		30 0 0 0 00
		Declared a 3,000-share (30%) stock dividend.		

Assets = Liabilities + Equity
$$-30,000$$
$$+30,000$$

This transaction decreases retained earnings and increases contributed capital by $30,000. On the date of payment the company debits Common Stock Dividend Distributable and credits Common Stock for $30,000. The effects from a large stock dividend on balance sheet accounts are similar to those for a small stock dividend except there is no effect on contributed capital in excess of par.

Stock Splits

A **stock split** is the distribution of additional shares to stockholders according to their percent ownership. Splits can be done in any ratio, including 2-for-1, 3-for-1, or higher. Stock splits reduce the par or stated value per share and increase the number of outstanding shares. A 2-for-1 split doubles the number of outstanding shares and halves the par value per share. Our feature company, **Crocs, Inc.** had a 2-for-1 stock split in 2007. They doubled the number of outstanding shares and halved the par value per stock.

To illustrate, CompTec has 100,000 outstanding shares of $20 par value common stock with a current market value of $88 per share. A 2-for-1 stock split replaces 100,000 shares of $20 par value stock with 200,000 shares of $10 par value stock. Market value is reduced from $88 per share to about $44 per share. *The split does not affect any balance sheet amounts or any individual stockholder's percent ownership.* Both the Paid-In Capital and Retained Earnings accounts are unchanged by a split, and *no journal entry is made.* The only effect on the accounts is a change in the stock account description. CompTec's 2-for-1 split on its $20 par value stock means that after the split, it changes its stock account title to Common Stock, $10 Par Value. This stock's description on the balance sheet also changes to reflect the additional issued and outstanding shares and the new par value.

HOW YOU DOIN'?   Answers—p. 552

4. How does a stock dividend impact assets and retained earnings?
5. What distinguishes a large stock dividend from a small stock dividend?
6. What amount of retained earnings is capitalized for a small stock dividend?

Dividends on Preferred Stock

Some companies have both common and preferred stock outstanding. Dividends are usually allocated to preferred stockholders before common stockholders. The dividends allocated to preferred stockholders are usually expressed as a dollar amount per share or a percent applied to par value. For example, a 9% preferred stock would pay dividends of 9% of the preferred stock's total par value. A preference for dividends does *not* ensure dividends. If the directors do not declare a dividend, neither the preferred nor the common stockholders receive one.

LO4 Distribute dividends between common stock and preferred stock.

Cumulative or Noncumulative Dividend   Most preferred stocks carry a cumulative dividend right. Holders of **cumulative preferred stock** have a right to be paid both the current and all prior periods' unpaid dividends before any dividend is paid to common stockholders. When preferred stock is cumulative and the directors either do not declare a dividend to preferred stockholders or declare one that does not cover the total amount of cumulative dividend, the unpaid dividend amount is called **dividend in arrears.** These amounts only become a liability if the board of directors declares another dividend. Holders of **noncumulative preferred stock** have no right to prior periods' unpaid dividends if they were not declared in those prior periods.

To illustrate the difference between cumulative and noncumulative preferred stock, assume that a corporation's outstanding stock includes (1) 1,000 shares of $100 par, 9% preferred stock—yielding $9,000 per year in potential dividends, and (2) 4,000 shares of $50 par value common stock. During 2010, the first year of operations, the directors declare total cash dividends of $5,000. Common shareholders receive no dividends since the $5,000 dividend declared is less than the preferred stock's potential dividend of $9,000. In year 2011, the directors declare cash dividends of $42,000. See Exhibit 21.5 for the allocation of dividends for these two years. Allocation of year 2011 dividends depends on whether the preferred stock is noncumulative or cumulative. With noncumulative preferred, the preferred stockholders never receive the $4,000 potential dividend skipped in 2010. If the preferred stock is cumulative, the $4,000 dividend in arrears from 2010 is paid in 2011, before any other dividends are paid.

Exhibit 21.5		Preferred	Common	Total
Allocation of Dividends (noncumulative vs. cumulative preferred stock)	**Preferred Stock Is Noncumulative**			
	Year 2010	$ 5,000	$ 0	$ 5,000
	Year 2011			
	Step 1: Current year's preferred dividend	$ 9,000		
	Step 2: Remainder to common		$33,000	$42,000
	Preferred Stock Is Cumulative			
	Year 2010	$ 5,000	$ 0	$ 5,000
	Year 2011			
	Step 1: Dividend in arrears from 2010	$ 4,000		
	Step 2: Current year's preferred dividend	9,000		
	Step 3: Remainder to common		$29,000	
	Totals for year 2011	$13,000	$29,000	$42,000

A liability for a dividend does not exist until the directors declare a dividend. If a preferred dividend date passes and the corporation's board fails to declare the dividend on its cumulative preferred stock, the dividend in arrears is not a liability. The *full-disclosure principle* requires a corporation to report (usually in a note) the amount of preferred dividends in arrears as of the balance sheet date.

Participating or Nonparticipating Dividend   **Nonparticipating preferred stock** has a feature that limits dividends to a maximum amount each year. This maximum is often stated as a percent of the stock's par value or as a specific dollar amount per share. Once preferred stockholders receive this amount, the common stockholders receive any and all additional dividends. **Participating preferred stock** allows preferred stockholders to share with common stockholders in any dividends paid in excess of the percent or dollar amount stated on the preferred stock. Corporations rarely issue participating preferred stock.

HOW YOU DOIN'?   Answer—p. 552

7. A corporation has issued and outstanding (i) 9,000 shares of $50 par value, 10% cumulative, nonparticipating preferred stock and (ii) 27,000 shares of $10 par value common stock. No dividends have been declared for the two prior years. During the current year, the corporation declares $288,000 in dividends. The amount paid to common shareholders is (*a*) $243,000. (*b*) $153,000. (*c*) $135,000.

Treasury Stock

Corporations buy shares of their own stock for several reasons: (1) to use their shares to acquire another corporation, (2) to purchase shares to avoid a hostile takeover of the company, (3) to reissue them to employees as compensation, and (4) to maintain a strong market for their stock or to show management confidence in the current price.

A corporation's reacquired shares are called **treasury stock,** which is like unissued stock in several ways: (1) neither treasury stock nor unissued stock is an asset, (2) neither receives cash dividends or stock dividends, and (3) neither includes voting rights. However, treasury stock differs from unissued stock in one major way: The corporation can resell treasury stock at less than par value without having the buyers incur a liability, if the stock was originally issued at par value or higher.

LO5 Record purchases and sales of treasury stock.

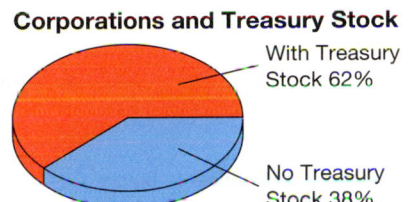

Corporations and Treasury Stock

With Treasury Stock 62%

No Treasury Stock 38%

Purchasing Treasury Stock

Purchasing treasury stock reduces the corporation's assets and equity by equal amounts. (We describe the *cost method* of accounting for treasury stock, which is the most widely used method. The *par value* method is another method explained in advanced courses.) To illustrate, Exhibit 21.6 shows Cyber Corporation's account balances *before* any treasury stock purchase (Cyber has no liabilities).

Assets		Stockholders' Equity	
Cash	$ 30,000	Common stock—$10 par; 10,000 shares	
Other assets	95,000	authorized, issued, and outstanding	$100,000
		Retained earnings	25,000
Total assets	$125,000	Total stockholders' equity	$125,000

Exhibit 21.6

Account Balances *before* Purchasing Treasury Stock

Cyber then purchases 1,000 of its own shares for $11,500 on May 1, which is recorded as follows.

May	1	Treasury Stock, Common	11 5 0 0 00	
		Cash		11 5 0 0 00
		Purchased 1,000 treasury shares at $11.50 per share.		

Assets = Liabilities + Equity
−11,500   −11,500

This entry reduces equity through the debit to the Treasury Stock account, which is a contra equity account. Exhibit 21.7 shows account balances *after* this transaction.

> Treasury stock does not carry voting or dividend rights.

Assets		Stockholders' Equity	
Cash	$ 18,500	Common stock—$10 par; 10,000 shares	
Other assets	95,000	authorized and issued; 1,000 shares in treasury	$100,000
		Retained earnings, $11,500 restricted by	
		treasury stock purchase	25,000
		Less cost of treasury stock	**(11,500)**
Total assets	$113,500	Total stockholders' equity	$113,500

Exhibit 21.7

Account Balances *after* Purchasing Treasury Stock

The treasury stock purchase reduces Cyber's cash, total assets, and total equity by $11,500 but does not reduce the balance of either the Common Stock or the Retained Earnings account. The equity reduction is reported by deducting the cost of treasury stock in the equity section. Also, two disclosures are evident. First, the stock description reveals that 1,000 issued shares are in treasury, leaving only 9,000 shares still outstanding. Second, the description for retained earnings reveals that it is partly restricted.

> The Treasury Stock account is *not* an asset. This contra equity account is a reduction to the equity section.

> A treasury stock purchase is also called a *stock buyback*.

Demonstration Problem 1

Barton Corporation began operations on January 1, 2010. The following transactions relating to stockholders' equity occurred in the first two years of the company's operations.

2010

Jan. 1   Authorized the issuance of 2 million shares of $5 par value common stock and 100,000 shares of $100 par value, 10% cumulative, preferred stock.

Jan. 2   Issued 200,000 shares of common stock for $12 cash per share.

Jan. 3   Issued 100,000 shares of common stock in exchange for a building valued at $820,000 and merchandise inventory valued at $380,000.

Jan. 5   Issued 12,000 shares of preferred stock for $110 cash per share.

2011

June 4   Issued 100,000 shares of common stock for $15 cash per share.

Note: Journal entries to record the above transactions are shown in the Demonstration Problem in Chapter 20.

Required

Prepare a table showing dividend allocations and dividends per share for 2010 and 2011 assuming Barton declares the following cash dividends: 2010, $50,000, and 2011, $300,000. Round dividends per share to the nearest cent.

Planning the Solution

- Compute the number of common and preferred shares outstanding.
- Prepare a table similar to Exhibit 21.5 showing dividend allocations for 2010 and 2011.

Solution to Demonstration Problem 1

Dividend allocation table: The potential dividend on preferred shares is $120,000, computed as 12,000 × $100 × 10%.

	Common	Preferred
2010 ($50,000)		
Preferred—current year (12,000 shares × $100 × 10% = $120,000)	$ 0	$ 50,000
Common—remainder (300,000 shares outstanding)	0	0
Total for the year	$ 0	$ 50,000
2011 ($300,000)		
Preferred—dividend in arrears from 2010 ($120,000 − $50,000)	$ 0	$ 70,000
Preferred—current year	0	120,000
Common—remainder (400,000 shares outstanding)	110,000	0
Total for the year	$110,000	$190,000
Dividends per share		
2010 ($0/300,000); ($50,000/12,000)	$ 0.00	$ 4.17
2011 ($110,000/400,000); ($190,000/12,000)	$ 0.28	$ 15.83

Demonstration Problem 2

Precision Company began year 2010 with the following balances in its stockholders' equity accounts.

Common stock—$10 par, 500,000 shares authorized,	
200,000 shares issued and outstanding	$2,000,000
Paid-in capital in excess of par, common stock	1,000,000
Retained earnings	5,000,000
Total	$8,000,000

All outstanding common stock was issued for $15 per share when the company was created. Prepare journal entries to account for the following transactions during year 2010.

Jan. 10 The board declared a $0.10 cash dividend per share to shareholders of record Jan. 28.
Feb. 15 Paid the cash dividend declared on January 10.
Mar. 31 Declared a 20% stock dividend. The market value of the stock is $18 per share.
May 1 Distributed the stock dividend declared on March 31.
July 1 Purchased 30,000 shares of treasury stock at $20 per share.
Sept. 1 Sold 20,000 treasury shares at $26 cash per share.
Dec. 1 Sold the remaining 10,000 shares of treasury stock at $7 cash per share.

Planning the Solution

- Calculate the total cash dividend to record by multiplying the cash dividend declared by the number of shares as of the date of record.
- Decide whether the stock dividend is a small or large dividend. Then analyze each event to determine the accounts affected and the appropriate amounts to be recorded.
- Account for the purchase of treasury stock. Analyze both reissuances to determine if they sold above or below cost.

Solution to Demonstration Problem 2

2010				
Jan.	10	Retained Earnings	20 000 00	
		Common Dividend Payable		20 000 00
		Declared a $0.10 per share cash dividend.		
Feb.	15	Common Dividend Payable	20 000 00	
		Cash		20 000 00
		Paid $0.10 per share cash dividend.		
Mar.	31	Retained Earnings	720 000 00	
		Common Stock Dividend Distributable		400 000 00
		Paid-In Capital in Excess of Par Value, Common Stock		320 000 00
		Declared a small stock dividend of 20% or		
		40,000 shares; market value is $18 per share.		
May	1	Common Stock Dividend Distributable	400 000 00	
		Common Stock		400 000 00
		Distributed 40,000 shares of common stock.		
July	1	Treasury Stock, Common	600 000 00	
		Cash		600 000 00
		Purchased 30,000 common shares at $20 per share.		
Sept.	1	Cash	520 000 00	
		Treasury Stock, Common		400 000 00
		Paid-In Capital, Treasury Stock		120 000 00
		Sold 20,000 treasury shares at $26 per share.		
Dec.	1	Cash	70 000 00	
		Paid-In Capital, Treasury Stock	120 000 00	
		Retained Earnings	10 000 00	
		Treasury Stock, Common		200 000 00
		Sold 10,000 treasury shares at $7 per share.		

Summary

LO1 Compute and record corporate income tax. Corporations pay federal, state, and local taxes on their income. Corporations typically make quarterly estimated tax payments and then adjust their tax liability to an amount based on their actual taxable income for that year.

LO2 Record transactions involving cash dividends. Cash dividends involve three events. On the date of declaration, the directors bind the company to pay the dividend. A dividend declaration reduces retained earnings and creates a current liability. On the date of record, recipients of the dividend are identified. On the date of payment, cash is paid to stockholders and the current liability is removed.

LO3 Account for stock dividends and stock splits. Neither a stock dividend nor a stock split alters the value of the company. However, the value of each share is less due to the distribution of additional shares. The distribution of additional shares is according to individual stockholders' ownership percent. Small stock dividends (≤25%) are recorded by capitalizing retained earnings equal to the market value of distributed shares. Large stock dividends (>25%) are recorded by capitalizing retained earnings equal to the par or stated value of distributed shares. Stock splits do not yield journal entries but do yield changes in the description of stock.

LO4 Distribute dividends between common stock and preferred stock. Preferred stockholders usually hold the right to dividend distributions before common stockholders. When preferred stock is cumulative and dividends are in arrears, the amount in arrears must be distributed to preferred before any dividends are distributed to common.

LO5 Record purchases and sales of treasury stock. When a corporation purchases its own previously issued stock, it debits the cost of these shares to Treasury Stock. Treasury stock is subtracted from equity in the balance sheet. If treasury stock is reissued, any proceeds in excess of cost are credited to Paid-In Capital, Treasury Stock. If the proceeds are less than cost, they are debited to Paid-In Capital, Treasury Stock to the extent a credit

balance exists. Any remaining amount of proceeds less than cost is debited to Retained Earnings.

LO6 Describe events that can affect retained earnings. Many companies face statutory and contractual restrictions on retained earnings. Corporations can voluntarily appropriate retained earnings to inform others about their disposition. Prior period adjustments are corrections of errors in prior financial statements.

LO7 Prepare a statement of retained earnings. This statement summarizes the events that impacted retained earnings during the period. These events include net income or loss and cash or stock dividends. Selected treasury stock transactions and prior period adjustments also appear on the statement of retained earnings.

LO8 Prepare a statement of stockholders' equity. This statement lists the beginning and ending balances of each equity account and describes the changes that occur during the period.

LO9 Compute earnings per share and describe its use. A company with a simple capital structure computes basic EPS by dividing net income less any preferred dividends by the weighted-average number of outstanding common shares. A company with a complex capital structure must usually report both basic and diluted EPS.

LO10 Compute price-earnings ratio and describe its use. A common stock's price-earnings (PE) ratio is computed by dividing the stock's market value (price) per share by its EPS. A stock's PE is based on expectations that can prove to be better or worse than eventual performance.

LO11 Compute dividend yield and explain its use. Dividend yield is the ratio of a stock's annual cash dividends per share to its market value (price) per share. Dividend yield can be compared with the yield of other companies to determine whether the stock is expected to be an income or growth stock.

Guidance Answers to HOW YOU DOIN'?

1. Common Dividend Payable is a current liability account.

2. The date of declaration, date of record, and date of payment.

3. A dividend is a legal liability at the date of declaration, on which date it is recorded as a liability.

4. A stock dividend does not transfer assets to stockholders, but it does require an amount of retained earnings to be transferred to a contributed capital account(s).

5. A small stock dividend is 25% or less of the previous outstanding shares. A large stock dividend is more than 25%.

6. Retained earnings equal to the distributable shares' market value should be capitalized for a small stock dividend.

7. (b)

Total cash dividend	$288,000
To preferred shareholders	135,000*
Remainder to common shareholders	$153,000

* 9,000 × $50 × 10% × 3 years = $135,000.

8. (b)

9. No. The shares are an investment for Southern Co. and are issued and outstanding shares for Northern Corp.

10. Treasury stock does not affect the number of authorized or issued shares, but it reduces the outstanding shares.

11. (a)

Key Terms

Appropriated retained earnings (p. 548) Retained earnings separately reported to inform stockholders of funding needs.

Basic earnings per share (p. 548) Net income less any preferred dividends and then divided by weighted-average common shares outstanding.

Changes in accounting estimates (p. 548) Change in an accounting estimate that results from new information, subsequent developments, or improved judgment that impacts current and future periods.

Complex capital structure (p. 549) Capital structure that includes outstanding rights or options to purchase common stock, or securities that are convertible into common stock.

Cumulative preferred stock (p. 543) Preferred stock on which undeclared dividends accumulate until paid; common stockholders cannot receive dividends until cumulative dividends are paid.

Date of declaration (p. 540) Date the directors vote to pay a dividend.

Date of payment (p. 540) Date the corporation makes the dividend payment.

Date of record (p. 540) Date directors specify for identifying stockholders to receive dividends.

Diluted earnings per share (p. 549) Earnings per share calculation that requires dilutive securities be added to the denominator of the basic EPS calculation.

Dilutive securities (p. 549) Securities having the potential to increase common shares outstanding; examples are options, rights, convertible bonds, and convertible preferred stock.

Dividend in arrears (p. 544) Unpaid dividend on cumulative preferred stock; must be paid before any regular dividends on preferred stock and before any dividends on common stock.

Dividend yield (p. 549) Ratio of the annual amount of cash dividends distributed to common shareholders relative to the common stock's market value (price).

Earnings per share (EPS) (p. 548) Amount of income earned by each share of a company's outstanding common stock; also called *net income per share*.

Estimated tax liability (p. 538) The amount a corporation expects to pay in income taxes for a specific year.

Large stock dividend (p. 541) Stock dividend that is more than 25% of the previously outstanding shares.

Noncumulative preferred stock (p. 544) Preferred stock on which the right to receive dividends is lost for any period when dividends are not declared.

Nonparticipating preferred stock (p. 544) Preferred stock on which dividends are limited to a maximum amount each year.

Participating preferred stock (p. 544) Preferred stock that shares with common stockholders any dividends paid in excess of the percent stated on preferred stock.

Payout ratio (p. 549) Cash dividends declared on common stock divided by net income.

Price-earnings (PE) ratio (p. 549) Ratio of a company's current market value per share to its earnings per share; also called *price-to-earnings*.

Prior period adjustment (p. 547) Correction of an error in a prior year that is reported in the statement of retained earnings (or statement of stockholders' equity) net of any income tax effects.

Restricted retained earnings (p. 547) Retained earnings not available for dividends because of legal or contractual limitations.

Retained earnings deficit (p. 540) Debit (abnormal) balance in Retained Earnings; occurs when cumulative losses and dividends exceed cumulative income; also called *accumulated deficit*.

Simple capital structure (p. 549) Capital structure that consists of only common stock and nonconvertible preferred stock; consists of no dilutive securities.

Small stock dividend (p. 541) Stock dividend that is 25% or less of a corporation's previously outstanding shares.

Statement of retained earnings (p. 547) Report of changes in retained earnings over a period; adjusted for increases (net income), for decreases (dividends and net loss), and for any prior period adjustment.

Statement of stockholders' equity (p. 548) Financial statement that lists the beginning and ending balances of each major equity account and describes all changes in those accounts.

Stock dividend (p. 541) Corporation's distribution of its own stock to its stockholders without the receipt of any payment.

Stock split (p. 543) Occurs when a corporation calls in its stock and replaces each share with more than one new share; decreases both the market value per share and any par or stated value per share.

Taxable income (p. 538) A corporation's total revenues under tax laws minus its total expenses under tax laws.

Treasury stock (p. 545) Corporation's own stock that it reacquired and still holds.

Multiple Choice Quiz   Answers on p. 565   mhhe.com/wildCA2e

Additional Multiple Choice Quizzes are available at the book's Website.

1. A company's board of directors votes to declare a cash dividend of 75¢ per share. The company has 15,000 shares authorized, 10,000 issued, and 9,500 shares outstanding. The total amount of the cash dividend is
   a. $375
   b. $4,125
   c. $7,125
   d. $7,500
   e. $11,250

2. A company issued 7% preferred stock with a $100 par value. This means that
   a. Preferred shareholders have a guaranteed dividend.
   b. The amount of the potential dividend is $7 per year per preferred share.

c. Preferred shareholders are entitled to 7% of the annual income.

d. The market price per share will approximate $100 per share.

e. Only 7% of the total contributed capital can be preferred stock.

3. A corporation had 50,000 shares of $20 per value common stock outstanding on July 1. Later that same day the board of directors declared a 10% stock dividend when the market value of each share was $27. The entry to record this dividend includes a

a. Debit of $100,000 to Retained Earnings.

b. Debit of $135,000 to Retained Earnings.

c. Debit of $100,000 to Common Stock Dividend Receivable.

d. Credit of $135,000 to Common Stock Dividend Receivable.

e. No entry is needed.

4. The following data are reported about a company's stockholders' equity accounts.

Common stock $10 par value, 20,000 shares authorized, and 10,000 shares issued	$100,000
Contributed capital in excess of par value, Common stock	50,000
Retained earnings	25,000
Treasury stock, 1,000 shares	11,500

The treasury shares were all purchased at the same price. The cost per share of the treasury stock is

a. $1.15

b. $1.28

c. $11.50

d. $10.50

e. $10.00

5. A company had a beginning balance in retained earnings of $43,000. It had net income of $6,000 and declared and paid out cash dividends of $5,625 in the current period. The ending balance in retained earnings equals

a. $108,625

b. $(12,625)

c. $11,375

d. $43,375

e. $(11,375)

Discussion Questions

1. Identify and explain the importance of the three dates relevant to corporate dividends.

2. Why do companies purchase their own stock?

3. How does declaring a stock dividend affect the corporation's assets, liabilities, and total equity? What are the effects of the eventual distribution of that stock?

4. What is the difference between a stock dividend and a stock split?

5. Courts have ruled that a stock dividend is not taxable income to stockholders. What justifies this decision?

6. How does the purchase of treasury stock affect the purchaser's assets and total equity?

7. Why do laws place limits on treasury stock purchases?

8. How are EPS results computed for a corporation with a simple capital structure?

---

connect™

QUICK STUDY

QS 21–1
Computing actual tax liability
LO1

Kane Company reports taxable income of $411,000 in 2010. Using the tax rates in Exhibit 21.1, compute Kane Company's tax liability for 2010.

QS 21–2
Journal entries for estimated tax payments   **LO1**

Refer to the information in QS 21-1. Assume that Kane Company expects to make $411,000 in taxable income in 2010. Prepare the journal entry Kane Company will record for each quarterly estimated tax payment in 2010.

QS 21–3
Accounting for cash dividends
LO2

Prepare journal entries to record the following transactions for Fletcher Corporation.

May 15   Declared a $54,000 cash dividend payable to common stockholders.
June 31   Paid the dividend declared on May 15.

On December 15 Zortok Company declared a $0.50 per share cash dividend. This dividend is paid on January 15 of the following year. The company has 20,000 shares authorized, 9,000 shares issued, and 8,000 shares of common stock outstanding. Prepare the journal entries to record the (*a*) dividend declaration and (*b*) dividend payment.

QS 21–4
Accounting for cash dividends   **LO2**

The stockholders' equity section of Jun Company's balance sheet as of April 1 follows. On April 2, Jun declares and distributes a 10% stock dividend. The stock's per share market value on April 2 is $20 (prior to the dividend). Prepare the stockholders' equity section immediately after the stock dividend.

QS 21–5
Accounting for small stock dividends   **LO3**

Common stock—$5 par value, 375,000 shares	
authorized, 200,000 shares issued and outstanding	$1,000,000
Paid-in capital in excess of par value, common stock	600,000
Retained earnings	833,000
Total stockholders' equity	$2,433,000

Clement Corporation declared a 35% stock dividend on November 1. The shares for this stock dividend were distributed one month later on December 1. The following data were available on November 1 just *before* the dividend.

QS 21–6
Accounting for large stock dividends   **LO3**

Retained earnings	$750,000
Shares issued and outstanding	60,000
Market value per share	$15
Par value per share	$5

Prepare the journal entries to record the (*a*) stock dividend declaration on November 1 and (*b*) stock issuance on December 1.

Stockholders' equity of Ernst Company consists of 80,000 shares of $5 par value, 8% cumulative preferred stock and 250,000 shares of $1 par value common stock. Both classes of stock have been outstanding since the company's inception. Ernst did not declare any dividends in the prior year, but it now declares and pays a $110,000 cash dividend at the current year-end. Determine the amount distributed to each class of stockholders for this two-year-old company.

QS 21–7
Distribute dividends between classes of shareholders   **LO4**

Shenzi Company has 1,000 shares of $50 par value, 4.5% cumulative, nonparticipating preferred stock outstanding and 10,000 shares of $10 par value common stock outstanding. Shenzi paid total cash dividends of $1,000 in its first year of operation. Compute the dollar amount of cash dividend that Shenzi must pay to preferred stockholders in the second year before any dividend is paid to common stockholders.

QS 21–8
Distribute dividends between classes of shareholders   **LO4**

On May 3, Zirbal Corporation purchased 4,000 shares of its own stock for $36,000 cash. On November 4, Zirbal reissued 850 shares of this treasury stock for $8,500. Prepare the May 3 and November 4 journal entries to record Zirbal's purchase and reissuance of treasury stock.

QS 21–9
Purchase and sale of treasury stock   **LO5**

Refer to the information in QS 21-9. Assume that on December 1, Zirbal Corporation reissued another 1,300 shares of treasury stock for $10,400. Prepare the journal entry to record the December 1 reissuance of treasury stock.

QS 21–10
Purchase and sale of treasury stock   **LO5**

AllCOM reports the following information for its current year. What is AllCOM's ending retained earnings balance?

QS 21–11
Events that affect retained earnings   **LO6**

Retained earnings, December 31 (prior year)	$250,000
Cost of goods sold	90,000
Other operating expenses, including income taxes	54,000
Cash dividends declared and paid	30,800
Correction for understatement of net income in prior	
period (inventory error), net of tax	23,000
Stock dividends declared and distributed	20,000
Net income	36,000

Exercise 21–8
Recording and reporting treasury
stock transactions   **LO5**

On October 10, the stockholders' equity of Sherman Systems appears as follows.

Common stock—$10 par value, 72,000 shares authorized, issued, and outstanding	$ 720,000
Paid-in capital in excess of par value, common stock	216,000
Retained earnings	864,000
Total stockholders' equity	$1,800,000

1. Prepare journal entries to record the following transactions for Sherman Systems.

     a. Purchased 5,000 shares of its own common stock at $25 per share on October 11.

     b. Sold 1,000 treasury shares on November 1 for $31 cash per share.

Check   (1c) Dr. Retained Earnings, $14,000

     c. Sold all remaining treasury shares on November 25 for $20 cash per share.

2. Explain how Sherman's equity section changes after the October 11 treasury stock purchase, and prepare the revised equity section of its balance sheet at that date.

Exercise 21–9
Preparing a statement of
retained earnings   **LO7**

The following information is available for Amos Company for the year ended December 31, 2010.

     a. Balance of retained earnings, December 31, 2009, prior to discovery of error, $1,375,000.

     b. Cash dividends declared and paid during 2010, $43,000.

     c. It neglected to record 2008 depreciation expense of $55,500, which is net of $4,500 in income taxes.

     d. Amos earned $126,000 in 2010 net income.

Prepare a 2010 statement of retained earnings for Amos Company.

Exercise 21–10
Basic earnings per share   **LO9**

Ecker Company reports $2,700,000 of net income for 2010 and declares $390,000 of cash dividends on its preferred stock for 2010. At the end of 2010, the company had 678,000 weighted-average shares of common stock outstanding.

Check   (2) $3.41

1. What amount of net income is available to common stockholders for 2010?

2. What is the company's basic earnings per share for 2010?

Exercise 21–11
Basic earnings per share   **LO9**

Kelley Company reports $960,000 of net income for 2010 and declares $130,000 of cash dividends on its preferred stock for 2010. At the end of 2010, the company had 379,000 weighted-average shares of common stock outstanding.

1. What amount of net income is available to common stockholders for 2010?

2. What is the company's basic earnings per share for 2010?

Exercise 21–12
Describe events that can affect
retained earnings   **LO6**

A corporation began the current year with $250,000 of unappropriated retained earnings. During the current year it earned $120,000 of net (after-tax) income, declared $75,000 of cash dividends, paid $50,000 in cash dividends, and purchased treasury stock costing $40,000. Calculate the current year-end balance in retained earnings.

Exercise 21–13
Prepare a statement of
retained earnings   **LO7**

Dawls Corporation reported stockholders' equity on December 31 of the prior year as follows:

Common stock, $5 par value, 1,000,000 shares authorized, 500,000 shares issued	$2,500,000
Contributed capital in excess of par, common stock	1,000,000
Retained earnings	3,000,000

The following selected transactions occurred during the current year.

Feb. 15   The board of directors declared a 5% stock dividend to stockholders of record on March 1, payable March 20. The stock was selling for $8 per share.

Mar. 9   Paid the stock dividend of February 15.

May 1   A cash dividend of $0.30 per share was declared by the board of directors to stockholders of record on May 20, payable June 1.

June 1   Paid the cash dividend of May 1.

Aug. 20   The board decided to split the stock 4-for-1, effective on September 1.

On December 15 Zortok Company declared a $0.50 per share cash dividend. This dividend is paid on January 15 of the following year. The company has 20,000 shares authorized, 9,000 shares issued, and 8,000 shares of common stock outstanding. Prepare the journal entries to record the (*a*) dividend declaration and (*b*) dividend payment.

QS 21-4
Accounting for cash dividends **LO2**

The stockholders' equity section of Jun Company's balance sheet as of April 1 follows. On April 2, Jun declares and distributes a 10% stock dividend. The stock's per share market value on April 2 is $20 (prior to the dividend). Prepare the stockholders' equity section immediately after the stock dividend.

QS 21-5
Accounting for small stock dividends **LO3**

Common stock—$5 par value, 375,000 shares	
authorized, 200,000 shares issued and outstanding	$1,000,000
Paid-in capital in excess of par value, common stock	600,000
Retained earnings	833,000
Total stockholders' equity	$2,433,000

Clement Corporation declared a 35% stock dividend on November 1. The shares for this stock dividend were distributed one month later on December 1. The following data were available on November 1 just *before* the dividend.

QS 21-6
Accounting for large stock dividends **LO3**

Retained earnings	$750,000
Shares issued and outstanding	60,000
Market value per share	$15
Par value per share	$5

Prepare the journal entries to record the (*a*) stock dividend declaration on November 1 and (*b*) stock issuance on December 1.

Stockholders' equity of Ernst Company consists of 80,000 shares of $5 par value, 8% cumulative preferred stock and 250,000 shares of $1 par value common stock. Both classes of stock have been outstanding since the company's inception. Ernst did not declare any dividends in the prior year, but it now declares and pays a $110,000 cash dividend at the current year-end. Determine the amount distributed to each class of stockholders for this two-year-old company.

QS 21-7
Distribute dividends between classes of shareholders **LO4**

Shenzi Company has 1,000 shares of $50 par value, 4.5% cumulative, nonparticipating preferred stock outstanding and 10,000 shares of $10 par value common stock outstanding. Shenzi paid total cash dividends of $1,000 in its first year of operation. Compute the dollar amount of cash dividend that Shenzi must pay to preferred stockholders in the second year before any dividend is paid to common stockholders.

QS 21-8
Distribute dividends between classes of shareholders **LO4**

On May 3, Zirbal Corporation purchased 4,000 shares of its own stock for $36,000 cash. On November 4, Zirbal reissued 850 shares of this treasury stock for $8,500. Prepare the May 3 and November 4 journal entries to record Zirbal's purchase and reissuance of treasury stock.

QS 21-9
Purchase and sale of treasury stock **LO5**

Refer to the information in QS 21-9. Assume that on December 1, Zirbal Corporation reissued another 1,300 shares of treasury stock for $10,400. Prepare the journal entry to record the December 1 reissuance of treasury stock.

QS 21-10
Purchase and sale of treasury stock **LO5**

AllCOM reports the following information for its current year. What is AllCOM's ending retained earnings balance?

QS 21-11
Events that affect retained earnings **LO6**

Retained earnings, December 31 (prior year)	$250,000
Cost of goods sold	90,000
Other operating expenses, including income taxes	54,000
Cash dividends declared and paid	30,800
Correction for understatement of net income in prior	
period (inventory error), net of tax	23,000
Stock dividends declared and distributed	20,000
Net income	36,000

QS 21–12
Accounting for changes in estimates; error adjustments
LO6

Answer the following questions related to a company's activities for the current year:

1. A review of the notes payable files discovers that three years ago the company reported the entire amount of a payment (principal and interest) on an installment note payable as interest expense. This mistake had a material effect on the amount of income in that year. How should the correction be reported in the current year financial statements?

2. After using an expected useful life of seven years and no salvage value to depreciate its office equipment over the preceding three years, the company decided early this year that the equipment will last only two more years. How should the effects of this decision be reported in the current year financial statements?

QS 21–13
Basic earnings per share   **LO9**

Murray Company reports net income of $770,000 for the year. It has no preferred stock, and its weighted-average common shares outstanding is 280,000 shares. Compute its basic earnings per share.

QS 21–14
Basic earnings per share   **LO9**

Epic Company earned net income of $900,000 this year. The number of common shares outstanding during the entire year was 400,000, and preferred shareholders received a $20,000 cash dividend. Compute Epic Company's basic earnings per share.

connect™

EXERCISES

Exercise 21–1
Compute and record corporate income tax transactions   **LO1**

Nitzu Company expects to earn $327,000 of taxable income in 2010.

Required

1. Using the tax rates in Exhibit 21.1, compute Nitzu's estimated tax liability for 2010.

2. Prepare the journal entry Nitzu will record each quarter in 2010 when it pays that quarter's estimated tax payment.

3. Assume that Nitzu's actual tax liability for 2010 is $111,015. Prepare the journal entry to adjust Nitzu's tax liability to the actual amount owed for 2010.

4. Assume that Nitzu's actual tax liability for 2010 is $109,997. Prepare the journal entry to adjust Nitzu's tax liability to the actual amount owed for 2010.

Exercise 21–2
Cash and stock dividends and stock splits   **LO2   LO3**

Prepare journal entries to record the following separate transactions for four companies.

1. Declared a $0.40 per share cash dividend on 200,000 shares of preferred stock outstanding.

2. Declared and distributed a 12% stock dividend on 800,000 shares of $5 par value common stock outstanding. Market price per common share on this date was $25.

3. Declared and distributed a 2-for-1 stock split on 500,000 shares of $10 par value common stock outstanding.

4. Declared and distributed a 30% stock dividend on 400,000 common shares of $5 par value common stock outstanding. Market price per common share on this date was $20.

Exercise 21–3
Distribute dividends between common stock and preferred stock   **LO4**

Since its inception, Xtreme Sports has had $100,000 of 8% nonparticipating, preferred stock outstanding and $500,000 of common stock outstanding. In the company's first year of operation, no dividends were paid. During the second year, Xtreme Sports paid cash dividends of $30,000. Determine the dividend amounts to be distributed to the common shareholders and to the preferred shareholders assuming the preferred stock is

1. Noncumulative.

2. Cumulative.

On June 30, 2010, Sharper Corporation's common stock is priced at $62 per share before any stock dividend or split, and the stockholders' equity section of its balance sheet appears as follows.

Common stock—$10 par value, 120,000 shares authorized, 50,000 shares issued and outstanding	$ 500,000
Paid-in capital in excess of par value, common stock	200,000
Retained earnings	660,000
Total stockholders' equity	$1,360,000

Exercise 21–4
Stock dividends and splits   **LO3**

1. Assume that the company declares and immediately distributes a 50% stock dividend. This event is recorded by capitalizing retained earnings equal to the stock's par value. Answer these questions about stockholders' equity as it exists *after* issuing the new shares.

  a. What is the retained earnings balance?

  b. What is the amount of total stockholders' equity?

  c. How many shares are outstanding?

Check   (1b) $1,360,000

2. Assume that the company implements a 3-for-2 stock split instead of the stock dividend in part 1. Answer these questions about stockholders' equity as it exists *after* issuing the new shares.

  a. What is the retained earnings balance?

  b. What is the amount of total stockholders' equity?

  c. How many shares are outstanding?

(2a) $660,000

3. Explain the difference, if any, to a stockholder from receiving new shares distributed under a large stock dividend versus a stock split.

The stockholders' equity of TVX Company at the beginning of the day on February 5 follows.

Common stock—$10 par value, 150,000 shares authorized, 60,000 shares issued and outstanding	$ 600,000
Paid-in capital in excess of par value, common stock	425,000
Retained earnings	550,000
Total stockholders' equity	$1,575,000

Exercise 21–5
Stock dividends and per share book values   **LO3**

On February 5, the directors declare a 20% stock dividend distributable on February 28 to the February 15 stockholders of record. The stock's market value is $40 per share on February 5 before the stock dividend. The stock's market value is $33.40 per share on February 28.

1. Prepare entries to record both the dividend declaration and its distribution.

2. One stockholder owned 800 shares on February 5 before the dividend. Compute the book value per share and total book value of this stockholder's shares immediately before and after the stock dividend of February 5. (In this case, define book value per share as total stockholders' equity divided by the number of issued and distributable shares.)

Check   (2) Book value per share: before, $26.250; after, $21.875

3. Compute the total market value of the investor's shares in part 2 as of February 5 and February 28.

York's outstanding stock consists of (a) 80,000 shares of noncumulative 7.5% preferred stock with a $5 par value and (b) 200,000 shares of common stock with a $1 par value. During its first four years of operation, the corporation declared and paid the following total cash dividends.

2010	$ 20,000
2011	28,000
2012	200,000
2013	350,000

Exercise 21–6
Dividends on common and noncumulative preferred stock   **LO4**

Determine the amount of dividends paid each year to each of the two classes of stockholders. Also compute the total dividends paid to each class for the four years combined.

Check   Total paid to preferred, $108,000

Use the data in Exercise 21-6 to determine the amount of dividends paid each year to each of the two classes of stockholders assuming that the preferred stock is cumulative. Also determine the total dividends paid to each class for the four years combined.

Exercise 21–7
Dividends on common and cumulative preferred stock   **LO4**

Exercise 21-8
Recording and reporting treasury stock transactions   LO5

On October 10, the stockholders' equity of Sherman Systems appears as follows.

Common stock—$10 par value, 72,000 shares authorized, issued, and outstanding	$ 720,000
Paid-in capital in excess of par value, common stock	216,000
Retained earnings	864,000
Total stockholders' equity	$1,800,000

1. Prepare journal entries to record the following transactions for Sherman Systems.

   a. Purchased 5,000 shares of its own common stock at $25 per share on October 11.

   b. Sold 1,000 treasury shares on November 1 for $31 cash per share.

Check   (1c) Dr. Retained Earnings, $14,000

   c. Sold all remaining treasury shares on November 25 for $20 cash per share.

2. Explain how Sherman's equity section changes after the October 11 treasury stock purchase, and prepare the revised equity section of its balance sheet at that date.

Exercise 21-9
Preparing a statement of retained earnings   LO7

The following information is available for Amos Company for the year ended December 31, 2010.

   a. Balance of retained earnings, December 31, 2009, prior to discovery of error, $1,375,000.

   b. Cash dividends declared and paid during 2010, $43,000.

   c. It neglected to record 2008 depreciation expense of $55,500, which is net of $4,500 in income taxes.

   d. Amos earned $126,000 in 2010 net income.

Prepare a 2010 statement of retained earnings for Amos Company.

Exercise 21-10
Basic earnings per share   LO9

Ecker Company reports $2,700,000 of net income for 2010 and declares $390,000 of cash dividends on its preferred stock for 2010. At the end of 2010, the company had 678,000 weighted-average shares of common stock outstanding.

   1. What amount of net income is available to common stockholders for 2010?

Check   (2) $3.41

   2. What is the company's basic earnings per share for 2010?

Exercise 21-11
Basic earnings per share   LO9

Kelley Company reports $960,000 of net income for 2010 and declares $130,000 of cash dividends on its preferred stock for 2010. At the end of 2010, the company had 379,000 weighted-average shares of common stock outstanding.

   1. What amount of net income is available to common stockholders for 2010?

   2. What is the company's basic earnings per share for 2010?

Exercise 21-12
Describe events that can affect retained earnings   LO6

A corporation began the current year with $250,000 of unappropriated retained earnings. During the current year it earned $120,000 of net (after-tax) income, declared $75,000 of cash dividends, paid $50,000 in cash dividends, and purchased treasury stock costing $40,000. Calculate the current year-end balance in retained earnings.

Exercise 21-13
Prepare a statement of retained earnings   LO7

Dawls Corporation reported stockholders' equity on December 31 of the prior year as follows:

Common stock, $5 par value, 1,000,000 shares authorized, 500,000 shares issued	$2,500,000
Contributed capital in excess of par, common stock	1,000,000
Retained earnings	3,000,000

The following selected transactions occurred during the current year.

Feb. 15   The board of directors declared a 5% stock dividend to stockholders of record on March 1, payable March 20. The stock was selling for $8 per share.

Mar. 9   Paid the stock dividend of February 15.

May   1   A cash dividend of $0.30 per share was declared by the board of directors to stockholders of record on May 20, payable June 1.

June 1   Paid the cash dividend of May 1.

Aug. 20   The board decided to split the stock 4-for-1, effective on September 1.

Sept. 1   Stock split 4-for-1.
Dec. 31   Earned a net income of $800,000 for the current year.

Prepare a statement of retained earnings as of December 31 of the current year.

Marble Corporation had the following balances in its stockholders' equity accounts at December 31, 2009.

Exercise 21-14
Prepare a statement of
stockholders' equity   **LO8**

Common stock, $10 par, 50,000 shares authorized, 20,000 shares issued	$200,000
Paid-In capital in excess of par value, common	250,000
Retained earnings	500,000
Treasury stock, 1,000 shares	(20,000)
Total stockholders' equity	$930,000

The following transactions occurred during 2010.

Feb. 3   Sold and issued 3,000 shares of common stock for $22 per share.
May 10   Declared a $0.50 per share dividend on common stock. (*Hint:* Remember treasury stock does not participate in dividends.)
Oct. 12   Sold 500 shares of the treasury stock for $20 per share.
Dec. 31   Net income for the year was $75,000.

Prepare a statement of stockholders' equity for 2010 using the form below.

MARBLE CORPORATION
Statement of Stockholders' Equity

	Common Stock	Contributed Capital in Excess of Par Value, Common	Retained Earnings	Treasury Stock	Total
Balance, December 31, 2009	$200,000	$250,000	$500,000	$(20,000)	$930,000
Balance, December 31, 2010					

---

connect

Kohler Corporation reports the following components of stockholders' equity on December 31, 2009.

PROBLEM SET A

Problem 21-1A
Cash dividends, treasury
stock, and statement of
retained earnings
LO2 LO5 LO7

Common stock—$10 par value, 100,000 shares authorized, 40,000 shares issued and outstanding	$400,000
Paid-in capital in excess of par value, common stock	60,000
Retained earnings	270,000
Total stockholders' equity	$730,000

In year 2010, the following transactions affected its stockholders' equity accounts.

Jan. 1   Purchased 4,000 shares of its own stock at $20 cash per share.
Jan. 5   Directors declared a $2 per share cash dividend payable on Feb. 28 to the Feb. 5 stockholders of record.

Feb. 28   Paid the dividend declared on January 5.

July   6   Sold 1,500 of its treasury shares at $24 cash per share.

Aug. 22   Sold 2,500 of its treasury shares at $17 cash per share.

Sept. 5   Directors declared a $2 per share cash dividend payable on October 28 to the September 25 stockholders of record.

Oct. 28   Paid the dividend declared on September 5.

Dec. 31   Closed the $388,000 credit balance (from net income) in the Income Summary account to Retained Earnings.

Required

1. Prepare journal entries to record each of these transactions for 2010.

Check   (2) Retained earnings, Dec. 31, 2010, $504,500.

2. Prepare a statement of retained earnings for the year ended December 31, 2010.

3. Prepare the stockholders' equity section of the company's balance sheet as of December 31, 2010.

Problem 21–2A

Equity analysis—journal entries and account balances

LO2   LO3

At September 30, the end of Beijing Company's third quarter, the following stockholders' equity accounts are reported.

Common stock, $12 par value	$360,000
Paid-in capital in excess of par value, common stock	90,000
Retained earnings	320,000

In the fourth quarter, the following entries related to its equity accounts are recorded.

Date		Account	Debit	Credit
Oct.	2	Retained Earnings	60 000 00	
		Common Dividend Payable		60 000 00
Oct.	25	Common Dividend Payable	60 000 00	
		Cash		60 000 00
Oct.	31	Retained Earnings	75 000 00	
		Common Stock Dividend Distributable		36 000 00
		Paid-In Capital in Excess of Par Value, Common Stock		39 000 00
Nov.	5	Common Stock Dividend Distributable	36 000 00	
		Common Stock, $12 Par Value		36 000 00
Dec.	1	Memo—Change the title of the common stock account		
		to reflect the new par value of $4.		
Dec.	31	Income Summary	210 000 00	
		Retained Earnings		210 000 00

Required

1. Explain each journal entry.

2. Complete the following table showing the equity account balances at each indicated date.

	Oct. 2	Oct. 25	Oct. 31	Nov. 5	Dec. 1	Dec. 31
Common stock	$_____	$_____	$_____	$_____	$_____	$_____
Common stock dividend distributable	_____	_____	_____	_____	_____	_____
Paid-in capital in excess of par, common stock	_____	_____	_____	_____	_____	_____
Retained earnings	_____	_____	_____	_____	_____	_____
Total equity	$_____	$_____	$_____	$_____	$_____	$_____

Check   Total equity: Oct. 2, $710,000; Dec. 31, $920,000

The equity sections from Atticus Group's 2009 and 2010 year-end balance sheets follow.

Problem 21-3A
Analysis of changes in
stockholders' equity accounts
LO2 LO3 LO5 LO6

Stockholders' Equity (December 31, 2009)	
Common stock—$4 par value, 100,000 shares authorized, 40,000 shares issued and outstanding	$160,000
Paid-in capital in excess of par value, common stock	120,000
Retained earnings	320,000
Total stockholders' equity	$600,000

Stockholders' Equity (December 31, 2010)	
Common stock—$4 par value, 100,000 shares authorized, 47,400 shares issued, 3,000 shares in treasury	$189,600
Paid-in capital in excess of par value, common stock	179,200
Retained earnings ($30,000 restricted by treasury stock)	400,000
	768,800
Less cost of treasury stock	(30,000)
Total stockholders' equity	$738,800

The following transactions and events affected its equity accounts during year 2010.

Jan.   5 Declared a $0.50 per share cash dividend, date of record January 10.
Mar. 20 Purchased treasury stock for cash.
Apr.   5 Declared a $0.50 per share cash dividend, date of record April 10.
July   5 Declared a $0.50 per share cash dividend, date of record July 10.
July 31 Declared a 20% stock dividend when the stock's market value is $12 per share.
Aug. 14 Issued the stock dividend that was declared on July 31.
Oct.   5 Declared a $0.50 per share cash dividend, date of record October 10.

Required

1. How many common shares are outstanding on each cash dividend date?
2. What is the total dollar amount for each of the four cash dividends?
3. What is the amount of the capitalization of retained earnings for the stock dividend?
4. What is the per share cost of the treasury stock purchased?
5. How much net income did the company earn during year 2010?

Check (3) $88,800
(4) $10
(5) $248,000

Weiss Company began year 2010 with the following balances in its stockholders' equity accounts.

Problem 21-4A
Dividends, treasury stock,
statement of retained earnings,
statement of stockholders' equity
LO2 LO3 LO5 LO7 LO8

Common stock—$10 par, 500,000 shares authorized, 200,000 shares issued and outstanding	$2,000,000
Paid-in capital in excess of par, common stock	1,000,000
Retained earnings	5,000,000
Total	$8,000,000

All outstanding common stock was issued for $15 per share when the company was created. Weiss Company reported net income of $288,000 during 2010. The following equity transactions occurred during 2010.

Jan. 10 The board declared a $0.10 cash dividend per share to shareholders of record Jan. 28.
Feb. 15 Paid the cash dividend declared on January 10.
Mar. 31 Declared a 20% stock dividend. The market value of the stock is $18 per share.
May   1 Distributed the stock dividend declared on March 31.
July   1 Purchased 30,000 shares of treasury stock at $20 per share.
Sept. 1 Sold 20,000 treasury shares at $26 cash per share.
Dec.   1 Sold 5,000 shares of treasury stock at $7 cash per share.

Required

1. Prepare journal entries to account for the transactions during 2010.
2. Prepare a statement of retained earnings for the year ended December 31, 2010.
3. Prepare a statement of stockholders' equity for the year ended December 31, 2010.

PROBLEM SET B

Problem 21-1B

Cash dividends, treasury stock, and statement of retained earnings

LO2   LO5   LO7

Balthus Corp. reports the following components of stockholders' equity on December 31, 2009.

Common stock—$1 par value, 320,000 shares authorized, 200,000 shares issued and outstanding	$ 200,000
Paid-in capital in excess of par value, common stock	1,400,000
Retained earnings	2,160,000
Total stockholders' equity	$3,760,000

It completed the following transactions related to stockholders' equity in year 2010.

Jan. 10   Purchased 40,000 shares of its own stock at $12 cash per share.
Mar. 2   Directors declared a $1.50 per share cash dividend payable on March 31 to the March 15 stockholders of record.
Mar. 31   Paid the dividend declared on March 2.
Nov. 11   Sold 24,000 of its treasury shares at $13 cash per share.
Nov. 25   Sold 16,000 of its treasury shares at $9.50 cash per share.
Dec. 1   Directors declared a $2.50 per share cash dividend payable on January 2 to the December 10 stockholders of record.
Dec. 31   Closed the $1,072,000 credit balance (from net income) in the Income Summary account to Retained Earnings.

Required

1. Prepare journal entries to record each of these transactions for 2010.

2. Prepare a statement of retained earnings for the year ended December 31, 2010.

3. Prepare the stockholders' equity section of the company's balance sheet as of December 31, 2010.

Check   (2) Retained earnings, Dec. 31, 2010, $2,476,000

Problem 21-2B

Equity analysis—journal entries and account balances

LO2   LO3

At December 31, the end of Chilton Communication's third quarter, the following stockholders' equity accounts are reported.

Common stock, $10 par value	$ 960,000
Paid-in capital in excess of par value, common stock	384,000
Retained earnings	1,600,000

In the fourth quarter, the following entries related to its equity accounts are recorded.

Jan.	17	Retained Earnings	96 0 0 0 00	
		Common Dividend Payable		96 0 0 0 00
Feb.	5	Common Dividend Payable	96 0 0 0 00	
		Cash		96 0 0 0 00
Feb.	28	Retained Earnings	252 0 0 0 00	
		Common Stock Dividend Distributable		120 0 0 0 00
		Paid-In Capital in Excess of Par Value, Common Stock		132 0 0 0 00
Mar.	14	Common Stock Dividend Distributable	120 0 0 0 00	
		Common Stock, $10 Par Value		120 0 0 0 00
Mar.	25	Memo—Change the title of the common stock account		
		to reflect the new par value of $5.		
Mar.	31	Income Summary	720 0 0 0 00	
		Retained Earnings		720 0 0 0 00

Required

1. Explain each journal entry.

2. Complete the following table showing the equity account balances at each indicated date.

	Jan. 17	Feb. 5	Feb. 28	Mar. 14	Mar. 25	Mar. 31
Common stock	$_____	$_____	$_____	$_____	$_____	$_____
Common stock dividend distributable	_____	_____	_____	_____	_____	_____
Paid-in capital in excess of par, common stock	_____	_____	_____	_____	_____	_____
Retained earnings	_____	_____	_____	_____	_____	_____
Total equity	$_____	$_____	$_____	$_____	$_____	$_____

Check Total equity: Jan. 17, $2,848,000; Mar. 31, $3,568,000

The equity sections from Hovo Corporation's 2009 and 2010 balance sheets follow.

Problem 21-3B

Analysis of changes in stockholders' equity accounts

LO2 LO3 LO5 LO6

Stockholders' Equity (December 31, 2009)

Common stock—$20 par value, 30,000 shares authorized, 17,000 shares issued and outstanding	$340,000
Paid-in capital in excess of par value, common stock	60,000
Retained earnings	270,000
Total stockholders' equity	$670,000

Stockholders' Equity (December 31, 2010)

Common stock—$20 par value, 30,000 shares authorized, 19,000 shares issued, 1,000 shares in treasury	$380,000
Paid-in capital in excess of par value, common stock	104,000
Retained earnings ($40,000 restricted by treasury stock)	295,200
	779,200
Less cost of treasury stock	(40,000)
Total stockholders' equity	$739,200

The following transactions and events affected its equity accounts during year 2010.

Feb. 15 Declared a $0.40 per share cash dividend, date of record five days later.
Mar. 2 Purchased treasury stock for cash.
May 15 Declared a $0.40 per share cash dividend, date of record five days later.
Aug. 15 Declared a $0.40 per share cash dividend, date of record five days later.
Oct. 4 Declared a 12.5% stock dividend when the stock's market value is $42 per share.
Oct. 20 Issued the stock dividend that was declared on October 4.
Nov. 15 Declared a $0.40 per share cash dividend, date of record five days later.

Required

1. How many common shares are outstanding on each cash dividend date?

2. What is the total dollar amount for each of the four cash dividends?

3. What is the amount of the capitalization of retained earnings for the stock dividend?

4. What is the per share cost of the treasury stock purchased?

5. How much net income did the company earn during year 2010?

Check (3) $84,000
(4) $40
(5) $136,000

XTech Company began 2010 with the following balances in its stockholders' equity accounts:

Common stock, $10 par, 1 million shares authorized, 300,000 shares issued and outstanding	$ 3,000,000
Paid-in capital in excess of par, common stock	1,500,000
Retained earnings	7,500,000
Total	$12,000,000

Problem 21-4B

Dividends, treasury stock, statement of retained earnings, statement of stockholders' equity

LO2 LO3 LO5 LO7 LO8

All outstanding common stock was issued for $15 per share when the company was created. XTech Company reported net income of $432,000 for 2010. The following transactions occurred during 2010.

Jan. 10   The board of directors declared a $0.15 cash dividend per share to shareholders of record on Jan. 28.
Feb. 15   Paid the cash dividend declared on January 10.
Mar. 31   Declared a 15% stock dividend; the market value of the stock is $27 per share.
May   1   Distributed the stock dividend declared on March 31.
July   1   Purchased 45,000 shares of treasury stock at $30 per share.
Sept. 1   Sold 30,000 treasury shares at $39 cash per share.
Dec.   1   Sold 5,000 shares of treasury stock at $14 cash per share.

Required

1. Prepare journal entries to account for the 2010 transactions.
2. Prepare a statement of retained earnings for the year ended December 31, 2010.
3. Prepare a statement of stockholders' equity for the year ended December 31, 2010.

BEYOND THE NUMBERS

REPORTING IN ACTION
LO2   LO5   LO9

BTN 21-1   Refer to **Best Buy**'s financial statements in Appendix A to answer the following.

1. What is the total amount of cash dividends paid to common stockholders for the years ended March 1, 2008, and March 3, 2007?
2. Identify and compare basic EPS amounts across years 2008, 2007, and 2006. Identify and comment on any marked changes.
3. Does Best Buy hold any treasury stock as of March 1, 2008? As of March 3, 2007?

Fast Forward

4. Access Best Buy's financial statements for fiscal years ending after March 1, 2008, from its Website (**BestBuy.com**) or the SEC's EDGAR database (**www.SEC.gov**). Has the number of common shares outstanding increased since March 1, 2008? Has Best Buy increased the total amount of cash dividends paid compared to the total amount for fiscal year 2008?

COMPARATIVE ANALYSIS
LO9   LO10   LO11

® RadioShack.

BTN 21-2   Key comparative figures for both Best Buy and **RadioShack** follow.

Key Figures	Best Buy	RadioShack
Net income (in millions)	$1,407	$236.8
Cash dividends declared per common share	$ 0.46	$ 0.25
Common shares outstanding (in millions)	410.6	131.1
Weighted-average common shares outstanding (in mil.)	439.9	134.6
Market value (price) per share	$36.24	$12.48

Required

1. Compute the basic earnings per share for each company using these data.
2. Compute the dividend yield for each company using these data. Does the dividend yield of either company characterize it as an income or growth stock? Explain.
3. Compute, compare, and interpret the price-earnings ratio for each company using these data.

ETHICS CHALLENGE
LO6

BTN 21-3   You are the accountant for an Internet start-up company. Your boss, the company's founder, is very concerned with reporting high net income. He suggests you not record depreciation expense on several of the company's assets. "Look, we need good income in order to borrow more money to finance our company's growth. A few years from now, after our investments pay off, we can adjust our retained earnings account to correct this error. No harm, no foul."

Required

How should you respond to your boss's suggestion?

BTN 21-4   Teams are to select an industry, and each team member is to select a different company in that industry. Each team member then is to acquire the selected company's financial statements (or Form 10-K) from the SEC EDGAR site (www.SEC.gov). Use these data to identify basic EPS. Use the financial press (or finance.yahoo.com) to determine the market price of this stock, and then compute the price-earnings ratio. Communicate with teammates via a meeting, e-mail, or telephone to discuss the meaning of this ratio, how companies compare, and the industry norm. The team must prepare a single memorandum reporting the ratio for each company and identifying the team conclusions or consensus. The memorandum is to be duplicated and distributed to the instructor and teammates.

WORKPLACE COMMUNICATION
LO10

Make a transparency of each team's memo for a class discussion.

BTN 21-5   Access the February 25, 2009, filing of the 2008 calendar-year 10-K report of **McDonald's** (ticker MCD) from www.SEC.gov. (*Hint:* Consider the statement of cash flows.)

TAKING IT TO THE NET
LO1   LO2   LO5

Required

1. What total amount of cash did McDonald's pay in 2008 to purchase treasury stock?
2. What amount did McDonald's pay out in cash dividends for 2008?
3. What was McDonald's income tax expense for 2008?

BTN 21-6   This activity requires teamwork to reinforce understanding of accounting for treasury stock.

1. Write a brief team statement (*a*) generalizing what happens to a corporation's financial position when it engages in a stock "buyback" and (*b*) identifying reasons that a corporation would engage in this activity.
2. Assume that an entity acquires 100 shares of its $100 par value common stock at a cost of $134 cash per share. Discuss the entry to record this acquisition. Next, assign *each* team member to prepare *one* of the following entries (assume each entry applies to all shares):
   a. Reissue treasury shares at cost.
   b. Reissue treasury shares at $150 per share.
   c. Reissue treasury shares at $120 per share; assume the contributed capital account from treasury shares has a $1,500 balance.
   d. Reissue treasury shares at $120 per share; assume the contributed capital account from treasury shares has a $1,000 balance.
   e. Reissue treasury shares at $120 per share; assume the contributed capital account from treasury shares has a zero balance.
3. In sequence, each member is to present his/her entry to the team and explain the *similarities* and *differences* between that entry and the previous entry.

TEAMWORK IN ACTION
LO5

Instructor should be sure each team accurately completes part 1 before proceeding.

BTN 21-7   Read the chapter's opening feature about **Crocs, Inc.** The company has not paid cash dividends since its inception.

ENTREPRENEURS IN BUSINESS
LO2   LO3

Required

1. Why do you think Crocs, Inc., has not paid cash dividends?
2. Explain why the board of directors of Crocs, Inc., might consider declaring a stock dividend before it pays a cash dividend.

---

1. c; $0.75 × 9,500 shares = $7,125
2. b; $100 × 7% = $7 potential dividend
3. b; $27,000 × 50,000 × 10% = $135,000 reduction in retained earnings
4. c; $11,500/1,000 shares = $11.50 per share
5. d; $43,000 + $6,000 − $5,625 = $43,375

ANSWERS TO MULTIPLE CHOICE QUIZ

A Look Back

Chapter 21 focused on corporate equity transactions, including stock repurchases and dividends. We also explained how to report and analyze income, earnings per share, and retained earnings.

A Look at This Chapter

This chapter describes the accounting for and analysis of bonds. We explain their characteristics, payment patterns, interest computations, retirement, and reporting requirements.

A Look Ahead

Chapter 23 focuses on reporting and analyzing a company's cash flows. Special emphasis is directed at the statement of cash flows.

Chapter 22

Long-Term Bonds

Learning Objectives

LO 1   Compare bond financing with stock financing.

LO 2   Prepare entries to record bond issuance and bond interest expense.

LO 3   Compute and record amortization of bond discount.

LO 4   Compute and record amortization of bond premium.

LO 5   Record the retirement of bonds.

LO 6   Prepare entries to account for bond sinking funds.

LO 7   Assess debt features and their implications.

LO 8   Compute the debt-to-equity ratio and explain its use.

LO 9   *Appendix 22A*—Describe bond amortization using effective interest amortization.

LO 10   *Appendix 22B*—Describe the accrual of bond interest when bond payments do not align with accounting periods.

"I wanted to create a product that inner-city kids would relate to"—James Lindsay

Hip-Hop Financing

PHILADELPHIA—James "Fly" Lindsay and his three sisters were raised by their mother in North Philadelphia. "We were poor," explains Lindsay, "but we were rich in the values that she [mother] set forth." One of those values was education—Lindsay was the first in his family to attend college—and another was the commitment to community. "You have everyone taking away, but you have to give back," insists Lindsay.

Lindsay decided to give back by launching his own business. "I wanted to have a chip company that kids from the hood could relate to," he explains. But Lindsay knew that success depended on securing financing and then planning for long-term liabilities. "Between family and friends," explains Lindsay, "we put our dollars together and made it happen." With $40,000 in financing, he launched **Rap Snacks** [**RapSnacks.com**], a maker of snack foods with a twist: Lindsay would sell his snacks with rappers on the wrappers. The snacks would be targeted to urban youth immersed in hip-hop culture. The snack wrappers, importantly, would include positive messages to the kids such as "Stay in School," "Respect Yourself," and "Money equals Education." Lindsay hopes they

instill a craving for success, commitment, and entrepreneurship.

Lindsay insists that urban youth need to learn about business and how it can help a community. Basic accounting principles and financing concepts such as bonds and notes are like another language to urban youth, he explains. Lindsay struggles to change that and more. "You can make money," says Lindsay, "but also have a social responsibility to where you came from." Actor and rapper Lil' Romeo has recently taken a lead in funding Rap Snacks.

Making investments in urban youth is a priority, says Lindsay. He continually works to convey knowledge of business financing, with the belief that urban youth can be successful. He manages his own company's long-term liabilities, interest payments, and collateral agreements, and is confident that urban youth can do the same. Understanding liabilities is not easy, says Lindsay, but the costs of not understanding are more severe—and more of the same—for the kids. "It feels good to make a difference," says Lindsay, "and set an example for the kids."

[Sources: *Rap Snacks Website*, January 2009; *Entrepreneur*, July 2003; *Philadelphia Inquirer*, October 2002; *Source Magazine*, June 2001; *Maxim*, March 2002; *Business Review*, September 2007; *PR Newswire*, September 2007]

Individuals, companies, and governments issue bonds to finance their activities. In return for financing, bonds promise to repay the lender with interest. This chapter explains the basics of bonds and the accounting for their issuance and retirement.

The chapter also describes other sources of long-term financing. Appendices to this chapter discuss effective interest amortization and accrual of bond interest.

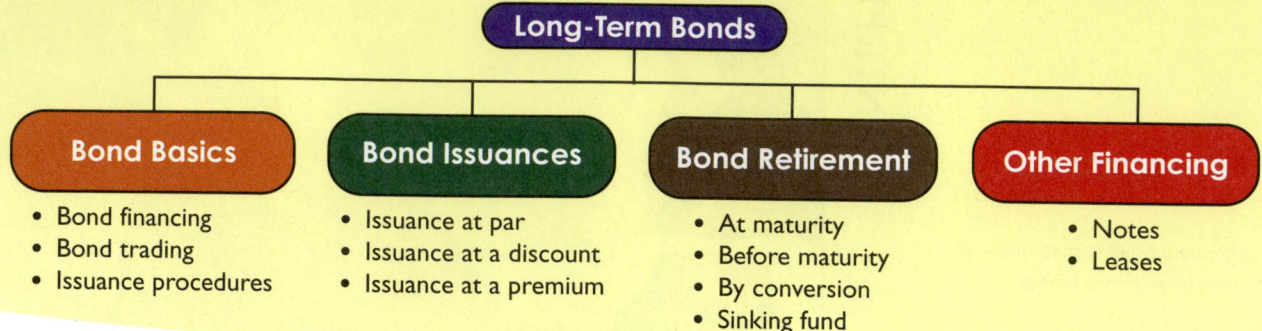

Long-Term Bonds

Bond Basics	**Bond Issuances**	**Bond Retirement**	**Other Financing**
• Bond financing • Bond trading • Issuance procedures	• Issuance at par • Issuance at a discount • Issuance at a premium	• At maturity • Before maturity • By conversion • Sinking fund	• Notes • Leases

Basics of Bonds

Like notes payable, bonds payable represent debt owed to lenders. This section explains the basics of bonds and a company's motivation for issuing them.

Bond Financing

LO1 Compare bond financing with stock financing.

Projects that demand large amounts of money often are funded from bond issuances. The bond issuer, or borrower, receives money from investors and repays those investors in the future. A **bond** is its issuer's written promise to repay an amount identified as the par value of the bond, plus interest. An unsecured bond, or debenture, is backed only by the issuer's general credit standing.

Ballot Box

Advantages of Bonds Bond financing has three main advantages:

1. *Bonds do not affect owner control.* Equity financing reflects ownership in a company, whereas bond financing does not. A person who contributes $1,000 of a company's $10,000 equity financing typically controls one-tenth of all owner decisions. A person who holds a $1,000 bond has no ownership right.

2. *Interest on bonds is tax deductible.* Bond interest payments are tax deductible for the issuer. Equity payments to owners, dividends for example, are not. To illustrate, assume that a corporation with no bond financing earns $15,000 in income *before* paying taxes at a 40% tax rate, which amounts to $6,000 ($15,000 × 40%) in taxes. If a portion of its financing is in bonds, however, the resulting bond interest is deducted in computing taxable income. That is, if bond interest expense is $10,000, the taxes owed would be $2,000 ([$15,000 − $10,000] × 40%), which is less than the $6,000 owed with no bond financing.

3. *Bonds can increase return on equity.* A company that earns a higher return with borrowed funds than it pays in interest on those funds increases its return on equity. This process is called *financial leverage* or *trading on the equity.*

To illustrate the third point, consider Magnum Co., which has $1 million in outstanding equity and is planning a $500,000 expansion to meet increasing demand for its product. Magnum predicts the $500,000 expansion will yield $125,000 in additional income before paying any interest. It currently earns $100,000 per year and has no interest expense. Magnum is considering three plans. Plan A is to not expand. Plan B is to expand and raise $500,000 from equity financing. Plan C is to expand and issue $500,000 of bonds that pay 10% annual interest ($50,000). Exhibit 22.1 shows how these three plans affect Magnum's net income, equity, and return on equity (net income/equity). The owner(s) will earn a higher return on equity if expansion occurs. Moreover, the best expansion plan is to issue bonds. Projected net income under Plan C ($175,000) is smaller than under Plan B ($225,000), but the return on equity is larger because of less equity investment. Plan C has another advantage if income is taxable. This illustration reflects a general rule: *Return on equity increases when the expected rate of return from the new assets is higher than the rate of interest expense on the debt financing.*

	Plan A Do Not Expand	Plan B Equity Financing	Plan C Bond Financing
Income before interest expense	$ 100,000	$ 225,000	$ 225,000
Interest expense	—	—	(50,000)
Net income	$ 100,000	$ 225,000	$ 175,000
Equity	$1,000,000	$1,500,000	$1,000,000
Return on equity	10.0%	15.0%	17.5%

Exhibit 22.1

Financing with Bonds versus Equity

Disadvantages of Bonds Bond financing has two main disadvantages:

1. *Bonds can decrease return on equity.* When a company earns a lower return with the borrowed funds than it pays in interest, it decreases its return on equity. This downside risk of financial leverage arises when a company has periods of low income or net losses.

2. *Bonds require payment of both periodic interest and the par value at maturity.* Bond payments can be a burden when income and cash flow are low. Equity financing, in contrast, does not require any payments because cash withdrawals (dividends) are paid at the discretion of the owner (or board).

A company must weigh the disadvantages and advantages of bond financing when deciding whether to issue bonds to finance operations.

Bond Trading

Bonds can be readily bought and sold. A large number of bonds trade on both the New York Exchange and the American Exchange. A bond *issue* consists of a number of bonds, usually in denominations of $1,000 or $5,000, and is sold to many different lenders. After bonds are issued, they often are bought and sold by investors, meaning that any particular bond probably has a number of owners before it matures. Since bonds are exchanged (bought and sold) in the market, they have a market value (price). For convenience, bond market values are expressed as a percent of their par (face) value.

The **par value of a bond,** also called the *face amount* or *face value,* is paid at a specified future date known as the bond's *maturity date.* For example, a company's bonds might be trading at 103½, meaning they can be bought or sold for 103.5% of their par value. Bonds can also trade below par value. For instance, if a company's bonds are trading at 95, they can be bought or sold at 95% of their par value.

IN THE NEWS

Quotes The bond quote here is interpreted (left to right) as **Bonds,** issuer name; **Rate,** contract interest rate (7%); **Mat,** matures in year 2025 when principal is paid; **Yld,** yield rate (5.9%) of bond at current price; **Vol,** daily dollar worth ($130,000) of trades (in 1,000s); **Close,** closing price (119.25) for the day as percent of par value; **Chg,** change (+1.25) in closing price from prior day's close.

Bonds	Rate	Mat	Yld	Vol	Close	Chg
IBM	7	25	5.9	130	119¼	+1¼

Bond-Issuing Procedures

State and federal laws govern bond issuances. Bond issuers also want to ensure that they do not violate any of their existing contracts when issuing bonds. Authorization of bond issuances includes the number of bonds authorized, their par value, and the contract interest rate. The legal document (contract) identifying the rights and obligations of both the bondholders and the issuer is called the **bond indenture.**

Bond Issuances

This section explains accounting for bond issuances at par, below par (discount), and above par (premium). It also describes how to amortize a discount or premium and record bonds issued between interest payment dates.

The bond issuer pays the interest rate specified in the indenture. This is called the **contract rate,** also known as the *coupon rate, stated rate,* or *nominal rate.* The annual interest paid is determined by multiplying the bond par value by the contract rate. The contract rate is usually stated on an annual basis, even if interest is paid semiannually. For example, if a company issues a $1,000, 8% bond paying interest semiannually, it pays annual interest of $80 (8% × $1,000) in two semiannual payments of $40 each.

Issuing Bonds at Par

LO2 Prepare entries to record bond issuance and bond interest expense.

To illustrate an issuance of bonds at par value, suppose a company receives authorization to issue $800,000 par value of 9%, 20-year bonds dated January 1, 2010. The bonds mature on December 31, 2029, and pay interest semiannually on each June 30 and December 31. This means the issuer will pay $36,000 ($800,000 × 9% × ½ year) of interest every six months over the 20-year bond life. If the bonds are sold at par value, the issuer records the bond issuance as:

Assets = Liabilities + Equity
+800,000   +800,000

2010 Jan.	1	Cash	800 0 0 0 00	
		Bonds Payable		800 0 0 0 00
		Issued bonds at par.		

This entry reflects increases in the issuer's cash *and* long-term liabilities.

The issuer records the first semiannual interest payment as follows.

Assets = Liabilities + Equity
−36,000   −36,000

2010 June	30	Bond Interest Expense	36 0 0 0 00	
		Cash		36 0 0 0 00
		Paid semiannual interest (9% × $800,000 × ½ year).		

The issuer pays and records its semiannual interest obligation every six months until the bonds mature. When the bonds mature, the issuer records its payment of principal as:

Assets = Liabilities + Equity
−800,000   −800,000

2029 Dec.	31	Bonds Payable	800 0 0 0 00	
		Cash		800 0 0 0 00
		Paid bond principal at maturity.		

Bond Discount or Premium

Bonds can be issued at a price other than par value. The price of a bond at issuance depends on the bond market's expectations of the risk of lending to the issuer. The bond's **market rate** of interest is the rate lenders are willing to accept (and borrowers are willing to pay) for a particular bond and its risk level. Lenders require higher market interest rates for riskier bonds. Market interest rates are also usually higher on bonds that mature over a longer time period. This is because of greater risk of negative events occurring over a longer time period.

IN THE NEWS

Ratings Game   Many bond buyers rely on rating services to assess bond risk. The best known are **Standard & Poor's** and **Moody's.** These services focus on the issuer's financial statements and other factors in setting ratings. Standard & Poor's ratings, from best quality to default, are AAA, AA, A, BBB, BB, B, CCC, CC, C, and D. Ratings can include a plus (+) or minus (−) to show relative standing within a category.

Many bond issuers try to set a contract rate of interest equal to the market rate they expect on the bond issuance date. When the contract rate and market rate are equal, as in our previous example, a bond sells at par value. When contract rate and market rate are not equal, a bond does not sell at par value. Instead, it is sold at a *premium* above par value or at a *discount* below par value. Exhibit 22.2 shows the relation between the contract rate, market rate, and a bond's issue price.

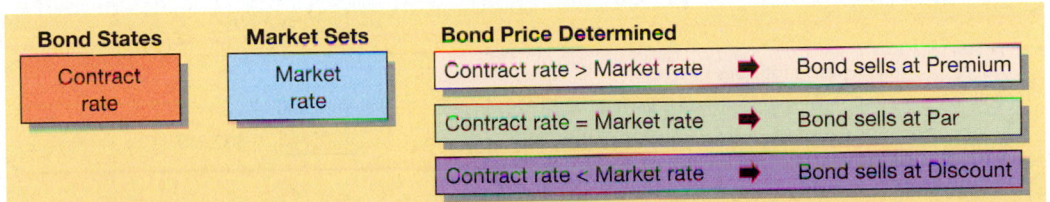

Bond States	Market Sets	Bond Price Determined	
Contract rate	Market rate	Contract rate > Market rate ➡	Bond sells at Premium
		Contract rate = Market rate ➡	Bond sells at Par
		Contract rate < Market rate ➡	Bond sells at Discount

Exhibit 22.2

Relation between Bond Issue Price, Contract Rate, and Market Rate

HOW YOU DOIN'?

Answers—p. 584

1. Unsecured bonds backed only by the issuer's general credit standing are called (*a*) serial bonds, (*b*) debentures, (*c*) registered bonds, or (*d*) convertible bonds.

2. How do you compute the amount of interest a bond issuer pays in cash each year?

3. When the contract rate is above the market rate, do bonds sell at a premium or a discount? Do purchasers pay more or less than the par value of the bonds?

Issuing Bonds at a Discount

A **discount on bonds payable** occurs when a company issues bonds with a contract rate less than the market rate. This means that the issue price is less than par value. The discount represents additional interest expense. To illustrate, assume that **Fila** offers to issue bonds with a $100,000 par value, an 8% annual contract rate (paid semiannually), and a five-year life. Also assume that the market rate for Fila bonds is 10%. These bonds then will sell at a discount since the contract rate is less than the market rate. Investors can earn 10% on similar investments so they will not pay full par value for these bonds. They will pay a lower price that earns them an effective interest rate of 10%. The exact issue price for these bonds is 92.277 (or 92.277% of par value). These bonds obligate the issuer to pay two separate types of future cash flows.

LO3 Compute and record amortization of bond discount.

1. Par value of $100,000 cash at the end of the bonds' five-year life.
2. Cash interest payments of $4,000 (4% × $100,000) at the end of each semiannual period during the bonds' five-year life.

The exact pattern of cash flows for the Fila bonds is shown in Exhibit 22.3.

	$4,000	$4,000	$4,000	$4,000		$4,000	$4,000	$100,000 $4,000
0	6 mo.	12 mo.	18 mo.	24 mo.	. . .	48 mo.	54 mo.	60 mo.

Exhibit 22.3

Cash Flows for Fila Bonds

We see that Fila's cash payments are not affected by the bond being issued at a discount. When Fila accepts $92,277 cash for its bonds on the issue date of December 31, 2010, it records the sale as follows.

Assets = Liabilities + Equity
+92,277   +100,000
           −7,723

2010					
Dec.	31	Cash	92 2 7 7 00	
		Discount on Bonds Payable	7 7 2 3 00	
		Bonds Payable		100 0 0 0 00
		Sold bonds at a discount on their issue date.		

These bonds are reported in the long-term liability section of Fila's December 31, 2010, balance sheet as shown in Exhibit 22.4. A discount is deducted from the par value of bonds to yield the **carrying (book) value of bonds.** Discount on Bonds Payable is a contra liability account. It has a normal debit balance. It represents additional interest expense Fila will eventually record.

Exhibit 22.4

Balance Sheet Presentation of Bond Discount

> Long-term liabilities
> Bonds payable, 8%, due December 31, 2015 . . . . $100,000
> **Less discount on bonds payable** . . . .   <u>7,723</u> $92,277

Amortizing a Bond Discount

Fila receives $92,277 for its bonds; in return it must pay bondholders $100,000 after five years (plus semiannual interest payments). The $7,723 discount is part of the interest cost of using the $92,277 for five years. The other part of Fila's interest expense is the $40,000 paid in 10 interest payments of $4,000 each. The total bond interest expense is the sum of the 10 interest payments and the bond discount, or $47,723.

The total $47,723 bond interest expense must be allocated across the 10 semiannual periods in the bonds' life, and the bonds' carrying value must be updated at each balance sheet date. The bonds' carrying value increases as the bonds approach their maturity date. This is done by the straight-line method (or the effective interest method in Appendix 22A). Both methods systematically reduce the bond discount to zero over the five-year life. This process is called *amortizing a bond discount*.

Zero-coupon bonds do not pay periodic interest (contract rate is zero). These bonds always sell at a discount because their 0% contract rate is always below the market rate.

Straight-Line Method

The **straight-line bond amortization** method allocates an equal portion of the total bond interest expense to each interest period. To apply the straight-line method to Fila's bonds, we divide the total bond interest expense of $47,723 by 10 (the number of semiannual periods in the bonds' life). This gives a bond interest expense of $4,772 per period (all computations, including those for assignments, are rounded to the nearest whole dollar). Alternatively, we can find this number by first dividing the $7,723 discount by 10, which yields the $772 amount of discount to be amortized each interest period. When the $772 is added to the $4,000 cash payment, the bond interest expense for each period is $4,772. Fila's journal entry to record bond interest expense and update the balance of the bond liability account at the end of *each* of the 10 semiannual interest periods (June 30, 2011, through December 31, 2015) is

Discount ÷ periods

Par value × contract rate

2011–2015				
June 30 and Dec. 31	Bond Interest Expense	4 7 7 2 00	
	Discount on Bonds Payable		7 7 2 00
	Cash		4 0 0 0 00
	To record semiannual interest and discount		
	amortization (straight-line method).		

Exhibit 22.5 shows the pattern of decreases in the Discount on Bonds Payable account and the pattern of increases in the bonds' carrying value. The following points summarize the discount bonds' straight-line amortization.

1. At issuance, the $100,000 par value consists of the $92,277 cash received by the issuer plus the $7,723 discount.

2. During the bonds' life, the (unamortized) discount decreases each semiannual period by the $772 amortization ($7,723/10), and the carrying value (par value less unamortized discount) increases each period by $772.

3. At maturity, the unamortized discount equals zero, and the carrying value equals the $100,000 par value that the issuer pays the holder.

Semiannual Period-End		Unamortized Discount*	Carrying Value†
(0)	12/31/2010	$7,723	$ 92,277
(1)	6/30/2011	6,951	93,049
(2)	12/31/2011	6,179	93,821
(3)	6/30/2012	5,407	94,593
(4)	12/31/2012	4,635	95,365
(5)	6/30/2013	3,863	96,137
(6)	12/31/2013	3,091	96,909
(7)	6/30/2014	2,319	97,681
(8)	12/31/2014	1,547	98,453
(9)	6/30/2015	775	99,225
(10)	**12/31/2015**	0‡	100,000

The two columns always sum to par value for a discount bond.

* Total bond discount (of $7,723) less accumulated periodic amortization ($772 per semiannual interest period).

† Bond par value (of $100,000) less unamortized discount.

‡ Adjusted for rounding.

Exhibit 22.5

Straight-Line Amortization of Bond Discount

Notice that the issuer incurs a $4,772 bond interest expense each period but pays only $4,000 cash. The $772 unpaid portion of this expense is added to the bonds' carrying value. (The total $7,723 unamortized discount is "paid" when the bonds mature; $100,000 is paid at maturity but only $92,277 was received at issuance.) The issuer ends up borrowing at the market rate of interest at the date of bond issuance.

HOW YOU DOIN'?   Answers—p. 584

Five-year, 6% bonds with a $100,000 par value are issued at a price of $91,893. Interest is paid semiannually, and the bonds' market rate is 8% on the issue date. Use this information to answer the following questions:

4. Are these bonds issued at a discount or a premium? Explain your answer.

5. What is the issuer's journal entry to record the issuance of these bonds?

6. What is the amount of bond interest expense recorded at the first semiannual period using the straight-line method?

Issuing Bonds at a Premium

When the contract rate of bonds is higher than the market rate, the bonds sell at a price higher than par value. The amount by which the bond price exceeds par value is the **premium on bonds.** To illustrate, assume that **Adidas** issues bonds with a $100,000 par value, a 12% annual contract rate, semiannual interest payments, and a five-year life. Also assume that the market rate for Adidas bonds is 10% on the issue date. Since investors can earn only 10% on similar investments, they will be willing to pay more than par value for Adidas bonds. They will pay a price that earns them 10% on their investment. The Adidas bonds will sell at a premium because the contract rate is higher than the market rate. The exact issue price for these bonds is 107.72 (or 107.72% of par value). These bonds obligate the issuer to pay out two separate future cash flows.

LO4 Compute and record amortization of bond premium.

1. Par value of $100,000 cash at the end of the bonds' five-year life.

2. Cash interest payments of $6,000 (6% × $100,000) at the end of each semiannual period during the bonds' five-year life.

The exact pattern of cash flows for the Adidas bonds is shown in Exhibit 22.6.

							$100,000
$6,000	$6,000	$6,000	$6,000		$6,000	$6,000	$6,000
0	6 mo.	12 mo.	18 mo.	24 mo.	...	48 mo.	54 mo.	60 mo.

Exhibit 22.6

Cash Flows for Adidas Bonds

Adidas's cash payments are not affected by the bond being issued at a premium. When Adidas accepts $107,720 cash for its bonds on the issue date of December 31, 2010, it records this transaction as follows.

Assets = Liabilities + Equity
+107,720   +100,000
             +7,720

2010					
Dec.	31	Cash	107 7 2 0 00		
		Premium on Bonds Payable		7 7 2 0 00	
		Bonds Payable			100 0 0 0 00
		Sold bonds at a premium on their issue date.			

These bonds are reported in the long-term liability section of Adidas's December 31, 2010, balance sheet as shown in Exhibit 22.7. A premium is added to par value to yield the carrying (book) value of bonds. Premium on Bonds Payable is an adjunct (also called *accretion*) liability account.

Exhibit 22.7

Balance Sheet Presentation of Bond Premium

Long-term liabilities
Bonds payable, 12%, due December 31, 2013 .... $100,000
Plus premium on bonds payable **7,720** $107,720

Amortizing a Bond Premium

Adidas receives $107,720 for its bonds; in return, it pays bondholders $100,000 after five years (plus semiannual interest payments). The $7,720 premium not repaid to issuer's bondholders at maturity reduces the issuer's expense of using the $107,720 for five years. The total bond interest expense ($52,280) is the sum of the 10 interest payments ($60,000) less the bond premium ($7,720). The premium is subtracted because it will not be paid to bondholders when the bonds mature. Total bond interest expense is allocated over the 10 semiannual periods using the straight-line method (or the effective interest method in Appendix 22A).

> A premium decreases Bond Interest Expense while a discount increases it.

Straight-Line Method

The straight-line method allocates an equal portion of total bond interest expense to each of the bonds' semiannual interest periods. To apply this method to the Adidas bonds, we divide the five years' total bond interest expense of $52,280 by 10 (the number of semi-annual periods in the bonds' life). This gives a total bond interest expense of $5,228 per semi-annual period. Adidas's entry to record bond interest expense and update the balance of the bond liability account for *each* semiannual period (June 30, 2011, through December 31, 2015) is:

Assets = Liabilities + Equity
−6,000   −772   −5,228

Premium ÷ periods →

Par value × contract rate →

2011–2015				
June 30 and Dec. 31	Bond Interest Expense	5 2 2 8 00	
	Premium on Bonds Payable	7 7 2 00	
	Cash		6 0 0 0 00
	To record semiannual interest and premium		
	amortization (straight-line method).		

Exhibit 22.8

Straight-Line Amortization of Bond Premium

Semiannual Period-End	Unamortized Premium*	Carrying Value†
(0) 12/31/2010	$7,720	$107,720
(1) 6/30/2011	6,948	106,948
(2) 12/31/2011	6,176	106,176
(3) 6/30/2012	5,404	105,404
(4) 12/31/2012	4,632	104,632
(5) 6/30/2013	3,860	103,860
(6) 12/31/2013	3,088	103,088
(7) 6/30/2014	2,316	102,316
(8) 12/31/2014	1,544	101,544
(9) 6/30/2015	772	100,772
(10) 12/31/2015	0	100,000

> During the bond's life, carrying value is adjusted to par and the amortized premium to zero.

* Total bond premium (of $7,720) less accumulated periodic amortization ($772 per semiannual interest period).

† Bond par value (of $100,000) plus unamortized premium.

Exhibit 22.8 shows the pattern of decreases in the unamortized Premium on Bonds Payable account and in the bonds' carrying value. The following points summarize straight-line amortization of the premium bonds.

1. At issuance, the $100,000 par value plus the $7,720 premium equals the $107,720 cash received by the issuer.

2. During the bonds' life, the (unamortized) premium decreases each period by the $772 amortization ($7,720/10), and the carrying value decreases each period by the same $772.

3. At maturity, the unamortized premium equals zero, and the carrying value equals the $100,000 par value that the issuer pays the holder.

HOW YOU DOIN'?

Answers—p. 584

On December 31, 2010, a company issues 16%, 10-year bonds with a par value of $100,000. Interest is paid each June 30 and December 31. The bonds are sold to yield a 14% annual market rate at an issue price of $110,592. Use this information to answer questions 7 through 9:

7. Are these bonds issued at a discount or a premium? Explain your answer.

8. Using the straight-line method to allocate bond interest expense, the issuer records the second interest payment (on December 31, 2011) with a debit to Premium on Bonds Payable in the amount of (a) $7,470, (b) $530, (c) $8,000, or (d) $400.

9. How are these bonds reported in the long-term liability section of the issuer's balance sheet as of December 31, 2011?

Bond Retirement

This section describes the retirement of bonds (1) at maturity, (2) before maturity, and (3) by conversion to stock.

Bond Retirement at Maturity

The carrying value of bonds at maturity always equals par value. For example, both Exhibits 22.5 (a discount) and 22.8 (a premium) show that the carrying value of bonds at the end of their lives equals par value. The retirement of these $100,000 face value bonds at maturity, assuming interest is already paid and entered, is recorded as follows:

LO5 Record the retirement of bonds.

2015					
Dec.	31	Bonds Payable	100 000 00	
		Cash		100 000 00
		To record retirement of bonds at maturity.		

Assets = Liabilities + Equity
−100,000 −100,000

Bond Retirement before Maturity

Issuers sometimes wish to retire some or all of their bonds before maturity. For instance, if interest rates decline significantly, an issuer may wish to replace high-interest-paying bonds with new low-interest bonds. Two common ways to retire bonds before maturity are to (1) exercise a **call option** or (2) purchase them on the open market. In the first instance, an issuer can reserve the right to retire bonds early by issuing callable bonds. The bond indenture can give the issuer an option to *call* the bonds before they mature by paying the par value plus a *call premium* to bondholders. In the second case, the issuer retires bonds by repurchasing them on the open market at their current price. When bonds are retired, the issuer rarely pays a price that exactly equals their carrying value. When a difference exists between the bonds' carrying value and the amount paid, the issuer records a gain or loss equal to the difference. This gain or loss is reported as income on the income statement of the issuer.

To illustrate the accounting for retiring callable bonds, assume that a company issued callable bonds at their par value of $100,000. The call option requires the issuer to pay a call premium of $3,000 to bondholders in addition to the par value. On July 1, 2010, the issuer calls these bonds and pays $103,000 to bondholders. The issuer recognizes a $3,000 loss from the difference between the bonds' carrying value of $100,000 and the retirement price of $103,000. The issuer records this bond retirement as:

July	1	Bonds Payable	100 000 00	
		Loss on Bond Retirement	3 000 00	
		Cash		103 000 00
		To record retirement of bonds before maturity.		

Assets = Liabilities + Equity
−103,000 −100,000 −3,000

An issuer usually must call all bonds when it exercises a call option. To retire as many or as few bonds as it desires, an issuer can purchase them on the open market. If it retires less than the entire class of bonds, it recognizes a gain or loss for the difference between the carrying value of those bonds retired and the amount paid to acquire them.

Bond Retirement by Conversion

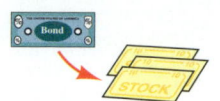

Convertible Bond

Holders of convertible bonds have the right to convert their bonds to stock. When conversion occurs, the bonds' carrying value is transferred to equity accounts and no gain or loss is recorded. The market prices of the bonds and stock are *not* relevant to this entry. To illustrate, assume that on January 1 the $100,000 par value bonds of **Converse**, with a carrying value of $100,000, are converted to 15,000 shares of $2 par value common stock. The entry to record this conversion is:

Assets = Liabilities + Equity
−100,000   +30,000
              +70,000

Jan.	1	Bonds Payable	100 0 0 0 00	
		Common Stock, $2 Par Value		30 0 0 0 00
		Paid-In Capital in Excess of Par Value		70 0 0 0 00
		To record retirement of bonds by conversion.		

HOW YOU DOIN'?

Answers—p. 584

10. Six years ago, a company issued $500,000 of 6%, eight-year bonds at a price of 95. The current carrying value is $493,750. The company decides to retire 50% of these bonds by buying them on the open market at a price of 102½. What is the amount of gain or loss on retirement of these bonds?

11. Holders of Shadow Mountain Inc. $50,000 par value convertible bonds, with a carrying value of $50,000, decide to convert to 12,000 shares of $2 par value common stock. What is the debit or credit amount to Paid-In Capital in Excess of Par Value?

Bond Sinking Funds

L06 Prepare entries to account for bond sinking funds.

The dollar amount of par values that bond issuers have to repay at maturity can be large. To ensure that issuers have the necessary cash to retire bonds at their maturity, bond indentures often require issuers to establish a **bond sinking fund.** Issuers make contributions to the bond sinking fund, and these contributions are invested in stocks, bonds, or other securities. At the bonds' maturity date the balance in the bond sinking fund is used to pay the par value of the bonds.

For example, suppose that **Reebok** issues bonds with a par value of $100,000 on January 1, 2010. The bonds mature in five years, on December 31, 2014. The bond indenture requires Reebok to make four contributions of $22,000 each, at the beginning of each year, starting on January 1, 2010. The entry to record this contribution on January 1, 2010, is

Assets = Liabilities + Equity
+25,000
−25,000

2010 Jan.	1	Bond Sinking Fund	22 0 0 0 00	
		Cash		22 0 0 0 00
		Contribution to bond sinking fund.		

Assume Reebok invests each year's contributions in an account that earns 5% interest. For 2010 Reebok will earn $1,100 of investment income ($22,000 × 5%). At the end of 2010 Reebok makes the following journal entry to record investment income earned during the year.

Assets = Liabilities + Equity
+1,100   +1,100

2010 Dec.	31	Bond Sinking Fund	1 1 0 0 00	
		Bond Sinking Fund Income		1 1 0 0 00
		Income earned by bond sinking fund.		

This process is repeated for the next three years. However, Reebok's investment income will not be $1,100 each year. For example, in 2011 Reebok's investment income will equal $2,255, as computed in Exhibit 22.9.

2010 contribution to bond sinking fund	$22,000
2010 bond sinking fund income	1,100
2011 contribution to bond sinking fund	22,000
Bond Sinking Fund balance at beginning of 2011	$45,100
2011 sinking fund income = $45,100 $\times$ 5% = $2,255	

Exhibit 22.9

Bond Sinking Fund Income

The balance in the bond sinking fund at each year-end is reported as an asset in the Investments section on Reebok's balance sheet. The bond sinking fund income is reported on Reebok's income statement each year.

On December 31, 2014, the bonds mature. The balance in the Bond Sinking Fund account is $100,000. Reebok makes the following entry to retire the bonds.

> Any balance remaining in the Bond Sinking Fund after the bonds are paid off is returned to the Cash account.

2014				
Dec.	31	Bonds Payable	100 000 00	
		Bond Sinking Fund		100 000 00
		Record retirement of bonds with sinking fund.		

Assets = Liabilities + Equity
−100,000 −100,000

Other Types of Long-Term Financing

This section describes other types of long-term financing a business can use.

Notes Payable

Like bonds, notes are issued to obtain assets such as cash. Unlike bonds, notes are usually transacted with a *single* lender, like a bank. The note issuer initially records the note at its face value minus any discount or plus any premium. The accounting over the life of the note is like that for a bond.

Installment Notes An **installment note** is an obligation requiring a series of payments to the lender. Installment notes are common for franchises and other businesses when lenders and borrowers agree to spread payments over several periods.

Mortgage Notes A **mortgage** is a legal agreement that helps protect a lender if a borrower fails to make required payments. A mortgage gives the lender a right to be paid from the cash proceeds of the sale of a borrower's assets in the mortgage. A legal document, called a *mortgage contract,* describes the mortgage terms. Mortgage notes are especially popular in the purchase of homes and the acquisition of plant assets. Accounting for mortgage notes is similar to that for bonds and other notes.

Operating Leases

The long-term financings discussed above require the borrower to show a liability on its balance sheet. Certain types of financing allow the borrower access to assets, without showing a financing liability on the balance sheet. A **lease** is a contractual agreement between a *lessor* (asset owner) and a *lessee* (asset renter or tenant). The contract grants the lessee the right to use the asset for a period of time in return for cash (rent) payments. Nearly one-fourth of all equipment purchases is financed with leases. The advantages of lease financing include the lack of an immediate large cash payment and the potential to deduct rental payments in computing taxable income.

DEBT FEATURES AND THE DEBT-TO-EQUITY RATIO

Features of Bonds and Notes

LO7 Assess debt features and their implications.

This section describes common features of debt securities.

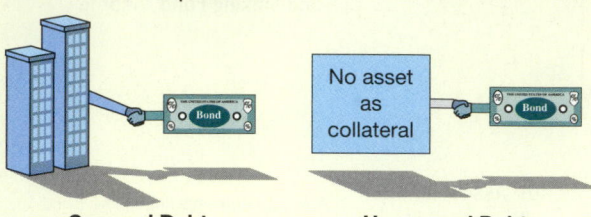

Secured Debt   **Unsecured Debt**

Secured or Unsecured   **Secured bonds** have specific assets of the issuer pledged (or *mortgaged*) as collateral. This gives bondholders added protection against the issuer's default. If the issuer fails to pay interest or par value, the secured holders can demand that the collateral be sold and the proceeds used to pay the obligation. **Unsecured bonds,** also called *debentures,* are backed by the issuer's general credit standing. Unsecured debt is riskier than secured debt. *Subordinated debentures* are liabilities that are not repaid until the claims of the more senior, unsecured (and secured) liabilities are settled.

Term or Serial   **Term bonds** are scheduled to mature on one date. **Serial bonds** mature at more than one date (often in series) and thus are usually repaid over a number of periods. For instance, $100,000 of serial bonds might mature at the rate of $10,000 each year from 6 to 15 years after they are issued.

IN THE NEWS

Munis   More than a million municipal bonds, or "munis," exist, and many are tax exempt. Munis are issued by state, city, town, and county governments to pay for public projects including schools, libraries, roads, bridges, and stadiums.

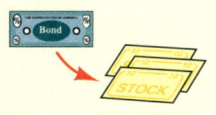

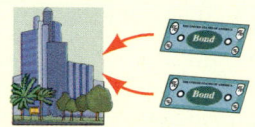

Convertible Debt   **Callable Debt**

Convertible and/or Callable   **Convertible bonds** (and notes) can be exchanged for a fixed number of shares of the issuing corporation's common stock. Convertible debt offers holders the potential to participate in future increases in stock price. Holders still receive periodic interest while the debt is held and the par value if they hold the debt to maturity. In most cases, the holders decide whether and when to convert debt to stock. **Callable bonds** (and notes) have an option exercisable by the issuer to retire them at a stated dollar amount before maturity.

IN THE NEWS

Junk Bonds   Junk bonds are company bonds with low credit ratings due to a higher than average likelihood of default. On the upside, the high risk of junk bonds can yield high returns if the issuer survives and repays its debt.

Debt-to-Equity Ratio

LO8 Compute the debt-to-equity ratio and explain its use.

It is useful to know a company's level of debt, especially in relation to total equity. This helps us assess the risk of a company's financing structure. A company financed mainly with debt is more risky because liabilities must be repaid—usually with periodic interest—whereas equity financing does not. A measure to assess the risk of a company's financing structure is the **debt-to-equity ratio** (see Exhibit 22.10).

Exhibit 22.10

Debt-to-Equity Ratio

$$\text{Debt-to-equity} = \frac{\text{Total liabilities}}{\text{Total equity}}$$

The debt-to-equity ratio varies across companies and industries. Industries that are more variable tend to have lower ratios, while more stable industries are less risky and tend to have higher ratios. To apply the debt-to-equity ratio, let's look at this measure for **Six Flags** in Exhibit 22.11.

($ millions)	2006	2005	2004
Total liabilities	$2,811	$2,799	$2,816
Total equity	$ 376	$ 694	$ 826
Debt-to-equity	7.5	4.0	3.4
Industry debt-to-equity	1.2	1.1	0.9

Exhibit 22.11

Debt-to-Equity Ratio for Six Flags

Six Flags' 2006 debt-to-equity ratio is 7.5, meaning that debtholders contributed $7.5 for each $1 contributed by equityholders. This implies a fairly risky financing structure for Six Flags. A similar concern is drawn from a comparison of Six Flags with its competitors, where the 2006 industry ratio is 1.2. Analysis across the years also shows that Six Flags' financing structure has grown increasingly risky over the past few years. Given its declining revenues and increasing operating expenses over the past few years (see its annual report), Six Flags is increasingly at risk of financial distress.

Demonstration Problem

Water Sports Company (WSC) patented and successfully test-marketed a new product. To expand its ability to produce and market the new product, WSC needs to raise $400,000 of financing. On January 1, 2010, the company obtained the money as follows.

WSC issued five-year bonds with a par value of $400,000. The bonds have a 12% annual contract rate and pay interest on June 30 and December 31. The bonds' annual market rate is 10% as of January 1, 2010. The bonds were issued at a price of $430,881.

Required

1. For the bonds, (*a*) prepare the January 1, 2010, journal entry to record their issuance; (*b*) prepare an amortization table using the straight-line method; (*c*) prepare the June 30, 2010, journal entry to record the first interest payment; and (*d*) prepare a journal entry to record retiring the bonds at a $416,000 call price on January 1, 2012.

2.[A]Redo parts 1(*b*), 1(*c*), and 1(*d*) assuming the bond premium is amortized using the effective interest method.

Planning the Solution

- The bonds are issued at a premium. This means they are originally recorded at a price above par value. Amortization reduces their carrying value to par value on the bonds' maturity date.

- Prepare an amortization table like Exhibit 22.8 (and Exhibit 22A.2) and use it to get the numbers needed for the journal entry. Also use the table to find the carrying value as of the date of the bonds' retirement that you need for the journal entry.

Solution to Demonstration Problem

Part 1: Straight-line amortization

a. Journal entry for January 1, 2010, issuance.

2010					
Jan.	1	Cash	430 881 00		
		Premium on Bonds Payable		30 881 00	
		Bonds Payable		400 000 00	
		Sold bonds at a premium.			

b. Straight-line amortization table for premium bonds.

Semiannual Period-End		Unamortized Premium	Carrying Value
(0)	1/1/2010	$30,881	$430,881
(1)	6/30/2010	27,793	427,793
(2)	12/31/2010	24,705	424,705
(3)	6/30/2011	21,617	421,617
(4)	12/31/2011	18,529	418,529
(5)	6/30/2012	15,441	415,441
(6)	12/31/2012	12,353	412,353
(7)	6/30/2013	9,265	409,265
(8)	12/31/2013	6,177	406,177
(9)	6/30/2014	3,089	403,089
(10)	12/31/2014	0*	400,000

* Adjusted for rounding.

c. Journal entry for June 30, 2010, bond payment.

2010 June	30	Bond Interest Expense	20 9 1 2 00	
		Premium on Bonds Payable	3 0 8 8 00	
		Cash		24 0 0 0 00
		Paid semiannual interest on bonds.		

d. Journal entry for January 1, 2012, bond retirement.

2012 Jan.	1	Bonds Payable	400 0 0 0 00	
		Premium on Bonds Payable	18 5 2 9 00	
		Cash		416 0 0 0 00
		Gain on Retirement of Bonds		2 5 2 9 00
		To record bond retirement (carrying value as of Dec. 31, 2011).		

Part 2: Effective interest amortization[A]

a. Effective interest amortization table for premium bonds.

	Semiannual Interest Period	(A) Cash Interest Paid 6% × $400,000	(B) Interest Expense 5% × Prior (E)	(C) Premium Amortization (A) − (B)	(D) Unamortized Premium Prior (D) − (C)	(E) Carrying Value $400,000 + (D)
(0)	1/1/2010				$30,881	$430,881
(1)	6/30/2010	$ 24,000	$ 21,544	$ 2,456	28,425	428,425
(2)	12/31/2010	24,000	21,421	2,579	25,846	425,846
(3)	6/30/2011	24,000	21,292	2,708	23,138	423,138
(4)	12/31/2011	24,000	21,157	2,843	20,295	420,295
(5)	6/30/2012	24,000	21,015	2,985	17,310	417,310
(6)	12/31/2012	24,000	20,866	3,134	14,176	414,176
(7)	6/30/2013	24,000	20,709	3,291	10,885	410,885
(8)	12/31/2013	24,000	20,544	3,456	7,429	407,429
(9)	6/30/2014	24,000	20,371	3,629	3,800	403,800
(10)	12/31/2014	24,000	20,200*	3,800	0	400,000
		$240,000	$209,119	$30,881		

* Adjusted for rounding.

b. Journal entry for June 30, 2010, bond payment.

2010					
June	30	Bond Interest Expense	21 5 4 4 00		
		Premium on Bonds Payable	2 4 5 6 00		
		Cash		24 0 0 0 00	
		Paid semiannual interest on bonds.			

c. Journal entry for January 1, 2012, bond retirement.

2012					
Jan.	1	Bonds Payable	400 0 0 0 00		
		Premium on Bonds Payable	20 2 9 5 00		
		Cash		416 0 0 0 00	
		Gain on Retirement of Bonds		4 2 9 5 00	
		To record bond retirement (carrying value as of Dec. 31, 2011).			

Effective Interest Amortization

APPENDIX 22A

Effective Interest Amortization of a Discount Bond

Accounting standards allow use of the straight-line method only when its results do not differ materially from those obtained using the effective interest method. Under the **effective interest method,** bond interest expense for a period equals the carrying value of the bond at the beginning of that period multiplied by the market rate on the bond when issued.

Exhibit 22A.1 shows an effective interest amortization table for the Fila bonds (as described in Exhibit 22.3). The key difference between the effective interest and straight-line methods lies in computing bond

LO9 Describe bond amortization using effective interest amortization.

Exhibit 22A.1

Effective Interest Amortization of Bond Discount

Bonds: $100,000 Par Value, Semiannual Interest Payments, Five-Year Life, 4% Semiannual Contract Rate, 5% Semiannual Market Rate					
Semiannual Interest Period-End	(A) Cash Interest Paid	(B) Bond Interest Expense	(C) Discount Amortization	(D) Unamortized Discount	(E) Carrying Value
(0) 12/31/2010				$7,723	$ 92,277
(1) 6/30/2011	$4,000	$4,614	$ 614	7,109	92,891
(2) 12/31/2011	4,000	4,645	645	6,464	93,536
(3) 6/30/2012	4,000	4,677	677	5,787	94,213
(4) 12/31/2012	4,000	4,711	711	5,076	94,924
(5) 6/30/2013	4,000	4,746	746	4,330	95,670
(6) 12/31/2013	4,000	4,784	784	3,546	96,454
(7) 6/30/2014	4,000	4,823	823	2,723	97,277
(8) 12/31/2014	4,000	4,864	864	1,859	98,141
(9) 6/30/2015	4,000	4,907	907	952	99,048
(10) 12/31/2015	4,000	4,952	952	0	100,000
	$40,000	$47,723	$7,723		

Column (**A**) is par value ($100,000) multiplied by the semiannual contract rate (4%).

Column (**B**) is prior period's carrying value multiplied by the semiannual market rate (5%) at issuance.

Column (**C**) is the difference between interest paid and bond interest expense, or [(B) − (A)].

Column (**D**) is the prior period's unamortized discount less the current period's discount amortization.

Column (**E**) is par value less unamortized discount, or [$100,000 − (D)].

interest expense. Instead of assigning an equal amount of bond interest expense to each period, the effective interest method assigns a bond interest expense amount that increases over the life of a discount bond. **Both methods allocate the *same* $47,723 of total bond interest expense over the bonds' life, but in different patterns.** Specifically, the amortization table in Exhibit 22A.1 shows that the balance of the discount (column D) is amortized until it reaches zero. Also, the bonds' carrying value (column E) changes each period until it equals par value at maturity. Compare columns D and E to the corresponding columns in Exhibit 22.5 to see the amortization patterns. Total bond interest expense is $47,723, consisting of $40,000 of semiannual cash payments and $7,723 of the original bond discount, the same for both methods.

Except for differences in amounts, journal entries recording the expense and updating the liability balance are the same under the effective interest method and the straight-line method. We can use the numbers in Exhibit 22A.1 to record each semiannual entry during the bonds' five-year life (June 30, 2011, through December 31, 2015). For instance, we record the interest payment at the end of the first semiannual period as:

Assets = Liabilities + Equity
−4,000   +614   −4,614

2011 June	30	Bond Interest Expense	46 1 4 00	
		Discount on Bonds Payable		6 1 4 00
		Cash		4 0 0 0 00
		To record semiannual interest and discount amortization		
		(effective interest method).		

Effective Interest Amortization of a Premium Bond

Exhibit 22A.2 shows the amortization table using the effective interest method for the Adidas bonds (as described in Exhibit 22.6). Column A lists the semiannual cash payments. Column B shows the amount of bond interest expense, computed as the 5% semiannual market rate at issuance multiplied by the beginning-of-period carrying value. The amount of cash paid in column A is larger than the

Exhibit 22A.2

Effective Interest Amortization of Bond Premium

			Bonds: $100,000 Par Value, Semiannual Interest Payments, Five-Year Life, 6% Semiannual Contract Rate, 5% Semiannual Market Rate				
	Semiannual Interest Period-End		(A) Cash Interest Paid	(B) Bond Interest Expense	(C) Premium Amortization	(D) Unamortized Premium	(E) Carrying Value
7	(0)	12/31/2010				$7,720	$107,720
8	(1)	6/30/2011	$6,000	$5,386	$ 614	7,106	107,106
9	(2)	12/31/2011	6,000	5,355	645	6,461	106,461
10	(3)	6/30/2012	6,000	5,323	677	5,784	105,784
11	(4)	12/31/2012	6,000	5,289	711	5,073	105,073
12	(5)	6/30/2013	6,000	5,254	746	4,327	104,327
13	(6)	12/31/2013	6,000	5,216	784	3,543	103,543
14	(7)	6/30/2014	6,000	5,177	823	2,720	102,720
15	(8)	12/31/2014	6,000	5,136	864	1,856	101,856
16	(9)	6/30/2015	6,000	5,093	907	949	100,949
17	(10)	12/31/2015	6,000	5,051*	949	0	100,000
18			$60,000	$52,280	$7,720		

Column (A) is par value ($100,000) multiplied by the semiannual contract rate (6%).

Column (B) is prior period's carrying value multiplied by the semiannual market rate (5%) at issuance.

Column (C) is the difference between interest paid and bond interest expense, or [(A) − (B)].

Column (D) is the prior period's unamortized premium less the current period's premium amortization.

Column (E) is par value plus unamortized premium, or [$100,000 + (D)].

* Adjusted for rounding.

bond interest expense because the cash payment is based on the higher 6% semiannual contract rate. The excess cash payment over the interest expense reduces the carrying value of the liability. This is the premium amortization. These amounts are shown in column C. Column E shows the carrying value after deducting the amortized premium in column C from the prior period's carrying value. Column D shows the premium's reduction by periodic amortization. When the issuer makes the first semiannual interest payment, the entry is:

2011 June	30	Bond Interest Expense	5 3 8 6 00	
		Premium on Bonds Payable	6 1 4 00	
		Cash		6 0 0 0 00
		To record semiannual interest and premium		
		amortization (effective interest method).		

Assets = Liabilities + Equity
−6,000   −614   −5,386

Similar entries with different amounts are recorded at each payment date until the bond matures at the end of 2015. The effective interest method yields decreasing amounts of bond interest expense and increasing amounts of premium amortization over the bonds' life.

Accruing Bond Interest Expense

APPENDIX
22B

Accruing Bond Interest Expense

If a bond's interest period does not coincide with the issuer's accounting period, an adjusting entry is needed to recognize bond interest expense accrued since the most recent interest payment. To illustrate, assume that the Adidas bonds described in Exhibit 22.6 are sold on the stated issue date of September 1, 2010, instead of December 31, 2010. Further assume that interest payments will be made each February 28 and August 30. This means no interest payments have been made as of December 31, 2010. As a result, four months' interest (and premium amortization) accrue before the end of the 2010 calendar year. Adidas must make an entry to record this interest and update the bonds' carrying value. Interest for this period equals $3,485, or 4/6 of the first six months' interest of $5,228 ($6,000 − $772). Also, the premium amortization is $515, or 4/6 of the first six months' straight-line amortization of $772. The sum of the bond interest expense and the amortization is $4,000 ($3,485 + $515), which equals 4/6 of the $6,000 cash payment due on February 28, 2011. Adidas records these effects with an adjusting entry at December 31, 2010:

LO10 Describe the accrual of bond interest when bond payments do not align with accounting periods.

> Computation of accrued bond interest may use months instead of days for simplicity purposes. For example, the accrued interest computation for the Adidas bonds is based on months.

2010 Dec.	31	Bond Interest Expense	3 4 8 5 00	
		Premium on Bonds Payable	5 1 5 00	
		Interest Payable		4 0 0 0 00
		To record four months' accrued interest		
		and premium amortization.		

Assets = Liabilities + Equity
            −515   −3,485
            +4,000

Similar entries are made on each December 31 throughout the bonds' five-year life. When the $6,000 cash payment occurs on each February 28 interest payment date, Adidas must recognize bond interest expense and amortization for January and February. It must also eliminate the interest payable liability created by the December 31 adjusting entry. For example, Adidas records its payment on February 28, 2011, as:

Assets = Liabilities + Equity
−6,000   −4,000   −1,743
         −257

2011					
Feb.	28	Interest Payable	4 0 0 0 00		
		Bond Interest Expense ($5,228 × ⅖)	1 7 4 3 00		
		Premium on Bonds Payable ($772 × ⅖)	2 5 7 00		
		Cash			6 0 0 0 00
		To record 2 months' interest and amortization and			
		eliminate accrued interest liability.			

The interest payments made each August 31 are recorded as usual because the entire six-month interest period is included within this company's calendar-year reporting period.

Summary

LO1 Compare bond financing with stock financing. Bond financing is used to fund business activities. Advantages of bond financing versus stock include (1) no effect on owner control, (2) tax savings, and (3) increased earnings due to financial leverage. Disadvantages include (1) interest and principal payments and (2) amplification of poor performance.

LO2 Prepare entries to record bond issuance and bond interest expense. When bonds are issued at par, Cash is debited and Bonds Payable is credited for the bonds' par value. At bond interest payment dates (usually semiannual), Bond Interest Expense is debited and Cash credited; the latter for an amount equal to the bond par value multiplied by the bond contract rate.

LO3 Compute and record amortization of bond discount. Bonds are issued at a discount when the contract rate is less than the market rate, making the issue (selling) price less than par. When this occurs, the issuer records a credit to Bonds Payable (at par) and debits both Discount on Bonds Payable and Cash. The amount of bond interest expense assigned to each period is computed using either the straight-line or effective interest method.

LO4 Compute and record amortization of bond premium. Bonds are issued at a premium when the contract rate is higher than the market rate, making the issue (selling) price greater than par. When this occurs, the issuer records a debit to Cash and credits both Premium on Bonds Payable and Bonds Payable (at par). The amount of bond interest expense assigned to each period is computed using either the straight-line or effective interest method. The Premium on Bonds Payable is allocated to reduce bond interest expense over the life of the bonds.

LO5 Record the retirement of bonds. Bonds are retired at maturity with a debit to Bonds Payable and a credit to Cash at par value. The issuer can retire the bonds early by exercising a call

option or purchasing them in the market. Bondholders can also retire bonds early by exercising a conversion feature on convertible bonds. The issuer recognizes a gain or loss for the difference between the amount paid and the bonds' carrying value.

LO6 Prepare entries to account for bond sinking funds. Bond indentures sometimes require issuers to contribute money to bond sinking funds to ensure the issuer can repay the bonds' par value at maturity. These contributions are recorded with a debit to Bond Sinking Fund and a credit to Cash. Any income the fund earns is recorded with a debit to Bond Sinking Fund and a credit to Bond Sinking Fund Income.

LO7 Assess debt features and their implications. Certain bonds are secured by the issuer's assets; other bonds, called *debentures,* are unsecured. Serial bonds mature at different points in time; term bonds mature at one time. Registered bonds have each bondholder's name recorded by the issuer; bearer bonds are payable to the holder. Convertible bonds are exchangeable for shares of the issuer's stock. Callable bonds can be retired by the issuer at a set price. Debt features alter the risk of loss for creditors.

LO8 Compute the debt-to-equity ratio and explain its use. Both creditors and equity holders are concerned about the relation between the amount of liabilities and the amount of equity. A company's financing structure is at less risk when the debt-to-equity ratio is lower, as liabilities must be paid and usually with periodic interest.

LO9ᴬ Describe bond amortization using effective interest amortization. The effective interest method assigns a bond interest expense amount that increases over the life of a discount bond.

LO10ᴮ Describe the accrual of bond interest when bond payments do not align with accounting periods. Issuers record the interest accrued when the accounting period does not coincide with debt payment dates.

Guidance Answers to **HOW YOU DOIN'?**

1. (b)

2. Multiply the bond's par value by its contract rate of interest.

3. Bonds sell at a premium when the contract rate exceeds the market rate and the purchasers pay more than their par value.

4. The bonds are issued at a discount, meaning that issue price is less than par value. A discount occurs because the bond contract rate (6%) is less than the market rate (8%).

5.

Cash.....................................	91,893
Discount on Bonds Payable...................	8,107
Bonds Payable	100,000

6. $3,811 (Total bond interest expense of $38,107 divided by 10 periods; or the $3,000 semiannual cash payment plus the $8,107 discount divided by 10 periods.)

7. The bonds are issued at a premium, meaning issue price is higher than par value. A premium occurs because the bonds' contract rate (16%) is higher than the market rate (14%).

8. (*b*) For each semiannual period: $10,592/20 periods = <u>$530</u> premium amortization.

9.

Bonds payable, 16%, due 12/31/2020	$100,000
Plus premium on bonds payable	<u>9,532</u>* $109,532

* Original premium balance of $10,592 less $530 and $530 amortized on 6/30/2011 and 12/31/2011, respectively.

10. $9,375 loss. Computed as the difference between the repurchase price of $256,250 [50% of ($500,000 × 102.5%)] and the carrying value of $246,875 (50% of $493,750).

11. $26,000 credit. $50,000 convertible bonds less $24,000 par value of common stock = $26,000 Paid in Capital.

Key Terms

Bond (p. 568) Written promise to pay the bond's par (or face) value and interest at a stated contract rate; often issued in denominations of $1,000.

Bond indenture (p. 569) Contract between the bond issuer and the bondholders; identifies the parties' rights and obligations.

Bond sinking fund (p. 576) A fund designed to accumulate assets to pay a bond's maturity value.

Call option (p. 575) The right of a bond issuer to retire bonds early.

Callable bonds (p. 578) Bonds that give the issuer the option to retire them at a stated amount prior to maturity.

Carrying (book) value of bonds (p. 572) Net amount at which bonds are reported on the balance sheet; equals the par value of the bonds less any unamortized discount or plus any unamortized premium; also called *carrying amount* or *book value*.

Contract rate (p. 570) Interest rate specified in a bond indenture (or note); multiplied by the par value to determine the interest paid each period; also called *coupon rate, stated rate*, or *nominal rate*.

Convertible bonds (p. 578) Bonds that bondholders can exchange for a set number of the issuer's shares.

Debt-to-equity ratio (p. 578) Defined as total liabilities divided by total equity; shows the proportion of a company financed by non-owners (creditors) in comparison with that financed by owners.

Discount on bonds payable (p. 571) Difference between a bond's par value and its lower issue price or carrying value; occurs when the contract rate is less than the market rate.

Effective interest method (p. 581) Allocates interest expense over the bond life to yield a constant rate of interest; interest expense for a period is found by multiplying the balance of the liability at the beginning of the period by the bond market rate at issuance; also called *interest method*.

Installment note (p. 577) Liability requiring a series of periodic payments to the lender.

Lease (p. 577) Contract specifying the rental of property.

Market rate (p. 570) Interest rate that borrowers are willing to pay and lenders are willing to accept for a specific lending agreement given the borrowers' risk level.

Mortgage (p. 577) Legal loan agreement that protects a lender by giving the lender the right to be paid from the cash proceeds from the sale of a borrower's assets identified in the mortgage.

Par value of a bond (p. 569) Amount the bond issuer agrees to pay at maturity and the amount on which cash interest payments are based; also called *face amount* or *face value* of a bond.

Premium on bonds (p. 573) Difference between a bond's par value and its higher carrying value; occurs when the contract rate is higher than the market rate; also called *bond premium*.

Secured bonds (p. 578) Bonds that have specific assets of the issuer pledged as collateral.

Serial bonds (p. 578) Bonds consisting of separate amounts that mature at different dates.

Straight-line bond amortization (p. 572) Method allocating an equal amount of bond interest expense to each period of the bond life.

Term bonds (p. 578) Bonds scheduled for payment (maturity) at a single specified date.

Unsecured bonds (p. 578) Bonds backed only by the issuer's credit standing; almost always riskier than secured bonds; also called *debentures*.

Multiple Choice Quiz

Answers on p. 595   mhhe.com/wildCA2e

Additional Multiple Choice Quizzes are available at the book's Website.

1. A bond traded at 97½ means that:
  a. The bond pays 97½% interest.
  b. The bond trades at $975 per $1,000 bond.
  c. The market rate of interest is below the contract rate of interest for the bond.
  d. The bonds can be retired at $975 each.
  e. The bond's interest rate is 2½%.

2. A bondholder that owns a $1,000, 6%, 15-year bond has:
  a. The right to receive $1,000 at maturity.
  b. Ownership rights in the bond issuing entity.
  c. The right to receive $60 per month until maturity.
  d. The right to receive $1,900 at maturity.
  e. The right to receive $600 per year until maturity.

3. A company issues 8%, 20-year bonds with a par value of $500,000. The current market rate for the bonds is 8%. The amount of interest owed to the bondholders for each semiannual interest payment is:
   a. $40,000.
   b. $0.
   c. $20,000.
   d. $800,000.
   e. $400,000.

4. A company issued 5-year, 5% bonds with a par value of $100,000. The company received $95,735 for the bonds. Using the straight-line method, the company's interest expense for the first semiannual interest period is:
   a. $2,926.50.
   b. $5,853.00.
   c. $2,500.00.
   d. $5,000.00.
   e. $9,573.50.

5. A company issued 8-year, 5% bonds with a par value of $350,000. The company received proceeds of $373,745. Interest is payable semiannually. The amount of premium amortized for the first semiannual interest period, assuming straight-line bond amortization, is:
   a. $2,698.
   b. $23,745.
   c. $8,750.
   d. $9,344.
   e. $1,484.

Superscript letter $^{A\,(B)}$ denotes assignments based on Appendix 22A (22B).

Discussion Questions

1. What is the main difference between a bond and a share of stock?

2. What is the advantage of issuing bonds instead of obtaining financing from the company's owners?

3. What is a bond indenture? What provisions are usually included in it?

4. What are the *contract* rate and the *market* rate for bonds?

5. What factors affect the market rates for bonds?

6.^{A}Does the straight-line or effective interest method produce an interest expense allocation that yields a constant rate of interest over a bond's life? Explain.

7. What is the issue price of a $2,000 bond sold at 98¼? What is the issue price of a $6,000 bond sold at 101½?

8. Describe the debt-to-equity ratio and explain how creditors and owners would use this ratio to evaluate a company's risk.

9. What obligation does an entrepreneur (owner) have to investors that purchase bonds to finance the business?

10. What is the purpose of a bond sinking fund?

11. What is an operating lease? How does a lessee account for an operating lease?

12. Refer to **Best Buy**'s annual report in Appendix A. Is there any indication that Best Buy has issued bonds?

13. Refer to the statement of cash flows for **RadioShack** in Appendix A. For the year ended December 31, 2007, what was the amount of principal payments on long-term debt?

QUICK STUDY

QS 22-1
Bond computations—straight-line
LO2   LO3

Enviro Company issues 8%, 10-year bonds with a par value of $250,000 and semiannual interest payments. On the issue date, the annual market rate for these bonds is 10%, which implies a selling price of 87½. The straight-line method is used to allocate interest expense.
   1. What are the issuer's cash proceeds from issuance of these bonds?
   2. What total amount of bond interest expense will be recognized over the life of these bonds?
   3. What is the amount of bond interest expense recorded on the first interest payment date?

QS 22-2
Bond computations—straight-line
LO2   LO4

Garcia Company issues 10%, 15-year bonds with a par value of $240,000 and semiannual interest payments. On the issue date, the annual market rate for these bonds is 8%, which implies a selling price of 117¼. The straight-line method is used to allocate interest expense.
   1. What are the issuer's cash proceeds from issuance of these bonds?
   2. What total amount of bond interest expense will be recognized over the life of these bonds?
   3. What amount of bond interest expense is recorded on the first interest payment date?

QS 22-3
Journalize bond issuance   **LO2**

Prepare the journal entry for the issuance of the bonds in both QS 22-1 and QS 22-2. Assume that both bonds are issued for cash on January 1, 2010.

On July 1, 2010, Advocate Company exercises an $8,000 call option (plus par value) on its outstanding bonds that have a carrying value of $416,000 and par value of $400,000. The company exercises the call option after the semiannual interest is paid on June 30, 2010. Record the entry to retire the bonds.

QS 22-4
Bond retirement by call option
LO5

On January 1, 2010, the $2,000,000 par value bonds of Spitz Company with a carrying value of $2,000,000 are converted to 1,000,000 shares of $1.00 par value common stock. Record the entry for the conversion of the bonds.

QS 22-5
Bond retirement by stock conversion **LO5**

Enter the letter of the description A through F that best fits each term or phrase 1 through 6.

A. Is unsecured; backed only by the issuer's credit standing.

B. Has varying maturity dates for amounts owed.

C. Identifies rights and responsibilities of the issuer and the bondholders.

D. Can be exchanged for shares of the issuer's stock.

E. Maintains a separate asset account from which bondholders are paid at maturity.

F. Pledges specific assets of the issuer as collateral.

1. _____ Serial bond   **4.** _____ Bond indenture

2. _____ Secured bond   **5.** _____ Sinking fund bond

3. _____ Convertible bond   **6.** _____ Debenture

QS 22-6
Bond features and terminology
LO7

Compute the debt-to-equity ratio for each of the following companies. Which company appears to have a riskier financing structure? Explain.

QS 22-7
Debt-to-equity ratio **LO8**

	Atlanta Company	Spokane Company
Total liabilities	$429,000	$ 548,000
Total equity	572,000	1,827,000

Refer to the information in QS 22-2. Assume the bond indenture requires Garcia Company to pay $11,122 per year into a bond sinking fund. Garcia invests these payments in an account that earns 5% interest each year. These payments are made at the beginning of each year. The bonds were issued on January 1, 2010.

1. Record the entry for the first sinking fund deposit on January 1, 2010.

2. Record the entry for the first year's investment income.

3. Record the entry Garcia will make to retire the bonds on December 31, 2024. Assume the bond sinking fund balance before retiring the bonds is $240,000.

QS 22-8
Bond sinking fund **LO6**

Refer to the information in QS 22-1. Assume that Enviro Company uses the effective interest method to allocate interest expense.

1. What are the issuer's cash proceeds from issuance of the bonds?

2. What total amount of bond interest expense will be recognized over the life of these bonds?

3. What is the amount of bond interest expense recorded on the first interest payment date?

QS 22-9[A]
Bond computations-effective interest **LO3**

Refer to the information in QS 22-2. Assume that Garcia Company uses the effective interest method to allocate interest expense.

1. What are the issuer's cash proceeds from issuance of the bonds?

2. What total amount of bond interest expense will be recognized over the life of these bonds?

3. What is the amount of bond interest expense recorded on the first interest payment date?

QS 22-10[A]
Bond computations-effective interest **LO9**

A corporation plans to invest $1 million in oil exploration. The corporation is considering two plans to raise the money. Under plan 1, $1 million of bonds with a contract rate of interest of 6% would be issued. Under plan 2, 50,000 additional shares of common stock would be issued at $20 per share. The corporation expects to earn $700,000 per year before bond interest and income taxes. Compute the return on equity for each of the two financing plans. Assume an income tax rate of 35%.

QS 22-11
Compare bond and stock financing **LO1**

EXERCISES

Exercise 22–1
Recording bond issuance and interest   **LO2**

On January 1, 2010, Boston Enterprises issues bonds that have a $3,400,000 par value, mature in 20 years, and pay 9% interest semiannually on June 30 and December 31. The bonds are sold at par.

1. How much interest will Boston pay (in cash) to the bondholders every six months?

2. Prepare journal entries to record (*a*) the issuance of bonds on January 1, 2010; (*b*) the first interest payment on June 30, 2010; and (*c*) the second interest payment on December 31, 2010.

3. Prepare the journal entry for issuance assuming the bonds are issued at (*a*) 98 and (*b*) 102.

Exercise 22–2
Straight-line amortization of bond discount; retiring bonds
LO2   LO3   LO5

Tano issues bonds with a par value of $180,000 on January 1, 2010. The bonds' annual contract rate is 8%, and interest is paid semiannually on June 30 and December 31. The bonds mature in three years. The annual market rate at the date of issuance is 10%, and the bonds are sold for $170,862.

1. What is the amount of the discount on these bonds at issuance?

2. How much total bond interest expense will be recognized over the life of these bonds?

3. Prepare an amortization table like the one in Exhibit 22.5 for these bonds; use the straight-line method to amortize the discount.

4. Prepare the journal entry to record the bonds' retirement at maturity.

Exercise 22–3^A
Effective interest amortization of bond discount; retiring bonds
LO3   LO5

Stanford issues bonds dated January 1, 2010, with a par value of $500,000. The bonds' annual contract rate is 9%, and interest is paid semiannually on June 30 and December 31. The bonds mature in three years. The annual market rate at the date of issuance is 12%, and the bonds are sold for $463,140.

1. What is the amount of the discount on these bonds at issuance?

2. How much total bond interest expense will be recognized over the life of these bonds?

3. Prepare an amortization table like the one in Exhibit 22A.1 for these bonds; use the effective interest method to amortize the discount.

4. Prepare the journal entry to record the bonds' retirement at maturity.

Exercise 22–4
Straight-line amortization of bond premium; retiring bonds
LO4   LO5

Quatro Co. issues bonds dated January 1, 2010, with a par value of $400,000. The bonds' annual contract rate is 13%, and interest is paid semiannually on June 30 and December 31. The bonds mature in three years. The annual market rate at the date of issuance is 12%, and the bonds are sold for $409,850.

1. What is the amount of the premium on these bonds at issuance?

2. How much total bond interest expense will be recognized over the life of these bonds?

3. Prepare an amortization table like the one in Exhibit 22.9 for these bonds; use the straight-line method to amortize the premium.

4. Prepare the journal entry to record the bonds' retirement at maturity.

Exercise 22–5^A
Effective interest amortization of bond premium   **LO4**

Refer to the bond details in Exercise 22-4 and prepare an amortization table like the one in Exhibit 22A.2 for these bonds using the effective interest method to amortize the premium.

Exercise 22–6
Computing bond interest; recording bond issuance
LO2   LO3

Brigham Company issues bonds with a par value of $800,000 on their stated issue date. The bonds mature in 10 years and pay 6% annual interest in semiannual payments. On the issue date, the annual market rate for the bonds is 8%.

1. What is the amount of each semiannual interest payment for these bonds?

2. How many semiannual interest payments will be made on these bonds over their life?

3. Use the interest rates given to determine whether the bonds are issued at par, at a discount, or at a premium.

4. The bonds are issued for $691,287. Prepare the journal entry to record the bonds' issuance.

Citywide Company issues bonds with a par value of $150,000 on their stated issue date. The bonds mature in five years and pay 10% annual interest in semiannual payments. On the issue date, the annual market rate for the bonds is 8%.

1. What is the amount of each semiannual interest payment for these bonds?

2. How many semiannual interest payments will be made on these bonds over their life?

3. Use the interest rates given to determine whether the bonds are issued at par, at a discount, or at a premium.

4. The bonds are issued for $162,172. Prepare the journal entry to record the bonds' issuance.

Exercise 22–7
Computing bond interest;
recording bond issuance
LO2   LO4

On January 1, 2010, Shay issues $700,000 of 10%, 15-year bonds at a price of 97¾. Six years later, on January 1, 2016, Shay retires 20% of these bonds by buying them on the open market at 104½. All interest is accounted for and paid through December 31, 2015, the day before the purchase. The straight-line method is used to amortize any bond discount.

1. How much does the company receive when it issues the bonds on January 1, 2010?

2. What is the amount of the discount on the bonds at January 1, 2010?

3. How much amortization of the discount is recorded on the bonds for the entire period from January 1, 2010, through December 31, 2015?

4. What is the carrying (book) value of the bonds as of the close of business on December 31, 2015? What is the carrying value of the 20% soon-to-be-retired bonds on this same date?

5. How much did the company pay on January 1, 2016, to purchase the bonds that it retired?

6. What is the amount of the recorded gain or loss from retiring the bonds?

7. Prepare the journal entry to record the bond retirement at January 1, 2016.

Exercise 22–8
Bond computations,
straight-line amortization,
and bond retirement
LO2   LO3   LO5

Check   (6) $8,190 loss

Duval Co. issues four-year bonds with a $100,000 par value on June 1, 2010, at a price of $95,948. The annual contract rate is 7%, and interest is paid semiannually on November 30 and May 31.

1. Prepare an amortization table like the one in Exhibit 22.5 for these bonds. Use the straight-line method of interest amortization.

2. Prepare journal entries to record the first two interest payments and to accrue interest as of December 31, 2010.

Exercise 22–9
Straight-line amortization and
accrued bond interest expense
LO2   LO3

Montclair Company is considering a project that will require a $500,000 loan. It presently has total liabilities of $220,000, and total assets of $610,000.

1. Compute Montclair's (a) present debt-to-equity ratio and (b) the debt-to-equity ratio assuming it borrows $500,000 to fund the project.

2. Evaluate and discuss the level of risk involved if Montclair borrows the funds to pursue the project.

Exercise 22–10
Applying debt-to-equity ratio
LO8

Refer to the information in Exercise 22-6. Assume the bonds were issued on January 1, 2010. The bond agreement requires Brigham Company to make $80,000 deposits into a bond sinking fund at the beginning of each of the next 10 years (starting on January 1, 2010). The deposits are invested in an account that earns investment income of $5,245 in 2010. The bond sinking fund account contains $14,711 after retiring the bonds on December 31, 2019. Prepare the journal entries for Brigham to record the following bond sinking fund transactions.

1. The deposit of cash into the bond sinking fund on January 1, 2010.

2. The investment income from the bond sinking fund for 2010.

3. The bond retirement on December 31, 2019.

4. The return of the remaining balance in the bond sinking fund on December 31, 2019, to the Cash account.

Exercise 22–11
Bond sinking fund transactions
LO6

PROBLEM SET A

Problem 22-1A

Straight-line amortization of bond discount and bond premium

LO2 LO3 LO4

mhhe.com/wildCA2e

Check (3) $4,143,552

(4) 12/31/2011 carrying value, $3,528,920

Hillside issues $4,000,000 of 6%, 15-year bonds dated January 1, 2010, that pay interest semiannually on June 30 and December 31. The bonds are issued at a price of $3,456,448.

Required

1. Prepare the January 1, 2010, journal entry to record the bonds' issuance.
2. For each semiannual period, compute (*a*) the cash payment, (*b*) the straight-line discount amortization, and (*c*) the bond interest expense.
3. Determine the total bond interest expense to be recognized over the bonds' life.
4. Prepare the first two years of an amortization table like Exhibit 22.5 using the straight-line method.
5. Prepare the journal entries to record the first two interest payments.
6. Assume that the bonds are issued at a price of $4,895,980. Repeat parts 1 through 5.

Problem 22-2A

Straight-line amortization of bond premium **LO1 LO4**

mhhe.com/wildCA2e

Check (2) 6/30/2012 carrying value, $252,668

Ellis issues 6.5%, five-year bonds dated January 1, 2010, with a $250,000 par value. The bonds pay interest on June 30 and December 31 and are issued at a price of $255,333. The annual market rate is 6% on the issue date.

Required

1. Calculate the total bond interest expense over the bonds' life.
2. Prepare a straight-line amortization table like Exhibit 22.8 for the bonds' life.
3. Prepare the journal entries to record the first two interest payments.

Problem 22-3A^A

Effective interest amortization of bond premium **LO2 LO4**

Check (2) 6/30/2012 carrying value, $252,865

Refer to the bond details in Problem 22-2A.

Required

1. Compute the total bond interest expense over the bonds' life.
2. Prepare an effective interest amortization table like the one in Exhibit 22A.2 for the bonds' life.
3. Prepare the journal entries to record the first two interest payments.

Problem 22-4A

Straight-line amortization of bond discount **LO2 LO3**

Check (2) $97,819

(3) 12/31/2011 carrying value, $308,589

Legacy issues $325,000 of 5%, four-year bonds dated January 1, 2010, that pay interest semiannually on June 30 and December 31. They are issued at $292,181 and their market rate is 8% at the issue date.

Required

1. Prepare the January 1, 2010, journal entry to record the bonds' issuance.
2. Determine the total bond interest expense to be recognized over the bonds' life.
3. Prepare a straight-line amortization table like the one in Exhibit 22.5 for the bonds' first two years.
4. Prepare the journal entries to record the first two interest payments.

Analysis Component

5. Assume the market rate on January 1, 2010, is 4% instead of 8%. Without providing numbers, describe how this change affects the amounts reported on Legacy's financial statements.

Problem 22-5A^A

Effective interest amortization of bond discount **LO2 LO3**

Check (2) $97,819

(3) 12/31/2011 carrying value, $307,308

mhhe.com/wildCA2e

Refer to the bond details in Problem 22-4A.

Required

1. Prepare the January 1, 2010, journal entry to record the bonds' issuance.
2. Determine the total bond interest expense to be recognized over the bonds' life.
3. Prepare an effective interest amortization table like the one in Exhibit 22A.1 for the bonds' first two years.
4. Prepare the journal entries to record the first two interest payments.

Ike issues $180,000 of 11%, three-year bonds dated January 1, 2010, that pay interest semiannually on June 30 and December 31. They are issued at $184,566. The market rate of interest is 10% at the issue date.

Required

1. Prepare the January 1, 2010, journal entry to record the bonds' issuance.
2. Determine the total bond interest expense to be recognized over the bonds' life.
3. Prepare an effective interest amortization table like Exhibit 22A.2 for the bonds' first two years.
4. Prepare the journal entries to record the first two interest payments.
5. Prepare the journal entry to record the bonds' retirement on January 1, 2012, at 98.

Analysis Component

6. Assume that the market rate on January 1, 2010, is 12% instead of 10%. Without presenting numbers, describe how this change affects amounts reported on Ike's financial statements.

Problem 22–6A[A]

Effective interest amortization of bond premium; retiring bonds

LO2 LO4 LO5

Check (3) 6/30/2011 carrying
value, $182,448

(5) $5,270 gain

mhhe.com/wildCA2e

At the end of the current year, the following information is available for both the Pulaski Company and the Scott Company:

	Pulaski Company	Scott Company
Total assets	$900,000	$450,000
Total liabilities	360,000	240,000
Total equity	540,000	210,000

Required

1. Compute the debt-to-equity ratio for both companies.
2. Comment on your results and discuss the riskiness of each company's financing structure.

Problem 22–7A

Applying the debt-to-equity ratio

LO8

Romero issues $3,400,000 of 10%, 10-year bonds dated January 1, 2010, that pay interest semiannually on June 30 and December 31. The bonds are issued at a price of $3,010,000.

Required

1. Prepare the January 1, 2010, journal entry to record the bonds' issuance.
2. For each semiannual period, compute (a) the cash payment, (b) the straight-line discount amortization, and (c) the bond interest expense.
3. Determine the total bond interest expense to be recognized over the bonds' life.
4. Prepare the first two years of an amortization table like Exhibit 22.5 using the straight-line method.
5. Prepare the journal entries to record the first two interest payments.
6. Assume that the bonds are issued at a price of $4,192,932. Repeat parts 1 through 5.

PROBLEM SET B

Problem 22–1B

Straight-line amortization of bond discount and bond premium

LO2 LO3 LO4

Check (3) $3,790,000

(4) 6/30/2011 carrying value,
$3,068,500

Ripkin Company issues 9%, five-year bonds dated January 1, 2010, with a $320,000 par value. The bonds pay interest on June 30 and December 31 and are issued at a price of $332,988. Their annual market rate is 8% on the issue date.

Required

1. Calculate the total bond interest expense over the bonds' life.
2. Prepare a straight-line amortization table like Exhibit 22.8 for the bonds' life.
3. Prepare the journal entries to record the first two interest payments.

Problem 22–2B

Straight-line amortization of bond premium

LO2 LO4

Check (2) 6/30/2012 carrying
value, $326,493

Problem 22-3B[A]

Effective interest amortization of bond premium; computing bond price   **LO2   LO4**

Check (2) 6/30/2012 carrying value, $327,136

Refer to the bond details in Problem 22-2B.

Required

1. Compute the total bond interest expense over the bonds' life.
2. Prepare an effective interest amortization table like the one in Exhibit 22A.2 for the bonds' life.
3. Prepare the journal entries to record the first two interest payments.

Problem 22-4B

Straight-line amortization of bond discount   **LO2   LO3**

Check (2) $257,506

(3) 6/30/2011 carrying value, $202,646

Gomez issues $240,000 of 6%, 15-year bonds dated January 1, 2010, that pay interest semiannually on June 30 and December 31. They are issued at $198,494, and their market rate is 8% at the issue date.

Required

1. Prepare the January 1, 2010, journal entry to record the bonds' issuance.
2. Determine the total bond interest expense to be recognized over the life of the bonds.
3. Prepare a straight-line amortization table like the one in Exhibit 22.5 for the bonds' first two years.
4. Prepare the journal entries to record the first two interest payments.

Problem 22-5B[A]

Effective interest amortization of bond discount   **LO2   LO3**

Check (2) $257,506;

(3) 6/30/2011 carrying value, $200,803

Refer to the bond details in Problem 22-4B.

Required

1. Prepare the January 1, 2010, journal entry to record the bonds' issuance.
2. Determine the total bond interest expense to be recognized over the bonds' life.
3. Prepare an effective interest amortization table like the one in Exhibit 22A.1 for the bonds' first two years.
4. Prepare the journal entries to record the first two interest payments.

Problem 22-6B[A]

Effective interest amortization of bond premium; retiring bonds   **LO2   LO4   LO5**

Check (3) 6/30/2011 carrying value, $479,202

(5) $3,088 loss

Valdez issues $450,000 of 13%, four-year bonds dated January 1, 2010, that pay interest semiannually on June 30 and December 31. They are issued at $493,608, and their market rate of interest is 10% at the issue date.

Required

1. Prepare the January 1, 2010, journal entry to record the bonds' issuance.
2. Determine the total bond interest expense to be recognized over the bonds' life.
3. Prepare an effective interest amortization table like the one in Exhibit 22A.2 for the bonds' first two years.
4. Prepare the journal entries to record the first two interest payments.
5. Prepare the journal entry to record the bonds' retirement on January 1, 2011, at 106.

Analysis Component

6. Assume that the market rate on January 1, 2010, is 14% instead of 10%. Without presenting numbers, describe how this change affects amounts reported on Valdez's financial statements.

Problem 22-7B

Applying the debt-to-equity ratio   **LO8**

At the end of the current year, the following information is available for both Atlas Company and Bryan Company.

	Atlas Company	Bryan Company
Total assets	$180,000	$750,000
Total liabilities	81,000	562,500
Total equity	99,000	187,500

Required

1. Compute the debt-to-equity ratio for both companies.
2. Comment on your results and discuss what they imply about the relative riskiness of these companies.

(This serial problem began in Chapter 1 and continues through most of the book. If previous chapter segments were not completed, the serial problem can begin at this point. It is helpful, but not necessary, for you to use the Working Papers that accompany the book.)

SP 22   Adriana Lopez has consulted with her local banker and is considering financing an expansion of her business by obtaining a long-term bank loan. Selected account balances at March 31, 2011, for Success Systems follow.

Total assets	$147,529	Total liabilities	$1,050	Total equity	$146,479

SERIAL PROBLEM

Success Systems

Required

1. The bank has offered a long-term secured note to Success Systems. The bank's loan procedures require that a client's debt-to-equity ratio not exceed 0.8. As of March 31, 2011, what is the maximum amount that Success Systems could borrow from this bank (rounded to nearest dollar)?
2. If Success Systems borrows the maximum amount allowed from the bank, what percentage of assets would be financed (*a*) by debt, and (*b*) by equity?
3. What are some factors Lopez should consider before borrowing the funds?

BEYOND THE NUMBERS

BTN 22-1   Refer to **Best Buy**'s financial statements in Appendix A to answer the following.
1. Identify the items that make up Best Buy's long-term debt at March 1, 2008. (*Hint:* See note 4.)
2. How much annual cash interest must Best Buy pay on the 2.25% convertible subordinated debt?
3. Did it have any additions to long-term debt that provided cash for the year-end March 1, 2008?

REPORTING IN ACTION
LO1   LO2

Fast Forward

4. Access Best Buy's financial statements for the years ending after March 1, 2008, from its Website (**BestBuy.com**) or the SEC's EDGAR database (**www.SEC.gov**). Has it issued additional long-term debt since the year-end March 1, 2008? If yes, indentify the amount(s).

BTN 22-2   Key comparative figures ($ millions) for both **Best Buy** and **RadioShack** follow.

	Best Buy		RadioShack	
Key Figures	**Current Year**	**Prior Year**	**Current Year**	**Prior Year**
Total assets	$12,758	$13,570	$1,990	$2,070
Total liabilities	8,274	7,369	1,220	1,416
Total equity	4,484	6,201	770	654

COMPARATIVE ANALYSIS
LO8

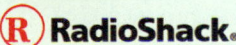

Required

1. Compute the debt-to-equity ratio for Best Buy and RadioShack for both the current year and the prior year.
2. Use the ratio you computed in part 1 to determine which company's financing structure is less risky. Assume an industry average of 1.1 for debt-to-equity.

ETHICS CHALLENGE
LO1

BTN 22-3   Brevard County needs a new county government building that would cost $24 million. The politicians feel that voters will not approve a municipal bond issue to fund the building since it would increase taxes. They opt to have a state bank issue $24 million of tax-exempt securities to pay for the building construction. The county then will make yearly lease payments (of principal and interest) to repay the obligation. Unlike conventional municipal bonds, the lease payments are not binding obligations on the county and, therefore, require no voter approval.

Required

1. Do you think the actions of the politicians and the bankers in this situation are ethical?
2. How do the tax-exempt securities used to pay for the building compare in risk to a conventional municipal bond issued by Brevard County?

WORKPLACE COMMUNICATION
LO4

BTN 22-4   Your business associate mentions that she is considering investing in corporate bonds currently selling at a premium. She says that since the bonds are selling at a premium, they are highly valued and her investment will yield more than the going rate of return for the risk involved. Reply with a memorandum to confirm or correct your associate's interpretation of premium bonds.

TAKING IT TO THE NET
LO7

BTN 22-5   Access the April 2, 2009, filing of the 10-K report of **Home Depot** for the year ended February 1, 2009, from **www.SEC.gov** (Ticker: HD). Refer to Home Depot's balance sheet, including its Note 2 (on long-term debt).

Required

1. Identify Home Depot's long-term liabilities and the amounts for those liabilities from Home Depot's balance sheet at February 1, 2009.
2. Home Depot reported in 2004 that it "issued $1.0 billion of 3¾% senior notes due September 15, 2009, at a discount of $5 million with interest payable semiannually on March 15 and September 15 each year."
   a. Why would Home Depot issue $1 billion of its notes for only $995 million?
   b. How much cash interest must Home Depot pay each March 15 and September 15 on these notes?

TEAMWORK IN ACTION
LO3   **LO4**

BTN 22-6[A]   Break into teams and complete the following requirements related to effective interest amortization for a premium bond.

1. Each team member is to independently prepare a blank table with proper headings for amortization of a bond premium. When all have finished, compare tables and ensure all are in agreement.

Parts 2 and 3 require use of these facts: On January 1, 2010, BC issues $100,000, 9%, five-year bonds at 104.1. The market rate at issuance is 8%. BC pays interest semiannually on June 30 and December 31.

2. In rotation, *each* team member must explain how to complete *one* line of the bond amortization table, including all computations for his or her line. (Round amounts to the nearest dollar.) All members are to fill in their tables during this process. You need not finish the table; stop after all members have explained a line.
3. In rotation, *each* team member is to identify a separate column of the table and indicate what the final number in that column will be and explain the reasoning.

> Rotate teams to report on parts 4 and 5. Consider requiring entries for issuance and interest payments.

4. Reach a team consensus as to what the total bond interest expense on this bond issue will be if the bond is not retired before maturity.
5. As a team, prepare a list of similarities and differences between the amortization table just prepared and the amortization table if the bond had been issued at a discount.

ENTREPRENEURS IN BUSINESS
LO1

BTN 22-7   James "Fly" Lindsay is the owner of **Rap Snacks**. Assume that Lindsay's franchise program currently has $250,000 in equity; and he is considering a $100,000 expansion to meet increased demand. The $100,000 expansion would yield $16,000 in additional annual income before interest expense. Assume that Lindsay's franchise program currently earns $40,000 annual income before interest expense of $10,000, yielding a return on equity of 12% ($30,000/$250,000). To fund the expansion, Lindsay is considering the issuance of a 10-year, $100,000 note with annual interest payments (the principal due at the end of 10 years).

Required

1. Using return on equity as the decision criterion, show computations to support or reject Lindsay's expansion if interest on the $100,000 note is (*a*) 10%, (*b*) 15%, (*c*) 16%, (*d*) 17%, and (*e*) 20%.

2. What general rule do the results in part 1 illustrate?

Chapter 23

Cash Flow Reporting

A Look Back

Chapter 22 focused on accounting for bonds. We also described bond characteristics, payment patterns, interest computations, and retirement and reporting requirements.

A Look at This Chapter

This chapter focuses on reporting and analyzing cash inflows and cash outflows. We emphasize how to prepare and interpret the statement of cash flows.

A Look Ahead

Chapter 24 focuses on tools to help us analyze financial statements. We also describe the use of ratio analysis to assess the liquidity, efficiency, solvency, and profitability of a company.

Learning Objectives

LO 1	Explain the purpose of cash flow information.
LO 2	Distinguish between operating, investing, and financing activities.
LO 3	Describe the format of the statement of cash flows.
LO 4	Prepare a statement of cash flows.
LO 5	Compute cash flows from operating activities using the indirect method.
LO 6	Determine cash flows from both investing and financing activities.
LO 7	Analyze the statement of cash flows.
LO 8	Compute and apply the cash flow on total assets ratio.
LO 9	*Appendix 23A*–Compute cash flows from operating activities using the direct method.

"We don't sell products...we sell relationships"
—Michael Woods (Ramona Woods on right)

Hair-Raising Cash Flows

GREENSBORO, NC—Although cash may not *be* king, it certainly improves the King's health. Just ask Michael and Ramona Woods, entrepreneurial cofounders of **Ashtae Products (ASHTAE.com),** a multicultural hair-care products and services company. The husband-and-wife team opened Ashtae, named after daughters Ashley and Taylore, in 1995—and revenues now exceed $5 million per year.

But early on, all was not well in the kingdom. "We did everything wrong when we started our business," says Ramona. Cash flow was a constant battle for fledgling Ashtae, as cash flows ran short despite growing profits. "Our mortgage went into foreclosure. Our cars were repossessed," recalls Ramona. "I had to take the bus with two little kids. Sometimes I didn't have the money for the bus . . . we did so much wrong."

Michael and Ramona learned the importance of cash flows the hard way. "We failed to realize that knowing how to sell and make money doesn't mean you know how to keep it," says Michael. Cash outflows for inventory often yielded negative cash flows for Ashtae in spite of growing sales and profits.

Managing cash was a constant struggle. The couple eventually learned how to monitor and control cash flows associated with each of its operating, investing, and financing activities. They discovered, says Michael, how "to plan for the various stages of growth" and to manage cash flows.

This chapter focuses on cash flows—its measurement, presentation, analysis, and interpretation. It describes how to analyze separately the cash flows related to operating, investing, and financing activities. Michael and Ramona know firsthand the importance of scrutinizing and overseeing cash flows. Says Ramona, "We had to learn to draw the line . . . [to achieve] a profitable business." With healthy cash flows today, the outlook for King Michael and Queen Ramona is promising. As Michael puts it, "WOW! That is the only word that can describe our performance."

[Sources: *Ashtae Website*, May 2009; *The Business Journal*, July 2005, January 2005, and December 2004]

Profitability is a main goal of most managers, but not the only goal. A company cannot achieve or maintain profits without carefully managing cash. Managers and other users of information pay close attention to a company's cash position and the events and transactions affecting cash. This chapter explains how we prepare, analyze, and interpret a statement of cash flows. It also discusses the importance of cash flow information for predicting future performance and making managerial decisions. More generally, effectively using the statement of cash flows is crucial for managing and analyzing the operating, investing, and financing activities of businesses.

Cash Flow Reporting

Basics of Cash Flow Reporting
- Purpose
- Measurement
- Classification
- Format
- Preparation

Cash Flows from Operating
- Indirect and direct methods of reporting
- Application of indirect method of reporting
- Summary of indirect method adjustments

Cash Flows from Investing
- Three-stage process of analysis
- Analysis of noncurrent assets
- Analysis of other assets

Cash Flows from Financing
- Three-stage process of analysis
- Analysis of noncurrent liabilities
- Analysis of equity

Basics of Cash Flow Reporting

This section describes the basics of cash flow reporting, including its purpose, measurement, classification, format, and preparation.

Purpose of the Statement of Cash Flows

LO1 Explain the purpose of cash flow information.

The purpose of the **statement of cash flows** is to report all major cash receipts (inflows) and cash payments (outflows) during a period. This includes separately identifying the cash flows related to operating, investing, and financing activities. The statement of cash flows does more than simply report changes in cash. It is the detailed disclosure of individual cash flows that makes this statement useful to users. Information in this statement helps users answer questions such as these:

- How does a company obtain its cash?
- Where does a company spend its cash?
- What explains the change in the cash balance from the beginning to the end of the year?

The statement of cash flows addresses important questions such as these by summarizing, classifying, and reporting a company's cash inflows and cash outflows for each period.

Measurement of Cash Flows

Cash flows are defined to include both *cash* and *cash equivalents*. The statement of cash flows explains the difference between the beginning and ending balances of cash and cash equivalents. We continue to use the phrases *cash flows* and the *statement of cash flows,* but we must remember that both phrases refer to both cash and cash equivalents. Recall that a cash equivalent must satisfy two criteria: (1) be readily convertible to a known amount of cash and (2) be sufficiently close to its maturity so its market value is unaffected by interest rate changes. In most cases, a debt security must be within three months of its maturity to satisfy these criteria. Companies must disclose and follow a clear policy for determining cash and cash equivalents and apply it consistently from period to period. **American Express**, for example, defines its cash equivalents as "time deposits and other highly liquid investments with original maturities of 90 days or less."

Cash and Cash Equivalents

IN THE NEWS

Cash Flow   "A lender must have a complete understanding of a borrower's cash flows to assess both the borrowing needs and repayment sources. This requires information about the major types of cash inflows and outflows. I have seen many companies, whose financial statements indicate good profitability, experience severe financial problems because the owners or managers lacked a good understanding of cash flows."
—Mary E. Garza, **Bank of America**.

Classification of Cash Flows

Since cash and cash equivalents are combined, the statement of cash flows does not report transactions between cash and cash equivalents such as cash paid to purchase cash equivalents and cash received from selling cash equivalents. However, all other cash receipts and cash payments are classified and reported on the statement as operating, investing, or financing activities. Individual cash receipts and payments for each of these three categories are labeled to identify their originating transactions or events. A net cash inflow (source) occurs when the receipts in a category exceed the payments. A net cash outflow (use) occurs when the payments in a category exceed the receipts.

LO2   Distinguish between operating, investing, and financing activities.

Operating Activities   **Operating activities** include those transactions and events that determine net income. Examples are the production and purchase of merchandise, the sale of goods and services to customers, and the expenditures to administer the business. Not all items in income, such as unusual gains and losses, are operating activities (we discuss these exceptions later in the chapter). Exhibit 23.1 lists the more common cash inflows and outflows from operating activities.

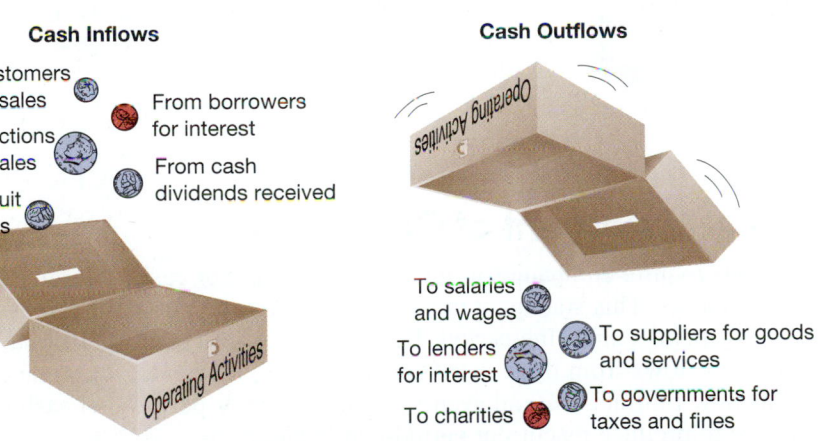

Exhibit 23.1

Cash Flows from Operating Activities

Investing Activities   **Investing activities** generally include those transactions and events that affect long-term assets, namely, the purchase and sale of long-term assets. They also include the (1) purchase and sale of short-term investments other than cash equivalents and (2) lending and collecting money for notes receivable. Exhibit 23.2 lists examples of cash flows from investing

Common errors include misclassification of *cash dividends received* and *cash interest received* as investing activities and *cash interest paid* as financing. The FASB requires these cash flows be reported as operating activities.

Exhibit 23.2

Cash Flows from Investing Activities

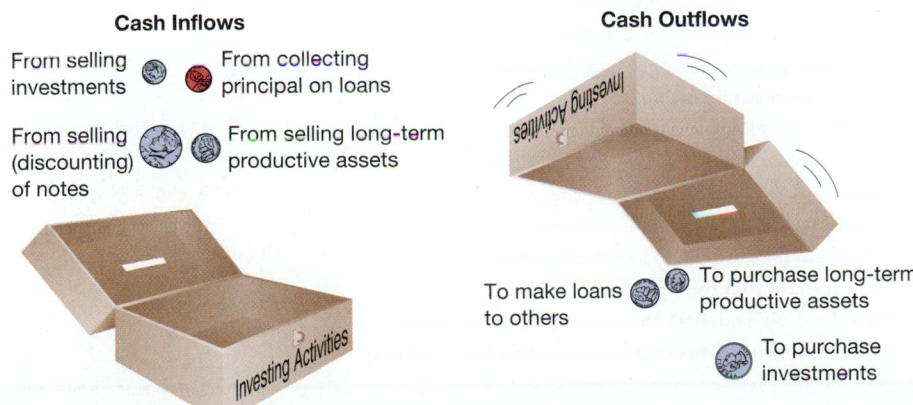

activities. Proceeds from collecting the principal amounts of notes deserve special mention. If the note results from sales to customers, its cash receipts are classified as operating activities whether short term or long term. If the note results from a loan to another party apart from sales, however, the cash receipts from collecting the note principal are classified as an investing activity. The FASB requires the collection of interest on loans be reported as an operating activity.

Financing Activities   **Financing activities** include those transactions and events that affect long-term liabilities and equity. Examples are (1) obtaining cash from issuing debt and repaying the amounts borrowed and (2) receiving cash from or distributing cash to owners. These activities involve transactions with a company's owners and creditors. They also often involve borrowing and repaying principal amounts relating to both short- and long-term debt. Notice that payments of interest expense are classified as operating activities. Also, cash payments to settle credit purchases of merchandise, whether on account or by note, are operating activities. Exhibit 23.3 lists examples of cash flows from financing activities.

> Interest paid on a loan is classified as an operating activity, but payments of loan principal are financing activities.

Exhibit 23.3

Cash Flows from Financing Activities

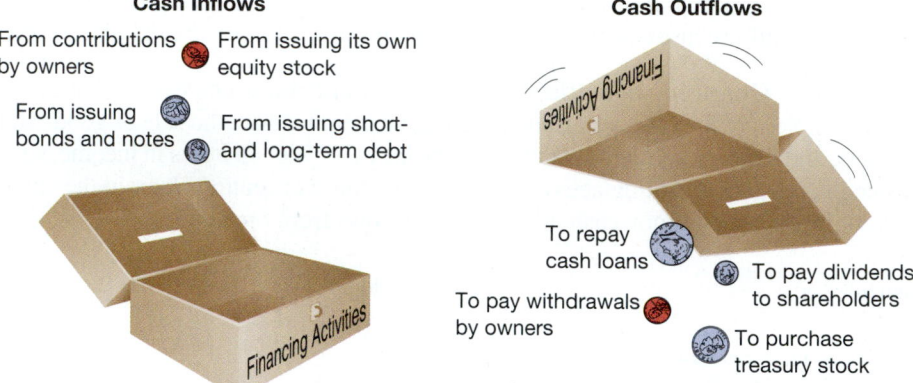

Format of the Statement of Cash Flows

LO3   Describe the format of the statement of cash flows.

Accounting standards require companies to include a statement of cash flows in a complete set of financial statements. This statement must report information about a company's cash receipts and cash payments during the period. Exhibit 23.4 shows the usual format. A company must report cash flows from three activities: operating, investing, and financing. The statement explains how transactions and events impact the prior period-end cash (and cash equivalents) balance to produce its current period-end balance.

Exhibit 23.4

Format of the Statement of Cash Flows

COMPANY NAME Statement of Cash Flows For *period* Ended *date*	
Cash flows from operating activities	
[List of individual inflows and outflows]	
Net cash provided (used) by operating activities	$ #
Cash flows from investing activities	
[List of individual inflows and outflows]	
Net cash provided (used) by investing activities	#
Cash flows from financing activities	
[List of individual inflows and outflows]	
Net cash provided (used) by financing activities	#
Net increase (decrease) in cash	$ #
Cash (and equivalents) balance at prior period-end	#
Cash (and equivalents) balance at current period-end	$ #

Preparing the Statement of Cash Flows

Preparing a statement of cash flows involves five steps:

1. Compute the net increase or decrease in cash.
2. Compute and report net cash provided (used) by operating activities (using either the direct or indirect method; both are explained).
3. Compute and report net cash provided (used) by investing activities.
4. Compute and report net cash provided (used) by financing activities.
5. Compute net cash flow by combining net cash provided (used) by operating, investing, and financing activities and then *prove it* by adding it to the beginning cash balance to show that it equals the ending cash balance. Important noncash investing and financing activities are disclosed in either a note or a separate schedule to the statement.

LO4 Prepare a statement of cash flows.

Step 1: Compute net increase or decrease in cash

Step 2: Compute net cash from operating activities

The first step to compute the net increase or net decrease in cash is a simple but crucial computation. It equals the current period's cash balance minus the prior period's cash balance. This is the *bottom-line* figure for the statement of cash flows and is a check on the accuracy of one's work. The information we need to prepare a statement of cash flows comes from various sources including comparative balance sheets at the beginning and end of the period, and an income statement for the period.

Step 3: Compute net cash from investing activities

A company's cash receipts and cash payments are recorded in the Cash account in its general ledger. The Cash account is therefore a natural place to look for information about cash flows from operating, investing, and financing activities. To illustrate, review the summarized Cash T-account of Genesis, Inc., in Exhibit 23.5. Individual cash transactions are summarized in this Cash account according to the major types of cash receipts and cash payments. For instance, only the total of cash receipts from all customers is listed. Individual cash transactions underlying these totals can number in the thousands. Accounting software programs are available to provide summarized cash accounts.

Step 4: Compute net cash from financing activities

Preparing a statement of cash flows from Exhibit 23.5 requires determining whether an individual cash inflow or outflow is an operating, investing, or financing activity, and then listing each by activity. This yields the statement shown in Exhibit 23.6. However, preparing the

Step 5: Prove and report beginning and ending cash balances

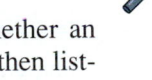

Accounting System:		
File Edit Maintain Tasks Analysis Options Reports Window Help		

Cash

Balance, Dec. 31, 2009	12,000	
Receipts from customers	570,000	Payments for merchandise 319,000
Receipts from asset sales	12,000	Payments for wages and operating expenses 218,000
Receipts from stock issuance ..	15,000	Payments for interest 8,000
		Payments for taxes 5,000
		Payments for assets 10,000
		Payments for bond retirement 18,000
		Payments for dividends 14,000
Balance, Dec. 31, 2010	17,000	

Sales	Purchases	General Ledger	Payroll	Inventory	Company	Analysis

Exhibit 23.5

Summarized Cash Account

Exhibit 23.6

Statement of Cash Flows—
Direct Method

GENESIS
Statement of Cash Flows
For Year Ended December 31, 2010

Cash flows from operating activities		
Cash received from customers	$570,000	
Cash paid for merchandise	(319,000)	
Cash paid for wages and other operating expenses	(218,000)	
Cash paid for interest	(8,000)	
Cash paid for taxes	(5,000)	
Net cash provided by operating activities		$20,000
Cash flows from investing activities		
Cash received from sale of plant assets	12,000	
Cash paid for purchase of plant assets	(10,000)	
Net cash provided by investing activities		2,000
Cash flows from financing activities		
Cash received from issuing stock	15,000	
Cash paid to retire bonds	(18,000)	
Cash paid for dividends	(14,000)	
Net cash used in financing activities		(17,000)
Net increase in cash		$ 5,000
Cash balance at prior year-end		12,000
Cash balance at current year-end		$17,000

statement of cash flows from an analysis of the summarized Cash account has two limitations. First, most companies have many individual cash receipts and payments, making it difficult to review them all. Accounting software minimizes this burden, but it is still a task requiring professional judgment for many transactions. Second, the Cash account does not usually carry an adequate description of each cash transaction, making assignment of all cash transactions according to activity difficult.

Information to Prepare the Statement Rather than from a summarized Cash account, information to prepare the statement of cash flows usually comes from four sources:

1. Comparative balance sheets.
2. Current income statement.
3. Statement of retained earnings.
4. Additional information.

Comparative balance sheets are used to compute changes in noncash accounts from the beginning to the end of the period. The current income statement is used to help compute cash flows from operating activities. Additional information often includes details on transactions and events that help explain both the cash flows and noncash investing and financing activities. We show how to use this information to prepare the direct method of cash flows in Appendix 23A.

IN THE NEWS

e-Cash Every credit transaction on the Net leaves a trail that a hacker or a marketer can pick up. Enter e-cash—or digital money. The encryption of e-cash protects your money from snoops and thieves and cannot be traced, even by the issuing bank.

Cash Flows from Operating

Indirect and Direct Methods of Reporting

Cash flows provided (used) by operating activities are reported in one of two ways: the *direct method* or the *indirect method*. **These two different methods apply only to the cash flows from operating activities section.**

The **direct method** separately lists each major item of operating cash receipts (such as cash received from customers) and each major item of operating cash payments (such as cash paid for merchandise). The cash payments are subtracted from cash receipts to determine the net cash provided (used) by operating activities. The operating activities section of Exhibit 23.6 reflects the direct method of reporting operating cash flows.

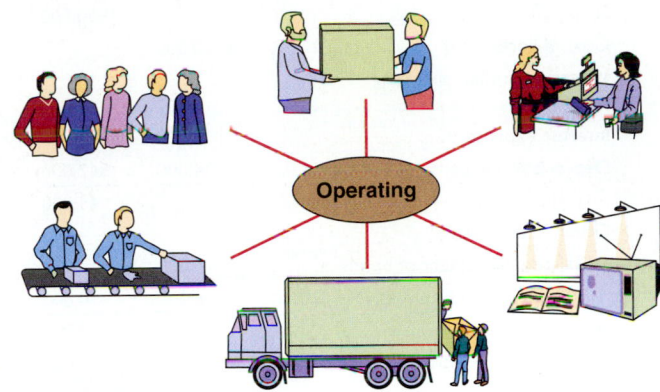

The **indirect method** reports net income and then adjusts it for items necessary to obtain net cash provided (used) by operating activities. It does *not* report individual items of cash inflows and cash outflows from operating activities. Instead, the indirect method reports the necessary adjustments to reconcile net income to net cash provided (used) by operating activities. The indirect method is most commonly used by big, publicly traded companies reporting their financial statements. The operating activities section for Genesis prepared under the indirect method is shown in Exhibit 23.7. We show how to compute the adjustments for Exhibit 23.7 in the next section.

Cash flows from operating activities		
Net income	$ 38,000	
Adjustments to reconcile net income to net cash provided by operating activities		
Increase in accounts receivable	(20,000)	
Increase in merchandise inventory	(14,000)	
Increase in prepaid expenses	(2,000)	
Decrease in accounts payable	(5,000)	
Decrease in interest payable	(1,000)	
Increase in income taxes payable	10,000	
Depreciation expense	24,000	
Loss on sale of plant assets	6,000	
Gain on retirement of bonds	(16,000)	
Net cash provided by operating activities		**$20,000**

Exhibit 23.7

Operating Activities Section—
Indirect Method

The net cash amount provided by operating activities is *identical* under both the direct and indirect methods. This equality always exists. The difference in these methods is with the computation and presentation of this amount. The FASB recommends the direct method, but because it is not required and the indirect method is arguably easier to compute, nearly all companies report operating cash flows using the indirect method.

To illustrate, we prepare the operating activities section of the statement of cash flows for Genesis. Exhibit 23.8 shows the December 31, 2009 and 2010, balance sheets of Genesis along with its 2010 income statement. We use this information to prepare a statement of cash flows that explains the $5,000 increase in cash for 2010 as reflected in its balance sheets. This $5,000 is computed as Cash of $17,000 at the end of 2010 minus Cash of $12,000 at the end of 2009. Genesis discloses additional information about 2010 transactions:

a. The accounts payable balances result from merchandise inventory purchases.

b. Purchased plant assets costing $70,000 by paying $10,000 cash and issuing $60,000 of bonds payable.

c. Sold plant assets with an original cost of $30,000 and accumulated depreciation of $12,000 for $12,000 cash, yielding a $6,000 loss.

Exhibit 23.8

Financial Statements

GENESIS Income Statement For Year Ended December 31, 2010		
Sales		$590,000
Cost of goods sold	$300,000	
Wages and other operating expenses	216,000	
Interest expense	7,000	
Depreciation expense	24,000	(547,000)
		43,000
Other gains (losses)		
Gain on retirement of bonds	16,000	
Loss on sale of plant assets	(6,000)	10,000
Income before taxes		53,000
Income taxes expense		(15,000)
Net income		$ 38,000

GENESIS Balance Sheets December 31, 2010 and 2009		
	2010	2009
Assets		
Current assets		
Cash	$ 17,000	$ 12,000
Accounts receivable	60,000	40,000
Merchandise inventory	84,000	70,000
Prepaid expenses	6,000	4,000
Total current assets	167,000	126,000
Long-term assets		
Plant assets	250,000	210,000
Accumulated depreciation	(60,000)	(48,000)
Total assets	$357,000	$288,000
Liabilities		
Current liabilities		
Accounts payable	$ 35,000	$ 40,000
Interest payable	3,000	4,000
Income taxes payable	22,000	12,000
Total current liabilities	60,000	56,000
Long-term bonds payable	90,000	64,000
Total liabilities	150,000	120,000
Equity		
Common stock, $5 par	95,000	80,000
Retained earnings	112,000	88,000
Total equity	207,000	168,000
Total liabilities and equity	$357,000	$288,000

d. Received cash of $15,000 from issuing 3,000 shares of common stock.

e. Paid $18,000 cash to retire bonds with a $34,000 book value, yielding a $16,000 gain.

f. Declared and paid cash dividends of $14,000.

> *The next section describes the indirect method. Appendix 23A describes the direct method. An instructor can choose to cover either one or both methods. Neither section depends on the other.*

Application of the Indirect Method of Reporting

LO5 Compute cash flows from operating activities using the indirect method.

Net income is computed using accrual accounting, which recognizes revenues when earned and expenses when incurred. Revenues and expenses do not necessarily reflect the receipt and payment of cash. The indirect method of computing and reporting net cash flows from operating activities involves adjusting the net income figure to obtain the net cash provided (used) by operating activities. This includes subtracting noncash increases (credits) from net income and adding noncash charges (debits) back to net income.

> *Noncash credits refer to revenue amounts reported on the income statement that are not collected in cash this period. Noncash charges refer to expense amounts reported on the income statement that are not paid this period.*

To illustrate, the indirect method begins with Genesis's net income of $38,000 and adjusts it to obtain net cash provided (used) by operating activities of $20,000. Exhibit 23.9 shows the results of the indirect method of reporting operating cash flows, which adjusts net income for three types of adjustments. There are adjustments ① to reflect changes in noncash current assets and current liabilities related to operating activities, ② to exclude income statement items involving operating activities that do not affect cash inflows or outflows, and ③ to eliminate gains and losses resulting

GENESIS Statement of Cash Flows For Year Ended December 31, 2010		
Cash flows from operating activities		
Net income	$38,000	
Adjustments to reconcile net income to net cash provided by operating activities		
Increase in accounts receivable	(20,000)	
Increase in merchandise inventory	(14,000)	
Increase in prepaid expenses	(2,000)	
Decrease in accounts payable	(5,000)	
Decrease in interest payable	(1,000)	
Increase in income taxes payable	10,000	
Depreciation expense	24,000	
Loss on sale of plant assets	6,000	
Gain on retirement of bonds	(16,000)	
Net cash provided by operating activities		$20,000
Cash flows from investing activities		
Cash received from sale of plant assets	12,000	
Cash paid for purchase of plant assets	(10,000)	
Net cash provided by investing activities		2,000
Cash flows from financing activities		
Cash received from issuing stock	15,000	
Cash paid to retire bonds	(18,000)	
Cash paid for dividends	(14,000)	
Net cash used in financing activities		(17,000)
Net increase in cash		$ 5,000
Cash balance at prior year-end		12,000
Cash balance at current year-end		$17,000

Exhibit 23.9

Statement of Cash Flows—
Indirect Method

① Adjustments for changes in current
assets and current liabilities.

} ② Adjustments for operating items
not providing or using cash

③ Adjustments for nonoperating items

Refer to Exhibit 23.8 and identify
the $5,000 change in cash. This
change is what the statement of
cash flows explains; it serves as a
check figure.

from investing and financing activities (not part of operating activities). This section describes each of these adjustments.

① Adjustments for Changes in Current Assets and Current Liabilities This section describes adjustments for changes in noncash current assets and current liabilities.

Adjustments for changes in noncash current assets.   Changes in noncash current assets are normally the result of operating activities. Examples are sales affecting accounts receivable and asset usage affecting prepaid rent. Decreases in noncash current assets yield the following adjustment:

Decreases in noncash current assets are added to net income.

To see the logic for this adjustment, consider that a decrease in a noncash current asset such as accounts receivable suggests more available cash at the end of the period compared to the beginning. This is so because a decrease in accounts receivable implies higher cash receipts than reflected in sales. We add these higher cash receipts (from decreases in noncash current assets) to net income when computing cash flow from operations.

In contrast, an increase in noncash current assets such as accounts receivable implies less cash receipts than reflected in sales. As another example, an increase in prepaid rent indicates that more cash is paid for rent than is deducted as rent expense. Increases in noncash current assets yield the following adjustment:

Increases in noncash current assets are subtracted from net income.

To illustrate, these adjustments are applied to the noncash current assets in Exhibit 23.8.

   Accounts receivable. Accounts Receivable *increase* $20,000, from a beginning balance of $40,000 to an ending balance of $60,000. This increase implies that Genesis collects less cash

Operating activities are typically those
that determine income, which are
often reflected in changes in current
assets and current liabilities.

than is reported in sales. That is, some of these sales were in the form of accounts receivable and that amount increased during the period. To see this it is helpful to use *account analysis*. This usually involves setting up a T-account and reconstructing its major entries to compute cash receipts or payments. The following reconstructed Accounts Receivable T-account reveals the lower amount of cash receipts compared to sales:

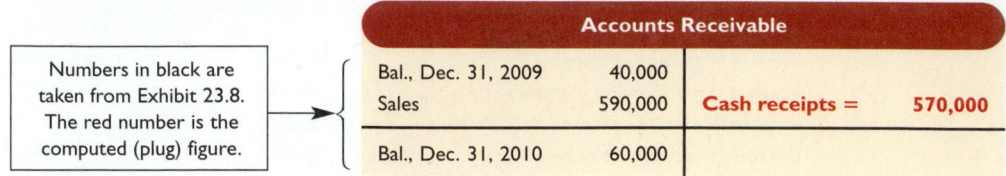

		Accounts Receivable		
Bal., Dec. 31, 2009	40,000			
Sales	590,000	**Cash receipts =**		**570,000**
Bal., Dec. 31, 2010	60,000			

Numbers in black are taken from Exhibit 23.8. The red number is the computed (plug) figure.

Notice that sales are $20,000 greater than the cash receipts. This $20,000—as reflected in the $20,000 increase in Accounts Receivable—is subtracted from net income when computing cash provided by operating activities (see Exhibit 23.9).

Merchandise inventory. Merchandise inventory *increases* by $14,000, from a $70,000 beginning balance to an $84,000 ending balance. This increase implies that Genesis had a larger amount of cash purchases than cost of goods sold. This larger amount of cash purchases is in the form of inventory, as reflected in the following account analysis:

		Merchandise Inventory	
Bal., Dec. 31, 2009	70,000		
Purchases =	**314,000**	Cost of goods sold	300,000
Bal., Dec. 31, 2010	84,000		

The amount by which purchases exceed cost of goods sold—as reflected in the $14,000 increase in inventory—is subtracted from net income when computing cash provided by operating activities (see Exhibit 23.9).

Prepaid expenses. Prepaid expenses *increase* $2,000, from a $4,000 beginning balance to a $6,000 ending balance, implying that Genesis's cash payments for operating expenses exceed its recorded expenses. These higher cash payments increase the amount of Prepaid Expenses, as reflected in its reconstructed T-account:

		Prepaid Expenses	
Bal., Dec. 31, 2009	4,000		
Cash payments =	**218,000**	Wages and other operating exp.	216,000
Bal., Dec. 31, 2010	6,000		

The amount by which cash payments exceed the recorded operating expenses—as reflected in the $2,000 increase in Prepaid Expenses—is subtracted from net income when computing cash provided by operating activities (see Exhibit 23.9).

Adjustments for changes in current liabilities.   Changes in current liabilities are normally the result of operating activities. An example is a purchase that affects accounts payable. Increases in current liabilities yield the following adjustment to net income when computing operating cash flows:

Increases in current liabilities are added to net income.

To see the logic for this adjustment, consider that an increase in the Accounts Payable account suggests that cash payments are less than the related (cost of goods sold) expense. As another example, an increase in wages payable implies that cash paid for wages is less than the recorded wages expense. Since the recorded expense is greater than the cash paid, we add the increase in wages payable to net income to compute net cash flow from operations.

Conversely, when current liabilities decrease, the following adjustment is required:

Decreases in current liabilities are subtracted from net income.

To illustrate, this adjustment is applied to the current liabilities in Exhibit 23.8.

Accounts payable. Accounts Payable *decrease* $5,000, from a beginning balance of $40,000 to an ending balance of $35,000. This decrease implies that cash payments to suppliers exceed purchases by $5,000 for the period, which is reflected in the reconstructed Accounts Payable T-account:

Accounts Payable			
		Bal., Dec. 31, 2009	40,000
Cash payments =	**319,000**	Purchases	314,000
		Bal., Dec. 31, 2010	35,000

The amount by which cash payments exceed purchases—as reflected in the $5,000 decrease in Accounts Payable—is subtracted from net income when computing cash provided by operating activities (see Exhibit 23.9).

Interest payable. Interest Payable *decreases* $1,000, from a $4,000 beginning balance to a $3,000 ending balance. This decrease indicates that cash paid for interest exceeds interest expense by $1,000, which is reflected in the Interest Payable T-account:

Interest Payable			
		Bal., Dec. 31, 2009	4,000
Cash paid for interest =	**8,000**	Interest expense	7,000
		Bal., Dec. 31, 2010	3,000

The amount by which cash paid exceeds recorded expense—as reflected in the $1,000 decrease in Interest Payable—is subtracted from net income (see Exhibit 23.9).

Income taxes payable. Income Taxes Payable *increase* $10,000, from a $12,000 beginning balance to a $22,000 ending balance. This increase implies that reported income taxes exceed the cash paid for taxes, which is reflected in the Income Taxes Payable T-account:

Income Taxes Payable			
		Bal., Dec. 31, 2009	12,000
Cash paid for taxes =	**5,000**	Income taxes expense	15,000
		Bal., Dec. 31, 2010	22,000

The amount by which cash paid falls short of the reported taxes expense—as reflected in the $10,000 increase in Income Taxes Payable—is added to net income when computing cash provided by operating activities (see Exhibit 23.9).

② **Adjustments for Operating Items Not Providing or Using Cash**   The income statement usually includes some expenses that do not reflect cash outflows in the period. Examples are depreciation, amortization, depletion, and bad debts expense. The indirect method for reporting operating cash flows requires that

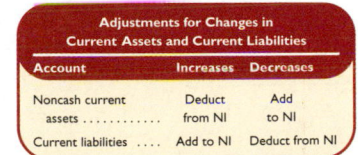

Expenses with no cash outflows are added back to net income.

To see the logic of this adjustment, recall that items such as depreciation, amortization, depletion, and bad debts originate from debits to expense accounts and credits to noncash accounts. These entries have *no* cash effect, and we add them back to net income when computing net cash flows from operations. Adding them back cancels their deductions.

Similarly, when net income includes revenues that do not reflect cash inflows in the period, the indirect method for reporting operating cash flows requires that

Revenues with no cash inflows are subtracted from net income.

We apply these adjustments to the Genesis operating items that do not provide or use cash.

Depreciation.   Depreciation expense is the only Genesis operating item that has no effect on cash flows in the period. We must add back the $24,000 depreciation expense to net income when computing cash provided by operating activities. (Remember that the cash outflow to acquire a plant asset is reported as an investing activity.)

③ **Adjustments for Nonoperating Items**   Net income often includes losses that are not part of operating activities but are part of either investing or financing activities. Examples are a loss from the sale of a plant asset and a loss from retirement of a bond payable. The indirect method for reporting operating cash flows requires that

Nonoperating losses are added back to net income.

To see the logic, consider that items such as a plant asset sale and a bond retirement are normally recorded by recognizing the cash, removing all plant asset or bond accounts, and recognizing any loss or gain. The cash received or paid is not part of operating activities but is part of either investing or financing activities. *No* operating cash flow effect occurs. However, because the nonoperating loss is a deduction in computing net income, we need to add it back to net income when computing cash flow from operations. Adding it back cancels the deduction.

Similarly, when net income includes gains not part of operating activities, the indirect method for reporting operating cash flows requires that

Nonoperating gains are subtracted from net income.

To illustrate these adjustments, we consider the nonoperating items of Genesis.

Loss on sale of plant assets.   Genesis reports a $6,000 loss on sale of plant assets as part of net income. This loss is a proper deduction in computing income, but it is *not part of operating activities*. Instead, a sale of plant assets is part of investing activities. Thus, the $6,000 nonoperating loss is added back to net income (see Exhibit 23.9). Adding it back cancels the loss. We later explain how to report the cash inflow from the asset sale in investing activities.

Gain on retirement of debt.   A $16,000 gain on retirement of debt is properly included in net income, but it is *not part of operating activities*. This means the $16,000 nonoperating gain must be subtracted from net income to obtain net cash provided by operating activities (see Exhibit 23.9). Subtracting it cancels the recorded gain. We later describe how to report the cash outflow to retire debt.

IN THE NEWS

Cash or Income   The difference between net income and operating cash flows can be large and reflects on the quality of earnings. This bar chart shows net income and operating cash flows of four companies. Operating cash flows can be either higher or lower than net income.

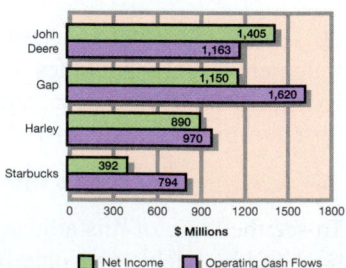

Summary of Adjustments for Indirect Method

Exhibit 23.10 summarizes the most common adjustments to net income when computing net cash provided (used) by operating activities under the indirect method.

Net Income

+ Decrease in noncash current asset
− Increase in noncash current asset
+ Increase in current liability*
− Decrease in current liability*

⎫ ① Adjustments for changes in current assets and current liabilities

+ Depreciation, depletion, and amortization

⎫ ② Adjustments for operating items not providing or using cash

+ Loss on disposal of long-term asset
+ Loss on retirement of debt
− Gain on disposal of long-term asset
− Gain on retirement of debt

⎫ ③ Adjustments for nonoperating items

Net cash provided (used) by operating activities

* Excludes current portion of long-term debt and any (nonsales-related) short-term notes payable—both are financing activities.

Exhibit 23.10

Summary of Common Adjustments for Indirect Method

The computations in determining cash provided (used) by operating activities are different for the indirect and direct methods, but the result is identical. Both methods yield the same $20,000 figure for cash from operating activities for Genesis; see Exhibits 23.6 and 23.9.

HOW YOU DOIN'?   Answers—p. 624

4. Determine net cash provided (used) by operating activities using the following data: net income, $74,900; decrease in accounts receivable, $4,600; increase in inventory, $11,700; decrease in accounts payable, $1,000; loss on sale of equipment, $3,400; payment of cash dividends, $21,500.

5. Why are expenses such as depreciation and amortization added to net income when cash flow from operating activities is computed by the indirect method?

6. A company reports net income of $15,000 that includes a $3,000 gain on the sale of plant assets. Why is this gain subtracted from net income in computing cash flow from operating activities using the indirect method?

Cash Flows from Investing

The third major step in preparing the statement of cash flows is to compute and report cash flows from investing activities. We normally do this by identifying changes in (1) all noncurrent asset accounts and (2) the current accounts for both notes receivable and investments in securities (excluding trading securities). We then analyze changes in these accounts to determine their effect, if any, on cash and report the cash flow effects in the investing activities section of the statement of cash flows. **Reporting of investing activities is identical under the indirect method and direct method.**

Three-Stage Process of Analysis

Information to compute cash flows from investing activities is usually taken from beginning and ending balance sheets and the income statement. We use a three-stage process to determine cash provided (used) by investing activities: (1) identify changes in investing-related accounts, (2) explain these changes using reconstruction analysis, and (3) report their cash flow effects.

Analysis of Noncurrent Assets

L06 Determine cash flows from both investing and financing activities.

Information about the Genesis transactions provided earlier reveals that the company both purchased and sold plant assets during the period. Both transactions are investing activities and are analyzed for their cash flow effects in this section.

> Investing activities include (1) purchasing and selling long-term assets, (2) lending and collecting on notes receivable, and (3) purchasing and selling short-term investments other than cash equivalents.

Plant Asset Transactions   The first stage in analyzing the Plant Assets account and its related Accumulated Depreciation is to identify any changes in these accounts from comparative balance sheets in Exhibit 23.8. This analysis reveals a $40,000 increase in plant assets from $210,000 to $250,000 and a $12,000 increase in accumulated depreciation from $48,000 to $60,000.

The second stage is to explain these changes. Items *b* and *c* of the additional information for Genesis (page 603) are relevant in this case. Recall that the Plant Assets account is affected by both asset purchases and sales, while its Accumulated Depreciation account is normally increased from depreciation and decreased from the removal of accumulated depreciation in asset sales. To explain changes in these accounts and to identify their cash flow effects, we prepare *reconstructed entries* from prior transactions; *they are not the actual entries by the preparer.*

To illustrate, item *b* reports that Genesis purchased plant assets of $70,000 by issuing $60,000 in bonds payable to the seller and paying $10,000 in cash. The reconstructed entry for analysis of item *b* follows:

Assets = Liabilities + Equity
+70,000   +60,000
−10,000

Reconstruction	Plant Assets	70,000	
	Bonds Payable		60,000
	Cash		**10,000**

This entry reveals a $10,000 cash outflow for plant assets and a $60,000 noncash investing and financing transaction involving bonds exchanged for plant assets.

Next, item *c* reports that Genesis sold plant assets costing $30,000 (with $12,000 of accumulated depreciation) for $12,000 cash, resulting in a $6,000 loss. The reconstructed entry for analysis of item *c* follows:

Assets = Liabilities + Equity
+12,000   −6,000
−30,000
+12,000

Reconstruction	**Cash**	**12,000**	
	Accumulated Depreciation	12,000	
	Loss on Sale of Plant Assets	6,000	
	Plant Assets		30,000

This entry reveals a $12,000 cash inflow from assets sold. The $6,000 loss is computed by comparing the asset book value (of $18,000) to the cash received and does not reflect any cash inflow or outflow. We also reconstruct the entry for Depreciation Expense using information from the income statement:

Assets = Liabilities + Equity
−24,000   −24,000

Reconstruction	Depreciation Expense	24,000	
	Accumulated Depreciation		24,000

This entry shows that Depreciation Expense results in no cash flow effect. These three reconstructed entries are reflected in the following plant asset and related T-accounts.

Plant Assets			
Bal., Dec. 31, 2009	210,000		
Purchase	**70,000**	**Sale**	**30,000**
Bal., Dec. 31, 2010	250,000		

Accumulated Depreciation—Plant Assets			
		Bal., Dec. 31, 2009	48,000
Sale	**12,000**	**Depr. expense**	**24,000**
		Bal., Dec. 31, 2010	60,000

This reconstruction analysis is complete in that the change in plant assets from $210,000 to $250,000 is fully explained by the $70,000 purchase and the $30,000 sale. Also, the change in accumulated depreciation from $48,000 to $60,000 is fully explained by depreciation expense of $24,000 and the removal of $12,000 in accumulated depreciation from an asset sale.

The third stage looks at the reconstructed entries for identification of cash flows. The two identified cash flow effects are reported in the investing section of the statement as follows (also see Exhibit 23.6 or 23.9):

Cash flows from investing activities	
Cash received from sale of plant assets	$12,000
Cash paid for purchase of plant assets	(10,000)

Also, the $60,000 portion of the purchase described in item *b* and financed by issuing bonds is a noncash investing and financing activity. It is reported in a note or in a separate schedule to the statement as follows:

Noncash investing and financing activity	
Purchased plant assets with issuance of bonds	$60,000

Analysis of Other Assets

Many other asset transactions (including those involving current notes receivable and investments in certain securities) are considered investing activities and can affect a company's cash flows. Since Genesis did not enter into other investing activities impacting assets, we do not need to extend our analysis to these other assets. If such transactions did exist, we would analyze them using the same three-stage process illustrated for plant assets.

HOW YOU DOIN'?   Answer—p. 624

7. Equipment costing $80,000 with accumulated depreciation of $30,000 is sold at a loss of $10,000. What is the cash receipt from this sale? In what section of the statement of cash flows is this transaction reported?

Cash Flows from Financing

The fourth major step in preparing the statement of cash flows is to compute and report cash flows from financing activities. We normally do this by identifying changes in all noncurrent liability accounts (including the current portion of any notes and bonds) and the equity accounts. These accounts include long-term debt, notes payable, bonds payable, common stock, and retained earnings. Changes in these accounts are then analyzed using available information to determine their effect, if any, on cash. Results are reported in the financing activities section of the statement. **Reporting of financing activities is identical under the direct method and indirect method.**

Three-Stage Process of Analysis

We again use a three-stage process to determine cash provided (used) by financing activities: (1) identify changes in financing-related accounts, (2) explain these changes using reconstruction analysis, and (3) report their cash flow effects.

Analysis of Noncurrent Liabilities

Information about Genesis provided earlier reveals two transactions involving noncurrent liabilities. We analyzed one of those, the $60,000 issuance of bonds payable to purchase plant assets. This transaction is reported as a significant noncash investing and financing activity in a note or a separate schedule to the statement of cash flows. The other remaining transaction involving noncurrent liabilities is the cash retirement of bonds payable.

> Financing activities generally refer to changes in the noncurrent liability and the equity accounts. Examples are (1) receiving cash from issuing debt or repaying amounts borrowed and (2) receiving cash from or distributing cash to owners.

Bonds Payable Transactions   The first stage in analysis of bonds is to review the comparative balance sheets from Exhibit 23.8. This analysis reveals an increase in bonds payable from $64,000 to $90,000.

The second stage explains this change. Item *e* of the additional information for Genesis (page 604) reports that bonds with a carrying value of $34,000 are retired for $18,000 cash, resulting in a $16,000 gain. These bonds were issued at their $18,000 par value. The reconstructed entry for analysis of item *e* follows:

Assets = Liabilities + Equity
−18,000   −34,000   +16,000

Reconstruction	Bonds Payable	34,000	
	Gain on retirement of debt...................		16,000
	Cash		**18,000**

This entry reveals an $18,000 cash outflow for retirement of bonds and a $16,000 gain from comparing the bonds payable carrying value to the cash received. This gain does not reflect any cash inflow or outflow. Also, item *b* of the additional information reports that Genesis purchased plant assets costing $70,000 by issuing $60,000 in bonds payable to the seller and paying $10,000 in cash. We reconstructed this entry when analyzing investing activities: It showed a $60,000 increase to bonds payable that is reported as a noncash investing and financing transaction. The Bonds Payable account reflects (and is fully explained by) these reconstructed entries as follows:

Bonds Payable			
		Bal., Dec. 31, 2009	64,000
Retired bonds	**34,000**	**Issued bonds**	**60,000**
		Bal., Dec. 31, 2010	90,000

The third stage is to report the cash flow effect of the bond retirement in the financing section of the statement as follows (also see Exhibit 23.6 or 23.9):

Cash flows from financing activities
Cash paid to retire bonds .... $(18,000)

Analysis of Equity

The Genesis information reveals two transactions involving equity accounts. The first is the issuance of common stock for cash. The second is the declaration and payment of cash dividends. We analyze both.

Common Stock Transactions   The first stage in analyzing common stock is to review the comparative balance sheets from Exhibit 23.8, which reveals an increase in common stock from $80,000 to $95,000.

The second stage explains this change. Item *d* of the additional information (page 604) reports that 3,000 shares of common stock are issued at par for $5 per share. The reconstructed entry for analysis of item *d* follows:

Assets = Liabilities + Equity
+15,000   +15,000

Reconstruction	**Cash**	**15,000**	
	Common Stock		15,000

This entry reveals a $15,000 cash inflow from stock issuance and is reflected in (and explains) the Common Stock account as follows:

Common Stock			
		Bal., Dec. 31, 2009	80,000
		Issued stock	**15,000**
		Bal., Dec. 31, 2010	95,000

The third stage discloses the cash flow effect from stock issuance in the financing section of the statement as follows (also see Exhibit 23.6 or 23.9):

Cash flows from financing activities	
Cash received from issuing stock	$15,000

Retained Earnings Transactions   The first stage in analyzing the Retained Earnings account is to review the comparative balance sheets from Exhibit 23.8. This reveals an increase in retained earnings from $88,000 to $112,000.

The second stage explains this change. Item *f* of the additional information (page 604) reports that cash dividends of $14,000 are paid. The reconstructed entry follows:

Reconstruction	Retained Earnings.............................	14,000		Assets = Liabilities + Equity
	Cash		**14,000**	−14,000 −14,000

This entry reveals a $14,000 cash outflow for cash dividends. Also note that the Retained Earnings account is impacted by net income of $38,000. (Net income was analyzed under the operating section of the statement of cash flows.) The reconstructed Retained Earnings account follows:

Retained Earnings			
		Bal., Dec. 31, 2009	88,000
Cash dividend	14,000	**Net income**	**38,000**
		Bal., Dec. 31, 2010	112,000

The third stage reports the cash flow effect from the cash dividend in the financing section of the statement as follows (also see Exhibit 23.6 or 23.9):

Cash flows from financing activities	
Cash paid for dividends	$(14,000)

> Financing activities not affecting cash flow include *declaration* of a cash dividend, *declaration* of a stock dividend, payment of a stock dividend, and a stock split.

We now have identified and explained all of the Genesis cash inflows and cash outflows and one noncash investing and financing transaction. Specifically, our analysis has reconciled changes in all noncash balance sheet accounts.

Proving Cash Balances

The fifth and final step in preparing the statement is to report the beginning and ending cash balances and prove that the *net change in cash* is explained by operating, investing, and financing cash flows. This step is shown here for Genesis.

> The following ratio helps assess whether operating cash flow is adequate to meet long-term obligations:
> **Cash coverage of debt** = Cash flow from operations divided by noncurrent liabilities.
> A low ratio suggests a higher risk of insolvency; a high ratio suggests a greater ability to meet long-term obligations.

Net cash provided by operating activities	$20,000
Net cash provided by investing activities	2,000
Net cash used in financing activities	(17,000)
Net increase in cash	**$ 5,000**
Cash balance at 2009 year-end	12,000
Cash balance at 2010 year-end	$17,000

The preceding table shows that the $5,000 net increase in cash, from $12,000 at the beginning of the period to $17,000 at the end, is reconciled by net cash flows from operating ($20,000 inflow), investing ($2,000 inflow), and financing ($17,000 outflow) activities. This is formally reported at the bottom of the statement of cash flows as shown in both Exhibits 23.6 and 23.9.

CASH FLOW ANALYSIS

Analyzing Cash Sources and Uses

LO7 Analyze the statement of cash flows.

Most managers stress the importance of understanding and predicting cash flows for business decisions. Creditors evaluate a company's ability to generate cash before deciding whether to lend money. Investors also assess cash inflows and outflows before buying and selling stock. Information in the statement of cash flows helps address these and other questions such as (1) How much cash is generated from or used in operations? (2) What expenditures are made with cash from operations? (3) What is the source of cash for debt payments? (4) What is the source of cash for distributions to owners? (5) How is the increase in investing activities financed? (6) What is the source of cash for new plant assets? (7) Why is cash flow from operations different from income? (8) How is cash from financing used?

To effectively answer these questions, it is important to separately analyze investing, financing, and operating activities. To illustrate, consider data from three different companies in Exhibit 23.11. These companies operate in the same industry and have been in business for several years.

Exhibit 23.11

Cash Flows of Competing Companies

($ thousands)	BMX	ATV	Trex
Cash provided (used) by operating activities	$90,000	$40,000	$(24,000)
Cash provided (used) by investing activities			
Proceeds from sale of plant assets			26,000
Purchase of plant assets	(48,000)	(25,000)	
Cash provided (used) by financing activities			
Proceeds from issuance of debt			13,000
Repayment of debt	(27,000)		
Net increase (decrease) in cash	$15,000	$15,000	$ 15,000

Each company generates an identical $15,000 net increase in cash, but its sources and uses of cash flows are very different. BMX's operating activities provide net cash flows of $90,000, allowing it to purchase plant assets of $48,000 and repay $27,000 of its debt. ATV's operating activities provide $40,000 of cash flows, limiting its purchase of plant assets to $25,000. Trex's $15,000 net cash increase is due to selling plant assets and incurring additional debt. Its operating activities yield a net cash outflow of $24,000. Overall, analysis of these cash flows reveals that BMX is more capable of generating future cash flows than is ATV or Trex.

Cash Flow on Total Assets

LO8 Compute and apply the cash flow on total assets ratio.

Cash flow information has limitations, but it can help measure a company's ability to meet its obligations, pay dividends, expand operations, and obtain financing. Users often compute and analyze a cash-based ratio similar to return on total assets except that its numerator is net cash flows from operating activities. The **cash flow on total assets** ratio is in Exhibit 23.12.

Exhibit 23.12

Cash Flow on Total Assets

$$\text{Cash flow on total assets} = \frac{\text{Cash flow from operations}}{\text{Average total assets}}$$

This ratio reflects actual cash flows and is not affected by accounting income recognition and measurement. It can help business decision makers estimate the amount and timing of cash flows when planning and analyzing operating activities.

To illustrate, the 2008 cash flow on total assets ratio for **Nike** is 15.6%—see Exhibit 23.13. Is a 15.6% ratio good or bad? To answer this question, we compare this ratio with the ratios of prior years (we could also compare its ratio with those of its competitors and the market). Nike's cash flow on total assets ratio for several prior years is in the second column of Exhibit 23.13. Results show that its 15.6% return is lower than each of the prior years' returns.

As an indicator of *earnings quality,* some analysts compare the cash flow on total assets ratio to the return on total assets ratio. Nike's return on total assets is provided in the third column of Exhibit 23.13. Nike's cash flow on total assets ratio exceeds its return on total assets in each of the five years, leading some analysts to infer that Nike's earnings quality is high for that period because more earnings are realized in the form of cash.

Year	Cash Flow on Total Assets	Return on Total Assets
2008	15.6%	15.1%
2007	17.6	14.0
2006	16.9	14.1
2005	17.9	13.8
2004	19.2	12.0

Exhibit 23.13

Nike's Cash Flow on Total Assets

Other Cash Flow Ratios

Analysts use various other cash-based ratios:

$$(1) \quad \text{Cash coverage of growth} = \frac{\text{Operating cash flow}}{\text{Cash outflow for plant assets}}$$

where a low ratio (less than 1) implies cash inadequacy to meet asset growth, whereas a high ratio implies cash adequacy for asset growth.

$$(2) \quad \text{Operating cash flow to sales} = \frac{\text{Operating cash flow}}{\text{Net sales}}$$

when this ratio substantially and consistently differs from the operating income to net sales ratio, the risk of accounting improprieties increases.

Demonstration Problem

Umlauf's comparative balance sheets, income statement, and additional information follow.

UMLAUF COMPANY
Balance Sheets
December 31, 2010 and 2009

	2010	2009
Assets		
Cash	$ 43,050	$ 23,925
Accounts receivable	34,125	39,825
Merchandise inventory	156,000	146,475
Prepaid expenses	3,600	1,650
Equipment	135,825	146,700
Accum. depreciation—		
Equipment	(61,950)	(47,550)
Total assets	$310,650	$311,025
Liabilities and Equity		
Accounts payable	$ 28,800	$ 33,750
Income taxes payable	5,100	4,425
Dividends payable	0	4,500
Bonds payable	0	37,500
Common stock, $10 par	168,750	168,750
Retained earnings	108,000	62,100
Total liabilities and equity	$310,650	$311,025

UMLAUF COMPANY
Income Statement
For Year Ended December 31, 2010

Sales		$446,100
Cost of goods sold	$222,300	
Other operating expenses	120,300	
Depreciation expense	25,500	(368,100)
		78,000
Other gains (losses)		
Loss on sale of equipment	(3,300)	
Loss on retirement of bonds	(825)	(4,125)
Income before taxes		73,875
Income taxes expense		(13,725)
Net income		$ 60,150

Additional Information

a. Equipment costing $21,375 with accumulated depreciation of $11,100 is sold for cash.

b. Equipment purchases are for cash.

c. Accumulated Depreciation is affected by depreciation expense and the sale of equipment.

d. The balance of Retained Earnings is affected by dividend declarations and net income.

e. All sales are made on credit.

f. All merchandise inventory purchases are on credit.

g. Accounts Payable balances result from merchandise inventory purchases.

h. Prepaid expenses relate to "other operating expenses."

Required

1. Prepare a statement of cash flows using the indirect method for year 2010.

2.^A Prepare a statement of cash flows using the direct method for year 2010.

Planning the Solution

- Prepare two blank statements of cash flows with sections for operating, investing, and financing activities using the (1) indirect method format and (2) direct method format.

- Compute the cash paid for equipment and the cash received from the sale of equipment using the additional information provided along with the amount for depreciation expense and the change in the balances of equipment and accumulated depreciation. Use T-accounts to help chart the effects of the sale and purchase of equipment on the balances of the Equipment account and the Accumulated Depreciation account.

- Compute the effect of net income on the change in the Retained Earnings account balance. Assign the difference between the change in retained earnings and the amount of net income to dividends declared. Adjust the dividends declared amount for the change in the Dividends Payable balance.

- Compute cash received from customers, cash paid for merchandise, cash paid for other operating expenses, and cash paid for taxes as illustrated in the chapter.

- Enter the cash effects of reconstruction entries to the appropriate section(s) of the statement.

- Total each section of the statement, determine the total net change in cash, and add it to the beginning balance to get the ending balance of cash.

Solution to Demonstration Problem

Supporting computations for cash receipts and cash payments.

(1)	*Cost of equipment sold	$ 21,375
	Accumulated depreciation of equipment sold	(11,100)
	Book value of equipment sold	10,275
	Loss on sale of equipment	(3,300)
	Cash received from sale of equipment	**$ 6,975**
	Cost of equipment sold	$ 21,375
	Less decrease in the equipment account balance	(10,875)
	Cash paid for new equipment	**$ 10,500**
(2)	Loss on retirement of bonds	$ 825
	Carrying value of bonds retired	37,500
	Cash paid to retire bonds	**$ 38,325**
(3)	Net income	$ 60,150
	Less increase in retained earnings	45,900
	Dividends declared	14,250
	Plus decrease in dividends payable	4,500
	Cash paid for dividends	**$ 18,750**
(4)^A	Sales	$ 446,100
	Add decrease in accounts receivable	5,700
	Cash received from customers	**$451,800**

[continued on next page]

[continued from previous page]

(5)ᴬ Cost of goods sold	....	$ 222,300
	Plus increase in merchandise inventory	9,525
	Purchases	231,825
	Plus decrease in accounts payable	4,950
	Cash paid for merchandise	$236,775
(6)ᴬ Other operating expenses	....	$ 120,300
	Plus increase in prepaid expenses	1,950
	Cash paid for other operating expenses	$122,250
(7)ᴬ Income taxes expense	....	$ 13,725
	Less increase in income taxes payable	(675)
	Cash paid for income taxes	$ 13,050

* Supporting T-account analysis for cash paid for new equipment follows:

Equipment			
Bal., Dec. 31, 2009	146,700		
Cash purchase	10,500	Sale	21,375
Bal., Dec. 31, 2010	135,825		

Accumulated Depreciation—Equipment			
		Bal., Dec. 31, 2009	47,550
Sale	11,100	Depr. expense	25,500
		Bal., Dec. 31, 2010	61,950

UMLAUF COMPANY
Statement of Cash Flows (Indirect Method)
For Year Ended December 31, 2010

Cash flows from operating activities		
Net income	$60,150	
Adjustments to reconcile net income to net cash provided by operating activities		
Decrease in accounts receivable	5,700	
Increase in merchandise inventory	(9,525)	
Increase in prepaid expenses	(1,950)	
Decrease in accounts payable	(4,950)	
Increase in income taxes payable	675	
Depreciation expense	25,500	
Loss on sale of plant assets	3,300	
Loss on retirement of bonds	825	
Net cash provided by operating activities		$79,725
Cash flows from investing activities		
Cash received from sale of equipment	6,975	
Cash paid for equipment	(10,500)	
Net cash used in investing activities		(3,525)
Cash flows from financing activities		
Cash paid to retire bonds payable	(38,325)	
Cash paid for dividends	(18,750)	
Net cash used in financing activities		(57,075)
Net increase in cash		$19,125
Cash balance at prior year-end		23,925
Cash balance at current year-end		$43,050

UMLAUF COMPANY Statement of Cash Flows (Direct Method) For Year Ended December 31, 2010		
Cash flows from operating activities		
Cash received from customers	$451,800	
Cash paid for merchandise	(236,775)	
Cash paid for other operating expenses	(122,250)	
Cash paid for income taxes	(13,050)	
Net cash provided by operating activities		$79,725
Cash flows from investing activities		
Cash received from sale of equipment	6,975	
Cash paid for equipment	(10,500)	
Net cash used in investing activities		(3,525)
Cash flows from financing activities		
Cash paid to retire bonds payable	(38,325)	
Cash paid for dividends	(18,750)	
Net cash used in financing activities		(57,075)
Net increase in cash		$19,125
Cash balance at prior year-end		23,925
Cash balance at current year-end		$43,050

23A Direct Method of Reporting Operating Cash Flows

LO9 Compute cash flows from operating activities using the direct method.

We compute cash flows from operating activities under the direct method by adjusting accrual-based income statement items to the cash basis. The usual approach is to adjust income statement accounts related to operating activities for changes in their related balance sheet accounts as follows:

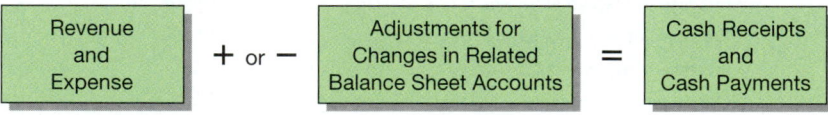

The framework for reporting cash receipts and cash payments for the operating section of the cash flow statement under the direct method is as in Exhibit 23A.1. We consider cash receipts first and then cash payments.

Operating Cash Receipts

A review of Exhibit 23.8 and the additional information reported by Genesis suggests only one potential cash receipt: sales to customers. This section, therefore, starts with sales to customers as reported on the income statement and then adjusts it as necessary to obtain cash received from customers to report on the statement of cash flows.

Cash Received from Customers
If all sales are for cash, the amount received from customers equals the sales reported on the income statement. When some or all sales are on account, however, we must adjust the amount of sales for the change in Accounts Receivable. It is often helpful to use *account analysis* to do this. This usually involves setting up a T-account and reconstructing its major entries, with emphasis on cash receipts and payments. To illustrate, we use a T-account that includes accounts

An accounts receivable increase implies cash received from customers is less than sales (the converse is also true).

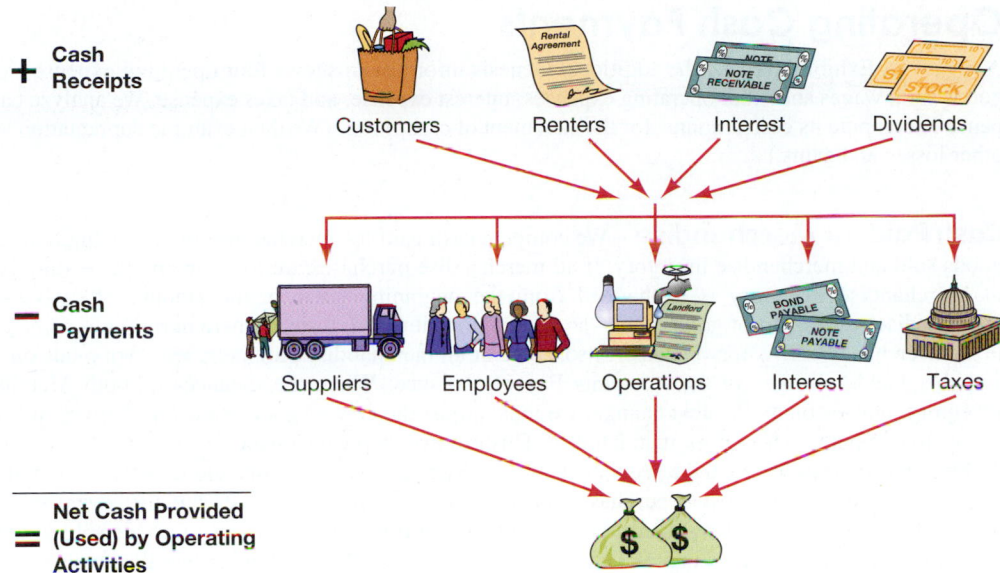

Exhibit 23A.1

Major Classes of Operating
Cash Flows

receivable balances for Genesis on December 31, 2009 and 2010. The beginning balance is $40,000 and the ending balance is $60,000. Next, the income statement shows sales of $590,000, which we enter on the debit side of this account. We now can reconstruct the Accounts Receivable account to determine the amount of cash received from customers as follows:

Accounts Receivable			
Bal., Dec. 31, 2009	40,000		
Sales	590,000	**Cash receipts =**	**570,000**
Bal., Dec. 31, 2010	60,000		

This T-account shows that the Accounts Receivable balance begins at $40,000 and increases to $630,000 from sales of $590,000, yet its ending balance is only $60,000. This implies that cash receipts from customers are $570,000, computed as $40,000 + $590,000 − [?] = $60,000. This computation can be rearranged to express cash received as equal to sales of $590,000 minus a $20,000 increase in accounts receivable. This computation is summarized as a general rule in Exhibit 23A.2. The statement of cash flows in Exhibit 23.6 reports the $570,000 cash received from customers as a cash inflow from operating activities.

> If the ending balance of accounts receivable is $20,000 (instead of $60,000), what is cash received from customers?
> *Answer:* $610,000

		+ Decrease in accounts receivable
Cash received from customers = Sales	—	or
		− Increase in accounts receivable

Exhibit 23A.2

Formula to Compute Cash
Received from Customers—
Direct Method

Other Cash Receipts   While Genesis's cash receipts are limited to collections from customers, we often see other types of cash receipts, most commonly cash receipts involving rent, interest, and dividends. We compute cash received from these items by subtracting an increase in their respective receivable or adding a decrease. For instance, if rent receivable increases in the period, cash received from renters is less than rent revenue reported on the income statement. If rent receivable decreases, cash received is more than reported rent revenue. The same logic applies to interest and dividends. The formulas for these computations are summarized later in this appendix.

> Net income and cash flows from operations are different. Net income is measured using accrual accounting. Cash flows from operations are measured using cash basis accounting.

Operating Cash Payments

A review of Exhibit 23.8 and the additional Genesis information shows four operating expenses: cost of goods sold; wages and other operating expenses; interest expense; and taxes expense. We analyze each expense to compute its cash amounts for the statement of cash flows. (We then examine depreciation and the other losses and gains.)

Cash Paid for Merchandise

We compute cash paid for merchandise by analyzing both cost of goods sold and merchandise inventory. If all merchandise purchases are for cash and the ending balance of Merchandise Inventory is unchanged from the beginning balance, the amount of cash paid for merchandise equals cost of goods sold—an uncommon situation. Instead, there normally is some change in the Merchandise Inventory balance. Also, some or all merchandise purchases are often made on credit, and this yields changes in the Accounts Payable balance. When the balances of both Merchandise Inventory and Accounts Payable change, we must adjust the cost of goods sold for changes in both accounts to compute cash paid for merchandise. This is a two-step adjustment.

First, we use the change in the account balance of Merchandise Inventory, along with the cost of goods sold amount, to compute cost of purchases for the period. An increase in merchandise inventory implies that we bought more than we sold, and we add this inventory increase to cost of goods sold to compute cost of purchases. A decrease in merchandise inventory implies that we bought less than we sold, and we subtract the inventory decrease from cost of goods sold to compute purchases. We illustrate the *first step* by reconstructing the Merchandise Inventory account of Genesis:

Merchandise Inventory			
Bal., Dec. 31, 2009	70,000		
Purchases =	**314,000**	Cost of goods sold	300,000
Bal., Dec. 31, 2010	84,000		

The beginning balance is $70,000, and the ending balance is $84,000. The income statement shows that cost of goods sold is $300,000, which we enter on the credit side of this account. With this information, we determine the amount for cost of purchases to be $314,000. This computation can be rearranged to express cost of purchases as equal to cost of goods sold of $300,000 plus the $14,000 increase in inventory.

The second step uses the change in the balance of Accounts Payable, and the amount of cost of purchases, to compute cash paid for merchandise. A decrease in accounts payable implies that we paid for more goods than we acquired this period, and we would then add the accounts payable decrease to cost of purchases to compute cash paid for merchandise. An increase in accounts payable implies that we paid for less than the amount of goods acquired, and we would subtract the accounts payable increase from purchases to compute cash paid for merchandise. The *second step* is applied to Genesis by reconstructing its Accounts Payable account:

Accounts Payable			
		Bal., Dec. 31, 2009	40,000
Cash payments =	**319,000**	Purchases	314,000
		Bal., Dec. 31, 2010	35,000

Its beginning balance of $40,000 plus purchases of $314,000 minus an ending balance of $35,000 yields cash paid of $319,000 (or $40,000 + $314,000 − [?] = $35,000). Alternatively, we can express cash paid for merchandise as equal to purchases of $314,000 plus the $5,000 decrease in accounts payable. The $319,000 cash paid for merchandise is reported on the statement of cash flows in Exhibit 23.6 as a cash outflow under operating activities.

We summarize this two-step adjustment to cost of goods sold to compute cash paid for merchandise inventory in Exhibit 23A.3.

If the ending balances of Inventory and Accounts Payable are $60,000 and $50,000, respectively (instead of $84,000 and $35,000), what is cash paid for merchandise?
Answer: $280,000

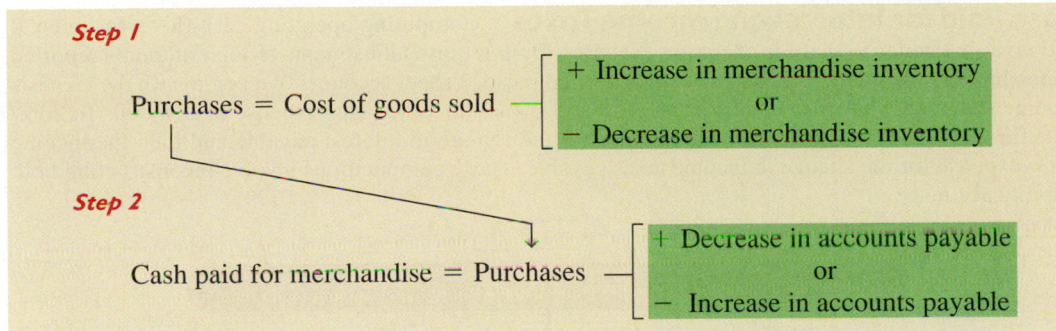

Cash Paid for Wages and Operating Expenses (excluding depreciation)   The

income statement of Genesis shows wages and other operating expenses of $216,000 (see Exhibit 23.8).
To compute cash paid for wages and other operating expenses, we adjust this amount for any changes in
their related balance sheet accounts. We begin by looking for any prepaid expenses and accrued liabilities
related to wages and other operating expenses in the balance sheets of Genesis in Exhibit 23.8. The balance sheets show prepaid expenses but no accrued liabilities. Thus, the adjustment is limited to the change
in prepaid expenses. The amount of adjustment is computed by assuming that all cash paid for wages and
other operating expenses is initially debited to Prepaid Expenses. This assumption allows us to reconstruct
the Prepaid Expenses account:

Prepaid Expenses			
Bal., Dec. 31, 2009	4,000		
Cash payments =	**218,000**	Wages and other operating exp.	216,000
Bal., Dec. 31, 2010	6,000		

Prepaid Expenses increase by $2,000 in the period, meaning that cash paid for wages and other operating
expenses exceeds the reported expense by $2,000. Alternatively, we can express cash paid for wages and
other operating expenses as equal to its reported expenses of $216,000 plus the $2,000 increase in prepaid
expenses.[1]

Exhibit 23A.4 summarizes the adjustments to wages (including salaries) and other operating expenses.
The Genesis balance sheet did not report accrued liabilities, but we include them in the formula to explain
the adjustment to cash when they do exist. A decrease in accrued liabilities implies that we paid cash for
more goods or services than received this period, so we add the decrease in accrued liabilities to the expense amount to obtain cash paid for these goods or services. An increase in accrued liabilities implies that
we paid cash for less than what was acquired, so we subtract this increase in accrued liabilities from the
expense amount to get cash paid.

> A decrease in prepaid expenses
> implies that reported expenses
> include an amount(s) that did
> not require a cash outflow in
> the period.

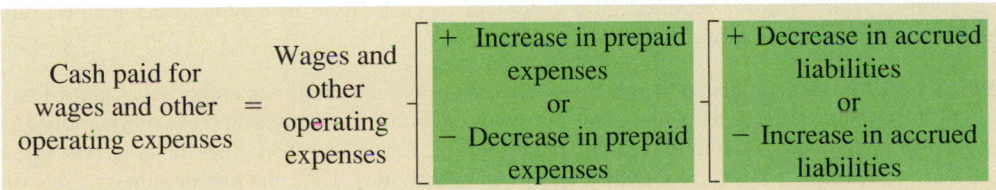

[1] The assumption that all cash payments for wages and operating expenses are initially debited to Prepaid
Expenses is not necessary for our analysis to hold. If cash payments are debited directly to the expense account,
the total amount of cash paid for wages and other operating expenses still equals the $216,000 expense plus the
$2,000 increase in Prepaid Expenses (which arise from end-of-period adjusting entries).

Cash Paid for Interest and Income Taxes   Computing operating cash flows for interest and taxes is similar to that for operating expenses. Both require adjustments to their amounts reported on the income statement for changes in their related balance sheet accounts. We begin with the Genesis income statement showing interest expense of $7,000 and income taxes expense of $15,000. To compute the cash paid, we adjust interest expense for the change in interest payable and then the income taxes expense for the change in income taxes payable. These computations involve reconstructing both liability accounts:

Interest Payable		
	Bal., Dec. 31, 2009	4,000
Cash paid for interest = 8,000	Interest expense	7,000
	Bal., Dec. 31, 2010	3,000

Income Taxes Payable		
	Bal., Dec. 31, 2009	12,000
Cash paid for taxes = 5,000	Income taxes expense	15,000
	Bal., Dec. 31, 2010	22,000

These accounts reveal cash paid for interest of $8,000 and cash paid for income taxes of $5,000. The formulas to compute these amounts are in Exhibit 23A.5. Both of these cash payments are reported as operating cash outflows on the statement of cash flows in Exhibit 23.6.

Exhibit 23A.5

Formulas to Compute Cash Paid for Both Interest and Taxes—Direct Method

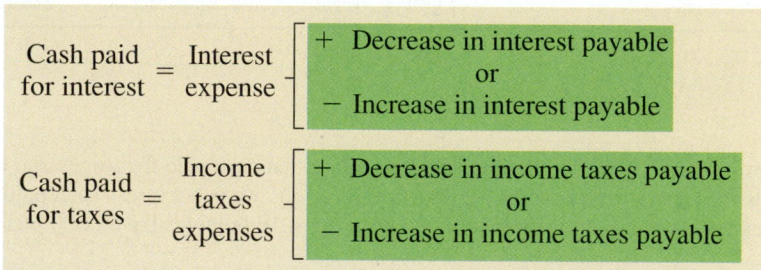

Analysis of Additional Expenses, Gains, and Losses   Genesis has three additional items reported on its income statement: depreciation, loss on sale of assets, and gain on retirement of debt. We must consider each for its potential cash effects.

Depreciation expense.   Depreciation expense is $24,000. It is often called a *noncash expense* because depreciation has no cash flows. Depreciation expense is an allocation of an asset's depreciable cost. The cash outflow with a plant asset is reported as part of investing activities when it is paid for. Thus, depreciation expense is *never* reported on a statement of cash flows using the direct method, nor is depletion or amortization expense.

Loss on sale of assets.   Sales of assets frequently result in gains and losses reported as part of net income, but the amount of recorded gain or loss does *not* reflect any cash flows in these transactions. Asset sales result in cash inflow equal to the cash amount received, regardless of whether the asset was sold at a gain or a loss. This cash inflow is reported under investing activities. Thus, the loss or gain on a sale of assets is *never* reported on a statement of cash flows using the direct method.

Gain on retirement of debt.   Retirement of debt usually yields a gain or loss reported as part of net income, but that gain or loss does *not* reflect cash flow in this transaction. Debt retirement results in cash outflow equal to the cash paid to settle the debt, regardless of whether the debt is retired at a gain or loss. This cash outflow is reported under financing activities; the loss or gain from retirement of debt is *never* reported on a statement of cash flows using the direct method.

The direct method is usually viewed as *user friendly* because less accounting knowledge is required to understand and use it.

Summary of Adjustments for Direct Method

Exhibit 23A.6 summarizes common adjustments for net income to yield net cash provided (used) by operating activities under the direct method.

Item	From Income Statement	Adjustments to Obtain Cash Flow Numbers	
Receipts			
From sales	Sales Revenue	+Decrease in Accounts Receivable / −Increase in Accounts Receivable	
From rent	Rent Revenue	+Decrease in Rent Receivable / −Increase in Rent Receivable	
From interest	Interest Revenue	+Decrease in Interest Receivable / −Increase in Interest Receivable	
From dividends	Dividend Revenue	+Decrease in Dividends Receivable / −Increase in Dividends Receivable	
Payments			
To suppliers	Cost of Goods Sold	+Increase in Inventory / −Decrease in Inventory	+Decrease in Accounts Payable / −Increase in Accounts Payable
For operations	Operating Expense	+Increase in Prepaids / −Decrease in Prepaids	+Decrease in Accrued Liabilities / −Increase in Accrued Liabilities
To employees	Wages (Salaries) Expense	+Decrease in Wages (Salaries) Payable / −Increase in Wages (Salaries) Payable	
For interest	Interest Expense	+Decrease in Interest Payable / −Increase in Interest Payable	
For taxes	Income Tax Expense	+Decrease in Income Tax Payable / −Increase in Income Tax Payable	

Exhibit 23A.6

Summary of Common Adjustments for Direct Method

Direct Method Format of Operating Activities Section

Exhibit 23.6 shows the Genesis statement of cash flows using the direct method. Major items of cash inflows and cash outflows are listed separately in the operating activities section. The format requires that operating cash outflows be subtracted from operating cash inflows to get net cash provided (used) by operating activities. The FASB recommends that the operating activities section of the statement of cash flows be reported using the direct method, which is considered more useful to financial statement users. *However, the FASB requires a reconciliation of net income to net cash provided (used) by operating activities when the direct method is used* (which can be reported in the notes). This reconciliation is similar to preparation of the operating activities section of the statement of cash flows using the indirect method.

Some preparers argue that it is easier to prepare a statement of cash flows using the indirect method. This likely explains its greater frequency in financial statements.

HOW YOU DOIN'?   Answers—p. 624

8. Net sales in a period are $590,000, beginning accounts receivable are $120,000, and ending accounts receivable are $90,000. What cash amount is collected from customers in the period?

9. The Merchandise Inventory account balance decreases in the period from a beginning balance of $32,000 to an ending balance of $28,000. Cost of goods sold for the period is $168,000. If the Accounts Payable balance increases $2,400 in the period, what is the cash amount paid for merchandise inventory?

10. Wages and other operating expenses total $112,000. Beginning-of-period prepaid expenses totaled $1,200, and its ending balance is $4,200. The end-of-period wages payable equal $5,600, whereas there were no accrued liabilities at period-end. How much cash is paid for wages and other operating expenses?

Summary

LO1 **Explain the purpose of cash flow information.** The main purpose of the statement of cash flows is to report the major cash receipts and cash payments for a period. This includes identifying cash flows as relating to either operating, investing, or financing activities. Most business decisions involve evaluating activities that provide or use cash.

LO2 **Distinguish between operating, investing, and financing activities.** Operating activities include transactions and events that determine net income. Investing activities include transactions and events that mainly affect long-term assets. Financing activities include transactions and events that mainly affect long-term liabilities and equity.

LO3 **Describe the format of the statement of cash flows.** The statement of cash flows separates cash receipts and payments into operating, investing, or financing activities.

LO4 **Prepare a statement of cash flows.** Preparation of a statement of cash flows involves five steps: (1) Compute the net increase or decrease in cash; (2) compute net cash provided (used) by operating activities (*using either the direct or indirect method*); (3) compute net cash provided (used) by investing activities; (4) compute net cash provided (used) by financing activities; and (5) report the beginning and ending cash balance and prove that it is explained by net cash flows. Noncash investing and financing activities are also disclosed.

LO5 **Compute cash flows from operating activities using the indirect method.** The indirect method for reporting net cash provided (used) by operating activities starts with net income and

then adjusts it for three items: (1) changes in noncash current assets and current liabilities related to operating activities, (2) revenues and expenses not providing (using) cash, and (3) gains and losses from investing and financing activities.

LO6 **Determine cash flows from both investing and financing activities.** Cash flows from both investing and financing activities are determined by identifying the cash flow effects of transactions and events affecting each balance sheet account related to these activities. All cash flows from these activities are identified when we can explain changes in these accounts from the beginning to the end of the period.

LO7 **Analyze the statement of cash flows.** To understand and predict cash flows, users stress identification of the sources and uses of cash flows by operating, investing, and financing activities. Emphasis is on operating cash flows since they derive from continuing operations.

LO8 **Compute and apply the cash flow on total assets ratio.** The cash flow on total assets ratio is defined as operating cash flows divided by average total assets. Analysis of current and past values for this ratio can reflect a company's ability to yield regular and positive cash flows. It is also viewed as a measure of earnings quality.

LO9[A] **Compute cash flows from operating activities using the direct method.** The direct method for reporting net cash provided (used) by operating activities lists major operating cash inflows less cash outflows to yield net cash inflow or outflow from operations.

Guidance Answers to   HOW YOU DOIN'?

1. No to both. The statement of cash flows reports changes in the sum of cash plus cash equivalents. It does not report transfers between cash and cash equivalents.

2. The three categories of cash inflows and outflows are operating activities, investing activities, and financing activities.

3. a. Investing   **c.** Financing   **e.** Operating
    b. Operating   **d.** Operating   **f.** Financing

4. $74,900 + $4,600 − $11,700 − $1,000 + $3,400 = $70,200

5. Expenses such as depreciation and amortization do not require current cash outflows. Therefore, adding these expenses back to net income eliminates these noncash items from the net income number, converting it to a cash basis.

6. A gain on the sale of plant assets is subtracted from net income because a sale of plant assets is not an operating activity; it is an investing activity for the amount of cash received from its sale. Also, such a gain yields no cash effects.

7. $80,000 − $30,000 − $10,000 = $40,000 cash receipt. The $40,000 cash receipt is reported as an investing activity.

8. $590,000 + ($120,000 − $90,000) = $620,000

9. $168,000 − ($32,000 − $28,000) − $2,400 = $161,600

10. $112,000 + ($4,200 − $1,200) − $5,600 = $109,400

Key Terms

Cash flow on total assets (p. 614) Ratio of operating cash flows to average total assets; not sensitive to income recognition and measurement; partly reflects earnings quality.

Direct method (p. 603) Presentation of net cash from operating activities for the statement of cash flows that lists major operating cash receipts less major operating cash payments.

Financing activities (p. 600) Transactions with owners and creditors that include obtaining cash from issuing debt, repaying amounts borrowed, and obtaining cash from or distributing cash to owners.

Indirect method (p. 603) Presentation that reports net income and then adjusts it by adding and subtracting items to yield net cash from operating activities on the statement of cash flows.

Investing activities (p. 599) Transactions that involve purchasing and selling of long-term assets, includes making and collecting notes receivable and investments in other than cash equivalents.

Operating activities (p. 599) Activities that involve the production or purchase of merchandise and the sale of goods or services

to customers, including expenditures related to administering the business.

Statement of cash flows (p. 598) A financial statement that lists cash inflows (receipts) and cash outflows (payments) during a period; arranged by operating, investing, and financing.

Multiple Choice Quiz   Answers on p. 639   mhhe.com/wildCA2e

Additional Multiple Choice Quizzes are available at the book's Website.

1. The statement of cash flows reports
   a. Assets, liabilities, and equity.
   b. Revenues, gains, expenses, and losses.
   c. Cash inflows and cash outflows for an accounting period.
   d. Equity, net income, and dividends.
   e. Changes in equity.

2. The appropriate section in the statement of cash flows for reporting the purchase of equipment for cash is
   a. Operating activities.
   b. Financing activities.
   c. Investing activities.
   d. None of these. This is not reported on the statement of cash flows.

3. The appropriate section in the statement of cash flows for reporting the cash payment of wages is
   a. Operating activities.
   b. Financing activities.
   c. Investing activities.
   d. None of these. This is not reported on the statement of cash flows.

4. A company had net cash flows from operations of $120,000, total cash flows of $500,000, and average total assets of $2,500,000. The cash flow on total assets ratio equals
   a. 4.8%.
   b. 5.0%.
   c. 20.0%.
   d. 20.8%.
   e. 24.0%.

5. A machine with a cost of $130,000 and accumulated depreciation of $85,000 is sold for $50,000 cash. The amount that should be reported as a source of cash under cash flows from investing activities is
   a. $50,000.
   b. $5,000.
   c. $45,000.
   d. Zero. This is an operating activity.
   e. Zero. This is a financing activity.

Superscript letter [A] *denotes assignments based on Appendix 23A*

Discussion Questions

1. What is the reporting purpose of the statement of cash flows? Identify at least two questions that this statement can answer.

2. Describe the direct method of reporting cash flows from operating activities.

3. When a statement of cash flows is prepared using the direct method, what are some of the operating cash flows?

4. Describe the indirect method of reporting cash flows from operating activities.

5. What are some investing activities reported on the statement of cash flows?

6. What are some financing activities reported on the statement of cash flows?

7. Where on the statement of cash flows is the payment of cash dividends reported?

8. Assume that a company purchases land for $100,000, paying $20,000 cash and borrowing the remainder with a long-term

note payable. How should this transaction be reported on a statement of cash flows?

9. On June 3, a company borrows $50,000 cash by giving its bank a 160-day, interest-bearing note. On the statement of cash flows, where should this be reported?

10. Is depreciation a source of cash flow?

11. Refer to **Best Buy**'s statement of cash flows in  Appendix A. (*a*) Which method is used to compute its net cash provided by operating activities? (*b*) While its balance sheet shows a decrease in receivables from fiscal years 2007 to 2008, why is this decrease in receivables added when computing net cash provided by operating activities for the year ended March 1, 2008?

12. Refer to **RadioShack**'s statement of ® **RadioShack**® cash flows in Appendix A. What are its cash flows from financing activities for the year ended December 31, 2007? List items and amounts.

QUICK STUDY

QS 23-1

Statement of cash flows

LO2   LO3

The statement of cash flows is one of the four primary financial statements.

1. Describe the content and layout of a statement of cash flows, including its three sections.

2. List at least three transactions classified as investing activities in a statement of cash flows.

3. List at least three transactions classified as financing activities in a statement of cash flows.

QS 23-2

Transaction classification by activity   **LO2**

Classify the following cash flows as operating, investing, or financing activities.

1. Sold long-term investments for cash.

2. Received cash payments from customers.

3. Paid cash for wages and salaries.

4. Purchased inventories for cash.

5. Paid cash dividends.

6. Issued common stock for cash.

7. Received cash interest on a note.

8. Paid cash interest on outstanding bonds.

9. Received cash from sale of land at a loss.

10. Paid cash for property taxes on building.

QS 23-3

Computing cash from operations (indirect)   **LO5**

Use the following information to determine this company's cash flows from operating activities using the indirect method.

KATAHN COMPANY Selected Balance Sheet Information December 31, 2010 and 2009		
	2010	**2009**
Current assets		
Cash	$84,650	$26,800
Accounts receivable	25,000	32,000
Inventory	60,000	54,100
Current liabilities		
Accounts payable	30,400	25,700
Income taxes payable	2,050	2,200

KATAHN COMPANY Income Statement For Year Ended December 31, 2010		
Sales		$515,000
Cost of goods sold		331,600
Gross profit		183,400
Operating expenses		
Depreciation expense	$ 36,000	
Other expenses	121,500	157,500
Income before taxes		25,900
Income taxes expense		7,700
Net income		$ 18,200

QS 23-4

Computing cash from asset sales

LO6

The following selected information is from Ellerby Company's comparative balance sheets.

At December 31	2010	2009
Furniture	$132,000	$ 184,500
Accumulated depreciation—Furniture	(88,700)	(110,700)

The income statement reports depreciation expense for the year of $18,000. Also, furniture costing $52,500 was sold for its book value. Compute the cash received from the sale of the furniture.

QS 23-5

Computing financing cash flows

LO6

The following selected information is from the Princeton Company's comparative balance sheets.

At December 31	2010	2009
Common stock, $10 par value	$105,000	$100,000
Paid-in capital in excess of par	567,000	342,000
Retained earnings	313,500	287,500

Princeton's net income for the year ended December 31, 2010, was $48,000.

1. Compute the cash received from the sale of its common stock during 2010.

2. Compute the cash paid for dividends during 2010.

Use the following balance sheets and income statement to answer QS 23-6 through QS 23-11.

Use the indirect method to prepare only the cash provided (used) from operating activities section of the statement of cash flows.

QS 23-6
Computing cash from operations (indirect) **LO5**

CRUZ, INC. Comparative Balance Sheets December 31, 2010		
	2010	**2009**
Assets		
Cash	$ 94,800	$ 24,000
Accounts receivable, net	41,000	51,000
Inventory	85,800	95,800
Prepaid expenses	5,400	4,200
Furniture	109,000	119,000
Accum. depreciation—Furniture	(17,000)	(9,000)
Total assets	$319,000	$285,000
Liabilities and Equity		
Accounts payable	$ 15,000	$ 21,000
Wages payable	9,000	5,000
Income taxes payable	1,400	2,600
Notes payable (long-term)	29,000	69,000
Common stock, $5 par value	229,000	179,000
Retained earnings	35,600	8,400
Total liabilities and equity	$319,000	$285,000

CRUZ, INC. Income Statement For Year Ended December 31, 2010		
Sales		$488,000
Cost of goods sold		314,000
Gross profit		174,000
Operating expenses		
Depreciation expense	$37,600	
Other expenses	89,100	126,700
Income before taxes		47,300
Income taxes expense		17,300
Net income		$ 30,000

Refer to the data in QS 23-6.
Furniture costing $55,000 is sold at its book value in 2010. Acquisitions of furniture total $45,000 cash, on which no depreciation is necessary because it is acquired at year-end. What is the cash inflow related to the sale of furniture?

QS 23-7
Computing cash from asset sales
LO6

Refer to the data in QS 23-6.
1. What amount of cash dividends is paid during 2010?
2. Assume that no additional notes payable are issued in 2010. What cash amount is paid to reduce the notes payable balance in 2010?

QS 23-8
Computing financing cash outflows **LO6**

Refer to the data in QS 23-6.
1. How much cash is received from sales to customers for year 2010?
2. What is the net increase or decrease in cash for year 2010?

QS 23-9^A
Computing cash received from customers **LO9**

Refer to the data in QS 23-6.
1. How much cash is paid to acquire merchandise inventory during year 2010?
2. How much cash is paid for operating expenses during year 2010?

QS 23-10^A
Computing operating cash outflows **LO9**

Refer to the data in QS 23-6.
Use the direct method to prepare the cash provided (used) from operating activities section of the statement of cash flows.

QS 23-11^A
Computing cash from operations (direct) **LO9**

QS 23-12

Analyses of sources
and uses of cash   **LO8**

Financial data from three competitors in the same industry follow.

1. Which of the three competitors is in the strongest position as shown by its statement of cash flows?

2. Analyze and discuss the strength of Peña's cash flow on total assets ratio to that of Garcia.

($ thousands)	Peña	Garcia	Piniella
Cash provided (used) by operating activities	$ 70,000	$ 60,000	$ (24,000)
Cash provided (used) by investing activities			
Proceeds from sale of operating assets			26,000
Purchase of operating assets	(28,000)	(34,000)	
Cash provided (used) by financing activities			
Proceeds from issuance of debt			23,000
Repayment of debt	(6,000)		
Net increase (decrease) in cash	$ 36,000	$ 26,000	$ 25,000
Average total assets	$ 790,000	$ 625,000	$ 300,000

QS 23-13

Computing cash flows from
operations (indirect)   **LO5**

For each of the following separate cases, compute cash flows from operations. The list includes all balance sheet accounts related to operating activities.

	Case A	Case B	Case C
Net income	$ 4,000	$100,000	$72,000
Depreciation expense	30,000	8,000	24,000
Accounts receivable increase (decrease)	40,000	20,000	(4,000)
Inventory increase (decrease)	(20,000)	(10,000)	10,000
Accounts payable increase (decrease)	24,000	(22,000)	14,000
Accrued liabilities increase (decrease)	(44,000)	12,000	(8,000)

QS 23-14

Computing cash flows from
investing   **LO6**

Compute cash flows from investing activities using the following information.

Sale of short-term investments	$ 6,000
Cash collections from customers	16,000
Purchase of used equipment	5,000
Depreciation expense	2,000

QS 23-15

Computing cash flows from
financing   **LO6**

Compute cash flows from financing activities using the following information.

Additional short-term borrowings	$20,000
Purchase of short-term investments	5,000
Cash dividends paid	16,000
Interest paid	8,000

connect

EXERCISES

Exercise 23-1

Cash flow from operations
(indirect)   **LO5**

Salud Company reports net income of $400,000 for the year ended December 31, 2010. It also reports $80,000 depreciation expense and a $20,000 gain on the sale of machinery. Its comparative balance sheets reveal a $40,000 increase in accounts receivable, $6,000 increase in accounts payable, $12,000 decrease in prepaid expenses, and $2,000 decrease in wages payable.

Required

Prepare only the operating activities section of the statement of cash flows for 2010 using the *indirect method.*

The following transactions and events occurred during the year. Assuming that this company uses the *indirect method* to report cash provided by operating activities, indicate where each item would appear on its statement of cash flows by placing an *x* in the appropriate column.

Exercise 23–2
Cash flow classification (indirect)
L05

	Operating Activities	Investing Activities	Financing Activities
a. Paid cash to purchase inventory.	___	___	___
b. Accounts receivable decreased in the year.	___	___	___
c. Sold equipment for cash, yielding a loss.	___	___	___
d. Recorded depreciation expense.	___	___	___
e. Income taxes payable increased in the year.	___	___	___
f. Declared and paid a cash dividend.	___	___	___
g. Accounts payable decreased in the year.	___	___	___
h. Paid cash to settle bond payable.	___	___	___
i. Prepaid expenses increased in the year.	___	___	___

The following transactions and events occurred during the year. Assuming that this company uses the *direct method* to report cash provided by operating activities, indicate where each item would appear on the statement of cash flows by placing an *x* in the appropriate column.

Exercise 23–3^A
Cash flow classification (direct)
L09

	Operating Activities	Investing Activities	Financing Activities	Not Reported on Statement or in Notes
a. Recorded depreciation expense.	___	___	___	___
b. Paid cash dividend that was declared in a prior period.	___	___	___	___
c. Sold inventory for cash.	___	___	___	___
d. Borrowed cash from bank by signing a 9-month note payable.	___	___	___	___
e. Paid cash to purchase a patent.	___	___	___	___
f. Paid cash toward accounts payable.	___	___	___	___
g. Collected cash from sales.	___	___	___	___
h. Paid cash to acquire treasury stock.	___	___	___	___

Olhstead Company's calendar-year 2010 income statement shows the following: Net Income, $374,000; Depreciation Expense, $44,000; Amortization Expense, $7,200; Gain on Sale of Plant Assets, $6,000. An examination of the company's current assets and current liabilities reveals the following changes (all from operating activities): Accounts Receivable decrease, $17,100; Merchandise Inventory decrease, $42,000; Prepaid Expenses increase, $4,700; Accounts Payable decrease, $8,200; Other Payables increase, $1,200. Use the *indirect method* to compute cash flow from operating activities.

Exercise 23–4
Cash flows from operating activities (indirect) **L05**

For each of the following three separate cases, use the information provided about the calendar-year 2010 operations of Alberto Company to compute the required cash flow information.

Exercise 23–5^A
Computation of cash flows (direct) **L09**

Case A: Compute cash received from customers:

Sales	$515,000
Accounts receivable, December 31, 2009	27,200
Accounts receivable, December 31, 2010	33,600

Case B: Compute cash paid for rent:

Rent expense	$139,800
Rent payable, December 31, 2009	7,800
Rent payable, December 31, 2010	6,200

Case C: Compute cash paid for merchandise:

Cost of goods sold	$525,000
Merchandise inventory, December 31, 2009	158,600
Accounts payable, December 31, 2009	66,700
Merchandise inventory, December 31, 2010	130,400
Accounts payable, December 31, 2010	82,000

Exercise 23–6

Cash flows from operating activities (indirect)   **LO5**

Use the following income statement and information about changes in noncash current assets and current liabilities to prepare the cash flows from operating activities section of the statement of cash flows using the *indirect* method.

ABBECK COMPANY		
Income Statement		
For Year Ended December 31, 2010		
Sales		$1,828,000
Cost of goods sold		991,000
Gross profit		837,000
Operating expenses		
Salaries expense	$245,535	
Depreciation expense	44,200	
Rent expense	49,600	
Amortization expenses—Patents	4,200	
Utilities expense	18,125	361,660
		475,340
Gain on sale of equipment		6,200
Net income		$ 481,540

Changes in current asset and current liability accounts for the year that relate to operations follow.

Accounts receivable	$30,500 increase	Accounts payable	$12,500 decrease
Merchandise inventory	25,000 increase	Salaries payable	3,500 decrease

---

Exercise 23–7ᴬ

Cash flows from operating activities (direct)   **LO9**

Refer to the information about Abbeck Company in Exercise 23-6.
Use the *direct method* to prepare the operating activities section of the statement of cash flows.

Exercise 23–8

Cash flows from investing activities   **LO6**

Use the following information to determine a company's cash flows from investing activities.

a. Equipment with a book value of $65,300 and an original cost of $133,000 was sold at a loss of $14,000.

b. Paid $89,000 cash for a new truck.

c. Sold land costing $154,000 for $198,000 cash, yielding a gain of $44,000.

d. Long-term investments in stock were sold for $60,800 cash, yielding a gain of $4,150.

Exercise 23–9

Cash flows from financing activities   **LO6**

Use the following information to determine a company's cash flows from financing activities.

a. Net income was $35,000.

b. Issued common stock for $64,000 cash.

c. Paid cash dividend of $14,600.

d. Paid $50,000 cash to settle a bond payable at its $50,000 maturity value.

e. Paid $12,000 cash to acquire its treasury stock.

f. Purchased equipment for $39,000 cash.

Arundel Company disclosed the following income statement and balance sheet information.

Exercise 23-10
Reporting and interpreting cash flows from operations (indirect)
L05 L08

Revenues	$100,000
Expenses	
Salaries expense	84,000
Utilities expense	14,000
Depreciation expense	14,600
Other expenses	3,400
Net loss	$(16,000)
Accounts receivable decrease	$ 24,000
Purchased a machine	10,000
Salaries payable increase	18,000
Other accrued liabilities decrease	8,000

Required

1. Prepare the operating activities section of the statement of cash flows for Arundel Company using the indirect method.

2. What were the major reasons that Arundel Company was able to report a net loss but positive cash flow from operations?

3. Of the potential causes of differences between cash flow from operations and net income, which are the most important to investors?

connect™

Forten Company, a merchandiser, recently completed its calendar-year 2010 operations. For the year, (1) all sales are credit sales, (2) all credits to Accounts Receivable reflect cash receipts from customers, (3) all purchases of inventory are on credit, (4) all debits to Accounts Payable reflect cash payments for inventory, and (5) Other Expenses are paid in advance and are initially debited to Prepaid Expenses. Forten's balance sheets and income statement follow:

PROBLEM SET A

Problem 23-1A
Statement of cash flows (indirect method)
L03 L04 L05 L06

FORTEN COMPANY
Comparative Balance Sheets
December 31, 2010 and 2009

	2010	2009
Assets		
Cash	$ 49,800	$ 73,500
Accounts receivable	65,810	50,625
Merchandise inventory	275,656	251,800
Prepaid expenses	1,250	1,875
Equipment	157,500	108,000
Accum. depreciation—Equipment	(36,625)	(46,000)
Total assets	$513,391	$439,800
Liabilities and Equity		
Accounts payable	$ 53,141	$114,675
Short-term notes payable	10,000	6,000
Long-term notes payable	65,000	48,750
Common stock, $5 par value	162,750	150,250
Paid-in capital in excess of par, common stock	37,500	0
Retained earnings	185,000	120,125
Total liabilities and equity	$513,391	$439,800

FORTEN COMPANY
Income Statement
For Year Ended December 31, 2010

Sales		$582,500
Cost of goods sold		285,000
Gross profit		297,500
Operating expenses		
Depreciation expense	$ 20,750	
Other expenses	132,400	153,150
Other gains (losses)		
Loss on sale of equipment		5,125
Income before taxes		139,225
Income taxes expense		24,250
Net income		$114,975

Additional Information on Year 2010 Transactions

a. The loss on the cash sale of equipment was $5,125 (details in *b*).

b. Sold equipment costing $46,875, with accumulated depreciation of $30,125, for $11,625 cash.

c. Purchased equipment costing $96,375 by paying $30,000 cash and signing a long-term note payable for the balance.

d. Borrowed $4,000 cash by signing a short-term note payable.

e. Paid $50,125 cash to reduce the long-term notes payable.

f. Issued 2,500 shares of common stock for $20 cash per share.

g. Declared and paid cash dividends of $50,100.

Check   Cash from operating activities, $40,900

Required

Prepare a complete statement of cash flows; report its operating activities using the *indirect method*.

Problem 23–2A[A]
Statement of cash flows (direct method)
LO3 LO4 LO6 LO9

Check   Cash used in financing activities, $(46,225)

Refer to Forten Company's financial statements and related information in Problem 23-1A.

Required

Prepare a complete statement of cash flows; report its operating activities according to the *direct method*.

Problem 23–3A
Statement of cash flows (indirect method)
LO3 LO4 LO5 LO6

mhhe.com/wildCA2e

Golden Corp., a merchandiser, recently completed its 2010 operations. For the year, (1) all sales are credit sales, (2) all credits to Accounts Receivable reflect cash receipts from customers, (3) all purchases of inventory are on credit, (4) all debits to Accounts Payable reflect cash payments for inventory, (5) Other Expenses are all cash expenses, and (6) any change in Income Taxes Payable reflects the accrual and cash payment of taxes. Golden's balance sheets and income statement follow.

GOLDEN CORPORATION
Comparative Balance Sheets
December 31, 2010 and 2009

	2010	2009
Assets		
Cash	$ 164,000	$107,000
Accounts receivable	83,000	71,000
Merchandise inventory	601,000	526,000
Equipment	335,000	299,000
Accum. depreciation—Equipment	(158,000)	(104,000)
Total assets	$1,025,000	$899,000
Liabilities and Equity		
Accounts payable	$ 87,000	$ 71,000
Income taxes payable	28,000	25,000
Common stock, $2 par value	592,000	568,000
Paid-in capital in excess of		
par value, common stock	196,000	160,000
Retained earnings	122,000	75,000
Total liabilities and equity	$1,025,000	$899,000

GOLDEN CORPORATION
Income Statement
For Year Ended December 31, 2010

Sales		$1,792,000
Cost of goods sold		1,086,000
Gross profit		706,000
Operating expenses		
Depreciation expense	$ 54,000	
Other expenses	494,000	548,000
Income before taxes		158,000
Income taxes expense		22,000
Net income		$ 136,000

Additional Information on Year 2010 Transactions

a. Purchased equipment for $36,000 cash.

b. Issued 12,000 shares of common stock for $5 cash per share.

c. Declared and paid $89,000 in cash dividends.

Required

Prepare a complete statement of cash flows; report its cash inflows and cash outflows from operating activities according to the *indirect method*.

Check Cash from operating activities, $122,000

Refer to Golden Corporation's financial statements and related information in Problem 23-3A.

Required

Prepare a complete statement of cash flows; report its cash flows from operating activities according to the *direct method*.

Problem 23-4A[A]

Statement of cash flows (direct method)

L03 L04 L06 L09

mhhe.com/wildCA2e

Check Cash used in financing activities, $(29,000)

Lansing Company's 2010 income statement and selected balance sheet data at December 31, 2009 and 2010 follow.

Problem 23-5A

Computing cash flows from operations (indirect) **L05**

LANSING COMPANY Selected Balance Sheet Accounts		
At December 31	**2010**	**2009**
Accounts receivable	$560,000	$580,000
Inventory	198,000	154,000
Accounts payable	440,000	460,000
Salaries payable	88,000	70,000
Utilities payable	22,000	16,000
Prepaid insurance	26,000	28,000
Prepaid rent	22,000	18,000

LANSING COMPANY Income Statement For Year Ended December 31, 2010	
Sales revenue	$97,200
Expenses	
Cost of goods sold	42,000
Depreciation expense	12,000
Salaries expense	18,000
Rent expense	9,000
Insurance expense	3,800
Interest expense	3,600
Utilities expense	2,800
Net income	$ 6,000

Required

Prepare the cash flows from operating activities section of the company's 2010 statement of cash flows using the indirect method.

Check Cash from operating activities, $(4,000)

Refer to the information in Problem 23-5A.

Required

Prepare the cash flows from operating activities section of the company's 2010 statement of cash flows using the direct method.

Problem 23-6A[A]

Computing cash flows from operations (direct) **L09**

Gazelle Corporation, a merchandiser, recently completed its calendar-year 2010 operations. For the year, (1) all sales are credit sales, (2) all credits to Accounts Receivable reflect cash receipts from customers, (3) all purchases of inventory are on credit, (4) all debits to Accounts Payable reflect cash payments for inventory, and (5) Other Expenses are paid in advance and are initially debited to Prepaid Expenses. Gazelle's balance sheets and income statement follow.

PROBLEM SET B

Problem 23-1B

Statement of cash flows (indirect method)

L03 L04 L05 L06

GAZELLE CORPORATION
Income Statement
For Year Ended December 31, 2010

Sales		$1,185,000
Cost of goods sold		595,000
Gross profit		590,000
Operating expenses		
Depreciation expense	$ 38,600	
Other expenses	362,850	
Total operating expenses		401,450
		188,550
Other gains (losses)		
Loss on sale of equipment		2,100
Income before taxes		186,450
Income taxes expense		28,350
Net income		$ 158,100

GAZELLE CORPORATION
Comparative Balance Sheets
December 31, 2010 and 2009

	2010	2009
Assets		
Cash	$123,450	$ 61,550
Accounts receivable	77,100	80,750
Merchandise inventory	240,600	250,700
Prepaid expenses	15,100	17,000
Equipment	262,250	200,000
Accum. depreciation—Equipment	(110,750)	(95,000)
Total assets	$607,750	$515,000
Liabilities and Equity		
Accounts payable	$ 17,750	$102,000
Short-term notes payable	15,000	10,000
Long-term notes payable	100,000	77,500
Common stock, $5 par	215,000	200,000
Paid-in capital in excess of		
par, common stock	30,000	0
Retained earnings	230,000	125,500
Total liabilities and equity	$607,750	$515,000

Additional Information on Year 2010 Transactions

a. The loss on the cash sale of equipment was $2,100 (details in *b*).

b. Sold equipment costing $51,000, with accumulated depreciation of $22,850, for $26,050 cash.

c. Purchased equipment costing $113,250 by paying $43,250 cash and signing a long-term note payable for the balance.

d. Borrowed $5,000 cash by signing a short-term note payable.

e. Paid $47,500 cash to reduce the long-term notes payable.

f. Issued 3,000 shares of common stock for $15 cash per share.

g. Declared and paid cash dividends of $53,600.

Required

Check Cash from operating activities, $130,200

Prepare a complete statement of cash flows; report its operating activities using the *indirect method*.

Problem 23–2B^A
Statement of cash flows
(direct method)
LO3 LO4 LO6 LO9

Check Cash used in financing activities, $51,100

Refer to Gazelle Corporation's financial statements and related information in Problem 23-1B.

Required

Prepare a complete statement of cash flows; report its operating activities according to the *direct method*.

Problem 23–3B
Statement of cash flows
(indirect method)
LO3 LO4 LO5 LO6

Satu Co., a merchandiser, recently completed its 2010 operations. For the year, (1) all sales are credit sales, (2) all credits to Accounts Receivable reflect cash receipts from customers, (3) all purchases of inventory are on credit, (4) all debits to Accounts Payable reflect cash payments for inventory, (5) Other Expenses are cash expenses, and (6) any change in Income Taxes Payable reflects the accrual and cash payment of taxes. Satu's balance sheets and income statement follow.

SATU COMPANY
Comparative Balance Sheets
December 31, 2010 and 2009

	2010	2009
Assets		
Cash	$ 58,750	$ 28,400
Accounts receivable	20,222	25,860
Merchandise inventory	165,667	140,320
Equipment	107,750	77,500
Accum. depreciation—Equipment	(46,700)	(31,000)
Total assets	$305,689	$241,080
Liabilities and Equity		
Accounts payable	$ 20,372	$157,530
Income taxes payable	2,100	6,100
Common stock, $5 par value	40,000	25,000
Paid-in capital in excess of		
par, common stock	68,000	20,000
Retained earnings	175,217	32,450
Total liabilities and equity	$305,689	$241,080

SATU COMPANY
Income Statement
For Year Ended December 31, 2010

Sales		$750,800
Cost of goods sold		269,200
Gross profit		481,600
Operating expenses		
Depreciation expense	$ 15,700	
Other expenses	173,933	189,633
Income before taxes		291,967
Income taxes expense		89,200
Net income		$202,767

Additional Information on Year 2010 Transactions

a. Purchased equipment for $30,250 cash.

b. Issued 3,000 shares of common stock for $21 cash per share.

c. Declared and paid $60,000 of cash dividends.

Required

Prepare a complete statement of cash flows; report its cash inflows and cash outflows from operating activities according to the *indirect method*.

Check Cash from operating activities, $57,600

Refer to Satu Company's financial statements and related information in Problem 23-3B.

Required

Prepare a complete statement of cash flows; report its cash flows from operating activities according to the *direct method*.

Problem 23–4B[A]
Statement of cash flows (direct method)
L03   L04   L06   L09

Check Cash provided by financing activities, $3,000

Salt Lake Company's 2010 income statement and selected balance sheet data at December 31, 2009 and 2010 follow.

Problem 23–5B
Computing cash flows from operations (indirect) **L05**

SALT LAKE COMPANY
Income Statement
For Year Ended December 31, 2010

Sales revenue	$156,000
Expenses	
Cost of goods sold	72,000
Depreciation expense	32,000
Salaries expense	20,000
Rent expense	5,000
Insurance expense	2,600
Interest expense	2,400
Utilities expense	2,000
Net income	$ 20,000

SALT LAKE COMPANY
Selected Balance Sheet Accounts

At December 31	2010	2009
Accounts receivable	$360,000	$300,000
Inventory	86,000	98,000
Accounts payable	240,000	260,000
Salaries payable	90,000	60,000
Utilities payable	20,000	0
Prepaid insurance	14,000	18,000
Prepaid rent	10,000	20,000

Required

Prepare the cash flows from operating activities section of the company's 2010 statement of cash flows using the indirect method.

Problem 23-6B[B]
Computing cash flows from operations (direct) **LO9**

Refer to the information in Problem 23-5B.

Required

Prepare the cash flows from operating activities section of the company's 2010 statement of cash flows using the direct method.

SERIAL PROBLEM

Success Systems

(This serial problem began in Chapter 1 and continues through most of the book. If previous chapter segments were not completed, the serial problem can begin at this point. It is helpful, but not necessary, for you to use the Working Papers that accompany the book.)

SP 23   Adriana Lopez, owner of Success Systems, decides to prepare a statement of cash flows for her business. (Although the serial problem allowed for various ownership changes in earlier chapters, we will prepare the statement of cash flows using the following financial data.)

SUCCESS SYSTEMS Income Statement For Three Months Ended March 31, 2011		
Computer services revenue		$31,850
Net sales		20,345
Total revenue		52,195
Cost of goods sold	$14,272	
Depreciation expense— Office equipment	625	
Depreciation expense— Computer equipment	1,250	
Wages expense	3,900	
Insurance expense	600	
Rent expense	2,625	
Computer supplies expense	2,075	
Advertising expense	800	
Mileage expense	512	
Repairs expense—Computer	1,200	
Total expenses		27,859
Net income		$24,336

SUCCESS SYSTEMS Comparative Balance Sheets December 31, 2010, and March 31, 2011		
	2011	**2010**
Assets		
Cash	$ 87,266	$ 80,260
Accounts receivable	24,400	5,800
Merchandise Inventory	680	0
Computer supplies	1,950	775
Prepaid insurance	1,200	1,800
Prepaid rent	875	875
Office equipment	10,000	10,000
Accumulated depreciation— Office equipment	(1,250)	(625)
Computer equipment	25,000	25,000
Accumulated depreciation— Computer equipment	(2,500)	(1,250)
Total assets	$147,621	$122,635
Liabilities and Equity		
Accounts payable	$ 0	$ 2,100
Wages payable	1,050	600
Unearned computer service revenue	0	2,500
Common stock	120,000	110,000
Retained earnings	26,571	7,435
Total liabilities and equity	$147,621	$122,635

Required

Prepare a statement of cash flows for Success Systems using the *indirect method* for the three months ended March 31, 2011. Recall that the owner Adriana Lopez contributed $10,000 to the business in exchange for additional stock in the first quarter of 2011 and has received $5,200 in cash dividends.

REPORTING IN ACTION
LO5   LO6   LO9

BTN 23-1   Refer to **Best Buy**'s financial statements in Appendix A to answer the following.

1. Is Best Buy's statement of cash flows prepared under the direct method or the indirect method? How do you know?

2. For each fiscal year 2008, 2007, and 2006, is the amount of cash provided by operating activities more or less than the cash paid for dividends?

3. What is the largest amount in reconciling the difference between net income and cash flow from operating activities in 2008? In 2007? In 2006?

4. Identify Best Buy's largest investing cash flow and largest financing cash flow in 2008 and in 2007.

Fast Forward

5. Obtain Best Buy's financial statements for a fiscal year ending after March 1, 2008, from either its Website (**BestBuy.com**) or the SEC's EDGAR database (**www.SEC.gov**). Since March 1, 2008, what are Best Buy's largest cash outflows and cash inflows in the investing and in the financing sections of its statement of cash flow?

COMPARATIVE ANALYSIS
LO7   LO8

BTN 23-2   Key comparative figures ($ millions) for **Best Buy** and **RadioShack** follow.

Key Figures	Best Buy			RadioShack		
	Current Year	1 Year Prior	2 Years Prior	Current Year	1 Year Prior	2 Years Prior
Operating cash flows	$ 2,025	$ 1,762	$ 1,740	$ 379	$ 315	$ 363
Total assets	12,758	13,570	11,864	1,990	2,070	2,205

Required

1. Compute the recent two years' cash flow on total assets ratios for both Best Buy and RadioShack.

2. What does the cash flow on total assets ratio measure?

3. Which company has the higher cash flow on total assets ratio for the periods shown?

4. Does the cash flow on total assets ratio reflect on the quality of earnings? Explain.

ETHICS CHALLENGE
LO1   LO7

BTN 23-3   Lisa Gish is preparing for a meeting with her banker. Her business is finishing its fourth year of operations. In the first year, it had negative cash flows from operations. In the second and third years, cash flows from operations were positive. However, inventory costs rose significantly in year 4, and cash flows from operations will probably be down 25%. Gish wants to secure a line of credit from her banker as a financing buffer. From experience, she knows the banker will scrutinize operating cash flows for years 1 through 4 and will want a projected number for year 5. Gish knows that a steady progression upward in operating cash flows for years 1 through 4 will help her case. She decides to use her discretion as owner and considers several business actions that will turn her operating cash flow in year 4 from a decrease to an increase over year 3.

Required

1. Identify two business actions Gish might take to improve cash flows from operations.

2. Comment on the ethics and possible consequences of Gish's decision to pursue these actions.

WORKPLACE COMMUNICATION
LO1

BTN 23-4   Your friend, Jessica Willard, recently completed the second year of her business and just received annual financial statements from her accountant. Willard finds the income statement and balance sheet informative but does not understand the statement of cash flows. She says the first section is especially confusing because it contains a lot of additions and subtractions that do not make sense to her.

Willard adds, "The income statement tells me the business is more profitable than last year and that's most important. If I want to know how cash changes, I can look at comparative balance sheets."

Required

Write a half-page memorandum to your friend explaining the purpose of the statement of cash flows. Speculate as to why the first section is so confusing and how it might be rectified.

TAKING IT TO THE NET

LO5   LO9

BTN 23-5   Access the March 23, 2009, filing of the 10-K report (for fiscal year ending January 31, 2009) of **J. Crew Group, Inc.**, at **www.SEC.gov**.

Required

1. Does J. Crew use the direct or indirect method to construct its consolidated statement of cash flows?
2. For the fiscal year ended January 31, 2009, what is the largest item in reconciling the net income to cash flow provided by operations?
3. In recent years J. Crew has recorded positive net income. Has the company been more successful in generating operating cash flows over this time period than in generating net income?
4. In the year ended January 31, 2009, what was the largest cash outflow for investing activities and for financing activities?
5. What items does J. Crew report as supplementary cash flow information?

TEAMWORK IN ACTION

LO1   LO4   LO5   LO9

BTN 23-6   Team members are to coordinate and independently answer one question within each of the following three sections. Team members should then report to the team and confirm or correct teammates' answers.

1. Answer *one* of the following questions about the statement of cash flows.
   a. What are this statement's reporting objectives?
   b. What two methods are used to prepare it? Identify similarities and differences between them.
   c. What steps are followed to prepare the statement?
   d. What types of analyses are often made from this statement's information?
2. Identify and explain the adjustment from net income to obtain cash flows from operating activities using the indirect method for *one* of the following items.
   a. Nonoperating gains and losses.
   b. Increases and decreases in noncash current assets.
   c. Increases and decreases in current liabilities.
3. [A]Identify and explain the formula for computing cash flows from operating activities using the direct method for *one* of the following items.
   a. Cash receipts from sales to customers.
   b. Cash paid for merchandise inventory.
   c. Cash paid for wages and operating expenses.
   d. Cash paid for interest and taxes.

> For teams of more than four, some pairing within teams is necessary. Use as an in-class activity or as an assignment. If used in class, specify a time limit on each part. Conclude with reports to the entire class, using team rotation. Each team can prepare responses on a transparency.

ENTREPRENEURS IN BUSINESS

LO1

BTN 23-7   Review the chapter's opener involving **Ashtae Products, Inc.**, to answer the following requirements.

Required

1. In a business such as Ashtae Products, monitoring cash flow is always a priority. Even though Ashtae has about $5 million in annual sales and earns a positive net income, explain how cash flow can lag behind earnings.
2. Ashtae is a closely held corporation. What are potential sources of financing for its future expansion?

1. c
2. c
3. a

4. a; $\dfrac{\$120,000}{\$2,500,000} = 4.8\%$

5. a

A Look Back

Chapter 23 focused on reporting and analyzing cash inflows and cash outflows. We explained how to prepare, analyze, and interpret the statement of cash flows.

A Look at This Chapter

This chapter emphasizes the analysis and interpretation of financial statement information. We learn to apply horizontal and vertical analyses to better understand company performance and financial condition.

A Look Ahead

Chapter 25 introduces us to managerial accounting. We discuss its purposes, concepts, and roles in helping managers gather and organize information for decisions. We also explain basic management principles.

Chapter

Comparative Financial Statement Analysis

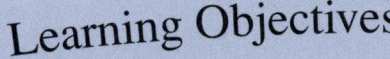

Learning Objectives

LO 1	Explain the purpose of analysis.
LO 2	Identify the building blocks of analysis.
LO 3	Describe standards for comparisons in analysis.
LO 4	Identify the tools of analysis.
LO 5	Explain and apply methods of horizontal analysis.
LO 6	Describe and apply methods of vertical analysis.
LO 7	Define and apply ratio analysis.
LO 8	Summarize and report results of financial statement analysis.

"What goes on at The Motley Fool . . . is similar to what goes on in a library"
—Tom Gardner (David Gardner on left)

Motley Fool

ALEXANDRIA, VA—In Shakespeare's Elizabethan comedy *As You Like It,* only the fool could speak truthfully to the King without getting his head lopped off. Inspired by Shakespeare's stage character, Tom and David Gardner vowed to become modern-day fools who tell it like it is. With under $10,000 in start-up money, the brothers launched **The Motley Fool (Fool.com).** And befitting of a Shakespearean play, the two say they are "dedicated to educating, amusing, and enriching individuals in search of the truth."

The Gardners do not fear the wrath of any King, real or fictional. They are intent on exposing the truth, as they see it, "that the financial world preys on ignorance and fear." As Tom explains, "There is such a great need in the general populace for financial information." Who can argue, given their brilliant success through practically every medium; including their Website, radio shows, newspaper columns, online store, investment newsletters, and global expansion.

Despite the brothers' best efforts, however, ordinary people still do not fully use information contained in financial statements. For instance, discussions keep appearing on The Motley Fool's online bulletin board that can be easily resolved using reliable and available accounting data. So, it would seem that the Fools must continue their work of "educating and enriching" individuals.

Resembling The Motley Fools' objectives, this chapter introduces horizontal and vertical analyses—tools used to reveal crucial trends and insights from financial information. It also expands on ratio analysis, which gives insight into a company's financial condition and performance. By arming ourselves with the information contained in this chapter and the investment advice of The Motley Fool, *we* can be sure to not play the fool in today's financial world.

[Sources: *Motley Fool Website,* January 2009; *Entrepreneur,* July 1997; *What to Do with Your Money Now,* June 2002; *USA Weekend,* July 2004; *Washington Post,* November 2007; *Money after 40,* April 2007]

This chapter shows how we use financial statements to evaluate a company's financial performance and condition. We explain financial statement analysis, its basic building blocks, the information available, standards for comparisons, and tools of analysis. Three major analysis tools are presented: horizontal analysis, vertical analysis, and ratio analysis. We apply each of these tools using **Best Buy**'s financial statements, and we introduce comparative analysis using **RadioShack**. This chapter expands and organizes the ratio analyses introduced at the end of each chapter.

Comparative Financial Statement Analysis

Basics of Analysis
- Purpose
- Building blocks
- Information
- Standards for comparisons
- Tools

Horizontal Analysis
- Comparative balance sheets
- Comparative income statements

Vertical Analysis
- Common-size balance sheet
- Common-size income statement

Ratio Analysis
- Liquidity and efficiency
- Solvency
- Profitability
- Market prospects
- Ratio summary

Basics of Analysis

Financial statement analysis applies analytical tools to general-purpose financial statements and related data for making business decisions. It involves transforming accounting data into more useful information. Financial statement analysis reduces our reliance on hunches, guesses, and intuition as well as our uncertainty in decision making. It does not lessen the need for expert judgment; instead, it provides us an effective and systematic basis for making business decisions. This section describes the purpose of financial statement analysis, its information sources, the use of comparisons, and some issues in computations.

Purpose of Analysis

LO1 Explain the purpose of analysis.

Internal users of accounting information are those involved in strategically managing and operating the company. They include managers, officers, internal auditors, consultants, budget directors, and market researchers. The purpose of financial statement analysis for these users is to provide strategic information to improve company efficiency and effectiveness in providing products and services.

External users of accounting information are *not* directly involved in running the company. They include shareholders, lenders, directors, customers, suppliers, regulators, lawyers, brokers, and the press. External users rely on financial statement analysis to make better and more informed decisions in pursuing their own goals.

We can identify other uses of financial statement analysis. Shareholders and creditors assess company prospects to make investing and lending decisions. A board of directors analyzes financial statements in monitoring management's decisions. Employees and unions use financial statements in labor negotiations. Suppliers use financial statement information in establishing credit terms. Customers analyze financial statements in deciding whether to establish supply relationships. Public utilities set customer rates by analyzing financial statements. Auditors use financial statements in assessing the "fair presentation" of their clients' financial results. Analyst services such as **Dun & Bradstreet**, **Moody's**, and **Standard & Poor's** use financial statements in making buy-sell recommendations and in setting credit ratings. The common goal of these users is to evaluate company performance and financial condition. This includes evaluating (1) past and current performance, (2) current financial position, and (3) future performance and risk.

Financial statement analysis tools are also used for personal financial investment decisions.

Financial statement analysis is a topic on the CPA, CMA, CIA, and CFA exams.

Building Blocks of Analysis

Financial statement analysis focuses on one or more elements of a company's financial condition or performance. Our analysis emphasizes four areas of inquiry—with varying degrees of importance. These four areas are described and illustrated in this chapter and are considered the *building blocks* of financial statement analysis:

LO2 Identify the building blocks of analysis.

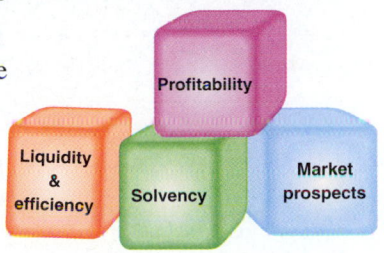

- **Liquidity** and **efficiency**—ability to meet short-term obligations and to efficiently generate revenues.
- **Solvency**—ability to generate future revenues and meet long-term obligations.
- **Profitability**—ability to provide financial rewards sufficient to attract and retain financing.
- **Market prospects**—ability to generate positive market expectations.

Applying the building blocks of financial statement analysis involves determining (1) the objectives of analysis and (2) the relative emphasis among the building blocks. We distinguish among these four building blocks to emphasize the different aspects of a company's financial condition or performance, yet we must remember that these areas of analysis are interrelated. For instance, a company's operating performance is affected by the availability of financing and short-term liquidity conditions. Similarly, a company's credit standing is not limited to satisfactory short-term liquidity but depends also on its profitability and efficiency in using assets. Early in our analysis, we need to determine the relative emphasis of each building block. Emphasis and analysis can later change as a result of evidence collected.

IN THE NEWS

Chips and Brokers   The phrase *blue chips* refers to stock of big, profitable companies. The phrase comes from poker, where the most valuable chips are blue. The term *brokers* refers to those who execute orders to buy or sell stock. The term comes from wine retailers—individuals who broach (break) wine casks.

Information for Analysis

Some users, such as managers and regulatory authorities, are able to receive special financial reports prepared to meet their analysis needs. However, most users must rely on **general-purpose financial statements** that include the (1) income statement, (2) balance sheet, (3) statement of stockholders' equity (or statement of retained earnings), (4) statement of cash flows, and (5) notes to these statements.

   Financial reporting refers to the communication of financial information useful for making investment, credit, and other business decisions. Financial reporting includes not only general-purpose financial statements but also information from SEC 10-K or other filings, press releases, shareholders' meetings, forecasts, management letters, auditors' reports, and Webcasts.

   Management's Discussion and Analysis (MD&A) is one example of useful information outside traditional financial statements. **Best Buy**'s MD&A (available at <u>BestBuy.com</u>), for example, begins with an overview and strategic initiatives. It then discusses operating results followed by liquidity and capital resources—roughly equivalent to investing and financing. The final few parts discuss special financing arrangements, key accounting policies, interim results, and the next year's outlook. The MD&A is an excellent starting point in understanding a company's business activities.

IN THE NEWS

Analysis Online   Many Websites offer free access and screening of companies by key numbers such as earnings, sales, and book value. For instance, **Standard & Poor's** has information for more than 10,000 stocks (<u>StandardPoor.com</u>).

Standards for Comparisons

LO3 Describe standards for comparisons in analysis.

When interpreting measures from financial statement analysis, we need to decide whether the measures indicate good, bad, or average performance. To make such judgments, we need standards (benchmarks) for comparisons that include the following:

- **■** *Intracompany*—The company under analysis can provide standards for comparisons based on its own prior performance and relations between its financial items. **Best Buy**'s current net income, for instance, can be compared with its prior years' net income and in relation to its revenues or total assets.
- **■** *Competitor*—One or more direct competitors of the company being analyzed can provide standards for comparisons. **Coca-Cola**'s profit margin, for instance, can be compared with **PepsiCo**'s profit margin.
- **■** *Industry*—Industry statistics can provide standards of comparisons. Such statistics are available from services such as **Dun & Bradstreet**, **Standard & Poor's**, and **Moody's**.
- **■** *Guidelines (rules of thumb)*—General standards of comparisons can develop from experience. Examples are the 2:1 level for the current ratio or 1:1 level for the acid-test ratio. Guidelines, or rules of thumb, must be carefully applied because context is crucial.

All of these comparison standards are useful when properly applied, yet measures taken from a selected competitor or group of competitors are often best. Intracompany and industry measures are also important. Guidelines or rules of thumb should be applied with care, and then only if they seem reasonable given past experience and industry norms.

Tools of Analysis

LO4 Identify the tools of analysis.

Three of the most common tools of financial statement analysis are

1. **Horizontal analysis**—Comparison of a company's financial condition and performance across time.
2. **Vertical analysis**—Comparison of a company's financial condition and performance to a base amount.
3. **Ratio analysis**—Measurement of key relations between financial statement items.

The remainder of this chapter describes these analysis tools and how to apply them.

HOW YOU DOIN'?
Answers—p. 661

  1. Who are the intended users of general-purpose financial statements?

  2. General-purpose financial statements consist of what information?

  3. Which of the following is *least* useful as a basis for comparison when analyzing ratios? (*a*) Company results from a different economic setting. (*b*) Standards from past experience. (*c*) Rule-of-thumb standards. (*d*) Industry averages.

  4. What is the preferred basis of comparison for ratio analysis?

Horizontal Analysis

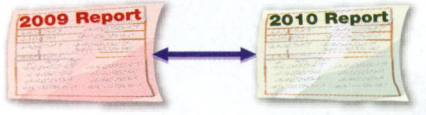

Analysis of any single financial number is of limited value. Instead, much of financial statement analysis involves identifying and describing relations between numbers, groups of numbers, and changes in those numbers. Horizontal analysis refers to examination of financial statement data *across time*. [The term *horizontal analysis* arises from the left-to-right (or right-to-left) movement of our eyes as we review comparative financial statements across time.]

Comparative Statements

Comparing amounts for two or more successive periods often helps in analyzing financial statements. **Comparative financial statements** facilitate this comparison by showing financial amounts in side-by-side columns on a single statement, called a *comparative format*. Using figures from **Best Buy**'s financial statements, this section explains how to compute dollar changes and percent changes for comparative statements.

LO5 Explain and apply methods of horizontal analysis.

Computation of Dollar Changes and Percent Changes   Comparing financial statements over relatively short time periods—two to three years—is often done by analyzing changes in line items. A change analysis usually includes analyzing absolute dollar amount changes and percent changes. Both analyses are relevant because dollar changes can yield large percent changes inconsistent with their importance. For instance, a 50% change from a base figure of $100 is less important than the same percent change from a base amount of $100,000 in the same statement. Reference to dollar amounts is necessary to retain a proper perspective and to assess the importance of changes. We compute the *dollar change* for a financial statement item as follows:

$$\text{Dollar change} = \text{Analysis period amount} - \text{Base period amount}$$

Analysis period is the point or period of time for the financial statements under analysis, and *base period* is the point or period of time for the financial statements used for comparison purposes. The prior year is commonly used as a base period. We compute the *percent change* by dividing the dollar change by the base period amount and then multiplying this quantity by 100 as follows:

$$\text{Percent change (\%)} = \frac{\text{Analysis period amount} - \text{Base period amount}}{\text{Base period amount}} \times 100$$

> What is a more significant change, a 70% increase on a $1,000 expense or a 30% increase on a $400,000 expense? *Answer:* The 30% increase.

We can always compute a dollar change, but we must be aware of a few rules in working with percent changes. To illustrate, look at four separate cases in this chart:

Case	Analysis Period	Base Period	Change Analysis Dollar	Change Analysis Percent
A	$ 1,500	$(4,500)	$ 6,000	—
B	(1,000)	2,000	(3,000)	—
C	8,000	—	8,000	—
D	0	10,000	(10,000)	(100%)

When a negative amount appears in the base period and a positive amount in the analysis period (or vice versa), we cannot compute a meaningful percent change; see cases A and B. Also, when no value is in the base period, no percent change is computable; see case C. Finally, when an item has a value in the base period and zero in the analysis period, the decrease is 100 percent; see case D.

> When there is a value in the base period and zero in the analysis period, the decrease is 100%. Why isn't the reverse situation an increase of 100%? *Answer:* A 100% increase of zero is still zero.

It is common when using horizontal analysis to compare amounts to either average or median values from prior periods (average and median values smooth out erratic or unusual fluctuations).[1] We also commonly round percents and ratios to one or two decimal places, but practice on this matter is not uniform. Computations are as detailed as necessary, which is judged by whether rounding potentially affects users' decisions. Computations should not be excessively detailed so that important relations are lost among a mountain of decimal points and digits.

---

[1] *Median* is the middle value in a group of numbers. For instance, if five prior years' incomes are (in 000s) $15, $19, $18, $20, and $22, the median value is $19. When there are two middle numbers, we can take their average. For instance, if four prior years' sales are (in 000s) $84, $91, $96, and $93, the median is $92 (computed as the average of $91 and $93).

Comparative Balance Sheets   Comparative balance sheets consist of balance sheet amounts from two or more balance sheet dates arranged side by side. Its usefulness is often improved by showing each item's dollar change and percent change to highlight large changes.

Analysis of comparative financial statements begins by focusing on items that show large dollar or percent changes. We then try to identify the reasons for these changes and, if possible, determine whether they are favorable or unfavorable. We also follow up on items with small changes when we expected the changes to be large.

Exhibit 24.1 shows comparative balance sheets for Best Buy. A few items stand out. Many asset categories substantially increase, which is probably not surprising because Best Buy is a growth company. Much of the increase in current assets is from the 16.9% increase in merchandise inventories. The long-term assets of property, equipment, and goodwill also increased.

We likewise see substantial increases on the financing side, the most notable ones being accounts payable and long-term liabilities totaling about $763 million. The increase in payables is related to the increase in cash.

> Spreadsheet programs can help with horizontal, vertical, and ratio analyses, including graphical depictions of financial relations.

> Business consultants use comparative statement analysis to provide management advice.

Exhibit 24.1

Comparative Balance Sheets

BEST BUY Comparative Balance Sheets March 1, 2008, and March 3, 2007				
(in millions)	2008	2007	Dollar Change	Percent Change
Assets				
Cash and cash equivalents	$ 1,438	$ 1,205	233	19.3%
Short-term investments	64	2,588	−2,524	−97.5
Receivables, net	549	548	1	0.2
Merchandise inventories	4,708	4,028	680	16.9
Other current assets	583	712	−129	−18.1
Total current assets	**7,342**	**9,081**	**−1,739**	**−19.1**
Property and equipment	5,608	4,904	704	14.4
Less accumulated depreciation	2,302	1,966	336	17.1
Net property and equipment	3,306	2,938	368	12.5
Goodwill	1,088	919	169	18.4
Trade name	102	81	21	25.9
Long-term investments	605	318	287	90.3
Other long-term assets, total	315	233	82	35.2
Total assets	**$12,758**	**$13,570**	**−812**	**−6.0**
Liabilities				
Accounts payable	$ 4,297	$ 3,934	363	9.2
Unredeemed gift card liabilities	531	496	35	7.1
Accrued compensation and related expenses	373	332	41	12.3
Accrued liabilities	1,535	1,520	15	1.0
Current port. of long-term debt	33	19	14	73.7
Total current liabilities	**6,769**	**6,301**	**468**	**7.4**
Long-term liabilities	878	478	400	83.7
Long-term debt	627	590	37	6.3
Total liabilities	**8,274**	**7,369**	**905**	**12.3**
Common stock	41	48	−7	−14.6
Additional paid-in capital	8	430	−422	−98.1
Retained earnings	3,933	5,507	−1,574	−28.6
Accumulated other comprehensive income	502	216	286	132.4
Total equity	**4,484**	**6,201**	**−1,717**	**−27.7**
Total liabilities & shareholders' equity	**$12,758**	**$13,570**	**−812**	**−6.0**

Comparative Income Statements   Comparative income statements are prepared similarly to comparative balance sheets. Amounts for two or more periods are placed side by side, with additional columns for dollar and percent changes. Exhibit 24.2 shows Best Buy's comparative income statements.

BEST BUY Comparative Income Statements For Years Ended March 1, 2008, and March 3, 2007				
(in millions, except per share data)	2008	2007	Dollar Change	Percent Change
Revenue	$40,023	$35,934	4,089	11.4%
Cost of revenue, total	30,477	27,165	3,312	12.2
Gross profit	9,546	8,769	777	8.9
Selling, general, and administrative expense	7,385	6,770	615	9.1
Operating income	2,161	1,999	162	8.1
Net interest income	67	131	−64	−48.9
Income before tax	2,228	2,130	98	4.6
Income tax—total	821	753	68	9.0
Net income	$ 1,407	$ 1,377	30	2.2
Basic earnings per share	3.2	2.86	0.3	11.9
Diluted earnings per share	3.12	2.79	0.3	11.8

Exhibit 24.2

Comparative Income Statements

Best Buy has substantial revenue growth of 11.4% in 2008. This finding helps support management's growth strategy as reflected in the comparative balance sheets. Best Buy also reveals some ability to control general and administrative expenses, which increased 9.1%. However, its cost of sales grew faster than its revenues, suggesting either an inability to control inventory costs or a less profitable product mix. Given its 11.4% increase in sales, we would have expected a greater net income growth than 2.2%.

Percent change can also be computed by dividing the current period by the prior period and subtracting 1.0. For example, the 11.4% revenue increase of Exhibit 24.2 is computed as: ($35,934/$30,848) − 1.

Vertical Analysis

Vertical analysis is a tool to evaluate individual financial statement items or a group of items in terms of a specific base amount. We usually define a key aggregate figure as the base, which for an income statement is usually revenue and for a balance sheet is usually total assets. This section explains vertical analysis and applies it to **Best Buy**. [The term *vertical analysis* arises from the up-down (or down-up) movement of our eyes as we review common-size financial statements. Vertical analysis is also called *common-size analysis*.]

Common-Size Statements

The comparative statements in Exhibits 24.1 and 24.2 show the change in each item over time, but they do not emphasize the relative importance of each item. We use **common-size financial statements** to reveal changes in the relative importance of each financial statement item. All individual amounts in common-size statements are redefined in terms of common-size percents. A *common-size percent* is measured by dividing each individual financial statement amount under analysis by its base amount:

$$\text{Common-size percent (\%)} = \frac{\text{Analysis amount}}{\text{Base amount}} \times 100$$

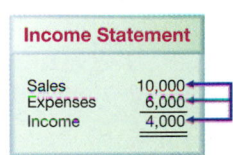

Income Statement	
Sales	10,000
Expenses	6,000
Income	4,000

LO6 Describe and apply methods of vertical analysis.

Common–Size Balance Sheets   Common-size statements express each item as a percent of a *base amount,* which for a common-size balance sheet is usually total assets. The base amount is assigned a value of 100%. (This implies that the total amount of liabilities plus equity equals 100% since this amount equals total assets.) We then compute a common-size percent for each asset, liability, and equity item using total assets as the base amount. When we present a company's successive balance sheets in this way, changes in the mixture of assets, liabilities, and equity are apparent.

Exhibit 24.3 shows common-size comparative balance sheets for Best Buy. Some relations that stand out on both a magnitude and percentage basis include (1) a decline to .5% in short-term investments as a percentage of assets, (2) an increase to 44.0% in property and equipment as a percentage of assets, (3) 4.7% increase in the percentage of accounts payable, (5) a 10.6% increase in total liabilities as a percentage of assets. Most of these changes are characteristic of a successful growth/stable company. The concern, if any, is whether Best Buy can continue to generate sufficient revenues and income to support its asset buildup within a very competitive industry.

Exhibit 24.3

Common-Size Comparative Balance Sheets

BEST BUY Common-Size Comparative Balance Sheets March 1, 2008, and March 3, 2007			Common-Size Percents*	
(in millions)	2008	2007	2008	2007
Assets				
Cash and cash equivalents	$ 1,438	$ 1,205	11.3%	8.9%
Short-term investments	64	2,588	0.5	19.1
Receivables, net	549	548	4.3	4.0
Merchandise inventories	4,708	4,028	36.9	29.7
Other current assets	583	712	4.6	5.2
Total current assets	**7,342**	**9,081**	**57.5**	**66.9**
Property and equipment	5,608	4,904	44.0	36.1
Less accumulated depreciation	2,302	1,966	18.0	14.5
Net property and equipment	3,306	2,938	25.9	21.7
Goodwill	1,088	919	8.5	6.8
Trade name	102	81	0.8	0.6
Long-term investments	605	318	4.7	2.3
Other long-term assets, total	315	233	2.5	1.7
Total assets	**$12,758**	**$13,570**		
Liabilities				
Accounts payable	$ 4,297	$ 3,934	33.7%	29.0%
Unredeemed gift card liabilities	531	496	4.2	3.7
Accrued compensation and related expenses	373	332	2.9	2.4
Accrued liabilities	1,535	1,520	12.0	11.2
Current port. of long-term debt	33	19	0.3	0.1
Total current liabilities	**6,769**	**6,301**	**53.1**	**46.4**
Long-term liabilities	878	478	6.9	3.5
Long-term debt	627	590	4.9	4.3
Total liabilities	**8,274**	**7,369**	**64.9**	**54.3**
Common stock	41	48	0.3	0.4
Additional paid-in capital	8	430	0.1	3.2
Retained earnings	3,933	5,507	30.8	40.6
Accumulated other comprehensive income	502	216	3.9	1.6
Total equity	**4,484**	**6,201**	**35.1**	**45.7**
Total liabilities & shareholders' equity	**$12,758**	**$13,570**		

* Percents are rounded to tenths and thus may not exactly sum to totals and subtotals.

Common-Size Income Statements Analysis also benefits from use of a common-size income statement. Revenues is usually the base amount, which is assigned a value of 100%. Each common-size income statement item appears as a percent of revenues. If we think of the 100% revenues amount as representing one sales dollar, the remaining items show how each revenue dollar is distributed among costs, expenses, and income.

Exhibit 24.4 shows common-size comparative income statements for each dollar of Best Buy's revenues. The past two years' common-size numbers are similar. The bad news is that gross profit lost .5 cent per revenue dollar—evidenced by the 24.4% to 23.9% decline in gross profit as a percentage of revenues. This is a concern given the price-competitive electronics market. Analysis here shows that common-size percents for successive income statements can uncover potentially important changes in a company's expenses. Evidence of no changes, especially when changes are expected, is also informative.

> International companies sometimes disclose "convenience" financial statements, which are statements translated in other languages and currencies. However, these statements rarely adjust for differences in accounting principles across countries.

Exhibit 24.4

Common-Size Comparative Income Statements

BEST BUY Common-Size Comparative Income Statements For Years Ended March 1, 2008, and March 3, 2007				
($ millions)	2008	2007	Common-Size Percents* 2008	2007
Revenue	$40,023	$35,934	100.0%	100.0%
Cost of revenue, total	30,477	27,165	76.1	75.6
Gross profit	**9,546**	**8,769**	**23.9**	**24.4**
Selling, general, and administrative expense	7,385	6,770	18.5	18.8
Operating income	**2,161**	**1,999**	**5.4**	**5.6**
Net interest income	67	131	0.2	0.4
Income before tax	**2,228**	**2,130**	**5.6**	**5.9**
Income tax—total	821	753	2.1	2.1
Net income	**$ 1,407**	**$ 1,377**	**3.5**	**3.8**

* Percents are rounded to tenths and thus may not exactly sum to totals and subtotals.

HOW YOU DOIN'?   Answers—p. 661

5. Which of the following is true for common-size comparative statements? (a) Each item is expressed as a percent of a base amount. (b) Total assets often are assigned a value of 100%. (c) Amounts from successive periods are placed side by side. (d) All are true. (e) None is true.

6. What is the difference between the percents shown on a comparative income statement and those shown on a common-size comparative income statement?

Ratio Analysis

Ratios are among the more widely used tools of financial analysis because they provide clues to and symptoms of underlying conditions. A ratio can help us uncover conditions and trends difficult to detect by inspecting individual components making up the ratio. Ratios, like other analysis tools, are usually future oriented; that is, they are often adjusted for their probable future trend and magnitude, and their usefulness depends on skillful interpretation.

A ratio expresses a mathematical relation between two quantities. It can be expressed as a percent, rate, or proportion. For instance, a change in an account balance from $100 to $250 can be expressed as (1) 150%, (2) 2.5 times, or (3) 2.5 to 1 (or 2.5:1). Computation of a ratio is a simple arithmetic operation, but its interpretation is not. To be meaningful, a ratio must refer to an economically important relation. For example, a direct and crucial relation exists between an item's sales price and its cost. Accordingly, the ratio of cost of goods sold to sales is meaningful. In contrast, no obvious relation exists between freight costs and the balance of long-term investments.

L07 Define and apply ratio analysis.

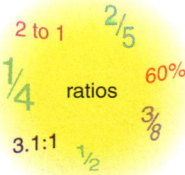

Some sources for industry norms are *Annual Statement Studies* by Robert Morris Associates, *Industry Norms & Key Business Ratios* by Dun & Bradstreet, *Standard & Poor's Industry Surveys,* and Reuters.com/finance.

This section describes an important set of financial ratios and its application. The selected ratios are organized into the four building blocks of financial statement analysis: (1) liquidity and efficiency, (2) solvency, (3) profitability, and (4) market prospects. All of these ratios were explained at relevant points in prior chapters. The purpose here is to organize and apply them under a summary framework. We use four common standards, in varying degrees, for comparisons: intracompany, competitor, industry, and guidelines.

Liquidity and Efficiency

Liquidity refers to the availability of resources to meet short-term cash requirements. It is affected by the timing of cash inflows and outflows along with prospects for future performance. Analysis of liquidity is aimed at a company's funding requirements. **Efficiency** refers to how productive a company is in using its assets. Efficiency is usually measured relative to how much revenue is generated from a certain level of assets.

Both liquidity and efficiency are important and complementary. If a company fails to meet its current obligations, its continued existence is doubtful. Viewed in this light, all other measures of analysis are of secondary importance. Although accounting measurements assume the company's continued existence, our analysis must always assess the validity of this assumption using liquidity measures. Moreover, inefficient use of assets can cause liquidity problems. A lack of liquidity often precedes lower profitability and fewer opportunities. It can foretell a loss of owner control. To a company's creditors, lack of liquidity can yield delays in collecting interest and principal payments or the loss of amounts due them. A company's customers and suppliers of goods and services also are affected by short-term liquidity problems. Implications include a company's inability to execute contracts and potential damage to important customer and supplier relationships. This section describes and illustrates key ratios relevant to assessing liquidity and efficiency.

Working Capital and Current Ratio   The amount of current assets less current liabilities is called **working capital,** or *net working capital.* A company needs adequate working capital to meet current debts, to carry sufficient inventories, and to take advantage of cash discounts. A company that runs low on working capital is less likely to meet current obligations or to continue operating. When evaluating a company's working capital, we must not only look at the dollar amount of current assets less current liabilities, but also at their ratio. The *current ratio* is defined as follows:

$$\text{Current ratio} = \frac{\text{Current assets}}{\text{Current liabilities}}$$

Exhibit 24.5

Best Buy's Working Capital and Current Ratio

Current ratio
RadioShack = 2.08
Industry = 1.6

($ millions)	2008	2007
Current assets	$7,342	$ 9,081
Current liabilities	6,769	6,301
Working capital	**$ 573**	**$2,780**
Current ratio		
$7,342/$6,769	**1.08 to 1**	
$9,081/$6,301		**1.44 to 1**

Drawing on information in Exhibit 24.1, **Best Buy**'s working capital and current ratio for both 2008 and 2007 are shown in Exhibit 24.5. **RadioShack** (2.08) and the Industry's current ratio of 1.6 is shown in the margin. Best Buy's 2008 ratio (1.08) is lower than any of the comparison ratios, and it appears to be in danger of defaulting on loan payments. A high current ratio suggests a strong liquidity position and an ability to meet current obligations. A company can, however, have a current ratio that is too high. An excessively high current ratio means that the company has invested too much in current assets compared to its current obligations. An excessive investment in current assets is not an efficient use of funds because current assets normally generate a low return on investment (compared with long-term assets).

Many users apply a guideline of 2:1 (or 1.5:1) for the current ratio in helping evaluate a company's debt-paying ability. A company with a 2:1 or higher current ratio is generally thought to be a good credit risk in the short run. Such a guideline or any analysis of the current ratio must recognize at least three additional factors: (1) type of business, (2) composition of current assets, and (3) turnover rate of current asset components.

Type of business.   A service company that grants little or no credit and carries few inventories can probably operate on a current ratio of less than 1:1 if its revenues generate enough cash to pay its current liabilities. On the other hand, a company selling high-priced clothing or furniture requires a higher ratio because of difficulties in judging customer demand and cash receipts. For instance, if demand falls, inventory may not generate as much cash as expected. Accordingly, analysis of the current ratio should include a comparison with ratios from successful companies in the same industry and from prior periods. We must also recognize that a company's accounting methods, especially choice of inventory method, affect the current ratio. For instance, when costs are rising, a company using LIFO tends to report a smaller amount of current assets than when using FIFO.

Composition of current assets.   The composition of a company's current assets is important to an evaluation of short-term liquidity. For instance, cash, cash equivalents, and short-term investments are more liquid than accounts and notes receivable. Also, short-term receivables normally are more liquid than inventory. Cash, of course, can be used to immediately pay current debts. Items such as accounts receivable and inventory, however, normally must be converted into cash before payment is made. An excessive amount of receivables and inventory weakens a company's ability to pay current liabilities. The acid-test ratio (see below) can help with this assessment.

Turnover rate of assets.   Asset turnover measures a company's efficiency in using its assets. One relevant measure of asset efficiency is the revenue generated. A measure of total asset turnover is revenues divided by total assets, but evaluation of turnover for individual assets is also useful. We discuss both receivables turnover and inventory turnover on the next page.

Acid–Test Ratio   Quick assets are cash, short-term investments, and current receivables. These are the most liquid types of current assets. The *acid-test ratio,* also called *quick ratio,* reflects on a company's short-term liquidity.

$$\text{Acid-test ratio} = \frac{\text{Cash + Short-term investments + Current receivables}}{\text{Current liabilities}}$$

Best Buy's acid-test ratio is computed in Exhibit 24.6. Best Buy's 2008 acid-test ratio (0.30) is less than of RadioShack (1.96), and less than the 1:1 common guideline for an acceptable acid-test ratio. As with analysis of the current ratio, we need to consider other factors. For instance, the frequency with which a company converts its current assets into cash affects its working capital requirements. This implies that analysis of short-term liquidity should also include an analysis of receivables and inventories, which we consider next.

($ millions)	2008	2007
Cash and equivalents	$1,438	$1,205
Short-term investments	64	2,588
Current receivables	549	548
Total quick assets	$2,051	$4,341
Current liabilities	$6,769	$6,301
Acid-test ratio		
$2,051/$6,769	0.30 to 1	
$4,341/$6,301		0.69 to 1

Exhibit 24.6

Acid-Test Ratio

Acid-test ratio
RadioShack = 1.96
Industry = 0.7

Accounts Receivable Turnover   We can measure how frequently a company converts its receivables into cash by computing the *accounts receivable turnover*. This ratio is defined as follows:

$$\text{Accounts receivable turnover} = \frac{\text{Net sales}}{\text{Average accounts receivable, net}}$$

Short-term receivables from customers are often included in the denominator along with accounts receivable. Also, accounts receivable turnover is more precise if credit sales are used for the numerator, but external users generally use net sales (or net revenues) because information about credit sales is typically not reported. Best Buy's 2008 accounts receivable turnover is computed as follows ($ millions):

Some users prefer using gross accounts receivable (before subtracting the allowance for doubtful accounts) to avoid the influence of a manager's bad debts estimate.

$$\frac{\$40,023}{(\$549 + \$548)/2} = 73.0 \text{ times}$$

Accounts receivable turnover
RadioShack = 17.1

Best Buy's value of 73.0 is larger than RadioShack's 17.1. Accounts receivable turnover is high when accounts receivable are quickly collected. A high turnover is favorable because it means the company need not commit large amounts of funds to accounts receivable. However, an accounts receivable turnover can be too high; this can occur when credit terms are so restrictive that they negatively affect sales volume.

Inventory Turnover   How long a company holds inventory before selling it will affect working capital requirements. One measure of this effect is *inventory turnover,* also called *merchandise turnover* or *merchandise inventory turnover,* which is defined as follows:

$$\text{Inventory turnover} = \frac{\text{Cost of goods sold}}{\text{Average inventory}}$$

Using Best Buy's cost of goods sold and inventories information, we compute its inventory turnover for 2008 as follows (if the beginning and ending inventories for the year do not represent the usual inventory amount, an average of quarterly or monthly inventories can be used).

$$\frac{\$30,477}{(\$4,708 + \$4,028)/2} = 6.98 \text{ times}$$

Best Buy's inventory turnover of 6.98 is higher than RadioShack's 3.05, and the industry's 4.5. A company with a high turnover requires a smaller investment in inventory than one producing the same sales with a lower turnover. Inventory turnover can be too high, however, if the inventory a company keeps is so small that it restricts sales volume.

Days' Sales Uncollected   Accounts receivable turnover provides insight into how frequently a company collects its accounts. Days' sales uncollected is one measure of this activity, which is defined as follows:

$$\text{Days' sales uncollected} = \frac{\text{Accounts receivable, net}}{\text{Net sales}} \times 365$$

Any short-term notes receivable from customers are normally included in the numerator. Best Buy's 2008 days' sales uncollected follows:

$$\frac{\$549}{\$40,023} \times 365 = 5.01 \text{ days}$$

RadioShack's 20.90 days are longer than the 5.01 days for Best Buy. Days' sales uncollected is more meaningful if we know company credit terms. A rough guideline states that days' sales uncollected should not exceed $1\frac{1}{3}$ times the days in its (1) credit period, *if* discounts are not offered or (2) discount period, *if* favorable discounts are offered.

Days' Sales in Inventory   *Days' sales in inventory* is a useful measure in evaluating inventory liquidity. Days' sales in inventory is linked to inventory in a way that days' sales uncollected is linked to receivables. We compute days' sales in inventory as follows:

$$\text{Days' sales in inventory} = \frac{\text{Ending inventory}}{\text{Cost of goods sold}} \times 365$$

Best Buy's days' sales in inventory for 2008 follows:

$$\frac{\$4,708}{\$30,477} \times 365 = 56.4 \text{ days}$$

Ending accounts receivable can be substituted for the average balance in computing accounts receivable turnover if the difference between ending and average receivables is small.

Inventory turnover
RadioShack = 3.05
Industry = 4.5

Days' sales uncollected
RadioShack = 20.90

Days' sales in inventory
RadioShack = 115.7

If the products in Best Buy's inventory are in demand by customers, this formula estimates that its inventory will be converted into receivables (or cash) in 56.4 days. If all of Best Buy's sales were credit sales, the conversion of inventory to receivables in 56.4 days *plus* the conversion of receivables to cash in 5.01 days implies that inventory will be converted to cash in about 61.41 days (56.4 + 5.01).

Total Asset Turnover

Total asset turnover reflects a company's ability to use its assets to generate sales and is an important indication of operating efficiency. The definition of this ratio follows:

$$\text{Total asset turnover} = \frac{\text{Net sales}}{\text{Average total assets}}$$

Best Buy's total asset turnover for 2008 follows and is greater than that for RadioShack.

$$\frac{\$40,023}{(\$12,758 + \$13,570)/2} = 3.04 \text{ times}$$

Total asset turnover
RadioShack = 2.09

HOW YOU DOIN'?   Answers—p. 661

7. Information from Paff Co. at Dec. 31, 2009, follows: cash, $820,000; accounts receivable, $240,000; inventories, $470,000; plant assets, $910,000; accounts payable, $350,000; and income taxes payable, $180,000. Compute its (a) current ratio and (b) acid-test ratio.

8. On Dec. 31, 2010, Paff Company (see question 7) had accounts receivable of $290,000 and inventories of $530,000. During 2010, net sales amounted to $2,500,000 and cost of goods sold was $750,000. Compute (a) accounts receivable turnover, (b) days' sales uncollected, (c) inventory turnover, and (d) days' sales in inventory.

Solvency

Solvency refers to a company's long-run financial viability and its ability to cover long-term obligations. All of a company's business activities—financing, investing, and operating—affect its solvency. Analysis of solvency is long term and uses less precise but more encompassing measures than liquidity. One of the most important components of solvency analysis is the composition of a company's capital structure. *Capital structure* refers to a company's financing sources. It ranges from relatively permanent equity financing to riskier or more temporary short-term financing. Assets represent security for financiers, ranging from loans secured by specific assets to the assets available as general security to unsecured creditors. This section describes the tools of solvency analysis. Our analysis focuses on a company's ability to both meet its obligations and provide security to its creditors *over the long run*. Indicators of this ability include *debt* and *equity* ratios, the relation between *pledged assets and secured liabilities*, and the company's capacity to earn sufficient income to *pay fixed interest charges*.

Debt and Equity Ratios

One element of solvency analysis is to assess the portion of a company's assets contributed by its owners and the portion contributed by creditors. This relation is reflected in the debt ratio. The *debt ratio* expresses total liabilities as a percent of total assets. The **equity ratio** provides complementary information by expressing total equity as a percent of total assets. **Best Buy**'s debt and equity ratios follow.

For analysis purposes, Minority Interest is usually included in equity.

($ millions)	2008	Ratios	
Total liabilities	$ 8,274	64.9%	[Debt ratio]
Total equity	4,484	35.1	[Equity ratio]
Total liabilities and equity	$12,758	100.0%	

Debt ratio :: Equity ratio
RadioShack = 61.3% :: 38.7%

Best Buy's financial statements reveal more debt than equity. A company is considered less risky if its capital structure (equity and long-term debt) contains more equity. One risk factor is the required payment for interest and principal when debt is outstanding. Another factor is the greater the stockholder financing, the more losses a company can absorb through equity before the assets become inadequate to satisfy creditors' claims. From the stockholders' point of view, if a company earns a return on borrowed capital that is higher than the cost of borrowing, the difference represents increased income to stockholders. The inclusion of debt is described as *financial leverage* because debt can have the effect of increasing the return to stockholders. Companies are said to be highly leveraged if a large portion of their assets is financed by debt.

<aside>Bank examiners from the FDIC and other regulatory agencies use debt and equity ratios to monitor compliance with regulatory capital requirements imposed on banks and S&Ls.</aside>

Debt–to–Equity Ratio

The ratio of total liabilities to equity is another measure of solvency. We compute the ratio as follows:

$$\text{Debt-to-equity ratio} = \frac{\text{Total liabilities}}{\text{Total equity}}$$

Best Buy's debt-to-equity ratio for 2008 is

$$\$8,274/\$4,484 = 1.84$$

<aside>**Debt-to-equity**
RadioShack = 1.59
Industry = 0.99</aside>

Best Buy's 1.84 debt-to-equity ratio is greater than the 1.59 for RadioShack and the industry ratio of 0.99. Consistent with our inferences from the debt ratio, Best Buy's capital structure has more debt than equity, which increases risk. Recall that debt must be repaid with interest, while equity does not. These debt requirements can be burdensome when the industry and/or the economy experience a downturn. A larger debt-to-equity ratio also implies less opportunity to expand through use of debt financing.

Times Interest Earned

The amount of income before deductions for interest expense and income taxes is the amount available to pay interest expense. The following *times interest earned* ratio reflects the creditors' risk of loan repayments with interest.

<aside>The times interest earned ratio and the debt and equity ratios are of special interest to bank lending officers.</aside>

$$\text{Times interest earned} = \frac{\text{Income before interest expense and income taxes}}{\text{Interest expense}}$$

The larger this ratio, the less risky is the company for creditors. One guideline says that creditors are reasonably safe if the company earns its fixed interest expense two or more times each year. Best Buy's times interest earned ratio follows; its value suggests that its creditors have little risk of nonrepayment.

<aside>**Times interest earned**
RadioShack = 9.7</aside>

$$\frac{\$1,407 + \$49(\text{see statement of cash flows}) + \$821}{\$49} = 46.5$$

IN THE NEWS

Bears and Bulls   A *bear market* is a declining market. The phrase comes from bear-skin jobbers who often sold the skins before the bears were caught. The term *bear* was then used to describe investors who sold shares they did not own in anticipation of a price decline. A *bull market* is a rising market. This phrase comes from the once popular sport of bear and bull baiting. The term *bull* came to mean the opposite of *bear*.

Profitability

We are especially interested in a company's ability to use its assets efficiently to produce profits (and positive cash flows). **Profitability** refers to a company's ability to generate an adequate return on invested capital. Return is judged by assessing earnings relative to the level and sources of financing. Profitability is also relevant to solvency. This section describes key profitability measures and their importance to financial statement analysis.

Profit Margin   A company's operating efficiency and profitability can be expressed by two components. The first is *profit margin*, which reflects a company's ability to earn net income from sales. It is measured by expressing net income as a percent of sales (*sales* and *revenues* are similar terms). **Best Buy**'s profit margin follows:

$$\text{Profit margin} = \frac{\text{Net income}}{\text{Net sales}} = \frac{\$1,407}{\$40,023} = 3.5\%$$

Profit margin
RadioShack = 5.6%

To evaluate profit margin, we must consider the industry. For instance, an appliance company might require a profit margin between 10% and 15%; whereas a retail supermarket might require a profit margin of 1% or 2%. Both profit margin and *total asset turnover* make up the two basic components of operating efficiency. These ratios reflect on management because managers are ultimately responsible for operating efficiency. The next section explains how we use both measures to analyze return on total assets.

Return on Total Assets   *Return on total assets* is defined as follows.

$$\text{Return on total assets} = \frac{\text{Net income}}{\text{Average total assets}}$$

Best Buy's 2008 return on total assets is

$$\frac{\$1,407}{(\$12,758 + \$13,570)/2} = 10.7\%$$

Return on total assets
RadioShack = 11.7%
Industry = 3.0

Best Buy's 10.7% return on total assets is lower than that for many businesses and also lower than RadioShack's return of 11.7% and the industry's 3.0% return. We also should evaluate any trend in the rate of return.

The following equation shows the important relation between profit margin, total asset turnover, and return on total assets.

$$\text{Profit margin} \times \text{Total asset turnover} = \text{Return on total assets}$$

or

$$\frac{\text{Net income}}{\text{Net sales}} \times \frac{\text{Net sales}}{\text{Average total assets}} = \frac{\text{Net income}}{\text{Average total assets}}$$

Both profit margin and total asset turnover contribute to overall operating efficiency, as measured by return on total assets. If we apply this formula to Best Buy, we get

$$3.5\% \times 3.04 = 10.7\% \text{ (with rounding)}$$

RadioShack: 5.6% × 2.09 = 11.7%

This analysis shows that RadioShack's superior return on assets versus that of Best Buy is driven mainly by its higher profit margin.

Return on Common Stockholders' Equity   Perhaps the most important goal in operating a company is to earn net income for its owner(s). *Return on common stockholders' equity* measures a company's success in reaching this goal and is defined as follows:

$$\text{Return on common stockholders' equity} = \frac{\text{Net income} - \text{Preferred dividends}}{\text{Average common stockholders' equity}}$$

Best Buy's 2008 return on common stockholders' equity is computed as follows:

$$\frac{\$1,407 - \$0}{(\$4,484 + \$6,201)/2} = 26.3\%$$

The denominator in this computation is the book value of common equity (including minority interest). In the numerator, the dividends on cumulative preferred stock are subtracted whether they are declared or are in arrears. If preferred stock is noncumulative, its dividends are subtracted only if declared.

Market Prospects

Market prospects reflect expectations (both good and bad) about a company's future performance as assessed by users and other interested parties. Market measures are useful for analyzing corporations with publicly traded stock. These market measures use stock price, which reflects the market's (public's) expectations for the company. This includes expectations of both company return and risk—as the market perceives it.

Price–Earnings Ratio   Computation of the *price-earnings ratio* follows:

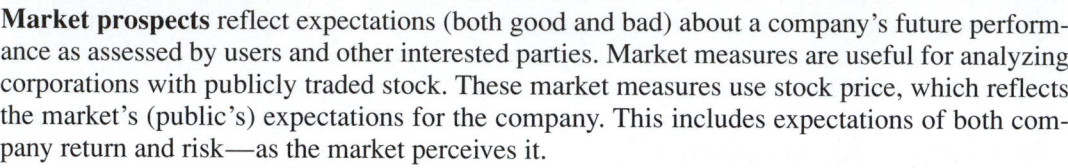

$$\text{Price-earnings ratio} = \frac{\text{Market price per common share}}{\text{Earnings per share}}$$

> PE ratio can be viewed as an indicator of the market's expected growth and risk for a stock. High expected risk suggests a low PE ratio. High expected growth suggests a high PE ratio.

Predicted earnings per share for the next period is often used in the denominator of this computation. Reported earnings per share for the most recent period is also commonly used. In both cases, the ratio is used as an indicator of the future growth and risk of a company's earnings as perceived by the stock's buyers and sellers.

    The market price of **Best Buy**'s common stock at the start of fiscal year 2009 was $27.87. Using Best Buy's $3.20 basic earnings per share, we compute its price-earnings ratio as follows (some analysts compute this ratio using the median of the low and high stock price).

$$\frac{\$27.87}{\$3.20} = 8.7$$

> Some investors avoid stocks with high PE ratios under the belief they are "overpriced." Alternatively, some investors *sell these stocks short*—hoping for price declines.

Best Buy's price-earnings ratio is higher than that for **RadioShack**. Best Buy's ratio likely reflects investors' expectations of continued growth but normal earnings.

Dividend Yield   *Dividend yield* is used to compare the dividend-paying performance of different investment alternatives. We compute dividend yield as follows:

$$\text{Dividend yield} = \frac{\text{Annual cash dividends per share}}{\text{Market price per share}}$$

Best Buy's dividend yield, based on its fiscal year-end market price per share of $27.87 and its policy of $0.46 cash dividends per share, is computed as follows.

$$\frac{\$0.46}{\$27.87} = 1.6\%$$

Some companies do not declare and pay dividends because they wish to reinvest the cash.

Summary of Ratios

Exhibit 24.7 summarizes the major financial statement analysis ratios illustrated in this chapter and throughout the book. This summary includes each ratio's title, its formula, and the purpose for which it is commonly used.

Exhibit 24.7

Financial Statement Analysis Ratios

Ratio	Formula	Measure of
Liquidity and Efficiency		
Current ratio	$= \dfrac{\text{Current assets}}{\text{Current liabilities}}$	Short-term debt-paying ability
Acid-test ratio	$= \dfrac{\text{Cash} + \text{Short-term investments} + \text{Current receivables}}{\text{Current liabilities}}$	Immediate short-term debt-paying ability
Accounts receivable turnover	$= \dfrac{\text{Net sales}}{\text{Average accounts receivable, net}}$	Efficiency of collection
Inventory turnover	$= \dfrac{\text{Cost of goods sold}}{\text{Average inventory}}$	Efficiency of inventory management
Days' sales uncollected	$= \dfrac{\text{Accounts receivable, net}}{\text{Net sales}} \times 365$	Liquidity of receivables
Days' sales in inventory	$= \dfrac{\text{Ending inventory}}{\text{Cost of goods sold}} \times 365$	Liquidity of inventory
Total asset turnover	$= \dfrac{\text{Net sales}}{\text{Average total assets}}$	Efficiency of assets in producing sales
Solvency		
Debt ratio	$= \dfrac{\text{Total liabilities}}{\text{Total assets}}$	Creditor financing and leverage
Equity ratio	$= \dfrac{\text{Total equity}}{\text{Total assets}}$	Owner financing
Debt-to-equity ratio	$= \dfrac{\text{Total liabilities}}{\text{Total equity}}$	Debt versus equity financing
Times interest earned	$= \dfrac{\text{Income before interest expense and income taxes}}{\text{Interest expense}}$	Protection in meeting interest payments
Profitability		
Profit margin ratio	$= \dfrac{\text{Net income}}{\text{Net sales}}$	Net income in each sales dollar
Gross margin ratio	$= \dfrac{\text{Net sales} - \text{Cost of goods sold}}{\text{Net sales}}$	Gross margin in each sales dollar
Return on total assets	$= \dfrac{\text{Net income}}{\text{Average total assets}}$	Overall profitability of assets
Return on common stockholders' equity	$= \dfrac{\text{Net income} - \text{Preferred dividends}}{\text{Average common stockholders' equity}}$	Profitability of owner investment
Book value per common share	$= \dfrac{\text{Shareholders' equity applicable to common shares}}{\text{Number of common shares outstanding}}$	Liquidation at reported amounts
Basic earnings per share	$= \dfrac{\text{Net income} - \text{Preferred dividends}}{\text{Weighted-average common shares outstanding}}$	Net income per common share
Market Prospects		
Price-earnings ratio	$= \dfrac{\text{Market price per common share}}{\text{Earnings per share}}$	Market value relative to earnings
Dividend yield	$= \dfrac{\text{Annual cash dividends per share}}{\text{Market price per share}}$	Cash return per common share

9. Which ratio best reflects a company's ability to meet immediate interest payments? (*a*) Debt ratio. (*b*) Equity ratio. (*c*) Times interest earned.

10. Which ratio best measures a company's success in earning net income for its owner(s)? (*a*) Profit margin. (*b*) Return on common stockholders' equity. (*c*) Price-earnings ratio. (*d*) Dividend yield.

11. If a company has net sales of $8,500,000, net income of $945,000, and total asset turnover of 1.8 times, what is its return on total assets?

ANALYSIS REPORTING

LO8 Summarize and report results of financial statement analysis.

Understanding the purpose of financial statement analysis is crucial to the usefulness of any analysis. This understanding leads to efficiency of effort, effectiveness in application, and relevance in focus. The purpose of most financial statement analyses is to reduce uncertainty in business decisions through a rigorous and sound evaluation. A *financial statement analysis report* helps by directly addressing the building blocks of analysis and by identifying weaknesses in inference by requiring explanation: It forces us to organize our reasoning and to verify its flow and logic. A report also serves as a communication link with readers, and the writing process reinforces our judgments and vice versa. Finally, the report helps us (re)evaluate evidence and refine conclusions on key building blocks. A good analysis report usually consists of six sections:

1. **Executive summary**—brief focus on important analysis results and conclusions.
2. **Analysis overview**—background on the company, its industry, and its economic setting.
3. **Evidential matter**—financial statements and information used in the analysis, including ratios, trends, comparisons, statistics, and all analytical measures assembled; often organized under the building blocks of analysis.
4. **Assumptions**—identification of important assumptions regarding a company's industry and economic environment, and other important assumptions for estimates.
5. **Key factors**—list of important favorable and unfavorable factors, both quantitative and qualitative, for company performance; usually organized by areas of analysis.
6. **Inferences**—forecasts, estimates, interpretations, and conclusions drawing on all sections of the report.

We must remember that the user dictates relevance, meaning that the analysis report should include a brief table of contents to help readers focus on those areas most relevant to their decisions. All irrelevant matter must be eliminated. For example, decades-old details of obscure transactions and detailed miscues of the analysis are irrelevant. Ambiguities and qualifications to avoid responsibility or hedging inferences must be eliminated. Finally, writing is important. Mistakes in grammar and errors of fact compromise the report's credibility.

Demonstration Problem

Use the following financial statements of Precision Co. to complete these requirements.

1. Prepare comparative income statements showing the percent increase or decrease for year 2010 in comparison to year 2009.
2. Prepare common-size comparative balance sheets for years 2010 and 2009.
3. Compute the following ratios as of December 31, 2010, or for the year ended December 31, 2010, and identify its building block category for financial statement analysis.

a. Current ratio
b. Acid-test ratio
c. Accounts receivable turnover
d. Days' sales uncollected
e. Inventory turnover
f. Debt ratio

g. Debt-to-equity ratio
h. Times interest earned
i. Profit margin ratio
j. Total asset turnover
k. Return on total assets
l. Return on common stockholders' equity

PRECISION COMPANY
Comparative Balance Sheets
December 31, 2010 and 2009

	2010	2009
Assets		
Current assets		
Cash	$ 79,000	$ 42,000
Short-term investments	65,000	96,000
Accounts receivable, net	120,000	100,000
Merchandise inventory	250,000	265,000
Total current assets	514,000	503,000
Plant assets		
Store equipment, net	400,000	350,000
Office equipment, net	45,000	50,000
Buildings, net	625,000	675,000
Land	100,000	100,000
Total plant assets	1,170,000	1,175,000
Total assets	$1,684,000	$1,678,000
Liabilities		
Current liabilities		
Accounts payable	$ 164,000	$ 190,000
Short-term notes payable	75,000	90,000
Taxes payable	26,000	12,000
Total current liabilities	265,000	292,000
Long-term liabilities		
Notes payable (secured by		
mortgage on buildings)	400,000	420,000
Total liabilities	665,000	712,000
Stockholders' Equity		
Common stock, $5 par value	475,000	475,000
Retained earnings	544,000	491,000
Total stockholders' equity	1,019,000	966,000
Total liabilities and equity	$1,684,000	$1,678,000

PRECISION COMPANY
Comparative Income Statements
For Years Ended December 31, 2010 and 2009

	2010	2009
Sales	$2,486,000	$2,075,000
Cost of goods sold	1,523,000	1,222,000
Gross profit	963,000	853,000
Operating expenses		
Advertising expense	145,000	100,000
Sales salaries expense	240,000	280,000
Office salaries expense	165,000	200,000
Insurance expense	100,000	45,000
Supplies expense	26,000	35,000
Depreciation expense	85,000	75,000
Miscellaneous expenses	17,000	15,000
Total operating expenses	778,000	750,000
Operating income	185,000	103,000
Interest expense	44,000	46,000
Income before taxes	141,000	57,000
Income taxes	47,000	19,000
Net income	$ 94,000	$ 38,000
Earnings per share	$ 0.99	$ 0.40

Planning the Solution

• Set up a four-column income statement; enter the 2010 and 2009 amounts in the first two columns and then enter the dollar change in the third column and the percent change from 2009 in the fourth column.

• Set up a four-column balance sheet; enter the 2010 and 2009 year-end amounts in the first two columns and then compute and enter the amount of each item as a percent of total assets.

• Compute the required ratios using the data provided. Use the average of beginning and ending amounts when appropriate (see Exhibit 24.7 for definitions).

Solution to Demonstration Problem

1.

PRECISION COMPANY
Comparative Income Statements
For Years Ended December 31, 2010 and 2009

	2010	2009	Increase (Decrease) in 2010 Amount	Increase (Decrease) in 2010 Percent
Sales	$2,486,000	$2,075,000	$411,000	19.8%
Cost of goods sold	1,523,000	1,222,000	301,000	24.6
Gross profit	963,000	853,000	110,000	12.9
Operating expenses				
Advertising expense	145,000	100,000	45,000	45.0
Sales salaries expense	240,000	280,000	(40,000)	(14.3)
Office salaries expense	165,000	200,000	(35,000)	(17.5)

[continued on next page]

[continued from previous page]

Insurance expense	100,000	45,000	**55,000**	**122.2**
Supplies expense	26,000	35,000	**(9,000)**	**(25.7)**
Depreciation expense	85,000	75,000	**10,000**	**13.3**
Miscellaneous expenses	17,000	15,000	**2,000**	**13.3**
Total operating expenses	778,000	750,000	**28,000**	**3.7**
Operating income	185,000	103,000	**82,000**	**79.6**
Interest expense	44,000	46,000	**(2,000)**	**(4.3)**
Income before taxes	141,000	57,000	**84,000**	**147.4**
Income taxes	47,000	19,000	**28,000**	**147.4**
Net income	$ 94,000	$ 38,000	**$ 56,000**	**147.4**
Earnings per share	$ 0.99	$ 0.40	**$ 0.59**	**147.5**

2.

PRECISION COMPANY
Common-Size Comparative Balance Sheets
December 31, 2010 and 2009

	December 31		Common-Size Percents	
	2010	2009	2010*	2009*
Assets				
Current assets				
Cash	$ 79,000	$ 42,000	4.7%	2.5%
Short-term investments	65,000	96,000	3.9	5.7
Accounts receivable, net	120,000	100,000	7.1	6.0
Merchandise inventory	250,000	265,000	14.8	15.8
Total current assets	514,000	503,000	30.5	30.0
Plant assets				
Store equipment, net	400,000	350,000	23.8	20.9
Office equipment, net	45,000	50,000	2.7	3.0
Buildings, net	625,000	675,000	37.1	40.2
Land	100,000	100,000	5.9	6.0
Total plant assets	1,170,000	1,175,000	69.5	70.0
Total assets	$1,684,000	$1,678,000	100.0	100.0
Liabilities				
Current liabilities				
Accounts payable	$ 164,000	$ 190,000	9.7%	11.3%
Short-term notes payable	75,000	90,000	4.5	5.4
Taxes payable	26,000	12,000	1.5	0.7
Total current liabilities	265,000	292,000	15.7	17.4
Long-term liabilities				
Notes payable (secured by mortgage on buildings)	400,000	420,000	23.8	25.0
Total liabilities	665,000	712,000	39.5	42.4
Stockholders' Equity				
Common stock, $5 par value	475,000	475,000	28.2	28.3
Retained earnings	544,000	491,000	32.3	29.3
Total stockholders' equity	1,019,000	966,000	60.5	57.6
Total liabilities and equity	$1,684,000	$1,678,000	100.0	100.0

* Columns do not always exactly add to 100 due to rounding.

3. **Ratios for 2010:**

   a. Current ratio: $514,000/$265,000 = 1.9:1 (liquidity and efficiency)

   b. Acid-test ratio: ($79,000 + $65,000 + $120,000)/$265,000 = 1.0:1 (liquidity and efficiency)

   c. Average receivables: ($120,000 + $100,000)/2 = $110,000
   Accounts receivable turnover: $2,486,000/$110,000 = 22.6 times (liquidity and efficiency)

   d. Days' sales uncollected: ($120,000/$2,486,000) × 365 = 17.6 days (liquidity and efficiency)

   e. Average inventory: ($250,000 + $265,000)/2 = $257,500
   Inventory turnover: $1,523,000/$257,500 = 5.9 times (liquidity and efficiency)

   f. Debt ratio: $665,000/$1,684,000 = 39.5% (solvency)

g. Debt-to-equity ratio: $665,000/$1,019,000 = 0.65 (solvency)

h. Times interest earned: $185,000/$44,000 = 4.2 times (solvency)

i. Profit margin ratio: $94,000/$2,486,000 = 3.8% (profitability)

j. Average total assets: ($1,684,000 + $1,678,000)/2 = $1,681,000
Total asset turnover: $2,486,000/$1,681,000 = 1.48 times (liquidity and efficiency)

k. Return on total assets: $94,000/$1,681,000 = 5.6% or 3.8% × 1.48 = 5.6% (profitability)

l. Average total common equity: ($1,019,000 + $966,000)/2 = $992,500
Return on common stockholders' equity: $94,000/$992,500 = 9.5% (profitability)

Summary

LO1 Explain the purpose of analysis. The purpose of financial statement analysis is to help users make better business decisions. Internal users want information to improve company efficiency and effectiveness in providing products and services. External users want information to make better and more informed decisions in pursuing their goals. The common goals of all users are to evaluate a company's (1) past and current performance, (2) current financial position, and (3) future performance and risk.

LO2 Identify the building blocks of analysis. Financial statement analysis focuses on four "building blocks" of analysis: (1) liquidity and efficiency—ability to meet short-term obligations and efficiently generate revenues; (2) solvency—ability to generate future revenues and meet long-term obligations; (3) profitability—ability to provide financial rewards sufficient to attract and retain financing; and (4) market prospects—ability to generate positive market expectations.

LO3 Describe standards for comparisons in analysis. Standards for comparisons include (1) intracompany—prior performance and relations between financial items for the company under analysis; (2) competitor—one or more direct competitors of the company; (3) industry—industry statistics; and (4) guidelines (rules of thumb)—general standards developed from past experiences and personal judgments.

LO4 Identify the tools of analysis. The three most common tools of financial statement analysis are (1) horizontal analysis—comparing a company's financial condition and performance across time; (2) vertical analysis—comparing a company's financial condition and performance to a base amount such as revenues or total

assets; and (3) ratio analysis—using and quantifying key relations among financial statement items.

LO5 Explain and apply methods of horizontal analysis. Horizontal analysis is a tool to evaluate changes in data across time. Comparative statements show amounts for two or more successive periods, often with changes disclosed in both absolute and percent terms.

LO6 Describe and apply methods of vertical analysis. Vertical analysis is a tool to evaluate each financial statement item or group of items in terms of a base amount. Two tools of vertical analysis are common-size statements and graphical analyses. Each item in common-size statements is expressed as a percent of a base amount. For the balance sheet, the base amount is usually total assets, and for the income statement, it is usually sales.

LO7 Define and apply ratio analysis. Ratio analysis provides clues to and symptoms of underlying conditions. Ratios, properly interpreted, identify areas requiring further investigation. A ratio expresses a mathematical relation between two quantities such as a percent, rate, or proportion. Ratios can be organized into the building blocks of analysis: (1) liquidity and efficiency, (2) solvency, (3) profitability, and (4) market prospects.

LO8 Summarize and report results of financial statement analysis. A financial statement analysis report is often organized around the building blocks of analysis. A good report separates interpretations and conclusions of analysis from the information underlying them. An analysis report often consists of six sections: (1) executive summary, (2) analysis overview, (3) evidential matter, (4) assumptions, (5) key factors, and (6) inferences.

Guidance Answers to HOW YOU DOIN'?

1. General-purpose financial statements are intended for a variety of users interested in a company's financial condition and performance—users without the power to require specialized financial reports to meet their specific needs.

2. General-purpose financial statements include the income statement, balance sheet, statement of stockholders' (owner's) equity, and statement of cash flows plus the notes related to these statements.

3. *a*

4. Data from one or more direct competitors are usually preferred for comparative purposes.

5. *d*

6. Percents on comparative income statements show the increase or decrease in each item from one period to the next. On common-size comparative income statements, each item is shown as a percent of net sales or revenues for that period.

7. (*a*) ($820,000 + $240,000 + $470,000)/
($350,000 + $180,000) = 2.9 to 1.
(*b*) ($820,000 + $240,000)/($350,000 + $180,000) = 2:1.

8. (*a*) $2,500,000/[($290,000 + $240,000)/2] = 9.43 times.
(*b*) ($290,000/$2,500,000) × 365 = 42 days.
(*c*) $750,000/[($530,000 + $470,000)/2] = 1.5 times.
(*d*) ($530,000/$750,000) × 365 = 258 days.

9. *c*

10. *b*

11. Profit margin × Total asset turnover = Return on total assets

$$\frac{\$945,000}{\$8,500,000} \times 1.8 = 20\%$$

Key Terms

Common-size financial statement (p. 647) Statement that expresses each amount as a percent of a base amount. In the balance sheet, total assets is usually the base and is expressed as 100%. In the income statement, net sales is usually the base.

Comparative financial statements (p. 645) Statement with data for two or more successive periods placed in side-by-side columns, often with changes shown in dollar amounts and percents.

Efficiency (p. 650) Company's productivity in using its assets; usually measured relative to how much revenue a certain level of assets generates.

Equity ratio (p. 653) Portion of total assets provided by equity, computed as total equity divided by total assets.

Financial reporting (p. 643) Process of communicating information relevant to investors, creditors, and others in making investment, credit, and business decisions.

Financial statement analysis (p. 642) Application of analytical tools to general-purpose financial statements and related data for making business decisions.

General-purpose financial statements (p. 643) Statements published periodically for use by a variety of interested parties; includes the income statement, balance sheet, statement of shareholder's equity

(or statement of retained earnings for a corporation), statement of cash flows, and notes to these statements.

Horizontal analysis (p. 644) Comparison of a company's financial condition and performance across time.

Liquidity (p. 650) Availability of resources to meet short-term cash requirements.

Market prospects (p. 656) Expectations (both good and bad) about a company's future performance as assessed by users and other interested parties.

Profitability (p. 654) Company's ability to generate an adequate return on invested capital.

Ratio analysis (p. 644) Determination of key relations between financial statement items as reflected in numerical measures.

Solvency (p. 653) Company's long-run financial viability and its ability to cover long-term obligations.

Vertical analysis (p. 644) Evaluation of each financial statement item or group of items in terms of a specific base amount.

Working capital (p. 650) Current assets minus current liabilities at a point in time.

Multiple Choice Quiz   Answers on p. 675   mhhe.com/wildCA2e

Additional Multiple Choice Quizzes are available at the book's Website.

1. A company's sales in 2009 were $300,000 and in 2010 were $351,000. Using 2009 as the base year, the percentage increase in sales for 2010 is:
  a. 17%
  b. 85%
  c. 100%
  d. 157%
  e. 48%

Use the following information for questions 2 through 5.

GALLOWAY COMPANY
Balance Sheet
December 31, 2010

Assets

Cash	$ 86,000
Accounts receivable	76,000
Merchandise inventory	122,000
Prepaid insurance	12,000
Long-term investments	98,000
Plant assets, net	436,000
Total assets	$830,000

Liabilities and Equity

Current liabilities	$124,000
Long-term liabilities	90,000
Common stock	300,000
Retained earnings	316,000
Total liabilities and equity	$830,000

2. What is Galloway Company's current ratio?
  a. 0.69
  b. 1.31
  c. 3.88
  d. 6.69
  e. 2.39

3. What is Galloway Company's acid-test ratio?
  a. 2.39
  b. 0.69
  c. 1.31
  d. 6.69
  e. 3.88

4. What is Galloway Company's debt ratio?
  a. 25.78%
  b. 100.00%
  c. 74.22%
  d. 137.78%
  e. 34.74%

5. What is Galloway Company's equity ratio?
  a. 25.78%
  b. 100.00%
  c. 34.74%
  d. 74.22%
  e. 137.78%

Discussion Questions

1. What is the difference between comparative financial statements and common-size comparative statements?

2. Which items are usually assigned a 100% value on (*a*) a common-size balance sheet and (*b*) a common-size income statement?

3. Explain the difference between financial reporting and financial statements.

4. What three factors would influence your evaluation as to whether a company's current ratio is good or bad?

5. Suggest several reasons why a 2:1 current ratio might not be adequate for a particular company.

6. Why is working capital given special attention in the process of analyzing balance sheets?

7. What does the number of days' sales uncollected indicate?

8. What does a relatively high accounts receivable turnover indicate about a company's short-term liquidity?

9. Why is a company's capital structure, as measured by debt and equity ratios, important to financial statement analysts?

10. How does inventory turnover provide information about a company's short-term liquidity?

11. What ratios would you compute to evaluate management performance?

12. Why would a company's return on total assets be different from its return on common stockholders' equity?

13. Use **Best Buy**'s financial statements in Appendix A to compute its return on total assets for the years ended March 1, 2008, and March 3, 2007. Total assets at February 25, 2006, were $11,864 (in millions).

---

connect

Which of the following items (1) through (9) are part of financial reporting but are *not* included as part of general-purpose financial statements? (1) stock price information and analysis, (2) statement of cash flows, (3) management discussion and analysis of financial performance, (4) income statement, (5) company news releases, (6) balance sheet, (7) financial statement notes, (8) statement of shareholders' equity, (9) prospectus.

QUICK STUDY

QS 24-1
Financial reporting **LO1**

What are four possible standards of comparison used to analyze financial statement ratios? Which of these is generally considered to be the most useful? Which one is least likely to provide a good basis for comparison?

QS 24-2
Standard of comparison **LO3**

Use the following information for Owens Corporation to determine (1) the 2009 and 2010 common-size percents for cost of goods sold using net sales as the base.

QS 24-3
Common-size and trend percents
LO5 LO6

($ thousands)	2010	2009
Net sales	$101,400	$58,100
Cost of goods sold	55,300	30,700

Compute the annual dollar changes and percent changes for each of the following accounts.

QS 24-4
Horizontal analysis **LO5**

	2010	2009
Short-term investments	$110,000	$80,000
Accounts receivable	22,000	25,000
Notes payable	30,000	0

Match the ratio to the building block of financial statement analysis to which it best relates.

QS 24-5
Building blocks of analysis
LO2 LO4 LO7

A. Liquidity and efficiency
B. Solvency
C. Profitability
D. Market prospects

1. _____ Gross margin ratio
2. _____ Acid-test ratio
3. _____ Equity ratio
4. _____ Return on total assets
5. _____ Dividend yield
6. _____ Book value per common share
7. _____ Days' sales in inventory
8. _____ Accounts receivable turnover
9. _____ Debt-to-equity
10. _____ Times interest earned

QS 24-6
Identifying financial ratios
L04 L07

1. Which two short-term liquidity ratios measure how frequently a company collects its accounts?
2. What measure reflects the difference between current assets and current liabilities?
3. Which two ratios are key components in measuring a company's operating efficiency? Which ratio summarizes these two components?

QS 24-7
Ratio interpretation
L07

For each ratio listed, identify whether the change in ratio value from 2009 to 2010 is usually regarded as favorable or unfavorable.

Ratio	2010	2009	Ratio	2010	2009
1. Profit margin	10%	9%	5. Accounts receivable turnover	6.7	5.5
2. Debt ratio	43%	39%	6. Basic earnings per share	$1.25	$1.10
3. Gross margin	32%	44%	7. Inventory turnover	3.4	3.6
4. Acid-test ratio	1.20	1.05	8. Dividend yield	4%	3.2%

QS 24-8
Defining financial ratios
L07 L08

Match each of the following terms A through J with the appropriate formulas 1 through 10.

A. Days' sales in inventory
B. Dividend yield
C. Total asset turnover
D. Inventory turnover
E. Return on common stockholders' equity

F. Gross margin ratio
G. Days' sales uncollected
H. Profit margin ratio
I. Times interest earned
J. Debt ratio

1. _____ $\dfrac{\text{Net income} - \text{preferred dividends}}{\text{Average common stockholders' equity}}$

2. _____ $\dfrac{\text{Accounts receivable}}{\text{Net sales}} \times 365$

3. _____ $\dfrac{\text{Total liabilities}}{\text{Total assets}}$

4. _____ $\dfrac{\text{Income before interest expense and income taxes}}{\text{Interest expense}}$

5. _____ $\dfrac{\text{Annual cash dividends per share}}{\text{Market price per share}}$

6. _____ $\dfrac{\text{Net sales} - \text{Cost of goods sold}}{\text{Net sales}}$

7. _____ $\dfrac{\text{Cost of goods sold}}{\text{Average inventory}}$

8. _____ $\dfrac{\text{Net sales}}{\text{Average total assets}}$

9. _____ $\dfrac{\text{Net income}}{\text{Net sales}}$

10. _____ $\dfrac{\text{Ending inventory}}{\text{Cost of goods sold}} \times 365$

EXERCISES

Exercise 24-1
Computation and analysis of trend percents **L05**

connect

Compute trend percents for the following accounts, using 2007 as the base year. State whether the situation as revealed by the trends appears to be favorable or unfavorable for each account.

	2011	2010	2009	2008	2007
Sales	$282,700	$270,700	$252,500	$234,460	$150,000
Cost of goods sold	128,100	121,980	115,180	106,340	67,000
Accounts receivable	18,000	17,200	16,300	15,100	9,000

Common-size percents for Danian Company's sales, cost of goods sold, and expenses follow. Determine whether net income increased, decreased, or remained unchanged in this three-year period. Assume that sales increased by 3.7% in 2009 and by 4.9% from 2008 levels.

Exercise 24–2
Determination of income effects from common-size percents   **LO5   LO6**

Common-Size Percents			
	2010	2009	2008
Sales	100.0%	100.0%	100.0%
Cost of goods sold	67.7	61.2	58.4
Total expenses	14.4	13.9	14.2

Express the following comparative income statements in common-size percents and assess whether or not this company's situation has improved in the most recent year.

Exercise 24–3
Common-size percent computation and interpretation   **LO6**

MULAN CORPORATION Comparative Income Statements For Years Ended December 31, 2010 and 2009		
	2010	2009
Sales	$657,386	$488,400
Cost of goods sold	427,301	286,202
Gross profit	230,085	202,198
Operating expenses	138,051	94,750
Net income	$ 92,034	$107,448

The following information is available for Orkay Company and Lowes Company, similar firms operating in the same industry. Write a half-page report comparing Orkay and Lowes using the available information. Your discussion should include their ability to meet current obligations and to use current assets efficiently.

Exercise 24–4
Analysis of short-term financial condition   **LO7   LO8**

	Orkay			Lowes		
	2010	2009	2008	2010	2009	2008
Current ratio	1.6	1.7	2.0	3.1	2.6	1.8
Acid-test ratio	0.9	1.0	1.1	2.7	2.4	1.5
Accounts receivable turnover	29.5	24.2	28.2	15.4	14.2	15.0
Merchandise inventory turnover	23.2	20.9	16.1	13.5	12.0	11.6
Working capital	$60,000	$48,000	$42,000	$121,000	$93,000	$68,000

Caren Company and Revlon Company are similar firms that operate in the same industry. Revlon began operations in 2009 and Caren in 2006. In 2011, both companies pay 7% interest on their debt to creditors. The following additional information is available.

Exercise 24–5
Analysis of efficiency and financial leverage   **LO7   LO8**

	Caren Company			Revlon Company		
	2011	2010	2009	2011	2010	2009
Total asset turnover	3.0	2.7	2.9	1.6	1.4	1.1
Return on total assets	6.9%	9.5%	8.7%	5.8%	5.5%	5.2%
Profit margin ratio	2.3%	2.4%	2.2%	2.7%	2.9%	2.8%
Sales	$400,000	$370,000	$386,000	$200,000	$160,000	$100,000

Write a half-page report comparing Caren and Revlon using the available information. Your analysis should include their ability to use assets efficiently to produce profits. Also comment on their success in employing financial leverage in 2011.

Exercise 24–6
Common-size percents
LO6

Nabisco Company's year-end balance sheets follow. Express the balance sheets in common-size percents. Round amounts to the nearest one-tenth of a percent. Analyze and comment on the results.

At December 31	2010	2009	2008
Assets			
Cash	$ 36,229	$ 42,780	$ 44,562
Accounts receivable, net	106,073	76,377	57,087
Merchandise inventory	137,408	98,929	62,038
Prepaid expenses	11,548	11,003	4,903
Plant assets, net	335,317	311,062	272,710
Total assets	$626,575	$540,151	$441,300
Liabilities and Equity			
Accounts payable	$157,577	$ 94,024	$ 57,087
Long-term notes payable secured by mortgages on plant assets	116,618	127,962	99,478
Common stock, $10 par value	163,500	163,500	163,500
Retained earnings	188,880	154,665	121,235
Total liabilities and equity	$626,575	$540,151	$441,300

Exercise 24–7
Liquidity analysis LO7

Refer to Nabisco Company's balance sheets in Exercise 24-6. Analyze its year-end short-term liquidity position at the end of 2010, 2009, and 2008 by computing (1) the current ratio and (2) the acid-test ratio. Comment on the ratio results. (Round ratio amounts to two decimals.)

Exercise 24–8
Liquidity analysis and
interpretation LO7

Refer to the Nabisco Company information in Exercise 24-6. The company's income statements for the years ended December 31, 2010 and 2009, follow. Assume that all sales are on credit and then compute: (1) days' sales uncollected, (2) accounts receivable turnover, (3) inventory turnover, and (4) days' sales in inventory. Comment on the changes in the ratios from 2009 to 2010. (Round amounts to one decimal.)

For Year Ended December 31	2010		2009	
Sales		$685,000		$557,000
Cost of goods sold	$417,850		$356,265	
Other operating expenses	207,282		141,971	
Interest expense	8,175		8,960	
Income taxes	12,900		12,450	
Total costs and expenses		646,207		519,646
Net income		$ 38,793		$ 37,354
Earnings per share		$ 2.37		$ 2.28

Exercise 24–9
Risk and capital structure analysis
LO7

Refer to the Nabisco Company information in Exercises 24-6 and 24-8. Compare the company's long-term risk and capital structure positions at the end of 2010 and 2009 by computing these ratios: (1) debt and equity ratios, (2) debt-to-equity ratio, and (3) times interest earned. Comment on these ratio results.

Exercise 24–10
Efficiency and
profitability analysis LO7

Refer to Nabisco Company's financial information in Exercises 24-6 and 24-8. Evaluate the company's efficiency and profitability by computing the following for 2010 and 2009: (1) profit margin ratio, (2) total asset turnover, and (3) return on total assets. Comment on these ratio results.

Refer to Nabisco Company's financial information in Exercises 24-6 and 24-8. Additional information about the company follows. To help evaluate the company's profitability, compute and interpret the following ratios for 2010 and 2009: (1) return on common stockholders' equity, (2) price-earnings ratio on December 31, and (3) dividend yield.

Exercise 24–11
Profitability analysis   **LO7**

Common stock market price, December 31, 2010	$30.00
Common stock market price, December 31, 2009	28.00
Annual cash dividends per share in 2010	0.28
Annual cash dividends per share in 2009	0.24

connect

Selected comparative financial statements of Astalon Company follow.

PROBLEM SET A

Problem 24–1A
Ratios and common-size statements   **LO5   LO6   LO7**

mhhe.com/wildCA2e

ASTALON COMPANY Comparative Income Statements For Years Ended December 31, 2010, 2009, and 2008			
	2010	**2009**	**2008**
Sales	$526,304	$403,192	$279,800
Cost of goods sold	316,835	255,624	179,072
Gross profit	209,469	147,568	100,728
Selling expenses	74,735	55,640	36,934
Administrative expenses	47,367	35,481	23,223
Total expenses	122,102	91,121	60,157
Income before taxes	87,367	56,447	40,571
Income taxes	16,250	11,572	8,236
Net income	$ 71,117	$ 44,875	$ 32,335

ASTALON COMPANY Comparative Balance Sheets December 31, 2010, 2009, and 2008			
	2010	**2009**	**2008**
Assets			
Current assets	$ 48,242	$ 38,514	$ 51,484
Long-term investments	0	800	3,620
Plant assets, net	92,405	97,259	58,047
Total assets	$140,647	$136,573	$113,151
Liabilities and Equity			
Current liabilities	$ 20,534	$ 20,349	$ 19,801
Common stock	69,000	69,000	51,000
Other paid-in capital	8,625	8,625	5,667
Retained earnings	42,488	38,599	36,683
Total liabilities and equity	$140,647	$136,573	$113,151

Required

1. Compute each year's current ratio. (Round ratio amounts to one decimal.)
2. Express the income statement data in common-size percents. (Round percents to two decimals.)

Problem 24–2A

Transactions, working capital, and liquidity ratios **LO7**

mhhe.com/wildCA2e

Check May 22: Current ratio, 2.23; Acid-test ratio, 1.37

May 29: Current ratio, 2.00; Working capital, $462,000

Page Corporation began the month of May with $884,000 of current assets, a current ratio of 2.6:1, and an acid-test ratio of 1.5:1. During the month, it completed the following transactions (the company uses a perpetual inventory system).

May	2	Purchased $70,000 of merchandise inventory on credit.
	8	Sold merchandise inventory that cost $60,000 for $130,000 cash.
	10	Collected $30,000 cash on an account receivable.
	15	Paid $31,000 cash to settle an account payable.
	17	Wrote off a $5,000 bad debt against the Allowance for Doubtful Accounts account.
	22	Declared a $1 per share cash dividend on its 67,000 shares of outstanding common stock.
	26	Paid the dividend declared on May 22.
	27	Borrowed $85,000 cash by giving the bank a 30-day, 10% note.
	28	Borrowed $100,000 cash by signing a long-term secured note.
	29	Used the $185,000 cash proceeds from the notes to buy new machinery.

Required

Prepare a table showing Page's (1) current ratio, (2) acid-test ratio, and (3) working capital, after each transaction. Round ratios to two decimals.

Problem 24–3A

Calculation of financial statement ratios **LO7**

mhhe.com/wildCA2e

Selected year-end financial statements of Cadet Corporation follow. (All sales were on credit; selected balance sheet amounts at December 31, 2009, were inventory, $56,900; total assets, $219,400; common stock, $85,000; and retained earnings, $52,348.)

CADET CORPORATION
Income Statement
For Year Ended December 31, 2010

Sales	$456,600
Cost of goods sold	297,450
Gross profit	159,150
Operating expenses	99,400
Interest expense	3,900
Income before taxes	55,850
Income taxes	22,499
Net income	$ 33,351

CADET CORPORATION
Balance Sheet
December 31, 2010

Assets		Liabilities and Equity	
Cash	$ 20,000	Accounts payable	$ 21,500
Short-term investments	8,200	Accrued wages payable	4,400
Accounts receivable, net	29,400	Income taxes payable	3,700
Notes receivable (trade)*	7,000	Long-term note payable, secured	
Merchandise inventory	34,150	by mortgage on plant assets	67,400
Prepaid expenses	2,700	Common stock	85,000
Plant assets, net	147,300	Retained earnings	66,750
Total assets	$248,750	Total liabilities and equity	$248,750

* These are short-term notes receivable arising from customer (trade) sales.

Required

Check Acid-test ratio, 2.2 to 1; Inventory turnover, 6.5

Compute the following: (1) current ratio, (2) acid-test ratio, (3) days' sales uncollected, (4) inventory turnover, (5) days' sales in inventory, (6) debt-to-equity ratio, (7) times interest earned, (8) profit margin ratio, (9) total asset turnover, (10) return on total assets, and (11) return on common stockholders' equity.

Summary information from the financial statements of two companies competing in the same industry follows.

Problem 24-4A
Comparative ratio
analysis   **L08   L07**

	Karto Company	Bryan Company		Karto Company	Bryan Company
Data from the current year-end balance sheets			**Data from the current year's income statement**		
Assets			Sales	$790,000	$897,200
Cash	$ 19,500	$ 36,000	Cost of goods sold	588,100	634,500
Accounts receivable, net	36,400	53,400	Interest expense	7,600	19,000
Current notes receivable (trade)	9,400	7,600	Income tax expense	15,185	24,769
Merchandise inventory	84,740	134,500	Net income	$179,115	$218,931
Prepaid expenses	6,200	7,250	Basic earnings per share	$ 4.71	$ 5.58
Plant assets, net	350,000	307,400			
Total assets	$506,240	$546,150			
			Beginning-of-year balance sheet data		
Liabilities and Equity			Accounts receivable, net	$ 26,800	$ 51,200
Current liabilities	$ 63,340	$ 73,819	Current notes receivable (trade)	0	0
Long-term notes payable	82,485	99,000	Merchandise inventory	55,600	107,400
Common stock, $5 par value	190,000	196,000	Total assets	408,000	422,500
Retained earnings	170,415	177,331	Common stock, $5 par value	190,000	196,000
Total liabilities and equity	$506,240	$546,150	Retained earnings	124,300	95,600

Required

1. For both companies compute the (*a*) current ratio, (*b*) acid-test ratio, (*c*) accounts (including notes) receivable turnover, (*d*) inventory turnover, (*e*) days' sales in inventory, and (*f*) days' sales uncollected. Identify the company you consider to be the better short-term credit risk and explain why.

2. For both companies compute the (*a*) profit margin ratio, (*b*) total asset turnover, (*c*) return on total assets, and (*d*) return on common stockholders' equity. Assuming that each company paid cash dividends of $3.50 per share and each company's stock can be purchased at $85 per share, compute their (*e*) price-earnings ratios and (*f*) dividend yields. Identify which company's stock you would recommend as the better investment and explain why.

Check   (1) Bryan: Accounts
receivable turnover, 16.0; Inventory
turnover, 5.2

(2) Karto: Profit margin,
22.7%; PE, 18.0

Selected comparative financial statement information of Danno Corporation follows.

PROBLEM SET B

Problem 24-1B
Ratios and common-size
statements   **L05   L06   L07**

DANNO CORPORATION Comparative Income Statements For Years Ended December 31, 2010, 2009, and 2008			
	2010	2009	2008
Sales	$392,000	$300,304	$208,400
Cost of goods sold	235,984	190,092	133,376
Gross profit	156,016	110,212	75,024
Selling expenses	55,664	41,442	27,509
Administrative expenses	35,280	26,427	17,297
Total expenses	90,944	67,869	44,806
Income before taxes	65,072	42,343	30,218
Income taxes	12,103	8,680	6,134
Net income	$ 52,969	$ 33,663	$ 24,084

DANNO CORPORATION
Comparative Balance Sheets
December 31, 2010, 2009, and 2008

	2010	2009	2008
Assets			
Current assets	$ 53,776	$ 42,494	$ 55,118
Long-term investments	0	400	4,110
Plant assets, net	99,871	106,303	64,382
Total assets	$153,647	$149,197	$123,610
Liabilities and Equity			
Current liabilities	$ 22,432	$ 22,230	$ 21,632
Common stock	70,000	70,000	52,000
Other paid-in capital	8,750	8,750	5,778
Retained earnings	52,465	48,217	44,200
Total liabilities and equity	$153,647	$149,197	$123,610

Required

1. Compute each year's current ratio. (Round ratio amounts to one decimal.)

2. Express the income statement data in common-size percents. (Round percents to two decimals.)

Problem 24-2B

Transactions, working capital, and liquidity ratios **LO7**

Check June 3: Current ratio, 2.88; Acid-test ratio, 2.40

June 30: Working capital, $(20,000); Current ratio, 0.97

Menardo Corporation began the month of June with $600,000 of current assets, a current ratio of 2.5:1, and an acid-test ratio of 1.4:1. During the month, it completed the following transactions (the company uses a perpetual inventory system).

June	1	Sold merchandise inventory that cost $150,000 for $240,000 cash.
	3	Collected $176,000 cash on an account receivable.
	5	Purchased $300,000 of merchandise inventory on credit.
	7	Borrowed $200,000 cash by giving the bank a 60-day, 8% note.
	10	Borrowed $240,000 cash by signing a long-term secured note.
	12	Purchased machinery for $550,000 cash.
	15	Declared a $1 per share cash dividend on its 160,000 shares of outstanding common stock.
	19	Wrote off a $10,000 bad debt against the Allowance for Doubtful Accounts account.
	22	Paid $24,000 cash to settle an account payable.
	30	Paid the dividend declared on June 15.

Required

Prepare a table showing the company's (1) current ratio, (2) acid-test ratio, and (3) working capital after each transaction. Round ratios to two decimals.

Problem 24-3B

Calculation of financial statement ratios **LO7**

Selected year-end financial statements of Steele Corporation follow. (All sales were on credit; selected balance sheet amounts at December 31, 2009, were inventory, $55,900; total assets, $249,400; common stock, $105,000; and retained earnings, $17,748.)

STEELE CORPORATION
Income Statement
For Year Ended December 31, 2010

Sales	$447,600
Cost of goods sold	298,150
Gross profit	149,450
Operating expenses	98,500
Interest expense	4,600
Income before taxes	46,350
Income taxes	18,672
Net income	$ 27,678

STEELE CORPORATION
Balance Sheet
December 31, 2010

Assets		Liabilities and Equity	
Cash	$ 8,000	Accounts payable	$ 25,500
Short-term investments	8,000	Accrued wages payable	3,000
Accounts receivable, net	28,800	Income taxes payable	4,000
Notes receivable (trade)*	8,000	Long-term note payable, secured	
Merchandise inventory	34,150	by mortgage on plant assets	63,400
Prepaid expenses	2,750	Common stock, $5 par value	105,000
Plant assets, net	150,300	Retained earnings	39,100
Total assets	$240,000	Total liabilities and equity	$240,000

* These are short-term notes receivable arising from customer (trade) sales.

Required

Compute the following: (1) current ratio, (2) acid-test ratio, (3) days' sales uncollected, (4) inventory turnover, (5) days' sales in inventory, (6) debt-to-equity ratio, (7) times interest earned, (8) profit margin ratio, (9) total asset turnover, (10) return on total assets, and (11) return on common stockholders' equity.

Check Acid-test ratio, 1.6 to 1;
Inventory turnover, 6.6

Summary information from the financial statements of two companies competing in the same industry follows.

Problem 24-4B
Comparative
ratio analysis   L08   L07

	Crisco Company	Silas Company			Crisco Company	Silas Company
Data from the current year-end balance sheets				**Data from the current year's income statement**		
Assets				Sales	$394,600	$668,500
Cash	$ 21,000	$ 37,500		Cost of goods sold	291,600	481,000
Accounts receivable, net	78,100	71,500		Interest expense	6,900	13,300
Current notes receivable (trade)	12,600	10,000		Income tax expense	6,700	14,300
Merchandise inventory	87,800	83,000		Net income	34,850	62,700
Prepaid expenses	10,700	11,100		Basic earnings per share	1.16	1.84
Plant assets, net	177,900	253,300				
Total assets	$388,100	$466,400				
				Beginning-of-year balance sheet data		
Liabilities and Equity				Accounts receivable, net	$ 73,200	$ 74,300
Current liabilities	$100,500	$ 98,000		Current notes receivable (trade)	0	0
Long-term notes payable	85,650	62,400		Merchandise inventory	106,100	81,500
Common stock, $5 par value	150,000	170,000		Total assets	384,400	444,000
Retained earnings	51,950	136,000		Common stock, $5 par value	150,000	170,000
Total liabilities and equity	$388,100	$466,400		Retained earnings	50,100	110,700

Required

1. For both companies compute the (a) current ratio, (b) acid-test ratio, (c) accounts (including notes) receivable turnover, (d) inventory turnover, (e) days' sales in inventory, and (f) days' sales uncollected. Identify the company you consider to be the better short-term credit risk and explain why.

2. For both companies compute the (a) profit margin ratio, (b) total asset turnover, (c) return on total assets, and (d) return on common stockholders' equity. Assuming that each company paid cash dividends of $1.10 per share and each company's stock can be purchased at $25 per share, compute their (e) price-earnings ratios and (f) dividend yields. Identify which company's stock you would recommend as the better investment and explain why.

Check (1) Crisco: Accounts receivable turnover, 4.8; Inventory turnover, 3.0

(2) Silas: Profit margin, 9.4%; PE, 13.6

SERIAL PROBLEM

Success Systems

*(This serial problem began in Chapter 1 and continues through most of the book. If previous chapter seg-
ments were not completed, the serial problem can begin at this point. It is helpful, but not necessary, to use
the Working Papers that accompany the book.)*

SP 24   Use the following selected data from Success Systems' income statement for the three months
ended March 31, 2011, and from its March 31, 2011, balance sheet to complete the requirements below:
computer services revenue, $25,160; net sales (of goods), $18,693; total sales and revenue, $43,853; cost
of goods sold, $14,052; net income, $18,686; quick assets, $100,205; current assets, $105,209; total assets, $129,909; current liabilities, $875; total liabilities, $875; and total equity, $129,034.

Required

1. Compute the gross margin ratio (both with and without services revenue) and net profit margin ratio.
2. Compute the current ratio and acid-test ratio.
3. Compute the debt ratio and equity ratio.
4. What percent of its assets are current? What percent are long term?

BEYOND THE NUMBERS

REPORTING IN ACTION
LO5   LO6   LO8

BTN 24–1   Refer to **Best Buy**'s financial statements in Appendix A to answer the following.

1. Compute common-size percents for fiscal years 2008 and 2007 for the following categories of assets:
(*a*) total current assets, (*b*) property and equipment, net, and (*c*) intangible assets. (Round to the nearest tenth of a percent.)
2. Comment on any significant changes across the years for the income statement trends computed in
part 1 and the balance sheet percents computed in part 2.

Fast Forward

3. Access Best Buy's financial statements for fiscal years ending after March 1, 2008, from Best Buy's
Website (**BestBuy.com**) or the SEC database (**www.SEC.gov**). Update your work for parts 1, 2, and 3
using the new information accessed.

COMPARATIVE ANALYSIS
LO3   LO6

(R) **RadioShack.**

BTN 24–2   Key figures for **Best Buy**, and **RadioShack** for fiscal year 2007 follow.

($ millions)	Best Buy	RadioShack
Cash and equivalents	$ 1,205	$ 472
Accounts receivable, net	548	248
Inventories	4,028	752
Retained earnings	5,507	1,781
Cost of sales	27,165	2,544
Revenues	35,934	4,778
Total assets	13,570	2,070

Required

1. Compute common-size percents for each of the companies using the data provided. (Round percents
to one decimal.)
2. Which company retains a higher portion of cumulative net income in the company?
3. Which company has a higher gross margin ratio on sales?
4. Which company holds a higher percent of its total assets as inventory?

BTN 24-3   As Beacon Company controller, you are responsible for informing the board of directors about its financial activities. At the board meeting, you present the following information.

ETHICS CHALLENGE
LO5   LO6   LO7

	2010	2009	2008
Sales trend percent	147.0%	135.0%	100.0%
Selling expenses to sales	10.1%	14.0%	15.6%
Sales to plant assets ratio	3.8 to 1	3.6 to 1	3.3 to 1
Current ratio	2.9 to 1	2.7 to 1	2.4 to 1
Acid-test ratio	1.1 to 1	1.4 to 1	1.5 to 1
Inventory turnover	7.8 times	9.0 times	10.2 times
Accounts receivable turnover	7.0 times	7.7 times	8.5 times
Total asset turnover	2.9 times	2.9 times	3.3 times
Return on total assets	10.4%	11.0%	13.2%
Return on stockholders' equity	10.7%	11.5%	14.1%
Profit margin ratio	3.6%	3.8%	4.0%

After the meeting, the company's CEO holds a press conference with analysts in which she mentions the following ratios.

	2010	2009	2008
Sales trend percent	147.0%	135.0%	100.0%
Selling expenses to sales	10.1%	14.0%	15.6%
Sales to plant assets ratio	3.8 to 1	3.6 to 1	3.3 to 1
Current ratio	2.9 to 1	2.7 to 1	2.4 to 1

Required

1. Why do you think the CEO decided to report 4 ratios instead of the 11 prepared?
2. Comment on the possible consequences of the CEO's reporting of the ratios selected.

BTN 24-4   Each team is to select a different industry, and each team member is to select a different company in that industry and acquire its financial statements. Use those statements to analyze the company, including at least one ratio from each of the four building blocks of analysis. When necessary, use the financial press to determine the market price of its stock. Communicate with teammates via a meeting, e-mail, or telephone to discuss how different companies compare to each other and to industry norms. The team is to prepare a single one-page memorandum reporting on its analysis and the conclusions reached.

WORKPLACE COMMUNICATION
LO2   LO7   LO8

BTN 24-5   Access the February 19, 2008, filing of the 2007 10-K report of the **Hershey Foods Corporation** (ticker HSY) at **www.SEC.gov** and complete the following requirements.

TAKING IT TO THE NET
LO4   LO7   LO8

Required

Compute or identify the following profitability ratios of Hershey for its years ending December 31, 2007, *and* December 31, 2006. Interpret its profitability using the results obtained for these two years.

1. Profit margin ratio.
2. Gross profit ratio.
3. Return on total assets. (Total assets in 2005 were $4,262,699.)

4. Return on common stockholders' equity. (Total shareholders' equity in 2005 was $1,016,380.)

5. Basic earnings per common share.

TEAMWORK IN ACTION

LO2 LO5 LO6 LO7

Pairing within teams may be necessary for part 2. Use as an in-class activity or as an assignment. Consider presentations to the entire class using team rotation with transparencies.

BTN 24-6   A team approach to learning financial statement analysis is often useful.

Required

1. Each team should write a description of horizontal and vertical analysis that all team members agree with and understand. Illustrate each description with an example.

2. *Each* member of the team is to select *one* of the following categories of ratio analysis. Explain what the ratios in that category measure. Choose one ratio from the category selected, present its formula, and explain what it measures.

   a. Liquidity and efficiency   **c.** Profitability

   b. Solvency   **d.** Market prospects

3. Each team member is to present his or her notes from part 2 to teammates. Team members are to confirm or correct other teammates' presentation.

ENTREPRENEURS IN BUSINESS

LO5 LO6 LO7 LO8

BTN 24-7   Assume that David and Tom Gardner of The Motley Fool (Fool.com) have impressed you since you first heard of their rather improbable rise to prominence in financial circles. You learn of a staff opening at The Motley Fool and decide to apply for it. Your resume is successfully screened from the thousands received and you advance to the interview process. You learn that the interview consists of analyzing the following financial facts and answering analysis questions. (*Note:* The data are taken from a small merchandiser in outdoor recreational equipment.)

	2010	2009	2008
Sales trend percents	137.0%	125.0%	100.0%
Selling expenses to sales	9.8%	13.7%	15.3%
Sales to plant assets ratio	3.5 to 1	3.3 to 1	3.0 to 1
Current ratio	2.6 to 1	2.4 to 1	2.1 to 1
Acid-test ratio	0.8 to 1	1.1 to 1	1.2 to 1
Merchandise inventory turnover	7.5 times	8.7 times	9.9 times
Accounts receivable turnover	6.7 times	7.4 times	8.2 times
Total asset turnover	2.6 times	2.6 times	3.0 times
Return on total assets	8.8%	9.4%	11.1%
Return on equity	9.75%	11.50%	12.25%
Profit margin ratio	3.3%	3.5%	3.7%

Required

Use these data to answer each of the following questions with explanations.

1. Is it becoming easier for the company to meet its current liabilities on time and to take advantage of any available cash discounts? Explain.

2. Is the company collecting its accounts receivable more rapidly? Explain.

3. Is the company's investment in accounts receivable decreasing? Explain.

4. Is the company's investment in plant assets increasing? Explain.

5. Is the owner's investment becoming more profitable? Explain.

6. Did the dollar amount of selling expenses decrease during the three-year period? Explain.

1. a; ($351,000/$300,000) × 100 =
117% − 100% = 17%

2. e; ($86,000 + $76,000 + $122,000 + $12,000)/
$124,000 = 2.39

3. c; ($86,000 + $76,000)/$124,000 = 1.31

4. a; ($124,000 + $90,000)/$830,000 = 25.78%

5. d; ($300,000 + $316,000)/$830,000 = 74.22%

ANSWERS TO MULTIPLE CHOICE QUIZ

A Look Back

Chapter 24 described the analysis and interpretation of financial statement information. We applied ratio analysis to better understand company performance and financial condition.

A Look at This Chapter

We begin our study of managerial accounting by explaining its purpose and describing its major characteristics. We also discuss cost concepts and describe how they help managers gather and organize information for making decisions. The reporting of manufacturing activities is also discussed.

A Look Ahead

Chapter 26 describes how we measure costs assigned to certain types of projects. We also explain the procedures used to determine costs using a job order costing system.

Chapter 25

Managerial Accounting Concepts and Principles

Learning Objectives

LO 1 Explain the purpose and nature of managerial accounting.

LO 2 Describe the lean business model.

LO 3 Describe accounting concepts useful in classifying costs.

LO 4 Define product and period costs and explain how they impact financial statements.

LO 5 Explain how balance sheets and income statements for manufacturing and merchandising companies differ.

LO 6 Compute cost of goods sold for a manufacturer.

LO 7 Explain manufacturing activities and the flow of manufacturing costs.

LO 8 Prepare a manufacturing statement and explain its purpose and links to financial statements.

LO 9 Compute cycle time and cycle efficiency, and explain their importance to production management.

"Find a niche and stay focused"
—Brian Taylor

No Naked Popcorn

ELK GROVE VILLAGE, IL—As a hungry college student, Brian Taylor liked to eat popcorn. Lots of it. Bored with "naked popcorn," Brian began experimenting with seasonings such as nacho cheese, cajun, jalapeño, and apple cinnamon. After he shared his concoctions with friends, dorm mates, and others, the demand for Brian's seasonings ballooned. In less than two years, Brian had the number one shake-on popcorn seasoning in the market, **Kernel Season's** (<u>KernelSeasons.com</u>).

Brian launched Kernel Season's with $7,000 he earned from giving tennis lessons and selling knives. In the beginning, he gave away his popcorn seasonings to local theaters to build awareness. Just like his college friends, moviegoers loved the all-natural, low-calorie seasonings. Soon theaters across the country were asking for his seasonings, and Brian worked hard to meet demand. "I was the only employee," explains Brian. "I made sales and shipped orders. I was figuring it out as I went along."

Well, business is now popping. Fourteen varieties of Kernel Season's are available in over 14,000 movie theaters and 15,000 grocery stores. Annual sales now exceed $5 million, and Brian is on Inc.com's "30 under 30," a list of America's coolest young entrepreneurs.

Brian believes college is the best time to start a new business. "Risk is low, and banks understand young entrepreneurs are trying to get things going," explains Brian. But Brian emphasizes that understanding basic managerial principles, product and period costs, manufacturing statements, and cost flows is equally crucial. "[I was] dedicated to business classes," says Brian, including my "accounting class." Brian uses managerial accounting information from his production process to monitor and control costs and to assess new business opportunities, including Kernel Season's apparel. Brian further stresses that company success and growth require him to develop budgets, monitor product performance, and make quick decisions.

Brian believes entrepreneurs fill a void by creating a niche. However, financial success depends on monitoring and controlling operations to best meet customer needs. Brian cautions would-be entrepreneurs to "stay focused" because in the absence of applying managerial accounting principles and concepts, it's just naked popcorn.

[Sources: *Kernel Season's Website,* January 2009; *Lake County News Sun,* October 2003; *Female Entrepreneur,* July/August 2003; *Chicago Tonight* interview, August 2007; *StartupNation.com,* May 2007; *Inc.com Website,* May 2008]

Managerial accounting, like financial accounting, provides information to help users make better decisions. However, managerial accounting and financial accounting differ in important ways, which this chapter explains. This chapter also compares the accounting and reporting practices used by manufacturing and merchandising companies. A merchandising company sells products without changing their condition. A manufacturing company buys raw materials and turns them into finished products for sale to customers. A third type of company earns revenues by providing services rather than products. The skills, tools, and techniques developed for measuring a manufacturing company's activities apply to service companies as well. The chapter concludes by explaining the flow of manufacturing activities and preparing the manufacturing statement.

Managerial Accounting Concepts and Principles

Managerial Accounting Basics
- Purpose of managerial accounting
- Nature of managerial accounting
- Managerial accounting in business

Managerial Cost Concepts
- Types of cost classifications
- Identification of cost classification
- Cost concepts for service companies

Reporting Manufacturing Activities
- Balance sheet
- Income statement
- Flow of activities
- Manufacturing statement

Managerial Accounting Basics

Purpose of Managerial Accounting

LO1 Explain the purpose and nature of managerial accounting.

Managerial accounting provides financial and nonfinancial information to an organization's managers. Information from the financial accounting system is incomplete for internal decision makers who manage organizations.

Much of managerial accounting involves gathering information about costs for planning and control decisions. The purpose of managerial accounting is to provide information to aid managers in their planning and control decisions.

Planning involves setting goals and making plans to achieve them. **Control** is the process of monitoring planning decisions and evaluating an organization's activities and employees.

Managers use information to plan and control business activities. Managers must plan a company's future. They seek to take advantage of opportunities or to overcome obstacles. They also try to control activities and ensure their effective and efficient implementation. Managerial accounting information helps these internal users make both planning and control decisions. In the next section we describe important characteristics of managerial accounting information. In later chapters, we explain how managers also use this information to direct and improve business operations.

Nature of Managerial Accounting

Managerial accounting has its own special characteristics. To understand these characteristics, we compare managerial accounting to financial accounting; they differ in at least seven important ways. These differences are summarized in Exhibit 25.1.

Managerial accounting systems are flexible. Managers decide what information they want and how it is reported. Managerial accounting information is not typically provided to external users and is not audited. This means managerial accounting information can be obtained more quickly. Managerial accounting also regularly includes predictions of conditions and events. For example, one important managerial accounting report is a budget. **Budgets** commonly predict revenues, expenses, and other items. Managerial accounting's focus on future events makes it useful in planning activities and in evaluating and controlling current activities.

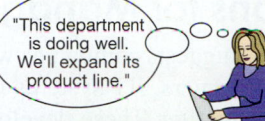

	Financial Accounting	Managerial Accounting
1. Users and decision makers	Investors, creditors, and other users external to the organization	Managers, employees, and decision makers internal to the organization
2. Purpose of information	Assist external users in making investment, credit, and other decisions	Assist managers in making planning and control decisions
3. Flexibility of practice	Structured and often controlled by GAAP	Relatively flexible (no GAAP constraints)
4. Timeliness of information	Often available only after an audit is complete	Available quickly without the need to wait for an audit
5. Time dimension	Focus on historical information with some predictions	Many projections and estimates; historical information also presented
6. Focus of information	Emphasis on whole organization	Emphasis on an organization's projects, processes, and subdivisions
7. Nature of information	Monetary information	Mostly monetary; but also nonmonetary information (such as quality measures)

Managerial Accounting in Business

Because of changes in the business environment, the importance of managerial accounting tools continues to increase. This section describes some of these changes and their impact on managerial accounting.

Lean Business Model   There is an increased emphasis on *customers* as the most important constituent of a business. Customers expect to derive a certain value for the money they spend to buy products and services. This implies that companies adopt a **customer orientation,** which means that employees understand and adapt to the changing needs and wants of their customers.

Many companies have responded by adopting the **lean business model,** whose goal is to *eliminate waste* while "satisfying the customer" and "providing a positive return" to the company.

Lean Practices   **Continuous improvement** rejects the notions of "good enough" or "acceptable" and challenges employees and managers to continuously experiment with new and improved business practices. This has led companies to adopt practices such as total quality management (TQM) and just-in-time (JIT) manufacturing. The philosophy underlying both practices is continuous improvement; the difference is in the focus.

Total quality management focuses on quality improvement and applies this standard to all aspects of business activities. Goals of a TQM process include reduced waste, better inventory control, fewer defects, and continuous improvement. Just-in-time concepts have similar goals. In doing so, managers and employees seek to uncover waste in business activities including accounting activities such as payroll and disbursements.

Just-in-time manufacturing is a system that acquires inventory and produces only when needed. JIT companies manufacture products only after they receive a customer order (a *demand-pull* system) and then deliver the customer's requirements on time.

LO2 Describe the lean business model.

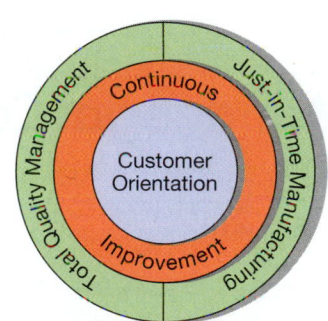

IN THE NEWS

Global Lean   **Toyota Motor Corporation** pioneered lean manufacturing, and it has since spread to other manufacturers throughout the world. The goals include improvements in quality, reliability, inventory turnover, productivity, exports, and—above all—sales and income.

Implications for Managerial Accounting

A customer focus suggests companies will provide goods or services tailored to the specific demands of their customers. JIT systems increase the importance of timely and accurate cost and performance information. These developments impact how the managerial accounting system collects and reports information.

The remainder of this book looks carefully at managerial accounting information, how to gather it, and how managers use it. We consider concepts used to determine the cost of products and services and topics like budgeting, break-even analysis, product costing, profit planning, and cost analysis.

HOW YOU DOIN'?   Answers—p. 695

1. Managerial accounting produces information (*a*) to meet internal users' needs, (*b*) to meet a user's specific needs, (*c*) often focusing on the future, or (*d*) all of these.

2. What is the difference between the intended users of financial and managerial accounting?

3. Do generally accepted accounting principles (GAAP) control and dictate managerial accounting?

4. What is the basic objective for a company practicing total quality management?

IN THE NEWS

Code of Ethics   The **Institute of Management Accountants** (IMA), the professional association for management accountants, has issued a code of ethics to help accountants involved in solving ethical dilemmas. The IMA's Statement of Ethical Professional Practice requires that management accountants be competent, maintain confidentiality, act with integrity, and communicate information in a fair and credible manner.

The IMA provides a "road map" for resolving ethical conflicts. It suggests that an employee follow the company's policies on how to resolve such conflicts. If the conflict remains unresolved, an employee should contact the next level of management (such as the immediate supervisor) who is not involved in the ethical conflict.

Managerial Cost Concepts

LO3 Describe accounting concepts useful in classifying costs.

Organizations incur many different types of costs. We can classify costs on the basis of their (1) behavior, (2) traceability, (3) controllability, (4) relevance, and (5) function. This section explains each concept for assigning costs to products and services.

Types of Cost Classifications

Classification by Behavior   Costs can be classified as fixed or variable. A **fixed cost** does not change with changes in the volume of activity (within a range of activity known as an activity's *relevant range*). For example, straight-line depreciation on equipment is a fixed cost. A **variable cost** changes when the volume of activity changes. Sales commissions computed as a percent of sales revenue are variable costs. Additional examples of fixed and variable costs for a bike manufacturer are provided in Exhibit 25.2. **Mixed costs** are a combination of fixed and variable costs. Equipment rental often includes a fixed cost for some minimum amount and a variable cost based on amount of usage. Classification of costs by behavior is helpful in short-term decision making. We discuss common short-term managerial decisions in Chapter 29.

Exhibit 25.2

Fixed and Variable Costs

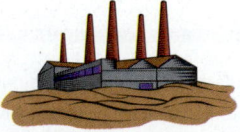

Fixed Cost: Rent for Rocky Mountain Bikes' building is $22,000, and doesn't change with the number of bikes produced.

Variable Cost: Cost of bicycle tires is variable with the number of bikes produced—this cost is $15 per pair.

Classification by Traceability

A **cost object** is a product, process, department, or customer to which costs are assigned. **Direct costs** are traceable to a single cost object. For example, if a product is a cost object, its material and labor costs are usually directly traceable. **Indirect costs** cannot be traced to a single cost object. An example of an indirect cost is a maintenance plan that benefits two or more departments. Exhibit 25.3 identifies examples of both direct and indirect costs for the maintenance department in a manufacturing plant. Classification of costs by traceability is useful for cost allocation. This is discussed in Chapter 27.

Exhibit 25.3

Direct and Indirect Costs of a Maintenance Department

Direct Costs		Indirect Costs	
• Salaries of maintenance department employees	• Materials purchased by maintenance department	• Factory accounting	• Factory light and heat
• Equipment purchased by maintenance department	• Maintenance department equipment depreciation	• Factory administration	• Factory internal audit
		• Factory rent	• Factory intranet
		• Factory managers' salary	• Insurance on factory

Classification by Controllability

A cost can be **controllable** or **not controllable.** Whether a cost is controllable or not depends on the employee's responsibilities, as shown in Exhibit 25.4. For example, investments in machinery are controllable by upper-level managers but not lower-level managers. Many daily operating expenses such as overtime often are controllable by lower-level managers. Classifying costs by controllability is especially useful for assigning responsibility to and evaluating managers.

Senior Manager
Controls costs of investment in land, buildings, and equipment.

Supervisor
Controls daily expenses such as supplies, maintenance, and overtime.

Exhibit 25.4

Controllability of Costs

Classification by Relevance

A **sunk cost** has already been incurred and cannot be avoided or changed. It is irrelevant to future decisions. One example is the cost of a company's office equipment previously purchased. An **out-of-pocket cost** requires a future outlay of cash and is relevant for decision making. Future purchases of equipment involve out-of-pocket costs. A discussion of relevant costs must also consider opportunity costs. An **opportunity cost** is the potential benefit lost by choosing a specific action from two or more alternatives. One example is a student giving up wages from a job to attend evening classes. Consideration of opportunity cost is important when the manager must choose between alternatives. This is discussed in Chapter 29.

Classification by Function

Another cost classification (for manufacturers) is capitalization as inventory or to expense as incurred. Costs capitalized as inventory are called **product costs,** which refer to expenditures necessary and integral to finished products. They include direct materials, direct labor, and indirect manufacturing costs called *overhead costs*. Product costs pertain to activities carried out to manufacture the product. Costs expensed are called **period costs,** which refer to expenditures identified more with a time period than with finished products. They include selling and general administrative expenses. Period costs pertain to activities that are not part of the manufacturing process. A distinction between product and period costs is important because period costs are expensed in the income statement and product costs are assigned to inventory on the balance sheet until that inventory is sold. An ability to understand and identify product costs and period costs is crucial to using and interpreting a *manufacturing statement* described later in this chapter.

LO4 Define product and period costs and explain how they impact financial statements.

Exhibit 25.5 shows the different effects of product and period costs. Period costs flow directly to the current income statement as expenses. They are not reported as assets. Product costs are first assigned to inventory. Their final treatment depends on when inventory is sold or disposed of. Product costs assigned to finished goods that are sold in year 2009 are reported on the 2009 income statement as part of cost of goods sold. Product costs assigned to unsold inventory are carried forward on the balance sheet at the end of year 2009. These amounts could be in any or all of raw materials, goods in process, or finished goods inventories. If this inventory is sold in year 2010, product costs assigned to it are reported as part of cost of goods sold in that year's income statement.

Only costs of production and purchases are classified as product costs. Product costs are either on the income statement as part of cost of goods sold or on the balance sheet as inventory. Period costs appear only on the income statement under operating expenses. See Exhibit 25.5.

Exhibit 25.5

Period and Product Costs in
Financial Statements

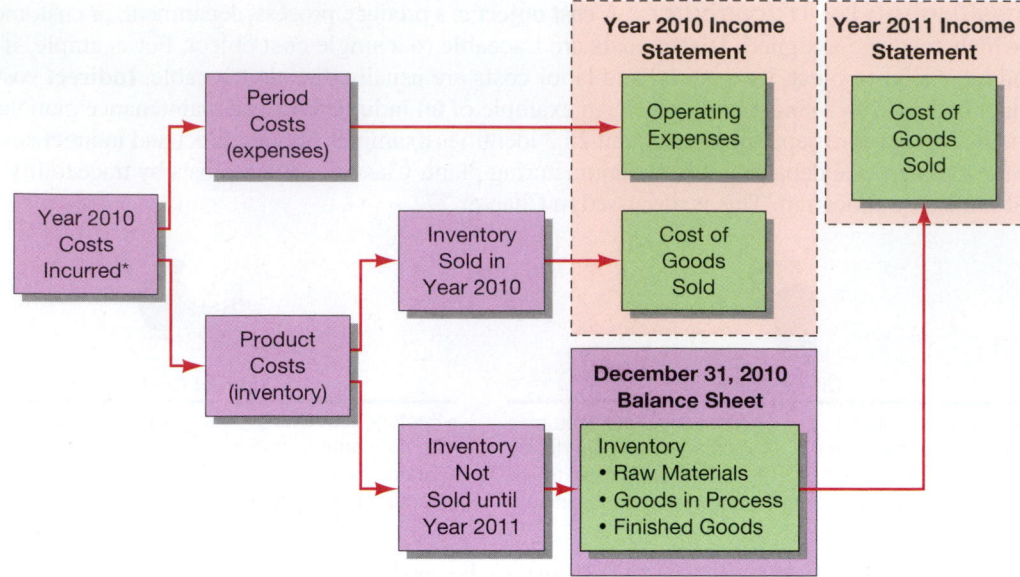

* This diagram excludes costs to acquire assets other than inventory.

Identification of Cost Classification

A cost can be classified using any one (or combination) of the five different means described here. To do this we must understand costs and operations. Potential multiple classifications are shown in Exhibit 25.6 using different costs incurred in manufacturing mountain bikes. The finished bike is the cost object. Proper allocation of these costs and the managerial decisions based on cost data depend on a correct cost classification.

Exhibit 25.6

Examples of Multiple
Cost Classifications

Cost Item	By Behavior	By Traceability	By Function
Bicycle tires	Variable	Direct	Product
Wages of assembly worker*	Variable	Direct	Product
Advertising	Fixed	Indirect	Period
Production manager's salary	Fixed	Indirect	Product
Office depreciation	Fixed	Indirect	Period

* Although an assembly worker's wages are classified as variable costs, their actual behavior depends on how workers are paid and whether their wages are based on a union contract (such as piece rate or monthly wages).

Cost Concepts for Service Companies

The cost concepts described are generally applicable to service organizations. For example, consider **Southwest Airlines**. Its cost of beverages for passengers is a variable cost based on number of passengers. The cost of leasing an aircraft is fixed with respect to number of passengers. We can also trace a flight crew's salary to a specific flight whereas we likely cannot trace wages for the ground crew to a specific flight. Classification by function (such as product versus period costs) is not relevant to service companies because services are not inventoried. Instead, costs incurred by a service firm are expensed in the reporting period when incurred.

Service Costs

- Beverages and snacks
- Cleaning fees
- Pilot and co-pilot salaries
- Attendant salaries
- Fuel and oil costs
- Travel agent fees
- Ground crew salaries

HOW YOU DOIN'?   Answers—p. 695

5. Which type of cost behavior increases total costs when volume of activity increases?

6. How could traceability of costs improve managerial decisions?

Reporting Manufacturing Activities

Manufacturing activities differ from both selling merchandise and providing services. Merchandisers buy goods ready for sale while manufacturers produce goods from materials and labor. **Payless** is a merchandising company. It buys and sells shoes without physically changing them. **Adidas** manufactures shoes, apparel, and accessories. It purchases materials such as leather, cloth, dye, plastic, rubber, glue, and laces and then uses employees' labor to convert these materials to products. **Southwest Airlines** is a service company that transports people and items.

Since their activities differ, the financial statements for manufacturing companies also differ slightly. This section compares manufacturer's and merchandiser's financial statements.

Manufacturer's Balance Sheet

Manufacturers carry several unique assets and usually have three inventories instead of the single inventory that merchandisers carry. Exhibit 25.7 shows three different inventories in the current asset section of the balance sheet for Rocky Mountain Bikes, a manufacturer. The three inventories are raw materials, goods in process, and finished goods.

L05 Explain how balance sheets and income statements for manufacturing and merchandising companies differ.

Raw Materials Inventory **Raw materials inventory** are the goods a company acquires to use in making products. It uses raw materials in two ways: directly and indirectly. Most raw materials physically become part of a product and are identified with specific units or batches of a product. Raw materials used directly in a product are called *direct materials*. Other materials used to support production processes are sometimes not as clearly identified with specific units or batches of product. These materials are called **indirect materials.** Items used as indirect materials often appear on a

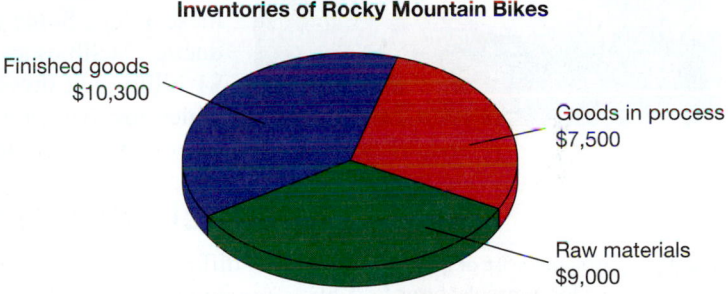

Inventories of Rocky Mountain Bikes

Finished goods $10,300

Goods in process $7,500

Raw materials $9,000

Exhibit 25.7

Balance Sheet for a Manufacturer

ROCKY MOUNTAIN BIKES Balance Sheet December 31, 2010			
Assets		**Liabilities and Equity**	
Current assets		Current liabilities	
Cash	$ 11,000	Accounts payable	$ 14,000
Accounts receivable, net	30,150	Wages payable	540
Raw materials inventory	**9,000**	Interest payable	2,000
Goods in process inventory	**7,500**	Income taxes payable	32,600
Finished goods inventory	**10,300**	Total current liabilities	49,140
Factory supplies	350	Long-term liabilities	
Prepaid insurance	300	Long-term notes payable	50,000
Total current assets	68,600	Total liabilities	99,140
Plant assets			
Small tools	1,100	Stockholders' equity	
Delivery equipment, net	5,000	Common stock, $1.20 par	24,000
Office equipment, net	1,300	Paid-in capital	76,000
Factory machinery, net	65,500	Retained earnings	49,760
Factory building, net	86,700	Total stockholders' equity	149,760
Land	9,500	Total liabilities and equity	$248,900
Total plant assets, net	169,100		
Intangible assets (patents), net	11,200		
Total assets	$248,900		

balance sheet as factory supplies or are included in raw materials. Some direct materials are classified as indirect materials when their costs are low (insignificant). For instance, keeping detailed records of the amount of glue used to manufacture one shoe is not cost beneficial. Glue instead would be an indirect cost.

Goods in Process Inventory   Manufacturers also hold **goods in process inventory,** also called *work in process inventory.* It consists of products in the process of being manufactured but not yet complete. The amount of goods in process inventory depends on the type of production process. If the time required to produce a unit of product is short, the goods in process inventory is likely small. If weeks or months are needed to produce a unit, the goods in process inventory is usually larger.

Finished Goods Inventory   Manufacturers also own **finished goods inventory,** which consists of completed products ready for sale. This inventory is similar to merchandise inventory owned by a merchandising company. A merchandiser often uses the term *merchandise* inventory; a manufacturer often uses the term *finished goods* inventory. Manufacturers also often own unique plant assets such as small tools, factory buildings, factory equipment, and patents to manufacture products. The balance sheet in Exhibit 25.7 shows that Rocky Mountain Bikes owns all of these assets. Some manufacturers invest millions or even billions of dollars in production facilities and patents. **Briggs & Stratton**'s recent balance sheet shows about $1 billion net investment in land, buildings, machinery and equipment, much of which involves production facilities. It manufactures more racing engines than any other company in the world.

Manufacturer's Income Statement

LO6 Compute cost of goods sold for a manufacturer.

The main difference between a manufacturer's income statement and that of a merchandiser involves the items making up cost of goods sold. Exhibit 25.8 compares the computation of cost of goods sold for a manufacturer (Rocky Mountain Bikes) and a merchandiser (Tele-Mart). A merchandiser adds cost of goods *purchased* to beginning merchandise inventory and then subtracts ending merchandise inventory to get cost of goods sold. A manufacturer adds cost of goods *manufactured* to beginning finished goods inventory and then subtracts ending finished goods inventory to get cost of goods sold.

Exhibit 25.8

Cost of Goods Sold for a Merchandiser and Manufacturer

Merchandising Company (Tele-Mart)		Manufacturing Company (Rocky Mtn. Bikes)	
Cost of goods sold		Cost of goods sold	
Beginning *merchandise* inventory	$ 14,200	**Beginning *finished goods* inventory**	$ 11,200
Cost of merchandise *purchased*	234,150	**Cost of goods *manufactured***	170,500
Goods available for sale	248,350	Goods available for sale	181,700
Less ending *merchandise* inventory	12,100	**Less ending *finished goods* inventory**	10,300
Cost of goods sold	$236,250	Cost of goods sold	$171,400

* Cost of goods manufactured is reported in the income statement of Exhibit 25.9. We show later in this chapter how to derive cost of goods manufactured from the manufacturing statement.

Although the cost of goods sold computations are similar, the numbers in these computations reflect different activities. A merchandiser's cost of goods purchased is the cost of buying products to be sold. A manufacturer's cost of goods manufactured is the sum of direct materials, direct labor, and factory overhead costs incurred in producing products. The remaining income statement sections are similar. The remainder of this section further explains these three manufacturing costs.

Direct Materials **Direct materials** are tangible components of a finished product. **Direct material costs** are the expenditures for direct materials that are traced through the manufacturing process to finished goods. Examples of direct materials in manufacturing a mountain bike include its tires, seat, frame, pedals, brakes, cables, gears, and handlebars. The chart in the margin shows that direct materials generally make up about 45% of manufacturing costs in today's products, but this amount varies across industries and companies.

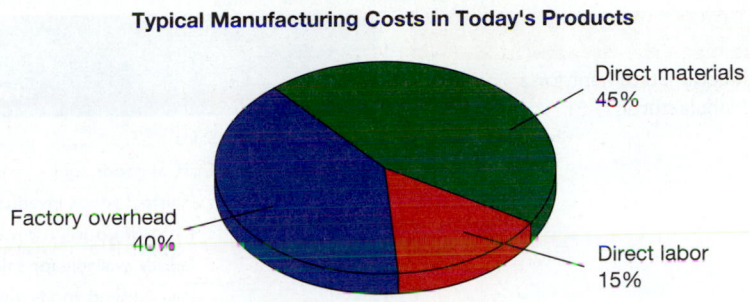

Typical Manufacturing Costs in Today's Products

Direct materials 45%

Factory overhead 40%

Direct labor 15%

Direct Labor **Direct labor** refers to the efforts of employees who physically convert materials to finished product. **Direct labor costs** are the wages and salaries for direct labor that are traced through the manufacturing process to finished goods. Examples of direct labor in manufacturing a mountain bike include operators directly involved in converting raw materials into finished products (welding, painting, forming) and assembly workers who attach materials such as tires, seats, pedals, and brakes to the bike frames. Costs of other workers on the assembly line who assist direct laborers are classified as **indirect labor costs. Indirect labor** refers to manufacturing workers' efforts not linked to specific units or batches of the product. Indirect labor costs are part of factory overhead.

Factory Overhead **Factory overhead** consists of all manufacturing costs that are not direct materials or direct labor. Factory overhead is also called *manufacturing overhead.* **Factory overhead costs** cannot be traced to finished goods. These costs include indirect materials and indirect labor. Overtime paid to direct laborers is also included in overhead because overtime is due to delays, interruptions, or constraints not necessarily identifiable to a specific product or batches of product. Factory overhead costs also include maintenance of the mountain bike factory, supervision of its employees, repairing manufacturing equipment, factory utilities (water, gas, electricity), production manager's salary, factory rent, depreciation on factory buildings and equipment, factory insurance, property taxes on factory buildings and equipment, and factory accounting and legal services. Factory overhead does *not* include selling and administrative expenses because they are not incurred in manufacturing products. These expenses are called *period costs.* They are recorded as expenses on the income statement when incurred.

Prime and Conversion Costs Direct material costs and direct labor costs are also called **prime costs**—expenditures directly associated with the manufacture of finished goods. Direct labor costs and overhead costs are called **conversion costs**—expenditures incurred in the process of converting raw materials to finished goods. Direct labor costs are considered both prime costs and conversion costs.

Reporting Performance Exhibit 25.9 shows the income statement for Rocky Mountain Bikes. Its operating expenses include sales salaries, office salaries, and depreciation of delivery and office equipment. Operating expenses do not include manufacturing costs such as factory workers' wages and depreciation of production equipment and the factory buildings. Manufacturers treat costs such as depreciation and rent as product costs if they are related to manufacturing. These manufacturing costs are reported as part of cost of goods manufactured and included in cost of goods sold. We explained why and how this is done in the section Classification by Function.

HOW YOU DOIN'? Answers—p. 695

7. What are the three types of inventory on a manufacturing company's balance sheet?

8. How does cost of goods sold differ for merchandising versus manufacturing companies?

ROCKY MOUNTAIN BIKES
Income Statement
For Year Ended December 31, 2010

Sales			$310,000
Cost of goods sold			
Finished goods inventory, Dec. 31, 2009		$ 11,200	
Cost of goods manufactured		**170,500**	
Goods available for sale		181,700	
Less finished goods inventory, Dec. 31, 2010		10,300	
Cost of goods sold			171,400
Gross profit			138,600
Operating expenses			
Selling expenses			
Sales salaries expense	18,000		
Advertising expense	5,500		
Delivery wages expense	12,000		
Shipping supplies expense	250		
Insurance expense—Delivery equipment	300		
Depreciation expense—Delivery equipment	2,100		
Total selling expenses		38,150	
General and administrative expenses			
Office salaries expense	15,700		
Miscellaneous expense	200		
Bad debts expense	1,550		
Office supplies expense	100		
Depreciation expense—Office equipment	200		
Interest expense	4,000		
Total general and administrative expenses		21,750	
Total operating expenses		59,900	
Income before income taxes		78,700	
Income taxes expense		32,600	
Net income		$ 46,100	
Net income per common share (20,000 shares)		$ 2.31	

Flow of Manufacturing Activities

LO7 Explain manufacturing activities and the flow of manufacturing costs.

To understand manufacturing and its reports, we must first understand the flow of manufacturing activities and costs. Exhibit 25.10 shows the flow of manufacturing activities for a manufacturer. This exhibit has three important sections: *materials activity, production activity,* and *sales activity.* We explain each activity in this section.

Materials Activity   The far left side of Exhibit 25.10 shows the flow of raw materials. Manufacturers usually start a period with some beginning raw materials inventory left from the previous period. The company then buys more raw materials in the current period. Adding these purchases to beginning inventory gives total raw materials available for use in production. These raw materials are then either used in production in the current period or remain in inventory at the end of the period for use in future periods.

Production Activity   The middle section of Exhibit 25.10 describes production activity. Four factors come together in production: beginning goods in process inventory, direct materials, direct labor, and overhead. Beginning goods in process inventory consists of partly assembled products from the previous period. Production activity results in products that are either finished or remain unfinished at the period-end. The cost of finished products makes up the cost of goods manufactured for the current period. Unfinished products are identified as ending

The series of activities that add value to a company's products or services is called a **value chain.**

Exhibit 25.10
Activities and Cost Flows in Manufacturing

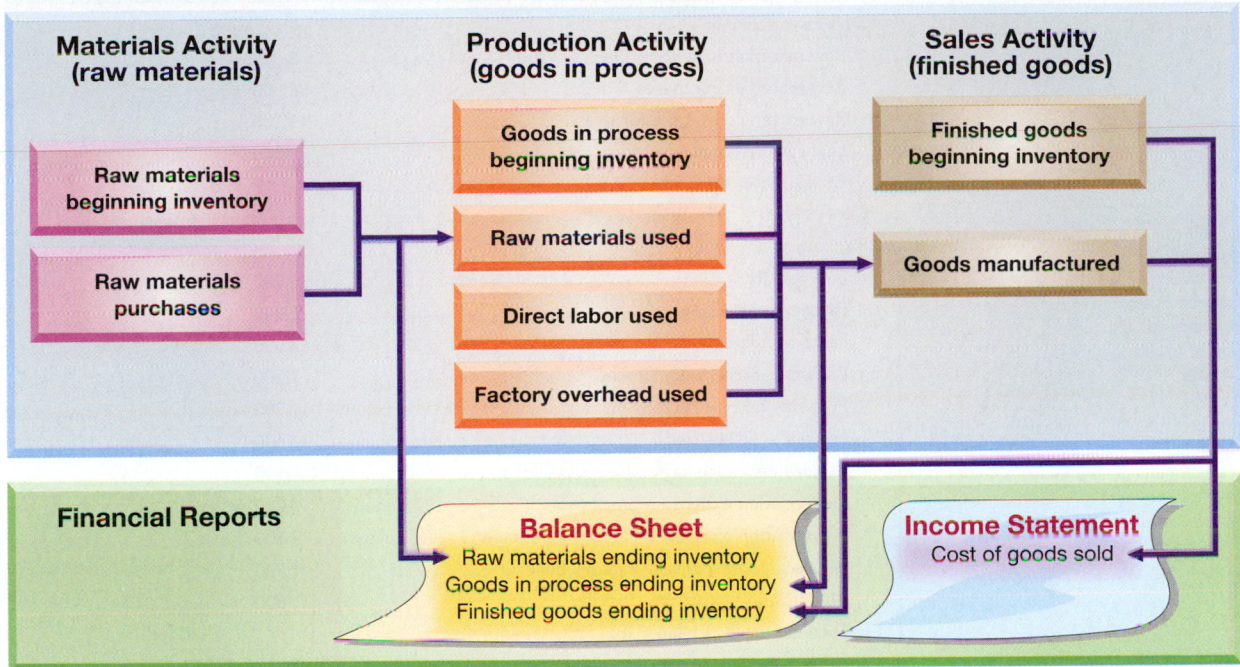

goods in process inventory. The cost of unfinished products consists of direct materials, direct labor, and factory overhead, and is reported on the current period's balance sheet. The costs of both finished goods manufactured and goods in process are *product costs*.

Sales Activity   The company's sales activity is portrayed in the far right side of Exhibit 25.10. Newly completed units are combined with beginning finished goods inventory to make up total finished goods available for sale in the current period. The cost of finished products sold is reported on the income statement as cost of goods sold. The cost of products not sold is reported on the current period's balance sheet as ending finished goods inventory.

Manufacturing Statement

A company's manufacturing activities are described in a **manufacturing statement,** also called the *schedule of manufacturing activities* or the *schedule of cost of goods manufactured.* The manufacturing statement summarizes the types and amounts of costs incurred in a company's manufacturing process. Exhibit 25.11 shows the manufacturing statement for Rocky Mountain Bikes. The statement is divided into four parts: *direct materials, direct labor, overhead,* and *computation of cost of goods manufactured.* We describe each of these parts in this section.

L08 Prepare a manufacturing statement and explain its purpose and links to financial statements.

① The manufacturing statement begins by computing direct materials used. We start by adding beginning raw materials inventory of $8,000 to the current period's purchases of $86,500. This yields $94,500 of total raw materials available for use. A physical count of inventory shows $9,000 of ending raw materials inventory. This implies a total cost of raw materials used during the period of $85,500 ($94,500 total raw materials available for use − $9,000 ending inventory). (*Note:* All raw materials are direct materials for Rocky Mountain Bikes.)

"My boss wants us to appeal to a younger and hipper crowd. So, I'd like to get a tattoo that says-- 'Accounting rules!'"

Exhibit 25.11

Manufacturing Statement

Direct material and direct labor costs increase with increases in production volume and are called *variable costs*. Overhead can be both variable and fixed. When overhead costs vary with production, they are called *variable overhead*. When overhead costs don't vary with production, they are called *fixed overhead*. Manufacturers sometimes report variable and fixed overhead separately in the manufacturing statement to provide more information to managers about cost behavior.

ROCKY MOUNTAIN BIKES
Manufacturing Statement
For Year Ended December 31, 2010

Direct materials			
① Raw materials inventory, Dec. 31, 2009		$ 8,000	
Raw materials purchases		86,500	
Raw materials available for use		94,500	
Less raw materials inventory, Dec. 31, 2010		9,000	
Direct materials used			$ 85,500
② **Direct labor**			60,000
Factory overhead			
Indirect labor		9,000	
Factory supervision		6,000	
Factory utilities		2,600	
Repairs—Factory equipment		2,500	
Property taxes—Factory building		1,900	
③ Factory supplies used		600	
Factory insurance expired		1,100	
Depreciation expense—Small tools		200	
Depreciation expense—Factory equipment		3,500	
Depreciation expense—Factory building		1,800	
Amortization expense—Patents		800	
Total factory overhead			30,000
Total manufacturing costs			175,500
Add goods in process inventory, Dec. 31, 2009			2,500
④ Total cost of goods in process			178,000
Less goods in process inventory, Dec. 31, 2010			7,500
Cost of goods manufactured			$170,500

② The second part of the manufacturing statement reports direct labor costs. Rocky Mountain Bikes had total direct labor costs of $60,000 for the period. This amount includes payroll taxes and fringe benefits.

③ The third part of the manufacturing statement reports overhead costs. The statement lists each important factory overhead item and its cost. Total factory overhead cost for the period is $30,000. Some companies report only *total* factory overhead on the manufacturing statement and attach a separate schedule listing individual overhead costs.

④ The final section of the manufacturing statement computes and reports the *cost of goods manufactured*. (Total manufacturing costs for the period are $175,500 [$85,500 + $60,000 + $30,000], the sum of direct materials used and direct labor and overhead costs incurred.) This amount is first added to beginning goods in process inventory. This gives the total goods in process inventory of $178,000 ($175,500 + $2,500). We then compute the current period's cost of goods manufactured of $170,500 by taking the $178,000 total goods in process and subtracting the $7,500 cost of ending goods in process inventory that consists of direct materials, direct labor, and factory overhead. The cost of goods manufactured amount is also called *net cost of goods manufactured* or *cost of goods completed*. Exhibit 25.9 shows that this item and amount are listed in the Cost of Goods Sold section of Rocky Mountain Bikes' income statement.

A managerial accounting system records costs and reports them in various reports that eventually determine financial statements. Exhibit 25.12 shows how overhead costs flow through the system: from an initial listing of specific costs, to a partial manufacturing statement, to the reporting on the income statement.

Management uses information in the manufacturing statement to plan and control the company's manufacturing activities. To provide timely information for decision making, the statement is often prepared monthly, weekly, or even daily. In anticipation of release of its

Exhibit 25.12

Overhead Cost Flows across Accounting Reports

Rocky Mountain Bikes
Factory Overhead Costs
For Year Ended December 31, 2010

Indirect labor	$ 9,000
Supervision	6,000
Other overhead items*	15,000
Total overhead	**$30,000**

*Overhead items are listed in Exhibit 25.11.

Rocky Mountain Bikes
Manufacturing Statement
For Year Ended December 31, 2010

Direct materials	$ 85,500
Direct labor	60,000
Factory overhead	**30,000**
Total manuf. costs	175,500
Beg. goods in process	2,500
Total goods in process	178,000
End. goods in process	(7,500)
Cost of goods manuf.	**$170,500**

Rocky Mountain Bikes
Income Statement
For Year Ended December 31, 2010

Sales	$310,000
Cost of goods sold	
Beg. finished goods	11,200
Cost of goods manuf.	**170,500**
End. finished goods	(10,300)
Cost of goods sold	171,400
Gross profit	138,600
Expenses	59,900
Income taxes	32,600
Net income	$ 46,100

Rocky Mountain Bikes
Balance Sheet–PARTIAL
December 31, 2010

Cash	$11,000
Accounts receivable, net	30,150
Raw materials inventory	**9,000**
Goods in process inventory	**7,500**
Finished goods inventory	**10,300**
Factory supplies	350
Prepaid insurance	300
Total current assets	$68,600

much-hyped iPhone, **Apple** grew its inventory of Flash-based memory chips, a critical component, and its finished goods inventory. The manufacturing statement contains information useful to external users but is not a general-purpose financial statement. Companies rarely publish the manufacturing statement because managers view this detailed information potentially harmful to them if released to competitors.

HOW YOU DOIN'?

Answers—p. 695

9. A manufacturing statement (*a*) computes cost of goods manufactured for the period, (*b*) computes cost of goods sold for the period, or (*c*) reports operating expenses incurred for the period.

10. Are companies required to report a manufacturing statement?

11. How are both beginning and ending goods in process inventories reported on a manufacturing statement?

CYCLE TIME AND CYCLE EFFICIENCY

As lean manufacturing practices help companies move toward just-in-time manufacturing, it is important for these companies to reduce the time to manufacture their products and to improve manufacturing efficiency. One metric that measures that time element is **cycle time (CT)**. A definition of cycle time is in Exhibit 25.13.

LO9 Compute cycle time and cycle efficiency, and explain their importance to production management.

$$\text{Cycle time} = \text{Process time} + \text{Inspection time} + \text{Move time} + \text{Wait time}$$

Exhibit 25.13

Cycle Time

Process time is the time spent producing the product. *Inspection time* is the time spent inspecting (1) raw materials when received, (2) goods in process while in production, and (3) finished goods prior to shipment. *Move time* is the time spent moving (1) raw materials from storage to production and (2) goods in process from factory location to another factory location. *Wait time* is the time that an order or job sits with no production applied to it; this can be due to order delays, bottlenecks in production, and poor scheduling.

Process time is considered **value-added time** because it is the only activity in cycle time that adds value to the product from the customer's perspective. The other three time activities are considered **non-value-added time** because they add no value to the customer.

Companies strive to reduce non-value-added time to improve **cycle efficiency (CE)**. Cycle efficiency is the ratio of value-added time to total cycle time—see Exhibit 25.14.

Exhibit 25.14

Cycle Efficiency

$$\text{Cycle efficiency} = \frac{\text{Value-added time}}{\text{Cycle time}}$$

To illustrate, assume that Rocky Mountain Bikes receives and produces an order for 500 Tracker® mountain bikes. Assume that the following times were measured during production of this order.

Process time	1.8 days
Inspection time	0.5 days
Move time	0.7 days
Wait time	3.0 days

In this case, cycle time is 6.0 days, computed as 1.8 days + 0.5 days + 0.7 days + 3.0 days. Also, cycle efficiency is 0.3, or 30%, computed as 1.8 days divided by 6.0 days. This means that Rocky Mountain Bikes spends 30% of its time working on the product (value-added time). The other 70% is spent on non-value-added activities.

If a company has a CE of 1, it means that its time is spent entirely on value-added activities. If the CE is low, the company should evaluate its production process to see if it can identify ways to reduce non-value-added activities. The 30% CE for Rocky Mountain Bikes is low and its management should look for ways to reduce non-value-added activities.

Demonstration Problem 1: Cost Behavior and Classification

Understanding the classification and assignment of costs is important. Consider a company that manufactures computer chips. It incurs the following costs in manufacturing chips and in operating the company.

1. Plastic board used to mount the chip, $3.50 each.
2. Assembly worker pay of $15 per hour to attach chips to plastic board.
3. Salary for factory maintenance workers who maintain factory equipment.
4. Factory supervisor pay of $55,000 per year to supervise employees.
5. Real estate taxes paid on the factory, $14,500.
6. Real estate taxes paid on the company office, $6,000.
7. Depreciation costs on machinery used by workers, $30,000.
8. Salary paid to the chief financial officer, $95,000.
9. Advertising costs of $7,800 paid to promote products.
10. Salespersons' commissions of $0.50 for each assembled chip sold.
11. Management has the option to rent the manufacturing plant to six local hospitals to store medical records instead of producing and assembling chips.

Classify each cost in the following table according to the categories listed in the table header. A cost can be classified under more than one category. For example, the plastic board used to mount chips is classified as a direct material product cost and as a direct unit cost.

Cost	Period Costs	Product Costs			Unit Cost Classification		Sunk Cost	Opportunity Cost
	Selling and Administrative	Direct Material (prime cost)	Direct Labor (prime and conversion)	Factory Overhead (conversion cost)	Direct	Indirect		
1. Plastic board used to mount the chip, $3.50 each		✔			✔			

Solution to Demonstration Problem 1

Cost*	Period Costs	Product Costs			Unit Cost Classification		Sunk Cost	Opportunity Cost
	Selling and Administrative	Direct Material (prime cost)	Direct Labor (prime and conversion)	Factory Overhead (conversion cost)	Direct	Indirect		
1.		✔			✔			
2.			✔		✔			
3.				✔		✔		
4.				✔		✔		
5.				✔		✔		
6.	✔							
7.				✔		✔	✔	
8.	✔							
9.	✔							
10.	✔							
11.								✔

* Costs 1 through 11 refer to the 11 cost items described at the beginning of the problem.

Demonstration Problem 2: Reporting for Manufacturers

A manufacturing company's balance sheet and income statement differ from those for a merchandising or service company.

Required

1. Fill in the [BLANK] descriptors on the partial balance sheets for both the manufacturing company and the merchandising company. Explain why a different presentation is required.

Manufacturing Company

ADIDAS GROUP
Partial Balance Sheet
December 31, 2010

Current assets	
Cash	$10,000
[BLANK]	8,000
[BLANK]	5,000
[BLANK]	7,000
Supplies	500
Prepaid insurance	500
Total current assets	$31,000

Merchandising Company

PAYLESS SHOE OUTLET
Partial Balance Sheet
December 31, 2010

Current assets	
Cash	$ 5,000
[BLANK]	12,000
Supplies	500
Prepaid insurance	500
Total current assets	$18,000

2. Fill in the [**BLANK**] descriptors on the income statements for the manufacturing company and the merchandising company. Explain why a different presentation is required.

Manufacturing Company

ADIDAS GROUP Partial Income Statement For Year Ended December 31, 2010	
Sales	$200,000
Cost of goods sold	
Finished goods inventory, Dec. 31, 2009	10,000
[**BLANK**]	120,000
Goods available for sale	130,000
Finished goods inventory, Dec. 31, 2010	(7,000)
Cost of goods sold	123,000
Gross profit	$ 77,000

Merchandising Company

PAYLESS SHOE OUTLET Partial Income Statement For Year Ended December 31, 2010	
Sales	$190,000
Cost of goods sold	
Merchandise inventory, Dec. 31, 2009	8,000
[**BLANK**]	108,000
Goods available for sale	116,000
Merchandise inventory, Dec. 31, 2010	(12,000)
Cost of goods sold	104,000
Gross profit	$ 86,000

3. The manufacturer's cost of goods manufactured is the sum of (a) _____, (b) _____, and (c) _____ costs incurred in producing the product.

Solution to Demonstration Problem 2

1. Inventories for a manufacturer and for a merchandiser.

Manufacturing Company

ADIDAS GROUP Partial Balance Sheet December 31, 2010	
Current assets	
Cash	$10,000
Raw materials inventory	8,000
Goods in process inventory	5,000
Finished goods inventory	7,000
Supplies	500
Prepaid insurance	500
Total current assets	$31,000

Merchandising Company

PAYLESS SHOE OUTLET Partial Balance Sheet December 31, 2010	
Current assets	
Cash	$ 5,000
Merchandise inventory	12,000
Supplies	500
Prepaid insurance	500
Total current assets	$18,000

Explanation: A manufacturing company must control and measure three types of inventories: raw materials, goods in process, and finished goods. In the sequence of making a product, the raw materials move into production—called *goods in process inventory*—and then to finished goods. All raw materials and goods in process inventory at the end of each accounting period are considered current assets. All unsold finished inventory is considered a current asset at the end of each accounting period. The merchandising company must control and measure only one type of inventory, purchased goods.

2. Cost of goods sold for a manufacturer and for a merchandiser.

Manufacturing Company

ADIDAS GROUP Partial Income Statement For Year Ended December 31, 2010		
Sales		$200,000
Cost of goods sold		
Finished goods inventory, Dec. 31, 2009	10,000	
Cost of goods manufactured	120,000	
Goods available for sale	130,000	
Finished goods inventory, Dec. 31, 2010	(7,000)	
Cost of goods sold	123,000	
Gross profit		$ 77,000

Merchandising Company

PAYLESS SHOE OUTLET Partial Income Statement For Year Ended December 31, 2010		
Sales		$190,000
Cost of goods sold		
Merchandise inventory, Dec. 31, 2009	8,000	
Cost of purchases	108,000	
Goods available for sale	116,000	
Merchandise inventory, Dec. 31, 2010	(12,000)	
Cost of goods sold	104,000	
Gross profit		$ 86,000

Explanation: Manufacturing and merchandising companies use different reporting terms. In particular, the terms *finished goods* and *cost of goods manufactured* are used to reflect the production of goods, yet the concepts and techniques of reporting cost of goods sold for a manufacturing company and merchandising company are similar.

3. A manufacturer's cost of goods manufactured is the sum of (a) *direct material,* (b) *direct labor,* and (c) *factory overhead* costs incurred in producing the product.

Demonstration Problem 3: Manufacturing Statement

The following account balances and other information are from SUNN Corporation's accounting records for year-end December 31, 2010. Use this information to prepare (1) a table listing factory overhead costs, (2) a manufacturing statement (show only the total factory overhead cost), and (3) an income statement.

Advertising expense	$ 85,000	Goods in process inventory, Dec. 31, 2009	$	8,000
Amortization expense—Factory patents	16,000	Goods in process inventory, Dec. 31, 2010		9,000
Bad debts expense	28,000	Income taxes		53,400
Depreciation expense—Office equipment	37,000	Indirect labor		26,000
Depreciation expense—Factory building	133,000	Interest expense		25,000
Depreciation expense—Factory equipment	78,000	Miscellaneous expense		55,000
Direct labor	250,000	Property taxes on factory equipment		14,000
Factory insurance expired	62,000	Raw materials inventory, Dec. 31, 2009		60,000
Factory supervision	74,000	Raw materials inventory, Dec. 31, 2010		78,000
Factory supplies used	21,000	Raw materials purchases		313,000
Factory utilities	115,000	Repairs expense—Factory equipment		31,000
Finished goods inventory, Dec. 31, 2009	15,000	Salaries expense		150,000
Finished goods inventory, Dec. 31, 2010	12,500	Sales		1,630,000

Planning the Solution

- Analyze the account balances and select those that are part of factory overhead costs.
- Arrange these costs in a table that lists factory overhead costs for the year.
- Analyze the remaining costs and select those related to production activity for the year; selected costs should include the materials and goods in process inventories and direct labor.
- Prepare a manufacturing statement for the year showing the calculation of the cost of materials used in production, the cost of direct labor, and the total factory overhead cost. When presenting overhead cost on this statement, report only total overhead cost from the table of overhead costs for the year. Show the costs of beginning and ending goods in process inventory to determine cost of goods manufactured.
- Organize the remaining revenue and expense items into the income statement for the year. Combine cost of goods manufactured from the manufacturing statement with the finished goods inventory amounts to compute cost of goods sold for the year.

WORKPLACE COMMUNICATION

BTN 25-3 Write a one-page memorandum to a prospective college student about salary expectations for graduates in business. Compare and contrast the expected salaries for accounting (including different subfields such as public, corporate, tax, audit, and so forth), marketing, management, and finance majors. Prepare a graph showing average starting salaries (and those for experienced professionals in those fields if available). To get this information, stop by your school's career services office; libraries also have this information. The Website JobStar.org (click on *Salary Info*) also can get you started.

TAKING IT TO THE NET

LO1 LO2

BTN 25-4 Managerial accounting professionals follow a code of ethics. As a member of the Institute of Management Accountants, the managerial accountant must comply with the Statement of Ethical Professional Practice.

Required

1. Identify, print, and read the Statement of Ethical Professional Practice posted at www.IMAnet.org. (Search using "ethical professional practice")

2. What four overarching ethical principles underlie the IMA's statement?

3. Describe the courses of action the IMA recommends in resolving ethical conflicts.

TEAMWORK IN ACTION

LO7 LO8

BTN 25-5 The following calendar-year information is taken from the December 31, 2010, adjusted trial balance and other records of Dahlia Company.

Advertising expense	$ 19,125	Direct labor	650,750
Depreciation expense—Office equipment	8,750	Indirect labor	60,000
Depreciation expense—Selling equipment	10,000	Miscellaneous production costs	8,500
Depreciation expense—Factory equipment	32,500	Office salaries expense	100,875
Factory supervision	122,500	Raw materials purchases	872,500
Factory supplies used	15,750	Rent expense—Office space	21,125
Factory utilities	36,250	Rent expense—Selling space	25,750
Inventories		Rent expense—Factory building	79,750
Raw materials, December 31, 2009	177,500	Maintenance expense—Factory equipment	27,875
Raw materials, December 31, 2010	168,125	Sales	3,275,000
Goods in process, December 31, 2009	15,875	Sales discounts	57,500
Goods in process, December 31, 2010	14,000	Sales salaries expense	286,250
Finished goods, December 31, 2009	164,375		
Finished goods, December 31, 2010	129,000		

Required

1. *Each* team member is to be responsible for computing **one** of the following amounts. You are not to duplicate your teammates' work. Get any necessary amounts from teammates. Each member is to explain the computation to the team in preparation for reporting to class.

    a. Materials used.

    b. Factory overhead.

    c. Total manufacturing costs.

    d. Total cost of goods in process.

    e. Cost of goods manufactured.

2. Check your cost of goods manufactured with the instructor. If it is correct, proceed to part (3).

3. *Each* team member is to be responsible for computing **one** of the following amounts. You are not to duplicate your teammates' work. Get any necessary amounts from teammates. Each member is to explain the computation to the team in preparation for reporting to class.

    a. Net sales.

    b. Cost of goods sold.

    c. Gross profit.

    d. Total operating expenses.

    e. Net income or loss before taxes.

Provide teams with transparencies and markers for presentation purposes.

ENTREPRENEURS IN BUSINESS

LO1   LO2   LO3

BTN 25-6   Brian Taylor of Kernel Season's must understand his manufacturing costs to effectively operate and succeed as a profitable and efficient company.

Required

1. What are the three main categories of manufacturing costs that Brian must monitor and control? Provide examples of each.
2. How can Brian make the Kernel Season's manufacturing process more cost-effective? Provide examples of two useful managerial measures of time and efficiency.
3. What are four goals of a total quality management process? How can Kernel Season's use TQM to improve its business activities?

ANSWERS TO MULTIPLE CHOICE QUIZ

1. c
2. b
3. b
4. a
5. e; Beginning finished goods inventory + Cost of goods manufactured (COGM) − Ending finished goods inventory = Cost of goods sold
$6,000 + COGM − $3,200 = $7,500
COGM = $4,700

A Look Back

Chapter 25 introduced the basics of managerial accounting, including cost concepts. It also described how to summarize and report production activities.

A Look at This Chapter

We begin this chapter by describing a cost accounting system. We then explain the procedures used to determine costs using a job order costing system. We conclude with a discussion of over- and underapplied overhead.

A Look Ahead

The remaining chapters focus on decisions managers must make and how managerial accounting helps with those decisions. The first of these, Chapter 27, describes measuring departmental performance and responsibility accounting.

Chapter 26

Job Order Cost Accounting

Learning Objectives

LO 1 Explain the cost accounting system.

LO 2 Describe important features of job order production.

LO 3 Explain job cost sheets and how they are used in job order cost accounting.

LO 4 Describe and record the flow of materials costs in job order cost accounting.

LO 5 Describe and record the flow of labor costs in job order cost accounting.

LO 6 Describe and record the flow of overhead costs in job order cost accounting.

LO 7 Compute predetermined overhead rates and apply overhead costs to jobs.

LO 8 Determine adjustments for overapplied and underapplied factory overhead.

"Being successful is having a vision which you are excited to follow without the fear of failure"
—Hank Julicher

Working the Field

PHILADELPHIA, PA—One size fits all? Not when it comes to synthetic turf for athletic fields—this according to Hank Julicher, founder of **Sprinturf** (**Sprinturf.com**). "Not all fields are exactly alike, because no two owners have the same exact needs," insists Hank. "Many variables must be considered, including playing requirements, climate, and financial considerations." Designing, installing, and servicing synthetic turf systems are Sprinturf's mission.

"There is much more to a playing field than just the surface," explains Hank. "Many would argue that the base is the most important—it needs the strength to support athletes and vehicles, while still being able to drain over 20″ of rainfall per hour." For this, Sprinturf relies on its all-rubber infill system for its installations. Still, understanding customer needs is key. In extremely hot, arid climates, Sprinturf uses light-colored rubber infill to reduce the temperature of playing surfaces. In cold areas, Sprinturf offers solutions to reduce snow and ice buildup. Hank has put in fields from Utah State University to University of Montana to Long Beach City College. While a touchdown is worth 6 points on every Sprinturf field, each field is otherwise unique.

Manufacturers of custom products, such as that from Sprinturf, use state-of-the-art job order cost accounting to track costs. This includes tracking the cost of materials, labor and overhead, and managing those expenses. To help control costs and ensure product quality, Sprinturf does not outsource any part of the design or installation process. Controlling all aspects of the process enables it to better isolate costs and avoid the run-away costs often experienced by start-ups that fail to use costing techniques. Recruiting top-notch personnel and experienced supervisors also helps control labor costs. Reflecting the unique nature of each field, each installation is videotaped to ensure it is done exactly according to customer specifications.

Hank Julicher stresses cost control as vital to Sprinturf's success. "To take on two 800-pound gorillas in our industry, we had to be more creative, efficient, and cost-effective to win," explains Hank. "We just hung in there until the public recognized our quality and value." This winning formula has led to product growth that any team would envy.

[Sources: *Sprinturf Website*, January 2009; *Entrepreneur*, 2007; *PanStadia*, February and November 2005]

This chapter introduces a cost accounting system for assigning costs to the flow of goods through a production process. We then describe the details of a *job order cost accounting system*. Job order costing is frequently used by manufacturers of custom products or providers of custom services. Manufacturers that use job order costing typically base it on a perpetual inventory system, which provides a continuous record of materials, goods in process, and finished goods inventories.

Job Order Cost Accounting

Job Order Cost Accounting	Job Order Cost Flows and Reports	Adjustment of Underapplied or Overapplied Overhead
• Cost accounting system • Job order production • Events in job order costing • Job cost sheet	• Materials cost flows and documents • Labor cost flows and documents • Overhead cost flows and documents • Summary of cost flows	• Underapplied overhead • Overapplied overhead

Job Order Cost Accounting

This section describes a cost accounting system and job order production and costing.

Cost Accounting System

LO1 Explain the cost accounting system.

Many companies use a cost accounting system to generate timely and accurate inventory information. A **cost accounting system** uses a *perpetual* inventory system, which continuously updates records for costs of materials, goods in process, and finished goods inventories. A cost accounting system also provides timely information about inventories and manufacturing costs per unit of product. This is especially helpful for managers' efforts to control costs and determine selling prices. (A **general accounting system** uses a *periodic* inventory system. Its use is declining as competitive forces and customer demands have increased pressures on companies to better manage inventories.)

The two basic types of cost accounting systems are *job order cost accounting* and *process cost accounting*. We describe job order cost accounting in this chapter. Process cost accounting is explained in advanced courses.

Job Order Production

LO2 Describe important features of job order production.

Many companies produce products individually designed to meet the needs of a specific customer. Each customized product is manufactured separately and its production is called **job order production,** or *job order manufacturing*. Examples of such products include special-order machines, a factory building, custom jewelry, wedding invitations, and artwork.

The production activities for a customized product represent a **job.** The principle of customization applies to both manufacturing *and* service companies. Most service companies perform a custom service for a specific customer. Examples of such services include an accountant auditing a client's financial statements, an interior designer remodeling an office, a wedding consultant planning and supervising a reception, and a lawyer defending a client. Whether the setting is manufacturing or services, job order operations involve meeting the needs of customers by producing or performing custom jobs. With job order production, each customer order likely differs from another in some important respect.

IN THE NEWS

Some companies use **process operations,** the mass production of products in a continuous flow of steps. Examples include **Exxon Mobil** (oil), **Kellogg** (cereals), **Coca-Cola** (soft drinks), **Penn Racquet Sports** (tennis balls), and **Hershey** (chocolate). Process operations typically require process costing, which focuses on the process itself, not the individual job or job lot. Process costing assigns costs to similar products that are mass-produced in a continuous process. Process costing is studied in advanced managerial accounting courses.

When a job involves producing more than one unit of a custom product, it is often called a **job lot.** Products produced as job lots could include benches for a church, imprinted T-shirts for a 10K race or company picnic, or advertising signs for a chain of stores. Although these orders involve more than one unit, the volume of production is typically low, such as 50 benches, 200 T-shirts, or 100 signs.

Events in Job Order Costing

A customer order for a custom product causes the company to begin work on a job.

The first step is to predict the cost to complete the job. This cost depends on the product design prepared by either the customer or the producer. The second step is to negotiate a sales price and decide whether to pursue the job. The selling price is determined by market factors. Producers evaluate the market price, compare it to cost, and determine whether the expected profit on the job is reasonable. If the profit is not reasonable, the producer determines a desired **target cost.** The third step is for the producer to schedule production of the job to meet the customer's needs and to fit within its own production constraints. This work schedule should consider workplace facilities including equipment, personnel, and supplies. Once this schedule is complete, the producer can place orders for raw materials. Production occurs as materials and labor are applied to the job.

An overview of job order production activity is shown in Exhibit 26.1. This exhibit shows the March production activity of Road Warriors, which manufactures security-equipped cars and trucks. The company converts any vehicle by adding security items such as alarms, reinforced exterior, bulletproof glass, and bomb detectors. The company began by catering to high-profile celebrities, but it now caters to anyone who desires added security in a vehicle.

Job order production for Road Warriors requires materials, labor, and overhead costs. Recall that direct materials are goods used in manufacturing that are clearly identified with a particular job. Similarly, direct labor is effort devoted to a particular job. Overhead costs support production of more than one job. Common overhead items are depreciation on factory buildings and equipment, factory supplies, supervision, maintenance, cleaning, and utilities.

Exhibit 26.1

Job Order Production Activities

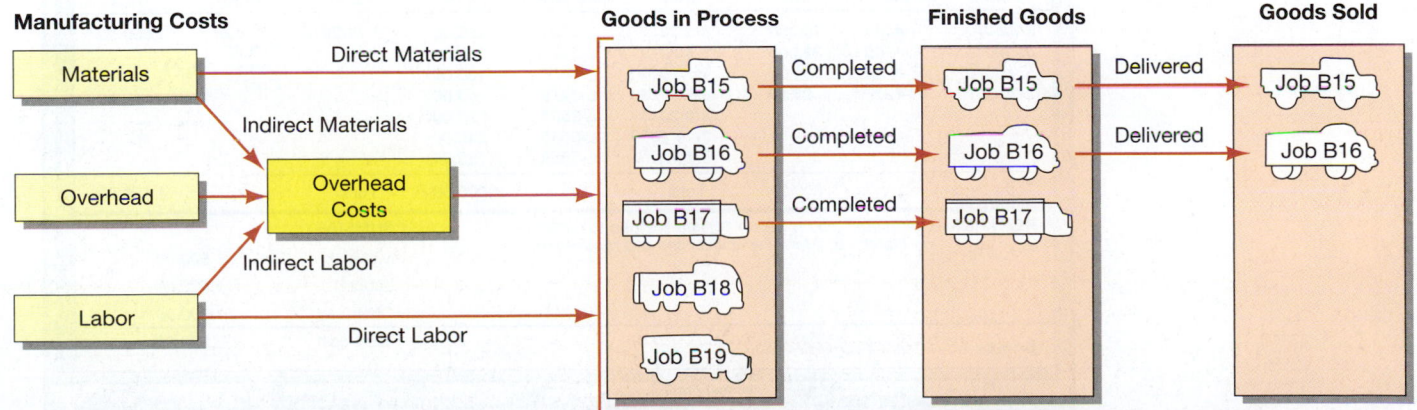

Exhibit 26.1 shows that materials, labor, and overhead are added to Jobs B15, B16, B17, B18, and B19 during March. Road Warriors completed Jobs B15, B16, and B17 in March and delivered Jobs B15 and B16 to customers. At the end of March, Jobs B18 and B19 remain in goods in process inventory and Job B17 is in finished goods inventory. Both labor and materials costs are also separated into their direct and indirect components. Their indirect amounts are added to overhead. Total overhead cost is then allocated to the various jobs.

IN THE NEWS

Custom Design   Managers once saw companies as the center of a solar system orbited by suppliers and customers. Now the customer has become the center of the business universe. **Nike** allows custom orders over the Internet, enabling customers to select materials, colors, and to personalize their shoes with letters and numbers. Soon consumers may be able to personalize almost any product, from cellular phones to appliances to furniture.

Job Cost Sheet

LO3   Explain job cost sheets and how they are used in job order cost accounting.

General ledger accounts usually do not provide all the accounting information that managers of job order cost operations need. To plan and control production activities, managers often require more detailed data. Such detailed data are usually stored in subsidiary records controlled by general ledger accounts. Subsidiary records store information about raw materials, overhead costs, jobs in process, finished goods, and other items. This section describes the use of these records.

A major aim of a **job order cost accounting system** is to determine the cost of producing each job or job lot. In the case of a job lot, the system also aims to compute the cost per unit. The accounting system must include separate records for each job to accomplish this, and it must capture information about costs incurred and charge these costs to each job.

A **job cost sheet** is a separate record maintained for each job. Exhibit 26.2 shows a job cost sheet for an alarm system that Road Warriors produced for a customer. This job cost sheet identifies the customer, the job number assigned, the product, and key dates. Costs incurred

Exhibit 26.2

Job Cost Sheet

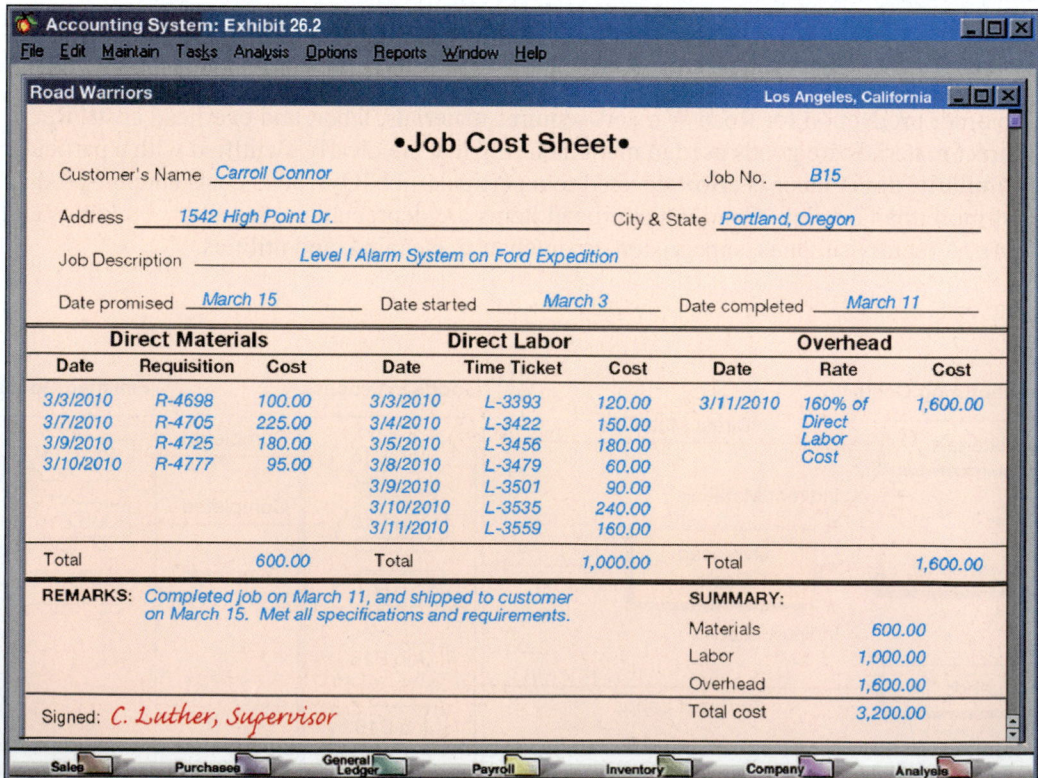

on the job are immediately recorded on this sheet. When the job is complete, the supervisor enters the date of completion, records any remarks, and signs the sheet. The job cost sheet in Exhibit 26.2 classifies costs as direct materials, direct labor, or overhead. It shows that a total of $600 in direct materials is added to Job B15 on four different dates. It also shows seven entries for direct labor costs that total $1,000. Road Warriors *allocates* (also termed *applies, assigns,* or *charges*) factory overhead costs of $1,600 to this job using an allocation rate of 160% of direct labor cost (160% × $1,000)—we discuss overhead allocation later in this chapter.

While a job is being produced, its accumulated costs are kept in the general ledger account **Goods in Process Inventory.** The collection of job cost sheets for all jobs in process makes up a subsidiary ledger controlled by the Goods in Process Inventory account. Managers use job cost sheets to monitor costs incurred to date and to predict and control costs for each job.

When a job is finished, its job cost sheet is completed and moved from the jobs in process file to the finished jobs file. This latter file acts as a subsidiary ledger controlled by the general ledger account **Finished Goods Inventory.** When a finished job is delivered to a customer, the job cost sheet is moved to a permanent file supporting the total cost of goods sold. This permanent file contains records from both current and prior periods.

HOW YOU DOIN'?

Answers—p. 729

1. Which of these products is likely to involve job order production? (*a*) inexpensive watches, (*b*) racing bikes, (*c*) bottled soft drinks, or (*d*) athletic socks.

2. What is the difference between a job and a job lot?

3. Which of these statements is correct? (*a*) The collection of job cost sheets for unfinished jobs makes up a subsidiary ledger controlled by the Goods in Process Inventory account, (*b*) Job cost sheets are financial statements provided to investors, or (*c*) A separate job cost sheet is maintained in the general ledger for each job in process.

4. What three costs are normally accumulated on job cost sheets?

Job Order Cost Flows and Reports

Materials Cost Flows and Documents

This section focuses on the flow of materials costs and the related documents in a job order cost accounting system. We begin by examining Exhibit 26.3. When materials are first received from suppliers, employees count and inspect them and record the items' quantity and cost on a **receiving report.** The receiving report is the *source document* for recording materials received in both a materials ledger card and in the general ledger. In nearly all job order cost systems, **materials ledger cards** (or files) are perpetual records that are updated each time materials are purchased and each time materials are issued for use in production.

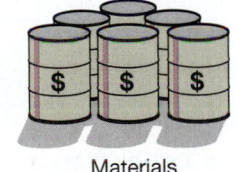

Materials

LO4 Describe and record the flow of materials costs in job order cost accounting.

To illustrate the purchase of materials, Road Warriors acquired $450 of wiring and related materials on March 4, 2010. This purchase is recorded as follows.

Mar.	4	Raw Materials Inventory—M-347	450 00		
		Accounts Payable		450 00	
		To record purchase of materials for production.			

Assets = Liabilities + Equity
+450   +450

Exhibit 26.3 shows that materials can be requisitioned (requested) for use either on a specific job (direct materials) or as overhead (indirect materials). Cost of direct materials flows from the materials ledger card to the job cost sheet. The cost of indirect materials flows from the materials ledger card to the Indirect Materials account in the factory overhead ledger, which is a subsidiary ledger controlled by the Factory Overhead account in the general ledger.

Exhibit 26.3

Materials Cost Flows through Subsidiary Records

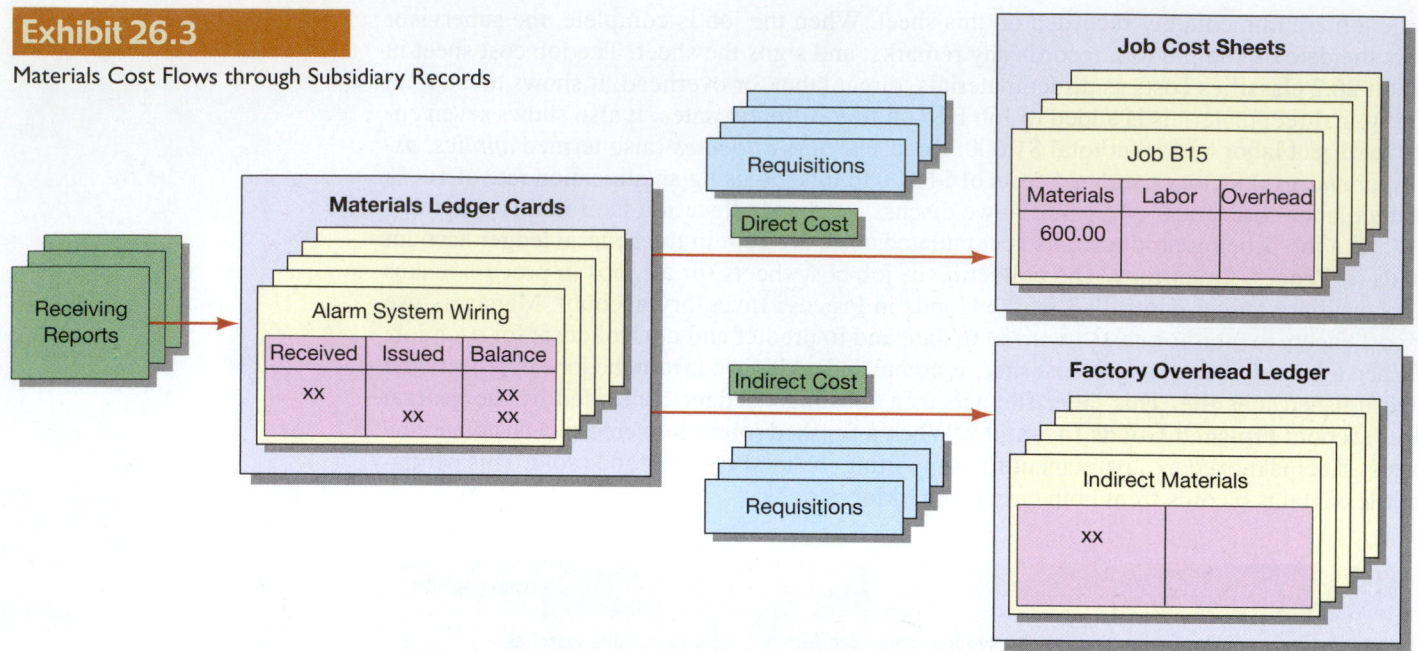

Exhibit 26.4 shows a materials ledger card for material received and issued by Road Warriors. The card identifies the item as alarm system wiring and shows the item's stock number, its location in the storeroom, information about the maximum and minimum quantities that should be available, and the reorder quantity. For example, alarm system wiring is issued and recorded on March 7, 2010. The job cost sheet in Exhibit 26.2 showed that Job B15 used this wiring.

Exhibit 26.4

Materials Ledger Card

Road Warriors

Item ___Alarm system wiring___   Stock No. ___M–347___   Location in Storeroom ___Bin 137___

Maximum quantity ___5 units___   Minimum quantity ___1 unit___   Quantity to reorder ___2 units___

	Received				Issued				Balance		
Date	Receiving Report Number	Units	Unit Price	Total Price	Requi- sition Number	Units	Unit Price	Total Price	Units	Unit Price	Total Price
									1	225.00	225.00
3/ 4/2010	C-7117	2	225.00	450.00					3	225.00	675.00
3/ 7/2010					R–4705	1	225.00	225.00	2	225.00	450.00

When materials are needed in production, a production manager prepares a **materials requisition** and sends it to the materials manager. The requisition shows the job number, the type of material, the quantity needed, and the signature of the manager authorized to make the requisition. Exhibit 26.5 shows the materials requisition for alarm system wiring for Job B15. To see how this requisition ties to the flow of costs, compare the information on the requisition with the March 7, 2010, data in Exhibits 26.2 and 26.4.

The use of alarm system wiring on Job B15 yields the following entry (locate this cost item in the job cost sheet shown in Exhibit 26.2).

Assets = Liabilities + Equity
+225
−225

Mar.	7	Goods in Process Inventory—Job B15		2 2 5 00	
		Raw Materials Inventory—M-347			2 2 5 00
		To record use of material on Job B15.			

Exhibit 26.5

Materials Requisition

Road Warriors

MATERIALS REQUISITION NUMBER R–4705

Job No.	B15	Date	3/7/2010
Material Stock No.	M–347	Material Description	Alarm system wiring
Quantity Requested	1	Requested By	C. Luther

= =

Quantity Provided	1	Date Provided	3/7/2010
Filled By	M. Bateman	Material Received By	C. Luther
Remarks			

IN THE NEWS

Materials Fraud   The Association of Certified Fraud Examiners reports that the typical employee "billing" billing fraud costs employers about $100,000 per incident. Examples of these schemes include creating a phony company and billing the employer for nonexistent goods or services and purchasing personal items and sending invoices to the employer for payment.

This entry is posted both to its general ledger accounts and to subsidiary records. Posting to subsidiary records includes a debit to a job cost sheet and a credit to a materials ledger card. (*Note:* An entry to record use of indirect materials is the same as that for direct materials *except* the debit is to Factory Overhead. In the subsidiary factory overhead ledger, this entry is posted to Indirect Materials.)

Labor Cost Flows and Documents

Exhibit 26.6 shows the flow of labor costs from clock cards and the Factory Payroll account to subsidiary records of the job order cost accounting system. Recall that costs in subsidiary records give detailed information needed to manage and control operations.

The flow of costs in Exhibit 26.6 begins with **clock cards.** Employees commonly use these cards to record the number of hours worked, and they serve as source documents for entries to record labor costs. Clock card data on the number of hours worked is used at the end of each pay period to determine total labor cost. This amount is then debited to the Factory Payroll account, a temporary account containing the total payroll cost (both direct and indirect). Payroll cost is later allocated to both specific jobs and overhead.

According to clock card data, workers earned $1,500 for the week ended March 5. The accrual and payment of these wages are recorded as follows.

L05 Describe and record the flow of labor costs in job order cost accounting.

Labor

Mar.	6	Factory Payroll	1 5 0 0 00	
		Cash		1 5 0 0 00
		To record the weekly payroll.		

Assets = Liabilities + Equity
−1,500   −1,500

To assign labor costs to specific jobs and to overhead, we must know how each employee's time is used and its costs. Source documents called **time tickets** usually capture these data. Employees regularly fill out time tickets to report how much time they spent on each job. An employee who works on several jobs during a day completes a separate time ticket for each job. Tickets are also prepared for time charged to overhead as indirect labor. A supervisor signs an employee's time ticket to confirm its accuracy.

In the accounting equation, we treat accounts such as Factory Overhead and Factory Payroll as temporary accounts, which hold various expenses until they are allocated to balance sheet or income statement accounts.

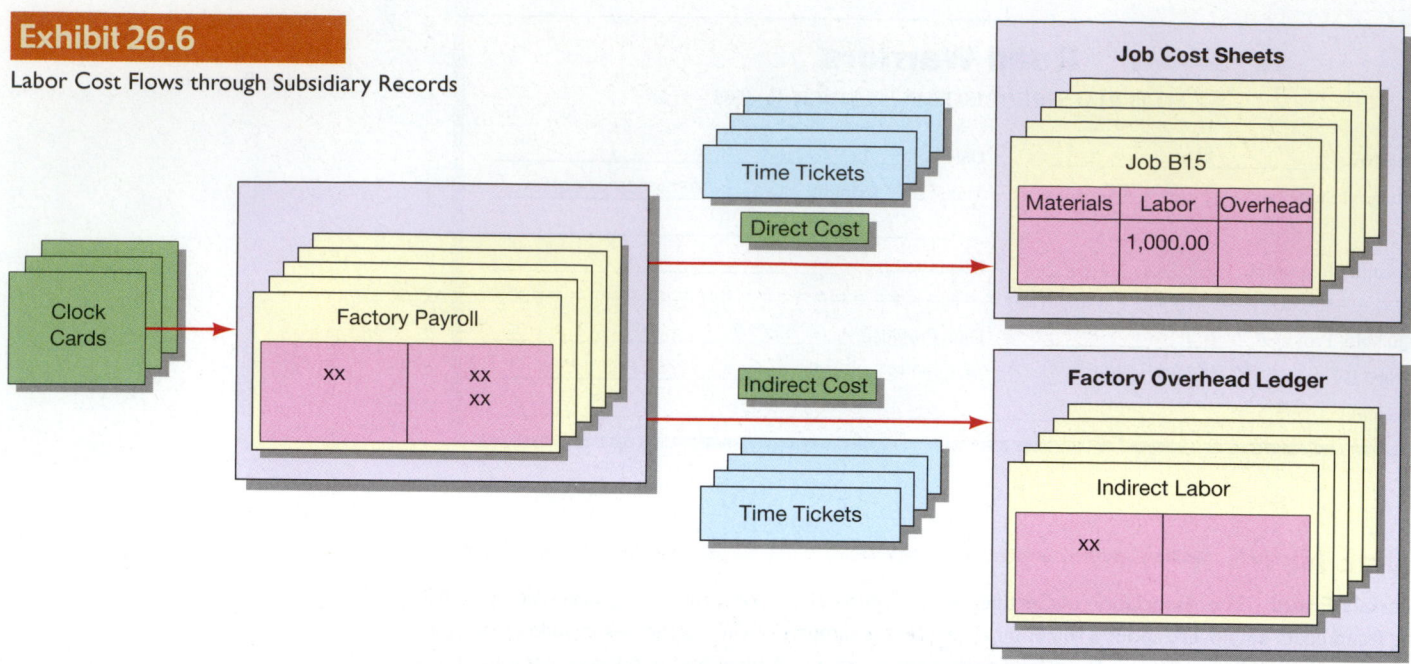

Exhibit 26.6

Labor Cost Flows through Subsidiary Records

Exhibit 26.7 shows a time ticket reporting the time a Road Warrior employee spent working on Job B15. The employee's supervisor signed the ticket to confirm its accuracy. The hourly rate and total labor cost are computed after the time ticket is turned in. To see the effect of this time ticket on the job cost sheet, look at the entry dated March 8, 2010, in Exhibit 26.2.

Exhibit 26.7

Time Ticket

> ## Road Warriors
>
> ### TIME TICKET   L–3479
>
> Job No. _____ *B15* _____   Date _____ *3/8/2010* _____
>
> Employee Name _____ *T. Zeller* _____   Employee Number _____ *3969* _____
>
> **TIME AND RATE INFORMATION:**
>
> Start Time _____ *9:00* _____   Finish Time _____ *12:00* _____
>
> Elapsed Time _____ *3.0* _____   Hourly Rate _____ *$20.00* _____   Total Cost _____ *$60.00* _____
>
> Approved By _____ *C. Luther* _____
>
> Remarks _____

When time tickets report labor used on a specific job, this cost is recorded as direct labor. The following entry records the data from the time ticket in Exhibit 26.7.

Assets = Liabilities + Equity
+60   +60

Mar.	8	Goods in Process Inventory—Job B15	60 00	
		Factory Payroll		60 00
		To record direct labor used on Job B15.		

The debit in this entry is posted both to the general ledger account and to the appropriate job cost sheet. (*Note:* An entry to record indirect labor is the same as for direct labor *except* that it debits Factory Overhead and credits Factory Payroll. In the subsidiary factory overhead ledger, the debit in this entry is posted to the Indirect Labor account.)

Overhead Cost Flows and Documents

Factory overhead (or simply overhead) cost flows are shown in Exhibit 26.8. Factory overhead includes all production costs other than direct materials and direct labor. Two sources of overhead costs are indirect materials and indirect labor. These costs are recorded from requisitions for indirect materials and time tickets for indirect labor. Two other sources of overhead are (1) vouchers authorizing payments for items such as supplies or utilities and (2) adjusting entries for costs such as depreciation.

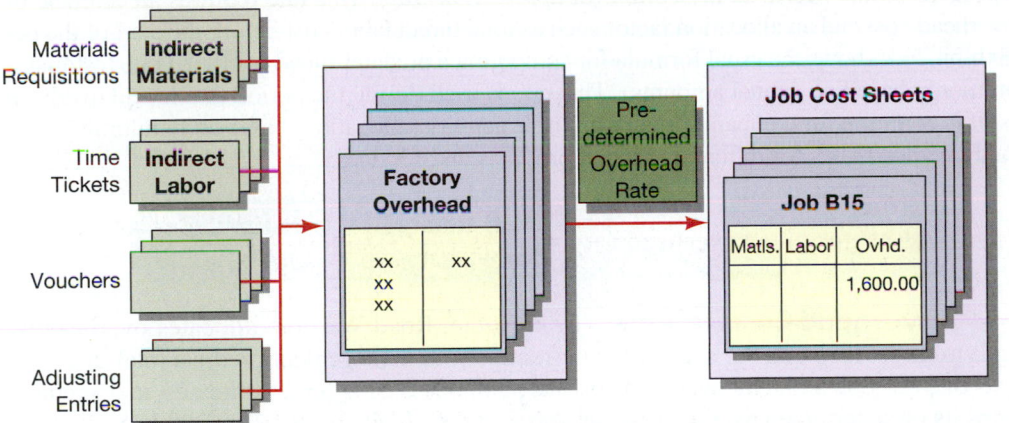

Exhibit 26.8

Overhead Cost Flows through Subsidiary Records

Factory overhead usually includes many different costs and, thus, a separate account for each is often maintained in a subsidiary factory overhead ledger. This ledger is controlled by the Factory Overhead account in the general ledger. Factory Overhead is a temporary account that accumulates costs until they are allocated to jobs.

Recall that overhead costs are recorded with debits to the Factory Overhead account and with credits to other accounts such as Cash, Accounts Payable, and Accumulated Depreciation—Equipment. In the subsidiary factory overhead ledger, the debits are posted to their respective accounts such as Depreciation Expense—Equipment, Insurance Expense—Warehouse, or Amortization Expense—Patents.

To illustrate the recording of overhead, the following two entries reflect the depreciation of factory equipment and the accrual of utilities, respectively, for the week ended March 6.

L06 Describe and record the flow of overhead costs in job order cost accounting.

Mar.	6	Factory Overhead		600 00	
		Accumulated Depreciation—Equipment			600 00
		To record depreciation on factory equipment.			
Mar.	6	Factory Overhead		250 00	
		Utilities Payable			250 00
		To record the accrual of factory utilities.			

Assets = Liabilities + Equity
−600   −600

Assets = Liabilities + Equity
           +250   −250

Allocating Overhead Costs

Exhibit 26.8 shows that overhead costs flow from the Factory Overhead account to job cost sheets. Because overhead is made up of costs not directly associated with specific jobs or job lots, we cannot determine the dollar amount incurred on a specific job. We know, however, that overhead costs represent a necessary part of business activities. If a job cost is to include all

L07 Compute predetermined overhead rates and apply overhead costs to jobs.

costs needed to complete the job, some amount of overhead must be included. Given the difficulty in determining the overhead amount for a specific job, however, we allocate overhead to individual jobs in some reasonable manner.

We generally allocate overhead by linking it to another factor used in production, such as direct labor or machine hours. The factor to which overhead costs are linked is known as the *allocation base*. A manager must think carefully about how many and which allocation bases to use. This managerial decision influences the accuracy with which overhead costs are allocated to individual jobs. In Exhibit 26.2, overhead is expressed as 160% of direct labor. We then allocate overhead by multiplying 160% by the estimated amount of direct labor on the jobs.

Computing Predetermined Overhead Rates We cannot wait until the end of a period to allocate overhead to jobs because perpetual inventory records demand up-to-date costs. Instead, we must predict overhead in advance and assign it to jobs so that a job's total costs can be estimated before its completion. This estimated cost is useful for managers in many decisions including setting prices. Estimating overhead in advance requires a **predetermined overhead rate,** also called *predetermined overhead allocation* (or *application*) *rate*. This rate requires an estimate of total overhead cost and an allocation factor such as total direct labor cost before the start of the period. Exhibit 26.9 shows the usual formula for computing a predetermined overhead rate (estimates are commonly based on annual amounts). This rate is used during the period to allocate overhead to jobs. It is common for companies to use multiple activity (allocation) bases and multiple predetermined overhead rates for different types of products and services.

> The predetermined overhead rate is computed at the start of the period and is used throughout the period to allocate overhead to jobs.

Exhibit 26.9

Predetermined Overhead Allocation Rate Formula

$$\text{Predetermined overhead rate} = \frac{\text{Estimated overhead costs}}{\text{Estimated activity base}}$$

Applying Overhead Costs to Jobs To illustrate, Road Warriors allocates overhead by linking it to direct labor. At the start of the current period, management predicts total direct labor costs of $125,000 and total overhead costs of $200,000. Using these estimates, management computes its predetermined overhead rate as 160% of direct labor cost ($200,000 ÷ $125,000). Reviewing the job order cost sheet in Exhibit 26.2, we see that $1,000 of direct labor went into Job B15. We then use the predetermined overhead rate of 160% to allocate $1,600 (160% × $1,000) of overhead to this job. The entry to record this allocation is

Assets = Liabilities + Equity
+1,600   +1,600

Mar.	11	Goods in Process Inventory—Job B15	1 6 0 0 00	
		Factory Overhead		1 6 0 0 00
		To assign overhead to Job B15.		

Since the allocation rate for overhead is estimated at the start of a period, the total amount assigned to jobs during a period rarely equals the amount actually incurred. We explain how this difference is treated later in this chapter.

Summary of Cost Flows

We showed journal entries for charging Goods in Process Inventory (Job B15) with the cost of (1) direct materials requisitions, (2) direct labor time tickets, and (3) factory overhead. We made separate entries for each of these costs, but they are usually recorded in one entry. Specifically, materials requisitions are often collected for a day or a week and recorded with a single entry summarizing them. The same is done with labor time tickets. When summary entries are made, supporting schedules of the jobs charged and the types of materials used provide the basis for postings to subsidiary records.

To show all production cost flows for a period and their related entries, we again look at Road Warriors' activities. Exhibit 26.10 shows costs linked to all of Road Warriors' production activities for March. Road Warriors did not have any jobs in process at the beginning of March, but it did apply materials, labor, and overhead costs to five new jobs in March. Jobs B15 and B16 are completed and delivered to customers in March, Job B17 is completed but not delivered, and Jobs B18 and B19 are still in process. Exhibit 26.10 also shows purchases of raw materials for $2,750, labor costs incurred for $5,300, and overhead costs of $6,720.

The upper part of Exhibit 26.11 shows the flow of these costs through general ledger accounts and the end-of-month balances in key subsidiary records. Arrow lines are numbered to show the

Exhibit 26.10

Job Order Costs of All Production Activities

ROAD WARRIORS
Job Order Manufacturing Costs
For Month Ended March 31, 2010

Explanation	Materials	Labor	Overhead Incurred	Overhead Allocated	Goods in Process	Finished Goods	Cost of Goods Sold
Job B15	$ 600	$1,000		$1,600			$3,200
Job B16	300	800		1,280			2,380
Job B17	500	1,100		1,760		$3,360	
Job B18	150	700		1,120	$1,970		
Job B19	250	600		960	1,810		
Total job costs	1,800	4,200		$6,720	$3,780	$3,360	$5,580
Indirect materials	550		$ 550				
Indirect labor		1,100	1,100				
Other overhead			5,070				
Total costs used in production	2,350	$5,300	$6,720				
Ending materials inventory	1,400						
Materials available	3,750						
Less beginning materials inventory	(1,000)						
Materials purchased	$2,750						

Exhibit 26.11

Job Order Cost Flows and Ending Job Cost Sheets

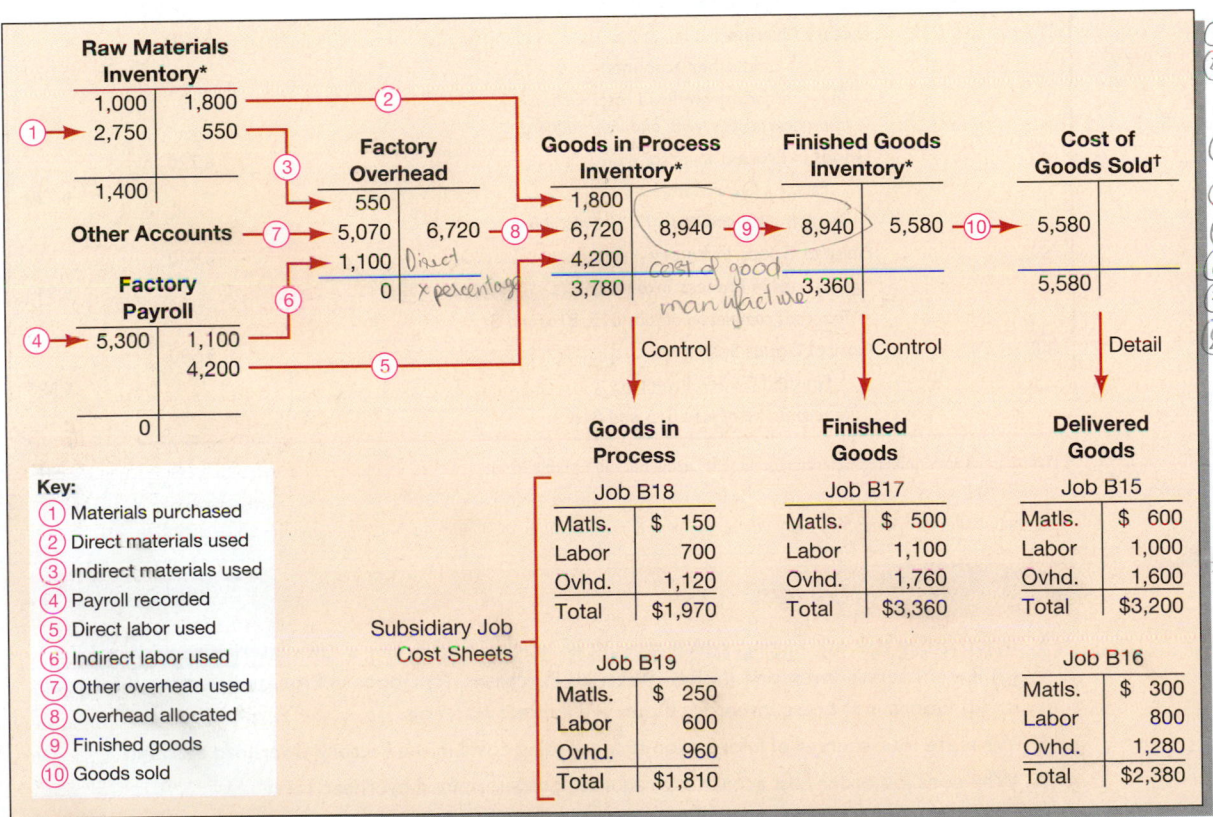

* The ending balances in the inventory accounts are carried to the balance sheet.
† The Cost of Goods Sold balance is carried to the income statement.

flows of costs for March. Each numbered cost flow reflects several entries made in March. The lower part of Exhibit 26.11 shows summarized job cost sheets and their status at the end of March. The sum of costs assigned to the jobs in process ($1,970 + $1,810) equals the $3,780 balance in Goods in Process Inventory shown in Exhibit 26.10. Also, costs assigned to Job B17 equal the $3,360 balance in Finished Goods Inventory. The sum of costs assigned to Jobs B15 and B16 ($3,200 + $2,380) equals the $5,580 balance in Cost of Goods Sold.

Exhibit 26.12 shows each cost flow with a single entry summarizing the actual individual entries made in March. Each entry is numbered to link with the arrow lines in Exhibit 26.11.

Exhibit 26.12

Entries for Job Order Production Costs*

①	Raw Materials Inventory..............................	2,750	
	Accounts Payable		2,750
	Acquired materials on credit for factory use.		
②	Goods in Process Inventory	1,800	
	Raw Materials Inventory		1,800
	To assign costs of direct materials used.		
③	Factory Overhead	550	
	Raw Materials Inventory		550
	To record use of indirect materials.		
④	Factory Payroll	5,300	
	Cash (and other accounts)		5,300
	To record salaries and wages of factory workers (including various payroll liabilities).		
⑤	Goods in Process Inventory	4,200	
	Factory Payroll		4,200
	To assign costs of direct labor used.		
⑥	Factory Overhead	1,100	
	Factory Payroll		1,100
	To record indirect labor costs as overhead.		
⑦	Factory Overhead	5,070	
	Cash (and other accounts)		5,070
	To record factory overhead costs such as insurance, utilities, rent, and depreciation.		
⑧	Goods in Process Inventory	6,720	
	Factory Overhead.............................		6,720
	To apply overhead at 160% of direct labor.		
⑨	Finished Goods Inventory	8,940	
	Goods in Process Inventory......................		8,940
	To record completion of Jobs B15, B16, and B17.		
⑩	Cost of Goods Sold	5,580	
	Finished Goods Inventory		5,580
	To record sale of Jobs B15 and B16.		

Actual overhead is debited to Factory Overhead. *Allocated* overhead is credited to Factory Overhead.

* Transactions are numbered to be consistent with arrow lines in Exhibit 26.11.

HOW YOU DOIN'?

Answers—p. 729

5. In job order cost accounting, which account is debited in recording a raw materials requisition? (*a*) Raw Materials Inventory, (*b*) Raw Materials Purchases, (*c*) Goods in Process Inventory if for a job, or (*d*) Goods in Process Inventory if they are indirect materials.

6. What are four sources of information for recording costs in the Factory Overhead account?

7. Why does job order cost accounting require a predetermined overhead rate?

8. What events result in a debit to Factory Payroll? What events result in a credit?

Adjustment of Underapplied or Overapplied Overhead

Refer to the debits in the Factory Overhead account in Exhibit 26.11 (or Exhibit 26.12). The total cost of factory overhead incurred during March is $6,720 ($550 + $5,070 + $1,100). The $6,720 exactly equals the amount assigned to goods in process inventory (see arrow line ⑧). Therefore, the overhead incurred equals the overhead applied in March. This rarely happens. The predetermined overhead rate is determined using estimated amounts before the period begins, and estimates rarely equal the exact amounts actually incurred. This section explains what we do when too much or too little overhead is applied to jobs.

Underapplied Overhead

When less overhead is applied than is actually incurred, the remaining debit balance in the Factory Overhead account at the end of the period is called **underapplied overhead.** To illustrate, assume that Road Warriors actually incurred *other overhead costs* of $5,550 instead of the $5,070 shown in Exhibit 26.11. This yields an actual total overhead cost of $7,200 in March. Since the amount of overhead applied was only $6,720, the Factory Overhead account is left with a $480 debit balance as shown in the ledger account in Exhibit 26.13.

LO8 Determine adjustments for overapplied and underapplied factory overhead.

Factory Overhead				Acct. No. 540
Date	**Explanation**	**Debit**	**Credit**	**Balance**
Mar. 31	Indirect materials cost	550		550 Dr.
31	Indirect labor cost	1,100		1,650 Dr.
31	Other overhead cost	5,550		7,200 Dr.
31	Overhead costs applied to jobs		6,720	480 Dr.

Exhibit 26.13

Underapplied Overhead in the Factory Overhead Ledger Account

The $480 debit balance reflects manufacturing costs not assigned to jobs. This means that the balances in Goods in Process Inventory, Finished Goods Inventory, and Cost of Goods Sold do not include all production costs incurred. When the underapplied overhead amount is immaterial, it is allocated (closed) to the Cost of Goods Sold account with the following adjusting entry.

Mar.	31	Cost of Goods Sold		4 8 0 00	
		Factory Overhead			4 8 0 00
		To adjust for underapplied overhead costs.			

Assets = Liabilities + Equity
                              −480
                              +480

The $480 debit (increase) to Cost of Goods Sold reduces income by $480. (When the underapplied (or overapplied) overhead is significant, the amount is normally allocated to the Cost of Goods Sold, Finished Goods Inventory, and Goods in Process Inventory accounts. This process is covered in advanced courses.)

Overapplied Overhead

When the overhead applied in a period exceeds the overhead incurred, the resulting credit balance in the Factory Overhead account is called **overapplied overhead.** We debit Factory Overhead and credit Cost of Good Sold for the amount of overapplied overhead at the end of the period.

HOW YOU DOIN'?   Answers—p. 729

9. In a job order cost accounting system, why does the Factory Overhead account usually have an overapplied or underapplied balance at period-end?

10. When the Factory Overhead account has a debit balance at period-end, does this reflect overapplied or underapplied overhead?

Demonstration Problem

The following information reflects Walczak Company's job order production activities for May.

Raw materials purchases	$16,000
Factory payroll cost	15,400
Overhead costs incurred	
Indirect materials	5,000
Indirect labor	3,500
Other factory overhead	9,500

Walczak's predetermined overhead rate is 150% of direct labor cost. Costs are allocated to the three jobs worked on during May as follows.

	Job 401	Job 402	Job 403
In-process balances on April 30			
Direct materials	$3,600		
Direct labor	1,700		
Applied overhead	2,550		
Costs during May			
Direct materials	3,550	$3,500	$1,400
Direct labor	5,100	6,000	800
Applied overhead	?	?	?
Status on May 31	Finished (sold)	Finished (unsold)	In process

Required

1. Determine the total cost of:
   a. The April 30 inventory of jobs in process.
   b. Materials used during May.
   c. Labor used during May.
   d. Factory overhead incurred and applied during May and the amount of any over- or underapplied overhead on May 31.
   e. Each job as of May 31, the May 31 inventories of both goods in process and finished goods, and the goods sold during May.

2. Prepare summarized journal entries for the month to record:
   a. Materials purchases (on credit), the factory payroll (paid with cash), indirect materials, indirect labor, and the other factory overhead (paid with cash).
   b. Assignment of direct materials, direct labor, and overhead costs to the Goods in Process Inventory account. (Use separate debit entries for each job.)
   c. Transfer of each completed job to the Finished Goods Inventory account.
   d. Cost of goods sold.
   e. Removal of any underapplied or overapplied overhead from the Factory Overhead account. (Assume the amount is not material.)

3. Prepare a manufacturing statement for May.

Planning the Solution

- Determine the cost of the April 30 goods in process inventory by totaling the materials, labor, and applied overhead costs for Job 401.
- Compute the cost of materials used and labor by totaling the amounts assigned to jobs and to overhead.
- Compute the total overhead incurred by summing the amounts for the three components. Compute the amount of applied overhead by multiplying the total direct labor cost by the predetermined overhead rate. Compute the underapplied or overapplied amount as the difference between the actual cost and the applied cost.

- Determine the total cost charged to each job by adding the costs incurred in April (if any) to the cost of materials, labor, and overhead applied during May.
- Group the costs of the jobs according to their completion status.
- Record the direct materials costs assigned to the three jobs, using a separate Goods in Process Inventory account for each job; do the same for the direct labor and the applied overhead.
- Transfer costs of Jobs 401 and 402 from Goods in Process Inventory to Finished Goods.
- Record the costs of Job 401 as cost of goods sold.
- Record the transfer of underapplied overhead from the Factory Overhead account to the Cost of Goods Sold account.
- On the manufacturing statement, remember to include the beginning and ending goods in process inventories and to deduct the underapplied overhead.

Solution to Demonstration Problem

I. Total cost of

a. April 30 inventory of jobs in process (Job 401).

Direct materials	$3,600
Direct labor	1,700
Applied overhead	2,550
Total cost	$7,850

b. Materials used during May.

Direct materials	
Job 401	$ 3,550
Job 402	3,500
Job 403	1,400
Total direct materials	8,450
Indirect materials	5,000
Total materials used	$13,450

c. Labor used during May.

Direct labor	
Job 401	$ 5,100
Job 402	6,000
Job 403	800
Total direct labor	11,900
Indirect labor	3,500
Total labor used	$15,400

d. Factory overhead incurred in May.

Actual overhead	
Indirect materials	$ 5,000
Indirect labor	3,500
Other factory overhead	9,500
Total actual overhead	18,000
Overhead applied (150% × $11,900)	17,850
Underapplied overhead	$ 150

e. Total cost of each job.

	401	402	403
In-process costs from April			
Direct materials	$ 3,600		
Direct labor	1,700		
Applied overhead*	2,550		
Cost incurred in May			
Direct materials	3,550	$ 3,500	$1,400
Direct labor	5,100	6,000	800
Applied overhead*	7,650	9,000	1,200
Total costs	$24,150	$18,500	$3,400

* Equals 150% of the direct labor cost.

Total cost of the May 31 inventory of goods in process (Job 403) = $3,400

Total cost of the May 31 inventory of finished goods (Job 402) = $18,500

Total cost of goods sold during May (Job 401) = $24,150

2. Journal entries.

a.

Raw Materials Inventory	16,000	
Accounts Payable		16,000
To record materials purchases.		
Factory Payroll	15,400	
Cash		15,400
To record factory payroll.		
Factory Overhead	5,000	
Raw Materials Inventory		5,000
To record indirect materials.		
Factory Overhead	3,500	
Factory Payroll		3,500
To record indirect labor.		
Factory Overhead	9,500	
Cash		9,500
To record other factory overhead.		

b. Assignment of costs to Goods in Process Inventory.

Goods in Process Inventory (Job 401)	3,550	
Goods in Process Inventory (Job 402)	3,500	
Goods in Process Inventory (Job 403)	1,400	
Raw Materials Inventory		8,450
To assign direct materials to jobs.		
Goods in Process Inventory (Job 401)	5,100	
Goods in Process Inventory (Job 402)	6,000	
Goods in Process Inventory (Job 403)	800	
Factory Payroll		11,900
To assign direct labor to jobs.		
Goods in Process Inventory (Job 401)	7,650	
Goods in Process Inventory (Job 402)	9,000	
Goods in Process Inventory (Job 403)	1,200	
Factory Overhead		17,850
To apply overhead to jobs.		

c. Transfer of completed jobs to Finished Goods Inventory.

Finished Goods Inventory	42,650	
Goods in Process Inventory (Job 401)		24,150
Goods in Process Inventory (Job 402)		18,500
To record completion of jobs.		

d.

Cost of Goods Sold	24,150	
Finished Goods Inventory		24,150
To record sale of Job 401.		

e.

Cost of Goods Sold	150	
Factory Overhead		150
To assign underapplied overhead.		

3.

WALCZAK COMPANY Manufacturing Statement For Month Ended May 31		
Direct materials		$ 8,450
Direct labor		11,900
Factory overhead		
Indirect materials	$5,000	
Indirect labor	3,500	
Other factory overhead	9,500	18,000
Total production costs		38,350
Add goods in process, April 30		7,850
Total cost of goods in process		46,200
Less goods in process, May 31		3,400
Less underapplied overhead		150
Cost of goods manufactured		$42,650

> Note how underapplied overhead is reported. Overapplied overhead is similarly reported, but is added.

Summary

LO1 Explain the cost accounting system. A cost accounting system records production activities using a perpetual inventory system, which continuously updates records for transactions and events that affect inventory costs.

LO2 Describe important features of job order production. Certain companies called *job order manufacturers* produce custom-made products for customers. These customized products are produced in response to a customer's orders. A job order manufacturer produces products that usually are different and, typically, produced in low volumes. The production systems of job order companies are flexible and are not highly standardized.

LO3 Explain job cost sheets and how they are used in job order cost accounting. In a job order cost accounting system, the costs of producing each job are accumulated on a separate job cost sheet. Costs of direct materials, direct labor, and overhead are accumulated separately on the job cost sheet and then added to determine the total cost of a job. Job cost sheets for jobs in process, finished jobs, and jobs sold make up subsidiary records controlled by general ledger accounts.

LO4 Describe and record the flow of materials costs in job order cost accounting. Costs of materials flow from receiving reports to materials ledger cards and then to either job cost sheets or the Indirect Materials account in the factory overhead ledger.

LO5 Describe and record the flow of labor costs in job order cost accounting. Costs of labor flow from clock cards to the Factory Payroll account and then to either job cost sheets or the Indirect Labor account in the factory overhead ledger.

LO6 Describe and record the flow of overhead costs in job order cost accounting. Overhead costs are accumulated in the Factory Overhead account that controls the subsidiary factory overhead ledger. Then, using a predetermined overhead rate, overhead costs are charged to jobs.

LO7 Compute predetermined overhead rates and apply overhead costs to jobs. Perpetual inventory systems require overhead costs to be estimated and assigned to jobs before the job's completion. This requires a predetermined overhead rate, which is computed as the total estimated overhead costs for a period divided by the total estimated activity base for the period. The activity base might be direct labor hours or machine hours, or their costs.

LO8 Determine adjustments for overapplied and underapplied factory overhead. At the end of each period, the Factory Overhead account usually has a residual debit (underapplied overhead) or credit (overapplied overhead) balance. If the balance is not material, it is transferred to Cost of Goods Sold, but if it is material, it is allocated to Goods in Process Inventory, Finished Goods Inventory, and Cost of Goods Sold.

Guidance Answers to HOW YOU DOIN'?

1. *b*

2. A job is a special order for a custom product. A job lot consists of a quantity of identical, special-order items.

3. *a*

4. Three costs normally accumulated on a job cost sheet are direct materials, direct labor, and factory overhead.

5. *c*

6. Four sources of factory overhead are materials requisitions, time tickets, vouchers, and adjusting entries.

7. Since a job order cost accounting system uses perpetual inventory records, overhead costs must be assigned to jobs before the end of a period. This requires the use of a predetermined overhead rate.

8. Debits are recorded when wages and salaries of factory employees are paid or accrued. Credits are recorded when direct labor costs are assigned to jobs and when indirect labor costs are transferred to the Factory Overhead account.

9. Overapplied or underapplied overhead usually exists at the end of a period because application of overhead is based on esti-mates of overhead and another variable such as direct labor. Estimates rarely equal actual amounts incurred.

10. A debit balance reflects underapplied factory overhead.

Key Terms

Clock card (p. 719) Source document used to record the number of hours an employee works and to determine the total labor cost for each pay period.

Cost accounting system (p. 714) Accounting system for manufacturing activities based on the perpetual inventory system.

Finished Goods Inventory (p. 717) Account that controls the finished goods files, which acts as a subsidiary ledger (of the Inventory account) in which the costs of finished goods that are ready for sale are recorded.

General accounting system (p. 714) Accounting system for manufacturing activities based on the *periodic* inventory system.

Goods in Process Inventory (p. 717) Account in which costs are accumulated for products that are in the process of being produced but are not yet complete; also called *work in process inventory.*

Job (p. 714) Production of a customized product or service.

Job cost sheet (p. 716) Separate record maintained for each job.

Job lot (p. 715) Production of more than one unit of a customized product or service.

Job order cost accounting system (p. 716) Cost accounting system to determine the cost of producing each job or job lot.

Job order production (p. 714) Production of special-order products; also called *customized production.*

Materials ledger card (p. 717) Perpetual record updated each time units are purchased or issued for production use.

Materials requisition (p. 718) Source document production managers use to request materials for production; used to assign materials costs to specific jobs or overhead.

Overapplied overhead (p. 725) Amount by which the overhead applied to production in a period using the predetermined overhead rate exceeds the actual overhead incurred in a period.

Predetermined overhead rate (p. 722) Rate established prior to the beginning of a period that relates estimated overhead to another variable, such as estimated direct labor, and is used to assign overhead cost to production.

Process operations (p. 715) Mass production of products in a continuous flow of steps.

Receiving report (p. 717) Form used to report that ordered goods are received and to describe their quantity and condition.

Target cost (p. 715) Maximum allowable cost for a product or service; defined as expected selling price less the desired profit.

Time ticket (p. 719) Source document used to report the time an employee spent working on a job or on overhead activities and then to determine the amount of direct labor to charge to the job or the amount of indirect labor to charge to overhead.

Underapplied overhead (p. 725) Amount by which overhead incurred in a period exceeds the overhead applied to that period's production using the predetermined overhead rate.

Multiple Choice Quiz
Answers on p. 747
mhhe.com/wildCA2e

Additional Multiple Choice Quizzes are available at the book's Website.

1. A company's predetermined overhead allocation rate is 150% of its direct labor costs. How much overhead is applied to a job that requires total labor costs of $30,000?
   a. $15,000
   b. $30,000
   c. $45,000
   d. $60,000
   e. $75,000

2. A company's cost accounting system uses direct labor costs to apply overhead to goods in process and finished goods inventories. Its production costs for the period are: direct materials, $45,000; direct labor, $35,000; and overhead applied, $38,500. What is its predetermined overhead allocation rate?
   a. 10%
   b. 110%

   c. 86%
   d. 91%
   e. 117%

3. A company's ending inventory of finished goods has a total cost of $10,000 and consists of 500 units. If the overhead applied to these goods is $4,000, and the predetermined overhead rate is 80% of direct labor costs, how much direct materials cost was incurred in producing these 500 units?
   a. $10,000
   b. $ 6,000
   c. $ 4,000
   d. $ 5,000
   e. $ 1,000

4. A company's Goods in Process Inventory T-account follows.

Goods in Process Inventory			
Beginning balance	9,000		
Direct materials	94,200		
Direct labor	59,200	?	Finished goods
Overhead applied	31,600		
Ending balance	17,800		

The cost of units transferred to Finished Goods inventory is

a. $193,000
b. $211,800
c. $185,000
d. $144,600
e. $176,200

5. At the end of its current year, a company learned that its over-head was underapplied by $1,500 and that this amount is not considered material. Based on this information, the company should
a. Close the $1,500 to Finished Goods Inventory.
b. Close the $1,500 to Cost of Goods Sold.
c. Carry the $1,500 to the next period.
d. Do nothing about the $1,500 because it is not material and it is likely that overhead will be overapplied by the same amount next year.
e. Carry the $1,500 to the Income Statement as "Other Expense."

Discussion Questions

1. Why must a company estimate the amount of factory overhead assigned to individual jobs or job lots?

2. The chapter used a percent of labor cost to assign factory over-head to jobs. Identify another factor (or base) a company might reasonably use to assign overhead costs.

3. What information is recorded on a job cost sheet? How do management and employees use job cost sheets?

4. In a job order cost accounting system, what records serve as a subsidiary ledger for Goods in Process Inventory? For Finished Goods Inventory?

5. What journal entry is recorded when a materials manager re-ceives a materials requisition and then issues materials (both direct and indirect) for use in the factory?

6. How does the materials requisition help safeguard a company's assets?

7. What is the difference between a clock card and a time ticket?

8. What events cause debits to be recorded in the Factory Overhead account? What events cause credits to be recorded in the Factory Overhead account?

9. What account(s) is(are) used to eliminate overapplied or un-derapplied overhead from the Factory Overhead account, as-suming the amount is not material?

10. Assume that **Apple** produces a batch of 1,000 iPods. Does it account for this as 1,000 individual jobs or as a job lot? Explain (consider costs and benefits).

11. Why must a company prepare a predetermined overhead rate when using job order cost accounting?

12. How would a hospital apply job order costing? Explain.

13. **Harley-Davidson** manufactures 30 custom-made, **Harley-Davidson** luxury-model motorcycles. Does it account for these motorcycles as 30 individual jobs or as a job lot? Explain.

---

connect™

A company incurred the following manufacturing costs this period: direct labor, $468,000; direct materi-als, $354,500; and factory overhead, $117,000. Compute overhead cost as a percent of (1) direct labor and (2) direct materials. Round percents to the nearest whole number.

QUICK STUDY

QS 26–1
Factory overhead rates **L07**

Determine which products are most likely to be manufactured as a job and which as a job lot.
1. A hand-crafted table.
2. A 90-foot motor yacht.
3. Wedding dresses for a chain of stores.
4. A custom-designed home.
5. Hats imprinted with company logo.
6. Little League trophies.

QS 26–2
Jobs and job lots **L02**

QS 26–3

Job cost computation   **LO3**

The following information is from the materials requisitions and time tickets for Job 9-1005 completed by Great Bay Boats. The requisitions are identified by code numbers starting with the letter Q and the time tickets start with W. At the start of the year, management estimated that overhead cost would equal 110% of direct labor cost for each job. Determine the total cost on the job cost sheet for Job 9-1005.

Date	Document	Amount
7/1/2010	Q-4698	$1,250
7/1/2010	W-3393	600
7/5/2010	Q-4725	1,000
7/5/2010	W-3479	450
7/10/2010	W-3559	300

QS 26–4

Direct materials journal entries

LO4

During the current month, a company that uses a job order cost accounting system purchases $50,000 in raw materials for cash. It then uses $12,000 of raw materials indirectly as factory supplies and uses $32,000 of raw materials as direct materials. Prepare entries to record these three transactions.

QS 26–5

Direct labor journal entries   **LO5**

During the current month, a company that uses a job order cost accounting system incurred a monthly factory payroll of $80,000, paid in cash. Of this amount, $40,000 is classified as indirect labor and the remainder as direct labor. Prepare entries to record these transactions.

QS 26–6

Factory overhead journal entries

LO6   LO7

During the current month, a company that uses a job order cost accounting system incurred a monthly factory payroll of $175,000, paid in cash. Of this amount, $44,000 is classified as indirect labor and the remainder as direct for the production of a job lot. Factory overhead is applied at 90% of direct labor. Prepare the entry to apply factory overhead to this job lot.

QS 26–7

Entry for over- or underapplied overhead

LO7   LO8

A company allocates overhead at a rate of 150% of direct labor cost. Actual overhead cost for the current period is $950,000, and direct labor cost is $600,000. Prepare the entry to close over- or underapplied overhead to cost of goods sold.

EXERCISES

connect™

Exercise 26–1

Documents in job order cost accounting

LO2   LO3   LO4   LO5   LO6

The left column lists the titles of documents and accounts used in job order cost accounting. The right column presents short descriptions of the purposes of the documents. Match each document in the left column to its numbered description in the right column.

A. Factory Payroll account

B. Materials ledger card

C. Time ticket

D. Voucher

E. Materials requisition

F. Factory Overhead account

G. Clock card

_____ **1.** Shows amount of time an employee works on a job.

_____ **2.** Temporarily accumulates incurred labor costs until they are assigned to specific jobs or to overhead.

_____ **3.** Shows only total time an employee works each day.

_____ **4.** Perpetual inventory record of raw materials received, used, and available for use.

_____ **5.** Shows amount approved for payment of an overhead or other cost.

_____ **6.** Temporarily accumulates the cost of incurred overhead until the cost is assigned to specific jobs.

_____ **7.** Communicates the need for materials to complete a job.

As of the end of June, the job cost sheets at Racing Wheels, Inc., show the following total costs accumulated on three custom jobs.

Exercise 26-2
Analysis of cost flows
LO2 LO4 LO5 LO6 LO7

	Job 102	Job 103	Job 104
Direct materials	$15,000	$33,000	$27,000
Direct labor	8,000	14,200	21,000
Overhead	4,000	7,100	10,500

Job 102 was started in production in May and the following costs were assigned to it in May: direct materials, $6,000; direct labor, $1,800; and overhead, $900. Jobs 103 and 104 are started in June. Overhead cost is applied with a predetermined rate based on direct labor cost. Jobs 102 and 103 are finished in June, and Job 104 is expected to be finished in July. No raw materials are used indirectly in June. Using this information, answer the following questions.

1. What is the cost of the raw materials requisitioned in June for each of the three jobs?

2. How much direct labor cost is incurred during June for each of the three jobs?

3. What predetermined overhead rate is used during June?

4. How much total cost is transferred to finished goods during June?

Check (4) $81,300

In December 2009, Shire Computer's management establishes the year 2010 predetermined overhead rate based on direct labor cost. The information used in setting this rate includes estimates that the company will incur $747,500 of overhead costs and $575,000 of direct labor cost in year 2010. During March 2010, Shire began and completed Job No. 13-56.

Exercise 26-3
Overhead rate; costs
assigned to jobs LO6 LO7

1. What is the predetermined overhead rate for year 2010?

2. Use the information on the following job cost sheet to determine the total cost of the job.

Check (2) $22,710

JOB COST SHEET

Customer's Name	Keiser Co.				Job No.	13-56	
Job Description	5 plasma monitors—61 inch						

	Direct Materials			Direct Labor		Overhead Costs Applied	
Date	Requisition No.	Amount		Time-Ticket No.	Amount	Rate	Amount
Mar. 8	4-129	$5,000		T-306	$ 700		
Mar. 11	4-142	7,020		T-432	1,250		
Mar. 18	4-167	3,330		T-456	1,250		
Totals							

Lorenzo Company uses a job order cost accounting system that charges overhead to jobs on the basis of direct material cost. At year-end, the Goods in Process Inventory account shows the following.

Exercise 26-4
Analysis of costs assigned to
goods in process LO5 LO7

Accounting System

File Edit Maintain Tasks Analysis Options Reports Window Help

Goods in Process Inventory Acct. No. 121

Date	Explanation	Debit	Credit	Balance
2010				
Dec. 31	Direct materials cost	1,500,000		1,500,000
31	Direct labor cost	300,000		1,800,000
31	Overhead costs	600,000		2,400,000
31	To finished goods		2,350,000	50,000

Sales   Purchases   General Ledger   Payroll   Inventory   Company   Analysis

1. Determine the overhead rate used (based on direct material cost).

2. Only one job remained in the goods in process inventory at December 31, 2010. Its direct materials cost is $30,000. How much direct labor cost and overhead cost are assigned to it?

Check (2) Direct labor cost, $8,000

Exercise 26-5

Cost flows in a job order
cost system

LO3 LO4 LO5 LO6 LO7

The following information is available for Lock-Safe Company, which produces special-order security products and uses a job order cost accounting system.

	April 30	May 31
Inventories		
Raw materials	$43,000	$ 52,000
Goods in process	10,200	21,300
Finished goods	63,000	35,600
Activities and information for May		
Raw materials purchases (paid with cash)		210,000
Factory payroll (paid with cash)		345,000
Factory overhead		
Indirect materials		15,000
Indirect labor		80,000
Other overhead costs		120,000
Sales (received in cash)		1,400,000
Predetermined overhead rate based on direct labor cost		70%

Compute the following amounts for the month of May.

Check   (3) $625,400

1. Cost of direct materials used.
2. Cost of direct labor used.
3. Cost of goods manufactured.
4. Cost of goods sold.*
5. Gross profit.
6. Overapplied or underapplied overhead.

* Do not consider any underapplied or overapplied overhead.

Exercise 26-6

Journal entries for a job order
cost accounting system

LO4 LO5 LO6 LO7 LO8

Use information in Exercise 26-5 to prepare journal entries for the following events in May.

1. Raw materials purchases for cash.
2. Direct materials usage.
3. Indirect materials usage.
4. Factory payroll costs in cash.
5. Direct labor usage.
6. Indirect labor usage.
7. Factory overhead excluding indirect materials and indirect labor (record credit to Other Accounts).
8. Application of overhead to goods in process.
9. Transfer of finished jobs to the finished goods inventory.
10. Sale and delivery of finished goods to customers for cash (record unadjusted cost of sales).
11. Allocation (closing) of overapplied or underapplied overhead to Cost of Goods Sold.

Exercise 26-7

Factory overhead computed,
applied, and adjusted

LO6 LO7 LO8

In December 2009, Infovision established its predetermined overhead rate for movies produced during year 2010 by using the following cost predictions: overhead costs, $1,680,000, and direct labor costs, $480,000. At year-end 2010, the company's records show that actual overhead costs for the year are $1,652,000. Actual direct labor cost had been assigned to jobs as follows.

Movies completed and released	$425,000
Movies still in production	50,000
Total actual direct labor cost	$475,000

1. Determine the predetermined overhead rate for year 2010.
2. Set up a T-account for overhead and enter the overhead costs incurred and the amounts applied to movies during the year using the predetermined overhead rate.

Check   (3) $10,500 overapplied

3. Determine whether overhead is overapplied or underapplied (and the amount) during the year.
4. Prepare the adjusting entry to allocate any over- or underapplied overhead to Cost of Goods Sold.

In December 2009, Cardozo Company established its predetermined overhead rate for jobs produced during year 2010 by using the following cost predictions: overhead costs, $750,000, and direct labor costs, $625,000. At year end 2010, the company's records show that actual overhead costs for the year are $830,000. Actual direct labor cost had been assigned to jobs as follows.

Exercise 26-8
Factory overhead computed, applied, and adjusted
LO6   LO7   LO8

Jobs completed and sold	$513,750
Jobs in finished goods inventory	102,750
Jobs in goods in process inventory	68,500
Total actual direct labor cost	$685,000

1. Determine the predetermined overhead rate for year 2010.

2. Set up a T-account for Factory Overhead and enter the overhead costs incurred and the amounts applied to jobs during the year using the predetermined overhead rate.

3. Determine whether overhead is overapplied or underapplied (and the amount) during the year.

4. Prepare the adjusting entry to allocate any over- or underapplied overhead to Cost of Goods Sold.

Check   (3) $8,000 underapplied

Sunrise Company applies factory overhead based on direct labor costs. The company incurred the following costs during 2010: direct materials costs, $650,000; direct labor costs, $3,000,000; and factory overhead costs applied, $1,800,000.

Exercise 26-9
Overhead rate calculation, allocation, and analysis
LO4   LO5   LO6   LO7

1. Determine the company's predetermined overhead rate for year 2010.

2. Assuming that the company's $71,000 ending Goods in Process Inventory account for year 2010 had $20,000 of direct labor costs, determine the inventory's direct materials costs.

3. Assuming that the company's $490,000 ending Finished Goods Inventory account for year 2010 had $250,000 of direct materials costs, determine the inventory's direct labor costs and its overhead costs.

Check   (3) $90,000 overhead costs

Deschamps Company's ending Goods in Process Inventory account consists of 5,000 units of partially completed product, and its Finished Goods Inventory account consists of 12,000 units of product. The factory manager determines that Goods in Process Inventory includes direct materials cost of $10 per unit and direct labor cost of $7 per unit. Finished goods are estimated to have $12 of direct materials cost per unit and $9 of direct labor cost per unit. The company established the predetermined overhead rate using the following predictions: estimated direct labor cost, $300,000, and estimated factory overhead, $375,000. The company allocates factory overhead to its goods in process and finished goods inventories based on direct labor cost. During the period, the company incurred these costs: direct materials, $535,000; direct labor, $290,000; and factory overhead applied, $362,500.

Exercise 26-10
Costs allocated to ending inventories
LO4   LO5   LO6   LO7

1. Determine the predetermined overhead rate.

2. Compute the total cost of the two ending inventories.

3. Compute cost of goods sold for the year (assume no beginning inventories and no underapplied or overapplied overhead).

Check   (3) Cost of goods sold, $671,750

connect

Ciolino Co.'s March 31 inventory of raw materials is $80,000. Raw materials purchases in April are $500,000, and factory payroll cost in April is $363,000. Overhead costs incurred in April are: indirect materials, $50,000; indirect labor, $23,000; factory rent, $32,000; factory utilities, $19,000; and factory equipment depreciation, $51,000. The predetermined overhead rate is 50% of direct labor cost. Job 306 is sold for $635,000 cash in April. Costs of the three jobs worked on in April follow.

PROBLEM SET A

Problem 26-1A
Production costs computed and recorded; reports prepared
LO3   LO4   LO5
LO6   LO7   LO8

	Job 306	Job 307	Job 308
Balances on March 31			
Direct materials	$ 29,000	$ 35,000	
Direct labor	20,000	18,000	
Applied overhead	10,000	9,000	
Costs during April			
Direct materials	135,000	220,000	$100,000
Direct labor	85,000	150,000	105,000
Applied overhead	?	?	?
Status on April 30	Finished (sold)	Finished (unsold)	In process

Required

1. Determine the total of each production cost incurred for April (direct labor, direct materials, and applied overhead), and the total cost assigned to each job (including the balances from March 31).

2. Prepare journal entries for the month of April to record the following.

   a. Materials purchases (on credit), factory payroll (paid in cash), and actual overhead costs including indirect materials and indirect labor. (Factory rent and utilities are paid in cash.)

   b. Assignment of direct materials, direct labor, and applied overhead costs to the Goods in Process Inventory.

   c. Transfer of Jobs 306 and 307 to the Finished Goods Inventory.

   d. Cost of goods sold for Job 306.

   e. Revenue from the sale of Job 306.

   f. Assignment of any underapplied or overapplied overhead to the Cost of Goods Sold account. (The amount is not material.)

3. Prepare a manufacturing statement for April (use a single line presentation for direct materials and show the details of overhead cost).

4. Compute gross profit for April. Show how to present the inventories on the April 30 balance sheet.

Check   (2f) $5,000 underapplied

(3) Cost of goods manufactured, $828,500

Analysis Component

5. The over- or underapplied overhead is closed to Cost of Goods Sold. Discuss how this adjustment impacts business decision making regarding individual jobs or batches of jobs.

Problem 26–2A

Source documents, journal entries, overhead, and financial reports

LO4 LO5 LO6 LO7 LO8

Farina Bay's computer system generated the following trial balance on December 31, 2010. The company's manager knows something is wrong with the trial balance because it does not show any balance for Goods in Process Inventory but does show balances for the Factory Payroll and Factory Overhead accounts.

	Debit	Credit
Cash	$102,000	
Accounts receivable	75,000	
Raw materials inventory	80,000	
Goods in process inventory	0	
Finished goods inventory	15,000	
Prepaid rent	3,000	
Accounts payable		$ 17,000
Notes payable		25,000
Common stock		50,000
Retained earnings		271,000
Sales		373,000
Cost of goods sold	218,000	
Factory payroll	68,000	
Factory overhead	115,000	
Operating expenses	60,000	
Totals	$736,000	$736,000

After examining various files, the manager identifies the following six source documents that need to be processed to bring the accounting records up to date.

Materials requisition 21-3010:	$10,200 direct materials to Job 402
Materials requisition 21-3011:	$18,600 direct materials to Job 404
Materials requisition 21-3012:	$5,600 indirect materials
Labor time ticket 6052:	$36,000 direct labor to Job 402
Labor time ticket 6053:	$23,800 direct labor to Job 404
Labor time ticket 6054:	$8,200 indirect labor

Jobs 402 and 404 are the only units in process at year-end. The predetermined overhead rate is 200% of direct labor cost.

Required

1. Use information on the six source documents to prepare journal entries to assign the following costs.

   a. Direct materials costs to Goods in Process Inventory.

   b. Direct labor costs to Goods in Process Inventory.

   c. Overhead costs to Goods in Process Inventory.

   d. Indirect materials costs to the Factory Overhead account.

   e. Indirect labor costs to the Factory Overhead account.

2. Determine the revised balance of the Factory Overhead account after making the entries in part 1. Determine whether there is any under- or overapplied overhead for the year. Prepare the adjusting entry to allocate any over- or underapplied overhead to Cost of Goods Sold, assuming the amount is not material.

Check (2) $9,200 underapplied overhead

3. Prepare a revised trial balance.

(3) T. B. totals, $736,000

4. Prepare an income statement for year 2010 and a balance sheet as of December 31, 2010.

(4) Net income, $85,800

Analysis Component

5. Assume that the $5,600 on materials requisition 21-3012 should have been direct materials charged to Job 404. Without providing specific calculations, describe the impact of this error on the income statement for 2010 and the balance sheet at December 31, 2010.

Widmer Watercraft's predetermined overhead rate for year 2010 is 200% of direct labor. Information on the company's production activities during May 2010 follows.

a. Purchased raw materials on credit, $200,000.

b. Paid $126,000 cash for factory wages.

c. Paid $15,000 cash to a computer consultant to reprogram factory equipment.

d. Materials requisitions record use of the following materials for the month.

Problem 26-3A
Source documents, journal entries, and accounts in job order cost accounting
LO4 LO5 LO6 LO7 LO8

Job 136	$ 48,000
Job 137	32,000
Job 138	19,200
Job 139	22,400
Job 140	6,400
Total direct materials	128,000
Indirect materials	19,500
Total materials used	$147,500

e. Time tickets record use of the following labor for the month.

Job 136	$ 12,000
Job 137	10,500
Job 138	37,500
Job 139	39,000
Job 140	3,000
Total direct labor	102,000
Indirect labor	24,000
Total	$126,000

f. Applied overhead to Jobs 136, 138, and 139.

g. Transferred Jobs 136, 138, and 139 to Finished Goods.

h. Sold Jobs 136 and 138 on credit at a total price of $525,000.

i. The company incurred the following overhead costs during the month (credit Prepaid Insurance for expired factory insurance).

Depreciation of factory building	$68,000
Depreciation of factory equipment	36,500
Expired factory insurance	10,000
Accrued property taxes payable	35,000

j. Applied overhead at month-end to the Goods in Process (Jobs 137 and 140) using the predetermined overhead rate of 200% of direct labor cost.

Required

1. Prepare a job cost sheet for each job worked on during the month. Use the following simplified form.

Job No. _____

Materials . . . . $ _____

Labor . . . . _____

Overhead . . . . _____

Total cost . . . . $ _____

Check   (2f) Cr. Factory Overhead, $177,000

2. Prepare journal entries to record the events and transactions *a* through *j*.

3. Set up T-accounts for each of the following general ledger accounts, each of which started the month with a zero balance: Raw Materials Inventory; Goods in Process Inventory; Finished Goods Inventory; Factory Payroll; Factory Overhead; Cost of Goods Sold. Then post the journal entries to these T-accounts and determine the balance of each account.

4. Prepare a report showing the total cost of each job in process and prove that the sum of their costs equals the Goods in Process Inventory account balance. Prepare similar reports for Finished Goods Inventory and Cost of Goods Sold.

Check   (4) Finished Goods Inventory, $139,400

Problem 26–4A

Overhead allocation and adjustment using a predetermined overhead rate

LO6   LO7   LO8

mhhe.com/wildCA2e

In December 2009, Yerbury Company's manager estimated next year's total direct labor cost assuming 50 persons working an average of 2,000 hours each at an average wage rate of $25 per hour. The manager also estimated the following manufacturing overhead costs for year 2010.

Indirect labor	$ 319,200
Factory supervision	240,000
Rent on factory building	140,000
Factory utilities	88,000
Factory insurance expired	68,000
Depreciation—Factory equipment	480,000
Repairs expense—Factory equipment	60,000
Factory supplies used	68,800
Miscellaneous production costs	36,000
Total estimated overhead costs	$1,500,000

At the end of 2010, records show the company incurred $1,520,000 of actual overhead costs. It completed and sold five jobs with the following direct labor costs: Job 201, $604,000; Job 202, $563,000; Job 203, $298,000; Job 204, $716,000; and Job 205, $314,000. In addition, Job 206 is in process at the end of 2010 and had been charged $17,000 for direct labor. No jobs were in process at the end of 2009. The company's predetermined overhead rate is based on direct labor cost.

Required

1. Determine the following.
  a. Predetermined overhead rate for year 2010.
  b. Total overhead cost applied to each of the six jobs during year 2010.
  c. Over- or underapplied overhead at year-end 2010.

Check   (1c) $12,800 underapplied

(2) Cr. Factory Overhead $12,800

2. Assuming that any over- or underapplied overhead is not material, prepare the adjusting entry to allocate any over- or underapplied overhead to Cost of Goods Sold at the end of year 2010.

If the working papers that accompany this book are unavailable, do not attempt to solve this problem.
Sager Company manufactures variations of its product, a technopress, in response to custom orders from
its customers. On May 1, the company had no inventories of goods in process or finished goods but held
the following raw materials.

Problem 26–5A
Production transactions;
subsidiary records; and source
documents
**LO3   LO4   LO5
LO6   LO7   LO8**

Material M	. . . .	200 units @ $250 =	$50,000
Material R	. . . .	95 units @ 180 =	17,100
Paint	. . . .	55 units @ 75 =	4,125
Total cost	. . . .		$71,225

On May 4, the company began working on two technopresses: Job 102 for Worldwide Company and Job
103 for Reuben Company.

Required

Follow the instructions in this list of activities and complete the sheets provided in the working papers.

a. Purchased raw materials on credit and recorded the following information from receiving reports and
invoices.

> Receiving Report No. 426, Material M, 250 units at $250 each.
> Receiving Report No. 427, Material R, 90 units at $180 each.

Instructions: Record these purchases with a single journal entry and post it to general ledger
T-accounts, using the transaction letter *a* to identify the entry. Enter the receiving report information
on the materials ledger cards.

b. Requisitioned the following raw materials for production.

> Requisition No. 35, for Job 102, 135 units of Material M.
> Requisition No. 36, for Job 102, 72 units of Material R.
> Requisition No. 37, for Job 103, 70 units of Material M.
> Requisition No. 38, for Job 103, 38 units of Material R.
> Requisition No. 39, for 15 units of paint.

Instructions: Enter amounts for direct materials requisitions on the materials ledger cards and the job
cost sheets. Enter the indirect material amount on the materials ledger card and record a debit to the
Indirect Materials account in the subsidiary factory overhead ledger. Do not record a journal entry at
this time.

c. Received the following employee time tickets for work in May.

> Time tickets Nos. 1 to 10 for direct labor on Job 102, $90,000.
> Time tickets Nos. 11 to 30 for direct labor on Job 103, $65,000.
> Time tickets Nos. 31 to 36 for equipment repairs, $19,250.

Instructions: Record direct labor from the time tickets on the job cost sheets and then debit indirect
labor to the Indirect Labor account in the subsidiary factory overhead ledger. Do not record a journal
entry at this time.

d. Paid cash for the following items during the month: factory payroll, $174,250, and miscellaneous over-
head items, $102,000.

Instructions: Record these payments with journal entries and then post them to the general ledger accounts. Also record a debit in the Miscellaneous Overhead account in the subsidiary factory overhead
ledger.

e. Finished Job 102 and transferred it to the warehouse. The company assigns overhead to each job with
a predetermined overhead rate equal to 80% of direct labor cost.

Instructions: Enter the allocated overhead on the cost sheet for Job 102, fill in the cost summary section of the cost sheet, and then mark the cost sheet "Finished." Prepare a journal entry to record the
job's completion and its transfer to Finished Goods and then post it to the general ledger accounts.

f. Delivered Job 102 and accepted the customer's promise to pay $400,000 within 30 days.

Instructions: Prepare journal entries to record the sale of Job 102 and the cost of goods sold. Post them to the general ledger accounts.

g. Applied overhead to Job 103 based on the job's direct labor to date.

Instructions: Enter overhead on the job cost sheet but do not make a journal entry at this time.

Check (h) Dr. Goods in Process Inventory, $71,050

h. Recorded the total direct and indirect materials costs as reported on all the requisitions for the month.

Instructions: Prepare a journal entry to record these costs and post it to general ledger accounts.

i. Recorded the total direct and indirect labor costs as reported on all time tickets for the month.

Instructions: Prepare a journal entry to record these costs and post it to general ledger accounts.

j. Recorded the total overhead costs applied to jobs.

Check Balance in Factory Overhead, $1,625 Cr., overapplied

Instructions: Prepare a journal entry to record the allocation of these overhead costs and post it to general ledger accounts.

PROBLEM SET B

Problem 26–1B

Production costs computed and recorded; reports prepared

LO3 LO4 LO5
LO6 LO7 LO8

Tavella Co.'s August 31 inventory of raw materials is $150,000. Raw materials purchases in September are $400,000, and factory payroll cost in September is $220,000. Overhead costs incurred in September are: indirect materials, $30,000; indirect labor, $14,000; factory rent, $20,000; factory utilities, $12,000; and factory equipment depreciation, $30,000. The predetermined overhead rate is 50% of direct labor cost. Job 114 is sold for $380,000 cash in September. Costs for the three jobs worked on in September follow.

	Job 114	Job 115	Job 116
Balances on August 31			
Direct materials	$ 14,000	$ 18,000	
Direct labor	18,000	16,000	
Applied overhead	9,000	8,000	
Costs during September			
Direct materials	100,000	170,000	$ 80,000
Direct labor	30,000	68,000	120,000
Applied overhead	?	?	?
Status on September 30	Finished (sold)	Finished (unsold)	In process

Required

1. Determine the total of each production cost incurred for September (direct labor, direct materials, and applied overhead), and the total cost assigned to each job (including the balances from August 31).

2. Prepare journal entries for the month of September to record the following.

  a. Materials purchases (on credit), factory payroll (paid in cash), and actual overhead costs including indirect materials and indirect labor. (Factory rent and utilities are paid in cash.)

  b. Assignment of direct materials, direct labor, and applied overhead costs to Goods in Process Inventory.

  c. Transfer of Jobs 114 and 115 to the Finished Goods Inventory.

  d. Cost of Job 114 in the Cost of Goods Sold account.

  e. Revenue from the sale of Job 114.

Check (2f) $3,000 overapplied

  f. Assignment of any underapplied or overapplied overhead to the Cost of Goods Sold account. (The amount is not material.)

(3) Cost of goods manufactured, $500,000

3. Prepare a manufacturing statement for September (use a single line presentation for direct materials and show the details of overhead cost).

4. Compute gross profit for September. Show how to present the inventories on the September 30 balance sheet.

Analysis Component

5. The over- or underapplied overhead adjustment is closed to Cost of Goods Sold. Discuss how this adjustment impacts business decision making regarding individual jobs or batches of jobs.

Swisher Company's computer system generated the following trial balance on December 31, 2010. The company's manager knows that the trial balance is wrong because it does not show any balance for Goods in Process Inventory but does show balances for the Factory Payroll and Factory Overhead accounts.

Problem 26–2B
Source documents, journal entries, overhead, and financial reports
L04   L05   L06   L07   L08

	Debit	Credit
Cash	$ 48,000	
Accounts receivable	42,000	
Raw materials inventory	26,000	
Goods in process inventory	0	
Finished goods inventory	9,000	
Prepaid rent	3,000	
Accounts payable		$ 10,500
Notes payable		13,500
Common stock		30,000
Retained earnings		87,000
Sales		180,000
Cost of goods sold	105,000	
Factory payroll	16,000	
Factory overhead	27,000	
Operating expenses	45,000	
Totals	$321,000	$321,000

After examining various files, the manager identifies the following six source documents that need to be processed to bring the accounting records up to date.

Materials requisition 94-231:	$4,600 direct materials to Job 603
Materials requisition 94-232:	$7,600 direct materials to Job 604
Materials requisition 94-233:	$2,100 indirect materials
Labor time ticket 765:	$5,000 direct labor to Job 603
Labor time ticket 766:	$8,000 direct labor to Job 604
Labor time ticket 777:	$3,000 indirect labor

Jobs 603 and 604 are the only units in process at year-end. The predetermined overhead rate is 200% of direct labor cost.

Required

1. Use information on the six source documents to prepare journal entries to assign the following costs.
   a. Direct materials costs to Goods in Process Inventory.
   b. Direct labor costs to Goods in Process Inventory.
   c. Overhead costs to Goods in Process Inventory.
   d. Indirect materials costs to the Factory Overhead account.
   e. Indirect labor costs to the Factory Overhead account.

2. Determine the revised balance of the Factory Overhead account after making the entries in part 1. Determine whether there is under- or overapplied overhead for the year. Prepare the adjusting entry to allocate any over- or underapplied overhead to Cost of Goods Sold, assuming the amount is not material.

Check   (2) $6,100 underapplied overhead

3. Prepare a revised trial balance.

(3) T. B. totals, $321,000

4. Prepare an income statement for year 2010 and a balance sheet as of December 31, 2010.

(4) Net income, $23,900

Analysis Component

5. Assume that the $2,100 indirect materials on materials requisition 94-233 should have been direct materials charged to Job 604. Without providing specific calculations, describe the impact of this error on the income statement for 2010 and the balance sheet at December 31, 2010.

Problem 26–3B

Source documents, journal
entries, and accounts in job
order cost accounting

LO4 LO5 LO6 LO7 LO8

Prescott Company's predetermined overhead rate is 200% of direct labor. Information on the company's
production activities during September 2010 follows.

a. Purchased raw materials on credit, $125,000.

b. Paid $84,000 cash for factory wages.

c. Paid $11,000 cash for miscellaneous factory overhead costs.

d. Materials requisitions record use of the following materials for the month.

Job 487	$30,000
Job 488	20,000
Job 489	12,000
Job 490	14,000
Job 491	4,000
Total direct materials	80,000
Indirect materials	12,000
Total materials used	$92,000

e. Time tickets record use of the following labor for the month.

Job 487	$ 8,000
Job 488	7,000
Job 489	25,000
Job 490	26,000
Job 491	2,000
Total direct labor	68,000
Indirect labor	16,000
Total	$84,000

f. Allocated overhead to Jobs 487, 489, and 490.

g. Transferred Jobs 487, 489, and 490 to Finished Goods.

h. Sold Jobs 487 and 489 on credit for a total price of $340,000.

i. The company incurred the following overhead costs during the month (credit Prepaid Insurance for expired factory insurance).

Depreciation of factory building	$37,000
Depreciation of factory equipment	21,000
Expired factory insurance	7,000
Accrued property taxes payable	31,000

j. Applied overhead at month-end to the Goods in Process (Jobs 488 and 491) using the predetermined
overhead rate of 200% of direct labor cost.

Required

1. Prepare a job cost sheet for each job worked on in the month. Use the following simplified form.

Job No. _____	
Materials	$ _____
Labor	_____
Overhead	_____
Total cost	$ _____

2. Prepare journal entries to record the events and transactions *a* through *j*.

3. Set up T-accounts for each of the following general ledger accounts, each of which started the month with a zero balance: Raw Materials Inventory, Goods in Process Inventory, Finished Goods Inventory, Factory Payroll, Factory Overhead, Cost of Goods Sold. Then post the journal entries to these T-accounts and determine the balance of each account.

4. Prepare a report showing the total cost of each job in process and prove that the sum of their costs equals the Goods in Process Inventory account balance. Prepare similar reports for Finished Goods Inventory and Cost of Goods Sold.

Check (2f) Cr. Factory Overhead, $118,000

(4) Finished Goods Inventory, $92,000

In December 2009, Pavelka Company's manager estimated next year's total direct labor cost assuming 50 persons working an average of 2,000 hours each at an average wage rate of $15 per hour. The manager also estimated the following manufacturing overhead costs for year 2010.

Problem 26–4B
Overhead allocation and adjustment using a predetermined overhead rate
LO6 LO7 LO8

Indirect labor	$159,600
Factory supervision	120,000
Rent on factory building	70,000
Factory utilities	44,000
Factory insurance expired	34,000
Depreciation—Factory equipment	240,000
Repairs expense—Factory equipment	30,000
Factory supplies used	34,400
Miscellaneous production costs	18,000
Total estimated overhead costs	$750,000

At the end of 2010, records show the company incurred $725,000 of actual overhead costs. It completed and sold five jobs with the following direct labor costs: Job 625, $354,000; Job 626, $330,000; Job 627, $175,000; Job 628, $420,000; and Job 629, $184,000. In addition, Job 630 is in process at the end of 2010 and had been charged $10,000 for direct labor. No jobs were in process at the end of 2009. The company's predetermined overhead rate is based on direct labor cost.

Required

1. Determine the following.
   a. Predetermined overhead rate for year 2010.
   b. Total overhead cost applied to each of the six jobs during year 2010.
   c. Over- or underapplied overhead at year-end 2010.

2. Assuming that any over- or underapplied overhead is not material, prepare the adjusting entry to allocate any over- or underapplied overhead to Cost of Goods Sold at the end of year 2010.

Check (1c) $11,500 overapplied

(2) Dr. Factory Overhead, $11,500

If the working papers that accompany this book are unavailable, do not attempt to solve this problem.
King Company produces variations of its product, a megatron, in response to custom orders from its customers. On June 1, the company had no inventories of goods in process or finished goods but held the following raw materials.

Problem 26–5B
Production transactions; subsidiary records; and source documents
LO3 LO4 LO5
LO6 LO7 LO8

Material M	120 units @ $200 =	$24,000
Material R	80 units @ 160 =	12,800
Paint	44 units @ 72 =	3,168
Total cost		$39,968

On June 3, the company began working on two megatrons: Job 450 for Encinita Company and Job 451 for Fargo, Inc.

Required

Follow instructions in this list of activities and complete the sheets provided in the working papers.

a. Purchased raw materials on credit and recorded the following information from receiving reports and invoices.

> Receiving Report No. 20, Material M, 150 units at $200 each.
> Receiving Report No. 21, Material R, 70 units at $160 each.

Instructions: Record these purchases with a single journal entry and post it to general ledger T-accounts, using the transaction letter *a* to identify the entry. Enter the receiving report information on the materials ledger cards.

b. Requisitioned the following raw materials for production.

> Requisition No. 223, for Job 450, 80 units of Material M.
> Requisition No. 224, for Job 450, 60 units of Material R.
> Requisition No. 225, for Job 451, 40 units of Material M.
> Requisition No. 226, for Job 451, 30 units of Material R.
> Requisition No. 227, for 12 units of paint.

Instructions: Enter amounts for direct materials requisitions on the materials ledger cards and the job cost sheets. Enter the indirect material amount on the materials ledger card and record a debit to the Indirect Materials account in the subsidiary factory overhead ledger. Do not record a journal entry at this time.

c. Received the following employee time tickets for work in June.

> Time tickets Nos. 1 to 10 for direct labor on Job 450, $40,000.
> Time tickets Nos. 11 to 20 for direct labor on Job 451, $32,000.
> Time tickets Nos. 21 to 24 for equipment repairs, $12,000.

Instructions: Record direct labor from the time tickets on the job cost sheets and then debit indirect labor to the Indirect Labor account in the subsidiary factory overhead ledger. Do not record a journal entry at this time.

d. Paid cash for the following items during the month: factory payroll, $84,000, and miscellaneous overhead items, $36,800.

Instructions: Record these payments with journal entries and post them to the general ledger accounts. Also record a debit in the Miscellaneous Overhead account in the subsidiary factory overhead ledger.

e. Finished Job 450 and transferred it to the warehouse. The company assigns overhead to each job with a predetermined overhead rate equal to 70% of direct labor cost.

Instructions: Enter the allocated overhead on the cost sheet for Job 450, fill in the cost summary section of the cost sheet, and then mark the cost sheet "Finished." Prepare a journal entry to record the job's completion and its transfer to Finished Goods and then post it to the general ledger accounts.

f. Delivered Job 450 and accepted the customer's promise to pay $290,000 within 30 days.

Instructions: Prepare journal entries to record the sale of Job 450 and the cost of goods sold. Post them to the general ledger accounts.

g. Applied overhead cost to Job 451 based on the job's direct labor used to date.

Instructions: Enter overhead on the job cost sheet but do not make a journal entry at this time.

h. Recorded the total direct and indirect materials costs as reported on all the requisitions for the month.

Instructions: Prepare a journal entry to record these costs and post it to general ledger accounts.

Check   (h) Dr. Goods in Process
Inventory, $38,400

i. Recorded the total direct and indirect labor costs as reported on all time tickets for the month.

   Instructions: Prepare a journal entry to record these costs and post it to general ledger accounts.

j. Recorded the total overhead costs applied to jobs.

   Instructions: Prepare a journal entry to record the allocation of these overhead costs and post it to general ledger accounts.

Check   Balance in Factory Overhead, $736 Cr., overapplied

SERIAL PROBLEM

Success Systems

(This serial problem began in Chapter 1 and continues through most of the book. If previous chapter segments were not completed, the serial problem can begin at this point. It is helpful, but not necessary, for you to use the Working Papers that accompany the book.)

SP 26   The computer workstation furniture manufacturing that Adriana Lopez started in January is progressing well. As of the end of June, Success Systems' job cost sheets show these total costs accumulated on three furniture jobs.

	Job 6.02	Job 6.03	Job 6.04
Direct materials	$3,000	$6,600	$5,400
Direct labor	1,600	2,840	4,200
Overhead	800	1,420	2,100

Job 6.02 was started in production in May, and these costs were assigned to it in May: direct materials, $1,200; direct labor, $360; and overhead, $180. Jobs 6.03 and 6.04 were started in June. Overhead cost is applied with a predetermined rate based on direct labor costs. Jobs 6.02 and 6.03 are finished in June, and Job 6.04 is expected to be finished in July. No raw materials are used indirectly in June.

Required

1. What is the cost of the raw materials used in June for each of the three jobs and in total?

2. How much total direct labor cost is incurred in June?

3. What predetermined overhead rate is used in June?

4. How much cost is transferred to finished goods inventory in June?

Check   (1) Total materials, $13,800

(3) 50%

BEYOND THE NUMBERS

REPORTING IN ACTION

BTN 26-1   **Best Buy**'s financial statements and notes in Appendix A provide evidence of growth potential in its domestic sales.

Required

1. Identify at least two types of costs that will predictably increase as a percent of sales with growth in domestic sales.

2. Explain why you believe the types of costs identified for part 1 will increase, and describe how you might assess Best Buy's success with these costs. (*Hint:* You might consider the gross margin ratio.)

Fast Forward

3. Access Best Buy's 10-K for a fiscal year ending after March 1, 2008, from its Website [BestBuy.com] or the SEC's EDGAR database [www.SEC.gov]. Review and report its growth in sales along with its cost and income levels (including its gross margin ratio).

ETHICS CHALLENGE
LO6

BTN 26-2   An accounting professional requires at least two skill sets. The first is to be technically competent. Knowing how to capture, manage, and report information is a necessary skill. Second, the ability to assess manager and employee actions and biases for accounting analysis is another skill. For instance, knowing how a person is compensated helps anticipate information biases. Draw on these skills and write a one-half page memo to the financial officer on the following practice of allocating overhead.

Background: Assume that your company sells portable housing to both general contractors and the government. It sells jobs to contractors on a bid basis. A contractor asks for three bids from different manufacturers. The combination of low bid and high quality wins the job. However, jobs sold to the government are bid on a cost-plus basis. This means price is determined by adding all costs plus a profit based on cost at a specified percent, such as 10%. You observe that the amount of overhead allocated to government jobs is higher than that allocated to contract jobs. These allocations concern you and motivate your memo.

> Students could compare responses and discuss differences in concerns with allocating overhead.

WORKPLACE COMMUNICATION
LO1   LO2   LO3

BTN 26-3   Assume that you are preparing for a second interview with a manufacturing company. The company is impressed with your credentials but has indicated that it has several qualified applicants. You anticipate that in this second interview, you must show what you offer over other candidates. You learn the company currently uses a periodic inventory system and is not satisfied with the timeliness of its information and its inventory management. The company manufactures custom-order holiday decorations and display items. To show your abilities, you plan to recommend that it use a cost accounting system.

Required

> Have students present a mock interview, one assuming the role of the president of the company and the other the applicant.

In preparation for the interview, prepare notes outlining the following:
1. Your cost accounting system recommendation and why it is suitable for this company.
2. A general description of the documents that the proposed cost accounting system requires.
3. How the documents in part 2 facilitate the operation of the cost accounting system.

TAKING IT TO THE NET
LO1   LO2

BTN 26-4   Many contractors work on custom jobs that require a job order costing system.

Required

Access the Website **AMSI.com** and click on *The Construction Manager*. Prepare a one-page memorandum for the CEO of a construction company providing information about the job order costing software this company offers. Would you recommend that the company purchase this software?

TEAMWORK IN ACTION
LO2

BTN 26-5   Consider the activities undertaken by a medical clinic in your area.

Required

1. Do you consider a job order cost accounting system appropriate for the clinic?
2. Identify as many factors as possible to lead you to conclude that it uses a job order system.

ENTREPRENEURS IN BUSINESS
LO2

BTN 26-6   Refer to the chapter opener regarding Hank Julicher and his company, **Sprinturf**. All successful businesses track their costs, and it is especially important for start-up businesses to monitor and control costs.

Required

1. Assume that Sprinturf uses a job order costing system. For the three basic cost categories of direct materials, direct labor, and overhead, identify at least two typical costs that would fall into each category for Sprinturf.

2. Assume a local high school expresses an interest in purchasing a synthetic field installation from Sprinturf. The high school's budget will allow them to pay no more than $600,000 for the field. How can Sprinturf use job cost information to assess whether to pursue this opportunity?

---

1. c; $30,000 × 150% = $45,000

2. b; $38,500/$35,000 = 110%

3. e; Direct materials + Direct labor + Overhead =
Total cost;
Direct materials + ($4,000/.80) + $4,000 =
$10,000
Direct materials = $1,000

4. e; $9,000 + $94,200 + $59,200 + $31,600 −
Finished goods inventory = $17,800
Thus, finished goods inventory = $176,200

5. b

ANSWERS TO MULTIPLE CHOICE QUIZ

A Look Back

Chapter 26 described the job order cost accounting system and the procedures used to determine costs in that system.

A Look at This Chapter

This chapter describes managerial reports useful in directing a company's activities. It also describes responsibility accounting, measuring departmental performance, and allocating common costs across departments.

A Look Ahead

Chapter 28 explains the importance of budgeting. It also describes the flexible budget and its preparation.

Chapter 27

Departmental and Responsibility Accounting

Learning Objectives

LO 1 Explain departmentalization and the role of departmental accounting.

LO 2 Distinguish between direct and indirect expenses.

LO 3 Identify bases for allocating indirect expenses to departments.

LO 4 Prepare departmental income statements.

LO 5 Prepare departmental contribution reports.

LO 6 Explain controllable costs and responsibility accounting.

LO 7 Analyze investment centers using return on total assets.

"Treat customers like gold and have fun doing it."
—Jim Bonaminio

The Wizard of Odd

FAIRFIELD, OH—Jim Bonaminio built his roadside produce stand while living in an abandoned gas station. "I would get up and leave at 4 in the morning to buy everything fresh [and] my wife opened the market at 8 a.m.," recalls Jim. "By 10 o'clock at night, we'd be sitting on the bed balancing the register receipts . . . we worked seven days a week." The fruit of those early efforts is **Jungle Jim's International Market** (**JungleJims.com**). Jim and his wife now serve more than 50,000 customers each week, and annual sales are near $100 million.

Jungle Jim's is arguably America's wackiest supermarket. Yet there is a plan to Jim's madness. Instead of trying to beat the big chains at the price-squeezing game, Jim's is a funhouse maze of a store. A seven-foot Elvis lion sings "Jailhouse Rock," an antique fire engine rests atop cases of hot sauce, port-a-potties lead to fancy restrooms, and Robin Hood greets customers with English food set within a 30-foot-tall Sherwood Forest. This is just a sampling. Jim also created a "Foodie Tram" using the old monorail acquired from Paramount's Kings Island.

"If you don't go out on a limb, then you're just like everybody else," insists Jim. "The stuff I've collected—all sorts of weird stuff—gets reused. We make it fit into the craziness." Despite the wackiness, his store's defining trait is specialty food departments reflecting over 70 countries. Jungle Jim's stocks more than 140,000 items, including 1,600 cheeses, 8,500 wines, 800 beers, 1,000 hot sauces, and an entire acre of produce! More than several dozen ethnic departments make up his 300,000-square-foot store.

This diversity of departments requires cost management. Jim has successfully merged cost controls and departmental and individual responsibility into his store. He closely monitors direct, indirect, and controllable costs and allocates them to departments and products. Jim knows how departments and products are performing and their contribution margins.

Yet cost management has not curtailed Jim's fun-loving approach to business. "I'm trying to create something that has never been done," says Jim. "I just want to see if I can do it and have fun."

[Sources: *Jungle Jim's Website*, May 2009; *BusinessWeek*, April 2005; *Country Living*, November 2004; *Miamian*, Summer 2004; *Design*, May 2004; *Smithsonian*, October 2000; *Plain Dealer*, November 2004]

The chapter introduces managerial accounting reports useful in managing a company's activities and explains how and why management divides companies into departments. This chapter also describes how common costs are allocated across departments and explains how departmental performance is measured.

Departmental and Responsibility Accounting

Departmental Accounting
- Motivation for departmentalization
- Departmental evaluation
- Departmental reporting and analysis

Departmental Expense Allocation
- Direct and indirect expenses
- Allocation of indirect expenses
- Departmental income statements
- Departmental contribution to overhead

Responsibility Accounting
- Controllable versus direct costs
- Responsibility accounting system

This chapter describes and illustrates allocation of costs for performance evaluation. We begin with departmental accounting and expense allocations and conclude with responsibility accounting.

Departmental Accounting

Companies are divided into *departments,* also called *subunits,* when they are too large to be managed effectively as a single unit. Managerial accounting for departments has two main goals. The first is to set up a **departmental accounting system** to provide information for managers to evaluate the profitability or cost effectiveness of each department's activities. The second goal is to set up a **responsibility accounting system** to control costs and expenses and evaluate managers' performances by assigning costs and expenses to the managers responsible for controlling them. Departmental and responsibility accounting systems are related and share much information.

Motivation for Departmentalization

LO1 Explain departmentalization and the role of departmental accounting.

Many companies are so large and complex that they are broken into separate divisions for efficiency and/or effectiveness purposes. Divisions then are usually organized into separate departments. When a company is departmentalized, each department is often placed under the direction of a manager. As a company grows, management often divides departments into new departments so that responsibilities for a department's activities do not overwhelm the manager's ability to oversee and control them. A company also creates departments to take advantage of the skills of individual managers. Departments are broadly classified as either operating or service departments.

Departmental Evaluation

When a company is divided into departments, managers need to know how each department is performing. The accounting system must supply information about resources used and outputs achieved by each department. This requires a system to measure and accumulate revenue and expense information for each department whenever possible.

Departmental information is rarely distributed publicly because of its potential usefulness to competitors. Information about departments is prepared for internal managers to help control operations, appraise performance, allocate resources, and plan strategy. If a department is highly profitable, management may decide to expand its operations, or if a department is performing poorly, information about revenues or expenses can suggest useful changes.

More companies are emphasizing customer satisfaction as a main responsibility of many departments. This has led to changes in the measures reported. Increasingly, financial measurements are being supplemented with quality and customer satisfaction indexes. **Motorola**, for instance, uses two key measures: the number of defective parts per million parts produced and the percent of orders delivered on time to customers.

Financial information used to evaluate a department depends on whether it is evaluated as a profit center or a cost center. A **profit center** incurs costs and generates revenues; selling departments are often evaluated as profit centers. A **cost center** incurs costs without directly generating revenues. The manufacturing departments of a manufacturer and its service departments such as accounting, advertising, and purchasing are all cost centers.

Evaluating managers' performance depends on whether they are responsible for profit centers or cost centers. Profit center managers are judged on their abilities to generate revenues in excess of the department's costs. They are assumed to influence both revenue generation and cost incurrence. Cost center managers are judged on their abilities to control costs by keeping them within a satisfactory range under an assumption that they only influence costs. Selling departments are often treated as *revenue centers;* their managers are responsible for maximizing sales revenues.

IN THE NEWS

Nonfinancial Measures   A majority of companies now report nonfinancial performance measures to management. Common measures are cycle time, defect rate, on-time deliveries, inventory turnover, customer satisfaction, and safety. When nonfinancial measures are used with financial measures, the performance measurement system resembles a *balanced scorecard.* Many of these companies also use activity-based management as part of their performance measurement system.

Departmental Reporting and Analysis

Companies use various measures (financial and nonfinancial) and reporting formats to evaluate their departments. The type and form of information depend on management's focus and philosophy. **Hewlett-Packard**'s statement of corporate objectives, for instance, indicates that its goal is to satisfy customer needs. Its challenge is to set up managerial accounting systems to provide relevant feedback for evaluating performance in terms of its stated objectives. Also, the means used to obtain information about departments depend on how extensively a company uses computer and information technology.

HOW YOU DOIN'?
Answers—p. 763

1. What is the difference between a departmental accounting system and a responsibility accounting system?
2. Service departments (a) manufacture products, (b) make sales directly to customers, (c) produce revenues, (d) assist operating departments.
3. Explain the difference between a cost center and a profit center. Cite an example of each.

Departmental Expense Allocation

When a company computes departmental profits, it confronts some accounting challenges that involve allocating its expenses across its operating departments.

Direct and Indirect Expenses

Direct expenses are costs readily traced to a department because they are incurred for that department's sole benefit. They require no allocation across departments. For example, the salary of an employee who works in only one department is a direct expense of that one department.

LO2 Distinguish between direct and indirect expenses.

Indirect expenses are costs that are incurred for the joint benefit of more than one department and cannot be readily traced to only one department. For example, if two or more departments share a single building, all enjoy the benefits of the expenses for rent, heat, and light. Indirect expenses are allocated across departments benefiting from them when we need information about departmental profits. Ideally, we allocate indirect expenses by using a cause-effect relation. When we cannot identify cause-effect relations, we allocate each indirect expense on a basis approximating the relative benefit each department receives. Measuring the benefit for each department from an indirect expense can be difficult.

> Utility expense has elements of both direct and indirect expenses.

Illustration of Indirect Expense Allocation

To illustrate how to allocate an indirect expense, we consider a retail store that purchases janitorial services from an outside company. Management allocates this cost across the store's three departments according to the floor space each occupies. Costs of janitorial services for a recent month are $300. Exhibit 27.1 shows the square feet of floor space each department occupies. The store computes the percent of total square feet allotted to each department and uses it to allocate the $300 cost.

Exhibit 27.1

Indirect Expense Allocation

Department	Square Feet	Percent of Total	Allocated Cost
Jewelry	2,400	60%	$180
Watch repair	600	15	45
China and silver	1,000	25	75
Totals	4,000	100%	$300

Specifically, because the jewelry department occupies 60% of the floor space, 60% of the total $300 cost is assigned to it. The same procedure is applied to the other departments. When the allocation process is complete, these and other allocated costs are deducted from the gross profit for each department to determine net income for each. One consideration in allocating costs is to motivate managers and employees to behave as desired. As a result, a cost incurred in one department might be best allocated to other departments when one of the other departments caused the cost.

Allocation of Indirect Expenses

> **LO3** Identify bases for allocating indirect expenses to departments.

This section describes how to identify the bases used to allocate indirect expenses across departments. No standard rule identifies the best basis because expense allocation involves several factors, and the relative importance of these factors varies across departments and organizations. Judgment is required, and people do not always agree.

Wages and Salaries

Employee wages and salaries can be either direct or indirect expenses. If their time is spent entirely in one department, employee wages are direct expenses of that department. However, if employees work for the benefit of more than one department, their wages are indirect expenses and must be allocated across the departments benefited. An employee's contribution to a department usually depends on the number of hours worked in contributing to that department. Thus, a reasonable basis for allocating employee wages and salaries is the *relative amount of time spent in each department*. In the case of a supervisor who manages more than one department, recording the time spent in each department may not always be practical. Instead, a company can allocate the supervisor's salary to departments on the basis of the number of employees in each department—a reasonable basis if a supervisor's main task is managing people. Another basis of allocation is on sales across departments, also a reasonable basis if a supervisor's job reflects on departmental sales.

Rent and Related Expenses

Rent expense for a building is reasonably allocated to a department on the basis of floor space it occupies. Location can often make some floor space more valuable than other space. Thus, the allocation method can charge departments that occupy more valuable space a higher expense per square foot. Ground floor retail space, for instance, is often more valuable than basement or upper-floor space because all customers pass departments near the entrance but fewer go beyond the first floor. When no precise measures of floor space values exist, basing allocations on data such as customer traffic and real estate assessments is helpful. When a company owns its building, its expenses for depreciation, taxes, insurance, and other related building expenses are allocated like rent expense.

Advertising Expenses   Effective advertising of a department's products increases its sales and customer traffic. Moreover, advertising products for some departments usually helps other departments' sales because customers also often buy unadvertised products. Thus, many stores treat advertising as an indirect expense allocated on the basis of each department's proportion of total sales. For example, a department with 10% of a store's total sales is assigned 10% of advertising expense. Another method is to analyze each advertisement to compute the Web/newspaper space or TV/radio time devoted to the products of a department and charge that department for the proportional costs of advertisements. Management must consider whether this more detailed and costly method is justified.

Equipment and Machinery Depreciation   Depreciation on equipment and machinery used only in one department is a direct expense of that department. Depreciation on equipment and machinery used by more than one department is an indirect expense to be allocated across departments. Accounting for each department's depreciation expense requires a company to keep records showing which departments use specific assets. The number of hours that a department uses equipment and machinery is a reasonable basis for allocating depreciation.

Utilities Expenses   Utilities expenses such as heating and lighting are usually allocated on the basis of floor space occupied by departments. This practice assumes their use is uniform across departments. When this is not so, a more involved allocation can be necessary, although there is often a trade-off between the usefulness of more precise allocations and the effort to compute them.

Service Department Expenses   To generate revenues, operating departments require support services provided by departments such as personnel, payroll, advertising, and purchasing. Such service departments are typically evaluated as cost centers because they do not produce revenues. (Evaluating them as profit centers requires the use of a system that "charges" user departments a price that then serves as the "revenue" generated by service departments.) Employee morale suffers when allocations are perceived as unfair. Thus, it is important to carefully design and explain the allocation of service department costs. A departmental accounting system can accumulate and report costs incurred directly by each service department for this purpose. The system then allocates a service department's expenses to operating departments benefiting from them. Exhibit 27.2 shows some commonly used bases for allocating service department expenses to operating departments.

> When a service department "charges" its user departments within a company, a *transfer pricing system* must be set up to determine the "revenue" from its services provided.

Exhibit 27.2

Bases for Allocating Service Department Expenses

Service Department	Common Allocation Bases
Office expenses	Number of employees or sales in each department
Personnel expenses	Number of employees in each department
Payroll expenses	Number of employees in each department
Advertising expenses	Sales or amount of advertising charged directly to each department
Purchasing costs	Dollar amounts of purchases or number of purchase orders processed
Cleaning expenses	Square feet of floor space occupied
Maintenance expenses	Square feet of floor space occupied

Departmental Income Statements

An income statement can be prepared for each operating department once expenses have been assigned to it. Its expenses include both direct expenses and its share of indirect expenses. For this purpose, compiling all expenses incurred in service departments before assigning them to operating departments is useful. We illustrate the steps to prepare departmental income

LO4 Prepare departmental income statements.

statements using **A-1 Hardware** and its five departments. Two of them (office and purchasing) are service departments and the other three (hardware, housewares, and appliances) are operating (selling) departments. Allocating costs to operating departments and preparing departmental income statements involves four steps.

Step 1   Step 1 accumulates direct expenses for each service and operating department as shown in Exhibit 27.3. Direct expenses include salaries, wages, and other expenses that each department incurs but does not share with any other department. This information is accumulated in departmental expense accounts.

Exhibit 27.3

Step 1: Direct Expense Accumulation

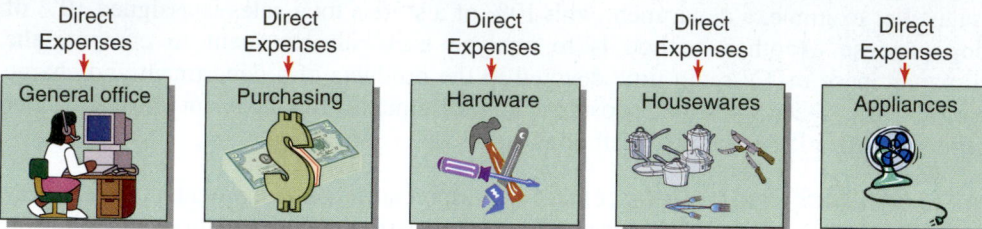

Step 2   Step 2 allocates indirect expenses across all departments using the allocation base identified for each expense as shown in Exhibit 27.4. Indirect expenses can include items such as depreciation, rent, advertising, and any other expenses that cannot be directly assigned to a department. Indirect expenses are recorded in expense accounts, and costs are allocated using a *departmental expense allocation spreadsheet* described in step 3.

Exhibit 27.4

Step 2: Indirect Expense Allocation

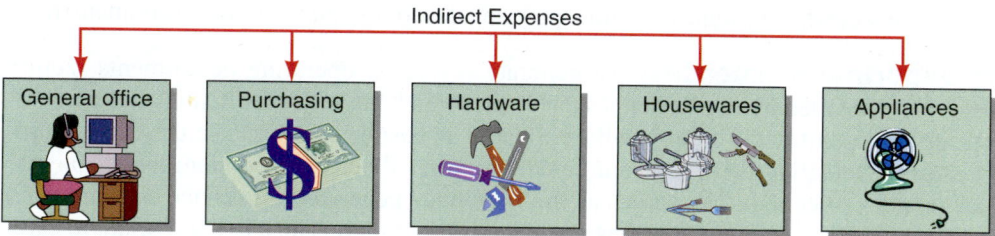

Step 3   Step 3 allocates expenses of the service departments (office and purchasing) to the operating departments. Exhibit 27.5 reflects the allocation of service department expenses using the allocation base(s).

Exhibit 27.5

Step 3: Service Department Expense Allocation to Operating Departments

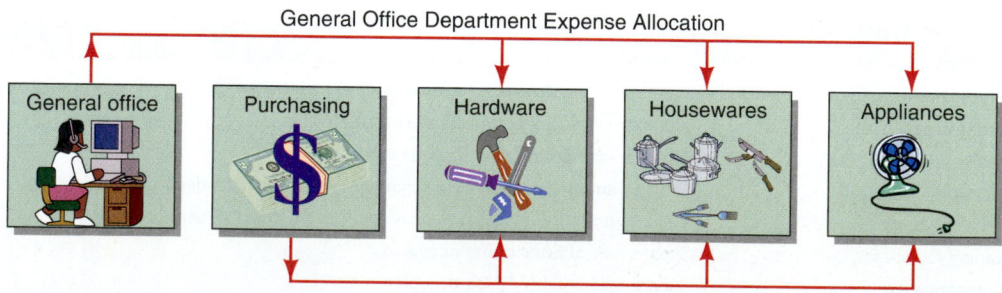

Computations for both steps 2 and 3 are commonly made using a departmental expense allocation spreadsheet as shown in Exhibit 27.6. The first two sections of this spreadsheet list direct expenses and indirect expenses by department. The third section lists the service department expenses and their allocations to operating departments. The allocation bases are identified in the second column, and total expense amounts are reported in the third column.

Exhibit 27.6

Departmental Expense Allocation Spreadsheet

	File Edit View Insert Format Tools Data Window Help						

A-1 HARDWARE
Departmental Expense Allocations
For Year Ended December 31, 2010

	Allocation Base	Expense Account Balance	General Office Dept.	Purchasing Dept.	Hardware Dept.	House- wares Dept.	Appliances Dept.
Direct expenses							
Salaries expense......................	Payroll records	$51,900	$13,300	$8,200	$15,600	$ 7,000	$ 7,800
Depreciation—Equipment.......	Depreciation records	1,500	500	300	400	100	200
Supplies expense....................	Requisitions.............................	900	200	100	300	200	100
Indirect expenses							
Rent expense	Amount and value of space..	12,000	600	600	4,860	3,240	2,700
Utilities expense.....................	Floor space..............................	2,400	300	300	810	540	450
Advertising expense...............	Sales..	1,000			500	300	200
Insurance expense..................	Value of insured assets	2,500	400	200	900	600	400
Total department expenses		72,200	15,300	9,700	23,370	11,980	11,850
Service department expenses							
General office department.....	Sales..		(15,300)		7,650	4,590	3,060
Purchasing department	Purchase orders.....................			(9,700)	3,880	2,630	3,190
Total expenses allocated to operating departments................		$72,200	$ 0	$ 0	$34,900	$19,200	$18,100

The departmental expense allocation spreadsheet is useful in implementing the first three steps. To illustrate, first (step 1) the three direct expenses of salaries, depreciation, and supplies are accumulated in each of the five departments.

Second (step 2), the four indirect expenses of rent, utilities, advertising, and insurance are allocated to all departments using the allocation bases identified. For example, consider rent allocation. Exhibit 27.7 lists the five departments' square footage of space occupied. The two service departments (office and purchasing) occupy 25% of the total space (3,000 sq. feet/12,000 sq. feet). However, they are located near the back of the building, which is of lower value than space near the front that is occupied by operating departments. Management estimates that space near the back accounts for $1,200 of the total rent expense of $12,000. Exhibit 27.8 shows how we allocate the $1,200 rent expense between these two service departments in proportion to their

Exhibit 27.7

Departments' Square Footages

General office	1,500 sq. ft.
Purchasing	1,500 sq. ft.
Hardware	4,050 sq. ft.
Housewares	2,700 sq. ft.
Appliances	2,250 sq. ft.
Total	12,000 sq. ft.

square footage. We then allocate the remaining $10,800 of rent expense to the three operating departments as shown in Exhibit 27.9. We continue step 2 by allocating the $2,400 of utilities expense to all departments based on the square footage occupied as shown in

Exhibit 27.8

Allocating Indirect (Rent) Expense to Service Departments

Department	Square Feet	Percent of Total	Allocated Cost
General office	1,500	50.0%	$ 600
Purchasing	1,500	50.0	600
Totals	3,000	100.0%	$1,200

Exhibit 27.9

Allocating Indirect (Rent) Expense to Operating Departments

Department	Square Feet	Percent of Total	Allocated Cost
Hardware	4,050	45.0%	$ 4,860
Housewares	2,700	30.0	3,240
Appliances	2,250	25.0	2,700
Totals	9,000	100.0%	$10,800

Exhibit 27.10. The rows in Exhibit 27.6 for rent and utilities expenses show the amounts from Exhibits 27.8, 27.9, and 27.10. The allocations of the two other indirect expenses of advertising and insurance are similarly computed. Note that because advertising expense is allocated on the basis of sales and because service departments do not have sales, it is allocated only to the three operating departments.

Exhibit 27.10

Allocating Indirect (Utilities) Expense to All Departments

Department	Square Feet	Percent of Total	Allocated Cost
General office	1,500	12.50%	$ 300
Purchasing	1,500	12.50	300
Hardware	4,050	33.75	810
Housewares	2,700	22.50	540
Appliances	2,250	18.75	450
Totals	12,000	100.00%	$2,400

Third (step 3), total expenses of the two service departments are allocated to the three operating departments using the allocation bases shown in the final three rows of Exhibit 27.6.

Step 4   When the departmental expense spreadsheet is complete, the amounts in the operating department columns are used to prepare departmental income statements as shown in Exhibit 27.11. These income statements are prepared for profit centers only. This exhibit uses

Exhibit 27.11

Departmental Income Statements

A-1 HARDWARE
Departmental Income Statements
For Year Ended December 31, 2010

	Hardware Department	Housewares Department	Appliances Department	Combined
Sales	$119,500	$71,700	$47,800	$239,000
Cost of goods sold	73,800	43,800	30,200	147,800
Gross profit	45,700	27,900	17,600	91,200
Operating expenses				
Salaries expense	15,600	7,000	7,800	30,400
Depreciation expense—Equipment	400	100	200	700
Supplies expense	300	200	100	600
Rent expense	4,860	3,240	2,700	10,800
Utilities expense	810	540	450	1,800
Advertising expense	500	300	200	1,000
Insurance expense	900	600	400	1,900
Share of general office expenses	7,650	4,590	3,060	15,300
Share of purchasing expenses	3,880	2,630	3,190	9,700
Total operating expenses	34,900	19,200	18,100	72,200
Net income (loss)	**$ 10,800**	**$ 8,700**	**$ (500)**	**$19,000**

the spreadsheet for its operating expenses; information on sales and cost of goods sold comes from departmental records.

Departmental Contribution to Overhead

Data from departmental income statements are not always best for evaluating each department's performance, especially when indirect expenses are a large portion of total expenses and when weaknesses in assumptions and decisions in allocating indirect expenses can markedly affect net income. In these and other cases, we might better evaluate department performance using the **departmental contribution to overhead,** which is a report of the amount of sales less *direct* expenses.[1]

The upper half of Exhibit 27.12 shows a departmental contribution to overhead as part of an expanded income statement. This format is common when reporting departmental contributions to overhead. Using the information in Exhibits 27.11 and 27.12, we can evaluate the profitability of the three operating departments. For instance, let's compare the performance of the appliances department as described in these two exhibits. Exhibit 27.11 shows a $500 net loss resulting from this department's operations, but Exhibit 27.12 shows a $9,500 positive contribution to overhead, which is 19.9% of sales. The contribution of the appliances department is not as large as that of the other selling departments, but a $9,500 contribution to overhead is better than a $500 loss. This tells us that the appliances department is not a money loser. On the contrary, it is contributing $9,500 toward defraying total indirect expenses of $40,500.

LO5 Prepare departmental contribution reports.

A-1 HARDWARE Income Statement Showing Departmental Contribution to Overhead For Year Ended December 31, 2010				
	Hardware Department	**Housewares Department**	**Appliances Department**	**Combined**
Sales	$119,500	$ 71,700	$47,800	$239,000
Cost of goods sold	73,800	43,800	30,200	147,800
Gross profit	45,700	27,900	17,600	91,200
Direct expenses				
Salaries expense	15,600	7,000	7,800	30,400
Depreciation expense—Equipment	400	100	200	700
Supplies expense	300	200	100	600
Total direct expenses	16,300	7,300	8,100	31,700
Departmental contributions to overhead	**$29,400**	**$20,600**	**$ 9,500**	**$59,500**
Indirect expenses				
Rent expense				10,800
Utilities expense				1,800
Advertising expense				1,000
Insurance expense				1,900
General office department expense				15,300
Purchasing department expense				9,700
Total indirect expenses				40,500
Net income				**$19,000**
Contribution as percent of sales	24.6%	28.7%	19.9%	24.9%

Exhibit 27.12

Departmental Contribution to Overhead

---

[1] A department's contribution is said to be "to overhead" because of the practice of considering all indirect expenses as overhead. Thus, the excess of a department's sales over direct expenses is a contribution toward at least a portion of its total overhead.

4. If a company has two operating (selling) departments (shoes and hats) and two service departments (payroll and advertising), which of the following statements is correct? (*a*) Wages incurred in the payroll department are direct expenses of the shoe department, (*b*) Wages incurred in the payroll department are indirect expenses of the operating departments, or (*c*) Advertising department expenses are allocated to the other three departments.

5. Which of the following bases can be used to allocate supervisors' salaries across operating departments? (*a*) Hours spent in each department, (*b*) number of employees in each department, (*c*) sales achieved in each department, or (*d*) any of the above, depending on which information is most relevant and accessible.

6. What three steps are used to allocate expenses to operating departments?

7. An income statement showing departmental contribution to overhead (*a*) subtracts indirect expenses from each department's revenues, (*b*) subtracts only direct expenses from each department's revenues, or (*c*) shows net income for each department.

Responsibility Accounting

LO6 Explain controllable costs and responsibility accounting.

Departmental accounting reports often provide data used to evaluate a department's performance, but are they useful in assessing how well a department *manager* performs? Neither departmental income nor its contribution to overhead may be useful because many expenses can be outside a manager's control. Instead, we often evaluate a manager's performance using responsibility accounting reports that describe a department's activities in terms of **controllable costs.**[2] A cost is controllable if a manager has the power to determine or at least significantly affect the amount incurred. **Uncontrollable costs** are not within the manager's control or influence.

Controllable versus Direct Costs

Controllable costs are not always the same as direct costs. Direct costs are readily traced to a department, but the department manager might or might not control their amounts. For example, department managers often have little or no control over depreciation expense because they cannot affect the amount of equipment assigned to their departments. Also, department managers rarely control their own salaries. However, they can control or influence items such as the cost of supplies used in their department. When evaluating managers' performances, we should use data reflecting their departments' outputs along with their controllable costs and expenses.

Distinguishing between controllable and uncontrollable costs depends on the particular manager and time period under analysis. For example, the cost of property insurance is usually not controllable at the department manager's level but by the executive responsible for obtaining the company's insurance coverage. Likewise, this executive might not control costs resulting from insurance policies already in force. However, when a policy expires, this executive can renegotiate a replacement policy and then controls these costs. Therefore, all costs are controllable at some management level if the time period is sufficiently long. We must use good judgment in identifying controllable costs.

---

[2] The terms *cost* and *expense* are often used interchangeably in managerial accounting, but they are not necessarily the same. *Cost* often refers to the monetary outlay to acquire some resource that can have present and future benefit. *Expense* usually refers to an expired cost. That is, as the benefit of a resource expires, a portion of its cost is written off as an expense.

Responsibility Accounting System

A *responsibility accounting system* uses the concept of controllable costs to assign managers the responsibility for costs and expenses under their control. Prior to each reporting period, a company prepares plans that identify costs and expenses under each manager's control. These plans are called **responsibility accounting budgets.** To ensure the cooperation of managers and the reasonableness of budgets, managers should be involved in preparing their budgets.

A responsibility accounting system also involves performance reports. A **responsibility accounting performance report** accumulates and reports costs and expenses that a manager is responsible for and their budgeted amounts. Management's analysis of differences between budgeted amounts and actual costs and expenses often results in corrective or strategic managerial actions. Upper-level management uses performance reports to evaluate the effectiveness of lower-level managers in controlling costs and expenses and keeping them within budgeted amounts. Responsibility accounting does not place blame. Instead, responsibility accounting is used to identify opportunities for improving performance.

A responsibility accounting system recognizes that control over costs and expenses belongs to several levels of management. We illustrate this by considering the organization chart in Exhibit 27.13. The lines in this chart connecting the managerial positions reflect channels of authority. For example, the four department managers of this consulting firm (benchmarking, cost management, outsourcing, and service) are responsible for controllable costs and expenses incurred in their departments, but these same costs are subject to the overall control of the vice president (VP) for operational consulting. Similarly, this VP's costs are subject to the control of the executive vice president (EVP) for operations, the president, and, ultimately, the board of directors.

At lower levels, managers have limited responsibility and relatively little control over costs and expenses. Performance reports for low-level management typically cover few controllable costs. Responsibility and control broaden for higher-level managers; therefore, their reports span a wider range of costs. However, reports to higher-level managers seldom contain the details reported to their subordinates but are summarized for two reasons: (1) lower-level managers are often responsible for these detailed costs and (2) detailed reports can obscure broader, more important issues facing a company.

Exhibit 27.14 shows summarized performance reports for the three management levels identified in Exhibit 27.13. Exhibit 27.14 shows that costs under the control of the benchmarking department manager are totaled and included among controllable costs of the VP for operational consulting. Also, costs under the control of the VP are totaled and included among controllable costs of the EVP for operations. In this way, a responsibility accounting system provides relevant information for each management level.

Technological advances increase our ability to produce vast amounts of information that often exceeds our ability to use it. Good managers select relevant data for planning and controlling the areas under their responsibility. A good responsibility accounting system makes every effort to provide relevant information to the right person (the one who controls the cost) at the right time (before a cost is out of control).

Exhibit 27.13

Organizational Responsibility Chart

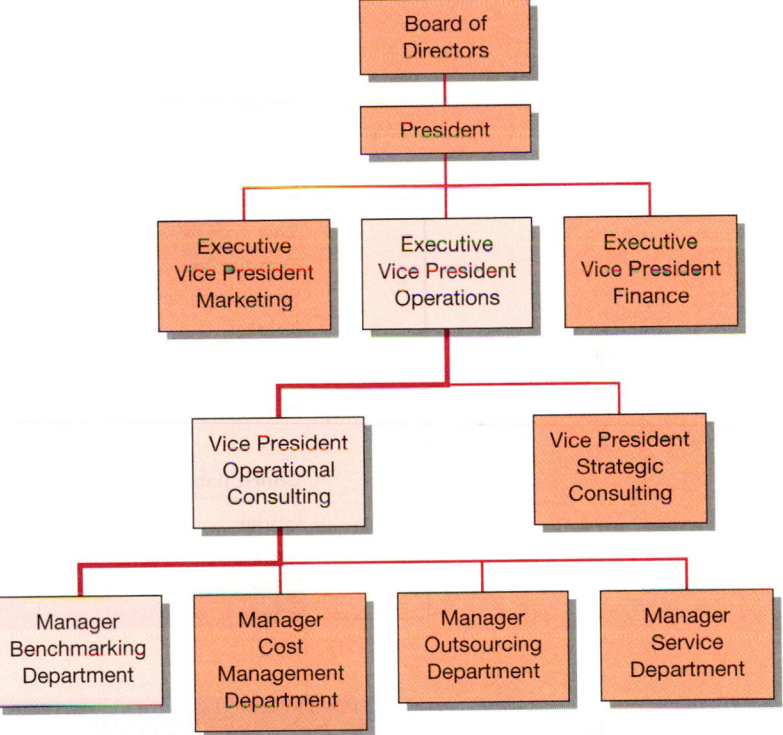

A responsibility accounting system usually divides a company into subunits called *responsibility centers*. The manager of each center is evaluated on how well the center performs, as reported in responsibility accounting reports.

QS 27-4
Basis for cost allocation
LO3   LO4

For each of the following types of indirect expenses and service department expenses, identify one allocation basis that could be used to distribute it to the departments indicated.
1. Computer service expenses of production scheduling for operating departments.
2. General office department expenses of the operating departments.
3. Maintenance department expenses of the operating departments.
4. Electric utility expenses of all departments.

QS 27-5
Computing performance
measures   **LO7**

A company's shipping division (an investment center) has sales of $2,700,000, net income of $216,000, and average invested assets of $2,000,000. Compute the division's return on invested assets. State your answer as a percentage with one decimal place.

---

connect

EXERCISES

Exercise 27-1
Departmental expense allocations
LO3

Woh Che Co. has four departments: materials, personnel, manufacturing, and packaging. In a recent month, the four departments incurred three shared indirect expenses. The amounts of these indirect expenses and the bases used to allocate them follow.

Indirect Expense	Cost	Allocation Base
Supervision	$ 82,500	Number of employees
Utilities	50,000	Square feet occupied
Insurance	22,500	Value of assets in use
Total	$155,000	

Departmental data for the company's recent reporting period follow.

Department	Employees	Square Feet	Asset Values
Materials	27	25,000	$ 6,000
Personnel	9	5,000	1,200
Manufacturing	63	55,000	37,800
Packaging	51	15,000	15,000
Total	150	100,000	$60,000

Check   (2) Total of $29,600 assigned to Materials Dept.

(1) Use this information to allocate each of the three indirect expenses across the four departments.
(2) Prepare a summary table that reports the indirect expenses assigned to each of the four departments.

Exercise 27-2
Rent expense allocated to
departments   **LO3**

Truck Market pays $130,000 rent each year for its two-story building. The space in this building is occupied by five departments as specified here.

Paint department	1,440 square feet of first-floor space
Engine department	3,360 square feet of first-floor space
Window department	2,016 square feet of second-floor space
Electrical department	960 square feet of second-floor space
Accessory department	1,824 square feet of second-floor space

Check   Allocated to Paint Dept., $25,350

The company allocates 65% of total rent expense to the first floor and 35% to the second floor, and then allocates rent expense for each floor to the departments occupying that floor on the basis of space occupied. Determine the rent expense to be allocated to each department. (Round percents to the nearest one-tenth and dollar amounts to the nearest whole dollar.)

Overland Cycle Shop has two service departments (advertising and administration) and two operating departments (cycles and clothing). During 2010, the departments had the following direct expenses and occupied the following amount of floor space.

Exercise 27–3
Departmental expense allocation spreadsheet   **LO3   LO4**

Department	Direct Expenses	Square Feet
Advertising	$ 18,000	1,120
Administrative	25,000	1,400
Cycles	103,000	7,140
Clothing	15,000	4,340

The advertising department developed and distributed 120 advertisements during the year. Of these, 90 promoted cycles and 30 promoted clothing. The store sold $350,000 of merchandise during the year. Of this amount, $273,000 is from the cycles department and $77,000 is from the clothing department. The utilities expense of $64,000 is an indirect expense to all departments. Prepare a departmental expense allocation spreadsheet for Overland Cycle Shop. The spreadsheet should assign (1) direct expenses to each of the four departments, (2) the $64,000 of utilities expense to the four departments on the basis of floor space occupied, (3) the advertising department's expenses to the two operating departments on the basis of the number of ads placed that promoted a department's products, and (4) the administrative department's expenses to the two operating departments based on the amount of sales. Provide supporting computations for the expense allocations.

Check   Total expenses allocated to Cycles Dept., $177,472

The following is a partially completed lower section of a departmental expense allocation spreadsheet for Cozy Bookstore. It reports the total amounts of direct and indirect expenses allocated to its five departments. Complete the spreadsheet by allocating the expenses of the two service departments (advertising and purchasing) to the three operating departments.

Exercise 27–4
Service department expenses allocated to operating departments   **LO4**

File Edit View Insert Format Tools Data Window Help

		Allocation of Expenses to Departments					
	Allocation Base	Expense Account Balance	Advertising Dept.	Purchasing Dept.	Books Dept.	Magazines Dept.	Newspapers Dept.
5 Total department expenses..........		$698,000	$24,000	$34,000	$425,000	$90,000	$125,000
6 **Service department expenses**							
7 Advertising department.............Sales			?		?	?	?
8 Purchasing department.............Purch. orders				?	?	?	?
9 Total expenses allocated to							
10 operating departments..............		?	$ 0	$ 0	?	?	?

Sheet1 Sheet2 Sheet3

Advertising and purchasing department expenses are allocated to operating departments on the basis of dollar sales and purchase orders, respectively. Information about the allocation bases for the three operating departments follows.

Department	Sales	Purchase Orders
Books	$495,000	516
Magazines	198,000	360
Newspapers	207,000	324
Total	$900,000	1,200

Check   Total expenses allocated to Books Dept., $452,820

Exercise 27–5
Indirect payroll expense allocated to departments   **L03**

Jessica Porter works in both the jewelry department and the hosiery department of a retail store. Porter assists customers in both departments and arranges and stocks merchandise in both departments. The store allocates Porter's $30,000 annual wages between the two departments based on a sample of the time worked in the two departments. The sample is obtained from a diary of hours worked that Porter kept in a randomly chosen two-week period. The diary showed the following hours and activities spent in the two departments. Allocate Porter's annual wages between the two departments.

Selling in jewelry department	51 hours
Arranging and stocking merchandise in jewelry department	6 hours
Selling in hosiery department	12 hours
Arranging and stocking merchandise in hosiery department	7 hours
Idle time spent waiting for a customer to enter one of the selling departments	4 hours

Check   Assign $7,500 to Hosiery

Exercise 27–6
Managerial performance evaluation   **L06**

Maryanne Dinardo manages an auto dealership's service department. The recent month's income statement for her department follows. (1) Analyze the items on the income statement and identify those that definitely should be included on a performance report used to evaluate Dinardo's performance. List them and explain why you chose them. (2) List and explain the items that should definitely be excluded. (3) List the items that are not definitely included or excluded and explain why they fall into that category.

Revenues		
Sales of parts	$ 72,000	
Sales of services	105,000	$177,000
Costs and expenses		
Cost of parts sold	30,000	
Building depreciation	9,300	
Income taxes allocated to department	8,700	
Interest on long-term debt	7,500	
Manager's salary	12,000	
Payroll taxes	8,100	
Supplies	15,900	
Utilities	4,400	
Wages (hourly)	16,000	
Total costs and expenses		111,900
Departmental net income		$ 65,100

Exercise 27–7
Investment center analysis   **L07**

You must prepare a return on investment analysis for the regional manager of Fast & Great Burgers. This growing chain is trying to decide which outlet of two alternatives to open. The first location (A) requires a $1,000,000 investment and is expected to yield annual net income of $160,000. The second location (B) requires a $600,000 investment and is expected to yield annual net income of $108,000. Compute the return on investment for each Fast & Great Burgers alternative and then make your recommendation in a one-half page memorandum to the regional manager. (The chain currently generates an 18% return on total assets.)

connect

PROBLEM SET A

Problem 27–1A
Allocation of building occupancy costs to departments   **L03**

mhhe.com/wildCA2e

National Bank has several departments that occupy both floors of a two-story building. The departmental accounting system has a single account, Building Occupancy Cost, in its ledger. The types and amounts of occupancy costs recorded in this account for the current period follow.

Depreciation—Building	$18,000
Interest—Building mortgage	27,000
Taxes—Building and land	9,000
Gas (heating) expense	3,000
Lighting expense	3,000
Maintenance expense	6,000
Total occupancy cost	$66,000

The building has 4,000 square feet on each floor. In prior periods, the accounting manager merely divided the $66,000 occupancy cost by 8,000 square feet to find an average cost of $8.25 per square foot and then charged each department a building occupancy cost equal to this rate times the number of square feet that it occupied.

   Diane Linder manages a first-floor department that occupies 1,000 square feet, and Juan Chiro manages a second-floor department that occupies 1,800 square feet of floor space. In discussing the departmental reports, the second-floor manager questions whether using the same rate per square foot for all departments makes sense because the first-floor space is more valuable. This manager also references a recent real estate study of average local rental costs for similar space that shows first-floor space worth $30 per square foot and second-floor space worth $20 per square foot (excluding costs for heating, lighting, and maintenance).

Required

1. Allocate all occupancy costs to the Linder and Chiro departments using the current allocation method.
2. Allocate the depreciation, interest, and taxes occupancy costs to the Linder and Chiro departments in proportion to the relative market values of the floor space. Allocate the heating, lighting, and maintenance costs to the Linder and Chiro departments in proportion to the square feet occupied (ignoring floor space market values).

Check   (2) Total occupancy cost to Linder, $9,600

Analysis Component

3. Which allocation method would you prefer if you were a manager of a second-floor department? Explain.

Williams Co. began operations in January 2010 with two operating (selling) departments and one service (office) department. Its departmental income statements follow.

Problem 27–2A
Departmental income statements; forecasts **LO3   LO4**

mhhe.com/wildCA2e

WILLIAMS COMPANY Departmental Income Statements For Year Ended December 31, 2010			
	Clock	**Mirror**	**Combined**
Sales	$130,000	$55,000	$185,000
Cost of goods sold	63,700	34,100	97,800
Gross profit	66,300	20,900	87,200
Direct expenses			
Sales salaries	20,000	7,000	27,000
Advertising	1,200	500	1,700
Store supplies used	900	400	1,300
Depreciation—Equipment	1,500	300	1,800
Total direct expenses	23,600	8,200	31,800
Allocated expenses			
Rent expense	7,020	3,780	10,800
Utilities expense	2,600	1,400	4,000
Share of office department expenses	10,500	4,500	15,000
Total allocated expenses	20,120	9,680	29,800
Total expenses	43,720	17,880	61,600
Net income	$ 22,580	$ 3,020	$ 25,600

Williams plans to open a third department in January 2011 that will sell paintings. Management predicts that the new department will generate $50,000 in sales with a 55% gross profit margin and will require the following direct expenses: sales salaries, $8,000; advertising, $800; store supplies, $500; and equipment depreciation, $200. It will fit the new department into the current rented space by taking some square footage from the other two departments. When opened the new painting department will fill one-fifth of the space presently used by the clock department and one-fourth used by the mirror department. Management does not predict any increase in utilities costs, which are allocated to the departments in proportion to occupied space (or rent expense). The company allocates office department expenses to the operating departments in proportion to their sales. It expects the painting department to increase total office department expenses by $7,000. Since the painting department will bring new customers into the store, management expects sales in both the clock and mirror departments to increase by 8%. No changes for those departments' gross profit percents or their direct expenses are expected except for store supplies used, which will increase in proportion to sales.

Check   2011 forecasted combined
net income (sales), $43,472
($249,800)

Required

Prepare departmental income statements that show the company's predicted results of operations for calendar year 2011 for the three operating (selling) departments and their combined totals. (Round percents to the nearest one-tenth and dollar amounts to the nearest whole dollar.)

Problem 27-3A

Responsibility accounting
performance reports; controllable
and budgeted costs   **LO5**   **LO6**

Billie Whitehorse, the plant manager of Travel Free's Indiana plant, is responsible for all of that plant's costs other than her own salary. The plant has two operating departments and one service department. The camper and trailer operating departments manufacture different products and have their own managers. The office department, which Whitehorse also manages, provides services equally to the two operating departments. A budget is prepared for each operating department and the office department. The company's responsibility accounting system must assemble information to present budgeted and actual costs in performance reports for each operating department manager and the plant manager. Each performance report includes only those costs that a particular operating department manager can control: raw materials, wages, supplies used, and equipment depreciation. The plant manager is responsible for the department managers' salaries, utilities, building rent, office salaries other than her own, and other office costs plus all costs controlled by the two operating department managers. The annual departmental budgets and actual costs for the two operating departments follow.

	Budget			Actual		
	Campers	**Trailers**	**Combined**	**Campers**	**Trailers**	**Combined**
Raw materials	$195,000	$275,000	$ 470,000	$194,200	$273,200	$ 467,400
Employee wages	104,000	205,000	309,000	106,600	206,400	313,000
Dept. manager salary	43,000	52,000	95,000	44,000	53,500	97,500
Supplies used	33,000	90,000	123,000	31,700	91,600	123,300
Depreciation—Equip.	60,000	125,000	185,000	60,000	125,000	185,000
Utilities	3,600	5,400	9,000	3,300	5,000	8,300
Building rent	5,700	9,300	15,000	5,300	8,700	14,000
Office department costs	68,750	68,750	137,500	67,550	67,550	135,100
Totals	$513,050	$830,450	$1,343,500	$512,650	$830,950	$1,343,600

The office department's annual budget and its actual costs follow.

	Budget	Actual
Plant manager salary	$ 80,000	$ 82,000
Other office salaries	32,500	30,100
Other office costs	25,000	23,000
Totals	$137,500	$135,100

Required

1. Prepare responsibility accounting performance reports like those in Exhibit 27.14 that list costs controlled by the following:

Check   (1a) $500 total over budget

   a. Manager of the camper department.

   b. Manager of the trailer department.

(1c) Indiana plant controllable
costs, $1,900 total under
budget

   c. Manager of the Indiana plant.

In each report, include the budgeted and actual costs and show the amount that each actual cost is over or under the budgeted amount.

Analysis Component

2. Did the plant manager or the operating department managers better manage costs? Explain.

Quality Furniture Company allocates its overhead expenses of $12,500 to its two departments on the basis of sales.

Problem 27–4A
Allocation of overhead costs
LO3

	Dept. 1	Dept. 2	Combined
Revenues from sales	$182,000	$78,000	$260,000
Direct salaries	42,250	22,750	65,000

Required

1. Determine the overhead expenses allocated to Departments 1 and 2 on the basis of sales.

2. In the future, Quality Furniture Company is considering allocating its indirect expenses on the basis of direct salaries. Determine the overhead expense allocation to Departments 1 and 2 assuming it is allocated on the basis of direct salaries.

Analysis Component

3. If you were the manager of Department 1, which allocation method would you prefer?

Harmon's has several departments that occupy all floors of a two-story building that includes a basement floor. Harmon rented this building under a long-term lease negotiated when rental rates were low. The departmental accounting system has a single account, Building Occupancy Cost, in its ledger. The types and amounts of occupancy costs recorded in this account for the current period follow.

PROBLEM SET B

Problem 27–1B
Allocation of building occupancy
costs to departments   **LO3**

Building rent	$400,000
Lighting expense	25,000
Cleaning expense	40,000
Total occupancy cost	$465,000

The building has 7,500 square feet on each of the upper two floors but only 5,000 square feet in the basement. In prior periods, the accounting manager merely divided the $465,000 occupancy cost by 20,000 square feet to find an average cost of $23.25 per square foot and then charged each department a building occupancy cost equal to this rate times the number of square feet that it occupies.

Jordan Style manages a department that occupies 2,000 square feet of basement floor space. In discussing the departmental reports with other managers, she questions whether using the same rate per square foot for all departments makes sense because different floor space has different values. Style checked a recent real estate report of average local rental costs for similar space that shows first-floor space worth $40 per square foot, second-floor space worth $20 per square foot, and basement space worth $10 per square foot (excluding costs for lighting and cleaning).

Required

1. Allocate all occupancy costs to Style's department using the current allocation method.

2. Allocate the building rent cost to Style's department in proportion to the relative market value of the floor space. Allocate to Style's department the lighting and heating costs in proportion to the square feet occupied (ignoring floor space market values).

Check   (2) Total costs allocated to
Style's Dept., $22,500

Analysis Component

3. Which allocation method would you prefer if you were a manager of a basement department?

Problem 27–2B
Departmental income
statements; forecasts **LO3 LO4**

Bonanza Entertainment began operations in January 2010 with two operating (selling) departments and one service (office) department. Its departmental income statements follow.

BONANZA ENTERTAINMENT Departmental Income Statements For Year Ended December 31, 2010			
	Movies	**Video Games**	**Combined**
Sales	$600,000	$200,000	$800,000
Cost of goods sold	420,000	154,000	574,000
Gross profit	180,000	46,000	226,000
Direct expenses			
Sales salaries	37,000	15,000	52,000
Advertising	12,500	6,000	18,500
Store supplies used	4,000	1,000	5,000
Depreciation—Equipment	4,500	3,000	7,500
Total direct expenses	58,000	25,000	83,000
Allocated expenses			
Rent expense	41,000	9,000	50,000
Utilities expense	7,380	1,620	9,000
Share of office department expenses	56,250	18,750	75,000
Total allocated expenses	104,630	29,370	134,000
Total expenses	162,630	54,370	217,000
Net income (loss)	$ 17,370	$ (8,370)	$ 9,000

Bonanza plans to open a third department in January 2011 that will sell compact discs. Management predicts that the new department will generate $300,000 in sales with a 35% gross profit margin and will require the following direct expenses: sales salaries, $18,000; advertising, $10,000; store supplies, $2,000; and equipment depreciation, $1,200. The company will fit the new department into the current rented space by taking some square footage from the other two departments. When opened, the new compact disc department will fill one-fourth of the space presently used by the movie department and one-third of the space used by the video game department. Management does not predict any increase in utilities costs, which are allocated to the departments in proportion to occupied space (or rent expense). The company allocates office department expenses to the operating departments in proportion to their sales. It expects the compact disc department to increase total office department expenses by $10,000. Since the compact disc department will bring new customers into the store, management expects sales in both the movie and video game departments to increase by 8%. No changes for those departments' gross profit percents or for their direct expenses are expected, except for store supplies used, which will increase in proportion to sales.

Required

Check 2011 forecasted movies net income (sales), $52,450 ($648,000)

Prepare departmental income statements that show the company's predicted results of operations for calendar year 2011 for the three operating (selling) departments and their combined totals. (Round percents to the nearest one-tenth and dollar amounts to the nearest whole dollar.)

Problem 27–3B
Responsibility accounting
performance reports; controllable
and budgeted costs **LO5 LO6**

Britney Brown, the plant manager of LMN Co.'s Chicago plant, is responsible for all of that plant's costs other than her own salary. The plant has two operating departments and one service department. The refrigerator and dishwasher operating departments manufacture different products and have their own managers. The office department, which Brown also manages, provides services equally to the two operating departments. A monthly budget is prepared for each operating department and the office department. The company's responsibility accounting system must assemble information to present budgeted and actual costs in performance reports for each operating department manager and the plant manager. Each performance report includes only those costs that a particular operating department manager can control: raw materials, wages, supplies used, and equipment depreciation. The plant manager is responsible for the department managers' salaries, utilities, building rent, office salaries other than her own, and other office costs plus all costs controlled by the two operating department managers. The April departmental budgets and actual costs for the two operating departments follow.

	Budget			Actual		
	Refrigerators	Dishwashers	Combined	Refrigerators	Dishwashers	Combined
Raw materials	$400,000	$200,000	$ 600,000	$385,000	$202,000	$ 587,000
Employee wages	170,000	80,000	250,000	174,700	81,500	256,200
Dept. manager salary	55,000	49,000	104,000	55,000	46,500	101,500
Supplies used	15,000	9,000	24,000	14,000	9,700	23,700
Depreciation—Equip.	53,000	37,000	90,000	53,000	37,000	90,000
Utilities	30,000	18,000	48,000	34,500	20,700	55,200
Building rent	63,000	17,000	80,000	65,800	16,500	82,300
Office department costs	70,500	70,500	141,000	75,000	75,000	150,000
Totals	$856,500	$480,500	$1,337,000	$857,000	$488,900	$1,345,900

The office department's budget and its actual costs for April follow.

	Budget	Actual
Plant manager salary	$ 80,000	$ 85,000
Other office salaries	40,000	35,200
Other office costs	21,000	29,800
Totals	$141,000	$150,000

Required

1. Prepare responsibility accounting performance reports like those in Exhibit 27.14 that list costs controlled by the following:

    a. Manager of the refrigerator department.

    b. Manager of the dishwasher department.

    c. Manager of the Chicago plant.

In each report, include the budgeted and actual costs for the month and show the amount by which each actual cost is over or under the budgeted amount.

Check   (1a) $11,300 total under budget

(1c) Chicago plant controllable costs, $3,900 total over budget

Analysis Component

2. Did the plant manager or the operating department managers better manage costs? Explain.

Robinson Electric Company allocates its overhead expenses of $45,500 to its two departments on the basis of direct salaries.

Problem 27-4B
Allocation of overhead costs
LO3

	Dept. 1	Dept. 2	Combined
Direct salaries	$ 25,250	$ 39,750	$ 65,000
Revenues from sales	122,000	138,000	260,000

Required

1. Determine the overhead expenses allocated to Departments 1 and 2 on the basis of direct salaries.

2. In the future, Robinson Electric Company is considering allocating its indirect expenses on the basis of revenue from sales. Determine the overhead expense allocation to Departments 1 and 2 assuming it is allocated on the basis of sales revenue.

Analysis Component

3. If you were the manager of Department 2, which allocation method would you prefer?

BEYOND THE NUMBERS

**REPORTING IN
ACTION**

LO6

BTN 27-1   Review **Best Buy**'s income statement in Appendix A and identify its revenues for the years ended March 1, 2008, March 3, 2007, and February 25, 2006. Assume Best Buy reports the following product revenue mix. (Assume that its product revenue mix is the same for each of the three years reported when answering the requirements.)

Home Office	Entertainment Software	Consumer Electronics	Appliances	Services
34%	17%	36%	6%	7%

Required

1. Compute the amount of revenue from each of its product lines for the years ended March 1, 2008, March 3, 2007, and February 25, 2006.
2. If Best Buy wishes to evaluate each of its product lines, how can it allocate its operating expenses to each of them to determine each product line's profitability?

Fast Forward

3. Access Best Buy's form 10-K for a fiscal year ending after March 1, 2008, from its Website (**BestBuy.com**) or the SEC's EDGAR database (**www.SEC.gov**). Compute its revenues for its product lines for the most recent year(s). Compare those results to those from part 1. How has its product mix changed?

ETHICS CHALLENGE

LO4

BTN 27-2   Senior Security Co. offers a range of security services for senior citizens. Each type of service is considered within a separate department. Mary Pincus, the overall manager, is compensated partly on the basis of departmental performance by staying within the quarterly cost budget. She often revises operations to make sure departments stay within budget. Says Pincus, "I will not go over budget even if it means slightly compromising the level and quality of service. These are minor compromises that don't significantly affect my clients, at least in the short term."

Required

1. Is there an ethical concern in this situation? If so, which parties are affected? Explain.
2. Can Mary Pincus take action to eliminate or reduce any ethical concerns? Explain.
3. What is Senior Security's ethical responsibility in offering professional services?

**WORKPLACE
COMMUNICATION**

LO2

BTN 27-3   Improvement Station is a national home improvement chain with more than 100 stores throughout the country. The manager of each store receives a salary plus a bonus equal to a percent of the store's net income for the reporting period. The following net income calculation is on the Denver store manager's performance report for the recent monthly period.

Sales	$2,500,000
Cost of goods sold	800,000
Wages expense	500,000
Utilities expense	200,000
Home office expense	75,000
Net income	$ 925,000
Manager's bonus (0.5%)	$ 4,625

In previous periods, the bonus had also been 0.5%, but the performance report had not included any charges for the home office expense, which is now assigned to each store as a percent of its sales.

Required

Assume that you are the national office manager. Write a one-half page memorandum to your store managers explaining why home office expense is in the new performance report.

BTN 27–4 Many companies extend the idea of responsibility accounting to corporate responsibility. Download Best Buy's 2008 Corporate Responsibility Report from http://www.bestbuyinc.com/assets/ corporate_reponsibility/08_report/CSR_2008_Final.pdf. Use information found in the "Key Performance Indicators" section of this report to answer the following questions.

TAKING IT TO THE NET

L06

Required

1. What four criteria does Best Buy use in determining its key performance indicators (metrics)?

2. What three broad categories of key performance indicators does Best Buy use in measuring performance?

3. Fill in the blanks below with information on Best Buy's performance on several key indicators for 2008. The first indicator is shown as an example.

Revenue	$40,023	$ millions
Employee total donations	_____	$ millions
Employee total volunteer hours	_____	hours
Carbon savings per year	_____	Pounds CO_2
Tons of electronics recycled/reused	_____	Tons
Overall customer satisfaction	_____	%
Checkout process satisfaction	_____	%

BTN 27–5 Jungle Jim's International Market has grown considerably since Jim Bonaminio began with his roadside produce stand. Jim now operates a gigantic supermarket with many departments and activities.

ENTREPRENEURS IN BUSINESS

L04

Required

1. How can Jim Bonaminio use departmental income statements to assist him in understanding and controlling his supermarket operations?

2. Are departmental income statements always the best measure of a department's performance? Explain.

BTN 27–6 Your center's usual return on total assets is 19%. You are considering two new investments for your center. The first requires a $250,000 average investment and is expected to yield annual net income of $50,000. The second requires a $1 million average investment with an expected annual net income of $175,000. Do you pursue either?

YOU CALL IT

1. b; [$641,250/($356,250 + $641,250 + $427,500)] × $150,000 = $67,500

2. c

3. a

4. b

5. a; $100,000/$500,000 = 20%

ANSWERS TO MULTIPLE CHOICE QUIZ

	Department X	Department Y	Department Z
Sales	$500,000	$200,000	$350,000
Cost of goods sold	350,000	75,000	150,000
Gross profit	150,000	125,000	200,000
Direct expenses	50,000	20,000	75,000
Departmental contribution	$100,000	$105,000	$125,000

A Look Back

Chapter 27 focused on cost allocation and performance measurement. We identified ways to measure and analyze a company's departments and its managers.

A Look at This Chapter

This chapter describes flexible budgets, variance analysis, and standard costs. It explains how each is used to control and monitor business activities.

A Look Ahead

Chapter 29 shows how both costs and sales behavior are useful to managers in performing cost-volume-profit analysis.

Chapter 28

Budgets and Standard Costing

Learning Objectives

LO 1	Compare fixed and flexible budgets.
LO 2	Prepare a flexible budget and interpret a flexible budget performance report.
LO 3	Define *standard costs* and explain their computation and uses.
LO 4	Describe variances and what they reveal about performance.
LO 5	Compute materials, labor, and overhead variances.
LO 6	Analyze changes in sales from expected amounts.

"Look at each part of the process and improve it"
—Chris Martin

Good Vibrations

NAZARETH, PA—Eric Clapton. Paul McCartney. Johnny Cash. Jimi Hendrix. What do these musical legends have in common? All played guitars manufactured by the **Martin Guitar Company** (**MartinGuitar.com**). Martin manufactures high-quality guitars and recently sold its millionth. This family-owned company, headed by Christian (Chris) F. Martin, has prospered by hurdling challenges facing all manufacturers—materials quality, product design, quality control, manufacturing methods, and new investment.

Chris' entrepreneurial spirit stimulated innovative product design and growth while adhering closely to product quality. Understanding cost analysis and variances, flexible and fixed budgets, and standard costs helps his company control its production process. Martin's "X" bracing system is a key part of the distinctive Martin guitar tone. The company also embraces continuous improvement. Recently it began a lean manufacturing project to improve production efficiency, work flow, and cycle time in one of its plants.

Martin Guitar adheres to tight standards variances. Vince Gentilcore, Martin's director of quality, classi-fies production problems into three types: materials, process, and employee. Developing managerial accounting systems to evaluate its performance on each of these dimensions is key. "[Defects] in wood affect yield, productivity, and costs of quality," explains Vince. "We have exacting specifications and controls in place to detect problems; we don't allow material to go into a guitar that doesn't satisfy our requirements." As for process, he closely monitors the company's computer-controlled machines to ensure excessive tool wear does not impair product quality. Another key to process control, explains Vince, is "the moisture content of the wood, which we track on a regular basis." Regarding employee costs, Chris Martin explains that "we have work quotas; we know how much labor costs and how long it takes."

Achieving high standards is the goal at Martin Guitar. "We're trying to make the best," proclaims Chris. "We are doing so much more volume today, even with all those competitors. [Our workers] hold the company to an extraordinarily high standard." With standards like these, Chris' company produces a pretty tune.

[Sources: *Martin Guitar Website,* January 2009; *Quality Digest,* November 2007; *Modern Guitars Magazine,* December and March 2005; For a virtual tour of Martin Guitars see MartinGuitar.com/visit/vtour.php]

Budgeting helps organize and formalize management's planning activities. This chapter extends the study of budgeting to look more closely at the use of budgets to evaluate performance. Evaluations are important for controlling and monitoring business activities. This chapter also describes and illustrates the use of standard costs and variance analyses. These managerial tools are useful for both evaluating and controlling organizations and for the planning of future activities.

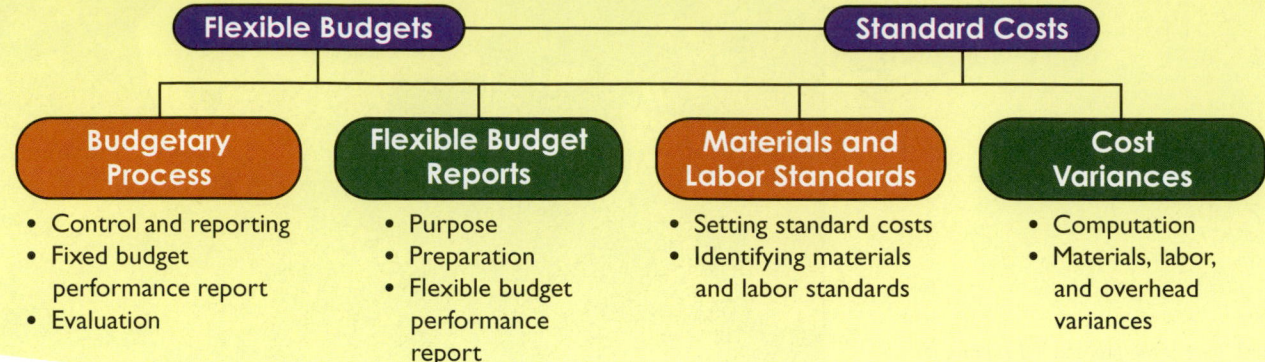

Flexible Budgets — **Standard Costs**

Budgetary Process
- Control and reporting
- Fixed budget performance report
- Evaluation

Flexible Budget Reports
- Purpose
- Preparation
- Flexible budget performance report

Materials and Labor Standards
- Setting standard costs
- Identifying materials and labor standards

Cost Variances
- Computation
- Materials, labor, and overhead variances

Section 1—Flexible Budgets

This section introduces fixed budgets and fixed budget performance reports. It then introduces flexible budgets and flexible budget performance reports and illustrates their advantages.

Budgetary Process

A master budget reflects management's planned objectives for a future period. The preparation of a master budget is based on a predicted level of activity such as sales volume for the budget period. This section discusses the effects on the usefulness of budget reports when the actual level of activity differs from the predicted level.

Budgetary Control and Reporting

Budgetary control refers to management's use of budgets to monitor and control a company's operations. This includes using budgets to see that planned objectives are met. **Budget reports** contain relevant information that compares actual results to planned activities. This comparison is motivated by a need to both monitor performance and control activities. Budget reports are sometimes viewed as progress reports, or *report cards,* on management's performance in achieving planned objectives. These reports can be prepared at any time and for any period. Three common periods for a budget report are a month, quarter, and year.

The budgetary control process involves at least four steps: (1) develop the budget from planned objectives, (2) compare actual results to budgeted amounts and analyze any differences, (3) take corrective and strategic actions, and (4) establish new planned objectives and prepare a new budget. Budget reports and related documents are effective tools for managers to obtain the greatest benefits from this budgetary process.

Fixed Budget Performance Report

In a fixed budgetary control system, the master budget is based on a single prediction for sales volume or other activity level. The budgeted amount for each cost essentially assumes that a specific (or *fixed*) amount of sales will occur. A **fixed budget,** also called *static budget,* is based on a single predicted amount of sales or other measure of activity.

OPTEL Fixed Budget Performance Report For Month Ended January 31, 2010	Fixed Budget	Actual Results	Variances*
Sales (in units)	10,000	12,000	
Sales (in dollars)	$100,000	$125,000	$25,000 F
Cost of goods sold			
Direct materials	10,000	13,000	3,000 U
Direct labor	15,000	20,000	5,000 U
Overhead			
Factory supplies	2,000	2,100	100 U
Utilities	3,000	4,000	1,000 U
Depreciation—Machinery	8,000	8,000	0
Supervisory salaries	11,000	11,000	0
Selling expenses			
Sales commissions	9,000	10,800	1,800 U
Shipping expenses	4,000	4,300	300 U
General and administrative expenses			
Office supplies	5,000	5,200	200 U
Insurance expenses	1,000	1,200	200 U
Depreciation—Office equipment	7,000	7,000	0
Administrative salaries	13,000	13,000	0
Total expenses	88,000	99,600	11,600 U
Income from operations	$ 12,000	$ 25,400	$13,400 F

Exhibit 28.1

Fixed Budget Performance Report

* F = Favorable variance and U = Unfavorable variance.

One benefit of a budget is its usefulness in comparing actual results with planned activities. Information useful for analysis is often presented for comparison in a performance report. As shown in Exhibit 28.1, a **fixed budget performance report** for Optel compares actual results for January 2010 with the results expected under its fixed budget that predicted 10,000 (composite) units of sales. Optel manufactures inexpensive eyeglasses, frames, contact lenses, and related supplies. For this report, its production volume equals sales volume (its inventory level did not change).

This type of performance report designates differences between budgeted and actual results as variances. We see the letters F and U located beside the numbers in the third number column of this report. Their meanings are as follows:

F = **Favorable variance**   When compared to budget, the actual cost or revenue contributes to a *higher* income. That is, actual revenue is higher than budgeted revenue, or actual cost is lower than budgeted cost.

U = **Unfavorable variance**   When compared to budget, the actual cost or revenue contributes to a *lower* income; actual revenue is lower than budgeted revenue, or actual cost is higher than budgeted cost.

This convention is common in practice and is used throughout this chapter.

Budget Reports for Evaluation

A primary use of budget reports is as a tool for management to monitor and control operations. Evaluation by Optel management is likely to focus on a variety of questions that might include these:

■ Why is actual income from operations $13,400 higher than budgeted?
■ Are amounts paid for each expense item too high?
■ Is manufacturing using too much direct material?
■ Is manufacturing using too much direct labor?

IN THE NEWS

Green Budget   Budget reporting and evaluation are used at the **Environmental Protection Agency (EPA)**. It regularly prepares performance plans and budget requests that describe performance goals, measure outcomes, and analyze variances.

The performance report in Exhibit 28.1 provides little help in answering these questions because actual sales volume is 2,000 units higher than budgeted. A manager does not know if this higher level of sales activity is the cause of variations in total dollar sales and expenses or if other factors have influenced these amounts. This inability of fixed budget reports to adjust for changes in activity levels is a major limitation of a fixed budget performance report. That is, it fails to show whether actual costs are out of line due to a change in actual sales volume or some other factor.

Flexible Budget Reports

Purpose of Flexible Budgets

LO1 Compare fixed and flexible budgets.

To help address limitations with the fixed budget performance report, particularly from the effects of changes in sales volume, management can use a flexible budget. A **flexible budget,** also called a *variable budget,* is a report based on predicted amounts of revenues and expenses corresponding to the actual level of output. Flexible budgets are useful both before and after the period's activities are complete.

A flexible budget prepared before the period is often based on several levels of activity. Budgets for those different levels can provide a "what if" look at operations. The different levels often include both a best case and worst case scenario. This allows management to make adjustments to avoid or lessen the effects of the worst case scenario.

A flexible budget prepared after the period helps management evaluate past performance. It is especially useful for such an evaluation because it reflects budgeted revenues and costs based on the actual level of activity. Thus, comparisons of actual results with budgeted performance are more likely to identify the causes of any differences. This can help managers focus attention on real problem areas and implement corrective actions. This is in contrast to a fixed budget, whose primary purpose is to assist managers in planning future activities and whose numbers are based on a single predicted amount of budgeted sales or production.

Preparation of Flexible Budgets

LO2 Prepare a flexible budget and interpret a flexible budget performance report.

A flexible budget is designed to reveal the effects of volume of activity on revenues and costs. To prepare a flexible budget, management relies on the distinctions between fixed and variable costs. Recall that the cost per unit of activity remains constant for variable costs so that the total amount of a variable cost changes in direct proportion to a change in activity level. The total amount of fixed cost remains unchanged regardless of changes in the level of activity within a relevant (normal) operating range. (Assume that costs can be reasonably classified as variable or fixed within a relevant range.)

When we create the numbers constituting a flexible budget, we express each variable cost either as a constant amount per unit of sales or as a percent of a sales dollar. In the case of a fixed cost, we express its budgeted amount as the total amount expected to occur at any sales volume within the relevant range.

Exhibit 28.2 shows a set of flexible budgets for Optel in January 2010. Seven of its expenses are classified as variable costs. Its remaining five expenses are fixed costs. These classifications result from management's investigation of each expense. Variable and fixed expense categories are *not* the same for every company, and we must avoid drawing conclusions from specific

Exhibit 28.2

Flexible Budgets

OPTEL Flexible Budgets For Month Ended January 31, 2010	Flexible Budget Variable Amount per Unit	Total Fixed Cost	Flexible Budget for Unit Sales of 10,000	Flexible Budget for Unit Sales of 12,000	Flexible Budget for Unit Sales of 14,000
Sales	$10.00		$100,000	$120,000	$140,000
Variable costs					
Direct materials	1.00		10,000	12,000	14,000
Direct labor	1.50		15,000	18,000	21,000
Factory supplies	0.20		2,000	2,400	2,800
Utilities	0.30		3,000	3,600	4,200
Sales commissions	0.90		9,000	10,800	12,600
Shipping expenses	0.40		4,000	4,800	5,600
Office supplies	0.50		5,000	6,000	7,000
Total variable costs	4.80		48,000	57,600	67,200
Contribution margin	$ 5.20		$ 52,000	$ 62,400	$ 72,800
Fixed costs					
Depreciation—Machinery		$ 8,000	8,000	8,000	8,000
Supervisory salaries		11,000	11,000	11,000	11,000
Insurance expense		1,000	1,000	1,000	1,000
Depreciation—Office equipment		7,000	7,000	7,000	7,000
Administrative salaries		13,000	13,000	13,000	13,000
Total fixed costs		$40,000	40,000	40,000	40,000
Income from operations			$ 12,000	$ 22,400	$ 32,800

cases. For example, depending on the nature of a company's operations, office supplies expense can be either fixed or variable with respect to sales.

The layout for the flexible budgets in Exhibit 28.2 follows a *contribution margin format*—beginning with sales followed by variable costs and then fixed costs. Both the expected individual and total variable costs are reported and then subtracted from sales. The difference between sales and variable costs equals contribution margin. The expected amounts of fixed costs are listed next, followed by the expected income from operations before taxes.

The first and second number columns of Exhibit 28.2 show the flexible budget amounts for variable costs per unit and each fixed cost for any volume of sales in the relevant range. The third, fourth, and fifth columns show the flexible budget amounts computed for three different sales volumes. For instance, the third column's flexible budget is based on 10,000 units. These numbers are the same as those in the fixed budget of Exhibit 28.1 because the expected volumes are the same for these two budgets.

Recall that Optel's actual sales volume for January is 12,000 units. This sales volume is 2,000 units more than the 10,000 units originally predicted in the master budget. When differences between actual and predicted volume arise, the usefulness of a flexible budget is apparent. For instance, compare the flexible budget for 10,000 units in the third column (which is the same as the fixed budget in Exhibit 28.1) with the flexible budget for 12,000 units in the fourth column. The higher levels for both sales and variable costs reflect nothing more than the increase in sales activity. Any budget analysis comparing actual with planned results that ignores this information is less useful to management.

To illustrate, when we evaluate Optel's performance, we need to prepare a flexible budget showing actual and budgeted values at 12,000 units. Thus, a flexible budget yields an "apples to apples" comparison because budgeted activity levels are the same as the actual. As part of a complete profitability analysis, managers could compare the actual income of $25,400 (from

Exhibit 28.1) with the $22,400 income expected at the actual sales volume of 12,000 units (from Exhibit 28.2). This results in a total income variance of $3,000 to be explained and interpreted. This variance is markedly different from the $13,400 variance identified in Exhibit 28.1 using a fixed budget. After receiving the flexible budget based on January's actual volume, management must determine what caused this $3,000 difference. The next section describes a flexible budget performance report that provides guidance in this analysis.

Flexible Budget Performance Report

A **flexible budget performance report** lists differences between actual performance and budgeted performance based on actual sales volume or other activity level. This report helps direct management's attention to those costs or revenues that differ substantially from budgeted amounts. Exhibit 28.3 shows Optel's flexible budget performance report for January. We prepare this report after the actual volume is known to be 12,000 units. This report shows a $5,000 favorable variance in total dollar sales. Because actual and budgeted volumes are both 12,000 units, the $5,000 sales variance must have resulted from a higher than expected selling price. Further analysis of the facts surrounding this $5,000 sales variance reveals a favorable sales variance per unit of nearly $0.42 as shown here:

Actual average price per unit (rounded to cents)	$125,000/12,000 = $10.42
Budgeted price per unit	$120,000/12,000 = 10.00
Favorable sales variance per unit	$5,000/12,000 = $ 0.42

The other variances in Exhibit 28.3 also direct management's attention to areas where corrective actions can help control Optel's operations. Each expense variance is analyzed as the sales variance was. We can think of each expense as the joint result of using a given number of units of input and paying a specific price per unit of input.

Exhibit 28.3

Flexible Budget
Performance Report

OPTEL Flexible Budget Performance Report For Month Ended January 31, 2010	Flexible Budget	Actual Results	Variances*
Sales (12,000 units)	$120,000	$125,000	**$5,000 F**
Variable costs			
Direct materials	12,000	13,000	**1,000 U**
Direct labor	18,000	20,000	**2,000 U**
Factory supplies	2,400	2,100	**300 F**
Utilities	3,600	4,000	**400 U**
Sales commissions	10,800	10,800	**0**
Shipping expenses	4,800	4,300	**500 F**
Office supplies	6,000	5,200	**800 F**
Total variable costs	57,600	59,400	**1,800 U**
Contribution margin	62,400	65,600	**3,200 F**
Fixed costs			
Depreciation—Machinery	8,000	8,000	**0**
Supervisory salaries	11,000	11,000	**0**
Insurance expense	1,000	1,200	**200 U**
Depreciation—Office equipment	7,000	7,000	**0**
Administrative salaries	13,000	13,000	**0**
Total fixed costs	40,000	40,200	**200 U**
Income from operations	$ 22,400	$ 25,400	**$3,000 F**

* F = Favorable variance and U = Unfavorable variance.

Each variance in Exhibit 28.3 is due in part to a difference between *actual price* per unit of input and *budgeted price* per unit of input. This is a **price variance.** Each variance also can be due in part to a difference between *actual quantity* of input used and *budgeted quantity* of input. This is a **quantity variance.** We explain more about this breakdown, known as **variance analysis,** later in the standard costs section.

Section 2—Standard Costs

Standard costs are preset costs for delivering a product or service under normal conditions. These costs are established by personnel, engineering, and accounting studies using past experiences and data. Management uses these costs to assess the reasonableness of actual costs incurred for producing the product or service. When actual costs vary from standard costs, management follows up to identify potential problems and take corrective actions.

LO3 Define *standard costs* and explain their computation and uses.

Standard costs are often used in preparing budgets because they are the anticipated costs incurred under normal conditions. Terms such as *standard materials cost, standard labor cost,* and *standard overhead cost* are often used to refer to amounts budgeted for direct materials, direct labor, and overhead.

Materials and Labor Standards

This section explains how to set materials and labor standards and how to prepare a standard cost card.

Setting Standard Costs

We illustrate standard costs by using the example of G-Max, a company that makes specialty golf equipment and accessories for individual customers.

The standard materials cost is the standard quantity of each material (1 lb. of titanium) to manufacture one unit multiplied by the standard cost per unit of input ($1 per pound). The standard labor cost is the standard quantity of hours of labor (1 hour) needed to manufacture multiplied by the standard wage rate per hour ($8 per hour).

The standard overhead cost per unit is the predetermined overhead rate used to assign standard overhead costs to products or services produced. This predetermined rate is usually based on some overhead allocation base (such as standard labor cost, standard labor hours, or standard machine hours). Standard overhead costs are, therefore, average per unit costs based on the predicted activity level.

As an example, G-max selects a standard overhead rate by estimating the overhead for the month and then divides by its expected production volume. They choose direct labor hours as the overhead allocation base.

G-Max managers predict a production volume of 4,000 clubheads in May. At this volume they budget $8,000 as May total overhead ($4,000 variable overhead and $4,000 fixed overhead). This choice implies a $2 per unit average overhead cost (computed as $8,000/4,000 hours). Since

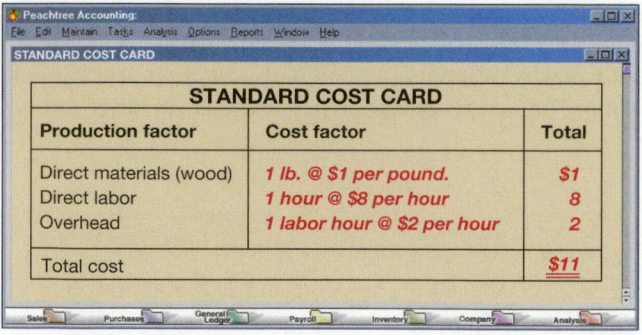

STANDARD COST CARD		
Production factor	**Cost factor**	**Total**
Direct materials (wood)	*1 lb. @ $1 per pound.*	$1
Direct labor	*1 hour @ $8 per hour*	8
Overhead	*1 labor hour @ $2 per hour*	2
Total cost		$11

G-Max has a standard of one direct labor hour per unit, the predetermined standard overhead rate for May is $2 per standard direct labor hour (computed as $8,000/4,000 direct labor hours).

The standard costs of direct materials, direct labor, and overhead are shown in Exhibit 28.4 for G-Max in what is called a *standard cost card*.

Identifying Standard Costs

Managerial accountants, engineers, personnel administrators, and other managers combine their efforts to set standard costs. To identify standards for direct labor costs, we can conduct time and motion studies for each labor operation in the process of providing a product or service. From these studies, management can learn the best way to perform the operation and then set the standard labor time required for the operation under normal conditions. Similarly, standards for materials are set by studying the quantity, grade, and cost of each material used. Standards for overhead costs are explained later in the chapter.

Regardless of the care used in setting standard costs and in revising them as conditions change, actual costs frequently differ from standard costs, often as a result of one or more factors. For instance, the actual quantity of material used can differ from the standard, or the price paid per unit of material can differ from the standard. Quantity and price differences from standard amounts can also occur for labor. That is, the actual labor time and actual labor rate can vary from what was expected. The same analysis applies to overhead costs.

IN THE NEWS

Cruis'n Standards   The **Corvette** consists of hundreds of parts for which engineers set standards. Various types of labor are also involved in its production, including machining, assembly, painting, and welding, and standards are set for each. Actual results are periodically compared with standards to assess performance.

Cost Variances

LO4 Describe variances and what they reveal about performance.

A **cost variance,** also simply called a *variance,* is the difference between actual and standard costs. A cost variance can be favorable or unfavorable. A variance from standard cost is considered favorable if actual cost is less than standard cost. It is considered unfavorable if actual cost is more than standard cost.[1]

Cost Variance Computation

Management needs information about the factors causing a cost variance, but first it must properly compute the variance. In its most simple form, a cost variance (CV) is computed as the difference between actual cost (AC) and standard cost (SC) as shown in Exhibit 28.5.

---

[1] Short-term favorable variances can sometimes lead to long-term unfavorable variances. For instance, if management spends less than the budgeted amount on maintenance or insurance, the performance report would show a favorable variance. Cutting these expenses can lead to major losses in the long run if machinery wears out prematurely or insurance coverage proves inadequate.

Exhibit 28.5

Cost Variance Formulas

> **Cost Variance (CV) = Actual Cost (AC) − Standard Cost (SC)**
>
> where:
>
> **Actual Cost (AC) = Actual Quantity (AQ) × Actual Price (AP)**
> **Standard Cost (SC) = Standard Quantity (SQ) × Standard Price (SP)**

A cost variance is further defined by its components. Actual quantity (AQ) is the input (material or labor) used to manufacture the quantity of output. Standard quantity (SQ) is the expected input for the quantity of output. Actual price (AP) is the amount paid to acquire the input (material or labor), and standard price (SP) is the expected price.

Two main factors cause a cost variance: (1) the difference between actual price and standard price results in a *price* (or rate) *variance* and (2) the difference between actual quantity and standard quantity results in a *quantity* (or usage or **efficiency**) *variance*. To assess the impacts of these two factors on a cost variance, we use the formula in Exhibit 28.6.

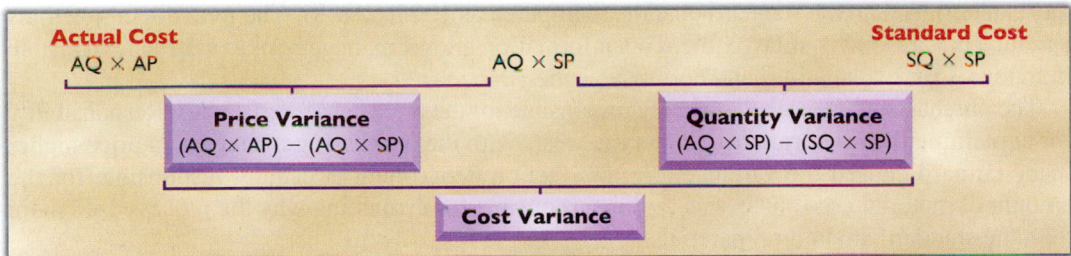

Exhibit 28.6

Price Variance and Quantity Variance Formulas

These formulas identify the sources of the cost variance. Managers sometimes find it useful to apply an alternative (but equivalent) computation for the price and quantity variances as shown in Exhibit 28.7.

> **Price Variance (PV) = [Actual Price (AP) − Standard Price (SP)] × Actual Quantity (AQ)**
>
> **Quantity Variance (QV) = [Actual Quantity (AQ) − Standard Quantity (SQ)] × Standard Price (SP)**

Exhibit 28.7

Alternative Price Variance and Quantity Variance Formulas

The results from applying the formulas in Exhibits 28.6 and 28.7 are identical.

Materials, Labor, and Overhead Variances

Materials Cost Variances During May 2010, G-Max budgeted to produce 4,000 clubheads (units). It actually produced only 3,500 units. It used 3,600 pounds of direct materials (titanium) costing $1.05 per pound, meaning its total materials cost was $3,780. This information allows us to compute both actual and standard direct materials costs for G-Max's 3,500 units and its direct materials cost variance as follows:

LO5 Compute materials, labor, and overhead variances.

Actual cost	3,600 lbs. @ $1.05 per lb.	= $3,780
Standard cost	3,500 lbs. @ $1.00 per lb.	= 3,500
Direct materials cost variance (unfavorable)		= **$ 280**

The materials price and quantity variances for these G-Max clubheads are computed and shown in Exhibit 28.8.

Exhibit 28.8

Materials Price and
Quantity Variances

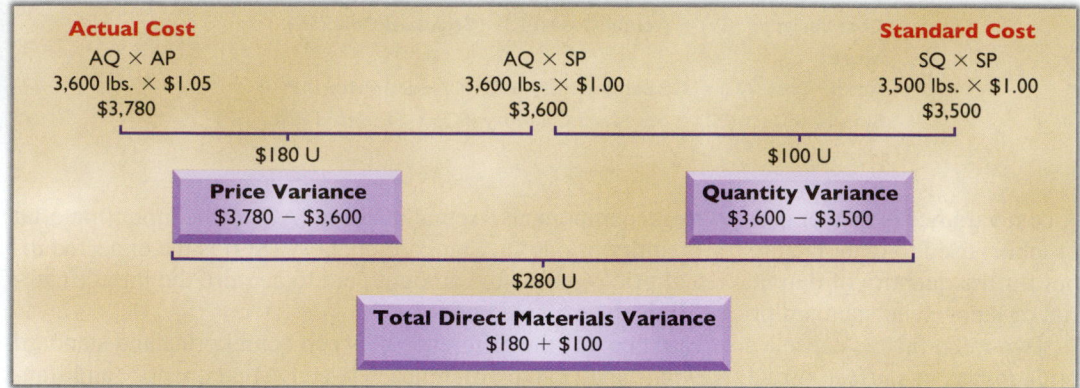

The $180 unfavorable price variance results from paying 5 cents more than the standard price, computed as 3,600 lbs. × $0.05. The $100 unfavorable quantity variance is due to using 100 lbs. more materials than the standard quantity, computed as 100 lbs. × $1. The total direct materials variance is $280 and is unfavorable. This information allows management to ask the responsible individuals for explanations and corrective actions.

The purchasing department is usually responsible for the price paid for materials. Responsibility for explaining the price variance in this case rests with the purchasing manager if a price higher than standard caused the variance. The production department is usually responsible for the amount of material used and in this case is responsible for explaining why the process used more than the standard amount of materials.

Variance analysis presents challenges. For instance, the production department could have used more than the standard amount of material because low quality material led to excessive waste. In this case, the purchasing manager is responsible for explaining why inferior materials were bought. However, the production manager is responsible for explaining what happened if analysis shows that waste was due to inefficiencies, not poor quality material.

Labor Cost Variances   Labor cost for a specific product or service depends on the number of hours worked (quantity) and the wage rate paid to employees (price). When actual amounts for a task differ from standard, the labor cost variance can be divided into a rate (price) variance and an efficiency (quantity) variance.

To illustrate, G-Max's direct labor standard for 3,500 units of its handcrafted clubheads is one hour per unit, or 3,500 hours at $8 per hour. Since only 3,400 hours at $8.30 per hour were actually used to complete the units, the actual and standard labor costs are

Actual cost	3,400 hrs. @ $8.30 per hr.	= $28,220
Standard cost	3,500 hrs. @ $8.00 per hr.	= 28,000
Direct labor cost variance (unfavorable)		= $ 220

This analysis shows that actual cost is merely $220 over the standard and suggests no immediate concern. Computing both the labor rate and efficiency variances reveals a different picture, however, as shown in Exhibit 28.9.

The analysis in Exhibit 28.9 shows that an $800 favorable efficiency variance results from using 100 fewer direct labor hours than standard for the units produced, but this favorable variance is more than offset by a wage rate that is $0.30 higher than standard. The personnel administrator or possibly the production manager needs to explain why the wage rate is higher than expected. The production manager should also explain how the labor hours were reduced.

Overhead Cost Variances   The **overhead cost variance** is the difference between the total overhead cost applied to products and the total overhead cost actually incurred. In this section, we show how to compute this variance. As noted on the standard cost card in Exhibit 28.4, G-Max applies its manufacturing overhead to its products at $2 per direct labor hour. This $2 rate includes $1 per hour for fixed manufacturing overhead and $1 per hour for variable manufacturing overhead.

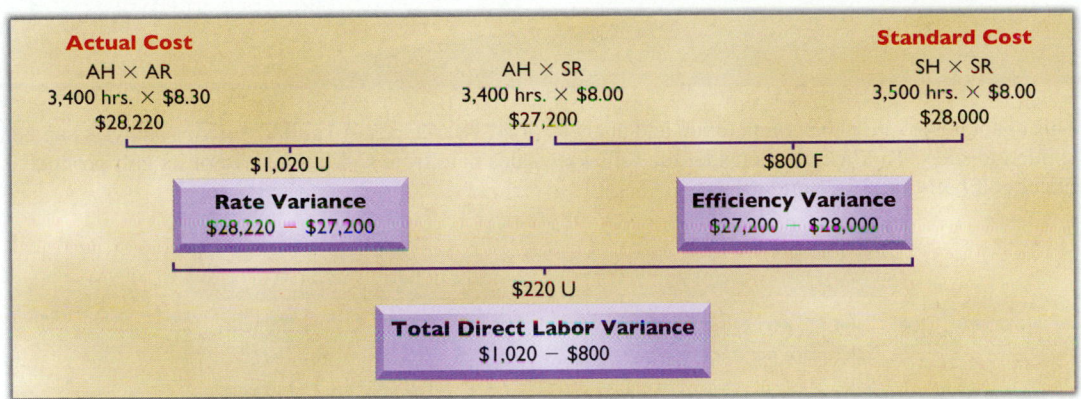

Exhibit 28.9

Labor Rate and
Efficiency Variances*

* AH is actual direct labor hours; AR is actual wage rate; SH is standard direct labor hours allowed for actual output; SR is standard wage rate.

Based on the actual production volume of 3,500 units, G-Max applied $7,000 of overhead to its products (3,500 units × $2 per unit). The actual manufacturing overhead was $7,650. The difference is an unfavorable variance of $650.

Applied manufacturing overhead to products:		
3,500 direct labor hours × $2 per hour		$7,000
Actual manufacturing overhead:		
Fixed costs	$4,000	
Variable costs	3,650	
Total		7,650
Unfavorable overhead cost variance		$(650)

The unfavorable overhead cost variance suggests that actual costs were greater than the amount allowed for the quantity of products produced.

Additional analysis of the components of the overall manufacturing overhead variance is covered in advanced courses. Two of the three variances computed for manufacturing overhead are the variable overhead spending and efficiency variances. The remaining component is the fixed overhead spending variance.

HOW YOU DOIN'?

Answers—p. 792

5. A standard cost (*a*) changes in direct proportion to changes in the level of activity, (*b*) is an amount incurred at the actual level of production for the period, or (*c*) is an amount incurred under normal conditions to provide a product or service.

6. What is a cost variance?

7. The following information is available for York Company.

Actual direct labor hours per unit	2.5 hours
Standard direct labor hours per unit	2.0 hours
Actual production (units)	2,500 units
Budgeted production (units)	3,000 units
Actual rate per hour	$3.10
Standard rate per hour	$3.00

The labor efficiency variance is (*a*) $3,750 U, (*b*) $3,750 F, or (*c*) $3,875 U.

8. Refer to question 7 above; the labor rate variance is (*a*) $625 F or (*b*) $625 U.

9. If a materials quantity variance is favorable and a materials price variance is unfavorable, can the total materials cost variance be favorable?

SALES VARIANCES

LO6 Analyze changes in sales from expected amounts.

This chapter explained the computation and analysis of cost variances. A similar variance analysis can be applied to sales. To illustrate, consider the following sales data from G-Max for two of its golf products, Excel golf balls and Big Bert® drivers.

	Budgeted	Actual
Sales of Excel golf balls (units)	1,000 units	1,100 units
Sales price per Excel golf ball	$ 10	$ 10.50
Sales of Big Bert® drivers (units)	150 units	140 units
Sales price per Big Bert® driver	$ 200	$ 190

Using this information, we compute both the *sales price variance* and the *sales volume variance* as shown in Exhibit 28.10. The total sales price variance is $850 unfavorable, and the total sales volume variance is $1,000 unfavorable. Neither variance implies anything positive about these two products. Further analysis of these total sales variances reveals that both the sales price and sales volume variances for Excel golf balls are favorable, meaning that both the unfavorable total sales price variance and the unfavorable total sales volume variance are due to the Big Bert driver.

Exhibit 28.10

Computing Sales Variances

Excel Golf Balls	Actual Results AS × AP	Flexible Budget AS × BP	Fixed Budget BS × BP
Sales dollars (balls)	(1,100 × $10.50) **$11,550**	(1,100 × $10) **$11,000**	(1,000 × $10) **$10,000**
	$550 F	$1,000 F	
	Sales Price Variance	**Sales Volume Variance**	
Big Bert® Drivers			
Sales dollars (drivers)	(140 × $190) **$26,600**	(140 × $200) **$28,000**	(150 × $200) **$30,000**
	$1,400 U	$2,000 U	
	Sales Price Variance	**Sales Volume Variance**	
Total	**$850 U**	**$1,000 U**	

* AS = actual sales units; AP = actual sales price; BP = budgeted sales price; BS = budgeted sales units (fixed budget).

Managers use sales variances for planning and control purposes. The sales variance information is used to plan future actions to avoid unfavorable variances. G-Max sold 90 total combined units (both balls and drivers) more than planned, but these 90 units were not sold in the proportion budgeted. G-Max sold fewer than the budgeted quantity of the higher-priced driver, which contributed to the unfavorable total sales variances. Managers use such detail to question what caused the company to sell more golf balls and fewer drivers. Managers also use this information to evaluate and even reward their salespeople. Extra compensation is paid to salespeople who contribute to a higher profit margin.

Demonstration Problem

Pacific Company provides the following information about its budgeted and actual results for June 2010. Although the expected June volume was 25,000 units produced and sold, the company actually produced and sold 27,000 units as detailed here:

	Budget (25,000 units)	Actual (27,000 units)
Selling price	$5.00 per unit	$5.23 per unit
Variable costs (per unit)		
Direct materials	1.24 per unit	1.12 per unit
Direct labor	1.50 per unit	1.40 per unit
Factory supplies	0.25 per unit	0.37 per unit
Utilities	0.50 per unit	0.60 per unit
Selling costs	0.40 per unit	0.34 per unit
Fixed costs (per month)		
Depreciation—Machinery	$3,750	$3,710
Depreciation—Building	2,500	2,500
General liability insurance	1,200	1,250
Property taxes on office equipment	500	485
Other administrative expense	750	900

Standard costs based on expected output of 25,000 units

	Per Unit of Output	Quantity to Be Used	Total Cost
Direct materials, 4 oz. @ $0.31 per oz.	$1.24/unit	100,000 oz.	$31,000
Direct labor, 0.25 hr. @ $6.00 per hr.	1.50/unit	6,250 hrs.	37,500
Overhead	1.00/unit		25,000

Actual costs incurred to produce 27,000 units

	Per Unit of Output	Quantity Used	Total Cost
Direct materials, 4 oz. @ $0.28 per oz.	$1.12/unit	108,000 oz.	$30,240
Direct labor, 0.20 hr. @ $7.00 per hr.	1.40/unit	5,400 hrs.	37,800
Overhead	1.20/unit		32,400

Standard costs based on expected output of 27,000 units

	Per Unit of Output	Quantity to Be Used	Total Cost
Direct materials, 4 oz. @ $0.31 per oz.	$1.24/unit	108,000 oz.	$33,480
Direct labor, 0.25 hr. @ $6.00 per hr.	1.50/unit	6,750 hrs.	40,500
Overhead			26,500

Required

1. Prepare June flexible budgets showing expected sales, costs, and net income assuming 20,000, 25,000, and 30,000 units of output produced and sold.

2. Prepare a flexible budget performance report that compares actual results with the amounts budgeted if the actual volume had been expected.

3. Apply variance analysis for direct materials and for direct labor.

Planning the Solution

- Prepare a table showing the expected results at the three specified levels of output. Compute the variable costs by multiplying the per unit variable costs by the expected volumes. Include fixed costs at the given amounts. Combine the amounts in the table to show total variable costs, contribution margin, total fixed costs, and income from operations.

- Prepare a table showing the actual results and the amounts that should be incurred at 27,000 units. Show any differences in the third column and label them with an *F* for favorable if they increase income or a *U* for unfavorable if they decrease income.

- Using the chapter's format, compute these total variances and the individual variances requested:
  - Total materials variance (including the direct materials quantity variance and the direct materials price variance).
  - Total direct labor variance (including the direct labor efficiency variance and rate variance).

Solution to Demonstration Problem

1.

PACIFIC COMPANY Flexible Budgets For Month Ended June 30, 2010					
	Flexible Budget		**Flexible Budget for Unit Sales of 20,000**	**Flexible Budget for Unit Sales of 25,000**	**Flexible Budget for Unit Sales of 30,000**
	Variable Amount per Unit	**Total Fixed Cost**			
Sales	$5.00		$100,000	$125,000	$150,000
Variable costs					
Direct materials	1.24		24,800	31,000	37,200
Direct labor	1.50		30,000	37,500	45,000
Factory supplies	0.25		5,000	6,250	7,500
Utilities	0.50		10,000	12,500	15,000
Selling costs	0.40		8,000	10,000	12,000
Total variable costs	3.89		77,800	97,250	116,700
Contribution margin	$1.11		22,200	27,750	33,300
Fixed costs					
Depreciation—Machinery		$3,750	3,750	3,750	3,750
Depreciation—Building		2,500	2,500	2,500	2,500
General liability insurance		1,200	1,200	1,200	1,200
Property taxes on office equipment		500	500	500	500
Other administrative expense		750	750	750	750
Total fixed costs		$8,700	8,700	8,700	8,700
Income from operations			$ 13,500	$ 19,050	$ 24,600

2.

PACIFIC COMPANY Flexible Budget Performance Report For Month Ended June 30, 2010			
	Flexible Budget	**Actual Results**	**Variance***
Sales (27,000 units)	$135,000	$141,210	$6,210 F
Variable costs			
Direct materials	33,480	30,240	3,240 F
Direct labor	40,500	37,800	2,700 F
Factory supplies	6,750	9,990	3,240 U
Utilities	13,500	16,200	2,700 U
Selling costs	10,800	9,180	1,620 F
Total variable costs	105,030	103,410	1,620 F
Contribution margin	29,970	37,800	7,830 F
Fixed costs			
Depreciation—Machinery	3,750	3,710	40 F
Depreciation—Building	2,500	2,500	0
General liability insurance	1,200	1,250	50 U
Property taxes on office equipment	500	485	15 F
Other administrative expense	750	900	150 U
Total fixed costs	8,700	8,845	145 U
Income from operations	$ 21,270	$ 28,955	$7,685 F

* F = Favorable variance and U = Unfavorable variance.

3. Variance analysis of materials and labor costs.

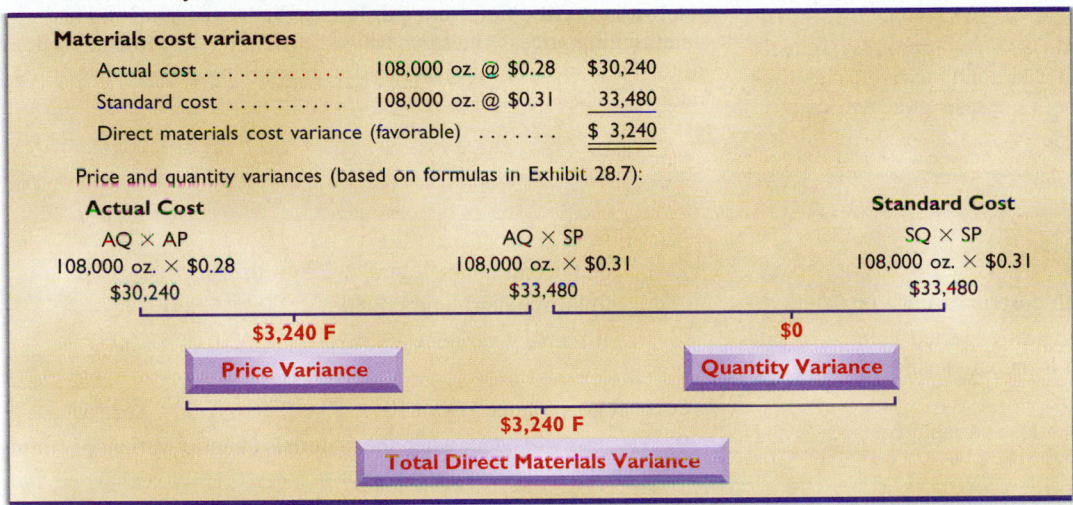

Materials cost variances

Actual cost	108,000 oz. @ $0.28	$30,240
Standard cost	108,000 oz. @ $0.31	33,480
Direct materials cost variance (favorable)		$ 3,240

Price and quantity variances (based on formulas in Exhibit 28.7):

Actual Cost   **Standard Cost**

AQ × AP   AQ × SP   SQ × SP
108,000 oz. × $0.28   108,000 oz. × $0.31   108,000 oz. × $0.31
$30,240 $33,480 $33,480

$3,240 F   **$0**

Price Variance   **Quantity Variance**

$3,240 F

Total Direct Materials Variance

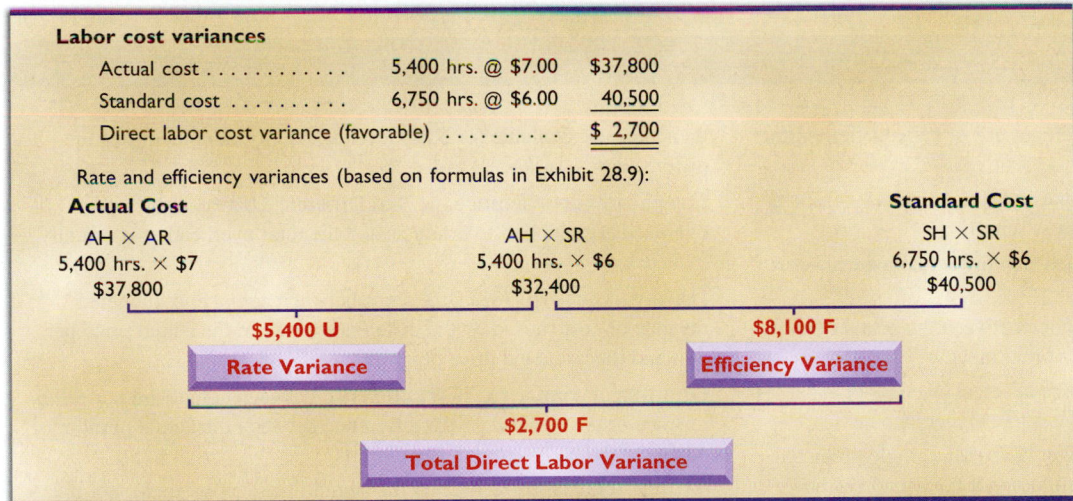

Labor cost variances

Actual cost	5,400 hrs. @ $7.00	$37,800
Standard cost	6,750 hrs. @ $6.00	40,500
Direct labor cost variance (favorable)		$ 2,700

Rate and efficiency variances (based on formulas in Exhibit 28.9):

Actual Cost   **Standard Cost**

AH × AR   AH × SR   SH × SR
5,400 hrs. × $7   5,400 hrs. × $6   6,750 hrs. × $6
$37,800 $32,400 $40,500

$5,400 U   **$8,100 F**

Rate Variance   **Efficiency Variance**

$2,700 F

Total Direct Labor Variance

Summary

LO1 **Compare fixed and flexible budgets.** A fixed budget shows the revenues and costs expected to occur at a specified volume level. If actual volume is at some other level, the amounts in the fixed budget do not provide a reasonable basis for evaluating actual performance. A flexible budget expresses variable costs in per unit terms so that it can be used to develop budgeted amounts for any volume level within the relevant range. Thus, managers compute budgeted amounts for evaluation after a period for the volume that actually occurred.

LO2 **Prepare a flexible budget and interpret a flexible budget performance report.** To prepare a flexible budget, we express each variable cost as a constant amount per unit of sales (or as a percent of sales dollar). In contrast, the budgeted amount of each fixed cost is expressed as a total amount expected to occur at any sales volume within the relevant range. The flexible budget is then determined using these computations and amounts for fixed and variable costs at the expected sales volume.

LO3 **Define *standard costs* and explain their computation and uses.** Standard costs are the normal costs that should be

incurred to produce a product or perform a service. They should be based on a careful examination of the processes used to produce a product or perform a service as well as the quantities and prices that should be incurred in carrying out those processes. On a performance report, standard costs (which are flexible budget amounts) are compared to actual costs, and the differences are presented as variances.

LO4 **Describe variances and what they reveal about performance.** Management can use variances to monitor and control activities. Total cost variances can be broken into price and quantity variances to direct management's attention to those responsible for quantities used and prices paid.

LO5 **Compute materials, labor, and overhead variances.** Materials and labor variances are due to differences between the actual costs incurred and the budgeted costs. The price (or rate) variance is computed by comparing the actual cost with the flexible budget amount that should have been incurred to acquire the actual quantity of resources. The quantity (or efficiency) variance is computed by comparing the flexible budget amount that should have been incurred to acquire the actual quantity of resources with the flexible budget amount that should have been incurred to acquire the standard quantity of resources.

LO6 **Analyze changes in sales from expected amounts.** Actual sales can differ from budgeted sales, and managers can investigate this difference by computing both the sales price and sales volume variances. The *sales price variance* refers to that portion of total variance resulting from a difference between actual and budgeted selling prices. The *sales volume variance* refers to that portion of total variance resulting from a difference between actual and budgeted sales quantities.

Guidance Answers to HOW YOU DOIN'?

1. *b*

2. The first step is classifying each cost as variable or fixed.

3. A fixed budget is prepared using an expected volume of sales or production. A flexible budget is prepared using the actual volume of activity.

4. Contribution margin equals sales less variable costs.

5. *c*

6. It is the difference between actual cost and standard cost.

7. *a*; Total actual hours: $2,500 \times 2.5 = 6,250$
Total standard hours: $2,500 \times 2.0 = 5,000$
Efficiency variance $= (6,250 - 5,000) \times \$3.00$
$= \$3,750$ U

8. *b*; Rate variance $= (\$3.10 - \$3.00) \times 6,250 = \$625$ U

9. Yes, this will occur when the materials quantity variance is more than the materials price variance.

Key Terms

Budgetary control (p. 778) Management use of budgets to monitor and control company operations.

Budget report (p. 778) Report comparing actual results to planned objectives; sometimes used as a progress report.

Cost variance (p. 784) Difference between the actual incurred cost and the standard cost.

Efficiency variance (p. 785) Difference between the actual quantity of an input and the standard quantity of that input.

Favorable variance (p. 779) Difference in actual revenues or expenses from the budgeted amount that contributes to a higher income.

Fixed budget (p. 778) Planning budget based on a single predicted amount of volume; unsuitable for evaluations if the actual volume differs from predicted volume.

Fixed budget performance report (p. 779) Report that compares actual revenues and costs with fixed budgeted amounts and identifies the differences as favorable or unfavorable variances.

Flexible budget (p. 780) Budget prepared (using actual volume) once a period is complete that helps managers evaluate past performance; uses fixed and variable costs in determining total costs.

Flexible budget performance report (p. 782) Report that compares actual revenues and costs with their variable budgeted amounts based on actual sales volume (or other level of activity) and identifies the differences as variances.

Overhead cost variance (p. 786) Difference between the total overhead cost applied to products and the total overhead cost actually incurred.

Price variance (p. 783) Difference between actual and budgeted revenue or cost caused by the difference between the actual price per unit and the budgeted price per unit.

Quantity variance (p. 783) Difference between actual and budgeted revenue or cost caused by the difference between the actual number of units and the budgeted number of units.

Standard costs (p. 783) Costs that should be incurred under normal conditions to produce a product or component or to perform a service.

Unfavorable variance (p. 779) Difference in revenues or costs, when the actual amount is compared to the budgeted amount, that contributes to a lower income.

Variance analysis (p. 783) Process of examining differences between actual and budgeted revenues or costs and describing them in terms of price and quantity differences.

Multiple Choice Quiz   Answers on p. 803   mhhe.com/wildCA2e

Additional Multiple Choice Quizzes are available at the book's Website.

1. Product A has a sales price of $10 per unit. Based on a 10,000-unit production level, the variable costs are $6 per unit and the fixed costs are $30,000. Using a flexible budget for 12,500 units, what is the budgeted operating income from Product A?
   a. $12,500
   b. $25,000
   c. $20,000
   d. $30,000
   e. $35,000

2. The costs that should be incurred under normal conditions to produce a specific product or component or to perform a specific service are
   a. Variable costs
   b. Fixed costs
   c. Standard costs
   d. Product costs
   e. Period costs

3. A company predicts its production and sales will be 24,000 units. At that level of activity, its fixed costs are budgeted at $300,000, and its variable costs are budgeted at $246,000. If its activity level declines to 20,000 units, what will be its fixed costs and its variable costs?
  a. Fixed, $300,000; Variable, $246,000
  b. Fixed, $250,000; Variable, $205,000
  c. Fixed, $300,000; Variable, $205,000
  d. Fixed, $250,000; Variable, $246,000
  e. Fixed, $300,000; Variable, $300,000

4. Using the following information about a single-product company, compute its total actual cost of direct materials used.
  • Direct materials standard cost: 5 lbs. × $2 per lb. = $10.
  • Total direct materials cost variance: $15,000 unfavorable.
  • Actual direct materials used: 300,000 lbs.
  • Actual units produced: 60,000 units.

  a. $585,000
  b. $600,000
  c. $300,000
  d. $315,000
  e. $615,000

5. A company uses four hours of direct labor to produce a product unit. The standard direct labor cost is $20 per hour. This period the company produced 20,000 units and used 84,160 hours of direct labor at a total cost of $1,599,040. What is its labor rate variance for the period?
  a. $83,200 Favorable
  b. $84,160 Unfavorable
  c. $84,160 Favorable
  d. $83,200 Unfavorable
  e. $ 960 Favorable

Discussion Questions

1. What limits the usefulness to managers of fixed budget performance reports?

2. Identify the main purpose of a flexible budget for managers.

3. Prepare a flexible budget performance report title (in proper form) for Spalding Company for the calendar year 2010. Why is a proper title important for this or any report?

4. What type of analysis does a flexible budget performance report help management perform?

5. In what sense can a variable cost be considered constant?

6. What department is usually responsible for a direct labor rate variance? What department is usually responsible for a direct labor efficiency variance? Explain.

7. What is a price variance? What is a quantity variance?

8. What is the purpose of using standard costs?

9. What is the predetermined standard overhead rate? How is it computed?

10. In general, variance analysis is said to provide information about _____ and _____ variances.

11. How can the manager of a music department of a **Best Buy** retail store use flexible budgets to enhance performance?

12. Is it possible for a retail store such as **Best Buy** to use variances in analyzing its operating performance? Explain.

---

connect™

Beech Company reports the following selected financial results for May. For the level of production achieved in May, the budgeted amounts would be: sales, $1,300,000; variable costs, $750,000; and fixed costs, $300,000. Prepare a flexible budget performance report for May.

Sales (150,000 units)	$1,275,000
Variable costs	712,500
Fixed costs	300,000

QUICK STUDY

QS 28–1
Flexible budget performance report **LO2**

Frontera Company's output for the current period results in a $20,000 unfavorable direct labor rate variance and a $10,000 unfavorable direct labor efficiency variance. Production for the current period was assigned a $400,000 standard direct labor cost. What is the actual total direct labor cost for the current period?

QS 28–2
Labor cost variances **LO4** **LO5**

Juan Company's output for the current period was assigned a $150,000 standard direct materials cost. The direct materials variances included a $12,000 favorable price variance and a $2,000 favorable quantity variance. What is the actual total direct materials cost for the current period?

QS 28–3
Materials cost variances
LO4 **LO5**

QS 28-4
Materials cost variances
LO4 LO5

For the current period, Kayenta Company's manufacturing operations yield a $4,000 unfavorable price variance on its direct materials usage. The actual price per pound of material is $78; the standard price is $77.50. How many pounds of material are used in the current period?

QS 28-5
Computing sales price and volume variances **LO6**

Farad Company specializes in selling used SUVs. During the first six months of 2010, the dealership sold 50 SUVs at an average price of $9,000 each. The budget for the first six months of 2010 was to sell 45 SUVs at an average price of $9,500 each. Compute the dealership's sales price variance and sales volume variance for the first six months of 2010.

---

connect™

EXERCISES

Exercise 28-1
Preparation of flexible budgets **LO1 LO2**

Tempo Company's fixed budget for the first quarter of calendar year 2010 reveals the following. Prepare flexible budgets following the format of Exhibit 28.2 that show variable costs per unit, fixed costs, and three different flexible budgets for sales volumes of 6,000, 7,000, and 8,000 units.

Sales (7,000 units)		$2,800,000
Cost of goods sold		
Direct materials	$280,000	
Direct labor	490,000	
Production supplies	175,000	
Plant manager salary	65,000	1,010,000
Gross profit		1,790,000
Selling expenses		
Sales commissions	140,000	
Packaging	154,000	
Advertising	125,000	419,000
Administrative expenses		
Administrative salaries	85,000	
Depreciation—Office equip.	35,000	
Insurance	20,000	
Office rent	36,000	176,000
Income from operations		$1,195,000

Check Income (at 6,000 units), $972,000

Exercise 28-2
Classification of costs as fixed or variable **LO1**

JPAK Company manufactures and sells mountain bikes. It normally operates eight hours a day, five days a week. Using this information, classify each of the following costs as fixed or variable. If additional information would affect your decision, describe the information.

a. Depreciation on tools   **e.** Management salaries   **i.** Gas used for heating
b. Pension cost   **f.** Incoming shipping expenses   **j.** Direct labor
c. Bike frames   **g.** Office supplies   **k.** Repair expense for tools
d. Screws for assembly   **h.** Taxes on property

Exercise 28-3
Preparation of a flexible budget performance report **LO1 LO2**

Solitaire Company's fixed budget performance report for June follows. The $315,000 budgeted expenses include $294,000 variable expenses and $21,000 fixed expenses. Actual expenses include $27,000 fixed expenses. Prepare a flexible budget performance report that shows any variances between budgeted results and actual results. List fixed and variable expenses separately.

	Fixed Budget	Actual Results	Variances
Sales (in units)	8,400	10,800	
Sales (in dollars)	$420,000	$540,000	$120,000 F
Total expenses	315,000	378,000	63,000 U
Income from operations	$105,000	$162,000	$ 57,000 F

Check Income variance, $21,000 F

Bay City Company's fixed budget performance report for July follows. The $647,500 budgeted expenses include $487,500 variable expenses and $160,000 fixed expenses. Actual expenses include $158,000 fixed expenses. Prepare a flexible budget performance report showing any variances between budgeted and actual results. List fixed and variable expenses separately.

	Fixed Budget	Actual Results	Variances
Sales (in units)	7,500	7,200	
Sales (in dollars)	$750,000	$737,000	$13,000 U
Total expenses	647,500	641,000	6,500 F
Income from operations	$102,500	$ 96,000	$ 6,500 U

Exercise 28-4
Preparation of a flexible budget performance report   **L01   L02**

Check   Income variance, $4,000 F

After evaluating Null Company's manufacturing process, management decides to establish standards of 3 hours of direct labor per unit of product and $15 per hour for the labor rate. During October, the company uses 16,250 hours of direct labor at a $247,000 total cost to produce 5,600 units of product. In November, the company uses 22,000 hours of direct labor at a $335,500 total cost to produce 6,000 units of product. (1) Compute the rate variance, the efficiency variance, and the total direct labor cost variance for each of these two months. (2) Interpret the October direct labor variances.

Exercise 28-5
Computation and interpretation of labor variances   **L04   L05**

Check   October rate variance, $3,250 U

Hart Company made 3,000 bookshelves using 22,000 board feet of wood costing $266,200. The company's direct materials standards for one bookshelf are 8 board feet of wood at $12 per board foot. (1) Compute the direct materials variances incurred in manufacturing these bookshelves. (2) Interpret the direct materials variances.

Exercise 28-6
Computation and interpretation of materials variances
L04   L05

Check   Price variance, $2,200 U

Comp Wiz sells computers. During May 2010, it sold 350 computers at a $1,200 average price each. The May 2010 budget included sales of 365 computers at an average price of $1,100 each. (1) Compute the sales price variance and the sales volume variance for May 2010. (2) Interpret the findings.

Exercise 28-7
Computing and interpreting sales variances   **L06**

connect

Trico Company set the following standard unit costs for its single product.

Direct materials (30 lbs. @ $4 per lb.)	$120.00
Direct labor (5 hrs. @ $14 per hr.)	70.00
Factory overhead—Variable (5 hrs. @ $8 per hr.)	40.00
Factory overhead—Fixed (5 hrs. @ $10 per hr.)	50.00
Total standard cost	$280.00

PROBLEM SET A

Problem 28-1A
Computation of materials and labor variances   **L04   L05**

mhhe.com/wildCA2e

The predetermined overhead rate is based on a planned operating volume of 80% of the productive capacity of 60,000 units per quarter. The following flexible budget information is available.

	Operating Levels		
	70%	80%	90%
Production in units	42,000	48,000	54,000
Standard direct labor hours	210,000	240,000	270,000
Budgeted overhead			
Fixed factory overhead	$2,400,000	$2,400,000	$2,400,000
Variable factory overhead	$1,680,000	$1,920,000	$2,160,000

During the current quarter, the company operated at 90% of capacity and produced 54,000 units of product; actual direct labor totaled 265,000 hours. Units produced are assigned the following standard costs:

Direct materials (1,620,000 lbs. @ $4 per lb.)	$ 6,480,000
Direct labor (270,000 hrs. @ $14 per hr.)	3,780,000
Factory overhead (270,000 hrs. @ $18 per hr.)	4,860,000
Total standard cost	$15,120,000

Actual costs incurred during the current quarter follow:

Direct materials (1,615,000 lbs. @ $4.10)	$ 6,621,500
Direct labor (265,000 hrs. @ $13.75)	3,643,750
Fixed factory overhead costs	2,350,000
Variable factory overhead costs	2,200,000
Total actual costs	$14,815,250

Check (1) Materials variances: Price, $161,500 U; Quantity, $20,000 F.
(2) Labor variances: Rate, $66,250 F; Efficiency, $70,000 F

Required

1. Compute the direct materials cost variance, including its price and quantity variances.
2. Compute the direct labor variance including its rate and efficiency variances.

Problem 28–2A
Preparation and analysis of a flexible budget   **LO1**   **LO2**

Phoenix Company's 2010 master budget included the following fixed budget report. It is based on an expected production and sales volume of 15,000 units.

PHOENIX COMPANY Fixed Budget Report For Year Ended December 31, 2010		
Sales		$3,000,000
Cost of goods sold		
Direct materials	$975,000	
Direct labor	225,000	
Machinery repairs (variable cost)	60,000	
Depreciation—Plant equipment	300,000	
Utilities ($45,000 is variable)	195,000	
Plant management salaries	200,000	1,955,000
Gross profit		1,045,000
Selling expenses		
Packaging	75,000	
Shipping	105,000	
Sales salary (fixed annual amount)	250,000	430,000
General and administrative expenses		
Advertising expense	125,000	
Salaries	241,000	
Entertainment expense	90,000	456,000
Income from operations		$ 159,000

Required

1. Classify all items listed in the fixed budget as variable or fixed. Also determine their amounts per unit or their amounts for the year, as appropriate.

Check (2) Budgeted income at 16,000 units, $260,000

2. Prepare flexible budgets (see Exhibit 28.2) for the company at sales volumes of 14,000 and 16,000 units.
3. The company's business conditions are improving. One possible result is a sales volume of approximately 18,000 units. The company president is confident that this volume is within the relevant range of existing capacity. How much would operating income increase over the 2010 budgeted amount of $159,000 if this level is reached without increasing capacity?

Check (4) Potential operating loss, $(144,000)

4. An unfavorable change in business is remotely possible; in this case, production and sales volume for 2010 could fall to 12,000 units. How much income (or loss) from operations would occur if sales volume falls to this level?

Refer to information in Problem 28-2A. Phoenix Company's actual income statement for 2010 follows.

PHOENIX COMPANY Statement of Income from Operations For Year Ended December 31, 2010		
Sales (18,000 units)		$3,648,000
Cost of goods sold		
Direct materials	$1,185,000	
Direct labor	278,000	
Machinery repairs (variable cost)	63,000	
Depreciation—Plant equipment	300,000	
Utilities (fixed cost is $147,500)	200,500	
Plant management salaries	210,000	2,236,500
Gross profit		1,411,500
Selling expenses		
Packaging	87,500	
Shipping	118,500	
Sales salary (annual)	268,000	474,000
General and administrative expenses		
Advertising expense	132,000	
Salaries	241,000	
Entertainment expense	93,500	466,500
Income from operations		$ 471,000

Problem 28-3A
Preparation and analysis
of a flexible budget
performance report   **LO1   LO2**

mhhe.com/wildCA2e

Required

1. Prepare a flexible budget performance report for 2010.

Analysis Component

2. Analyze and interpret both the (*a*) sales variance and (*b*) direct materials variance.

Check   (1) Variances: Fixed costs,
$36,000 U; Income, $9,000 F

Antuan Company set the following standard costs for one unit of its product. Capacity is 20,000 units per month.

Direct materials (6 lbs. @ $5 per lb.)	$ 30
Direct labor (2 hrs. @ $17 per hr.)	34
Overhead (2 hrs. @ $18.50 per hr.)	37
Total standard cost	$101

Problem 28-4A
Flexible budget preparation;
computation of materials and
labor variances   **LO4   LO5**

The company incurred the following actual costs when it operated at 75% of capacity in October.

Direct materials (91,000 lbs. @ $5.10 per lb.)	$ 464,100
Direct labor (30,500 hrs. @ $17.25 per hr.)	526,125
Overhead costs	560,500
Total costs	$1,550,725

Required

1. Compute the direct materials cost variance, including its price and quantity variances.

2. Compute the direct labor cost variance, including its rate and efficiency variances.

Check   (1) Materials variances: Price,
$9,100 U; Quantity, $5,000 U.
(2) Labor variances: Rate,
$7,625 U; Efficiency, $8,500 U

Problem 28-5A
Materials and labor variances
LO4   LO5

Kegler Company has set the following standard costs per unit for the product it manufactures.

Direct materials (15 lbs. @ $4 per lb.)	$ 60.00
Direct labor (3 hrs. @ $15 per hr.)	45.00
Overhead (3 hrs. @ $3.85 per hr.)	11.55
Total standard cost	$116.55

During May, the company operated at 90% of capacity and produced 9,000 units, incurring the following actual costs.

Direct materials (138,000 lbs. @ $3.75 per lb.)	$ 517,500
Direct labor (31,000 hrs. @ $15.10 per hr.)	468,100
Overhead costs	99,250
Total costs	$1,084,850

Check   (1) Materials variances:
Price, $34,500 F; Quantity,
$12,000 U.
(2) Labor variances:
Rate, $3,100 U; Efficiency,
$60,000 U.

Required

1. Compute the direct materials variance, including its price and quantity variances.
2. Compute the direct labor variance, including its rate and efficiency variances.

PROBLEM SET B

Problem 28-1B
Computation of materials and labor variances   **LO4   LO5**

Kryll Company set the following standard unit costs for its single product.

Direct materials (25 lbs. @ $4 per lb.)	$100.00
Direct labor (6 hrs. @ $8 per hr.)	48.00
Factory overhead—Variable (6 hrs. @ $5 per hr.)	30.00
Factory overhead—Fixed (6 hrs. @ $7 per hr.)	42.00
Total standard cost	$220.00

The predetermined overhead rate is based on a planned operating volume of 80% of the productive capacity of 60,000 units per quarter. The following flexible budget information is available.

	Operating Levels		
	70%	**80%**	**90%**
Production in units	42,000	48,000	54,000
Standard direct labor hours	252,000	288,000	324,000
Budgeted overhead			
Fixed factory overhead	$2,016,000	$2,016,000	$2,016,000
Variable factory overhead	1,260,000	1,440,000	1,620,000

During the current quarter, the company operated at 70% of capacity and produced 42,000 units of product; direct labor hours worked were 250,000. Units produced are assigned the following standard costs:

Direct materials (1,050,000 lbs. @ $4 per lb.)	$4,200,000
Direct labor (252,000 hrs. @ $8 per hr.)	2,016,000
Factory overhead (252,000 hrs. @ $12 per hr.)	3,024,000
Total standard cost	$9,240,000

Actual costs incurred during the current quarter follow:

Direct materials (1,000,000 lbs. @ $4.25)	$4,250,000
Direct labor (250,000 hrs. @ $7.75)	1,937,500
Fixed factory overhead costs	1,960,000
Variable factory overhead costs	1,200,000
Total actual costs	$9,347,500

Check (1) Materials variances: Price, $250,000 U; Quantity, $200,000 F.
(2) Labor variances: Rate, $62,500 F; Efficiency, $16,000 F

Required

1. Compute the direct materials cost variance, including its price and quantity variances.

2. Compute the direct labor variance, including its rate and efficiency variances.

Tohono Company's 2010 master budget included the following fixed budget report. It is based on an expected production and sales volume of 20,000 units.

Problem 28–2B
Preparation and analysis of a flexible budget **L01 L02**

TOHONO COMPANY		
Fixed Budget Report		
For Year Ended December 31, 2010		
Sales		$3,000,000
Cost of goods sold		
Direct materials	$1,200,000	
Direct labor	260,000	
Machinery repairs (variable cost)	57,000	
Depreciation—Machinery	250,000	
Utilities (25% is variable cost)	200,000	
Plant manager salaries	140,000	2,107,000
Gross profit		893,000
Selling expenses		
Packaging	80,000	
Shipping	116,000	
Sales salary (fixed annual amount)	160,000	356,000
General and administrative expenses		
Advertising	81,000	
Salaries	241,000	
Entertainment expense	90,000	412,000
Income from operations		$ 125,000

Required

1. Classify all items listed in the fixed budget as variable or fixed. Also determine their amounts per unit or their amounts for the year, as appropriate.

2. Prepare flexible budgets (see Exhibit 28.2) for the company at sales volumes of 18,000 and 24,000 units.

3. The company's business conditions are improving. One possible result is a sales volume of approximately 28,000 units. The company president is confident that this volume is within the relevant range of existing capacity. How much would operating income increase over the 2010 budgeted amount of $125,000 if this level is reached without increasing capacity?

4. An unfavorable change in business is remotely possible; in this case, production and sales volume for 2010 could fall to 14,000 units. How much income (or loss) from operations would occur if sales volume falls to this level?

Check (2) Budgeted income at 24,000 units, $372,400

(4) Potential operating loss, $(246,100)

Problem 28–3B
Preparation and analysis
of a flexible budget
performance report   **L01   L02**

Refer to information in Problem 28-2B. Tohono Company's actual income statement for 2010 follows.

TOHONO COMPANY Statement of Income from Operations For Year Ended December 31, 2010		
Sales (24,000 units)		$3,648,000
Cost of goods sold		
Direct materials	$1,400,000	
Direct labor	360,000	
Machinery repairs (variable cost)	60,000	
Depreciation—Machinery	250,000	
Utilities (variable cost, $64,000)	218,000	
Plant manager salaries	155,000	2,443,000
Gross profit		1,205,000
Selling expenses		
Packaging	90,000	
Shipping	124,000	
Sales salary (annual)	162,000	376,000
General and administrative expenses		
Advertising expense	104,000	
Salaries	232,000	
Entertainment expense	100,000	436,000
Income from operations		$ 393,000

Required

Check   (1) Variances: Fixed costs, $45,000 U; Income, $20,600 F

1. Prepare a flexible budget performance report for 2010.

Analysis Component

2. Analyze and interpret both the (*a*) sales variance and (*b*) direct materials variance.

Problem 28–4B
Flexible budget preparation;
computation of materials and
labor variances   **L04   L05**

SunCoast Company set the following standard costs for one unit of its product.

Direct materials (4.5 lb. @ $6 per lb.)	$27
Direct labor (1.5 hrs. @ $12 per hr.)	18
Overhead (1.5 hrs. @ $16 per hr.)	24
Total standard cost	$69

The company incurred the following actual costs when it produced 15,000 units in December.

Direct materials (69,000 lbs. @ $6.10)	$ 420,900
Direct labor (22,800 hrs. @ $12.30)	280,440
Overhead costs	355,260
Total costs	$1,056,600

Check   (1) Materials variances: Price, $6,900 U; Quantity, $9,000 U
(2) Labor variances: Rate, $6,840 U; Efficiency, $3,600 U

Required

1. Compute the direct materials cost variance, including its price and quantity variances.

2. Compute the direct labor cost variance, including its rate and efficiency variances.

Guadelupe Company has set the following standard costs per unit for the product it manufactures.

Direct materials (10 lbs. @ $3.00 per lb.)	$30.00
Direct labor (4 hr. @ $6 per hr.)	24.00
Overhead (4 hr. @ $2.50 per hr.)	10.00
Total standard cost	$64.00

During March, the company operated at 90% of capacity and produced 9,000 units, incurring the following actual costs.

Direct materials (92,000 lbs. @ $2.95 per lb.)	$271,400
Direct labor (37,600 hrs. @ $6.05 per hr.)	227,480
Overhead costs	81,700
Total costs	$580,580

Required

1. Compute the direct materials cost variance, including its price and quantity variances.
2. Compute the direct labor variance, including its rate and efficiency variances.

(This serial problem began in Chapter 1 and continues through most of the book. If previous chapter segments were not completed, the serial problem can begin at this point. It is helpful, but not necessary, for you to use the Working Papers that accompany the book.)

SP 28   Success Systems' second quarter 2011 fixed budget performance report for its computer furniture operations follows. The $174,150 budgeted expenses include $144,900 variable expenses and $29,250 fixed expenses. The actual expenses include $30,000 fixed expenses. Prepare a flexible budget performance report that shows any variances between budgeted results and actual results. List fixed and variable expenses separately.

	Fixed Budget	Actual Results	Variances
Desk sales (in units)	144	150	
Chair sales (in units)	72	80	
Desk sales (in dollars)	$162,000	$169,500	$7,500 F
Chair sales (in dollars)	$ 27,000	$ 30,000	$3,000 F
Total expenses	$174,150	$182,450	$8,300 U
Income from operations	$ 14,850	$ 17,050	$2,200 F

BTN 28–1   The usefulness of budgets, variances, and related analyses often depends on the accuracy of management's estimates of future sales activity.

Required

1. Identify and record the prior three years' sales (in dollars) for **Best Buy** using the financial statements in Appendix A.
2. Using the data in part 1, predict Best Buy's sales activity for the next two to three years. (If possible, compare your predictions to actual sales figures for these years.)

ETHICS CHALLENGE
LO4   LO5

BTN 28-2   Setting materials, labor, and overhead standards is challenging. If standards are set too low, companies might purchase inferior products and employees might not work to their full potential. If standards are set too high, companies could be unable to offer a quality product at a profitable rate and employees could be overworked. The ethical challenge is to set a high but reasonable standard. Assume that as a manager, you are asked to set the standard materials price and quantity for the new 1,000 CKB Mega-Max chip, a technically advanced product. To properly set the price and quantity standards, you assemble a team of specialists to provide input.

Required

Identify four types of specialists that you would assemble to provide information to help set the materials price and quantity standards. Briefly explain why you chose each individual.

WORKPLACE COMMUNICATION
LO4   LO5

BTN 28-3   The reason we use the words *favorable* and *unfavorable* when evaluating variances is made clear when we look at the closing of accounts. To see this, consider that (1) all variance accounts are closed at the end of each period (temporary accounts), (2) a favorable variance is always a credit balance, and (3) an unfavorable variance is always a debit balance. Write a one-half page memorandum to your instructor with three parts that answer the three following requirements. (Assume that variance accounts are closed to Cost of Goods Sold.)

Required

1. Does Cost of Goods Sold increase or decrease when closing a favorable variance? Does gross margin increase or decrease when a favorable variance is closed to Cost of Goods Sold? Explain.
2. Does Cost of Goods Sold increase or decrease when closing an unfavorable variance? Does gross margin increase or decrease when an unfavorable variance is closed to Cost of Goods Sold? Explain.
3. Explain the meaning of a favorable variance and an unfavorable variance.

TAKING IT TO THE NET
LO3

BTN 28-4   Access **iSixSigma**'s Website (**iSixSigma.com**) to search for and read information about *benchmarking* to complete the following requirements.

Required

1. Write a one-paragraph explanation (in layperson's terms) of benchmarking.
2. How does standard costing relate to benchmarking?

TEAMWORK IN ACTION
LO4

BTN 28-5   Many service industries link labor rate and time (quantity) standards with their processes. One example is the standard time to board an aircraft. The reason time plays such an important role in the service industry is that it is viewed as a competitive advantage: best service in the shortest amount of time. Although the labor rate component is difficult to observe, the time component of a service delivery standard is often readily apparent, for example, "Lunch will be served in less than five minutes, or it is free."

Required

Break into teams and select two service industries for your analysis. Identify and describe all the time elements each industry uses to create a competitive advantage.

ENTREPRENEURS IN BUSINESS
LO4   LO5

BTN 28-6   Entrepreneur Chris Martin of **Martin Guitar Company** (see chapter opener) uses a costing system with standard costs for direct materials, direct labor, and overhead costs. Two comments frequently are mentioned in relation to standard costing and variance analysis: "Variances are not explanations" and "Management's goal is not to minimize variances."

Required

Write Chris Martin a short memo interpreting these two comments.

1. c; Sales ($10 × $12,500 units)   = $125,000
Variable costs ($6 × 12,500 units) = (75,000)
Fixed costs   (30,000)
    Operating Income $ 20,000

2. c

3. c; Fixed costs remain at $300,000; Variable costs = ($246,000/24,000 units) × 20,000 units = $205,000.

4. e; Budgeted direct materials + Unfavorable variance = Actual cost of direct materials used; or 60,000 units × $10 per unit = $600,000 + $15,000 U = $615,000.

5. c; (AH × AR) − (AH × SR) = $1,599,040 − (84,160 hours × $20 per hour) = $84,160 F.

ANSWERS TO MULTIPLE CHOICE QUIZ

A Look Back

Chapter 28 described budgeting. It explained how managers use budgets to control and monitor business activities.

A Look at This Chapter

This chapter focuses on relevant information for managerial decisions. We show how information on costs and sales is useful in performing cost-volume-profit analyses. We then explain several procedures for making and evaluating short-term managerial decisions.

Chapter 29

Relevant Costing for Managerial Decisions

Learning Objectives

LO 1	Compute contribution margin and describe what it reveals about a company's cost structure.
LO 2	Compute break-even point for a single-product company.
LO 3	Prepare a contribution margin income statement.
LO 4	Describe several applications of cost-volume-profit analysis.
LO 5	Explain the steps in the managerial decision process.
LO 6	Describe the importance of relevant costs for short-term decisions.
LO 7	Evaluate short-term managerial decisions using relevant costs.

"Now batting, a 34-ounce Prairie Sticks double-dipped black maple bat!"—PA Announcer

Batter Up

RED DEER, CANADA—Jared Greenberg, of the Red Deer Riggers, and Dan Zinger of the Red Deer Stags, dream to make it to the major leagues . . . not as players, but as makers of baseball bats. Their start-up company, **Prairie Sticks Bat Company** (**PrairieSticks.com**), started in Jared's workshop with a hand lathe and a piece of wood when local amateur players had trouble getting maple bats from manufacturers. Jared says he began producing bats for his teammates and friends "just like you would do in your middle school shop class."

Prairie Sticks' bats are made from four different types of wood, each with different prices (the company also makes fungo bats and training bats). Jared and Dan use product contribution margins in determining their best sales mix. This is especially important given their constraints on machine hours and labor—they have only one hydraulic tracing lathe and no other employees that make bats.

This past year they sold 1,500 bats. With production growth comes new business questions. Do we take a one-time deal with a buyer? Do we scrap or rework unacceptable inventory? Do we make or buy certain raw materials? These questions need answers. Jared and Dan focus on relevant costs and incremental revenues for insight into answering those questions. If a customer wants a bat in a color Prairie Sticks does not stock, the company charges a higher price to cover the incremental cost of the new color. The company makes novelty bats, unusable for play but fine for gifts and awards, out of inferior wood. These novelty bats sell at reduced prices, but enable the company to avoid costly rework and processing costs. They also sell apparel and hats, made by outside manufacturers.

Prairie Sticks now makes bats for big leaguers. It uses the same wood as the major batmakers; and $100,000 worth of equipment, including the hydraulic lathe, can turn out an unfinished bat in less than two minutes. Soon, they hope to step to the plate to accept additional business.

A recent news release reported that a minor league player had been traded for "10 Prairie Sticks double-dipped maple bats, black," which led to major publicity and a surge in orders. "It's been crazy," says Jared. "[Since] this story has broken . . . we're on the verge of picking up our Major League vendor's license," explains Dan. That would be a tape-measure home run.

[Sources: *Prairie Sticks Bat Company Website,* January 2009; *AlbertaLocalNews.com,* May 2008; *Fox Sports on MSN.com,* May 2008; *Edmonton CityTV.com* interview, May 2008]

Successful managers use cost information when making their decisions. This chapter first shows how managers can use cost and sales information to understand how different strategies affect profit or loss. This analysis is useful in determining a company's break-even point. The chapter then examines common business decisions that require choosing between alternative courses of action. Analysis typically focuses on finding the alternative that offers the highest income from investment or the greatest reduction in costs. The chapter also explains several methods of analysis that can help managers make sound business decisions.

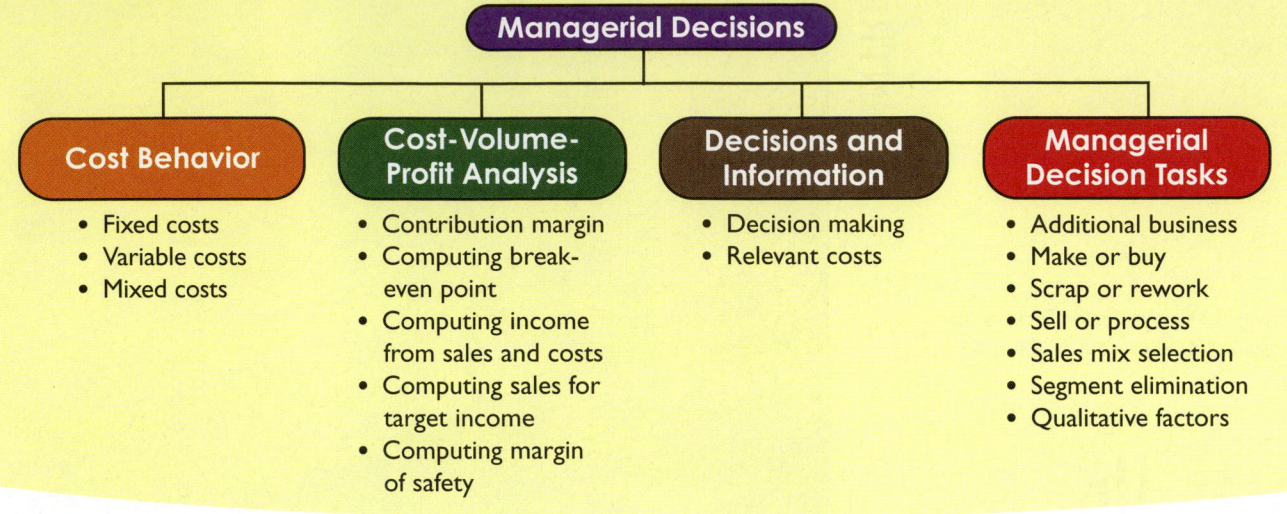

Managerial Decisions

Cost Behavior
- Fixed costs
- Variable costs
- Mixed costs

Cost-Volume-Profit Analysis
- Contribution margin
- Computing break-even point
- Computing income from sales and costs
- Computing sales for target income
- Computing margin of safety

Decisions and Information
- Decision making
- Relevant costs

Managerial Decision Tasks
- Additional business
- Make or buy
- Scrap or rework
- Sell or process
- Sales mix selection
- Segment elimination
- Qualitative factors

Identifying Cost Behavior

Planning a company's future activities and events is crucial to successful management. An important planning tool is **cost-volume-profit (CVP) analysis,** which helps predict how changes in costs and sales levels affect income. In its basic form, CVP analysis involves computing the sales level at which a company neither earns an income nor incurs a loss, called the *break-even point*. Managers use CVP analysis to answer questions like:

■ What sales volume is needed to earn a target income?

■ What is the change in income if selling prices decline and sales volume increases?

Cost-volume-profit analysis is useful in a wide range of business decisions. It requires management to classify all costs as either *fixed* or *variable* with respect to production or sales volume. We introduced cost behavior in Chapter 25 and review it briefly next.

IN THE NEWS

No Free Lunch   Hardly a week goes by without a company advertising a free product with the purchase of another. Examples are a free printer with a digital camera purchase or a free monitor with a computer purchase. Can these companies break even, let alone earn profits? We are reminded of the *no-free-lunch* adage, meaning that companies expect profits from the companion or add-on purchase to make up for the free product.

Fixed Costs

> Fixed costs are constant in total but vary (decline) per unit as more units are produced. Variable costs vary in total but are fixed per unit.

A *fixed cost* does not change when the volume of activity changes. For example, $5,000 in monthly rent paid for a factory building remains the same whether the factory operates with a single eight-hour shift or around the clock. Common examples of fixed costs include depreciation, property taxes, office salaries, and many service department costs.

Variable Costs

A *variable cost* changes in proportion to changes in volume of activity. The direct materials cost of a product is one example of a variable cost. If one unit of product requires materials costing

$20, total materials costs are $200 when 10 units of product are manufactured, $400 for 20 units, $600 for 30 units, and so on. Notice that variable cost *per unit* remains constant but the *total* amount of variable cost changes with the level of production. In addition to direct materials, common variable costs include direct labor (if employees are paid per unit), sales commissions, shipping costs, and some overhead costs.

Mixed Costs

A **mixed cost** includes both fixed and variable cost components. For example, compensation for sales representatives often includes a fixed monthly salary and a variable commission based on sales.

HOW YOU DOIN'?   Answers—p. 821

1. Which of the following statements is typically true? (*a*) Variable cost per unit increases as volume increases, or (*b*) fixed cost per unit decreases as volume increases.

2. Describe the behavior of a fixed cost.

3. If cost per unit of activity remains constant (fixed), why is it called a variable cost?

Cost–Volume Profit Analysis

Break-even analysis is a special case of cost-volume-profit analysis. This section describes how to compute the break-even point.

Contribution Margin and Its Measures

We explained how managers classify costs as being fixed or variable with respect to volume of activity. In manufacturing companies, volume of activity usually refers to the number of units produced. We then classify a cost as either fixed or variable, depending on whether total cost changes as the number of units produced changes. We can then compute a product's contribution margin. **Contribution margin per unit,** or *unit contribution margin,* is the amount a product's unit selling price exceeds its total unit variable cost. This excess amount contributes to covering fixed costs and generating profits on a per unit basis. Exhibit 29.1 shows the contribution margin per unit formula.

LO1 Compute contribution margin and describe what it reveals about a company's cost structure.

$$\text{Contribution margin per unit} = \text{Sales price per unit} - \text{Total variable cost per unit}$$

Exhibit 29.1

Contribution Margin per Unit

Managers often use a **contribution margin ratio,** which is the percent of a unit's selling price that exceeds total unit variable cost. It is the percent of each sales dollar that remains after deducting total unit variable cost. Exhibit 29.2 shows the formula for the contribution margin ratio.

$$\text{Contribution margin ratio} = \frac{\text{Contribution margin per unit}}{\text{Sales price per unit}}$$

Exhibit 29.2

Contribution Margin Ratio

To illustrate the use of contribution margin, let's consider Rydell, which sells footballs for $100 per unit and incurs variable costs of $70 per unit sold. Its fixed costs are $24,000 per month with monthly capacity of 1,800 units (footballs). Rydell's contribution margin per unit is $30, which is computed as follows.

Selling price per unit	$100
Variable cost per unit	70
Contribution margin per unit	$ 30

Its contribution margin ratio is 30%, computed as $30/$100. For each unit sold, Rydell has $30 that contribute to covering fixed cost and profit. For each $1 in sales, Rydell has $0.30 that contributes to fixed cost and profit.

LO2 Compute break-even point for a single-product company.

Computing Break-Even Point

The **break-even point** is the sales level at which a company neither earns a profit nor incurs a loss. The concept of break-even applies to most organizations, activities, and events. One of the most important items of information when launching a project is whether it will break even, that is, whether sales will at least cover total costs. The break-even point can be expressed in either units or dollars of sales.

We compute the break-even point using the formula in Exhibit 29.3. To illustrate break-even analysis, let's again look at Rydell, which sells footballs for $100 per unit and incurs $70 of variable costs per unit sold. Rydell's contribution margin per unit is $30 ($100 − $70). Its fixed costs are $24,000 per month. Rydell breaks even for the month when it sells 800 footballs ($24,000/$30).

Exhibit 29.3

Formula for Computing Break-Even Sales (in units)

$$\text{Break-even point in units} = \frac{\text{Fixed costs}}{\text{Contribution margin per unit}}$$

At a price of $100 per unit, monthly sales of 800 units yields sales dollars of $80,000 (called *break-even sales dollars*). This $80,000 break-even sales can be computed directly using the formula in Exhibit 29.4.

Exhibit 29.4

Formula for Computing Break-Even Sales (in dollars)

$$\text{Break-even point in dollars} = \frac{\text{Fixed costs}}{\text{Contribution margin ratio}}$$

Rydell's break-even point in dollars is computed as $24,000/0.30, or $80,000 of monthly sales. To verify that Rydell's break-even point equals $80,000 (or 800 units), we prepare a simplified income statement in Exhibit 29.5. It shows that the $80,000 revenue from sales of 800 units exactly equals the sum of variable and fixed costs.

Exhibit 29.5

Contribution Margin Income Statement at Break-Even Sales

> A *contribution margin income statement* groups variable and fixed expenses separately and reports the contribution margin.

RYDELL COMPANY Contribution Margin Income Statement (at Break-even) For Month Ended January 31, 2010	
Sales (800 units at $100 each)	$80,000
Variable costs (800 units at $70 each)	56,000
Contribution margin	24,000
Fixed costs	24,000
Net income	$ 0

LO3 Prepare a contribution margin income statement.

The statement in Exhibit 29.5 is called a *contribution margin income statement*. It differs from a conventional income statement in two ways. First, it separately classifies costs and expenses as variable or fixed. Second, it reports contribution margin (Sales − Variable costs). The contribution margin income statement format is used in this chapter's assignment materials because of its usefulness in CVP analysis.

> **HOW YOU DOIN'?**   Answers—p. 821
>
> 4. Fixed cost divided by the contribution margin ratio yields the (*a*) break-even point in dollars, (*b*) contribution margin per unit, or (*c*) break-even point in units.
>
> 5. A company sells a product for $90 per unit with variable costs of $54 per unit. What is the contribution margin ratio?
>
> 6. Refer to the information in question (5) above. If fixed costs for the period are $90,000, what is the break-even point in dollars?

Computing Income from Sales and Costs

Managers consider many strategies in planning business operations. An important question managers often need to answer is "What is the predicted income from a predicted level of sales?" To answer this, we look at four variables in CVP analysis. These variables and their relations to income (pretax) are shown in Exhibit 29.6. We use these relations to predict income from predicted sales and cost levels.

Sales
− Variable costs
Contribution margin
− Fixed costs
Income (pretax)

Exhibit 29.6

Income Relations in CVP Analysis

To illustrate, let's assume that Rydell's management expects to sell 1,500 units in January 2010. What will be January's income if this sales level is achieved? Following Exhibit 29.6, we compute Rydell's expected income in Exhibit 29.7.

RYDELL COMPANY Contribution Margin Income Statement (pretax) For Month Ended January 31, 2010	
Sales (1,500 units at $100 each)	$150,000
Variable costs (1,500 units at $70 each)	105,000
Contribution margin	45,000
Fixed costs	24,000
Income (pretax)	$ 21,000

Exhibit 29.7

Computing Expected Pretax Income from Expected Sales

The $21,000 income is pretax. To find the amount of *after-tax* income from selling 1,500 units, management must apply the proper tax rate. Assume that the tax rate is 25%. Then, we can prepare the after-tax contribution margin income statement shown in Exhibit 29.8.

RYDELL COMPANY Contribution Margin Income Statement (after tax) For Month Ended January 31, 2010	
Sales (1,500 units at $100 each)	$150,000
Variable costs (1,500 units at $70 each)	105,000
Contribution margin	45,000
Fixed costs	24,000
Pretax income	21,000
Income taxes (25%)	5,250
Net income (after tax)	$ 15,750

Exhibit 29.8

Computing Expected After-Tax Income from Expected Sales

Management then assesses whether this income is adequate for the assets invested. Management should also consider whether sales and income can be increased by raising or lowering prices. CVP analysis is a good tool for addressing these kinds of "what-if" questions.

Computing Sales for a Target Income

Many companies' annual plans are based on certain income targets (sometimes called *budgets*). Rydell's plan is to increase income by 10% over last year. When prior year income is known, Rydell easily computes its target income. CVP analysis helps to determine the sales level needed to achieve the target income. Computing this sales level is important because planning for the

"How many units must I sell to earn $50,000?"

year is then based on this level. We use the formula shown in Exhibit 29.9 to compute sales for a target *after-tax* income.

$$\text{Dollar sales at target after-tax income} = \frac{\text{Fixed costs} + \text{Target pretax income}}{\text{Contribution margin ratio}}$$

To illustrate, Rydell has monthly fixed costs of $24,000 and a 30% contribution margin ratio. Assume that it sets a target monthly after-tax income of $9,000 when the tax rate is 25%. This means the pretax income is targeted at $12,000 [$9,000/(1 − 0.25)] with a tax expense of $3,000. Using the formula in Exhibit 29.9, we find that $120,000 of sales is needed to produce a $9,000 after-tax income as shown in Exhibit 29.10.

$$\text{Dollar sales at target after-tax income} = \frac{\$24,000 + \$12,000}{30\%} = \$120,000$$

This means Rydell must sell 1,200 units ($120,000/$100).

Computing the Margin of Safety

All companies wish to do better than break even. The excess of expected sales over the break-even sales level is called a company's **margin of safety.** This is the amount that sales can drop before the company incurs a loss. To illustrate, if Rydell's expected sales are $100,000, the margin of safety is $20,000 above break-even sales of $80,000.

Management must assess whether the margin of safety is adequate in light of factors such as sales variability, competition, consumer tastes, and economic conditions.

IN THE NEWS

Eco-CVP   Ford Escape, Toyota Prius, and Honda Insight are hybrids. Many promise to save owners $1,000 or more a year in fuel costs relative to comparables and they generate less greenhouse gases. Are these models economically feasible? Analysts estimate that **Ford** can break even with its Escape when a $3,000 premium is paid over comparable gas-based models.

HOW YOU DOIN'?   Answers—p. 822

7. A company has fixed costs of $50,000 and a 25% contribution margin ratio. What dollar sales are necessary to achieve an after-tax net income of $120,000 if the tax rate is 20%? (*a*) $800,000, (*b*) $680,000, or (*c*) $600,000.

8. If a company's contribution margin ratio decreases from 50% to 25%, what can be said about unit sales needed to achieve the same target income level?

9. What is a company's margin of safety?

The rest of this chapter focuses on methods that use accounting information to make several important managerial decisions. Most of these are short-term decisions. This differs from methods used for longer-term managerial decisions that are described in Appendix C of this book.

Decisions and Information

This section explains how managers make decisions and the information relevant to those decisions.

Decision Making

Managerial decision making has five steps: (1) define the decision task, (2) identify alternative courses of action, (3) collect relevant information and evaluate each alternative, (4) select the preferred course of action, and (5) analyze and assess decisions made. These five steps are illustrated in Exhibit 29.11.

LO5 Explain the steps in the managerial decision process.

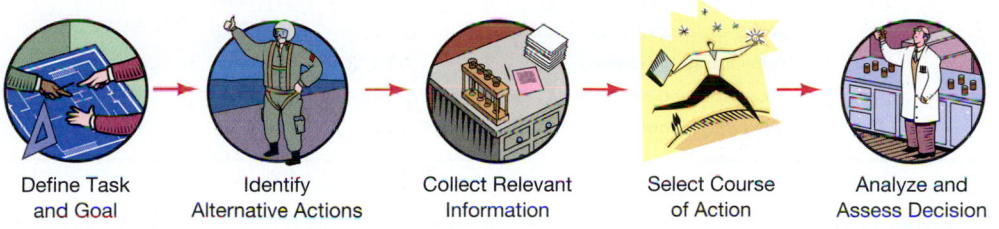

| Define Task and Goal | Identify Alternative Actions | Collect Relevant Information | Select Course of Action | Analyze and Assess Decision |

Exhibit 29.11

Managerial Decision Making

Both managerial and financial accounting information are important in most management decisions. The accounting system provides primarily *financial* information like performance reports and budget analyses for decision making. *Nonfinancial* information, like environmental effects, and social responsibility, is also relevant.

Relevant Costs

Most accounting systems provide historical costs. Although historical costs are important and useful for many tasks such as product pricing and the control and monitoring of business activities, an analysis of *relevant costs,* or *avoidable costs,* is often especially useful. We discuss three types of relevant costs: sunk costs, out-of-pocket costs, and opportunity costs.

LO6 Describe the importance of relevant costs for short-term decisions.

A *sunk cost* arises from a past decision and cannot be avoided or changed; it is irrelevant to future decisions. An example is the cost of computer equipment previously purchased by a company. Most allocated costs, including fixed overhead items such as depreciation and administrative expenses, are sunk costs.

An *out-of-pocket cost* requires a future outlay of cash and is relevant for current and future decision making. For instance, future purchases of computer equipment involve out-of-pocket costs.

An *opportunity cost* is the potential benefit lost by taking a specific action when two or more alternative choices are available. An example is a student giving up wages from a job to attend summer school. Companies continually must choose from alternative courses of action. For instance, a company might be approached by a customer to make a special product. A decision to accept or reject the special order must consider the profit to be made from the special order and the profit given up by devoting time and resources to this order instead of pursuing an alternative project. The profit given up is an opportunity cost.

Management must also consider the relevant benefits associated with a decision. **Relevant benefits** refer to the additional or *incremental* revenue generated by selecting a particular course of action over another. For instance, a student must decide the relevant benefits of taking one course over another. In sum, both relevant costs and relevant benefits are crucial to managerial decision making.

Managerial Decision Tasks

LO7 Evaluate short-term managerial decisions using relevant costs.

Many different tasks require analyzing alternative actions and making decisions. We describe several different types of decisions in this section. We set these tasks in the context of **FasTrac**, an exercise supplies and equipment manufacturer. *We treat each of these decision tasks as separate from each other.*

Additional Business

FasTrac is operating at its normal level of 80% of full capacity. At this level, it produces and sells approximately 100,000 units of product annually. Its per unit and annual total costs are shown in Exhibit 29.12.

Exhibit 29.12

Selected Operating Income Data

	Per Unit	Annual Total
Sales (100,000 units)	$10.00	$1,000,000
Direct materials	(3.50)	(350,000)
Direct labor	(2.20)	(220,000)
Overhead	(1.10)	(110,000)
Selling expenses	(1.40)	(140,000)
Administrative expenses	(0.80)	(80,000)
Total costs and expenses	(9.00)	(900,000)
Operating income	$ 1.00	$ 100,000

A current buyer of FasTrac's products wants to purchase 10,000 more units of its product and export them to another country. This buyer offers to pay $8.50 per unit, or $1.50 less than the current price. FasTrac is considering the proposal because this sale would be several times larger than any single previous sale and it would use idle capacity. Since the units will be exported this new business will not affect current domestic sales.

Management needs to know whether accepting the offer will increase net income. The analysis in Exhibit 29.13 shows that if management uses per unit historical costs, it would reject the sale because it yields a loss. However, historical costs are *not* relevant to this decision. Instead, management should use **incremental costs,** also called *differential costs.* These are the additional costs incurred if a company pursues a certain course of action. FasTrac's incremental costs are those related to the added volume (10,000 units) that this new order would bring.

Exhibit 29.13

Analysis of Additional Business Using Historical Costs

	Per Unit	Total
Sales (10,000 additional units)	$ 8.50	$ 85,000
Direct materials	(3.50)	(35,000)
Direct labor	(2.20)	(22,000)
Overhead	(1.10)	(11,000)
Selling expenses	(1.40)	(14,000)
Administrative expenses	(0.80)	(8,000)
Total costs and expenses	(9.00)	(90,000)
Operating loss	$(0.50)	**$(5,000)**

To make its decision, FasTrac must analyze the costs of this new business in a different manner. The following information regarding the order is available:

■ Manufacturing 10,000 additional units requires direct materials of $3.50 per unit and direct labor of $2.20 per unit (same as for all other units).

■ Manufacturing 10,000 additional units adds $5,000 of incremental overhead costs for power, packaging, and indirect labor (all variable costs).

■ Incremental commissions and selling expenses from this sale of 10,000 additional units would be $2,000 (all variable costs).

■ Incremental administrative expenses of $1,000 for clerical efforts are needed (all fixed costs) with the sale of 10,000 additional units.

We show in Exhibit 29.14 how accepting this new business will affect FasTrac's income.

	Current Business	Additional Business	Combined
Sales	$1,000,000	$ 85,000	$1,085,000
Direct materials	(350,000)	(35,000)	(385,000)
Direct labor	(220,000)	(22,000)	(242,000)
Overhead	(110,000)	(5,000)	(115,000)
Selling expenses	(140,000)	(2,000)	(142,000)
Administrative expense	(80,000)	(1,000)	(81,000)
Total costs and expenses	(900,000)	(65,000)	(965,000)
Operating income	$ 100,000	$ 20,000	$ 120,000

Exhibit 29.14

Analysis of Additional Business Using Relevant Costs

The analysis of relevant costs in Exhibit 29.14 suggests that the additional business be accepted. It would add $85,000 of revenue and add only $65,000 of costs. This would yield $20,000 of additional pretax income. More generally, FasTrac would increase its income with any price above $6.50 per unit ($65,000 incremental cost/10,000 additional units).

The key point is that management must not blindly use historical costs, especially allocated overhead costs. Instead, the accounting system needs to provide information about the incremental costs to be incurred if the additional business is accepted.

Make or Buy

The decision to make or buy a component for a current product is common and depends on incremental costs. To illustrate, FasTrac has excess productive capacity it can use to manufacture Part 417, a component of the main product it sells. The part is currently purchased and delivered to the plant at a cost of $1.20 per unit. FasTrac estimates that making one unit of Part 417 would cost $0.45 for direct materials, $0.50 for direct labor, and an unknown amount for overhead. The task is to determine how much overhead to add to these costs so we can decide whether to make or buy Part 417. If FasTrac's normal predetermined overhead application rate is 100% of direct labor cost, we might be tempted to conclude that overhead cost is $0.50 per unit, computed as 100% of the $0.50 direct labor cost. We would then mistakenly conclude that total cost is $1.45 ($0.45 of materials + $0.50 of labor + $0.50 of overhead). A wrong decision in this case would be to conclude that the company is better off buying the part at $1.20 each than making it for $1.45 each.

Only incremental overhead costs are relevant in this situation. Thus, we must compute an *incremental overhead rate*. Incremental overhead costs might include, for example, additional power for operating machines, extra supplies, added cleanup costs, materials handling, and quality control. We can prepare a per unit analysis in this case as shown in Exhibit 29.15.

If incremental overhead costs are less than $0.25 per unit, the total cost of making the component is less than the purchase price of $1.20. FasTrac's decision rule is to make the part at any incremental overhead cost less than $0.25 per unit. FasTrac must also consider several nonfinancial factors in the make or buy decision. These can include product quality, timeliness of delivery (especially in a just-in-time setting), reactions of customers and suppliers, and other intangibles such as employee morale and workload. It must also consider whether making the part requires incremental fixed costs to expand plant capacity. When these added factors are considered, small cost differences may not matter.

	Make	Buy
Direct materials	$0.45	—
Direct labor	0.50	—
Overhead costs	**[?]**	**—**
Purchase price	—	$1.20
Total incremental costs	**$0.95 + [?]**	**$1.20**

Exhibit 29.15

Make or Buy Analysis

IN THE NEWS

Make or Buy Services   Companies apply make or buy decisions to their services. Many now outsource their payroll activities to a payroll service provider. It is argued that the prices paid for such services are close to what it costs them to do it, but without the headaches.

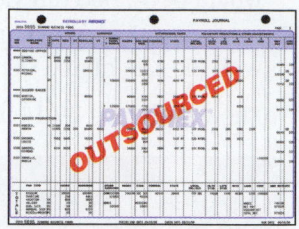

Scrap or Rework

Sometimes companies manufacture products that do not meet their quality standards. Managers often must decide whether to scrap or rework products in process. Costs already incurred in manufacturing substandard units are sunk costs. Sunk costs are irrelevant in any decision on whether to sell the substandard units as scrap or to rework them to meet quality standards.

    To illustrate, assume that FasTrac has 10,000 defective units of a product that have already cost $1 per unit to manufacture. These units can be sold as is (as scrap) for $0.40 each, or they can be reworked for $0.80 per unit and then sold for their full price of $1.50 each. Should FasTrac sell the units as scrap or rework them?

    To make this decision, management must recognize that the already incurred manufacturing costs of $1 per unit are sunk (unavoidable). These costs are *entirely irrelevant* to the decision. In addition, we must include all costs of reworking defects, including interfering with normal operations, in our analysis. For instance, if FasTrac reworks the defects it cannot manufacture 10,000 *new* units with an incremental cost of $1 per unit and a selling price of $1.50 per unit. Thus, it incurs an opportunity cost equal to the lost $5,000 net return from making and selling 10,000 new units. This opportunity cost is the difference between the $15,000 revenue (10,000 units × $1.50) from selling these new units and their $10,000 manufacturing costs (10,000 units × $1). Our analysis is in Exhibit 29.16.

Exhibit 29.16

Scrap or Rework Analysis

	Scrap	Rework
Sale of scrapped/reworked units	$ 4,000	$15,000
Less costs to rework defects		(8,000)
Less opportunity cost of not making new units		**(5,000)**
Incremental net income	**$4,000**	**$ 2,000**

The analysis shows a $2,000 net income difference in favor of scrapping the defects. If we had not included the opportunity costs of $5,000, the rework option would have shown an income of $7,000 instead of $2,000. This would have shown a net income difference of $3,000 in favor of reworking the defects, mistakenly making the reworking appear more favorable than scrapping.

HOW YOU DOIN'?

Answers—p. 822

10. A company receives a special order for 200 units that requires stamping the buyer's name on each unit, yielding an additional fixed cost of $400 to its normal costs. Without the order, the company is operating at 75% of capacity and produces 7,500 units of product at the following costs:

Direct materials	$37,500
Direct labor	60,000
Overhead (30% variable)	20,000
Selling expenses (60% variable)	25,000

The special order will not affect normal unit sales and will not increase fixed overhead and selling expenses. Variable selling expenses on the special order are reduced to one-half the normal amount. The price per unit necessary to earn $1,000 on this order is (*a*) $14.80, (*b*) $15.80, (*c*) $19.80, (*d*) $20.80, or (*e*) $21.80.

11. What are the incremental costs of accepting additional business?

Sell or Process

The managerial decision to sell partially completed products as is or to process them further for sale depends on relevant costs. To illustrate, suppose that FasTrac has 40,000 units of partially finished Product Q. It has already spent $0.75 per unit to manufacture these 40,000 units ($30,000 total cost). FasTrac can sell the 40,000 units to another manufacturer as raw material for $50,000. Alternatively, it can process them further and produce finished products X, Y, and Z at an incremental cost of $2 per unit. The added processing yields the products and revenues shown in Exhibit 29.17. FasTrac must decide whether the added revenues from selling finished products X, Y, and Z exceed the added costs of finishing them.

Exhibit 29.18 shows the two-step analysis for this decision. First, FasTrac computes its incremental revenue from further processing Q into products X, Y, and Z. This amount is the difference between the $220,000 revenue from the further processed products and the $50,000 FasTrac will give up by not selling Q as is (a $50,000 opportunity cost). Second, FasTrac computes its incremental costs from further processing Q into X, Y, and Z. This amount is $80,000 (40,000 units × $2 incremental cost). The analysis shows that FasTrac can earn incremental net income of $90,000 by further processing Q. (Notice that the earlier incurred $30,000 manufacturing cost for the 40,000 units of Product Q does not appear in Exhibit 29.18 because it is a sunk cost and is irrelevant to the decision.)

Product	Price	Units	Revenues
Product X	$4.00	10,000	$ 40,000
Product Y	6.00	22,000	132,000
Product Z	8.00	6,000	48,000
Spoilage	—	2,000	0
Totals		40,000	$220,000

Revenue if processed	$220,000
Revenue if sold as is	(50,000)
Incremental revenue	170,000
Cost to process	(80,000)
Incremental net income	**$ 90,000**

HOW YOU DOIN'?   Answers—p. 822

12. A company has already incurred a $1,000 cost in partially producing its four products. Their selling prices when partially and fully processed follow with additional costs necessary to finish these partially processed units:

Product	Unfinished Selling Price	Finished Selling Price	Further Processing Costs
Alpha	$300	$600	$150
Beta	450	900	300
Gamma	275	425	125
Delta	150	210	75

Which product(s) should *not* be processed further: (*a*) Alpha, (*b*) Beta, (*c*) Gamma, or (*d*) Delta?

13. Under what conditions is a sunk cost relevant to decision making?

Sales Mix Selection

When a company sells a mix of products, some will be more profitable than others. Management often concentrates sales efforts on more profitable products. If production facilities or other factors are limited, increasing the production and sale of one product usually requires reducing the production and sale of others. Here, management must identify the most profitable combination, or **sales mix** of products. To identify the best sales mix, management must know the *contribution margin* of each product, the facilities required to produce each product, any constraints on these facilities, and its markets. Recall that a product's contribution margin equals its selling price minus its variable costs.

IN THE NEWS

Companies such as **Gap**, **Abercrombie & Fitch**, and **American Eagle** must continuously monitor and manage the sales mix of their product lists. Selling their products in hundreds of countries and territories further complicates their decision process. The contribution margin of each product is crucial to their product mix strategies.

To illustrate, assume that FasTrac makes and sells products A and B. The same machines are used to produce both products. A and B have the following selling prices and variable costs per unit:

	Product A	Product B
Selling price per unit	$5.00	$7.50
Variable costs per unit	3.50	5.50
Contribution margin per unit	$1.50	$2.00

Variable costs are included in the analysis because they are the incremental costs of producing these products within the existing capacity of 100,000 machine hours per month. We consider three separate cases.

Case 1: Assume that (1) each product requires 1 machine hour per unit for production and (2) the markets for these products are unlimited. Under these conditions, FasTrac should produce only Product B because of its larger contribution margin of $2 per unit. At full capacity, FasTrac would produce $200,000 of total contribution margin per month, computed as $2 per unit times 100,000 machine hours.

Case 2: Assume that (1) Product A requires 1 machine hour per unit, (2) Product B requires 2 machine hours per unit, and (3) the markets for these products are unlimited. Under these conditions, FasTrac should produce only Product A because it has a contribution margin of $1.50 per machine hour compared with only $1 per machine hour for Product B. Exhibit 29.19 shows the relevant analysis.

Exhibit 29.19

Sales Mix Analysis

	Product A	Product B
Selling price per unit	$5.00	$7.50
Variable costs per unit	3.50	5.50
Contribution margin per unit	$1.50	$2.00
Machine hours per unit	1.0	2.0
Contribution margin per machine hour	**$1.50**	**$1.00**

At its full capacity of 100,000 machine hours, FasTrac would produce 100,000 units of Product A, yielding $150,000 of total contribution margin per month. In contrast, if it uses all 100,000 hours to produce Product B, only 50,000 units would be produced yielding a contribution margin of $100,000. These results suggest that when a company faces excess demand and limited capacity, only the most profitable product per input should be manufactured.

Case 3: The need for a mix of different products arises when market demand does not allow a company to sell all that it produces. For instance, assume that (1) Product A requires 1 machine hour per unit, (2) Product B requires 2 machine hours per unit, and (3) the market for Product A is limited to 80,000 units. Under these conditions, FasTrac should produce no more than 80,000 units of Product A. This would leave another 20,000 machine hours of capacity for making Product B. FasTrac should use this spare capacity to produce 10,000 units of Product B. This sales mix would maximize FasTrac's total contribution margin per month at an amount of $140,000.

Segment Elimination

When a segment such as a department or division is performing poorly, management must consider eliminating it. Segment information on either net income (loss) or its contribution to overhead is not sufficient for this decision. Instead, we must look at the segment's avoidable expenses and unavoidable expenses. **Avoidable expenses,** also called *escapable expenses,* are amounts the company would not incur if it eliminated the segment. **Unavoidable expenses,** also called *inescapable expenses,* are amounts that would continue even if the segment is eliminated.

To illustrate, FasTrac considers eliminating its treadmill division because its $48,300 total expenses are higher than its $47,800 sales. Classification of this division's operating expenses into avoidable or unavoidable expenses is shown in Exhibit 29.20.

	Total	Avoidable Expenses	Unavoidable Expenses
Cost of goods sold	$30,000	$30,000	—
Direct expenses			
Salaries expense	7,900	7,900	—
Depreciation expense—Equipment	200	—	$ 200
Indirect expenses			
Rent and utilities expense	3,150	—	3,150
Advertising expense	400	400	—
Insurance expense	400	300	100
Service department costs			
Share of office department expenses	3,060	2,200	860
Share of purchasing expenses	3,190	1,000	2,190
Total	**$48,300**	**$41,800**	**$6,500**

Exhibit 29.20

Classification of Segment Operating Expenses for Analysis

FasTrac's analysis shows that it can avoid $41,800 expenses if it eliminates the treadmill division. Because this division's sales are $47,800, eliminating it will cause FasTrac to lose $6,000 of income ($47,800 − $41,800). *Our decision rule is that a segment is a candidate for elimination if its revenues are less than its avoidable expenses.* FasTrac should not eliminate its treadmill division. Avoidable expenses can be viewed as the costs to generate this segment's revenues.

When considering elimination of a segment, we must assess its impact on other segments. A segment could be unprofitable on its own, but might contribute to other segments' revenues and profits. It is possible then to continue a segment even when its revenues are less than its avoidable expenses. Similarly, a profitable segment might be discontinued if its space, assets, or staff can be more profitably used by expanding existing segments or by creating new ones. Our decision to keep or eliminate a segment requires a more complex analysis than simply looking at a segment's performance report. Such reports provide useful information, but they do not provide all the information necessary for this decision.

Qualitative Decision Factors

Managers must consider qualitative factors in their decisions. Consider a decision on whether to buy a component from an outside supplier or continue to make it. Several qualitative decision factors must be considered. For example, the quality, delivery, and reputation of the proposed supplier are important. The effects from deciding not to make the component can include potential layoffs and lower worker morale. Consider another situation in which a company is considering a one-time sale to a new customer at a special low price. Qualitative factors to consider in this situation include the effects of a low price on the company's image and the threat that regular customers might demand a similar price. The company must also consider whether this customer is really a one-time customer. If not, can it continue to offer this low price in the long run? Clearly, management cannot rely solely on financial data to make such decisions.

HOW YOU DOIN'? Answers—p. 822

14. What is the difference between avoidable and unavoidable expenses?

15. A segment is a candidate for elimination if (*a*) its revenues are less than its avoidable expenses, (*b*) it has a net loss, (*c*) its unavoidable expenses are higher than its revenues.

Demonstration Problem 1

Sport Caps Co. manufactures and sells caps for different sporting events. The fixed costs of operating the company are $150,000 per month, and the variable costs are $5 per cap. The caps are sold for $8 per unit. The fixed costs provide a production capacity of up to 100,000 caps per month.

Required

1. Use the formulas in the chapter to compute the following:
   a. Contribution margin per cap.
   b. Break-even point in terms of the number of caps produced and sold.
   c. Amount of net income at 30,000 caps sold per month (ignore taxes).
   d. Amount of net income at 85,000 caps sold per month (ignore taxes).
   e. Number of caps to be produced and sold to provide $45,000 of after-tax income, assuming an income tax rate of 25%.
2. Use the formulas in the chapter to compute the
   a. Contribution margin ratio.
   b. Break-even point in terms of sales dollars.
   c. Amount of net income at $250,000 of sales per month (ignore taxes).
   d. Amount of net income at $600,000 of sales per month (ignore taxes).
   e. Dollars of sales needed to provide $45,000 of after-tax income, assuming an income tax rate of 25%.

Planning the Solution

- Identify the formulas in the chapter for the required items expressed in units and solve them using the data given in the problem.
- Identify the formulas in the chapter for the required items expressed in dollars and solve them using the data given in the problem.

Solution to Demonstration Problem 1

1. a. Contribution margin per cap $= $ Selling price per unit $-$ Variable cost per unit
   $= \$8 - \$5 = \underline{\$3}$

   b. Break-even point in caps $= \dfrac{\text{Fixed costs}}{\text{Contribution margin per cap}} = \dfrac{\$150,000}{\$3} = \underline{50,000 \text{ caps}}$

   c. Net income at 30,000 caps sold $= $ (Units $\times$ Contribution margin per unit) $-$ Fixed costs
   $= (30,000 \times \$3) - \$150,000 = \underline{\$(60,000) \text{ loss}}$

   d. Net income at 85,000 caps sold $= $ (Units $\times$ Contribution margin per unit) $-$ Fixed costs
   $= (85,000 \times \$3) - \$150,000 = \underline{\$105,000 \text{ profit}}$

   e. Pretax income $= \$45,000/(1 - 0.25) = \$60,000$
   Income taxes $= \$60,000 \times 25\% = \$15,000$

   Units needed for $45,000 income $= \dfrac{\text{Fixed costs} + \text{Target pretax income}}{\text{Contribution margin per cap}}$
   $= \dfrac{\$150,000 + \$60,000}{\$3} = \underline{70,000 \text{ caps}}$

2. a. Contribution margin ratio $= \dfrac{\text{Contribution margin per unit}}{\text{Selling price per unit}} = \dfrac{\$3}{\$8} = \underline{0.375}, \text{ or } \underline{37.5\%}$

b. Break-even point in dollars $= \dfrac{\text{Fixed costs}}{\text{Contribution margin ratio}} = \dfrac{\$150,000}{37.5\%} = \underline{\$400,000}$

c. Net income at sales of $250,000 = (Sales $\times$ Contribution margin ratio) $-$ Fixed costs
$= (\$250,000 \times 37.5\%) - \$150,000 = \underline{\$(56,250) \text{ loss}}$

d. Net income at sales of $600,000 = (Sales $\times$ Contribution margin ratio) $-$ Fixed costs
$= (\$600,000 \times 37.5\%) - \$150,000 = \underline{\$75,000 \text{ income}}$

e. Dollars of sales to yield
$45,000 after-tax income
$= \dfrac{\text{Fixed costs} + \text{Target pretax income}}{\text{Contribution margin ratio}}$
$= \dfrac{\$150,000 + \$60,000}{37.5\%} = \underline{\$560,000}$

Demonstration Problem 2

Determine the appropriate action in each of the following managerial decision situations.

1. Packer Company is operating at 80% of its manufacturing capacity of 100,000 product units per year. A chain store has offered to buy an additional 10,000 units at $22 each and sell them to customers so as not to compete with Packer Company. The following data are available.

Costs at 80% Capacity	Per Unit	Total
Direct materials	$ 8.00	$ 640,000
Direct labor	7.00	560,000
Overhead (fixed and variable)	12.50	1,000,000
Totals	$27.50	$2,200,000

In producing 10,000 additional units, fixed overhead costs would remain at their current level but incremental variable overhead costs of $3 per unit would be incurred. Should the company accept or reject this order?

2. Green Company uses Part JR3 in manufacturing its products. It has always purchased this part from a supplier for $40 each. It recently upgraded its own manufacturing capabilities and has enough excess capacity (including trained workers) to begin manufacturing Part JR3 instead of buying it. The company prepares the following cost projections of making the part, assuming that overhead is allocated to the part at the normal predetermined rate of 200% of direct labor cost.

Direct materials	$11
Direct labor	15
Overhead (fixed and variable) (200% of direct labor)	30
Total	$56

The required volume of output to produce the part will not require any incremental fixed overhead. Incremental variable overhead cost will be $17 per unit. Should the company make or buy this part?

3. Gold Company's manufacturing process causes a relatively large number of defective parts to be produced. The defective parts can be (a) sold for scrap, (b) melted to recover the recycled metal for reuse, or (c) reworked to be good units. Reworking defective parts reduces the output of other good units because no excess capacity exists. Each unit reworked means that one new unit cannot be produced. The following information reflects 500 defective parts currently available.

Proceeds of selling as scrap	$2,500
Additional cost of melting down defective parts	400
Cost of purchases avoided by using recycled metal from defects	4,800
Cost to rework 500 defective parts	
Direct materials	0
Direct labor	1,500
Incremental overhead	1,750
Cost to produce 500 new parts	
Direct materials	6,000
Direct labor	5,000
Incremental overhead	3,200
Selling price per good unit	40

Should the company melt the parts, sell them as scrap, or rework them?

Planning the Solution

- Determine whether Packer Company should accept the additional business by finding the incremental costs of materials, labor, and overhead that will be incurred if the order is accepted. Omit fixed costs that the order will not increase. If the incremental revenue exceeds the incremental cost, accept the order.

- Determine whether Green Company should make or buy the component by finding the incremental cost of making each unit. If the incremental cost exceeds the purchase price, the component should be purchased. If the incremental cost is less than the purchase price, make the component.

- Determine whether Gold Company should sell the defective parts, melt them down and recycle the metal, or rework them. To compare the three choices, examine all costs incurred and benefits received from the alternatives in working with the 500 defective units versus the production of 500 new units. For the scrapping alternative, include the costs of producing 500 new units and subtract the $2,500 proceeds from selling the old ones. For the melting alternative, include the costs of melting the defective units, add the net cost of new materials in excess over those obtained from recycling, and add the direct labor and overhead costs. For the reworking alternative, add the costs of direct labor and incremental overhead. Select the alternative that has the lowest cost. The cost assigned to the 500 defective units is sunk and not relevant in choosing among the three alternatives.

Solution to Demonstration Problem 2

1. This decision involves accepting additional business. Since current unit costs are $27.50, it appears initially as if the offer to sell for $22 should be rejected, but the $27.50 cost includes fixed costs. When the analysis includes only *incremental* costs, the per unit cost is as shown in the following table. The offer should be accepted because it will produce $4 of additional profit per unit (computed as $22 price less $18 incremental cost), which yields a total profit of $40,000 for the 10,000 additional units.

Direct materials	$ 8.00
Direct labor	7.00
Variable overhead (given)	3.00
Total incremental cost	$18.00

2. For this make or buy decision, the analysis must not include the $13 nonincremental overhead per unit ($30 − $17). When only the $17 incremental overhead is included, the relevant unit cost of manufacturing the part is shown in the following table. It would be better to continue buying the part for $40 instead of making it for $43.

Direct materials	$11.00
Direct labor	15.00
Variable overhead	17.00
Total incremental cost	$43.00

3. The goal of this scrap or rework decision is to identify the alternative that produces the greatest net benefit to the company. To compare the alternatives, we determine the net cost of obtaining 500 marketable units as follows:

Incremental Cost to Produce 500 Marketable Units	Sell as Is	Melt and Recycle	Rework Units
Direct materials			
New materials	$ 6,000	$6,000	
Recycled metal materials		(4,800)	
Net materials cost		1,200	
Melting costs		400	
Total direct materials cost	6,000	1,600	
Direct labor	5,000	5,000	$1,500
Incremental overhead	3,200	3,200	1,750
Cost to produce 500 marketable units	14,200	9,800	3,250
Less proceeds of selling defects as scrap	(2,500)		
Opportunity costs*			5,800
Net cost	$11,700	$9,800	$9,050

The incremental cost of 500 marketable parts is smallest if the defects are reworked.

* The $5,800 opportunity cost is the lost contribution margin from not being able to produce and sell 500 units because of reworking, computed as ($40 − $28.40) × 500 units.

Summary

LO1 Compute contribution margin and describe what it reveals about a company's cost structure. Contribution margin per unit is a product's sales price less its total variable costs. Contribution margin ratio is a product's contribution margin per unit divided by its sales price. Unit contribution margin is the amount received from each sale that contributes to fixed costs and income. The contribution margin ratio reveals what portion of each sales dollar is available as contribution to fixed costs and income.

LO2 Compute break-even point for a single-product company. A company's break-even point for a period is the sales volume at which total revenues equal total costs. To compute a break-even point in terms of sales units, we divide total fixed costs by the contribution margin per unit. To compute a break-even point in terms of sales dollars, divide total fixed costs by the contribution margin ratio.

LO3 Prepare a contribution margin income statement. A contribution margin income statement classifies costs and expenses as variable or fixed. It also reports the contribution margin.

LO4 Describe several applications of cost-volume-profit analysis. Cost-volume-profit analysis can be used to predict what can happen under alternative strategies concerning sales volume, selling prices, variable costs, or fixed costs. Applications include "what-if" analysis, computing sales for a target income, and break-even analysis.

LO5 Explain the steps in the managerial decision process. The five steps are: (1) define the decision task; (2) identify alternatives; (3) collect relevant information and evaluate alternatives; (4) select a course of action; and (5) analyze decisions made.

LO6 Describe the importance of relevant costs for short-term decisions. A company must rely on relevant costs pertaining to alternative courses of action rather than historical costs. Out-of-pocket expenses and opportunity costs are relevant because these are avoidable; sunk costs are irrelevant because they result from past decisions and are therefore unavoidable. Managers must also consider the relevant benefits associated with alternative decisions.

LO7 Evaluate short-term managerial decisions using relevant costs. Relevant costs are useful in making decisions such as to accept additional business, make or buy, and sell as is or process further. For example, the relevant factors in deciding whether to produce and sell additional units of product are incremental costs and incremental revenues from the additional volume.

Guidance Answers to HOW YOU DOIN'?

1. *b*

2. A fixed cost remains unchanged in total amount regardless of output levels. However, fixed *cost per unit* declines with increased output.

3. Such a cost is considered variable because the *total* cost changes in proportion to volume changes.

4. *a*

5. ($90 − $54)/$90 = 40%

6. $90,000/40% = $225,000

7. a; Two steps are required for explanation:

(1) Pretax income = $120,000/(1 − 0.20) = $150,000

(2) $\dfrac{\$50,000 + \$150,000}{25\%} = \$800,000$

8. If the contribution margin ratio decreases from 50% to 25%, unit sales would have to double.

9. A company's margin of safety is the excess of the predicted sales level over its break-even sales level.

10. *e*; Variable costs per unit for this order of 200 units follow:

Direct materials ($37,500/7,500)	$ 5.00
Direct labor ($60,000/7,500)	8.00
Variable overhead [(0.30 × $20,000)/7,500]	0.80
Variable selling expenses [(0.60 × $25,000 × 0.5)/7,500]	1.00
Total variable costs per unit	$14.80

Cost to produce special order: (200 × $14.80) + $400

= $3,360.

Price per unit to earn $1,000: ($3,360 + $1,000)/200 = $21.80.

11. They are the additional (new) costs of accepting new business.

12. *d*;

	Incremental benefits		Incremental costs
Alpha	$300 ($600 − $300)	>	$150 (given)
Beta	$450 ($900 − $450)	>	$300 (given)
Gamma	$150 ($425 − $275)	>	$125 (given)
Delta	$ 60 ($210 − $150)	<	$ 75 (given)

13. A sunk cost is *never* relevant because it results from a past decision and is already incurred.

14. Avoidable expenses are ones a company will not incur by eliminating a segment; unavoidable expenses will continue even after a segment is eliminated.

15. *a*

Key Terms

Avoidable expense (p. 817) Expense (or cost) that is relevant for decision making; expense that is not incurred if a department, product, or service is eliminated.

Break-even point (p. 808) Output level at which sales equals fixed plus variable costs; where income equals zero.

Contribution margin per unit (p. 807) Amount that the sale of one unit contributes toward recovering fixed costs and earning profit; defined as sales price per unit minus variable expense per unit.

Contribution margin ratio (p. 807) Product's contribution margin divided by its sale price.

Cost-volume-profit (CVP) analysis (p. 806) Planning method that includes predicting the volume of activity, the costs incurred, sales earned, and profits received.

Incremental cost (p. 812) Additional cost incurred only if a company pursues a specific course of action.

Margin of safety (p. 810) Excess of expected sales over the level of break-even sales.

Mixed cost (p. 807) Cost that behaves like a combination of fixed and variable costs.

Relevant benefits (p. 811) Additional or incremental revenue generated by selecting a particular course of action over another.

Sales mix (p. 815) Ratio of sales volumes for the various products sold by a company.

Unavoidable expense (p. 817) Expense (or cost) that is not relevant for business decisions; an expense that would continue even if a department, product, or service is eliminated.

Multiple Choice Quiz   **Answers on p. 837**   **mhhe.com/wildCA2e**

Additional Multiple Choice Quizzes are available at the book's Website.

1. A company's only product sells for $150 per unit. Its variable costs per unit are $100, and its fixed costs total $75,000. What is its contribution margin per unit?
   a. $50
   b. $250
   c. $100
   d. $150
   e. $25

2. Using information from question 1, what is the company's break-even point in units?
   a. 500 units
   b. 750 units
   c. 1,500 units
   d. 3,000 units
   e. 1,000 units

3. A product sells for $400 per unit and its variable costs per unit are $260. The company's fixed costs are $840,000. If the

company desires $70,000 pretax income, what is the required dollar sales?
   a. $2,400,000
   b. $200,000
   c. $2,600,000
   d. $2,275,000
   e. $1,400,000

4. A company inadvertently produced 3,000 defective MP3 players. The players cost $12 each to produce. A recycler offers to purchase the defective players as they are for $8 each. The production manager reports that the defects can be corrected for $10 each, enabling them to be sold at their regular market price of $19 each. The company should:
   a. Correct the defect and sell them at the regular price.
   b. Sell the players to the recycler for $8 each.
   c. Sell 2,000 to the recycler and repair the rest.

d. Sell 1,000 to the recycler and repair the rest.

e. Throw the players away.

5. A company's productive capacity is limited to 480,000 machine hours. Product X requires 10 machine hours to produce; and Product Y requires 2 machine hours to produce. Product X sells for $32 per unit and has variable costs of $12 per unit; Product Y sells for $24 per unit and has variable costs of

$10 per unit. Assuming that the company can sell as many of either product as it produces, it should:

a. Produce X and Y in the ratio of 57% and 43%.

b. Produce X and Y in the ratio of 83% X and 17% Y.

c. Produce equal amounts of Product X and Product Y.

d. Produce only Product X.

e. Produce only Product Y.

Discussion Questions

1. How is cost-volume-profit analysis useful?

2. What is a variable cost? Identify two variable costs.

3. When output volume increases, do variable costs per unit increase, decrease, or stay the same within the relevant range of activity? Explain.

4. When output volume increases, do fixed costs per unit increase, decrease, or stay the same within the relevant range of activity? Explain.

5. Define and describe *contribution margin* per unit.

6. Define and explain the *contribution margin ratio*.

7. In cost-volume-profit analysis, what is the estimated profit at the break-even point?

8. Each of two similar companies has sales of $20,000 and total costs of $15,000 for a month. Company A's total costs include $10,000 of variable costs and $5,000 of fixed costs. If Company B's total costs include $4,000 of variable costs and $11,000 of fixed costs, which company will enjoy more profit if sales double?

9. _____ of _____ reflects expected sales in excess of the level of break-even sales.

10. **Apple** produces iPods for sale. Identify some of the variable and fixed product costs associated with that production. [*Hint:* Limit costs to product costs.]

11. What is an out-of-pocket cost? What is an opportunity cost? Are opportunity costs recorded in the accounting records?

12. Why are sunk costs irrelevant in deciding whether to sell a product in its present condition or to make it into a new product through additional processing?

13. Identify the incremental costs incurred by **Best Buy** for shipping one additional iPod from a warehouse to a retail store along with the store's normal order of 75 iPods.

14. Identify the five steps involved in managerial decision making.

15. Assume that **Apple** manufactures and sells 500,000 units of a product at $30 per unit in domestic markets. It costs $20 per unit to manufacture ($13 variable cost per unit, $7 fixed cost per unit). Can you describe a situation under which the company is willing to sell an additional 25,000 units of the product in an international market at $15 per unit?

16. What is the difference between an opportunity cost and a sunk cost?

---

connect

Determine whether each of the following is best described as a fixed, variable, or mixed cost with respect to product units.

1. Rubber used to manufacture athletic shoes.

2. Maintenance of factory machinery.

3. Packaging expense.

4. Wages of an assembly-line worker paid on the basis of acceptable units produced.

5. Factory supervisor's salary.

6. Taxes on factory building.

7. Depreciation expense of warehouse.

QUICK STUDY

QS 29–1
Cost behavior identification   **LO1**

Compute and interpret the contribution margin ratio using the following data: sales, $5,000; total variable cost, $3,000.

QS 29–2
Contribution margin ratio   **LO1**

SBD Phone Company sells its cordless phone for $90 per unit. Fixed costs total $162,000, and variable costs are $36 per unit. Determine (1) contribution margin per unit and (2) break-even point in units.

QS 29–3
Contribution margin per unit and break-even units   **LO1   LO2**

QS 29-4
Contribution margin ratio and break-even dollars **LO1   LO2**

Refer to QS 29-3. Determine (1) contribution margin ratio and (2) break-even point in dollars.

QS 29-5
CVP analysis and target income **LO4**

Refer to QS 29-3. Assume that SBD Phone Co. is subject to a 30% income tax rate. Compute the units of product that must be sold to earn after-tax income of $140,000.

QS 29-6
Selection of sales mix **LO6   LO7**

Excel Memory Company can sell all units of computer memory X and Y that it can produce, but it has limited production capacity. It can produce two units of X per hour *or* three units of Y per hour, and it has 4,000 production hours available. Contribution margin is $5 for Product X and $4 for Product Y. What is the most profitable sales mix for this company?

QS 29-7
Analysis of incremental costs **LO6   LO7**

Kando Company incurs a $9 per unit cost for Product A, which it currently manufactures and sells for $13.50 per unit. Instead of manufacturing and selling this product, Kando can purchase Product B for $5 per unit and sell it for $12 per unit. If it does so, unit sales would remain unchanged and $5 of the $9 per unit costs assigned to Product A would be eliminated. Should the company continue to manufacture Product A or purchase Product B for resale?

QS 29-8
Scrap or rework **LO6   LO7**

Erin Company has the choice of either selling 1,000 defective units as scrap or rebuilding them. The company could sell the defective units as they are for $4 per unit. Alternatively, it could rebuild them with incremental costs of $1 per unit for materials, $2 per unit for labor, and $1.50 per unit for overhead, and then sell the rebuilt units for $8.00 each. What should the company do?

QS 29-9
Additional business **LO6   LO7**

Thompson Company had the following results of operations for the past year.

Sales (16,000 units at $10)		$ 160,000
Direct materials and direct labor	$96,000	
Overhead (20% variable)	16,000	
Selling and administrative expenses (all fixed)	32,000	(144,000)
Operating income		$ 16,000

A foreign company (whose sales will not affect Thompson's market) offers to buy 4,000 units at $7.50 per unit. In addition to variable manufacturing costs, selling these units would increase fixed overhead by $600 and selling and administrative costs by $300. What will be the change in Thompson's profits if it accepts the offer?

QS 29-10
Sell or process further **LO6   LO7**

Jacob processes three different products that can either be sold "as is" or processed further. Listed below are sales and additional cost data. Which product should not be processed further?

Product	Sales Value with No Further Processing	Additional Processing Costs	Sales Value after Further Processing
Acta	$1,350	$900	$2,700
Corda	450	225	630
Fando	900	450	1,800

QS 29-11
Make or buy **LO6   LO7**

Alpha Co. can produce a unit of Beta for the following costs.

Direct material	$ 8
Direct labor	24
Overhead	40
Total costs per unit	$72

An outside supplier offers to provide Alpha with all the Beta units it needs at $60 per unit. If Alpha buys from the supplier, Alpha will still incur 40% of its overhead. Should Alpha make product Beta or instead buy product Beta from the outside supplier?

connect™

Emily Company management predicts that it will incur fixed costs of $160,000 and earn pretax income of $164,000 in the next period. Its expected contribution margin ratio is 25%. Use this information to compute the amounts of (1) total dollar sales and (2) total variable costs.

EXERCISES

Exercise 29–1
Predicting sales and variable costs using contribution margin   **L01**

Bloom Company manufactures a single product that sells for $180 per unit and whose total variable costs are $135 per unit. The company's annual fixed costs are $562,500. Use this information to compute the company's (a) contribution margin, (b) contribution margin ratio, (c) break-even point in units, and (d) break-even point in dollars of sales.

Exercise 29–2
Contribution margin and break-even   **L01   L02**

Refer to Exercise 29-2. (1) Prepare a contribution margin income statement for Bloom Company showing sales, variable costs, and fixed costs at the break-even point. (2) If Bloom's fixed costs increase by $135,000, what amount of sales (in dollars) is needed to break even? Explain.

Exercise 29–3
Income reporting and break-even analysis
L01   L02   L03

Bloom Company's management (in Exercise 29-2) targets an annual after-tax income of $810,000. The company is subject to a 20% income tax rate. Assume that fixed costs remain at $562,500. Compute the (1) unit sales to earn the target after-tax net income and (2) dollar sales to earn the target after-tax net income.

Exercise 29–4
Computing sales to achieve target income   **L04**

Bloom Company's sales manager (in Exercise 29-2) predicts that annual sales of the company's product will soon reach 40,000 units and its price will increase to $200 per unit. According to the production manager, the variable costs are expected to increase to $140 per unit but fixed costs will remain at $562,500. The income tax rate is 20%. What amounts of pretax and after-tax income can the company expect to earn from these predicted changes? (*Hint:* Prepare a forecasted contribution margin income statement as in Exhibit 29.8.)

Exercise 29–5
Forecasted income statement
L03   L04

Check   Forecast income, $1,470,000

Nombre Company management predicts $390,000 of variable costs, $430,000 of fixed costs, and a pretax income of $155,000 in the next period. Management also predicts that the contribution margin per unit will be $9. Use this information to compute the (1) total expected dollar sales for next period and (2) number of units expected to be sold next period.

Exercise 29–6
Predicting unit and dollar sales
L04

Cassie Company expects to sell 200,000 units of its product next year, which would generate total sales of $17 million. Management predicts that pretax net income for next year will be $1,250,000 and that the contribution margin per unit will be $25. Use this information to compute next year's total expected (a) variable costs and (b) fixed costs.

Exercise 29–7
Computation of variable and fixed costs   **L04**

Farrow Co. expects to sell 150,000 units of its product in the next period with the following results.

Exercise 29–8
Decision to accept additional business or not   **L06   L07**

Sales (150,000 units)	$2,250,000
Costs and expenses	
Direct materials	300,000
Direct labor	600,000
Overhead	150,000
Selling expenses	225,000
Administrative expenses	385,500
Total costs and expenses	1,660,500
Net income	$ 589,500

The company has an opportunity to sell 15,000 additional units at $12 per unit. The additional sales would not affect its current expected sales. Direct materials and labor costs would be the same for the additional units as they are for the regular units. However, the additional volume would create the following incremental costs: (1) total overhead would increase by 15% and (2) administrative expenses would increase by $64,500. Prepare an analysis to determine whether the company should accept or reject the offer to sell additional units at the reduced price of $12 per unit.

Check   Income increase, $3,000

Exercise 29–9
Make or buy decision
LO6   LO7

Check $35,750 increased costs to buy

Gilberto Company currently manufactures one of its crucial parts at a cost of $4.45 per unit. This cost is based on a normal production rate of 65,000 units per year. Variable costs are $1.95 per unit, fixed costs related to making this part are $65,000 per year, and allocated fixed costs are $58,500 per year. Allocated fixed costs are unavoidable whether the company makes or buys the part. Gilberto is considering buying the part from a supplier for a quoted price of $3.50 per unit guaranteed for a three-year period. Should the company continue to manufacture the part, or should it buy the part from the outside supplier? Support your answer with analyses.

Exercise 29–10
Sell or process decision
LO6   LO7

Cobe Company has already manufactured 28,000 units of Product A at a cost of $28 per unit. The 28,000 units can be sold at this stage for $700,000. Alternatively, it can be further processed at a $420,000 total additional cost and be converted into 5,600 units of Product B and 11,200 units of Product C. Per unit selling price for Product B is $105 and for Product C is $70. Prepare an analysis that shows whether the 28,000 units of Product A should be processed further or not.

Exercise 29–11
Analysis of income effects from eliminating departments
LO6   LO7

Suresh Co. expects its five departments to yield the following income for next year.

	File Edit View Insert Format Tools Data Window Help				
		Dept. M	Dept. N	Dept. O	Dept. P	Dept. T
1						
2	Sales	$63,000	$ 35,000	$56,000	$42,000	$ 28,000
3	Expenses					
4	Avoidable	9,800	36,400	22,400	14,000	37,800
5	Unavoidable	51,800	12,600	4,200	29,400	9,800
6	Total expenses	61,600	49,000	26,600	43,400	47,600
7	Net income (loss)	$ 1,400	$(14,000)	$29,400	$ (1,400)	$(19,600)
8						

Sheet1 / Sheet2 / Sheet3

Check   Total income (loss):
(2) $(21,000), (3) $7,000

Recompute and prepare the departmental income statements (including a combined total column) for the company under each of the following separate scenarios: Management (1) does not eliminate any department, (2) eliminates departments with expected net losses, and (3) eliminates departments with sales dollars that are less than avoidable expenses. Explain your answers to parts 2 and 3.

Exercise 29–12
Sales mix determination and analysis   **LO6   LO7**

Colt Company owns a machine that can produce two specialized products. Production time for Product TLX is two units per hour and for Product MTV is five units per hour. The machine's capacity is 2,750 hours per year. Both products are sold to a single customer who has agreed to buy all of the company's output up to a maximum of 4,700 units of Product TLX and 2,500 units of Product MTV. Selling prices and variable costs per unit to produce the products follow. Determine (1) the company's most profitable sales mix and (2) the contribution margin that results from that sales mix.

	Product TLX	Product MTV
Selling price per unit	$15.00	$9.50
Variable costs per unit	4.80	5.50

Check   (2) $55,940

Marsden manufactures a cat food product called Special Export. Marsden currently has 10,000 bags of Special Export available. The variable production costs per bag are $1.80 and total fixed costs are $10,000. The cat food can be sold as it is for $9 per bag or be processed further into Prime Cat Food and Feline Surprise at an additional $2,000 cost. The additional processing will yield 10,000 bags of Prime Cat Food and 3,000 bags of Feline Surprise, which can be sold for $8 and $6 per bag, respectively. Determine (1) whether Marsden should sell its 10,000 bags of Special Export or process it further into Prime and Feline Surprise and (2) the total gross profit from processing Special Export further.

Exercise 29–13
Sell or process further
LO6   LO7

Parker Plumbing has received a special one-time order for 1,500 faucets (units) at $5 per unit. Parker currently produces and sells 7,500 units at $6 each. This level represents 75% of its capacity. Production costs for these units are $4.50 per unit, which includes $3 variable cost and $1.50 fixed cost. To produce the special order, a new machine needs to be purchased at a cost of $1,000 with a zero salvage value. Management expects no other changes in costs as a result of the additional production. Determine whether Parker Plumbing should accept the special order.

Exercise 29–14
Additional business   **LO6   LO7**

Zims Company must decide between scrapping or rebuilding units that do not pass inspection. The company has 15,000 such units that cost $6 per unit to manufacture. The units were built to satisfy a special order, which must still be satisfied if the defective units are scrapped. The units can be sold as scrap for $2.50 each or they can be reworked for $4.50 each and sold for the full price of $9 each. If the units are sold as scrap, the company will have to build 15,000 replacement units and sell them at the full price.

Exercise 29–15
Scrap or rework   **LO6   LO7**

Required

1. What is the net return (income) from selling the units as scrap?
2. What is the net return (income) from reworking and selling the units?
3. Should the company sell the units as scrap or rework them?

Fung Company is planning to introduce a new portable TV to its existing product line. Management must decide whether to make the TV case or buy it from an outside supplier. The lowest outside price is $100. If the case is produced internally, the company will have to purchase new equipment that will yield annual depreciation of $130,000. The company will also need to rent a new production facility at $200,000 a year. At 20,000 cases per year, a preliminary analysis of production costs shows the following:

Exercise 29–16
Make or buy   **LO6   LO7**

	Per Case
Direct materials	$ 40.00
Direct labor	32.00
Variable overhead	10.00
Equipment depreciation	6.50
Building rental	10.00
Allocated fixed overhead	7.50
Total cost	$106.00

Required

1. Determine whether the company should make the cases or buy them from the outside supplier.
2. What other factors, besides cost, should the company consider?

PROBLEM SET A

Problem 29–1A

Contribution margin income statement and contribution margin ratio   **LO1   LO3**

The following costs result from the production and sale of 1,000 drum sets manufactured by Tom Thompson Company for the year ended December 31, 2010. The drum sets sell for $500 each. The company has a 25% income tax rate.

Variable production costs	
Plastic for casing	$ 17,000
Wages of assembly workers	82,000
Drum stands	26,000
Variable selling costs	
Sales commissions	15,000
Fixed manufacturing costs	
Taxes on factory	5,000
Factory maintenance	10,000
Factory machinery depreciation	40,000
Fixed selling and administrative costs	
Lease of equipment for sales staff	10,000
Accounting staff salaries	35,000
Administrative management salaries	125,000

Check   (1) Net income, $101,250

Required

1. Prepare a contribution margin income statement for the company.

2. Compute its contribution margin per unit and its contribution margin ratio.

Analysis Component

3. Interpret the contribution margin and contribution margin ratio from part 2.

Problem 29–2A

Break-even analysis   **LO1   LO2   LO3**

Xcite Equipment Co. manufactures and markets a number of rope products. Management is considering the future of Product XT, a special rope for hang gliding, that has not been as profitable as planned. Since Product XT is manufactured and marketed independently of the other products, its total costs can be precisely measured. Next year's plans call for a $200 selling price per 100 yards of XT rope. Its fixed costs for the year are expected to be $270,000, up to a maximum capacity of 700,000 yards. Forecasted variable costs are $140 per 100 yards of XT rope.

Required

Check   (1) Break-even sales, 4,500 units or $900,000

1. Estimate Product XT's break-even point in terms of (a) sales units and (b) sales dollars.

2. Prepare a contribution margin income statement showing sales, variable costs, and fixed costs for Product XT at the break-even point.

Problem 29–3A

Break-even analysis; income targeting and forecasting   **LO1   LO2   LO3   LO4**

Astro Co. sold 20,000 units of its only product and incurred a $50,000 loss (ignoring taxes) for the current year as shown below. During a planning session for year 2011's activities, the production manager notes that variable costs can be reduced 50% by installing a machine that automates several operations. To obtain these savings, the company must increase its annual fixed costs by $200,000. The maximum output capacity of the company is 40,000 units per year.

ASTRO COMPANY	
Contribution Margin Income Statement	
For Year Ended December 31, 2010	
Sales	$1,000,000
Variable costs	800,000
Contribution margin	200,000
Fixed costs	250,000
Net loss	$ (50,000)

Required

1. Compute the break-even point in dollar sales for year 2010.

2. Compute the predicted break-even point in dollar sales for year 2011 assuming the machine is installed and there is no change in unit sales price.

3. Prepare a forecasted contribution margin income statement for 2011 that shows the expected results with the machine installed. Assume that the unit sales price and the number of units sold will not change and no income taxes.

Check (3) Net income, $150,000

4. Compute the sales level required in both dollars and units to earn $140,000 of after-tax income in 2011 with the machine installed and no change in unit sales price. Assume that the income tax rate is 30%. (*Hint:* Use the procedures in Exhibit 29.9.)

(4) Required sales, $1,083,333 or 21,667 units (rounded)

5. Prepare a forecasted contribution margin income statement that shows the results at the sales level computed in part 4. Assume an income tax rate of 30%.

(5) Net income, $140,000 (rounded)

Vanna Co. produces and sells two products, T and O. It manufactures these products in separate factories and markets them through different channels. They have no shared costs. This year, Vanna sold 50,000 units of each product. Sales and costs for each product follow.

Problem 29–4A
Break-even analysis, different cost structures, and income calculations **LO1 LO2**

	Product T	Product O
Sales	$2,000,000	$2,000,000
Variable costs	1,600,000	250,000
Contribution margin	400,000	1,750,000
Fixed costs	125,000	1,475,000
Income before taxes	275,000	275,000
Income taxes (32% rate)	88,000	88,000
Net income	$ 187,000	$ 187,000

Required

1. Compute the break-even point in dollar sales for each product.

2. Assume that the company expects sales of each product to decline to 30,000 units next year with no change in unit sales price. Prepare forecasted financial results for next year following the format of the contribution margin income statement as shown above with columns for each of the two products (assume a 32% tax rate). Also, assume that any loss before taxes yields a 32% tax savings.

Check (2) After-tax income: T, $78,200; O, $(289,000)

3. Assume that the company expects sales of each product to increase to 60,000 units next year with no change in unit sales price. Prepare forecasted financial results for next year following the format of the contribution margin income statement as shown above with columns for each of the two products (assume a 32% tax rate).

(3) After-tax income: T, $241,400; O, $425,000

Analysis Component

4. If sales greatly decrease, which product would experience a greater loss? Explain.

5. Describe some factors that might have created the different cost structures for these two products.

This year Bertrand Company sold 40,000 units of its only product for $25 per unit. Manufacturing and selling the product required $200,000 of fixed manufacturing costs and $325,000 of fixed selling and administrative costs. Its per unit variable costs follow.

Problem 29–5A
Analysis of price, cost, and volume changes for contribution margin and net income
LO1 LO2 LO3 LO4

Material	$8.00
Direct labor (paid on the basis of completed units)	5.00
Variable overhead costs	1.00
Variable selling and administrative costs	0.50

Next year the company will use new material, which will reduce material costs by 50% and direct labor costs by 60% and will not affect product quality or marketability. Management is considering an increase in the unit sales price to reduce the number of units sold because the factory's output is nearing its annual output capacity of 45,000 units. Two plans are being considered. Under plan 1, the company will keep the price at the current level and sell the same volume as last year. This plan will increase income because of the reduced costs from using the new material. Under plan 2, the company will increase price by 20%. This plan will decrease unit sales volume by 10%. Under both plans 1 and 2, the total fixed costs and the variable costs per unit for overhead and for selling and administrative costs will remain the same.

Required

Check (1) Break-even: Plan 1,
         $750,000; Plan 2, $700,000

         (2) Net income: Plan 1,
         $122,500; Plan 2, $199,500

1. Compute the break-even point in dollar sales for both (a) plan 1 and (b) plan 2.
2. Prepare a forecasted contribution margin income statement with two columns showing the expected results of plan 1 and plan 2. The statements should report sales, total variable costs, contribution margin, total fixed costs, income before taxes, income taxes (30% rate), and net income.

Problem 29-6A
Analysis of income effects of additional business **L06 L07**

mhhe.com/wildCA2e

Jones Products manufactures and sells to wholesalers approximately 400,000 packages per year of underwater markers at $6 per package. Annual costs for the production and sale of this quantity are shown in the table.

Direct materials	$ 576,000
Direct labor	144,000
Overhead	320,000
Selling expenses	150,000
Administrative expenses	100,000
Total costs and expenses	$1,290,000

A new wholesaler has offered to buy 50,000 packages for $5.20 each. These markers would be marketed under the wholesaler's name and would not affect Jones Products' sales through its normal channels. A study of the costs of this additional business reveals the following:

- Direct materials costs are 100% variable.
- Per unit direct labor costs for the additional units would be 50% higher than normal because their production would require overtime pay at one-and-one-half times the usual labor rate.
- 25% of the normal annual overhead costs are fixed at any production level from 350,000 to 500,000 units. The remaining 75% of the annual overhead cost is variable with volume.
- Accepting the new business would involve no additional selling expenses.
- Accepting the new business would increase administrative expenses by a $5,000 fixed amount.

Required

Prepare a three-column comparative income statement that shows the following:

1. Annual operating income without the special order (column 1).
2. Annual operating income received from the new business only (column 2).
3. Combined annual operating income from normal business and the new business (column 3).

Check Operating income:
       (1) $1,110,000, (2) $126,000

Problem 29-7A
Analysis of sales mix strategies
L06 L07

Edgerron Company is able to produce two products, G and B, with the same machine in its factory. The following information is available.

	Product G	Product B
Selling price per unit	$120	$160
Variable costs per unit	40	90
Contribution margin per unit	$ 80	$ 70
Machine hours to produce 1 unit	0.4 hours	1.0 hours
Maximum unit sales per month	600 units	200 units

The company presently operates the machine for a single eight-hour shift for 22 working days each month. Management is thinking about operating the machine for two shifts, which will increase its productivity by another eight hours per day for 22 days per month. This change would require $15,000 additional fixed costs per month.

Required

1. Determine the contribution margin per machine hour that each product generates.

2. How many units of Product G and Product B should the company produce if it continues to operate with only one shift? How much total contribution margin does this mix produce each month?

3. If the company adds another shift, how many units of Product G and Product B should it produce? How much total contribution margin would this mix produce each month? Should the company add the new shift? Explain.

4. Suppose that the company determines that it can increase Product G's maximum sales to 700 units per month by spending $12,000 per month in marketing efforts. Should the company pursue this strategy and the double shift? Explain.

Check   Units of Product G: (2) 440, (3) 600, (4) 700

Elegant Decor Company's management is trying to decide whether to eliminate Department 200, which has produced losses or low profits for several years. The company's 2010 departmental income statement shows the following.

Problem 29-8A
Analysis of possible elimination of a department   L06   L07

ELEGANT DECOR COMPANY Departmental Income Statements For Year Ended December 31, 2010			
	Dept. 100	Dept. 200	Combined
Sales	$436,000	$290,000	$726,000
Cost of goods sold	262,000	207,000	469,000
Gross profit	174,000	83,000	257,000
Operating expenses			
Direct expenses			
Advertising	17,000	12,000	29,000
Store supplies used	4,000	3,800	7,800
Depreciation—Store equipment	5,000	3,300	8,300
Total direct expenses	26,000	19,100	45,100
Allocated expenses			
Sales salaries	65,000	39,000	104,000
Rent expense	9,440	4,720	14,160
Bad debts expense	9,900	8,100	18,000
Office salary	18,720	12,480	31,200
Insurance expense	2,000	1,100	3,100
Miscellaneous office expenses	2,400	1,600	4,000
Total allocated expenses	107,460	67,000	174,460
Total expenses	133,460	86,100	219,560
Net income (loss)	$ 40,540	$ (3,100)	$ 37,440

In analyzing whether to eliminate Department 200, management considers the following:

a. The company has one office worker who earns $600 per week, or $31,200 per year, and four salesclerks who each earn $500 per week, or $26,000 per year.

b. The full salaries of two salesclerks are charged to Department 100. The full salary of one sales clerk is charged to Department 200. The salary of the fourth clerk, who works half-time in both departments, is divided evenly between the two departments.

c. Eliminating Department 200 would avoid the sales salaries and the office salary currently allocated to it. However, management prefers another plan. Two salesclerks have indicated that they will be quitting soon. Management believes that their work can be done by the other two clerks if the one office worker works in sales half-time. Eliminating Department 200 will allow this shift of duties. If this change is implemented, half the office worker's salary would be reported as sales salaries and half would be reported as office salary.

d. The store building is rented under a long-term lease that cannot be changed. Therefore, Department 100 will use the space and equipment currently used by Department 200.

e. Closing Department 200 will eliminate its expenses for advertising, bad debts, and store supplies; 70% of the insurance expense allocated to it to cover its merchandise inventory; and 25% of the miscellaneous office expenses presently allocated to it.

Required

1. Prepare a three-column report that lists items and amounts for (a) the company's total expenses (including cost of goods sold)—in column 1, (b) the expenses that would be eliminated by closing Department 200—in column 2, and (c) the expenses that will continue—in column 3.

2. Prepare a forecasted annual income statement for the company reflecting the elimination of Department 200 assuming that it will not affect Department 100's sales and gross profit. The statement should reflect the reassignment of the office worker to one-half time as a salesclerk.

Analysis Component

3. Reconcile the company's combined net income with the forecasted net income assuming that Department 200 is eliminated (list both items and amounts). Analyze the reconciliation and explain why you think the department should or should not be eliminated.

PROBLEM SET B

Problem 29-1B

Contribution margin income statement and contribution margin ratio **LO1 LO3**

The following costs result from the production and sale of 12,000 CD sets manufactured by Gilmore Company for the year ended December 31, 2010. The CD sets sell for $18 each. The company has a 25% income tax rate.

Variable manufacturing costs	
Plastic for CD sets	$ 1,500
Wages of assembly workers	30,000
Labeling	3,000
Variable selling costs	
Sales commissions	6,000
Fixed manufacturing costs	
Rent on factory	6,750
Factory cleaning service	4,520
Factory machinery depreciation	20,000
Fixed selling and administrative costs	
Lease of office equipment	1,050
Systems staff salaries	15,000
Administrative management salaries	120,000

Required

1. Prepare a contribution margin income statement for the company.

2. Compute its contribution margin per unit and its contribution margin ratio.

Analysis Component

3. Interpret the contribution margin and contribution margin ratio from part 2.

Problem 29-2B

Break-even analysis
LO1 LO2 LO3

Hip-Hop Co. manufactures and markets several products. Management is considering the future of one product, electronic keyboards, that has not been as profitable as planned. Since this product is manufactured and marketed independently of the other products, its total costs can be precisely measured. Next year's plans call for a $350 selling price per unit. The fixed costs for the year are expected to be $42,000, up to a maximum capacity of 700 units. Forecasted variable costs are $210 per unit.

Required

1. Estimate the keyboards' break-even point in terms of (a) sales units and (b) sales dollars.

2. Prepare a contribution margin income statement showing sales, variable costs, and fixed costs for keyboards at the break-even point.

Problem 29-3B

Break-even analysis; income targeting and forecasting
LO1 LO2 LO3 LO4

Rivera Co. sold 20,000 units of its only product and incurred a $50,000 loss (ignoring taxes) for the current year as shown below. During a planning session for year 2011's activities, the production manager notes that variable costs can be reduced 50% by installing a machine that automates several operations. To obtain these savings, the company must increase its annual fixed costs by $150,000. The maximum output capacity of the company is 40,000 units per year.

RIVERA COMPANY
Contribution Margin Income Statement
For Year Ended December 31, 2010

Sales	$750,000
Variable costs	600,000
Contribution margin	150,000
Fixed costs	200,000
Net loss	$ (50,000)

Required

1. Compute the break-even point in dollar sales for year 2010.

2. Compute the predicted break-even point in dollar sales for year 2011 assuming the machine is installed and no change in unit sales price. (Round the change in variable costs to a whole number.)

3. Prepare a forecasted contribution margin income statement for 2011 that shows the expected results with the machine installed. Assume that the unit sales price and the number of units sold will not change and no income taxes.

4. Compute the sales level required in both dollars and units to earn $140,000 of after-tax income in 2011 with the machine installed and no change in unit sales price. Assume that the income tax rate is 30%. (*Hint:* Use the procedure in Exhibit 29.9 to compute the required sales level in dollars.)

5. Prepare a forecasted contribution margin income statement that shows the results at the sales level computed in part 4. Assume an income tax rate of 30%.

Check (3) Net income, $100,000

(4) Required sales, $916,667 or 24,445 units (rounded)

(5) Net income, $140,000 (rounded)

Mingei Co. produces and sells two products, BB and TT. It manufactures these products in separate factories and markets them through different channels. They have no shared costs. This year, Mingei Co. sold 50,000 units of each product. Sales and costs for each product follow.

Problem 29–4B
Break-even analysis, different cost structures, and income calculations
LO1 LO2 LO3 LO4

	Product BB	Product TT
Sales	$800,000	$800,000
Variable costs	560,000	100,000
Contribution margin	240,000	700,000
Fixed costs	100,000	560,000
Income before taxes	140,000	140,000
Income taxes (32% rate)	44,800	44,800
Net income	$ 95,200	$ 95,200

Required

1. Compute the break-even point in dollar sales for each product.

2. Assume that the company expects sales of each product to decline to 33,000 units next year with no change in unit sales price. Prepare forecasted financial results for next year following the format of the contribution margin income statement as shown above with columns for each of the two products (assume a 32% tax rate, and that any loss before taxes yields a 32% tax savings).

3. Assume that the company expects sales of each product to increase to 64,000 units next year with no change in unit sales price. Prepare forecasted financial results for next year following the format of the contribution margin income statement as shown above with columns for each of the two products (assume a 32% tax rate).

Check (2) After-tax income: BB, $39,712; TT, $(66,640)

(3) After-tax income: BB, $140,896; TT, $228,480

Analysis Component

4. If sales greatly increase, which product would experience a greater increase in profit? Explain.

5. Describe some factors that might have created the different cost structures for these two products.

Problem 29–5B
Analysis of price, cost, and volume changes for contribution margin and net income
LO1 LO2 LO3 LO4

This year Best Company earned a disappointing 5.6% after-tax return on sales from marketing 100,000 units of its only product. The company buys its product in bulk and repackages it for resale at the price of $20 per unit. Best incurred the following costs this year.

Total variable unit costs	$800,000
Total variable packaging costs	$100,000
Fixed costs	$950,000
Income tax rate	25%

The marketing manager claims that next year's results will be the same as this year's unless some changes are made. The manager predicts the company can increase the number of units sold by 80% if it reduces the selling price by 20% and upgrades the packaging. This change would increase variable packaging costs by 20%. Increased sales would allow the company to take advantage of a 25% quantity purchase discount on the cost of the bulk product. Neither the packaging change nor the volume discount would affect fixed costs, which provide an annual output capacity of 200,000 units.

Required

Check (1) Break-even for new strategy, $1,727,273

(2) Net income: Existing strategy, $112,500; New strategy, $475,500

1. Compute the break-even point in dollar sales under the (a) existing business strategy and (b) new strategy that alters both unit sales price and variable costs.

2. Prepare a forecasted contribution margin income statement with two columns showing the expected results of (a) the existing strategy and (b) changing to the new strategy. The statements should report sales, total variable costs (unit and packaging), contribution margin, fixed costs, income before taxes, income taxes, and net income. Also determine the after-tax return on sales for these two strategies.

Problem 29–6B
Analysis of income effects of additional business LO6 LO7

Windmire Company manufactures and sells to local wholesalers approximately 300,000 units per month at a sales price of $4 per unit. Monthly costs for the production and sale of this quantity follow.

Direct materials	$384,000
Direct labor	96,000
Overhead	288,000
Selling expenses	120,000
Administrative expenses	80,000
Total costs and expenses	$968,000

A new out-of-state distributor has offered to buy 50,000 units next month for $3.44 each. These units would be marketed in other states and would not affect Windmire's sales through its normal channels. A study of the costs of this new business reveals the following:

- Direct materials costs are 100% variable.
- Per unit direct labor costs for the additional units would be 50% higher than normal because their production would require time-and-a-half overtime pay to meet the distributor's deadline.
- Twenty-five percent of the normal annual overhead costs are fixed at any production level from 250,000 to 400,000 units. The remaining 75% is variable with volume.
- Accepting the new business would involve no additional selling expenses.
- Accepting the new business would increase administrative expenses by a $4,000 fixed amount.

Required

Prepare a three-column comparative income statement that shows the following:

Check Operating income:
(1) $232,000, (2) $44,000

1. Monthly operating income without the special order (column 1).
2. Monthly operating income received from the new business only (column 2).
3. Combined monthly operating income from normal business and the new business (column 3).

Problem 29–7B
Analysis of sales mix strategies
LO6 LO7

Sung Company is able to produce two products, R and T, with the same machine in its factory. The following information is available.

	Product R	Product T
Selling price per unit	$60	$80
Variable costs per unit	20	45
Contribution margin per unit	$40	$35
Machine hours to produce 1 unit	0.4 hours	1.0 hours
Maximum unit sales per month	550 units	175 units

The company presently operates the machine for a single eight-hour shift for 22 working days each month. Management is thinking about operating the machine for two shifts, which will increase its productivity by another eight hours per day for 22 days per month. This change would require $3,250 additional fixed costs per month.

Required

1. Determine the contribution margin per machine hour that each product generates.

2. How many units of Product R and Product T should the company produce if it continues to operate with only one shift? How much total contribution margin does this mix produce each month?

3. If the company adds another shift, how many units of Product R and Product T should it produce? How much total contribution margin would this mix produce each month? Should the company add the new shift? Explain.

4. Suppose that the company determines that it can increase Product R's maximum sales to 675 units per month by spending $4,500 per month in marketing efforts. Should the company pursue this strategy and the double shift? Explain.

Check Units of Product R: (2) 440, (3) 550, (4) 675

Esme Company's management is trying to decide whether to eliminate Department Z, which has produced low profits or losses for several years. The company's 2010 departmental income statement shows the following.

Problem 29-8B
Analysis of possible elimination of a department **LO6 LO7**

ESME COMPANY
Departmental Income Statements
For Year Ended December 31, 2010

	Dept. A	Dept. Z	Combined
Sales	$700,000	$175,000	$875,000
Cost of goods sold	461,300	125,100	586,400
Gross profit	238,700	49,900	288,600
Operating expenses			
Direct expenses			
Advertising	27,000	3,000	30,000
Store supplies used	5,600	1,400	7,000
Depreciation—Store equipment	14,000	7,000	21,000
Total direct expenses	46,600	11,400	58,000
Allocated expenses			
Sales salaries	70,200	23,400	93,600
Rent expense	22,080	5,520	27,600
Bad debts expense	21,000	4,000	25,000
Office salary	20,800	5,200	26,000
Insurance expense	4,200	1,400	5,600
Miscellaneous office expenses	1,700	2,500	4,200
Total allocated expenses	139,980	42,020	182,000
Total expenses	186,580	53,420	240,000
Net income (loss)	$ 52,120	$ (3,520)	$ 48,600

In analyzing whether to eliminate Department Z, management considers the following items:

a. The company has one office worker who earns $500 per week or $26,000 per year and four salesclerks who each earn $450 per week or $23,400 per year.

b. The full salaries of three salesclerks are charged to Department A. The full salary of one salesclerk is charged to Department Z.

c. Eliminating Department Z would avoid the sales salaries and the office salary currently allocated to it. However, management prefers another plan. Two salesclerks have indicated that they will be quitting soon. Management believes that their work can be done by the two remaining clerks if the one office worker works in sales half time. Eliminating Department Z will allow this shift of duties. If this change is implemented, half the office worker's salary would be reported as sales salaries and half would be reported as office salary.

d. The store building is rented under a long-term lease that cannot be changed. Therefore, Department A will use the space and equipment currently used by Department Z.

e. Closing Department Z will eliminate its expenses for advertising, bad debts, and store supplies; 65% of the insurance expense allocated to it to cover its merchandise inventory; and 30% of the miscellaneous office expenses presently allocated to it.

Required

1. Prepare a three-column report that lists items and amounts for (a) the company's total expenses (including cost of goods sold)—in column 1, (b) the expenses that would be eliminated by closing Department Z—in column 2, and (c) the expenses that will continue—in column 3.

2. Prepare a forecasted annual income statement for the company reflecting the elimination of Department Z assuming that it will not affect Department A's sales and gross profit. The statement should reflect the reassignment of the office worker to one-half time as a salesclerk.

Analysis Component

3. Reconcile the company's combined net income with the forecasted net income assuming that Department Z is eliminated (list both items and amounts). Analyze the reconciliation and explain why you think the department should or should not be eliminated.

Check   (1) Total expenses: (a) $826,400, (b) $181,960

(2) Forecasted net income without Department Z, $55,560

BEYOND THE NUMBERS

REPORTING IN ACTION
LO1   LO4

BTN 29-1   **Best Buy** offers services to customers that help them use products they purchase from Best Buy. One of these services is its Geek Squad, which is Best Buy's 24-Hour Computer Support Task Force. As you complete the following requirements, assume that the Geek Squad uses many of Best Buy's existing resources such as its purchasing department and its buildings and equipment.

Required

1. Identify several of the variable, mixed, and fixed costs that the Geek Squad is likely to incur in carrying out its services.

2. Assume that Geek Squad revenues are expected to grow by 25% in the next year. How do you expect the costs identified in part 1 to change, if at all?

3. How is your answer to part 2 different from many of the examples discussed in the chapter? (*Hint:* Consider how the contribution margin ratio changes as volume—sales or customers served—increases.)

ETHICS CHALLENGE
LO1

BTN 29-2   Labor costs of an auto repair mechanic are seldom based on actual hours worked. Instead, the amount paid a mechanic is based on an industry average of time estimated to complete a repair job. The repair shop bills the customer for the industry average amount of time at the repair center's billable cost per hour. This means a customer can pay, for example, $120 for two hours of work on a car when the actual time worked was only one hour. Many experienced mechanics can complete repair jobs well under the industry average. The average data are compiled by engineering studies and surveys conducted in the auto repair business. Assume that you are asked to complete such a survey for a repair center. The survey calls for objective input, and many questions require detailed cost data and analysis. The mechanics and owners know you have the survey and encourage you to complete it in a way that increases the average billable hours for repair work.

Required

Write a one-page memorandum to the mechanics and owners that describes the direct labor analysis you will undertake in completing this survey.

WORKPLACE COMMUNICATION

BTN 29-3   Access and review the entrepreneurial information at **Business Owner's Toolkit** [Toolkit.cch.com]. Access and review its *New Business Cash Needs Estimate* under the **Business Tools/Business Finance** menu bar or similar worksheets related to controls of cash and costs.

Required

Write a one-half page report that describes the information and resources available at the Business Owner's Toolkit to help the owner of a start-up business to control and monitor its costs.

BTN 29-4   Many companies must determine whether to internally produce their component parts or to outsource them. Further, some companies now outsource key components to international providers. Access the Website **BizBrim.com** and review the available information on outsourcing—especially as it relates to both the advantages and the negative effects of outsourcing.

TAKING IT TO THE NET
LO1 LO4

Required

1. What does Bizbrim identify as the major advantages and the major disadvantages of outsourcing?
2. Does it seem that Bizbrim is generally in favor of or opposed to outsourcing? Explain.

BTN 29-5   A local movie theater owner explains to you that ticket sales on weekends and evenings are strong, but attendance during the weekdays, Monday through Thursday, is poor. The owner proposes to offer a contract to the local grade school to show educational materials at the theater for a set charge per student during school hours. The owner asks your help to prepare a CVP analysis listing the cost and sales projections for the proposal. The owner must propose to the school's administration a charge per child. At a minimum, the charge per child needs to be sufficient for the theater to break even.

TEAMWORK IN ACTION
LO2 LO4

Required

Your team is to prepare two separate lists of questions that enable you to complete a reliable CVP analysis of this situation. One list is to be answered by the school's administration, the other by the owner of the movie theater.

BTN 29-6   Jared Greenberg and Dan Zinger of **Prairie Sticks Bat Company** make baseball bats. They must decide on the best sales mix. Assume their company has a capacity of 80 hours of lathe/processing time available each month and it makes two types of bats, Deluxe and Premium. Information on these bats follows.

ENTREPRENEURS IN BUSINESS
LO7

	Deluxe	Premium
Selling price per bat	$70	$90
Variable costs per bat	$40	$50
Lathe/processing minutes per bat	6 minutes	12 minutes

Required

1. Assume the markets for both models of bats are unlimited. How many Deluxe bats and how many Premium bats should the company make each month? Explain. How much total contribution margin does this mix produce each month?
2. Assume the market for Deluxe bats is limited to 600 bats per month, with no market limit for Premium bats. How many Deluxe bats and how many Premium bats should the company make each month? Explain. How much total contribution margin does this mix produce each month?

Appendix A

Financial Statement Information

This appendix includes financial information for (1) **Best Buy** and (2) **RadioShack**. This information is taken from their annual 10-K reports filed with the SEC. An **annual report** is a summary of a company's financial results for the year along with its current financial condition and future plans. This report is directed to external users of financial information, but it also affects the actions and decisions of internal users.

A company uses an annual report to showcase itself and its products. Many annual reports include attractive photos, diagrams, and illustrations related to the company. The primary objective of annual reports, however, is the *financial section,* which communicates much information about a company, with most data drawn from the accounting information system. The layout of an annual report's financial section is fairly established and typically includes the following:

- Letter to Shareholders
- Financial History and Highlights
- Management Discussion and Analysis
- Management's Report on Financial Statements and on Internal Controls
- Report of Independent Accountants (Auditor's Report) and on Internal Controls
- Financial Statements
- Notes to Financial Statements
- List of Directors and Officers

This appendix provides the financial statements for Best Buy (plus selected notes) and RadioShack. The appendix is organized as follows:

- **Best Buy A-2** through **A-20**   ■ **RadioShack A-21** through **A-26**

Many assignments at the end of each chapter refer to information in this appendix. We encourage readers to spend time with these assignments; they are especially useful in showing the relevance and diversity of financial accounting and reporting.

> *Special note:* The SEC maintains the EDGAR (**E**lectronic **D**ata **G**athering, **A**nalysis, and **R**etrieval) database at **www.sec.gov**. The **Form 10-K** is the annual report form for most companies. It provides electronically accessible information. The **Form 10-KSB** is the annual report form filed by "small businesses." It requires slightly less information than the Form 10-K. One of these forms must be filed within 90 days after the company's fiscal year-end. (Forms 10-K405, 10-KT, 10-KT405, and 10-KSB405 are slight variations of the usual form due to certain regulations or rules.)

Financial Report

Selected Financial Data

The following table presents our selected financial data. Certain prior-year amounts have been reclassified to conform to the current-year presentation. In fiscal 2004, we sold our interest in Musicland. All fiscal years presented reflect the classification of Musicland's financial results as discontinued operations.

Five-Year Financial Highlights

$ in millions, except per share amounts

Fiscal Year	2008	2007	2006	2005	2004
Consolidated Statements of Earnings Data					
Revenue	$40,023	$35,934	$30,848	$27,433	$24,548
Operating income	2,161	1,999	1,644	1,442	1,304
Earnings from continuing operations	1,407	1,377	1,140	934	800
Loss from discontinued operations, net of tax	—	—	—	—	(29)
Gain (loss) on disposal of discontinued operations, net of tax	—	—	—	50	(66)
Net earnings	1,407	1,377	1,140	984	705
Per Share Data					
Continuing operations	$3.12	$2.79	$2.27	$1.86	$1.61
Discontinued operations	—	—	—	—	(0.06)
Gain (loss) on disposal of discontinued operations	—	—	—	0.10	(0.13)
Net earnings	3.12	2.79	2.27	1.96	1.42
Cash dividends declared and paid	0.46	0.36	0.31	0.28	0.27
Common stock price:					
High	53.90	59.50	56.00	41.47	41.80
Low	41.85	43.51	31.93	29.25	17.03
Operating Statistics					
Comparable store sales gain	2.9%	5.0%	4.9%	4.3%	7.1%
Gross profit rate	23.9%	24.4%	25.0%	23.7%	23.9%
Selling, general and administrative expenses rate	18.5%	18.8%	19.7%	18.4%	18.6 %
Operating income rate	5.4%	5.6%	5.3%	5.3%	5.3%
Year-End Data					
Current ratio	1.1	1.4	1.3	1.4	1.3
Total assets	$12,758	$13,570	$11,864	$10,294	$8,652
Debt, including current portion	816	650	596	600	850
Total shareholders' equity	4,484	6,201	5,257	4,449	3,422
Number of stores					
Domestic	971	873	774	694	631
International	343	304	167	144	127
Total	1,314	1,177	941	838	758
Retail square footage (000s)					
Domestic	37,511	34,092	30,874	28,513	26,699
International	11,069	9,419	4,652	4,057	3,587
Total	48,580	43,511	35,526	32,570	30,286

Fiscal 2007 included 53 weeks. All other periods presented included 52 weeks.

Consolidated Balance Sheets
$ in millions, except per share amounts

	March 1, 2008	March 3, 2007
Assets		
Current Assets		
Cash and cash equivalents	$ 1,438	$ 1,205
Short-term investments	64	2,588
Receivables	549	548
Merchandise inventories	4,708	4,028
Other current assets	583	712
Total current assets	7,342	9,081
Property and Equipment		
Land and buildings	732	705
Leasehold improvements	1,752	1,540
Fixtures and equipment	3,057	2,627
Property under capital lease	67	32
	5,608	4,904
Less accumulated depreciation	2,302	1,966
Net property and equipment	3,306	2,938
Goodwill	1,088	919
Tradenames	97	81
Equity and Other Investments	605	338
Other Assets	320	213
Total Assets	$12,758	$13,570
Liabilities and Shareholders' Equity		
Current Liabilities		
Accounts payable	$ 4,297	$ 3,934
Unredeemed gift card liabilities	531	496
Accrued compensation and related expenses	373	332
Accrued liabilities	975	990
Accrued income taxes	404	489
Short-term debt	156	41
Current portion of long-term debt	33	19
Total current liabilities	6,769	6,301
Long-Term Liabilities	838	443
Long-Term Debt	627	590
Minority Interests	40	35
Shareholders' Equity		
Preferred stock, $1.00 par value: Authorized — 400,000 shares; Issued and outstanding — none	—	—
Common stock, $.10 par value: Authorized — 1.0 billion shares; Issued and outstanding — 410,578,000 and 480,655,000 shares, respectively	41	48
Additional paid-in capital	8	430
Retained earnings	3,933	5,507
Accumulated other comprehensive income	502	216
Total shareholders' equity	4,484	6,201
Total Liabilities and Shareholders' Equity	$12,758	$13,570

See Notes to Consolidated Financial Statements.

BEST BUY

BEST BUY

Consolidated Statements of Earnings

$ in millions, except per share amounts

For the Fiscal Years Ended	March 1, 2008	March 3, 2007	February 25, 2006
Revenue	$40,023	$35,934	$30,848
Cost of goods sold	30,477	27,165	23,122
Gross profit	9,546	8,769	7,726
Selling, general and administrative expenses	7,385	6,770	6,082
Operating income	2,161	1,999	1,644
Other income (expense)			
Investment income and other	129	162	107
Interest expense	(62)	(31)	(30)
Earnings before income tax expense, minority interest and equity in loss of affiliates	2,228	2,130	1,721
Income tax expense	815	752	581
Minority interest in earnings	(3)	(1)	—
Equity in loss of affiliates	(3)	—	—
Net earnings	$ 1,407	$ 1,377	$ 1,140
Earnings per share			
Basic	$ 3.20	$ 2.86	$ 2.33
Diluted	$ 3.12	$ 2.79	$ 2.27
Weighted-average common shares outstanding (in millions)			
Basic	439.9	482.1	490.3
Diluted	452.9	496.2	504.8

See Notes to Consolidated Financial Statements.

BEST BUY

Consolidated Statements of Cash Flows
$ in millions

For the Fiscal Years Ended	March 1, 2008	March 3, 2007	February 25, 2006
Operating Activities			
Net earnings	$1,407	$1,377	$1,140
Adjustments to reconcile net earnings to total cash provided by operating activities:			
Depreciation	580	509	456
Stock-based compensation	105	121	132
Deferred income taxes	74	82	(151)
Excess tax benefits from stock-based compensation	(24)	(50)	(55)
Other, net	(3)	21	1
Changes in operating assets and liabilities, net of acquired assets and liabilities:			
Receivables	12	(70)	(43)
Merchandise inventories	(562)	(550)	(457)
Other assets	42	(47)	(11)
Accounts payable	221	320	385
Other liabilities	74	185	165
Income taxes	99	(136)	178
Total cash provided by operating activities	2,025	1,762	1,740
Investing Activities			
Additions to property and equipment, net of $80, and $75 non-cash capital expenditures in fiscal 2008 and 2006, respectively	(797)	(733)	(648)
Purchases of investments	(8,501)	(4,789)	(4,561)
Sales of investments	10,935	5,095	4,362
Acquisitions of businesses, net of cash acquired	(89)	(421)	—
Change in restricted assets	(85)	63	47
Other, net	1	5	46
Total cash provided by (used in) investing activities	1,464	(780)	(754)
Financing Activities			
Repurchase of common stock	(3,461)	(599)	(772)
Issuance of common stock under employee stock purchase plan and for the exercise of stock options	146	217	292
Dividends paid	(204)	(174)	(151)
Repayments of debt	(4,353)	(84)	(69)
Proceeds from issuance of debt	4,486	96	36
Excess tax benefits from stock-based compensation	24	50	55
Other, net	(16)	(19)	(10)
Total cash used in financing activities	(3,378)	(513)	(619)
Effect of Exchange Rate Changes on Cash	122	(12)	27
Increase in Cash and Cash Equivalents	233	457	394
Cash and Cash Equivalents at Beginning of Year	1,205	748	354
Cash and Cash Equivalents at End of Year	$1,438	$1,205	$ 748
Supplemental Disclosure of Cash Flow Information			
Income taxes paid	$ 644	$ 804	$ 547
Interest paid	49	14	16

See Notes to Consolidated Financial Statements.

Consolidated Statements of Changes in Shareholders' Equity

$ and shares in millions

	Common Shares	Common Stock	Additional Paid-In Capital	Retained Earnings	Accumulated Other Comprehensive Income	Total
Balances at February 26, 2005	**493**	**$49**	**$936**	**$3,315**	**$149**	**$4,449**
Net earnings	—	—	—	1,140	—	1,140
Other comprehensive income, net of tax:						
Foreign currency translation adjustments	—	—	—	—	101	101
Unrealized gains on available-for-sale investments	—	—	—	—	11	11
Total comprehensive income						1,252
Stock options exercised	9	1	256	—	—	257
Tax benefit from stock options exercised and employee stock purchase plan	—	—	55	—	—	55
Issuance of common stock under employee stock purchase plan	1	—	35	—	—	35
Stock-based compensation	—	—	132	—	—	132
Common stock dividends, $0.31 per share	—	—	—	(151)	—	(151)
Repurchase of common stock	(18)	(1)	(771)	—	—	(772)
Balances at February 25, 2006	**485**	**49**	**643**	**4,304**	**261**	**5,257**
Net earnings	—	—	—	1,377	—	1,377
Other comprehensive loss, net of tax:						
Foreign currency translation adjustments	—	—	—	—	(33)	(33)
Unrealized losses on available-for-sale investments	—	—	—	—	(12)	(12)
Total comprehensive income						1,332
Stock options exercised	7	1	167	—	—	168
Tax benefit from stock options exercised and employee stock purchase plan	—	—	47	—	—	47
Issuance of common stock under employee stock purchase plan	1	—	49	—	—	49
Stock-based compensation	—	—	121	—	—	121
Common stock dividends, $0.36 per share	—	—	—	(174)	—	(174)
Repurchase of common stock	(12)	(2)	(597)	—	—	(599)
Balances at March 3, 2007	**481**	**48**	**430**	**5,507**	**216**	**6,201**
Net earnings	—	—	—	1,407	—	1,407
Other comprehensive income (loss), net of tax:						
Foreign currency translation adjustments	—	—	—	—	311	311
Unrealized losses on available-for-sale investments	—	—	—	—	(25)	(25)
Total comprehensive income						1,693
Cumulative effect of adopting a new accounting standard (Note 8)	—	—	—	(13)	—	(13)
Stock options exercised	4	—	93	—	—	93
Tax benefit from stock options exercised and employee stock purchase plan	—	—	17	—	—	17
Issuance of common stock under employee stock purchase plan	1	—	53	—	—	53
Stock-based compensation	—	—	105	—	—	105
Common stock dividends, $0.46 per share	—	—	—	(204)	—	(204)
Repurchase of common stock	(75)	(7)	(690)	(2,764)	—	(3,461)
Balances at March 1, 2008	**411**	**$41**	**$ 8**	**$3,933**	**$502**	**$4,484**

See Notes to Consolidated Financial Statements.

Notes to Consolidated Financial Statements

$ in millions, except per share amounts or as otherwise noted

1.   Summary of Significant Accounting Policies
Description of Business

Best Buy is a specialty retailer of consumer electronics, home office products, entertainment software, appliances and related services, with fiscal 2008 revenue of $40.0 billion.

We operate two reportable segments: Domestic and International. The Domestic segment is comprised of all states, districts and territories of the U.S. and includes store, call center and online operations of Best Buy, Best Buy Mobile, Geek Squad, Magnolia Audio Video, Pacific Sales Kitchen and Bath Centers ("Pacific Sales") and Speakeasy ("Speakeasy").

The International segment is comprised of all Canada store, call center and online operations, including Best Buy, Future Shop and Geek Squad; all China store, call center and online operations, including Best Buy, Geek Squad and Jiangsu Five Star Appliance Co. ("Five Star"). The International segment offers products and services similar to those offered by our Domestic segment. However, Canada Best Buy stores do not carry appliances. Further, our China Best Buy store and Five Star stores do not carry entertainment software. At the end of fiscal 2008, the International segment operated 131 Future Shop stores and 51 Best Buy stores in Canada, and 160 Five Star stores and one Best Buy store in China.

In support of our retail store operations, we also maintain Web sites for each of our brands (BestBuy.com, BestBuy.ca, BestBuy.com.cn, BestBuyMobile.com, Five-Star.cn, FutureShop.ca, GeekSquad.com, GeekSquad.ca, MagnoliaAV.com, PacificSales.com, and Speakeasy.net).

Use of Estimates in the Preparation of Financial Statements

The preparation of financial statements in conformity with accounting principles generally accepted in the United States ("GAAP") requires us to make estimates and assumptions. These estimates and assumptions affect the reported amounts in the consolidated balance sheets and statements of earnings, as well as the disclosure of contingent liabilities. Future results could be materially affected if actual results were to differ from these estimates and assumptions.

Fiscal Year

Our fiscal year ends on the Saturday nearest the end of February. Fiscal 2008 and 2006 each included 52 weeks, and fiscal 2007 included 53 weeks.

Cash and Cash Equivalents

Cash primarily consists of cash on hand and bank deposits. Cash equivalents primarily consist of money market accounts and other highly liquid investments with an original maturity of three months or less when purchased. The amounts of cash equivalents at March 1, 2008, and March 3, 2007, were $871 and $695, respectively, and the weighted-average interest rates were 4.1% and 4.8%, respectively.

Outstanding checks in excess of funds on deposit (book overdrafts) totaled $159 and $183 at March 1, 2008, and March 3, 2007, respectively, and are reflected as current liabilities in our consolidated balance sheets.

Merchandise Inventories

Merchandise inventories are recorded at the lower of cost, using either the average cost or first-in, first-out method, or market. Inbound freight-related costs from our vendors are included as part of the net cost of merchandise inventories. Also included in the cost of inventory are certain vendor allowances that are not a reimbursement of specific, incremental and identifiable costs to promote a vendor's products. Other costs associated with acquiring, storing and transporting merchandise inventories to our retail stores are expensed as incurred and included in cost of goods sold.

Our inventory loss reserve represents anticipated physical inventory losses (e.g., theft) that have occurred since the last physical inventory date. Independent physical inventory

$ in millions, except per share amounts or as otherwise noted

counts are taken on a regular basis to ensure that the inventory reported in our consolidated financial statements is properly stated. During the interim period between physical inventory counts, we reserve for anticipated physical inventory losses on a location-by-location basis.

Our markdown reserve represents the excess of the carrying value, typically average cost, over the amount we expect to realize from the ultimate sale or other disposal of the inventory. Markdowns establish a new cost basis for our inventory. Subsequent changes in facts or circumstances do not result in the reversal of previously recorded markdowns or an increase in that newly established cost basis.

Restricted Assets

Restricted cash and investments in debt securities totaled $408 and $382, at March 1, 2008, and March 3, 2007, respectively, and are included in other current assets or equity and other investments in our consolidated balance sheets. Such balances are pledged as collateral or restricted to use for vendor payables, general liability insurance, workers' compensation insurance and warranty programs.

Property and Equipment

Property and equipment are recorded at cost. We compute depreciation using the straight-line method over the estimated useful lives of the assets. Leasehold improvements are depreciated over the shorter of their estimated useful lives or the period from the date the assets are placed in service to the end of the initial lease term. Leasehold improvements made significantly after the initial lease term are depreciated over the shorter of their estimated useful lives or the remaining lease term, including renewal periods, if reasonably assured. Accelerated depreciation methods are generally used for income tax purposes.

When property is fully depreciated, retired or otherwise disposed of, the cost and accumulated depreciation are removed from the accounts and any resulting gain or loss is reflected in the consolidated statement of earnings.

Repairs and maintenance costs are charged directly to expense as incurred. Major renewals or replacements that substantially extend the useful life of an asset are capitalized and depreciated.

Costs associated with the acquisition or development of software for internal use are capitalized and amortized over the expected useful life of the software, from three to seven years. A subsequent addition, modification or upgrade to internal-use software is capitalized only to the extent that it enables the software to perform a task it previously did not perform. Capitalized software is included in fixtures and equipment. Software maintenance and training costs are expensed in the period incurred.

Property under capital lease is comprised of buildings and equipment used in our retail operations and corporate support functions. The related depreciation for capital lease assets is included in depreciation expense. The carrying value of property under capital lease was $54 and $26 at March 1, 2008, and March 3, 2007, respectively, net of accumulated depreciation of $13 and $6, respectively.

During the fourth quarter of fiscal 2007, we removed from our fixed asset balance $621 of fully depreciated assets that were no longer in service. This asset adjustment was based primarily on an analysis of our fixed asset records and certain other validation procedures and had no net impact on our fiscal 2007 consolidated balance sheet, statement of earnings or statement of cash flows.

Goodwill and Intangible Assets

Goodwill

Goodwill is the excess of the purchase price over the fair value of identifiable net assets acquired in business combinations accounted for under the purchase method. We do not amortize goodwill but test it for impairment annually, or when indications of potential impairment exist, utilizing a fair value approach at the reporting unit level. A reporting unit is the operating segment, or a business unit one level below that operating segment, for which discrete financial information is prepared and regularly reviewed by segment management.

$ in millions, except per share amounts or as otherwise noted

Tradenames

We have indefinite-lived intangible assets related to our Pacific Sales and Speakeasy tradenames which are included in the Domestic segment. We also have indefinite-lived intangible assets related to our Future Shop and Five Star tradenames, which are included in the International segment.

We determine fair values utilizing widely accepted valuation techniques, including discounted cash flows and market multiple analyses. During the fourth quarter of fiscal 2008, we completed our annual impairment testing of our goodwill and tradenames, using the valuation techniques as described above, and determined there was no impairment.

Investments

Debt Securities

Short-term and long-term investments in debt securities are comprised of auction-rate securities, variable-rate demand notes, asset-backed securities, municipal debt securities and commercial paper. In accordance with SFAS No. 115, *Accounting for Certain Investments in Debt and Equity Securities,* and based on our ability to market and sell these instruments, we classify auction-rate securities and other investments in debt securities as available-for-sale and carry them at fair value. Auction-rate securities are intended to behave like short-term debt instruments because their interest rates are reset periodically through an auction process, typically at intervals of 7, 28 and 35 days. Investments in these securities can be sold for cash at par value on the auction date if the auction is successful. Substantially all of our auction-rate securities are AAA/Aaa-rated and collateralized by student loans, which are guaranteed 95% to 100% by the U.S. government. We also hold auction-rate securities that are in the form of municipal revenue bonds, the vast majority of which are AAA/Aaa-rated and insured by bond insurers. We do not have any investments in securities that are collateralized by assets that include mortgages or subprime debt. Our intent with these investments is not to hold these securities to maturity, but to use the periodic

auction feature to provide liquidity as needed. See Note 3, *Investments,* for further information.

In accordance with our investment policy, we place our investments in debt securities with issuers who have high-quality credit and limit the amount of investment exposure to any one issuer. The primary objective of our investment activities is to preserve principal and maintain a desired level of liquidity to meet working capital needs. We seek to preserve principal and minimize exposure to interest-rate fluctuations by limiting default risk, market risk and reinvestment risk.

Marketable Equity Securities

We also invest in marketable equity securities and classify them as available-for-sale. Investments in marketable equity securities are included in equity and other investments in our consolidated balance sheets, and are reported at fair value based on quoted market prices. All unrealized holding gains and losses are reflected net of tax in accumulated other comprehensive income in shareholders' equity.

Other Investments

We also have investments that are accounted for on either the cost method or the equity method that we include in equity and other investments in our consolidated balance sheets.

We review the key characteristics of our debt, marketable equity securities and other investments portfolio and their classification in accordance with GAAP on an annual basis, or when indications of potential impairment exist. If a decline in the fair value of a security is deemed by management to be other-than-temporary, we write down the cost basis of the investment to fair value, and the amount of the write-down is included in net earnings.

Income Taxes

We account for income taxes using the asset and liability method. Under this method, deferred tax assets and liabilities are recognized for the estimated future tax consequences attributable to differences between the

$ in millions, except per share amounts or as otherwise noted

financial statement carrying amounts of existing assets and liabilities and their respective tax bases, and operating loss and tax credit carryforwards. Deferred tax assets and liabilities are measured pursuant to tax laws using rates we expect to apply to taxable income in the years in which we expect those temporary differences to be recovered or settled. We recognize the effect of a change in income tax rates on deferred tax assets and liabilities in our consolidated statement of earnings in the period that includes the enactment date. We record a valuation allowance to reduce the carrying amounts of deferred tax assets if it is more likely than not that such assets will not be realized.

Long-Term Liabilities

The major components of long-term liabilities at March 1, 2008, and March 3, 2007, included long-term rent-related liabilities, unrecognized tax benefits recorded pursuant to FIN No. 48, deferred compensation plan liabilities, advances received under vendor alliance programs and self-insurance reserves.

Revenue Recognition

We recognize revenue when the sales price is fixed or determinable, collectibility is reasonably assured and the customer takes possession of the merchandise, or in the case of services, at the time the service is provided. Revenue is recognized for store sales when the customer receives and pays for the merchandise at the point of sale. For online sales, we estimate and defer revenue and the related product costs for shipments that are in-transit to the customer. Revenue is recognized at the time we estimate the customer receives the product. Customers typically receive goods within a few days of shipment. Such amounts were immaterial at March 1, 2008, and March 3, 2007. Amounts billed to customers for shipping and handling are included in revenue.

Revenue is reported net of estimated sales returns and excludes sales taxes. We estimate our sales returns reserve based on historical return rates. Our sales returns reserve was $101 and $104, at March 1, 2008, and March 3, 2007, respectively.

Gift Cards

We sell gift cards to our customers in our retail stores, through our Web sites, and through selected third parties. We do not charge administrative fees on unused gift cards, and our gift cards do not have an expiration date. We recognize revenue from gift cards when: (i) the gift card is redeemed by the customer, or (ii) the likelihood of the gift card being redeemed by the customer is remote ("gift card breakage"), and we determine that we do not have a legal obligation to remit the value of unredeemed gift cards to the relevant jurisdictions. We determine our gift card breakage rate based upon historical redemption patterns. Based on our historical information, the likelihood of a gift card remaining unredeemed can be determined 24 months after the gift card is issued. At that time, we recognize breakage income for those cards for which the likelihood of redemption is deemed remote and we do not have a legal obligation to remit the value of such unredeemed gift cards to the relevant jurisdictions. Gift card breakage income is included in revenue in our consolidated statements of earnings.

We began recognizing gift card breakage income during the third quarter of fiscal 2006. Gift card breakage income was as follows in fiscal 2008, 2007 and 2006:

	2008	2007	2006
Gift card breakage income	$34	$46	$43

Due to the resolution of certain legal matters associated with gift card liabilities, we recognized $19 and $27 of gift card breakage income in fiscal 2007 and 2006, respectively, that related to prior fiscal years.

BEST BUY

BEST BUY

$ in millions, except per share amounts or as otherwise noted

Cost of Goods Sold and Selling, General and Administrative Expenses

The following table illustrates the primary costs classified in each major expense category:

Cost of Goods Sold	SG&A

• Total cost of products sold including:
  — Freight expenses associated with moving merchandise inventories from our vendors to our distribution centers;
  — Vendor allowances that are not a reimbursement of specific, incremental and identifiable costs to promote a vendor's products; and
  — Cash discounts on payments to merchandise vendors;
• Cost of services provided including;
  — Payroll and benefits costs for services employees; and
  — Cost of replacement parts and related freight expenses;
• Physical inventory losses;
• Markdowns;
• Customer shipping and handling expenses;
• Costs associated with operating our distribution network, including payroll and benefit costs, occupancy costs, and depreciation;
• Freight expenses associated with moving merchandise inventories from our distribution centers to our retail stores; and
• Promotional financing costs.
	• Payroll and benefit costs for retail and corporate employees;
	• Occupancy costs of retail, services and corporate facilities;
	• Depreciation related to retail, services and corporate assets;
	• Advertising;
	• Vendor allowances that are a reimbursement of specific, incremental and identifiable costs to promote a vendor's products;
	• Charitable contributions;
	• Outside service fees;
	• Long-lived asset impairment charges; and
	• Other administrative costs, such as credit card service fees, supplies, and travel and lodging.

Advertising Costs

Advertising costs, which are included in SG&A, are expensed the first time the advertisement runs. Advertising costs consist primarily of print and television advertisements as well as promotional events. Net advertising expenses were $684, $692 and $644 in fiscal 2008, 2007 and 2006, respectively. Allowances received from vendors for advertising of $156, $140 and $123, in fiscal 2008, 2007 and 2006, respectively, were classified as reductions of advertising expenses.

Stock-Based Compensation

At the beginning of fiscal 2006, we early-adopted the fair value recognition provisions of SFAS No. 123 (revised 2004), *Share-Based Payment* (123(R)), requiring us to recognize expense related to the fair value of our stock-based compensation awards. We elected the modified prospective transition method as permitted by SFAS No. 123(R). Under this transition method, stock-based compensation expense in fiscal 2008, 2007 and 2006 included: (i) compensation expense for all

$ in millions, except per share amounts or as otherwise noted

stock-based compensation awards granted prior to, but not yet vested as of February 26, 2005, based on the grant date fair value estimated in accordance with the original provisions of SFAS No. 123, *Accounting for Stock-Based Compensation;* and (ii) compensation expense for all stock-based compensation awards granted subsequent to February 26, 2005, based on the grant-date fair value estimated in accordance with the provisions of SFAS No. 123(R). We recognize compensation expense on a straight-line basis over the requisite service period of the award (or to an employee's eligible retirement date, if earlier). Total stock-based compensation expense included in our consolidated statements of earnings for fiscal 2008, 2007 and 2006 was $105 ($72, net of tax), $121 ($82, net of tax) and $132 ($87, net of tax), respectively. In accordance with the modified prospective transition method of SFAS No. 123(R), financial results for prior periods have not been restated.

2. Acquisitions

Speakeasy, Inc.

On May 1, 2007, we acquired Speakeasy for $103 in cash, or $89 net of cash acquired, which included transaction costs and the repayment of $5 of Speakeasy's debt. We acquired Speakeasy, an independent U.S. broadband, voice, data and information technology services provider, to strengthen our portfolio of technology solutions. We accounted for the acquisition using the purchase method in accordance with SFAS No. 141, *Business Combinations.* Accordingly, we recorded the net assets at their estimated fair values, and included operating results in our Domestic segment from the date of acquisition. We allocated the purchase price on a preliminary basis using information then available. The allocation of the purchase price to the assets and liabilities acquired will be finalized no later than the first quarter of fiscal 2009. The premium we paid in excess of the fair value of the net assets acquired was primarily

for the expected synergies we believe Speakeasy will generate by providing new technology solutions for our existing and future customers, as well as to obtain Speakeasy's skilled, established workforce. None of the goodwill is deductible for tax purposes.

The preliminary purchase price allocation, net of cash acquired, was as follows:

Receivables	$ 8
Property and equipment	7
Other assets	25
Tradename	6
Goodwill	74
Current liabilities	(31)
Total	$ 89

Jiangsu Five Star Appliance Co., Ltd.

On June 8, 2006, we acquired a 75% interest in Five Star for $184, which included a working capital injection of $122 and transaction costs. Five Star is an appliance and consumer electronics retailer and had 131 stores located in eight of China's 34 provinces on the date of acquisition. We made the investment in Five Star to further our international growth plans, to increase our knowledge of Chinese customers and to obtain an immediate retail presence in China. We have a contractual commitment to acquire the remaining 25% interest within the next several years, subject to Chinese government approval. The acquisition was accounted for using the purchase method in accordance with SFAS No. 141. Accordingly, we recorded the net assets at their estimated fair values, and included operating results in our International segment from the date of acquisition. We allocated the purchase price on a preliminary basis using information then available. The allocation of the purchase price to the assets and liabilities acquired was finalized in the first quarter of fiscal 2008. There was no significant adjustment to the preliminary purchase price allocation. None of the goodwill is deductible for tax purposes.

BEST BUY

$ in millions, except per share amounts or as otherwise noted

The final purchase price allocation, net of cash acquired, was as follows:

Restricted cash	$ 204
Merchandise inventories	109
Property and equipment	78
Other assets	80
Tradename	21
Goodwill	22
Accounts payable	(368)
Other current liabilities	(35)
Debt	(64)
Long-term liabilities	(1)
Minority interests [1]	(33)
Total	$ 13

[1]   The minority owners' proportionate share of assets and liabilities were recorded at historical carrying values.

The minority owners' proportionate share of net earnings was $3 and $1 in fiscal 2008 and 2007, respectively.

Five Star owns a 40% interest in, and purchases appliances from, Jiangsu Heng Xin Ge Li Air Conditioner Sales Co., Ltd. Purchases from this affiliate were $65 and $43 in fiscal 2008 and 2007, respectively. At March 1, 2008, and March 3, 2007, $22 and less than $1, respectively, was due to this affiliate for the purchase of appliances.

3.   Investments

Investments were comprised of the following:

	March 1, 2008	March 3, 2007
Short-term investments		
Debt securities	$ 64	$2,588
Equity and other investments		
Debt securities	$417	$ 318
Marketable equity securities	172	4
Other investments	16	16
Total equity and other investments	$605	$ 338

Debt Securities

The following table presents the fair values, related weighted-average interest rates (taxable equivalent) and major security types for our investments:

	March 1, 2008		March 3, 2007	
	Fair Value	Weighted-Average Interest Rate	Fair Value	Weighted-Average Interest Rate
Short-term investments	$ 64	4.94%	$2,588	5.68%
Long-term investments	417	7.60%	318	5.68%
Total	$481		$2,906	
Auction-rate securities	$417		$2,377	
Municipal debt securities	—		506	
Commercial paper	64		—	
Variable-rate demand notes and asset-backed securities	—		23	
Total	$481		$2,906	

The carrying values of our investments were at fair value at March 1, 2008, and March 3, 2007. As discussed in Note 1, our investments include auction-rate securities, the interest rates of which are reset through an auction process, most commonly at intervals of 7, 28 and 35 days. The same auction process has historically provided a means by which we may rollover the investment or sell these securities at par in order to provide us with liquidity as needed. At March 1, 2008, we had $417 (par value) of auction-rate securities.

Marketable Equity Securities

The carrying values of our investments in marketable equity securities at March 1, 2008, and March 3, 2007,

$ in millions, except per share amounts or as otherwise noted

were $172 and $4, respectively. The increase in marketable equity securities since March 3, 2007, was primarily due to our investment in The Carphone Warehouse Group PLC ("CPW"), Europe's leading independent retailer of mobile phones and services. During the second quarter of fiscal 2008, we purchased in the open market 26.1 million shares of CPW common stock for $183, representing nearly 3% of CPW's outstanding shares.

Net unrealized losses, net of tax, included in accumulated other comprehensive income were ($25) and ($1) at March 1, 2008, and March 3, 2007, respectively.

Other Investments

The aggregate carrying values of investments accounted for on either the cost method or the equity method, at March 1, 2008, and March 3, 2007, were $16 and $16, respectively.

4. Debt

Short-term debt consisted of the following:

	March 1, 2008	March 3, 2007
Revolving credit facilities, secured and unsecured, variable interest rates ranging from 3.5% to 8.0% at March 1, 2008	$ 156	$ 20
Notes payable to banks, secured, paid October 2007	—	21
Total short-term debt	$ 156	$ 41

Fiscal Year	2008	2007
Maximum month-end outstanding during the year	$1,955	$ 78
Average amount outstanding during the year	$ 655	$ 57
Weighted-average interest rate	4.5%	5.3%

Long-term debt consisted of the following:

	March 1, 2008	March 3, 2007
Convertible subordinated debentures, unsecured, due 2022, interest rate 2.25%	$ 402	$402
Financing lease obligations, due 2009 to 2023, interest rates ranging from 3.0% to 6.5%	197	171
Capital lease obligations, due 2010 to 2026, interest rates ranging from 5.1% to 8.8%	51	24
Other debt, due 2010 to 2022, interest rates ranging from 2.6% to 8.8%	10	12
Total long-term debt	660	609
Less: current portion	(33)	(19)
Total long-term debt, less current portion	$ 627	$590

Certain debt is secured by property and equipment with a net book value of $87 and $80 at March 1, 2008, and March 3, 2007, respectively.

Credit Facilities

On June 26, 2007, we entered into a $3,000 bridge loan facility with Goldman Sachs Credit Partners L.P. (the "Bridge Facility"), concurrent with the execution of agreements to purchase $3,000 of shares of our common stock in the aggregate pursuant to our ASR program. See Note 5, *Shareholders' Equity*, for further information on the ASR program. We initially borrowed $2,500 under the Bridge Facility and used $500 of our existing cash and investments to fund the ASR program. Effective July 11, 2007, we reduced the amount we could borrow under the Bridge Facility to $2,500.

$ in millions, except per share amounts or as otherwise noted

	2008	2007	2006
Revenue			
Domestic	$33,328	$31,031	$27,380
International	6,695	4,903	3,468
Total revenue	$40,023	$35,934	$30,848
Operating Income			
Domestic	$ 1,999	$ 1,900	$ 1,588
International	162	99	56
Total operating income	2,161	1,999	1,644
Other income (expense)			
Investment income and other	129	162	107
Interest expense	(62)	(31)	(30)
Earnings from operations before income tax expense, minority interest and equity in loss of affiliates	$ 2,228	$ 2,130	$ 1,721
Assets			
Domestic	$ 8,194	$10,614	$ 9,722
International	4,564	2,956	2,142
Total assets	$12,758	$13,570	$11,864

10. Contingencies and Commitments

Contingencies

We are involved in various other legal proceedings arising in the normal course of conducting business. We believe the amounts provided in our consolidated financial statements, as prescribed by GAAP, are adequate in light of the probable and estimable liabilities. The resolution of those other proceedings is not expected to have a material impact on our results of operations or financial condition.

Commitments

We engage Accenture LLP ("Accenture") to assist us with improving our operational capabilities and reducing our costs in the information systems, procurement and human resources areas. Our future contractual obligations to Accenture are expected to range from $76 to $272 per year through 2012, the end of the periods under contract. Prior to our engagement of Accenture, a significant portion of these costs were incurred as part of normal operations.

We had outstanding letters of credit for purchase obligations with a fair value of $90 at March 1, 2008.

At March 1, 2008, we had commitments for the purchase and construction of facilities valued at approximately $45. Also, at March 1, 2008, we had entered into lease commitments for land and buildings for 104 future locations. These lease commitments with real estate developers provide for minimum rentals ranging from 5 to 20 years, which if consummated based on current cost estimates, will approximate $72 annually over the initial lease terms. These minimum rentals are reported in the future minimum lease payments included in Note 6, *Leases*.

In April 2008, CompUSA, Inc. accepted our offer to acquire the rights to 17 leases for $13.5. Pending approval from the landlords, we expect to take possession of all sites by June 2008. The total square footage related to these leases is approximately 453,000 square feet, or an average of approximately 27,000 square feet per site. The remaining minimum lease terms range from 3 to 14 years, however, all leases include renewal options for an additional 5 to 20 years. The sites are located throughout the U.S., primarily in western states, and we anticipate utilizing these sites over the next two fiscal years for planned new stores for both Best Buy and Pacific Sales.

Alabama Albertville, Alexander City, Andalusia, Arab, Ardmore, Athens, Atmore, Attalla, Bay Minette, Bayou La Batre, Bessemer, Birmingham, Butler, Calera, Camden, Center Point, Centre, Childersburg, Clanton, Cullman, Daphne, Decatur, Demopolis, Dothan, Enterprise, Fairfield, Fairhope, Florence, Foley, Fort Payne, Gadsden, Gardendale, Gulf Shores, Guntersville, Haleyville, Hamilton, Hartselle, Hoover, Huntsville, Jackson, Jasper, Leeds, Linden, Luverne, Madison, Marion, Mobile, Montgomery, Moulton, Northport, Opelika, Opp, Oxford, Pelham, Pell City, Phenix City, Piedmont, Prattville, Robertsdale, Rogersville, Russellville, Saraland, Scottsboro, Selma, Sumiton, Sylacauga, Tallassee, Thomasville, Troy, Tuscaloosa *Alaska* Anchorage, Bethel, Cordova, Craig, Eagle River, Fairbanks, Glennallen, Haines, Homer, Juneau, Kenai, Ketchikan, Kodiak, Petersburg, Seward, Sitka, Skagway, Soldotna, Valdez, Wasilla *Arizona* Ajo, Apache Junction, Avondale, Benson, Bullhead City, Camp Verde, Casa Grande, Chandler, Chino Valley, Colorado City, Coolidge, Cottonwood, Douglas, Flagstaff, Florence, Fort Mohave, Fountain Hills, Gilbert, Glendale, Greenvalley, Heber, Holbrook, Kayenta, Kingman, Lake Havasu, Lakeside, Maricopa, Mesa, Miami, Morenci, New River, Nogales, Oro Valley, Parker, Payson, Peoria, Phoenix, Prescott, Prescott Valley, Quartzsite, Safford, San Manuel, Scottsdale, Sedona, Show Low, Sierra Vista, Springerville, St. Johns, Sun City, Surprise, Taylor, Tempe, Thatcher, Tuba City, Tucson, Wickenburg, Willcox, Yuma *Arkansas* Arkadelphia, Ash Flat, Batesville, Beebe, Benton, Bentonville, Berryville, Brinkley, Bryant, Cabot, Camden, Cave City, Clarksville, Clinton, Conway, Danville, De Queen, De Witt, Dumas, El Dorado, Fayetteville, Flippin, Forrest City, Fort Smith, Glenwood, Harrison, Heber Springs, Hope, Hot Springs, Jacksonville, Jasper, Jonesboro, Little Rock, Magnolia, Malvern, Mammoth Springs, Marshall, Melbourne, Mena, Mountain Home, Mountain View, North Little Rock, Nashville, Newport, Paragould, Paris, Pine Bluff, Prescott, Rogers, Russellville, Salem, Searcy, Sheridan, Siloam Springs, Springdale, Star City, Stuttgart, Van Buren, West Helena, West Memphis, Wynne *California* Agoura, Alameda, Albany, Alhambra, Alta Loma, Alturas, American Canyon, Anaheim, Anaheim Hills, Anderson, Angels Camp, Antioch, Apple Valley, Arcadia, Arcata, Arnold, Arroyo Grande, Atascadero, Atwater, Auburn, Avalon, Azusa, Bakersfield, Baldwin Park, Barstow, Beaumont, Bell, Belmont, Benicia, Berkeley, Beverly Hills, Big Bear Lake, Bishop, Blue Jay, Blythe, Brawley, Brea, Buellton, Buena Park, Burbank, Burlingame, Calexico, California City, Camarillo, Canoga Park, Canyon Country, Capitola, Carlsbad, Carmichael, Carpinteria, Carson, Castro Valley, Cathedral City, Cerritos, Chatsworth, Chico, Chino, Chino Hills, Chula Vista, Citrus Heights, City of Industry, Clearlake, Cloverdale, Clovis, Coachella, Coalinga, Colton, Colusa, Compton, Concord, Corcoran, Corning, Corona, Corte Madera, Costa Mesa, Covina, Crescent City, Crestline, Culver City, Cupertino, Cypress, Daly City, Dana Point, Danville, Davis, Del Mar, Delano, Desert Hot Springs, Diamond Bar, Dinuba, Downey, Duarte, Dublin, E Los Angeles, El Cajon, El Centro, El Cerrito, El Monte, Elk Grove, Emeryville, Encinitas, Encino, Escondido, Eureka, Fairfield, Fall River Mills, Fallbrook, Folsom, Fontana, Foothill Ranch, Fortuna, Foster City, Fountain Valley, Freedom, Fremont, Fresno, Fort Bragg, Fullerton, Garberville, Garden Grove, Gardena, Gilroy, Glendale, Glendora, Goleta, Gonzales, Granada Hills, Grass Valley, Greenfield, Grover Beach, Hanford, Harbor City, Hawthorne, Hayward, Hemet, Hercules, Hesperia, Highland, Hollister, Hollywood, Huntington Beach, Huntington Park, Indio, Inglewood, Irvine, Jackson, King City, La Habra, La Jolla, La Mesa, La Mirada, La Puente, La Quinta, La Verne, Lafayette, Laguna Hills, Laguna Niguel, Lake Elsinore, Lake Isabella, Lakeport, Lakewood, Lancaster, Lawndale, Lemoore, Lincoln Heights, Livermore, Lodi, Lompoc, Long Beach, Los Alamitos, Los Angeles, Los Banos, Los Gatos, Los Osos, Lynwood, Madera, Malibu, Mammoth Lakes, Manhattan Beach, Manteca, Marina Del Rey, Martinez, Marysville, Maywood, Merced, Milpitas, Mission Hills, Modesto, Mojave, Monrovia, Montclair, Montebello, Monterey, Monterey Park, Montrose, Moorpark, Moreno Valley, Morgan Hill, Morro Bay, Mountain View, Mount Shasta, Murrieta, Napa, National City, Newbury Park, Newhall, Newport Beach, North Highlands, North Hollywood, Northridge, Norwalk, Novato, Oakdale, Oakhurst, Oakland, Oakley, Oceanside, Ojai, Ontario, Orange, Orangevale, Orland, Oroville, Oxnard, Pacifica, Palm Desert, Palm Springs, Palmdale, Palo Alto, Panorama City, Paradise, Paramount, Pasadena, Paso Robles, Patterson, Perris, Petaluma, Phelan, Pico Rivera, Pinole, Pittsburg, Placentia, Placerville, Pleasant Hill, Pleasanton, Pollock Pines, Pomona, Porterville, Poway, Quincy, Ramona, Rancho Cordova, Rancho Cucamonga, Rancho Santa Margarita, Red Bluff, Redding, Redlands, Redondo Beach, Redwood City, Reedley, Rialto, Ridgecrest, Rio Vista, Riverbank, Riverside, Rocklin, Rohnert Park, Rolling Hills, Rosamond, Rosemead, Roseville, Rowland Heights, Sacramento, Salinas, San Bernardino, San Bruno, San Clemente, San Diego, San Dimas, San Francisco, San Jose, San Leandro, San Luis Obispo, San Marcos, San Mateo, San Pablo, San Pedro, San Rafael, San Ramon, Sanger, Santa Ana, Santa Barbara, Santa Clara, Santa Cruz, Santa Maria, Santa Monica, Santa Paula, Santa Rosa, Santee, Saugus, Scotts Valley, Seal Beach, Seaside, Sebastopol, Selma, Sherman Oaks, Signal Hill, Simi, San Juan Capistrano, Soledad, Sonoma, Sonora, South Gate, South Lake Tahoe, South Pasadena, South San Francisco, Spring Valley, Stockton, Studio City, Sun Valley, Sunnyvale, Susanville, Sylmar, Taft, Tehachapi, Temecula, Temple City, Thousand Oaks, Torrance, Tracy, Truckee, Tujunga, Tulare, Turlock, Tustin, Twentynine Palms, Ukiah, Union City, Upland, Vacaville, Valencia, Vallejo, Valley Springs, Van Nuys, Venice, Ventura, Victorville, Visalia, Vista, Walnut Creek, Wasco, Watsonville, Weaverville, West Covina, West Hollywood, West Los Angeles, West Sacramento, Westchester, Westminster, Whittier, Willits, Willows, Wilmington, Windsor, Woodland, Woodland Hills, Yorba Linda, Yreka, Yuba City, Yucaipa, Yucca Valley *Colorado* Alamosa, Arvada, Aspen, Aurora, Avon, Bayfield, Bennett, Boulder, Brighton, Broomfield, Buena Vista, Burlington, Canon City, Castle Rock, Castle Rock, Centennial, Center, Colorado Springs, Conifer, Cortez, Craig, Crested Butte, Denver, Durango, Elizabeth, Englewood, Estes Park, Evergreen, Flagler, Fort Collins, Fountain, Fraser, Frisco, Glenwood Spring, Golden, Grand Junction, Greeley, Greenwood Village, Gunnison, Highlands Ranch, Holyoke, Idaho Springs, La Junta, Lafayette, Lakewood, Lamar, Limon, Littleton, Longmont, Loveland, Meeker, Monte Vista, Montrose, Monument, Northglenn, Pagosa Springs, Paonia, Parachute, Parker, Pueblo, Rifle, Salida, Springfield, Steamboat Springs, Sterling, Thornton, Westminster, Woodland Park, Wray, Yuma *Connecticut* Avon, Barkhamsted, Bloomfield, Branford, Bridgeport, Bristol, Canaan, Cheshire, Clinton, Cos Cob, Cromwell, Danbury, Derby, East Haven, Enfield, Fairfield, Farmington, Glastonbury, Groton, Guilford, Hamden, Hartford, Manchester, Meriden, Middletown, Milford, Naugatuck, New Britain, New Canaan, New Haven, New London, New Milford, Newington, Newtown, North Haven, Norwalk, Norwich, Old Saybrook, Orange, Plainfield, Putnam, Ridgefield, Riverside, Southbury, Southington, Stamford, Torrington, Trumbull, Vernon, Wallingford, Waterbury, Waterford, Watertown, West Hartford, Westport, Wethersfield, Willimantic, Wilton, Windsor, *D.C.* Washington *Delaware* Bear, Claymont, Dover, Georgetown, Middletown, Milford, New Castle, Newark, Rehoboth Beach, Seaford, Smyrna, Wilmington *Florida* Alachua, Altamonte, Altamonte Springs, Apopka, Arcadia, Atlantic Beach, Auburndale, Avon Park, Bartow, Bayonet Point, Belle Glade, Belleview, Big Pine Key, Boca Raton, Bonita Springs, Boynton Beach, Bradenton, Brandon, Branford, Brooksville, Callaway, Cape Coral, Casselberry, Century, Chiefland, Chipley, Clearwater, Clermont, Clewiston, Cocoa, Cocoa Beach, Cooper City, Coral Gables, Coral Springs, Crawfordville, Crestview, Crystal River, Davie, Daytona Beach, Deerfield, Deerfield Beach, Defuniak Springs, Deland, Delray Beach, Deltona, Destin, Dunnellon, Englewood, Fernandina Beach, Florida City, Fort Lauderdale, Fort Myers, Fort Pierce, Fort Walton Beach, Gainesville, Greenacres, Gulf Breeze, Haines City, Hialeah, Hilliard, Holiday, Hollywood, Homestead, Homosassa, Immokalee, Indiantown, Inverness, Jacksonville, Jensen Beach, Jupiter, Key Largo, Key West, Keystone Heights, Kissimmee, Lady Lake, Lake City, Lake Mary, Lake Placid, Lake Wales, Lake Worth, Lakeland, Lantana, Largo, Lauderdale Lakes, Lauderhill, Leesburg, Lehigh Acres, Live Oak, Longwood, Lutz, Macclenny, Madison, Marathon, Marco Island, Margate, Marianna, Mary Esther, Melbourne, Merritt Island, Miami, Miami Beach, Milton, Miramar, Monticello, Mount Dora, North Fort Myers, North Miami Beach, Naples, Navarre, New Port Richey, New Smyrna Beach, Niceville, Oakland Park, Ocala, Ocoee, Okeechobee, Orange City, Orange Park, Orlando, Ormond Beach, Oviedo, Palatka, Palm Bay, Palm Beach Garden, Palm Coast, Palm Harbor, Panama City, Pembroke Pines, Pensacola, Perry, Plant City, Plantation, Pompano Beach, Port Charlotte, Port Orange, Port Richey, Port St. Joe, Port St. Lucie, Punta Gorda, Riverview, Royal Palm Beach, Ruskin, Sanford, Santa Rosa Beach, Sarasota, Satellite Beach, Sebastian, Sebring, Seffner, Seminole, South Daytona, Spring Hill, St. Augustine, St. Cloud, St. Petersburg, Starke, Stuart, Sunrise, Tallahassee, Tampa, Tarpon Springs, Temple Terrace, Tequesta, Titusville, Venice, Vero Beach, Wauchula, Wellington, West Palm Beach, Weston, Wildwood, Wilton Manors, Winter Haven, Winter Park, Winter Springs, Zephyrhills *Georgia* Adel, Albany, Alpharetta, Americus, Athens, Atlanta, Augusta, Austell, Bainbridge, Barnesville, Baxley, Blairsville, Blakely, Blue Ridge, Brunswick, Buford, Cairo, Calhoun, Canton, Carrollton, Cartersville, Cedartown, Centerville, Chamblee, Chatsworth, Clayton, Cleveland, Columbus, Commerce, Conyers, Cordele, Cornelia, Covington, Cumming, Cuthbert, Dahlonega, Dalton, Dawson, Dawsonville, Decatur, Donalsonville, Douglas, Douglasville, Dublin, Duluth, East Ellijay, Elberton, Fayetteville, Fitzgerald, Folkston, Forest Park, Forsyth, Fort Gaines, Fort Oglethorpe, Fort Valley, Gainesville, Griffin, Hampton, Hartwell, Hazlehurst, Hiawassee, Hinesville, Hiram, Homerville, Jackson, Jasper, Jesup, Kennesaw, Lafayette, Lagrange, Lawrenceville, Lilburn, Lincolnton, Lithonia, Macon, Madison, Marietta, Martinez, Mc Rae, McDonough, Metter, Milledgeville, Monroe, Monticello, Morrow, Moultrie, Nashville, Newnan, Norcross, Oakwood, Peachtree City, Perry, Quitman, Richmond Hill, Riverdale, Rockmart, Rome, Roswell, Royston, Savannah, Smyrna, Snellville, St. Marys, St. Simons Island, Statesboro, Stockbridge, Stone Mountain, Summerville, Suwanee, Sylvania, Sylvester, Thomaston, Thomasville, Thomson, Tifton, Toccoa, Trenton, Union City, Valdosta, Vidalia, Villa Rica, Warner Robins, Washington, Waycross, Winder, Woodbury, Woodstock *Hawaii* Aiea, Ewa Beach, Haleiwa, Hilo, Honolulu, Kahului, Kailua, Kailua-Kona, Kamuela, Kaneohe, Kapolei, Kihei, Lahaina, Lihue, Mililani, Wahiawa, Waianae, Waipahu *Idaho* American Falls, Blackfoot, Boise, Bonners Ferry, Buhl, Burley, Caldwell, Chubbuck, Coeur d'Alene, Cottonwood, Driggs, Emmett, Grangeville, Hailey, Idaho Falls, Lewiston, McCall, Meridian, Montpelier, Moscow, Mountain Home, Nampa, Orofino, Pocatello, Post Falls, Rexburg, Rigby, Salmon, Sandpoint, Twin Falls, Wendell *Illinois* Aledo, Alton, Anna, Antioch, Arcola, Arlington Heights, Arthur, Aurora, Bartlett, Batavia, Belleville, Belvidere, Bensenville, Benton, Berwyn, Bloomingdale, Bloomington, Blue Island, Bolingbrook, Bourbonnais, Burbank, Calumet City, Canton, Carbondale, Carlinville, Carmi, Centralia, Champaign, Channahon, Chester, Chicago, Chicago Heights, Cicero, Collinsville, Crystal Lake, Danville, Decatur, Des Plaines, Dixon, Dolton, Downers Grove, Du Quoin, Dwight, East Peoria, East St. Louis, Effingham, El Paso, Elgin, Elk Grove Village, Eureka, Evanston, Fairbury, Fairfield, Fairview Heights, Flora, Fox Lake, Frankfort, Freeport, Galesburg, Geneseo, Gibson City, Glen Carbon, Glen Ellyn, Glencoe, Glenview, Granite City, Greenville, Gurnee, Harrisburg, Havana, Highland, Highland Park, Hoffman Estates, Homer Glen, Homewood, Hoopeston, Jacksonville, Jerseyville, Joliet, Kankakee, Kewanee, La Grange, Lake Zurich, Lansing, Lemont, Lincoln, Litchfield, Lake in the Hills, Lombard, Machesney Park, Macomb, Marengo, Marion, Markham, Mascoutah, Matteson, Mattoon, McHenry, Melrose Park, Mendota, Midlothian, Moline, Montgomery, Morris, Mount Vernon, Mundelein, Naperville, Nashville, Niles, Norridge, North Riverside, Oak Lawn, Oak Park, Olney, Ottawa, Palatine, Palos Heights, Paris, Pekin, Peoria, Peru, Petersburg, Pontiac, Princeton, Quincy, Robinson, Rochelle, Rockford, Round Lake Beach, Salem, Sandwich, Savanna, Savoy, Schaumburg, Seneca, Shiloh, Skokie, South Elgin, South Holland, Sparta, Springfield, St. Charles, Staunton, Sterling, Streator, Sullivan, Sycamore, Tinley Park, Tuscola, Urbana, Vernon Hills, Villa Park, Virden, Waterloo, Watseka, Waukegan, West Dundee, Wheaton, Wheeling, Willowbrook, Wilmington, Wood River, Yorkville, Zion *Indiana* Anderson, Angola, Argos, Auburn, Aurora, Avon, Batesville, Bedford, Berne, Bicknell, Bloomington, Bluffton, Brazil, Bremen, Brook, Brookville, Brownsburg, Brownstown, Cannelton, Carmel, Clarksville, Columbia City, Columbus, Corydon, Covington, Crawfordsville, Crown Point, Decatur, Demotte, Elkhart, Elwood, Evansville, Fishers, Fort Wayne, Fowler, Frankfort, Franklin, Gary, Goshen, Greencastle, Greenfield, Greensburg, Greenwood, Griffith, Hammond, Hobart, Huntington, Indianapolis, Jasper, Kendallville, Knox, Kokomo, La Porte, Lafayette, Lagrange, Lebanon, Ligonier, Linton, Madison, Marion, Martinsville, Merrillville, Michigan City, Mishawaka, Monticello, Mooresville, Muncie, Munster, Nappanee, New Albany, New Carlisle, New Castle, New Haven, Noblesville, North Manchester, North Vernon, Paoli, Peru, Petersburg, Plainfield, Plymouth, Portage, Portland, Princeton, Rensselaer, Richmond, Rising Sun, Rochester, Rockport, Rockville, Rushville, Schererville, Seymour, Shelbyville, South Bend, Syracuse, Terre Haute, Tipton, Valparaiso, Vincennes, W Lafayette, Wabash, Warsaw, Washington, Winamac, Winchester *Iowa* Adel, Altoona, Ames, Ankeny, Atlantic, Belle Plaine, Boone, Carroll, Cedar Falls, Cedar Rapids, Chariton, Charles City, Cherokee, Clarinda, Clinton, Coralville, Council Bluffs, Cresco, Creston, Davenport, Decorah, Denison, Des Moines, Dubuque, Dyersville, Eagle Grove, Estherville, Fairfield, Fort Dodge, Fort Madison, Garner, Glenwood, Greenfield, Grinnell, Hampton, Harlan, Humboldt, Independence, Iowa City, Iowa Falls, Jefferson, Keokuk, Knoxville, Le Mars, Logan, Manchester, Maquoketa, Marengo, Marshalltown, Mason City, Mount Pleasant, Muscatine, New Hampton, Newton, Orange City, Osage, Osceola, Ottumwa, Pella, Perry, Pocahontas, Red Oak, Rock Valley, Sac City, Sheldon, Sioux Center, Sioux City, Spencer, Spirit Lake, Stuart, Vinton, Washington, Waterloo, Webster City, West Burlington, West Des Moines, West Union, Winterset *Kansas* Abilene, Anthony, Arkansas City, Atchison, Atwood, Bonner Springs, Burlington, Chanute, Clay Center, Colby, Columbus, Concordia, Derby, Dodge City, El Dorado, Ellsworth, Emporia, Fort Scott, Garden City, Garnett, Girard, Goodland, Great Bend, Hays, Hillsboro, Horton, Hutchinson, Independence, Iola, Junction City, Kansas City, Lawrence, ... Lenexa, Liberal, Manhattan, McPherson, Mission, Newton, Oakley, Olathe, Osage City, Osawatomie, Ottawa, Overland Park, Parsons, Pittsburg, Pratt, Salina, Scott City, Seneca, Shawnee Mission, ... Wellington, Wichita, Winfield *Kentucky* Alexandria, Ashland, Barbourville, Bardstown, Bardwell, Beaver Dam, Berea, Bowling Green, Brandenburg, Cadiz, Campbellsville, Campton, Carrollton, ... City, Columbia, ... Danville, Dry Ridge, Elizabethtown, Erlanger, Falmouth, Flemingsburg, Florence, Frankfort, Franklin, Georgetown, Glasgow, Grayson, Hazard, Henderson, Hopkinsville, Jackson, ... La Grange, Latonia, Leb... Lexington, London, Louisville, Madisonville, Mayfield, Maysville, Middlesboro, Monticello, Morehead, Morgantown, Mount Sterling, Mount Vernon, Murray, Newport, Nichol... Owensboro, Paducah, Paris, Pike... Pineville, Prestonsburg, Princeton, Radcliff, Richmond, Russell Springs, Russellville, Salyersville, Scottsville, Shelbyville, Somerset, South Williamson, Stanton, Taylorsville, Warsaw, West Liberty, Whitley City, Williams... Winchester *Louisiana* Abbeville, Alexandria, Bastrop, Baton Rouge, Bogalusa, Bossier City, Boutte, Crowley, Cut Off, Denham Springs, Deridder, Eunice, Franklinton, G... Hammond, Harahan, Harvey, Houma, Jea... Jena, Jennings, Kenner, Kentwood, La Place, Lafayette, Lake Charles, Leesville, Mandeville, Mansfield, Many, Metairie, Minden, Monroe, Morgan City, Natchit... New Iberia, New Orleans, New Roads, Oakdale, Opelousas, Pineville, Plaquemine, Rayne, Ruston, Shreveport, Slidell, Springhill, St. Francisville, Sulphur, Thibodaux, Ville Platte, West Monroe, Westwego, Winfield, Winnsboro, Zachary *Maine* Auburn, Augusta, Bangor, Bar Harbor, Belfast, Biddeford, Boothbay Harbor, Brunswick, Bucksport, Damariscotta, Dover-Foxcroft, Ellsworth, Falmouth, Farmington, Fort Kent, Lewiston, Machias, Madawaska, Mexico, Millinocket, Oxford, Portland, Presque Isle, Rockland, Sanford, Skowhegan, South Portland, Standish, Topsham, Waterville, Wells, Windham *Maryland* Aberdeen, Annapolis, Baltimore, Bel Air, Beltsville, Bethesda, Bowie, Burtonsville, Cambridge, Catonsville, Charlotte Hall, Chestertown, Clinton, Cockeysville, College Park, Columbia, Denton, Derwood, Dunkirk, Easton, Edgewood, Eldersburg, Elkton, Ellicott City, Frederick, Gaithersburg, Germantown, Glen Burnie, Greenbelt, Hagerstown, Hampstead, Hanover, Hyattsville, Kensington, La Plata, La Vale, Largo, Laurel, Leonardtown, Lexington Park, ... Mount Airy, Oakland, Ocean City, Odenton, Olney, Owings Mills, Oxon Hill, Pasadena, Pocomoke City, Potomac, Prince Frederick, Randallstown, Reisterstown, Rockville, Salisbury, Severna Park, Silver Spring, Stevensville, Thurmont, Towson, Waldorf, Westminster, Wheaton *Massachusetts* Acton, Andover, Ashland, Athol, Auburn, Bedford, Beverly, Billerica, Boston, Braintree, Bridgewater, Brockton, Burlington, Cambridge, Chelmsford, Chicopee, Danvers, Dedham, Dorchester, East Boston, East Walpole, East Wareham, Fairhaven, Fall River, Falmouth, Fitchburg, Foxboro, Framingham, Gardner, Greenfield, Harrington, Hadley, Haverhill, Holyoke, Hyannis, Kingston, Lanesborough, Lenox, Leominster, Lowell, Lynn, Malden, Marlborough, Marshfield, Medford, Milford, Natick, New Bedford, Newton, North Adams, North Attleboro, North Dartmouth, Northampton, Orleans, Peabody, Pittsfield, Plymouth, Quincy, Raynham, Revere, Roslindale, Saugus, South Attleboro, South Boston, South Dennis, South Easton, South Lawrence, South Yarmouth, Southbridge, Springfield, Stoneham, Stoughton, Sudbury, Swampscott, Swansea, Taunton, Vineyard Haven, Waltham, Watertown, Webster, Westfield, Westford, Whitinsville, Wilmington, Woburn, Worcester *Michigan* Adrian, Albion, Allegan, Alpena, Ann Arbor, Auburn Hills, Bad Axe, Battle Creek, Bay City, Bellaire, Belleville, Benton Harbor, Big Rapids, Birmingham, Bloomfield, Boyne City, Brighton, Brooklyn, Brown City, Burton, Byron Center, Cadillac, Canton, Caro, Carson City, Cass City, Center Line, Charlevoix, Cheboygan, Chesaning, Clinton Township, Clio, Coldwater, Commerce, Davison, Dearborn, Dearborn Heights, Detroit, Dowagiac, Eastpointe, Eaton Rapids, Escanaba, Evart, Farmington Hills, Farmington, Fenton, Ferndale, Flint, Frankenmuth, Fremont, Gaylord, Grand Blanc, Grand Haven, Grand Rapids, Grayling, Greenville, Grosse Pointe, Hastings, Hemlock, Highland Park, Holland, Houghton Lake, Howell, Imlay City, Ionia, Iron Mountain, Ironwood, Ishpeming, Jackson, Jenison, Jonesville, Kalamazoo, Kalkaska, Kentwood, Lake Orion, L'Anse, Lansing, Lapeer, Lincoln Park, Livonia, Ludington, Madison Heights, Manistee, Manistique, Marine City, Marquette, Marshall, Midland, Milford, Monroe, Mount Pleasant, Munising, Muskegon, Newberry, Niles, Novi, Oak Park, Okemos, Oscoda, Owosso, Petoskey, Pinconning, Plainwell, Pontiac, Port Huron, Portage, Redford, Reed City, Rochester, Rogers City, Roseville, Royal Oak, Saginaw, Sandusky, Sault St. Marie, Shelby, South Haven, Southfield, Southgate, St. Ignace, St. Johns, Standish, Stanton, Sturgis, Suttons Bay, Tawas City, Three Oaks, Three Rivers, Traverse City, Troy, Tuscola, Vassar, Washington Township, Waterford, Wayne, Westland, White Cloud, White Pigeon, Whitehall, Woodhaven, Wyoming, Ypsilanti *Minnesota* Ada, Aitkin, Albany, Albert Lea, Alexandria, Apple Valley, Austin, Baxter, Bemidji, Benson, Blaine, Bloomington, Brooklyn Center, Burnsville, Cambridge, Chanhassen, Coon Rapids, Cottage Grove, Crystal, Detroit Lakes, Duluth, Eagan, Eden Prairie, Elk River, Erskine, Fairmont, Faribault, Fergus Falls, Forest Lake, Golden Valley, Grand Marais, Grand Rapids, Hibbing, Hilltop, Hutchinson, International Falls, Jackson, Lake City, Le Sueur, Little Falls, Mankato, Maple Grove, Marshall, Minneapolis, Minnetonka, Montevideo, Monticello, Moorhead, Moose Lake, Mora, Morris, New Ulm, North Branch, Ortonville, Owatonna, Park Rapids, Pipestone, Redwood Falls, Richfield, Rochester, Roseau, Roseville, Saint Cloud, Saint Paul, Savage, Shakopee, Sleepy Eye, St. Cloud, St. James, St. Louis Park, St. Paul, Stillwater, Thief River Falls, Vadnais Heights, Virginia, Walker, Warroad, Waseca, Wayzata, Willmar, Windom, Winona, Woodbury, Worthington, Young America *Mississippi* Amory, Batesville, Biloxi, Booneville, Brookhaven, Canton, Carthage, Clarksdale, Cleveland, Clinton, Columbia, Columbus, Corinth, Crystal Springs, D'Iberville, Flora, Greenville, Greenwood, Grenada, Gulfport, Hattiesburg, Houston, Jackson, Laurel, Lucedale, Magee, McComb, Mendenhall, Meridian, Monticello, Morton, Natchez, New Albany, Ocean Springs, Olive Branch, Oxford, Pascagoula, Pearl, Philadelphia, Picayune, Pontotoc, Poplarville, Prentiss, Purvis, Quitman, Ridgeland, Senatobia, Southaven, Starkville, Tupelo, Tylertown, Vicksburg, Waynesboro, West Point, Wiggins, Yazoo City *Missouri* Alton, Arnold,

RADIOSHACK

RadioShack.

RadioShack Corporation | **Financial Reports**

CONSOLIDATED BALANCE SHEETS
RadioShack Corporation and Subsidiaries

(In millions, except for share amounts)	December 31, 2007	December 31, 2006
Assets		
Current assets:		
Cash and cash equivalents	$ 509.7	$ 472.0
Accounts and notes receivable, net	256.0	247.9
Inventories	705.4	752.1
Other current assets	95.7	127.6
Total current assets	1,566.8	1,599.6
Property, plant and equipment, net	317.1	386.3
Other assets, net	105.7	84.1
Total assets	$ 1,989.6	$ 2,070.0
Liabilities and Stockholders' Equity		
Current liabilities:		
Short-term debt, including current maturities of long-term debt	$ 61.2	$ 194.9
Accounts payable	257.6	254.5
Accrued expenses and other current liabilities	393.5	442.2
Income taxes payable	35.7	92.6
Total current liabilities	748.0	984.2
Long-term debt, excluding current maturities	348.2	345.8
Other non-current liabilities	123.7	86.2
Total liabilities	1,219.9	1,416.2
Commitments and contingent liabilities		
Stockholders' equity:		
Preferred stock, no par value, 1,000,000 shares authorized:		
Series A junior participating, 300,000 shares designated and none issued	—	—
Common stock, $1 par value, 650,000,000 shares authorized; 191,033,000 shares issued	191.0	191.0
Additional paid-in capital	108.4	92.6
Retained earnings	1,992.1	1,780.9
Treasury stock, at cost; 59,940,000 and 55,196,000 shares, respectively	(1,516.5)	(1,409.1)
Accumulated other comprehensive loss	(5.3)	(1.6)
Total stockholders' equity	769.7	653.8
Total liabilities and stockholders' equity	$ 1,989.6	$ 2,070.0

CONSOLIDATED STATEMENTS OF INCOME
RadioShack Corporation and Subsidiaries

| (In millions, except per share amounts) | Year Ended December 31, | | | | | |
| | 2007 | | 2006 | | 2005 | |
	Dollars	% of Revenues	Dollars	% of Revenues	Dollars	% of Revenues
Net sales and operating revenues	$4,251.7	100.0%	$4,777.5	100.0%	$5,081.7	100.0%
Cost of products sold (includes depreciation amounts of $10.0 million, $10.7 million and $10.3 million, respectively)	2,225.9	52.4	2,648.1	55.4	2,815.0	55.4
Gross profit	2,025.8	47.6	2,129.4	44.6	2,266.7	44.6
Operating expenses:						
Selling, general and administrative	1,538.5	36.2	1,810.7	37.9	1,803.3	35.5
Depreciation and amortization	102.7	2.4	117.5	2.5	113.5	2.2
Impairment of long-lived assets and other charges	2.7	—	44.3	0.9	—	—
Total operating expenses	1,643.9	38.6	1,972.5	41.3	1,916.8	37.7
Operating income	381.9	9.0	156.9	3.3	349.9	6.9
Interest income	22.6	0.5	7.4	0.1	5.9	0.1
Interest expense	(38.8)	(0.9)	(44.3)	(0.9)	(44.5)	(0.8)
Other income (loss)	0.9	—	(8.6)	(0.2)	10.2	0.2
Income before income taxes	366.6	8.6	111.4	2.3	321.5	6.4
Income tax provision	129.8	3.0	38.0	0.8	51.6	1.0
Income before cumulative effect of change in accounting principle	236.8	5.6	73.4	1.5	269.9	5.4
Cumulative effect of change in accounting principle, net of $1.8 million tax benefit in 2005	—	—	—	—	(2.9)	(0.1)
Net income	$ 236.8	5.6%	$ 73.4	1.5%	$ 267.0	5.3%3

Net income per share

Basic:

Income before cumulative effect of change in accounting principle	$ 1.76	$ 0.54	$ 1.82
Cumulative effect of change in accounting principle, net of taxes	—	—	(0.02)
Basic income per share	$ 1.76	$ 0.54	$ 1.80
Assuming dilution:			
Income before cumulative effect of change in accounting principle	$ 1.74	$ 0.54	$ 1.81
Cumulative effect of change in accounting principle, net of taxes	—	—	(0.02)
Diluted income per share	$ 1.74	$ 0.54	$ 1.79
Shares used in computing income per share:			
Basic	134.6	136.2	148.1
Diluted	135.9	136.2	148.8

CONSOLIDATED STATEMENTS OF STOCKHOLDERS' EQUITY AND COMPREHENSIVE INCOME
RadioShack Corporation and Subsidiaries

(In millions)	Shares at December 31,			Dollars at December 31,		
	2007	2006	2005	2007	2006	2005
Common stock						
Beginning and end of year	191.0	191.0	191.0	$ 191.0	$ 191.0	$ 191.0
Treasury stock						
Beginning of year	(55.2)	(56.0)	(32.8)	$(1,409.1)	$(1,431.6)	$ (859.4)
Purchase of treasury stock	(8.7)	—	(25.3)	(208.5)	—	(625.8)
Issuance of common stock	0.5	0.6	1.2	12.8	18.6	31.8
Exercise of stock options and grant of stock awards	3.5	0.2	0.9	88.3	3.9	21.8
End of year	(59.9)	(55.2)	(56.0)	$(1,516.5)	$(1,409.1)	$(1,431.6)
Additional paid-in capital						
Beginning of year				$ 92.6	$ 87.7	$ 82.7
Issuance of common stock				6.2	(5.7)	3.5
Excercise of stock options and grant of stock awards				(8.4)	(1.7)	(5.0)
Stock option compensation				10.7	12.0	—
Net stock-based compensation income tax benefits				7.3	0.3	6.5
End of year				$ 108.4	$ 92.6	$ 87.7
Retained earnings						
Beginning of year				$ 1,780.9	$ 1,741.4	$1,508.1
Net income				236.8	73.4	267.0
Implementation of FIN 48				7.2	—	—
Common stock cash dividends declared				(32.8)	(33.9)	(33.7)
End of year				$ 1,992.1	$ 1,780.9	$1,741.4
Accumulated other comprehensive (loss) income						
Beginning of year				$ (1.6)	$ 0.3	$ (0.3)
Pension adjustments, net of tax				0.4	(1.0)	—
Other comprehensive (loss) income				(4.1)	(0.9)	0.6
End of year				$ (5.3)	$ (1.6)	$ 0.3
Total stockholders' equity				$ 769.7	$ 653.8	$ 588.8
Comprehensive income						
Net income				$ 236.8	$ 73.4	$ 267.0
Other comprehensive (loss) income, net of tax:						
Foreign currency translation adjustments				(4.0)	0.3	(0.4)
Amortization of gain on cash flow hedge				(0.1)	(0.1)	(0.1)
Unrealized (loss) gain on securities				—	(1.1)	1.1
Other comprehensive (loss) income				(4.1)	(0.9)	0.6
Comprehensive income				$ 232.7	$ 72.5	$ 267.6

CONSOLIDATED STATEMENTS OF CASH FLOWS
RadioShack Corporation and Subsidiaries

(In millions)	Year Ended December 31, 2007	2006	2005
Cash flows from operating activities:			
Net income	$ 236.8	$ 73.4	$ 267.0
Adjustments to reconcile net income to net cash provided by operating activities:			
Depreciation and amortization	112.7	128.2	123.8
Cumulative effect of change in accounting principle	—	—	4.7
Impairment of long-lived assets and other charges	2.7	44.3	—
Stock option compensation	10.7	12.0	—
Reversal of unrecognized tax benefits	(11.9)	—	—
Deferred income taxes	16.5	(32.7)	(74.0)
Other non-cash items	(9.0)	5.1	(2.9)
Provision for credit losses and bad debts	0.4	0.4	0.1
Changes in operating assets and liabilities:			
Accounts and notes receivable	(0.7)	61.8	(68.2)
Inventories	46.8	212.8	38.8
Other current assets	5.3	2.5	28.5
Accounts payable, accrued expenses, income taxes payable and other	(31.3)	(193.0)	45.1
Net cash provided by operating activities	379.0	314.8	362.9
Cash flows from investing activities:			
Additions to property, plant and equipment	(45.3)	(91.0)	(170.7)
Proceeds from sale of property, plant and equipment	1.5	11.1	226.0
Other investing activities	1.8	0.6	(16.0)
Net cash (used in) provided by investing activities	(42.0)	(79.3)	39.3
Cash flows from financing activities:			
Purchases of treasury stock	(208.5)	—	(625.8)
Sale of treasury stock to employee benefit plans	—	10.5	30.1
Proceeds from exercise of stock options	81.3	1.7	17.4
Payments of dividends	(32.8)	(33.9)	(33.7)
Changes in short-term borrowings and outsanding checks in excess of cash balances, net	10.7	42.2	(4.0)
Reductions of long-term borrowings	(150.0)	(8.0)	(0.1)
Net cash (used in) provided by financing activities	(299.3)	12.5	(616.1)
Net increase (decrease) in cash and cash equivalents	37.7	248.0	(213.9)
Cash and cash equivalents, beginning of period	472.0	224.0	437.9
Cash and cash equivalents, end of period	$ 509.7	$ 472.0	$ 224.0
Supplemental cash flow information:			
Interest paid	$ 42.6	$ 44.0	$ 43.4
Income taxes paid	112.2	52.9	158.5

RADIOSHACK

Appendix B

Accounting Principles

Learning Objectives

LO 1	Describe a rules-based and a principles-based approach toward accounting standards.
LO 2	Define the primary objective of financial reporting.
LO 3	Discuss qualitative characteristics of useful accounting information.
LO 4	Describe assumptions underlying useful accounting information.
LO 5	Explain principles of useful accounting information.
LO 6	Describe constraints on useful accounting information.

For accounting information to be useful, it must possess certain qualitative characteristics. The purpose of this appendix is to provide a conceptual framework for accounting principles that is desirable for accounting information.

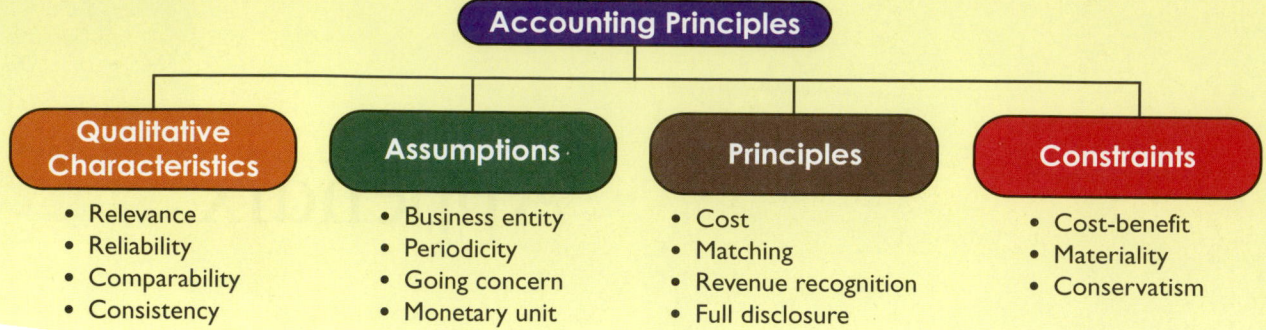

Accounting Principles

Qualitative Characteristics
- Relevance
- Reliability
- Comparability
- Consistency

Assumptions
- Business entity
- Periodicity
- Going concern
- Monetary unit

Principles
- Cost
- Matching
- Revenue recognition
- Full disclosure

Constraints
- Cost-benefit
- Materiality
- Conservatism

Rules–Based versus Principles–Based Accounting

LO1 Describe a rules-based and a principles-based approach toward accounting standards.

U.S. accounting practices are often viewed as *rules-based* (as mentioned in Chapter 1). This means that companies are required to apply technical, specific, and detailed rules in preparing financial statements and reports. A *principles-based* approach is sometimes argued as preferable. A principles-based system would develop and apply broad, fundamental concepts for accounting. Companies would have more flexibility in preparing principles-based financial statements to meet the intent of the accounting principle rather than just the specific accounting rule.

For example, a broad accounting principle might be that a company must report all debt it might have to repay. Certain executives of **Enron** were able to mislead investors by not reporting some of its debt. While many of Enron's reports technically followed rules-based standards, the reports failed to adequately disclose all of its debts. As another example, a broad principle might be that a company must report all of its building leases that it is contractually obligated to pay as a liability on its balance sheet. Executives of many retail companies (such as **Wal-Mart** and **Payless Shoe Source**) follow the rules-based standards of accounting for leases. Their balance sheets generally fail to comprehensively report all of the leases that each company is required to pay. In both instances, while the rules are technically followed, the accounting has not achieved the intent of the standards.

Sarbanes-Oxley Act and Principles-Based Accounting

As a result of the Enron scandal and other abuses of rules-based accounting practices, the **Sarbanes-Oxley Act** requires the **Securities and Exchange Commission,** the government group that establishes financial reporting requirements, to study the feasibility of shifting to a more "principles-based" approach. The **Financial Accounting Standards Board,** the private group that sets standards for accounting practice, has also proposed changes designed to create a more principles-based approach to accounting standards. Many accounting experts believe that a change to principles-based standards will force companies preparing financial statements to focus on the intent of accounting standards rather than just technical compliance with the rules. On the other side of the debate, some accounting experts worry that a shift to principles-based standards will lead to lawsuits as shareholders and companies fight over the true intent of the standards.

A principles-based system requires a sound conceptual framework. To more fully understand the principles-based approach, the existing conceptual framework of accounting principles is presented in this appendix.

Objectives of Financial Reporting

LO2 Define the primary objective of financial reporting.

External financial statements users, such as investors and creditors, use accounting information in financial reports to make decisions (such as whether to buy or sell a stock or extend a loan). To assist in decision making, accounting reports must possess useful information.

The primary objective of financial reporting is to provide useful economic information to assist decision makers. There are many elements of accounting information. Exhibit B.1 provides a pyramid detailing the framework of qualitative characteristics, assumptions, principles, and constraints for providing useful accounting information.

The objective of financial reporting is to provide useful accounting information to decision makers.

Qualitative Characteristics of Accounting Information
To be useful to decision makers, accounting information should have the following characteristics:

1. Relevance
a. Predictive Value (helps with forecasts)
b. Feedback Value (corrects or confirms forecasts)
c. Timely (available when needed)

2. Reliability
a. Verifiable (can be verified by an independent party)
b. Representational Faithfulness (reports what happened)
c. Neutrality (information is not biased)

3. Comparability
(Different companies use similar accounting principles and methods)

4. Consistency
(Same company uses the same accounting principles and methods each year)

Assumptions	Principles	Constraints
1. Business Entity (business is accounted for separately from its owner and other business entities)	**1. Cost** (accounting information is based on cash or equal-to-cash basis)	**1. Cost-Benefit** (benefits to accounting information users is greater than the cost to prepare it)
2. Periodicity (the life of a company can be divided up into smaller reportable time periods)	**2. Matching** (expenses are recorded as incurred to generate revenues)	**2. Materiality** (transactions too small to make an impact on a decision maker are recorded in the most cost-beneficial way)
3. Going Concern (entity will continue operating instead of being closed or sold)	**3. Revenue Recognition** (revenue recorded when earned and realizable)	**3. Conservatism** (select accounting methods that are least likely to overstate assets and income)
4. Monetary Unit (transactions expressed in monetary units)	**4. Full Disclosure** (any information that can influence the judgment of a decision maker is reported)	

Exhibit B.1

Elements of Useful Accounting Information

Qualitative Characteristics of Useful Accounting Information

As noted in Exhibit B.1, to be useful, accounting information must be relevant, reliable, comparable, and consistent across time. Exhibit B.2 provides an illustration of these qualitative characteristics.

Relevance

To provide useful information, that information must be **relevant** to the decision maker. Information is relevant if it would make a difference in a business decision. Information is relevant when it helps users predict the future (*predictive value*) or evaluate the past (*feedback value*) and is received in time to affect their decisions (*timeliness*).

LO3 Discuss qualitative characteristics of useful accounting information.

Reliability

Information is **reliable** if users can depend on it to be free from bias and error. Reliable information is *verifiable* and *faithfully represents* the substance of the underlying economic transaction. If **Best Buy** sold a television for $4,000, it should be reported in its sales revenue as

Exhibit B.2

Qualitative Characteristics of Useful Accounting Information

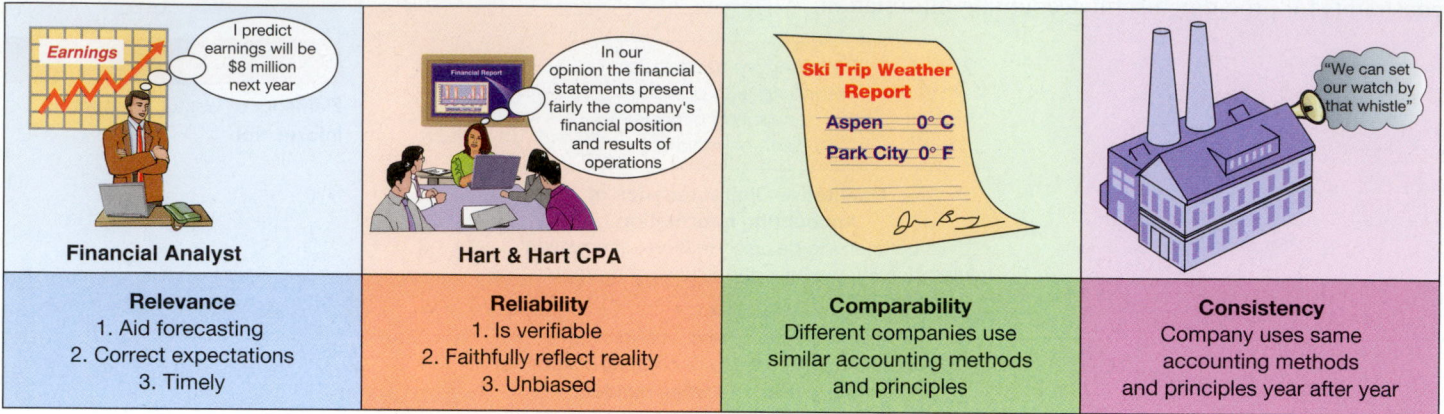

Relevance	Reliability	Comparability	Consistency
1. Aid forecasting 2. Correct expectations 3. Timely	1. Is verifiable 2. Faithfully reflect reality 3. Unbiased	Different companies use similar accounting methods and principles	Company uses same accounting methods and principles year after year

$4,000. Reliable accounting information is neutral, or free from bias. In other words, accounting information should not be designed to lead accounting information users to accept or reject any specific decision alternative.

Comparability

Information is **comparable** if it helps users to identify differences and similarities between companies. Comparability is possible only if companies follow similar accounting methods and practices. However, even if all companies uniformly follow the same accounting practices, comparable reports do not result if the practices are not appropriate. For example, comparable information would not be provided if all companies were to ignore the useful lives of their assets and depreciate all assets over two years.

Comparability is often harder for cross-country comparisons. Suppose we want to make an investment in an automobile manufacturer such as **Daimler Chrysler**, a German company, or **Toyota**, a Japanese company. Since each of these countries has its own set of accounting rules and methods, a direct comparison will be difficult. The **International Accounting Standards Board** has been established to help harmonize accounting practices across countries.

Consistency

Accounting information users generally look at multiple time periods of a company's financial statements to see if there are any noticeable trends. To make this comparison over multiple periods, the same accounting principles and methods should be used in each period. Otherwise, it is hard to know if changes over time are due to real fundamental changes in financial performance or are simply because the company changed the way it accounted for certain items. Applying the same accounting information methods and practices over time is known as **consistency.**

Underlying Accounting Assumptions

LO4 Describe assumptions underlying useful accounting information.

Four assumptions underlie the overall objective of providing useful information to decision makers. These are the business entity assumption, the periodicity assumption, the going concern assumption, and the monetary unit assumption.

Business Entity Assumption

The **business entity assumption** means that a business is accounted for separately from other business entities, including its owner. The reason for this principle is that separate information about each business is necessary for good decisions. A business entity can take one of three legal forms: *proprietorship, partnership,* or *corporation.*

Abuse of the business entity assumption was a main culprit in the collapse of **Enron.**

Periodicity Assumption

A component of providing relevant and useful information is that it must be timely. Useful information must reach decision makers frequently and promptly. To provide timely information, accounting systems prepare reports at regular intervals. This results in an accounting process impacted by the periodicity (or time period) principle. The **periodicity assumption** is that an organization's activities can be divided into specific time periods such as a month, a three-month quarter, a six-month interval, or a year.

"RadioShack announces earnings per share of . . ."

Going-Concern Assumption

The **going-concern assumption** means that accounting information reflects an assumption that the business will continue operating instead of being closed or sold. This implies, for example, that a factory facility is reported at cost instead of, say, liquidation values that assume immediate, involuntary closure.

IN THE NEWS

Principles and Scruples   Auditors, directors, and lawyers are using principles to improve accounting reports. Examples include financial restatements at **Delphi**, accounting reviews at **Echostar**, and expense adjustments at **Electronic Data Systems**. Principles-based accounting has led accounting firms to drop clients deemed too risky.

Monetary Unit Assumption

The **monetary unit assumption** means that we can express transactions and events in monetary, or money, units. Money is the common denominator in business. Examples of monetary units are the dollar in the United States, Canada, Australia, and Singapore; the pound sterling in the United Kingdom; and the peso in Mexico, the Philippines, and Chile. The monetary unit assumption also means that financial statement amounts are typically not adjusted for the effects of inflation.

> For currency conversion:
> **www.xe.com**

HOW YOU DOIN'?   Answers—p. B-8

1. Why is it important to have comparable accounting methods between companies?
2. Why is the business entity assumption important?
3. Why is the going-concern assumption important?

Accounting Principles

Accounting relies on four key principles (as illustrated in Exhibit B.1): cost, matching, revenue recognition, and full disclosure.

LO5   Explain principles of useful accounting information.

Cost Principle

The **cost principle** means that accounting information is based on actual cost. Cost is measured on a cash or equal-to-cash basis. This means if cash is given for a service, the transaction's cost is measured as the amount of cash paid. If something besides cash is exchanged (such as a car traded for a truck), the transaction's cost is measured as the cash value of what is given up or received. The cost principle emphasizes reliability, and information based on cost is considered objective. To illustrate, suppose a company pays $5,000 for equipment. The cost principle requires that this purchase be recorded at a cost of $5,000. It makes no difference if the owner thinks this equipment is now worth $7,000.

> The cost principle is also called the *historical cost principle.*

Matching Principle

The **matching principle** prescribes that expenses be reported in the same period and on the same income statement as the revenues that were earned as a result of those expenses. To illustrate, suppose a business provides traffic consulting services to a municipal client. All of the expenses (consultant labor, computer use, copies, travel, presentation preparation, use of office space) incurred to complete those consulting services should be recorded in the same period as the consulting services.

   Sometimes, it is difficult to match each expense with its related revenue. There are three general guidelines that are used in applying the matching principle (with examples):

Guideline	Example
• Cause and effect	Expenses directly incurred to generate revenue such as consultant labor
• Systematic and rational allocation	Depreciation of office equipment and office space
• Immediate recognition of some costs with uncertain future benefits	Advertising, salary of consultant's supervisor

Revenue Recognition Principle

Revenue (sales) is the amount received from selling products and services. The **revenue recognition principle** provides guidance on when a company must recognize revenue. To *recognize* revenue means to record it. If revenue is recognized too early, a company would look more profitable than it is. If revenue is recognized too late, a company would look less profitable than it is. The following three concepts are important to revenue recognition. (1) *Revenue is recognized when earned.* The earnings process is normally complete when services are performed or a seller transfers ownership of products to the buyer. (2) *Proceeds from selling products and services need not be in cash.* A common noncash proceed received by a seller is a customer's promise to pay at a future date, called *credit sales.* (3) *Revenue is measured by the cash received plus the cash value of any other items received.*

> When a bookstore sells a text-book on credit is its earnings process complete? *Answer:* The bookstore can record sales for these books minus an amount expected for book returns.

IN THE NEWS

Revenues for the **New England Patriots** football team include ticket sales, television and cable broadcasts, radio rights, concessions, and advertising. Revenues from ticket sales are earned when the Patriots play each game. Advance ticket sales are not revenues; instead, they represent a liability until the Patriots play the game for which the ticket was sold.

Full Disclosure Principle

Companies have many choices on what information to report. The **full disclosure principle** requires that all accounting information important enough to affect a decision be presented. Such accounting information may be disclosed in the financial statements, footnotes to the financial statements, or as supplementary information. There is always the possibility that too much information or too much detail will overwhelm the user. Therefore, companies try to be clear but concise.

Accounting Constraints

LO6 Describe constraints on useful accounting information.

All of the assumptions and principles discussed thus far help accountants provide useful information to decision makers. However, providing all of this quality information can be too costly to the company. There is a balance between providing sufficient information to the decision maker without being too costly to the company preparing the accounting information. There are three constraints to providing useful information to the decision maker: cost-benefit, materiality, and conservatism.

Cost-Benefit

The benefit to decision makers of receiving accounting information must be worth the cost of providing it. The **cost-benefit** trade-off suggests that information will be provided only if the benefits to users outweigh the costs of preparing and disclosing it.

However, the costs and benefits are not always easy to compute. Moreover, the costs are usually borne by the company, and the benefits are received by a diverse set of decision makers across the world. Still, it is useful to try to carefully consider the costs and benefits before producing or requiring the disclosure of additional accounting information.

Materiality

Materiality asks the question: Is the item big enough to make an impact on the decision maker? If the item is not big enough to make a difference, then **generally accepted accounting principles (GAAP)** do not have to be followed. To illustrate, if **RadioShack** makes a $10 mistake in recording an expense when its overall expenses are $10 billion, the $10 error is most likely not a material item and GAAP need not be followed.

Conservatism

Conservatism suggests that when faced with two equally plausible accounting method choices (or estimates), the company should choose the accounting method (or estimate) that is least likely to overstate assets and income or to understate liabilities and expenses. Managers are generally optimistic, and this constraint offsets that optimism to help present a more conservative view of a company's financial position. The general concept can be summarized in this way: if in doubt, recognize all losses but do not recognize any gains.

A common example of conservatism is in the valuation of inventory. Inventories are usually recorded at their cost. However, if the market value of the inventory falls below its cost, conservatism requires that inventories be written down to the market value. To illustrate, consider a company that sells computer systems. Due to the quick technology advances and declining prices of new computer hardware, if a computer does not sell relatively quickly, the market value can fall below the cost to manufacture and sell it. Due to conservatism, the computer is written down to its market value.

HOW YOU DOIN'?   Answers—p. B-8

4. Why is the revenue recognition principle important?

5. Do you think a $10 million error would be material in a company with $100 million in sales?

Summary

LO1 **Describe a rules-based and a principles-based approach toward accounting standards.** The rules-based approach implies that companies are required to apply technical, specific, and detailed rules in preparing financial statements and reports. The principles-based approach develops and applies broad, overarching, and fundamental concepts for accounting.

LO2 **Define the primary objective of financial reporting.** The primary objective of accounting is to provide useful economic information to assist decision makers to make decisions.

LO3 **Discuss qualitative characteristics of useful accounting information.** The qualitative characteristics of useful accounting information are that the information must be relevant, reliable, comparable, and consistent. Information is relevant if it would make a difference in a decision. Reliable information is information that can be depended on. Companies can be compared to each other if they use the same accounting methods and principles. Consistency is met when firms apply the same accounting methods and principles year after year.

LO4 **Describe assumptions underlying useful accounting information.** There are several underlying assumptions to support the overall objective of providing useful information to decision makers including the business entity assumption, the periodicity assumption, the going concern assumption, and the monetary unit assumption.

LO5 **Explain principles of useful accounting information.** Accounting principles help make accounting information useful to decision makers. They include the cost, matching, revenue recognition, and full disclosure principles.

LO6 **Describe constraints on useful accounting information.** There are three constraints to providing useful information to decision makers. The benefits of the accounting information must be greater than the costs, the accounting information must be material, and the accounting choices must be conservative.

1. Comparable accounting information provides a similar measuring stick for both companies to assess their relative financial performance. If companies have different accounting methods, there is no way to compare them. It would be like comparing apples to oranges.

2. Users desire information about the performance of a specific entity. If information is mixed between two or more entities, its usefulness decreases.

3. Many of the elements of the financial statements assume that company will continue in operation. This allows them to be valued at cost on the balance sheet rather than being sold at liquidation prices.

4. The revenue recognition principle gives guidelines of when to recognize (record) revenue. This is important; for example, if revenue is recognized too early, the financial statements report revenue sooner than it should and the business looks more profitable than it is. The reverse is also true.

5. Yes, this would be considered to be a material item since it represents 10% of the firm's sales, suggesting it would make a difference on a decision maker's decisions.

Key Terms

Business entity assumption (p. B-4) Concept that assumes a business will be accounted for separately from its owner(s) and any other entity.

Comparability (p. B-4) A qualitative characteristic of accounting information suggesting that information is more useful if it can be related to an industry or competitor benchmark.

Conservatism (p. B-7) Concept that prescribes use of the less optimistic estimate when two estimates are about equally likely.

Consistency (p. B-4) A qualitative characteristic of accounting information that prescribes use of the same accounting method(s) and practice(s) over time so that financial statements are comparable across periods.

Cost-benefit (p. B-7) A constraint of useful accounting information prescribing that information will be provided only if the benefits to users outweigh the costs of preparation.

Cost principle (p. B-5) Accounting principle that prescribes financial statement information to be based on actual costs incurred in business transactions.

Financial Accounting Standards Board (FASB) (p. B-2) Independent group of full-time members responsible for setting accounting rules.

Full disclosure principle (p. B-6) Principle that prescribes financial statements (including notes) to report all relevant information about an entity's operations and financial condition.

Generally Accepted Accounting Principles (GAAP) (p. B-7) Rules that specify acceptable accounting practices.

Going-concern assumption (p. B-5) Concept that prescribes financial statements to reflect the assumption that the business will continue operating indefinitely.

International Accounting Standards Board (IASB) (p. B-4) Group that identifies preferred accounting practices and encourages global acceptance; issues International Financial Reporting Standards (IFRS).

Matching principle (p. B-6) Prescribes expenses to be reported in the same period as the revenues that were earned as a result of the expenses.

Materiality (p. B-7) Prescribes that accounting for items that markedly impact financial statements, and any inferences drawn from them, adhere to GAAP.

Monetary unit assumption (p. B-5) Concept that assumes transactions and events can be expressed in money units.

Periodicity assumption (p. B-5) The life of a company can be divided up into smaller, reportable time periods.

Relevance (p. B-3) A qualitative characteristic of accounting information that prescribes that information be useful, understandable, timely, and pertinent for decision making.

Reliability (p. B-3) The principle that information is verifiable and faithfully represents the substance of the underlying economic transaction.

Revenue recognition principle (p. B-6) The principle prescribing that revenue is recognized when earned.

Sarbanes-Oxley Act (p. B-2) Created the *Public Company Accounting Oversight Board,* regulates analyst conflicts, imposes corporate governance requirements, enhances accounting and control disclosures, impacts insider transactions and executive loans, establishes new types of criminal conduct, and expands penalties for violations of federal securities laws.

Securities and Exchange Commission (SEC) (p. B-2) Federal agency Congress has charged to set reporting rules for organizations that sell ownership shares to the public.

Multiple Choice Quiz
Answers on p. B-12   mhhe.com/wildCA2e

Additional Multiple Choice Quizzes are available at the book's Website.

1. The principle that prescribes that a business be accounted for separately and distinctly from its owner or owners is known as the:
   a. Matching principle.
   b. Business entity assumption.
   c. Going-concern assumption.
   d. Revenue recognition principle.
   e. Cost principle.

2. The rule that prescribes financial statements reflect the assumption that the business will continue operating instead of being closed or sold, unless evidence shows that it will not continue, is the:
   a. Going-concern assumption.
   b. Business entity assumption.
   c. Matching principle.
   d. Cost Principle.
   e. Monetary unit assumption.

3. To include the personal assets and transactions of a business's owner in the records and reports of the business would conflict with the:
   a. Matching principle.
   b. Realization principle.
   c. Business entity assumption.
   d. Going-concern assumption.
   e. Revenue recognition principle.

4. The accounting principle that prescribes accounting information be based on actual cost and requires assets and services to be recorded initially at the cash or cash-equivalent amount given in exchange, is the:
   a. Accounting equation.
   b. Cost principle.

   c. Going-concern assumption.
   d. Revenue recognition principle.
   e. Business entity assumption.

5. The qualitative characteristic of reliability:
   a. Means that information is supported by independent, unbiased evidence.
   b. Means that information can be based on what the preparer thinks is true.
   c. Means that financial statements should contain information that is optimistic.
   d. Means that a business may not reorganize revenue until cash is received.
   e. All of the above.

Discussion Questions

1. Describe the four key qualitative characteristics of useful accounting information.
2. Why is the business entity assumption important?
3. Why is the matching principle important?
4. What are the three basic forms of business organization?
5. What does the reliability characteristic imply for information reported in financial statements?
6. A business reports its own office stationery on the balance sheet at its $400 cost, although it cannot be sold for more than

$10 as scrap paper. Which accounting principle(s) justifies this treatment?
7. What is **Best Buy**'s revenue recognition policy (as detailed in the footnotes to its financial statements [page A-11])?
8. By examining **RadioShack**'s financial statements in Appendix A, what evidence is there that the company follows the matching principle?

connect

Identify the following characteristics of useful accounting information as being a component of either Relevant (R) or Reliable (L). (*Hint:* Refer to Exhibit B.1.)

1. Timeliness
2. Verifiable
3. Representational Faithfulness

4. Predictive Value
5. Feedback Value
6. Neutrality

QUICK STUDY

QS B–1
Identifying characteristics of accounting information   **LO3**

Fill in the blanks with appropriate accounting terminology.

1. Accounting information is _____ if different companies use similar accounting principles.
2. Information is _____ if it would make a difference in a business decision.
3. Accounting information is _____ if the same company uses the same accounting methods year after year.
4. Information is reliable if users can depend on it to be free from _____ and error.

QS B–2
Terminology of the characteristics of accounting information   **LO3**

Identify the appropriate assumption underlying useful accounting information for each description 1 through 4.

1. Hancock Hats reports its sales on a monthly basis.
2. Joann Hancock, owner of Hancock Hats, keeps the accounting records of her business separate from her personal accounts.
3. Hancock Hats reports its financial statements assuming it will continue to be in business for the foreseeable future.
4. Hancock Hats expresses its financial statements using the U.S. dollar.

QS B–3
Assumptions underlying useful accounting information   **LO4**

Identify the appropriate accounting principle for each description 1 through 4.

1. Callahan's Castles records expenses incurred to produce revenues in the accounting period.
2. Callahan's Castles discloses all information about pension expenses that can influence the decision maker.
3. Callahan's Castles records sales on its toy castles when they are delivered to the customer.
4. Callahan's Castles records its computer equipment at its acquisition cost.

QS B–4
Principles of useful accounting information   **LO5**

QS B–5

Constraints of useful accounting information   **LO6**

Fill in the blanks with appropriate accounting terminology.

1. _____ suggests that transactions that are too small to make an impact on a decision maker are recorded in the most cost beneficial way.

2. Conservatism suggests that accounting methods be selected that are least likely to _____ assets and income.

3. The _____-benefit constraint suggests that the benefits to receiving accounting information than the costs to prepare it.

---

connect

EXERCISES

Exercise B–1

Identifying accounting principles or assumptions   **LO4   LO5**

Identify which general accounting principle best describes each of the following practices.

a. In December 2009, Chavez Landscaping received a customer's order and cash prepayment to install sod at a new house that would not be ready for installation until March 2010. Chavez should record the revenue from the customer order in March 2010, not in December 2009.

b. If $51,000 cash is paid to buy land, the land is reported on the buyer's balance sheet at $51,000.

c. Jo Keene owns both Sailing Passions and Dockside Supplies. In preparing financial statements for Dockside Supplies, Keene makes sure that the expense transactions of Sailing Passions are kept separate from Dockside's statements.

Exercise B–2

Rules-based vs. principles-based accounting   **LO1   LO3**

Target Corporation follows accounting rules in reporting its lease obligations. However, the vast majority of Target's obligations for its store leases are not reported as liabilities on Target's balance sheet. Similar to other retail establishments, Target structures its leases to avoid reporting lease liabilities on the balance sheet.

1. Why does Target Corp. wish to avoid reporting its store leases on the balance sheet?

2. Would a principles-based approach continue to allow Target Corp. to avoid reporting its store leases on the balance sheet?

3. Which qualitative characteristic(s) of accounting information is violated when Target Corp. avoids reporting its store leases on the balance sheet?

Exercise B–3

Identifying accounting principles   **LO4   LO5**

Match each of the numbered descriptions with the principle it best reflects. Indicate your answer by writing the letter for the appropriate principle in the blank space next to each description.

A. Cost principle

B. Business entity principle

C. Revenue recognition principle

D. Going-concern principle

_____ **1.** Financial statements reflect the assumption that the business continues operating.

_____ **2.** Every business is accounted for separately from its owner or owners.

_____ **3.** Revenue is recorded only when the earnings process is complete.

_____ **4.** Information is based on actual costs incurred in transactions.

Exercise B–4

Identifying accounting principles and assumptions   **LO4   LO5**

You are reviewing the accounting records of Cathy's Antiques, owned by Cathy Miller. You have uncovered the following situations. Cite the appropriate accounting principle or assumption and suggest an action for each separate item.

1. In August, a check for $500 was written to Wee Day Care Center; this amount represents child care for her son Brandon.

2. Cathy plans a Going Out of Business Sale for May, since she will be closing her business for a month-long vacation in June. She plans to reopen July 1 and will continue operating Cathy's Antiques indefinitely.

3. Cathy received a shipment of pine furniture from Quebec, Canada; the invoice was stated in Canadian dollars.

4. Joseph Clark paid $1,500 for a dining table; the amount was recorded as revenue. The table will be delivered to Mr. Clark in six weeks.

Match each of the numbered transactions to the accounting terms A through E applicable to recording and reporting them.

A. Business entity assumption

B. Reliability

C. Cost principle

D. Monetary unit assumption

E. Revenue recognition principle

_____ **1.** An insurance company receives insurance premiums for six future months' worth of coverage.

_____ **2.** A building is for sale at $480,000; an appraisal is given for $450,000.

_____ **3.** Helen Cho, a sole proprietor, pays for her daughter's preschool out-of-business funds.

_____ **4.** Mayan Imports receives a shipment from Mexico; the invoice is stated in pesos.

_____ **5.** To make the balance sheet look better, Helen Cho added several thousand dollars to the Equipment account that she believed was undervalued.

Exercise B–5
Identifying accounting principles and assumptions
LO3 LO4 LO5

Fill in the blanks with the appropriate accounting terms or phrases.

1. _____ means that a company applies the same concept year after year.

2. For information to be relevant, it should have predictive or feedback _____, and it must be presented in a _____ manner.

3. _____ is the quality of information that suggests it can be depended on to represent reality, be verifiable and not be biased.

4. _____ means that two companies can be assessed relative to each other.

Exercise B–6
Identifying qualitative characteristics **LO3**

---

1. Pagnozzi Properties is trying to decide if it needs to install a new accounting system to keep track of every detailed construction cost. The cost of the system will be $20,000 and the benefits are uncertain.

2. Gary Peters makes a $20 mistake when accounting for travel expenses. He has a question of whether this mistake needs to be corrected since it is relatively small.

3. Manuel Sanchez wants to know which accounting choice to make when accounting for consulting expenses at the end of the year. He decides that when in doubt, it would be better to understate rather than overstate net income.

In each case 1 through 3, identify the constraint that each of these statements addresses.

Exercise B–7
Identifying constraints of providing useful information **LO6**

---

1. Inventory is reported at market value when cost is lower.

2. Computers costing less than $1,000 are immediately expensed even though their useful life is three years.

3. The auditors of Dietrich Co. found an error of $50 in its financial statements and decide to restate their financial statements; Dietrich has sales revenue of $15 million.

4. To appropriately account for the pension liability, Ziebart Co. installs an abnormally expensive system to track employees, their health, and their pension status. Ziebart argues that this system is necessary to comply with accounting guidelines.

Indicate the accounting constraint, if any, that is violated by each practice.

Exercise B–8
Identifying constraints violated **LO6**

---

connect™ ——

Identify the accounting assumption, principle, or constraint that best describes the accounting practices at Ben Wallace Company.

1. Land is valued at its original purchase price rather than its appraised value.

2. Ben Wallace Company issues financial statements every three months.

3. Expenses are allocated to the appropriate revenues each accounting period.

4. All relevant financial information is disclosed in the financial reports.

PROBLEM SET A

Problem B–1A
Identify accounting assumptions, principles, or constraints
LO4 LO5 LO6

5. Personal computers costing less than $1,000 are expensed in the current period even though their useful life is three years.

6. The CEO's personal business records are kept separate from the company's records.

7. The U.S. dollar is the unit of currency used in financial reports.

Problem B-2A

Identifying assumptions, principles, or constraints violated
LO4   LO5   LO6

Presented below are transactions that occurred during 2010.

1. Susan Scholz, the president of Lake of the Ozarks cabin properties, buys a computer for personal use and charges it to her company's expense account.

2. In preparation of its financial statements, Ettredge Inc. omitted information about its method of accounting for accounts receivable.

3. To make its profits look better, Shanghai Automotive booked sales before its cars were shipped.

4. Jose Martinez reports all of its assets and liabilities at liquidation value, even though the company does not expect to go out of business in the foreseeable future.

5. Tom Hapgood writes up his inventory on the balance sheet since its market value is higher than its cost.

Required

For each of the above transactions, identify the assumption, principle, or constraint that has been violated.

PROBLEM SET B

Problem B-1B

Identify accounting assumptions, principles, or constraints
LO4   LO5   LO6

Identify the accounting assumption, principle, or constraint that best describes the accounting practices at Steve Hill Company.

1. Financial statements are prepared each year.

2. Market value changes after an asset's purchase are not recorded in the accounts.

3. Notes and supplementary information are included with the financial statements.

4. The factory is not reported at liquidation value. (Do not use the cost principle.)

5. Manufactured toys are not recorded as revenues until they have been sold and shipped.

6. Requires that generally accepted accounting principles be followed for all material items.

Problem B-2B

Identifying assumptions, principles, or constraints violated
LO4   LO5   LO6

Danny Manning and Larry Brown are accountants for the Engineering Institute. They disagree over the following transactions that occurred during 2010. Larry disagrees with Danny on each of the transactions below.

1. The Engineering Institute finds a bargain for a commercial-grade plotter and pays $3,000. Danny argues that if they had bought it from the dealer, they would have paid $4,000. Danny suggests they record the plotter for $4,000.

2. Timothy West, president of the Engineering Institute, used his company expense account to purchase a new BMW for his personal use. Danny argues that since the president is also the owner of the Engineering Institute, it really does not matter who paid for it.

3. Depreciation for the year was $114,000. Danny argues that since net income is expected to be lower in the current fiscal year, they should just charge it as an expense next year.

4. Danny suggests that the Engineering Institute value its equipment on its balance sheet at its liquidation value, which is $50,000 less than cost.

5. The Engineering Institute signed a lease on its offices for the next five years. A lease liability is not included on the company's balance sheet. Danny doesn't think such information needs to be disclosed.

Required

For each of the above transactions, identify why Larry disagrees. Also identify the assumption, principle, or constraint that has been violated.

ANSWERS TO MULTIPLE CHOICE QUIZ

1. b
2. a
3. c

4. b
5. a

Glossary

Accelerated depreciation method Method that produces larger depreciation charges in the early years of an asset's life and smaller charges in its later years. *(p. 452)*

Account Record within an accounting system in which increases and decreases are entered and stored in a specific asset, liability, equity, revenue, or expense. *(pp. 23 & 44)*

Account balance Difference between total debits and total credits (including the beginning balance) for an account. *(p. 47)*

Accounting Information and measurement system that identifies, records, and communicates relevant information about a company's business activities. *(p. 4)*

Accounting cycle Recurring steps performed each accounting period, starting with analyzing transactions and continuing through the post-closing trial balance (or reversing entries). *(p. 137)*

Accounting equation Equality involving a company's assets, liabilities, and equity; Assets = Liabilities + Equity; also called *balance sheet equation*. *(p. 22)*

Accounts payable ledger Subsidiary ledger listing individual creditor (supplier) accounts. *(p. 294)*

Accounts receivable Amounts due from customers for credit sales; backed by the customer's general credit standing. *(p. 370)*

Accounts receivable ledger Subsidiary ledger listing individual customer accounts. *(p. 267)*

Accounts receivable turnover Measure of both the quality and liquidity of accounts receivable; indicates how often receivables are received and collected during the period; computed by dividing net sales by average accounts receivable. *(p. 380)*

Accrual basis accounting Accounting system that recognizes revenues when earned and expenses when incurred; the basis for GAAP. *(p. 104)*

Accrued expenses Costs incurred in a period that are both unpaid and unrecorded; adjusting entries for recording accrued expenses involve increasing expenses and increasing liabilities. *(p. 109)*

Accrued revenues Revenues earned in a period that are both unrecorded and not yet received in cash (or other assets); adjusting entries for recording accrued revenues involve increasing assets and increasing revenues. *(p. 324)*

Adjusted trial balance List of accounts and balances prepared after period-end adjustments are recorded and posted. *(p. 110)*

Adjusting entry Journal entry at the end of an accounting period to bring an asset or liability account to its proper amount and update the related expense or revenue account. *(p. 106)*

Aging of accounts receivable Process of classifying accounts receivable by how long they are past due for purposes of estimating uncollectible accounts. *(p. 378)*

Allowance for Doubtful Accounts Contra asset account with a balance approximating uncollectible accounts receivable; also called *Allowance for Uncollectible Accounts*. *(p. 375)*

Allowance method Procedure that (a) estimates and matches bad debts expense with its sales for the period and/or (b) reports accounts receivable at estimated realizable value. *(p. 374)*

Amortization Process of allocating the cost of an intangible asset to expense over its estimated useful life. *(p. 460)*

Annual financial statements Financial statements covering a one-year period; often based on a calendar year, but any consecutive 12-month (or 52-week) period is acceptable. *(p. 105)*

Appropriated retained earnings Retained earnings separately reported to inform stockholders of funding needs. *(p. 548)*

Assets Resources a business owns or controls that are expected to provide current and future benefits to the business. *(p. 22)*

Authorized depository A bank that can accept payroll deposits from its own checking account customers. *(p. 234)*

Authorized stock Total amount of stock that a corporation's charter authorizes it to issue. *(p. 518)*

Average cost See *weighted average*. *(p. 428)*

Avoidable expense Expense (or cost) that is relevant for decision making; expense that is not incurred if a department, product, or service is eliminated. *(p. 817)*

Bad debts Accounts of customers who do not pay what they have promised to pay; an expense of selling on credit; also called *uncollectible accounts*. *(p. 373)*

Balance column account Account with debit and credit columns for recording entries and another column for showing the balance of the account after each entry. *(p. 80)*

Balance sheet Financial statement that lists types and dollar amounts of assets, liabilities, and equity at a specific date. *(p. 29)*

Bank reconciliation Report that explains the difference between the book (company) balance of cash and the cash balance reported on the bank statement. *(p. 186)*

Bank statement Bank report on the depositor's beginning and ending cash balances, and a listing of its changes, for a period. *(p. 185)*

Basic earnings per share Net income less any preferred dividends and then divided by weighted-average common shares outstanding. *(p. 548)*

Betterments Expenditures to make a plant asset more efficient or productive; also called *improvements. (p. 456)*

Blank endorsement Depositor signs the back of the check and the check is payable to the bearer of the check. *(p. 184)*

Bond Written promise to pay the bond's par (or face) value and interest at a stated contract rate; often issued in denominations of $1,000. *(p. 568)*

Bond indenture Contract between the bond issuer and the bondholders; identifies the parties' rights and obligations. *(p. 569)*

Bond sinking fund A fund designed to accumulate assets to pay a bond's maturity value. *(p. 576)*

Book value Asset's acquisition costs less its accumulated depreciation (or depletion, or amortization); also sometimes used synonymously as the *carrying value* of an account. *(pp. 109 & 450)*

Book value per common share Recorded amount of equity applicable to common shares divided by the number of common shares outstanding. *(p. 523)*

Book value per preferred share Equity applicable to preferred shares (equals its call price [or par value if it is not callable] plus any cumulative dividends in arrears) divided by the number of preferred shares outstanding. *(p. 523)*

Break-even point Output level at which sales equals fixed plus variable costs; where income equals zero. *(p. 808)*

Budget Formal statement of future plans, usually expressed in monetary terms. *(p. 678)*

Budget report Report comparing actual results to planned objectives; sometimes used as a progress report. *(p. 778)*

Budgetary control Management use of budgets to monitor and control company operations. *(p. 778)*

Business entity assumption Concept that assumes a business will be accounted for separately from its owner(s) and any other entity. *(pp. 11 & B-4)*

Call option The right of a bond issuer to retire bonds early. *(p. 575)*

Call price Amount that must be paid to call and retire a callable preferred stock or a callable bond. *(p. 523)*

Callable bonds Bonds that give the issuer the option to retire them at a stated amount prior to maturity. *(p. 578)*

Callable preferred stock Preferred stock that the issuing corporation, at its option, may retire by paying the call price plus any dividends in arrears. *(p. 523)*

Canceled checks Checks that the bank has paid and deducted from the depositor's account. *(p. 186)*

Capital expenditures Additional costs of plant assets that provide material benefits extending beyond the current period; also called *balance sheet expenditures. (p. 456)*

Capital stock General term referring to a corporation's stock used in obtaining capital (owner financing). *(p. 518)*

Carrying (book) value of bonds Net amount at which bonds are reported on the balance sheet; equals the par value of the bonds less any unamortized discount or plus any unamortized premium; also called *carrying amount* or *book value. (p. 572)*

Cash Includes currency, coins, and amounts on deposit in bank checking or savings accounts. *(p. 178)*

Cash basis accounting Accounting system that recognizes revenues when cash is received and recognizes expenses as cash is paid; not consistent with GAAP. *(p. 104)*

Cash disbursements journal Special journal normally used to record all payments of cash; also called *cash payments journal. (p. 294)*

Cash discount Reduction in the price of merchandise granted by a seller to a buyer when payment is made within the discount period. *(p. 263)*

Cash equivalents Short-term, investment assets that are readily convertible to a known cash amount or sufficiently close to their maturity date (usually within 90 days) so that market value is not sensitive to interest rate changes. *(p. 339)*

Cash flow on total assets Ratio of operating cash flows to average total assets; not sensitive to income recognition and measurement; partly reflects earnings quality. *(p. 614)*

Cash Over and Short Income statement account used to record cash overages and cash shortages arising from errors in cash receipts or payments. *(p. 179)*

Cash receipts journal Special journal normally used to record all receipts of cash. *(p. 270)*

Change in an accounting estimate Change in an accounting estimate that results from new information, subsequent developments, or improved judgment that impacts current and future periods. *(pp. 454 & 548)*

Chart of accounts List of accounts used by a company; includes an identification number for each account. *(p. 76)*

Check Document signed by a depositor instructing the bank to pay a specified amount to a designated recipient. *(p. 184)*

Check register Another name for a cash disbursements journal when the journal has a column for check numbers. *(pp. 169 & 294)*

Circular E IRS federal income tax withholding tables. *(p. 210)*

Classified balance sheet Balance sheet that presents assets and liabilities in relevant subgroups, including current and noncurrent classifications. *(p. 349)*

Clock card Source document used to record the number of hours an employee works and to determine the total labor cost for each pay period. *(p. 719)*

Closing entries Entries recorded at the end of each accounting period to transfer end-of-period balances in revenue, gain, expense, loss, and withdrawal (dividend for a corporation) accounts to the capital account (to retained earnings for a corporation). *(p. 134)*

Closing process Necessary end-of-period steps to prepare the accounts for recording the transactions of the next period. *(p. 133)*

Columnar journal Journal with more than one column. *(p. 266)*

Common stock Corporation's basic ownership share; also called *capital stock* or *contributed capital. (p. 518)*

Common-size financial statement Statement that expresses each amount as a percent of a base amount. In the balance sheet, total assets is usually the base and is expressed as 100%. In the income statement, net sales revenue is usually the base. *(p. 647)*

Comparability A qualitative characteristic of accounting information suggesting that information is more useful if it can be related to an industry or competitor benchmark. *(p. B-4)*

Comparative financial statement Statement with data for two or more successive periods placed in side-by-side columns, often with changes shown in dollar amounts and percents. *(p. 645)*

Complex capital structure Capital structure that includes outstanding rights or options to purchase common stock, or securities that are convertible into common stock. *(p. 549)*

Conservatism concept Concept that prescribes the less optimistic estimate when two estimates are about equally likely. *(pp. 423 & B-4)*

Consistency concept Concept that prescribes use of the same accounting method(s) over time so that financial statements are comparable across periods. *(pp. 421 & B-4)*

Continuous improvement Concept requiring every manager and employee to continually look to improve operations. *(p. 679)*

Contra account Account linked with another account and having an opposite normal balance; reported as a subtraction from the other account's balance. *(pp. 51 & 108)*

Contract rate Interest rate specified in a bond indenture (or note); multiplied by the par value to determine the interest paid each period; also called *coupon rate, stated rate,* or *nominal rate. (p. 570)*

Contribution margin per unit Amount that the sale of one unit contributes toward recovering fixed costs and earning profit; defined as sales price per unit minus variable expense per unit. *(p. 807)*

Contribution margin ratio Product's contribution margin divided by its sale price. *(p. 807)*

Control Process of monitoring planning decisions and evaluating the organization's activities and employees. *(p. 678)*

Controllable costs Costs that a manager has the power to control or at least strongly influence. *(pp. 681 & 758)*

Controlling account General ledger account, the balance of which (after posting) equals the sum of the balances in its related subsidiary ledger. *(p. 267)*

Conversion costs Expenditures incurred in converting raw materials to finished goods; includes direct labor costs and overhead costs. *(p. 685)*

Convertible bonds Bonds that bondholders can exchange for a set number of the issuer's shares. *(p. 578)*

Convertible preferred stock Preferred stock with an option to exchange it for common stock at a specified rate. *(p. 522)*

Copyright Right giving the owner the exclusive privilege to publish and sell musical, literary, or artistic work during the creator's life plus 70 years. *(p. 462)*

Corporation Business that is a separate legal entity under state or federal laws with owners called *shareholders* or *stockholders. (p. 11)*

Cost All normal and reasonable expenditures necessary to get an asset in place and ready for its intended use. *(p. 449)*

Cost accounting system Accounting system for manufacturing activities based on the perpetual inventory system. *(p. 714)*

Cost-benefit A constraint of useful accounting information prescribing that information will only be provided if the benefits to users outweigh the costs of preparation. *(p. B-7)*

Cost center Department that incurs costs but generates no revenues; common example is the accounting or legal department. *(p. 751)*

Cost object Product, process, department, or customer to which costs are assigned. *(p. 681)*

Cost of goods sold Cost of inventory sold to customers during a period; also called *cost of sales. (p. 322)*

Cost principle Accounting principle that prescribes financial statement information to be based on actual costs incurred in business transactions. *(p. B-5)*

Cost variance Difference between the actual incurred cost and the standard cost. *(p. 784)*

Cost-volume-profit (CVP) analysis Planning method that includes predicting the volume of activity, the costs incurred, sales earned, and profits received. *(p. 806)*

Credit Recorded on the right side; an entry that decreases asset and expense accounts, and increases liability, revenue, and most equity accounts; abbreviated Cr. *(p. 46)*

Credit memorandum Notification that the sender has credited the recipient's account in the sender's records. *(p. 265)*

Credit period Time period that can pass before a customer's payment is due. *(pp. 263 & 289)*

Credit terms Description of the amounts and timing of payments that a buyer (debtor) agrees to make in the future. *(p. 263 & 288)*

Creditors Individuals or organizations entitled to receive payments. *(p. 22)*

Cumulative preferred stock Preferred stock on which undeclared dividends accumulate until paid; common stockholders cannot receive dividends until cumulative dividends are paid. *(p. 543)*

Current assets Cash and other assets expected to be sold, collected, or used within one year or the company's operating cycle, whichever is longer. *(p. 351)*

Current liabilities Obligations due to be paid or settled within one year or the company's operating cycle, whichever is longer. *(p. 351)*

Customer orientation Company position that its managers and employees be in tune with the changing wants and needs of consumers. *(p. 679)*

Cycle efficiency (CE) A measure of production efficiency, which is defined as value-added (process) time divided by total cycle time. *(p. 690)*

Cycle time (CT) A measure of the time to produce a product or service, which is the sum of process time, inspection time, move time, and wait time; also called *throughput time. (p. 689)*

Date of declaration Date the directors vote to pay a dividend. *(p. 540)*

Date of payment Date the corporation makes the dividend payment. *(p. 540)*

Date of record Date directors specify for identifying stockholders to receive dividends. *(p. 540)*

Days' sales in inventory Estimate of number of days needed to convert inventory into receivables or cash; equals ending inventory divided by cost of goods sold and then multiplied by 365; also called *days' stock on hand.* *(p. 423)*

Days' sales uncollected Measure of the liquidity of receivables computed by dividing the current balance of receivables by the annual credit (or net) sales and then multiplying by 365; also called *days' sales in receivables.* *(p. 652)*

Debit Recorded on the left side; an entry that increases asset and expense accounts, and decreases liability, revenue, and most equity accounts; abbreviated Dr. *(p. 46)*

Debit memorandum Notification that the sender has debited the recipient's account in the sender's records. *(p. 289)*

Debt ratio Ratio of total liabilities to total assets; used to reflect risk associated with a company's debts. *(p. 695)*

Debt-to-equity ratio Defined as total liabilities divided by total equity; shows the proportion of a company financed by non-owners (creditors) in comparison with that financed by owners. *(p. 578)*

Declining-balance method Method that determines depreciation charge for the period by multiplying a depreciation rate (often twice the straight-line rate) by the asset's beginning-period book value. *(p. 452)*

Departmental accounting system Accounting system that provides information useful in evaluating the profitability or cost effectiveness of a department. *(p. 750)*

Departmental contribution to overhead Amount by which a department's revenues exceed its direct expenses. *(p. 757)*

Depletion Process of allocating the cost of natural resources to periods when they are consumed and sold. *(p. 459)*

Deposits in transit Deposits recorded by the company but not yet recorded by its bank. *(p. 187)*

Deposit ticket Lists items such as currency, coins, and checks deposited and their corresponding dollar amounts. *(p. 183)*

Depreciation Expense created by allocating the cost of plant and equipment to periods in which they are used; represents the expense of using the asset. *(pp. 108 & 449)*

Diluted earnings per share Earnings per share calculation that requires dilutive securities be added to the denominator of the basic EPS calculation. *(p. 549)*

Dilutive securities Securities having the potential to increase common shares outstanding; examples are options, rights, convertible bonds, and convertible preferred stock. *(p. 549)*

Direct costs Costs incurred for the benefit of one specific cost object. *(p. 681)*

Direct expenses Expenses traced to a specific department (object) that are incurred for the sole benefit of that department. *(p. 751)*

Direct labor Efforts of employees who physically convert materials to finished product. *(p. 685)*

Direct labor costs Wages and salaries for direct labor that are separately and readily traced through the production process to finished goods. *(p. 685)*

Direct material Raw material that physically becomes part of the product and is clearly identified with specific products or batches of product. *(p. 685)*

Direct material costs Expenditures for direct material that are separately and readily traced through the production process to finished goods. *(p. 685)*

Direct method Presentation of net cash from operating activities for the statement of cash flows that lists major operating cash receipts less major operating cash payments. *(p. 603)*

Direct write-off method Method that records the loss from an uncollectible account receivable at the time it is determined to be uncollectible; no attempt is made to estimate bad debts. *(p. 374)*

Discount on bonds payable Difference between a bond's par value and its lower issue price or carrying value; occurs when the contract rate is less than the market rate. *(p. 571)*

Discount period Time period in which a cash discount is available and the buyer can make a reduced payment. *(pp. 263 & 289)*

Dividend in arrears Unpaid dividend on cumulative preferred stock; must be paid before any regular dividends on preferred stock and before any dividends on common stock. *(p. 544)*

Dividend yield Ratio of the annual amount of cash dividends distributed to common shareholders relative to the common stock's market value (price). *(p. 549)*

Double-entry accounting Accounting system in which each transaction affects at least two accounts and has at least one debit and one credit. *(p. 47)*

Earnings per share (EPS) Amount of income earned by each share of a company's outstanding common stock; also called *net income per share.* *(p. 548)*

Effective interest method Allocates interest expense over the bond life to yield a constant rate of interest; interest expense for a period is found by multiplying the balance of the liability at the beginning of the period by the bond market rate at issuance; also called *interest method.* *(p. 581)*

Efficiency Company's productivity in using its assets; usually measured relative to how much revenue a certain level of assets generates. *(p. 691)*

Efficiency variance Difference between the actual quantity of an input and the standard quantity of that input. *(p. 785)*

Electronic funds transfer (EFT) Use of electronic communication to transfer cash from one party to another. *(p. 185)*

Employee Someone whose work is under the direction of an employer. *(p. 206)*

Employee earnings records Record of an employee's net pay, gross pay, deductions, and year-to-date payroll information. *(p. 216)*

Employee's Withholding Allowance Certificate (Form W-4) A form which shows an employee's withholding allowances. *(p. 206)*

Employer identification number (EIN) A number issued by the federal government that uniquely identifies a business. *(p. 232)*

Employer's Quarterly Unemployment Tax Report A report filed with the state that shows an employer's unemployment taxes owed. *(p. 241)*

Endorsement A written authorization transferring ownership of a check. *(p. 184)*

EOM Abbreviation for *end of month;* used to describe credit terms for credit transactions. *(p. 263)*

Equity Owner's claim on the assets of a business; equals the residual interest in an entity's assets after deducting liabilities; also called *net assets. (p. 23)*

Equity ratio Portion of total assets provided by equity, computed as total equity divided by total assets. *(p. 653)*

Estimated tax liability The amount a corporation expects to pay in income taxes for a specific year. *(p. 538)*

Ethics Codes of conduct by which actions are judged as right or wrong, fair or unfair, honest or dishonest. *(p. 9)*

Events Those happenings that affect an entity's accounting equation *and* can be reliably measured. *(p. 23)*

Expanded accounting equation Assets = Liabilities + Equity; Equity equals [Owner capital − Owner withdrawals + Revenues − Expenses] for a noncorporation; Equity equals [Contributed capital + Retained earnings + Revenues − Expenses] for a corporation where dividends are subtracted from retained earnings. *(p. 23)*

Expenses Outflows or using up of assets as part of operations of a business to generate sales. *(p. 23)*

External transactions Exchanges of economic value between one entity and another entity. *(p. 23)*

External users Persons using accounting information who are not directly involved in running the organization. *(p. 6)*

Extraordinary repairs Major repairs that extend the useful life of a plant asset beyond prior expectations; treated as a capital expenditure. *(p. 457)*

Factory overhead Factory activities supporting the production process that are not direct material or direct labor; also called *overhead* and *manufacturing overhead. (p. 685)*

Factory overhead costs Expenditures for factory overhead that cannot be separately or readily traced to finished goods; also called *overhead costs. (p. 685)*

Favorable variance Difference in actual revenues or expenses from the budgeted amount that contributes to a higher income. *(p. 779)*

Federal depository bank Bank authorized to accept deposits of amounts payable to the federal government. *(p. 234)*

Federal Insurance Contributions Act (FICA) Taxes Taxes assessed on both employers and employees; for Social Security and Medicare programs. *(pp. 207 & 232)*

Federal Reserve Bank A bank that can accept payroll deposits from any business. *(p. 234)*

Federal unemployment taxes (FUTA) Payroll taxes on employers assessed by the federal government to support its unemployment insurance program. *(p. 232)*

Financial accounting Area of accounting mainly aimed at serving external users. *(p. 6)*

Financial Accounting Standards Board (FASB) Independent group of full-time members responsible for setting accounting rules. *(pp. 10 & B-2)*

Financial reporting Process of communicating information relevant to investors, creditors, and others in making investment, credit, and business decisions. *(p. 643)*

Financial statement analysis Application of analytical tools to general-purpose financial statements and related data for making business decisions. *(p. 642)*

Financing activities Transactions with owners and creditors that include obtaining cash from issuing debt, repaying amounts borrowed, and obtaining cash from or distributing cash to owners. *(p. 600)*

Finished goods inventory Account that controls the finished goods files, which acts as a subsidiary ledger (of the Inventory account) in which the costs of finished goods that are ready for sale are recorded. *(pp. 684 & 717)*

First-in, first-out (FIFO) Method to assign cost to inventory that assumes items are sold in the order acquired; earliest items purchased are the first sold. *(p. 418)*

Fiscal year Consecutive 12-month (or 52-week) period chosen as the organization's annual accounting period. *(p. 105)*

Fixed budget Planning budget based on a single predicted amount of volume; unsuitable for evaluations if the actual volume differs from predicted volume. *(p. 778)*

Fixed budget performance report Report that compares actual revenues and costs with fixed budgeted amounts and identifies the differences as favorable or unfavorable variances. *(p. 779)*

Fixed cost Cost that does not change with changes in the volume of activity. *(p. 680)*

Flexible budget Budget prepared (using actual volume) once a period is complete that helps managers evaluate past performance; uses fixed and variable costs in determining total costs. *(p. 780)*

Flexible budget performance report Report that compares actual revenues and costs with their variable budgeted amounts based on actual sales volume (or other level of activity) and identifies the differences as variances. *(p. 782)*

FOB Abbreviation for *free on board;* the point when ownership of goods passes to the buyer; *FOB shipping point* (or *factory*) means the buyer pays shipping costs and accepts ownership of goods when the seller transfers goods to carrier; *FOB destination* means the seller pays shipping costs and buyer accepts ownership of goods at the buyer's place of business. *(p. 290)*

Form 940 IRS form used to report an employer's federal unemployment taxes (FUTA) on an annual filing basis. *(p. 241)*

Form 940-EZ The Employer's Annual Federal Unemployment Tax Return. This shows the amount of FUTA tax the employer owes for the year. *(p. 241)*

Form 941 IRS form filed to report FICA taxes owed and remitted. *(p. 236)*

Form 8109 A preprinted Federal Tax Deposit Coupon. It is used when an employer deposits money into a federal depository bank. *(p. 235)*

Form 8109-B A Federal Tax Deposit Coupon used by new businesses or when the business does not have a supply of preprinted Forms 8109. *(p. 235)*

Form SS-4 An Internal Revenue Service form filed by a business in order to receive an employer identification number. *(p. 238)*

Form W-2 Annual report by an employer to each employee showing the employee's wages subject to FICA and federal income taxes along with amounts withheld. *(p. 239)*

Form W-3 The Transmittal of Wage and Tax Statements form. This form reports the total wages and tax withholding information for all the employer's employees for the year. *(p. 239)*

Form W-4 Withholding allowance certificate, filed with the employer, identifying the number of withholding allowances claimed. *(p. 206)*

Franchises Privileges granted by a company or government to sell a product or service under specified conditions. *(p. 462)*

Full disclosure principle Principle that prescribes financial statements (including notes) to report all relevant information about an entity's operations and financial condition. *(pp. 399 & B-6)*

General accounting system Accounting system for manufacturing activities based on the *periodic* inventory system. *(p. 714)*

General and administrative expenses Expenses that support the operating activities of a business. *(p. 348)*

General journal All-purpose journal for recording the debits and credits of transactions and events. *(pp. 77 & 266)*

General partner Partner who assumes unlimited liability for the debts of the partnership; responsible for partnership management. *(p. 487)*

General partnership Partnership in which all partners have mutual agency and unlimited liability for partnership debts. *(p. 487)*

Generally Accepted Accounting Principles (GAAP) Rules that specify acceptable accounting practices. *(pp. 10 & B-7)*

General-purpose financial statements Statements published periodically for use by a variety of interested parties; includes the income statement, balance sheet, statement of owner's equity (or statement of retained earnings for a corporation), statement of cash flows, and notes to these statements. *(p. 643)*

Going-concern assumption Concept that prescribes financial statements to reflect the assumption that the business will continue operating indefinitely. *(p. B-5)*

Goods in process inventory Account in which costs are accumulated for products that are in the process of being produced but are not yet complete; also called *work in process inventory*. *(pp. 684 & 717)*

Goodwill Amount by which a company's (or a segment's) value exceeds the value of its individual assets less its liabilities. *(p. 462)*

Gross margin (See *gross profit*.) *(p. 322)*

Gross margin ratio Gross margin (net sales minus cost of goods sold) divided by net sales; also called *gross profit ratio*. *(p. 657)*

Gross pay Total compensation earned by an employee. *(p. 206)*

Gross profit Net sales minus cost of goods sold; also called *gross margin*. *(p. 322)*

Gross profit method Procedure to estimate inventory when the past gross profit rate is used to estimate cost of goods sold, which is then subtracted from the cost of goods available for sale. *(p. 430)*

Horizontal analysis Comparison of a company's financial condition and performance across time. *(p. 644)*

Impairment Diminishment of an asset value. *(p. 454)*

Income (See *net income*.)

Income statement Financial statement that subtracts expenses from revenues to yield a net income or loss over a specified period of time; also includes any gains or losses. *(p. 29)*

Income Summary Temporary account used only in the closing process to which the balances of revenue and expense accounts (including any gains or losses) are transferred; its balance is transferred to the capital account (or retained earnings for a corporation). *(p. 133)*

Incremental cost Additional cost incurred only if a company pursues a specific course of action. *(p. 812)*

Indefinite useful life Asset life that is not limited by legal, regulatory, contractual, competitive, economic, or other factors. *(p. 460)*

Independent contractor Someone who does a job for an employer, but decides how to do the work. *(p. 206)*

Indirect costs Costs incurred for the benefit of more than one cost object. *(p. 681)*

Indirect expenses Expenses incurred for the joint benefit of more than one department (or cost object). *(p. 752)*

Indirect labor Efforts of production employees who do not work specifically on converting direct materials into finished products and who are not clearly identified with specific units or batches of product. *(p. 685)*

Indirect labor costs Labor costs that cannot be physically traced to production of a product or service; included as part of overhead. *(p. 685)*

Indirect material Material used to support the production process but not clearly identified with products or batches of product. *(p. 683)*

Indirect method Presentation that reports net income and then adjusts it by adding and subtracting items to yield net cash from operating activities on the statement of cash flows. *(p. 603)*

Individual employee earnings records Records that summarize each employee's earnings, deductions, and net pay during each calendar year. *(p. 216)*

Installment note Liability requiring a series of periodic payments to the lender. *(pp. 401 & 577)*

Intangible assets Long-term assets (resources) used to produce or sell products or services; usually lack physical form and have uncertain benefits. *(pp. 351 & 460)*

Interest Charge for using money (or other assets) loaned from one entity to another. *(p. 396)*

Interim financial statements Financial statements covering periods of less than one year; usually based on one-, three-, or six-month periods. *(pp. 105 & 430)*

Internal controls or **Internal control system** All policies and procedures used to protect assets, ensure reliable accounting, promote efficient operations, and urge adherence to company policies. *(p. 160)*

Internal transactions Activities within an organization that can affect the accounting equation. *(p. 23)*

Internal users Persons using accounting information who are directly involved in managing the organization. *(p. 5)*

International Accounting Standards Board (IASB) Group that identifies preferred accounting practices and encourages global acceptance; issues International Financial Reporting Standards (IFRS). *(pp. 10 & B-4)*

Inventory Goods a company owns and expects to sell in its normal operations. *(p. 286)*

Inventory turnover Number of times a company's average inventory is sold during a period; computed by dividing cost of goods sold by average inventory; also called *merchandise turnover*. *(p. 423)*

Investing activities Transactions that involve purchasing and selling of long-term assets; includes making and collecting notes receivable and investments in other than cash equivalents. *(p. 599)*

Investment center Center of which a manager is responsible for revenues, costs, and asset investments. *(p. 760)*

Investment center return on total assets Center net income divided by average total assets for the center. *(p. 760)*

Invoice Itemized record of goods prepared by the vendor that lists the customer's name, items sold, sales prices, and terms of sale. *(pp. 167 & 287)*

Invoice approval Document containing a checklist of steps necessary for approving the recording and payment of an invoice; also called *check authorization*. *(p. 168)*

Job Production of a customized product or service. *(p. 714)*

Job cost sheet Separate record maintained for each job. *(p. 716)*

Job lot Production of more than one unit of a customized product or service. *(p. 715)*

Job order cost accounting system Cost accounting system to determine the cost of producing each job or job lot. *(p. 716)*

Job order production Production of special-order products; also called *customized production*. *(p. 714)*

Journal Record in which transactions are entered before they are posted to ledger accounts; also called *book of original entry*. *(p. 74)*

Journalizing Process of recording transactions in a journal. *(p. 74)*

Just-in-time (JIT) manufacturing Process of acquiring or producing inventory only when needed. *(p. 679)*

Land improvements Assets that increase the benefits of land, have a limited useful life, and are depreciated. *(p. 448)*

Large stock dividend Stock dividend that is more than 25% of the previously outstanding shares. *(p. 541)*

Last-in, first-out (LIFO) Method to assign cost to inventory that assumes costs for the most recent items purchased are sold first and charged to cost of goods sold. *(p. 419)*

Lean business model Practice of eliminating waste while meeting customer needs and yielding positive company returns. *(p. 679)*

Lease Contract specifying the rental of property. *(pp. 462 & 577)*

Leasehold Rights the lessor grants to the lessee under the terms of a lease. *(p. 462)*

Leasehold improvements Alterations or improvements to leased property such as partitions and storefronts. *(p. 462)*

Ledger Record containing all accounts (with amounts) for a business; also called *general ledger*. *(p. 74)*

Lessee Party to a lease who secures the right to possess and use the property from another party (the lessor). *(p. 462)*

Lessor Party to a lease who grants another party (the lessee) the right to possess and use its property. *(p. 462)*

Liabilities Creditors' claims on an organization's assets; involves a probable future payment of assets, products, or services that a company is obligated to make due to past transactions or events. *(p. 22)*

Licenses (See *franchises*.) *(p. 462)*

LIFO conformity rule If LIFO is used for tax reporting it must also be used for financial reporting. *(p. 421)*

Limited liability company (LLC) Organization form that combines select features of a corporation and a limited partnership; provides limited liability to its members (owners), is free of business tax, and allows members to actively participate in management. *(p. 488)*

Limited liability partnership Partnership in which a partner is not personally liable for malpractice or negligence unless that partner is responsible for providing the service that resulted in the claim. *(p. 487)*

Limited partners Partners who have no personal liability for partnership debts beyond the amounts they invested in the partnership. *(p. 487)*

Limited partnership Partnership that has two classes of partners: limited partners and general partners. *(p. 487)*

Liquid assets Resources such as cash that are easily converted into other assets or used to pay for goods, services, or liabilities. *(p. 178)*

Liquidating cash dividend Distribution of assets that returns part of the original investment to stockholders; deducted from contributed capital accounts. *(p. 533)*

Liquidity Availability of resources to meet short-term cash requirements. *(pp. 178 & 643)*

List price Catalog (full) price of an item before any trade discount is deducted. *(p. 287)*

Long-term investments Long-term assets not used in operating activities such as notes receivable and investments in stocks and bonds. *(p. 351)*

Long-term liabilities Obligations not due to be paid within one year or the operating cycle, whichever is longer. *(p. 351)*

Look-back rule A rule used to classify business as monthly or semiweekly depositors. *(p. 234)*

Lower of cost or market (LCM) Required method to report inventory at market replacement cost when that market cost is lower than recorded cost. *(p. 422)*

Maker of the note Entity who signs a note and promises to pay it at maturity. *(p. 396)*

Managerial accounting Area of accounting mainly aimed at serving the decision-making needs of internal users; also called *management accounting*. *(pp. 5 & 678)*

Manufacturing statement Report that summarizes the types and amounts of costs incurred in a company's production process for a period; also called *cost of goods manufacturing statement*. *(p. 687)*

Margin of safety Excess of expected sales over the level of break-even sales. *(p. 810)*

Market prospects Expectations (both good and bad) about a company's future performance as assessed by users and other interested parties. *(p. 643)*

Market rate Interest rate that borrowers are willing to pay and lenders are willing to accept for a specific lending agreement given the borrowers' risk level. *(p. 570)*

Market value per share Price at which stock is bought or sold. *(p. 518)*

Matching principle Prescribes expenses to be reported in the same period as the revenues that were earned as a result of the expenses. *(pp. 105, 374, & B-6)*

Materiality Prescribes that accounting for items that markedly impact financial statements, and any inferences drawn from them, adhere to GAAP. *(p. B-7)*

Materiality constraint Prescribes that accounting for items that significantly impact financial statements and any inferences from them strictly adhere to GAAP. *(p. 374)*

Materials ledger card Perpetual record updated each time units are purchased or issued for production use. *(p. 717)*

Materials requisition Source document production managers use to request materials for production; used to assign materials costs to specific jobs or overhead. *(p. 718)*

Maturity date of a note Date when a note's principal and interest are due. *(p. 397)*

Merchandise (See *merchandise inventory.*) *(p. 262)*

Merchandise inventory Goods that a company owns and expects to sell to customers; also called *merchandise* or *inventory*. *(pp. 286 & 317)*

Merchandiser Entity that earns net income by buying and selling merchandise. *(pp. 262 & 286)*

Merit rating Rating assigned to an employer by a state based on the employer's record of employment. *(p. 232)*

Minimum legal capital Amount of assets defined by law that stockholders must (potentially) invest in a corporation; usually defined as par value of the stock; intended to protect creditors. *(p. 519)*

Mixed cost Cost that behaves like a combination of fixed and variable costs. *(pp. 680 & 807)*

Modified Accelerated Cost Recovery System (MACRS) Depreciation system required by federal income tax law. *(p. 454)*

Monetary unit assumption Concept that assumes transactions and events can be expressed in money units. *(p. B-5)*

Mortgage Legal loan agreement that protects a lender by giving the lender the right to be paid from the cash proceeds from the sale of a borrower's assets identified in the mortgage. *(pp. 403 & 577)*

Multiple-step income statement Income statement format that shows subtotals between sales and net income, categorizes expenses, and often reports the details of net sales and expenses. *(p. 347)*

Mutual agency Legal relationship among partners whereby each partner is an agent of the partnership and is able to bind the partnership to contracts within the scope of the partnership's business. *(p. 487)*

Natural resources Assets physically consumed when used; examples are timber, mineral deposits, and oil and gas fields; also called *wasting assets*. *(p. 459)*

Net income Amount earned after subtracting all expenses necessary for and matched with sales for a period; also called *income, profit,* or *earnings*. *(p. 23)*

Net loss Excess of expenses over revenues for a period. *(p. 23)*

Net pay Gross pay less all deductions; also called *take-home pay*. *(p. 213)*

Net purchases Net cost of merchandise purchased; computed as purchases minus purchase discounts, minus purchase returns and allowances, plus transportation-in. *(pp. 290 & 322)*

Net realizable value Expected selling price (value) of an item minus the cost of making the sale. *(p. 414)*

Net sales Net amount of merchandise sold; computed as sales minus sales returns and allowances minus sales discounts. *(p. 322)*

Noncumulative preferred stock Preferred stock on which the right to receive dividends is lost for any period when dividends are not declared. *(p. 544)*

Nonparticipating preferred stock Preferred stock on which dividends are limited to a maximum amount each year. *(p. 544)*

No-par value stock Stock class that has not been assigned a par (or stated) value by the corporate charter. *(p. 519)*

Non-value-added time The portion of cycle time that is not directed at producing a product or service; equals the sum of inspection time, move time, and wait time. *(p. 690)*

Note payable Liability expressed by a written promise to pay a definite sum of money on demand or on a specific future date(s). *(p. 400)*

Operating activities Activities that involve the production or purchase of merchandise and the sale of goods or services to customers, including expenditures related to administering the business. *(p. 599)*

Operating cycle Normal time between paying cash for merchandise or employee services and receiving cash from customers. *(p. 350)*

Opportunity cost Potential benefit lost by choosing a specific action from two or more alternatives. *(p. 681)*

Ordinary repairs Repairs to keep a plant asset in normal, good operating condition; treated as a revenue expenditure and immediately expensed. *(p. 456)*

Organization expenses (costs) Costs such as legal fees and promoter fees to bring an entity into existence. *(p. 517)*

Out-of-pocket cost Cost incurred or avoided as a result of management's decisions. *(p. 681)*

Outstanding checks Checks written and recorded by the depositor but not yet paid by the bank at the bank statement date. *(p. 187)*

Overapplied overhead Amount by which the overhead applied to production in a period using the predetermined overhead rate exceeds the actual overhead incurred in a period. *(p. 725)*

Overhead cost variance Difference between the total overhead cost applied to products and the total overhead cost actually incurred. *(p. 786)*

Owner, capital Account showing the owner's claim on company assets; equals owner investments plus net income (or less net losses) minus owner withdrawals since the company's inception; also referred to as *equity*. *(p. 23)*

Owner investment Assets put into the business by the owner. *(p. 23)*

Owner withdrawals (See *withdrawals*.) *(p. 23)*

Paid-in capital Total amount of cash and other assets a corporation receives from its stockholders in exchange for its stock. *(p. 519)*

Paid-in capital in excess of par value Amount received from issuance of stock that is in excess of the stock's par value. *(p. 520)*

Par value Value assigned a share of stock by the corporate charter when the stock is authorized. *(p. 519)*

Par value of a bond Amount the bond issuer agrees to pay at maturity and the amount on which cash interest payments are based; also called *face amount* or *face value* of a bond. *(p. 569)*

Par value stock Class of stock assigned a par value by the corporate charter. *(p. 519)*

Participating preferred stock Preferred stock that shares with common stockholders any dividends paid in excess of the percent stated on preferred stock. *(p. 544)*

Partner return on equity Partner net income divided by average partner equity for the period. *(p. 499)*

Partnership contract Agreement among partners that sets terms under which the affairs of the partnership are conducted; also called *articles of partnership* if in writing. *(p. 486)*

Partnership liquidation Dissolution of a partnership by (1) selling noncash assets and allocating any gain or loss according to partners' income-and-loss ratio, (2) paying liabilities, and (3) distributing any remaining cash according to partners' capital balances. *(p. 497)*

Patent Exclusive right granted to its owner to produce and sell an item or to use a process for 17 years. *(p. 461)*

Payout ratio Cash dividends declared on common stock dividend by net income. *(p. 549)*

Payee of the note Entity to whom a note is made payable. *(p. 396)*

Payroll bank account Bank account used solely for paying employees; each pay period an amount equal to the total employees' net pay is deposited in it and the payroll checks are drawn on it. *(p. 214)*

Payroll deductions Amounts withheld from an employee's gross pay; also called *withholdings*. *(p. 209)*

Payroll register Record for a pay period that shows the pay period dates, regular and overtime hours worked, gross pay, net pay, and deductions. *(p. 213)*

Period costs Expenditures identified more with a time period than with finished products costs; includes selling and general administrative expenses. *(p. 681)*

Periodic inventory system Method that records the cost of inventory purchased but does not continuously track the quantity available or sold to customers; records are updated at the end of each period to reflect the physical count and costs of goods available. *(pp. 371 & 415)*

Periodicity assumption (or principle) Assumption that an organization's activities can be divided into specific time periods such as months, quarters, or years. *(p. B-5)*

Permanent accounts Accounts that reflect activities related to one or more future periods; balance sheet accounts whose balances are not closed; also called *real accounts*. *(p. 133)*

Perpetual inventory system Method that maintains continuous records of the cost of inventory available and the cost of goods sold. *(p. 415)*

Petty cash Small amount of cash in a fund to pay minor expenses; accounted for using an imprest system. *(p. 180)*

Planning Process of setting goals and preparing to achieve them. *(p. 678)*

Plant assets Tangible long-lived assets used to produce or sell products and services; also called *property, plant and equipment (PP&E)* or *fixed assets*. *(pp. 107 & 446)*

Plant asset age Estimated by dividing accumulated depreciation expense. *(p. 464)*

Plant asset useful life Equals the plant asset cost divided by depreciation expense. It is the length of time an asset will be productively used in the operations of a business. *(p. 463)*

Post-closing trial balance List of permanent accounts and their balances from the ledger after all closing entries are journalized and posted. *(p. 137)*

Posting Process of transferring journal entry information to the ledger; computerized systems automate this process. *(p. 74)*

Posting reference (PR) column A column in journals in which individual ledger account numbers are entered when entries are posted to those ledger accounts. *(p. 78)*

Predetermined overhead rate Rate established prior to the beginning of a period that relates estimated overhead to another variable, such as estimated direct labor, and is used to assign overhead cost to production. *(p. 722)*

Preemptive right Stockholders' right to maintain their proportionate interest in a corporation with any additional shares issued. *(p. 518)*

Preferred stock Stock with a priority status over common stockholders in one or more ways, such as paying dividends or distributing assets. *(p. 522)*

Premium on bonds Difference between a bond's par value and its higher carrying value; occurs when the contract rate is higher than the market rate; also called *bond premium*. *(p. 573)*

Premium on stock (See *paid-in capital in excess of par value*.) *(p. 520)*

Prepaid expenses Items paid for in advance of receiving their benefits; classified as assets. *(p. 106)*

Price-earnings (PE) ratio Ratio of a company's current market value per share to its earnings per share; also called *price-to-earnings*. *(p. 549)*

Price variance Difference between actual and budgeted revenue or cost caused by the difference between the actual price per unit and the budgeted price per unit. *(p. 783)*

Prime costs Expenditures directly identified with the production of finished goods; include direct materials costs and direct labor costs. *(p. 685)*

Principal of a note Amount that the signer of a note agrees to pay back when it matures, not including interest. *(p. 396)*

Principles of internal control Principles prescribing management to establish responsibility, maintain records, insure assets, separate recordkeeping from custody of assets, divide responsibility for related transactions, apply technological controls, and perform reviews. *(p. 160)*

Prior period adjustment Correction of an error in a prior year that is reported in the statement of retained earnings (or statement of stockholders' equity) net of any income tax effects. *(p. 547)*

Process operations Mass production of products in a continuous flow of steps. *(p. 715)*

Product costs Costs that are capitalized as inventory because they produce benefits expected to have future value; include direct materials, direct labor, and overhead. *(p. 681)*

Pro forma financial statements Statements that show the effects of proposed transactions and events as if they had occurred. *(p. 133)*

Profit center Business unit that incurs costs and generates revenues. *(p. 751)*

Profit margin Ratio of a company's net income to its net sales; the percent of income in each dollar of revenue; also called *net profit margin*. *(p. 655)*

Profitability Company's ability to generate an adequate return on invested capital. *(p. 643)*

Promissory note (or note) Written promise to pay a specified amount either on demand or at a definite future date; is a *note receivable* for the lender but a *note payable* for the lendee. *(p. 396)*

Proxy Legal document giving a stockholder's agent the power to exercise the stockholder's voting rights. *(p. 517)*

Purchase discount Term used by a purchaser to describe a cash discount granted to the purchaser for paying within the discount period. *(p. 288)*

Purchase order Document used by the purchasing department to place an order with a seller (vendor). *(pp. 168 & 287)*

Purchase requisition Document listing merchandise needed by a department and requesting it be purchased. *(pp. 166 & 286)*

Purchases journal Journal normally used to record all purchases on credit. *(p. 292)*

Quantity variance Difference between actual and budgeted revenue or cost caused by the difference between the actual number of units and the budgeted number of units. *(p. 783)*

Ratio analysis Determination of key relations between financial statement items as reflected in numerical measures. *(p. 644)*

Raw materials inventory Goods a company acquires to use in making products. *(p. 683)*

Realizable value Expected proceeds from converting an asset into cash. *(p. 375)*

Receiving report Form used to report that ordered goods are received and to describe their quantity and condition. *(pp. 167, 287 & 717)*

Recordkeeping Part of accounting that involves recording transactions and events, either manually or electronically; also called *bookkeeping*. *(p. 4)*

Relevance A qualitative characteristic of accounting information that prescribes that information be useful, understandable, timely and pertinent for decision making. *(p. B-3)*

Relevant benefits Additional or incremental revenue generated by selecting a particular course of action over another. *(p. 811)*

Reliability The principle that information is verifiable and faithfully represents the substance of the underlying economic transaction. *(p. B-3)*

Responsibility accounting budget Report of expected costs and expenses under a manager's control. *(p. 759)*

Responsibility accounting performance report Responsibility report that compares actual costs and expenses for a department with budgeted amounts. *(p. 759)*

Responsibility accounting system System that provides information that management can use to evaluate the performance of a department's manager. *(p. 750)*

Restricted retained earnings Retained earnings not available for dividends because of legal or contractual limitations. *(p. 547)*

Restrictive endorsement The depositor transfers the check to a specific person, business, or bank for a specific purpose. *(p. 184)*

Retailer Intermediary that buys products from manufacturers or wholesalers and sells them to consumers. *(p. 262)*

Retained earnings Cumulative income less cumulative losses and dividends. *(p. 519)*

Retained earnings deficit Debit (abnormal) balance in Retained Earnings; occurs when cumulative losses and dividends exceed cumulative income; also called *accumulated deficit*. *(p. 548)*

Return on total assets *(p. 655)*

Revenue expenditures Expenditures reported on the current income statement as an expense because they do not provide benefits in future periods. *(p. 456)*

Revenue recognition principle The principle prescribing that revenue is recognized when earned. *(pp. 105 & B-6)*

Revenues Gross increase in equity from a company's business activities that earn income; also called *sales*. *(p. 23)*

Reversing entries Optional entries recorded at the beginning of a period that prepare the accounts for the usual journal entries as if adjusting entries had not occurred in the prior period. *(p. 356)*

S corporation Corporation that meets special tax qualifications so as to be treated like a partnership for income tax purposes. *(p. 488)*

Salary A fixed amount of compensation paid or received on a regular basis, such as every two weeks, monthly, or annually. *(p. 208)*

Sales discount Term used by a seller to describe a cash discount granted to buyers who pay within the discount period. *(p. 262)*

Sales journal Journal normally used to record sales of goods on credit. *(p. 266)*

Sales mix Ratio of sales volumes for the various products sold by a company. *(p. 815)*

Salvage value Estimate of amount to be recovered at the end of an asset's useful life; also called *residual value* or *scrap value*. *(p. 449)*

Sarbanes-Oxley Act Created the *Public Company Accounting Oversight Board*, regulates analyst conflicts, imposes corporate governance requirements, enhances accounting and control disclosures, impacts insider transactions and executive loans, establishes new types of criminal conduct, and expands penalties for violations of federal securities laws. *(pp. 9 & B-2)*

Schedule of accounts payable List of the balances of all accounts in the accounts payable ledger and their total. *(p. 294)*

Schedule of accounts receivable List of the balances for all accounts in the accounts receivable ledger and their total. *(p. 268)*

Secured bonds Bonds that have specific assets of the issuer pledged as collateral. *(p. 578)*

Securities and Exchange Commission (SEC) Federal agency Congress has charged to set reporting rules for organizations that sell ownership shares to the public. *(pp. 9 & B-2)*

Self-employment tax Social Security and Medicare taxes for persons who operate their own businesses. *(p. 208)*

Selling expenses Expenses of promoting sales, such as displaying and advertising merchandise, making sales, and delivering goods to customers. *(p. 347)*

Serial bonds Bonds consisting of separate amounts that mature at different dates. *(p. 578)*

Shareholders Owners of a corporation; also called *stockholders*. *(p. 11)*

Signature card Includes the signatures of each person authorized to sign checks on the bank account. *(p. 183)*

Simple capital structure Capital structure that consists of only common stock and nonconvertible preferred stock; consists of no dilutive securities. *(p. 549)*

Single-step income statement Income statement format that includes cost of goods sold as an expense and shows only one subtotal for total expenses. *(p. 349)*

Small stock dividend Stock dividend that is 25% or less of a corporation's previously outstanding shares. *(p. 541)*

Solvency Company's long-run financial viability and its ability to cover long-term obligations. *(p. 643)*

Source documents Source of information for accounting entries that can be in either paper or electronic form; also called *business papers*. *(p. 75)*

Special journal Any journal used for recording and posting transactions of a similar type. *(p. 266)*

Specific identification Method to assign cost to inventory when the purchase cost of each item in inventory is identified and used to compute cost of inventory. *(p. 417)*

Standard costs Costs that should be incurred under normal conditions to produce a product or component or to perform a service. *(p. 783)*

State unemployment taxes (SUTA) State payroll taxes on employers to support its unemployment programs. *(p. 232)*

Stated value stock No-par stock assigned a stated value per share; this amount is recorded in the stock account when the stock is issued. *(p. 519)*

Statement of cash flows A financial statement that lists cash inflows (receipts) and cash outflows (payments) during a period; arranged by operating, investing, and financing. *(p. 598)*

Statement of owner's equity Report of changes in equity over a period; adjusted for increases (owner investment and net income) and for decreases (withdrawals and net loss). *(p. 29)*

Statement of partners' equity Financial statement that shows total capital balances at the beginning of the period, any additional investment by partners, the income or loss of the period, the partners' withdrawals, and the partners' ending capital balances; also called *statement of partners' capital*. *(p. 493)*

Statement of retained earnings Report of changes in retained earnings over a period; adjusted for increases (net income), for decreases (dividends and net loss), and for any prior period adjustment. *(p. 547)*

Statement of stockholders' equity Financial statement that lists the beginning and ending balances of each major equity account and describes all changes in those accounts. *(p. 548)*

Stock dividend Corporation's distribution of its own stock to its stockholders without the receipt of any payment. *(p. 541)*

Stock split Occurs when a corporation calls in its stock and replaces each share with more than one new share; decreases both the market value per share and any par or stated value per share. *(p. 543)*

Stockholders' equity A corporation's equity; also called *shareholders' equity* or *corporate capital*. *(p. 519)*

Straight-line depreciation Method that allocates an equal portion of the depreciable cost of plant asset (cost minus salvage) to each accounting period in its useful life. *(pp. 108 & 450)*

Straight-line bond amortization Method allocating an equal amount of bond interest expense to each period of the bond life. *(p. 572)*

Subsidiary ledger List of individual sub-accounts and amounts with a common characteristic; linked to a controlling account in the general ledger. *(p. 267)*

Sunk cost Cost already incurred and cannot be avoided or changed. *(p. 681)*

T-account Tool used to show the effects of transactions and events on individual accounts. *(p. 46)*

Target cost Maximum allowable cost for a product or service; defined as expected selling price less the desired profit. *(p. 715)*

Taxable income A corporation's total revenues under tax laws minus its total expenses under tax laws. *(p. 538)*

Temporary accounts Accounts used to record revenues, expenses, and withdrawals (dividends for a corporation); they are closed at the end of each period; also called *nominal accounts*. *(p. 133)*

Term bonds Bonds scheduled for payment (maturity) at a single specified date. *(p. 578)*

Time ticket Source document used to report the time an employee spent working on a job or on overhead activities and then to determine the amount of direct labor to charge to the job or the amount of indirect labor to charge to overhead. *(p. 719)*

Times interest earned ratio Ratio of income before interest expense (and any income taxes) divided by interest expense; reflects risk of covering interest commitments when income varies. *(p. 403)*

Total asset turnover Measure of a company's ability to use its assets to generate sales; computed by dividing net sales by average total assets. *(p. 463)*

Total quality management (TQM) Concept calling for all managers and employees at all stages of operations to strive toward higher standards and reduce number of defects. *(p. 679)*

Trade discount Reduction from a list or catalog price that can vary for wholesalers, retailers, and consumers. *(p. 288)*

Trademark or **trade (brand) name** Symbol, name, phrase, or jingle identified with a company, product, or service. *(p. 462)*

Transportation-In Freight costs paid by the buyer. *(p. 287)*

Treasury stock Corporation's own stock that it reacquired and still holds. *(p. 545)*

Trial balance List of accounts and their balances at a point in time; total debit balances equal total credit balances. *(p. 55)*

Unadjusted trial balance List of accounts and balances prepared before accounting adjustments are recorded and posted. *(p. 110)*

Unavoidable expense Expense (or cost) that is not relevant for business decisions; an expense that would continue even if a department, product, or service is eliminated. *(p. 817)*

Unclassified balance sheet Balance sheet that broadly groups assets, liabilities, and equity accounts. *(p. 349)*

Uncontrollable costs Costs that a manager does not have the power to determine or strongly influence. *(p. 758)*

Underapplied overhead Amount by which overhead incurred in a period exceeds the overhead applied to that period's production using the predetermined overhead rate. *(p. 725)*

Unearned revenue Liability created when customers pay in advance for products or services; earned when the products or services are later delivered. *(pp. 52 & 324)*

Unfavorable variance Difference in revenues or costs, when the actual amount is compared to the budgeted amount, that contributes to a lower income. *(p. 779)*

Units-of-production depreciation Method that charges a varying amount to depreciation expense for each period of an asset's useful life depending on its usage. *(p. 451)*

Unlimited liability Legal relationship among general partners that makes each of them responsible for partnership debts if the other partners are unable to pay their shares. *(p. 487)*

Unsecured bonds Bonds backed only by the issuer's credit standing; almost always riskier than secured bonds; also called *debentures*. *(p. 578)*

Useful life Length of time an asset will be productively used in the operations of a business; also called *service life*. *(p. 449)*

Value-added time The portion of cycle time that is directed at producing a product or service; equals process time. *(p. 690)*

Value chain Sequential activities that add value to an entity's products or services; includes design, production, marketing, distribution, and service. *(p. 686)*

Variable cost Cost that changes in proportion to changes in the activity output volume. *(p. 680)*

Variance analysis Process of examining differences between actual and budgeted revenues or costs and describing them in terms of price and quantity differences. *(p. 783)*

Vendee Buyer of goods or services. *(p. 167)*

Vendor Seller of goods or services. *(pp. 161 & 287)*

Vertical analysis Evaluation of each financial statement item or group of items in terms of a specific base amount. *(p. 644)*

Voucher Internal file used to store documents and information to control cash disbursements and to ensure that a transaction is properly authorized and recorded. *(p. 164)*

Voucher register Journal (referred to as *book of original entry*) in which all vouchers are recorded after they have been approved. *(p. 169)*

Voucher system Procedures and approvals designed to control cash disbursements and acceptance of obligations. *(p. 164)*

Wage bracket withholding table Table of the amounts of income tax withheld from employees' wages. *(p. 210)*

Wages Money paid or received for work or services by the hour, day, or week or by the number of units produced. *(p. 208)*

Weighted average Method to assign inventory cost to sales; the cost of available-for-sale units is divided by the number of units available to determine per unit cost prior to each sale that is then multiplied by the units sold to yield the cost of that sale. *(p. 428)*

Wholesaler Intermediary that buys products from manufacturers or other wholesalers and sells them to retailers or other wholesalers. *(p. 262)*

Withdrawals Payment of cash or other assets from a proprietorship or partnership to its owner or owners. *(p. 23)*

Withholding allowance This determines the amount of federal income taxes to withhold from an employee's pay. *(p. 206)*

Workers' compensation insurance An insurance program that provides benefits to workers who are injured on the job. *(p. 233)*

Work sheet Spreadsheet used to draft an unadjusted trial balance, adjusting entries, adjusted trial balance, and financial statements. *(p. 128)*

Working capital Current assets minus current liabilities at a point in time. *(p. 650)*

Working papers Analyses and other internal documents prepared by accountants when organizing information for formal reports and financial statements. *(p. 128)*

Workplace fraud The deliberate misuse of an employer's assets for an employee's personal gain. *(p. 158)*

Credits

Index

Note: Page numbers followed by *n* indicate material in footnotes.

Chart of Accounts

Following is a typical chart of accounts. Each company has its own unique accounts and numbering system.

Assets

Current Assets

101 Cash
102 Petty cash
103 Cash equivalents
104 Short-term investments
105 Market adjustment, _____ securities (S-T)
106 Accounts receivable
107 Allowance for doubtful accounts
108 Legal fees receivable
109 Interest receivable
110 Rent receivable
111 Notes receivable
119 Merchandise inventory
120 _____ inventory
121 _____ inventory
124 Office supplies
125 Store supplies
126 _____ supplies
128 Prepaid insurance
129 Prepaid interest
131 Prepaid rent
132 Raw materials inventory
133 Goods in process inventory, _____
134 Goods in process inventory, _____
135 Finished goods inventory

Long-Term Investments

141 Long-term investments
142 Market adjustment, _____ securities (L-T)
144 Investment in _____
145 Bond sinking fund

Plant Assets

151 Automobiles
152 Accumulated depreciation—Automobiles
153 Trucks
154 Accumulated depreciation—Trucks
155 Boats
156 Accumulated depreciation—Boats
157 Professional library
158 Accumulated depreciation—Professional library
159 Law library
160 Accumulated depreciation—Law library
161 Furniture
162 Accumulated depreciation—Furniture
163 Office equipment
164 Accumulated depreciation—Office equipment
165 Store equipment
166 Accumulated depreciation—Store equipment
167 _____ equipment
168 Accumulated depreciation—_____ equipment
169 Machinery
170 Accumulated depreciation—Machinery
173 Building _____
174 Accumulated depreciation—Building _____
175 Building _____
176 Accumulated depreciation—Building _____
179 Land improvements _____
180 Accumulated depreciation—Land improvements _____
181 Land improvements _____
182 Accumulated depreciation—Land improvements _____
183 Land

Natural Resources

185 Mineral deposit
186 Accumulated depletion—Mineral deposit

Intangible Assets

191 Patents
192 Leasehold
193 Franchise
194 Copyrights
195 Leasehold improvements
196 Licenses
197 Accumulated amortization—_____

Liabilities

Current Liabilities

201 Accounts payable
202 Insurance payable
203 Interest payable
204 Legal fees payable
207 Office salaries payable
208 Rent payable
209 Salaries payable
210 Wages payable
211 Accrued payroll payable
214 Estimated warranty liability
215 Income taxes payable
216 Common dividend payable
217 Preferred dividend payable
218 State unemployment taxes payable
219 Employee federal income taxes payable
221 Employee medical insurance payable
222 Employee retirement program payable
223 Employee union dues payable
224 Federal unemployment taxes payable
225 FICA taxes payable
226 Estimated vacation pay liability

Unearned Revenues

230 Unearned consulting fees
231 Unearned legal fees
232 Unearned property management fees
233 Unearned _____ fees
234 Unearned _____ fees
235 Unearned janitorial revenue
236 Unearned _____ revenue
238 Unearned rent

Notes Payable

240 Short-term notes payable
241 Discount on short-term notes payable
245 Notes payable
251 Long-term notes payable
252 Discount on long-term notes payable

Long-Term Liabilities

253 Long-term lease liability
255 Bonds payable
256 Discount on bonds payable
257 Premium on bonds payable
258 Deferred income tax liability

Equity

Owner's Equity

301 _____, Capital
302 _____, Withdrawals
303 _____, Capital
304 _____, Withdrawals
305 _____, Capital
306 _____, Withdrawals

Paid-In Capital

307 Common stock, $ _____ par value
308 Common stock, no-par value
309 Common stock, $ _____ stated value
310 Common stock dividend distributable
311 Paid-in capital in excess of par value, Common stock
312 Paid-in capital in excess of stated value, No-par common stock
313 Paid-in capital from retirement of common stock
314 Paid-in capital, Treasury stock
315 Preferred stock
316 Paid-in capital in excess of par value, Preferred stock

Retained Earnings

318 Retained earnings
319 Cash dividends (or Dividends)
320 Stock dividends

Other Equity Accounts

321 Treasury stock, Common
322 Unrealized gain—Equity
323 Unrealized loss—Equity

Revenues

401 _____ fees earned
402 _____ fees earned
403 _____ services revenue
404 _____ services revenue
405 Commissions earned
406 Rent revenue (or Rent earned)
407 Dividends revenue (or Dividend earned)
408 Earnings from investment in _____
409 Interest revenue (or Interest earned)
410 Sinking fund earnings
413 Sales
414 Sales returns and allowances
415 Sales discounts

Cost of Sales

Cost of Goods Sold

502 Cost of goods sold
505 Purchases
506 Purchases returns and allowances
507 Purchases discounts
508 Transportation-in

Manufacturing

520 Raw materials purchases
521 Transportation-in on raw materials
530 Factory payroll
531 Direct labor
540 Factory overhead
541 Indirect materials
542 Indirect labor
543 Factory insurance expired
544 Factory supervision
545 Factory supplies used
546 Factory utilities
547 Miscellaneous production costs
548 Property taxes on factory building
549 Property taxes on factory equipment
550 Rent on factory building
551 Repairs, factory equipment
552 Small tools written off
560 Depreciation of factory equipment
561 Depreciation of factory building

Standard Cost Variance

580 Direct material quantity variance
581 Direct material price variance
582 Direct labor quantity variance
583 Direct labor price variance
584 Factory overhead cost variance

Expenses

Amortization, Depletion, and Depreciation

601 Amortization expense—_____
602 Amortization expense—_____
603 Depletion expense—_____
604 Depreciation expense—Boats
605 Depreciation expense—Automobiles
606 Depreciation expense—Building _____
607 Depreciation expense—Building _____
608 Depreciation expense—Land improvements _____
609 Depreciation expense—Land improvements _____
610 Depreciation expense—Law library
611 Depreciation expense—Trucks
612 Depreciation expense—_____ equipment
613 Depreciation expense—_____ equipment
614 Depreciation expense—_____
615 Depreciation expense—_____

Employee-Related Expenses

620 Office salaries expense
621 Sales salaries expense
622 Salaries expense
623 _____ wages expense
624 Employees' benefits expense
625 Payroll taxes expense

Financial Expenses

630 Cash over and short
631 Discounts lost
632 Factoring fee expense
633 Interest expense

Insurance Expenses

635 Insurance expense—Delivery equipment
636 Insurance expense—Office equipment
637 Insurance expense—_____

Rental Expenses

640 Rent expense
641 Rent expense—Office space
642 Rent expense—Selling space
643 Press rental expense
644 Truck rental expense
645 _____ rental expense

Supplies Expenses

650 Office supplies expense
651 Store supplies expense
652 _____ supplies expense
653 _____ supplies expense

Miscellaneous Expenses

655 Advertising expense
656 Bad debts expense
657 Blueprinting expense
658 Boat expense
659 Collection expense
661 Concessions expense
662 Credit card expense
663 Delivery expense
664 Dumping expense
667 Equipment expense
668 Food and drinks expense
671 Gas and oil expense
672 General and administrative expense
673 Janitorial expense
674 Legal fees expense
676 Mileage expense
677 Miscellaneous expenses
678 Mower and tools expense
679 Operating expense
680 Organization expense
681 Permits expense
682 Postage expense
683 Property taxes expense
684 Repairs expense—_____
685 Repairs expense—_____
687 Selling expense
688 Telephone expense
689 Travel and entertainment expense
690 Utilities expense
691 Warranty expense
695 Income taxes expense

Gains and Losses

701 Gain on retirement of bonds
702 Gain on sale of machinery
703 Gain on sale of investments
704 Gain on sale of trucks
705 Gain on _____
706 Foreign exchange gain or loss
801 Loss on disposal of machinery
802 Loss on exchange of equipment
803 Loss on exchange of _____
804 Loss on sale of notes
805 Loss on retirement of bonds
806 Loss on sale of investments
807 Loss on sale of machinery
808 Loss on _____
809 Unrealized gain—Income
810 Unrealized loss—Income

Clearing Accounts

901 Income summary
902 Manufacturing summary

A. K. A.

The same financial statement sometimes receives different titles. Below are some of the more common aliases.*

Balance Sheet	Statement of Financial Position Statement of Financial Condition
Income Statement	Statement of Income Operating Statement Statement of Operations Statement of Operating Activity Earnings Statement Statement of Earnings Profit and Loss (P&L) Statement
Statement of Cash Flows	Statement of Cash Flow Cash Flows Statement Statement of Changes in Cash Position Statement of Changes in Financial Position
Statement of Owner's Equity	Statement of Changes in Owner's Equity Statement of Changes in Owner's Capital Statement of Shareholders' Equity[†] Statement of Changes in Shareholders' Equity[†] Statement of Stockholders' Equity and Comprehensive Income[†] Statement of Changes in Capital Accounts[†]

* The term **Consolidated** often precedes or follows these statement titles to reflect the combination of different entities, such as a parent company and its subsidiaries.
[†]Corporation only.

We thank Dr. Louella Moore from Arkansas State University for suggesting this listing.

MANAGERIAL ANALYSES AND REPORTS

① Cost Types

Variable costs:	Cost changes in proportion to volume of activity	p. 680
Fixed costs:	Cost does not change in proportion to volume of activity	p. 680
Mixed costs:	Cost consists of both a variable and a fixed element	p. 680

② Cost Sources

Direct materials:	Raw materials costs directly linked to finished product	p. 685
Direct labor:	Employee costs directly linked to finished product	p. 685
Overhead:	Costs indirectly linked to processing finished product	p. 721

③ Costing Systems

Job order costing:	Costs assigned to each unit or batch of units	p. 714
Process costing:	Costs assigned to similar products that are mass-produced in a continuous manner	p. 714

④ Costing Ratios

Contribution margin ratio = (Net sales − Variable costs)/Net sales	p. 807
Predetermined overhead rate = Estimated overhead costs/Estimated activity base	p. 722
Break-even point in units = Fixed costs/Contribution margin per unit	p. 808

⑤ Planning and Control Metrics

Cost variance = Actual cost − Standard (budgeted) cost	p. 785
Sales (revenue) variance = Actual sales − Standard (budgeted) sales	p. 788

⑥ Capital Budgeting

Payback period = Time expected to recover investment cost	p. C-3
Accounting rate of return = Expected annual net income/Average annual investment	p. C-6
Net present value (NPV) = Present value of cash flows − Investment cost	p. C-7
NPV rule: 1. Compute net present value (NPV in $)	
2. If NPV ≥ 0, then accept project; If NPV < 0, then reject project	p. C-7
Internal rate 1. Compute internal rate of return (IRR in %)	
of return: 2. If IRR ≥ hurdle rate, accept project; If IRR < hurdle rate, reject project	p. C-9

⑦ Costing Terminology

Relevant range:	Organization's normal range of operating activity	p. 680
Direct cost:	Cost incurred for the benefit of one cost object	p. 681
Indirect cost:	Cost incurred for the benefit of more than one cost object	p. 681
Product cost:	Cost that is necessary and integral to finished products	p. 681
Period cost:	Cost identified more with a time period than with finished products	p. 681
Overhead cost:	Cost not separately or directly traceable to a cost object	p. 681
Relevant cost:	Cost that is pertinent to a decision	p. 811
Opportunity cost:	Benefit lost by choosing an action from two or more alternatives	p. 681
Sunk cost:	Cost already incurred that cannot be avoided or changed	p. 681
Standard cost:	Cost computed using standard price and standard quantity	p. 783
Cost variance:	Difference between actual cost and budgeted (standard) cost	p. 784
Budget:	Formal statement of an organization's future plans	p. 678
Break-even point:	Sales level at which an organization earns zero profit	p. 808
Incremental cost:	Cost incurred only if the organization undertakes certain action	p. 812

⑧ Standard Cost Variances

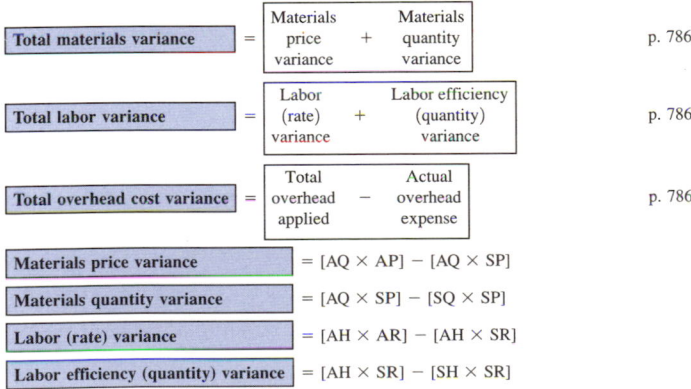

Total materials variance	=	Materials price variance	+	Materials quantity variance	p. 786
Total labor variance	=	Labor (rate) variance	+	Labor efficiency (quantity) variance	p. 786
Total overhead cost variance	=	Total overhead applied	−	Actual overhead expense	p. 786

Materials price variance	= [AQ × AP] − [AQ × SP]
Materials quantity variance	= [AQ × SP] − [SQ × SP]
Labor (rate) variance	= [AH × AR] − [AH × SR]
Labor efficiency (quantity) variance	= [AH × SR] − [SH × SR]

where
AQ is actual quantity of materials; AP is actual price of materials; AH is actual hours of labor; AR is actual rate of wages; SQ is standard quantity of materials; SP is standard price of materials; SH is standard hours of labor; SR is standard rate of wages.

Manufacturing Statement
For _period_ Ended _date_

Direct materials		
Raw materials inventory, Beginning	$	#
Raw materials purchases		#
Raw materials available for use		#
Raw materials inventory, Ending		(#)
Direct materials used............................		#
Direct labor		#
Overhead costs		
Total overhead costs		#
Total manufacturing costs		#
Add goods in process inventory, Beginning		#
Total cost of goods in process		#
Deduct goods in process inventory, Ending		(#)
Cost of goods manufactured	$	#

Contribution Margin Income Statement
For _period_ Ended _date_

Net sales (revenues)	$	#
Total variable costs		#
Contribution margin		#
Total fixed costs		#
Net income	$	#

Flexible Budget
For _period_ Ended _date_

	Flexible Budget		Flexible Budget for Unit Sales of #
	Variable Amount per Unit	Fixed Cost	
Sales (revenues)	$ #		$ #
Variable costs			
Examples: Direct materials, Direct labor, ...			
Other variable costs	#		#
Total variable costs	#		#
Contribution margin	$ #		#
Fixed costs			
Examples: Depreciation, Manager		$ #	#
salaries, Administrative salaries		#	#
Total fixed costs		$ #	#
Income from operations			$ #

Fixed Budget Performance Report
For _period_ Ended _date_

	Fixed Budget	Actual Performance	Variances[†]
Sales: In units	#	#	
In dollars	$ #	$ #	$ # F or U
Cost of sales:			
Direct costs	#	#	# F or U
Indirect costs	#	#	# F or U
Selling expenses:			
(Examples: Commissions, ...	#	#	# F or U
Shipping expenses)	#	#	# F or U
General and administrative expenses:			
(Examples: Administrative salaries)	#	#	# F or U
Total expenses	$ #	$ #	$ # F or U
Income from operations	$ #	$ #	$ # F or U

[†]F = Favorable variance; U = Unfavorable variance.

FUNDAMENTALS

① Accounting Equation

Assets	=	Liabilities	+	Equity

Debit for increases (↑)	Credit for decreases (↓)	Debit for decreases (↓)	Credit for increases (↑)	Debit for decreases (↓)	Credit for increases (↑)

Owner's Capital*	−	Owner's Withdrawals*	+	Revenues	−	Expenses

Dr. for decreases (↓)	Cr. for increases (↑)	Dr. for increases (↑)	Cr. for decreases (↓)	Dr. for decreases (↓)	Cr. for increases (↑)	Dr. for increases (↑)	Cr. for decreases (↓)

▢ Indicates normal balance.

*Comparable corporate accounts are Common Stock (Paid-In Capital) and Dividends.

② Accounting Cycle

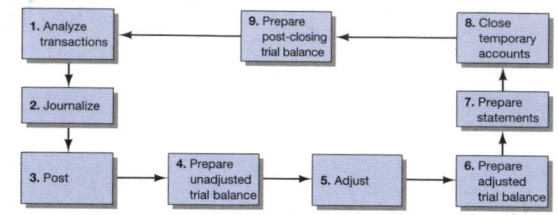

1. Analyze transactions
2. Journalize
3. Post
4. Prepare unadjusted trial balance
5. Adjust
6. Prepare adjusted trial balance
7. Prepare statements
8. Close temporary accounts
9. Prepare post-closing trial balance

③ Adjustments and Entries

Type	Adjusting Entry	
Prepaid Expenses	Dr. Expense	Cr. Asset*
Unearned Revenues	Dr. Liability	Cr. Revenue
Accrued Expenses	Dr. Expense	Cr. Liability
Accrued Revenues	Dr. Asset	Cr. Revenue

*For depreciation, credit Accumulated Depreciation (contra asset).

④ 4-Step Closing Process

1. Close revenue accounts to Income Summary.
2. Close expense accounts to Income Summary.
3. Close the Income Summary account to the owner's capital account.
4. Close the Withdrawals account to the owner's capital account.

⑤ Accounting Concepts

Characteristics	Assumptions	Principles	Constraints
Relevance	Business entity	Historical cost	Cost-benefit
Reliability	Periodicity	Matching	Materiality
Comparability	Going concern	Revenue recognition	Conservatism
Consistency	Monetary unit	Full disclosure	

⑥ Ownership of Inventory

	Ownership Transfers When Goods Passed To	Transportation Costs Paid By
FOB Shipping Point	Carrier	Buyer
FOB Destination	Buyer	Seller

⑦ Inventory Costing Methods

Specific Identification
First-In, First-Out (FIFO)
Last-In, First-Out (LIFO)
Weighted-Average

⑧ Depreciation and Depletion

Straight-Line: $\dfrac{\text{Cost} - \text{Salvage value}}{\text{Useful life in periods}} \times \text{Periods expired}$

Units-of-Production: $\dfrac{\text{Cost} - \text{Salvage value}}{\text{Useful life in units}} \times \text{Units produced}$

Declining-Balance: $\text{Rate*} \times \text{Beginning-of-period book value}$
*Rate is often double the straight-line rate, or $2 \times (1/\text{useful life})$

Depletion: $\dfrac{\text{Cost} - \text{Salvage value}}{\text{Total capacity in units}} \times \text{Units extracted}$

⑨ Interest Computation

$\text{Interest} = \text{Principal (face)} \times \text{Rate} \times \text{Time}$

⑩ Bad Debts Estimation

Bad Debts Estimation
_or_

Income Statement Focus

Balance Sheet Focus
_or_

Percent of Sales [Emphasis on Matching]

Percent of Receivables [Emphasis on Realizable Value]

Aging of Receivables [Emphasis on Realizable Value]

Sales × Rate = Bad Debts Expense

Accounts Receivable × Rate = Allowance for Doubtful Accounts

Accounts Receivable (by Age) × Rates (by Age) = Allowance for Doubtful Accounts

---

ANALYSES

① Liquidity and Efficiency

$\text{Current ratio} = \dfrac{\text{Current assets}}{\text{Current liabilities}}$ — p. 650

$\text{Working capital} = \text{Current assets} - \text{Current liabilities}$ — p. 650

$\text{Acid-test ratio} = \dfrac{\text{Cash} + \text{Short-term investments} + \text{Current receivables}}{\text{Current liabilities}}$ — p. 651

$\text{Accounts receivable turnover} = \dfrac{\text{Net sales}}{\text{Average accounts receivable}}$ — p. 651

$\text{Credit risk ratio} = \dfrac{\text{Allowance for doubtful accounts}}{\text{Accounts receivable}}$ — p. 381

$\text{Inventory turnover} = \dfrac{\text{Cost of goods sold}}{\text{Average inventory}}$ — p. 652

$\text{Days' sales uncollected} = \dfrac{\text{Accounts receivable}}{\text{Net sales}} \times 365^*$ — p. 652

$\text{Days' sales in inventory} = \dfrac{\text{Ending inventory}}{\text{Cost of goods sold}} \times 365^*$ — p. 652

$\text{Total asset turnover} = \dfrac{\text{Net sales}}{\text{Average total assets}}$ — p. 653

$\text{Plant asset useful life} = \dfrac{\text{Plant asset cost}}{\text{Depreciation expense}}$ — p. 463

$\text{Plant asset age} = \dfrac{\text{Accumulated depreciation}}{\text{Depreciation expense}}$ — p. 464

*360 days is also commonly used.

② Solvency

$\text{Debt ratio} = \dfrac{\text{Total liabilities}}{\text{Total assets}}$ $\quad$ $\text{Equity ratio} = \dfrac{\text{Total equity}}{\text{Total assets}}$ — p. 657

$\text{Debt-to-equity} = \dfrac{\text{Total liabilities}}{\text{Total equity}}$ — p. 654

$\text{Times interest earned} = \dfrac{\text{Income before interest expense and income taxes}}{\text{Interest expense}}$ — p. 654

$\text{Cash coverage of growth} = \dfrac{\text{Cash flow from operations}}{\text{Cash outflow for plant assets}}$ — p. 615

$\text{Cash coverage of debt} = \dfrac{\text{Cash flow from operations}}{\text{Total noncurrent liabilities}}$ — p. 613

③ Profitability

$\text{Profit margin ratio} = \dfrac{\text{Net income}}{\text{Net sales}}$ — p. 655

$\text{Gross margin ratio} = \dfrac{\text{Net sales} - \text{Cost of goods sold}}{\text{Net sales}}$ — p. 322

$\text{Return on total assets} = \dfrac{\text{Net income}}{\text{Average total assets}}$ — p. 655

$= \text{Profit margin ratio} \times \text{Total asset turnover}$ — p. 655

$\text{Return on common stockholders' equity} = \dfrac{\text{Net income} - \text{Preferred dividends}}{\text{Average common stockholders' equity}}$ — p. 655

$\text{Book value per common share} = \dfrac{\text{Stockholders' equity applicable to common shares}}{\text{Number of common shares outstanding}}$ — p. 523

$\text{Basic earnings per share} = \dfrac{\text{Net income} - \text{Preferred dividends}}{\text{Weighted-average common shares outstanding}}$ — p. 549

$\text{Cash flow on total assets} = \dfrac{\text{Cash flow from operations}}{\text{Average total assets}}$ — p. 614

$\text{Payout ratio} = \dfrac{\text{Cash dividends declared on common stock}}{\text{Net income}}$ — p. 549

④ Market

$\text{Price-earnings ratio} = \dfrac{\text{Market price per common share}}{\text{Earnings per share}}$ — p. 656

$\text{Dividend yield} = \dfrac{\text{Annual cash dividends per share}}{\text{Market price per share}}$ — p. 656

1.

award:
**2 out of
2 points**

Select the building block of financial statement analysis to the ratio to which it best relates.

1.	Gross margin ratio	**Profitability** ✓
2.	Acid-test ratio	**Liquidity and Efficiency** ✓
3.	Equity ratio	**Solvency** ✓
4.	Return on total assets	**Profitability** ✓
5.	Dividend yield	**Market Prospects** ✓
6.	Book value per common share	**Profitability** ✓
7.	Days' sales in inventory	**Liquidity and Efficiency** ✓
8.	Accounts receivable turnover	**Liquidity and Efficiency** ✓
9.	Debt-to-equity	**Solvency** ✓
10.	Times interest earned	**Solvency** ✓

eBook Links (3)

Worksheet	Learning Objective: 24-02 Identify the building blocks of analysis.	Learning Objective: 24-07 Define and apply ratio analysis.
Difficulty: Easy	Learning Objective: 24-04 Identify the tools of analysis.	

2.

award:
**2 out of
2 points**

Match each of the following terms A through J with the appropriate formulas 1 through 10.

A. Days' sales in inventory
B. Dividend yield
C. Total asset turnover
D. Inventory turnover

F. Gross margin ratio
G. Days' sales uncollected
H. Profit margin ratio
I. Times interest earned

E. Return on common stockholders' equity   J. Debt ratio

1. **E.** ✅
$$\frac{\text{Net income} - \text{preferred dividends}}{\text{Average common stockholders' equity}}$$

2. **G.** ✅
$$\frac{\text{Accounts receivable}}{\text{Net sales}} \times 365$$

3. **J.** ✅
$$\frac{\text{Total liabilities}}{\text{Total assets}}$$

4. **I.** ✅
$$\frac{\text{Income before interest expense and income taxes}}{\text{Interest expense}}$$

5. **B.** ✅
$$\frac{\text{Annual cash dividends per share}}{\text{Market price per share}}$$

6. **F.** ✅
$$\frac{\text{Net sales} - \text{Cost of goods sold}}{\text{Net sales}}$$

7. **D.** ✅
$$\frac{\text{Cost of goods sold}}{\text{Average inventory}}$$

8. **C.** ✅
$$\frac{\text{Net sales}}{\text{Average total assets}}$$

9. **H.** ✅
$$\frac{\text{Net income}}{\text{Net sales}}$$

10. **A.** ✅
$$\frac{\text{Ending inventory}}{\text{Cost of goods sold}} \times 365$$

3.

award:
**2 out of
2 points**

Selected comparative financial statements of Astalon Company follow:

ASTALON COMPANY
Comparative Income Statements

For Years Ended December 31, 2010, 2009, and 2008					
	2010		2009		2008
Sales	$ 550,945	$	422,069	$	292,900
Cost of goods sold	331,669		267,592		187,456
Gross profit	219,276		154,477		105,444
Selling expenses	78,234		58,246		38,663
Administrative expenses	49,585		37,142		24,311
Total expenses	127,819		95,388		62,974
Income before taxes	91,457		59,089		42,470
Income taxes	17,011		12,113		8,621
Net income	$ 74,446	$	46,976	$	33,849

ASTALON COMPANY
Comparative Balance Sheets
December 31, 2010, 2009, and 2008

	2010		2009		2008
Assets					
Current assets	$ 52,420	$	41,012	$	54,824
Long-term investments	0		700		4,100
Plant assets, net	95,869		102,282		60,375
Total assets	$ 148,289	$	143,994	$	119,299
Liabilities and Equity					
Current liabilities	$ 21,650	$	21,455	$	20,877
Common stock	68,000		68,000		50,000
Other paid-in capital	8,500		8,500		5,556
Retained earnings	50,139		46,039		42,866

Total liabilities and equity	$	148,289	$	143,994	$	119,299

Requirement 1:
Compute each year's current ratio. (**Round your answers to 1 decimal place.**)

Current ratio December 31, 2010:	2.4	to	1.0
Current ratio December 31, 2009:	1.9	to	1.0
Current ratio December 31, 2008:	2.6	to	1.0

Requirement 2:
Express the income statement data in common-size percents. (**Round your answers to 2 decimal places. Omit the "%" sign in your response.**)

ASTALON COMPANY Common-Size Comparative Income Statements For Years Ended December 31, 2010, 2009, and 2008			
	2010	2009	2008
Sales	100.00 %	100.00 %	100.00 %
Cost of goods sold	60.20	63.40	64.00
Gross profit	39.80	36.60	36.00
Selling expenses	14.20	13.80	13.20
Administrative expenses	9.00	8.80	8.30
Total expenses	23.20	22.60	21.50
Income before taxes	16.60	14.00	14.50
Income taxes	3.09	2.87	2.94
Net income	13.51 %	11.13 %	11.56 %

eBook Links (3)

Worksheet	Learning Objective: 24-05 Explain and apply methods of horizontal analysis.	Learning Objective: 24-07 Define and apply ratio

4.

Selected year-end financial statements of Cadet Corporation follow. (All sales were on credit; selected balance sheet amounts at December 31, 2009, were inventory, $56,900; total assets, $259,400; common stock, $90,000; and retained earnings, $53,348.)

CADET CORPORATION Income Statement For Year Ended December 31, 2010		
Sales	$	456,600
Cost of goods sold		297,550
Gross profit		159,050
Operating expenses		99,300
Interest expense		4,600
Income before taxes		55,150
Income taxes		22,217
Net income	$	32,933

CADET CORPORATION Balance Sheet December 31, 2010				
Assets			**Liabilities and Equity**	
Cash	$	12,000	Accounts payable	$ 25,500
Short-term investments		9,400	Accrued wages payable	4,400
Accounts receivable, net		29,200	Income taxes payable	2,900
Notes receivable (trade)*		5,000	Long-term note payable, secured by mortgage on plant assets	69,400

Merchandise inventory		42,150	Common stock			90,000
Prepaid expenses		3,050	Retained earnings			59,900
Plant assets, net		151,300				
Total assets	$	252,100	Total liabilities and equity	$		252,100

* These are short-term notes receivable arising from customer (trade) sales.

Required:
Compute the following (Use 365 days in a year. Do not round interim calculations. Round your answers to 1 decimal place. Omit the "%" sign in your response):

1. Current ratio	3.1 ✓	to	1 ✓
2. Acid-test ratio	1.7 ✓	to	1 ✓
3. Days' sales uncollected	27.3 ✓	days	
4. Inventory turnover	6.0 ✓	times	
5. Days' sales in inventory	51.7 ✓	days	
6. Debt-to-equity ratio	.8 ✓	to	1 ✓
7. Times interest earned	13.0 ✓	times	
8. Profit margin ratio	7.2 ✓	%	
9. Total asset turnover	1.8 ✓	times	
10. Return on total assets	13.1 ✓	%	
11. Return on common stockholders' equity	22.0 ✓	%	

[The following information applies to the questions displayed below.]
Summary information from the financial statements of two companies competing in the same industry follows:

	Karto Company		Bryan Company			Karto Company
Data from the current year-end balance sheets					**Data from the current year's income state**	
Assets					Sales	$ 780,
Cash	$	20,500	$	34,000	Cost of goods sold	590,
Accounts receivable, net		35,400		53,400	Interest expense	8,
Current notes receivable (trade)		9,100		7,000	Income tax expense	14,
Merchandise		84,540		130,500	Net income	$ 166,

inventory

						Basic earnings per share	$	
Prepaid expenses		5,700		7,400				
Plant assets, net		310,000		312,400				
Total assets	$	465,240	$	544,700				

						Beginning-of-year balance sheet data		
Liabilities and Equity						Accounts receivable, net	$	30,
Current liabilities	$	69,340	$	103,300		Current notes receivable (trade)		
Long-term notes payable		78,192		55,508		Merchandise inventory		55,
Common stock, $5 par value		170,000		226,000		Total assets		398,
Retained earnings		147,708		159,892		Common stock, $5 par value		170,
Total liabilities and equity	$	465,240	$	544,700		Retained earnings		114,

5.

award:
1 out of
1 point

Requirement 1:
For both companies compute the (*a*) current ratio, (*b*) acid-test ratio, (*c*) accounts (including notes) receivable turnover, (*d*) inventory turnover, (*e*) days' sales in inventory, and (*f*) days' sales uncollected. (Use 365 days in a year. Do not round interim calculations. Round your answers to 1 decimal place.)

	Karto Company	Bryan Company

a.	Current ratio	2.2 ⊘ to	1 ⊘		2.2 ⊘ to	1 ⊘
b.	Acid-test ratio	.9 ⊘ to	1 ⊘		.9 ⊘ to	1 ⊘
c.	Accounts receivable turnover	20.7 ⊘ times			15.9 ⊘ times	
d.	Inventory turnover	8.4 ⊘ times			5.2 ⊘ times	
e.	Days' sales in inventory	52.3 ⊘ days			75.3 ⊘ days	
f.	Days' sales uncollected	20.8 ⊘ days			24.2 ⊘ days	

eBook Links (2)

Worksheet	Learning Objective: 24-07 Define and apply ratio analysis.
Difficulty: Hard	Learning Objective: 24-08 Summarize and report results of financial statement analysis.

Requirement 1:
For both companies compute the (*a*) current ratio, (*b*) acid-test ratio, (*c*) accounts (including notes) receivable turnover, (*d*) inventory turnover, (*e*) days' sales in inventory, and (*f*) days' sales uncollected. (**Use 365 days in a year. Do not round interim calculations. Round your answers to 1 decimal place.**)

		Karto Company			Bryan Company	
a.	Current ratio	2.2	to 1		2.2	to 1
b.	Acid-test ratio	.9	to 1		.9	to 1
c.	Accounts receivable turnover	20.7	times		15.9	times
d.	Inventory turnover	8.4	times		5.2	times
e.	Days' sales in inventory	52.3	days		75.3	days
f.	Days' sales uncollected	20.8	days		24.2	days

Explanation:
Karto Company:

Current ratio:

$$\frac{\$155,240^*}{\$69,340} = 2.2 \text{ to } 1$$

*$20,500 + $35,400 + $9,100 + $84,540 + $5,700 = $155,240

Acid-test ratio:

$$\frac{\$65,000^*}{\$69,340} = .9 \text{ to } 1$$

*$20,500 + $35,400 +$9,100 = $65,000

Accounts receivable turnover:

$$\frac{\$780,000}{(\$35,400 + \$9,100 + \$30,800)/2} = 20.7 \text{ times}$$

Inventory turnover:

$$\frac{\$590,100}{(\$84,540 + \$55,600)/2} = 8.4 \text{ times}$$

Days' sales in inventory:

$$\frac{\$84,540}{\$590,100} \times 365 = 52.3 \text{ days}$$

Days' sales uncollected:

$$\frac{\$35,400 + \$9,100}{\$780,000} \times 365 = 20.8 \text{ days}$$

Bryan Company:

Current ratio:

$$\frac{\$232,300^{**}}{\$103,300} = 2.2 \text{ to } 1$$

**$34,000 + $53,400 + $7,000 + $130,500 + $7,400 = $232,300

Acid-test ratio:

$$\frac{\$94,400^{**}}{\$103,300} = .9 \text{ to } 1$$

**$34,000 + $53,400 + $ 7,000 = $94,400

Accounts receivable turnover:

$$\frac{\$910,200}{(\$53,400 + \$7,000 + \$54,200)/2} = 15.9 \text{ times}$$

Inventory turnover:

$$\frac{\$632,500}{(\$130,500 + \$111,400)/2} = 5.2 \text{ times}$$

Days' sales in inventory:

$$\frac{\$130{,}500}{\$632{,}500} \times 365 = 75.3 \text{ days}$$

Days' sales uncollected:

$$\frac{\$53{,}400 + \$7{,}000}{\$910{,}200} \times 365 = 24.2 \text{ days}$$

6.

award:
**1 out of
1 point**

Requirement 2:
For both companies compute the (*a*) profit margin ratio, (*b*) total asset turnover, (*c*) return on total assets, and (*d*) return on common stockholders' equity. Assuming that each company paid cash dividends of $3.90 per share and each company's stock can be purchased at $105 per share, compute their (*e*) price-earnings ratios and (*f*) dividend yields. (**Round your answers to 2 decimal places. Omit the "%" sign in your response.**)

	Karto Company	Bryan Company
a. Profit margin ratio	21.28 %	25.88 %
b. Total asset turnover	1.81 times	1.90 times
c. Return on total assets	38.46 %	49.22 %
d. Return on common stockholders' equity	55.15 %	66.13 %
e. Price-earnings ratio	21.52	20.15
f. Dividend yield	3.71 %	3.71 %

company's maximum manufacturing cycle time. (**Round your answer to the nearest whole number.**)

Maximum manufacturing cycle time	26 ± 1 days

Explanation:

2(a):
Manufacturing cycle efficiency (8.0 days/ 27.1 days) = .30

3:
Maximum manufacturing cycle time = 8 days / .31 = 26 days

Oakwood Company produces oak bookcases to customer order. Oakwood received an order from a customer to produce 5,000 bookcases. The following information is available for the production of the bookcases.

Process time	8.0 days
Inspection time	.7 days
Move time	3.4 days
Wait time	15.0 days

Requirement 1:
Compute the company's manufacturing cycle time. **(Round your answers to 1 decimal place.)**

Process time	8.0	days
Inspection time	.7	days
Move time	3.4	days
Wait time	15.0	days
Manufacturing cycle time	27.1	days

Requirement 2:
(a)Compute the company's manufacturing cycle efficiency. **(Enter your answer as ratios and not percentages. For example, enter "50%" as "0.50". Round your answer to 2 decimal places.)**

Manufacturing cycle efficiency	.30

(b)Interpret your answer.

Oakwood is spending 30% of its time in value-added activities, and 70% of its time on non-value-added activities.

Requirement 3:
Assume that Oakwood wishes to increase its manufacturing cycle efficiency to .31. Compute the

Requirement 3:

Assume that 1,600 drum sets are produced in the next month. What do you predict will be the total cost of plastic for the casings and the per-unit cost of the plastic for the casings? (**Round your total cost to the nearest dollar amount. Round your per-unit cost to 2 decimal places. Omit the "$" sign in your response.**)

Total cost	$	25,376
Per-unit cost	$	15.86

Requirement 4:

Assume that 1,600 drum sets are produced in the next month. What do you predict will be the total cost of property taxes and the per-unit cost of the property taxes? (**Round your per-unit cost to 2 decimal places. Omit the "$" sign in your response.**)

Total cost	$	6,600
Per-unit cost	$	4.13

Explanation:

2:

Per unit cost = Total cost / 1,400 drum sets

3:

If 1,600 drum sets are produced, we would expect the cost of the plastic for the casings to increase to $25,376 (1,600 drum sets × $15.86/set), but the cost per unit will stay at $15.86 per drum set. Variable costs increase in total as the number of units produced increases, but the unit cost remains constant.

4:

If 1,600 drum sets are produced, we would expect the cost of the property taxes to remain at $6,600 because it is a fixed cost. However, the cost per unit will decrease to $4.13/drum set ($6,600 drum sets / 1,600 sets). Fixed costs do not change in total as production increases, but the unit cost will decrease as production increases.

9.

Costs		Variable	Fixed		Product	Period	
Plastic for casing	$	22,200		$	22,200		
Wages of assembly workers		83,000	$ 0		83,000	$	0
Property taxes on factory		0	6,600		6,600		0
Accounting staff salaries		0	31,000		0		31,000
Drum stands (1,400 stands outsourced)		28,000	0		28,000		0
Rent cost of equipment for sales staff		0	12,000		0		12,000
Upper management salaries		0	160,000		0		160,000
Annual flat fee for maintenance service		0	18,000		18,000		0
Sales commissions—$16 per unit	$	22,400	0		0	$	22,400
Machinery depreciation		0	40,000		40,000		0

Requirement 2:
Compute the manufacturing cost per drum set. (**Round your per-unit cost to 2 decimal places. Omit the "$" sign in your response.**)

DrumBeat		
Calculation of Manufacturing Cost per Drum Set		
For Year Ended December 31, 2010		
Item	Total cost	Per unit cost
Variable Production Costs		
Plastic for Casing	$ 22,200	$ 15.86
Wages of Assembly Workers	83,000	59.29
Drum Stands	28,000	20.00
Total variable costs	133,200 ± 0.1	95.15 ± 0.1
Fixed Production Costs		
Property Taxes on Factory	6,600	4.71
Annual Fee for Maintenance Service	18,000	12.86
Machinery Depreciation	40,000	28.57
Total fixed costs	64,600 ± 0.1	46.14 ± 0.1
Total manufacturing cost	$ 197,800 ± 0.1	$ 141.29 ± 0.1

Requirement 2:
Identify the correct statement(s) from below: **(Select all that apply.)**

⊗ ☑   Most Fixed costs are indirect.

⊗ ☐   Most Variable costs are direct.

⊘ ☐   Most Indirect costs are fixed.

⊘ ☑   Most Direct costs are variable.

8.
award:
1 out of
1 point

Listed here are the total costs associated with the production of 1,400 drum sets manufactured by DrumBeat. The drum sets sell for $1,000 each.

Costs	Cost by Behavior		Cost by Function	
	Variable	Fixed	Product	Period
Plastic for casing—$22,200	$22,200		$22,200	
Wages of assembly workers—$83,000				
Property taxes on factory—$6,600				
Accounting staff salaries—$31,000				
Drum stands (1,400 stands outsourced)—$28,000				
Rent cost of equipment for sales staff—$12,000				
Upper management salaries—$160,000				
Annual flat fee for maintenance service—$18,000				
Sales commissions—$16 per unit				
Machinery depreciation—$40,000				

Requirement 1:
Classify each cost and its amount as (a) either fixed or variable and (b) either product or period (the first cost is completed as an example). **(Leave no cells blank - be certain to enter "0" wherever required. Omit the "$" sign in your response.)**

	Cost by Behavior	Cost by Function

manufacturing companies will simply classify all employee benefits as indirect and overhead.

Wages to assembly workers:
Direct labor is a prime and conversion cost because this labor force is in direct contact with the product in the conversion process.

6.
award:
1 out of
1 point

Requirement 1:
Classify each cost (a) as either fixed or variable and (b) as either direct or indirect by entering a X in appropriate column. **(Select "NA" for not applicable.)**

(a)Fixed or Variable

Product Cost	Cost by Behavior	
	Variable	Fixed
Annual flat fee paid for office security	NA	X
Leather cover for soccer balls	X	NA
Lace to hold the leather together	X	NA
Wages of assembly workers	X	NA
Taxes on factory	NA	X
Coolants for machinery	NA	X
Machinery depreciation	NA	X

(b)Direct or Indirect

Product Cost	Cost by Traceability	
	Direct	Indirect
Annual flat fee paid for office security	NA	X
Leather cover for soccer balls	X	NA
Lace to hold the leather together	NA	X
Wages of assembly workers	X	NA
Taxes on factory	NA	X
Coolants for machinery	NA	X
Machinery depreciation	NA	X

7.

as prime for one company and conversion for another. Select "NA" for not applicable.)

Cost	Product Cost Prime	Product Cost Conversion	Period Cost
Direct materials used	X	NA	NA
State and federal income taxes	NA	NA	X
Payroll taxes for production supervisor	NA	X	NA
Amortization of patents on factory machine	NA	X	NA
Accident insurance on factory workers	X	X	NA
Wages to assembly workers	X	X	NA
Factory utilities	NA	X	NA
Small tools used	NA	X	NA
Bad debts expense	NA	NA	X
Depreciation—Factory building	NA	X	NA
Advertising	NA	NA	X
Office supplies used	NA	NA	X

Requirement 2:

Classify each product cost as either a direct cost or an indirect cost using the product as the cost object by a entering X in appropriate column. **(Certain costs that can be classified as direct for one company and indirect for another. Select "NA" for not applicable.)**

Cost	Direct Cost	Indirect Cost
Direct materials used	X	NA
State and federal income taxes	NA	NA
Payroll taxes for production supervisor	NA	X
Amortization of patents on factory machine	NA	X
Accident insurance on factory workers	X	X
Wages to assembly workers	X	NA
Factory utilities	NA	X
Small tools used	NA	X
Bad debts expense	NA	NA
Depreciation—Factory building	NA	X
Advertising	NA	NA
Office supplies used	NA	NA

Explanation:

Accident insurance on factory workers:

There are certain costs that can be classified as direct for one company and indirect for another. The specific classification depends on the materiality and cost benefit of tracking. For example, some companies track employee benefits for direct and indirect workers. Yet, some

award:
1 out of
1 point

Requirement 2:

The company starts reporting measures such as the percent of defective products and the number of units scrapped. **(Select all that apply.)**

- ☑ Total quality management (TQM)
- ☐ Just-in-time (JIT) system
- ☑ Continuous improvement (CI)
- ☐ Customer orientation (CO)

eBook Link

Check All That Apply	Difficulty: Easy	Learning Objective: 25-02 Describe the lean business model.

4.
award:
1 out of
1 point

Requirement 3:

The company starts measuring inventory turnover and discontinues elaborate inventory records. Its new focus is to pull inventory through the system.

- ⦿ Just-in-time (JIT) system
- ○ Customer orientation (CO)
- ○ Total quality management (TQM)
- ○ Continuous improvement (CI)

5.
award:
1 out of
1 point

Georgia Pacific, a manufacturer, incurs the following costs.

Requirement 1:

Classify each cost as either a product or a period cost by entering a X in appropriate column. If a product cost, identify it as a prime and/or conversion cost. **(Certain costs that can be classified**

1.
award:
2 out of
2 points

Both managerial accounting and financial accounting provide useful information to decision makers. Place X to indicate in the following chart the most likely source of information for each business decision (a decision can require major input from both sources). **(Select "NA" for not applicable.)**

Business Decision	Primary Information Source	
	Managerial	Financial
Report financial performance to board of directors	X	X
Estimate product cost for a new line of shoes	X	NA
Plan the budget for next quarter	X	NA
Measure profitability of all individual stores	X	X
Prepare financial reports according to GAAP	NA	X
Determine amount of dividends to pay stockholders	X	X
Determine location and size for a new plant	X	NA
Evaluate a purchasing department's performance	X	NA

2.
award:
0.33 out of
1 point

Requirement 1:
The company starts reporting measures on customer complaints and product returns from customers. **(Select all that apply.)**

⊗☑ Total quality management (TQM)

●☐ Just-in-time (JIT) system

⊗☑ Continuous improvement (CI)

●☑ Customer orientation (CO)

eBook Link

| **Check All That Apply** | Difficulty: Easy | Learning Objective: 25-02 Describe the lean business model. |

3.

Explanation:
Retained earnings ($271,120 + $89,520) = 360,640

23.
award:
0 out of
1 point

Requirement 5:
Assume that the $5,720 on materials requisition 21-3012 should have been direct materials charged to Job 404.
Without providing specific calculations, which of the following statement(s) is true? **(Select all that apply.)**

- ☐ It will yield a $5,720 decrease in retained earnings on the balance sheet when the error is corrected.

- ☐ Since Job 404 is in process at the end of the period, there will be no effect on goods in process inventory and total assets..

- ☐ Since Job 404 is in process at the end of the period, goods in process inventory and total assets would both be overstated on the balance sheet.

- ☑ Since Job 404 is in process at the end of the period, goods in process inventory and total assets would both be understated on the balance sheet.

- ☑ It will yield a $5,720 increase in retained earnings on the balance sheet when the error is corrected.

Requirement 4a:
Prepare an income statement for year 2010. (**Negative amounts should be indicated by a minus sign. Omit the "$" sign in your response.**)

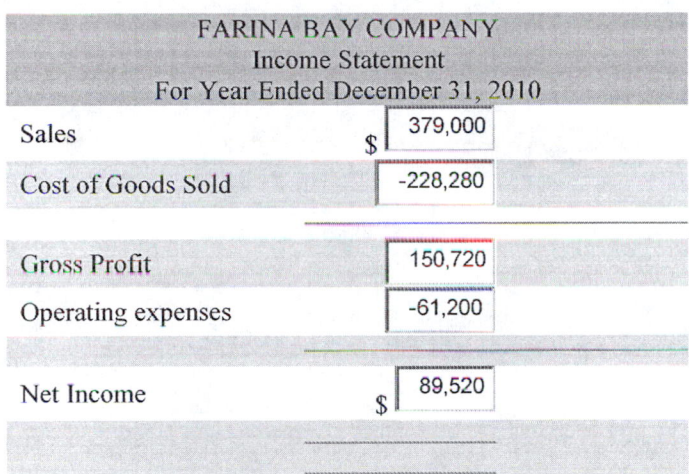

FARINA BAY COMPANY Income Statement For Year Ended December 31, 2010	
Sales	$ 379,000
Cost of Goods Sold	-228,280
Gross Profit	150,720
Operating expenses	-61,200
Net Income	$ 89,520

Requirement 4b:
Prepare a balance sheet as of December 31, 2010. (**Omit the "$" sign in your response.**)

FARINA BAY COMPANY Balance Sheet December 31, 2010				
Assets			Liabilities and Equity	
Cash		$ 103,200	Accounts Payable	$
Accounts Receivable		76,200	Notes Payable	
Inventories			Total liabilities	$
Raw Material Inventory	$ 45,480			
Goods in Process Inventory	210,840		Common Stock	
Finished Goods Inventory	16,200	272,520	Retained Earnings	$ 3
Prepaid Rent		3,120	Total stockholders' equity	4
Total assets		$ 455,040	Total Liabilities and Equity	$ 4

Notes Payable		25,600
Common Stock		51,200
Retained Earnings		271,120
Sales		379,000
Cost of Goods Sold	228,280	
Factory Payroll	0	
Factory Overhead	0	
Operating Expenses	61,200	
Totals	$ 744,520	$ 744,520

Explanation:

Raw materials inventory

Balance per trial balance	$	81,200
Less: Amounts recorded for Jobs 402 and 404		(30,000)
Less: Indirect materials		(5,720)
Ending balance	$	45,480

Goods in process inventory

	Job 402	Job 404	Total
Direct materials	$ 10,800	$ 19,200	$ 30,000
Direct labor	35,880	24,400	60,280
Overhead	71,760	48,800	120,560
Total cost	$ 118,440	$ 92,400	$ 210,840

Revised Factory Overhead account	
Ending balance from trial balance	$ 116,200
Applied to jobs 402 and 404	-120,560
Additional indirect materials	5,720
Additional indirect labor	8,320
Underapplied Overhead	$ 9,680

19.
award:
1 out of
1 point

Requirement 2b:

Prepare the adjusting entry to allocate any over- or underapplied overhead to Cost of Goods Sold, assuming the amount is not material. (Omit the "$" sign in your response.)

Date	General Journal	Debit	Credit
Dec. 31	Cost of Goods Sold	9,680	
	Factory Overhead		9,680

20.
award:
0 out of
0 points

Requirement 3:

Prepare a revised trial balance. (Leave no cells blank - be certain to enter "0" wherever required. Omit the "$" sign in your response.)

FARINA BAY COMPANY Trial Balance December 31,2010		
	Debit	Credit
Cash	$ 103,200	
Accounts Receivable	76,200	
Raw Materials Inventory	45,480	
Goods in Process Inventory	210,840	
Finished Goods Inventory	16,200	
Prepaid Rent	3,120	
Accounts Payable		$ 17,600

Use information on the six source documents to prepare journal entries to assign the following costs. (**Omit the "$" sign in your response.**)

(a) Direct materials costs to Goods in Process Inventory.

Date	General Journal	Debit	Credit
Dec. 31	Goods in Process Inventory	30,000	
	Raw Materials Inventory		30,000

(b) Direct labor costs to Goods in Process Inventory.

Date	General Journal	Debit	Credit
Dec. 31	Goods in Process Inventory	60,280	
	Factory Payroll		60,280

(c) Overhead costs to Goods in Process Inventory.

Date	General Journal	Debit	Credit
Dec. 31	Goods in Process Inventory	120,560	
	Factory Overhead		120,560

(d) Indirect materials costs to the Factory Overhead account.

Date	General Journal	Debit	Credit
Dec. 31	Factory Overhead	5,720	
	Raw Materials Inventory		5,720

(e) Indirect labor costs to the Factory Overhead account.

Date	General Journal	Debit	Credit
Dec. 31	Factory Overhead	8,320	
	Factory Payroll		8,320

18.
award:
0 out of
0 points

Requirement 2a:
Determine the revised balance of the Factory Overhead account after making the entries in requirement 1. Determine whether there is any under- or overapplied overhead for the year. (**Negative amounts should be indicated by a minus sign. Omit the "$" sign in your response.**)

Finished goods (Job 307)	$	296,800
Total inventories	$	888,800

Explanation:
Presentation of inventories on the April 30 balance sheet

Beginning raw materials inventory	$	160,000
Purchases		500,000
Direct materials used		(300,000)
Indirect materials used		(38,000)
Ending raw materials inventory	$	322,000

16.
award:
1 out of
1 point

Requirement 5:
Which of the following statement(s) is true? (**Select all that apply.**)

- [ ] Profits at the job (and batch) level are understated if the overhead is underapplied.

- [ ] Profits at the job (and batch) level are overstated if the overhead is overapplied.

- [x] Profits at the job (and batch) level are overstated if the overhead is underapplied.

- [x] Profits at the job (and batch) level are understated if the overhead is overapplied.

17.
award:
1 out of
1 point

Requirement 1:

Cost of goods manufactured (306 & 307)	$	442,800

14.
award:
0 out of
0 points

Requirement 4a:
Compute gross profit for April. (**Omit the "$" sign in your response.**)

Gross profit	$	231,800

Explanation:
Gross profit on the income statement for the month ended April 30

Sales	$	400,000
Cost of goods sold ($146,000 + $22,200)		(168,200)
Gross profit	$	231,800

15.
award:
1 out of
1 point

Requirement 4b:
Show how to present the inventories on the April 30 balance sheet.(**Omit the "$" sign in your response.**)

Inventories		
Raw materials	$	322,000
Goods in process (Job 308)	$	270,000

jobs

Overhead incurred				
Indirect materials	$	38,000		
Indirect labor		14,000		
Factory rent		22,000		
Factory utilities		16,000		
Factory equip. depreciation		31,000		121,000
Underapplied overhead			$	22,200

13.
award:
1 out of
1 point

Requirement 3:
Prepare a manufacturing statement for April (use a single line presentation for direct materials and show the details of overhead cost.) (**Negative amounts should be indicated by a minus sign. Omit the "$" sign in your response.**)

CIOLINO COMPANY Manufacturing Statement For Month Ended April 30		
Direct Materials Used		$ 300,000
Direct Labor Used		247,000
Factory overhead		
Indirect Materials	$ 38,000	
Indirect Labor	14,000	
Factory Rent	22,000	
Factory Utilities	16,000	
Depreciation of Equipment	31,000	121,000
Total manufacturing costs		668,000
Goods in Process March 31 (306 & 307)		67,000
Total cost of goods in process		735,000
Goods in Process April 30 (308)		-270,000
Deduct : Underapplied Overhead		-22,200

		Debit	Credit
Raw Materials Inventory			300,000

		Debit	Credit
Goods in Process Inventory		247,000	
Factory Payroll			247,000

		Debit	Credit
Goods in Process Inventory		98,800	
Factory Overhead			98,800

(c) Transfer of Jobs 306 and 307 to the Finished Goods Inventory.

General Journal	Debit	Credit
Finished Goods Inventory	442,800	
Goods in Process Inventory		442,800

(d) Cost of goods sold for Job 306.

General Journal	Debit	Credit
Cost of Goods Sold	146,000	
Finished Goods Inventory		146,000

(e) Revenue from the sale of Job 306.

General Journal	Debit	Credit
Cash	400,000	
Sales		400,000

(f) Assignment of any underapplied or overapplied overhead to the Cost of Goods Sold account. (The amount is not material.)

General Journal	Debit	Credit
Cost of Goods Sold	22,200	
Factory Overhead		22,200

Explanation:

(c)

($146,000 + $296,800) = $442,800

(f)

Overhead applied to	$ 98,800

Total costs	$	146,000	$	296,800	$	270,000	$ 712,800

12.
award:
1 out of
1 point

Requirement 2:
Prepare journal entries for the month of April to record the following. (**Omit the "$" sign in your response.**)

(a) Materials purchases (on credit), factory payroll (paid in cash), and actual overhead costs including indirect materials and indirect labor. (Factory rent and utilities are paid in cash.)

General Journal	Debit	Credit
Raw Materials Inventory	500,000	
Accounts Payable		500,000
Factory Payroll	220,000	
Cash		220,000
Factory Overhead	38,000	
Raw Materials Inventory		38,000
Factory Overhead	14,000	
Factory Payroll		14,000
Factory Overhead	22,000	
Cash		22,000
Factory Overhead	16,000	
Cash		16,000
Factory Overhead	31,000	
Accumulated Depreciation		31,000

(b) Assignment of direct materials, direct labor, and applied overhead costs to the Goods in Process Inventory.

General Journal	Debit	Credit
Goods in Process Inventory	300,000	

Underapplied	$	6,300	

Explanation:

Factory Overhead			
Incurred	461,690	Applied*	455,390
Underapplied	6,300		

*Overhead applied to jobs = 113% × $403,000 = $455,390

10.
award:
0 out of
0 points

Requirement 4:
Prepare the adjusting entry to allocate any over- or underapplied overhead to Cost of Goods Sold. (**Omit the "$" sign in your response.**)

Date	General Journal	Debit	Credit
Dec. 31	Cost of Goods Sold	6,300	
	Factory Overhead		6,300

11.
award:
1 out of
1 point

Requirement 1:
Determine the total of each production cost incurred for April (direct labor, direct materials, and applied overhead), and the total cost assigned to each job (including the balances from March 31). (**Leave no cells blank - be certain to enter "0" wherever required. Omit the "$" sign in your response.**)

	306	307	308	April Total
Balances from March	$ 34,000	$ 33,000	$ 0	$ 67,000
For April				
Direct materials	$ 70,000	$ 170,000	$ 60,000	$ 300,000
Direct labor	30,000	67,000	150,000	247,000
Applied overhead	12,000	26,800	60,000	98,800
Total costs added in April	112,000	263,800	270,000	645,800

Requirement 1:
Determine the predetermined overhead rate for year 2010. (**Round your answer to the nearest whole percent. Omit the "%" sign in your response.**)

Overhead rate	113 %

Explanation:
Predetermined overhead rate

Estimated overhead costs	$450,000
Estimated direct labor costs	$400,000
Rate (Overhead/Direct labor)	113%

8.

Requirement 2:
Prepare T-account for Factory Overhead and enter the overhead costs incurred and the amounts applied to jobs during the year using the predetermined overhead rate. (**Use rounded overhead rate. Round your answers to the nearest dollar amount. Omit the "$" sign in your response.**)

Factory Overhead		
Incurred	461,690	Applied	455,390

Explanation:
Applied:
Overhead applied to jobs = 113% × $403,000 = $455,390

9.

Requirement 3:
Determine whether overhead is overapplied or underapplied (and the amount) during the year. (**Input the amount as positive value. Use the rounded overhead rate. Round your answer to the nearest dollar amount. Omit the "$" sign in your response.**)

1. Raw materials purchases for cash.
2. Direct materials usage.
3. Indirect materials usage.
4. Factory payroll costs in cash.
5. Direct labor usage.
6. Indirect labor usage.
7. Factory overhead excluding indirect materials and indirect labor (record credit to Other Accounts).
8. Application of overhead to goods in process.
9. Transfer of finished jobs to the finished goods inventory.
10. Sale and delivery of finished goods to customers for cash (record unadjusted cost of sales).
11. Allocation (closing) of overapplied or underapplied overhead to Cost of Goods Sold.

Event	General Journal	Debit	Credit
1.	Raw Materials Inventory	182,000	
	Cash		182,000
2.	Goods in Process Inventory	152,000	
	Raw Materials Inventory		
3.	Factory Overhead	8,000	
	Raw Materials Inventory		8,000
4.	Factory Payroll	280,000	
	Cash		280,000
5.	Goods in Process Inventory	199,000	
	Factory Payroll		199,000
6.	Factory Overhead	81,000	
	Factory Payroll		81,000
7.	Factory Overhead	92,000	
	Other Accounts		92,000
8.	Goods in Process Inventory	109,450	
	Factory Overhead		109,450
9.	Finished Goods Inventory	449,950	
	Goods in Process Inventory		449,950
10.	Cash	1,400,000	
	Sales		
	Cost of Goods Sold	478,450	
	Finished Goods Inventory		478,450
11.	Cost of Goods Sold	71,550	
	Factory Overhead		71,550

7.

Total cost of the job	$	22,508

Explanation:

1:

$$\text{Rate} = \frac{\text{Estimated overhead costs}}{\text{Estimated direct labor}} = \frac{\$770,000}{\$590,000} = 131\%$$

2:

Direct materials	$	15,000
Direct labor		3,250
Overhead ($3,250 × 131%)		4,258
Total cost of Job No. 13-56	$	22,508

6.
award:
0 out of
0 points

The following information is available for Lock-Safe Company, which produces special-order security products and uses a job order cost accounting system.

	April 30	May 31
Inventories		
Raw materials	$37,000	$ 59,000
Goods in process	9,300	19,800
Finished goods	63,000	34,500
Activities and information for May		
Raw materials purchases (paid with cash)		182,000
Factory payroll (paid with cash)		280,000
Factory overhead		
Indirect materials		8,000
Indirect labor		81,000
Other overhead costs		92,000
Sales (received in cash)		1,400,000
Predetermined overhead rate based on direct labor cost		55%

Required:
Prepare journal entries for the following events in May. (Omit the "$" sign in your response.)

	Total transferred cost	$ 35,000	$ 87,160	$ 122,160

5.
award:
0 out of
0 points

In December 2009, Shire Computer's management establishes the year 2010 predetermined overhead rate based on direct labor cost. The information used in setting this rate includes estimates that the company will incur $770,000 of overhead costs and $590,000 of direct labor cost in year 2010. During March 2010, Shire began and completed Job No. 13-56.

Requirement 1:
What is the predetermined overhead rate for year 2010? (**Round your answer to the nearest whole percent. Omit the "%" sign in your response.**)

Overhead rate	131 %

Requirement 2:
Use the information on the following job cost sheet to determine the total cost of the job. (**Use the rounded overhead rate. Round your answer to the nearest dollar amount. Omit the "$" sign in your response.**)

JOB COST SHEET

Customer's Name: Keiser Co.   Job No. 13-56.

Job Description: 5 plasma monitors—61 inch

		Direct Materials		Direct Labor		Overhead Costs Applied	
Date	Requisition No.	Amount	Time-Ticket No.	Amount		Rate	Amount
Mar. 8	4-129	$ 5,000	T-306	$ 660			
Mar. 11	4-142	6,600	T-432	1,330			
Mar. 18	4-167	3,400	T-456	1,260			
Totals							

Explanation:
Direct labor cost incurred in the month equals the total direct labor costs accumulated on the three jobs less the amount of direct labor cost assigned to Job 102 in May:

Job 102	$	10,000		
Less prior costs		(3,600)	$	6,400
Job 103				29,300
Job 104				42,000
Total direct labor			$	77,700

Requirement 3:
What predetermined overhead rate is used during June? (Omit the "%" sign in your response.)

Overhead rate	20 %

4.
award:
0 out of
0 points

Requirement 4:
How much total cost is transferred to finished goods during June? (Omit the "$" sign in your response.)

Total transferred cost	$ 122,160

Explanation:
The cost transferred to finished goods in June equals the total costs of the two completed jobs for the month, which are Jobs 102 and 103:

	Job 102	Job 103	Total
Direct materials	$ 23,000	$ 52,000	$ 75,000
Direct labor	10,000	29,300	39,300
Overhead	2,000	5,860	7,860

1.
award:
0 out of
0 points

Requirement 1:
What is the cost of the raw materials requisitioned in June for each of the three jobs? (Omit the "$" sign in your response.)

Job 102	$	10,000
Job 103	$	52,000
Job 104	$	63,000

Explanation:
The cost of direct materials requisitioned in the month equals the total direct materials costs accumulated on the three jobs less the amount of direct materials cost assigned to Job 102 in May:

Job 102	$	23,000		
Less prior costs		(13,000)	$	10,000
Job 103				52,000
Job 104				63,000
Total materials used (requisitioned)			$	125,000

2.
award:
0 out of
0 points

Requirement 2:
How much direct labor cost is incurred during June for each of the three jobs? (Omit the "$" sign in your response.)

Job 102	$	6,400
Job 103	$	29,300
Job 104	$	42,000